The Duel

PAKISTAN ON THE FLIGHT PATH OF AMERICAN POWER

TARIQ ALI

Scribner

NEW YORK   LONDON   TORONTO   SYDNEY

SCRIBNER
A Division of Simon & Schuster, Inc.
1230 Avenue of the Americas
New York, NY 10020

First Scribner hardcover edition September 2008

SCRIBNER and design are registered trademarks of
The Gale Group, Inc., used under license
by Simon & Schuster, Inc., the publisher of this work.

For information about special discounts for bulk purchases,
please contact Simon & Schuster Special Sales:
1-800-456-6798 or business@simonandschuster.com

Designed by Kyoko Watanabe
Text set in Adobe Garamond

Manufactured in the United States of America

1   3   5   7   9   10   8   6   4   2

Library of Congress Cataloging-in-Publication Data
Ali, Tariq.
Pakistan on the flight path of American power / Tariq Ali.
—1st Scribner hardcover ed.
p.   cm.
1. Pakistan—Politics and government. I. Title.
DS384.A769 2008
954.9105—dc22   2008018358

ISBN-13: 978-1-4165-6101-9
ISBN-10: 1-4165-6101-3

Map on p. xiv is courtesy of the *New Left Review.*

for
Tahira, Tauseef, Kamila, and Mishael,
four generations of Lahoris

CONTENTS

Preface   IX

1. Pakistan at Sixty: A Conflagration of Despair   I

2. Rewinding Pakistan: Birth of Tragedy   29

3. The Washington Quartet:
   The Man Who Would Be Field Marshal   50

4. The Washington Quartet:
   The General Who Lost a Country   70

5. The Washington Quartet:
   The Soldier of Islam   97

6. The Washington Quartet:
   The General as Chief Executive   134

7. The House of Bhutto: Daughter of the West   159

8. On the Flight Path of American Power   191

9. Operation Enduring Freedom:
   Mirage of the "Good" War   217

10. Can Pakistan Be Recycled?   249

    Index   279

PREFACE

BOOKS HAVE A DESTINY. THIS IS MY THIRD STUDY OF PAKISTAN. The first, *Pakistan: Military Rule or People's Power?*, was written in 1969 and predicted the breakup of the state. It was banned in Pakistan. Critics of every persuasion, even those who liked the book, thought it was going too far in suggesting that the state could disintegrate, but a few years later that is exactly what happened. Just over a decade later I wrote *Can Pakistan Survive?* The question mark was not unimportant but nonetheless struck a raw nerve in General Zia's Pakistan, where to even pose the question was unacceptable. The general himself was extremely angry about its publication, as were sections of the bureaucracy, willing instruments of every despotism. Zia attacked both me and the book at a press conference in India, which was helpful and much appreciated by the publisher's sales department. That book too was banned, but to my delight was shamelessly pirated in many editions in Pakistan. They don't ban books anymore, or at least not recently, which is a relief and a small step forward.

When I left in 1963, the country consisted of West and East Pakistan. Eight years later the East defected and became Bangladesh. The population of the Western wing was then 40–45 million. It has grown phenomenally ever since and is now approaching the 200 million mark. The under-thirties constitute a majority.

This book centers on the long duel between a U.S.-backed politico-military elite and the citizens of the country. In earlier years the State Department would provide the seconds for the duel, but with U.S.

troops now in neighboring Afghanistan and U.S. bombs falling on homes inside Pakistan, the conflict is assuming a more direct form. Were it to proceed further, as some have been arguing in Washington, there is a distinct possibility that serious cracks would threaten the much-vaunted unity of the Pakistan military high command. The relationship with Washington, always controversial in the country, now threatens the Pakistan army. Political commentators in the United States together with a cabal of mimics in Pakistan regularly suggest that an Islamist revolution is incubating in a country that is seriously threatened by "jihadi terrorists." The only function of such a wild assertion is to invite a partial U.S. occupation and make the jihadi takeover a self-fulfilling prophecy.

The most important aspect of the duel is not the highly publicized conflict in Waziristan, but the divide between the majority of the people and their corrupt, uncaring rulers. This duel is often fought without weapons, sometimes in the mind, but it never goes away. An important reason for the deep hostility to the United States has little to do with religion, but is based on the knowledge that Washington has backed every military dictator who has squatted on top of the country. With Pakistan once again a strategic asset, the fear is that Washington will do so again, since it regards the military as the only functioning institution in the country, without showing any signs of comprehension as to why this is the case. This book might help in this regard.

What explains my continuing interest in Pakistan? I was born and educated there. Most of my family still lives there, and in periods when I haven't been banned from entering the country, I visit regularly. I enjoy running into old friends and acquaintances, especially now that most of them have retired from important positions and can speak openly and laugh again. I never feel alone in Pakistan. Something of me stayed behind in the soil and the trees and the people so even in bad times I am welcome.

I love the mountains. At least they can't be skyscrapered and forced to look like Dubai. Palm trees, Gulf kitsch, and the Himalayas don't mix, not that it prevents some from trying. The cityscapes are something else. They have greatly changed over the years; new unplanned and poorly designed buildings have wrecked most of the larger towns.

In Islamabad, the capital, one of the U.S. architects who built the city in the late sixties, Edward Stone, was unhappy with the site because it sat on a geological fault line and had weak soil. He advised that no building higher than three stories should ever be built there. He was ignored by the military dictator of the day. When a massive earthquake hit the country in 2005, buildings trembled all over Islamabad. I was there during the aftershocks, which were bad enough.

It was not only the earthquake that hurt Pakistan. This latest tragedy brought other wounds to the surface. A deeper and darker malaise, barely noticed by the elite and taken for granted by most citizens, had infected the country and was now publicly visible. The earthquake that killed tens of thousands of people shone a light on a country tainted by corrupted bureaucrats, army officers, and politicians, by governments rotten to the core, by protected mafias, and by the bloated profits of the heroin industry and the arms trade. Add to this the brutal hypocrisy of the Islamist parties, which exploit the state religion, and the picture is complete. Many ordinary people on the street, unsurprised by tales of privilege and graft, viewed the disaster in this context. At a state school in Lahore, students collecting toys for the children who'd survived the tragedy were asked whom they would like to address them. They voted unanimously against any politician, army officer, or civilian bureaucrat. They wanted a doctor.

None of this, of course, explains the urge to keep writing about a country. The reason is simple. However much I despise the callousness, corruption, and narcissism of a degenerate ruling elite, I have never allowed that to define my attitude toward the country. I have always harbored a deep respect and affection for the common people, whose instincts and intelligence, despite high levels of illiteracy, consistently display a much sounder appreciation of what the country requires than those who have lorded it over them since 1947. Any independent-minded Pakistani journalist or writer will confirm this view.

The people cannot be blamed for the tragedies that have afflicted their country. They are not to blame for the spirit of hopelessness and inescapable bondage that sometimes overcomes them. The surprise is that more of them don't turn to extremist religious groups, but they have generally remained stubbornly aloof from all that, which is highlighted

in every election, including the latest, held in February 2008. Given the
chance, they vote in large majorities for those who promise social change
and reforms and against those in power. They are always disappointed.

COLIN ROBINSON, my long-standing editor, first at Verso, later at the
New Press, and now at Scribner, was strongly convinced that I should
write this book long before I was. His persistence paid off. His instincts
were better than mine. As I was working on the book, Mary-Kay
Wilmers, stern janitor of the *London Review of Books,* plucked a lengthy
extract from the work-in-progress on Benazir Bhutto's return home. It
was, as readers will discover, sharply critical. Two weeks after I delivered
it, as I was working on this manuscript, Bhutto was assassinated. Sentiment dictated I soften the prose, but despite my sadness and anger at
her death, I resisted. As the German writer Lessing once remarked,
"The man who presents truth in all sorts of masks and disguises may
be her pander, but never her lover." And truth usually visits Pakistan in
whispers. We owe it to the people to speak our minds. The death of
Benazir, whom I knew well over many years, was undoubtedly tragic.
But not sufficient reason to change my assessment. That she handed
over her party to her husband till her son came of age was a sad reflection on the state of democratic politics in Pakistan and confirmed my
judgment. The country needs a break from uniforms and dynasties.

My thanks are due to numerous people in Pakistan from all walks
of life, from peasants and trade unionists to generals, civil servants, and
old friends, who spoke without inhibition during my trips over the last
few years. Naming them would not necessarily be construed as friendly.
Thanks also, as always, to Susan Watkins, my companion for almost
three decades, a friendly but firm editor of the *New Left Review,* as many
contributors (myself included) have discovered.

When I began to write this book a London friend asked, "Isn't it
reckless to start a book while the dice is still in the air?" If I waited for
the dice to fall, I would never have written anything on Pakistan.

TARIQ ALI
APRIL 5, 2008

The Duel

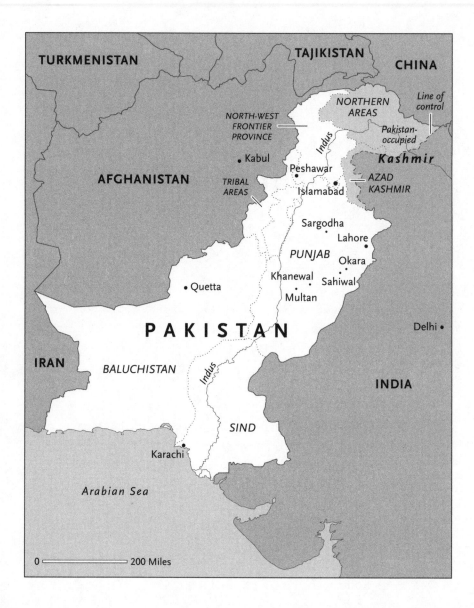

1

PAKISTAN AT SIXTY

A Conflagration of Despair

THE TWENTIETH CENTURY WAS NOT KIND TO PAKISTAN. THE LAST three decades, in particular, had witnessed a shallow and fading state gradually being reduced to the level of a stagnant and treacherous swamp. Business, official and unofficial, flourished at various points, but without the aid of education, technology, or science. A tiny number of people acquired gigantic fortunes, and the opening of a Porsche showroom in Islamabad in 2005 was greeted with loud hurrahs and celebrated as one indicator among others of a country that had, at long last, achieved modernity. What was forgotten were the latest malnutrition statistics that revealed a startling fact: the height of the average citizen was on the decline. According to the latest United Nations Population Fund figures, 60 percent of children under five were moderately or severely stunted.

Few among the rich cared about the underprivileged. The needs of ordinary people, their tattered lives, the retreat to religion, a thriving black market, armed clashes between different Muslim factions, war on the western frontier, and assassination of political leaders—none of this affected the rich too much. The thunder of money drowned out all other noises. Most of the mainstream political parties, like their Western cousins, no longer subscribed to programs rooted in ideology, but instead became dependent on cronyism, clientilism, and soulless followers. The organizational goal has become strictly personal: sinecures, money, power, and unquestioning obedience to the leader or, in some cases, to the army as collective leader. Notables in each party are hostile to every genuine talent. Political positions as well as parliamentary seats are rarely determined on merit. A pure character or a sharp intellect is virtually a disqualification.

When an individual turns sixty s/he gazes in the mirror and is either pleased or filled with discomfort. It's a great pity that a country cannot view itself in similar fashion. It becomes necessary for someone else—artist, poet, filmmaker, or writer—to become the mirror.

The sixtieth anniversary year of Pakistan, 2007, when power appeared to be draining away from the dictator, seemed a good moment to observe the country firsthand. The cities of the plain are best avoided in August, when the rains come and transform them into a huge steam bath. When I lived there, we usually fled to the mountains, where the Himalayan breezes keep the atmosphere permanently refreshed. In 2007 I stayed put. The monsoon season can be hazardous but needs to be experienced once in a while, simply to access the old memory bank. The real killer is a debilitating humidity. Relief arrives in short bursts: a sudden stillness followed by the darkening of the sky, thunderclaps sounding like distant bombs, then the hard rain. Rivers and tributaries quickly overflow. Flash floods make cities impassable. Sewage runs through slums and wealthier neighborhoods alike. Stench transcends class barriers, and even those accustomed to leaping from air-conditioned rooms to air-conditioned cars can't completely escape the smell.

The contrast between climate and the hopeless world of official politics could not be more striking. The latter is a desert. The reliction is complete. Not even an imaginary oasis in sight. Popular disillusionment and resentment is widespread. The large hoardings promoting the cult of the Big Leader (General Musharraf)/Small Leader (provincial shadows with no personality of their own) have assumed a nauseating and nightmarish quality. One of the older sources of official legitimacy—the cultivation of anti-Indian/anti-Hindu fervor—has also run dry. August 14, the country's red-letter day marking its independence, is even more artificial and irritating than before. A cacophony of meaningless slogans impress nobody, as countless clichés of chauvinistic self-adulation in newspaper supplements compete for space with stale photographs of the country's founder, Mohammed Ali Jinnah, and the eternal poet laureate, Allama Iqbal, that have been seen on hundreds of previous occasions. Add to this banal panel discussions in the videosphere, all reminding us of what Jinnah had said or not said. As ever, this is accompanied by a great deal of whinging about how the perfidious Lord Mountbatten and his "promiscuous" wife, Edwina (her love affair with Indian leader Jawaharlal Nehru is treated as a political event by Pakistani blowhards), had favored India when it came to a division of the spoils. It's true, but who cares now? The odd couple can't be blamed for the wreck that the country has become. In private, of course, there is much more soul-searching, and one often hears a surprising collection of people who now feel the state should never have been founded.

Several years after the breakup of the country in 1971, I wrote a book called *Can Pakistan Survive?* It was publicly denounced and banned by the dictator of the day, General Zia-ul-Haq, the worst ever in the country's history. Under his watch the country was heavily "Islamized," its political culture brutalized with dissidents flogged in public. His ghastly legacy appears to have left a permanent mark. My book was pirated in many editions and, as I was later told, read carefully by a number of generals. In it I argued that if the state carried on in the same old way, some of the minority provinces left behind might also defect, leaving the Punjab alone, strutting like a cock on a dunghill. Many who bitterly denounced me as a traitor and renegade are now asking the same question. It's too late for regrets, I tell them. The country is here to stay. It's not the mystical "ideology of Pakistan" or even religion that guarantees its survival, but two other factors: its nuclear capacity and the support it receives from Washington. Were the latter to decide that Pakistan needed a soft balkanization—for instance, the detachment of the North-West Frontier Province and its merger with a NATO-occupied Afghanistan—then China might feel obliged to step in to preserve the existing state. One of the basic contradictions confronting the country has become even more pronounced: thousands of villages and slums remain without electricity or running water. The wooden plow coexists with the atomic pile. This is the real scandal.

On the country's sixtieth birthday (as on its twentieth and fortieth anniversaries) an embattled military regime was fighting for its survival: an external war was being waged on its western frontier, while at home it was being tormented by jihadis, lawyers, and judges. None of this seemed to make much impact on the young daredevils in Lahore, who were determined to commemorate the day in their own fashion. Early in the morning, young males on motorbikes, bull and bullfighter in one, took over the streets to embark on what has become an annual suicide race. As if the only thing worth celebrating is their right to die. Only five managed it in 2007, a much lower figure than in previous years. Maybe this is a rational way to mark a conflict in which more than a million people hacked each other to death as the decaying British Empire prepared to scuttle off home.

Meanwhile another uniformed despot was taking the salute at a military parade in Islamabad to mark Independence Day, mouthing a bad speech written by a bored bureaucrat that failed to stifle the yawns of the surrounding sycophants. Even the F-16s in proud formation failed to excite the audience. Flags were waved by schoolchildren, a band played the national anthem, the whole show was broadcast live, then it was over.

The West prefers to view Pakistan through a single optic. European and North American papers give the impression that the main, if not the only, problem confronting Pakistan is the power of the bearded fanatics skulking in the Hindu Kush, who, as the papers see it, are on the verge of taking over the country. In this account, all that has stopped a jihadi finger from finding its way to the nuclear trigger has been General Musharraf. It was already clear in 2007 that he might drown in a sea of troubles, and so the helpful U.S. State Department pushed out an overinflated life raft in the shape of Benazir Bhutto. But what, some of us were asking months before the tragedy of her assassination in December 2007, if they were to sink together?

In fact, the threat of a jihadi takeover of Pakistan is remote. There is no possibility of a coup by religious extremists unless the army wants one, as in the 1980s, when General Zia-ul-Haq handed over the Ministries of Education and Information to the Jamaat-e-Islami, with dire results: Islamist gangs extinguished all democratic opposition on the campuses, and Jamaati propagandists became embedded in the media. Serious problems confront Pakistan, but these are usually ignored in Washington, by both the administration and the financial institutions. The lack of a basic social infrastructure encourages hopelessness and despair, but only a tiny minority turns to armed jihad.

During periods of military rule in Pakistan three groups get together: military leaders, a corrupt claque of fixer-politicians, and businessmen eyeing juicy contracts or state-owned land. Each is by now sufficiently versed in deception and well trained in concealing petty rivalries and jealousies for the sake of the greater bad. The bond that unites them is money and the primitive accumulation of property in town and country. Politicians ill-favored by the military wonder what they've done wrong and queue up to correct misunderstandings and win acceptance. The country's ruling elite has spent the last sixty years defending its ill-gotten wealth and privilege, and the Supreme Leader (uniformed or not) is invariably intoxicated by their flattery.

What of the official opposition? Alas, the system specializes in producing MNAs (Members of the National Assembly) who, in the main, are always on the lookout for ready cash. Brutal and coarse with raucous voices and a sly cunning, they're experts in cultivating paymasters who become dependent on them. They would be intensely comic figures were they not so dangerous: silkily affectionate when their needs are met, merciless when frustrated. What have the people done to deserve this?

Corruption envelops Pakistan like a sheet of water. The late Benazir Bhutto and her widower, Asif Ali Zardari, had, after two terms in office, accumulated assets of $1.5 billion. The twice prime minister Nawaz Sharif and his brother, with their intimate knowledge of the business cycle, probably netted double that amount. Given the inspiration from above, lesser politicians, bureaucrats on every level, and their counterparts in the armed services have had little trouble in building their own piles. The poor bear the burden, but the middle classes are also affected. Lawyers, doctors, teachers, small businessmen, and traders are crippled by a system in which patronage and bribery are trump cards. Some escape—twenty thousand Pakistani doctors are working in the United States alone—but others come to terms with the system and accept compromises that make them deeply cynical about themselves and everyone else.

MEANWHILE THE ISLAMISTS, while far removed from state power, are busy picking up supporters. The persistent and ruthless missionaries of Tablighi Jamaat (TJ) are especially effective. The name *Tabligh* means the "propagation of true Islam," and the sect has many similarities with born-again Christian fundamentalists in the United States. Sinners from every social group, desperate for purification, queue to join. TJ headquarters in Pakistan are situated in a large mission in Raiwind. Once a tiny village surrounded by fields of wheat, corn, and mustard seed, it is now a fashionable suburb of Lahore, where the Sharif brothers built a Gulf-style palace when they were in power in the 1990s. The TJ was founded in the 1920s by Maulana Ilyas, a cleric who trained at the orthodox Sunni seminary in Deoband, in Uttar Pradesh. At first, its missionaries were concentrated in northern India, but today large groups are in North America and Western Europe. The TJ hopes to get planning permission to build a mosque in East London next to the site of the 2012 Olympic Games. It would be the largest mosque in Europe. In Pakistan, TJ influence is widespread. Penetrating the national cricket team and recruiting stars has been its most conspicuous success: Inzamam-ul-Haq and Mohammad Yousuf are activists for the cause at home, while Mushtaq Ahmed works hard in their interest in Britain. Another triumph was the post-9/11 recruitment of Junaid Jamshed, the charismatic lead singer of Pakistan's first successful pop group, Vital Signs. He renounced his past and now sings only devotional songs—*naats*.

The Tablighis stress their nonviolence and insist they are merely broadcasting the true faith to help people find the correct path in life. This may be so, but it is clear that some younger male recruits, bored with all the dogma, ceremonies, and ritual, are more interested in getting their hands on a Kalashnikov. Many commentators believe that the Tablighi missionary camps are fertile recruiting grounds for armed groups active on the western frontier and in Kashmir.

The establishment has been slow to challenge the interpretation of Islam put forward by groups such as Tablighi. It is not groups of this sort that threaten Musharraf's rule. It is the legal profession that has fought the regime to a virtual standstill. On March 9, 2007, Musharraf suspended Iftikhar Muhammad Chaudhry, the chief justice of the Supreme Court, pending an investigation. The accusations against Chaudhry were contained in a letter from Naeem Bokhari, a pro-government lawyer. Curiously, the letter was widely circulated—I received a copy via e-mail. I wondered whether something was afoot, but decided the letter was just sour grapes. Not so: it soon became clear that it was part of a plan. The letter began with a few personal complaints before extravagant rhetoric took over:

> My Lord, the dignity of lawyers is consistently being violated by you. We are treated harshly, rudely, brusquely and nastily. We are not heard. We are not allowed to present our case. There is little scope for advocacy. The words used in the Bar Room for Court No. 1 are "the slaughter house." We are cowed down by aggression from the Bench, led by you. All we receive from you is arrogance, aggression and belligerence.

The following passage should have alerted me to what was really going on:

> I am pained at the wide publicity to cases taken up by My Lord in the Supreme Court under the banner of Fundamental Rights. The proceedings before the Supreme Court can conveniently and easily be referred to the District and Sessions Judges. I am further pained by the media coverage of the Supreme Court on the recovery of an [abducted] female. In the Bar Room, this is referred to as a "media circus."

Chief Justice Chaudhry was beginning to embarrass the regime. He had found against the government on a number of key issues, including the rushed privatization of the Pakistan Steel Mills in Karachi, a pet project of the then prime minister, Shaukat "Shortcut" Aziz. The case was reminiscent of Yeltsin's Russia. Economists had estimated that the industry was worth $5 billion. Seventy-five percent of the shares were sold for $362 million in a thirty-minute auction to a friendly consortium consisting of Arif Habib Securities (Pakistan), al-Tuwairqi (Saudi Arabia), and the Magnitogorsk Iron & Steel Works Open JSC (Russia). The privatization wasn't popular with the military, and the retiring chairman, Haq Nawaz Akhtar, complained that "the plant could have fetched more money if it were sold as scrap." The general perception was that the president and the prime minister had helped out their friends. A frequenter of the stock exchange told me in Karachi that Arif Habib Securities, which now owns 20 percent of Pakistan Steel Mills, was set up as a front company for Shaukat Aziz. Tuwairqi, the Saudi steel giant, acquired 40 percent. Musharraf is reportedly on close terms with this company and had previously turned up to open a steel plant set up by the group on 220 acres of land rented from the adjoining Pakistan Steel Mills. Now they have a stake in the whole thing.

After the Supreme Court insisted that "disappeared" political activists be produced in court and refused to dismiss rape cases, some in Islamabad worried that the chief justice might even declare the military presidency unconstitutional. Paranoia set in. Measures had to be taken. The general and his cabinet decided to frighten Chaudhry by suspending him. On March 9, 2007, the chief justice was arrested and kept in solitary confinement for several hours, manhandled by intelligence operatives, and traduced on state television. But instead of caving in and accepting a generous resignation settlement, the judge insisted on defending himself, triggering a remarkable movement in defense of an independent judiciary. This was surprising. Pakistani judges are notoriously conservative and have legitimized every coup with a bogus "doctrine of necessity" ruling. When Musharraf took over, a handful of judges refused to swear an oath of loyalty and resigned, but not Chaudhry, who was elevated to the Supreme Court a year later, in January 2000, and became chief justice in 2005. Prior to this appointment, little or nothing indicated that he was a judicial activist.

When I visited Pakistan in April 2007, the protests were getting bigger every day. Initially confined to the country's eighty thousand lawyers and several dozen judges, unrest soon spread beyond them, which was again unusual in a country whose people have become increasingly alienated from elite rule. But the lawyers were marching in defense of the constitutional separation of powers. Street demonstrations occurred in virtually every city, and the sight of men in black being confronted by cordons of armed policemen became commonplace. The independent TV stations—Geo, Indus, Aaj, and others—provided daily coverage of events. Musharraf and his ministers were subjected to sharp and critical interviews that must have made the president yearn for the comparative safety of CNN and BBC World. The general would regularly upbraid journalists for not treating him with the same deference shown to Bush and European leaders by Western networks.

This delightfully old-fashioned struggle involved neither money nor religion, but principle. Careerists from the opposition (some of whom had organized thuggish assaults on the Supreme Court when in power) tried to make the cause their own. "Don't imagine they've all suddenly changed," Abid Hasan Manto, one of the country's most respected lawyers, told me. "They're cut from the same cloth as the rest of the elite. On the other hand, when the time comes, almost anything can act as a spark."

Most people in the Islamabad bureaucracy soon recognized that they had made a gigantic blunder in arresting Chaudhry. But as often happens in a crisis, instead of acknowledging this and moving to correct it, the perpetrators decided on a show of strength. The first targets were independent TV channels. In Karachi and other cities in the south, three channels suddenly went dark as they were screening reports on the demonstrations. There was popular outrage. On May 5 Chaudhry drove from Islamabad to give a speech in Lahore, stopping at every town en route to meet supporters; it took twenty-six hours to complete a journey that normally takes three or four. In Islamabad, Musharraf plotted a counterstrike.

The judge was due to visit Karachi, the country's largest city, a sprawling, anarchic mass of 15 million people, on May 12. Political power in Karachi rests in the hands of the MQM (Muttahida Qaumi Movement/United National Movement), an unsavory outfit created in 1984 during Zia's dictatorship. It began life in 1978 as a student group set up by Altaf Hussain with a membership restricted to Urdu-speaking students in the Sind. These were the children of Muslim refugees who had fled India in 1947 and sought a new home in Pakistan. Many remained poor and suffered from job discrimination. The new organization played on these resentments and gave them voice, but soon acquired notoriety for its involvement in protection rackets and other kinds of violence. It has supported Musharraf loyally through every crisis.

Its leader, Altaf Hussain, fled the country in the 1990s to avoid prosecution. He was given asylum in Britain and now guides the movement from a safe perch in London, fearful of retribution from his many opponents were he to return. In a video address to his followers in Karachi just prior to Chaudhry's arrival, he said, "If conspiracies are hatched to end the present democratically elected government, then each and every worker of MQM . . . will stand firm and defend the democratic government." On Islamabad's instructions, the MQM leaders decided to prevent the judge from leaving the airport and addressing his supporters, who were assaulted in different parts of the city. Almost fifty people were killed. After footage of the violence was screened on Aaj TV, the station was attacked by armed MQM volunteers, who shot at the building for six whole hours and set cars in the parking lot on fire.

Senior police officers, the chief minister, and the governor all failed to intervene, and a successful general strike followed, which further isolated the regime. A devastating report, *Carnage in Karachi,* published in August 2007 by the Human Rights Commission of Pakistan, confirmed in great detail what everyone already knew: the police and army had been ordered to stand by while armed MQM members went on the rampage:

> . . . a matter of grave concern from the perspective of the institutional integrity of the state is the virtual withdrawal of the state's security apparatus for almost 20 hours and the actual takeover of the city by armed cadres of more than one political party. The spectacle of a *disarmed* police force operating on the direction of *armed* cadres was highly disturbing, especially since key officers of the state were reduced to expressing their helplessness.

Musharraf, trying desperately to keep a grip on the country, was now confronted with the possibility that a popular movement in defense of the chief justice might become uncontrollable, especially if the events in Karachi were repeated elsewhere. Fearful of the consequences of further repression, he had little alternative but to sound a retreat. The chief justice's appeal against his suspension was finally admitted and heard by the Supreme Court. On July 20 a unanimous decision reinstated him, and shamefaced government lawyers were seen leaving the precincts in a hurry. A reinvigorated court got down to business. Hafiz Abdul Basit was a "disappeared" prisoner arrested for "terrorism" without any specific charge. The chief justice summoned Tariq Pervez, the director general of Pakistan's Federal Investigation Agency, and asked him politely where the prisoner was being kept. Pervez replied that he had no idea and had never even heard of Basit. The chief justice instructed the police chief to produce Basit in court within forty-eight hours: "Either produce the detainee or get ready to go to jail." Two days later Basit was produced and then released, after the police failed to present any substantial evidence against him. Washington and London were not happy. They were convinced that Basit was a terrorist who should have been kept in prison indefinitely, as he certainly would have been in Britain or the United States.

The Supreme Court then decided to consider six petitions challenging Musharraf's decision to contest the presidency without relinquishing his command of the army. Even though parliament had passed the President to Hold Another Office Act in 2004 to circumvent a challenge to Musharraf's decision to stay on as army chief while president, the Supreme Court had accepted an appeal against this decision, saying that the language of the amended law was not in conformity with the constitution. There was also the question of term limits: Pakistan's constitution permits the president only two terms in office. Musharraf had assumed the presidency in June 2001. This was followed by a referendum in 2002 that he claimed was a "democratic mandate" and therefore, his opponents argued, constituted a second term. An added problem was that he was over sixty and, according to government rules, should therefore have retired as chief of army staff. Having done so, he would then have faced a two-year bar on any government employee seeking elected office. Unsurprisingly, there was much nervousness in Islamabad. The president's supporters threatened dire consequences if the Court ruled against him. But to declare a state of emergency would have required the support of the army, and at that stage, soon after the Karachi killings, informal soundings had revealed a reluctance to intervene on the part of the generals. Their polite excuse at the time was that they were too heavily committed to the "war on terror" to be able to devote resources to preserve law and order in the cities. They would later, with a bit of encouragement from the U.S. embassy, change their minds.

As THE JUDICIAL crisis temporarily ended, a more somber one loomed. Most of today's jihadi groups are the mongrel offspring of Pakistani and Western intelligence outfits, born in the 1980s when General Zia was in power and waging the West's war against the godless Russians, who were then occupying Afghanistan. It was then that state patronage of Islamist groups began. One beneficiary was the cleric Maulana Abdullah, who was allotted land to build a madrassa in the heart of Islamabad, not far from the government buildings. Soon the area was increased so that two separate facilities (for male and female students) could be constructed, together with an enlarged Lal Masjid, or Red Mosque. State money was provided for all this, and the government was the technical owner of the property.

During the 1980s and 1990s this complex became a transit camp for young jihadis on their way to fight in Afghanistan and, later, Kashmir. Abdullah made no secret of his beliefs. He was sympathetic to the Saudi Wahhabi interpretation of Islam and during the Iraq-Iran war was only too happy to encourage the killing of Shia "heretics" in Pakistan. Shia constitute 20 percent of the Muslim population in Pakistan, and prior to Zia's dictatorship there was little hostility between them and the majority of the Sunnis. Abdullah's patronage of ultrasectarian, anti-Shia terror groups led to his own assassination in October 1998. Members of a rival Muslim faction killed him soon after he had finished praying in his own mosque.

His sons, Abdul Rashid Ghazi and Abdul Aziz, then took control of the mosque and religious schools. The government agreed that Aziz would lead the Friday congregation. His sermons were often supportive of Al Qaeda, though he was more careful about his language after 9/11. Senior civil servants and military officers often attended Friday prayers. The better-educated and soft-spoken Rashid, with his lean, haggard face and ragged beard, was left to act as spin doctor and was effective in charming visiting foreign and local journalists.

But after November 2004, when the army, under heavy U.S. pressure, launched an offensive in the tribal areas bordering Afghanistan, relations between the brothers and the government became tense. Aziz in particular was livid. When, according to Rashid, "a retired colonel of the Pakistan army approached us with a written request for a fatwa clarifying the Sharia perspective on the army waging a war on the tribal people," Aziz did not waste any time. He issued a fatwa declaring that the killing of its own people by a Muslim army is *haram* (forbidden), "that any army official killed during the operation should not be given a Muslim burial," and that "the militants who die while fighting the Pakistan army are martyrs." Within days of its publication the fatwa had been publicly endorsed by almost five hundred "religious scholars." Despite heavy pressure from the mosque's patrons in the ISI (Inter-Services Intelligence), Pakistan's military intelligence, the brothers refused to withdraw it. The government response was surprisingly muted. Aziz's official status as the mosque's imam was ended and an arrest warrant issued against him, but it was never served, and the brothers were allowed to carry on as usual. Perhaps the ISI thought they might still prove useful.

Set up in 1948 with officers of the three services of the Pakistan military, the ISI was originally a routine intelligence directorate specializing in the gathering and analysis of information and focused largely on India and local "Communist subversion." Its size and budget grew at a phenomenal rate during the first Afghan war against the Soviet Union. It worked closely with U.S., French, and British intelligence services during that period and, as described later in this book, played a central role in arming and training the mujahideen and, later, infiltrating the Taliban into Afghanistan. With a level of autonomy no greater than that allowed the CIA or the DIA in the United States, the ISI operated throughout with the official approval of the military high command.

Earlier in 2004 the government had claimed to have uncovered a terrorist plot to bomb military installations, including the GHQ (general headquarters) in Rawalpindi and state buildings in Islamabad, on August 14. Machine guns and explosives were found in Abdul Rashid Ghazi's car. New warrants were issued against the brothers and they were arrested. At this point the religious affairs minister, Ijaz-ul-Haq, General Zia's son, persuaded his colleagues to pardon the clerics in return for a written apology pledging that they wouldn't become involved in the armed struggle. Rashid claimed the whole plot had been scripted to please the West and in a newspaper article asked the religious affairs minister to provide proof that the minister had supposedly asked for the undertaking. There was no response.

In January 2007, the brothers decided to shift their focus from foreign to domestic policy and demanded an immediate implementation of Sharia law. Until then they had been content to denounce U.S. policies in the Muslim world and America's local point man, Musharraf, for helping dismantle the Taliban government in Afghanistan. They did not publicly support the three attempts that had recently been made on Musharraf's life, but it was hardly a secret that they regretted his survival. The statement they issued in January was intended as an open provocation to the regime. Aziz spelled out his program: "We will never permit dance and music in Pakistan. All those interested in such activities should shift to India. We are tired of waiting. It is Sharia or martyrdom." They felt threatened by the government's demolition of two mosques that had been built illegally on public land. When they received notices announcing the demolition of parts of the Red Mosque and the women's seminary, the brothers dispatched dozens of women students in black burkas to occupy a children's library next to their seminary. The intelligence agencies appeared to be taken aback, but quickly negotiated an end to the occupation.

The brothers continued to test the authorities. Sharia was implemented in the gender-segregated madrassas (religious schools) housed in the mosque complex, and there was a public bonfire of books, CDs, and DVDs. Then the women from the madrassa directed their fire against Islamabad's upmarket brothels, targeting Aunty Shamim, a well-known procuress who provided "decent" girls for indecent purposes, and whose clients included the local great and good, a number of them moderate religious leaders. Aunty ran the brothel like an office: she kept office hours and shut up shop at midday on Friday so that clients could go to the nearest mosque, which was the Lal Masjid. The morality brigades raided the brothel and "freed" the women. Most of the girls were educated, some were single parents, others were widows, all were desperately short of funds. The office hours suited them. Aunty Shamim fled town, and her workers sought similar employment elsewhere, while the madrassa girls celebrated an easy victory.

Emboldened by their triumph, the brothers next decided to take on Islamabad's upmarket massage parlors, not all of which were sex joints, and some of which were staffed by Chinese citizens. Six Chinese women were abducted in late June and taken to the mosque. The Chinese ambassador was not pleased. He informed President Hu Jintao, who was even less pleased, and Beijing made it clear that it wanted its citizens freed without delay. Government fixers arrived at the mosque to plead the strategic importance of Sino-Pakistan relations, and the women were released. The massage industry promised that henceforth only men would massage other men. Honor was satisfied, even though the deal directly contradicted the Sharia, which usually decrees the death penalty for homosexuality. The liberal press depicted the antivice campaign as the Talibanization of Pakistan, which annoyed the Lal Masjid clerics. "Rudy Giuliani, when he became mayor of New York, closed the brothels," Rashid said. "Was that also Talibanization?" Rashid, were he alive, would have strongly supported the "resignation" of Governor Spitzer.

Angered and embarrassed by the kidnapping of the Chinese women, Musharraf demanded a resolution to the crisis. The Saudi ambassador to Pakistan, Ali Saeed Awadh Asseri, arrived at the mosque and spent ninety minutes with the brothers. They were welcoming but told him that all they wanted was the implementation of Saudi laws in Pakistan. Surely he agreed? The ambassador declined to meet the press after the visit, so his response remains unrecorded. His mediation a failure, Plan B was set in motion.

On July 3, the paramilitary Rangers began to lay barbed wire at the end of the street in front of the mosque. Some madrassa students opened fire, shot a Ranger dead, and for good measure torched the neighboring Environment Ministry. Security forces responded the same night with tear gas and machine guns. The next morning the government declared a curfew in the area, and a weeklong siege of the mosque began, with television networks beaming images across the world. Rashid, infatuated with publicity, must have been pleased. The brothers thought that keeping women and children hostage inside the compound might save them. But some were released and Aziz was arrested as he tried to escape in a burka, only to be released quietly a week later and allowed to return to his village.

On July 10, paratroopers finally stormed the complex. Rashid and at least a hundred others died in the ensuing clashes. Eleven soldiers were also killed and more than forty wounded. Several police stations were attacked, and ominous complaints came from the tribal areas. Maulana Faqir Mohammed, a leading Taliban supporter, told thousands of armed tribesmen, "We beg Allah to destroy Musharraf, and we will seek revenge for the Lal Masjid atrocities." This view was reiterated by Osama bin Laden, who declared Musharraf an "infidel" and said that "removing him is now obligatory for Muslims."

I was in Pakistan in September 2007 when suicide bombers hit military targets, among them a bus carrying ISI employees, to avenge Rashid's death. But in the country as a whole the reaction was muted. The leaders of the MMA (Muttahida Majlis-e-Amal), a coalition of religious parties that governed the Frontier Province and shares power in Baluchistan, made ugly public statements, but took no action. Only a thousand people marched in the demonstration called in the provincial capital, Peshawar, the day after the deaths. This was the largest protest march, and even here the mood was subdued. There was no shrill glorification of the martyrs. The contrast with the campaign to reinstate the chief justice could not have been more pronounced. Three weeks later, more than one hundred thousand people gathered in the Punjabi city of Kasur to observe the 250th anniversary of the death of the great seventeenth-century poet Bulleh Shah, one in a distinguished line of Sufi poets who promoted skepticism, denounced organized religion, and avoided all forms of orthodoxy. For Bulleh Shah a mullah should be compared to a barking dog or a crowing cock. In response to a question from a believer as to his own religious identity, the poet replied:

Who knows what I am,
Neither a believer in the mosque,
Nor an unbeliever worshipping clay,
Neither Moses nor Pharaoh,
Neither sinner nor saint;
Who knows what I am . . .

That this and similar poems are regularly performed throughout Pakistan is one indication that jihadis are not popular in most of the country. Nor is the government. The mosque episode raised several important questions that remain unanswered. Why did the government not act in January when the vigilantes first poured out? How did the clerics accumulate such a large store of weapons without the knowledge of the government? Was the ISI aware that the mosque concealed an arsenal? If so, why did they keep it quiet? What were the relations between the clerics and government agencies? Why was Aziz released and allowed to return to his village without being charged?

I wondered if I might find answers to these questions in Peshawar, the capital of the North-West Frontier Province, a few miles from the Khyber Pass and Afghanistan. I had not visited the city for over a quarter of a century, not since it had become the headquarters of the anti-Soviet jihad in the 1980s and its governor, a close colleague of General Zia's, had defended the heroin trade. On that occasion in 1973 I had crossed the Afghan border and returned without a passport, just to see if it could still be done. Pleased with my success I then took a bus to Rawalpindi. I still remember the thrill of catching sight of a bloodred sunset filling the sky as we crossed the river Indus on the bridge at Attock.

The old bridge always brings back memories of childhood and youth. The sight of the turbulent waters below helps recall the history that had, in the shape of successive conquerors from Europe and Central Asia, marched through here on its way south and long before Alexander. How many soldiers had died making the crossing on makeshift rafts? The Mogul emperor Akbar had built a giant fort just upstream from where the Kabul River merged noisily with its more famous cousin. Its strategic aim was to house a garrison that could ward off invaders and crush local rebellions and, no doubt, tax merchants.

Thirty-four years later, on my way by car from Islamabad, I could not suppress my excitement. I stopped the car to take a look at the river and the fort above. The fort is now a notorious political prison, a torture center used by successive Pakistan governments and not just the military kind. I tried but could not see the two black rocks that, as I remembered, jutted from the river just below the fort. Where were they? Perhaps they could only be seen from the old nineteenth-century bridge, a masterpiece of Victorian engineering, surrounded by Mogul ruins, including an old gravestone labeled "prostitute's tomb" (a punishment inflicted by a queen on her husband's favorite mistress) that used to make us giggle as children.

The two rocks had been named after two brothers, Kamal-ud-Din and Jamal-ud-Din, who were flung down from their peak into the river below on the orders of the great Mogul emperor. Akbar's toleration of dissent has been greatly exaggerated. Its true that while the Catholic Inquisition was sowing terror in Europe, Akbar, himself a Muslim, ruled that "anyone is to be allowed to go over to a religion that pleases him." The interreligious debates he organized in Agra included Hindus, Muslims, Christians, Parsis, Jains, Jews, and the atheists of the Carvaka school, who argued that Brahmans had established ceremonies for the dead only "as a means of livelihood" for themselves.

But Akbar sometimes flouted his own injunctions when his power was challenged. Hence his deep anger with the rebellious Pashtuns from Waziristan and their challenging philosophy. The brothers were members of a sixteenth-century Muslim sect, the Roshnais, "Enlightened Ones," founded by their father, Pir Roshan. They rejected all revealed religions and hence the Koran. They argued against the mediation of prophets or kings. The Creator was alone and each person should relate to Him as an individual.* Religion was a personal matter between Allah and a believer.

Akbar was busy trying to create his own synthetic religion as a way of bridging various confessional and class divides and uniting India. The persecution of this sect, however, was not the outcome of ideological

---

*Similar ideas were floating around Christian Europe at the time and were subsequently deployed by Oliver Cromwell to topple Charles I and execute him.

rivalry. The Enlightened Ones were popular among the peasantry in the region, and their approach to life was often used to justify rebellions against the central authority. The Mogul king, who founded the city of Peshawar as a military and trading base, regarded this as intolerable.

Peshawar, now a city of over 3 million, has trebled in size over the last thirty years. Most of its new inhabitants consist of three generations of refugees, a result of the interconnected Afghan wars unleashed by the big powers (the Soviet Union and the United States respectively) in the twentieth and twenty-first centuries. The colonial city built by the British was designed as a cantonment town, to house a garrison that protected the northwestern frontier of British India against czarist and Bolshevik intrigues. This function has been preserved and expanded.

Peshawar remains a border city, but it is not the case, as the *New York Times* reported on January 18, 2008, that "for centuries, fighting and lawlessness have been part of the fabric of this frontier town." This view is derived from the minstrel of the British Empire, Rudyard Kipling, whose descriptions were mistakenly read as history. In a dispatch from Peshawar, a location he characterized as "the city of evil countenances," to the *Civil and Military Gazette* in Lahore on March 28, 1885, hostility to the British presence was described as follows:

> Under the shop lights in front of the sweet-meat and *ghee* seller's booths, the press and dins of words is thickest. Faces of dogs, swine, weasels and goats, all the more hideous for being set on human bodies, and lighted with human intelligence, gather in front of the ring of lamp-light, where they may be studied for half-an-hour at a stretch. Pathans, Afridis, Logas, Kohistanis, Turcomans, and a hundred other varieties of the turbulent Afghan race, are gathered in the vast human menagerie between the Gate and the Ghor Kutri. As an Englishman passes, they will turn to scowl upon him, and in many cases to spit fluently to the ground after he has passed. One burly big-paunched ruffian, with shaven head and a neck creased and dimpled with rolls of fat, is specially zealous in this religious rite—contenting himself with no perfunctory performance, but with a wholesouled expectoration, that must be as refreshing to his comrades, as it is disgusting to the European, sir. . . . But he is only

one of twenty thousand. The main road teems with magnificent
scoundrels and handsome ruffians; all giving the on-looker the
impression of wild beasts held back from murder and violence, and
chafing against the restraint.

There was little trouble during the nineteenth and twentieth centuries, except when wars were being waged by the British Empire in
Afghanistan. Although the British, attempting to crush and defuse a
nationalist current demanding independence, had imposed military
rule and were administering heavy punishments for trivial offenses in
the frontier province, the largest movement during the twentieth century was explicitly peaceful. Ghaffar Khan and Dr. Khan Sahib, two
brothers from a landed family in Charsadda, decided to launch a political, nonviolent struggle against the British in 1930. The Redshirt
movement, as it became known (because of the color of the shirts worn
by its supporters rather than any other affinities; their inspiration was
Gandhi not Lenin), spread rapidly throughout the region. Ghaffar
Khan and his volunteers visited every single village to organize the peasants against the empire and branches of the movement emerged even
in the remotest village.

The British authorities, stung by the growth of support for this
organization, were determined it should be "nipped in the bud." This
led to the notorious massacre in the Qissa Khwani (Storytellers) bazaar
in 1930, when a thousand or so Redshirts who had gathered to welcome Congress leaders were informed that the authorities had refused
to let the leaders enter the province. The Congress held a mass meeting and called for an immediate boycott of British-owned shops. The
governor ordered the arrest of Ghaffar Khan and others under Section
144, a legal clause in the public-order ordinance prohibiting the assembly of more than four people in public spaces, a law still much used in
South Asia. The demonstrators refused to move, and troops opened
fire, killing two hundred activists. More people poured out onto the
streets, their numbers compelling the troops to withdraw. Peshawar was
under the control of its people for four whole days without any violence prior to the entry of British military reinforcements. The massacre and its aftermath were described by a colonial officer, Sir Herbert

Thompson, as a typical case of "a child astonished by its own tantrum, returning to the security of the nanny's hand."*

Despite the extensive use of policy spies and infiltrated agents, the British could not bring forward a single charge of violence against Ghaffar Khan and his supporters, but this did not prevent them from continually harassing, imprisoning, and maltreating the leaders and activists. The Qissa Khwani massacre increased support for the Redshirts, and because, despite his Muslim beliefs, Ghaffar Khan believed in a unified and secular India, he came to the attention of Mahatma Gandhi and Jawaharlal Nehru. The Redshirts formally applied to join the Congress Party and were admitted. The result was a Congress presence in the province that led to the party winning successive elections from 1937 onward. Nehru would later write in his autobiography:

> It was surprising how this Pathan accepted the idea of non-violence, far more so in theory than many of us. And it was because he believed in it that he managed to impress his people with the importance of remaining peaceful in spite of provocation. . . . [T]he self-discipline that the frontier people showed in 1930 and subsequent years has been something amazing.

This area with a large Muslim majority preferred to remain aloof from the Muslim League and the idea of Pakistan, though the League would acquire a base in the province with the help of the imperial bureaucracy and police force and a combination of chicanery and violence. The British, who had assiduously encouraged the division between the Hindu and Muslim communities, were confused and irritated by the Redshirts. In the work of another British colonial officer, Sir Olaf Caroe, this was expressed in the form of a reactionary mysticism. Caroe's generally interesting history of the Pashtun (Pathan to the colonists) people contains oddities such as "It is hard to see how the

---

*Quoted in *The Pathan Unarmed* by Mukulika Banerjee (Oxford, 2000). This work by an Indian scholar, the most comprehensive history of the Redshirt movement and its leaders, is ignored by most Pakistani historians and social anthropologists because it contradicts the founding myths of the country.

Pathan tradition could reconcile itself for long to Hindu leadership, by so many regarded as smooth-faced, pharisaical and double-dealing. . . . How then could he have associated himself with a party under Indian, even Brahmin, inspiration . . ." There is more nonsense along similar lines. Those Pashtuns who were not prepared to fall into line with the British were dealt with brutally.

A U.S. journalist who witnessed the conflict interviewed Mahatma Gandhi. "What," he asked the Indian leader, "do you think of Western civilization?" The old fox smiled. "It would be a good idea," he replied, the treatment of Pashtun nationalists foremost in his mind. British agents would bribe the tribes while their propagandists spread rumors that Ghaffar Khan, a pious Muslim, was a secret Brahman. Congress leaders were barred from visiting the province while all doors were opened for the pro-British Muslim League. That this special benevolence on the part of the British was repeatedly rejected by a majority of the Pashtuns is an indication of the strength of Ghaffar Khan's movement. His ideas of nonviolence and a unified, independent India went deep. It would take decades of bribery and repression (including after the birth of Pakistan) to wrench them out of the soil, with disastrous consequences.

An imperial stereotype of the "childlike" but "noble savage" Pathan pervades much of colonial literature, including Kipling's short stories and his repressed homoerotic novel *Kim*. Having convinced themselves that these ancient warrior tribes were incapable of rational thought and needed to be spoon-fed forever, the British were genuinely surprised when this turned out not to be the case. In colonial historiography, violence and Pashtun could never be opposites.

The tensions and violent undercurrents that mark Peshawar today have little to do with previous centuries, but are a direct result of the continuing wars in neighboring Afghanistan, whose impact on Pakistan, China, and the United States/European Union is discussed in a subsequent chapter. Pakistan's North-West Frontier Province (NWFP) is the only province named geographically and thus denied its ethnic Pashtun identity.

Since October 2002, the MMA, a united front consisting of the Jamaat-e-Islami (JI) and the Jamiat-Ulema-e-Islam (JUI), together with four minor religious sects, has governed here, though losing badly in 2008. Though it has at times dominated the NWFP, the Islamist coalition won only 15 percent of the national vote in 2002, their highest ever, but still far removed from winning power nationally through the ballot box. The two parties are different in character. Of the two parties, the JI was more rigid in its interpretation of religion. It had been founded in Lahore in 1941 as a riposte to the Muslim League and the Pakistan Resolution and was viewed by its founder, Abul Ala Maududi (1903–79), as a "counter-League." Maududi was highly regarded as a theologian, and his links with the Wahhabis of Saudi Arabia predated the formation of Pakistan. The JUI was based in the North-West Frontier and Baluchistan. Its leader, Mufti Mahmud (1919–80), was a wily political operator, capable of alliances with secular nationalists to further his aims. The origins of this group lay in the Deoband seminary that was regarded as the home of Sunni orthodoxy in prepartition India. Both parties saw the birth of Pakistan as a secular nationalist conspiracy against the "real truths of Islam."

The JI is probably the best-organized political grouping in the country. Its internal structure was modeled on that of traditional Communist parties, and it retains a cell structure in every major city to this day. The JUI was more traditional, confined to the border provinces, and dependent on kinship structures. During the Cold War the JI, through its close links with Saudi Arabia, was firmly committed to the West, while the JUI flirted with the pro-Soviet groups in Pakistan. Today both claim to be hostile to Washington, but the differences are largely tactical and local. Both parties would probably be prepared for a serious deal with Washington and, like the Muslim Brotherhood in Egypt, view how the pro-NATO Islamists run Turkey as a possible model for future relations. The notion that these are hard-core Islamists hell-bent on imposing a caliphate is frivolous. Prevented from any real autonomy in the socioeconomic sphere, they have chosen to assert their Islamist identity by agitating for the Sharia laws, targeting coeducational institutions such as the University of Peshawar (where gender relations have been relatively relaxed since the foundation of the country), painting out women on advertising billboards, threatening video shops, etc.

During a sixty-minute debate with a JI ideologue on CNBC (Pakistan) a few years ago, I asked why they were so obsessed with women. Why not leave them alone? Why try and obliterate their images? His reply was reminiscent of that of a radical feminist from the seventies (when campaigns against pornography and sex parlors were much in vogue): "We do not like women being treated as sex objects. Do you?" I admitted I didn't either, but surely painting over them was hardly a solution. And what about men? I inquired politely. Were they not sex objects as well? At this point the host of the show hurriedly moved on to safer territory. He assumed I was referring to male homosexuality, forbidden by the Koran, which is widespread throughout the country and has strong roots in the Frontier regions, which some trace back to Alexander's invasion and the Greeks that stayed behind. There are other and more mundane reasons. However, I was not merely referring to homosexuality but men as sex objects for women. Why should this be tolerated? I was hoping to move on and discuss the mushrooming of sex videos and porn since the MMA electoral triumph, but there was no more time.

The general disgust with traditional politics has created a moral vacuum, which is filled by pornography and religiosity of various sorts. In some areas religion and pornography go together: the highest sales of porn videos are in Peshawar and Quetta, strongholds of the religious parties. Taliban leaders in Pakistan target video shops, but the dealers merely go underground. Nor should it be imagined that the bulk of the porn comes from the West. There is a thriving clandestine industry in Pakistan, with its own local stars, male and female. Sexual frustration has the country in thrall.

To DISCUSS THE state of the NWFP, I met with a group of local intellectuals, journalists, and secular nationalist politicians, some of them heirs of the old Redshirt tradition even though the shirts are now somewhat soiled. Ghaffar Khan's son and grandson were infected with the disease that afflicts traditional Pakistani politicians, being bereft of principle or program, cutting deals with the military and the Muslim League to further Awami National Party (ANP) interests. We were meeting at the Ghaffar Khan Centre, which is both party headquarters and a library and meeting place. The discussion centered on the MMA, the Taliban, and the U.S./EU occupation of Afghanistan. The view here was that the MMA had only won because they were backed by the military and had equated a vote for them with a vote for the Koran. This was no doubt partially true, but left the tarnished record of the ANP's period in office out of the equation. Understandable enough given the location and circumstances, but something that needs to be addressed if they are to move forward again. This is the only secular force in the region with a sprinkling of cadres who are still capable of seeing the larger picture. They realize they need a strategic plan, and that continually shifting positions and political somersaults spell disaster. The written program of the party has not changed much over the years—land reforms, social justice, etc.—but the remoteness of all this from its practice has led to a great deal of cynicism. In addition, the party has now abandoned its anti-imperialist rhetoric and, like the Bhutto family's Pakistan Peoples Party (PPP), is banking its hopes on a prolonged U.S. presence in the region to get rid of its religious opponents.

Some of the key problems confronting the Frontier Province relate to neighboring Afghanistan. Afrasiab Khattak, the most intelligent leader of the ANP, believes that the worst period in the region's history began during General Zia's dictatorship, when the country was awash with heroin, Western and Mossad agents, and unlimited weaponry and cash to fight the Soviet troops then encamped in Afghanistan. This is true, but some of the principal leaders of the ANP, including Ajmal Khattak, wholeheartedly backed the Soviet intervention and settled down in Afghanistan for the duration. This was, alas, a common view of much of what passed for the left in Pakistan at that time. Some well-known Pakistani commentators who supported the U.S./NATO occupation in 2001 had reacted with a similar enthusiasm when Soviet troops moved southward across the Oxus in 1979.

THE FAILURE OF the NATO occupation has revived the Taliban as well as the trade in heroin and destabilized northwestern Pakistan. The indiscriminate bombing raids by U.S. drones have killed too many innocent civilians, and the culture of revenge remains strong in the region. The corruption and cronyism that are the hallmarks of the NATO-installed Karzai government have grown like an untreated tumor and alienated many Afghans who had welcomed the toppling of Mullah Omar and hoped for better times. Instead they have witnessed landgrabs and the construction of luxury villas by Karzai's colleagues. Western funds designed to aid some reconstruction were rapidly siphoned off to build fancy homes for the native enforcers. In year two of the occupation there was a gigantic housing scandal. Cabinet ministers awarded themselves and favored cronies prime real estate in Kabul, where land prices reached a high point after the occupation since the occupiers and their camp followers had to live in the style to which they had become accustomed. Karzai's colleagues built their large villas, protected by NATO troops, in full view of the poor.

Not all the Pashtun tribes in Pakistan and Afghanistan have recognized the Durand Line imposed by the British. And so, when anti-NATO guerrillas flee to the tribal areas under Pakistani control, they are not handed over to Islamabad, but are fed and clothed till they go back or are protected like the Al Qaeda leaders. This is what the fighting in South Waziristan is largely about. Washington wants to see more bodies and feels that Musharraf's deals with tribal elders border on capitulation to the Taliban. This makes the Americans angry because Pakistan's military actions are paid for directly by CENTCOM (United States Central Command) and they feel they are not getting value for their money. This is not to mention the $10 billion Pakistan has received since 9/11 for signing up for the "war on terror."

The problem is that some elements within Pakistani military intelligence feel that they can take Afghanistan back once Operation Enduring Freedom has come to an end. For this reason they refuse to give up their links with some of the guerrilla leaders. They even think that the United States might ultimately favor such an action, and as is known, Karzai has put out serious feelers to the Taliban. I doubt whether this is possible since other players are in the region. Iranian influence is strong in Herat and western Afghanistan. The Northern Alliance receives Russian weapons. India is the largest regional power. The only lasting settlement would be a regional guarantee of Afghan stability and the formation of a national government after a NATO withdrawal.

Even if Washington accepted a cleansed version of the Taliban, the others will not, and a new set of civil conflicts could only lead to disintegration this time. Were this to happen, the Pashtuns on both sides of the Durand Line might opt to create their own state and further bifurcate Pakistan. It sounds extremely far-fetched today, but what if the confederation of tribes that is Afghanistan were to split up into little statelets, each under the protection of a larger power?

BACK IN THE heart of Pakistan the most difficult and explosive issue remains social and economic inequality. This is not unrelated to the increase in the number of madrassas. If there were a half-decent state education system, poor families might not feel the need to hand over a son or daughter to the clerics in the hope that at least one child will be clothed, fed, and educated. Were there even the semblance of a health system, many would be saved from illnesses contracted as a result of fatigue and poverty. No government since 1947 has done much to reduce inequality. The notion that the late Benazir Bhutto, perched on Musharraf's shoulder, equaled progress is as risible as Nawaz Sharif's imagining that millions of people would turn out to receive him when he arrived at Islamabad airport in July 2007. The outlook is bleak. There is no serious political alternative to military rule.

I spent my last day in Karachi with fishermen in a village near Korangi Creek. The government has signed away the mangroves where shellfish and lobsters flourish, and land is being reclaimed to build Diamond City, Sugar City, and other monstrosities on the Gulf model. The fishermen have been campaigning against these encroachments, but with little success. "We need a tsunami," one of them half joked. We talked about their living conditions. "All we dream of is schools for our children, medicines and clinics in our villages, clean water and electricity in our homes," one woman said. "Is that too much to ask for?" Nobody even mentioned religion.

And religion was barely mentioned in the elections that took place in February 2008. It had been generally assumed that these would be royally rigged, but Musharraf's successor at GHQ, General Ashfaq Kayani, instructed the ISI and its notorious "election cell" not to interfere with the process. This had a dramatic impact. Despite the boycott by some parties and the generally low turnout (40 percent or less), those who did vote treated the polls as a referendum on Musharraf and voted against his faction of the Muslim League. The joint victors were the Sharif brothers and, as the BBC reported, the "widower Bhutto," preferring this to his proper name. Musharraf should have resigned, but insisted on hanging on to power, helped by the U.S. ambassador, who summoned the widower to remind him of the deal done with his late wife. There is little doubt that the dynastic politicians, both the widower and the grandson of Ghaffar Khan, will do Washington's bidding, if what is demanded is not completely irrational.

2

Rewinding Pakistan
Birth of Tragedy

It started badly. For three hellish months a multiform, irrational mood gripped parts of India. There was a great deal of bloodshed as Hindus, Muslims, and Sikhs in northern and eastern India—Punjab and Bengal—slaughtered each other in preparation for the big day: August 14, 1947, when India would hurriedly be partitioned by a collapsing empire. There was little joy as people on both sides in northern and eastern India, still in a daze, counted their dead and thought of the homes they had left behind. A flood of refugees swamped cities on both sides of the divide. Some Muslims from Delhi and elsewhere who had fled to Pakistan were already disappointed and wanted to go back, only to find their homes and shops had been occupied by others. Old railway stations in new Pakistan were packed with men and women dead to the world, lying on the ground, their makeshift bedding often dyed with blood, soiled with urine and excrement. All were hungry. Some had contracted cholera. Others were desperate for water. There were not enough refugee camps, let alone other facilities. Those who made the decisions had not foreseen the scale of the disaster. It was difficult to predict what might happen next.

It was the same on the other side. Most Sikhs and Hindus from what was now Western Pakistan had fled to India. Mass rapes were common. Men from all three communities regularly targeted young girls between the ages of ten and sixteen. How many died? How many children disappeared? How many women were abducted? The estimates of the dead vary between a million and 2 million. Nobody knows. One grave can contain a whole family, and cremations conceal the numbers. These days they would call it ethnic cleansing or genocide. In 1947–48 they spoke of "an outbreak of communal violence."

Partitions along ethnic or religious lines usually result in mutually inflicted violence, but the politicians of that time had no understanding of the magnitude of what they had prepared. Astonishingly, given the shrewd and effective barrister that he was, Mohammed Ali Jinnah, or the Quaid-i-Azam,* the leader of the new country, seemed unaware of the logic of his own arguments. As late as May 1946, Jinnah had not believed that the creation of a Muslim state separated from India would lead to the partition of Bengal or the Punjab, where the three communities lived in roughly equal numbers, with Muslims more predominant in western Punjab. He had argued that splitting these two provinces "would lead to disastrous results." This was certainly true, but it was pure fantasy to imagine that this could be avoided once a partition along religious lines had been agreed to. The Great Leader thought of Pakistan as a smaller version of India with one small difference: the Muslims would be a majority. He had not thought of asking himself why Hindus and Sikhs should now accept what he had refused to countenance: living under a majority composed of another religious group.

Confronted with a mass influx of refugees, a panic-stricken Muslim League leadership in Karachi now told Indian Muslims that the new state was not intended for all Muslims but only those from east Punjab. The Muslims in Delhi and Uttar Pradesh (UP) should stay where they were. This was bluntly asserted by Pakistan's first prime minister, Liaquat Ali Khan, himself a scion of the UP gentry. What he really meant was that there was no place for middle- and lower-middle-class Muslims from the named regions. Nobody paid any attention. Muslim refugees from Delhi and other areas continued to pour into the new country. The creation of a "separate homeland" for India's

---

*"Great Leader" in English (imagine it in German)—the honorific bestowed on Jinnah by his followers.

Muslims had been taken seriously by the lower orders. They had no idea that it was a state for landlords alone. It's not that many Muslims wished to leave their ancestral villages and towns in search of an uncertain future. The pogroms, real and threatened, left them no alternative.

The Muslim League, a creation of Muslim conservatives, was founded in 1906 when a Muslim delegation sought and obtained a meeting with the British viceroy, Lord Minto. They pledged loyalty to the empire and demanded job quotas and separate electorates for Muslims. Underlying it all was the fear of Muslim professionals that they would lose out badly to the Hindu majority unless the British agreed to positive discrimination. The League's politics varied as did its social composition, and not until 1940 did it pass the Lahore Resolution, demanding a separate state for Indian Muslims, but clearly not all Muslims, since this was not considered feasible.

A conflict of myriad wills sometimes results in the creation of something that nobody willed. At best it can be an approximation of what was desired. At worst a meaningless by-product. So it came about that on the morning of August 14, 1947, a group of surprised men woke to find themselves at the helm of a new Muslim state—Pakistan. They were gathered in Karachi, its then capital. Once a small Sindhi fishing village, it had grown to house parts of the Royal Indian Navy and its population had accordingly increased. Few of them had believed that this would ever come about. In private they whispered to each other that the idea of Pakistan had largely been a bargaining ploy to win institutional safeguards for the large Muslim minority in postindependence India.

Events took another course. Now they had a country. They were, in the main, bandwagon careerists from landed Muslim families who had eagerly collaborated with the British Empire and only lately joined the Muslim League. Their brain cells had become rusty from lack of use. In the old days the "great" imperial bureaucracy had done most of the thinking for them. Their task was to convey orders or transmit ideas received from above to their subordinates. Confronted with actual independence, their lack of substance became apparent. In years to come most of them would dispense with reason altogether, resort to force, and back ambition-soaked generals desperate for power, while bemoaning the fickleness of democracy, which had, in reality, never been given a chance. The reason was never hidden. A structural contradiction lay at the heart of the new country. Religious affinity was the only rationale for uniting West Pakistan and its Muslim-majority provinces—Punjab, Sind, Baluchistan and North-West Frontier—with East Pakistan, which was the Muslim-majority slice of Bengal. The result was one sovereign state consisting of two territorial units separated not only by geographical distance but by linguistic, cultural, social, and ethnic differences that had no commonality other than religion and the state airline. Across this artificial structure, where the center of "national" power was separated from the majority of the population by over one thousand miles of hostile Indian territory, there lay the army and the civil service, both of which treated the Bengali majority as if they were colonial subjects. The absurd attempt to impose Urdu as the lingua franca of the new state had to be abandoned when angry Bengali crowds rioted as they confronted Jinnah on his first and last visit to Dhaka in 1948. The Bengalis, unlike the Punjabis, refused to permit any downgrading of their language. The formative years of Pakistan witnessed a squalid attempt by the new rulers to prevent a majority of citizens in the country from playing a part in determining its future. The Bengalis had to be kept under control, and this became the guiding principle of Jinnah's heirs. For this reason they delayed the adoption of a new constitution for almost a decade, fearing that franchise would give the Bengali majority an advantage.

By this time another "great thing" had come into play: the United States of America was slowly taking over the role of the British Empire. Its needs were different, its method of functioning favored indirect rule via pliant politicians or generals, and as time progressed it would become equally demanding. It was never to be a question of objectively evaluating Pakistan's real needs. As in the case of its British predecessor, U.S. interests were paramount.

Looking back on this period now, it's clear that even though an influential section of the imperial bureaucracy in India was citing the idea of "Muslim civilization versus Hindu civilization" to promote separation on the familiar lines of "two distinct nations," it was, in fact, the Second World War that proved to be decisive in the partitioning of the subcontinent. During the war, when the hub of the British Empire was fighting for its existence, the Congress Party of Mahatma Gandhi and Jawaharlal Nehru demanded immediate independence so that a free India could determine whether it should participate in the war effort. The British were angered by the request and refused. The Congress contemptuously broke off relations with the British and boycotted its institutions. The colonial power was even less pleased when after the fall of Singapore to the Japanese in February 1942 Gandhi proposed and launched a "Quit India" movement in August. An offer from the British cabinet pledging independence at the end of the war was rejected with a biting phrase—"a blank cheque from a failing bank," retorted Gandhi, who was convinced the British would lose in Asia and independence might have to be negotiated with the Japanese.

In polar contrast, the Muslim League had always remained on the British side. It was firmly supportive of the war effort. The British responded in kind. Pakistan was, in effect, a big thank-you present to the Muslim League. Had the Congress Party adopted a similar strategy, the result might well have been different. It is an intriguing counterfactual notion. Once the idea of a division had been agreed on, all movements that became an obstruction were gently discouraged. One of the least discussed aspects of the twenty months preceding partition was a wave of strikes that swept India, putting class above separatism. In the Punjab, Muslim peasants were ranged against Muslim landlords. The most important of these strikes was the naval mutiny in February 1946 that had paralyzed the Royal Indian Navy, evoking the specter of the naval mutinies that had heralded the 1917 Russian Revolution and the triumph of Lenin's Bolshevik Party. Ships were occupied and the strike spread from Bombay to Karachi and Madras. Rear Admiral Godfrey threatened to bomb his own battleships, but his was impotent rage. The Strike Committee comprised Hindus, Muslims, and Sikhs. All were united. Then the politicians stepped in and both the Congress Party and the Muslim League backed the British and helped defuse the strike. Nehru was unhappy. "The choice was a difficult one," he said of his decision.

Jinnah's appeal to the naval ratings was also straightforwardly communal: "I call upon the Muslims to stop and create no further trouble until we are in a position to handle this very difficult situation." A general strike in solidarity with the sailors paralyzed Bombay and crippled industry. British-led troops and police opened fire, killing five hundred people. The politicians were shamefaced, but muted in their criticisms. The poet Sahir Ludhianvi asked, "O leaders of our nation tell us / Whose blood is this? / Who died?"*

In addition to the naval uprising, three hundred sepoys mutinied in Jabalpur, and in March that same year the Gurkha soldiers raised the flag of revolt at Dehra Dun. In April, ten thousand policemen went on strike. Gandhi now became nervous and referred to the united Hindu-Muslim strikes as "an unholy combination." To support them, he argued, meant "delivering India to the rabble. I would not wish to live up to 125 to witness that consummation. I would rather perish in flames."† The acclivity of class tensions helped determine the fate of the subcontinent. Everyone was in a hurry now lest the situation become uncontrollable for all three sides—the British, the Congress Party, and the Muslim League. The deal was done in a hurry.

A sprinkling of lawyers and a clutch of clever businessmen (more interested in influence and increasing their assets than achieving greatness) had provided the Muslim League with brains and cash, but they were never in control of the organization. The principal leaders were all men of a conservative temperament, though modern in outlook.‡ Few had ever been involved in the civil disobedience movements or helped organize peasants or trade unions. Aware that their nationalist credentials were limited, they had staged a few token protests, such as Direct Action Day a few months before the British left. As a result they were able to spend a few hours in prison, about which they would talk for the rest of their lives.

In London, on the eve of partition, an emergency Labour cabinet

---

*It has always struck me as odd that no Indian filmmaker, inspired by Eisenstein's classic *Battleship Potemkin,* has put this most dramatic mutiny on the screen, whereas there have been several movies about the 1857 uprising against the British.

†*Harijan,* April 7, 1946.

‡Jinnah himself had no truck with religion as such, but like Ben-Gurion and the Zionist leadership in Palestine, he used it to carve out a state. Unlike his Israeli counterparts, he did not permit religious laws to govern the private lives of the citizens.

assembled in a somber mood at 10 Downing Street. Presided over by Prime Minister Clement Attlee, it was devoted exclusively to the growing crisis in India. The secretary of state for India was despondent. The search for a last-minute way to stem the flow of blood resulting from the amputation had proved unsuccessful. The minutes reported, "Mr Jinnah was very bitter and determined. He seemed to the Secretary of State like a man who knew that he was going to be killed and therefore insisted on committing suicide to avoid it." Surely he was not alone. The refusal of Congress Party leaders to accept a number of proposals that might have preserved the unity of the subcontinent had left him with no other alternative.

As late as March 1946, Jinnah had been prepared for an honorable compromise, but the visionless and arrogant Congress Party leaders (Gandhi, an honorable exception in this case, had suggested that Jinnah become the first prime minister of a united India) had prevaricated and then the opportunity was lost forever. Had Jinnah been able to peer a few years ahead, he might well have abandoned the experiment. The dust never settled on the state he had created. Jinnah was surrounded by a swarm of excited young men who were in the habit of talking of a "new spirit" without ever being able to explain what it meant. It is too late to turn the clock back now, but it certainly needs to be readjusted to South Asian time.

THE BIRTH OF Pakistan was considered, by most of its supporters, as a great achievement, but the danger of embracing "great achievements" is only understood when the greatness, if ever it really existed, lies buried in the past. It takes decades for most modern states to acquire an identity. Pakistan's rulers, attempting to stamp one by force, downgraded the existing identities of the regions comprised within the new state. Punjabis, Pashtuns, Bengalis, Sindhis, and Baluchis were, in the main, Muslims, but religion, while important culturally, was but one aspect of their overall identity. It was not strong enough to override all else. Historically, for most of these nationalities, Islam was essentially a set of rituals. It appealed to emotions, it made people feel part of a wider history. For the peasants, the interpreters of the true faith were not mullahs, but the great mystic poets whose verses were sung and celebrated in each region. In the early decades of the new state, religion was never ideological except for a handful of clerics and the two small political parties discussed in the previous chapter, the orthodox Jamaat-e-Islami (JI, or the Islam Party) and Jamiat-Ulema-e-Islam (JUI, or Party of Islamic Scholars). Even these organizations and others had espoused universalism and had opposed the creation of a separate Muslim state, referring to Jinnah as Kafir-i-Azam (the Great Infidel), which reportedly amused him a great deal. Pushed by the turn of events, both groups rapidly reconciled themselves to the new reality, and the former became a stern guardian of the "ideology of Pakistan" against secularists, Communists, liberals, and anyone who felt that things were going seriously wrong.

THE HORRORS OF partition could not be addressed by those responsible for the division. It was left to poets and novelists to express the suffering of the many. Three of them produced work that has remained peerless. One was Faiz Ahmed Faiz (1911–84), who together with Pablo Neruda and Nazim Hikmet formed the much celebrated triumvirate of radical twentieth-century poets who shared a common experience of imprisonment and exile. Faiz was one of the greatest South Asian poets of the modern period. A Punjabi by birth, he wrote mainly in Urdu. "The Dawn of Freedom," composed soon after the massacres of August 1947, reflected a widespread sadness, despair, and anger:

> *This pockmarked daybreak,*
> *Dawn gripped by night,*
> *This is not that much-awaited light*
> *For which friends set out filled with hope*
> *That somewhere in the desert of the sky*
> *The stars would reach a final destination,*
> *The ship of grief would weigh anchor. . . .*
>
> *Our leaders' style is changing,*
> *Sexual pleasures permitted, sadness for separation forbidden,*

This cure does not help the fevered liver, heartburn or the
  unsettled eye.
That sweet morning breeze
Where did it come from?
Where did it disappear?
The roadside lamp has no news;
The heavy night weighs the same
The heart and eye await deliverance;
Forward, we have not yet reached our goal. . . .

Saadat Hasan Manto (1912–55), one of the most gifted Urdu short-story writers produced by the subcontinent, took an even more detached view of the killings. Like Faiz, he too was able to turn painful events into great literature. He took no sides. He wrote with a passionate detachment, depicting the summer of 1947 as a state of utter madness. For Manto, it was a crisis of human nature, a sharp decline in moral conduct and behavior, and this shaped the structure of his stories about partition. The fear that gripped northern India in the months leading up to partition profoundly affected most people.* Manto's stories help us understand how and why.

Manto died in Lahore when I was eleven years old. I never met him and have always wished I had. In later photographs his melancholy is striking. He appears exhausted, the consequence of unhappiness and a ravaged liver; but earlier portraits reveal an intelligent and mischievous face, sparkling eyes, and an impudence almost bursting through the thick glass of his spectacles, mocking the custodians of morality, the practitioners of confessional politics, or the commissariat of the Progressive Writers. "Do your worst," he appears to be telling them. "I

---

*My mother, for instance, an active member of the Communist Party at the time and proud of her correspondence with Jawaharlal Nehru, would often recall how in April 1947, heavily pregnant with my sister and alone at home, she was disturbed by a loud knock on the front door. As she opened the door, she was overcome by panic. She thought she was about to be murdered. In front of her stood the giant figure of a Sikh. He saw the fear on her face, understood, and spoke to her in a soft, reassuring voice. All he wanted was the exact location of a particular house on a nearby road. My mother gave him the directions. He thanked her warmly and left. She was overpowered by shame. How could she of all people, without a trace of communal prejudice, have reacted in that fashion? She was not alone.

don't care." He could never write to please or produce formulaic literature in the name of "socialist realism."

Manto wrote "Toba Tek Singh" immediately after partition. The setting is the Lahore *pagalkhana* (lunatic asylum). When whole cities are being ethnically cleansed, how can the asylums escape? Bureaucrats organizing the transfer of power tell the Hindu and Sikh lunatics that they will be forcibly transferred to institutions in India. The inmates rebel. They embrace each other, weeping. They will not be willingly parted and have to be forced onto the trucks carrying them to new asylums. One of them, a Sikh, is so overcome by rage that he dies on the demarcation line that now divides Pakistan from India. Confronted by so much insanity in the real world, Manto found normality in the asylum. The city he loved was Bombay, but he was forced to move to Lahore. He would later write:

> My heart is heavy with grief today. A strange listlessness has enveloped me. More than four years ago when I said farewell to my other home, Bombay, I experienced the same kind of sadness. There was a strange listlessness in the air much like that created by the forlorn cries of kites flying purposelessly in the skies of early summer. Even the slogans of "Long Live Pakistan" and "Long Live Quaid-e-Azam" fell on the ear with a melancholy thud.
>
> The airwaves carried the poetry of Iqbal on their shoulders, as it were, night and day and felt bored and exhausted by the weight of their burden. The feature programs had weird themes: how to make shoes . . . how to propagate poultry . . . how many refugees had come to the camps and how many were still there.

Faiz belonged to the region that became Pakistan. Manto migrated from India. Amrita Pritam, a Sikh by birth (1919–2005), was younger than both of them. She was born in Gujranwala, a small Punjabi town, but was educated in Lahore. Her father was a schoolteacher who also wrote poetry. Amrita wrote in Punjabi (the divine language of the Sikhs) and published an acclaimed first collection when she was seventeen. She did not want to leave Lahore and her many Muslim friends, but was swept across the new border by the merciless tide of history.

Traumatized by the partition, which would mark much of her work, she invoked Waris Shah (1706–98), the great mystical love poet of the Punjab, whose epic *Heer and Ranjha,* a ballad of impossible love, parental tyranny, and forced marriage, remains a great favorite on both sides of the Punjabi divide and is performed as regularly as Shakespeare. Pritam described the division of the Punjab as a poison that had destroyed a common culture:

> *I ask Waris Shah today:*
> *"Speak up from your grave,*
> *From your Book of Love unfurl*
> *A new and different page.*
> *One daughter of the Punjab did scream*
> *You covered our walls with your laments."*
> *Millions of daughters weep today*
> *And call out to Waris Shah:*
> *"Arise you chronicler of our inner pain*
> *And look now at your Punjab;*
> *The forests are littered with corpses*
> *And blood flows down the Chenab."*
> *Our five rivers lie poisoned*
> *Their waters irrigate the earth. . . .*

Poets and writers stirred the dissatisfaction that stalked Pakistan. They shattered the self-image of the leadership, but to no avail. The Muslim League confiscated the heritage of the late Muhammad Iqbal (1877–1938), a great poet from a preceding generation, educated at Heidelberg and heavily influenced by German philosophy, which explains his later attraction to metaphysics. Iqbal wrote much about Islam and was a believer but never pious and, in the tradition of the Sufi poets of the Punjab, was contemptuous of mullahs. When he was alive, the preachers villified him as an "apostate," "heretic," and "infidel." After his death they mummified him into an icon of the new state, a cultural equivalent of the Great Leader, and thus considerably reduced the impact of his poetry by presenting him as a crude revivalist. Some of us who came of age in the first decades of Pakistan were

alienated by this image. Only later did the radical literary critic Sibte
Hassan rebuke us for our philistinism and teach us to appreciate Iqbal's
poetry and his "hidden" poems. One such remains apposite, though
written about an earlier kind of globalization than the one we live in
today:

> *Monarchy, you know, is coercion*
> *Trade, is coercion too*
> *The shopkeepers stall integral to throne and crown;*
> *Profit from trade, tribute from occupation,*
> *The world-conqueror is also a merchant*
> *Killing without war a strategy;*
> *In the rotation of his machines lurks death.*

Alongside the hidden or explicit critiques of the poets, the new
country faced serious problems. How would it function in the absence
of the imperial parent? What were its global priorities, and, most
important, where was the cash coming from? Unsurprisingly, India had
claimed the giant's share of the combined state's assets. There was also
the question of personnel. Who would run the army and the civil service, two crucial bequests of the British Empire? Some of Jinnah's colleagues were fond of recounting a popular anecdote from the Mogul
period, considered the high point of Muslim rule despite the fact that
virtually all the Mogul rulers, much addicted to the pleasures of wine,
women, and hashish, could hardly be described as model Muslims. A
Mogul emperor is said to have summoned a highly respected scholar to
the audience chamber in the palace and informed him, "I wish to make
you the *qadi* [a chief justice with wide-ranging administrative powers]
of this city." The learned man responded, "Your majesty, I am not fit
for this post." A surprised ruler asked why this should be the case. The
scholar replied, "Consider whether what I have just said is true or false.
If it is true, then accept it. If it is a lie, then reflect whether it is permis-
sible to make a liar the chief justice of this fair city."
      But few people in the new state confessed to not being fit for the
positions on offer. This state had been created, after all, to make it easier for them to get all the jobs without competition from Hindus and

Sikhs. It now became their unflinching duty to keep permanent vigil and ensure that the lower classes of the Muslim population never received an education that might lead them to challenge their monopoly of power. This continuity has been carefully maintained.

Even in those trying times, during the first months after independence, most of the people at the top were mainly thinking about themselves. Young Pakistanis should have no illusions. The situation has worsened considerably, but there never was a golden age.

Take the Great Leader, Jinnah. A revealing portrait of his priorities emerges from a confidential report by Paul H. Alling, the Connecticut Yankee sent as the first U.S. ambassador to the new country. While presenting his credentials, Alling informed his hosts that the United States was "appreciative of the difficulties which beset a new nation" and was "deeply sympathetic with the many problems which face Pakistan." Clearly this sympathy had its limits: the Joint Chiefs of Staff had contemptuously rejected an earlier request from the Pakistan government asking Washington for $2 billion to modernize the army.

Nonetheless the ambassador was invited to a picnic with Jinnah and his sister, Fatima. Assuming that important matters of state might be discussed, Alling prepared himself as best he could and joined the siblings on the governor-general's launch close to their beach cottage on Sandspit. The discussion centered on nation building of a special variety. Jinnah was widely regarded as a fop, a somewhat prim and very proper Edwardian gentleman, far removed from the world of vulgar commerce and the mass struggles for independence. Decorum mattered a great deal to him. This was less true of Fatima, a thin woman with a drawn, careworn face who knew that her brother did not have long to live and the future needed to be secured. Given the refusal of his estranged daughter to leave Bombay, Fatima ran the household. As turbaned waiters were serving tea and cucumber sandwiches, Jinnah wanted to know how the ambassador was getting on with the acquisition of property for the new embassy and staff. Alling explained that they had a tentative program and everything was under control:

Both he and his sister then inquired whether we were interested in their house "Flagstaff" which he had told me a few days previously was available for purchase. I explained that our negotiations for the purchase of an Ambassador's residence at No 1 Bonus Road had progressed so far—before we had knowledge that "Flagstaff" was available—that it had proved impossible to withdraw.

He then asked if "Flagstaff" would not be suitable for the use of other personnel of the Embassy. In reply I said that we had, of course, explored that possibility but that our building expert felt he could not justify the purchase of such an extensive property for any of the subordinate personnel. I added that actually we were inter-ested only in purchasing a few small houses or flats whereupon he said he would send us details of one or two such properties. I could sense, however, that Mr Jinnah and his sister were disappointed that we had been unable to purchase "Flagstaff."*

The Father of the Nation died soon after in September 1948. Alling had left for another posting a few months earlier. Several weeks before his departure, a thoughtful State Department sent Jinnah a small gift as a token of their esteem. Four ceiling fans, twelve inches in diameter, arrived at Flagstaff and were accepted. The embassy surveyors' work had not been entirely in vain.

It was not an auspicious beginning either for the country or its rela-tions with Washington. In the years that followed, "Flagstaffing" would reach epidemic proportions, with politicians and senior armed services personnel competing with each other for unearned income. Meanwhile the ruling elite would sigh with relief and happiness at being accepted as servitors in a Washington heaven, their country now a U.S. satrapy in a continent racked, for most of the twentieth century, by colonial wars and revolutions. Milton's Satan was convinced that it was "better to reign in hell than serve in heaven." Pakistan's rulers proved it was possible to do both.

Jinnah had become the governor-general of Pakistan without hav-ing ever created a substantial party organization, let alone one of a mass

---

*The Ambassador in Karachi (Paul H. Alling) to the Secretary of State (Marshall), March 22, 1948, 845F.00/3–2248, cited in M. S. Venkataramani, *The American Role in Pakistan* (Lahore: 1984).

character. The United Provinces in India, one of the main regions of
the Muslim middle classes for whom he spoke, was not included in the
new state. Largely a stranger to the present provinces of West Pakistan,
he simply confirmed the provincial landlords and feudalists in power as
the representatives of his party there. The result was that the ruling elite
in Pakistan never possessed a reliable political party capable of controlling the masses. The Muslim League soon became a clutch of corrupt
and quarrelsome caciques who discredited it permanently. Pakistan was
thus, from the outset, firmly dominated by its civilian bureaucracy and
the army, both of which had faithfully served the British. The top echelons of each were composed of an exclusive English-educated elite,
handpicked and trained for their tasks by the British Empire. In the first
decade after partition, the civilian bureaucracy exercised political paramountcy in Pakistan. The CSP—Civil Service of Pakistan—comprised
a closed oligarchy of five hundred functionaries commanding the state.
Indeed, the two masterful heads of state of this period, Ghulam
Mohammad (1951–55) and Iskander Mirza (1955–58), were co-opted
directly from its ranks. They manipulated the token parliamentarism of
the time, until it became so discredited that in 1958 a military coup was
engineered, which brought General Ayub Khan to the presidency.

Given that Pakistan had been created in the name of religion, new
questions arose. What would be the nature of the new state? Could a
state created for one religious community be nonreligious? Jinnah was
staunchly secular. In a memorable address to the Pakistan Constituent
Assembly on August 11, 1947, he left no room whatsoever for any
doubt:

> . . . every one of you, no matter to what community he belongs, no
> matter what relations he had with you in the past, no matter what
> his colour, caste or creed, is first, second and last a citizen of this
> State with equal rights, privileges and obligations. . . . I cannot
> emphasise it too much. We should begin to work in that spirit and
> in course of time all these angularities of the majority and minority
> communities—the Hindu community and the Muslim community—because even as regards Muslims you have Pathans, Punjabis,
> Shias, Sunnis and so on—will vanish . . . you are free; you are free

to go to your temples, you are free to go to your mosques or to any
other places of worship in this State of Pakistan . . . you will find
that in course of time Hindus would cease to be Hindus and Muslims would cease to be Muslims, not in the religious sense, because
that is the personal faith of each individual, but in the political sense
as citizens of the state.

This attempt to institutionalize a Muslim nationalism dissociated
from religion was analogous to Zionism. Ben-Gurion, Golda Meir,
Moshe Dayan, and all the other implacable and ironhearted creators of
a Jewish state were not religious. The same was, more or less, true of a
number of Muslim League leaders. This was one reason why the more
serious Islamist organizations in India, the Jamaat-e-Islami, led by
Maulana Maududi, and the Majlis-i-Ahrar, had both opposed the
demand for Pakistan to be "un-Islamic." The Majlis had been set up in
1929 and was linked to the Congress Party. Its key founder, Maulana
Abul Kalam Azad, refused to accept Pakistan and became a leader of
the Indian Congress Party and a close friend of Nehru's. The Ahraris
believed in a composite nationalism and had been long aligned with the
Congress Party, but key figures split with Azad and decided to shift to
Pakistan. Like Maududi, they loathed Jinnah. He was trying to steal
their flock. For them the idea of a secular nationalist Muslim state was
"a creature of the devil." They migrated to Pakistan and gave battle.
    The headquarters of the Islamist groups had been in what was now
India. Had they been consistent in their beliefs, they would have stayed
there propagating the idea of a world Islamic caliphate. It was not as if
India were ever going to be denuded of Muslims, however hard the
Hindu fundamentalists might try to bring this about. Some venerated
Muslim leaders such as Maulana Abul Kalam Azad were members of
the new Indian government. Azad had reduced the Muslims of Delhi
to tears with his famous address pleading with them to stay on: "How
can you bear to leave this our city, our Chandni Chowk, all that our
forebears helped to build. . . ." But Maududi and the Ahraris chose
Pakistan. Having done so, they were determined to purify it of all un-
Islamic influences, and of these there were many, starting with the
Great Leader himself. So began a long battle for the soul of the new

state. The terrain chosen by the Islamists was faith. They ignored non-Muslims since they were unbelievers and should be treated as such without any nonsense of equal citizenship. None of the Islamist groups, however, could agree on what constituted an Islamic state, though Saudi Arabia came close to being a model for many orthodox Sunni Muslims. Shia divines would hark back to the form of government during the Prophet's lifetime, but there was never any agreement on the precise functions of the state or the composition of those who controlled it. What the followers of Maududi and the Ahrar leadership and smaller groups did agree on was that the Muslim League was led by a bunch of infidels, and that the country's first foreign minister, Zafarullah Khan, was an apostate who deserved death. Why? Because, they argued, he belonged to the heretical Ahmediyya sect, which had no place in the Islamic community. Having opposed the creation of Pakistan, these worthies were now determined to prove their loyalty to the new state by sprinkling hydrochloric acid on the impure.

A campaign against the Ahmediyya community began with the birth of Pakistan and was the first episode in the long duel between Islamists and the state for control of the country. Islamic history is replete with "heretical sects" and reform movements from the earliest days after the death of the Prophet Muhammad. During the nineteenth century a self-proclaimed Mahdi (a controversial notion in Islam, a redeemer who will make himself known before the Day of Judgment) emerged in the Sudan at the head of a giant mass movement, created a guerrilla army, and defeated the British at Khartoum in 1885. Poor General Charles Gordon was martyred in the process.

Mirza Ghulam Ahmed (MGA), the founder of the Ahmediyya sect, was far removed from any notion of an armed struggle against British imperialism. He was born in Qadian in 1835, the grandson of a Muslim general who had fought under the legendary Sikh ruler Maharaja Ranjit Singh. In a subcontinent riven with religious controversy and Islam under attack by Christian missionaries as well as Arya Samajists (a Hindu reform movement), Mirza Ghulam Ahmed became a religious scholar, mired himself in Persian and Arabic manuscripts and books on early Islam, and developed an interesting synthesis in a lengthy four-volume defense of his faith and dozens of other works, including one on Muslim philosophy that greatly impressed the Russian novelist Tolstoy. Unsurprisingly, the gifted scholar acquired a large following. No Elmer Gantry was he. His view that Islam in India had become obsessed with rituals and forgotten the content was close to the mark.

Had he confined himself to scholarship, Mirza G. undoubtably would have become a popular figure among Indian Muslims, but an overimmersion in any faith can sometimes have a hallucinatory impact, as Joan of Arc and Teresa of Ávila have demonstrated in the past. In 1882, MGA told his followers that he had received a divine revelation entrusting him with a special mission. This was dangerous territory and challenged Islamic tradition, according to which only the founder of the faith could be so blessed. MGA persisted, however, and as the recipient of divine messages he demanded recognition from his followers of this new status.

According to Ahmed, the revelation he'd received went like this: Jesus, son of Mary, had not died on the cross, had not ascended to heaven, but had rather been rescued off the cross by an intrepid band of disciples, cured of his wounds, and helped to escape from Palestine. He reached Kashmir, where he lived a long and happy life and died a natural death. This is strong stuff, but the revelation ended on a truly surreal note.

The rescue of Jesus and his asylum in Kashmir negated any idea of a literal Resurrection. What it meant was that someone else with all the attributes of Jesus would one day appear among the followers of the Prophet of Islam. This had now come to pass. Mirza Ghulam Ahmed, he announced, was none other than that person and should accordingly be greeted and treated as the Messiah, whose arrival had been foretold. He also declared himself a Mahdi. Ahmed declared he would wage the jihad of reason and defeat the opponents of Islam through argument and not violence.

Mainstream Islam responded to this with a shower of fatwas, but the Ahmediyya sect continued to win adherents over the years and was in 1901 registered as a separate Muslim sect. The founder died in 1908 and was succeeded by another scholar as the caliph. On the latter's death Mirza G.'s son, Mirza Bashir-ud-din, became the head of the organization. This, as is so often the case with sects, led to a split. A group that accepted the teaching but rejected the claims of prophethood seceded and set up their own group in Lahore.

In 1947, according to their own estimates, there were over two hundred thousand Ahmediyyas in both factions. They became known for their missionary zeal abroad, and Ahmediyya missions were active in East and South Africa, where they achieved some success. Like the Baha'is in neighboring Iran, they looked after their own, had a much higher level of education than the rest of the country, and made sure that none of their number was ever in serious need of food or shelter. They were represented in virtually every sphere of public life. Their philanthropy was appreciated by many people who were far removed from their interpretation of Islam. The poet Iqbal, who understood Islamic philosophy and history better than most, was certainly impressed by Ahmediyya scholarship and worked with them in some areas.

The Islamist groups began a violent campaign against them, attacking their meetings, killing an Ahmediyya army major, demanding the sacking of the foreign minister, and insisting that the sect be declared non-Muslim. This could easily have been stopped, but sections of the Muslim League leadership in the Punjab, reeking of opportunism, jumped on the bandwagon, including the oily-tongued, Oxford-educated Mian Mumtaz Daultana, who had flirted mildly with Communism during his youth. Daultana effectively prevented the police from providing protection to the besieged Ahmediyya community. In 1953, serious riots broke out, Ahmediyya shops were looted and mosques attacked, and some members of the community lost their lives. As a nine-year-old it was my first encounter with irrationality. Just below our apartment in Lahore was a Bata shoe store, owned by an Ahmediyya, whose son was at school with me. Returning from school one day, I saw it being attacked by armed hoodlums. Nobody was hurt, but it was a frightening experience.

An angry provincial governor called on the army to intervene. Martial law was declared in Lahore. General Azam gave orders to shoot rioters on sight. Within twenty-four hours the crisis was over. Maulana Maududi and others were tried for treason, and Maududi was sentenced to death, which was later commuted.

A court of inquiry was established to inquire into the cause of the disturbances. It was presided over by Justice Munir and Justice Kayani. The published report, I have often argued, is a classic of its type, a modern masterpiece of political literature. It should become part of the national curriculum if a serious state education system is ever established. The two judges began to question Muslim clerics from rival schools, and different factions testified as to what they thought constituted a Muslim state and their definition of a Muslim. With each new reply the judges found it difficult to conceal their incredulity, some of which was reflected in their report. All the groups concurred in the view that a secular state was impermissible and that non-Muslims could not be treated as equal citizens. This raised a new problem:

> The question, therefore, whether a person is or is not a Muslim will be of fundamental importance, and it was for this reason that we asked most of the leading ulama [religious scholars] to give their definition of a Muslim, the point being that if the ulama of the various sects believed the Ahmadis to be *kafirs* [unbelievers], they must have been quite clear in their minds not only about the grounds of such belief but also about the definition of a Muslim because the claim that a certain person or community is not within the pale of Islam implies an exact conception of what a Muslim is. The result of this part of the inquiry, however, has been anything but satisfactory, and if considerable confusion exists in the mind of our ulama on such a simple matter, one can easily imagine what the differences on more complicated matters will be. . . .
>
> Keeping in view the several definitions given by the ulama, need we make any comment except that no two learned divines are agreed on this fundamental. If we attempt our own definition as each learned divine has done and that definition differs from that given by all others, we unanimously go out of the fold of Islam. And if we adopt the definition given by any one of the ulama, we remain Muslims according to the view of that alim, but kafirs according to the definition of everyone else.*

Report of the Court of Inquiry on the Punjab Disturbances of 1953 (Lahore: 1954).

The demand to declare the Ahmediyyas infidels faded from public view. No government took it seriously, and threats to the community receded. Ironically, it was Prime Minister Zulfiqar Ali Bhutto, under political siege by a combined opposition in 1976, who thought he would outflank the Islamist parties by implementing three of their old demands: a ban on alcohol, Friday and not Sunday as the official holiday, and, more serious, declaring the Ahmediyyas a non-Muslim sect. This craven capitulation could only strengthen those who had first proposed these measures. Ahmediyyas remain Muslims in India, Britain, France, Germany, East Africa, but not in Pakistan. The late Pakistani physicist Dr. Abdus Salam was the only Muslim scientist to win the Nobel Prize. That he was an Ahmedi would make the preceding sentence inaccurate in Pakistan.

The Pakistan envisaged by Jinnah never took off. The geographical entity died on the killing fields of East Pakistan. Over 70 percent of Pakistanis were born after the debacle of 1971. Amnesia prevails. Few have any idea what took place or even that there was once another country. The country's name was the brainchild of Chaudhry Rahmat Ali, an Indian Muslim studying in London during the thirties and evidently with time on his hands. He played around with the initials of Muslim majority areas in India: *P* represented the Punjab, *A* was for Afghanistan, *K* was Kashmir, *S* represented Sind. Unfortunately, *pak* also means "pure" but, more interesting, there was no *B* for Bengal or Baluchistan. Could a nuclear Pakistan dominated by the military fragment still further, and if so, what might be the consequences for the region as a whole? Whose interests would another division serve? Those without knowledge or understanding of their own history are fated to repeat it. What follows is an attempt to explain the past and the present in the hope of a better future.

3

THE WASHINGTON QUARTET
The Man Who Would Be
Field Marshal

IN OCTOBER 1958, A DECADE AFTER THE GREAT LEADER'S DEATH, the political system he had set in place received its first shock. The Pakistan Army, backed by Washington, decided on a preemptive strike against democracy and declared martial law. Some months later at a public poetry reading, most of the participants confined themselves to reciting love poems. When it was his turn, the Punjabi poet Ustad Daman began to recite a poem about birds twittering. Some of us shouted from the audience, "For Allah's sake, say something!" This unseemly provocation elicited an extemporized couplet:

Now each day is sweet and balmy,
Wherever you look, the army.

Cheered by the large crowd, he was then picked up by the police a few hours later and held in custody for a week or so. Pakistan had changed.

How and why did this happen? Within a year of the country's founding, the Great Leader was dead, leaving behind a set of notables—mainly landed gentry sometimes doubling as hereditary religious leaders (Pirs, Makhdooms, etc.)—who sometimes wondered how they were going to muddle through. The new rulers were soon confronted with two contradictions, one of them serious.

The first of these concerned the political geography of the new country. It was divided in two parts, East and West, separated from each other by a thousand miles of India and having little in common except religion, and sometimes not even that. If Islam constituted a nationality (as the Muslim League insisted but as orthodox Islamists initially resisted), this was always going to be its big test. Sixty percent of the population was in East Pakistan, with their own language, tradition, culture, diet, and time zone. The overwhelming bulk of the bureaucracy and army was from or based in West Pakistan. The reason was simple. The Punjab had been the "sword arm" of the raj especially after the conclusion of the Sikh Wars of the nineteenth century. A large share of the native soldiery came from the most economically backward parts of the subcontinent; the army was considered a step up by poor peasant families groaning under the yoke of native landlords. The British virtually restricted recruitment to the countryside. They were suspicious of the urban petit bourgeois and saw the Bengalis as the epitome of this layer, loquacious and unreliable, who had to be kept out.

In 1933, General Sir George MacMunn (1869–1952), a doughty warrior from the Scottish lowlands, wrote a quaint tract entitled *The Martial Races of India,* replete with imperial justifications for the pattern of recruitment to the British Indian army:

> The staunch old yeoman who came into the Indian commissioned ranks via the rank and file, or the young Indian landowner made the Indian officer as we know him. . . . The clever young men of the Universities were quite unfitted for military work . . . the army officers had long realised that the Indian intelligentsia would never make officers.

This rule was relaxed during the Second World War when expediency dictated the entry of educated officers, and a number of undesirables (including even Communists after Hitler's invasion of the Soviet Union) were hastily recruited to assist the war effort in India and Britain.

Postwar pruning got rid of most of this layer. Others left voluntarily. Staunch yeomen and younger sons of the landed gentry remained.

The British Indian army was shaken during the war. The fall of Singapore to the Japanese had pierced the myth of British invulnerability. There was no fail-safe inoculation against the nationalist disease, and a number of officers and soldiers (some of them from the "martial races") captured by the Japanese defected and set up the Indian National Army, which fought alongside their captors against the British on the basis of wrongheaded nationalist logic according to which "the enemy of my enemy is my friend," something that is almost always never the case. Empires old and new have no friends. They only have interests. The civil conflicts during partition also colored the thinking of Indian officers in the north. They had witnessed appalling massacres that they were helpless to prevent, largely because the imperial power feared that divided loyalties would lead to chaos if there was a breakup of the army along communal lines. For that reason the military was not encouraged to intervene in order to stop the massacres. At best, the army offered some limited protection to refugees on both sides.

This army itself was partitioned along communal lines, creating two different command structures, each temporarily under the control of a British general. Consequently, the new Pakistan army maintained most of the old colonial traditions with continuity preserved in the first instance by the appointment of General Sir Frank Messervy and subsequently Sir Douglas Gracey, a colonial veteran, as its first two commanders in chief. In addition, over five hundred other British officers stayed behind to give the new fighting force a much-needed boost. This created some resentment. In 1950, a small group of more nationalist-minded officers (including a general, Akbar Khan), together with an even tinier collection of Communist intellectuals, discussed a possible coup d'état to topple the pro-West government. The half-baked plot was uncovered, and the participants (including the poet Faiz Ahmed Faiz and the literary critics Sibte Hassan and Sajjad Zaheer) were sent to prison, and the infinitesimal Pakistan Communist Party was banned.

In contrast to Hindu and Sikh detachments, no all-Muslim units had been allowed in the colonial army, a decision dating back to the 1857 anti-British uprising for which the imperial power wrongly held the old Muslim aristocracy exclusively responsible. In fact, it was a proto-nationalist rebellion by Indians of every stripe against the new conquerors. The old recruitment policy persisted till well after partition. Few Bengalis were recruited to the Pakistan army. The policy was changed much later with the partially successful, if politically disastrous, Islamization during the late seventies and eighties that is discussed in a subsequent chapter and whose effects are still present.

The first Pakistani military chief met all MacMunn's criteria. General Ayub Khan was tall, mustachioed, and well built. He was from tried and tested stock, the son of a risaldar major (a noncommissioned officer), and regarded by his superiors as an obedient and trustworthy soldier. He was to fully justify that trust, remaining loyal first to the British and later to the United States throughout his years in military politics. He reached the top effortlessly, helped by fate: General Iftikhar, due to succeed Gracey and generally regarded as a sharper and more independent-minded officer, perished in an air crash in 1949. It would be unfair to single out Ayub Khan as the only native conservative-minded and submissive, pro-British senior officer in the new Pakistan army. Few of his well-trained contemporaries were any different. The same could be said about their Indian counterparts. Reading through the prolix and self-serving memoirs of postindependence generals on both sides of the Indo-Pak divide is tedious and unrewarding. The books are revealing, however, in that they provide an insight to the psychology of the generals. The golden age, for most of them, lies firmly in the past, with gimlets (gin cocktails) at lunchtime or a postsunset whiskey with their pink-skinned superiors. That they had not been allowed membership in exclusive whites-only clubs till after independence did not bother them unduly. They had got used to the social apartheid. At their happiest fighting alongside and working under British officers, they would treasure those times for the rest of their lives. Ayub Khan, for instance, had been among an early batch of young native cadets sent to Sandhurst when the "Indianization" of the army had become necessary. He would later proudly recall that he was "the first foreign cadet to be promoted Corporal and given two stripes."

A majority of ruling Pakistani politicians too had grown up serving the British. Like their old mentors, they regarded the ordinary people with a mixture of repugnance and fear. Small wonder that senior civil servants and military officers, true heirs of the departed colonial power, treated the politicians with contempt. On this front, the difference with India could not have been more pronounced. In India the political leadership had been forged over three decades of continuous nationalist struggles and long periods of imprisonment. No general or civil servant would have had the nerve to challenge a first-generation Congress leader. Had he lived longer, Jinnah might possibly have stamped his authority on the two institutions—the army and the civil service— that dwarfed the Muslim League on every level, but his deputy, Liaquat Ali Khan, prime minister and Leader of the Nation (Quaid-i-Millat) and himself a refugee, lacked the same authority over his own party and the country. The Punjabi landlords who dominated the Muslim League and were desperate to gain total control viewed the prime minister as an unnecessary impediment to their own rise, and there is little doubt that it was they who had him assassinated while he was addressing a large crowd in the municipal park in Rawalpindi in October 1951. His assassin, Said Akbar, was immediately shot dead by the police on the orders of Najaf Khan, a senior police officer and factotum of the then inspector general of police, Khan Qurban Ali Khan, who in turn was a close friend of senior Punjabi landlord-politicians.

Liaquat's assassination symbolized the deep-rooted antagonisms that had developed between the local gentry and the refugee "interlopers" who had crossed the river Jumna and made their way to the Muslim homeland. Some of the wealthier refugees would later regret their decision to come to Pakistan, but the less privileged had no alternative. They were driven out of their villages and towns. That the refugees tended to be more cultured and better educated than their unwilling hosts soon became another point of contention. They were strongly embedded in the civil service of Pakistan, and this created resentments. Their linguistic affectations and mannerisms were constantly caricatured, and they in turn found it difficult to conceal their contempt for the wooden-headed and uncouth Sindhi and Punjabi politicians. The cold-blooded decision to bump off Liaquat was partly intended as a shot across the bows of his fellow migrants. The message was simple: you are here on sufferance and don't forget that this country belongs to us. So much for "the homeland of Islam in the subcontinent." Worse was yet to come.

General Ayub Khan was in London when Liaquat was assassinated, and later described, somewhat disingenuously, his shock on meeting the new prime minister, Khwaja Nazimudin, and cabinet: "Not one of them mentioned Liaquat Ali's name, nor did I hear a word of sympathy or regret from any one of them. Governor-General Ghulam Mohammad seemed equally unaware of the fact that the country had lost an eminent and capable Prime Minister. . . . I wondered how callous, cold-blooded and selfish people could be. . . . I got the distinct impression that they were all feeling relieved that the only person who might have kept them under control had disappeared from the scene."

That the country's senior politicians did not copiously weep was to their credit. Having approved the removal of their colleague, it would have been gross hypocrisy on their part to do so. But it seems unlikely that General Ayub's intelligence chiefs had not informed him of who was behind the assassination. This being so, why did he not act at the time and insist that the rogues responsible organize an immediate general election? He was, of course, preoccupied elsewhere, engaged in political intrigues of his own with the defense secretary, Iskander Mirza, a former general turned senior bureaucrat. Mirza was an astute manipulator. He took advantage of the weakness of the political leadership, ousted a mentally decaying, foulmouthed fellow bureaucrat, Ghulam Mohammad, and took over as governor-general, the country's head of state.

Mirza ruled with a heavy hand, and when the Bengalis toppled a Muslim League government after provincial polls in 1954, the governor-general removed the elected government and imposed Governor's Rule throughout East Pakistan. It was the first step toward the disintegration of the country and the militarization of its political culture. It is a sad story that I have written about in some detail elsewhere.* Here it is sufficient to stress that the alienation of the eastern half of the country began early and got worse each consecutive year. The prejudice of Pun-

---

*Pakistan: Military Rule or People's Power? (London and New York: 1970).

jabi officers and civil servants against the Bengalis mirrored British prejudices during the colonial period.

As with others who would follow him, Mirza's overconfidence brought about his political demise. He had presided over the introduction of a new constitution in 1956 declaring Pakistan an Islamic republic and himself as its first president. Mirza and Ayub together institutionalized Pakistan's role as a U.S. satrapy by joining a network of Cold War security arrangements known as the Baghdad Pact and the Southeast Asia Treaty Organization (SEATO), designed to defend U.S. interests in both regions. Ayub had negotiated directly with Washington to secure the military aid program of 1953–54 and Pakistan admittance to the "free world" together with South Korea, South Vietnam, and Thailand.

The writer Saadat Hasan Manto, bemused by what was taking place, wrote a set of nine satirical "Letters to Uncle Sam." The fourth was written on February 21, 1954, a year before his death:

Dear Uncle:

I wrote to you only a few days ago and here I am writing again. My admiration and respect for you are going up at the same rate as your progress towards a decision to grant military aid to Pakistan. I tell you I feel like writing a letter a day to you.

Regardless of India and the fuss it is making, you must sign a military pact with Pakistan because you are seriously concerned about the stability of the world's largest Islamic state since our mullah is the best antidote to Russian communism. Once military aid starts flowing you should arm these mullahs. They would also need American-made rosaries and prayer-mats, not to forget small stones that they use to soak up the after-drops following nature's call. . . . I think the only purpose of military aid is to arm these mullahs. I am your Pakistani nephew and I know your moves. Everyone can now become a smartass thanks to your style of playing politics.

If this gang of mullahs is armed in the American style, the Soviet Union that hawks communism and socialism in our country will have to shut shop. I can visualise the mullahs, their hair trimmed with American scissors and their pyjamas stitched by American machines in strict conformity with the *Sharia*. The stones they use for their after-drops [of urine] will also be American, untouched by human hand, and their prayer-mats, too, will be American. Everyone will then become your camp-follower, owing allegiance to you and none else.*

Pakistan's servile leaders were supportive of the Anglo-French-Israeli invasion of Egypt in 1956. This was totally unnecessary, and one can only assume that they thought the United States would, however reluctantly, fall in line behind the adventure, which it did not. Their support for the war on Nasser's Egypt inflamed public opinion and created a wave of anger that led to mass demonstrations throughout the country. Interestingly, the Jamaat-e-Islami played no part in these mobilizations. Political parties now began to demand an exit from the security pacts and a neutral foreign policy. These demands were popular. Mirza and Ayub were apprehensive that the country's first general election, scheduled for April 1959, might produce a coalition that would take Pakistan out of the security pacts and toward a nonaligned foreign policy, like neighboring India. The United States was even more nervous over such a prospect and encouraged a military takeover.

Mirza, ever arrogant, thought he could run the show with Ayub as his loyal sidekick. He underestimated the autonomy of the army. Simply because General Ayub had, until then, supported every measure he had proposed, the president assumed he would be able to maintain complete control. On Mirza's initiative, the Pakistan army seized power on October 7, 1958. A cabinet dominated by generals was appointed together with a few nonparty civilians. These included Mohammed Shoaib, a veteran U.S. agent, as finance minister; a brilliant lawyer, Manzur Qadir, as foreign minister; and an unknown young Sindhi, Zulfiqar Ali Bhutto, as minister for commerce. The response of the West was supportive, and the *New York Times,* while deploring the suspension of the constitution, was nonetheless hopeful:

---

*"Letters to Uncle Sam," translated into English by Khalid Hassan, the letters were first published by Alhamra Press, Islamabad, a few weeks before 9/11.

"In Pakistan both President Mirza and the army's head General Ayub Khan have stated clearly that what they propose and wish to do is to establish in due course a fine, honest, and democratic government. There is no reason to doubt their sincerity."*

A few weeks later three generals called on the president and read out to him his political obituary. A shaken Iskander Mirza left the country forever and became an exile in London, where he later died.

General Ayub Khan became Pakistan's first military dictator. Within six months all political parties and trade unions had been banned, and the largest chain of opposition newspapers, Progressive Papers Limited, was taken over by the government without a whimper of opposition from the tame Pakistani press or its Western counterparts. A secret Ministry of Education directive was issued in August 1959. Its aim was to "stop the infiltration of communist literature into the country and to prohibit its publication and circulation within the country." All educational institutions were instructed to "undertake a survey of books in university and college/school libraries to ensure that all objectionable materials are withdrawn." The delighted Islamists cheered the announcement. As a dictatorship, Pakistan became an even stauncher member of the free world. General Ayub told the first meeting of his cabinet, "As far as you are concerned, there is only one embassy that matters in this country: the American embassy." The United States reciprocated with a statement endorsed unanimously by the National Security Council (NSC) that noted "the presence of important U.S. security facilities in Pakistan" and gave full backing to the military takeover of the country:

> The political instability which was characteristic of previous governments and seriously impeded the effectiveness of U.S. efforts in Pakistan has been replaced by a relatively stable martial law regime. . . . The present political situation should be conducive to the furtherance of U.S. objectives. . . . In view of the present stability, even though achieved by fiat, the problem has changed from one

---

*New York Times, editorial, October 12, 1958.

of short-term urgency, requiring us to reckon with individual politicians in one crisis after another, to one which allows us to take a longer-range view of Pakistan's potential. . . . We give special emphasis to assuring the Pakistan government of our sympathetic interest in and support for its proposed economic and social reforms.

This was simply a case of putting immediate U.S. interests above all else—an imperial failing since ancient times. The NSC statement supporting the military dictatorship ran counter to an extremely astute analysis that was also on the table. A top-secret report from the Office of Intelligence and Research Analysis of the State Department written in December 1958 bluntly stated the consequences of backing the military dictatorship:

> . . . a prolonged period of military rule, which Ayub apparently contemplates, could intensify provincial and class tensions. It would probably disillusion the intellectuals, teachers, journalists, lawyers and the broad run of the middle class whose deepest political desire has been to see Pakistan match India's record of democracy and avoid degenerating to the level of a Middle Eastern or Latin American dictatorship.
> . . . only under a democratic system would East Pakistan, with its greater population, appear to be able to match the greater military and bureaucratic weight of West Pakistan. . . . The prospect of prolonged suppression of political freedom under military domination would intensify the risk of such an increase in tension and discontent in East Pakistan as perhaps to jeopardize the unity of the two wings of the country.

Those who made similar arguments inside Pakistan were denounced as "pro-Indian traitors" or "Communist agents." Ayub Khan, who soon promoted himself to field marshal, differed on this assessment of democracy and came up with a novel explanation. In an early radio broadcast to the nation, the military dictator informed his bewildered "fellow countrymen" that "we must understand that democracy cannot work in a hot climate. To have democracy we must have a cold climate like Britain." Few doubted his sincerity on this matter.

Remarks of this sort did little to diminish Ayub's popularity in the West. He became a great favorite of the press in Britain and the United States. His bluff exterior charmed the notorious showgirl Christine Keeler (they splashed together in the pool at Cliveden during a Commonwealth Prime Ministers' Conference in 1961), and the saintly Kingsley Martin of the *New Statesman* published a groveling interview. Meanwhile opposition voices were silenced and political prisoners were tortured.

In 1962, Ayub decided that the time had come to widen his appeal. He took off his uniform, dressed in native gear, and, addressing a forced gathering of peasants assembled by their landlords, announced that there would soon be presidential elections and he hoped people would support him. The bureaucracy organized a political party, the Convention Muslim League, and careerists flocked to join it. The election took place in 1965, and the polls had to be rigged to ensure the field marshal's triumph. His opponent, Fatima Jinnah (the aged sister of the Great Leader), fought a spirited campaign but to no avail; family links did not count for as much in those days. The handful of bureaucrats who refused to help "adjust" the election results were offered early retirement.

Meanwhile, Western backing for the regime continued apace. The arguments used in its support related principally to the "economic development" taking place, which was supposedly transforming Pakistan from a rural to an urban economy and paving the way for the modernization of the country. This was certainly the view of Finance Minister Mohammed Shoaib, who was so close to Washington that it sometimes received the minutes of cabinet meetings, together with Shoaib's assessments, before they were even seen by its own members. Shoaib was given strong backing by many visiting stars from the U.S. academe. Gustav Papanek from Harvard fully approved the state establishment of enterprises that could then be turned over to private entrepreneurs and wrote in praise of the "free market economy" that "through a combination of incentives and obstacles produced an environment in which success was likely only for the ruthless individual . . .

whose economic behaviour was not too different from their robber baron counterparts of 19th century Western industrialisation."* Robber barons they certainly were, but unlike their European counterparts they enjoyed the support of a fiscal and economic system that diverted the productive wealth produced by agriculture via a network of subsidies into manufacturing.

The resulting redistribution was at the expense of the peasantry, but few cared. The U.S. economic advisers echoed Papanek's view that "great inequalities were necessary in order to create industry and industrialists," and that the growth generated in this fashion would lead to a "real improvement for the lower income groups." This is what later, in the era of globalization, became known as the trickle-down effect. It did not work then as it does not work now. The upper-income groups in the towns paid no taxes and illegally moved their money abroad. Little was invested in the productive nonagricultural sector. Even the official planning commission set up by the government bewailed the bad habits of the city elite in West Pakistan. Keith B. Griffin, an Oxford economist well versed in the economic problems confronting the country, produced a report showing that between 63 percent and 83 percent of savings transferred from agriculture were wasted in nonproductive extravagances, i.e., the sumptuous style cultivated by the nouveaux riches. Griffin went on to point out that in West Pakistan "the potential surplus of these savings units was used to consume more, to buy more ornaments, jewellery and consumer durables and to bid up the prices of real estate and farm lands, helping their owners to disinvest. Often such surplus was devoted to luxury house construction or to open up one more retail store in the already crowded streets and bazaars."†

The greater inequalities accepted by the Neanderthal Harvard Group were creating new divisions in the country as a whole. In the West wing of the country the elite flaunted its new wealth without shame. There was no shortage of critical comment, but few of the crit-

---

*Gustav F. Papanek, *Pakistan's Development: Social Goals and Private Incentives* (Cambridge, MA: 1967).

†Keith B. Griffin, "Financing Development Plans in Pakistan," *Pakistan Development Review*, Winter 1965.

ics took the imbalance this was creating with the East wing very seriously. The Bengalis, naturally, were not pleased with this state of affairs. In addition to being punished politically simply because they were a majority, they now saw moneys accrued by jute production in their region, the export of which had provided a balance of payments surplus during the boom created by the Korean War, disappearing into the coffers of West Pakistan. The stark contrast between the West and East wings of the country created the basis of the national movement in Bengal. The demands of the nationalist Awami League were a local version of "no taxation without representation."

As the tenth anniversary of the field marshal's reign approached, a sycophantic intelligentsia and a myopic bureaucracy began to prepare the celebrations, known as the Decade of Development. The Ministry of Information decided on a trumpet call in the shape of a book. It was thought that Pakistan's soldier-statesman would be further legitimized on the world stage by the publication of his memoirs. Ayub Khan's *Friends Not Masters: A Political Autobiography* was published by Oxford University Press in 1967 to great acclaim in the Western press and nothing short of sycophantic hysteria in the government-controlled media at home.*

The biography's publication was linked to the dictator's growing unpopularity. A military adventure against India in 1965 had ended in disaster. Ayub, always cautious in these matters, was reluctant to authorize a strike against India. Bhutto and a number of senior generals convinced him that a preemptive strike would take the Indians by surprise and that Operation Grand Slam would liberate Kashmir, the disputed and divided province claimed by both sides after 1947. Ayub finally

---

*Ayub's information secretary, Altaf Gauhar, a crafty, cynical courtier, had ghosted a truly awful book: stodgy, crude, verbose, and full of half-truths. It backfired badly and was soon being viciously satirized in clandestine pamphlets on university campuses. Ayub had in Chairman Mao mode suggested that Pakistanis "should study this book, understand and act upon it. . . . It contains material which is for the good of the people." But in China there was universal literacy so people could read the wretched *Little Red Book*. In Pakistan over 75 percent of the population was illiterate, and of the rest only a tiny elite could read English. An Urdu edition was produced but bought only by government employees. It was not considered necessary to waste money on a Bengali edition, the only sensible decision of the period.

agreed. India was taken by surprise and Pakistani forces came close to achieving their strategic objectives, but serious operational and organizational failures halted the advance, giving India time to move its troops forward and push Pakistan back, but only after the largest tank battle since the Second World War. Sixty Pakistani tanks were captured intact after the Indian victory.

Ayub was forced to travel to Tashkent, where the Soviet prime minister, Aleksey Kosygin, brokered a cease-fire deal between the two countries. Zulfiqar Ali Bhutto, by this time a mercurial foreign minister, resigned soon afterward, alleging that secret protocols attached to the Tashkent Treaty amounted to a betrayal of the Kashmiri people's right to self-determination. This turned out not to have been the case, but it had become a useful weapon at mass meetings. When, a year later, I asked Bhutto why he had pushed Ayub to wage an unwinnable war, his reply took me aback: "It was the only way to weaken the bloody dictatorship. The regime will crack wide open fairly soon." Bhutto had by this time decided to organize his own political grouping, and the Pakistan Peoples Party (PPP) was founded in 1966.* From the beginning the party line was to destroy the Ayub regime. In 1967, Bhutto began to address a series of large meetings throughout the country and was arrested. His confidence was high. Knowing full well that his cell was bugged, he would, during meetings with his lawyer, Mahmud Ali Kasuri, provoke the military. "General Musa's days as governor of West Pakistan are numbered. We'll dress him in a skirt and make him dance on the streets like a monkey," was one of the few insults that were printable.

In response to the growing opposition in the country the regime decided that a distraction was needed. In October 1968 lavish celebrations to commemorate the tenth anniversary of the dictatorship were in progress. The Karachi daily *Dawn* competed with the government press by publishing sixty-nine photographs of the field marshal in a single issue. The citizens were triumphantly informed that in Karachi, a city with only three bottled-milk outlets, the consumer could choose

---

*For an account of my own involvement during an early stage of the new party's manifesto and relations with Bhutto, see *Clash of Fundamentalisms: Crusades, Jihads and Modernity* (London and New York: 2003), 240–44.

among Bubble Up, Canada Dry, Citra Cola, Coca-Cola, Double Cola, Kola Kola, Pepsi-Cola, Perri Cola, Fanta, Hoffman's Mission, and 7UP. In Lahore a reporter from the government newspaper *Pakistan Times* slobbered over a fashion show:

> The mannequins received a big hand from the elegant crowd as they moved up and down the brightly lit catwalk modelling the dresses. Some of the creations which the audience warmly applauded were "Romantica," "Raja's Ransom," "Sea Nymph" and "Hello Officer." . . . The Eleganza '69 look was defined as a blend of the soft and the severe.

But the bread and circuses became a public relations disaster. On November 7, 1968, students in Rawalpindi and Dhaka surprised the government and themselves by marching out onto the streets. They demanded freedom and the restoration of democracy, recalling the words of the Martinican poet Aimé Césaire:

> *It was an evening in November . . .*
> *And suddenly shouts lit up the silence;*
> *We had attacked, we the slaves; we, the*
> *Dung-underfoot, we the animals with patient hooves . . .*

Soon student action committees were springing up across both parts of the country. This was the "unfashionable" 1968, far removed from the glamour of Europe and the United States. It was also different in character. The gap between the actions of the Pakistani students and workers and the actual conquest of state power was much narrower than in France or Italy, let alone the United States or Britain. No democratic institutions existed in Pakistan. Political parties were relatively weak. The movement was stronger than them.

The scale of the uprising was breathtaking: during five months of continuous struggles that began on November 7, 1968, and ended on March 26, 1969, some 10–15 million people had participated in the struggle across East and West Pakistan. The state responded with its customary brutality. There were mass arrests and the dictatorship ordered the police to "kill rioters" on sight. Several students died during the first few weeks. In the two months that followed, workers, lawyers, small shopkeepers, prostitutes, and government clerks joined the protests. Stray dogs with *Ayub* painted on their back became a special target for armed police.

But here too the two halves of the country saw a marked disparity in the degree of repression. A few hundred died in West Pakistan. Nearly two thousand perished in Bengal. More than in the Punjab, Sind, North-West Frontier, and Baluchistan put together. One of the most moving aspects of this insurrection was the unity it imposed from below. When students died in the West, barefoot women students of Dhaka in the East marched in silence in a show of respect and solidarity. These six months were the only period in the history of united Pakistan where ordinary people on both sides of the country genuinely felt close to each other. I know this from personal experience. For three months, from March to May 1969, I traveled extensively in both parts of Pakistan, addressing meetings large and small and talking to student leaders and antidictatorship politicians, poets, and trade union leaders. The mood was joyous. The country had never been so full of hope before or since.

In those few months, the Pakistani people spoke freely. All that they had kept repressed since 1947 poured out. And the movement was not without humor. For hundreds of years the Punjabi word *chamcha* (spoon) has been used to denote a stooge. The origins of this are obscure. Some argue that it goes back to the arrival of the British. Local potentates who had hitherto subscribed to the art of eating delicately with their fingers had abandoned tradition and begun to use spoons and forks. Whatever the truth, the demonstrators started greeting pro-regime civil servants and politicians with spoons, the size depending on the self-importance that the dignitary attached to himself and popular estimates (usually accurate) of the degree of his sucking up to power at home or in Washington. When Ayub or his ministers arrived, they were greeted by gigantic homemade spoons as well as hundreds of the normal variety bought in the bazaar and used as cymbals to enliven proceedings.

The meetings I attended in East Bengal were particularly heated. I could see before my eyes the large gulf that separated the two wings of Pakistan. I argued that a voluntary socialist and democratic federation was the only thing that could save the country. This view sounds utopian today, but in those heady days everything seemed possible.

On a hot and humid afternoon in April 1969 I was taken to address the students of Dhaka University under the *amtala* tree on the campus. Many a political movement had been born in this symbolic space. Here, the students had, after a spate of fiery speeches, decided to fight the dictatorship. They would not let me speak in Urdu and voted, by an overwhelming majority (which included Nicholas Tomalin of the *Sunday Times*), that I speak in English, suggesting wryly that I learn Bengali for the next time. It is a beautiful language and I promised I would, even though I half knew that there never would be a next time. Every political instinct told me that Bengali national aspirations were about to be crushed by the army, that it would rather destroy Pakistan than permit any meaningful autonomy, let alone accept a confederation. I made this point forcefully to the students that day. This being the case, I told them, why not go for complete independence? Take over your country. Done quickly, it might avoid the bloodshed to come. There was a hush. The audience looked at me in amazement. Someone from the other side, a Punjabi to boot, had mentioned the word *independence*. Then they cheered and chanted slogans, before carrying me on their shoulders back to my car.

The "Lal salaams" (red salutes) were still ringing in my ears when I was taken that same day to meet Sheikh Mujibur Rahman, the leader of the nationalist, but still staunchly parliamentarian, Awami League. In March 1965, the Awami League, in the person of the sheikh, had dropped a bombshell with what became the famous Six Point plan for regional autonomy (discussed in the following chapter). The opposition West Pakistani leaders were so shocked that they accused the Ayub regime's most Machiavellian civil servant, Altaf Gauhar, of having drafted the plan to split the anti-Ayub opposition.

This marked the beginning of the gulf between Bengali nationalism and the West Pakistani opposition parties. The abyss widened over the years, and the united struggle against the dictatorship was just a passing phase. Sheikh Mujibur Rahman knew my own sympathies were on the left and that I was closer to the Bengali peasant leader Maulana Bhashani, who had taken me on a tour of the villages and small towns of the Eastern province a few weeks previously. Bhashani had told me then of his meetings in China with Chou En-lai, who had pleaded with him not to weaken Ayub Khan since he was a friend of China's. The majority of Pakistani Maoists had loyally followed this advice, but Bhashani had realized that to support Ayub meant political suicide. He had joined the movement, but it was already too late.

Sheikh Mujib now reminded me that I had recently referred to him as "Chiang Kai-Sheikh" and muttered something about Mao backing Ayub Khan. Nonetheless he greeted me warmly and came straight to the point.

"Is it true that you said what they told me you said today?"

I nodded.

"You are sure they will use force. How sure?"

I explained that my certainty did not come from any hard information from those in power or even through understanding their psychology, but from one hard fact. The primary export commodities of East Bengal were vital to the economy of West Pakistan. Autonomy would mean the loss of financial control for the West. Sheikh Mujib listened attentively, but did not seem fully convinced. Perhaps he thought he could maneuver his way to power via a deal with the military chiefs. His party was pro-West and had, only recently, stressed its closeness to Washington and security pacts. He may have believed that Washington would compel the Pakistani military to play ball. Later when Nixon and Kissinger "tilted toward" Islamabad, it was a bitter cup for him to swallow. Mujib felt he had been badly betrayed.

The movement in 1968 was overwhelmingly secular, nationalist, and anti-imperialist. The student wing of the Jamaat-e-Islami would sometimes try to disrupt meetings, including two of mine in Rawalpindi and Multan, occasionally by force, but were swept aside by waves of students chanting various versions of "Socialism is on its way" and "Death to Maududi," the latter a reference to the leader and principal theologian of the Islamists, patronized by the Saudi royal family and a committed supporter of the United States.

The war in Vietnam had struck a deep chord among Pakistanis of virtually all social classes, and the poet Habib Jalib was wildly cheered on platforms we shared that year when he recited:

Global defenders of human rights,
Why the silence?
Where are you?
Speak!
Humanity is on the rack
Vietnam is on fire,
Vietnam is on fire

Jalib would then turn on the rulers of Pakistan and warn them that if they carried on as before, the Vietnamese fire might spread to "where you are" and "clouds filled with dynamite will pour down on you."

A detailed survey of the casualties revealed the scale of the mobilizations. November 1968: 4 deaths and over 1,000 arrests; December 1968: 11 deaths, 1,530 arrests; January 1969: 57 deaths, 4,710 arrests, and 1,424 injured; February 1969: 47 deaths, 100 arrests, and 12 injured; March 1969: 90 deaths, 356 arrests, and 40 injured. These figures were based on press releases from the government and were generally regarded as a considerable underestimation. It had by now become obvious to the military high command that blanket repression was not deterring the crowds. They had lost their fear of death. When this happens, revolution becomes a possibility.

Railway workers in the Punjab had begun to sabotage rail tracks to prevent troop movements, and in East Bengal police stations were attacked and armories raided. A week later, the generals in GHQ called on their field marshal with sad faces but firm instructions. Ayub did not hesitate. He surrendered. His resignation was announced that same day. His successor, General Yahya (a particular pronunciation means "fuck-fuck" in Punjabi) Khan, took over and immediately announced that the country's first-ever general election would be held in December 1970. A euphoric fever gripped the country. Clashing cymbals, cheering crowds, and loud drumbeats marked the fall of Ayub Khan, who had, as Bhutto later recalled, been considering elevating himself to an even higher position than field marshal:

During the "golden era" of Ayub Khan an earnest proposal was made to him by an eminent personality to declare a hereditary monarchy in Pakistan and to make himself the first monarch. Ayub Khan took the proposal seriously. He formed a two-man Supreme Council of Nawab of Kalabagh and myself to examine it. We returned the proposal together with its blue-print to Ayub Khan within a week with the recommendations that he should forget it altogether. Ayub Khan's observations were "bhehtar sallah" (good advice). He added however, "It is not all that senseless."*

This jovial Sandhurst-trained officer, secular in outlook, fond of the odd drink, and used to obeying orders, had, alas, been overpromoted. Now he was gone. His overdependence on Washington and his own Svengalis had brought him down.

What lay ahead? Just three years previously, Karl von Vorys, a political science professor at the University of Pennsylvania, had concluded a 341-page book on Pakistan with these words:

"Just six years ago Mohammad Ayub Khan took the helm of the State of Pakistan. Since then he has many accomplishments to his credit. The disintegration of the country, an acute threat in 1958, seems rather remote now."† At least one sentence was accurate.

---

*Zulfiqar Ali Bhutto, *If I Am Assassinated* (New Delhi: 1979).

†Karl von Vorys, *Political Development in Pakistan* (Princeton: 1965).

4

THE WASHINGTON QUARTET

The General
Who Lost a Country

THE PAKISTAN ARMY PRIDES ITSELF ON BEING A UNIFYING FORCE, without which Pakistan would disappear. The history about to be recounted suggests that the opposite is the truth. In March 1969, Ayub passed control of the country to General Yahya Khan, who promised a free election within a year and, fearing the revival of the mass movement, kept his word. Before returning to the twisted narrative of Pakistani history, a pen portrait summarizing the place and function of the army might be helpful to the reader.

The army's oft-repeated claim that it is independent of "vested interests" had finally been exposed. Ayub Khan had played politics and enrolled the landed gentry in his Muslim League. His son had utilized the military umbrella to become a businessman and had amassed a small fortune. Indeed, the whole historical role of the military and bureaucratic state apparatus that Pakistan "inherited" from British rule in India had now emerged into the light of day for many Pakistanis of the '68 generation. This role was in many ways a peculiarly central and concentrated one in Pakistan, setting it off from the military regimes that exist in various Asian and African countries today.

The Japanese invasion and occupation of Southeast Asia during the

Second World War temporarily smashed the old colonial apparatuses of government—which had anyway never had a large indigenous quotient—in Burma, Indonesia, and elsewhere. After the war, there was little chance for the imperial powers to reconstitute these, and considerable sections of the armed forces and civil services that emerged in the postindependence period had participated in a national liberation struggle against either Japanese or European oppressors.

In Africa, on the other hand, the colonial administrations were usually staffed so thoroughly by the colonizing power itself that the civilian bureaucracy and—above all—the army had to build up virtually from scratch after independence was granted. On the Indian subcontinent, however, neither of these patterns prevailed. Here, a large and locally recruited civil service was an absolute necessity, since the British could not hope to staff themselves the bulk of the administrative system necessary to control such an immense population. The same situation obliged them simultaneously to create an extremely large Indian army, whose junior and some senior officers were recruited from the feudal aristocracy of the subcontinent. Lord Curzon's Memorandum on Army Commissions for Indians stated in 1900 that indigenous officers "should be confined to the small class of nobility or gentry . . . [and] should rest upon aristocracy of birth." Such an officer corps would serve "to gratify legitimate ambitions, and to attach the higher ranks of Indian society, and more especially the old aristocratic families, to the British Government by closer and more cordial ties."*

On the whole the scheme worked pretty well until the end of the Second World War. Indian troops performed sterling service for their imperialist masters in both world wars, and in relentless domestic repression at home. No other colonial power could boast of such a capacious sepoy force. A precondition of its success was, of course, the ethnic heterogeneity of India, which allowed the British to recruit their mercenary army from selected "martial races"—mainly Punjabis, Sikhs, Pathans, Rajputs, Jats, and Dogras—who could be relied on to keep down the other subject nationalities of the empire.

---

*See C. H. Phillips, ed., *Select Documents on the History of India and Pakistan* (London: 1962), 4: 518–20.

However, in India the Congress Party had led a strong independence movement from the 1920s onward that built a mass organization in the countryside and succeeded in levering Britain out of its imperial suzerainty after it had been fatally weakened by the Second World War. The Congress was then able itself to knit the state together and dominate a parliamentary system that has survived ever since.

The scenario in Pakistan was very different. The Muslim League was always an extremely weak organization by comparison. Originally created by Islamic princes and nobles in 1906 "to foster a sense of loyalty to the British government among the Muslims of India" (to cite from its statement of aims), it was captured by the educated Muslim middle class led by Jinnah in the 1930s and for a brief period was in alliance with the Congress Party. However, its main thrust was always anti-Hindu rather than anti-British. It collaborated with the raj during the Second World War and received a separate state from it in 1947, without having seriously struggled for independence. This change was itself stage-managed by the bureaucracy, which initially wielded most of the real power. However, once in the saddle, Ayub surrounded himself with a clique of cronies and increasingly made his regime into a personal dictatorship, rather than institutionalizing corporate military rule. A decade later Ayub's regime had become so immensely unpopular that it provoked the largest social upheaval in the history of the country. It was henceforward useless to the ruling class. Thus, in the emergency of early 1969, with masses on the streets in Rawalpindi, Lahore, Karachi, Dhaka, and Chittagong, and continuous strikes and riots in both East and West, the army dislodged Ayub and finally assumed direct political command.

The Yahya interregnum represented the end of a slow shift in the intrastate complex of power from the civilian to the military apparatus. Naturally, the civil service remained influential within the government: key civilian bureaucrats still concerned themselves with those manifold problems of running the state machine and the economy that were beyond the competence of the army officers. But the military were now the senior partner.

Already in 1971, the Pakistan army constituted a force of three hundred thousand troops, mostly recruited from those sections of the

Punjabi and Pathan peasantry who traditionally provided infantry for the British. Seventy thousand of them were deployed in Bengal. The officer corps, from the critical rank of lieutenant colonel upward, was a select elite screened with the utmost care for its class background and political outlook. The generals, brigadiers, and colonels of the Pakistan army are scions (usually younger sons) of the feudal aristocracy and gentry of Punjab and the North-West Frontier, with a sprinkling of wealthy immigrants from Gujarat and Hyderabad. The impeccable social credentials and accents of this group, which so entrance Western journalists, reveal their past. They were trained as imperial recruits in Sandhurst or Dehra Dun. The Punjabi regiments engaged in repression in Bengal thus included units who once practiced their trade under General Gracey in Vietnam. General Tikka Khan, who later became known as the butcher of Dhaka, was a veteran of Montgomery's army in the North African campaign. General "Tiger" Niazi, who signed the act of surrender to India in December 1971, later wrote with pride in his memoirs that the nickname Tiger "was given to me by Brigadier Warren, Commander, 161 Infantry Brigade, for my exploits in Burma during World War Two."* This was the situation at the time of the military offensive against the Eastern portion of Pakistan by its own army.

MEANWHILE, THE ignominious departure of Ayub Khan had shifted the struggle from the streets to electoral campaigning. Two political parties dominated the scene. In the West, the Peoples Party, led by Zulfiqar Ali Bhutto, had absorbed some of the most courageous and intelligent leaders and activists of the 1968–69 movement. They were aware that the country's mood of unfocused euphoria could not go on. It required a political outcome. For this a party was essential, and all the other parties were either discredited or irrelevant in the larger scheme

---

*A. A. K. Niazi, *The Betrayal of East Pakistan* (Karachi: 1999). What this and other self-serving memoirs of the period reveal is that most of the Pakistani generals involved in this tragedy have learned nothing and forgotten nothing. All they can contemplate is their own navels. Everyone else is to blame but them. There were no war crimes, no massacres. If anything, the military and its Bengali Razakar units (collaborators) were the victims.

of things. Bhutto had sown the seeds and he would reap the rewards. In the East, the bulk of the Maoist left that had supported Ayub Khan because of his links with China collapsed. The weaknesses of the traditional pro-Moscow left, strong in the media, weak on the streets, left the field wide-open to the Awami League. This party had defended Bengali autonomy and won over the movement to this cause. It became the voice of Bengali nationalism and was politically prepared for the onslaught that was being planned in Islamabad.

In 1947, the predominantly Hindu trader and landlord class of East Bengal migrated to West Bengal, which was and is a part of India, leaving their businesses and lands behind them. From the start this vacuum was filled by Bihari Muslim refugees from the United Provinces of India and non-Bengali businessmen from the Western portion of Pakistan. The economic exploitation of East Bengal, which began immediately after partition, led to an annual extraction of some 3 billion rupees (approximately $300 million) from the East by West Pakistani capital. The most important foreign-exchange earner was jute, a crop produced in East Pakistan that accounted for over 50 percent of exports. This money was spent on private consumption and capital investment in West Pakistan. The sums granted for development projects by the central government offer an interesting case study of discrimination. Between 1948 and 1951, $130 million were sanctioned for development. Of this, only 22 percent went to East Pakistan. From 1948 to 1969 the value of the resources transferred from the East amounted to $2.6 billion. The West Pakistan economy was heavily dependent on East Bengal, partly as a field for investment, but above all as a mine of subsidies and as a captive market. The Six Points demanded by the Awami League included both political and economic autonomy and directly threatened the immediate business interests of West Pakistani capitalists and their supporters embedded in the military and the civil service. The Six Points were:

1. A federal system of government, parliamentary in nature and based on adult franchise.
2. Federal government to deal only with defense and foreign affairs. All other subjects to be dealt with by the federating states.

3. Either two separate, but freely convertible, currencies for the two parts of the country or one currency for the whole country. In this case effective constitutional measures to be taken to prevent flight of capital from East to West Pakistan.
4. Power of taxation and revenue collection to be vested in the federating units and not at the center.
5. Separate accounts for foreign-exchange earnings of the two parts of the country under control of the respective governments.
6. The setting up of a militia or paramilitary force for East Pakistan.

These demands were both a response to the exploitation cited above and a serious attempt to maintain the unity of Pakistan via a new constitutional arrangement. When reproached by foreign correspondents for being "unreasonable," Sheikh Mujibur Rahman would become extremely irritated: "Is the West Pakistan government not aware that I am the only one able to save East Pakistan from communism? If they make the decision to fight, I shall be pushed out of power and the Naxalite types [Maoists] will intervene in my name. If I make too many concessions, I shall lose my authority. I am in a very difficult situation."*

The Six Points represented the charter of the aspirant Bengali bourgeoisie; it articulated their desire to create their own regional state apparatus and to have an equal share of the capitalist cake. But this was precisely the reason why the dominant bloc in West Pakistan was opposed to them. The Pakistan army was organically hostile to the prospect of a Bengali civilian government because of the danger that it would reduce the lavish military apparatus that had been a built-in feature of the Islamabad regime since Ayub seized power in October 1958. Some idea of the enormous stake the Pakistani officer corps had in retaining the status quo is reflected in that military expenditures over the preceding decade (1958–68) had absorbed no less than 60 percent of the total state budget. In the fiscal year of 1970 alone, some $625 million were allocated for the armed forces. The shortsighted West Pakistani political leaders who failed to appreciate this would soon become

---

Le Monde (Paris), March 31, 1971. The interview had been conducted some weeks earlier by an Agence France-Presse correspondent.

the victims of the same machine, for the army was not seriously in favor of any government that might challenge the imbalance between social and military expenditure.

To their credit the Awami League politicians had repeatedly denounced these colossal outlays on a military machine that was overwhelmingly non-Bengali and saturated from top to bottom with racist and religious chauvinism against the Bengalis, who had traditionally been regarded as dark, weak, and infected with Hinduism. For its part, the Pakistani business class had its own material reasons for resisting the Six Points. Business interests in the West no longer regarded the East as an optimal field of investment. Bengal remained of vital importance to them, both as a captive market and as a source of foreign exchange. In the late sixties, between 40 percent and 50 percent of West Pakistan's exports were taken by the East at monopoly prices. Where else could West Pakistani capitalism have disposed of its high-cost manufactures?

The Awami League won widespread political support in East Bengal for two important reasons. First, it grasped the importance of the national question: it saw clearly the subcolonial status of East Pakistan. Second, political parties of the extreme left, which gave opportunistic support to the Ayub dictatorship because of the latter's "friendship" with China, failed. The Maoist wing of the National Awami Party (NAP) insisted, with Chinese backing, that the Ayub regime had "certain anti-imperialist features" and was therefore in some ways to be preferred to bourgeois democracy.

Thus the Awami League could present itself as the only meaningful opposition force in the province. It constantly carried out propaganda in favor of its Six Points; it called for free elections, and it organized demonstrations against the Ayub dictatorship. Some of its leaders, including Mujibur Rahman, were consequently arrested, which only increased their popularity. When the anti-Ayub upsurge resulted in the fall of the dictator and his replacement by the Yahya junta in early 1969, it was hardly surprising that the Awami League reaped the benefits. Yet it could still not disavow its heritage. In the weeks before the army persuaded Ayub to retire, the Awami League eagerly participated in the "constitutional" talks at the Round Table Conferences called by Ayub to reach a compromise. It had fueled the mass movement and witnessed the anger of Bengali peasants and workers; even so it remained tied to its parliamentarist past.

THE YAHYA MILITARY regime, unable to quell the mass upheaval in both parts of the country, was forced to promise a general election on the basis of adult franchise. Its advisers evidently believed it could concede this as a diversionary tactic. They were confident that the bureaucracy, from long experience in such matters, would be able to manipulate the results satisfactorily. To give the latter some time to prepare itself, the elections were postponed—ostensibly because of the cyclone disaster in late 1970, which claimed two hundred thousand Bengali lives. But the failure of the army to provide any adequate flood relief only intensified the deep anger of the Bengali people. When the different Maoist factions in East Bengal decided to boycott the elections, which were finally held in December 1970, the Awami League was given a free hand and won a tidal victory. Of the 169 seats allocated to East Pakistan in the National Assembly, the League won 167. It also gained 291 out of the 343 seats in the provincial parliament. Its bloc in the National Assembly gave it an overall majority throughout the country and entitled it to form the central government. Such a prospect traumatized the West Pakistani ruling oligarchy. Given that the Awami League had fought the elections on the basis of the Six Points and had indeed on occasion surpassed them in its electoral rhetoric, it was clear that the army would try to prevent a meeting of the National Assembly. In this they were greatly helped, if not led, by Zulfiqar Ali Bhutto, who refused to countenance a Pakistan government led by the majority party.

Bhutto's Pakistan Peoples Party had triumphed in the western portion of the country and should have negotiated a settlement with the victors. Instead Bhutto sulked and told his party to boycott a meeting of the new parliament that had been called in Dhaka, the capital of East Pakistan, and thus provided the army with breathing space to prepare a military assault. He coined the slogan "Idhar Hum, Udhar Tum" (Here It's Us, There It's You), making it clear that, like the military, he was not interested in sharing power. This made a split inevitable. Bengal now went into noncooperation mode. A wave of strikes paralyzed the province. Even in the army cantonments the tension was deeply felt. For instance, when the Awami League decided on noncooperation, all the Bengali cooks, servants, and laundrymen left the cantonments; in the food markets the vendors refused to sell soldiers any food, and Bengali cars visiting cantonments had their numbers published in the *People* newspaper. At one stage the situation became so desperate that special nourishment for the officers had to be flown out from West Pakistan.

EVEN BEFORE THE formal invasion took place on March 25, 1971, hundreds of Bengali lives had been lost at the hands of what was seen as an oppressor army dispatched by West Pakistan. Some of the generals involved at the time have subsequently written that Mujib, frightened of his own people, asked the army to crush the movement, but that this, in reality, was a trap to make them even more unpopular. What a tangled web they weave, those who practice to deceive.

These earlier demonstrations of the army's brute power should have convinced the Awami League politicians of what was likely to follow unless they prepared the Bengali people for a protracted struggle. This they refused to do, despite the evident desire of the masses, expressed in thunderous slogans at Awami League meetings, for a total break with Pakistan. The rising tide of popular political consciousness was already clear in the enormous meetings that took place throughout the province both before and after the general election of 1970. At every stage the citizens assimilated the lessons of the past much more rapidly than their parliamentarist leaders and showed their willingness to fight the colonial state in East Bengal. At every stage they were again and again checked by the visceral constitutionalism of the Awami League leadership. This conflict between the mass movement and the tame reformism of its official guides was all the more tragic in that the existing organizations of the left were localized or discredited and thus not in a position to influence the course of the struggle decisively.

Ranajit Roy, a respected Indian press commentator, candidly noted a common element of Indo-Pakistani establishment politics in expressing his sympathy for Sheikh Mujibur Rahman: "The Awami League leadership in many ways corresponds to the leadership of our own Congress—a leadership which, with the backing of peaceful agitation, sought to arrive and ultimately succeeded in arriving at compromises with our colonialist masters. Our independence was the result of an understanding with the British masters. Sheikh Mujibur hoped to pull off a comparable deal with Islamabad. Like the Congress Party in India, the Awami League does not have the stomach for the type of war circumstances have forced Bangla Desh to wage."

These musings, of course, unwittingly pointed to an important difference between British and Pakistani colonialism in the subcontinent. British imperialism was able to grant a political decolonization because it nowhere meant the abandonment of its real economic empire, whose central segments were Malayan rubber and tin, Middle Eastern oil and South African gold, and Indian plantations. But the loss of political control of East Bengal affected the vital interests of the impoverished and wretched subcolonialism of Islamabad directly. For the weaker a colonial power, the more dependent it is on formal political possession of its subject territories. The history of the twentieth century has a striking lesson for us in this respect.

The European imperialism that waged the longest and most stubborn war for the retention of its overseas possessions was not industrialized England, France, or even Belgium. It was the small, backward, and predominantly agrarian society of Portugal. Lisbon fought a ferocious and unremitting campaign in Africa to keep Angola, Mozambique, and Guinea because of the enormous economic and ideological importance of these colonies. The subcolonialism of Portugal, whose own economy had been deeply penetrated by the capital investment of the advanced powers, furnished an instructive comparison with that of Pakistan. Neither had much politico-economic room for maneuvering; both were in their different ways consequently driven to extreme and unmediated measures of repression.

These led to a massive crisis for both countries: the breakup of one as documented in this book and a serious split in the army of the other. Portuguese majors and colonels were in the vanguard of the popular movement that toppled Salazar's Estado Novo in the democratic revolution of 1974.

Any objective assessment of the Awami League, which is still a major party in Bangladesh, would conclude that it has been a secular, but conservative party since its birth. Its formative years, like those of its West Pakistani siblings, were dominated by parliamentary maneuver and intrigue. Its main social roots have always been in the functionaries, teachers, petty traders, and shopkeepers who proliferate in East Bengali society. Its founder, H. S. Suhrawardy, who for a short time succeeded in becoming Pakistan's prime minister, distinguished himself in 1956 by supporting the Anglo-French-Israeli invasion of Egypt. He became one of the most articulate defenders of imperialist interests in Pakistan and American policy in Asia as a whole. Left-wing parties and organizations in East Pakistan who opposed these policies were physically attacked by Awami League "volunteers" and had their meetings broken up with monotonous regularity. Suhrawardy's other notable achievement was to supervise the fusion of the provinces of Baluchistan, Sind, and the North-West Frontier into a single territorial unit dominated completely by Punjab. In this way he showed his respect for the "autonomy" of the West Pakistani provinces.

After 1958, Suhrawardy played a dissident role during the early years of the Ayub dictatorship and was imprisoned for a short time as a result; but his opposition was always limited to the bourgeois constitutionalist framework. Suhrawardy's undoubted talents—he was a proficient lawyer, an artful political manipulator, and a glib conversationalist—placed him head and shoulders above the rest of the Awami League leadership. His ambitions were, however, far removed from Bengali independence: his aim was to make the Awami League an all-Pakistan electoral machine, capable of winning power as a "national" party and thus catapulting H. S. Suhrawardy into the highest-possible office. His untimely death in 1963 put an end to this dream.

It is essential to recall this early history to understand the later attitudes of the Awami League. It continued to play an oppositional role during the remaining years of the Ayub dictatorship. Ayub himself more than once considered the idea of reaching some compromise with its leaders and incorporating them into the central government, but the gangster politicians from the East Pakistani underworld, on whom Ayub had relied for so long to maintain "law and order" in Bengal, constantly and successfully sabotaged this plan, as it would have meant the end of their own political careers.

The Awami League was thus offered no choice but to continue as an oppositional force. It joined a multiparty alliance (Combined Opposition Parties) in 1964 to field a candidate against Ayub, but the elections were rigged by the army and the civil service and the field marshal was returned with a comfortable majority. As a result the country suffered an inner breakdown, but nobody in power noticed. From now on the Awami League, however reluctantly, would be pushed in a different direction, leaving it with few options but to challenge the military head-on. The hopes of the transatlantic press rested on a military dictator. Some weeks before the military was unleashed against 75 million Bengalis, the *Economist* was representative of this mainstream opinion and approved of General Yahya: "It is also likely that the President will do his best to stay the army's hand. So far he has proved a model soldier in politics, remaining aloof from the electioneering and releasing all political prisoners after the election."

Jinnah's Pakistan died on March 26, 1971, with East Bengal drowned in blood. Two senior West Pakistanis had, to their credit, resigned in protest against what was about to happen. Admiral Ahsan and General Yaqub left the province after their appeals to Islamabad had been rejected. Both men had strongly opposed a military solution. Bhutto, on the other hand, backed the invasion. "Thank God, Pakistan has been saved," he declared, aligning himself with the disaster that lay ahead. Rahman was arrested and several hundred nationalist and left-wing intellectuals, activists, and students were killed in a carefully organized massacre. The lists of victims had been prepared with the help of local Islamist vigilantes, whose party, the Jamaat-e-Islami, had lost badly in the elections. Soldiers were told that Bengalis were relatively recent converts to Islam and hence not "proper Muslims"—their genes needed improving. This was the justification for the campaign of mass rape.

In Dhaka, Mujibur Rahman waited at home to be arrested. Many of his colleagues went underground. The military shelled Dhaka University. Artillery units flattened working-class districts; trade-union and newspaper offices were burned to the ground. Soldiers invaded the women's hostel on the university campus, raping and killing many res-

idents. With the help of the intelligence agencies and local collaborators, mainly Islamist activists, lists of nationalist and Communist intellectuals had been prepared (as in Indonesia in 1965), and they were
now picked up and killed. Some had been close friends of mine. I was
both sad and angry. I had predicted this tragedy, while hoping it might
be avoided. Immediately after the December 1970 general election I
wrote, "Will the Pakistan Army and the capitalist barons of West Pakistan allow these demands to go through? The answer is quite clearly
no. What will probably happen is that in the short-term Mujibur
Rehman will be allowed to increase East Pakistan's percentage of
import and export licenses and will be allocated a larger share of foreign capital investment. These are the 'concessions' which the Army
will be prepared to make in the coming few months. If Rehman accepts
them, he will be allowed to stay in power. If not, it will be back to business as usual in the shape of the Army. Of course there is no doubt that
in the event of another military coup there will be no holding back the
immense grievances of Bengal and the desire for an independent Bengal will increase a hundredfold."*

The Bengali political leaders had not prepared the people for this
onslaught. Had they done so, many lives might have been saved. Bengali policemen and soldiers had been waiting for the word from above
to desert with their weapons and defend their people. It was the death
knell of Jinnah's Pakistan. Bangladesh (Bengali nation) was about to be
born. The struggle that now erupted between the Bengali liberation
forces and the armed might of West Pakistani capital represented both
a continuation of the mass movement that erupted in 1968–69 and a
qualitative break.

There were two distinguishing features of politics in East Bengal
from the beginning of 1971: on the one hand, the enthusiastic participation of the people in every level of an escalating social and
national struggle; and on the other, the political deficiencies of the petit
bourgeois notabilities of the Awami League, whose whole tradition of
compromise and maneuver rendered them incapable of providing lead-

---

*"Pakistan: After the December Elections, What Next?" *Red Mole,* January 1, 1971, 10.

ership in a real independence movement. Mujib had addressed a mass meeting of nearly a million people on March 7, 1971, where he had fulminated against the delays and intrigues but refused to declare independence. Ordinary Bengalis paid the price for his prevarications.

Operation Searchlight was brutal, but ineffective. Killing students and intellectuals did not lead to the quick and clear victory sought by the Pakistani generals. Once the initial attack had failed, the military with the help of local Islamist volunteers (members of the Jamaat-e-Islami) began to kill Hindus—there were 10 million of them in East Pakistan— and burn their homes. Tens of thousands were exterminated. These were war crimes according to any international law.*

All this was taking place while most pro-Yahya Western governments averted their eyes and hoped for the best. As news of the offensive spread, the predominantly Bengali East Pakistan Rifles mutinied. Much was made in later propaganda by Islamabad about how the West Pakistan commander Colonel Janjua was woken up by a Bengali subordinate, taken to his office in his pajamas, sat down in the commanding officer's chair, and executed by his batman. It was ugly, but what civil war is not? Few asked how had it come about that the only Bengali company in the country had a non-Bengali commander? It was part of the problem.

Guerrilla units emerged in different parts of the province, representing different political factions but united in the struggle for independence. The strongest of these was the Mukti Bahini (Liberation

---

*The Nuremberg Principles, as formulated by the International Law Commission, left no room for doubt. They defined war crimes as:

> Violations of the laws or customs of war which include, but are not limited to, murder, ill-treatment or deportation to slave-labor or for any other purpose of civilian population of or in occupied territory, murder or ill-treatment of prisoners of war, or persons on the seas, killing of hostages, plunder of public or private property, wanton destruction of cities, towns, or villages, or devastation not justified by military necessity.

Crimes against humanity were:

> Murder, extermination, enslavement, deportation and other inhuman acts done against any civilian population, or persecutions on political, racial or religious grounds, when such acts are done or such persecutions are carried on in execution of or in connection with any crime against peace or any war crime.

Army), led largely by Awami League nationalists, but others operated locally, including groups inspired by Che Guevara and led by Tipu Biswas and Abdul Matin. These militants had been left with no other choice. The ruling elites in both India and Pakistan wanted a rapid conclusion to the struggle. This did not happen. Supreme power in Islamabad at this stage was exercised by a small circle of military officers, flanked by a few civilian advisers and accomplices. Yahya Khan himself had become a dim and slothful figurehead. Reports would later emerge of how late one night while intoxicated, he had rushed out stark naked onto the streets of Peshawar roaring with laughter, chased by his favorite mistress (widely known as "General" Rani), and had to be escorted back indoors by his unsurprised guards. This was at the height of the war. None of this would have mattered if he had been successful, but failure stared the army in the face.

The clique that ruled behind him and was conducting the war included five senior generals and a few civil servants, none of whom were distinguished for their competence. In his memoirs, General Gul Hassan, a senior officer at the time, recounts the chaos in GHQ during the war: dispatches full of lies, cover-ups designed to conceal military failures, the overextension of military units that left Dhaka vulnerable, and so on. Viewed coldly as a military operation, it was a disaster. General "Tiger" Niazi, commandant of East Pakistan, had boasted that he would crush the rebellion within weeks, but this braggadocio was to no avail. Gul Hassan could barely conceal his contempt for Niazi, who he felt was no more than "company commander material." Hassan himself was not a great strategic thinker and came up with a madcap scheme to open a second front. This entailed a strategic thrust against India on its western frontiers. He argued that the best way to save East Pakistan now was via a full-scale war that would lead to a UN/U.S./China intervention to impose a global cease-fire. The risk here was that if, as was likely, this did not happen, then West Pakistan too might go up in smoke. His more friendly superiors patted him on the back for clever thinking but rejected the idea.* They were not totally stupid. The com-

---

Memoirs of Gul Hassan Khan (Karachi: 1993).

plete control of the state by the army now raised more fundamental questions.

The Pakistan army and civil bureaucracy have always enjoyed a relative autonomy from the landlords and businessmen of West Pakistan. But the converse does not hold. The latter were heavily dependent on the military-bureaucratic complex that dominated the state. This process had been accelerated by the mass upsurge of 1968–69. The oligarchy in the West became more and more acutely aware of its dependence on the continued strength of the military and civilian state machine. The army and its cohesion was thus needed as a political rallying point over and above its purely repressive functions. The Six Points of March 1971 had struck at the heart of oligarchic rule in the West. This explains the frenzied refusal to compromise with the Awami League, the ferocity of the action against the East, and the remarkable degree of unanimity in West Pakistani ruling circles in immediately supporting the coup of March 25. It also explains the fidelity of the United States and its British adjutants to the military regime, despite the fact that it had jeopardized "stability" in Bengal.

The United States did try to inflect the Pakistani dictatorship toward "moderation," while shoring it up otherwise. Critical voices in Washington were annoyed by the threat posed to their global interests by the narrow national egoism of the Pakistan army. They were also nervous that the debacle in the East might destabilize the hitherto solid command structure of the Pakistani military.

Steeped in British conventions, the senior officers had hitherto always respected strict hierarchy of rank. Both Ayub and Yahya, when they assumed power in 1958 and 1969 respectively, were commander in chief of the army and formally acted in an ex officio capacity. A Middle Eastern– or Latin American–style putsch by radical younger generals or colonels would have represented a sharp rupture with this whole tradition. Such an eventuality was avoided in the nick of time after the crushing defeat of December 1971, when the domestic situation had already greatly deteriorated and the junior ranks were restive because of the ineptitude of the high command.

The war in Bangladesh had badly shaken the Pakistani economy, which had been depressed anyway since 1968. Foreign exchange had drastically dwindled, while prices and unemployment rose in tandem. Jute exports had naturally collapsed, precipitating steep falls on the Karachi stock exchange. This grave economic crisis was, of course, caused by the cost of the expeditionary force in Bengal. Press estimates calculated this at something like $2 million a day (the equivalent of $40 million today), a massive burden when added to West Pakistan's chronic import deficit of $140 million dollars ($2.8 billion today) a month. The Islamabad regime was thus faced with a domestic squeeze it had not bargained for when it embarked on its genocidal operations in March. It unilaterally suspended payments on its foreign debts and needed further large infusions of U.S. aid to ward off total bankruptcy.

New dangers loomed on other fronts. It soon became clear to the Indian government, led by Indira Gandhi, that a protracted struggle in East Bengal could have critical repercussions inside India in West Bengal. The latter province had been in the throes of a profound social crisis for three years now. Peasant uprisings and generalized social unrest had made the border province a powder keg. The Indian ruling elite, although far stronger than its Pakistani counterpart, was well aware of this and nervous that the infection might spread. Many reading this account today will be surprised by the thought that anyone in power ever feared a "Red revolution," but they did. The strength of the Communist Party (Marxist) and Maoist groups to its left worried successive Indian governments.

This was one of the main reasons that Mrs. Gandhi was quick in her demagogic response to the events in East Bengal. Every opposition party in India had been urging New Delhi to intervene more forcefully. However, Indira Gandhi's policy was to prop up the Awami League, while repeatedly disarming guerrillas crossing the border and instituting strict political control over the so-called "training camps" set up on Indian soil. Although it enjoyed great military superiority, the Indian government was initially daunted by the prospect of an intervention in East Bengal. It would anger the United States and China and might plunge the whole region into a turmoil that New Delhi feared it might not be able to control. Indeed, even if the Awami League succeeded in establishing what Indira Gandhi referred to as a "secular and democratic state" in East Bengal, the weakness of the indigenous elite and the virtual absence of a developed state apparatus would have posed the question of some sort of a revolutionary solution with great rapidity.

THE MOST EFFECTIVE political force in West Bengal itself at that time (as today) was undoubtedly the Communist Party of India (Marxist), or CPI(M), with its tens of thousands of militants and millions of supporters. The centrist inclinations of this party were in full view even then as it formed a coalition state government in the province, though once governor's rule was imposed and the center took charge, it allowed itself more revolutionary rhetoric. Its leaders stated that Indira Gandhi and Yahya Khan represented equally reactionary social and political forces, which was a bit unfair. They argued that just as East Bengal was specially exploited by West Pakistan, so "West Bengal was especially exploited by the Indian Centre." The logical conclusion to this view was to develop a strategy for a United Socialist Bengal. But to think in such terms necessitated a break with the past, and this the CPI(M) could not do. Perhaps it was a utopian notion, and perhaps it was the strong utopian streak in me that led me later, and quite independently of the CPI(M), to raise the demand for a United Socialist Bengali Republic. I found myself being denounced as an "ultraleft adventurist," a criticism that, on thinking back, possibly contained a germ of truth. At the time it seemed a reasonable enough response to military dictators, compromised politicians, and ignoble businessmen.

It was as an "ultraleft adventurer" that I arrived on a pitch-dark night in Calcutta in 1971, disguised as a Hindu trader. My aim was to meet up with a courier from the war zone and cross the border with him into East Pakistan and establish direct contact with the Bengali resistance. I had shaved off my mustache for the first and last time and barely recognized myself. I was traveling on a fake British passport that had once belonged to a man called Muttabir Thakur, a Bengali trader from Brick Lane in the East End of London. I had no idea who he was, but he had volunteered to surrender his passport to help the Bengali struggle. I was at that time still a Pakistani citizen and was aware that then, as now, a Pakistani passport did not facilitate a quick entry into most countries and especially not India.

For some unfathomable reason, Sophie, the French militant who had dyed my hair in Paris, had given it and my eyebrows a reddish tint so that when I looked in the mirror, I saw someone resembling a Hollywood serial killer. I was carrying a revolver gifted indirectly by the IRA for this journey, which I had packed in my suitcase together with some ammunition.

At Bombay airport the immigration officer asked me a routine question: "What is your father's name?" I had memorized Thakur's address in Calcutta, but had stupidly not foreseen this question. I panicked, blurting out, "Mohammed." The immigration officer was shocked, but before he could say anything, an elderly, ample-girthed Parsi lady queuing up behind me, evidently touched that a Hindu boy's father had been named Mohammed, defused the situation by exclaiming, "How sweet!" Everyone smiled, my papers were stamped, and Customs did not bother to open my suitcase.

I had arrived determined to cross the border and establish contact with the guerrilla band of Abdul Matin and Tipu Biswas, who represented the most sympathetic, Guevarist wing of the Bengali left. One of their supporters had translated Che Guevara's *Guerrilla Warfare* into Bengali, and it was now being read by soldiers in the Mukti Bahini, the official liberation army, which included former Bengali soldiers and officers of the Pakistan army. Matin and Biswas's irregulars were said to be operating in Pabna, in the heart of the province between the Ganges and the Brahmaputra rivers, as well as in the northeast of the province, in the region of Sylhet and Mymensingh. This last had been the epicenter of the great Tebhaga peasant uprising for rent reductions in 1945–47, the most militant social revolt of the rural poor in the subcontinent to that date. The tradition had certainly not disappeared. A courier from the Bengali maquis met me in Calcutta. He must have been only eighteen years old, but his composure and authority belied his youth. He impressed me greatly. He told me that the resistance was growing and maturing every day and had succeeded in paralyzing the port towns of Chittagong and Khulna, thus reducing interzonal trade to a trickle. "Soon we will take Santa Clara and then Havana," he said with a smile, the closest he came to revealing his political identity. In those days, given the diversity of groups engaged in the resistance, it was better not to pry too deeply into political affiliations, especially if one was a Punjabi from West Pakistan.

His instructions were to take me across the border, from where others would be responsible for my transportation. He insisted that we could not travel with any weapons in case we were stopped and searched by the Indian border police. So, reluctantly, I left the revolver behind. As we moved in the direction of the border, we began to encounter roadblocks and signs of heavy Indian troop movements and tanks. The border was obviously being sealed off. We were warned by activists en route that border crossings were virtually impossible. There was no option but to abort the mission. The courier kept his cool. He left me at a safe location in Calcutta and returned. I never discovered his real name. Some years later a Bengali friend told me that he was dead.

Over breakfast one morning at the Great Eastern, a dilapidated but atmospheric relic of the raj in central Calcutta, I was chatting with friends when an English journalist, Peter Hazelhurst of the *Times,* walked over and stared at me. I looked up, gave no sign of recognition, and turned away. We all fell quiet and buried our faces in newsprint. Hazelhurst hovered around, then returned to our table. He said something to me but I ignored him. He now insisted that he had recognized my voice, congratulated me on the effectiveness otherwise of my disguise, and threatened to expose my presence unless I gave him an exclusive interview as to what I was doing there. I was trapped and agreed. Afterward he gave me twenty-four hours to get out and helped to throw pursuers off the scent by writing I was heavily bearded and heading for Delhi. In fact I went to the airport and hopped on the first flight to London. In the interview I had raised the desirability of a United Red Bengal, a beacon for the whole region, a spark that would set the prairie on fire. Words came easily in those days. Hazelhurst agreed that a Red Bengal would alarm Delhi even more than Islamabad and reported me accurately, a rare enough occurrence at the time. These stray reflections stirred a hornet's nest. The Maoist groups, in particular, saw this as a "petty-bourgeois nationalist deviation." The prospect of a united Bengal was viewed with equal alarm by Washington, which perceived it as a stepping-stone to the possible Vietnamization of South Asia. This became clear when, astonishingly but to my immense delight, the following editorial appeared in the *New York Times*:

> Mr. Ali's radical vision of chaos on the Indian subcontinent cannot be taken lightly. . . .
>
> A prolonged guerrilla conflict in East Pakistan would have profound repercussions in the neighboring violence-prone Indian state of West Bengal, already shaken by the influx of more than three million refugees from the Pakistani Army's campaign of terror. Prime Minister Indira Gandhi is under mounting pressure to intervene to try to check this threat to India's own internal peace and integrity.
>
> It is obviously in nobody's interest to allow the Bengali "spark" to explode into a major international conflict, one which might speedily involve the major powers. Nor is it wise to permit the situation in East Pakistan to continue to fester, inviting the gradual political disintegration of the entire subcontinent.
>
> To deprive Tariq Ali and his like of their "big opportunity" it is essential that Pakistan's President Yahya Khan come to terms speedily with the more moderate Sheik Mujibur Rahman and his Awami League, which won an overwhelming popular mandate in last December's national and state elections. Such an accommodation with East Pakistan's elected representatives should be a prerequisite for the resumption of U.S. aid, except for relief assistance, to Pakistan.*

But Yahya Khan was out of it by now. It was Mrs. Gandhi, the Indian prime minister, who would deprive us of our "big opportunity." It had become obvious to New Delhi that the Pakistan army could not hold the province for long, and if the guerrilla war persisted, the Awami League leadership might be bypassed by more radical elements. Accordingly, on December 3, 1971, the Indian army crossed the East Bengal border, were greeted as liberators, were helped by the local population, and advanced toward the capital, Dhaka. Within a

---

*"Bengal Is the Spark," editorial, *New York Times*, June 2, 1971.

fortnight they had compelled "Tiger" Niazi to surrender himself and the rest of his command. Pakistan lost half its navy, a quarter of its air force, and just under a third of its army. The rout was complete. Within weeks Sheikh Mujibur Rahman had been released from a West Pakistani prison and flown to Dhaka via London. Washington, fearing chaos in his absence, had pressured Islamabad for his swift release. A defeated leadership had little choice but to oblige. East Bengal now became Bangladesh, a country of 70 million people. Within several weeks the Indian army had left, leaving the new state to construct its own apparatus.

The ferocious cyclone that had struck East Bengal in 1970, a year before the Pakistan army, had claimed two hundred thousand lives. Nature was kinder than the war. Sheikh Mujibur Rahman insisted that 3 million Bengalis had been killed in the war. The Pakistan army disputed these figures without supplying their own. A senior State Department mandarin, presumably relying on U.S. intelligence reports, wrote that "one million people were killed in Bengal between March and December [1971]. Some four million families—up to 20 million people—appear to have fled their homes, nearly half of them to refuge in India. Between one and two million houses were destroyed."* These are shocking figures, dwarfing the massacres at the time of partition and even the appalling Bengal famine of 1943. General A. O. Mitha, with the help of the U.S. military, had created the Special Services Group (SSG) in the sixties. Its purpose was to carry out specialist missions behind enemy lines (India), and its commandos had been sent to East Pakistan long before March 1971. In his memoirs, Mitha describes being stationed in Calcutta as a young officer and witnessing the heartrending plight of the famine victims. The same general, this time part of the war machine, exonerated the military commanders and blamed the politicians for the bloodbath.

Back in Islamabad, General Hameed, the man responsible for the prosecution of the war and on behalf of the high command, addressed all the officers in GHQ to explain why they had surrendered and lost

---

*Phillips Talbot, "The Subcontinent: Ménage à Trois," *Foreign Affairs* 50, no. 4 (July 1972), 698–710.

half the country. Thirty years later, Mitha, who had thought the meeting was a bad idea but had to attend, described the scene when Hameed invited questions:

> All hell broke loose. Majors, Lt. Colonels, Brigadiers screamed and shouted at him and called him and Yahya filthy names. The gist of what they shouted was that the reason for the defeat was that all senior officers were interested in was getting more and more plots and more and more land. . . . Hameed tried to calm them down but nobody would listen to him now, so he walked out.*

General Gul Hassan, who was at the same meeting, wrote in his memoirs, "One incessant demand I vaguely recall was that all officers' messes should be declared dry." He was convinced that a group of conspirators in the army were planning to use the SSG to either arrest or kill Bhutto when he returned to Islamabad from New York, where he had been addressing the United Nations Security Council. Gul Hassan noted:

> I do not know what role was contemplated for the SSG in Rawalpindi, but I can state categorically that the one purpose it was not intended for was to furnish a guard of honour to Bhutto at the airport. Had this drama been staged, it would have smacked of a re-enactment of our military action in Dhaka. Whether the President [Yahya Khan] was a party to this design, I am in no position to say. General Mitha, with his potent credentials, was the obvious choice to set this plot in train. . . . The discipline of the Army was on the verge of snapping and the repugnant odour of anarchy was in the air. . . . The induction of a company of the SSG, by no stretch of imagination for a Samaritan role, was a move so reckless that, had it materialised, it could have dispatched the country into oblivion.†

---

*Major General A. O. Mitha, *Unlikely Beginnings: A Soldier's Life* (Karachi: 2003).
†*Memoirs of Lt. Gen. Gul Hassan Khan* (Karachi: Oxford University Press, 1993).

In his memoirs, General Mitha denied the charge and accused Gul Hassan of pandering to Bhutto and "lying." What none of them could deny was that their fun-loving president, General Yahya Khan, had presided over a monumental political and military disaster. Having successfully liquidated the old state, he was now asked to relinquish power. His reign had lasted less than three years. The debate as to the inevitability of this loss continues to this day within the military elite, and a hard-line view of the conflict insists that it was all an Indian plot and Pakistan will have its revenge in Kashmir provided it is permitted "strategic depth" in Afghanistan. Action based on half-baked ideas of this variety might, on the contrary, lead to a repeat performance of 1971 and further dent, if not destroy, the state.

What would happen to a remaindered Pakistan? The overwhelming electoral success of the Awami League had stunned Bhutto. It utterly upset his plans for taking power. He had emerged as the most vociferous defender of the traditional hegemony of West Pakistan, had hysterically denounced the Six Points, and after confabulations with top army generals had whipped up an intensely chauvinistic atmosphere in Punjab to prepare his supporters for war.

In the 1970 elections in West Pakistan, Bhutto's Pakistan Peoples Party (PPP) had emerged as the largest Western party in the new constituent assembly. But smaller parties had also emerged with significant regional bases in Baluchistan and the North-West Frontier, and Bhutto knew that at best he would be a junior partner in any coalition government at the center. If the Awami League chose to govern alone, he would be acknowledged only as the leader of West Pakistan. Bhutto had won the elections in Punjab and Sind after his party had campaigned on a radical platform promising massive land reforms, extensive nationalization, food, clothing, and shelter for all, universal education, and an end to the economic power of the twenty-two families who, according to the Planning Commission, controlled 70 percent of the country's industrial capital, 80 percent of banking, and 90 percent of the insurance industry. These were improbable promises. Because of the virtual eclipse of the left, he was able, for a while, to don the socialist mantle. People close to him at the time, experienced veterans of the caliber of Meraj Mohammad Khan, Mukhtar Rana, Dr. Mubashir Hassan (the first finance minister in the PPP government), would later reveal that the radical rhetoric was little more than a mask designed to win and retain power. It was never meant seriously, and Bhutto would often laugh at the early descriptions of him in the Western press as an Asian Fidel Castro. It undoubtedly tickled his vanity, but his ideas and plans were far removed from any revolution. If anything, he believed in a form of social autocracy on the Lee Kuan Yew pattern in Singapore. A city-state could not, however, provide a model for even the new, reduced Pakistan.

Bhutto's party organization was an improvised assemblage of feudalists, racketeers, lawyers, and bandwagon petit bourgeois together with some of the most dedicated student activists who had helped topple the dictatorship. Its electoral success owed a great deal to Bhutto's deals with powerful landlord cliques in the provinces (his pact with leading Sindhi feudalists, of which he was one, was particularly notorious). However, the PPP also reflected, captured, and confiscated the genuine popular aspirations for social transformation of towns and villages. He made his party the only possible conduit for change and had destroyed the stranglehold of traditional landlord politics in the Punjab. For the first time peasants defied their patrons and voted for Bhutto.

According to the wits in Lahore's teahouses, "even a rabid dog on the PPP ticket" would have won that year. This was proved by the election of Ahmed Raza Kasuri, one of Bhutto's early and more eccentric supporters, who would later be a turncoat and accuse his former leader of murder. I remember well, in 1969, Bhutto arriving at a wedding in Lahore, preceded by Ahmed Raza in butler mode announcing, "Everyone, please rise for Chairman Bhutto, who is about to arrive," a remark that caused much merriment and was greeted with ribaldry.

So great was the enthusiasm and so deep the desire for social change that in those early months a great deal could have been accomplished. That the chairman of the Peoples Party was no visionary was revealed by his attitude to East Pakistan. Serious class tensions within Bhutto's electoral bloc and the hollowness of its party organization meant that the only cement to hold it together was a popular national chauvinism as embodied in the language and style of its leader.

The generals who had lost the war and some of their junior officers hated references to themselves by critics of every hue as "wine-soaked generals and bloodthirsty colonels." Nor were they alone. West Pakistani bureaucrats, state television executives, and numerous others who had been caught up in the euphoria unleashed by the chauvinism were now afflicted with a deep melancholy. Instead of calmly evaluating what had happened, they retreated into a fantasy world, occasionally quoting the poetry of Faiz to enliven otherwise dull and dreadful memoirs. They were careful never to mention the three grief-stricken poems Faiz wrote about blood-soaked East Bengal after 1971, the voice of a nation that had lost its tongue. The second of these was a bittersweet plea for truth and forgiveness:

This is how my sorrow became visible:
Its dust, piling up for years in my heart,
finally reached my eyes,

the bitterness now so clear that
I had to listen when my friend
told me to wash my eyes with blood.

Everything at once was tangled in blood—
each face, each idol, red everywhere.
Blood swept over the sun, washing away its gold.

The moon erupted with blood, its silver extinguished.
The sky promised a morning of blood,
and the night wept only blood.

The trees hardened into crimson pillars.
All flowers filled their eyes with blood.
and every glance was an arrow,

each pierced image blood. This blood
—a river crying out for martyrs—
flows on in longing. And in sorrow, in rage, in love.

*

Let it flow. Should it be dammed up,
there will only be hatred cloaked in colours of death.
Don't let this happen, friends,
bring all my tears back instead,
a flood to purify my dust-filled eyes,
to wash this blood forever from my eyes.

Finally realizing the scale of the disaster they had brought on themselves, a battered army leadership now turned to a patrician political leader, Zulfiqar Ali Bhutto, to manage the rump state and help them out of their mess. At this point the "relative autonomy" of the military had ceased to exist. That they would ever return to power seemed unimaginable. It is not often in history that a political leader is given a chance to look ahead and stamp a vision, a new imprint, on the future of his country. History offered Bhutto that chance. Would he take it?

THE WASHINGTON QUARTET
The Soldier of Islam

THE HEADLINES IN THE YEAR 1972 WERE GRABBED BY EAST PAK-
istan becoming Bangladesh. But the impact of the disintegration of
the old state on West Pakistan should not be underestimated. The three
minority provinces—Baluchistan, Frontier, and Sind—felt orphaned
and began to resent the center. The presence of Bengal in Pakistan
had provided them with a protective umbrella in the sense that they
always felt that if they combined with Bengal, they could outvote the
Punjab. Now they were alone. Nor should it be imagined that everyone in the Punjab was happy with what had taken place. The enthusiasm for Bhutto demonstrated in the 1970 elections never entirely
disappeared, but it began to wane. The passionate social and political atmosphere I had experienced immediately after the fall of the dictatorship in 1969 had become polluted by the knowledge of the
atrocities in East Pakistan. The racism directed against the darker-
skinned Bengalis was much stronger among sections of the English-
educated elite. The common people were troubled. Their living
conditions were no different from those of their former compatriots
in East Pakistan.

The war had diminished the revolutionary ardor of the students,
workers, and urban poor. They had demonstrated that the power of a

military dictatorship and its capacity to resist popular pressures had been greatly overrated. It was they who had sacrificed lives to wrest the instruments of power from the dictatorship, only to experience their own leaders collaborating with the generals to crush an insurgent population of East Pakistan, with disastrous results. The effect of this was twofold. It created enormous political confusion and led to the disappearance of the mass spontaneity that had characterized the uprising of 1968–69.

The PPP's politics too had become tangled up in the blood of Bengal. However it was justified to their supporters, it still did not seem right. But despite the change in mood, their supporters still expected something positive from the PPP. The longing for social change, for freer intellectual and political life and space to breathe, would never disappear.

In 1972, Bhutto was the unchallengeable leader of a truncated Pakistan. He knew that the only way to rekindle the movement and enthuse his supporters was by implementing the reforms that had been promised in the election manifesto of the Peoples Party, the demands that had been summarized in a popular chant against the Jamaat-e-Islami. When Islamist sloganeers asked, "What does Pakistan mean?" their activists would reply in unison, "There is only one Allah and he is Allah." The response of PPP militants to the same question was less abstract: "Food, clothing, and shelter." This had become the electoral battle cry of Bhutto's party, had won him the majority in West Pakistan, had left the Islamists fuming but impotent. In his first address to the new Pakistan, Bhutto pledged, "My dear countrymen, my dear friends, my dear students, laborers, peasants . . . all those of you who fought for Pakistan. . . . We are facing the worst crisis in our country's life, a deadly crisis. We have to pick up the pieces, very small pieces, but we will make a new Pakistan, a prosperous and progressive Pakistan."

HOW WOULD THIS deadly crisis be resolved? Everything favored Bhutto and the Pakistan Peoples Party. The military high command was totally discredited, the right-wing parties isolated, and the two provinces not under PPP control—Frontier and Baluchistan—were governed by a coalition of secular nationalists led by the National Awami Party (now the Awami National Party—ANP) and the JUI, which were both committed to social reforms and an independent foreign policy. The JUI was not at that time making the implementation of the Sharia (Islamic laws) a precondition for anything.

Despite the promises and the propitious circumstances for honoring them, little was actually delivered to the majority of citizens. The country became oversaturated with PPP propaganda, the cult of the leader, and dehydrated ideas. Change was purely cosmetic, as symbolized by Bhutto's decision to design special military-style uniforms for party leaders and members of the government that were compulsory for official occasions. The sight of some overweight ministers ridiculously garbed created a great deal of amusement. Few were aware that the inspiration for this artificial grandeur came from Benito Mussolini rather than local bandleaders. The nub of the matter was that Bhutto was a man of few convictions. His opinions were never firm and settled. What he lacked in this department was overcompensated for by his sharp wit and intelligence, but that was never enough.

The balance sheet of Bhutto's five years in office is not edifying. From January to April 1972, he ruled the country as chief martial law administrator, and in that capacity he issued the Economic Reform Order on January 3, 1972, under which the banks, insurance companies, and seventy other industrial enterprises, large and small, were nationalized by the government. These included the medium-size steel foundry in Lahore owned by the Sharif family, which made them Bhutto's enemies for the rest of his life. Simultaneously, trade unions were given more rights than ever before and encouraged to keep a watch on industry. This was undoubtedly radical and broke the power of the twenty-two families that had dominated the country's economy, but was it effective without more generalized reforms in other spheres of life?

In domestic politics, two key issues mattered most to people at the time. A majority of the population was rural, and the stranglehold of landlords in the countryside stifled agriculture. The land ceiling (amount of land permitted to large landowners) was reduced, but in such a way as to make the change ineffective, and the usual allowances were made exempting orchards, stud farms, stock rearing, and *shikar-gahs* (hunting grounds) from the new assessments.* Even staunchly pro-PPP commentators in the press expressed their disappointment. They had hoped that, if nothing else, Bhutto would free Pakistan (as Nehru had done in India) from the multifarious survivors of feudalism that impeded the country's modernization.

Why did he not do so? The size of his own landholdings was not a deterrent. His cousin Mumtaz Bhutto was the big landowner in the family. He was a leader of the PPP and at the time favored radical reforms. What held Bhutto back was political opportunism. He had defeated the Punjabi landlords electorally. The loyalty of this social layer was to itself and its property. Many of them happily jumped ship and clambered aboard Bhutto's shiny, new vessel. Within six months some of the largest landlords in the country had aligned themselves with Bhutto. To keep them in line, the threat of land reform was used as the sword of Damocles. It was one of Bhutto's more serious errors. It had been taken for granted that health care, child care, and education would improve under the new dispensation. The statistics suggested otherwise. The infant mortality rate in 1972, one of the highest on the continent, was 120 per 1,000 live births. The figures were exactly the same in 1977. There was a marginal rise in literacy, but the elite structure of education remained unchanged.

In the absence of change, the indiscriminate nationalizations antagonized capitalists large and small without bringing any real improvement to the lives of urban dwellers. It resulted in increasing the weight of the state bureaucracy, encouraged cronyism and massive corruption, and scared off the industrialists, who fled with their capital to the Gulf, East Africa, London, and New York. Some would never return. Industrial output declined. This suggested that piecemeal reform would not work. Selective nationalizations of public utilities together with a stringent tax regime and tough regulation might have been more beneficial.

The second issue related to the army. The army's political role was never that of a lobby trying to influence government, as is the case, for

---

*See Tariq Ali, *Can Pakistan Survive?* (London: 1983), pp. 102–4, for a more detailed critique.

instance, in the United States, but a permanent conspiracy trying to replace the government. Bhutto knew this better than most. Yet he did little to change the existing structures, instead setting up his own paramilitary organization, the Federal Security Force, a praetorian guard led by ex-general and fantasist Akbar Khan, who had been imprisoned for planning a coup in league with Communist intellectuals in the fifties. This antagonized the military high command while leaving it intact. There were purges, with a thousand officers prematurely retired from the army and several hundred civil servants sacked for "corruption." Recognition that the two institutions needed reform was not enough. Its overall impact was to subordinate the civilian bureaucracy to executive power, which made things worse, not better.

A new constitution was drafted by one of the country's most distinguished lawyers, Mian Mahmud Ali Kasuri, who, as minister of law, was one of the few people capable of resisting Bhutto. Kasuri strongly opposed a presidential system and pressed for a federal parliamentary solution that made the executive accountable to parliament. Bhutto finally accepted this but insisted on provisions that made it virtually impossible for the National Assembly to remove a prime minister, a task assumed happily later on by the army. The new constitution came into force in August 1973. Despite the recent experience of losing Bengal, the Peoples Party leadership backed Bhutto when he dismissed the elected governments in Frontier and Baluchistan, accusing the National Awami Party leaders of "treason," and had them arrested and tried on spurious charges. They were accused of being involved in a plot with the Soviet Union and Iraq to break up Pakistan and Iran. The only plot that existed had been hatched by the Iranian and Pakistani intelligence services to crush the autonomous governments in Pakistan because the Shah of Iran regarded them as "subversive."

Bhutto's fatal flaw was a refusal to share power within his party and without. Had he done so with Sheikh Mujibur Rahman, it would have made it difficult, if not impossible, for the army to invade Bengal and destroy the old state. Had he been more farsighted he would have brought the provincial leaders of the National Awami Party into the central government. His refusal to surrender a monopoly of power would be his undoing. Its immediate consequences were disastrous.

The two elected leaders of Baluchistan, Ghaus Bux Bizenjo and Ataullah Mengal, the governor and chief minister of their province, were in prison. I knew both of them well, and during a lengthy conversation with Mengal in 1981, he described the problems that had confronted them:

> When I was in Mach jail in Baluchistan, our situation was brought home to me very vividly. A prison warder is the lowest-paid government employee. There were one hundred twenty warders in this prison, but only eleven of them were Baluch. If anyone had stated this, he would have been denounced as a traitor. When we took office in 1972, there was a total of twelve thousand government employees in twenty-two grades. Only three thousand were Baluch. There are only a few hundred Baluch in the entire Pakistan army. The Baluch regiment has no Baluch in it! The Kalat Scouts was a paramilitary force raised during the Ayub dictatorship. There were only two people from Kalat recruited to its ranks. . . . If you land at Quetta airport today and visit the city, you will soon realize that ninety-five percent of the police constables have been brought from the outside. When we tried to correct the balance, Bhutto and his Punjabi aide Khar organized a police strike against our government. This merely added fuel to the fire of nationalism. The students, in particular, wanted to go the whole way. Bizenjo and I told them, "These are temporary phases. We don't have another alternative." Governments, military regimes, have come and gone, but they have shared one attitude in common. They have mistreated and oppressed the Baluch.

The Baluch resented the overthrow of their government in 1973 and within weeks several hundred students and activists had fled to the mountains. The more radical nationalists among them led by the Marxist-Leninist-Guevarist leaders of the Marri tribe organized the Baluch Peoples Liberation Front (BPLF) and fought back by unleashing an insurgency that lasted four years. Bhutto sent in the predominantly Punjabi army, thus revealing his own incapacity to deal with a political crisis for which he was responsible. The rehabilitation of the discredited military that this represented was another serious error. To achieve victory the army required help, which came in the shape of HueyCobra helicopter gunships supplied by the Shah of Iran and flown by Iranian pilots. In the nineteenth century the British had imposed national boundaries dividing Baluchistan into Iranian, Afghan, and British Indian segments, disrupting the easygoing tribal nomadism of the region. The Shah was fearful that the rebellion would cross borders and disrupt his kingdom. The West backed Bhutto because it feared an autonomous Baluchistan might come under Soviet influence and the Soviet navy might use the port at Gwadar to further its global ambitions. The army finally succeeded in crushing the rebellion, but at some cost. The brutality of the campaign left the province smoldering with resentment.*

THE CRISIS IN Baluchistan dented Bhutto's standing in the country. Through this inability to cope with the real problems of the new Pakistan, the PPP demonstrated its futility. Many felt that the tragic lessons of Bengal had not been learned. It was back to business as usual, but this time under a civilian autocrat. State television projected Bhutto as it had Field Marshal Ayub. The print media was kept under strict surveillance, and internal debates and discussion were being actively discouraged inside the Peoples Party. The word of the leader was sufficient. This led to some resignations and, later, police repression against PPP dissidents. It was a confession of political bankruptcy. Had inner-party democracy prevailed, Bhutto as well as his party and the country would have benefited greatly. Instead the intelligence agencies were strengthened and given free range to spy and report back on the activities of rival political parties.

Bhutto had derived all his nightmares and fears from his experience

---

*A small group of middle-class Punjabi socialists defended the honor of their province by joining the Baluch resistance. One of them, Johnny Das, the son of a senior air force officer of Hindu origin, was captured, tortured, and killed. The others survived. They included the brothers Asad and Rashid Rehman (the former was the legendary guerrilla leader Chakar Khan), Najam Sethi (currently editor of the *Daily Times*), and the journalist Ahmed Rashid. This was undoubtedly their finest hour.

as a cabinet minister in Field Marshal Ayub's government. He was aware of how the intelligence agencies tortured opponents and, on rare occasions, killed political prisoners. He had observed firsthand the ironfisted feudal and backward Nawab of Kalabagh, Ayub's governor in West Pakistan, treating the province as a fiefdom. In his own villages, Kalabagh did not permit schools lest the peasants get ideas above their station. Bhutto feared but also respected his authoritarian style.

Instead of making a clean break with this past, Bhutto molded it to serve his own political needs. He did so not out of a conscious desire to mimic Ayub or Kalabagh, but because he feared the rise of a new opposition. Deeply insecure psychologically, he saw imaginary enemies everywhere. Self-defense, self-love, self-preservation, and sycophancy became the overpowering characteristics of his administration. None of this was necessary. Not even his enemies disputed that he was the most gifted political leader that the country had ever produced. Intellectually he was light-years ahead of any general or politician. His grasp of world politics was based on a deep reading of history. He had studied international law under Hans Kelsen at Berkeley, and both in California and at Oxford his precociousness left a mark on his tutors. The tragedy was in his imagining that his intellectual superiority made him infallible, and this made him his own worst enemy. The majority of his supporters were poor. What they wanted, above all, was an equality of opportunity for their children. Even if this craving was difficult to satisfy immediately, a start could have been made and the foundations laid for modernizing the country. There was to be no beginning, and so when the end came, all that people remembered was a courageous individual who had spoken on their behalf against their traditional oppressors. They understood that this was important, but also knew that it was not enough. On one occasion in Larkana, his hometown in Sind, peasant leaders and activists came to speak with him. For a whole hour they poured out their bitterness about promises he had made and not kept and how PPP landlords were not interested in implementing any reforms. Bhutto heard them out and then asked, "Now tell me this and be completely honest. Can you think of any other prime minister who would have met you and sat quietly listening to your complaints?" The peasant leaders laughed and cheered and the meeting came to an end.

They deserved better. The generation that had propelled Bhutto to power contained enormous reserves: it was rich in political passion, generous, idealistic, and this allowed it to visualize a better future for everyone. Morally exhausted now by the events in Bengal, silencing self-doubts and surfing on the wave of chauvinism promoted from above, the poor still hoped that conditions would change for the better in what was left of their country. They were disappointed. The predicament of Pakistan has never been that of an enlightened leadership marooned in a sea of primitive people. It has usually been the opposite.

What of the defeated army? It was not uncommon in those days to encounter a street wisdom: if only Bhutto had executed six or seven generals, all would have been well. Even if this had been desirable, how could Bhutto have ordered such an act? He had, after all, supported the military intervention in East Pakistan. Had he agreed to participate in the National Assembly after the 1970 elections and had he accepted Mujib as the prime minister of the country, it would have been difficult for the army to intervene. Had they done so, then West Pakistan too might have risen in arms, and that would have created a completely different situation. Soldiers encouraged to rape Bengali women and shoot Bengali civilians might have been more restrained in the Punjab, from where they had come.

The majority view in the Punjab was that drunk and incompetent generals combined with an Indian military intervention had lost them Pakistan. As I have argued, this was a simplistic and chauvinist view that ignored the structural exploitation of East Bengal by a predominantly West Pakistan–based elite. Given his own position on the conflict, Bhutto could not have tried the generals for treason and executed them, but he could certainly have transformed the basic structure of the colonial army by drastically reducing its size and instituting a more democratic command structure. There would have been widespread support for any such change in 1972–73.

Instead, and in keeping with his character, Bhutto tinkered with the army by retiring some senior generals and favoring others. He appointed General Tikka Khan, a "hero" of the war against Bengal, as the new commander in chief, and on his retirement in 1976, he leapfrogged Zia-ul-Haq over the heads of five senior generals and appointed him as army chief. Bhutto regarded him as a loyal simpleton. This was inaccurate, but even if it had been true, it would not have mattered much. To concentrate on the personnel rather than reforming the institution was a fatal error. Bhutto paid for it with his life. The country continues to suffer.

Far from being a useful idiot, Zia always reminded me of Dickens's inspired creation Uriah Heep, the hideous clerk in *David Copperfield*. A hypocrite whose body language stressed his humbleness while masking his ambition. His closest general-in-arms, K. M. Arif, referred to him without irony as "a practicing Muslim, he was a model of humility." General Saeed Qadir, another close colleague, listed "humbleness" as one of his boss's positive attributes and "hypocrisy" as one of his weaknesses, failing to link one to the other. Like many of his more senior colleagues, Zia had come of age in the British Indian army. Born in Jullundhur in 1924 and educated in Delhi, he moved to Pakistan after partition and was fond of stressing his "humble origins" in contrast to those who hailed from the gentry. Nor was he ever hesitant in praising the leader who had entrusted him with command of the army.

After training at Fort Leavenworth in Kansas during the early sixties, Brigadier Zia-ul-Haq was dispatched to Jordan in late 1968 to help train the locals in the art of suppressing popular uprisings. The target in this case were the Palestinians, who comprised a majority of the country's population and were in a turbulent mood after the six-day Israeli blitzkrieg in June 1967 had destroyed the Egyptian and Syrian armies, occupied large tracts of Palestine and Gaza, and delivered a fatal blow to Arab nationalism, which never recovered. The Palestinians realized they had to fight for themselves and correctly perceived Jordan as a weak link. The monarchy had become extremely unpopular after the Israeli triumph, and its overthrow would have provided the Palestinians with a state. It was not to be. In September 1970, Zia led the Jordanian troops to crush the Palestinian uprising. Between five and seven thousand Palestinians were killed. General Moshe Dayan noted that King Hussein "killed more Palestinians in eleven days than Israel could kill in twenty years." The month became known as Black September. Zia was awarded the highest Jordanian honor and returned home in triumph. Soon afterward he was promoted and posted as a corp commander in Kharian, a military city in the Punjab. According to friends, the Black September operation was one aspect of his past that he would never discuss, but clearly it was treated as a routine operation even by Bhutto, who publicly defended the Palestine Liberation Organization (PLO).

The poor may have felt instinctively that Bhutto was on their side (the elite never forgave him for encouraging this view and for the nationalizations), but few measures were ever enacted to justify their confidence. His style of government was authoritarian; his personal vindictiveness was corrosive. Under his watch the Inter-Services Intelligence (ISI) set up the notorious "election cell" to help the government "win" elections by threatening opposition candidates and ensuring that local bureaucrats rigged the ballot in favor of the government. This desperate opportunism created the basis for what followed after him. He attempted to fight the religious opposition by stealing their clothes: he banned the sale of alcohol, made Friday a public holiday, and declared the Ahmediyya sect to be non-Muslim (a long-standing demand of the Jamaat-e-Islami that had, till then, been treated by most politicians with contempt). By accepting the battleground determined by his enemies, he was bound to lose. These measures did not help him, but damaged the country by legitimizing confessional politics.

What a contrast this was to the mood in 1972 when Bhutto had addressed a giant rally in Lahore. He habitually carried a silver flask containing whiskey that he would mix with water and sip at public meetings. On this occasion a well-orchestrated group of Islamist militants strategically placed stood up the minute he mixed his drink and started shouting, "What are you drinking?" Bhutto held up the glass and replied, "Sherbet." The crowd laughed. The indignant hecklers were enraged. "Look, people," they said, "your leader is drinking *sharab* [liquor] not sherbet." An angry Bhutto roared back, "Fine. I am drinking *sharab*. Unlike you sisterfuckers I don't drink the blood of our people." The people rose to their feet and chanted in Punjabi, "Long may our Bhutto live, long may our Bhutto drink."

• • •

FEW PAKISTANI politicians were as obsessed with world politics as was Bhutto. All his knowledge was put to the test soon after he came to power in a truncated state crippled by defeat. Bhutto successfully concluded an agreement with Mrs. Gandhi in Simla that led to the release of ninety thousand Pakistan soldiers taken prisoner after the 1971 surrender in Dhaka. Soon after, he organized the Islamic Summit in Lahore, whose main function was to make the recognition of Bangladesh palatable to the army, but this was not enough to silence the self-doubt and fill the vacuum left by the loss of East Bengal. Pakistan's survival as a nation, Bhutto now decided, was dependent on nuclear parity with India.

"We will eat grass for a thousand years," he had shouted at a public meeting in Rawalpindi after India announced its first nuclear test, "but we will make the bomb." He knew perfectly well which section of the population would dine on grass for a millennium, but felt that a new Pakistan required a sense of pride and achievement. Unable to deliver food, clothing, education, health, and shelter, he would work hard at giving the people a bomb. This was to be the cornerstone of a new Pakistani nationalism that had not been possible before the amputation of Bengal. It was a deadly decision.

The plan to acquire a nuclear device could only be carried out nocturnally, under cover of a total information blackout and with Bhutto as the presiding genius. He saw this as a supreme and redeeming act. It was all meant to be a secret, but an early meeting with the country's physicists could not have taken place in a more inappropriate location, of the sort that Bhutto usually favored for clandestine trysts. It was on the estate of Nawab Sadiq Hussain Qureshi, a large landlord in Multan. The city was known for the delicacy and sweetness of its mangoes, a burning-hot wind that blew in the summer months, Sufi shrines, and a tradition of exquisite tile-making that went back to the early Mogul period. Qureshi was a recent supporter of Bhutto's (and a second cousin of mine) and could be relied upon to maintain secrecy.

The country's senior scientists, less than half a dozen men, were incredulous when informed as to why they had been summoned. This was empty talk, they said to each other, a hashish-induced fantasy. Dr. I. H. Usmani, chairman of the Pakistan Atomic Energy Commission, was openly skeptical. He knew that India was two decades ahead of Pakistan and that "Pakistan just didn't have the infrastructure for that kind of programme. I'm not talking about the ability to get 10kg of plutonium. I'm talking of the real infrastructure. Pakistan totally lacked a metallurgy industry. But if you're playing political poker and have no cards, you have to go on betting."

Bhutto was reminded of the low standard of most of the country's science graduates. It was impossible, he was told, he should forget it. Instead Bhutto ignored them and went over their heads to a younger, eager group of physicists, men such as Munir Ahmed Khan, Samar Mubarakmand, and Sultan Bashiruddin Mahmood, who were hungry for success and state patronage. They were only too happy to be lured into the surrealistic enterprise by a political leader whose mind was possessed by the vision of a mushroom cloud over the Pakistani desert. Soon they would be joined by another Muslim nationalist, A. Q. Khan, a postpartition refugee from India filled with hatred for that country. These were the men who built the Pakistani bomb, and in remote Kahuta, Bhutto's nuclear state was born. The nuclear facility remains there to this day.

While the scientists were happily working away, Bhutto's high-handedness in neighboring Islamabad had united all his opponents under the umbrella of the Pakistan National Alliance. An election was eagerly awaited. Despite all his mistakes Bhutto would probably have won the 1977 elections without state interference, though with a much-reduced majority. This is generally agreed. His more sycophantic adherents in the state bureaucracy and the ISI were not prepared to take any risk. The manipulation was so blatant and crude that the opposition came out on the streets, and neither Bhutto's sarcasm nor his wit was enough to allay the crisis. Nor was the United States. Washington had always regarded Bhutto as unreliable and untrustworthy and was unimpressed by the pretensions of his flaccid party or the large crowds that came to hear him. Now it became fearful that he would acquire the bomb. It wanted him out and soon.

In June 1977, on the verge of being toppled by the military, Bhutto told parliament, "I know the bloodhounds are after my blood," and denounced the U.S. secretary of state, Cyrus Vance, for interfering in the internal affairs of Pakistan. In his death-cell memoir, *If I Am Assassinated*, he alleged that Henry Kissinger had warned him, during one of his visits to Pakistan in August 1976, that unless he desisted on the nuclear question, "We will make a horrible example out of you." Both Kissinger and Bhutto could be economical with the truth, but the remark has recently been confirmed. A journalist in the Pakistan financial paper *Business Recorder* cites a senior Pakistani foreign official (on condition of anonymity) present on the occasion:

> . . . Kissinger waited for a while, and said in a cultured tone, "Basically I have come not to advise, but to warn you. USA has numerous reservations about Pakistan's atomic programme; therefore you have no way out, except agreeing to what I say." Bhutto smiled and asked, "Suppose I refuse, then what?" Henry Kissinger became dead serious.
>
> He locked his eyes on Bhutto's and spewed out deliberately, "Then we will make a horrible example of you!" Bhutto's face flushed. He stood up, extended his hand towards Kissinger and said, "Pakistan can live without the US President. Now your people will have to find some other ally in this region." Bhutto then turned and went out.*

If this is accurate, then we have to ask, what happened between February and August 1976? On February 26 that year, while Bhutto was in New York attending the United Nations, a meeting was organized with the secretary of state. The declassified memorandum of conversation offers some interesting insights. Bhutto's attempts to offer ultraloyal advice on how the United States should have dealt with the Cuban intervention in Angola (via a firm military riposte) and related matters clearly irritated Kissinger, who asked if Bhutto had been speaking to Brzezinski. A rambling discussion on world politics and U.S. strategy follows in which the satrap expresses concern that the imperial power is seen as weak by its enemies, which is disorienting for its

---

*Business Recorder, January 29, 2008.

friends. Détente is viewed by Bhutto as having gone too far when "pip-squeak countries like Cuba" can score wins with ten thousand troops in Angola. "There were twelve thousand Cubans," corrects Kissinger as he deftly parries each thrust. It's obvious that for him the main reason for the meeting, apart from humoring Bhutto, is the nuclear issue. As the following extract reveals, each side was aware of the other's position, but the tone here is friendly (if occasionally servile on Bhutto's side) and far removed from any threats:

> BHUTTO: Mr. Secretary, I am sure you like the role we played in the Middle East debate.
> THE SECRETARY (KISSINGER): Yes. That was appreciated. If I spoke vehemently on the topic of détente, Angola, and the erosion of central authority, I did so because I believe you were one of the world leaders who understands us.
> BHUTTO: After that remark I don't want to provoke you by mentioning nuclear reactors.
> THE SECRETARY: . . . What concerns us is how reprocessing facilities are used at a certain point. I told you last year that we appreciated that you were forgoing a nuclear capability. This placed us in a good position and gave us arguments to assist you in other ways.

The discussion continues with Kissinger stressing his concern that once a nuclear reprocessing plant was built it could easily develop in another direction, and Bhutto pleading disingenuously that in such a case the West could easily bring pressure to bear that could stop that. Kissinger remains unconvinced. When Bhutto explains that Pakistan had pledged never to misuse the reprocessing facilities, his interlocutor points out that he is not interested in "words, but concerned with realities." The country with the facilities could easily abrogate a binational agreement whenever it wished.

Earlier Bhutto had been informed that the United States was quite happy to provide Iran with nuclear reprocessing plants that could be used by Pakistan and other states in the region. This brilliant idea had matured in the heads of two senior officials in the Ford administration who would resurface in a later Republican administration: Dick Cheney, then chief of staff at the White House, and Donald Rumsfeld, the defense secretary. Cheney is a keen advocate today of bombing Iran's nuclear energy stations, an idea that has, till now, been vetoed by the Pentagon. That Cheney and Rumsfeld's plan might not have been entirely determined by U.S. strategic needs is mentioned in a recent study, whose authors point out that "the first proposed US nuclear deal with Iran would have been extremely lucrative for US corporations like Westinghouse and General Electric, which stood to earn $6.4 billion from the project."* Cheney and Rumsfeld were never great believers in self-renunciation. Strategic and business interests could never be separate for them.

Bhutto was not interested in playing second fiddle to Iran and rejected the idea, but he was also not seriously interested in a reprocessing plant. All he wanted was the bomb. That was the instruction he had given to Pakistani scientists. Clearly, between the two meetings with Kissinger the latter was informed by U.S. intelligence of what was really going on. Kissinger's realization that he was being lied to so blatantly prompted him to start playing the godfather. His rage was not just imperial, but also personal. From 1973 onward Kissinger had spearheaded a campaign to lift the U.S. arms embargo on Pakistan and had dispatched Henry Byroade as U.S. ambassador to accelerate the process and control the nuclear ambitions. Byroade later confirmed this in an interview with historian Niel M. Johnson:

JOHNSON: . . . So you left there in '73 and went to Pakistan.
BYROADE: That's right. I planned to retire, and Henry Kissinger talked me into going to Pakistan. I went there for one specific purpose, and I planned to stay about eighteen months. We'd had an arms embargo on Pakistan for about ten years, growing out of the India-Pakistan war. This had worked out in the long term to be, I thought, very unfair to Pakistan, because India turned to the Soviet Union for their armament needs, primar-

---

*Adrian Levy and Catherine Scott-Clark, *Deception* (London: 2008). This is the most complete and best-researched account to date of how Pakistan became a nuclear power.

ily, but also to a lot of other countries. . . . Kissinger said, "This is unfair, and we've got to lift that embargo, but it's not easy with the India lobby and all of that." So he said, "You go out there and stay long enough to be credible and come back and talk to people on the Hill about it, and see if we can lift that thing."

. . . You know, it's very easy to impose these things; India and Pakistan get into a war, our weapons are involved, so "bingo, embargo!" It was very proper, but when it came around to lifting it, it's something else. But we did during Bhutto's visit, and we did get a little flak from the Hill but not very much. So we lifted that and were able for the first time to start replenishing some of their equipment. I was then ready to come home, but Pakistan got involved in the nuclear business, which upset me no end. I stayed and struggled, trying to keep that from being a problem between us for two more years. I was there about four years.

JOHNSON: Four years, and Bhutto was still in power?

BYROADE: Bhutto was in trouble, deep trouble when I left, but he was still in power.

JOHNSON: General Zia, was he the one that was . . .

BYROADE: When I left, he was chief of staff, with, I think, no idea of taking over at that point.*

In 1976, Zia had been made chief of staff by Bhutto. It is possible, but unlikely, that Byroade, whose links with the U.S. military stretched back to the Second World War, had no idea of DIA/Pentagon contacts with Zia, which went back to his time in Fort Leavenworth and had been renewed in Jordan in 1970. Military coups in Pakistan are rarely, if ever, organized without the tacit or explicit approval of the U.S. embassy. Bhutto's "treachery" on the nuclear issue was the principal reason why the United States gave the green light for his removal.

On the night of July 4–5, 1977, to preempt an agreement between Bhutto and the opposition parties that would have entailed new gen-

---

*"Oral History Interview with Henry Byroade," 1988, Truman Library archives.

eral elections, General Zia struck. Having reached an agreement with
the United States that Bhutto's rule was intolerable, Zia was not prepared to tolerate a rapprochement between the two rival political
groups. He proclaimed martial law, declared himself chief martial law
administrator, promised new elections within ninety days, and placed
Bhutto "under protective custody." Bhutto was stunned. In January
1977 I had visited Pakistan and on my return written a series of three
short articles for the *Guardian* predicting a military takeover. This was
considered fantastical and the articles were not published. I had
repeated the argument to Benazir Bhutto in Oxford, to which she had
replied that her father might well be assassinated, but that there could
never be a coup "since Zia was in our pocket." I told her to let her father
know that in Pakistan no general was ever in the pocket of a civilian
politician.

The army had assumed there would be large public protests and
had been prepared to crush them, but was encouraged by the muted
response. As a result, Bhutto was released on July 28, 1977. He immediately embarked on a political tour of the country and was greeted
by large crowds. In Lahore, half a million people came out to receive
him, thus destroying the military's illusions that he was a discredited
and spent force. "Two men, one coffin" is what Zia's colleagues now
told him. Zia realized that Bhutto would win any election that was
not heavily rigged. Were this to happen, Zia's own future would be
truncated. This time he made sure that Bhutto would never be free
again.

On September 3, 1977, Bhutto was arrested in Lahore and charged
with "conspiracy to murder Ahmed Raza Kasuri," a former PPP member who had joined the opposition. In November 1974, a group of
gunmen had opened fire on a car carrying Kasuri and his father. The
latter died. Kasuri had accused Bhutto of being responsible, but a special inquiry tribunal had looked into the allegations and rejected them.
Kasuri then rejoined the Peoples Party and remained a member from
April 1976 to April 1977, but was refused a party nomination to contest the ill-fated March 1977 general elections. This rejection went
deep. After Zia's coup, Kasuri embarked on a private prosecution of
Bhutto, and this was now used by the military as a motive in a case of

alleged murder. On September 13, 1977, Bhutto was released on bail by two senior High Court judges—K. Samdani and Mazharul Huq. Four days later he was rearrested in Karachi by commandos under martial law regulations.

The trial for murder began in September 1977 before the Lahore High Court. The two judges who had granted bail were excluded from the bench. The acting chief justice, Maulvi Mushtaq, was a close personal friend of Zia's and his conduct at the trial was a travesty. Even journalists who disliked Bhutto were shocked by Mushtaq's vindictiveness. He had been ordered to insult and humiliate Bhutto, and he did so throughout the trial, which lasted till March 1978. Only hearsay evidence implicated Bhutto. One of the state witnesses was Masood Mahmood, a former boss of the Federal Security Force. He had been promised immunity, but ended up with a new identity, a great deal of money, and a luxury apartment in California, where he died in the late nineties. Foreign observers attending the trial included John Mathew, QC, and Ramsey Clark, former attorney general of the United States. Both agreed that in Britain and the United States such a case would never have come to trial since it was based on the uncorroborated evidence of pardoned accomplices.* Bhutto and four others were sentenced to death on March 18, 1978. An appeal against the judgment was heard in the Supreme Court on May 20, 1978, and continued for several months. Bhutto's appearance before the court shocked observers. He had lost a great deal of weight and looked haggard. His speech lasted three hours. He defended his political honor, refused to take the charge of murder seriously, and pointed the finger at Zia and his generals, who had decided to do away with him. He concluded by looking at the judges with contempt and saying, "Now you can hang me." The Supreme Court rejected the appeal by a 4–3 vote. One judge who was considered unreliable by the military was retired during the trial; a second was denied sick leave and a delay in the trial. He had to withdraw from the bench. Chief Justice Anwarul Haq was in communication with the military dictator every single day. A detailed two-hundred-page

---

*Ramsey Clark, "The Trial of Ali Bhutto and the Future of Pakistan," *Nation*, August 19–26, 1978.

dissenting opinion by Justice Safdar Shah provided a devastating rebuttal of the case brought forward by the state. Shah, with whom I spent many hours in London, revealed that he had been threatened before and during the case and told that his relations in the army would suffer unless he behaved himself. He told me, "I was ashamed to belong to a Supreme Court which did the bidding of the military."

Bhutto was hanged at 2 a.m. on April 4, 1979, in the district jail, Rawalpindi. The day before, he had been visited by his wife, Nusrat, and daughter, Benazir, for the last time. Both women had courageously been campaigning against the dictatorship and had been in and out of prison themselves. He told them how proud he was of his family. Neither woman was allowed to attend his funeral. Some years later the prison where Bhutto was hanged was demolished on Zia's orders.

Zia had the support of the military high command (with only a single general against) and, of course, the United States.* The notion that Zia would have gone through with the hanging had it been opposed by Washington is risible. U.S. operatives in the region (including the "anthropologist" and Afghan expert Louis Dupree) had told a number of senior Pakistani officials that Bhutto was dispensable and would soon be out of the way.

The Pakistani leader's judicial assassination transformed him into a martyr and ensured that his legacy would endure. Washington had assumed that with Bhutto out of the way the Pakistan army would abandon all notions of acquiring a nuclear identity. Here they miscalculated badly. In fact, Bhutto had retained political control of the nuclear facility, keeping the generals at a safe distance. One of Zia's first instructions was to authorize a total military takeover of Kahuta. Since 1971, the military had become obsessed with revenge. In return for the loss of Bangladesh, they were now going to make a determined effort to destabilize and capture Kashmir, a long-disputed territory to which both India and Pakistan laid claim and which is discussed in a subsequent chapter. It was almost as if they believed their own propaganda according to which "Hindus and traitors" had been responsible for the

*Ali, *Can Pakistan Survive?*

Bengali defection. The trauma of military defeat had left a permanent scar on the psyche of many officers unaccustomed to thinking for themselves. A debilitated military apparatus was prepared to take risks to restore its pride.

Bhutto's decision to respond to India's nuclear test by securing a "Muslim bomb" strongly appealed to the army as well as those whose financial help would be essential. These included Mu'ammar al-Gadhafi, the eccentric and unpredictable leader of Libya, who would sometimes fly over from Tripoli unannounced, causing havoc for the chief of protocol in Islamabad, to have breakfast with his dear friend Bhutto and find out how work on the bomb was proceeding. Of all the Arab leaders, Gadhafi alone had genuinely intervened to save Bhutto's life. Zia had promised him to commute the sentence, but later said he was overruled by his colleagues.

With Bhutto out of the way, the military could now control the entire nuclear process till success had been achieved. Whether they would have succeeded in hoodwinking Washington indefinitely—had not another major shift occurred in the region—remains an open question. But a geopolitical earthquake, the Soviet occupation of neighboring Afghanistan in December 1979, provided the cover for Pakistani scientists to mimic their Indian counterparts and split the atom. Zia himself was given a whitewash in the West. He was no longer a temporary necessity. From being viewed as a squalid and brutal military dictator, he was transformed into a necessary ally defending the frontiers of the free world against the godless Russians.

Religious affinity had done little to mitigate the hostility of Afghan leaders toward their neighbor to the east. The main reason was the Durand Line, a border imposed on the Afghans by the British Empire in 1893 to mark the frontier between British India and Afghanistan after the British had failed to subjugate the country. This arbitrary line through the mountains had purposefully divided the Pashtun population of the region. It was agreed at the time that, on the Hong Kong model, after a hundred years all of what became the North-West Frontier Province of British India would revert to Afghanistan. But no government in Kabul accepted the Durand Line any more than they accepted British, or, later, Pakistani, control over the territory.

• • •

IN JULY 1977, when Zia seized power, 90 percent of men and 98 percent of women in neighboring Afghanistan were illiterate; 5 percent of landowners (most of whom were also tribal leaders) held 45 percent of the cultivable land, and the country had the lowest per capita income of any in Asia. A majority of the people in the countryside were desperately poor. Comparisons with other countries seem absurd when the classification that matters is between those who eat twice a day, those who eat once, and the hungry. In these conditions it is hardly surprising that fatalism and religion become deep-rooted. The tiny intellectual elite—monarchists, liberals, republicans, Communists—that dominated political life in Kabul were heavily dependent on local traders, businessmen, and tribal leaders. Money from the former helped to bribe the latter. The Afghan rulers had preserved their independence and held the British at bay. For most of the twentieth century geography had dictated neutrality in the Cold War. The rulers were friendly with Moscow and New Delhi. Some Pashtun Hindus had relocated in Kabul rather than flee to India during partition, and the Afghan rulers were much more tolerant in religious matters than their neighbors.

By a strange quirk of history, the same year that Zia seized power, the Parcham (Flag) Communists in Afghanistan, who had backed the 1973 military coup by Prince Daud after which a republic was proclaimed, withdrew their support from Daud and were reunited with other Communist groups to form the People's Democratic Party of Afghanistan (PDPA). Despite its title, the new party was neither popular nor democratic. Its most influential cadres were strategically concentrated in the army and air force.

The regimes in neighboring countries became involved in the brewing crisis that now threatened Daud. The Shah of Iran feared a Communist takeover and, acting as a conduit for Washington, recommended firm action—large-scale arrests, executions, torture—and put units from Savak, his tried-and-tested torture agency, at Daud's disposal. The Shah tried to bribe Daud. If he recognized the Durand Line as a permanent frontier with Pakistan, Iran would give $3 billion to Afghanistan and ensure that Pakistan ceased all hostile actions in the tribal zones. Pakistani intelligence agencies had (even under Bhutto) been arming Afghan exiles while encouraging old-style tribal uprisings aimed at restoring the monarchy. Daud was tempted to accept the Shah's offer, but the Communists in the armed forces, fearing Iranian repression as in Baluchistan, organized a preemptive strike and took power in April 1978. Washington was in a panic. This increased tenfold as it became clear that its long-standing ally, the overconfident Shah, was about to be toppled together with his throne.

General Zia's dictatorship thus became the linchpin of U.S. strategy in the region, which is why Washington green-lighted Bhutto's execution and turned a blind eye to the country's nuclear program. The United States wanted a stable Pakistan, whatever the cost.

Zia understood his role well and instructed General Akhtar Abdul Rahman, his director general at the ISI, "The water in Afghanistan must be made to boil at the right temperature." Rahman, an efficient, bigoted, and cold-blooded officer, set up the Afghan Bureau of the ISI, which worked with U.S. intelligence agencies and was provided with unlimited supplies of funds and weaponry. Its aim was straightforward: to set a "bear trap," in the words of the U.S. national security adviser, Zbigniew Brzezinski, via a simple strategy to destabilize the Afghan government, in the hope that its Soviet protectors would be drawn into the conflict.

Plans of this sort often go awry (as in Cuba over five decades), but they succeeded in Afghanistan, primarily because of the weaknesses of the Afghan Communists: they had come to power through a military coup that hadn't involved any mobilization outside Kabul, yet they pretended this was a national revolution; their Stalinist political formation made them allergic to any form of accountability, and such ideas as drafting a charter of democratic rights or holding free elections to a constituent assembly never entered their heads. Ferocious factional struggles led, in September 1979, to a Mafia-style shoot-out at the Presidential Palace in Kabul, during which the prime minister, Hafizullah Amin, shot President Taraki dead. Amin claimed that 98 percent of the population supported his reforms but the 2 percent who opposed them had to be liquidated. The photographs of the victims were proudly published in the government press. Repression on this scale and of this

variety had never before been experienced in the country. Mutinies in
the army and uprisings in a number of towns resulted, and this time
they had nothing to do with Washington or General Zia, but reflected
genuine revulsion against the regime. Islamabad, of course, incited and
armed the religious opposition. One of the ideological weapons used
was a campaign against the PDPA's decision to make literacy compulsory for all Afghan women. This was publicized as a ferocious assault
on Islam and Afghan traditions.

FINALLY, AFTER TWO unanimous politburo decisions against intervention, the Soviet Union changed its mind, saying that it had "new
documentation." This is still classified, but it would not be surprising
in the least if the evidence consisted of forgeries suggesting that Amin
(who was educated at Columbia University in the United States) was a
CIA agent. Whatever it was, the politburo, with Yuri Andropov, then
head of the KGB, voting against, now decided to send troops into
Afghanistan. Its aim (not unlike that of the United States in 2001) was
to get rid of a discredited regime and replace it with a marginally less
repulsive one. The bear trap had worked. On Christmas Day in 1979,
a hundred thousand Soviet troops crossed the Oxus and rumbled into
Kabul. President Carter referred to the event as "the greatest threat to
peace since World War Two" and warned the Soviet leader, Leonid
Brezhnev, to "either withdraw or face serious consequences."

Given that Afghanistan, thanks to the Russians, had now become
fundamental to civilization, it was crucial for it to acquire a heroic
political history. This required outside help on various levels. Knights
in shining armor were dispatched to the region. Washington alerted
researchers and advisers from different agencies and think tanks. The
Rand Corporation reacted swiftly and decided that one of its more pre-
cocious staff members, a twenty-eight-year-old Japanese-American,
should be parachuted into Pakistan on a rapid reconnaissance mission.

Francis Fukuyama spent ten days in the country from May 25 to
June 5, 1980, as the guest of the director of military intelligence and
was provided with access to generals and senior civil servants. Pakistan
had earlier turned down a $400 million aid package offered by the

White House's national security adviser, Zbigniew Brzezinski, on the grounds that "it was peanuts" and informed Washington that it was looking forward to subsidies that, at the least, were on a scale similar to what was being provided to Egypt and Turkey. Why should Pakistan accept anything less? It was now a frontline state, and in pleasant anticipation of what this new status entailed, a number of senior members of the elite had opened bank accounts in far-flung tax havens.

The military top brass confided their innermost fears to Fukuyama. The Soviet Union might cross the Durand Line and detach a salient of their North-West Frontier Province. A carefully orchestrated Indo-Soviet-Afghan pincer movement with the aim of further fragmenting Pakistan "along ethnic lines" was always a possibility. The guilty conscience on Baluchistan was beginning to affect the brass.

Fukuyama accepted much of what he was told, since it tied in neatly with U.S. interests. In any case, he knew that history is never written by any particular authors but often emerges from the periphery to surprise the center. The Vietnamese victory of 1975 still haunted U.S. policy makers. This new history being made in the awesome environment of the Hindu Kush just needed occasional help to proceed along similar lines. Muddling through was not an option. Fukuyama summed up the pros and cons of a tighter U.S.-Pakistan embrace. The advantages were obvious:

(1) denial of Pakistani territory to the Soviet Union.
(2) the possibility of aiding the Afghan rebels militarily so as to raise the cost of the intervention for the Soviets and divert their attention from the Persian Gulf.
(3) the use of Pakistani facilities in connection with the planned Rapid Deployment Force.
(4) the demonstration of American reliability, especially with respect to the People's Republic of China.

The obvious drawbacks were not insurmountable: "(1) Adverse effects on U.S.-Indian relations; (2) a weakening of the credibility of the U.S. nonproliferation policy; (3) high economic costs and (4) commitment to a regime of questionable staying power."

Shrewdly, Fukuyama noted that the Sino-Pakistani relationship offered a model equilibrium:

> The Chinese have supported civilian and military regimes indifferently and have not attempted to influence Pakistan's internal character. As a consequence, they have never been called to account for the failures of a particular regime. . . . Unless the United States can emulate this behavior in some fashion, the liabilities may well exceed the benefits.*

This advice was more or less accepted and reinforced by Brzezinski's "realism." General Zia-ul-Haq, the worst of Pakistan's dictators, was about to be whitewashed and transformed into a plucky freedom fighter against the Evil Empire. The newspapers and television networks did their duty.

From 1980 to 1989, Afghanistan became the focal point of the Cold War. Millions crossed the Durand Line and settled in camps and cities in the NWFP, the largest influx—3.5 million refugees—a direct result of the Soviet occupation. The result was to be catastrophic for both countries. Nobody benefited from the Afghan war except for a tiny layer of heroin smugglers, civilian middlemen, the top brass of the Pakistan army, and politicians allied to all three. Weapons, heroin, drug dollars, NGOs assigned to "help" the refugees, and would-be jihadi warriors from Saudi Arabia, Egypt, and Algeria flooded the region. Pakistan's largest city and port became the center of the heroin trade. The poppy was cultivated in the north, transformed into powder, and packaged to Karachi, from where it was smuggled out to Europe and America. The modern city and its elite were graphically depicted in Kamila Shamsie's novel *Kartography*.

All the main Western intelligence agencies (including the Israelis) were present in Peshawar, near the Afghan frontier. It began to resemble a gold-rush town. The region would never again be the same. For the first time in Pakistan's history, the market and black-market rates

---

*Francis Fukuyama, "The Security of Pakistan: A Trip Report," September 1980, Rand, Santa Monica.

for the dollar were exactly the same. Weapons, including Stinger missiles, were sold to the mujahideen and illegal-arms dealers by Pakistani officers wanting to get rich quick. At a dinner in a London restaurant in 1986, Benazir Bhutto whispered in my ear that our generous host, a certain Sindhi gentleman, waxing eloquent on matters cultural, had a day job selling Stingers and Kalashnikovs. I asked him whether I could buy a missile and how much it would set me back. He was not in the least bit curious as to why I might need such a weapon.

"No problem at all," he said with a smile. "Fly to Karachi. I'll meet you at the airport. We'll drive out of the city and you can try one. Then we'll discuss a price." Unlike me, he was quite serious.

The heroin trade funded Pakistan's thriving black economy. General Fazle Haq, Zia's governor in the Frontier Province, publicly declared his indifference, arguing that since the heroin went abroad, Pakistanis weren't that bothered. The number of registered addicts in Pakistan grew from a few hundred in 1977 to over 2 million in 1987.* The growth of gang warfare in Karachi is directly linked to its becoming a center of the heroin trade.

As for Pakistan and its people, they languished. Zia wanted a total break with the past and reached out for religion, usually the first resort of a scoundrel. On December 2, 1978, the "soldier of Islam," as he often referred to himself, had denounced politicians "who did what they pleased in the name of Islam," then proclaimed that he was preparing to enforce true Islamic laws in the country. He announced the creation of Sharia courts, whose powers were limited but which could nonetheless pronounce whether a law was "Islamic or un-Islamic." Disputes between theologians began immediately, and a number of courts had to be rapidly reconstituted. Two months later Zia promulgated a number of new ordinances and presidential orders. According to these, all legal punishments related to alcohol consumption, adultery, theft, and burglary were to be replaced by the religious punishments prescribed by the Koran and early Islamic jurisprudence. Any Muslim caught drinking would be subjected to eighty lashes; an

---

*One of the banks through which the heroin mafia laundered money was the BCCI (Bank of Credit and Commerce International), now defunct.

unmarried couple caught fornicating would get one hundred lashes, but adultery involving married partners would lead to both being stoned to death; an offense against property would require amputation of the right hand from the wrist, and robbery would be punished by chopping off both hand and foot. These were Sunni prescriptions. The Shia theologians opposed amputating at the wrist, but were happy with removing all fingers and the thumb of the right hand. And as for the absurd demand so beloved of the Peoples Party, for food, clothes, and shelter, all this, according to General Zia, could not be provided by the state or private businesses, but only by God: "Any increase or decrease in your sustenance comes from Him. Trust in God and He will bestow upon you an abundance of good things in life."

All government employees were instructed to say their prayers regularly, and the relevant authorities were instructed to make all necessary arrangements for performing prayers in government buildings, airports, railway stations, and bus stops. A special ordinance was passed insisting on total reverence for Ramadan, and cinemas were to be closed during this period for three hours after the evening prayers. Pakistan had never known anything like it, and the results were mixed. Officially encouraged religiosity now became the norm, but with a massive increase in alcohol consumption and every drunkard claiming that he was resisting the dictatorship. The figures on adultery and the observance of fasts can never be established. The Taliban did not as yet exist, but the stage was being prepared. To the credit of the medical profession, doctors refused to preside over or perform "Islamic" amputations, and these particular punishments could never be implemented. Public and prison floggings, however, occurred regularly and further brutalized the country's fragile political culture.

Unsurprisingly, under Zia, the Jamaat-e-Islami, which had never won more than 5 percent of the vote anywhere in the country, was patronized by the government. Its cadres were sent to fight in Afghanistan, its armed student wing was encouraged to terrorize campuses in the name of Islam, its ideologues were ever present on TV and in the print media. The Inter-Services Intelligence were now instructed by the military leadership to assist the formation of other, more extreme jihadi groups, which carried out terrorist acts at home and abroad. Religious schools began to be established in the countryside, especially in the frontier provinces. Soon Zia too needed his own political party, and the bureaucracy set one up, the Pakistan Muslim League, with Zia's favorite protégés: the Sharif brothers and the Chaudhrys of Gujrat. Currently at each other's throats, they at that time combined their great strengths, one of which was the use of political power to assist the primitive but rapid accumulation of capital.

The Sharif family had become favorites of Zia's mainly because they had suffered under Bhutto and their hatred for him was unrestrained. Blacksmiths by trade, they had left India and sought refuge in the new Muslim homeland, settling down in Lahore. Muhammad Sharif, a hardworking, semipious disciplinarian, made sure his sons, Nawaz and Shahbaz, were provided with a proper education. The family had done well, their small steel foundries prospered, and if anything they were disinterested in politics. Their refusal to pay protection money to some of the more thuggish Bhutto supporters in Lahore led to their business being targeted and nationalized in 1972. The decision was economically stupid and politically counterproductive. A family of neutral small businessmen were transformed into lifelong enemies of the Bhutto family. The day Zia ordered Bhutto's execution, Muhammad Sharif and his sons gave thanks to Allah for responding so rapidly to their prayers. The oldest son, Nawaz, became a protégé of the general's and was made the leader of the *khaki* Muslim League. Transmogrified into politicians by the military, the Sharif family were ever grateful to General Zia. Their primary loyalty, however, was to their own business interests. The foundries had been returned to them but they were no longer enough. Political power was now harnessed to make huge profits largely through securing massive bank loans that were not repaid. This process started early and acquired new momentum after General Zia's unexpected death.

The second family to benefit from military regimes was the Chaudhry clan based in Gujrat. This is an old Punjabi town, located near the Chenab River, built by the Mogul emperor Akbar and garrisoned by Gujjars, traditionally belonging to a seminomadic caste of cowherds and goatherds (hence the city's name). The initial function of the town was to supply the Mogul armies with food and other necessities as they tramped through the region. The Jats, descended from migrant tribes, were farmers who acquired a taste for war and supplied soldiers to the Moguls and later, in much greater numbers, to the British and their successor armies. Some of them settled in the town as well, with constant rivalry between them and the Gujjars.

Gujrat acquired a reputation for craftsmanship—especially pottery—of a high quality during the Mogul period. Few signs of this are left except in the craft of forging currency and especially passports. Before electronic safeguards were introduced, a particular Gujrati craftsman reputedly produced passports and U.S. visas of such high quality that his clients were rarely detected. Such were his skills that government ministers sometimes used him to help their poorer clansmen escape to friendlier climes, an interesting example of self-indictment.

The Chaudhry clan were Jats, and especially during British rule when living standards declined, most of them were badly off and constantly in search of employment. The founding father was Chaudhry Zahoor Elahi. Most of his friends regarded him as a warmhearted and generous rogue. He belonged to Nat, a tiny village near Gujrat, dominated by criminal fraternities whose sense of solidarity left a deep mark on him. His father was much respected locally as an effective river bandit who earned his living by recycling stolen goods. Zahoor Elahi began his adult life as a police constable in British India, a background that could not have been more remote from that of the generals he would later serve.

In 1943, Zahoor Elahi was posted to the Sikh holy city of Amritsar. His brother Manzoor Elahi accompanied him in the hope of finding employment. Zahoor was respectful and worked hard, but also had an ear on permanent alert wherever he was, just in case fate decided to help out. One day he was in the police station when he heard that a local Hindu tradesman, who had infringed some law, was about to be raided.

Sensing an opportunity here, Zahoor Elahi visited the trader that same day and warned him. When the raid took place, the police found nothing. An investigation was launched, the treachery was discovered, and poor Zahoor was sacked from the force.

The businessman was sufficiently grateful to give money to both brothers. Manzoor Elahi was helped to set up a tiny handloom work-shop. Then came partition. The brothers returned to their village. One day Zahoor Elahi went to the Rehabilitation and Compensations office and demanded that they be recompensed for what they had lost (in reality very little). Like many others in those turbulent times, he exaggerated the claim. In those days it was thought that illegal gains should be converted into the most easily transportable commodity, which was either gold or jewelry. Zahoor Elahi displayed an unbridled passion for land and real estate, the genetic traces of which can still be seen in his progeny. He first obtained a large house in downtown Gujrat, in lieu of what was claimed to have been lost in Amritsar. He never looked back, skillfully deploying his natural gifts to gradually build up a large fortune. Once this had been achieved, to his credit he never forgot his past and maintained friendly relations with the local police and criminals, often bringing them together to explain that, despite a difference in profession, they had interests in common.

He was not the only booty politician in the country, but he was one of the most astute. He understood that in politics as well as everyday life, any person with an ounce of sense could reach a goal that gave the lie to his beginnings. Ethics were unnecessary. As befitted a small-town notable, he joined the Muslim League and began to rise in its ranks. With the impressive growth of his property portfolio, his regular pilgrimages to Mecca were combined with duty-free shopping. He always returned with trunkloads of presents for his friends, high and low.

He joined Field Marshal Ayub's Muslim League, the first of the *khaki* (the appellation derives from the color of their military uniforms) leagues that would become a tiny but important pillar of military rule in the country. He became a party stalwart, providing funds and busing in audiences to make the general feel popular at public meetings. For a self-made man to rise so high in Pakistan was unusual at that time. Others like him found poverty vexatious, but lacked initiative and networking skills. The process would become much more commonplace during the heroin bonanza some decades later, when the entrepreneurial spirit of the Chaudhrys and the Sharifs permeated the big cities and left a permanent mark on the political life of the country. It costs a great deal to become a prime minister.

As long as Bhutto was a cabinet minister in the military regime, Elahi played the sycophant, a role in which he had trained himself since his days as a young police constable. After Bhutto was sacked by Ayub and was still sulking in his tent thinking seriously about whether to organize a new political party, Elahi turned his back on the fallen minister. He did more. He became a key defender of Ayub inside the Muslim League and cajoled and bribed those who were tempted to leave with Bhutto and managed to keep most of them in the party. Bhutto was never one to forgive a slight, real or imagined. Once in power in 1972, he made it clear that he regarded the Chaudhrys of Gujrat as thieves and pimps who should be treated as such. Attempts by the Chaudhrys to broker a deal with the new leader via intermediaries close to him came to naught. Bhutto's hatred, once ablaze, always tended toward the indiscriminate. He had an elephant's memory, as many a civil servant who had avoided him during his years of disgrace was to discover. Zahoor Elahi bided his time. It came sooner than expected. He welcomed Zia's coup in 1977, developing close relations with the dictator and backing Bhutto's execution. He ostentatiously asked General Zia to make him a present of the "sacred pen" with which he had signed Bhutto's death warrant. The chief justice of the West Pakistan High Court, Maulvi Mushtaq Hussain, who had behaved abominably in court during Bhutto's trial for murder, had become a close friend of Zahoor Elahi's. In 1978, he was in Lahore lavishing his hospitality on the judge. Both men were in the car that was taking the judge back to his home in Lahore's Model Town district. A group of al-Zulfiqar gunmen opened fire. The judge, who was the target, ducked and avoided the bullet meant for him. Chaudhry was felled. Zahoor Elahi had not been the target, but al-Zulfiqar, embarrassed at missing the judge, claimed he was also on their list, which may have been true.

Whatever the truth, Zahoor Elahi became an instant martyr. The anniversary of his death is marked in Gujrat each year with great pomp and ceremony by his family (usually government ministers), and streets have been named after him. After his death, his oldest son, Chaudhry Shujaat Hussain, inherited the mantle and became a crucial power broker in General Zia's *khaki* Muslim League. Total power, however, continued to elude the Zahoor Elahi clan. The Sharif family had the Muslim League contract, but the Chaudhrys maintained family tradition by masking their resentment. They waited patiently. Their chance would come a decade later when another general, Pervez Musharraf, seized power.

But the Chaudhrys, along with the Sharifs, prospered well enough during the Zia years. So did the Pakistan army, to which the war in Afghanistan had given an enormous boost. It was a frontline ally of the United States against the godless Communists. And Zia and his generals knew only too well that without the financial and military support of the United States and also of China, Saudi Arabia, Israel, and Egypt, it would not have been so easy to win. The ISI and CIA watched and applauded as Russian technicians and their families were killed, disemboweled, and their heads displayed on posts. This was sweet revenge for Vietnam. Meanwhile Prince Turki bin Faisal, the Saudi chieftain promoting the war, dispatched Sheikh Osama bin Laden to Afghanistan to further advance the struggle by demonstrating to the Believers that the Saudis were behind them and not to worry too much about America. The story has been well documented, but what is not stressed often enough is how this war wrecked the northwestern regions of Pakistan. The consequences are still sharply felt.

The crude but effective ISI manuals used to fight Moscow are once again proving helpful, this time to the forces fighting the United States in Afghanistan today. One of the anti-Soviet commanders, Abdul Haq, told admiring Western journalists that the mujahideen did not actually target civilians, "but if I hit them, I don't care. . . . If my family lived near the Soviet embassy, I would hit it. I wouldn't care about them. If I am prepared to die, my son has to die for it, and my wife has to die for it." These "qualities" were then praised in the Western media as exhibitions of an indomitable warrior race. Robert Fisk, who reported on the conflict for the London *Times,* has written of the strict instructions to refer to the mujahideen as "freedom fighters," regardless of any of their activities.

Brigadier Mohammed Yousaf of the ISI, who was centrally involved in training the mujahideen and selecting Pakistani commandos to cross the border and fight alongside them, defended these tactics in 2003:

Next was sabotage and assassination from within . . . this included placing a bomb under the dining-room table of Kabul University in

late 1983. The explosion, in the middle of the meal, killed nine
Soviets, including a woman Professor. Educational institutions were
considered fair game as the staff were all communists indoctrinat-
ing their students with Marxist dogma . . . this was corrupting the
youth, turning them away from Islam.*

The same tactics and the same justifications, directed now against
the United States and NATO, are said to represent the "sickness" of
Islam and are traced back directly to the Koran or other Islamic teach-
ings. In which case, one might ask, how is it that jihadi manuals circu-
lating in the refugee camps and among the mujahideen were produced
at the University of Nebraska–Omaha?

The primers, which were filled with talk of jihad and featured
drawings of guns, bullets, soldiers and mines, have served since as
the Afghan school-system's core curriculum. Even the Taliban used
the American-produced books, though the radical movement
scratched out human faces in keeping with its strict fundamentalist creed.†

Meanwhile changes were taking place in the Soviet Union. With
the elevation of Mikhail Gorbachev to general secretary of the politburo in March 1985, it soon became obvious that the Soviet Union
would accept defeat in Afghanistan and withdraw its troops. I had a
surprising personal experience in this regard. At a UN-sponsored conference in Tashkent that spring, I was astonished when, after my
speech, which was extremely critical of the Soviet intervention in
Afghanistan and its aftermath, the younger members of the Soviet delegation, led by Yevgeni Primakov (subsequently head of the KGB and
briefly prime minister under Yeltsin), came up and hugged me, saying

---

*Mohammed Yousaf and Mark Adkin, *The Bear Trap: Afghanistan's Untold Story* (Lahore:
2003). Should be a recommended read for all NATO personnel in Afghanistan. Exactly the
same tactics are being used against them.

†Joe Stephens and David B. Ottaway, "The ABCs of Jihad in Afghanistan," *Washington Post,*
March 23, 2002.

they agreed with me and so did their new general secretary. When I reported this to various Pakistani friends, they became despondent. Some refused to believe this was possible. Today, many of them are equally committed to the U.S. occupation of Afghanistan and plead with the West to send more troops.*

The Soviet Union had accepted defeat and decided on a unilateral withdrawal from Afghanistan. Nonetheless, General Gromov wanted some guarantees for their Afghan supporters who were being left behind. The United States—its mission successful—was prepared to play ball. General Zia, however, was not. The Afghan war had gone to his head (as it had to that of Osama bin Laden and his colleagues), and he wanted his own people in power there. Zia dreamed of hoisting the crescent and star in Central Asian capitals. As the Soviet withdrawal got closer, Zia and the ISI made plans for the postwar settlement. During his rule Pakistan had built a nuclear bomb, and this, coupled with the Soviet defeat, had given Zia and the generals closest to him a new confidence and the feeling that they were invulnerable.

AND THEN ZIA went up in smoke. On August 17, 1988, he took five generals to the trial of a new U.S. Abrams M1/A1 tank at a military test range near Bahawalpur. Also present were a U.S. general and the U.S. ambassador, Arnold Raphael. The demonstration did not go well and everybody was grumpy. Zia offered the Americans a lift in his specially built C-130 aircraft, which had a sealed cabin to protect him from assassins. A few minutes after the plane took off, the pilots lost control and it crashed into the desert. All the passengers were killed. All that was left of Zia was his jawbone, which was duly buried in Islamabad (the nearby roundabout became known to cabbies as Jawbone Chowk). The cause of the crash remains a mystery. The U.S. National Archives contain 250 pages of documents relating to

---

*Ahmad Rashid, "Accept Defeat by Taliban, Pakistan Tells NATO," *Daily Telegraph*, November 30, 2006. Rashid writes, "To progress in Riga, Nato will have to enlist US support to call Pakistan's bluff, put pressure on Islamabad to hand over the Taliban leadership and put more troops in to fight the insurgency while persuading Mr Karzai to become more pro-active."

the incident, but they are still classified. Pakistani intelligence experts have informally told me that it was the Russians taking their revenge for Afghanistan or, in another variant, acting on behalf of Indian leader Rajiv Gandhi, whose mother, Indira, was assassinated by her Sikh bodyguards, who had apparently visited the Sikh training camps in Pakistan. A remarkable version was supplied by John Gunther Dean, a senior diplomat serving as U.S. ambassador to India. According to Barbara Crossette, the *New York Times* South Asia bureau chief at the time:

> In New Delhi in August 1988, a lot of history came together in Dean's mind. He had an immediate suspicion about who killed Zia, but his putative perpetrator was not on the list of possible conspirators then in circulation. Dean thought the plot to rid the world of General Zia bore the hallmarks of Israel, or specifically the Israeli intelligence agency, Mossad.
>
> Dean believed in "dissent through channels," not leaks. And, knowing what a controversy such a public accusation would unleash, and the effect it would have not only in the United States and South Asia but also in the wider Islamic world, he decided to go back to Washington to explain his theory in person to his superiors at the State Department. That act cost him his diplomatic career.*

Was Dean hinting that Mossad had blown up Zia to punish him for getting a bomb? Dean never spoke again so we don't know, but it seems unlikely. The Israelis had appreciated Zia's role in defeating the Palestinians in Jordan. Zia had allowed a Mossad presence in Peshawar during the Afghan war. Furthermore, he often thought of Pakistan as a Muslim equivalent of Israel:

> Pakistan is like Israel, an ideological state. Take out Judaism from Israel and it will collapse like a house of cards. Take Islam out of Pak-

---

*Barbara Crossette, "Who Killed Zia?" *World Policy Journal,* Fall 2005.

istan and make it a secular state: it would collapse. For the past four years we have been trying to bring Islamic values to the country.*

Most Pakistanis, as is their wont, blamed the CIA. Zia's son was convinced it was Murtaza Bhutto's group, "al-Zulfiqar." Zia's widow would whisper it was "our own people," meaning the army. Benazir Bhutto described it as "an act of God." The only fact they could all agree on was that he was dead. The mystery remains unsolved to this day. When foreign leaders were pleading with him to spare Zulfiqar Ali Bhutto's life, Zia had replied that nobody was indispensable, and "I am of the opinion that the higher you go, the harder you fall." The "soldier of Islam" had left behind his own epitaph.

---

*Quoted in the *Economist*, December 12, 1981. When in 1970 I first made this comparison in the very first sentence of *Pakistan: Military Rule or People's Power?* there was outrage, especially among right-wing Pakistanis. A decade later the analogy had become halal, or kosher.

6

THE WASHINGTON QUARTET

The General
as Chief Executive

WITH ZIA'S ASSASSINATION, THE SECOND PERIOD OF MILITARY rule in Pakistan came to an end. What followed was a longish civilian prologue to Musharraf's reign, unprecedented in the country's short history. For ten years members of two political dynasties—the Bhutto and Sharif families—ran the country in turn. This ten-year spell was an important phase in Pakistan's history. Tragically, neither Bhutto's daughter, Benazir, nor Zia's protégé, Nawaz Sharif, showed any ability to govern the country in interests other than their own. Clientilism, patronage, and corruption on a gigantic scale were the hallmarks of their weak regimes.

In November 1988, a thirty-five-year-old Benazir Bhutto had, much to the annoyance of the army, won the elections held a short time after Zia's demise. Despite strong Islamist opposition, she became the country's only woman prime minister. This had been the first real opportunity people had to show their anger at her father's execution. Her program pledged a few reforms to help the poor, but was far removed from the world of "food, clothes, and shelter for all." Her options were severely limited. Her enemies were embedded in the state apparatuses and she was politically weak. When I met her a few months after her triumph, she was refreshingly honest: "I can't do anything. The army on one side and the president [Ghulam Ishaq Khan, a former bureaucrat who had supported Zia against Bhutto] on the other." It was undoubtedly a difficult situation. My advice was to go on television and tell the people, explaining why she was virtually powerless. It was the only way to educate citizens. My other suggestion was to implement certain reforms that did not require billions. She should, at the least, attempt to set up girls' schools all over the country and repeal the disgraceful Hudood Ordinances, pushed through by Zia, that treated women as second-class citizens and equated rape with adultery. She nodded approvingly, but nothing was done. As prime minister, Benazir could not even avenge herself on Zia's ghost, let alone introduce a single legislative measure that mattered. The system Zia had put in place was never challenged. Most of her party hierarchy were so happy to be back in power that all they could think about was themselves. After an inconclusive twenty months in office, President Ishaq, using the enormous powers vested in him via Zia's Eighth Amendment to the 1973 constitution, dismissed Benazir's government in August 1990, accusing her of tolerating corruption and failing to control ethnic violence in her home province of Sind. There was little public response. In the elections that followed, Nawaz Sharif won a majority and became the new prime minister. He too fell out with the president and was dismissed from office in 1993. A former World Bank employee, Moin Qureshi, was appointed caretaker prime minister pending new elections in October 1993, which returned Benazir to power.

Meanwhile the crisis in Afghanistan continued even after the unilateral Soviet withdrawal in February 1989. The two countries had become intertwined. A leading member of the Soviet politburo, Yevgeni Primakov, had proposed a deal to stabilize Afghanistan whereby Moscow would gradually take the old Afghan leaders and cadres out of the country, leaving an intact structure for the government that followed. Pakistan rejected this sensible offer. Its foreign minister, Sahibzada Yaqub Khan, an old friend of Washington, wanted no compromise. Nor did his masters. The scent of blood was in their nostrils, and so the mujahideen factions were told to continue the war. A demoralized and defeated pro-Soviet Afghan army disintegrated rapidly, and most of the Afghan leadership ultimately fled abroad. The prime minister, Mohammad Najibullah, took refuge in the UN office. Large parts of Kabul were destroyed, after which the mujahideen groups, much to the dismay of their foreign friends, began to fight each other. Political disputes were settled with artillery. Different combinations of president and ministers were not able to restore order. There was no effective central government. Gunmen became "tax collectors" and trade came to a virtual standstill. The poppy alone remained sacrosanct.

During Benazir Bhutto's second term in office (1993–96) her minister of the interior, General Naseerullah Babar, together with the ISI, devised a plan to set up the Taliban as a politico-military force that could take over Afghanistan, a move only halfheartedly approved by the U.S. embassy. The truth was, once the Soviet Union had withdrawn its troops, Washington had lost interest in the country.

Benazir Bhutto's denials that her government was the main force supporting the Taliban were never convincing. In 1994, the last time I met her, she told me that all her government was doing was sending the Afghan refugees back to Afghanistan. What this gloss concealed was the heavy involvement of the ISI in the return journey. The Taliban (the word literally means "students") were children of Afghan refugees and poor Pathan families "educated" in the madrassas in the 1980s. They provided the shock troops, but were led by a handful of experienced mujahideen including Mullah Omar. Without Pakistan's support they could never have taken Kabul, although Mullah Omar, another fantasist, sometimes preferred to forget this reality, just as Sheikh Osama and Al Qaeda had convinced themselves that the defeat of the Russians was a jihadi victory, forgetting the key role of the infidels, without whose support the jihadis could never have won at all. Omar's faction was dominant, but the ISI never completely lost control of the organization. Islamabad kept its cool even when Omar's zealots asserted their independence by attacking the Pakistan embassy in Kabul in 1999 and, in the same year, his religious police interrupted a friendly soccer match between the two countries because the Pakistani players had arrived sporting long hair and shorts. Before a stunned crowd, the police caned the players, shaved their heads, and sent them back home. A return match in Islamabad was canceled.

General Hamid Gul, a staunchly pro-jihadi director general of the ISI during Benazir's first term, whom she had unsuccessfully attempted to remove, paid her a warm tribute after her assassination in 2007:

> It is not the jihadis who have killed her. She was rather protective of the jihadis in the past. Benazir was never soft on the Kashmir issue, let me tell you that. I served as the ISI director-general under her. The Taliban emerged during her second tenure in office and captured Kabul when she was still the prime minister. Her interior minister used to patronise them openly.*

Benazir Bhutto's second government ran into serious trouble when her carefully handpicked president, Farooq Leghari, a loyal and staunch PPP stalwart, became discontented. It was an old problem: corruption in high places. Visiting Islamabad in early 1996, I found the surface calm deceptive. As I was lunching with my mother in her favorite Islamabad restaurant, a jovial, mustachioed figure came over to greet us from an adjacent table. His wife, Benazir, was abroad on a state visit. Senator Asif Zardari, state minister for investment, responsible for entertaining the children in her absence, had brought them out for a special treat. An exchange of pleasantries ensued. I asked how things were proceeding in the country. "Fine," he replied with a charming grin. "All is well." He should have known better.

Behind closed doors in Islamabad, a palace coup was in motion. Benazir Bhutto was about to be luxuriously betrayed. Leghari was preparing to dismiss her government after secret consultations with the army and opposition leaders. During dinner that same week, a senior civil servant, extremely fond of Benazir, was in despair. The president, he said, had sought to defuse the crisis by asking for a special meeting with the prime minister. Benazir, characteristically, turned up with her husband. This annoyed Leghari: one of the subjects he wanted to discuss with her was her husband's legendary greed. Despite this, Leghari remained calm while attempting to convince the first couple that not

---

*"Get America Out of the Way and We'll Be OK," interview with Harinder Baweja, *Tehelka Magazine,* February 2, 2008.

only their political enemies were demanding action. The scale of the corruption and the corresponding decay of the administration had become a national scandal. Leghari was under pressure from the army and others to move against the government. To resist them he needed her help. He pleaded with her to discipline Zardari and a number of other ministers who were out of control. Zardari, stubborn as always in defense of his material interests, taunted the president: nobody in Pakistan, he said, including Leghari, was entirely clean. The threat was obvious: you touch us and we'll expose you.

Leghari felt the dignity of his office had been insulted. He went pale and began to tremble with anger. He suggested that the minister for investment leave the room. Benazir nodded and Zardari walked out. Leghari again entreated her to restrain her husband. She smiled and gave her president a lecture on loyalty and how much she valued it. The people who were complaining, she told him, were jealous of her husband's business acumen. They were professional whingers, has-beens, rogues resentful at being passed over. She made no concessions. She was not convinced that the army was planning a coup.

It's true that not every general is bursting to seize state power. General Asif Nawaz (chief of staff from 1991 to 1993) resisted the temptation despite advice to the contrary, and his sudden and unexpected death fueled the rumor mills in Islamabad. His widow and many others suspected murder.* His successor, General Wahid Kakar (1993–96) was to tell friends that the U.S. ambassador had made it clear that given the crisis, Washington would understand if firm action was taken. Kakar too remained outside politics, though the scale of corruption angered him, and on a famous occasion he is reported to have confronted Benazir Bhutto and complained about her husband's greed.

"Why don't you divorce him or have him bumped off?" asked the general.

"If you have any proof, General, sahib," Benazir purred in response, "please send it to me."

---

*A fascinating account of this episode and numerous others in Pakistan's military history is contained in Shuja Nawaz, *Crossed Swords: Pakistan, Its Army, and the Wars Within* (Karachi: 2008).

Kakar retired peacefully and was replaced by General Jehangir Karamat, another professional officer who refused to contemplate a coup.

Several months after dismissing Benazir, Leghari told me that this meeting, the last of many, had been decisive. He could no longer tolerate her excesses: if she continued in office, the army would intervene against democracy for the fourth time in the country's history. Reluctantly, he said, he decided to invoke the Eighth Amendment—Zia's gift to the nation—which gives the president powers to dismiss an elected government. New elections have to be held within ninety days.

Corruption was the main charge leveled against Benazir and Zardari. The couple were alleged to have used public office to amass a large private fortune—reckoned to be in the region of $1.5 billion—and transferred their assets abroad. Zardari was arrested, but his business associates remained loyal. One of them, the chairman of Pakistan Steel, committed suicide rather than give evidence against his former patron. Benazir's closest supporters insist that her political prestige was squandered by her husband, that he was a fraud, a poseur, a wastrel, a philanderer, and much worse. In March 1999, addressing a friendly gathering at an Islamabad seminar, Benazir defended her spouse. He was much misunderstood, she said, but before she could continue, the audience began to shake their heads in disapproval. "No! No! No!" they shouted. She paused and then said with a sigh, "I wonder why I always get the same reaction whenever I mention him."

Zardari was not the only reason for her unpopularity. The Peoples Party had done little for the poor, who were its natural constituency. Most of her ministers, at the national and provincial levels, were too busy lining their own pockets. Permanently surrounded by sycophants and cronies, she had become isolated from her electorate and oblivious to reality. The country was continuing to rot. A state that has never provided free education or health care and could no longer guarantee subsidized wheat, rice, or sugar rations to the poor or protect innocent lives from random killings in its largest city had created mass despair. In January 1999, a transport worker in Hyderabad who had not been paid for two years went to the Press Club, soaked himself in petrol, and set himself alight. He left behind a letter that read like an extract from an Upton Sinclair novel:

I have lost patience. Me and my fellow workers have been protesting the nonpayment of our salaries for a long time. But nobody takes any notice. My wife and mother are seriously ill and I have no money for their treatment. My family is starving and I am fed up with quarrels. I don't have the right to live. I am sure the flames of my body will reach the houses of the rich one day.

In the general election that followed Benazir's removal from power, the Peoples Party suffered a humiliating defeat. The Pakistani electorate may be largely semiliterate, but its political sophistication has never been in doubt. Disillusioned, apathetic, and weary, Benazir's supporters refused to vote for her, but they could not at that point bring themselves to vote for her enemy. Nawaz Sharif's Muslim League won a giant majority, winning two-thirds of the seats in the National Assembly, but 70 percent of the electorate stayed indoors.

The Sharif brothers were returned to power. Once again, Shahbaz, the younger but shrewder sibling, accepted family discipline and Nawaz became the prime minister. In 1998, Sharif made Pervez Musharraf army chief of staff in preference to the more senior general, Ali Kuli Khan. Sharif's reasoning may have been that Musharraf, from a middle-class, refugee background like himself, would be easier to manipulate than Ali Kuli, who came from a landed Pathan family in the NWFP and was a schoolfellow of President Farooq Leghari, whom Sharif didn't trust either because of the latter's PPP origins. Whatever the reasoning, it turned out to be a mistake of similar magnitude to Zulfiqar Ali Bhutto's when he leapfrogged General Zia over the head of five senior generals. Ali Kuli Khan, highly regarded by most of his colleagues, did not harbor political ambitions and, like his immediate predecessors, would probably have stayed out of politics.

On Bill Clinton's urging, Sharif pushed for a rapprochement with India. This accorded with his own business instincts. Travel and trade agreements were negotiated, land borders were opened, flights resumed, but before the next stage—loosening of travel restrictions and regular cross-border train services—could be reached, the Pakistan army began to assemble in the Himalayan foothills.

To put it mildly, the terrain in Kargil and the neighboring region is inhospitable and for at least half the year also inaccessible. The jagged peaks reach nineteen thousand feet, and winter temperatures average -60 degrees Celsius. When the snows melt, the fierce rocks make all movement extremely difficult. Officers and soldiers serving in the region regard it as a Siberian exile. An unwritten agreement between India and Pakistan from 1977 onward was that neither side would man posts from September 15 to April 15 each year. In 1999, the Pakistan army, hoping to isolate the Indians in Kashmir, decided to bin the agreement and launched a limited war that raised the specter of a nuclear exchange.

THE INDIANS, CLEARLY taken by surprise on discovering Pakistani troops and irregulars occupying heights on the Indian side, suffered serious reverses during the first few weeks of the conflict, but subsequently moved in crack regiments and artillery together with heavy air cover and began to inflict casualties, compelling Pakistan to withdraw from some areas. After three months of fighting from May to July 1999, neither side could claim total victory, but casualties were high (several thousand on both sides). In his memoirs, Musharraf grotesquely exaggerates Pakistan's "triumph," claiming his side won. In reality, another stupid idea had backfired on the Pakistani high command. A cease-fire was agreed to and each army returned to its side of the Line of Control that separates Pakistan-occupied Kashmir from that run by India.

There were, however, a few unpleasant reminders of the ideological fanaticism introduced into the Pakistan army during the Zia period. Compulsory prayers and preachers attached to units had begun to affect the soldiery. In December 2000, I was told by a former army officer in Lahore about a disturbing incident after the Kargil cease-fire. The Indians had informed their Pakistani counterparts that one of the peaks in Kargil-Drass was still occupied by Pakistani soldiers, contrary to the cease-fire agreement. A senior officer investigated and ordered the captain in charge of the peak to return to the Pakistani side of the Line of Control. The captain accused his senior officer and the military high command of betraying the Islamist cause and shot the officer dead. The Islamist officer was finally disarmed, tried by a secret court-martial, and executed.

WHY DID THE war take place at all? In private, the Sharif brothers told associates that the army was opposed to their policy of friendship with India and was determined to sabotage the process: the army had acted without clearance from the government. In his memoir, Musharraf insists that the army had kept the prime minister informed in briefings in January and February 1999. This ties in with what my informant (a former senior civil servant) who was present at the briefing told me. The slick video presentation by the GHQ had impressed Sharif. Naturally in the video the good guys won hands down. All Sharif asked at the end was "Can you do it quickly?"

The real reason for the war went back to the defeat in Dhaka. If the Americans could avenge Vietnam in Afghanistan, why not Pakistan in Kashmir? Ever since the 1990 victory in Kabul, the ISI had been infiltrating jihadis across the Line of Control into Indian-held Kashmir, trying to mimic the Afghan operation, but this time working on their own. They succeeded in destabilizing the province, but the Indian government responded with more troops, and ordinary Kashmiris were caught in the ugly crossfire. The Indian troops were undoubtedly brutal, but the jihadis, with their Wahhabi rhetoric, also antagonized important layers of the population. Islam in Kashmir had always been of the soft Sufi variety.

The Kargil war was designed to recapture the initiative. Looking back, it is truly staggering that Pakistan's military philosophers actually thought they could defeat India. Once the latter realized that this was a full-fledged assault, it recovered and sent in heavy artillery with air and helicopter cover. A naval offensive, prelude to a blockade, was also set in motion. With only six days of fuel left, the Napoléons in Pakistan's GHQ had no alternative but to accept a cease-fire. Sharif told Washington that he had been bounced into a war he didn't want, but did not oppose. Soon afterward, the Sharif family decided to get rid of Musharraf. Constitutionally, of course, the prime minister had the power to dismiss the chief of staff and appoint a new one, as Zulfiqar

Ali Bhutto had done in the 1970s when he appointed Zia. But the army then was weak, divided, and had been defeated in a major war; this was certainly not the case in 1999. Here it was only a stupid, if costly, adventure that had gone wrong.

SHARIF'S CANDIDATE TO succeed Musharraf was General Ziauddin Butt, head of the ISI, who was widely regarded as weak and incompetent. He was bundled off to Washington for vetting and while there is said to have pledged bin Laden's head on a platter. If Sharif had simply dismissed Musharraf, he might have had a better chance of success, but what he lacked in good sense his overclever brother tried to make up for in guile. Were the Sharif brothers really so foolish as to believe that the army was unaware of their intrigues, or were they misled by their belief in U.S. omnipotence? Clinton duly warned the Pakistan army that Washington would not tolerate a military coup in Pakistan. I remember chuckling at the time that this was a first in U.S.-Pakistan relations. Sharif relied too heavily on Clinton's warning. He should have checked with the Pentagon's Defense Intelligence Agency.

The tragicomic episode that followed is described accurately enough in Musharraf's memoir, *In the Line of Fire,* a book intended largely for Western eyes.* Musharraf describes how on October 11, 1999, he and his wife were flying back from Sri Lanka on a normal passenger flight when the pilot received instructions not to land. While the plane was still circling over Karachi, Nawaz Sharif summoned General Ziauddin Butt and in front of a TV crew swore him in as the new chief of staff. Meanwhile there was panic on Musharraf's plane, by now low on fuel. He contacted the commander of the Karachi garrison, the army took control of the airport, and the plane landed safely.

---

*Pervez Musharraf's *In the Line of Fire* (New York and London: 2005) gives the official version of what has been happening in Pakistan over the last six years. Whereas Altaf Gauhar injected nonsense of every sort into Ayub's memoirs, his son Humayun Gauhar, who worked with Musharraf on this book, has avoided the more obvious pitfalls. The general's raffish lifestyle is underplayed, but enough is in the book to suggest that he is not too easily swayed by religious or social obligations.

Simultaneously, military units surrounded the prime minister's house in Islamabad and arrested Nawaz Sharif. General Zia had been assassinated on a military flight; Musharraf took power on board a passenger plane.

So began the third extended period of military rule in Pakistan, initially welcomed by all Nawaz Sharif's political opponents (including Benazir Bhutto, long before her consecration as the Mother of Democracy) and some of his former colleagues. Musharraf was initially popular in Pakistan, and if he had pushed through reforms to provide an education for all children, with English as a compulsory second language (as in Malaysia) to break the elite's monopoly on higher education abroad, instituted land reforms to end the stranglehold of the gentry on large swathes of the countryside, tackled corruption in the armed forces and everywhere else, and ended the jihadi escapades in Kashmir and Pakistan as a prelude to a long-term deal with India, he might have left behind a positive legacy. Sadly and predictably, none of this was even attempted. Musharraf did, however, implement one important shift by permitting the emergence of independent TV stations and thus breaking the deadly stranglehold of state TV. This undoubtedly enhanced media freedom in the country. A number of the networks were challenging, critical, and not at all worried about offending those in authority. Musharraf lived to regret this concession.

In the political realm, he mimicked his military predecessors. Like them, he took off his uniform, went to a landlord-organized gathering in Sind, and entered politics. His party? The ever-*khaki*, ever-available courtesan known to the country as the Muslim League. His supporters? Chips off the old corrupt block he had denounced so vigorously on taking office and whose leaders he was prosecuting for large-scale corruption. The inevitable had happened. The Chaudhrys of Gujrat had split from the Sharif family and done a deal with the general. Chaudhry Shujaat Hussain, the minister of the interior and narcotic control in Nawaz Sharif's government, had decided that becoming a broker for the military was a far more rewarding occupation than a spell in opposition. The only surprise was that anyone was surprised.

• • •

THE FIRST MAJOR crisis to hit the Musharraf regime occurred on September 11, 2001. By pure chance, that very week the long-bearded General Mahmud Ahmad, director general of the ISI, was in Washington as a guest of the Pentagon. While the 9/11 attacks were occuring, General Ahmad was enjoying a relaxed breakfast at the Capitol with the chairmen of the Senate and House Intelligence committees, Senator Bob Graham (D) and Representative Porter Goss (R). The latter had worked for the CIA black-ops (clandestine operations) section for over ten years. In a discussion of terrorism, reference was made to Osama bin Laden's base in Afghanistan. In the interval between the two attacks on the World Trade Center, General Ahmad tried to convince his hosts that Mullah Omar was totally trustworthy and could be persuaded to disgorge Osama bin Laden. The meeting carried on in this vein until the second plane hit the WTC and everyone left. It is not known if Graham questioned his guest regarding information that, it was later revealed, his staff had received from an ISI operative in August that year, warning that the Twin Towers would soon be attacked.

The next day, General Ahmad, accompanied by Maleeha Lodhi, Pakistan's ambassador in Washington, was summoned to the State Department to receive the notorious ultimatum from Richard Armitage revealed by Musharraf in Washington to promote his memoir: either you're with us or you're against us, and "we'll bomb you into the Stone Age" if you resist. Musharraf was insistent that the threat had been made. Bush was sure that those words would not have been used. Ahmad and Armitage denied it had been said at their meeting. Musharraf then claimed he had other sources of information. Clearly something had been said, but had Musharraf exaggerated to impress his corps commanders that there was no option but to do Washington's bidding, or was it a simple ploy to increase sales of his book? Maleeha Lodhi's account of the meeting was altogether more diplomatic, as befitted her status:

> "The two of them were very tense," Ms. Lodhi said of Mr. Armitage and General Ahmad. "Armitage started out by saying: 'This is a grave moment. History begins today for the United States. We're

asking all our friends—you're not the only country we're speaking to—we're asking people whether they're with us or against us.'"*

The next day, the couple were sent for again, and Armitage handed the ISI boss a seven-point list of U.S. requirements from Pakistan for waging the coming war in Afghanistan. Without even looking closely at the printed sheet, Mahmud Ahmad put it in his pocket and said that he accepted everything. As some of the demands affected Pakistan's sovereignty, even Richard Armitage was taken aback and asked the ISI boss whether he needed to consult with General Musharraf before making any commitments. "Not necessary," replied General Ahmad. "He will agree with me." Ahmad's strong antipathy to the United States was hardly a secret. He was evidently in a hurry to get back home and convince his colleagues not to accept any of the demands. These were later published in *The 9/11 Commission Report*:

1. Stop Al Qaeda operatives at its border and end all logistical support for bin Laden.
2. Give the United States blanket overflight and landing rights for all necessary military and intelligence operations.
3. Provide territorial access to U.S. and allied military intelligence and other personnel to conduct operations against Al Qaeda.
4. Provide the United States with intelligence information.
5. Continue to publicly condemn the terrorist attacks.
6. Cut off all shipments of fuel to the Taliban and stop recruits from going to Afghanistan.
7. If the evidence implicated bin Laden and Al Qaeda, and the Taliban continued to harbor them, to break relations with the Taliban government.

This was a direct challenge to Pakistan's sovereignty, reducing it to the status of Britain. Musharraf later denied that he had agreed to the second and third points, but that was certainly not the view in Wash-

---

New York Times, August 4, 2007.

ington. Colin Powell informed the National Security Council that the Pakistanis had agreed to everything. What was not in the seven points but had been demanded in secret discussions was U.S. access to the nuclear facility. This Musharraf could not and did not accept, hence the endless campaign in the U.S. and European media on the jihadi "threat" to the weapons.

The Pakistani generals were faced with a difficult choice after September 11. If they did not agree to U.S. demands, Washington might follow the Israeli example and make an anti-Muslim pact with the religious extremists ruling India at the time. But if they kowtowed, the results could be catastrophic, given that Pakistani intelligence (ISI) had been funding fundamentalist groups in Pakistan since the Zia years (1977–88). Musharraf, backed by most of his generals, decided that it was necessary to withdraw from Kabul, to persuade his supporters in the Taliban not to resist U.S. occupation, and to open up Pakistan's military and air force bases to the United States. From these bases, the U.S.-led assault on Afghanistan was mounted in October 2001.

In truth, Musharraf did not always cooperate or accept every demand. He also had a sense of humor. Why otherwise would he have decided to attend the Non-Aligned Conference in Havana timed to open on September 11, 2006? At a meeting with Hugo Chávez, the Venezuelan president, Musharraf offered this advice: "You are far too aggressive with the Americans. Do as I do. Accept what they say and then do as you want."

MEANWHILE, THE embittered ISI chief and a colleague were dispatched to Kabul to inform the Taliban that war was coming unless they handed the Al Qaeda leadership over to Pakistan. Whatever happened, the Taliban were not to resist the occupation, but pack their bags, make themselves scarce, and disappear. All Pakistan military and air force personnel in Afghanistan were recalled. The impulsive Mahmud Ahmad did transmit this message, but added his own footnote. He told Mullah Omar that he disagreed with the command and thought the Taliban should fight back. Immediately on his return to Islamabad, Ahmad was fired, and more pliant officers were sent to talk the Taliban out of any crazed attempt to resist U.S. military power. Most of the leadership did as asked and agreed to bide their time. Mullah Omar chose to tie his fate to that of his honored Al Qaeda guest, and when last seen, this veteran of the anti-Soviet war, half lame and half blind, was on a motorbike heading for the mountains to make his great escape. Unlike Steve McQueen in the movie, the mullah is still at large. All the high-tech surveillance devices have so far not succeeded in tracking him down.

Musharraf's unstinting support for the U.S. after 9/11 prompted local wags to dub him Busharraf, and in March 2005 Condoleezza Rice described the U.S.-Pakistan relationship since 9/11 as "broad and deep." Had Musharraf not, after all, unraveled Pakistan's one military victory to please Washington? He would always insist that he only agreed to become Washington's surrogate because of State Department honcho Richard Armitage's Stone Age threat. What really worried Islamabad, however, was a threat Musharraf doesn't mention: if Pakistan had refused, the United States would have used the Indian bases that were on offer.

This decision almost cost Musharraf his life. The victory in Afghanistan had struck a deep chord among the more conservative sections of the army. Ever since the war against East Bengal, soldiers had been heavily indoctrinated with anti-Hindu propaganda. The Hindus were the enemy. They would destroy Pakistan at the first opportunity. Coupled to this was the Islamization within the army pushed through by Zia especially during the jihad against the Soviet army next door. To accept a U.S. occupation of a Muslim state that they had helped set up was too much for some of the officers. For some soldiers too it was a shameful defeat. At an open GHQ seminar headed "Fall of the Taliban," the now retired ISI brigadier Mohammed Yousaf, who had been invited as a participant, walked in and added the word *Government* after *Taliban*. He would not accept that it was all over. Nor was he wrong. Jihadi militants, helped by information from within the army, had decided to kill Musharraf. They felt betrayed. Their logic was simple: if it had been right to wage jihad against the Soviet infidels, why did the same not apply to the American infidels? The textbooks from the University of Nebraska had left a mark.

When Musharraf seized power in 1999, he had refused to move from his homely, colonial bungalow in Rawalpindi to the kitsch comfort of the President's House in Islamabad, which with its gilt furniture and tasteless decor owes more to Gulf State opulence than local tradition. The cities are close to each other, but far from identical. Islamabad, laid out in a grid pattern and overlooked by the Himalayan foothills, was built in the 1960s by General Ayub. He wanted a new capital remote from threatening crowds, but close to GHQ in Rawalpindi, which had been constructed by the British as a garrison town. After partition, it became the obvious place to situate the military headquarters of the new Pakistan.

One of the nineteenth-century British colonial expeditions to conquer Afghanistan (they all ended in disaster) was planned in Rawalpindi. From here, a century and a half later, the Washington-blessed jihad was launched against the hopeless Afghan Communists. From here, the U.S. demand to use Pakistan as a base for its operations in Afghanistan was discussed and agreed upon in September 2001.

For a short while after the U.S. occupation of Kabul, a misleading calm prevailed in Pakistan. I had predicted a rapid defeat of the Taliban, since that is what GHQ had decided, and suggested that the jihadi groups would regroup in Pakistan and, sooner or later, start punishing General Musharraf's regime. This began in 2002. An unreported attempt to kill Musharraf was followed by three big hits: the kidnapping and brutal murder of *Wall Street Journal* reporter Daniel Pearl; the assassination of the interior minister's brother; and the bombing of a church in the heart of Islamabad's tightly protected diplomatic enclave. In addition, targeted assassinations of middle-class professionals took place in Karachi. Over a dozen doctors belonging to the Shia minority were killed. These acts were a warning to Pakistan's military ruler: if you go too far in accommodating Washington, your head will also roll.

Were all these acts of terrorism actually carried out by hard-line groups such as Jaish-e-Mohammed and Harkatul Ansar, who often claim them? Probably, but this is not an entirely coherent assertion. These organizations were, after all, funded and armed by the state as late as the Kargil war. Turn them upside down and the rational kernel is revealed. It is the ISI whose blatant manipulation of these groups has been obvious to everyone in the country for a long time. Those sections of the ISI who patronized and funded these organizations were livid at "the betrayal of the Taliban."

Unless this is appreciated, the random and selective terrorism that shook the country after the fall of the Taliban becomes inexplicable. Musharraf, like Bhutto and Nawaz Sharif, inherited Zia's ISI, whose size and budget had massively expanded during the first Afghan war. Secretary of State Colin Powell's statement of March 3, 2002, exonerating the ISI from any responsibility for Pearl's disappearance and murder shocked many Pakistanis. Virtually everyone I spoke to in Pakistan at the time stated the exact opposite. Musharraf was obviously not involved, but he must have been informed of what was taking place. He had referred to Pearl as an "overintrusive journalist" caught up in "intelligence games," an indication that Musharraf did know something. Had he informed his bosses in Washington? And if so, why did Powell absolve the ISI? Pearl was lured to a fashionable restaurant in Karachi, kidnapped, then executed by his captors. A video showing Pearl's throat being slit was distributed to the Western media, and a gruesome clip was shown on CBS News.

The Pearl tragedy had shed some light on the darker recesses of the intelligence networks. He was a tough-minded, investigative (as opposed to embedded) journalist with a deep regard for the truth. While he showed little interest in political or social theories or ideologies, he was sensitive to the moral and human costs of their implementation. This applied as much to the "humanitarian intervention" in Kosovo as to clerical misrule in Iran, though his reports from Iran never followed the official Washington line. Some of his best pieces in the *Wall Street Journal* were reasoned and eloquent rejections of state propaganda, including U.S. propaganda about Kosovo used to justify the bombing of Yugoslavia. He proved that the Sudanese pharmaceutical factory—bombed on Bill Clinton's orders to distract attention from the Lewinsky affair—was exactly that and not a shady installation producing biological and chemical weapons as alleged by the White House.

When Pearl's death was announced, I remember thinking that the official U.S. response was rather subdued. What if the victim had been Thomas Friedman of the *New York Times*? Would Pervez Musharraf have been able to describe Friedman at a Washington press conference as "too intrusive," which is what he said about Pearl? It was as if Pearl had connived in his own murder. The brother of Pakistan's interior minister had been killed by an Islamist group a few weeks before Pearl. When, during a private meeting, the minister muttered something about Pearl bringing it on himself, a friend Pearl's widow had brought with her asked, "With all due respect, Mr. Minister, would you blame your brother for having been murdered just because he was driving the streets of Karachi?"

Pearl's journalism was sorely missed in the run-up to the Iraq war when propaganda flooded the television networks and the "paper of record" had become almost as uncritical and unquestioning as the Pakistani media had once been under General Zia's dictatorship. There was no mystery as to why Pearl had come to Pakistan in the first place; obviously to track the big story, to see if he could uncover the links between the intelligence services and indigenous terrorism. His newspaper—and indeed the State Department—were remarkably coy on this subject, refusing to disclose the leads that Pearl was pursuing. Contrary to stories that were circulated later, Daniel Pearl was a cautious journalist. His wife, Mariane, detailed the memos he sent to his paper, arguing that they should train and protect journalists reporting from danger zones.* They were ignored. Pearl refused to go to Afghanistan—the situation was too insecure—but he also knew that the real story was in Pakistan. He decided to investigate the links between Richard Reid, the shoe bomber, and Islamist groups in Pakistan. This was presumably what Musharraf thought "too intrusive." Pakistani officials more than once told Mariane that if Pearl had behaved like other foreign journalists, the tragedy might have been averted. Neither she nor the FBI experts who flew to Pakistan were able to decipher Pearl's notes, written in code and describing, one assumes, what he found out.

Any Western journalist, however friendly, who visits Pakistan is routinely watched and followed. This is an old intelligence habit, an article of faith, dating back to the country's founding (and before), and

---

*Mariane Pearl, *A Mighty Heart: The Brave Life and Death of My Husband* (New York and London: 2004), subsequently a Hollywood movie.

it goes on even when elected governments are in power. In the wake of the Afghan war the intelligence agencies became overstocked with cheap labor. The notion that Danny Pearl, beavering away on his own, setting up contacts with members of extremist groups, was not at the same time being carefully monitored by the secret services is incredible. In fact, it is unbelievable. And nobody in Pakistan believed it at the time or does now.

Circumstantial evidence suggested the involvement of the intelligence agencies in Pearl's death. There was no direct proof, but it was no secret in Pakistan that Omar Saeed Sheikh, the psychopath who set up the kidnapping, had intelligence connections. In 1994, ISI-spawned Islamist groups had infiltrated him into Kashmir. A specialist in kidnapping foreigners and keeping them as hostages, he masterminded an action of this kind in Delhi to secure the release from Tihar jail of Masood Azhar, leader of an Islamist group. The kidnapping succeeded, but so did Indian intelligence: after a shoot-out, Sheikh was captured. He slapped the senior police officer who arrested him and was beaten up in return. Five years later, in December 1999, his colleagues hijacked an Indian airliner on its way to Kandahar and threatened to kill everyone on board unless Sheikh and other "liberation fighters" were freed. They were.

What drove a Sylvester Stallone fan, born in East London in 1973, to become a religious fanatic? His parents had emigrated to Britain in 1968 with enough capital to establish a small garment business. Perfect Fashions did well enough for Omar to be sent to prep school. But his fondness for drink and thuggery worried his parents, who sent him back to the Land of the Pure. He didn't last long at Aitchison College, a top private school in Lahore: after a couple of years, he was expelled for "bullying." A contemporary described him to me as having had "strong psychopathic tendencies . . . even then," and said he was always threatening to kill other boys. He returned to London and was sent to school at Snaresbrook, where he was a contemporary of Nasser Hussain, the future England cricket captain. Omar was a keen chess player and arm wrestler, ever eager to demonstrate the latter skill in local pubs.

He did well at Snaresbrook and went to study statistics at the London School of Economics. A number of active Islamist groups were on campus, and Bosnia became their cause. The involvement of Western intellectuals in Bosnia has been well publicized, usually by themselves. Less well documented is that remnants of the Afghan mujahideen, including some of Osama's men, had been taken in U.S. transport planes to fight the holy war in the Balkans. In 1993, Sheikh went to Bosnia as part of a group of Muslim students from the LSE taking medicines and supplies to victims of the civil war. Here, he first established contact with the armed-struggle Islamist groups who converted him to their version of jihad. General Musharraf later claimed that Sheikh was a double agent who had been recruited by MI6 and sent to Bosnia. By January 2002 he was in Islamabad promising Daniel Pearl a much-sought-after interview with the clerical godfather of the shoe bomber.

Many questions about Pearl's death remain unanswered. The group that kidnapped and killed Pearl supposedly called itself the National Movement for the Restoration of Pakistani Sovereignty. One of its demands—the release of the Guantánamo prisoners—was obvious, but the second was extraordinary: the delivery of F-16s, which the United States had been paid for but had not delivered, to Pakistan. A jihadi group that supposedly regards the Musharraf regime as traitorous for selling out the Taliban endorsing a twenty-year-old demand of the military and state bureaucracy? Impossible.

Sheikh surrendered to the provincial home secretary (a former ISI officer) in Lahore on February 5, 2002. Officially he was arrested in Lahore a week later. None of these matters was raised at his trial in a closed court in Hyderabad in July 2002. He was sentenced to death, his fellow conspirators to life imprisonment. Both sides appealed, Sheikh against the death sentence, the state against the sentence of life imprisonment—rather than hanging—for the other three. Sheikh wrote a statement that was read out by his lawyer: "We'll see who will die first, me or the authorities who have arranged the death sentence for me. Musharraf should know that Almighty Allah is there and can get his revenge." The three attempts on Musharraf's life, two of which took place within a fortnight and one of which came close to success, indicated that Sheikh wasn't making an empty boast.

Heavy traffic often makes the ten-mile journey from Islamabad to Rawalpindi tortuous, unless you're the president and the highway has been cleared by a security detail. Even then, carefully orchestrated assassination attempts can play havoc with the schedule. The first happened on December 14, 2003. Moments after the general's motorcade passed over a bridge, a powerful bomb exploded and badly damaged the bridge, although no one was hurt. The armored limo, fitted with radar and an antibomb device, courtesy of the Pentagon, saved Musharraf's life. His demeanor at the time surprised observers. He was said to have been calm and cheerful, making jocular allusions to living in perilous times. Unsurprisingly, security had been high—decoys, last-minute route changes, etc.—but this didn't prevent another attempt a week later, on Christmas Day. This time two men driving cars loaded with explosives came close to success. The president's car was damaged, guards in cars escorting him were killed, but Musharraf was unhurt. Since his exact route and the time of his departure from Islamabad were heavily guarded secrets, the terrorists must have had inside information. If your security staff includes angry Islamists who see you as a traitor and want to blow you up, then, as the general states in his memoir, Allah alone can protect you. He has certainly been kind to Musharraf.

The culprits were discovered and tortured till they revealed details of the plot. Some junior military officers were also implicated. The key plotters were tried in secret and hanged. Amjad Farooqi, the supposed mastermind and a jihadi extremist, was shot dead by security forces. Two questions haunt both Washington and Musharraf's colleagues: How many of those involved remained undetected, and would the command structure of the army survive if a terrorist succeeded next time around? Musharraf didn't seem worried and adopted a jaunty, even boastful tone. Before 9/11 he was treated like a pariah abroad and beset by problems at home. How to fortify the will of a high command weakened by piety and corruption? How to deal with the corruption and embezzlement that had been a dominant feature of both the Sharif and Bhutto governments? Benazir Bhutto was already in self-exile in Dubai; the Sharif brothers had been arrested and Nawaz was charged with high treason. Washington rapidly organized an offer of asylum from Saudi Arabia, a state whose ruling family has institutionalized the theft of public funds. These questions soon disappeared from the agenda as the Chief Executive of Pakistan, a title more in keeping with the spirit of the age and preferable to the old-fashioned Chief Martial Law Administrator, began to settle down, adjust to the realities of elite existence, and prepare to make himself president.

As for Omar Saeed Sheikh, who could certainly reveal a great deal, he continues to live in a death cell in a Pakistani prison, chatting amiably to his guards and e-mailing newspaper editors in Pakistan to tell them that if he is executed, papers he has left behind will be published exposing the complicity of others. Perhaps this is a bluff, or perhaps he was a triple agent and was working for the ISI as well.

What the Pearl killing revealed was that Musharraf had not yet succeeded in establishing total control over the intelligence agencies. He would only do so after the attempts on his own life. General Ashfaq Kayani, another senior officer trained in the United States, was appointed director general of the ISI. He supervised the gathering of information that led to the capture of those in the army who had helped Musharraf's would-be assassins. Kayani was promoted to chief of army staff, replacing Musharraf in November 2007. In a dispatch from Carlotta Gall on January 7, 2008, the *New York Times* reflected the tremor of excitement felt in Washington:

> "He's loyal to Musharraf to the point where Musharraf is a liability and no longer an asset to the corporate body of the Pakistani military," said Bruce Riedel, a former C.I.A. and White House official who is an expert on Pakistan. "They will say: 'Thank you very much for your interest in security affairs. Here is your ticket out of the country.'"
>
> As he has risen through the military, General Kayani has impressed American military and intelligence officials as a professional, pro-Western moderate with few political ambitions.

Musharraf had been described in similar language ten years previously, but now his allies were not pleased. The foreign policy half of the apple was beginning to shrivel, but what of the other half? The Chaudhrys were permanently reaping the harvest of power. Musharraf's favorite prime minister, Shaukat "Shortcut" Aziz, formerly a senior executive of Citibank with close ties to the eighth-richest man in the world, the Saudi prince Al-Walid bin Talal, was spouting a great deal of nonsense. The model preferred by some Western commentators on permanent military rule with technocrats running the Finance Ministry has proved a total failure. Watching Aziz flattering the Chaudhrys with wild assertions of their genius in what passes for a parliament in Islamabad reminded one of a paid piper rather than an "impartial technocrat." One wondered what had recommended him in the first place. Whose choice was he? As it became clear that nothing much was going to change, a wave of cynicism engulfed the country.

The score-settling with perceived enemies at home was crude, and for that reason Musharraf's book, *In the Line of Fire,* caused a commotion in Pakistan, demonstrating that the title, at least, was accurate. A spirited controversy erupted in the media, something that could never have happened during previous periods of military rule. Scathing criticism came from ex-generals (Ali Kuli Khan's detailed rejoinder was published in most newspapers), opposition politicians, and pundits of every sort. In fact there was more state interference in the media during Nawaz Sharif's tenure than under Musharraf prior to the desperate state of emergency imposed in the fall of 2007. The level of debate in the Pakistani media is much higher than that in neighboring India, once greatly admired for its vigorous and critical press, but now taken over by a middle-class obsession with shopping and celebrity that has led to widespread trivialization of TV and most of the print media.

Musharraf was better than Zia and Ayub in many ways, but the more unpopular he became, the more he began to resort to the time-honored style of dictators. Human rights groups noticed a sharp rise in the number of political activists who were being "disappeared": four hundred in 2007 alone, including Sindhi nationalists and a total of twelve hundred in the province of Baluchistan, where the army has become trigger-happy once again. The war on terror has provided many leaders with the chance to sort out their domestic opponents, but that doesn't make it any better.

And then there is Operation Enduring Freedom in Afghanistan, where the only thing that endures is violence and the heroin trade. Despite the fake optimism sometimes evinced in the Western media, it is hardly a secret that it is a total mess. A revived Taliban is winning pop-ularity by resisting the occupation. NATO helicopters and soldiers are killing hundreds of civilians and describing them as "Taliban fighters." Hamid Karzai, the man with the nice shawls, is seen as a hopeless pup-pet, totally dependent on NATO troops. He has antagonized both the Pashtuns, who are turning to the Taliban once again in large numbers, and the warlords of the Northern Alliance, who openly denounce him and suggest it's time he was sent back to the States. In western Afghan-istan, only Iranian influence has preserved a degree of stability. If Ahmadinejad is provoked into withdrawing his support, Karzai will not last more than a week. Islamabad waits and watches. Military strategists are convinced that the United States has lost interest and NATO will soon leave. If that happens, Pakistan is unlikely to permit the Northern Alliance to take Kabul. Its army will move in again. A Pakistan veteran of the Afghan wars joked with me, "Last time we sent in the beards, but times have changed. This time, inshallah, we'll dress them all in Armani suits so it looks good on U.S. television."

The region remains fogbound. Pakistan's first military leader was seen off by a popular insurrection. The second was assassinated. What will happen to Musharraf? Once he took off his uniform and handed over the army to General Ashfaq Kayani, he left himself totally depen-dent on the goodwill of his successor and Washington. General Kayani's decision some weeks before the elections to withdraw all mil-itary personnel from civilian duties (army officers were running public utilities and numerous other nonmilitary institutions) may or may not have been a broad hint to his predecessor to follow suit, but its result was to stop the "election cell" of the ISI from "intervening" in the elec-tions. The "mother of all election victories" that Musharraf had pre-dicted could only have been achieved with the connivance of military intelligence. In previous years it was never a surprise when captains and majors accosted local or national politicians and civil servants to inform them what was required. Their absence meant that the Chaudhrys of Gujrat received a heavy blow, and senior ministers in Musharraf's cab-inet were defeated in the Punjab. I received a euphoric e-mail from an old friend: "The people know that the mouths of military dictators are the home of lies."

The February 2008 elections were viewed as a referendum on Musharraf's rule. Despite the low turnout, he lost badly. The PPP emerged as the largest party with eighty-seven seats, with the Sharif brothers' Muslim League winning sixty-six. The two old rivals between them had an overall majority. The Chaudhrys of Gujrat slumped to thirty-eight seats in the National Assembly, with serious allegations that at least ten of these were won through large-scale manipulation. The Islamists lost control of the Frontier Province to the secular PPP and ANP. Musharraf should have offered to resign as soon as the new parliament was in session, giving the newly elected national and provincial assemblies the opportunity to elect a new president.

His supporters insist that the Bush administration wanted him to continue in office, and U.S. ambassador Anne Patterson summoned the widower Bhutto to the embassy in Islamabad to remind him of the deal that had been agreed to by his late wife, that she was to become Musharraf's junior partner and not bargain with the Sharif brothers, whose Islamist sympathies made them suspect. The scale of the general's defeat, however, made such a prospect suicidal. Except for the most slavish pro-Bush Pakams (Pakistani-Americans), whose dross regularly pollutes the blogosphere, the serious advice Zardari received was that the days of the Republicans were numbered. Far better, in these conditions, to help Musharraf become a private citizen voluntarily before the Democrats got rid of him.

7

The House of Bhutto

Daughter of the West

ARRANGED MARRIAGES CAN BE A MESSY BUSINESS. DESIGNED principally as a means of accumulating wealth, circumventing undesirable flirtations, or transcending clandestine love affairs, they often don't work. Where both parties are known to loathe each other, only a rash parent, desensitized by the thought of short-term gain, will continue with the marriage knowing full well that it will end in misery and possibly violence. Occasionally the husband's side will agree to a wedding, pocket the dowry, and burn the bride. That this is equally true in political life became clear in the ill-fated attempt by Washington to tie Benazir Bhutto to Pervez Musharraf.

The single, strong parent in this case was a desperate State Department—with John Negroponte as the ghoulish go-between and British prime minister Gordon Brown as the blushing bridesmaid—fearful that if it did not push this through, both parties might soon be too old for recycling. The bride was certainly in a hurry, the groom less so. Brokers from both sides engaged in lengthy negotiations on the size of the dowry. Her broker was Rehman Malik, a former boss of Pakistan's FBI-equivalent FIA (Federal Investigation Agency), who was himself investigated for corruption by the National Accountability Bureau and served nearly a year in prison after Benazir's fall in 1996, then became one of her business partners and is currently under investigation (with her) by a Spanish court looking into a company called Petroline FZC, which made questionable payments to Iraq under Saddam Hussein. Documents, if genuine, show that she chaired the company. She may have been in a hurry, but she did not wish to be seen taking the arm of a uniformed president. He was not prepared to forgive her past. The couple's distaste for each other yielded to a mutual dependence on the United States. Neither party could say no, though Musharraf hoped the union could be effected inconspicuously. Fat chance.

Both parties made concessions. A popular opposition demand had been that Musharraf relinquish his military post before he stood for the presidency. Bhutto now agreed that he could take off his uniform after his "reelection" by the existing parliament, but it had to be before the next general election. (He did so, leaving himself dependent on the goodwill of his successor as army chief of staff.) He pushed through a legal ruling—yet another sordid first in the country's history—known as the National Reconciliation Ordinance, which withdrew all cases pending against politicians (these included Nawaz Sharif) accused of looting the national treasury. The ruling was crucial for Bhutto since she hoped that the money-laundering and corruption cases pending against her, her husband, and her fixer Iftikhar Malik in three European courts—Barcelona, Geneva, and London—would now be dismissed. The Spanish obliged, but the Swiss remain adamant and London bowed to the wishes of the Pakistani government.

Many Pakistanis—not just the mutinous and mischievous types who have to be locked up at regular intervals—were repelled, and coverage of "the deal" in the Pakistani media was universally hostile, except on state television. The "breakthrough" was loudly trumpeted in the West, however, and a whitewashed Benazir Bhutto was presented on U.S. networks and BBC TV news as the champion of Pakistani democracy—reporters loyally referred to her as "the former prime minister" rather than the fugitive politician facing corruption charges in several countries.

She had returned the favor in advance by expressing sympathy for the U.S. wars in Iraq and Afghanistan, lunching with the Israeli ambassador to the UN (a litmus test), and pledging to "wipe out terrorism" in her own country. In 1979, a previous military dictator had bumped off her father with Washington's approval, and perhaps she thought it would be safer to seek permanent shelter underneath the imperial umbrella. HarperCollins had paid her half a million dollars to write a new book. The working title she chose was *Reconciliation*. It was published posthumously and contained little that had not already been said by commentators on Islam, the types who appear on the approved list of Daniel Pipes and the Campus Watch folk. The real struggle was not between the world of Islam and the United States, but within Islam itself. Moderate Islam, as represented no doubt by herself, Hamid Karzai, Hosni Mubarak, and other modernists, did not pose a threat to any Western values. Nor does the Koran. Nor do most Muslims. Evil extremism had to be destroyed.* Like Musharraf's predecessors, he promised he would stay in power for a limited period, pledging in 2003 to resign as army chief of staff in 2004. Like his predecessors, he ignored his pledge. Martial law always begins with the promise of a new order that will sweep away the filth and corruption that marked the old one. In this case it toppled the civilian administrations of Benazir Bhutto and Nawaz Sharif. But "new orders" are not forward movements, more military detours that further weaken the shaky foundations of a country and its institutions. Within a decade the uniformed ruler will be overtaken by a new upheaval.

Dreaming of her glory days in the last century, Benazir wanted a large reception on her return. The general was unhappy. The intelligence agencies (as well as her own security advisers) warned her of the dangers. She had declared war on the terrorists, and they had threatened to kill her. But she was adamant. She wanted to demonstrate her popularity to the world and to her political rivals, including those inside her own fiefdom, the Pakistan Peoples Party (PPP). She had been living in self-exile in Dubai since 1996, occasionally

---

*To her credit, Bhutto generously acknowledged the help she had received from Husain Haqqani, a former Jamaat-e-Islami militant and Zia sympathizer who later became attached to the PPP and was Pakistan's ambassador to Sri Lanka, a post from which he was removed following a security breach. He subsequently obtained an academic post in the United States, acting simultaneously as an adviser to first Benazir and more recently Zardari. Haqqani's interests and those of the United States have always coincided, which is why, one assumes, he has been appointed the new Pakistani ambassador to the United States.

visiting London to shop and Washington to meet her contacts in the State Department. For a whole month before she boarded the Dubai-Karachi flight, the PPP busily recruited and paid volunteers from all over the country to welcome her. Up to two hundred thousand people lined the streets, but it was a far cry from the million who turned up in Lahore in 1986 when a very different Benazir had returned to challenge General Zia-ul-Haq. The plan had been to move slowly in the Bhuttomobile from Karachi airport to the tomb of the country's founder, Muhammed Ali Jinnah, where she would make a speech. It was not to be. As darkness fell, the bombers struck. Who they were and who sent them remains a mystery. She was unhurt, but 130 people died, including some of the policemen guarding her. The wedding reception had led to mayhem. Fingers were immediately pointed at jihadi groups in Pakistan, but the leader of the most prominent of these, Baitullah Masood, denied involvement. She herself singled out rogue elements from "within the government" and ex-military officers linked to the Taliban.

The general, while promising to collaborate with Benazir, was coolly making arrangements to prolong his stay at President's House. Even before her arrival, he had considered taking drastic action by imposing a state of emergency to dodge the obstacles that stood in his way, but his generals (and the U.S. embassy) seemed unconvinced by the timing. The bombing of Benazir's cavalcade reopened the debate. Pakistan, if not exactly the erupting volcano portrayed in the Western media, was being shaken by all sorts of explosions. The legal profession, up in arms at Musharraf's recent dismissal of the chief justice, had won a temporary victory, resulting in a fiercely independent Supreme Court. The independent TV networks continued to broadcast reports that challenged official propaganda. Investigative journalism is never popular with governments, and the general often contrasted the deference with which he was treated by the U.S. networks and BBC television with the "unruly" questioning inflicted on him by local journalists: it "misled the people." He had loved the coverage his book received in the United States and, in particular, his appearance with Jon Stewart on *The Daily Show*.

At home it was very different. He had become obsessed with the media coverage of the lawyers' revolt. A decline in his popularity had increased the paranoia. His advisers were people he had promoted. Generals who had expressed divergent opinions in what he referred to as "frank and informal get-togethers" had been retired. His political allies were worried that their opportunities to enrich themselves even further would be curtailed if they had to share power with Benazir.

What if the Supreme Court now declared his reelection by a dying and unrepresentative assembly illegal? To ward off disaster, the ISI had been preparing blackmail flicks: agents secretly filmed some of the Supreme Court judges in flagrante. But so unpopular had Musharraf become that even the sight of judicial venerables in bed might not have done the trick. It might even have increased their support.* Musharraf decided that blackmail wasn't worth the risk. Only firm action could "restore order"—i.e., save his skin. The usual treatment in these cases is a declaration of martial law. But what if the country is already being governed by the army chief of staff? The solution is simple. Treble the dose. Organize a coup within a coup. That is what Musharraf decided to do. Washington was informed a few weeks in advance, Downing Street somewhat later. Benazir's patrons in the West told her what was about to happen, and she, foolishly for a political leader who has just returned to her country, evacuated to Dubai.

On November 3, 2007, Musharraf, as chief of the army, suspended the 1973 constitution and imposed a state of emergency: all non-government TV channels were taken off the air, the mobile phone networks were jammed, paramilitary units surrounded the Supreme Court. The chief justice convened an emergency bench of judges, who—heroically—declared the new dispensation "illegal and unconstitutional." They were unceremoniously removed and put under house arrest. Pakistan's judges have usually been acquiescent. Those who in the past resisted military leaders were soon bullied out of it, so

---

*In 1968, when a right-wing, pro-military rag in Lahore published an attack on me, it revealed that I "had attended sex orgies in a French country house organised by [my] friend, the Jew Cohn-Bendit. All the fifty women in the swimming-pool were Jewish." Alas, this was totally false, but my parents were amazed at the number of people who congratulated them on my virility.

the decision of this chief justice took the country by surprise and won him great admiration. Global media coverage of Pakistan suggests a country of generals, corrupt politicians, and bearded lunatics; the struggle to reinstate the chief justice had presented a different picture.

Aitzaz Ahsan, a prominent member of the PPP, minister of the interior in Benazir's first government, and currently president of the Bar Association, was arrested and placed in solitary confinement. Several thousand political and civil rights activists were picked up. The former cricket hero, Imran Khan, a fierce and incorruptible opponent of the regime, was arrested, charged with "state terrorism"—for which the penalty is death or life imprisonment—and taken in handcuffs to a remote high-security prison. Musharraf, Khan argued, had begun yet another shabby chapter in Pakistan's history.

Lawyers were arrested all over the country; many were physically attacked by policemen. The order was to humiliate them, and the police obliged. A lawyer, "Omar," circulated an account of what happened:

> While I was standing talking to my colleagues, we saw the police go wild on the orders of a superior officer. In riot gear . . . brandishing weapons and sticks, about a hundred policemen attacked us . . . and seemed intensely happy at doing so. We all ran. Some of us who were not as nimble on their feet as others were caught by the police and beaten mercilessly. We were then locked in police vans used to transport convicted prisoners. Everyone was stunned at this show of brute force but it did not end. The police went on mayhem inside the court premises and court buildings. . . . Those of us who were arrested were taken to various police stations and put in lockups. At midnight, we were told that we were being shifted to jail. We could not get bail as our fundamental rights were suspended. Sixty lawyers were put into a police van ten feet by four feet wide and five feet in height. We were squashed like sardines. When the van reached the jail, we were told that we could not get [out] until orders of our detention were received by the jail authorities. Our older colleagues started to suffocate, some fainted, others started to panic because of claustrophobia. The police ignored our screams and refused to open the van doors. Finally, after three hours . . . we were let out and

taken to mosquito-infected barracks where the food given to us smelled like sewage water.

Geo, the largest Pakistani TV network, had long since located its broadcasting facilities in Dubai. It was a strange sensation watching the network in London when the screens were blank in Pakistan. On the first day of the emergency I saw Hamid Mir, a journalist loathed by the general, reporting from Islamabad and asserting that the U.S. embassy had given the green light to the coup because it regarded the chief justice as a nuisance and wrongly believed him to be "a Taliban sympathizer." Certainly no U.S. spokesperson or State Department adjunct in the Foreign Office criticized the dismissal of the eight Supreme Court judges or their arrest: that was the quid pro quo for Washington's insistence that Musharraf take off his uniform. If he was going to turn civilian, he wanted all the other rules twisted in his favor. A newly appointed stooge Supreme Court would soon help him with the rule-bending. As would the authorities in Dubai, who helpfully suspended Geo's facilities. Benazir Bhutto too, in the first few days after the state of emergency was declared, maintained an opportunist silence on the judiciary.

In the evening of that first day, and after several delays, a flustered General Musharraf, his hair badly dyed, appeared on TV, trying to look like the sort of leader who wants it understood that the political crisis is to be discussed with gravity and sangfroid. Instead, he came across as an inarticulate dictator fearful for his own political future. His performance as he broadcast to the nation, first in Urdu and then in English, was incoherent. The gist was simple: he had to act because the Supreme Court had "so demoralized our state agencies that we can't fight the war on terror" and the TV networks had become "totally irresponsible." "I have imposed emergency," he said halfway through his diatribe, adding, with a contemptuous gesture, "You must have seen it on TV." Was he being sarcastic, given that most channels had been shut down? Who knows? Mohammed Hanif, the sharp-witted head of the BBC's Urdu Service, which monitored the broadcast, confessed himself flummoxed when he wrote up what he heard. He had no doubt that the Urdu version of the speech was the general's own work. Hanif's deconstruction—

he quoted the general in Urdu and in English—deserved a broadcast all of its own:

> Here are some random things he said. And trust me, these things were said quite randomly. Yes, he did say, "Extremism *bahut* extreme *ho gaya hai* [extremism has become too extreme]. . . . Nobody is scared of us anymore. . . . Islamabad is full of extremists. . . . There is a government within government. . . . Officials are being asked to the courts. . . . Officials are being insulted by the judiciary."
>
> At one point he appeared wistful when reminiscing about his first three years in power: "I had total control." You were almost tempted to ask: "What happened then, uncle?" But obviously, uncle didn't need any prompting. He launched into his routine about three stages of democracy. He claimed he was about to launch the third and final phase of democracy (the way he said it, he managed to make it sound like the Final Solution). And just when you thought he was about to make his point, he took an abrupt turn and plunged into a deep pool of self-pity. This involved a long-winded anecdote about how the Supreme Court judges would rather attend a colleague's daughter's wedding than just get it over with and decide that he is a constitutional president. . . . I have heard some dictators' speeches in my life, but nobody has gone so far as to mention someone's daughter's wedding as a reason for imposing martial law on the country.
>
> When for the last few minutes of his speech he addressed his audience in the West in English, I suddenly felt a deep sense of humiliation. This part of his speech was scripted. Sentences began and ended. I felt humiliated that my president not only thinks that we are not evolved enough for things like democracy and human rights, but that we can't even handle proper syntax and grammar.

The English-language version put the emphasis on the "war on terror": Napoléon and Abraham Lincoln, he said, would have done what he did to preserve the "integrity of their country"—the mention of Lincoln was obviously intended for the U.S. market. In Pakistan's military academies the usual soldier heroes are Napoléon, de Gaulle, and Atatürk.

What did Benazir, now outmaneuvered, make of the speech as she watched it on TV in her Dubai sanctuary? She first said she was shocked, which was slightly disingenuous. Even if she had not explicitly been told in advance that an emergency would be declared, it was hardly a surprise. U.S. secretary of state Condoleezza Rice had already made a token public appeal to Musharraf not to take this course, indicating clearly what lay ahead. Yet for more than twenty-four hours Benazir Bhutto was unable to give a clear response. At one point she even criticized the chief justice for being too provocative.

Agitated phone calls from Pakistan persuaded her to return immediately to Karachi. To put her in her place, the authorities kept her plane waiting on the tarmac. When she finally reached the VIP lounge, her PPP colleagues told her that unless she denounced the emergency, the party would split. Outsmarted and abandoned by Musharraf, she couldn't take the risk of losing key figures in her own organization. And so she criticized the emergency and its perpetrator, established contact with the beleaguered opposition, and, as if putting on a new lipstick, declared that she would now lead the struggle to get rid of the dictator. She also tried to call on the chief justice to express her sympathy, but wasn't allowed near his residence.

She could have followed the example of her imprisoned colleague Aitzaz Ahsan, a senior minister in both her governments, but she was envious of him: he had become far too popular in Pakistan. He'd even had the nerve to go to Washington without her patronage, where he was politely received by society and inspected as a possible substitute should things go badly wrong. Not a single message had flowed from her BlackBerry to congratulate him on his victories in the struggle to reinstate the chief justice. Ahsan had advised her against any deal with Musharraf. When generals are against the wall, he is reported to have told her, they resort to desperate and irrational measures. Others who offered similar advice in gentler language were also batted away. She was the PPP's "chairperson for life" and brooded no dissent. That Ahsan had been proved right irritated her even more. Any notion of political morality had long ago been dumped. The very idea of a party with a consistent set of beliefs was regarded as ridiculous and outdated. Ahsan was now safe in prison, far from the madding hordes of Western journalists whom she received in style during the few days she spent under house arrest and afterward. She made a few polite noises about his imprisonment, but nothing more.

Sensing trouble, Washington dispatched a go-between at short notice to sort out the mess. Negroponte spent time with Musharraf and spoke to Benazir, still insisting that they make up and go through with the deal. She immediately toned down her criticisms, but the general was scathing and said in public that she would never win the elections scheduled for January 2008. Perhaps he thought the ISI would rig them in style as they had done so often in the past. Opinion polls revealed that her old rival Nawaz Sharif was well ahead of her. Musharraf's hasty pilgrimage to Mecca was no doubt an attempt to secure Saudi mediation in case he had to cut a deal with the Sharif brothers— who had been living in exile in Saudi Arabia—and sideline her completely. The Saudi king insisted that Nawaz Sharif should now be permitted to return to his country. Both sides denied that a deal was done, but Sharif returned to Pakistan soon afterward with Saudi blessings and an armor-plated Cadillac as a special gift from the king. There seemed little doubt that Riyadh would rather have him than Benazir.

With Pakistan still under a state of emergency and the largest media network refusing to sign the oath of allegiance that would allow them back on air, the vote scheduled for January could only have been a general's election. It was hardly a secret that the ISI and the civilian bureaucracy would decide who won and where, and because of this some of the opposition parties were considering not contesting the election. Nawaz Sharif told the press that he had in a long telephone call failed to persuade Benazir to join a boycott and thereby render the process null and void from the start. But once he was back in the country, he became less certain. His supporters insisted that their popularity in the Punjab had risen because of their refusal to deal with Musharraf, and a boycott would be counterproductive. Sharif accepted this view.

What would Benazir do now? Washington's leverage in Islamabad was limited, which is why they wanted her to be involved in the first place. "It's always better," the U.S. ambassador half joked at a reception, "to have two phone numbers in a capital." That may be so, but they could not guarantee her the prime ministership or even a fair election.

In his death cell, three decades previously, her father had mulled over similar problems and come to slightly different conclusions. *If I Am Assassinated*, Zulfiqar Ali Bhutto's last will and testament, contained some tart assessments whose meaning wasn't lost on his colleagues:

> I entirely agree that the people of Pakistan will not tolerate foreign hegemony. On the basis of the self-same logic, the people of Pakistan would never agree to an internal hegemony. The two hegemonies complement each other. If our people meekly submit to internal hegemony, a priori, they will have to submit to external hegemony. This is so because the strength and power of external hegemony is far greater than that of internal hegemony. If the people are too terrified to resist the weaker force, it is not possible for them to resist the stronger force. The acceptance of or acquiescence in internal hegemony means submission to external hegemony.

After Bhutto was hanged in April 1979, the text became semisacred among his supporters. But, when in power, Bhutto père had failed to develop any counterhegemonic strategy or institutions, other than the 1973 constitution, drafted by the veteran civil rights lawyer Mahmud Ali Kasuri (whose son Khurshid was until recently Musharraf's foreign minister). A personality-driven, autocratic style of governance had neutered the spirit of Bhutto's party, encouraged careerists, and finally paved the way for his enemies. He was the victim of a grave injustice; his death removed all the warts and transformed him into a martyr. More than half the country, mainly the poor, mourned his passing.

The tragedy led to the PPP's being treated as a family heirloom, which was unhealthy for both party and country. It provided the Bhuttos with a vote bank and large reserves. But the experience of her father's trial and death had radicalized and politicized his daughter. She would have preferred, she told me at the time, to be a diplomat. Her two brothers, Murtaza and Shahnawaz, were in London, having been forbidden to return home by their imprisoned father. The burden of trying to save her father's life fell on Benazir and her mother, Nusrat, and the courage they exhibited won them the silent respect of a frightened majority. They refused to cave in to General Zia's military dictatorship, which apart from anything else was invoking Islam to claw back rights won by women in previous decades. Benazir and Nusrat Bhutto were arrested and released several times. Their health began to suffer. Nusrat was allowed to leave the country to seek medical advice in 1982. Benazir was released a little more than a year later, thanks, in part, to U.S. pressure orchestrated by her old Harvard friend Peter Galbraith, who had useful contacts in the State Department. She later described the period in her memoir, *Daughter of the East* (1988); it included photo captions such as "Shortly after President Reagan praised the regime for making 'great strides towards democracy,' Zia's henchmen gunned down peaceful demonstrators marking Pakistan Independence Day. The police were just as brutal to those protesting at the attack on my jeep in January 1987."

Benazir moved to London, where her tiny Barbican flat in the heart of the old city became a center of opposition to the dictatorship, and here we often discussed a campaign to take on the generals. Benazir had built up her position by steadfastly and peacefully resisting the military and replying to every slander with a cutting retort. Her brothers had been operating on a different level. They set up an armed group, al-Zulfiqar, whose declared aim was to harass and weaken the regime by targeting "traitors who had collaborated with Zia." The principal volunteers were recruited inside Pakistan, and in 1980 they were provided with a base in Afghanistan, where the pro-Moscow Communists had taken power three years before. It is a sad story with a fair share of factionalism, show trials, petty rivalries, fantasies of every sort, and death for the group's less-fortunate members.

In March 1981, Murtaza and Shahnawaz Bhutto were placed on the FIA's most wanted list. They had hijacked a Pakistan International airliner soon after it left Karachi (a power cut had paralyzed the X-ray machines, enabling the hijackers to take their weapons on board); it was diverted to Kabul. Here Murtaza took over and demanded the release of political prisoners. A young military officer on board the flight was murdered. The plane refueled and went on to Damascus, where the legendary Syrian spymaster General Kholi took charge and ensured there were no more deaths. That American passengers were on the plane was a major consideration for the generals, and for that reason alone the prisoners in Pakistan were released and flown to Tripoli.

This was seen as a victory and welcomed as such by the PPP in Pakistan. For the first time the group began to be taken seriously. A key target inside the country was Maulvi Mushtaq Hussain, the chief justice of the High Court in Lahore, who had in 1978 sentenced Zulfiqar Ali Bhutto to death, and whose behavior in court (among other charges, he had accused Bhutto of "pretending to be a Muslim"—his mother was a Hindu convert) had enraged the entire Bhutto family. Mushtaq was in a friend's car being driven to his home in Lahore's Model Town area when al-Zulfiqar gunmen opened fire. The judge survived, but his friend and the driver died.

The friend was the founding father of the Chaudhrys of Gujrat: Chaudhry Zahoor Elahi, whom we have met earlier in this narrative. It is the next generation of Chaudhrys that currently provides Musharraf with civilian ballast: Zahoor Elahi's son Shujaat organized the split with Nawaz Sharif and created the splinter PML-Q to ease the growing pains of the new regime. He still fixes political deals and wanted an emergency imposed much earlier to circumvent the deal with Benazir. He was to be the mastermind of the general's election campaign. His cousin Pervez Elahi was chief minister of the Punjab; the latter's son, in turn, is busy continuing the family tradition by evicting tenants and buying up all the available land on the edge of Lahore.

The hijacking meanwhile had annoyed Moscow, and the regime in Afghanistan asked the Bhutto brothers to find another refuge. While in Kabul, they had married two Afghan sisters, Fauzia and Rehana Fasihudin, daughters of a senior official at the Afghan Ministry of Foreign Affairs. Together with their wives they now left the country and after a sojourn in Syria and possibly Libya ended up in Europe. The reunion with their sister took place on the French Riviera in 1985, a setting well suited to the lifestyles of all three siblings.

The young men feared General Zia's agents. Each had a young daughter. Shahnawaz lived in an apartment in Cannes. He had been in charge of the "military apparatus" of al-Zulfiqar, responsible for the purchase of weapons, and life in Kabul had exacted a heavier toll on him. He was edgy and nervous. Relations with his wife were stormy, and he told his sister that he was preparing for a divorce. "There's never been a divorce in the family. Your marriage wasn't even an arranged one. . . . You chose to marry Rehana. You must live with it" was Benazir's revealing reply, according to her memoir. This was to be her own attitude when her husband's philandering was brought to her notice. Then on July 18, 1985, Shahnawaz was found dead in his apartment. His wife claimed he had taken poison, but according to Benazir, nobody in the family believed her story; there had been violence in the room and his papers had been searched. Rehana looked immaculate, which disturbed the family. She was imprisoned for three months under the Good Samaritan law for not having gone to the assistance of a dying person. After her release she settled in the United States. "Had the CIA killed him as a friendly gesture towards their favourite dictator?" Benazir speculated. She raised another question too: had the sisters become ISI agents? The truth remains hidden. Not long afterward Murtaza divorced Fauzia, but kept custody of their three-year-old daughter, Fatima, and moved to Damascus. Here he had plenty of time for reflection and told friends that too many mistakes had been made in the struggle against the dictatorship. In 1986 he met Ghinwa Itaoui, a young teacher who had fled Lebanon after the Israeli invasion of 1982. She calmed him down and took charge of Fatima's education. They were married in 1989, and a son, Zulfiqar, was born the following year.

Benazir returned to Pakistan in 1986 and was greeted by large crowds, nearly a million people in Lahore, who came out to show their affection for her and to demonstrate their anger with the regime. She campaigned all over the country, but felt increasingly that for some of the more religious-minded a young, unmarried woman was not acceptable as a leader. How, for instance, could she visit Saudi Arabia without a husband? An offer of marriage from the Zardari family was accepted, and she married Asif in 1987. The Zardaris were small landowners. The father, Hakim Zardari, had been a supporter of the National Awami Party and owned some cinemas in Karachi. They were not wealthy but had enough to indulge Asif Zardari's passion for polo. He loved horses and women and was not interested in politics. Benazir told me that she was slightly nervous that it was an arranged marriage, but was hoping for the best. She had been worried that any husband would find it difficult to deal with the periods of separation her nomadic political life would entail, but this never bothered Zardari, who was perfectly capable of occupying himself.

A year later General Zia's plane blew up in midair. In the elections that followed the PPP won the largest number of seats. Benazir became prime minister, but was hemmed in by the army on one side and the president, the army's favorite bureaucrat, Ghulam Ishaq Khan, on the other. She told me at the time that she felt powerless. Being in power, it seemed, was satisfaction enough. She went on state visits: met and liked Mrs. Thatcher and later, with her new husband in tow, was received politely by the Saudi king. In the meantime, plots were afoot—the opposition was literally buying off some of her MPs—and in August 1990 her government was removed by presidential decree and Zia's protégés the Sharif brothers were back in power.

By the time she was reelected in 1993, she had abandoned all idea of reform, but that she was in a hurry to do something became clear when she appointed her husband minister for investment, making him responsible for all investment offers from home and abroad. The Pakistani press widely alleged that the couple accumulated $1.5 billion. The high command of the Pakistan Peoples Party now became a machine for making money, but without any trickle-down mechanism. This period marked the complete degeneration of the party. The single tradition that had been passed down since the foundation of the party was autocratic centralism. The leader's word was final. Like her father in this respect, Benazir never understood that debate is not only the best medium of confutation, of turning the ideological tables. It is also the most effective form of persuasion. The debate urgently needed to be shifted out of the paddock of religion and into a more neutral space. This never happened.

All that shamefaced party members could say on corruption, when I asked them during several visits to Pakistan, was "Everybody does it all over the world," thus accepting that the cash nexus was now all that mattered. Money was now the sacred center of all politics. In foreign policy Benazir's legacy was mixed. She refused to sanction an anti-Indian military adventure in Kargil on the Himalayan slopes, but to make up for it, as I wrote at the time,* her government pushed through the Taliban takeover in Kabul—which makes it doubly ironic that Washington and London were promoting her as a champion of democracy before her tragic demise.

Murtaza Bhutto had contested the elections from abroad and won a seat in the Sind provincial legislature. He returned home and expressed his unhappiness with his sister's agenda. Family gatherings became tense. Murtaza had his weaknesses, but he wasn't corrupt, and he argued in favor of the old party's radical manifesto. He made it clear that he regarded Zardari as an interloper whose only interest was money. Nusrat Bhutto suggested that Murtaza be made the chief minister of Sind; Benazir's response was to remove her mother as chairperson of the PPP. Any sympathy Murtaza may have felt for his sister turned to loathing. He no longer felt obliged to control his tongue and at every possible opportunity lambasted Zardari and the corrupt regime over which his sister presided. It was difficult to fault him on the facts. The incumbent chief minister of Sind was Abdullah Shah, one of Zardari's creatures. He began to harass Murtaza's supporters. Murtaza decided to confront the organ-grinder himself. According to some, he rang Zardari and invited him round for an informal chat to try to settle the problems within the family. Zardari agreed. As the two men were pacing the garden, Murtaza's retainers appeared and grabbed Zardari. Someone brought out a cutthroat razor and some warm water and Murtaza shaved off half of Zardari's mustache to the delight of the retainers, then told him to get lost. A fuming Zardari, who had probably feared much worse, was compelled to shave off the other half at home. The media, bemused, were informed that the new clean-shaven consort had accepted intelligence advice that the mustache made him too recognizable a target. Benazir's private version for friends was somewhat different. She said the kids disliked it because it prickled when he kissed them and so he dispensed with it for their sake. Both explanations were negated by Zardari's allowing it to grow again immediately afterward.

Some months later, in September 1996, as Murtaza and his

---

*London Review of Books, April 15, 1999.

entourage were returning home from a political meeting, they were ambushed, just outside their house, by some seventy armed policemen accompanied by four senior officers. A number of snipers were positioned in surrounding trees. The streetlights had been switched off. Murtaza clearly understood what was happening and got out of his car with his hands raised; his bodyguards were instructed not to use their weapons. Instead, the police opened fire. Seven men were killed, Murtaza among them. The fatal bullet had been fired at close range. The trap had carefully been laid, but as is the way in Pakistan, the crudeness of the operation—false entries in police logbooks, lost evidence, witnesses arrested and intimidated, the provincial PPP governor (regarded as untrustworthy) dispatched to a nonevent in Egypt, a policeman killed who was feared might talk—made it obvious that the decision to execute the prime minister's brother had been made at a high level. Shoaib Suddle, deputy inspector general of Sind when Murtaza was murdered, was charged with involvement in the killing, but the case was dismissed before it went to trial. He was subsequently promoted to inspector general by Zardari in April 2008. Two months later, he was appointed director general of the Intelligence Bureau in Islamabad.

While the ambush was being prepared, the police had sealed off Murtaza's house (from which his father had been lifted by Zia's commandos in 1977). The family inside felt something was wrong, and a remarkably composed Fatima Bhutto, age fourteen, rang her aunt at Prime Minister's House. The conversation that followed remains imprinted on her memory, and a few years ago she gave me an account of it. Zardari took her call.

FATIMA: I wish to speak to my aunt, please.
ZARDARI: It's not possible.
FATIMA: Why? [At this point, Fatima says she heard loud wails and
    what sounded like fake crying.]
ZARDARI: She's hysterical, can't you hear?
FATIMA: Why?
ZARDARI: Don't you know? Your father's been shot.

Fatima and Ghinwa found out where Murtaza had been taken and rushed out of the house. The street outside showed no sign that anything had happened: the scene of the killing had been wiped clean of all evidence, with no traces of blood or signs of disturbance. They drove straight to the hospital, but it was too late: Murtaza was already dead.

When Benazir arrived to attend her brother's funeral in Larkana, angry crowds stoned her limo. She had to retreat. In another unusual display of emotion, local people encouraged Murtaza's widow to attend the actual burial ceremony in defiance of Islamic tradition. According to Fatima, one of Benazir's hangers-on instigated legal proceedings against Ghinwa in a religious court for breaching Islamic law. Nothing was sacred.

Anyone who'd witnessed Murtaza's murder was arrested; one witness died in prison. When Fatima rang Benazir to ask why witnesses were being arrested and not the killers, she was told, "Look, you're very young. You don't understand things." Perhaps for this reason the kind aunt decided to encourage Fatima's blood mother, Fauzia, whom she had previously denounced as a murderer in the pay of General Zia, to come to Pakistan and claim custody of Fatima. No mystery as to who paid her fare from California. Fatima and Ghinwa Bhutto resisted and the attempt failed. Benazir then tried a softer approach and insisted that Fatima accompany her to New York, where she was going to address the UN Assembly. Ghinwa Bhutto approached friends in Damascus and had her two children flown out of the country. Fatima later discovered that Fauzia had been seen hobnobbing with Benazir in New York.

In November 1996 Benazir was once again removed from power, this time by her own president, Farooq Leghari, a PPP stalwart. He cited corruption, but what had also angered him was the ISI's crude attempt at blackmail—the intelligence agencies had photographed Leghari's daughter meeting a boyfriend and threatened to go public. The week Benazir fell, the chief minister of Sind, Abdullah Shah, who had helped organize Murtaza's murder, hopped on a motorboat and fled Karachi for the Gulf and then to the United States.

A judicial tribunal had been appointed by Benazir's government to inquire into the circumstances leading to Murtaza's death. Headed by a Supreme Court judge, it took detailed evidence from all parties. Murtaza's lawyers accused Zardari, Abdullah Shah, and two senior police officials of conspiracy to murder. Benazir (now out of power) accepted that there had been a conspiracy, but suggested that "the hidden hand responsible for this was President Farooq Ahmad Leghari." The intention, she said, was to "kill a Bhutto to get rid of a Bhutto." Nobody took this seriously. Given all that had happened, it was an incredible suggestion.

The tribunal said no legally acceptable evidence linked Zardari to the incident, but asserted, "This was a case of extra-judicial killings by the police," and concluded that such an incident could not have taken place without approval from the highest quarters. Nothing happened. Eleven years later, Fatima Bhutto publicly accused Zardari; she also claimed that many of those involved that day appear to have been rewarded for their actions. In an interview on an independent TV station just before the emergency was imposed, Benazir was asked to explain how her brother had bled to death outside his home while she was prime minister. She walked out of the studio.

A sharp op-ed piece by Fatima Bhutto appeared in the *Los Angeles Times* on November 14, 2007. She did not mince words:

Ms. Bhutto's political posturing is sheer pantomime. Her negotiations with the military and her unseemly willingness until just a few days ago to take part in Musharraf's regime have signaled once and for all to the growing legions of fundamentalists across South Asia that democracy is just a guise for dictatorship. . . .

My father was Benazir's younger brother. To this day, her role in his assassination has never been adequately answered, although the tribunal convened after his death under the leadership of three respected judges concluded that it could not have taken place without approval from a "much higher" political authority. . . .

I have personal reasons to fear the danger that Ms. Bhutto's presence in Pakistan brings, but I am not alone. The Islamists are waiting at the gate. They have been waiting for confirmation that the reforms for which the Pakistani people have been struggling have been a farce, propped up by the White House. Since Musharraf seized power in 1999, there has been an earnest grass-roots movement for democratic reform. The last thing we need is to be tied to a neocon agenda through a puppet "democrat" like Ms. Bhutto.

This elicited the following response from its target: "My niece is angry with me." Well, yes.

Musharraf may have withdrawn the corruption charges against Benazir, but three other cases were proceeding in Switzerland, Spain, and Britain. The latter two appear to have been dropped, but the Swiss court is refusing to close the case.

In July 2003, after an investigation lasting several years, Daniel Devaud, a Geneva magistrate, convicted Mr. and Mrs. Asif Ali Zardari, in absentia, of money laundering. They had accepted $15 million in bribes from two Swiss companies, SGS and Cotecna. The couple were sentenced to six months in prison and ordered to return $11.9 million to the government of Pakistan. "I certainly don't have any doubts about the judgments I handed down," Devaud told the BBC. Benazir appealed, thus forcing a new investigation. On September 19, 2005, she appeared in a Geneva court and tried to detach herself from the rest of the family. She hadn't been involved, she said: it was a matter for her husband and her mother, who was afflicted with Alzheimer's. She knew nothing of the accounts. And what of the agreement her agent Jens Schlegelmilch had signed according to which, in case of her and Zardari's death, the assets of Bomer Finance Company would be divvied out equally between the Zardari and Bhutto families? She knew nothing of that either. And the £120,000 diamond necklace in the bank vault paid for by Zardari? It was intended for her, but she had rejected the gift as "inappropriate." The case is still pending. In November 2007, Musharraf told Owen Bennett-Jones of the BBC World Service that his government would not interfere with the proceedings: "That's up to the Swiss government. Depends on them. It's a case in their courts."

In Britain the legal shenanigans concerned the $3.4 million Rockwood estate in Surrey, bought by offshore companies on behalf of Zardari in 1995 and refurbished to his exacting tastes. Zardari denied owning the estate. Then, when the court was about to instruct the liquidators to sell it and return the proceeds to the Pakistani government, Zardari came forward and accepted ownership. In 2006, Lord Justice Collins had ruled that, while he was not making any "findings of fact," there was a "reasonable prospect" that the Pakistani government might be able to establish that Rockwood had been bought and furnished with "the fruits of corruption." A close friend of Benazir Bhutto's informed me that she was genuinely not involved in this one, since Zardari wasn't thinking of spending much time there with her.

Even these fragments of the past emerged only fleetingly and rarely on television. What was interesting was the short memory of the U.S. press. In 1998, the *New York Times* had published a sharp and lengthy indictment of Bhutto-Zardari corruption. John F. Burns described how "Asif Ali Zardari turned his marriage to Ms. Bhutto into a source of virtually unchallengeable power" and went on to cite several cases of corruption. The first involved a gold bullion dealer in Dubai who had paid $10 million into one of Zardari's accounts in return for being awarded the monopoly on gold imports that were vital to Pakistan's jewelry industry. Two other cases involved France and, again, Switzerland:

In 1995, a leading French military contractor, Dassault Aviation, agreed to pay Mr. Zardari and a Pakistani partner $200 million for a $4 billion jet fighter deal that fell apart only when Ms. Bhutto's Government was dismissed. In another deal, a leading Swiss company hired to curb customs fraud in Pakistan paid millions of dollars between 1994 and 1996 to offshore companies controlled by Mr. Zardari and Ms. Bhutto's widowed mother, Nusrat. . . .

In 1994 and 1995, [Zardari] used a Swiss bank account and an American Express card to buy jewelry worth $660,000—including $246,000 at Cartier and Bulgari Corp. in Beverly Hills, Calif., in barely a month.*

Given the scale of the corruption, why was Washington so desperate? Daniel Markey, formerly of the State Department and currently senior fellow for India, Pakistan, and South Asia at the Council on Foreign Relations, explained why the United States had pushed the marriage of convenience: "A progressive, reform-minded, more cosmopolitan party in government would help the U.S." As their finances revealed, the Zardaris were certainly cosmopolitan.

---

*John F. Burns, "House of Graft: Tracing the Bhutto Millions . . . A Special Report," *New York Times*, January 9, 1998.

What then is at stake in Pakistan as far as Washington is concerned? "The concern I have," Robert Gates, the U.S. secretary for defense, told the world, "is that the longer the internal problems continue, the more distracted the Pakistani army and security services will be in terms of the internal situation rather than focusing on the terrorist threat in the frontier area." But one reason for the internal crisis has been Washington's overreliance on Musharraf and the Pakistani military. Washington's support and funding have given him the confidence to operate as he pleases. But the thoughtless Western military occupation of Afghanistan is obviously crucial, since the instability in Kabul seeps into Peshawar and the tribal areas between the two countries. The state of emergency targeted the judiciary, opposition politicians, and the independent media. All three groups were, in different ways, challenging the official line on Afghanistan and the "war on terror," the disappearance of political prisoners, and the widespread use of torture in Pakistani prisons. The issues were being debated on television in a much more open fashion than happens anywhere in the West, where a blanket consensus on Afghanistan drowns all dissent. Musharraf argued that civil society was hampering the war on terror. Hence the emergency. It's nonsense, of course. It's the war in the frontier regions that is creating dissent inside the army. Many do not want to fight. Hence the surrender of dozens of soldiers to Taliban guerrillas. This is the reason many junior officers are taking early retirement.

Western pundits blather on about the jihadi finger on the nuclear trigger. This is pure fantasy, reminiscent of a similar campaign almost three decades ago, when the threat wasn't the jihadis who were fighting alongside the West in Afghanistan, but nationalist military radicals. The cover story of *Time* magazine for June 15, 1979, dealt with Pakistan; a senior Western diplomat was quoted as saying that the big danger was "that there is another Gadhafi down there, some radical major or colonel in the Pakistani army. We could wake up and find him in Zia's place one morning and, believe me, Pakistan wouldn't be the only place that would be destabilized."

The Pakistan army is half a million strong. Its tentacles are everywhere: land, industry, public utilities, and so on. It would require a cataclysmic upheaval (a U.S. invasion and occupation, for example) for this army to feel threatened by a jihadi uprising. Two considerations unite senior officers: the unity of the organization and keeping politicians at bay. One reason is the fear that they might lose the comforts and privileges they have acquired after decades of rule; but they also have the deep aversion to democracy that is the hallmark of most armies. Unused to accountability within their own ranks, it's difficult for them to accept it in society at large.

As southern Afghanistan collapses into chaos, and as corruption and massive inflation take hold, the Taliban are gaining more and more recruits. The generals who once convinced Benazir that control of Kabul via the Taliban would give them "strategic depth" may have retired, but their successors know that the Afghans will not tolerate a long-term Western occupation. They hope for the return of a whitewashed Taliban. Instead of encouraging a regional solution that includes India, Iran, and Russia, the United States would prefer to see the Pakistan army as its permanent cop in Kabul. It won't work. In Pakistan itself the long night continues as the cycle restarts: military leadership promising reforms degenerates into tyranny, politicians promising social support to the people degenerate into oligarchs. Given that a better functioning neighbor is unlikely to intervene, Pakistan will oscillate between these two forms of rule for the foreseeable future. The people, who feel they have tried everything and failed, will return to a state of semisleep, unless something unpredictable rouses them again. This is always possible.

Before the story could move further, another tragedy struck Pakistan and the House of Bhutto. Determined to fulfill her part of the Faustian deal brokered in Washington, Benazir Bhutto, despite some hesitation, agreed to participate in an election regarded at the time as deeply flawed by virtually every independent commentator in Pakistan and by many in her own party.

She decided to begin her campaign in the country's military capital, Rawalpindi, where she arrived on December 27, 2007. She came to address a public meeting at Liaquat Bagh (formerly Municipal Park), a popular public space named after the country's first prime minister, Liaquat Ali Khan, who was killed there by an assassin in October 1951. The killer, Said Akbar, was immediately shot dead on the orders of a police officer involved in the plot. Not far from here, a colonial structure where nationalists were imprisoned once stood. This was Rawalpindi jail. Here, Benazir's father, Zulfiqar Ali Bhutto, was hanged in April 1979. The military tyrant responsible for his judicial murder made sure the site of the tragedy was destroyed as well.

The rally was not disrupted on this occasion, but the killers were waiting in the vicinity of her car. As she was about to leave, she decided on a last wave to her supporters and the television cameras. A bomb blew up and she appeared to have been felled by bullets fired at her car. The assassins, mindful of their failure in Karachi a month previously, had taken out double insurance this time. They wanted her dead at any cost. Government pathologists claimed that Bhutto caught her head on the sunroof of the car she was speaking from as she ducked inside, fracturing her skull, and that was the cause of her death. Her party disagreed. Scotland Yard was asked for help. After a brief investigation it concurred with the government report. Exhuming the body and a new postmortem would have been definitive, but Zardari refused to permit it.

Her death was greeted with anger throughout the country. The people of her home province, Sind, responded with violent demonstrations, targeting government buildings and cars of non-Sindhis. While the global media networks assumed, without any investigation, that she was killed by local jihadi terrorists or Al Qaeda, the crowds in Pakistan had different ideas and pointed accusing fingers at the president, while the streets resounded to chants of Peoples Party supporters: *"Amreeka ne kutta paala, vardi wallah, vardi wallah"* ("America trained a dog / the one in uniform, the one in uniform").

Even those sharply critical of Benazir Bhutto's behavior and policies—both while she was in office and more recently—were stunned and angered by her death. Indignation and fear stalked the country once again. This event made a crude rigging of the February 2008 elections virtually impossible. An odd coexistence of military despotism and anarchy created the conditions leading to her assassination. In the past, military rule was designed to preserve order—and did so for a few years. No longer. Today it creates disorder and promotes lawlessness. How else can one explain the sacking of the chief justice and other judges of the country's Supreme Court for attempting to hold the government's intelligence agencies and the police accountable to courts of law? Their replacements lack the backbone to do anything, let alone conduct a proper inquest into the misdeeds of the agencies to uncover the truth behind the carefully organized killing of a major political leader. Pakistan today is a conflagration of despair. It is assumed that the killers were jihadi fanatics. This may well be true, but were they acting on their own? Conspiracy theories mushroomed after her death. General Hamid Gul, a former director general of the ISI during Benazir's first prime ministership, told the media that despite promising the United States that she would hand over A. Q. Khan, the self-styled "father of the Pakistani bomb," for questioning and permit the entry of U.S. troops and planes to deal with Al Qaeda in Pakistan, she had "drifted from her agenda" after her arrival and the first attempt on her life. Hamid Gul insisted that "the Israeli lobby will never rest in peace until they have snatched our nuclear weapons. In the war against terror, Pakistan is the target." For this, according to General Gul, she was eliminated. This is a popular view among retired segments of the military and civilian bureaucracy, but is it credible?

It is certainly the case that Musharraf refused to send A. Q. Khan to Washington. Government officials told me that the United States was desperate to question Khan about his dealings with Iran, and what he said under questioning in the United States might be used as a pretext to bomb Iran's nuclear reactors. If Benazir Bhutto had agreed to this, which is possible, nothing suggests that she had undergone any political conversion after her return. She had hitched her future to the United States for a number of reasons. They would help whitewash her past and get her back into power, after which she would still need Washington's support to deal with the army. The United States as the sole imperial power was too powerful to oppose anyway, and those, like her late father, who did not do its bidding had ended up dead. For these reasons she had decided on a historic compromise and promised a rapid recognition of Israel as well, to appease Washington. This explains the unusual Israeli media coverage of her death as a "massive loss" and several full-page advertisements in the *New York Times* and other newspapers by a Los Angeles–based pro-Israeli organization, the Simon

Wiesenthal Center. A large picture of Bhutto was beneath the words "SUICIDE TERROR: What more will it take for the world to act?" and the ad called on the United Nations for a special session devoted to the issue. "Unless we put suicide bombing on the top of the international community's agenda, this virulent cancer could engulf us all," it reads. "The looming threat of WMDs in the hands of suicide bombers will dwarf the casualties already suffered in 30 countries." The ad demanded that the UN declare suicide bombings a "crime against humanity."

Benazir, according to some close to her, had been tempted to boycott the Pakistani elections, but had lacked the political courage to defy Washington, which was insisting that the elections go ahead as scheduled. She certainly had plenty of physical courage and had refused to be cowed by threats from local opponents. She chose to address an election rally in Liaquat Bagh. Her death further poisoned relations between the Pakistan Peoples Party and the army. That had started in 1977 when her father was removed by a military dictator and killed. Party activists, particularly in the province of Sind, were brutally tortured, humiliated, and, sometimes, disappeared or killed.

Pakistan's turbulent history, a result of continuous military rule and unpopular global alliances, confronts the ruling elite now with serious choices. They appear to have no positive aims. The overwhelming majority of the country disapproves of the government's foreign policy. They are angered by its lack of a serious domestic policy except for further enriching a callous and greedy elite that includes a swollen, parasitic military. Now they watch helplessly as politicians are shot dead in front of them.

I FIRST MET Benazir at her father's house in Clifton, Karachi, in 1969, when she was a fun-loving teenager, and eight years later at Oxford, when she invited me to speak at the Oxford Union when she was its president. At that time she was not particularly interested in politics and told me she had always wanted to be a diplomat. History and personal tragedy pushed her in another direction. Her father's death transformed her. She became a new person, determined to take on the military dictator of that time. We would endlessly discuss the future of the country in her tiny flat in London. She agreed that land reforms, mass education programs, a health service, and an independent foreign policy were constructive aims and crucial if the country was to be saved from the vultures in and out of uniform. Her constituency was the poor, and she was proud of that.

I was in regular communication with political activists and intellectuals in Lahore. Their virtually unanimous view was that since her return would be the first occasion for people to publicly mourn the execution of her father, at least half a million would come out to greet her. Having experienced firsthand the terrors of the Zia dictatorship, she was less sure about the turnout, and who can blame her. The country had been silenced by repression, but my instincts were the same as those of friends in Lahore. She asked me to write her speech. One day she rang. "Last night I dreamt I'd arrived in Lahore, the crowds were there, I went to the podium, opened my handbag, but the speech was missing. Can't you hurry up?" I did, and then we rehearsed it once a week before she left. Her Urdu was rudimentary, but when I suggested that she ask the assembled masses a question in Punjabi, she balked at the thought. The question was simple: *"Zia rehvay ya jahvay?"* (Should Zia stay or go?). Her pronunciation was abysmal. She would laugh and try again till it became as good as it was ever going to be. There was another moment of panic. "What should I do if they reply he should stay." This time I laughed. "They wouldn't be there if they felt that." Film footage shows her asking the question in Punjabi, and the affecting response of the crowd, which turned out to be closer to a million people strong. That campaign was the high point of her life, when a combination of political and physical courage created a wave of hope in the benighted country.

She changed again after becoming prime minister. In the early days, when I met her on a number of occasions in Islamabad, we would gently argue. In response to my numerous complaints, all she would say was that the world had changed. She couldn't be on the "wrong side" of history. And so, like many others, she made her peace with Washington. This finally led to the deal with Musharraf and her return home after more than a decade in exile. On a number of occasions she told me that she did not fear death. It was one of the dangers of playing politics in Pakistan. The last time we met was in the prime minister's residence in 1995, a year before she was dismissed from office for corruption. I asked whether she was worried by the threat of assassination. There had been an attempt already, she informed me, but the assassin, Aimal Kansi, almost blew himself up, but escaped. She smiled. I was astonished by the revelation.

Kansi was a former CIA agent recruited during the first Afghan war. He felt betrayed by the agency when they cut off his salary after the Russians left Afghanistan. His subsequent behavior resembled the script of *The Bourne Identity*. In 1993, Kansi returned to the United States, made his way to Langley, Virginia, waited with a sniper's rifle, and unleashed a deadly rampage, killing two CIA employees, including his former boss, and wounding several others. He returned to Pakistan and was on the most wanted list of the CIA and the FBI. In 1997, he was finally captured by FBI agents in a seedy hotel in Islamabad. He had been betrayed by his own bodyguards, the CIA having spent more than $3.5 million to pay informants and others to entrap him. He was extradited to the United States, where he was tried and killed by lethal injection. Till she told me, I had no idea that he had tried to kill her as well.

It is difficult to imagine any good coming out of the tragedy of her death, but there is one possibility. Pakistan desperately needs a political party that can give voice to the social needs of the bulk of the people. The Peoples Party, founded by Zulfiqar Ali Bhutto, was built by the activists of the only popular mass movement the country has known: students, peasants, and workers who fought for three months in 1968–69 to topple the country's first military dictator. They saw it as their party, and that feeling persists in some parts of the country to this day, despite everything.

Benazir's horrific death should have given her colleagues pause for reflection. To be dependent on a person or a family may be necessary at certain times, but it is a structural weakness, not a strength for a political organization. The Peoples Party needed to be refounded as a modern and democratic organization, open to serious debate and discussion, defending social and human rights, uniting the many disparate groups and individuals in Pakistan desperate for any halfway decent alternative, and coming forward with concrete proposals to stabilize occupied and war-torn Afghanistan. The Bhutto family should not have been asked for any more sacrifices. But it was not to be. When emotions run high, reason goes underground, and in Pakistan it can lie buried for a long time.

Six hours before she was executed, Mary, Queen of Scots, wrote to her brother-in-law, Henry III of France: "As for my son, I commend him to you in so far as he deserves, for I cannot answer for him." The year was 1587. On December 30, 2007, a conclave of feudal potentates gathered in the home of the slain Benazir Bhutto to hear her last will and testament being read out, its contents subsequently announced to the world media. Where Mary was tentative, her modern equivalent left no room for doubt. She could certainly answer for her son.

Her will specified that her nineteen-year-old boy, Bilawal Zardari, a student at Oxford University, should succeed her as chairperson of the party. Her husband, Asif Zardari (one of the most venal and discredited politicians in the country and still facing corruption charges in two European courts), would lead the party till Bilawal came of age. He would then become chairperson for life, as was the custom. That this is now official does not make it any less grotesque. The Peoples Party had now formally become a family heirloom, a property to be disposed of at the will of its proprietor.

Pakistan and the supporters of the party deserved something better than this distasteful, medieval charade. Benazir's last decision, alas, was in the same autocratic mode as its predecessors, an approach that would tragically cost her . . . her own life. Had she heeded the advice of some party leaders and not agreed to the Washington-brokered deal with Pervez Musharraf or, even later, decided to boycott his parliamentary election without cast-iron guarantees regarding her safety, she might still have been alive.

That most of the PPP inner circle consists of spineless timeservers leading frustrated and melancholy lives is no excuse for the farcical succession. All this could be transformed if inner-party democracy was implemented. A tiny layer of incorruptible and principled politicians are inside the party, but they have been sidelined. Dynastic politics is a sign of weakness, not strength. Benazir was fond of comparing her clan to the Kennedys, but chose to ignore the fact that the Democratic Party is not the instrument of any one family.

The issue of democracy is enormously important in a country that has been governed by the military for over half of its life. Pakistan is not a "failed state" in the sense of the Congo or Rwanda. It is a dysfunctional state and has been for almost four decades.

At the heart of this dysfunction is the domination by the army, and each period of military rule has made things worse. This has prevented the emergence of stable political institutions. Here the United States bears direct responsibility, since it has always regarded the military as the only institution it can do business with and, unfortunately, still does so. This rock has forced choppy waters into a headlong torrent.

The military's weaknesses are well-known and amply documented. But the politicians are not in a position to cast stones. After all, it was not Musharraf who pioneered the assault on the judiciary so conveniently overlooked by the U.S. deputy secretary of state, John Negroponte, and the British foreign secretary, David Miliband. The first attack on the Supreme Court was mounted by Nawaz Sharif's goons, who physically assaulted judges because they were angered by a decision that ran counter to their master's interests when he was prime minister.

Those who had hoped that, with Benazir's death, the Peoples Party might start a new chapter are likely to be disappointed. Zardari's ascendancy will almost certainly split the party over the next few years. He was loathed by many activists, who held him responsible for his wife's downfall. Now he is their leader.

The global consensus that jihadis or Al Qaeda killed Benazir Bhutto fell apart within a fortnight of her murder. It emerged that when Benazir asked the United States for a Karzai-style phalanx of privately contracted former U.S. marine bodyguards, the Pakistan government saw it as a breach of sovereignty and contemptuously rejected the suggestion. Hillary Clinton and Senator Joseph Biden, chairman of the Senate Foreign Relations Committee, publicly hinted that the convict's badge should be pinned on General Musharraf and not Al Qaeda for the murder, a sure sign that sections of the U.S. establishment were thinking it was time to dump the Pakistani president. He, of course, angrily denied any association with the Bhutto murder and asserted that even if she had survived, she would not have been able to handle the crisis in Pakistan:

The United States thought Benazir was the right person to fight terrorists. Who is the best person to fight? You need three qualities
today if you want to fight the extremists and the terrorists. Number
one, you must have the military with you. Well, she was very
unpopular with the military. Very unpopular. Number two, you
shouldn't be seen by the entire religious lobby to be alien—a nonreligious person. The third element: don't be seen as an extension of
the United States. Now I am branded as an extension, but not to the
extent she was. Pakistanis know that I can be tough. I can speak out
against Hillary Clinton. I can speak out against anyone. These are
the elements. You be the judge.*

Washington's problem is that, with Benazir dead, the only phone
number in Islamabad they can call is that of General Ashfaq Kayani, the
Fort Leavenworth–trained head of the army. Nawaz Sharif is regarded
in Washington as a lightweight and a Saudi poodle (his close business
and religious affinities with the kingdom are well-known) and hence
not 100 percent reliable, though, given the U.S.-Saudi alliance, poor
Sharif is puzzled as to why this should exclude him from consideration.
He and his brother are both ready to do Washington's bidding but
would prefer the Saudi king to Musharraf as the imperial messenger.

A temporary solution to the crisis was available. This would have
required General Musharraf's replacement as president by a less contentious figure, an all-party government of unity to prepare the basis
for genuine elections within six months, and the reinstatement of the
sacked Supreme Court judges to investigate Benazir's murder without
fear or favor. Musharraf has finally discarded his uniform and handed
over the military to Kayani. He should simultaneously have retired
from political life since it was the uniform that had led him to the presidency. It would have been a new start, but Pakistan's history is replete
with leaders who had no desire to besmirch themselves with new ideas.
Politics of the short term is always in command. This turbulent year
virtually telescoped the entire history of the country, barring a province

---

*Interview with *Newsweek,* January 12, 2008.

on the verge of defection. One of the more depressing features of the Pakistani military-bureaucratic elite—which has governed the country almost continuously since it was founded in 1947—is its startling lack of originality. It regularly repeats old mistakes. Never is this more obvious than during extended periods of direct or indirect military rule (1958–71, 1977–89, 1999–2008).

Social and political rank in much of today's world is determined by wealth. Power and money cohabit the same space. The result is a mutant democracy whose function is to seal off all possibilities of redistributing wealth and power or enhancing its own standing with the citizenry. Some exceptions remain. In China, for instance, the party hierarchy remains dominant, a partial reflection, perhaps, of the ancient mandarin tradition that insisted on educational qualifications as the principal criteria for social advancement. In Pakistan, the brightest kids dream of becoming stockbrokers in New York; the most ambitious imagine themselves in uniform. The immeasurable importance of the army determines the entire political culture of the country. The chief of staff is the single person on whom the gaze of the political community in Pakistan rests semipermanently. Next in line of importance is the U.S. ambassador. A failure to grasp this basic reality makes it genuinely difficult to understand the past or present of the country.

Throughout its sixty-year history, political life in Pakistan has been dominated by a series of clashes between general and politician, with civilian bureaucrats pretending to be impartial seconds, while mostly favoring the military. The final arbiter is usually Washington. The statistics reveal the winner. Bureaucrats and unelected politicians ran Pakistan for eleven years, the army has ruled the country for thirty-four years, and elected representatives have been in power for fifteen years. It is a dismal record, but it had Washington's strong approval as revealed by an inspection of each of the dictatorships in turn.

8

ON THE FLIGHT PATH OF
AMERICAN POWER

THE 9/11 COMMISSION REPORT, PUBLISHED IN JULY 2004, PRO-
nounced, among other things, that the Musharraf government was the
best if not the only hope for long-term stability in Pakistan and
Afghanistan. The turbulence required a strongman, and as long as Pakistan was on board in the "war against terror" and prepared to fight the
forces of extremism, the United States owed long-term and comprehensive support to a regime committed to "enlightened moderation."

The word association forces me to digress briefly and recall the late
conservative senator Barry Goldwater's dictum in his speech accepting
the Republican presidential nomination in 1964: "I would remind you
that extremism in the defense of liberty is no vice! And let me remind
you also that moderation in the pursuit of justice is no virtue." Malcolm X defended this view eloquently in one of his last public appearances, at which I was present. Leaving aside important differences of
how to interpret "liberty," this is also the view today of many who resist
the United States in Iraq and Afghanistan, though unfortunately most
of them would not agree with a 1981 assessment by the same senator
during a Senate speech in which he offered sage advice to his own party
that applied equally to the Washington-backed Afghan insurgents bat-
tling the godless Russians at the time:

On religious issues there can be little or no compromise. There is no position on which people are so immovable as their religious beliefs. There is no more powerful ally one can claim in a debate than Jesus Christ, or God, or Allah, or whatever one calls this supreme being. But like any powerful weapon, the use of God's name on one's behalf should be used sparingly. The religious factions that are growing throughout our land are not using their religious clout with wisdom. They are trying to force government leaders into following their position one hundred percent. If you disagree with these religious groups on a particular moral issue, they complain, they threaten you with a loss of money or votes or both.

I'm frankly sick and tired of the political preachers across this country telling me as a citizen that if I want to be a moral person, I must believe in A, B, C, and D. Just who do they think they are? And from where do they presume to claim the right to dictate their moral beliefs to me? And I am even more angry as a legislator who must endure the threats of every religious group who thinks it has some God-granted right to control my vote on every roll call in the Senate. I am warning them today: I will fight them every step of the way if they try to dictate their moral convictions to all Americans in the name of "conservatism."

These strictures had little real impact. Religious fundamentalism soon occupied the White House, and its equally fundamentalist enemy targeted Wall Street and the Pentagon. The advice of *The 9/11 Commission Report* was subsequently accepted by Congress and the Intelligence Reform and Terrorism Prevention Act of 2004 (Public Law 108–458). The recommendations in relation to Pakistan were put into effect by calling for a program of sustained U.S. aid to Pakistan and instructing the president to report to Congress what a long-term U.S. strategy to engage with and support would entail. This was followed in November 2005 by a subsidiary appraisal from the commissioners that offered only a C grade to U.S. efforts in encouraging Pakistan's anti-extremism policies and contained a warning that the country "remains a sanctuary and training ground for terrorists." This view, widespread in the United States and Europe, is regularly reflected in the media and appears to have infected the political culture of both regions.

Stanley Kurtz, a fellow of the Hudson Institute and Hoover Institution, recently wrote, "In a sense global Islam is now Waziristan writ large. . . . Waziristan now seeks to awaken the tribal jihadist side of the global Muslim soul." It is not uncommon to read gibberish of this variety from a number of neocon pundits. As suggested earlier in this book, their equivalents were expressing equally nonsensical views in the eighties when the tribal areas were regarded as freedom writ large and most Western journalists meekly followed "advice" and referred to the mujahideen as "freedom fighters." The same people continue to inhabit the same region. Once a necessary steamroller to defeat the Russians, now it appears that they themselves have to be steamrollered into oblivion. What has changed is the global priorities of the United States. This explains the new language. It is relatively easy for state intellectuals (those employed by instrumentalist think tanks and swathes of the academy) in the United States to somersault themselves into new positions and fall into line with imperial needs as required. It's much more difficult for client states to behave in exactly the same way. This explains the crisis that has erupted on Pakistan's western frontiers.

The British Empire was once embroiled in the same region. For them too Waziristan was evil writ large. Their ideologues (and later their Pakistani mimics) produced a great deal of literature on this rugged region, a crude anthropology to justify war and imperial domination. What is today ascribed to Islam alone was in those earlier times seen as a genetic characteristic of the Pashtun race and some of its more recalcitrant tribal components. Here is Mr. Temple, a senior British civil servant in 1855, sharing his opinions with his colleagues in terms and language that would have been appreciated by General Custer:

> Now these tribes are savages—noble savages perhaps—and not without some virtue and generosity, but still absolutely barbarians nevertheless. . . . In their eyes their one great commandment is blood for blood, and fire and sword for all infidels. . . . They are a sensual race . . . very avaricious . . . thievish and predatory to the last

degree. . . . The Pathan mother offers prayers that her son may be a successful robber. . . . It would never even occur to their minds that an oath on the Koran was binding. . . . They are fierce and bloodthirsty.*

Here is another cultivated imperial officer, Mr. Ibbetson, writing in 1881:

The true Pathan is perhaps the most barbaric of all the races with which we are brought into contact. . . . He is bloodthirsty, cruel and vindictive in the highest degree. . . . He does not know what truth or faith is. . . . It is easy to convict him out of his own mouth; here are some of his proverbs: "a Pathan's enmity smoulders like a dung fire"; "speak good words to an enemy very softly; gradually destroy him root and branch."

To demonstrate that the Scots were not going to be left behind, here is Mr. MacGregor a few years later:

. . . There is no doubt, like other Pathans, they would not shrink from any falsehood, however atrocious, to gain an end. Money could buy their services for the foulest deed.

The author who cites these dozens of similar references also reveals:

The Wazirs are Muhammadans of the Sunni sect, but, like any other Pathan tribe, they are not particularly strict in the performance of their religious duties. The mullahs have influence only as far as the observances of religion go, and are powerless in political matters, but the Wazirs are an especially democratic and independent people, and even their own Maliks [tribal leaders] have little real control over them.†

---

*Colonel H. C. Wylly, *From the Black Mountain to Waziristan* (London: 1912).
†Ibid.

The Afghan wars of the twentieth century changed all that and the mullahs became much more powerful, but what remains true is that the use of force, as the British discovered, can never be a permanent solution. Britain's successor state in the region carried on in similar fashion, first using mercenary tribesmen to invade Kashmir in 1948 and subsequently using them during the first Afghan war from 1979 to 1989. This raises interesting questions regarding the place occupied by Pakistan in relation to the United States.

For instance, whose interests are really being served by Pakistan's foreign policy from 1947 till today, give or take Zulfiqar Ali Bhutto's last few years in office? Is it the case that some senior cabinet ministers, generals, diplomats, and selected civil servants have often reported directly to Washington, circumventing their own respective chains of command? And, if so, why has this been the case for sixty years? It is not a pretty tale.

The Great Leader had tried to rent his house to the new world power and failed. His colleagues were altogether more ambitious. With Jinnah's encouragement the new rulers of Pakistan developed an early communal awareness that to survive they had to rent their country. An open auction was considered unrealistic. There was only one possible buyer. They were quite frank on this level and told Washington that after an initial fee of $2 billion to meet their "administrative expenses" for the first few years, they would still need "a regular source of finance" to keep going. This demand has been a constant of Pakistani politics. As their lobbyist in the United States in 1947, the shrewd, if foul-tongued, bureaucrat Ghulam Mohammed, doubling then as the country's first minister of finance, chose the Chase National Bank of New York. Jinnah sent a trusted aide, Laiq Ali, with a memorandum spelling out the country's needs to the bank chairman, Winthrop W. Aldrich. He read it carefully, improved its language, and suggested some changes, and then it was officially forwarded to Foggy Bottom.

When Laiq met State Department officials, he stressed that the new country "presently faced a Soviet threat on its Western frontier." This was a foolish fabrication as the State Department was well aware. The Soviet Union, wrecked by the war, was concentrating its energies on rebuilding the country and shoring up Eastern Europe. The United

States was busy securing Western Europe and Japan, as well as keeping an eye on China, where the Eighth Route Army was beginning to threaten a Communist victory. The offer to buy Pakistan and its armed forces in perpetuity had no real appeal at the time. An internal memorandum circulated by the Office for Near Eastern Affairs was blunt: "It was obvious from this approach that Pakistan was thinking in terms of the U.S. as a primary source of military strength, and since this would involve virtual U.S. military responsibility for the new Dominion, our reply to the Pakistan request was negative."

This was made clear to Laiq Ali, though a sweetener was offered in the shape of an emergency loan to help alleviate social needs. A dejected Laiq then asked if money could be made available for certain specialist development projects. When his American interlocutors queried if these had been worked out in detail, he responded that he had knowledge only of a projected paper mill, in which he himself was interested. Unfortunately the official documents do not minute the informal reactions of officials. Washington did not even bother responding to the generous Pakistani offer to sell its army.

Confronted with this unexpected rejection, the Great Leader's special envoy asked if some money could be provided to buy some blankets and medicines for the refugees from India. This request was also turned down, but with the possibility that the United States might sell army surplus to Pakistan at a rate considerably lower than the market price. All the while Laiq was cabling Jinnah that the talks were going well. The Great Leader must have had his doubts. He instructed a veteran pro-British Muslim League leader and later prime minister, Sir Feroze Khan Noon, then on his way to Turkey, to call on the U.S. ambassador in Ankara and exert a bit more pressure. "Darkness at Noon" (a sobriquet subsequently awarded him by the *Pakistan Times*) sprang to his task with alacrity and penned the following "confidential memorandum," so crude that it must have both appalled and entertained what was at the time a sophisticated State Department under George C. Marshall's leadership:

> The Mussalmans in Pakistan are against Communism. The Hindus have an Ambassador in Moscow, Mrs Pandit, who is the sister of the Hindu Prime Minister in Delhi, Mr Nehru, and the Russians have

got an Ambassador in Delhi, the Hindu capital. We the Mussul-
mans of Pakistan have no Ambassador in Moscow nor is there any
Ambassador in Karachi—our capital. . . . If USA help Pakistan to
become a strong and independent country . . . then the people of
Pakistan will fight to last man against Communism to keep their
freedom and preserve their way of life.

There was no response. A desperate Noon then appealed to the
Turkish government for military equipment, but they turned him
down and immediately informed Washington of their decision. The
reason for the indifference was not a mystery. The United States,
Britain, and the Soviet Union agreed that the single most important
country in the region was India. In 1948, Pakistan had attempted to
solve the dispute with India over Kashmir by force. Kashmir was a
Muslim-majority province in India, but its Hindu maharaja had signed
the papers of accession and joined the Indian federation without consulting the people. This created real anger, and to keep Kashmiri
nationalists on his side, the Indian prime minister, Jawaharlal Nehru,
had promised a referendum that would allow Kashmiris to determine
their own future. It never happened. An enormous literature exists on
this subject, and I have written about it elsewhere at some length.*
Here it is only necessary to recall that the irregulars dispatched by Pakistan to take Kashmir were the same "terror tribes" that occupy the
news headlines today. They were much less disciplined at the time.
They were led by Pakistan army officers but were often out of control.
Their untamed tribal egoism—looting and raping nuns en route—led
to military disaster, holding back the assault on Srinagar. Indian troops
secured the airport in that capital city, landed more troops, and the
fighting was soon over. The British generals commanding both armies
had had enough and refused to tolerate any escalation of the conflict.
A Line of Control was established and Kashmir was unfairly divided.
India obtained what its prime minister described as the "snowy bosom"
of this stunningly beautiful region, leaving Pakistan with what can only

---

*Clash of Fundamentalisms: Crusades, Jihads and Modernity (London and New York: 2002),
chapter 18, "The Story of Kashmir."

be referred to as its bony posterior. Since then the dispute has led to semipermanent tension between the two countries. Even at the height of the Cold War, by which time, as is outlined below, Pakistan had become its closest of allies, the United States maintained an even-handed approach to Kashmir, a clear signal that it was not prepared to jeopardize its long-term interests in South Asia.

Pakistan kept trying to sell itself. Jinnah, deeply hostile to the British Labour government, told the U.S. ambassador not to be "mis-led by the UK," which was pro-India, but to understand that Pakistan alone could be a crucial ally against Soviet expansionism. Jinnah, who must have overdosed on Rudyard Kipling's novels, insisted that Soviet agents were present in Kalat and Gilgit in search of a base in Baluchi-stan. It was pure fantasy. More of the same was on offer from Pakistan's foreign minister, Zafarullah Khan, in New York. His line was margin-ally more sophisticated. Accepting that India was the major power, he pleaded with the United States to shore up Pakistan, whose people were genetically anticommunist, since this was the best way to protect India against the Soviet Union, which would send its armies through the Khyber Pass. This ploy did not work either, but Pakistan's persistence would ultimately pay off.

During the Korean War (1950–53) the United States finally turned to Pakistan and slowly began to incorporate its military and bureau-cracy into its new security arrangements for the region. In 1953, for-mer Pakistani ambassador to the United States Mohammad Ali Bogra was prime minister and, while opening a General Motors assembly plant in Karachi, once again suggested that "ties of goodwill and friend-ship can be forged on a permanent basis."

The United States responded by sending wheat as "aid." It was in fact part of the U.S. government's domestic price-support scheme to reduce a large domestic wheat surplus. Simultaneously John Foster Dulles, the secretary of state, put out a statement branding Pakistan as "a bulwark for freedom in Asia." The Pakistani prime minister responded obsequiously.

The country's largest English-language daily, the *Pakistan Times,* was not impressed and blasted the statement editorially on July 27, 1953:

They [Pakistanis] will find it somewhat difficult to understand the meaning of the Prime Minister's assertion, on the occasion of the first US food ship, that Pakistan and America speak the "same language regarding the ideals of freedom and democracy." They will indeed find it hard to work out a common factor between their ideals of freedom and such concrete expressions of American foreign policy as innumerable strategic bases round the globe, open support to the crumbling Western Empires and their indigenous puppets in the Orient, alliance with such retrograde elements as the Kuomintang and the Rhee gang, and the strengthening of Wall Street's hold on various Middle Eastern economies. They will also wonder how to reconcile their cherished dreams of a democratic political and social order with the cruel realities of American life such as racial discrimination and the lynching of Negroes, persecution of intellectuals and witchhunting.*

Military pacts and aid came together and would soon be followed by military dictatorships. In September 1954, Pakistan publicly declared it had become a willing tool by joining the Southeast Asia Treaty Organization together with Thailand and the Philippines. Other Southeast Asian countries included the United States, Britain, France, Australia, and New Zealand. Exactly one year later, in September 1955, Pakistan joined another Western outfit known as the Baghdad Pact, which included King Faisal's Iraq, Iran, Turkey, and Britain. Naturally, all this took place without the benefit of a single general election in Pakistan. Public anger could not be registered democratically. A U.S. Senate report, "Technical Assistance: Final Report of Committee on Foreign Relations," published on March 12, 1957, confirmed what

---

*These newspapers were part of the Progressive Papers Ltd chain, which included an Urdu political-cultural weekly, *Lail-o-Nahar* (Day and Night). Set up in Lahore with Jinnah's support in 1946, the newspapers were, in fact, owned and edited by left-wing intellectuals, some of them sympathetic to or members of the tiny Pakistan Communist Party. They included the poet Faiz Ahmed Faiz, literary critics Sibte Hasan and Ahmed Nadeem Qasmi. My father, Mazhar Ali Khan, was the editor of the *Pakistan Times*. I recently found a letter in his archives from the U.S. ambassador disinviting him from dinner because of a "hostile" editorial on the United States. The entire chain, a permanent irritation to every regime, was taken over by the military dictatorship of Ayub Khan in April 1959.

many Pakistanis were beginning to suspect: "From a political view-point, U.S. military aid has strengthened Pakistan's armed services, *the greatest single stabilizing force in the country* [my italics—TA], and has encouraged Pakistan to participate in collective defense arrangements."

IN JULY 1959, General Ayub, now firmly in control, agreed to the establishment of a top-secret U.S. military base in Badaber, near Peshawar. The aim was to spy on the Soviet Union. In May of the following year, the Russians downed a U-2 spy plane that had taken off from Peshawar and captured the pilot, Gary Powers. When the United States denied the spy flights, the Russians produced the poor pilot. The Soviet leader, Nikita Khrushchev, entertaining General Maxwell Taylor at a banquet in Moscow, reportedly clambered onto the table in a rage and shouted, "You Americans are like dogs. You eat and shit in the same place." Khrushchev later addressed a press conference at which he announced that he knew where the plane had taken off from and that Peshawar was now a Soviet target, marked with a red circle. I remember well the panic that gripped the Pakistani military establishment, not to mention the brave burghers of Peshawar, some of whom hurriedly left the city. It was empty rocket-rattling, but it highlighted Pakistan's dependent status. A few years previously, the acting foreign minister, Zulfiqar Ali Bhutto, had asked the U.S. embassy whether he could visit the base. He was politely told it was out of bounds, but that the base commanders would be happy to serve him coffee and cakes in the cafeteria. Decades later a general could write about how "Pakistan felt deceived because the US had kept her in the dark about such clandestine spy operations launched from Pakistan's territory," but this was pious nonsense. Ayub Khan knew perfectly well that the USAF base was not a rest and recreation stop for crews en route to the Far East.

Following the U-2 incident, policy makers in Washington (always more concerned with India) suggested to Ayub Khan that the best way to safeguard the subcontinent against Communism was to set up a "joint defense" system. The general agreed and suggested this to the Indian prime minister, Jawaharlal Nehru, who had carefully kept India nonaligned in the Cold War. Nehru's response was a clear rejection. "Joint defense against who?" he asked frostily.

Ayub had done as he was asked, and his reward was an official state visit to Camelot in 1961, where he was given the red-carpet treatment, reserved for special clients. A presidential yacht transported him to Mount Vernon with the Kennedys. Later he addressed a joint session of Congress, saying, "The only people who will stand by you in Asia are the people of Pakistan—provided you are prepared to stand by them." This was not completely accurate, and the use of the word *people* enraged many back home. He was a dictator who had denied citizens the franchise, so they felt he had no right to speak for them. There was much anger and many poems written.

The following year India suffered a heavy defeat in the mysterious Sino-Indian border war launched by China to regain disputed territory that was of little significance. The short war was actually intended as a shot across Soviet bows via its Indian friend and was, in fact, the first real indication of a serious rift between the Soviet Union and China, though few interpreted it as such at the time. For the United States it was a case of "unprovoked Communist aggression" on the part of the Chinese. The United States and Britain began to provide the Indian armed forces with the latest weaponry. Ayub was livid but impotent. Not till a decade after Beijing's public break with Moscow did Washington begin to think seriously about cultivating China. And here Pakistan would prove extremely helpful as a go-between, a role its leaders always relished.

When it became obvious even to Ayub Khan that the United States would never back Pakistan militarily in any conflict with India, he began to get slightly nervous. Public opinion had been opposed to the security pacts for some time. After the Pakistan-Indian war of 1965 the United States stopped its military aid to Pakistan. This shook the military-bureaucratic regime to its core. Zulfiqar Ali Bhutto, the foreign minister, was sacked for demanding a new turn based on bilateral relations. He would later explain his position thus:

Each of Pakistan's multilateral and bilateral military commitments became useless the moment the United States unilaterally termi-

nated military assistance to Pakistan. With the removal of reciprocity, the agreements became void ipso facto. Notwithstanding this
incontestable position, the Government of Ayub Khan, committing
dereliction of its elementary duty to the people of Pakistan, refused
to renounce the agreements. It chose to endanger the security of
Pakistan without an iota of corresponding protection. It cannot be
forgotten that Pakistan assumed the liabilities of the Cold War in
return for military assistance and political support on Kashmir. The
military assistance ended three years ago and the political support
went earlier. The United States' position on Kashmir began to shift
imperceptibly since the first Sino-Indian conflict of October 1959.
This was established beyond doubt when Pakistan took the dispute
to the Security Council in 1964. The United States imposed an
embargo on the delivery of military equipment to Pakistan when
the country was struggling for its survival against an aggressor five
times its size. For three years a complete ban was placed on the sale
of weapons and spare parts to Pakistan. The government of a country in three military alliances had to run from pillar to post in search
of armaments and spare parts, from black market centers and notorious arms peddlers. Throughout this difficult period, Ayub Khan
refused to free the country from the burden of these obsolete
alliances. On the contrary, he permitted the United States' base in
Peshawar to operate until the expiry of its lease in July 1969. Not
even those countries which are the pillars of NATO would find it
possible to assume such onerous one-sided military obligations on
behalf of the United States or any other country.*

As this lengthy extract reveals, even in his most radical phase when
he was out of power, Pakistan's most intelligent and least provincial
political leader was obsessed with the idea of India as a primary enemy.
This had formed the cornerstone of the country's foreign policy since
1947. It affected how the country functioned internally and produced
a warped political culture. During a lengthy conversation with Bhutto

---

*Zulfiqar Ali Bhutto, *Pakistan and Alliances* (Lahore: 1972).

in the summer of 1969 at his Clifton residence in Karachi, I questioned him about this, pointing out that playing on national chauvinism did not advance any progressive cause. This was soon after the 1965 war with India, which he had strongly pushed for. "How else do you think we're going to get rid of this bloody army which rules the country? Defeat in this war weakened them. That's why the big movement succeeded."* Bhutto was capable of extreme forms of cynicism, but did he actually believe this? I don't know. Privately he was a great admirer of Jawaharlal Nehru's and had read all his books, one of which he referred to in his death-cell memoir. Perhaps he understood at some level that Jinnah had created a state but not a nation. Pakistani nationalism was incredibly weak, and Bengali, Pashtun, Sindhi, and Baluch identities were much stronger. Bengal would soon be detached, but the others remained. The only way of forging a Pakistani identity was by identifying an enemy. India or "the Hindu." It was crude, but largely ineffective outside the Punjab. Even there many were ready for a different message from the stale chauvinism and the constant sloganizing that "Kashmir is in danger" mouthed by most politicians to garner cheap support. And so "anti-Indianism" became a substitute for any genuine anticolonial nationalism, a problem India never had to confront. Despite the vast number of ethnicities, languages, and varied cultural traditions, with a sense of their own epic literature and place in the region, there was never any serious problem about the people considering themselves Indian, with a few temporary exceptions—Sikhs in the Punjab, tribals in Nagaland—resulting from the political stupidity of the ruling elite.

Reading speeches made by Pakistan's first batch of bureaucrats-

---

*Also present were Mustafa Khar and Mumtaz Bhutto, staunch members of the PPP. Our conversation rapidly changed course when General Yahya's son was announced. I had just written a savage "Letter from Pakistan" for the satirical magazine *Private Eye* in which I had denounced the son as well as the father. On seeing me, Yahya junior turned to Bhutto and asked, "Sir, who do you think writes these lies about my family in *Private Eye*?" Bhutto responded with a twinkle in his eye, "Ask Tariq. He lives there." Yahya junior looked at me. "I have no idea" was my response, "but I suspect it's their editor, Richard Ingrams, who knows a lot about this world." There was much merriment after Yahya junior departed. That this surreal conversation took place at all surprises me more now than it did at the time.

turned-politicians, one is struck by a permanent "inferiority complex" in relation to India. To counter the latter, they avoid mentioning that Pakistan has only a brief history. Instead they hark back to the Muslim warriors of the early medieval period and sometimes the Mogul emperors, though these were never a good role model for young Pakistan since religion mattered little to the emperors and even the pious Aurungzeb—the last of the great Moguls—preserved an imperial army led by Hindu generals and did not attempt to make the mosque the center of state power. And so Pakistani history was never written as a common history with the rest of India till 1947, but as a crude separatist account of Indian Muslims and their glorious past.

As the United States moved closer to India after the Sino-Indian border war in 1959, Pakistan made a concerted effort to develop friendly relations with China. Ayub Khan's trip to Beijing in 1964 prefigured Richard Nixon's a decade later. The "mass welcome" laid on by the Chinese went to Ayub's head, and long after he had been driven out by a genuine mass upsurge in his own country, he would watch home movies of his China triumph. Washington was not too pleased, but found the relationship useful, and Pakistanis working for the CIA were sometimes used to spy on China, including at least one pilot, known to me, who flew PIA passenger flights to China. The friendship was instrumental for both sides, and Pakistani bureaucrats and government ministers were often debriefed in Washington. The poet Habib Jalib joked in a long satirical poem entitled "Adviser" in which the eponymous hero says to the president:

> This is what I said to him:
> "China now our dearest friend
> On it does our life depend
> But the system that there prevails
> Do not go near it,
> Salute it from afar
> Salute it from afar"

In time the Chinese system too would be turned upside down, becoming a model for Asian capitalism and making a wholehearted embrace extremely desirable for Pakistan. Throughout, the cold war with India remained a constant. The official view that India rather than the structural crisis inherent in the Pakistani state since its foundation had led to the explosion in East Bengal remained embedded in official thinking, hardening into the basis for policy making. But it was impossible to ignore that in 1971 neither China nor the United States helped "save Pakistan," as had been predicted by some and hoped by others. They let it bleed. What was the dominant view in India?

Is it the case that the triumphalist Indian leadership was planning to eliminate West Pakistan as well? There are divergent views. The first is that of Indira Gandhi, the Indian prime minister at the time, as divulged to the author during a lengthy off-the-record discussion in 1984, some months before her assassination.

After a formal interview for a book on India that I was working on at the time,* Mrs. Gandhi turned to me and said, "Now my turn to ask you some questions. I've read your new book [*Can Pakistan Survive?*]. You know these generals and how they think and operate. I am being told by my people here that Pakistan is preparing a surprise attack on us in Kashmir. What do you think?" I was taken aback. The first thought that went through my mind was that a preemptive strike by India was being considered. I was blunt in my response, pointing out that with Pakistan heavily involved in running the mujahideen on behalf of the United States, it was inconceivable that they would want to open up a second front. It would be so irrational that even if some blowhards in the high command wanted to, it would immediately be vetoed by Washington. She persisted with her questioning, and I, in turn, refused to accept that any such plan existed or was possible. I had used the word *irrational* a great deal and she turned on me.

"I am amazed that someone like you thinks that generals are rational human beings."

I burst out laughing. There was a certain irony. I, with a near hydrophobic horror of military dictators, had been put in the position of "defending" the Pakistan army.

---

*The book was *The Nehrus and the Gandhis: An Indian Dynasty,* the latest edition of which was published in 2005.

"But this would be so irrational that it would be insane," I replied. "It would mean a state and its generals deciding to commit suicide. They will not do that, and I say this as someone who is completely opposed to them and am still persona non grata because of my views on what they did in Bengal."

The discussion then took an amazing turn.

"Let me tell you something," she said. "And this is about *our* generals. After Pakistan had surrendered, General Manekshaw walked into this very office and saluted me."

Mrs. Gandhi, like Zulfiqar Bhutto, was a good mimic, and her description was very diverting. What she then described surprised me a great deal. After the salute Manekshaw asked her whether the military high command had permission to "finish the job." This meant crossing the border and taking West Pakistan. Given the demoralized state of the Pakistan army, the outcome was preordained unless the Chinese and the United States entered the conflict.

"This being India," Mrs. Gandhi continued, "I thanked the general and said the cabinet would consider the suggestion."

She then summoned an urgent cabinet meeting.

"When I reported the military request, the ministers were initially very excited and many of them were prepared to go along with it. When the meeting began, I was alone. When it ended, I had a unanimous vote for an immediate cease-fire. I tell you this to show you that in India too generals can be very irrational. In Pakistan they run the country."

I repeated what I had said earlier, and discussion on this subject ended. She then told me that the Israelis had offered to carry out a lightning strike against Pakistan's nuclear reactor provided they could use an Indian air force base. "I turned down this offer. I told them we can do it ourselves if we wanted."

Our conversation concluded with her talking about Bhutto and his visit to Simla to sign the peace treaty after the war in Bangladesh and how nervous he had been. She asked after his children and asked me to convey her warm regards to Benazir.

"You know, I was in prison myself when they hanged Bhutto. It upset me a great deal. Had I been prime minister, I would not have let it happen." Mrs. Gandhi seemed very sure on this front.

The next day I was invited to an "off-the-record" discussion at the India International Centre, where I was staying with twenty or so people, mainly civil servants, intelligence officials, journalists representing the Soviet and American lobbies, etc. "We hear you had a very interesting discussion with our prime minister yesterday," said the chair. "That's what we want to discuss." For two hours they tried to convince me that I was wrong and that Pakistan was preparing a strike in Kashmir. I remained patient, explaining at great length why this was impossible given the Afghan involvement and given that General Zia was extremely unpopular in the Sind, Baluchistan, parts of the Frontier, and sections of the Punjab. Zia could not afford any crazy war that he would lose. That is why he was desperate at the moment for some form of rapprochement and kept turning up in India uninvited on the pretext of watching cricket matches. Most of the spooks present were not convinced, and finally I told them that if India wanted a preemptive strike against Pakistan, I couldn't stop them, but they should think up a better excuse since nobody in the world would believe India had been attacked first.

This story has an amusing footnote. Back in London several months later, I described this conversation to Benazir Bhutto. She listened carefully, then asked, "But why did you tell them that our generals weren't preparing an attack?" At that moment she reminded me most of her father. She too thought the best way to break the military's grip on politics was by helping them to be defeated in a war.

I recalled my Delhi conversations most vividly when I heard that Mrs. Gandhi was assassinated by her two Sikh bodyguards in October 1984. It later emerged that one of them had visited Sikh training camps in Pakistan. For though no frontal assault was being prepared, the desire for revenge among sections of the military never evaporated. Mrs. Gandhi's internal problems with the Sikh community were of her own making, and Pakistan took advantage of Sikh discontent by training Sikh terrorists. Could it be that the CIA and the DIA had obtained information from their agents inside the Indian establishment suggesting that the Indians were seriously considering a "preemptive strike" against Pakistan? This would certainly have destabilized the entire Afghan operation, not to mention the military dictatorship in Pakistan.

A high-powered secret decision might have made Washington get rid
of the Indian prime minister using Sikh hitmen trained in Pakistan.
That certainly was the view of senior civil servants in New Delhi, who
told me that the internal report submitted to the new prime minister
linked Pakistan to the assassins and had not been made public for fear
of creating a new war fever.

Further evidence in this vein was offered to me on a trip to Pakistan
in 2006. On the flight back to London I encountered an old acquaintance. I had first spotted him in the departure lounge at the airport,
surrounded by uniformed policemen as I waited to board the PIA
flight. He took a seat not far from me in the business class, which was
virtually empty. I was buried in a novel when he came and stood near
my seat. We exchanged salaams.

"Recognize me?" he asked.

"Forgive me," I replied, "I . . ."

"I never forgave you when you were young. Why should I now?
Look at me closely and try again."

I did as he asked. Slowly a picture formed of a pimply teenager who
many decades ago used to hang out with my gang of friends during the
delightful summer months we spent in the Himalayan foothills in
Nathiagali. I remembered his mother first as cooking the best semolina
halwa in the country, and that helped recall his name. He roared with
delight.

"What do you do these days?" I asked him.

"You're going to kill me."

"Try me."

"I was a senior security officer for Bhutto and later Zia."

"You served both."

"It was my job."

I sighed in despair. "And after that?"

He was now an even more senior intelligence officer, on his way to
a European conference to discuss better ways of combatting terrorism.

"Is OBL still alive?"

He didn't reply.

"When you don't reply, I'll assume the answer is yes."

I asked the question again. He didn't reply.

"Do you know where he is?"

He burst out laughing. "I don't, and even if I did, do you think I'd tell you?"

"No, but I thought I'd ask anyway. Does anyone know where he is?"

He shrugged his shoulders.

I insisted, "Nothing in our wonderful country is ever a secret. Someone must know."

"Three people know. Possibly four. You can guess who they are."

I could. "And Washington?"

"They don't want him alive?"

"And your boys can't kill him."

"Listen, friend, why should we kill the goose that lays the golden eggs?"

As long as Osama was alive, the official seemed to be saying, the flow of dollars would never stop. It sounded credible, but was it true? I shifted the conversation to another subject. Why had General Zia's assassination never been properly investigated? He shrugged his shoulders, saying Washington wasn't keen to dig any deeper. His own view was that the Russians were responsible. This is not an uncommon view among sections of Pakistani intelligence. For most of them the explanation is linked to Afghanistan: it was revenge by Moscow. I think this is pure fantasy. What my informant suggested was more original and contained a sting in the tail. According to him, the Russians owed the Indians a favor (he didn't explain why), and Indian prime minister Rajiv Gandhi (Indira's son) had asked for Zia's head.

"Why?" I inquired in as innocent a tone as I could muster.

"In return for his mother's death."

This was the only semiofficial confirmation I ever received from the Pakistani side regarding Mrs. Gandhi's assassination.

All this is in the past. The current obsession is with the nuclear status of both countries, which could, it is feared, lead to a wipeout of large parts of the subcontinent. The assessment of a "jihadi threat" to Pakistan's nuclear facilities is particularly virulent and not simply on the blogosphere. Otherwise intelligent people are making regular statements that border on hysteria. The following three samples are representative of this overreaction, and numerous others are even less restrained. Matthew Bunn of the Managing the Atom Project at Harvard has said:

> If you can have over forty heavily armed terrorists show up in the middle of Moscow and seize a theatre. How many might show up at some remote Pakistani nuclear weapon storage facility? This is a country that has you know substantial armed remnants of Al Qaeda still operating in the country, that are able to hold off big chunks of the Pakistani regular army and the frontier provinces for weeks at a time. If a huge Al Qaeda force arrives at one of these nuclear weapon storage facilities, what do the guards do? Do they fight, do they help? This strikes me as a very open question.

Art Brown, former CIA operations director, Asia, regards Musharraf as a vital asset without whom there might be serious trouble:

> I think that if Musharraf is removed from office, particularly if he is assassinated and there is a power grab, I think the control over the Pakistani nuclear program would obviously be a concern. We would be concerned over any government that had that kind of a program and lost its leader in a bloody coup. The laboratories themselves are probably less of a concern just because it would take longer to do something with those materials in the laboratories, take them out and sell them. We might be able to intercept that at some point, but the ready-made nuclear weapons that are sitting there in the Pakistani arsenal, those indeed could go out somebody's door and appear in our opponents' box overnight.

Robert Joseph, from the Arms Control section of the U.S. State Department, is equally worried:

> What concerns me the most is that a terrorist has to be successful only one time in terms of acquiring the material and acquiring the nuclear device and detonating that device on an American city or a city anywhere in the world. So what we need to do is have a comprehensive approach for dealing with that threat. We are emphasiz-

ing two key elements. One of course is prevention. So that we deny the terrorist access to fissile material or other weapons of mass destruction of related materials. We also need to put in place, and we are working hard, the protection capabilities, the ability to detect the transfer of this type of material for example. As well as to interdict this material.

Add to this the views of the nuclear historian Scott Sagan in his book and a new dimension emerges:

Pakistan is clearly the most serious concern in the short run. Pakistani weapons lack the advanced Permissive Actions Link (PALS) locks that make it difficult for a terrorist or other unauthorized individual to use a stolen nuclear weapon. In June 2001, Pakistani officials also acknowledged that there were no specialized Pakistani teams trained on how to seize or dismantle a nuclear weapon if one was stolen. No dedicated personnel reliability program (PRP) was in place to ensure the psychological stability and reliability of the officers and guards of Pakistan's nuclear forces. Instead, Pakistani soldiers and scientists with nuclear responsibilities were reviewed and approved for duty if they were not suspected of being Indian agents by the Inter Services Intelligence (ISI) agency.

This is what partially explains U.S. support for Pakistan's military leadership at the expense of democracy and democratic institutions. If we take each argument in turn, what is being said is either risible or applies to Israel and India as well. What if forty heavily armed ultra-right Jewish settlers tried to seize Israeli weapons of mass destruction? Or a small group of hard-core Hindu fundamentalists attempted the same in India? As in Pakistan, they would be apprehended and dealt with. None of these countries has a security force known for its softness to dissidents of any variety. As for "substantial armed remnants" of Al Qaeda, cited by Matthew Bunn, most intelligence reports put their number at well below five hundred. The Pakistan army is currently half a million strong.

And if Musharraf resigns or is removed from the presidency, the military high command would not be affected in the slightest. They would continue to control the security of the nuclear facilities. As for the acquisition of nuclear weapons by "a terrorist," this was much more likely in Russia under Yeltsin than in Pakistan today. After all, much of the fissile material obtained by Pakistan came from Western Europe. Sagan's points are far more relevant, but since he wrote his book in 2003, all the measures whose absence he noted, according to Pakistan's military security experts, are now in place, and the United States is aware of this. The loopholes that existed in terms of selling nuclear technology to friendly states have long since been sealed.

As I have suggested elsewhere in this book, the only way any jihadi groups could penetrate the nuclear facilities would be if the army wanted them to. This is virtually excluded as long as the military does not split, though the possibility of a rupture in the armed forces would be real if the United States insisted on expanding the Afghan war by occupying parts of Pakistan or systematically bombing Pashtun villages suspected of harboring "terrorists." Continuous U.S. pressure on Pakistan's stance toward Israel is also linked to the country's nuclear status. Pakistani officials are told that were they to recognize Israel, some of the pressure on the nuclear issue would dissipate.

Early in March 2008, Shireen Mazari, director general of the Institute of Strategic Studies, revealed that Washington had sent Pakistan a list of eleven demands. These included providing U.S. military and auxiliary staff the right to enter and leave the country without visa restrictions, to carry arms and wear uniforms throughout Pakistan; only U.S. jurisdiction would apply to U.S. nationals, as in Japan. They would also be free to import and export anything, as they currently can in Iraq. In addition to this they wanted free movement of all vehicles and aircraft and total immunity from all claims for damage of property or personnel. The demands were rejected. Mazari concluded her report with the following advice:

> So, for those who feel there is bonhomie and complete understanding between the Pakistan military and the US military, and the trouble only exists at the political level, it is time to do a serious rethink. The first step in dealing rationally with our indigenous terrorist

problem holistically and credibly is to create space between ourselves and the US. As the US adage goes: "There is no such thing as
a free lunch."*

Two months later, Dr. Mazari was unceremoniously sacked from
her job by the Foreign Office and given fifteen minutes to vacate her
office. She was even more angered by a call from Husain Haqqani,
ambassador designate to Washington, who arrived with a bouquet of
flowers to bid her farewell and apologize for the manner of her dismissal. Mazari was blunt in her response. "I know my independent
views have upset the U.S. lobby in Pakistan which dominates the PPP.
That's why I have been sacked."

If this is the prelude to something bigger, such as a partial U.S.
occupation of the North-West Frontier Province, it could trigger a
severe crisis in the army, already under strain carrying out CENTCOM
instructions on the Pakistan-Afghan border. The fallout could have
unpredictable consequences.

As FAR AS nuclear weapons are concerned, the double standards of the
West are not helpful and are viewed with contempt in most parts of the
world. Nonetheless it's a fact that neither India nor Pakistan benefits
from this weaponry, which has become a new form of sacred property.
The figures speak for themselves. Following the nuclear tests of 1998
the Indian government announced an allocation of $9.9 billion for
defense spending in 1999, an increase of 14 percent over the previous
year. Pakistan, in turn, raised its budget by 8.5 percent to $3.3 billion.
South Asia today is one of the world's most heavily militarized regions.
The Indian and Pakistani armies are two of the world's ten largest war
machines. There is a combined 6:1 ratio of soldiers to doctors. The
social costs of arms spending are horrendous.

It would be to the great advantage of both countries if the billions
spent on nuclear weapons were used to build schools, universities, and

---

*Shireen M. Mazari, "US Yearns for Pak Capitulation," *News* (Islamabad), March 8, 2008.

hospitals and to provide clean water in the villages. Rationality, alas, is the first victim when these two countries quarrel. During the military skirmishes in the snow deserts of Kargil, nuclear threats were exchanged by both states on thirteen separate occasions within three months. This was followed by new terrorist attacks in India. Pakistan denied any responsibility, but New Delhi was unconvinced.

On December 13, 2001, five suicide terrorists armed with automatic rifles, grenades, and explosives killed nine people and wounded two dozen others before being killed themselves in a forty-five-minute battle with security forces outside the Indian parliamentary building. Mercifully parliament wasn't in session that day. Had Indian politicians been killed in the attack, another war between the two states would have been a near certainty.

The Indian home minister, L. K. Advani, a leader of the Hindu-chauvinist Bharatiya Janata Party (BJP), which was then in power, pointed the finger at two well-known Islamist terror groups—Jaish-e-Mohammed and Lashkar-e-Taiba—created and backed by Pakistan's Inter-Services Intelligence. He described what had taken place as the "most alarming act of terrorism in the history of two decades of Pakistan-sponsored terrorism in India. . . . The terrorists and their mentors . . . [wanted] to wipe out the entire political leadership of India." This was clearly an invitation to a military response, and it led to an intense and sharp debate within the Indian elite as to whether they should hit back with a surgical strike on training camps in Pakistani-controlled Kashmir. In the end, thankfully, they decided not to do so.

The groups that attacked the Indian parliament were not only targeting India. Their aim was evidently to provoke a conflict between the two countries. They despised Musharraf for betraying the cause and siding with Washington after 9/11. Their hatred for "Hindu" India was nothing new and had been enhanced by BJP rule in that country. The tragedy is that they came so close to inciting a war. Senior Indian strategists argued that if the United States could bomb a country and change its government while searching for terrorists who ordered the hits on the Pentagon, why could India not do the same? The logic was impeccable, but the outcome could have been a catastrophe of massive proportions. Pakistan's rulers responded with a nuclear threat: if their country's sovereignty was threatened, they would not hesitate to use nuclear weapons. An ugly chill gripped the atmosphere.

Washington sought to reassure India. Simultaneously, it pressured Islamabad to shift rapidly into reverse gear. On January 12, 2002, Musharraf made a landmark speech. He offered India a no-war pact, denuclearization of South Asia, closure of the jihadi training camps in Pakistan, and a total transformation of Indo-Pak relations. While hard-line fundamentalist newspapers attacked him, the country remained calm. Not a bird twittered, not a dog barked. So much for the view that ordinary Pakistanis are obsessed with the "Islamic bomb." Pakistan's nuclear capacity had often been used by the jihadi groups as a guarantee of their untouchability. No longer. A positive response from India was vital and could have altered the entire political landscape to the benefit of both countries. But India refused to budge. Its spokesmen continued to mouth platitudes but insisted on "minimum nuclear deterrence" and refused the offer of a no-war pact.

By rejecting Pakistan's denuclearization offer, the Indian government exposed the hollowness of its professed commitment to nuclear disarmament. The folly was compounded by the test-firing of a new Agni missile on the eve of the Republic Day celebrations on January 26, 2002. Apart from being an irresponsible and provocative gesture, the test was a reaffirmation of New Delhi's resolve to proceed with nuclear armaments.

The advocates of a short sharp war against Pakistan are largely confined to the well-off, urban middle classes in India. The poor, in the main, do not favor conflict. They know the dangers it would create inside India with its 200 million Muslims. They know that wars don't come cheap and that they would bear the brunt of the suffering. Three hundred million Indians already live below the poverty line.

Even among the gung ho middle classes the desire for a war would fade were they faced with conscription and required to fight themselves. Unlike bin Laden's followers, these are armchair fundamentalists.

Meanwhile, the Pakistani and Indian armies are on full alert and confront each other across a mine-strewn border. The mines are especially concentrated in cultivated farmlands near the international border and the Line of Control in Kashmir. The local villagers will suffer the consequences for years to come. Already there have been numerous civilian casualties.

New Delhi sees itself as a potential world power. It craves a seat on the UN Security Council. It argues that if small European countries such as Britain and France can possess nuclear weapons, then why not India? The simplest response would be to extend nuclear disarmament and for Europe to initiate the process. The West seems unlikely to oblige. The U.S. military budget remains inflated and accounts for one-half of the world's expenditure on armaments. The old enemy no longer exists, but the Cold War scenarios remain in place. U.S. military planners continue to target Russia and China. The latest wave of NATO expansion that both preceded and followed the war in Yugoslavia hardened Russian opposition to nuclear disarmament. When NATO patrols the Black Sea, what price the "Partnership for Peace"?

Herein lies the crux of the problem. Unless the West begins nuclear disarmament, it has no moral or material basis on which to demand that others do the same. Only a twisted logic accepts that London and Paris can have the bomb, but New Delhi and Islamabad cannot. India and Pakistan are only too aware that nuclear rain and radiation are no respecters of frontiers. It is unlikely that they would resort to first use of these weapons, but that is not sufficient reassurance for the citizens of either country.

While Pakistan's principal preoccupation remains India, its senior partners in Washington have been trying hard to shift Islamabad's focus to the western frontier. This has briefly been discussed in an earlier chapter, but the impact of U.S.-occupied Afghanistan on Pakistan is such that it necessitates a more detailed mapping of the new turbulence afflicting the region.

9

OPERATION ENDURING FREEDOM
Mirage of the "Good" War

THE BUSH-CHENEY ERA IS DRAWING TO A CLOSE, BUT THEIR replacements, despite the debacle in Iraq, are unlikely to settle the American giant back to a digestive sleep. The leitmotif of Cheney's foreign policy was "either you're for us or for terrorism against us." The application of this line meant isolating, intimidating, or invading individual states that did not accept shelter under the U.S. umbrella.

In 2004, as the chaos in Iraq deepened, the war in Afghanistan became the "good war" by comparison. It had been legitimized by the UN—even if the resolution was not passed until after the bombs had finished falling—and backed by NATO. If tactical differences had sharpened over Iraq, they could be resolved in Afghanistan. First Zapatero in Spain, then Prodi in Italy, and most recently Rudd in Australia compensated for pulling troops out from Iraq by dispatching them to Kabul.* France and Germany could extol their peacekeeping or civilizing roles there. For the Scandinavians it became a feel-good war.

---

*Visiting Madrid, after Zapatero's election triumph of March 2008, I was informed by a senior government official that they had considered a total withdrawal from Afghanistan a few months before the elections but had been outmaneuvered by a U.S. promise to Spain that the head of its military was being proposed for commander of the NATO forces and a withdrawal from Kabul would disrupt this possibility. Spain drew back only to discover that they had been tricked.

Meanwhile, the number of Afghani civilians killed has exceeded nearly a hundredfold the 2,746 who died in Manhattan. Unemployment is around 60 percent, and maternal, infant, and child mortality levels are now the highest in the world. Opium production has soared, and the "Neo-Taliban" is growing stronger year by year. A CIA assessment of late 2006 painted a somber picture of Karzai and his regime as hopelessly corrupt and incapable of defending Afghanistan against the Taliban.* Increasingly Western commentators have evoked the specter of failure—usually to spur *encore un effort*. But all those who supported the folly must share the misfortune.

TWO PRINCIPAL ARGUMENTS, often overlapping, are put forward as to "what went wrong" in Afghanistan. For liberal interventionists, the answer can be summarized in two words: "not enough."† The invasion organized by Bush, Cheney, and Rumsfeld was done "on the cheap." The "light footprint" demanded by the Pentagon meant that too few troops were on the ground in 2001–2. Financial commitment to "nation-building" was insufficient. Though it may now be too late, the answer is to pour in more troops, more money—"multiple billions" over "many years," according to the U.S. ambassador in Kabul.‡ The second answer to what has gone wrong—advanced by Karzai, the White House, but also the Western media generally—can be summed up in one word: Pakistan. Neither of these arguments holds water.

As suicide bombings increased in Baghdad, Afghanistan became—for American Democrats keen to prove their "security" credentials—the "real front" of the war on terror, supported by every U.S. presidential candidate in the run-up to the 2008 elections, with Senator Barack Obama pressuring the White House to violate Pakistani sovereignty

---

*"C.I.A. Review Highlights Afghan Leader's Woes," *New York Times,* November 5, 2006.

†See inter alia "The Good War, Still to Be Won," *New York Times,* August 20, 2007; "Gates, Truth and Afghanistan," *New York Times,* February 12, 2008; Francis Fukuyama, ed., *Nation-Building: Beyond Afghanistan and Iraq* (Baltimore: 2006); and successive International Crisis Group reports.

‡*New York Times,* November 5, 2006.

whenever necessary. On March 15, 2007, for instance, Obama told
NBC, "If you look at what's happening in Afghanistan now, you are seeing the Taliban resurgent, you are seeing Al Qaeda strengthen itself. We
have not followed through on the good starts we made in Afghanistan,
partly because we took so many resources out and put them in Iraq. I
think it is very important for us to begin a planned redeployment from
Iraq, including targeting Afghanistan." A few months later on August 1,
with the Stars and Stripes providing a suitable backdrop, he addressed
the Woodrow Wilson Center in Washington and made it clear that if
necessary he would authorize U.S. troops to enter Pakistan on search-
and-destroy missions: "Let me make this clear. There are terrorists holed
up in those mountains who murdered three thousand Americans. They
are plotting to strike again. It was a terrible mistake to fail to act when
we had a chance to take out an Al Qaeda leadership meeting in 2005.
If we have actionable intelligence about high-value terrorist targets and
President Musharraf won't act, we will."

His embittered rival, Senator Hillary Clinton, was not going to let
him get away with this too easily. One of her staunchest supporters,
Senator Chris Dodd of Connecticut, rebuked Obama the same day (as
did the White House) and said, "It is dangerous and irresponsible to
leave even the impression that the United States would needlessly and
publicly provoke a nuclear power." A week later, during a Democratic presidential debate, Hillary Clinton rapped her rival on the knuck-
les while raising the specter of a jihadi finger on Pakistan's nuclear
trigger:

> Well, I do not believe people running for president should engage
> in hypotheticals, and it may well be that the strategy we have to pur-
> sue on the basis of actionable intelligence—but remember, we've
> had some real difficult experience with actionable intelligence. . . .
> But I think it is a very big mistake to telegraph that and to destabi-
> lize the Musharraf regime, which is fighting for its life against
> Islamic extremists, who are in bed with Al Qaeda and Taliban. And
> remember, Pakistan has nuclear weapons. The last thing we want is
> to have Al Qaeda–like followers in charge of Pakistan and having
> access to nuclear weapons. So, you can think big, but remember,

you shouldn't always say everything you think if you're running for president because it can have consequences across the world, and we don't need that right now.

With varying degrees of firmness, the occupation of Afghanistan is also supported by China, Iran, and Russia, though in the case of the latter, there was always a strong element of schadenfreude. Soviet veterans of the Afghan war were amazed to see their mistakes now being repeated by the United States, despite attempts to portray this as the ultimate humanitarian conflict. This did not prevent Russian veterans, especially helicopter pilots, from offering themselves as mercenaries in Afghanistan. Over two dozen are currently engaged in action over a terrain they know well.

Soon after its launching, the NATO war on Afghanistan was referred to—including by Cherie Blair and Laura Bush—as a "war to liberate the women of Afghanistan." Had this been true, it would have been a pathbreaking conflict: the first imperial war in human history to liberate women. But it wasn't true. This became obvious even before the harsh realities of the location had dispelled the haze of spin, intended in any case for the children-citizens at home to make them feel good about bombing another foreign land (though this did not convince Jenna Bush, who confided to Daniel Pearl's widow that she was opposed to the bombing of Afghanistan). And the latest reports from Afghan women's organizations paint a grim picture of the condition of women in NATO-occupied Afghanistan. They fared much better during the Russian period.

HISTORICALLY, ATTEMPTS by the more enlightened sections of the Afghan elite to improve the condition of the country were regularly sabotaged by the British Empire. Since the nineteenth century, all political and administrative power in Afghanistan as well as virtually all the land was under the control of the king, his nobles, and a mosaic of tribal chiefs. The king was seen as the symbol of Afghan unity and responsible for relations with foreign powers, but his effective authority was limited to the Pashtun region of the country. Most of the population were peasants and herdsmen, with artisans and traders, merchants and craftsmen concentrated in the old medieval towns that included Herat, Ghazni, Kandahar, and Kabul.

The two nineteenth-century British attempts to occupy the country ended in partial failure. After the retreat of the second expeditionary force in 1893, the British took over the country's foreign policy while agreeing to its status as a buffer state between British India and czarist Russia. This was accompanied by a further weakening of the buffer as the British divided the Pashtun tribes and their lands by drawing the Durand Line through the mountains as their semipermanent frontier with Afghanistan. The purpose of this was to weaken the Pashtun tribes and thus reduce their political potential, but also to make British India impregnable. Imposed by force, the treaty was meant to last a hundred years, after which the border would no longer exist and the lands would revert to Afghanistan, though this interpretation is, unsurprisingly, disputed by Pakistan.

During the twentieth century outside influences were indirect, as in the impact of the Russian and Kemalist revolutions after the collapse of czarism and the Ottoman Empire, respectively. In the second decade of the last century, a reforming monarch, Amanullah, proposed a constitution that included an elected parliament and the right of women to vote. The British imported T. E. Lawrence "of Arabia" to help organize a tribal revolt and topple the monarch. The propaganda campaign mounted by the British to convince tribal conservatives included doctored photographs of the Afghan queen, a proto-feminist, in a swimming costume.

Stagnation continued after the Second World War, and few considered the possibility of a republic, let alone a more radical outcome. Zahir Shah, the last king of Afghanistan, was a mild nationalist but with an intense dislike of the British Empire and had, for that reason, maintained friendly relations with Mussolini and the Third Reich till 1945.

When Zahir Shah, less of a despot than those who succeeded him, was removed in a palace coup by his cousin Daud in 1973 and exiled to the Italian Riviera, most observers agreed that the country had made surprisingly little progress over the preceding 150 years. Its rentier economy and landlocked status had made it heavily dependent on aid,

with a huge gulf between the wealthy elite and the bulk of the population. The modern world barely intruded even in the cities, with the
exception of Kabul. Five years later, Daud too was overthrown by his
erstwhile allies in a Communist-led coup d'état, thus ending the rule
of the Durranis. This regime too imploded. In 1979, to prevent its collapse, the Soviet Union sent the Red Army across the border to try to
save a crumbling and isolated regime. It was obvious at the time that
the entry of Soviet troops would bring a horrific counterreaction and
wreck the region for decades. Few, however, foresaw the speed with
which a once valued U.S. ally would be transformed into an unspeak-
able antagonist, creating mayhem in neighboring Pakistan, a country
that was vital to the whole operation in the first place, as it is again
today.

When the bombing began in October 2001, I argued the following
scenario:

> . . . the Taliban are effectively encircled and isolated. Their defeat is
> inevitable. Both Pakistan and Iran are ranged against them on two
> important borders. It is unlikely they will last more than a few
> weeks. Obviously some of their forces will go to the mountains and
> wait till the west withdraws before attacking the new regime, likely
> to be installed in Kabul when the octogenarian King Zahir Shah is
> moved from his comfortable Roman villa to less salubrious sur-
> roundings in the wreckage of Kabul.
>
> The Northern Alliance backed by the west is marginally less reli-
> gious than the Taliban, but its record on everything else is just as
> abysmal. Over the last year they have taken over the marketing of
> heroin on a large scale, making a mockery of Blair's claim that this
> war is also a war against drugs.
>
> The notion that they would represent an advance on the Taliban
> is laughable. Their first instinct will be revenge against their oppo-
> nents. However the Alliance has been weakened in recent days by
> the defection of Gulbuddin Hekmatyar, once the favourite "free-
> dom fighter" of the west, welcomed in the White House and Down-
> ing Street by Reagan and Thatcher.
>
> This man has now decided to back the Taliban against the infi-

del. Sustaining a new client state in Afghanistan will not be an easy affair given local and regional rivalries. General Musharraf has already told Pakistanis he will not accept a regime dominated by the Northern Alliance. This is hardly surprising since his army has been fighting the Alliance for over a decade.

Till now the Pakistan army (unlike its Arab counterparts) has avoided a coup mounted by captains and colonels. It has always been the generals who have seized power and kept the army united, largely by sharing out the pieces of silver.

It is an open question whether that will be enough on this occasion. A lot will depend on the aftermath of the current war. A major concern for the overwhelming majority of Pakistanis is that the Taliban, cornered and defeated in their own country, will turn on Pakistan and wreak havoc on its cities and social fabric. Peshawar, Quetta, Lahore and Karachi are especially vulnerable. By that time the west, having scored a "victory," will turn a blind eye to the mess left behind.

As for the supposed aim of this operation—the capture of Bin Laden—this is unlikely to be easy. He is well-protected in the remote Pamir mountains and might well disappear. But victory will still be proclaimed. The west will rely on the short memory of its citizens. But let us even suppose that Bin Laden is captured and killed. How will this help the "war against terrorism"? Other individuals will decide to mimic the events of September 11 in different ways.*

At that time the entire leadership of the Western world, with hardly an exception, was convinced that the bombing and occupation were right and necessary. That the "good war" has now turned bad is no longer disputed by the more knowledgeable analysts. There is, however, no agreed prescription for dealing with the problems, not least of which, for some, is the future of NATO, stranded far away from the Atlantic in a mountain fastness, whose people, after offering a small window of opportunity to the occupiers, realized it was a mistake and

---

*"Into Pakistan's Maelstrom," *Guardian,* October 10, 2001.

became stubbornly hostile to the occupation. As early as 2003, a special report commissioned by the U.S. Council on Foreign Relations painted a gloomy picture:

> Nineteen months after the defeat of the Taliban and its al-Qaeda allies, Afghanistan remains a long way from achieving the U.S. goal of a stable self-governing state that no longer serves as a haven for terrorists. Indeed, failure to stem deteriorating security conditions and to spur economic reconstruction could lead to a reversion to warlord-dominated anarchy and mark a major defeat for the U.S. war on terrorism. To prevent this from happening, the Task Force recommends that the United States strengthen the hand of President Hamid Karzai and intensify support for security, diplomatic, and economic reconstruction in Afghanistan. Although Karzai is trying to assert his authority outside Kabul, he lacks the means to compel compliance by recalcitrant warlords and regional leaders who control most of the countryside. Current policy for the 9,000 U.S. troops in Afghanistan rules out support for Karzai against the regional warlords and also active participation in the planned effort to demobilize the 100,000-strong militias. In the Afghan setting, where the United States has the primary military power, this approach is mistaken and leaves a dangerous security void outside Kabul, where the 4,800-strong International Security Assistance Force (ISAF) maintains the peace.

Five years later, on February 28, 2008, Admiral Michael McConnell, director of national intelligence, a firm supporter of Vice President Cheney, informed the Senate Armed Services Committee that U.S.-supported Hamid Karzai controlled under a third of Afghanistan and the Taliban controlled 11 percent and had a presence virtually everywhere. Asked whether the insurgency had been contained, the admiral could offer little solace: "I wouldn't say it's been contained. It's been sustained in the south; it's grown a bit in the east and the north." Given the extent of the crisis, can the United States afford to enlarge the scale and transform the style of Operation Enduring Freedom?

They certainly seem to think so at Fort Riley in Kansas, where selected U.S. troops and thirty-one Afghan soldiers were training in March 2008. The Afghans were present to help U.S. soldiers imbibe "cultural sensitivity." The Voice of America reported, "The training takes place in a mock Afghan village complete with so-called enactors, usually Afghan-Americans, who play the role of villagers and combatants. Soldiers must safely enter the village, locate the house of the insurgents and enter without harming any of the civilians who wander the streets nearby. . . . Lieutenant Colonel John Nagi, one of the authors of the U.S. military handbook on counterinsurgency, says gaining a better understanding of the Afghan people is a key factor in defeating Al Qaeda and the Taliban."*

But what if the Afghan people obstinately refuse to accept that a foreign occupation is in their interests and continue to help those resisting it? This elementary question tends to escape counterinsurgency experts, but should occupy minds in the Pentagon.

The initial war aim appeared to be limited to the capture of Osama bin Laden, dead or alive, and the destruction of Al Qaeda bases in Afghanistan. There was no deep hostility in the West to the Taliban regime prior to 9/11. Even immediately afterward it was made clear to Pakistan that if the Al Qaeda leaders were handed over, the regime could stay. Mullah Omar refused to hand over bin Laden on the grounds that he was a guest and no proof was available linking him to the attacks on the United States. Omar was, however, as *The 9/11 Commission Report* makes clear, prepared to carry on negotiations with the United States. The National Security Council had been toying with the idea of using 9/11 to invade Iraq, but Omar's refusal to capitulate immediately left the NSC with little option but to concentrate on Afghanistan. An avalanche of fear, hatred, and revenge now descended on the country. With Pakistan officially committed to the U.S. side, the Taliban regime in Kabul fell without a serious struggle. The reason so many zealots of the cause disbanded so rapidly was obvious. Pakistan forbade any frontal confrontation and, despite some ISI defections, got its way. The more recalcitrant Mullah Omar faction decided, of their own accord, to evac-

---

*Greg Flakus, "Afghan Soldiers Train at U.S. Army Base," Voice of America, March 25, 2008.

uate to the mountains and bide their time. This was why Kabul fell without a fight, the Northern Alliance heroes entering the town soon after the BBC's war correspondent.

Pakistan's key role in securing this "victory" was underplayed in the Western media. The public was told that elite Special Forces units and CIA "specialists" had liberated Afghanistan, and having triumphed here, they could now be sent on to Iraq. It was a gross miscalculation on every level. Once the situation began to unravel and could no longer be concealed, former U.S. ambassadors began to speak publicly of a lack of resources, not enough money and not enough soldiers. "We're tough, we're determined, we're relentless," the U.S. president informed the world in April 2002. "We will stay until the mission is done."

That same month a wave of new refugees fled from the terror of history and most of the Taliban middle cadres crossed the border into Pakistan to regroup and plan for what lay ahead. Zalmay Khalilzad, the Afghan-American proconsul in Afghanistan, now began the hard task of assembling a new government. It was impossible to transplant a whole generation of Americans (or Afghan-Americans) to run the country as the old colonial powers had done. Even then they had required local allies. Khalilzad knew that the United States could not run the country without the Northern Alliance, and he toned down the emancipatory rhetoric that had been used to justify the occupation.

The coalition constructed by Khalilzad was intended as an octopus with Karzai as its eye. Militias of rival groups, united only by opposition to the toppled Taliban, occupied Kabul, and their representatives had to be accommodated on every level. In these conditions it was difficult to install a surrogate regime. Meanwhile, U.S. forces stationed themselves in former Soviet bases and the prisons once again began to echo with the screams of tortured victims. The "Chicago boys" had brought the peace of the graveyard to Pinochet's Chile, the "Berkeley mafia" had injected "macroeconomic stability" in Suharto's Indonesia. Could the swarm of NGO locusts descending on Kabul pull off something similar in Afghanistan? Both Pinochet and Suharto had drowned the opposition in blood, with almost a million corpses in Indonesia. Afghanistan could not be subjugated in similar fashion, both because of its more "primitive" social structure based on tribal dominance and the institutionalized decentralization represented by the Northern Alliance. The chaos encountered in Afghanistan was closer to the Somalian debacle of 1993.

The Taliban regime had been a "purer" model of the Wahhabi state in Saudi Arabia. Repressive and cruel, it had nonetheless restored order in a country racked by foreign and civil wars since 1979. According to virtually every source, the rape that had been endemic in the country was ended with the public execution of rapists, though an overruled radical-feminist wing of the Taliban had suggested that castration would be sufficient punishment. Attempts were also being made to reduce the heroin output, with some success. On the economic front, Wahhabi Islam is perfectly at home with the neoliberal dispensation that rules the world. Koranic literalists can find passages in favor of free trade, and the Taliban delegation received full honors when they visited UNOCAL (now part of Chevron) headquarters in Texas. On December 17, 1997, the London *Daily Telegraph* headlined, "Oil Barons Court Taliban in Texas," and informed its readers that the bearded visitors were prepared to sign a "£2 billion contract with an American oil company to build a pipeline across the war-torn country" and, then more mysteriously noted, "The Islamic warriors appear to have been persuaded to close the deal, not through delicate negotiation but by old-fashioned Texan hospitality. . . . Dressed in traditional *salwar kameez*, Afghan waistcoats and loose, black turbans, the high-ranking delegation was given VIP treatment during the four-day stay." A deal was a deal regardless of sartorial differences, and the few images recording this event were later immortalized in Michael Moore's *Fahrenheit 9/11*. The pipeline project was delayed not so much by Taliban doubts, but by rival offers emanating from Russia and supported by Tehran. Despite this, the U.S. oil company was confident of its success, and a final deal was close to being stitched when the planes hit the Twin Towers.

What many Afghans now expected from a successor government was a similar level of order, without the repression and social restrictions, and a freeing of the country's spirit. What they were instead presented with was a melancholy spectacle that blasted all their hopes.

The problem was not a lack of funds but the Western state-building project itself. By its nature a top-down process, it aims to construct an army constituted not to defend the nation but to impose order on its own people, on behalf of outside powers; a civil administration that will have no control over planning, health, education, etc., all of which will be run by NGOs whose employees will be far better paid than the locals, and answerable not to the population but to their overseas sponsors; and a government whose foreign policy is identical to Washington's. In September 2006, a German correspondent in Kabul sent a dispatch home in which she explained the reasons for local hostility to the West and why so many Afghans were joining the resistance. The contrast between the wealth displayed by the occupiers, including corporate expense accounts that charged the cost of prostitutes to their firms, and the poverty of most Afghans created resentment and anger. Add to this the weekend partying in Kabul:

> Now hordes of Westerners are chauffeured to the ministries of a morning, and picked up in air-conditioned vehicles of an afternoon. The foreigners have brought new customs to the capital as well; jeans are now on sale, although many women still walk the streets in burkas. Every Thursday, before the Afghan weekend starts, UNHAS—the UN air service that transports embassy and aid organization employees around the country—registers a miraculous spike in passengers to Kabul from the provinces: It's party time! And the revelry behind the façades of the capital's aging mansions is as riotous as anything to be found in Berlin or New York.
>
> At a French shipping company's toga bash, men donned fake laurel wreaths, bared their torsos, wrapped themselves in sheets and pranced around like Roman emperors. At the garden party arranged by an international consulting firm, hundreds of foreigners whooped it up until the wee hours, dancing amid a decorative backdrop of camels.*

It is amazing colonial arrogance to fail to notice that an occupied country is no longer sovereign, even if the occupation has been legally

---

*Susanne Koelbl, "The Wild East," *Der Spiegel,* September 29, 2006.

sanctioned by the United Nations Security Council. How can any government in these conditions be considered legitimate?

The Bonn Conference organized two months after the occupation, from November 27 to December 5, 2001, could not discuss this central issue and instead became bogged down with power-sharing arrangements. Joschka Fischer, the German foreign minister, ignorant of the realities on the ground, pressed for a federal solution on the German model to neutralize separatist attractions, but this was not a problem. The contentious issue was who exercised power and where. To concentrate Western minds, components of the Northern Alliance organized at least three different coup attempts to topple Karzai in 2002–3. They were obstructed by NATO, providing a vivid illustration of both sovereignty and legitimacy to the population at large.

The reality on the ground was clear enough. After the fall of the Taliban government, four major armed groups reemerged as strong regional players. In the gas-rich and more industrialized north, bordering the Central Asian republics of Uzbekistan and Tajikistan, with his capital in Mazar-i-Sharif, the Uzbek warlord Rashid Dostum was in charge. Allied first to the Communists, later to the Taliban, and most recently NATO, General Dostum had reportedly demonstrated his latest loyalty by massacring hundreds of Taliban and Arab prisoners.

Not far from Dostum, in the mountainous northeast of the country, a region rich in emeralds, lapis lazuli, and opium, the late Ahmed Shah Massoud built his fighting organization of Tajiks, who regularly ambushed troops on the Salang Highway, which linked Kabul to Tashkent during the Soviet occupation. The most dynamic, if overpraised, guerrilla leader of the anti-Taliban groups, Massoud hailed from Panjshir province. During the anti-Russian war he had become a favorite pinup in Paris, usually portrayed as a rugged romantic, a Muslim, an anticommunist Che Guevara, a man of the people. His membership in the Jamaat-e-Islami, led by Burhanuddin Rabbani, and his own reactionary views on most social issues were barely mentioned. These were tiny defects at a time when Islamic groups were considered staunch allies of the West.

Had Massoud not been killed by a suicide bomber two days before 9/11, he would have been the most obvious candidate to head a post-

Taliban government. The French government issued a postage stamp
with his portrait, and NATO named Kabul airport after him. But Massoud could never have been as reliable a client as the transplanted
Hamid Karzai, and it is an open question whether the indigenous guerrilla leader would have accepted a lengthy foreign occupation or agreed
to permanent U.S. military bases in the country. He had been the leader
of the armed wing of Burhanuddin Rabbani's Islamist group, which
operated in tandem with an allied Islamist leader, Abdul Rasul Sayyaf.
Both men were lecturers in Sharia, or Islamic law, on the faculty at
Kabul University in 1973. Their movements were incubated and, until
1993, funded by Saudi Arabia, after which the latter gradually shifted
its support to the Taliban. Massoud maintained a semi-independence
during the Taliban period. To his supporters in the West he had presented an image of pure, incorruptible masculinity. It was not the same
at home. Rape and the heroin trade were not uncommon in areas under
his control. His supporters are currently in the government, but not as
reliable as Karzai, which worries NATO.

On the west, sheltered by neighboring Iran, lies the ancient city of
Herat, once a center of learning and culture where poets, artists, and
scholars flourished. Here, for over three centuries, important books
were written and illustrated, including the fifteenth-century classic
Miraj-nameh, an early medieval Islamic account of the Prophet's ascent
to heaven from the Dome of the Rock and the punishments he
observed as he passed through hell. Some European scholars maintain
that a Latin translation of this work inspired Dante. The book has
sixty-one paintings in all, created with great love for the Prophet of
Islam. He is depicted with Central Asian features and seen flying to
heaven on a magical steed, which has a woman's head. There are also
illustrations of a meeting with Gabriel and Adam, a sighting of houris
at the gates of paradise, and renderings of wine bibbers being punished
in hell. These stunning illustrations are accompanied by the exquisite
calligraphy of Malik Bakshi in the Uighur script.

The sophisticated culture required to produce such a work is a far
cry from modern Herat and its outlying regions, where the Shia warlord Ismail Khan today holds sway and where the majority of Hazaras
live. A former army captain inspired by the Islamic revolution in neigh-

boring Iran, Ismail achieved instant fame by leading a garrison revolt against the pro-Moscow regime in 1979. Backed by Tehran, he built up a strong force that united all the Shia groups and was to trouble the Russians throughout their stay. Tens of thousands of refugees from this region (where a Persian dialect is the spoken language) were given work, shelter, and training in Iran. From 1989 to 1992, the province was run on authoritarian lines. The harsh regime and Ismail Khan's half-witted effrontery began to alienate supporters. His high-tax and forced-conscription policies angered peasant families. When the Taliban took power in Kabul, support had already drained away from the warlord. Herat fell without a struggle. Ismail and his supporters quietly crossed the border to Iran, where they bided their time, to return in October 2001 under NATO cover.

Iran has certainly given covert support to the occupations of Iraq and Afghanistan, which removed their enemies from power. This proved more beneficial in Iraq, where pro-Iranian parties were given a large share in the Green Zone government. In Afghanistan the situation was different. Here the Tajiks make up 27 percent of the population; the Uzbeks and Hazaras, 8 and 7 percent respectively; and 54 percent of Afghans are Pashtuns, who live in the south and east of the country along the border with Pakistan. During the first Afghan war (1979–92) three militant Sunni groups acquired dominance, and soon after they took Kabul the tiny non-Muslim minority of Hindus and Sikhs, mainly shopkeepers and traders, were displaced. Some were killed. Ten thousand refugees fled to India. Gulbuddin Hekmatyar, an ISI asset, was provisioned by Pakistan and had been groomed by the Saudis to take over, but found himself confronted by Massoud and others. The jihad was long over and now the jihadis were at each other's throats. The brutal power struggle wrecked the country and had little to do with religion. They were, after all, all Muslims. Rather than matters of faith, what was at stake was control of the drug trade.

Meanwhile, serious problems confronted the occupying forces. The brutality of U.S. and British troops alienated the population, and talk of "victory" began to sound hollow to Afghan ears. By 2003–4 existing Taliban guerrilla factions were mounting serious resistance, attacking troop carriers, occasionally bringing down helicopters, and punishing collaborators. NATO retaliation resulted in extensive civilian casualties, leading to further disenchantment with the occupation. With some exceptions this was barely reported in the West. *Time* magazine became a serial offender (though it was by no means alone) by running unfiltered NATO spin, as typified by Tim McGirk's report of March 28, 2005, which summons every conceivable cliché to bang the drum for the official case:

> "The Taliban is a force in decline," says Major General Eric Olson, who conducted the U.S. military's counterinsurgency battle until last month. . . . The Taliban's fall has been a long time coming . . . what turned the tide? In a word, nation-building. . . . Last October's Presidential elections were crucial. . . . "It was a moral and psychological defeat for the Taliban," Olson told *Time*. . . . Now the Taliban is a busted flush. . . . Says Major Mike Myers, a spokesman for the U.S. forces in Kandahar, "The Taliban class of 2004 was smaller than the class of 2003." . . . In Kabul, Karzai is hoping that the Taliban are now demoralized enough to consider an amnesty. Soon, Karzai is expected to announce a "reconciliation" with all Taliban except Omar and his top commanders.

That this was pure propaganda must soon have become obvious to the editors of *Time*. Less than a year later, on February 26, 2006, an attempted assassination of Dick Cheney by the Taliban occurred while he was visiting the "secure" U.S. air base at Bagram (once an equally secure Soviet air base). Cheney's survival provoked some controversy on U.S. television when *Real Time* host Bill Maher expressed consternation that comments posted that same week on the Huffington Post website had been removed because "they expressed regret that the attack on Dick Cheney failed." Maher went on to say, "I have zero doubt that if Dick Cheney was not in power, people wouldn't be dying needlessly tomorrow. . . . I'm just saying if he did die, other people, more people would live. That's a fact." No European TV pundit would have dared to make this sort of comment in public. They were too cowed by the "war on terror."

Two U.S. soldiers and a mercenary ("contractor") died in the attack on Cheney, as did twenty other people working at the base. This episode alone should have focused the U.S. vice president's mind on the scale of the Afghan debacle. The casualty rates rose substantially in 2006 as NATO troops lost forty-six soldiers, shot down in helicopters or caught in clashes with what was now being referred to as the neo-Taliban. In the confrontation with their Afghan antagonists, the United States was facing a number of closely interrelated problems.

The first was the failure of "nation-building." Few tears were shed in Afghanistan and elsewhere when the Taliban fell, but the hopes aroused by Western demagogy did not last long. It soon became clear that the new transplanted elite would cream off a fair portion of the foreign aid and create its own criminal networks of graft and patronage. Then there were the NGOs. Even those sympathetic to the occupation had lost patience with these organizations. The Karzai government, of course, disliked them because it felt all the aid money should be channeled through the government. But disaffection with these organizations extended throughout the populace. In a state with hardly any stability, the notion of "civil society," which the NGOs were committed to building, had little appeal. In addition, the resources available to them provoked considerable resentment. "The NGOs," according to an experienced and well-versed U.S. academic, "brought scores of overpaid young people into their communities, where they flaunted their high salaries and new motor vehicles. Worse, their well-funded activities highlighted the poverty and ineffectiveness of the civil administration and discredited its local representatives in the eyes of the local populace."* Unsurprisingly, they began to be targeted by the insurgents and had to hire mercenary protection.

There are few signs that the $19 billion in "aid and reconstruction" money devoted to Afghanistan has served to ease the suffering of the majority of its people. The electricity supply is worse now than five years ago. As one commentator noted, "While foreigners and wealthy Afghans power air conditioners, hot-water heaters, computers and satellite televisions with private generators, average Kabulis suffered a sum-

---

*S. Frederick Starr, "Sovereignty and Legitimacy in Afghan Nation-Building," in Francis Fukuyama, ed., *Nation-Building: Beyond Afghanistan and Iraq* (Baltimore: 2006).

mer without fans and face a winter without heaters."* As a result, hundreds of homeless Afghans are literally freezing to death each winter.

Overall, "nation-building" in Afghanistan has so far produced only a puppet president dependent for his survival on foreign mercenaries, a corrupt and abusive police force, a "nonfunctioning" judiciary, a burgeoning criminal layer, and a deepening social and economic crisis. Even the West's own specialists and institutions concede much of this to be the case. It beggars belief to argue that more of the same will be the answer to Afghanistan's problems.

IN SEPTEMBER 2005, a quick-fix election was organized at high cost with the help of U.S. public relations firms. The lion's share of the profits was pocketed by the Rendon Group of Washington, D.C., which has received contracts worth millions of dollars. The elections were organized, at least partly, for the benefit of Western public opinion, but the realities on the ground soon overcame the temporary feel-good impact. NATO troops guarded polling booths in some areas and the Northern Alliance in others. There were widespread reports of coercion, and residents of Baghlan, Kapisa, and Herat provinces told reporters from the Pajhwok Afghan News agency that some polling agents, staff, and police officials had forced them to cast votes for particular candidates. Karzai had to vote in a special voting booth constructed inside the presidential palace.

The results failed to bolster support for NATO inside the country. While 12 million Afghan citizens were eligible to vote, just over 4 million did so. The violence preceding the elections symbolized the absurdity of the process. Though newly elected, President Karzai symbolized his own isolation, as well as an oft-tested instinct for self-preservation, by refusing to be guarded by a security detail from his own ethnic Pashtun base. He wanted and was given tough, Terminator-look-alike U.S. marines. They were later replaced by mercenaries or privatized soldiers.

In September 2006, exactly a year after the elections had been

---

*Barnett Rubin, "Saving Afghanistan," *Foreign Affairs*, January–February 2007, 8.

trumpeted as an enormous success in the Western media, an attempted bombing of the U.S. embassy came close to hitting its target. A CIA assessment that same month painted a somber picture, describing Karzai and his regime as hopelessly corrupt and incapable of defending Afghanistan against the Taliban. Ronald E. Neumann, the U.S. ambassador in Kabul, supported this view and told the *New York Times* that the United States faced "stark choices": a defeat could only be avoided through "multiple billions" over "multiple years."*

Like Neumann, others who still support the war in Afghanistan, which include the media and mainstream political parties throughout North America and Euroland, argue that more state-building on the style of postwar Japan and Western Europe would stabilize the country. Others argue that the model of imperial rule should follow the British style. Neither argument is tenable. Might Afghanistan have been secured with a limited Marshall Plan–style intervention, as is argued by numerous supporters of the war who blame the White House for not spending enough on social projects? It is, of course, possible that the construction of free schools and hospitals, subsidized homes for the poor, and the rebuilding of the social infrastructure that was destroyed after the withdrawal of Soviet troops in 1989 might have stabilized the country. But neither the United States nor their EU allies were seriously interested in such a project. It went against the grain of normal neocolonial policies. The Marshall Plan was a unique response to a severe crisis of confidence in a system that had been wrecked by a ferocious war. It was designed to secure Western Europe in the face of a supposed Communist threat. It was a special operation without precedent before or since: the first time in history that a victorious power (the United States) had helped to revive its economic rivals in order to confront a common enemy whose economic system was at the time perceived as a challenge. Afghanistan was an entirely different situation and was handled as a more traditional colonial operation. Mythmakers, often themselves British, suggested this be done on the British model of "good" imperialism rather than the crude and brutish variety

---

**New York Times, November 5, 2006.

of the Americans. This distinction was almost certainly lost on the benighted Afghans, who had long understood that while the British could be competent administrators, they were every bit as savage as their cousins across the Atlantic, a point demonstrated repeatedly throughout Africa, the Middle East, and India. Their record in assisting the development of the countries they occupied was equally bleak. In 1947, the year the British left India, 85 percent of India's economy was rural, and the overwhelming majority of midnight's children were illiterate. The colonial legacy was summarized crisply by the *Cambridge Economic History of India,* vol. 2, c. 1757–c. 1970:

> Capital formation (around 6 per cent of NDP) was inadequate to bring about rapid improvement in per capita income, which was about one-twentieth of the level then attained in developed countries. The average availability of food was not only deficient in quantity and quality, but, as recurrent famines underscored so painfully, also precarious. Illiteracy was a high 84 per cent and the majority (60 per cent) of children in the 6 to 11 age group did not attend school; mass communicable diseases (malaria, smallpox and cholera) were widespread and, in the absence of a good public health service and sanitation, mortality rates (27 per 1000) were very high. The problems of poverty, ignorance and disease were aggravated by the unequal distribution of resources between groups and regions.

Rory Stewart, who served as a colonial administrator in British-occupied southern Iraq, is angered by the stupidity of the occupiers in both Iraq and Afghanistan and not overimpressed by NGO civil-society imports to antique lands. He writes, for instance:

> Foreign policy experts will tell you that poor states lack the rule of law, a vibrant civil society, free media, a transparent civil service . . . employees of major international agencies commonly complain that Afghans or Iraqis or Kenyans "can't plan" or "can't implement."
>
> At its worst, this attitude is racist, bullying and ignorant. But there are less sinister explanations. As a diplomat, I was praised for

"realism" if I sent home critical telegrams. Now, working for a non-profit, I find that donor proposals encourage us to emphasize the negative aspects of local society. . . . Afghans and Iraqis are often genuinely courageous, charming, generous, inventive and honorable. Their social structures have survived centuries of poverty and foreign mischief and decades of war and oppression, and have enabled them to overcome almost unimaginable trauma. But to acknowledge this seems embarrassingly romantic or even patronizing.

Yet the only chance of rebuilding a nation like Iraq or Afghanistan in the face of insurgency or civil war is to identify, develop and use some of these traditional values. . . . This may be uncomfortable for the international community. A leader who can restore security, reconcile warring parties and shape the aspirations of a people may resemble an Ataturk more than a U.S. president. This is not a call for dictatorship. True progress must be sustained by the unconstrained wishes of the people. These should include, in Afghanistan, people with strong liberal values as much as conservative rural communities. These various desires must be protected from both the contorted control of an authoritarian state and the muffling effect of foreign aid.*

Stewart's writings have a touch of imperial romanticism, which might help him outlast many bitter disillusionments. A cool, philosophical frame of mind would immediately grasp that it is not aid alone that muffles but the imperial presence itself. It was always thus.

It is sometimes instructive to study history through the evolution of a city. Take Kabul, for instance, the site of numerous invasions and occupations over three thousand years, a few of them benign. Located in a valley, six thousand feet above sea level, it existed long before Christianity. Historically the city was at the crossroads of adjoining civilizations for countless centuries since it commanded the passes, as numerous conquerors starting with Alexander of Macedonia and followed by Sultan Mahmud, Genghis Khan, Babar, and those with less

*Rory Stewart, "The Value of Their Values," *New York Times*, March 7, 2007.

familiar names spent time here on their way to India. Babar loved this city and made it his capital for several years before marching southward. A passionate agriculturist, the founder of the Mogul dynasty, he supervised the irrigation of large tracts of land, planted orchards, and built gardens with artificial streams that made the summer heat and the dust-laden environment of the city more bearable.

The city was a triumph of medieval Mogul architecture. Ali Mardan Khan, a Mogul governor of the seventeenth century and a renowned architect and engineer specializing in public works, built a *char-chala* (four-sided) roofed and arcaded bazaar on the model of the markets that once existed, and occasionally still do, in a number of old Muslim cities, including Cairo, Damascus, Baghdad, Palermo, and Córdoba. It was regarded as unique in the region. Nothing on the same scale was built in Lahore or Delhi. This market was deliberately destroyed in 1842 by the Scottish general George Pollock's "Army of Retribution" (also remembered as among the worst killers, looters, and marauders ever to arrive in Afghanistan, a contest in which competition remains strong). Defeated in a number of cities and forced to evacuate Kabul, the British punished its citizens by removing the market from the map.

A century and a half later, soon after the withdrawal of the Russians, who had built their soulless, multistoried buildings to house their troops and other personnel outside the old city, the Afghan warlords and competing Islamic factions, now fighting each other, came close to destroying the city altogether. Jade Maiwand, a major shopping street that was cut through the center of the city in the 1970s, was reduced to rubble during the warfare of 1992–96. Ajmal Maiwandi, an Afghan-American architect, describes how Kabul has been transformed by history:

> The major destruction of Kabul occurred between 1992 and 1996 after the withdrawal of the Soviet Union in 1989 and the fall of Kabul to various warring factions in 1992. Throughout the war, the urban identity of Kabul was transformed continuously from a modern capital, to the military and political headquarters of an invading army, to the besieged seat of power of a puppet regime, to the frontlines of factional conflict resulting in the destruction of two-thirds of its urban mass, to the testing fields of religious fanaticism which

erased from the city the final layers of urban life, to the target of an international war on terrorism, to a secure gateway into Afghanistan for the internationally backed peace efforts, and presently, to a symbol of a new phase in international unilateralism.*

What Kabul will look like after NATO has left remains to be seen, but the large shantytown settlements that are springing up everywhere provide a clue. The city may well become a tourist attraction on the "planet of slums"[†] world tour.

Meanwhile architecture is far from the most important of the country's problems at the moment. The U.S. presence today is refracted largely through its military muscle, the air power lovingly referred to as "Big Daddy" by frightened, young U.S. soldiers on unwelcoming terrain, but which is far from paternal when it comes to discriminating between civilians and combatants. The real question is not so much Western arrogance, ugly though it is at the best of times, but what the alternative could be in a society where a Western intervention has unleashed similar opposition as have previous wars and occupations by the British and the Soviet Union. There is no simple solution, but what is clear is that an "international community" that thrives on double standards is seen by the population as part of the problem.[‡]

Profound difficulties are also to be found among the lucrative blooms in Afghanistan's luscious poppy fields. The NATO mission has made no serious attempt to bring about a significant reduction in the heroin trade. How could it? Karzai's own supporters, few in number though

---

*Dr. Ajmal Maiwandi, www.xs4all.nl/~jo/Maiwandi.html.

[†]Mike Davies, *Planet of Slums* (London and New York: 2006). This work is a brilliant account of how globalization is transforming our world.

[‡]A classic example of blindness and double standards was U.S. defense secretary Robert Gates's statement in Australia on February 24, 2008, when he was asked to comment on the entry of Turkish troops into Iraq to combat a Kurdish organization listed as "terrorist" by the "international community": "Our experiences in Iraq and Afghanistan show that military muscle should be complemented by efforts to address grievances held by minority groups. These economic and political measures are really important because after a certain point people become inured to military attacks. And if you don't blend them with these kinds of nonmilitary initiatives, then at a certain point the military efforts become less and less effective. . . . I would strongly urge Turkey to respect Iraq's sovereignty."

they are, would rapidly desert if any attempts were made to stop their trading activities. It would require massive state help to agriculture and cottage industries over many years to reduce the dependence on poppy farming. Ninety percent of the world's opium production is based in Afghanistan. UN estimates suggest that heroin accounts for 52 percent of the impoverished country's gross domestic product, and the opium sector of agriculture continues to grow apace. Indeed, these have been persistent allegations—just as persistently denied by their subject—that President Karzai's younger brother, Ahmad Wali Karzai, has become one of the richest drug barons in the country. At a meeting with Pakistan's president in 2006, when Karzai was bleating on about Pakistan's inability to stop cross-border smuggling, General Musharraf calmly suggested that perhaps Karzai should set an example by bringing his sibling under control. The hatred for each other of these two close allies of Washington is not a secret in this region.

Added to the opium problem are the corruptions of the elite, which grow each month like an untreated tumor. Western funds designed to aid reconstruction were siphoned off to build fancy homes for their native enforcers. As early as 2002, in a gigantic housing scandal, cabinet ministers awarded themselves and favored cronies prime real estate in Kabul. Land prices in the city had reached a high point after the occupation, when the occupiers, NGO employees, and their camp followers built large villas for themselves in full view of the poor.

Then there is, of course, the resistance. The "neo-Taliban" control at least twenty districts in Kandahar, Helmand, and Uruzgan provinces where NATO troops replaced U.S. soldiers. It is hardly a secret that many officials in these zones are closet supporters of the guerrilla fighters. The situation is out of control, as Western intelligence agencies active in the country are fully aware. When the occupation first began, Secretary of State Colin Powell explained that his model was Panama: "The strategy has to be to take charge of the whole country by military force, police, or other means." His knowledge of Afghanistan was clearly limited. Panama, populated by 3.5 million people, could not have been more different from Afghanistan, which has a population approaching 30 million and is geographically quite distinct. To even attempt a military occupation of the entire country would require a minimum of two hundred thousand troops. A total of eight thousand U.S. troops were dispatched to seal the victory; the four thousand "peacekeepers" sent by other countries rarely left Kabul or stationed themselves in more peaceful regions in the north of the country. The Germans concentrated on creating a police force, and the Italians, without any sense of irony, were busy "training an Afghan judiciary." The British, more hated by the Afghans than even the Americans, were in Helmand amid the poppy fields. Incapable of crushing the resistance, they tried to buy off the local resistance until this was vetoed by an enraged President Karzai.

Colin Powell's ignorance also extended to regional and ethnic complexities. During a closed meeting in Islamabad soon after the occupation, he openly failed to grasp the difference between ethnicity and ideology, happily equating Pashtun and Taliban. Khurshid Mahmood Kasuri, the Pakistan foreign minister, corrected the misapprehension by pointing out gently that two senior Foreign Office officials present at the meeting were Pashtuns, definitely not Taliban.

And lastly, while economic conditions failed to improve, NATO military strikes often targeted innocent civilians, leading to violent anti-American protests in the Afghan capital in 2006. What was initially viewed by some locals as a necessary police action against Al Qaeda following the 9/11 attacks is now perceived by a growing majority in the entire region as a full-fledged imperial occupation. The neo-Taliban is growing and creating new alliances not because its sectarian religious practices have become popular, but because it is the only available umbrella for national liberation. As the British and Russians discovered at a high cost in the preceding two centuries, Afghans never like being occupied.

The repression, striking blindly, leaves people with no option but to back those trying to resist, especially in a part of the world where the culture of revenge is strong. When a whole community feels threatened, it reinforces solidarity, regardless of the inadequacies of those who are fighting back. Many Afghans who detest the Taliban are so angered by the failures of NATO and the behavior of its troops that they will support any opposition. A related problem is the undisciplined nature of the mercenaries deployed to assist the NATO armies. They are not responsible to the military commanders, and even sympathetic observers admit that "their behavior, including alcohol consumption and the patronage of a growing number of brothels in Kabul (both very effectively prohibited to U.S. military personnel), is arousing public anger and resentment."* To this could be added numerous incidents of rape, unlawful killings of civilians, indiscriminate search-and-arrest missions, and the rough treatment of women by male soldiers. This has created a thirst for dignity that can be assuaged only by genuine independence.

The middle-cadre Taliban who fled across the border in November 2001 had regrouped and started low-level guerrilla activity by the following year, attracting a trickle of new recruits from madrassas and refugee camps in Pakistan. By 2003 the movement was starting to win active support in the mosques—first from village mullahs, in Zabul, Helmand, Ghazni, Paktika, and Kandahar, and then in the towns. From 2004 onward, increasing numbers of young Waziris were radicalized by the attacks by armed U.S. drones and Pakistani military and police incursions in the impoverished tribal areas. By 2006 there were reports of Kabul mullahs who had previously supported Karzai's allies but were now railing against the foreigners and the government; calls for jihad against the occupation were heard in the northeast border provinces of Takhar and Badakhshan.

But the largest pool of recruits, according to a well-informed recent estimate, has been "communities antagonized by the local authorities and security forces." In Kandahar, Helmand, and Uruzgan, Karzai's cronies—district and provincial governors, security and police chiefs— had enraged local people through harassment and extortion, if not by directing U.S. troops against them. In these circumstances, the Taliban were the only available defense. According to the same report, the Taliban themselves have claimed that families driven into refugee camps by indiscriminate U.S. airpower attacks on the villages have been the major source of recruits. By 2006 the movement was winning the support of traders and businessmen in Kandahar and led a mini "Tet offensive" there that year. One reason suggested for their increasing support

---

*Barnett R. Rubin, "Afghanistan: A U.S. Perspective," in *Crescent of Crisis,* ed. Ivo H. Daalder, Nicole Gnesotto, and Philip H. Gordon (Washington: 2006).

in towns is that the neo-Taliban have relaxed their strictures, for males at least—no longer demanding beards or banning music—and improved their propaganda (producing tapes and CDs of popular singers, and DVDs of U.S. and Israeli atrocities in Iraq, Lebanon, and Palestine).

The reemergence of the Taliban cannot therefore be blamed simply on Islamabad's failure to police the border or cut "command and control" links, as is sometimes claimed by Washington. While the ISI played a commanding role in the retreat of 2001, they no longer have the same degree of control over a more diffuse and widespread movement, for which the occupation itself has been the main recruiting sergeant. NATO's failure cannot therefore be blamed simply on the Pakistani government.

It is a traditional colonial ploy to blame "outsiders" for internal problems: Karzai specializes in this approach. If anything, the destabilization functions in the other direction: the war in Afghanistan has created a critical situation in two Pakistani frontier provinces. The Pashtun majority in Afghanistan has always had close links to its fellow Pashtuns in Pakistan. The present border was an imposition by the British Empire, but it has always remained porous. It is virtually impossible to build a Texan fence or an Israeli wall across the mountainous and largely unmarked twenty-five-hundred-kilometer border that separates the two countries. The solution is political, not military, and should be sought in the region, not in Washington or Brussels.

The cold winds of the Hindu Kush have, through the centuries, frozen both native reformer and foreign occupier. To succeed, a real peace process must be organically linked to the geography and ethnic composition of the country. Those who argue that all that is needed is to throw money at the Afghans to buy off the tribal elders, as the British used to do, have little idea of what is really happening on the ground. The resistance is assuming classical proportions. If one compares Elizabeth Rubin's graphic reports from Afghanistan in the *New York Times* with coverage from South Vietnam in the same newspaper forty years ago, remarkable similarities are apparent. Rubin, like David Halberstam in Vietnam, is alarmed by the high rate of civilian deaths caused by NATO: "The sheer tonnage of metal raining down on

Afghanistan was mind-boggling: a million pounds between January and September of 2007, compared with half-a-million in all of 2006." She later describes the war in Kunar province, where Afghan guerrillas maintain an astonishing level of attacks. American troops come under fire outside their own temporary headquarters:

> The bullets smacked the dirt in front of us. Kearney shoved me into a shack where an Afghan was cooking bread. A few more shots were fired. It was "One-Shot Freddy," as the soldiers refer to him, an insurgent shooter everyone had a theory about regarding the vintage of his gun, his identity, his tactics—but neither Kearney's scouts nor Shadow the drone could ever track him. I accidentally slashed my forearm on a nail in the shack and as I watched the blood pool I thought that if I had to live with Freddy and his ilk for months on end I, too, would see a forked tongue in every villager and start dreaming of revenge.*

Washington's strategic aims in Afghanistan can appear to be primarily focused these days on merely disciplining European allies who betrayed them in Iraq and testing others. In March 2008 the NATO secretary-general, Jaap Scheffer, was full of praise for the Croatians in Afghanistan: "The Croatian participation, and that goes for many other partners, is very important. One of the yardsticks . . . by which nations who are knocking on the door of NATO . . . are measured is are they willing to be a security exporter with us, not only a security consumer but also a security exporter? Croatia is clearly one of those nations who has a good track record of being a security exporter, and I'm happy to hear from my Montenegrin friend that Montenegro, I know that, is also in the process."

The Germans, still training the Afghan police force, would do well to consider whether the skills they are imparting to young Afghans in the "procedural elements of a transatlantic nation-building strategy" today will not be used against NATO tomorrow, as happens in Iraq

---

*Elizabeth Rubin, "Battle Company Is Out There," *New York Times,* February 24, 2008.

when newly minted soldiers, ordered to kill their own people, often desert to the other side.

Clearly the capture of the Al Qaeda leaders cannot be the main goal of the NATO occupiers. Even if the ISI located and handed the leaders over to Washington, NATO would not likely leave the country. To portray the invasion as a "war of self-defense" for NATO makes a mockery of international law, which was perverted to twist a flukishly successful attack by a tiny, terrorist Arab groupuscule into an excuse for an open-ended American military thrust into the Middle East and Central Asia.

Herein lie the reasons for the near unanimity among Western opinion makers that the occupation must not only continue but expand—"many billions over many years." The reasons are to be sought not in the mountain fastnesses of Afghanistan but in Washington and Brussels. As the *Economist* summarizes, "Defeat would be a body blow not only to the Afghans, but"—and more important, of course—"to the NATO alliance." As ever, geopolitics prevail over Afghan interests in the calculus of the big powers. The bases agreement signed by the United States with its appointee in Kabul in May 2005 gives the Pentagon the right to maintain a massive military presence in Afghanistan in perpetuity. That Washington is not seeking permanent bases in this fraught and inhospitable terrain simply for the sake of "democratization and good governance" was made clear by NATO's secretary-general Jaap Scheffer at the Brookings Institution in March 2008: the opportunity to site military facilities, and potentially nuclear missiles, in a country that borders China, Iran, and Central Asia was too good to miss.

More strategically, Afghanistan has become a central theater for uniting, and extending, the West's power, its political grip on the world order. On the one hand, it is argued, it provides an opportunity for the United States to shrug off its failures in imposing its will in Iraq and persuading its allies to play a broader role there. In contrast, as Obama and Clinton have stressed, America and its allies "have greater unity of purpose in Afghanistan. The ultimate outcome of NATO's effort to stabilize Afghanistan and U.S. leadership of that effort may well affect the cohesiveness of the alliance and Washington's ability to shape

NATO's future."* Beyond this, NATO strategists looking to the rise of China propose a vastly expanded role for the Western military alliance. Once focused on the Euro-Atlantic area, "in the 21st century NATO must become an alliance founded on the Euro-Atlantic area, designed to project systemic stability beyond its borders":

> The center of gravity of power on this planet is moving inexorably eastward. The Asia-Pacific region brings much that is dynamic and positive to this world, but as yet the rapid change therein is neither stable nor embedded in stable institutions. Until this is achieved, it is the strategic responsibility of Europeans and North Americans, and the institutions they have built, to lead the way . . . security effectiveness in such a world is impossible without both legitimacy and capability.†

The only way to protect the international system the West has built, the author continues, is to "reenergize" the transatlantic relationship: "There can be no systemic security without Asian security and there will be no Asian security without a strong role for the West therein."

At present these ambitions are still fantasies. In Afghanistan, angry street demonstrations occurred all over the country in protest of Karzai's signing the U.S. bases agreement—a clear indication, if one was still needed, that NATO will have to take Karzai with it if it withdraws.

Uzbekistan responded by asking the United States to withdraw its base and personnel from their country. The Russians and Chinese are reported to have protested strongly in private, and subsequently conducted joint military operations on each other's territory for the first time. "Concern over apparent U.S. plans for permanent bases in Afghanistan and Central Asia" was an important cause of their rapprochement. More limply, Iran responded by increasing export duties, bringing construction in Herat to a halt. In response to Karzai's pleas, Tehran proposed a treaty that would prohibit foreign intelligence oper-

---

*Paul Gallis, "NATO in Afghanistan," CRS Report for Congress, October 23, 2007.

†Julian Lindley-French, "Big World, Big Future, Big NATO," *NATO Review,* Winter 2005.

ations in each country against the other; hard to see how Karzai could have signed this with a straight face.

Washington's options are limited. The most favored solution, balkanization and the creation of ethnic protectorates, might not work in Afghanistan. The Kosovars and others in the former Yugoslavia were willing client-nationalists, but the Hazaras are perfectly happy with indirect Iranian protection, and Tehran does not favor partitioning Afghanistan. Nor do the Russians and their Central Asian allies, who sustain the Tajiks. Some U.S. intelligence officers have informally been discussing the creation of a Pashtun state that unites the tribes and dissolves the Durand Line, but this would destabilize Pakistan and Afghanistan to such a degree that the consequences would be unpredictable. In any event there appear to be no serious takers in either country at the moment.

If this is understood, then a second alternative, both preferable and more workable, becomes apparent. This would involve a withdrawal of all NATO forces either preceded or followed by a regional pact to ensure Afghan stability for the next ten years. Pakistan, Iran, India, Russia, and possibly China could guarantee and support a functioning national government pledged to preserving the ethnic and religious diversity of Afghanistan. A serious social and economic plan to rebuild the country and provide the basic necessities for its people would become a necessary prerequisite for stability.

This would not only be in the interests of Afghanistan, it would be seen as such by its people, exhausted by decades of endless war and two major foreign occupations. The NATO occupation has made such an arrangement much more difficult. Its predictable failure has revived the Taliban, uniting increasing numbers of poor Pashtuns under its umbrella. But a NATO withdrawal could facilitate a serious peace process. It might also benefit Pakistan, provided its military leaders abandoned foolish notions of "strategic depth" and viewed India not as an enemy but as a possible partner in creating a regional cohesion within whose framework many contentious issues could be resolved. Are Pakistan's military leaders and politicians capable of grasping the nettle and moving their country forward? Can they move out of the flight path of U.S. power?

In the meantime the instability in Afghanistan is seeping over the border into Pakistan. Even the secretary-general of NATO is beginning to understand the dangers inherent in this should it continue much longer. In a recent speech in Washington, Jaap Scheffer responded to a questioner by saying, "If instability in Pakistan and instability in the frontier means instability in Afghanistan, the opposite is also true. . . . We need to depart from the notion that Pakistan is not part of the solution, and we should not only brand Pakistan as part of the problem. . . . We have to do everything we can to assist and help the Pakistanis. . . . It's my intention that as soon as there is a new government in Pakistan, I intend to travel again to Islamabad to talk to the president, to talk to the government, to see how we can lift the level of our political dialogue in the interest of minimizing this cross-instability around the borderline there."

The new government in Pakistan inaugurated on March 26, 2008, has already made it clear that it intends to negotiate with the militants in Waziristan. John Negroponte and Richard A. Boucher, representing the U.S. State Department, were not warmly greeted when they arrived in Islamabad to meet Asif Zardari and Nawaz Sharif. The country's largest daily, the *News,* published an editorial, "Hands Off Please, Uncle Sam," that was extremely critical of U.S. interference in the country. Sharif too was surprisingly sharp, refusing to give Negroponte any guarantees or commitments on "fighting terrorism." Sharif told the press, "If America wants to see itself clean of terrorists, we also want that our villages and towns should not be bombed. We do not like the fact that our country is now a killing field. We will negotiate with the militants to try and stop all this." The problem for Pakistan's elected government is that without a settlement in Afghanistan, it will find it difficult to stabilize the tribal areas on its western frontier.

The insurgents in Afghanistan are growing more audacious every month. In June 2008, a guerrilla contingent on motorbikes attacked the prison in Kandahar and freed one thousand prisoners. An embarrassed Karzai immediately *blamed* Pakistan and threatened to cross the border and teach Islamabad a lesson.

In reality, the strategic needs of the United States are now destabilizing the region. What if the people of the region reject these imperial fantasies? Will they, like their states, also be dissolved and created anew?

10

CAN PAKISTAN BE RECYCLED?

IN FEBRUARY 2008, ONE OF AMERICA'S MOST VENERABLE THINK tanks, the Brookings Institution of Washington, D.C., organized an exercise in moral abstraction under the rubric "The U.S.-Pakistan Strategic Relationship." The panel at this event reflected the new pluralism, consisting largely of old friends. In this case, two military philosophers, General Anthony Zinni, onetime boss of U.S. CENTCOM, and General Jehangir Karamat, former chief of staff of the Pakistan army and onetime ambassador to Washington, flanked Richard Armitage, formerly of the State Department, who, as discussed earlier, gained enormous prestige in some quarters after 9/11 for threatening to reduce General Musharraf and Pakistan to the Stone Age. General Karamat, a decent and honorable empire-loyalist, who resisted temptation and never seized power in Pakistan, understood immediately what was expected of him on the Brookings platform. The strategic relationship was not about the inevitable strains in a sixty-year-old marriage, whose course and consequences I've attempted to outline in this book, but about the immediate needs of the United States, which have shaped Pakistani policy for decades.

"Ladies and gentlemen," began poor General Karamat, "the sort of questions that are being asked in terms of the U.S.-Pakistan relationship right now are what is really happening in Pakistan's western border areas, why is it happening, and what is Pakistan doing about it." He tried to explain as best he could that the situation was complex, Pak-

istan was not to blame for the expanding militancy and that the traditional tribal leaders had been virtually eliminated and replaced by militants. He warned gently against any attempt to erode Pakistan's
sovereignty because it would be counterproductive and concluded by
stressing the importance of the "strategic relationship that has a great
future."

General Zinni was at his patronizing worst. He knew the Pakistan
army well, he said. His first direct contact had been with a battalion
that fought in Somalia in the early nineties and had performed
extremely well in a difficult situation. He might have been General
Charles Gordon commending the courage of his Indian sepoys in helping to crush the Taiping rebellion in nineteenth-century China. Zinni
knew Karamat well and was pleased to inform the audience, "General
Karamat is a graduate of Leavenworth, the Leavenworth Hall of Fame
as a matter of fact. He takes pride in that, and I know that for a fact.
That kind of connection, that kind of communication, made our ability to communicate and operate with each other despite the political
climate much more effective." Zinni was effusive in describing how
helpful everyone had been on his 1999 trip to Pakistan when he had
arrived to help out on the Kargil war with India. In reality, the U.S.
general had come armed with an ultimatum from Bill Clinton: withdraw from Indian territory or else. Dennis Kux, another former State
Department official on the South Asia desk, describes what actually
happened:

> Taken aback and dismayed by the Kargil adventure, the U.S. gov-
> ernment responded vigorously—far more so than the Johnson
> administration had reacted during the early stages of the 1965
> Kashmir war. President Clinton telephoned Nawaz Sharif to urge
> him to have his forces withdrawn and sent Gen. Anthony Zinni to
> Islamabad to second this message directly with the prime minister
> and with Gen. Pervez Musharraf, who had replaced Karamat as
> chief of army staff. Brushing aside Pakistan's claim that it was not
> directly involved with the Kargil operation and lacked control over
> the mujahideen, the U.S. general urged Islamabad to see to it that
> the intruders pulled back across the Kashmir line of control. When

not even the Chinese, let alone the Americans, were willing to support the Pakistani position, Islamabad found itself internationally isolated . . . and decided to cut Pakistan's losses.*

It was thoughtful of Zinni not to rub this in on what was, after all, intended as a friendly occasion with a fixed purpose. Zinni backed Karamat's view that Pakistan should not be overpressured on its western border. It had lost a lot of soldiers already. In fact, though Zinni did not say so, more Pakistani than U.S. soldiers or mercenaries have died in the cross-border Afghan war. The Pakistani military deliberately underestimates its casualties. The army claims that one thousand troops were killed during the Waziristan campaigns in 2004 through 2006. When in Peshawar in 2007, I was repeatedly told by local journalists that the real figure was over three thousand killed and many thousands wounded.

The show came to life when Richard Armitage took the microphone. Cutting through diplomatic niceties, Armitage pointed out that Pakistan was in a mess, had been so since 1947, and was no longer a country but four countries (a reference to the country's four provinces) or a bit more if one saw Waziristan as Qaedistan. He accepted only partial U.S. responsibility for this state of affairs and isolated it to the U.S. mode of intervention during the Soviet-Afghan war: "We knew exactly what we were doing in Pakistan at the time, and we knew exactly what was going to happen in Afghanistan when we walked away. This was not a secret." In other words they knew perfectly well that they had handed the country to religious groups and the ISI. What they were doing was using Pakistan as a "Kleenex" (as a senior official informed Dennis Kux) or, more accurately, a "condom" as a retired and embittered general once described the "strategic relationship" to me. As I have repeatedly stressed in this book, U.S. priorities determined Pakistan's domestic and foreign policies from 1951 onward. The long period of foreplay culminated in the Afghan climax. So enthralled were the Pak-

---

*Dennis Kux, *The United States and Pakistan:1947–2000: Disenchanted Allies* (Washington and Baltimore: 2001). This is an extremely useful and sober, if not fully comprehensive, account of the "strategic relationship."

istani military by the experience that they became desperate to repeat it in Kashmir and Kargil, forgetting that a condom can't do it on its own.

Crucially, Armitage, like Zinni and Karamat before him, opposed as counterproductive the pressuring of the Pakistan government to permit U.S. troops to operate on Pakistani soil, a discussion that had been taking place behind closed doors in Washington for well over a year. U.S. presidential hopeful Senator Barack Obama had made an ill-judged intervention, publicly demonstrating his virility in military matters by supporting the hawks and calling for U.S. attacks inside Pakistan. Armitage said that he saw the future of Afghanistan related closely to a stable, democratic polity in Pakistan, but not a Venezuelan-style democracy, an odd remark given that there is no immediate possibility of this, but certainly revealing of his other preoccupation. None of this appeared to have had an impact on the White House. On April 12, 2008, the American president informed ABC News that the most dangerous area in the world now was neither Iraq nor Afghanistan, but Pakistan, because of the presence of Al Qaeda, who were preparing attacks on the United States. The logic was obvious though not spelled out: preparing public opinion for possible search-and-destroy missions inside Pakistan. The drones, on their own, were not sufficient. The problem, which neither Armitage nor the retired generals addressed at all, was the war in Afghanistan and the problems of governance in Kabul, where a regime fully supported and supervised by the United States is supposedly in charge.

The future of the two countries is certainly interrelated, but as the 2008 elections in Pakistan demonstrated and as some of us have been arguing for some time, the religious groups and parties have little mass support, let alone the armed-struggle jihadi currents. The crisis resulting from Operation Enduring Freedom is now creating havoc inside Pakistan and affecting morale in its army. The solution to this lies in Kabul and Washington. Islamabad and the EU are simply loyal auxiliaries with little real leverage to resolve the crisis.

Britain's most self-important viceroy to India, Lord Curzon, famously remarked that "no patchwork scheme will settle the Waziristan problem. . . . Not until the military steam-roller has passed over the country from end to end, will there be peace. But I do not want to be the person to start that machine." To expect the Pakistan army to do so, and as a result kill thousands of its own people from regions where it recruits soldiers, is to push it in a suicidal direction. Even the toughest command structure might find it difficult to maintain unity in these conditions.

Were this attempted directly by the United States, the Pakistan army would split, and hordes of junior officers would likely decamp to the mountains and resist. The military high command, regularly receiving reports of substantial numbers of soldiers surrendering to much smaller contingents of guerrillas, is well aware that the war in the Frontier Province is extremely unpopular among its troops. The soldiers surrender because they don't want to fight "America's war" or kill coreligionists. Junior officers have been taking early retirement to avoid a second tour of duty on the Afghan border. This being the case today, it is not difficult to imagine the result of a direct U.S. intervention inside Pakistan.

At the time of this writing, the Iraq war has cost $3 trillion. An all-out war inside Pakistan would require a great deal more. Were the Pakistan army to accept money and weaponry to become the steamroller referred to by Lord Curzon, the "jihadi finger on the nuclear trigger" so frequently cited by the West might well become a self-fulfilling prophecy. The regional solution, as I argued in the preceding chapter, is the only serious way out of this crisis.

Armitage accepted that religious extremism had little support in Pakistan, but stressed the crisis of leadership and governance, pointing out the lack of an obvious replacement for President Musharraf:

> Unfortunately, the late Benazir Bhutto had a chance as a democratically elected leader, and I think it not for nothing that she found herself in Dubai for a number of years, and Mr. Nawaz Sharif also has had his difficulties. I am not being particularly nasty, I am just pointing out the fact that one of the things that we have to deal with now is that we do not have a ready candidate for soldier of the month.

This view is not much different from my own, with the following proviso. The search for a military pinup to salvage a crisis should come to a permanent halt. The latest incumbent, like his predecessors, has been an abject failure, as the imposition of an emergency revealed. On this, Stephen Cohen, another Brookings expert who specializes in Pakistan, was much sharper in a preelection exchange with me on the *Financial Times* website:

> I'd say that more Americans now see [Musharraf] as a liability, and this begins with the US military who have encountered Pakistan-based Taliban. . . . At best I see Musharraf being eased out by a combination of the Pakistan army, which must find him now to be an embarrassment, and foreign supporters, including the US but certainly China and the Europeans who realise that Pakistan must have coherent and effective leadership to tackle its many problems, not least of which is the growing violence in the society.

While there is truth to this, Cohen, like most U.S. analysts, underestimates the way that continuous Washington-backed military interventions have wrecked the organic evolution of politics in Pakistan, leaving it in the hands of mediocre and mottled politicians who have, till now, shown few signs of learning from past mistakes and whose only skill is in the relentless pursuit of personal wealth. Musharraf signed his political death warrant when he joined up with one such political faction—the Chaudhrys of Gujrat—to help him retain power. It was a signal that, under his watch, nothing was going to change.

And yet, if the present cycle of Pakistani power struggles could be broken, it is not impossible that a new movement or party might emerge to fundamentally change the political system. A precedent of sorts has been established. Who would have predicted the eruption of a large lawyers' movement or Supreme Court judges breaking with tradition and refusing a carte blanche to a cornered military government? It happened when the regime had become discredited and the opposition parties ineffective. The judiciary, despite its limitations, filled the vacuum. The timing was right for the chief justice to accept legal challenges to an unpopular and corrupt regime. His actions reignited popular involvement in the political process, creating the basis for an opposition victory in the general elections of 2008.

It is indisputable that the joint victors of the February 2008 general elections—Bhutto's husband, Asif Zardari, and the Sharif brothers—are tried-and-tested failures. An atmosphere of stifling pusillanimity and conformity prevails inside their political parties where compromises and deals are the prerogative of the leader alone. They were elected primarily because, as is increasingly the case in the West as well, when policy differences in a globalized world are minute, electors tend to vote against the incumbent. Musharraf had outlasted his welcome. His cronies were unpopular. Large-scale manipulation having been vetoed by the new army chief of staff, the elections were cautiously rigged to deny any single party an overall majority in accordance with the U.S.-brokered deal with Benazir.

Benazir had agreed to become Musharraf's junior partner and work with him and also, if necessary, his favored Chaudhrys of Gujrat. This is why Anne Patterson, the latest U.S. ambassador to Pakistan, summoned the widower Zardari after his election victory and reminded him, no doubt in more diplomatic language, that he had inherited not only the Peoples Party from his wife but also her legacy. Musharraf's spin doctors piled the pressure on Zardari by informing the media that corruption cases against him in Europe and Pakistan had not been withdrawn. Only his wife had been given legal immunity. This was somewhat mean-spirited since they worked as a team and immunity for one should have applied to the other, but nothing is ever as straightforward as it seems. Finally, the charges in Pakistan were dropped.

A recycling of the country and its modernization is perfectly possible, but it requires large-scale structural reforms. To isolate Pakistan's problems to religious extremism and dual power in Waziristan or the possession of nuclear weapons is to miss the point, to become marooned in a landscape behind enemy lines. These issues, as I have made clear in preceding chapters, are not unimportant, but the problems relating to them are a direct result of doing Washington's bidding in previous decades. The imbalance is glaring. In 2001, when U.S. interest in the country resumed, debt and defense amounted to two-thirds of public spending—257 billion rupees ($4.2 billion) and 149.6 billion rupees ($2.5 billion) respectively, compared to total tax revenues of 414.2 billion rupees ($6.9 billion). In a country with one of the worst public education systems in Asia—70 percent of women and 41 percent of men are officially classified as illiterate—and with health care virtually nonexistent for over half the population, a mere 105.1 billion rupees ($1.75 billion) was left for overall development.

Throughout the nineties, the International Monetary Fund (IMF) had scolded civilian governments for failing to keep their restructuring promises. Musharraf's regime, by contrast, won admiring praise from 1999 onward for sticking to IMF guidelines "despite the hardships imposed on the public by austerity measures." Impoverishment and desperation in the burgeoning city slums and the countryside—still home to 67.5 percent of the population—were exacerbated further. Some 56 million Pakistanis, nearly 30 percent of the population, now live below the poverty line; the number has increased by 15 million since Musharraf seized power. Of Pakistan's four provinces, the Punjab, with around 60 percent of the population, has continued to dominate economically and politically, with Punjabis filling the upper echelons of the army and bureaucracy and channeling what development there is to local projects. Sind, with 23 percent of the population, and Baluchistan, with 5 percent, remain starved of funds, water, and power supplies, while the North-West Frontier's fortunes have increasingly been tied to the Afghan war and heroin economy.

A cash-flow crisis in May 2008 was temporarily resolved by a Saudi commitment to provide oil on long-term credit.

To PERMANENTLY continue as a satrapy is certainly not going to help Pakistan. Instead, a number of changes, if implemented, could set the country on the road to rapid economic development experienced elsewhere in Asia, while at the same time building and sustaining democratic structures at the level of the state.

First, serious land reform is required to disperse economic and political power to the countryside, reduce rural poverty, and provide aid and subsidies to farmers and peasant cooperatives. Farmers in the United States and Europe have been heavily subsidized, often to the detriment of agriculture in the third world. A subsidy program to small farmers in Pakistan could be of great benefit, but elite attachment to the current market-priorities global system militates against any such plan. Ownership of land is highly concentrated. Only 20 percent of all landholders own more than thirty-five acres, and less than 10 percent own more than one hundred acres. Eighty-six percent of households in Sind, 78 percent in Baluchistan, 74 percent in the Punjab, and 65 percent in the North-West Frontier Province own no land at all. Fifty-five percent of the country's total population of 170 million is landless. This inequity lies at the heart of rural poverty.

The problem is structural. The economy rests on a narrow production base, heavily dependent on the unreliable cotton crop and the low-value-added textile industry; irrigation supplies are deficient, and soil erosion and salinity are widespread. More damaging still are the crippling social relations in the countryside. Low productivity in agriculture can only be reversed through the implementation of serious land reforms, but the alliance between *khaki* state and local landlords makes this virtually impossible. As an Economist Intelligence Unit report on Pakistan noted:

> Change is hindered not least because the status quo suits the wealthy landowners who dominate the sector, as well as federal and provincial parliaments. Large landowners own 40 per cent of the arable land and control most of the irrigation system. Yet assessments by independent agencies, including the World Bank, show them to be less productive than smallholders. They are also poor taxpayers, heavy borrowers and bad debtors.*

The weak economy has been further skewed for decades now by Pakistan's vast military apparatus. For "security reasons," its detailed budget is never itemized in official statements: a single line records the overall sum. In Pakistan, the power of any elected body to probe into military affairs has always been strictly curtailed. The citizenry remains unaware of how the annual $2.5 billion is distributed between the army (550,000 strong, with over two thousand tanks and two armored

---

*Economist Intelligence Unit, *Pakistan, Afghanistan* (London: 2002), 26.

divisions); the air force (ten fighter squadrons of forty combat planes each, as well as French- and U.S.-made missile systems); and the navy (ten submarines, eight frigates)—let alone what is spent on nuclear weapons and delivery systems.

In these circumstances the most recent slogan of the Ministry of Culture, "Grow and Globalize," takes on a satirical, if not surrealist, hue. Unfortunately it is meant seriously. The idea behind it is the sale of large tracts of land to global agribusiness, as has been done in Brazil, while along the way transforming the peasants into employ-ees on short-term contracts. A civil servant from the Finance Min-istry in Islamabad was recently reported in the press as saying, "The era of land reform has gone and now the government wants to cre-ate new job opportunities through liberalization, privatization, and deregulation of the economy. There is no plan even to discuss land reforms in the upcoming planning document." In the face of this bru-tal new approach, the old-fashioned feudal landlords have been given a renewed lease on life. In Sind, for instance, they continue to admin-ister justice, dominate politics, rule their fiefdoms with an iron hand, and also, in their own fashion, provide for the common weal by not letting their peasants starve. Some, such as Mumtaz Bhutto (Benazir's uncle), openly contend that those who work their land are better off under a precapitalist system of this sort than under what is offered by globalization. Of course, they will not even consider a third alter-native of land redistribution to the poor.

Alongside agricultural reform, a functioning social infrastructure urgently needs to be created for the mass of the population. This requires a transformation on three levels: education, health, and cheap housing. Of these the first two should now be a strategic priority for any government. Figures released by the UN in 2007–8 place Pakistan 136th out of 177 on the Human Development Index, below Sri Lanka, India, the Maldives, and Myanmar. Illiteracy has actually increased and will continue to do so unless measures are taken. The official primary-school enrollment rate of 53 percent is the lowest in South Asia and is almost certainly an overestimate. The Ministry of Education, I was told in Islamabad, pays salaries to nonexistent teachers, charges overhead for deserted school buildings, and has various other scams that inflate the published figures. Even so, the official spending on education is 2.4 percent of GDP, considerably lower than that of Nepal. Despite the parlous state of primary education, more than 50 percent of the allocated nonrecurrent education budget goes unspent each year because of the poor capacity of the system. Many smaller towns have empty, dilapidated school buildings with few teachers. Given this, it is hardly a surprise that desperate, poor families are prepared to entrust their children to madrassas of the Isalamists, where they will be fed, clothed, and educated better than in what passes for a state system. The private educational network is both expensive and class-bound, sometimes rejecting children from poor backgrounds even when they have managed to borrow the money or obtained philanthropic aid. This massive shortcoming in Pakistani society is the responsibility of every government since 1947. The Bhuttos, father and daughter, were no better than Zia and Musharraf in this regard. A high-quality state system with English as a compulsory language (on the Malaysian model) would be an extremely popular measure in every province and would entirely transform the country.

Educational opportunities may be limited in Pakistan, but the poor have almost no health care. Recent figures show that there are just eight physicians and one dentist per ten thousand people and fewer than five hundred psychiatrists for a country with large numbers of traumatized and disturbed people. Malnutrition, acute respiratory illnesses, tuberculosis, preventable diseases of various types, are widespread. One in every eleven citizens suffers from diabetes. Given the lack of facilities, and with nearly three-quarters of Pakistan's specialist doctors working in the United States, government hospitals are a disgrace. Most medical practitioners work in their own clinics or private hospitals for the rich. No official statistics are provided, but Karachi, Lahore, and Islamabad together have up to a hundred or so well equipped of the latter. Conditions in state hospitals in the big cities are grim, and the lack of affordable medicine a permanent curse on the poor. The tragedy is continuous. The coalition government formed after the February 2008 elections announced its twenty top "ministries." These did not include "health and human development."

As for housing, the state provides none except for those currently in government service or the armed forces. The privatization of land in the military cantonments has meant, however, that new military colonies are being created in remote areas outside the cities.

The legal system too is skewed in favor of the wealthy. Recent events with the chief justices notwithstanding, most judges in Pakistan have been vacillating, cowardly, negligent, prejudiced, and above all corrupt. The Zia dictatorship frightened them into submission. His civilian heirs appointed political cronies with the result that, especially during the nineties, justice in Pakistan has never been blind; what was usually weighed in its scales was banknotes, with a few honorable exceptions. It was no secret in the country that in legal cases involving property or corporate claims, senior lawyers, when asked to name a fee, would simply ask the client how many judges he was prepared to buy.

The spate of recent Supreme Court activism that led to Pakistan's only judicial crisis does offer hope on this front, but it is worth remembering that the rot begins at the primary level. Judicial and legal reforms, including a complete separation of powers between the judiciary and the executive, would be a first step toward reviving a dysfunctional state. Proper salaries to reduce the need for "illegal" money would also be helpful. The restoration of the chief justice and his colleagues sacked by Musharraf is an important political issue. But even if the divisions on this question, both within the PPP and between it and Nawaz Sharif's Muslim League, were resolved and the judges reinstated, the structural problems would not go away.

It soon became clear that Zardari was more sympathetic to Musharraf than he was to judicial activists.

The "march" from Karachi to Islamabad was in reality a drive to the capital in cars and buses. It was large, but the government insisted there should neither be a sit-in or a permanent siege of parliament. The leaders capitulated and disbanded the assembly. The result has been to demoralize the movement. Where Musharraf failed, the widower has succeeded.

One of the proud boasts of the Musharraf regime was that it had provided the country with a free media for the first time in its history. This was only a partial exaggeration. Pakistan's first two military dictators had crushed the media in blatant fashion. Zulfiqar Ali Bhutto was not a great friend of press freedom, nor was Nawaz Sharif. While Benazir Bhutto did not interfere with the print media, both she and her husband offered nonstop advice to the programmers of PTV, the state television network, which was impossible to ignore. By way of contrast, Musharraf, during his early days as president, when he was brimming with self-confidence, ended the state monopoly of television. The airwaves were liberated. As a result a range of new stations mushroomed, often providing higher-quality news reportage and analysis than their counterparts in India or Britain. A cocky and arrogant General Musharraf did not imagine that he could ever be threatened by press freedom. He also knew that Pakistanis watched Indian cable channels and news bulletins much more than they did their own state TV. He recognized that reforming the antiquated broadcasting structure would benefit local businesses and create a healthy competition with channels abroad, and indeed this is what happened.

But Musharraf had underestimated the capacity of Pakistani journalists, especially a newer and younger generation untouched by the sleaze of the past, to pursue the truth. Historical crises such as the breakup of the country were, for the first time, openly discussed in the media, and the generals were confronted with hard questions. Inevitably a clampdown followed the early loosening of censorship. The independent media's coverage of the lawyers' revolt was one of the primary targets of the declaration of a state of emergency in 2007. Geo, the largest network, went off the air for many months. The government introduced regulatory procedures that seriously restricted news broadcasting. Musharraf insisted that to remain on air TV news stations had to sign a code of conduct whereby journalists who ridiculed him and other government officials would be subjected to fines and prison sentences. "The media should not agitate," Musharraf said. "It should join us in the war on terror." He was wistfully thinking of CNN and BBC World.

The newly elected government's minister for information announced in April 2008 that legislation was about to be introduced to restore complete media freedom.

The interrelationship between domestic and foreign policy in Pakistan has never been hidden. Instead of a foreign policy dependent on big powers, there should be a regional concentration on South Asia and the working out of a common approach to international relations. A rapprochement with India and the creation of a South Asian Union, a better and more coherent version of the EU, is in the long-term interests of the whole region. At a time when the United States is actively breaking up states and encouraging client nationalisms in such places as Kosovo, Croatia, and Kurdistan, regional cohesion offers a nonconfrontational solution to the Kashmir and Tamil disputes, a reduction in military expenditures, and an improvement in social standards in all countries in the area. It would also lead to a political strengthening of the region as a whole, allowing for healthier relationships with the United States and China. South Asia should not act as a buffer between these two great powers, but as a strong and independent region in its own right. Pakistan's relations with China are an important factor in this equation. In recent years they have been symbolized by a massive Chinese investment transforming Gwadar, a small fishing port on the Makran coast in Baluchistan, into a major port. China's vice premier, Wu Bangguo, was flown in to lay the foundation stone of the new development on March 22, 2002, four months after the U.S. occupation of Kabul. When completed later this year, Gwadar will be the largest deep-sea port in the region, providing the Chinese with an oil terminal close to the Persian Gulf, which supplies two-thirds of its energy. Some U.S. intelligence analysts are worried that Gwadar could become a Chinese naval base providing rapid access to the Indian Ocean. Such anxieties are reciprocal. With U.S. bases and armies now on China's borders in Afghanistan, Beijing is beginning to feel the tension. This was one of the reasons that the Chinese prime minister visited Pakistan in April 2005 to sign a set of twenty-two accords that were designed to boost bilateral relations. A year later Musharraf visited Beijing. The official agenda centered on trade and counterterrorism, but Afghanistan and Pakistan's desire for civil nuclear cooperation will have been discussed in great detail. China is regarded by many in the Pakistani military leadership as an "all-weather friend," a more reliable strategic and noninterfering partner than Washington, which has periodically embargoed the supply of military hardware; the final restrictions were only removed after 9/11.

The West's current obsession with Islam is related only partially to

9/11; the larger cause is oil, the bulk of which lies underneath lands inhabited by Muslims. In considering the meanings of Islam, Western analysts would do well to recognize it for what it is: a world religion that is in no sense monolithic. Both as a religion and a culture it encompasses numerous local traditions as different from each other as those in Senegal and Indonesia, South Asia and the Arabian Peninsula, the Maghreb and China. It contains all the colors of the rainbow and its culture has remained vibrant to this day. Saudi Arabia, Egypt, and Indonesia produced three of the finest novelists of the twentieth century, Abdelrahman Munif, Naguib Mahfouz, and Pramoedya Ananta Toer. South Asia has produced poets of matchless quality, including Ghalib, Iqbal, and Faiz. Senegal and Iran have given us an auteur cinema that compares to the best once produced in Europe and often superior to Hollywood. That this has to be spelled out in the twenty-first century points to the provincialism of the West, incapable of looking beyond its own interests and unaware of the world it traduces.

The political realm is murkier, but here also there are causes and consequences. Indonesia, the largest Muslim state in the world, once had the world's largest Communist Party, with a million members and sympathizers. They were wiped out by General Suharto with the blessings of today's Islamophobes.* Who crushed the Iraqi Communists with a leadership that included Sunni, Shia, Jew, and Christian? A U.S.-backed Saddam Hussein. Repression, the implosion of the Communist system, and the new economic orthodoxy produced a vacuum in many parts of the Islamic world. As a result, many turned to religion. A series of articles on Egypt in the *New York Times* in February 2008 highlighted middle-class unemployment as a major factor driving young people to the mosques. The same is true to a lesser extent in Pakistan. For some, religiosity eases the pain.

As for political Islam, it too comes in different shapes and colors. NATO's Islamists in Turkey, neoliberal to the core, are popular in the West. The Muslim Brotherhood in Egypt would be equally happy to work with the United States, but might disagree on Palestine, since

---

*Benedict Anderson, "Exit Suharto," *New Left Review,* March–April 2008.

Gaza is a neighbor. Elsewhere new forces and faces are emerging that have something in common. Muqtada, Haniya, Nasrallah, Ahmadinejad: each has risen by organizing the urban poor in their localities—Baghdad and Basra, Gaza and Jenin, Beirut and Sidon, Tehran and Shiraz. It is in the slums that Hamas, Hezbollah, the Sadr brigades, and the Basij have their roots. The contrast with the Hariris, Chalabis, Karzais, Allawis, on whom the West relies—overseas millionaires, crooked bankers, CIA bagmen—could not be starker. A radical wind is blowing from the alleys and shacks of the latter-day wretched of the earth, surrounded by the fabulous wealth of petroleum. The limits of this radicalism, so long as it remains captured by the Koran, are clear enough. The impulses of charity and solidarity are infinitely better than those of imperial greed and comprador submission, but so long as what they offer is social alleviation rather than reconstruction, they are sooner or later liable to recuperation by the existing order. Leaders with a vision capable of transcending national or communal divisions, with a sense of unity and the self-confidence to broadcast it, have yet to emerge.

There is, of course, Al Qaeda, but its importance in the general scheme of things is greatly overstated by the West. It unleashes sporadic terror attacks and kills innocents, but it does not pose any serious threat to U.S. power. It is not even remotely comparable to the anticolonial national liberation movements that tormented Britain, France, and the United States in Africa or Indochina during the last century. The current turmoil is still confined to those areas of the Middle East where for twenty years or more American power never significantly penetrated: the West Bank, Baathist Iraq, Khomeinist Iran. The real U.S. anchorage in the region lies elsewhere—in Egypt, Saudi Arabia, the Gulf States, and Jordan. There, despite being Muslims, America's traditional clients have held the line and are usually on hand to help out with regional problems. That Pakistan has been part of this group has been at its own cost.

It is foolish to speak, as many Western commentators do, of "global Islam" being "Waziristan writ large," when what is really meant is that the U.S./NATO war in Afghanistan is posing serious problems and that neo-Taliban groups are crossing the border and winning support in Pakistan. Referring to this phenomenon as an aspect of "global Islam" is about as accurate as referring to the judeocide of the Second World War as an aspect of "global Christianity."

An argument often used by Bernard Lewis is that the United States has become a scapegoat for the Muslim world to explain its own decline and problems. To put forward this argument at a time when the Western military or economic occupation of the Arab world, barring Syria and partially Lebanon, is virtually complete is somewhat disingenuous. The founders of Al Qaeda were incubated in Saudi Arabia and Egypt before being dispatched to wage jihad in Afghanistan by Zbigniew Brzezinski, now an adviser to Barack Obama in the 2008 presidential campaign. Pakistan's relations with Saudi Arabia have always been close, with the cash nexus, rather than religion, playing the bigger part. But the Saudi kingdom is also close to Washington. Surely Bernard Lewis is aware that King Faisal sincerely believed that the only way to defeat Nasser and the godless Communists was by making religion the central pillar of the Saudi social order and using it ruthlessly against the enemy. Islam was under threat and had to be defended on all fronts. This pleased his allies in Washington, who were tolerant even of his decision to impose an oil embargo against the West after the 1973 war, something that has never been attempted since.

Even after Saudi oil was fully nationalized in 1980, Washington's politico-military elite maintained their pledge to defend the existing Saudi regime and its state whatever the cost. Why, some people asked, could the Saudi state not defend itself? The answer was because the Saud clan, living in permanent fear, was haunted by the specter of the radical nationalists who had seized power in Egypt in 1952 and in Iraq six years later. The Sauds kept the size of the national army and air force to the barest minimum to minimize the risk of a coup d'état. Many of the armaments they have purchased to please the West lie rusting peacefully in desert warehouses.

For a decade and a half in the late 1970s and '80s, the Pakistan army, paid for by the Saudi treasury, sent in large contingents to protect the Saudi royal family in case of internal upheavals. Then, after the first Gulf War, the American military arrived. It is still there. U.S. air bases in Saudi Arabia and Qatar were used to launch the war against

Iraq. All pretense of independence had gone. The only thing the Saudi princes could do was to plead with the United States not to make public what was hardly a state secret. There was practically no TV coverage of planes taking off from Saudi Arabia bound for Iraq.

Linked to the "scapegoating" argument is a "new" idea that is also promoted by Muslims anxious to please, mainly in the U.S. academy. The struggle, they argue, is not between Islam and the United States but within Islam itself. All this means is that with the United States strongly backing and protecting its friends in the Muslim world, those who oppose client status are fighting back. As the nationalists and the left both have been virtually eliminated, this task has now fallen to Islamist groups of differing stripes. Al Qaeda is one such group, but is a tiny minority within the House of Islam. Nor is this new. Islam has never been united.* That is one reason why it lost Sicily and Spain in the medieval period. The only time it managed to unite its armies was under the Kurdish sultan Salah ad-Din to take back Jerusalem from the Crusaders in the twelfth century and return it to its former status as a city for all three peoples of the Book.

It is simply foolish to expect "Islam" to speak with one voice any more than Christianity or Judaism, Hinduism or Buddhism. The rise of recent Islamist movements with their extremist factions is a modern phenomenon, a product of the last fifty years of world history. It's a phase that will wither away, including in South Waziristan, if the military occupations of Muslim lands are ended. There are bigger problems in the world. To make Islam the scapegoat for U.S. foreign policy disasters is as destructive as the utilization of religion during the Cold War, when the United States itself for the first time stressed its own loyalty to religion. The reason was obvious. Religion was being used to mobilize support in the third world against the godless Communist enemy. President Truman used religion as a weapon against the Soviet Union. In 1952, the U.S. Supreme Court accepted a higher authority than itself when it ruled, "We are a religious people whose institutions presuppose a Supreme Being." The word *religious* rather than *Christian*

---

*I have explained this in some detail in *Clash of Fundamentalisms: Crusades, Jihads and Modernity* (New York and London: 2002).

was used precisely to make a common block with Muslims. President Eisenhower repeated all this in 1954: "Our government makes no sense unless it is founded on a deeply felt religious faith—and I don't care what it is."* In Pakistan and other Muslim states such as Egypt and Indonesia, the USIS openly supported the Muslim Brotherhood and the Jamaat-e-Islami and their student wings. As we have seen, this process reached its climax during the first Afghan war as General Zia, backed by Washington, created, armed, and trained specialist jihadi groups to wage the war against the godless in Afghanistan. Waziristan, in those years, was global anticommunism writ large. The United States could, or so it imagined, wash its hands and retire. The Pakistani state was lumbered with this unsavory legacy. Then came the 9/11 blowback, which, contrary to the views expressed by George W. Bush at the time, was not an attack on pure innocence by irrational evil, but the outcome of what had transpired in another epoch.

In 2003, after a lengthy trip to Pakistan, I wrote:

The Army is now the only ruling institution; its domination of the country is complete. How long can this be sustained? . . . The officer corps is no longer the exclusive domain of the landed gentry—a majority of officers come from urban backgrounds and are subject to the same influences and pressures as their civilian peers. Privileges have kept them loyal, but the processes that destroy politicians are already at work. Whereas in the recent past it was Nawaz Sharif and his brother, or Benazir Bhutto and her husband, who demanded kickbacks before making deals, it is now General Musharraf's office that sanctions key projects.

Of course, high—even stratospheric—levels of corruption are no bar to longevity, if a military regime has sufficiently intimidated its population and enjoys solid enough support in Washington, as the Suharto regime in Indonesia testifies. Can Musharraf look forward to this sort of reign? The fate of his dictatorship is likely to depend on the interaction of three main forces. First will be the

---

*Christian Century 71 (1954).

degree of internal cohesion of the Army itself. Historically, it has never split—vertically or horizontally—and its discipline in following a 180-degree turn in policy towards Afghanistan, whatever the sweeteners that have accompanied it, has so far been impressive. It is not impossible that one day some patriotic officer might deliver the country of its latest tyrant, as Zia was once mysteriously sent on his way to Gehenna; but for the minute, such an ending appears improbable. Having weathered the humiliation of its abandonment of the Taliban, the high command looks capable of brazening out any further acts of obeisance to orders from the Pentagon.

What of parliamentary opposition to military rule? Vexing though the upshot of the October 2002 election, for all its fraud, proved to be for Musharraf, the parties that dominate the political landscape in Pakistan offer little hope of rebellion against him. The cringing opportunism of the Bhutto and Sharif clans knows few limits. The Islamist front ensconced in Peshawar and Quetta is noisier, but not more principled—cash and perquisites quickly stilling most of its protests. Popular discontent remains massive, but lacks any effective channels of national expression. It would be good to think that their performances in office had discredited the PPP and Sharif's clique forever, but experience suggests that should the regime at any point start to crack, there is little to prevent these phoenixes of sleaze from arising once more, in the absence of any more progressive alternatives.

Finally, there is the American overlord itself. The Musharraf regime cannot aspire to play the same role as regional satrap that Zia once enjoyed. Pakistan has been ousted as imperial instrument in Afghanistan, and checked from compensating with renewed incursions in Kashmir. But if Islamabad has been forced into a more passive posture along its northern borders, its strategic importance for the US has, if anything, increased. For Washington has now made a huge political investment in the creation of a puppet regime in Kabul, to be guarded by US troops "for years to come," in the words of General Tommy Franks—not to speak of its continuing hunt for Osama bin Laden and his lieutenants. Pakistan is a vital flank in the pursuit of both objectives, and its top brass can look forward to the kind of lavish emoluments, public and private, that the Thai military received for their decades of collusion with the American war in Indochina. Still, Washington is pragmatic and knows that Benazir Bhutto and Nawaz Sharif were just as serviceable agents of its designs in Kabul as Zia himself. Should he falter domestically, Musharraf will be ditched without sentiment by the suzerain. The Pax Americana can wage war with any number of proxies. It will take an uprising on the scale of 1969 to shake Pakistan free of them.*

Events have not contradicted this analysis, with one exception. It was impossible to predict the pleasant if unexpected surprise that the country witnessed in the judicial upsurge. Its impact was a renewal of hope, and the effective media coverage of the movement left Musharraf exposed. He now needed a mixture of repression together with a civilian cover and had little option but to accept a U.S.-brokered deal with the late Benazir Bhutto. He was by now largely discredited in the country, and the imposition of the emergency was the last straw for many of his supporters. The assassination of Bhutto increased his unpopularity. Defeat soon followed.

However flawed the February 2008 general elections in Pakistan may have been, they were a blow to Musharraf as well as the Islamist alliance, which lost its stronghold to the secular Awami National Party, the heirs twice removed of old Ghaffar Khan, who had taught the Pashtuns to value nonviolence and to combat imperialism. The Peoples Party emerged as the largest party with 120 out of a total of 342 seats in the National Assembly, closely followed by the Sharif Muslim League with 90 seats and the ANP with 13. The pro-Musharraf Muslim League won 51 seats and the MQM 25. The defeat was decisive. Had there been no ballot rigging, it would have been a complete rout, especially for the MQM in Karachi, where violence and chicanery were on open display. The religious coalition obtained 6 members of parliament, and even if the Jamaat-e-Islami had not boycotted the election, their representation would not have been much higher.

---

* "The Colour Khaki," *New Left Review* 19 (January–February 2003).

Till the Bhutto assassination, the election campaign had been largely lackluster. The mainstream parties had few differences on ideological or policy grounds, either on the domestic or the international level. The Peoples Party had long abandoned its populism. The key interlinked issues were Musharraf's presidency and the reinstatement of the chief justice and others sacked during the emergency. The PPP was divided on this issue. One of its Punjabi veterans, Aitzaz Ahsan, was a central figure in the campaign to bring the judges back. Bhutto's widower, on the other hand, had been sentenced to years in prison by the same judiciary and loathed them. At a meeting of party leaders in April 2008, he made his views clear to Ahsan.

Leaving aside that the ANP, like the PPP, is not unfriendly to Washington, its electoral triumph in the Frontier Province confirms what some of us have consistently argued. The world's sixth most populous country and a nuclear state is not on the verge of a jihadi takeover. If neocons in the Bush administration or their successor want their prophecies of gloom and doom fulfilled, all they need to do is to occupy parts of Pakistan, destroy its nuclear facility, and impose a puppet regime. The hell that is Iraq would rapidly shift eastward. Definitely not recommended.

The delighted politicians of the PPP and the triumphant Muslim League rapidly agreed to form a coalition and divide the ministerial spoils. True to form, Nawaz Sharif, himself out of parliament, selected tried-and-trusted supporters or relatives for the work that lay ahead. Zardari, empowered by his widow, was able to choose the new prime minister. During her exile, Bhutto had selected an amiable and unquestioning Sindhi landlord as her proxy. He was widely expected to be the PPP choice. Makhdoom Amin Fahim, a pir-cum-landlord, politician and religious divine rolled into one, is hardly a social liberal. Uniquely, even for Pakistan, all his four brothers-in-law are the Koran. Fahim's family claims descent from the first Muslims to enter the subcontinent, the cohort of Muhammad bin Kasim who took Sind in 711. Women in early Islam owned and inherited property equally with men, a tradition that took root in parts of Sind. Landowners there devised an ingenious solution to prevent women from marrying outside the family, which could lead to the parcelization of the estates. The young heiresses were literally married off to the Koran—similar to nuns becoming brides of Christ. This preserved the girls' virginity, which in turn provided them with magic healing powers; but above all it ensured that the property remained under the control of their fathers and brothers. The problem posed by the four wealthy sisters of the PPP leader was thus piously solved.

Zardari decided against Fahim for geopolitical reasons. He felt a Punjabi landlord would be better placed to run the country and selected another divine-plus-politician from the saint-ridden city of Multan. The choice was Yousaf Raza Gillani, a politician well attuned to the spirit of the age and cut from the same cloth as many of his contemporaries. Gillani's qualities had been recognized by General Zia-ul-Haq, and like Nawaz Sharif, he became an early favorite of the dictator's, serving loyally on various committees designed to buttress the regime. After Zia's death, Gillani was a loyal supporter of the Muslim League, but fell out with Nawaz Sharif and joined the Peoples Party. He stayed with them and turned down offers from the Chaudhrys of Gujrat to jump ship and join their Muslim League. His instinct served him well in this case. His loyalty to the PPP when it was out of power has been handsomely rewarded by the party's godfather.

The immediate impact of the electoral defeat suffered by Musharraf's political factotums was to dispel the disillusionment and cynicism of the citizenry. The moral climate seemed to improve. But not for long. The fervor and naïveté soon turned to anger. The worm-eaten tongues of some politicians were soon back on display. Two major issues confronted the victors. The first concerned the judiciary. Nawaz Sharif had pledged that, if elected, his party would reverse the midnight actions carried out during the emergency and restore the chief justice of the Supreme Court and the other sacked judges to their former positions. Soon after their election triumph, the widower Bhutto and Nawaz Sharif met in Bhurban and publicly agreed that this would be a major priority and the judges would be brought back within thirty days of the new government taking office. There was general rejoicing in the country. Since November 3, 2007, until just after the election, the chief justice, Iftikhar Muhammad Chaudhry, had been a prisoner of the regime, detained in his house that was sealed off with barbwire barricades and a complement of riot police permanently on guard. His landlines were cut and his cell phones incapacitated by jamming devices. Colleagues and lawyers defending him were subjected to similar treatment. One of them, Aitzaz Ahsan, railed against the Bush regime in an op-ed in the *New York Times* on December 23, 2007:

> People in the United States wonder why extremist militants in Pakistan are winning. What they should ask is why does President Musharraf have so little respect for civil society—and why does he essentially have the backing of American officials?
>
> The White House and State Department briefings on Pakistan ignore the removal of the justices and all these detentions. Meanwhile, lawyers, bar associations and institutes of law around the world have taken note of this brave movement for due process and constitutionalism. They have displayed their solidarity for the lawyers of Pakistan. These include, in the United States alone, the American Bar Association, state and local bars stretching from New York and New Jersey to Louisiana, Ohio and California, and citadels of legal education like Harvard and Yale Law Schools.
>
> The detained chief justice continues to receive enormous recognition and acknowledgment. Harvard Law School has conferred on him its highest award, placing him on the same pedestal as Nelson Mandela and the legal team that argued Brown v. Board of Education. The National Law Journal has anointed him its lawyer of the year. The New York City Bar Association has admitted him as a rare honorary member. Despite all this, the Musharraf regime shows no sign of relenting.

The new government ordered the immediate release of the dismissed judges and the removal of all restrictions. This was widely seen as a prelude to their reinstatement. Musharraf and his backers in Washington panicked. If the chief justice and his colleagues resumed office, John Negroponte informed the new government (via Assistant Secretary of State Richard Boucher), Musharraf might be legally removed and that was unacceptable. He had to stay on, at least as long as Bush remained in the White House. His departure would be regarded as a setback in the war on terror.

This accelerated the political process and brought out into the open the differences on this issue between the PPP leadership and the Sharif brothers. At a subsequent meeting with U.S. officials in Dubai, in the presence of Musharraf and Benazir Bhutto's fixers, the latter were asked to confirm the exact nature of the deal agreed by the late Benazir with the Americans prior to her return to Pakistan. Her husband had been sidelined during that period and appeared to be unaware of all the details.

Asif Zardari had his own worries. The National Reconciliation Ordinance that pardoned corrupt politicians had been part of the deal between Bhutto and Musharraf. It was a much-hated ordinance and the Supreme Court was due to hear an appeal questioning its legality. Zardari, only too aware that this and the possibility that cases against him in European courts might be resurrected, capitulated. Simultaneously, U.S. officials in Pakistan offered inducements to the chief justice in the form of a senior position on the International Court of Justice with all the perks of the post or even an academic post in the United States. The chief justice told them that he was not interested.

Asif Zardari and Nawaz Sharif met in London in April 2008 to iron out their differences. Each was accompanied by trusted aides. Two elected Muslim League parliamentarians flanked Nawaz Sharif. Two unelected political fixers, Rehman Malik and Husain Haqqani (the first a submissive courtier, the second a crucial link to Washington), sat with Zardari. No consensus could be reached on the restoration of the judiciary and this inevitably produced cracks in the alliance. After consulting senior colleagues, Nawaz Sharif withdrew Muslim League ministers from the central government, citing disagreement on this issue. It is extremely rare in Pakistan for any politician to relinquish office on an issue of principle. Nawaz Sharif's popularity in the country soared. Zardari's action provoked the deepest indignation among the supporters of the judiciary and a number of senior figures in the PPP were clearly unhappy at the public embrace of Musharraf. But having accepted Zardari as their temporary leader they had rendered themselves powerless. As the party's guardian, the Bhutto family had deprived their ward of any intrinsic political identity and no group inside it was capable of formulating an independent political program. PPP politicians had grown so accustomed to the Bhutto harness that they could take no step without it. This is a pity. As I have argued earlier, the Bhutto family has long exhausted its historical function. Were the PPP to rid itself of this incubus, democracy could only be enhanced, even if it took a few years for its leaders and members to overcome their political numbness and become articulate again. In the meantime, the initiative lies entirely with Zardari and his close advisers. They make the key decisions, utilizing Prime Minister Gillani and the PPP cohort in parliament as a rubber stamp. For the moment this suits both Musharraf and Bush. What happens after their departure remains an open question.

The campaign to defend the judiciary was the first serious nationwide mass movement against the arbitrariness of military rule since 1969. The Supreme Court decisions that challenged the Musharraf regime had restored the country's self-respect. Its secular character had disproved the myth that jihadi terrorists were on the verge of taking over the country. But the judges were much less popular in the ruling circles of the United States and Europe, where elite opinion was neoimperialist in outlook and obsessed with occupation and war. Pakistan's judges were not regarded as helpful by these groups. Musharraf's use of emergency powers to dismiss the "turbulent" chief justice had accelerated the decomposition of the regime. For defending the civil rights of the poor, the chief justice was referred to by some Western liberal newspapers as a "judicial activist" or a "firebrand."

Washington and its allies regarded the war in Afghanistan and Pakistan's role in relation to it as the central priority. Everything else was seen as a diversion. What would be the attitude of the newly elected Pakistani politicians to the tempest in Afghanistan? Would they refrain from moves that might embarrass the United States and give Washington a free hand? In March 2008, Admiral Eric T. Olson, the head of the United States Special Operations Command, arrived in Islamabad for consultations with the Pakistan military and surprised locals by demanding a roundtable meeting with the country's elected leaders, another first in the country's history. Olson asked the politicians how they viewed the urgent U.S. need for cross-border incursions. None of the Pakistanis who responded regarded this as a good idea and they made their opposition very clear. The seniormost civil servant in the Frontier, Khalid Aziz, told Olson that "it would be extremely dangerous. It would increase the number of militants, it would become a war of liberation for the Pashtuns.They would say: 'We are being slaughtered. Our enemy is the United States.'"

For Nawaz Sharif the possibility of the killing of Pakistani citizens in the Frontier Province by U.S. troops ruled out this arrangement as a serious option. He believed that negotiations with the militants in Waziristan and a gradual military withdrawal from the area were essential to deter terrorist attacks in the large cities. The PPP was more equivocal on, but it too was firmly against, NATO raids inside Pakistan. The ANP leaders in the Frontier, who had hitherto been supportive of the U.S. presence in neighboring Afghanistan, were not prepared to give Washington a blank check and supported negotiations with Baitullah Masood, a pro-Taliban militia leader in South Waziristan, accused by the CIA of masterminding Benazir Bhutto's assassination, a claim denied by some of Bhutto's closest colleagues. Two senior ANP leaders, Asfandyar Wali Khan (the grandson of the late Ghaffar Khan) and Afrasiab Khattak, were summoned to Washington for meetings with National Security Adviser Stephen Hadley and John Negroponte. There was only one point on the agenda: cross-border raids. Washington was determined to find Pakistani politicians who would defend them. Both ANP leaders refused. Later, Khattak informed the *New York Times,* "We told them physical intervention into the tribal areas by the United States would be a blunder. It would create an atmosphere in which the terrorists would rally popular support." That this needed saying is worrying.

Owais Ghani the governor of the Frontier Province and, interestingly, a Musharraf appointee, also reiterated this view, "Pakistan will take care of its own problems, you take care of Afghanistan on your side. Pakistan is a sovereign state. NATO is in Afghanistan. It's time they did some soldiering."

On May 18, as if to underscore that the United States was not overly worried about the views of elected politicians, a Predator drone bombed Damadola in the Bajaur Agency in Pakistan and killed over a dozen people. The United States claimed that they had targeted and killed a "sig-

nificant leader." Akhundzada Chattan, the member of parliament from
the Bajaur Agency and a PPP veteran, called a press conference and
denounced the United States in strong language for "killing innocents."
Local PPP leaders backed him up strongly, especially when he repeatedly insisted that "the protest lodged by the Pakistan government against
the missile raid is not enough. The government should also sever diplomatic ties with the U.S. and expel its ambassador immediately."

Chattan said that a clear pattern had now been established. As soon
as the Pakistan government and the local insurgents began to talk to
one another and discuss a durable peace, NATO targeted the tribal
areas inside Pakistan and killed innocent people. He warned Washington to cease these activities and issued an appeal to the tribal elders, the
insurgents, the Pakistan army, and the new government to cast aside all
other differences and unite against "foreign aggression." This dissent in
the PPP suggests that Zardari's ascendancy is perhaps not as secure as
he might imagine. It is also another reminder that the decision of successive Pakistan governments to keep the tribal areas formally separate
from the rest of the country is counterproductive. Such an anomaly
prevents political parties and other organizations from functioning in
the region, leaving political control in the hands of tribal leaders, usually with dire results.

As if these developments on the Afghanistan border were not big
enough problems by themselves, the country as a whole is in the grip of
a food and power crisis that is creating severe difficulties in every city.
Inflation is out of control and was approaching 15 percent in May
2008. Gas, which is used for cooking in many homes, has risen by 30
percent in the past year. Wheat, the staple diet of most people, has seen
a 20 percent price hike since November 2007 and, while the UN's Food
and Agriculture Organization admits that the world's food stocks are at
record lows, there is an additional problem in Pakistan. Large quantities of wheat are being smuggled into Afghanistan to serve the needs of
the NATO armies. It is no secret in Pakistan that some of the smugglers
include the newly elected parliamentarians. Their triumphant, smiling
faces conceal odious calculations. Politics is a way to make money. The
few hopes aroused by the election have faded. The poor are the worst
hit, but middle-class families are also beginning to be affected.

• • •

POLITICS IN A land of perpetual dictatorships and corrupt politicians is undoubtedly depressing, but with some positive aspects. For one, politics has revived an interest in stories from the popular literature of an earlier period of Muslim rule in the region. The following tale, first told by a sixteenth-century storyteller, repeated to me in Lahore in 2007, sums up, with a few modifications, life in Pakistan today: A man is seriously dissatisfied with a junior magistrate's decision. The latter, irritated, taunts him to appeal to the *qadi* (a senior judge). The man replies, "But he's your brother, he won't listen to me." The magistrate says, "Go to the mufti [expert in Muslim law]." The man replies, "But he's your uncle." The magistrate says, "Go to the minister." The man replies, "He's your grandfather." The magistrate says, "Go to the king." The man replies, "Your niece is engaged to him." The magistrate, livid with anger, says, "Go to hell then." The man replies, "That's where your esteemed father reigns. He'll see to it I get no satisfaction there."

Official history is mainly composed of half-truths and outright lies, in which everything is attributed to well-meaning rulers and noble, pious sentiments. Those who write this are worshippers of accomplished facts, rallying to the side of victors. Sometimes a general, sometimes a politician. Success justifies everything. There is another history that refuses to be repressed.

Pakistan's satirists, writers, and poets generally refuse to silence their voices. They serve as the collective conscience of the country, and life without them would indeed be bleak. They often sight victory in times of defeat. The Punjabi poet and novelist Fakhar Zaman, who as a PPP activist served his time in prison during the Zia dictatorship, is one who refuses to relinquish hope:

How can he who lost his eyesight paint?
How can he who lost his hands sculpt?
How can he who lost his hearing compose music?
How can he whose tongue was cut out sing?
How can he whose hands are tied write poetry?
And how can he whose feet are fettered dance?

With muffled nose and mouth how can one inhale the scent of
flowers?
But all this has really happened:
Without eyes, we painted
Without hands, we sculpted statues
Without hearing, we composed music
Deprived of a tongue, we sang
Handcuffed, we wrote poetry
With fettered legs, we danced
And the fragrance of flowers pierced our muffled mouths and
nostrils.

INDEX

Abdullah, Maulana, 12
Advani, L. K., 214
"Adviser" (Jalib), 204
Afghanistan, 13, 118–19, 151, 170, 171,
    181, 186, 195, 221, 245, 276
    Soviet invasion of, 13, 17, 19, 25,
        117, 119, 120, 121, 122, 129–31,
        132, 135–36, 148, 186, 191, 193,
        195, 220, 222, 229, 231, 235,
        238, 239, 241, 251, 267
    U.S. invasion and occupation of, 19,
        22, 25, 26–27, 120, 130–31, 147,
        148, 152, 160, 191, 212, 216,
        217–20, 222–29, 231–48, 251,
        256, 264
    see also Taliban
Ahmad, Mahmud, 145–46, 147
Ahmed, Mirza Ghulam, 45–46
Ahmed, Mushtaq, 6
Ahmediyya sect, 45–49, 107
Ahsan, Admiral, 81
Ahsan, Aitzaz, 164, 167–68, 270, 272
Akbar, Emperor, 17–19, 125
Akbar, Said, 54, 181–82
Akhtar, Haq Nawaz, 8
Aldrich, Winthrop W., 195
Alexander the Great, 17, 24, 237
Ali, Chaudhry Rahmat, 49
Ali, Laiq, 195, 196
Alling, Paul H., 41–42
Al Qaeda, 13, 26, 136, 146, 148, 182,
    188, 210, 211, 219, 224, 225,
    241, 245, 252, 264, 265, 266
al-Tuwairqi, 8

Al-Walid bin Talal, 156
al-Zulfiqar, 128, 133, 170, 171
Amanullah, King of Afghanistan, 221
Amin, Hafizullah, 119, 120
Andropov, Yuri, 120
Angola, 79, 110, 111
Arif, K. M., 106
Arif Habib Securities, 8
Armitage, Richard, 145–46, 148, 249,
    251, 252
Asseri, Ali Saeed Awadh, 15
Atatürk, Mustafa Kemal, 166, 221, 237
Attlee, Clement, 35
Awami League, 62, 66, 74, 76, 77,
    78–79, 80, 81, 82–83, 84, 85, 86,
    90
Awami National Party (ANP), 24–25, 76,
    99, 101, 158, 172, 269
Ayub Khan, Mohammad, 43, 53, 56, 57,
    58, 59–60, 62–63, 65, 67, 68–69,
    70, 72, 73, 74, 75, 80, 81, 85,
    102, 103, 104, 105, 127, 128,
    143n, 149, 156, 199n, 200, 201,
    202, 204
Azad, Maulana Abul Kalam, 44, 47
Azhar, Masood, 152
Aziz, Abdul, 12–13, 14–16, 17
Aziz, Khalid, 275
Aziz, Shaukat, 7–8, 155–56

Babar, Naseerullah, 136, 127–38
Baghdad Pact, 56, 199
Baha'is, 47
Bahini, Mukti, 83, 88

Bajaur Agency, 275, 276
Baluchistan, 23, 93, 97, 98, 101, 102, 103, 121, 156, 198, 207, 262
Baluch Peoples Liberation Front (BPLF), 102
Bangladesh, 80, 116
    see also East Pakistan
Bashir-ud-din, Mirza, 46
Basit, Hafiz Abdul, 11
BBC, 28, 160, 162, 178, 226, 261
Bengal, 29, 30, 32, 35, 55–56, 65–66, 67, 68, 73, 74, 77, 78, 95, 97, 105
    1943 famine in, 91
Betrayal of East Pakistan, The (Niazi), 73n
Bharatiya Janata Party (BJP), 214
Bhashani, Maulana, 67
Bhutto, Benazir, 4, 5, 62, 63, 93, 114, 116, 123, 133, 134–35, 136, 137–39, 140, 144, 154, 163, 164, 165, 167–69, 171, 172–74, 175, 176–79, 181–82, 184–86, 207, 253, 255, 259, 269, 273
    assassination of, xiii, 4, 182–84, 186, 187, 188–89, 269, 270, 275
    in 2008 election, 27, 159–61, 168, 181–82, 184, 255, 270
Bhutto, Fatima, 175, 176, 177
Bhutto, Mumtaz, 100, 203n
Bhutto, Murtaza, 133, 169, 170, 171, 172, 174, 175–77
Bhutto, Nusrat, 116, 169, 174, 179
Bhutto, Shahnawaz, 169, 170, 171–72
Bhutto, Zulfiqar Ali, 49, 57, 63, 68–69, 73–74, 77, 81, 92, 93–94, 96, 101, 103–5, 107, 125, 127–28, 133, 140, 142–43, 150, 186, 195, 200, 201–3, 208, 259, 260–61
    arrest, trial, and execution of, 114–16, 119, 128, 169, 171, 182, 184, 185
    nuclear bomb acquired by, 108–13, 117, 119
Biden, Joseph, 188
bin Kasim, Muhammad, 270
bin Laden, Osama, 16, 129, 131, 136, 143, 145, 146, 208–9, 215, 268
Biswas, Tipu, 84, 88
Bizenjo, Ghaus Bux, 102
Black September, 106–7
Blair, Tony, 222
Bogra, Mohammad Ali, 198
Boucher, Richard A., 248, 272

Brezhnev, Leonid, 120
British Empire, 4, 19–22, 31, 32–33, 40, 51–52, 56, 70, 71, 79, 103, 117, 118, 126, 193–95, 220, 221
Brown, Art, 210
Brown, Gordon, 159
Brzezinski, Zbigniew, 110, 119, 121, 122, 265
Bulleh Shah, 16–17
Bunn, Matthew, 210, 211
Burma, 71, 73
Burns, John F., 179
Bush, George W., 145, 217, 218, 267, 270, 272
Bush, Jenna, 220
Butt, Ziauddin, 143
Byroade, Henry, 112–13

Can Pakistan Survive? (Ali), ix, 3
Carnage in Karachi, 10
Caroe, Olaf, 21–22
Carter, Jimmy, 120
CBS News, 150
CENTCOM, 26
Césaire, Aimé, 64
Chattan, Akhundzada, 276
Chaudhry Iftikhar Muhammad, 7, 8, 9–11, 271–72
Chaudhry Manzoor Elahi, 126, 128
Chaudhry Pervez Elahi, 171
Chaudhry Shujaat Hussain, 128, 144, 171
Chaudhry Zahoor Elahi, 126–28, 171
Chaudhrys of Gujrat, 125, 126, 128–29, 144, 155, 157, 158, 171, 254, 255
Chávez, Hugo, 147
Cheney, Dick, 112, 217, 218, 224, 232–33
China, 3, 15, 22, 67, 74, 84, 86, 121, 122, 129, 190, 196, 201, 202, 204, 205, 206, 216, 220, 245, 246, 247, 254, 262
Chou En-lai, 67
CIA, 13, 120, 129, 133, 172, 186, 204, 207, 218, 226, 235
Citibank, 156
Civil and Military Gazette, 19–20
Civil Service of Pakistan (CSP), 43
Clark, Ramsey, 115
Clinton, Bill, 140, 143, 150, 250
Clinton, Hillary, 188, 189, 219–20, 245
Cohen, Stephen, 254

Cold War, 23, 56, 118, 122, 198, 202, 216, 266
Collins, Lord Justice, 178
Combined Opposition Parties, 81
Congress Party, 20, 21, 22, 33, 34, 35, 44, 54, 72, 79
Convention Muslim League, 60
Council on Foreign Relations, 179
Croatia, 244, 262
Crossette, Barbara, 132
Crusades, 266
Cuba, 110, 111, 119
Culture, Pakistan Ministry of, 258
Curzon, Lord, 71, 252, 253

Daily Telegraph (London), 227
Daman, Ustad, 50
Daud, Prince of Afghanistan, 118–19, 221, 222
Daughter of the East (Benazir Bhutto), 170, 172
Daultana, Mian Mumtaz, 47
"Dawn of Freedom, The" (Faiz), 36–37
Dayan, Moshe, 44, 106
Defense Intelligence Agency (DIA), 13, 113, 143, 207
Devaud, Daniel, 178
Dhaka University, 66, 81
Dodd, Chris, 219
Dostum, Rashid, 229
Dulles, John Foster, 198
Dupree, Louis, 116
Durand Line, 26, 27, 117, 118, 121, 122, 221, 247

East Pakistan, ix, 32, 51, 55–56, 59, 62, 64, 72, 76, 77, 78–81, 94, 97, 105
   economic exploitation of, 74–75
   West Pakistan's invasion of, 78, 81–93, 97–98, 148, 205
   see also Bangladesh
Economist, 81, 245
Economist Intelligence Unit, 257
Education, Pakistan Ministry of, 4–5, 58, 258–59
Egypt, 23, 57, 80, 106, 121, 122, 129, 175, 263, 264, 265, 267
Eisenhower, Dwight D., 267
elections, Pakistani, xii
   of 1959, 57
   of 1964, 81

   of 1970, 68, 77, 93, 97, 105
   of 1977, 109, 114
   of 1988, 134, 173–74
   of 1990, 135
   of 1993, 135
   of 1999, 140
   of 2002, 268
   of 2008, 27–28, 158, 159–61, 168, 181–82, 184, 254–55, 269, 270, 271
Environment Ministry, Pakistani, 16
European Union, 22, 25

Faisal, King of Iraq, 199
Faisal, King of Saudi Arabia, 265
Faisal, Turki bin, Prince of Saudi Arabia, 129
Faiz, Faiz Ahmed, 36–37, 52, 95, 199*n*, 263
"Fall of the Taliban" (seminar), 148
Farenheit 9/11 (film), 227
Farooqi, Amjad, 154
Fasihudin, Fauzia, 171, 172, 176
Fasihudin, Rehana, 171, 172
Federal Bureau of Investigation (FBI), 151, 186
Federal Investigation Agency (FIA), 11, 159, 170
Federal Security Force, 101, 115
Finance Ministry, Pakistani, 156, 258
Fischer, Joschka, 229
Fisk, Robert, 129
Ford, Gerald, 111–12
France, 13, 49, 57, 79, 80, 179, 216, 217, 264
Franks, Tommy, 268
Friends Not Masters (Ayub Khan), 62
Fukuyama, Francis, 120–22

Gadhafi, Mu'ammar al-, 117, 180
Galbraith, Peter, 170
Gall, Carlotta, 155
Gandhi, Indira, 86, 87, 90, 108, 132, 205–6, 207
Gandhi, Mohandas, 20, 21, 22, 33, 34, 35
Gandhi, Rajiv, 132, 209
Gates, Robert, 180, 239*n*
Geo, 9, 165, 261
Germany, 49, 217, 241, 244–45
Ghalib, 263
Ghani, Owais, 275

Ghazi, Abdul Rashid, 12, 13, 14–16
Gillani, Yousaf Raza, 271, 274
Godfrey, J. H., 33
Goldwater, Barry, 191–92
Gorbachev, Mikhail, 130
Gordon, Charles, 45, 250
Goss, Porter, 145
Gracey, Douglas, 52, 73
Graham, Bob, 145
Great Britain, 10, 11, 13, 19–22, 31, 49,
    51, 53, 57, 60, 72, 80, 85, 115,
    160, 178, 197, 199, 216, 236,
    239, 241, 264
  see also British Empire
Griffin, Keith B., 61
Gromov, Boris V., 131
Guantánamo Bay, 153
Guardian, 114
Guerrilla Warfare (Guevara), 88
Guevara, Che, 84, 88, 229
Gul, Hamid, 183
Gulf War, 265

Hadley, Stephen, 275
Hameed, General, 91–92
Hanif, Mohammed, 165–66
Haq, Abdul, 129
Haq, Anwarul, 115
Haq, Fazle, 123
Haqqani, Husain, 161n, 273
Harkatul Ansar, 149
Hassan, Gul, 84, 92, 137
Hassan, Mubashir, 94
Hassan, Sibte, 40, 52
Hazelhurst, Peter, 89
Heer and Ranjha (Waris Shah), 39
Hekmatyar, Gulbuddin, 222, 231
Henry III, King of France, 187
Hindu Kush, 121, 243
Hindus, 18, 21, 29, 30, 31, 33, 38, 43,
    44, 45, 52, 72, 76, 83, 118, 148,
    171, 211
Hu Jintao, 15
Human Rights Commission of Pakistan,
    10
Huq, Mazharul, 115
Hussain, Altaf, 9, 10
Hussain, Maulvi Mushtaq, 128, 171
Hussain, Nasser, 152
Hussein, King of Jordan, 106
Hussein, Saddam, 160, 263

If I Am Assassinated (Zulfiqar Bhutto),
    110, 169
Iftikhar Khan, Mohammed, 53
Ijaz-ul-Haq, 14
Ilyas, Maulana, 6
India, ix, 6, 13, 14, 18, 19, 21, 26, 44,
    46, 49, 54, 56, 59, 70–72, 86, 91,
    100, 117, 126, 132, 140, 141,
    144, 147, 156, 179, 181, 197–98,
    200–201, 202, 204, 221, 247,
    258, 262
  civil service in, 71
  economy of, 236
  1857 mutiny in, 34n, 52–53
  nuclear weapons of, 108, 109, 209,
    211, 213–16
  Pakistan's wars with, 62–63, 73,
    141–43, 149, 197, 201, 203,
    205–6
  partition of, 3, 9, 29–31, 34–35, 37,
    38, 43, 149
  strikes in, 33–34
  in World War II, 32–33, 51–52, 71, 73
India International Centre, 207
Indian Congress Party, 44
Indian National Army, 51–52
Indonesia, 71, 82, 226, 267
Information, Pakistan Ministry of, 4–5,
    62
International Court of Justice, 273
International Law Commission, 83n
International Monetary Fund (IMF), 256
Inter-Services Intelligence (ISI), 13–14,
    16, 17, 27, 107, 119, 124, 129,
    131, 136–37, 142, 145, 146, 147,
    149–50, 152, 153, 155, 157, 163,
    168, 172, 176, 183, 211, 214,
    225, 231, 243, 245, 251
In the Line of Fire (Musharraf), 142, 145,
    156
Inzamam-ul-Haq, 6
Iqbal, Allama, 3
Iqbal, Muhammad, 39–40, 47, 263
Iran, 26, 47, 101, 103, 111–12, 118,
    150, 157, 181, 183, 199, 220,
    230, 245, 246–47, 263, 264
Iraq, 101, 160, 191, 199, 225, 236, 237,
    264, 265
Iraq-Iran War, 12
Iraq War, 151, 243, 244–45, 253, 270
Ishaq, President, 135

Islam, xi, 12–13, 27, 33, 35–36, 40, 43, 44–45, 53, 74, 107, 123–24, 215
  Ahmediyya sect of, 45–49
  in India's partition, 29–31
  Pakistan established for, 29–30, 55
  women in, 23–24
Islamabad, 4, 9, 12, 14–16, 26, 259
  2005 earthquake in, xi
Islamic Summit, 108
Islam Party, *see* Jamaat-e-Islami
Israel, 34*n*, 57, 80, 106, 122, 129, 132–33, 147, 160, 172, 183–84, 211, 212, 243
Italy, 217, 241
Itaoui, Ghinwa, 172

Jaish-e-Mohammed, 149, 214
Jalib, Habib, 68, 204
Jamaat-e-Islami (JI), 4–5, 22–24, 36, 44, 57, 67, 83, 107, 124, 161*n*, 229, 267, 269
Jamiat-Ulema-e-Islam (JUI), 22–23, 36, 99
Jamshed, Junaid, 6
Japan, 33, 52, 70–71, 212
Jinnah, Fatima, 41–42, 60
Jinnah, Mohammed Ali, 3, 30, 32, 33–34, 35, 36, 40, 41–44, 49, 50, 54, 72, 81, 162, 196, 198, 199*n*, 203
Johnson, Niel M., 112
Jordan, 106, 113, 264
Joseph, Robert, 210–11

Kabul, 26, 118, 119, 136, 147, 171, 181, 228, 233–34, 237, 262
Kabul University, 230
Kakar, Wahid, 138–39
Kansi, Aimal, 186
Karachi, Pakistan, 7–8, 9–11, 12, 27, 30, 122, 167
Karachi stock exchange, 86
Karamat, Jehangir, 139, 249, 250–51, 252
Kartography (Shamsie), 122
Karzai, Ahmad Wali, 240
Karzai, Hamid, 26, 157, 161, 218, 224, 229, 230, 232, 233, 235, 239, 240, 241, 246–47
Kashmir, 6, 12, 62, 63, 93, 116, 142, 195, 197, 198, 202, 203, 205, 207, 214, 215–16, 252, 262, 268

Kasuri, Ahmed Raza, 94, 114–15
Kasuri, Khurshid Mahmood, 169, 241
Kasuri, Mahmud Ali, 63, 101, 169
Kayani, Ashfaq, 27–28, 155, 157, 189
Kayani, Justice, 48
Keeler, Christine, 60
Kelsen, Hans, 104
KGB, 120, 130
Khalilzad, Zalmay, 226
Khan, Akbar, 52, 101
Khan, Ali Kuli, 140, 156
Khan, Ali Mardan, 238
Khan, A. Q., 109, 183
Khan, Chakar, 103*n*
Khan, Ghaffar, 20–21, 22, 24, 28, 269, 275
Khan, Ghulam Ishaq, 135, 173
Khan, Imran, 164
Khan, Ismail, 230, 231
Khan, Khan Qurban Ali, 54
Khan, Liaquat Ali, 30, 54, 55, 181
Khan, Meraj Mohammad, 93
Khan, Munir Ahmed, 109
Khan, Sahibzada Yaqub, 135
Khan, Tikka, 73, 105
Khan, Wali, 275
Khan, Zafarullah, 45, 198
Khattak, Afrasiab, 25, 275
Kholi, General, 170
Khrushchev, Nikita, 200
Khyber Pass, 17, 198
Kipling, Rudyard, 19–20, 22, 198
Kissinger, Henry, 67, 110–11, 112
Koran, 18, 24, 25, 123, 130, 161, 227, 264, 270, 271
Korean War, 62, 198
Kosovo, 150, 247, 262
Kosygin, Aleksey, 63
Kurtz, Stanley, 193
Kux, Dennis, 250–51

Lahore Resolution, 31
Lal Masjid, 12, 13, 15–16, 17
Lal salaams, 66
Lashkar-e-Taiba, 214
Lebanon, 172, 243, 265
Lee Kuan Yew, 94
Leghari, Benazir, 137
Leghari, Farooq, 137–38, 140, 176, 177
"Letters to Uncle Sam" (Manto), 56–57

Lewis, Bernard, 265
Libya, 117, 171
Lodhi, Maleeha, 145–46
Los Angeles Times, 177
Ludhianvi, Sahir, 34

McConnell, Michael, 224
McGirk, Tim, 232
MacMunn, George, 51, 53
Magnitogorsk Iron & Steel Works Open
     JSC, 8
Maher, Bill, 232
Mahfouz, Naguib, 263
Mahmood, Masood, 115
Mahmood, Sultan Bashiruddin, 109
Mahmud, Mufti, 23
Maiwandi, Ajmal, 238–39
Majlis-i-Ahrar, 44
Makhdoom Amin Fahim, 270, 271
Malik, Iftikhar, 160
Malik, Rehman, 159–60, 273
Manekshaw, General, 206
Manto, Abid Hasan, 9
Manto, Saadat Hassan, 37–38, 56–57
Mao Zedong, 62*n*, 67
Marri tribe, 102
Marshall, George C., 196
Marshall Plan, 235
Martial Races of India, The (MacMunn),
     51
Martin, Kingsley, 60
Mary, Queen of Scots, 187
Masood, Baitullah, 162, 275
Massoud, Ahmed Shah, 229–30
Mathew, John, 115
Matin, Abdul, 84, 88
Maududi, Abul Ala, 23, 67
Maududi, Maulana, 44, 45, 47
Mazari, Shireen, 212–13
Meir, Golda, 44
Members of the National Assembly
     (MNAs), 5
Mengal, Ataullah, 102
Messervy, Frank, 52
Miliband, David, 188
Minto, Lord, 31
Miraj-nameh, 230
Mirza, Iskander, 43, 55, 56, 57, 58
MI6, 153
Mitha, A. O., 91, 92
Moguls, 17–19, 108, 125–26, 204, 238

Mohammad, Ghulam, 43, 55, 195
Mohammad Reza Shah Pahlavi, 101,
     103, 118–19
Mohammed, Maulana Faqir, 16
Montgomery, Bernard, 73
Mossad, 132
Mountbatten, Edwina, 3
Mountbatten, Lord, 3
Mozambique, 79
Mubarak, Hosni, 161
Mubarakmand, Samar, 109
Muhammad, Prophet, 45
mujahideens, 123, 129, 130, 135, 153,
     205
Mukti Bahini (Liberation Army), 83–84
Munif, Abdelrahman, 263
Munir, Justice, 48
Musa, General, 63
Musharraf, Pervez, 2, 4, 8, 14, 16, 26, 27,
     140, 141, 145, 150–51, 153, 163,
     165–66, 167, 177, 178, 187, 188,
     189, 191, 211–12, 214, 215, 219,
     223, 240, 249, 250, 256, 259,
     260, 261, 262, 267–68, 272, 273,
     274
  attempts on life of, 14, 148, 149,
     153–54
  lawyers and judicial activists as threat
     to, 7–12, 16, 162, 164–67, 188,
     254, 260, 269
  rise to power by, 129, 143–44, 149
  September 11 response of, 146–47
  in 2008 election, 27–28, 158,
     159–60, 168, 254, 255, 269
Mushtaq, Maulvi, 115
Muslim Brotherhood, 23, 263, 267
Muslim League, 21, 23, 24, 28, 30, 31,
     33, 34, 39, 43, 44, 45, 47, 54, 55,
     70, 72, 125, 127, 128, 140, 144,
     260, 271, 273
Muttahida Majlis-e-Amal (MMA), 16,
     22–25
Muttahida Qaumi Movement/United
     National Movement (MQM),
     9–11

Nagi, John, 225
Najibullah, Mohammad, 136
Nasser, Gamal Abdel, 57, 265
National Assembly, Pakistan, 77, 101,
     105, 140, 269

National Awami Party (NAP), *see* Awami
    National Party
National Movement for the Restoration
    of Pakistani Sovereignty, 153
National Reconciliation Ordinance, 160,
    273
National Security Council, 58–59, 147
NATO, 3, 23, 25–27, 130, 157, 202,
    216, 217, 223, 229, 230, 231,
    241–42, 243, 244, 245–46, 248,
    263, 264, 275, 276
Nawaz, Asif, 138
Nazimudin, Khwaja, 55
NBC, 219
Negroponte, John, 159, 168, 188, 248,
    272, 275
Nehru, Jawaharlal, 3, 21, 33, 37*n*, 44,
    100, 196–97, 200–201, 203
Neumann, Ronald E., 235
New York Times, 19, 23, 57–58, 90, 132,
    150, 155, 179, 183, 235, 243–44,
    263, 272, 275
Niazi, "Tiger," 73, 84, 90
9/11 Commission Report, The, 16, 191,
    192, 225
Nixon, Richard, 67, 204
Non-Aligned Conference, 147
Noon, Feroze Khan, 196–97
Northern Alliance, 26, 157, 222, 223,
    226, 227
North-West Frontier Province, 3, 17,
    22–27, 32, 73, 80, 93, 97, 98,
    101, 117, 121, 122, 123, 158,
    213, 253, 256, 257

Obama, Barack, 218–19, 245, 252, 265
Office of Intelligence and Research
    Analysis, 59
Olson, Eric T., 274–75
Omar, Mullah, 26, 136, 145, 147–48, 225
Operation Enduring Freedom, *see*
    Afghanistan, U.S. invasion and
    occupation of
Operation Grand Slam, 62
Operation Searchlight, 83
Ottoman Empire, 221

Pajhwok Afghan News, 234
Pakistan, ix–xii
    agriculture in, 99–100
    antivice campaigns on, 24

army of, x, 2, 12, 13, 32, 52, 53, 57,
    66, 70, 72–73, 75–76, 77, 78,
    84–85, 88, 91, 102, 105, 108,
    114, 116, 122, 129, 134, 138,
    140, 141, 142–43, 163, 180–81,
    197, 206, 215, 253, 267
assassinations in, 1, 12, 149, 151; *see
    also* Bhutto, Benazir, assassination
    of; Zia-ul-Haq, Mohammad,
    death of
birth of, 31–32, 35, 41
black market in, 1, 122–23
bombings in, 16, 149, 150, 218
climate of, 2
Communists in, 23, 36, 37*n*, 52, 67,
    75, 101
constitutions of, 11, 32, 56, 135, 139
corruption in, 5–6, 7–12, 43, 101,
    137–39, 159, 160, 161, 164, 173,
    174, 176, 178, 187
cyclone disaster in, 77, 91
democratic politics in, xii, 4–5, 50,
    59–60, 64, 181, 188, 190
economic inequality in, 1–2, 5, 27,
    41, 53–54, 60–61, 107, 108, 185,
    276
economy of, 60–62, 67, 72, 74–76,
    85–86, 100, 255–59
education in, 1, 12, 27, 41, 48, 100,
    104, 108, 144, 185, 213, 256,
    258, 259
Egyptian invasion supported by, 57,
    80
elite vs. people in, ix, xi–xii, 1–2,
    5–6, 8
health care in, 27, 108, 185, 256,
    258
heroin trade in, xi, 17, 25, 122, 123,
    127, 156, 256
histories of, 204
housing in, 258, 259–60
India's wars with, 62–63, 73, 141–43,
    149, 197, 201, 203, 205–6
infant mortality in, 100
land reform in, 144, 185, 257, 258
literacy in, xi, 62*n*, 100, 140, 256,
    258
malnutrition in, 1
martial law declared in, 114, 161,
    166
mass rapes in, 29–30

Pakistan *(cont.)*
    media in, 5, 9, 10, 13, 16, 23–24,
        144, 156, 163, 174, 177, 180,
        198–99, 261
    military rule of, ix, x, xi, 2, 5, 8, 27,
        98, 114–17, 128, 134, 160–61,
        184, 185, 188, 190; *see also*
        Musharraf, Pervez; Pakistan, army
        of; Zia-ul-Haq, Mohammad
    monsoon season in, 2
    nationalizations in, 99, 107, 125
    1977 coup in, 114–16, 118, 128
    nuclear capacity of, 3, 4, 49, 108–13,
        117, 119, 132, 147, 180, 183, 206,
        209–12, 213–15, 219, 262, 270
    parliament of, 2
    poets of, 36–40, 50, 263, 277–78
    pornography in, 24
    privatization in, 7–8, 258, 260
    protests in, 8, 64–65, 170
    Qissa Khwani, 20–21
    religious groups in, x, xi, 1, 3, 4–5,
        6–7, 12–17, 27, 123–24, 242,
        254
    sex industry in, 14–15, 24
    sixtieth anniversary of, 2
    strikes in, 10, 72, 77–78
    Taliban movement in, 242, 254
    tax regime in, 100
    technology in, 1
    twentieth anniversary of, 4
    2005 earthquake in, xi
    unemployment in, 86
    U.S. arms embargo on, 112, 113,
        202, 262
    U.S. influence in, ix–x, 12, 13,
        27–28, 32, 50, 53, 56, 58–59,
        60–61, 67, 84, 85, 109–11,
        113–14, 116, 119, 120–21, 129,
        143, 145–47, 149, 150, 159,
        161, 179, 184, 187, 192,
        195–97, 198–99, 201–2, 226,
        251–52, 254, 255, 268–69, 270,
        272–73
    wheat smuggling from, 276
    see also Durand Line; India, partition of
Pakistan Atomic Energy Commission,
    108
Pakistan Constituent Assembly, 43
Pakistan Muslim League, 125
Pakistan National Alliance, 109

Pakistan Peoples Party (PPP), 25, 63, 73,
    77, 93, 94, 98, 100, 101, 103,
    104, 114, 124, 137, 139, 140,
    158, 161–62, 164, 167, 169, 171,
    173, 174, 175, 176, 182, 184,
    186, 188, 203n, 255, 260, 269,
    270, 271, 274, 276, 277
Pakistan Resolution, 23
Pakistan Steel Mills, 7–8, 139
Pakistan Times, 64, 196, 198–99
Palestine, 106, 243, 263–64
Palestine Liberation Organization, 107
Papanek, Gustav, 60–61
Party of Islamic Scholars, *see* Jamiat-
    Ulema-e-Islam
Pashtuns, 18, 25, 26, 27, 117, 220, 231,
    241, 243, 247
Pathan Unarmed, The (Banerjee), 21n
Pearl, Daniel, 149, 150–52, 153, 155, 220
Pearl, Mariane, 151, 220
People (newspaper), 78
People's Democratic Party of Afghanistan
    (PDPA), 118, 120
Pervez, Tariq, 11
Peshawar, University of, 23
Petroline FZC, 160
Planning Commission, 93
PML-Q, 171
Pollock, George, 238
Powell, Colin, 147, 240, 241
Powers, Gary, 200
Pramoedya Ananta Toer, 263
President to Hold Another Office Act
    (2004), 11
Primakov, Yevgeni, 130, 135
Pritam, Amrita, 38–39
Prodi, Romano, 217
Progressive Papers Limited, 58
Punjab, 29, 30, 33, 35, 39, 47, 68, 71,
    73, 93, 168, 171, 203

Qadir, Manzur, 57
Qadir, Saeed, 106
Qissa Khwani, 20–21
Quetta, Pakistan, 24, 102
"Quit India" movement, 33
Qureshi, Moin, 135
Qureshi, Nawab Sadiq Hussain, 108

Rabbani, Burhanuddin, 229, 230
Rahman, Akhtar Abdul, 119

Rahman, Mujibur, 66–67, 75, 76, 78–79, 81, 83, 90, 91, 101, 105
Rana, Mukhtar, 93
Rangers, Pakistani, 15–16
Raphael, Arnold, 131
Reagan, Ronald, 170, 222
Red Mosque, 12, 13, 14, 15–16, 17
Redshirt movement, 20
Rehman, Asad, 103n
Rehman, Rashid, 103n
Reid, Richard, 151
Rendon Group, 234
Rice, Condoleezza, 148, 167
Riedel, Bruce, 155
Robinson, Colin, xiii
Roshan, Pir, 18
Roshnais, 18–19
Roy, Ranajit, 78–79
Royal Indian Navy, 31, 33
Rubin, Elizabeth, 243–44
Rumsfeld, Donald, 112, 218
Russia, 7, 8, 181, 212, 216, 220, 221, 227, 231, 246, 247

Sagan, Scott, 211, 212
Sahib, Khan, 20
Salah ad-Din, 266
Salam, Abdus, 49
Salazar, António de Oliveira, 79
Samdani, K., 115
Saudi Arabia, 8, 12, 15, 23, 45, 67, 122, 129, 172, 173, 189, 227, 256, 264, 265–66
Savak, 118
Sayyaf, Abdul Rasul, 230
Scheffer, Jaap, 244, 245, 248
Schlegelmilch, Jens, 178
September 11, 2001, terrorist attacks of, 6, 13, 26, 57n, 145, 147, 148, 154, 214, 223, 225, 227, 229, 241, 249, 262–63, 267
Shah, Abdullah, 174, 176
Shah, Safdar, 116
Shah of Iran, 101, 103, 118–19
Shamim, Aunty, 14–15
Shamsie, Kamila, 122
Sharia, 14–16, 23, 57, 99, 123, 230
Sharif, Muhammad, 125
Sharif, Nawaz, 5, 6, 27, 28, 125, 134, 135, 140, 142, 143, 144, 150, 154, 156, 158, 160, 161, 168, 171, 173, 188, 189, 248, 250, 253, 255, 260, 261, 269, 270, 271, 273, 275
Sharif, Shahbaz, 5, 6, 28, 125, 142, 143, 154, 158, 255
Sharif family, 99, 127, 128–29, 134, 273
Sharif Muslim League, 269
Sheikh, Omar Saeed, 152–53, 155
Shias, 12, 43, 45, 124, 231, 263
Shoaib, Mohammed, 57, 60
Sikhs, 29, 33, 52
Singapore, 33, 52, 94
Singh, Maharaja Ranjit, 45
Six Point plan, 66, 74–75, 85, 93
Somalia, 227, 250
Southeast Asia Treaty Organization (SEATO), 56, 199
Soviet Union, 23, 26, 51, 56, 63, 101, 103, 197, 200, 201, 207, 209
  Afghanistan invaded by, 13, 17, 19, 25, 117, 119, 120, 121, 122, 129–31, 132, 135–36, 148, 186, 191, 193, 195, 220, 222, 229, 231, 235, 238, 239, 241, 251, 267
Spain, 160, 178, 217, 266
Special Service Group (SSG), 91, 92
State Department, U.S., ix, 4, 42, 59, 91, 132, 145, 148, 151, 159, 162, 165, 170, 179, 195, 196, 249, 250, 272
Stewart, Rory, 236–37
Suddle, Shoaib, 175
Sufis, 39, 108, 142
Suharto, Mohammed, 226, 263
Suhrawardy, H. S., 80
Sunday Times, 66
Sunnis, 12, 23, 43, 45, 124, 263
Supreme Council of Nawab of Kalabagh, 69, 104
Supreme Court, Pakistan, 7, 8, 9, 11–12, 115–16, 162, 163, 165, 166, 183, 188, 189, 254, 260, 273, 274
Switzerland, 160, 178, 179
Syria, 106, 171, 265

Tablighi Jamaat (TJ), 6
Taliban, 13, 16, 24, 25, 26–27, 124, 136, 146, 147–48, 157, 162, 165, 174, 180, 181, 219, 222, 224, 225, 227, 231, 241, 242, 243, 247, 254
Taraki, Nur Muhammad, 119

Tashkent Treaty, 63
Taylor, Maxwell, 200
Tebhaga peasant uprising, 88
Thakur, Muttabir, 87
Thatcher, Margaret, 173, 222
Thompson, Herbert, 20–21
Time, 180, 232
Times (London), 89, 129
"Toba Tek Singh" (Manto), 38
Tolstoy, Leo, 46
Tomalin, Nicholas, 66
Truman, Harry S., 266
Turkey, 23, 121, 196, 197, 199, 239*n*, 263

United Nations, 84, 110, 160, 176, 184, 202, 216, 228, 258, 276, 229, 240
United Nations Population Fund, 1
United States, 11, 23, 86, 195–96, 207
    Afghanistan invaded and occupied by, 19, 22, 25, 26–27, 120, 130–31, 146, 147, 148, 152, 160, 191, 212, 216, 217–20, 222–29, 231–48, 251, 256, 264
    influence of, on Pakistan, ix–x, 12, 13, 27–28, 32, 50, 53, 56, 58–59, 60–61, 67, 84, 85, 109–11, 113–14, 116, 119, 120–21, 129, 143, 145–47, 149, 150, 159, 161, 179, 184, 187, 192, 195–97, 198–99, 201–2, 251–52, 254, 255, 268–69, 270, 272–73
    Pakistan arms embargo of, 112, 113, 202, 262
    Pakistani doctors in, 5
    Pakistani hostility toward, ix
    in Suez crisis, 57
Usmani, I. H., 108–9
Uzbekistan, 229, 246

Vance, Cyrus, 109–10
Vietnam War, 67–68, 121, 129, 142, 243
von Vorys, Karl, 69

Wahhabism, 12, 23, 142, 227
Wall Street Journal, 149, 150

Waris Shah, 39
war on terror, 12, 26, 165, 166, 180, 191, 261
Warren, Brigadier, 73
Waziristan, 18, 242, 251
Westinghouse, 112
West Pakistan, ix, 43, 52, 59, 61, 62, 64, 65, 66, 72, 74–75, 76, 77, 94, 98, 104, 105, 128
    East Pakistan's invasion of, 78, 81–93, 97–98, 148, 205
    see also Pakistan
Wilmers, Mary-Kay, xiii
World War II, 32–33, 51–52, 70–71, 72, 73, 113, 221, 265
Wu Bangguo, 262

Yahya Khan, Agha Muhammad, 68, 70, 76, 77, 81, 83, 85, 87, 90, 92–93, 203*n*
Yaqub, General, 81
Yeltsin, Boris, 7, 130, 212
Yousaf, Mohammed, 129–30, 148
Yousuf, Mohammad, 6

Zaheer, Sajjad, 52
Zahir Shah, 221, 222
Zaman, Fakhar, 277–78
Zapatero, José Luis Rodríguez, 217
Zardari, Asif Ali, 5, 137, 138, 139, 158, 160, 161*n*, 172–73, 174, 175, 176, 178, 179, 182, 187, 188, 248, 255, 260, 270, 271, 273
Zardari, Bilawal, 187
Zardari, Hakim, 172
Zia-ul-Haq, Mohammad, ix, 3, 4, 9, 12, 17, 25, 106–7, 113, 114, 115, 116, 117, 118, 119, 120, 122, 123, 124–25, 128, 129, 131, 135, 140, 141, 143, 144, 147, 148, 151, 156, 161*n*, 162, 169–70, 176, 180, 185, 207, 208, 259, 260, 268, 269, 271, 277
    death of, 131–33, 134, 173, 209
Zinni, Anthony, 249, 250–51, 252

About the Author

Writer and filmmaker Tariq Ali was born in Lahore and studied politics and philosophy at Oxford University. He was a prominent leader of opposition to the war in Vietnam and more recently the war in Iraq. Today he writes regularly for a range of publications including the *Guardian*, the *Nation*, and the *London Review of Books* and is on the editorial board of *New Left Review*. He has written more than a dozen books including nonfiction such as *Can Pakistan Survive?*, *The Clash of Fundamentalisms*, *Bush in Babylon*, and *Pirates of the Caribbean*, and fiction including *Shadows of the Pomegranate Tree*, *The Book of Saladin*, *The Stone Woman*, and *A Sultan in Palermo*, as well as scripts for both stage and screen. He lives in London.

THE STRUCTURE OF
AMERICAN INDUSTRY

THE STRUCTURE OF
AMERICAN INDUSTRY

SOME CASE STUDIES

edited by

WALTER ADAMS, Ph.D.

Professor of Economics
Michigan State University

Third Edition

New York   *The Macmillan Company*

Preface to the Third Edition

Most Americans, it is fair to say, believe with Lord Keynes that, "individualism, if it can be purged of its defects and abuses, is the best safeguard of personal liberty in the sense that, compared with any other system, it greatly widens the field for the exercise of personal choice. It is also the best safeguard of the variety of life, which emerges precisely from this extended field of personal choice, and the loss of which is the greatest of all the losses of the homogeneous or totalitarian state. For this variety preserves the traditions which embody the most secure and successful choices of former generations; it colours the present with the diversification of its fancy; and, being the handmaid of experiment as well as of tradition and fancy, it is the most powerful instrument to better the future."

Despite their general commitment to this article of faith, Americans have not been averse to a constant and critical reappraisal of their industrial system. Especially in the last two decades—under the impact of war and recession, international upheaval and competitive co-existence—they have asked old questions with renewed vigor. Is competition compatible with efficiency? Is private initiative conducive to growth? Is a market-oriented economy sufficiently productive and progressive to assure success in the race for survival? Is a competitive organization of industry a guarantee both of maximum freedom and optimum performance?

While this book does not pretend to offer definitive solutions or final answers, it does present a comprehensive, up-to-date, and kaleidoscopic view of American industry. It affords us a laboratory for analyzing industries with diverse forms of market structure, various patterns of market behavior, and different types of market performance. The industries included in this volume are, of course, "individuals"—and, in that sense, unique—but they are also representative of significant segments of the industrial framework. An understanding of their organization and operation, therefore, is the first step toward critical comparison and valid generalization. Most important, such understanding is the basis for a rational formulation of desirable and feasible public policies.

In preparing this volume we have tried to eliminate the abstruse and abstract, the esoteric and scholastic. To make this book palatable to the student and citizen, the intelligent layman and interested observer, we have resisted the temptation of writing for the professional grandstand—that relatively small and brave fraternity which has the capacity (and fortitude) to tackle the more specialized economic literature. In other words, we have tried to minimize the technical trade jargon without sacrificing

v

accuracy or scholarship. This, at least, is our claim to enlightened product differentiation.

We can only hope that professors of economics and business, the legal profession, and the business community will accord this volume the same warm reception as the earlier editions, and that our friends overseas will regard it as a contribution to their understanding of American industry.

Walter Adams

East Lansing, Michigan

Contributors

Walter Adams, Professor of Economics, Michigan State University; consultant to various Congressional committees; erstwhile member of Attorney General's National Committee to Study the Antitrust Laws.

Carl Brehm, Assistant Professor of Economics, Michigan State University.

Joel B. Dirlam, Associate Professor of Economics, University of Connecticut; expert witness before various Congressional committees.

Horace M. Gray, Professor of Economics, University of Illinois; expert witness before various Congressional committees.

William F. Hellmuth, Professor of Economics and Dean of the College of Arts and Sciences, Oberlin College; expert witness before various Congressional committees.

James B. Hendry, Associate Professor of Economics, Michigan State University; erstwhile consultant to Senate Small Business Committee.

Charles H. Hession, Professor of Economics, Brooklyn College.

Alfred E. Kahn, Professor and Chairman of the Economics Department, Cornell University; expert witness before various Congressional committees; erstwhile member of Attorney General's National Committee to Study the Antitrust Laws.

Charles C. Killingsworth, University Professor of Labor & Industrial Relations, Michigan State University; arbitration expert in the steel, rubber, and automobile industries.

Willys R. Knight, Professor of Economics, Georgia State College.

Theodore J. Kreps, Professor, Graduate School of Business, Stanford University; consultant to various Congressional committees; former Staff Director, Joint Congressional Economic Committee.

Robert F. Lanzillotti, Professor of Economics, Washington State University; expert witness before various Congressional committees.

Irwin M. Stelzer, Vice President, Boni, Watkins, Jason & Company.

Richard B. Tennant, Economist, McKinsey & Company; formerly, Assistant Professor of Economics, Yale University.

Contents

1. Agriculture   W. R. Knight   1
2. The Cotton Textile Industry   I. M. Stelzer   42
3. The Bituminous Coal Industry   J. B. Hendry   74
4. The Residential Construction Industry   C. Brehm   113
5. The Steel Industry   W. Adams   144
6. The Aluminum Industry   R. F. Lanzillotti   185
7. The Chemical Industry   A. E. Kahn   233
8. The Petroleum Industry   J. B. Dirlam   277
9. The Automobile Industry   R. F. Lanzillotti   311
10. The Cigarette Industry   R. B. Tennant   357
11. The Motion Picture Industry   W. F. Hellmuth   393
12. The Metal Container Industry   C. H. Hession   430
13. The Airlines Industry   H. M. Gray   468
14. The Newspaper Industry   T. J. Kreps   509
15. Public Policy in a Free Enterprise Economy   W. Adams   533
16. Epilogue: Organized Labor in a Free Enterprise Economy   C. C. Killingsworth   564

THE STRUCTURE OF
AMERICAN INDUSTRY

Chapter 1

WILLYS R. KNIGHT

Agriculture

SECTION I: INTRODUCTION

Agriculture is an industry whose economic characteristics approach those of pure competition. That a highly competitive condition is no guarantor of a healthy state of affairs is revealed by a study of this industry. Neither farmers themselves, nor students of economics, can be content with its performance. Three leading economic problems plague American agriculture. The first concerns low productivity per worker—a condition which, although far from universal, accounts for the depressed condition of thousands of farm families. Largely because there are so many small-scale operators, the average net income of farmers is probably lower than that of any other large producer group in the American economy.[1]

The second problem afflicting agriculture concerns marked price instability for farm products. It is not unusual for the total value of individual crops produced in the nation to vary 20 per cent from one year to the next, and numerous instances could be found where the variation has been 40 per cent or more. Because agricultural prices generally fluctuate with a greater rapidity than do costs of production, farmers' incomes are quite unstable from year to year.

The third problem is a persistent, powerful tendency for agricultural production in the United States to expand faster than market demand would warrant—in other words, the chronic "surplus" conundrum.

---

[1] It has been reliably estimated that for the year 1957, whereas the average annual wage per employed factory worker in the United States was $4,284, the average annual earnings (including nonmoney income and government payments) per worker engaged in agriculture was only $1,793. (Data from United States Department of Agriculture, *The Farm Income Situation*, July 1958, p. 25.)

1

Historical Background

A look into this nation's agricultural history shows that small-scale farms have always been with us, in fact, much more so in the past than today. A network of small farms was established right from the outset of this country; the abundance of land (plus generous policies for its distribution) and the lack of cash markets for agricultural products favored this development.

It would be a mistake to imply that public authorities in all the colonies intended that this new land should be covered with small-scale, independent farmers. Indeed, various schemes of farming on a group basis were given a brief try and, too, in some areas the attempt was made to transplant to America something akin to a late-type European manorial system. Economic forces played a large role in upsetting these plans. Land was so abundant in supply that its market value was slight, and its possession failed to bring economic power and wealth, as had been the case in the more populated European countries. Viewed from the standpoint of men of that period, the problem came into focus as a "labor shortage." Because of the abundant opportunity which workmen had to set up farms of their own, low-wage labor was hard to find for work on the large estates. Prior to the importation of Negro slaves, several measures were tried in the hope of overcoming the "labor shortage," but without success.[2]

Besides the economic handicaps, other blows were dealt the manorial system as a result of the American Revolution; it brought a legal end to quitrents and primogeniture, two pillars of the system. Moreover, since the large property owners were generally loyal to the British Crown, many estates were confiscated by the Revolutionists and broken up for distribution. In short, although the major handicaps were economic, the legal blows hastened the end of large estates. Later, the combined effects of the Civil War and new developments in production undermined the large plantations in the South.

The land policy followed after the American Revolution continued to be liberal (low cost), particularly after 1830, enabling small-scale agriculture to be extended over vast new areas. During the period 1800–60, the mid-continent (which is the heartland of American agriculture) was settled, the

---

[2] From this experience there is an important lesson to be learned, namely that institutions and practices which have been stable in one area of the world frequently cannot be established in another where the economic environment is different. Too often people think that any economic arrangement may be instituted simply by the forceful exercise of government authority. Yet, time and again, economic forces (which are silent and unseen) bring the downfall of such action.

better soil areas bearing a price of $1.25 per acre, and the poorer areas going for less according to their desirability. Nearly all the agricultural land east of the Mississippi River, and a considerable amount immediately west of it, had passed into private ownership prior to 1860 under this low-price policy. Conditions for acquiring land were made even easier in 1862 with the passage of the Homestead Act which provided for free land to bona fide settlers. In summary, almost anyone could secure as his own, at little or no cost, as much land as he could utilize, somewhere in America, from the time of the first settlements around 1620 until as late as 1875.

Besides the land policy and the "labor shortage" which hampered large-scale efforts, there was another economic factor which helped to set the pattern of small-scale agriculture in America, namely the lack of cash markets.[3] Markets were lacking, of course, because nearly everyone lived on farms and supplied his own requirements for agricultural products. Each family found it desirable not to push farm output to its maximum, but rather to be productive along many lines (spinning, weaving, dress-making, herb gathering, food processing and preservation, soap making, hunting, etc.). Corn was the basic food and a relatively few acres of it sufficed each family.

Though these historical circumstances may explain their origins, they do not tell why a network of family-size farms still blankets America. The old circumstances which generated the system are gone; cash markets are now abundant, land is expensive, and machinery has largely eliminated the need for low-cost hired labor. Why has not agriculture taken a course of development similar to that of industry generally, that is, toward large-scale operations? Iron-making, too, was once a small-scale enterprise in America, but today it is only performed by big concerns. The best answer to the question seems to be that large farms have been unable thus far to demonstrate marked superiority, in terms of production efficiency, over well-managed, family-size farms.[4]

[3] Attention should be called to certain important exceptions, namely that substantial cash markets did exist (chiefly in Europe) for tobacco, cotton, rice, indigo, and furs, and it was precisely in these cases that ambitious entrepreneurs found the incentive to organize relatively large-scale business enterprises in early America. Before these market opportunities could be exploited, a way had to be found to overcome the labor shortage. After several ideas failed, a solution was found (in the case of agricultural ventures, although not for the fur business) in the form of Negro slaves. To a considerable extent it is still true today that farming ventures which employ many men (now found mainly in the Southwest) rely on a cheap labor supply.

[4] In the case of certain minor crops, known as "specialty crops," it may be that the large-scale farms are more efficient.

Rise of Commercial Farming

Since the middle of the nineteenth century, the major development in American agriculture has been a transition from self-sufficing to "commercial" agriculture.[5] Not all regions have shared in this evolutionary development to an equal degree; some of them, like the Southern Appalachians and the Ozarks, still contain many subsistence farms. In such areas the farm operators have few resources of land and capital with which to work, and output per worker is very low. Methods of farming are inefficient and, in many cases, habits of steady work seem to be lacking.[6] The farms are small in size, the soil poor or hilly, machinery lacking, and the material level of living is low. These farmers continue a way of life similar to that of pioneers of an earlier century. They constitute a substantial proportion of the small-scale operators found in American agriculture.

What is it that brought the change to commercial farming, overcoming the way of life of independence and self-sufficiency found on the small farms of earlier generations? It has been the appearance of cash markets for farm products which came in as urban centers developed. Why did urbanization arise? The chief instigator has been the rise of manufacturing industry.[7] To a lesser extent—yet vital in the cases of tobacco, wheat, and cotton—foreign markets comprised important cash markets. As long as this country consisted mainly of rural people, little specialization in agricultural production occurred (tobacco and cotton, with their large foreign markets at an early date, being the exceptions).

With the appearance of cash markets, farmers became anxious to step up production. They became cost conscious and interested in adopting scientific methods. Output per worker grew, and living levels rose, as a rule. Fluid milk, fruit, vegetable, and poultry production developed around urban centers, almost irrespective of the suitability of the physical environment. Besides its great impact on the *demand* for agricultural products, urbaniza-

---

[5] Commercial agriculture means production geared to cash markets. Since experience reveals that it pays to specialize, it also tends to mean the production of but one, or a few, products.

[6] There is probably more logic in the "laziness" of the self-sufficing farmers than is apparent on the surface. That is, it may well be that on these farms the marginal utility to be derived from devoting extra hours to productive work is so small that spending the time in leisure yields greater satisfaction.

[7] American leadership in the past seems to have greatly underestimated the impact of industrialization. Neither the extent of manufacturing development, nor the repercussions it would bring to agriculture and other spheres of American life, seem to have been anticipated by leaders in government, agriculture, business, or education.

tion affected agriculture in another respect which concerned the conditions of *supply*. It attracted labor away from the farms, thereby encouraging the farmers to reorganize their methods and adopt machinery in order to supply the market. Moreover, the pull of good jobs in the city caused the gradual abandonment of the little farms on the hillsides and on poor soils, leaving only the better situated farms in operation. The combined effect of these revolutionary forces was strongly in the direction of larger productivity per worker in agriculture.[8]

In addition to the impetus which it gave toward larger output and specialization, commercial agriculture brought many other changes for American farmers, some of which were unfortunate. Whereas, under the subsistence pattern he had been able to erect a little economic island for his family, insulated from market disturbances, now he became linked to the ebb and flow of supply-and-demand fluctuations which were sensitive to dynamic developments throughout the nation (and the world). No longer his own master under his vine and fig tree, he became an anxious listener to the latest market reports, a heated participant in tariff controversies and finally, an advocate of a nationally sponsored system of guaranteed "fair" agricultural prices and production control. Another unfortunate development, for which the shift to commercial agriculture was partly responsible has been the apparent breakdown of a rural society in the United States increasingly, rural people have become oriented toward cities for their recreation, education, church affiliation, etc.

On the other hand, commercial agriculture has brought great blessings to today's farmer; it has made possible high production levels (and thereby high real incomes) undreamed of by his forefathers—levels of living impossible of attainment on the old, highly diversified, subsistence homesteads While they have remained small in terms of ownership, management, and labor requirements, family-size farms in this new era of agriculture have been able to become truly large-scale in terms of output, if judged by the standards of the past. It has been comforting to the American ideals of freedom and individualism that, despite the trend in so many industries toward production units involving the disciplined, specialized, cooperative efforts of thousands of men under one business management, the great field of agriculture still offers a remunerative livelihood to a family-size enterprise (if conducted efficiently). The great strides in farm technology during the

[8] The urban influence (or lack of it) does not entirely determine the character of agriculture in a given region; physical factors such as soil, climate, and topography also modify it.

last century seem not to have placed the family-size farm at a disadvantage; in fact, it seems to have been strengthened, as a rule. At least, no super-efficient, large-scale system of farming now looms on the horizon.[9]

The Problem of Low Productivity

There is a wide variety in the levels of production existing among the units which make up American agriculture. (See Table 1.) Although one

TABLE 1

Number of Farms by Economic Classes, United States, 1950 and 1954

Types of Farms	Value of Sales Class Limits	Number of Farms 1950	1954
		Thousand	*Thousand*
Commercial		3,706.4	3,327.6
Class I	$25,000 and over	103.2	134.0
Class II	10,000 to 24,999	381.2	448.9
Class III	5,000 to 9,999	721.2	706.9
Class IV	2,500 to 4,999	882.3	812.0
Class V	1,200 to 2,499	901.3	763.3
Class VI	250 to 1,199 [a]	717.2	462.4
Other		1,672.8	1,455.4
Part time	250 to 1,199 [b]	639.2	574.6
Residential	Under 250	1,029.4	878.1
Abnormal [c]		4.2	2.7
Total		5,379.3	4,783.0

[a] The operator worked off the farm less than 100 days and the farm sales were greater than other family income.

[b] The operator worked off the farm 100 or more days and had other family income that exceeded farm sales, or other family income exceeded farm sales.

[c] Public and private institutional farms, community projects, etc.

Source: Census of Agriculture, 1950, 1954.

may expect, as a general rule, a well-managed, family-size farm in this decade to achieve a gross output of $10,000 or more, note that only a small minority are able to do so. (A *gross* output of $10,000 would yield, after

[9] Some pertinent information bearing on this matter is found in a provocative study of the dairy industry by C. R. Hoglund, *Economy of Improved Production Practices on Specialized Dairy Farms in Southeastern Michigan,* Ag. Econ. 491, April 1952, Michigan State College Agricultural Experiment Station, East Lansing, Michigan. According to Hoglund, the economies to be had by shifting from a one- to a two-man farm are almost negligible, assuming *usual* production practices. Upon the adoption of the best practices, the economies of the shift might amount to as much as a 14 per cent reduction in costs per unit of output. In any case, the economies of a three-man farm over a two-man one were estimated to be hardly appreciable.

deducting production expenses, an income for family living of about $5,000.)
A surprising number—over a million—of the "commercial" farms had gross
sales of $2,500 or less in 1954! Observe, however, the marked shrinkage
(about 25 per cent) in the number of low-productivity enterprises between
1950 and 1954. This is a very favorable trend judged from an economist's
point of view.

Beside the commercial agriculture group, there are a large number of
part-time and residential farms. They may be excluded from a discussion
of agriculture's problem situations because the people living on these farms
supplement their incomes substantially with pensions, investments, and nonfarm jobs. They are not really farm people.

Of the real, bona fide, small-scale operators there are a large number of
"welfare" cases; it has been estimated that about 20 per cent are overage,
3 per cent underage, 3 per cent widows, and nearly 5 per cent are disabled.[10]
Additional economic help for these people must come chiefly from welfare
agencies, not from farming employment.

Nevertheless, after making these allowances, as of 1954 about 800 thousand small-scale farms remain—farms operated by able-bodied men with
little or no outside income.[11] The average productivity per worker in this
group is estimated to be about a third as large as that of workers on medium-
size farms. These workers constitute one of the largest and most depressed
groups in the nation; and, it may be added, a similar situation (and for
similar reasons) exists among the farm population in many other countries
(e.g., Canada). This group constitutes a great reservoir of human resources
which, from an economic point of view, is underemployed. It has been
estimated that raising the productivity of the underemployed workers of
all kinds in American agriculture up to the level of the average man on
medium-size family farms would amount to an addition of 2.5 million workers to the nation's labor force.[12] The problem of underemployment in agriculture is found all across the nation, but it is concentrated much more in
some regions (notably the South) than in others.[13]

[10] For a concise, pertinent analysis of the small-scale farm problem, see the pamphlet
prepared for the Joint Committee on the Economic Report (U.S. Congress) by W. W.
Wilcox and W. E. Hendrix, *Underemployment of Rural Families,* Washington: Government Printing Office, 1951.

Also see *Low Production Farms,* Agric. Inform. Bulletin 108, Washington: U.S. Department of Agriculture, 1953.

[11] Hereafter in this chapter, when mention is made of the small-scale farm problem,
it is this group only to which the term applies.

[12] Wilcox and Hendrix, *op.cit.,* pp. 4, 5.

[13] Wilcox and Hendrix estimate that of the total number of underemployed farm
families, approximately 26 per cent are found in the North, 70 per cent in the South, and
4 per cent in the West. See Wilcox and Hendrix, *op.cit.,* p. 14.

Why is the number of small-scale operators so much larger, both absolutely and relatively, in some areas of America than in others? It does not seem to hinge on whether the farmer rents or owns his farm, or on the inherent abilities of racial or ethnic groups. It is connected with the amount of land, livestock, and equipment with which each farm operator has to work. Resources per operator vary widely among the various farming regions of the United States. (See Table 2.)

TABLE 2

Capital Investment and Average Net Farm Income of Typical Commercial
Family-Operated Farms, Selected Types in the United States

Types of Farms	Total Farm Capital, Jan. 1, 1956	Average Net Farm Income (1953–56)
	Dollars	Dollars
Dairy, Central Northeast	30,000	3,931
Hog-Beef Fattening, Corn Belt	60,460	6,805
Tobacco-Cotton, Coastal Plain, N. Car.	21,350	3,296
Cotton, Southern Piedmont	16,290	1,840
Cotton, Irrigated, High Plains, Tex.	88,540	10,408
Peanut-Cotton, Southern Coastal Plains	9,740	2,802
Winter Wheat, Southern Plains	76,540	5,092
Sheep Ranch, Northern Plains	81,770	4,912

Source: U.S. Department of Agriculture, *Farm Costs and Returns,* 1956.

The suggestion that comes to mind immediately is that farmers in the less productive areas need more access to capital funds with which to acquire sufficient resources. However, closer examination shows that it is not that simple; the ratio of labor to land is excessive in the areas dominated by small-scale farms, indicating that an out-migration of labor (rather than a heavy inflow of capital) is the thing primarily needed. Still, it would be a mistake to think that an additional capital inflow would serve no useful purpose; there is some undeveloped opportunity within agriculture (even in regions like the Southeast where the underemployment is most widespread), the development of which will require a large volume of investment funds.

One is led to wonder why it is, in the face of the great array of credit institutions—private banking, government, semigovernment, and cooperative credit institutions—that any farmer should lack adequate funds to exploit potentially profitable opportunities? It is true that much attention has been devoted, and a host of institutions created, during the last forty years, to provide farmers with adequate access to capital funds, and it is hard to conceive what else can be done. Actually, the heart of the problem is not a capital shortage; rather, experience and analysis have shown that the big limiting factor is the low level of managerial ability usually possessed by those who need more capital and cannot get it. In other words, no credit institution can hand out thousands of dollars to a farmer just because he needs it unless there is abundant evidence that he will use it wisely.[14] If additional capital is made available to many small-scale operators, it will have to be provided on a "supervised" basis; that is, some management direction from an outside source is needed—a ticklish and time-consuming matter for whatever agency or institution undertakes the job.

Probably the one most important reason why the small-scale farm problem is more serious in some regions than others is the differential rate of migration. Throughout American history, as well as that of other lands, more children are raised than are needed to replenish the labor supply in an agricultural society. Unless there is an out-migration, population pressure upon the land develops, resulting in the continued subdivision of good lands and the spread of farming onto marginal soils. Carried to its ultimate, the result is such a low output per worker, and therefore such low real incomes, that death rates rise to equal birth rates.

Consequently, there is an urgent need for nonfarm employment to absorb the surplus farm population. When such employment exists, particularly if it is nearby, the healthy flow from farm to city takes place, and that is probably a reason why statistics show farm productivity and living levels are highest in the vicinity of urban centers. However, distance alone does not explain the rate of migration; apparently education, income per family, health, and some other noneconomic factors bear upon it.[15]

Directly in line with the migration analysis just given, one finds in this nation that birth rates tend to be highest in those states where farm productivity is lowest, although this inverse relation between births and productivity is not perfect. In general, rural birth rates are about 20 per cent higher in the low-productivity states than in the high ones, and this tends to ag-

[14] It is entirely possible that the number of people who have enough managerial ability to handle large amounts of capital funds wisely is distinctly limited both in town and in the country. Surely, it is not assumed in manufacturing and commerce that *any* employee should be placed in a managerial position, responsible for large investment, just because he would like to be a manager. Yet, the assumption seems to exist in agriculture that anyone who wants to be a farm operator *can,* or *should,* somehow have access to all the capital needed to function on an adequate scale (which, in today's agriculture, would probably amount to $40,000 upwards per operator).

[15] The great differences in productivity between farmers in various regions of the United States are due, basically, not to natural or inherent factors, but rather to a host of things which go to make up the total culture of a group of people. There are numerous instances in the world where economically "backward" groups live adjacent to "progressive" ones.

gravate the man-land ratio in the poorer areas. It may also be noted that, as an average, the birth rate among farm people across the nation is twice that of city residents. Hence, a constant migration of the excess rural population to urban employment is essential if the small-scale farm problem is to be avoided.

The Problem of Price Instability

Leaving aside for the moment the problem of low productivity, there is to be considered that other great economic problem which afflicts agriculture, namely, the instability of agricultural prices (and the resultant wide variation in farm income). As farming has become increasingly commercial in nature, it has had to share the ups and downs of the national and international economy. These economic vicissitudes, usually originating in the nonfarm portion of the economy, have stricken farmers (raw material producers) with an accelerated effect. Agricultural prices, which link farmers to the total economy, have shown violent fluctuations, moving in the same direction (whether up or down) as the general price level but with a faster speed. To visualize how great the price variability has been, consider the price of hogs, for example, over the last thirty years. The average price received by farmers for hogs in 1924 was $7.34; in 1926, $11.79; in 1932, $3.34; in 1936, $9.37; in 1939, $6.23; in 1942, $13.04; in 1947, $24.10; in 1949, $18.10; in 1953, $21.60; in 1956, $14.50; and in 1958, about $21.00. Note that within a period of two or three years, the price would frequently change by 30 per cent or more.

To the farmer, market price—not steadiness of employment—constitutes the key to economic security.[16] Like it or not, his lot is tied to that of the city worker; when urban employment drops, agricultural prices tend to decline (due to lessened demand). Conversely, during years of urban prosperity, when consumers' incomes head upwards, the dollar volume of farm commodities marketed generally follows in a parallel manner. (See Fig. 1.)

The rapid rise in farmers' cash marketings since 1940 might suggest that rural people have enjoyed big earnings. Cases could be cited where this did not occur, but the general situation has been otherwise. In 1956 a careful estimate of hourly earnings [17] for work performed by operators and members of their families on typical commercial family-operated farms showed

---

[16] In this part of the chapter, which deals with the problem of price instability, it is assumed that attention is directed toward adequate size farms, not small-scale ones.

[17] Hourly labor earnings computed after deducting from farm income a reasonable charge for family-supplied capital. (Data from U.S. Department of Agriculture, *Farm Costs and Returns, 1956*, Agric. Inform. Bulletin 176, June 1957, pp. 38 ff.)

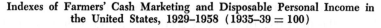

FIGURE 1

Indexes of Farmers' Cash Marketing and Disposable Personal Income in
the United States, 1929–1958 (1935–39 = 100)

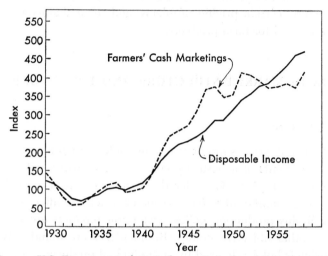

Source: U.S. Department of Agriculture, *Agricultural Statistics*, 1958.

the following: dairy farms, central Northeast, $.70; hog-beef raising, Corn
Belt, $.48; hog-beef fattening, Corn Belt, $1.15; tobacco-cotton, Coastal
Plain, North Carolina, $.79; cotton, southern Piedmont, $.31; cotton, irri-
gated, High Plains, Texas, $3.42; wheat-corn-livestock, northern Plains, $.34.
In all cases but one these returns were far below the average hourly wages
received by semiskilled workers in mass production industry at the time.

Chronic Surpluses

The reason why American farmers persistently produce in excess of market
requirements is to be found in the highly competitive structure of the industry. Each producer, being small in relation to the total, reasons that he
cannot influence market price in his favor, but that he can increase his net
income by cutting his production costs. To cut costs, he must adopt new
practices and buy new machinery. Almost inevitably, in order to achieve the
economies per unit of output which are possible with the improved technology, he must expand his scale of production. Moreover, the new equipment he buys makes it possible for him to produce much more than formerly
without additional physical strain. The pressure toward higher output persists even in the face of unfavorable prices (of which more will be said
later).

In this section a brief historical background of American agriculture was presented in order to bring into focus the origins of the three leading problems facing the industry. In the next section is found a discussion of the market structure, certain pricing problems, and some characteristics of the supply and demand for farm products.

SECTION II: MARKET STRUCTURE AND PRICE POLICY

Market Structure

The government price support program aside, agriculture meets rather well the requirements of a perfectly competitive industry, with certain exceptions (discussed later). Consider the characteristics of agriculture. (1) There are a *large number of sellers*, no one of which can affect market price perceptibly by his production policy. (2) *Farm products are standardized* and sold by rather objective grades. Brand names are found only seldom, and advertising is but rarely used by an individual producer in the endeavor to boost the demand for his output. It is true that groups of farmers engage in advertising programs occasionally; for example, Eastern apple growers advertise in the hope that people in their area will eat more "homegrown," rather than Washington apples. It is by no means clear that advertising of this sort is effective, however. (3) *Entry into the industry is easy.* There are no patents to hinder the adoption of the best methods of production or in choosing the item to be produced. New methods have been introduced by competitive producers as fast as they were willing and financially able to do so. As a result, methods of preparing the soil, planting, cultivating, and harvesting many field crops have been revolutionized in the last couple of generations. Ease of entry is also facilitated because capital requirements, though large from the point of view of a young man wishing to farm, are small when compared with those of many other industries. (4) *Prices of most farm products are determined on free markets* in which many offers from sellers and bids from buyers are made. Prices change frequently within the course of a trading day, and they are often quoted in cents (and, sometimes, fractions thereof), indicating that tiny changes in supply and demand are reflected in price.

The competitive market structure is reflected in the process of price determination, the actual day-to-day mechanics of which vary from product to product. Thus, the exact procedure of marketing and price determination vary in the cases of hogs, wheat, and apples, but in each instance price is finally determined in a highly competitive way. However, if government price support and acreage limitation are in effect, agriculture may no longer be considered as "highly competitive," according to the economist's meaning of this phrase.

Aside from the instances where the government price support and acreage limitation program restricts competition, there are certain other cases which suggest a monopoly element. *Formula* pricing of fluid milk under "Federal market orders"—replacing free-market pricing—has become widespread over the United States. It is doubtful, however, that the pricing system resulting from such orders has brought monopoly profits to dairy farmers because the restrictions laid down by Congress made the central object of the price formulas the achievement of *orderly* marketing rather than a premium return. In recent years, however, a rash of negotiated premiums over Federal milk order minimum prices has broken out which smack of a monopoly element. These premiums, although not derived from government pricing formulas, are nevertheless safeguarded by Federal marketing orders which effectively keep milk handlers from looking elsewhere for lower cost supplies of fluid milk.

In addition to the fluid milk case, those who doubt that agriculture is highly competitive often refer to the marketing practices of the California "Sunkist" growers as evidence of imperfect competition. Despite the manifestations of monopoly practices, competitive forces are preponderant in the production and marketing of oranges. It must be admitted that California orange growers advertise their brand name, that they have eliminated some degree of competition between themselves by forming one predominant marketing agency, and that oranges have been withheld occasionally from the market in the hope of securing a better price—practices hardly consistent with perfect competition. The real question, however, is whether the Sunkist program has been effective in securing a distinct premium price for growers as a result of their marketing and advertising program. The weight of evidence casts doubt on the program's effectiveness in influencing consumers to pay a premium for the product. The competitive factor that has acted to hold down prices of oranges has been the marked expansion of production in Florida, together with a big shift toward frozen concentrated juice as a marketing vehicle. Except for the temporary price spurts reflecting bad freezes in growing areas, the price of oranges since 1940 has failed to rise as much as prices for agricultural commodities generally. The "Sunkist" growers have not been able to differentiate their product in people's minds sufficiently to escape the downward pull of price.

Does a recitation of its highly competitive characteristics have much to do with the economic ills of the agricultural industry? Indeed, there is a bearing! The competitive engine explains the persistent tendency to over-produce (mentioned above). Also because of the *large number* engaged in the industry, it is virtually impossible (even through the medium of co-operative organization) for producers to achieve that regulation of output which would be necessary to achieve a stable price for their output. Be-cause of *product standardization* the individual producer has no chance to isolate himself from market disturbances and achieve a stable, adequate price for his output. The fact that prices are determined on *free markets*, in which a host of dynamic facts and fancies daily exert their influence without moderation, helps to explain why agricultural prices fluctuate so frequently and widely. Because of *ease of entry* it is possible for men to become farm-ers who—for reasons of either limited ability, poor health, laziness, old age, etc.—will never achieve output levels adequate for decent incomes. Truly, agriculture's basic economic ills are rooted deeply in the structure of the industry.

Structure of Prices

An examination of the price-making forces, supply and demand, will re-veal something of the behavior of agricultural prices and suggest a general view of the market outlook for the industry. Let us approach this subject from the viewpoint of a group of interested farmers who, worried by the long-continued weakness of agricultural prices, wonder if there is much prospect of a boost in the demand for their output in the future.

Long-Run Demand. The long-run demand for food [18] depends chiefly on the level of population in the United States. In view of the experience of the last couple of generations, it appears that rising incomes do not have a primary influence on total demand; per capita food consumption, whether measured in pounds or calories, is now estimated to be at the same level as in the first decade of this century. Since it is the *number* of people that makes the big difference, and since the national level of population is currently expanding at a rate of about 1.75 per cent a year, there is considerable hope of a substantial boost in the demand for agricultural products in the long run.

Leaving aside the domestic scene for the moment, it should be noted that foreign purchases of American farm products are more apt to decline than

---

[18] Space does not permit an examination of the demand for tobacco and cotton crops, the combined value of which normally amounts to about 9 per cent of the total farm output of this nation.

increase in the future, especially if Europe's East-West trade is revived.[19] Except for temporary increases associated with war periods, bona fide farm commodity exports have been declining since 1900. (Recently the volume shipped abroad has been large, but only because about two-fifths moved under some sort of government surplus disposal program.) With so many people in the world who are inadequately fed, it may seem strange that no great foreign demand for America's farm products is anticipated. The need exists but the means of payment are lacking.

What would a boost in income for poor people in the United States accomplish for agricultural demand? Available evidence indicates that demand would increase, but not markedly; therefore, as a long-run determinant, per capita income must be considered a factor of only secondary importance. Studies of consumer spending habits indicate that, if given more income, low-income groups would spend somewhat more for farm products, but they would not consume additional calories; rather they would eat slightly more of the animal products (like milk and beefsteak) and less bread, cornmeal, potatoes, and beans.[20]

Would wider dissemination of nutritional knowledge result in a large increase in the demand for farm products? Very likely it would not. Improving the diets of those who need it in America today will rarely require a greater expenditure of money because the most important barriers to overcome are ignorance and unwillingness to change food habits, not a lack of income. Actually, there are some reasons to believe that a wider spread of nutritional knowledge might cause a decline in the demand for food. In the first place, because there are many Americans who eat too much, a better understanding of nutrition might encourage them to curtail their food expenditures. Second, nutritional science teaches people the how and why of substituting less expensive foods for the more costly ones (fats, proteins, minerals, and vitamins of vegetable origin in place of nutrients from animal products). On balance, however, nutritional science and its wider dissemination are apt to be neutral factors in respect to the total demand for agricultural products in the years ahead.[21]

[19] Of total food products coming from American farms, the export market has taken about 10 per cent since 1946; this proportion is apt to decline to about 5 per cent in the years ahead, if prewar experience provides a reliable guide. For certain crops (wheat, cotton, and tobacco), export markets are much more important, however.

[20] This sort of substitution would mean a net increase in demand for farm products because it takes many more units of land, labor, and capital to produce a diet rich in animal foods than one of vegetable origin. Hence, a shift to the more expensive diet would mean an increased demand for the services farmers render, and more acreage would be needed.

[21] For a more comprehensive discussion of this subject, see T. W. Schultz, *The Economic Organization of Agriculture*, New York: McGraw-Hill, 1953, Chap. 6.

Will manufacturing industries ever consume a large share of the farm output for nonfood uses? It is entirely possible that industries may, though this prospect is not apparent in the foreseeable future. As matters now stand, farmers can be happy if new industrial uses are found fast enough to offset the replacement of farm products by synthetic fibers (which have cut deeply into the market for wool and cotton), by industrial processes which convert low-cost vegetable fats to replace soaps of animal-fat origin, etc. In short, it must be remembered that industrial technology is a two-edged sword—it cuts both ways!

In conclusion, what is the outlook in the long-run demand for food in this country? Assuming that the total population will continue to grow at the rate of 2.5 to 3 million per year, the result will be a substantial boost in the market requirements for agricultural products in, let us say, twenty years.

Long-Run Supply.   Will farm output expand faster than, or slower than, the expected population growth? Of course, no one can answer that question definitely. If farmers were to adopt generally all the good management practices that are known now, production could be increased much faster than the expected increase in consumers' needs. The hard thing to predict is how fast improved methods will be adopted. Leaving aside the impact of government controls, it appears that the improved technology will spread, and the total production of farm products in this country will gradually continue to rise, as it has in the past, even though agricultural prices were to decline from current levels. This increase is probable even though many small-scale operators and hired workers leave agriculture for jobs in cities. In other words, the increased output is expected to come in the future, as it has for some years past, from greater yields per acre, per worker, and per livestock unit, not from new areas and new workers being applied to farming.

Over the past thirty years this nation's population has increased about 45 per cent, whereas its index of total farm output for human consumption has risen 64 per cent. The large growth in production occurred despite a variety of Federal programs which have curtailed the acreage devoted to cultivation. Of course, a large volume of agricultural commodities has been made available for humans as a result of replacing horses and mules by tractors. Moreover, the efficiency of production per acre and per animal unit has been importantly increased over the last three decades. If a need should arise, production could be greatly expanded by increasing the number of acres devoted to crop production.

The outlook for agricultural demand twenty years ago (when a stationary population was expected soon) was much more gloomy than it is now because in the earlier period the ever-improving farm technology seemed to promise large and continued surpluses [22] of unmanageable proportions which would necessitate painful economic adjustments for many years to come. Farm groups have had a solid basis for fearing overproduction arising from improved technology because economic facts and analysis seem to indicate that, in view of the difficulty in transferring factors of production out of agriculture into other occupations, the greater supplies sent to market have tended to aid consumers more than they have benefited producers.

After surveying the long-run supply and demand conditions one may conclude that, whereas total population and food output are both expanding significantly, the situation of recent decades—wherein there is a tendency for agricultural production to grow slightly faster—is apt to continue in the foreseeable future.

Short-Run Demand.   The frequent and wide fluctuations in the short-run demand for farm products is at the heart of the problem of farm price and income stability. That the demand can fluctuate violently, in the short run, may be inferred from the marked instability of prices which is shown in Figure 2. This instability is due, almost entirely, to fluctuating demand, since production (also shown in Fig. 2) is relatively stable from year to year (except for years of severe drought such as 1934 and 1936).

FIGURE 2

Indexes of Farm Output and Prices Received by Farmers in the United States, 1919–1959 (1935–39 = 100)

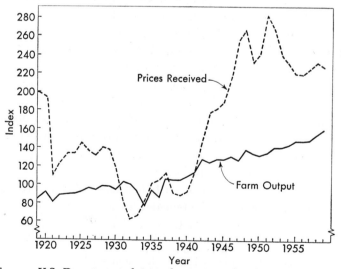

Source: U.S. Department of Agriculture, *Agricultural Statistics,* 1958.

[22] By "surplus" is meant a quantity of product that will not go into consumption at a given price. It does not mean an amount beyond the nation's capacity to consume in some form at some price; a surplus is a price phenomenon, basically, not a physical one.

Why does demand fluctuate so much? What determines the intensity of the short-run demand for agricultural products as a whole? Recalling that only a small proportion of the supply is sold abroad, it is clear that attention must be directed toward the forces underlying domestic demand. Both the facts and the theory of the matter indicate that domestic demand varies primarily with city consumers' incomes. (Note the parallelism between the volume of farmers' cash marketings and total disposable income in the nation—Figure 1.) Hence, whether farmers' markets are good depends mainly on the level of disposable income—not on the President, or Congress, on price support legislation, or men who are "sympathetic" with farmers' problems, or even the weather.

The fact that farmers' cash marketings soared upward after 1940 is evidence of a greatly stepped-up tempo of spending for farm products, and it seems to contradict a statement made earlier that the demand for agricultural products would not increase greatly if low-income groups were given more to spend. To resolve this apparent conflict, it is essential to differentiate between a rise in *money* income (due to general inflation) and one in *real* income. The upward surge in wage rates and other prices since 1942 has been primarily a *money* phenomenon, not a real one, and the marked increase in farmers' sales volume since that date is mainly a reflection of the impact of general monetary inflation in the agricultural marketplace.[23]

Before leaving the subject of demand, it is pertinent to consider the "elasticity of demand" for farm products. There are two aspects of it, namely *income*- and *price*-elasticity. Regarding the first, there has been a remarkable stability in the proportion of total consumer income spent on food over the past two decades which suggests that, at the retail level, income elasticity approaches unity. Increasingly, however, the consumer's dollars have been going for more processing-, packaging-, and marketing-costs. Hence, measured at the farm level, there is a different picture; studies indicate that the elasticity for food products as a whole is only about .2—in other words, very inelastic.[24] All this has a sober meaning to farmers in that they may expect only a small increase in the demand for their output as more Americans move into higher income brackets.

Regarding the second, it is believed that price-elasticity varies considerably from product to product; the demand for wheat, milk, and potatoes is

[23] Whereas the dominant increase in the demand for agricultural products is undoubtedly traceable to general monetary inflation, there is reason to believe that demand per capita increased slightly in real terms too.

[24] For a discussion of the income-elasticity for farm products with reference to its significance to farmers see Schultz, *op.cit.*, Chap. 5. For an exposition of the unit elasticity at the retail level see F. L. Thomsen, *Agricultural Marketing*, New York: McGraw-Hill, 1951, pp. 38–40.

said to be highly inelastic, while that for fruits is held to be elastic. For total food (and for total farm) products, the authorities hold at the farm level the demand is markedly inelastic. However, at the retail level there is some reason to believe that total demand may possess unit elasticity.[25] It is a pity that the demand for leading farm products is not elastic because, if it were, the problem of agricultural surpluses could be met by improving the efficiency of farm production; that is, by reducing the costs and selling prices, larger quantities of farm products could be marketed, still allowing normal profits for producers. But, alas, this is not the case.

Constant Short-Run Supply. Agriculture is rather unique among American industries in regard to its short-run supply character. The supply of all farm products coming on the market varies little from year to year, even though the demand for them may drop drastically. Does this violate economic principles? On first glance, economic theory seems to indicate that when demand declines, bringing a drop in market price, a curtailment of production is to be expected. However, further inquiry indicates that a drop in production may not occur, in the short-run, if most of the costs are fixed. This is the case with agriculture.

Most of the costs incurred by a farm operator do not vary with output. Real estate taxes, interest, and depreciation are all important costs, and they are fixed. The labor supply comes mostly from the operator's own family. The farmer cannot cut his costs by an appreciable amount, nor secure a higher price through curtailment of output. Only if a large number of farmers restrict production will price rise. This is not likely to happen, however, since it is usually to the individual farmer's interest to expand his own output if he thinks other farmers are reducing theirs. When every farmer calculates on that basis, the result, of course, is unrestricted production.

In a depression, when prices fall to a very low level, a farmer can find little alternative use for his labor. Consequently, he continues to farm as long as he can cover his variable costs. He may shift from one crop to another, but he cannot profitably shift his resources into a nonfarm use to any feasible degree. Moreover, if one farmer goes bankrupt, another takes his place. These factors help to explain the powerful tendency for agricultural production to remain at a high level even when confronted by a substantially lowered demand for farm products.

[25] For evidence that total demand is inelastic relative to the price factor see H. G. Halcrow, *Agricultural Policy of the United States*, New York: Prentice-Hall, 1953, Chap. 6. For evidence that unit elasticity seems to prevail at the retail level see Thomsen, *op.cit.*, p. 40.

Resource Allocation and the Price System

That the existence of highly competitive conditions does not assure a desirable state of affairs is illustrated by the improper allocation of resources in agriculture. The functioning of prices in connection with the problem of resource allocation needs careful consideration. A very important function of prices, in a predominantly free-enterprise economy, is to distribute land, labor, and capital among the various occupations and to place the proper quantities of these factors in such a way that they will make the greatest contribution to society's output (in terms of value). Recalling economic principles for the moment, one remembers that, under highly competitive conditions, profits guide production. Profits are determined by relative prices (market price of the product versus the average cost of production, which is, in effect, the sum of the factor prices). Each entrepreneur will endeavor to add successive "doses" of the factors of production as long as it is profitable to do so. The factors will tend to flow to those uses which yield the highest return. The factors will be distributed in such a manner that for each grade, its marginal productivity and financial remuneration will tend to be the same in all employments.

It might seem as though the price mechanism would do a good job of allocating resources in an industry which approaches perfect competition as closely as agriculture does. Yet, obviously, this is not the case. As was shown earlier, there is far too much labor employed in some segments of American agriculture. Also, it is probable that there is too little capital utilized in many agricultural areas. What is the trouble? Don't farmers respond to the movement of relative prices? This question cannot be answered categorically.

In the management of the farm enterprise, a farm operator *does* respond to the movement of relative prices. For example, past records show clearly that when the price of corn drops relative to the price of hogs, farmers find it profitable to feed hogs. As a result, they breed more hogs. As hogs get plentiful and feed scarce, hog prices fall and profits vanish. Farmers then cut back production. This results in a definite corn-hog cycle of about four years duration.

There are numerous other instances of this sort which could be cited to demonstrate that farmers watch prices and try to maximize their incomes by rearranging their production. But where new techniques and work habits must be learned (as in the case of expanding milk production in the South) the response of farmers is slow—even in the face of highly attractive prices.

In some other respects prices do not direct resources very well. One of these concerns the allocation of labor between agriculture and the rest of the economy. This pertains to the problem of the small-scale farm (underemployment, or excess labor in farming). During periods of full employment, this equilibrating mechanism (the price system) functions fairly well, but during times of unemployment it hardly works at all. Between 1940 and the end of 1954, a period of high employment, the farm population of the South declined 34 per cent, while for the rest of the nation the drop was 22 per cent; this exodus from the farms has continued since 1954.

The shift from farm to city is not an easy one, as a rule. It may be helpful to list the barriers which hinder such a shift.

1. *Unemployment in the Cities.* A higher wage level prevailing in cities will fail to attract rural workers away from farms if urban employers are not hiring additional labor.

2. *Cost of Movement.* Moving is expensive, particularly if the worker has a family. Partly for this reason, it is usually the young unmarried people who migrate from farm to city. Experience shows that a shift from farm to nonfarm work takes place most readily if the nonfarm work is nearby. In this case, the worker can continue to live on his farm. Eventually he is apt to move close to his work, as finances and other considerations permit.

3. *Race Prejudice.* Many of the excess workers in American agriculture are members of minority groups like Negroes, Mexicans, and American Indians. If they migrate to urban centers, they find themselves eligible only for lowly jobs, as a rule. While this is, of course, due largely to a lack of education and training, it is partly due to prejudice. Furthermore, these groups face severe housing problems in most urban centers.

4. *Lack of Education and Information.* Most of the excess rural workers have had inadequate school opportunities, and this handicaps them in finding good employment. Also, they lack information as to where and what job opportunities are in distant cities. Getting the less attractive jobs, lacking education, and acquaintance with the social customs of people in the cities, hearing others speak with a different dialect, being "looked down upon" occasionally by established city dwellers, the poor country worker often returns to his old surroundings, in spite of the lower income, in order to "feel at home" again. Migrating to the city is far more than an economic matter. It is the young farm people, especially those with a high school education, who adjust quickly to the life and manners of the cities and are assimilated easily.

5. *Labor Union Policies.* Unions frequently erect barriers to keep additional workers from entering the better paid city jobs. Thus, a man from the country, even though he possessed much skill in a trade, would have con-

siderable difficulty being admitted to any one of several trade unions, unless the demand for labor happened to be very strong at the time.

Other Problems. The second aspect of the problem of poor allocation of resources concerns the situation *within agriculture* itself. For many years the existence of the share-cropping system in the South, the primary region of surplus farm labor, constituted a barrier which made difficult the shifting of resources from one type of agriculture to another. The system would function for cotton production, but it was virtually impossible to apply it to such enterprises as dairy and beef enterprises. The share-cropping system has been receding rapidly over the past decade or two, and it no longer represents a major barrier.

One of the troublespots concerns the problem of rigid middleman costs which cause the price system to send a series of rather bewildering price signals to farmers. As a result, the price system fails to guide production as well as it theoretically should. Because marketing and processing margins for agricultural products are rather constant and wide (though not excessive), small changes in the demand for finished items cause large fluctuations in price at the farm level.[26] The demand for farm products is derived from consumers' purchases of the commodity in its final form. When the price of the finished product changes (as it frequently does), the price of the agricultural raw material moves with an accelerated effect. This is illustrated by the changing share of the consumer's dollar claimed by farm products over the course of the business cycle. The farmer's share in 1929 was 42 per cent; in 1932, 32 per cent; in 1940, 40 per cent; in 1946, 53 per cent; and in 1958, 40 per cent. Thus the acceleration principle, in times of recession, works its deadly effects on the raw material producing agricultural industries.

The trouble with sudden and large fluctuations in prices of farm products, in connection with the problem of resource allocation, is that these fluctuations make it difficult for a farmer to decide which commodity, and which level of output, would be most profitable for his production. Case after case could be cited where prices of individual agricultural commodities have varied by 20 per cent or more from one year to the next, and these fluctuations are rarely predictable (with any degree of accuracy, in terms of the extent of change and its timing). Imagine what effect a 20 per cent (or a 40 per cent, or even a 10 per cent) change in selling price would have on the farmer's profit margin! Planning production in terms of careful estimates of marginal costs and marginal revenues, as economic textbooks tend to sug-

[26] The acceleration principle is partly responsible for the marked instability in agricultural prices and income, a major problem. The acceleration factor is of secondary importance, however, as compared with the fluctuations in total demand. For a discussion of the way in which the acceleration principle works, see Thomsen, *op.cit.*, pp. 217–24,

gest, is out of the question. Although it would be a mistake to say that production economics principles have no bearing, still, it should be recognized that there is a large element of uncertainty necessarily involved in the planning of agricultural production which is at odds with the concept of logical resource allocation according to marginal costs and revenues.[27]

Summarizing this section, while there is evidence that agricultural resources of one kind and another do respond to the suggestions of the price system, that response is often slow and feeble. Very few informed observers today would recommend a free-market price system as an adequate device for guiding farm resources.

Government and the Price Structure

Due to unsatisfactory results of free-market pricing for farm products, Federal programs, principally centered around price objectives called "parity prices" (explained more fully in Section III of this chapter), were instituted during the New Deal period. Briefly, parity prices for farm products were defined by Congress as those which would bear the same relation to the prices of things farmers purchase as they bore in a chosen base period. For most products, the base period utilized was 1910–14. This was a period when agricultural prices stood relatively high when compared with costs of other commodities; hence, it was a happy choice from the farmers' point of view.

For the government to announce the parity price of an agricultural commodity as of any given date will not cause the market to adopt it. The interaction of supply and demand at that time may result in a price higher, or lower, than parity. To bring prices up to parity, when the market is lower, requires supplementary measures.

One of the measures tried during the last twenty years has been production control; it was hoped that, by preventing excessive production, agricultural prices would stay at the desired level. However, acreage control did not hold back production as anticipated because yields per acre tended to

[27] It would be difficult enough, in the formulation of output decisions, to decipher the meaning of current price movements; but, to make matters worse, it is on future marginal costs and revenue that production plans should be based, if the logical principles found in the textbooks were to be followed. For commodities like apples and citrus fruits, where production plans must be implemented many years in advance of the sale of the output—and the entrepreneur can learn but little of the production intentions of thousands of his competitors across this broad nation—there is necessarily a large element of gamble involved. Because it is almost impossible for the farmer to gauge the future with any degree of accuracy, factors like personal preference, prevailing neighborhood custom, and habitual procedure are found to bear a strong influence on production decisions.

increase enough to offset the effect. During a number of years it was found that the amounts of farm products coming to market would not go into consumption at prices approaching parity, in spite of acreage reduction. In order to cope with this situation, additional measures were devised and applied, chief of which was the crop loan and storage program, for which Congress appropriated money from time to time. Congress authorized the Commodity Credit Corporation (a Federal agency) to purchase surplus crops or to make nonrecourse loans (or to guarantee loans) to farmers for this purpose. Farmers who placed nonperishable items like wheat or cotton in approved storage received a loan rate which, in the late thirties, was about 60 per cent of parity. The program works the same today, except that it has been broadened to cover more products, and Congress has authorized loan rates at higher levels (usually 90 per cent of parity).

Obviously, this program swings into action only when the loan rate is above the free market price, and it tends to establish a floor under prices. In the early days of this program, it dovetailed nicely with the objectives of another plan, the "Ever Normal Granary," an idea which arose quite naturally from the experience of the bitter drought years, 1934 and 1936. The idea was, of course, that quantities of storable crops should be placed in warehouses during years of bumper harvest to be used later in lean years. Since the price support and storage program is normally called upon during years of large harvest, it made a fine partner for the Ever Normal Granary idea. However, the nation has not experienced severe droughts like those of the midthirties, and the granaries have been overflowing most of the time since then; the "ever normal" idea has been dropped as crop carryovers have stayed abnormally high.

Other programs were devised to remove quantities of products from the normal trade channels and to help dispose of surpluses. Federal funds were used to finance exports, school lunches, and free food for people on relief. These subsidy schemes were overshadowed by the foreign aid programs during and right after World War II which provided a marked stimulus to American exports of numerous farm products. As this foreign aid has tapered off and exports have tended to fall, the old schemes to help dispose of surpluses have all been revived and expanded full-scale.

The price support program was basically shifted during World War II to an *incentive* device for the expansion of production; the support level was increased to 90 per cent of parity and extended to a larger list of commodities. This high support level was originally intended for the duration of the war plus two years (the end of 1948). Before the lapse of high supports occurred, Congress extended them "temporarily" and enacted a new program which would become effective in 1950. The new law provided for a system of flexible supports and certain other commendable changes.[28] In most instances the new method of computing parity prices was more favorable to livestock and livestock products (which comprise over half of the output of American farms), but it meant lower supports for field crops (which had been relying on the support prices rather heavily in prior years). To illustrate, under the new formula the parity price for wheat would have been 20 per cent lower, and that for beef cattle 20 per cent higher, than under the old formula.

Congress in 1949, apparently interpreting the 1948 elections as a mandate from farmers that they wanted high supports, laid aside most of the 1948 amendments. It passed legislation which provided that, until the end of 1954, whichever of the two formulas yielded the higher price would be the one used in announcing the parity price for a "basic" commodity. In addition to this boost given to parity prices, Congress also directed that farm wage rates be included in computing a certain index used in the calculation of parity—the effect of this inclusion being to boost parity prices higher still. The law authorized a moderate reduction in supports for 1955 and a full-range permissive lowering for 1956 crops.

The prospect of significantly lower price props in 1956, at a time when agricultural markets were weakening from an excess of supply in relation to demand, precipitated considerable political pressure to do something to protect farm incomes. In response, Congress enacted the Soil Bank Program which provided that farm land could be placed in either an "acreage" or a "conservation" *reserve* upon request by an operator who would receive a government payment in return. The basic ideas were twofold: (1) to rapidly divert much farmland from intensive production to the growing of trees, and to curtail acreage of crops already in large surplus (wheat, cotton, corn, rice, tobacco and peanuts) in favor of more grasses and legumes; and (2) to encourage a wide variety of conservation practices so as to safeguard the productive base for possible future needs. After a year or two the acreage reserve was no longer continued, but the conservation reserve, a longer range pro-

---

[28] In the first place, the base for computing the index of prices received by farmers was changed from the 1910–14 period to a moving average of the most recent ten years; this was to take cognizance of long-run changes in demand and production costs. Secondly, for certain crops, price supports were to be lower after big harvests and higher after small ones, allowing prices to serve as production directives; the supports were to vary between 60 and 90 per cent of parity and were to average 75 per cent. Finally, the Secretary of Agriculture was authorized to support many farm products (formerly not included in the support program) at between zero and 90 per cent of parity, depending on numerous factors (in effect, forward price floors based on the administrator's best judgment).

gram, was kept intact. Surpluses continued to mount rapidly because farmers stepped up their output per acre, weather remained favorable, foreign demand tended to dwindle, and important loopholes were left in the law by the Congressional farm bloc. Despite the increased tempo of the various surplus disposal programs, by mid-1959 the Federal government had a staggering investment approaching nine billion dollars in surplus crops in storage—with a promise of more headed toward its bins from the fall harvest. Articles and speeches abounded on all sides to the effect that this costly Federal program could not, and should not, be allowed to continue much longer. Yet the verdict of twenty years' experience reveals that the farm population, although relatively few in numbers, wields strong influence in Congress. Nevertheless a crack in the ranks of farmers had become plainly evident by 1959 in that at least one major farm organization would no longer endorse a high support program. Yet neither major political party would at this time dare to attempt a frontal assault on the costly support system despite the fact that a crisis clearly looms on the horizon.

SECTION III: PUBLIC POLICY

In this section is found a brief review of the vast array of programs dealing with the economic ills of agriculture which have been tried in the past; also, some of the current programs—both those in use and those proposed —are described and analyzed.

Small-Scale Farm Problem

Except insofar as a general education policy helps to meet the need, the problem presented by the existence of thousands of small-scale farmers living at poverty or near-poverty levels has not been grappled with in a comprehensive manner via public programs at any time in American history. To a large extent this is because of a deep-seated belief that individuals can and should look after their own welfare. The marginal farm problem has persisted so long, however, that it has become increasingly apparent that a new deliberate program of some sort is needed—one that will have a three-phased approach: (1) to find and apply measures whereby the level of farm management practices may be elevated substantially; (2) to combine small acreages into adequate-size farming units in cases where good management capacity exists; and most important (3) to encourage and assist families to find nonfarm employment. There is a vast network of educational and credit agencies now serving agriculture in this country which have long endeavored to meet the first two of the needs enumerated, but it appears that they may have to try some new methods if the problem of small-scale farming is to be solved. As a first step, it appears that many of these families must be somehow inspired to desire a higher level of production (and living), and be made to believe that they can achieve it by their own efforts.

By and large, the public programs concerned to date with the small-scale operators have been directed toward helping them become more productive farmers, not aiding their transfer to other jobs. The various programs of the New Deal were of this nature (Resettlement Administration and Farm Security Administration). None of these efforts was of sufficient magnitude or duration to do more than dent the surface of the problem. What has really helped has been the high-level urban employment of the past two decades which has attracted many of these marginal operators right out of agriculture.

There is considerable agreement among economists that farm policy should not be directed toward upgrading all the small-scale farmers. If the low production farms were reorganized into adequate sized units, only a small proportion (probably under 20 per cent) of the surplus workers might profitably remain in agriculture. All of them cannot be employed effectively in agriculture because the market for farm products is rather inelastic. In fact, existing adequate-scale farmers can produce all the farm products the market will take at reasonable prices. Therefore, from an economic standpoint most small-scale farmers should be shifted to other branches of the economy, the demand for whose products has a greater income and price elasticity.

The shift from farm to nonfarm work takes place most readily when cities, with all their diverse employments, are nearby. In the Southeast, where most of the surplus labor is found, the greater development of cities hinges chiefly on a proportional growth of manufacturing enterprises; currently, a wave of industrialization is sweeping the area and this augurs well for its economic future in general, and for the excess farm population in particular. Additional development is needed, however, before one can say that the problem has been solved.

Every village threatened with a decline in its rural economy wants manufacturing firms to locate in its environs, but generally the logic of location economics would not indicate these villages as likely spots. In the great majority of cases, the human resources must migrate elsewhere in order to be fitted into more productive and remunerative settings. In a very few cases there may be natural resources which could be made the base for a revived economy if a large government development program were undertaken. An instance of this kind was the Tennessee River Valley Development. Through its unusually cheap and abundant supply of electricity it attracted certain kinds of industry (especially aluminum producers and atomic plants) to the area, and it aided in other respects also. But where are there more cases like this?

If little nonfarm employment can be developed in the vicinity of the surplus rural labor, then this labor will have to move to existing employment centers. To encourage migration, attention should be centered on the younger generation by providing its members with a good education through the high school level. By training them in skills useful in nonfarm work, by acquainting them with habits and conditions of life in other areas, by informing them where job opportunities exist, and by offering some financial assistance for traveling to the jobs, these young people can be induced to move. If these conditions were provided, coupled with continuous full employment in cities, it is possible that the problem of surplus agricultural labor would substantially disappear within another generation.

Contrary to the recommendations of many economists, diverse efforts have been made by the leaders who are closest to farmers to help *every* small-scale operator raise his output. This is largely due to the difference between a local and a national point of view. Consider the situation as seen by the county agricultural agent. His job is to help *all* farmers in the county. If he can help some small-scale farmer lift his output, he has performed his function. A county agent does not worry about the problem of too many agriculturists. From a local point of view, there is always room for another farmer to produce some type of product.

Likewise, the 4-H Club leader and the high-school teacher of agriculture try to encourage the rural youth to become good farmers, not to migrate as soon as possible away from agriculture. The various land-grant colleges with their schools of agriculture are also dominated by the idea of helping each and every farmer in their respective states. Generally, this tends to keep people in agriculture rather than facilitating movement into other occupations.

Sometimes, political leaders and publishers like to think of their regions as being inherently agricultural. They think of farming as the "good way of life." They fear the developments that may come from rising city populations, particularly those dominated by large numbers of industrial workers. In part, they fear this sort of development because it may result in a new complex of political, economic, and social leadership. Some of these people would like to hinder the spread of manufacturing to their areas. Judged by developments across the nation, however, general sentiment eventually swings toward maximizing economic development, including manufacturing, despite the perplexing social repercussions which may arise therefrom.

The farm policy predicament is well illustrated by the statement made to this writer by a Negro assistant county agent from Alabama. He said: "It may be true that the real hope of many small-scale Negro farmers in Alabama does not lie in agriculture at all. It may be true that there ought to be more manufacturing, commercial, and service employment in Alabama for these people; or, that there ought to be large migration to existing employment centers. However, I feel sure that a large expansion of nonfarm employment is not coming to Alabama very fast. Large migration is not feasible under existing uncertainty concerning employment, crowded city housing conditions, and social tensions created by the influx of poor rural Negroes into Northern cities. Therefore, my efforts have been aimed, and will continue to be aimed, in the direction of encouraging Negro farmers in Alabama to increase their livestock enterprises. This sort of program can be done by the farmers themselves anytime. It may result in only small improvements in their living levels. However, the solution recommended by economists depends on factors outside the control of these poor farmers, and the developments favored by economists may never come to pass. The program I am promoting will yield benefits *soon*." Thus, men who work at the "grass roots" are following policies which, from an aggregate point of view, may be of questionable long-run value; but it must be admitted that there is much sense in what they are doing.

Unstable Price Problem

Ever since the second half of the nineteenth century, most farm programs have been concerned with the matter of prices. Following the Civil War, agricultural prices took a tumble and farmers favored various "easy-money," inflationary programs such as the "greenback" and the "free silver" movements.

In the last quarter of the nineteenth century, farmers desired government regulation of the railroads and other big business which they believed were exploiting them. In the seventies and nineties, when farm prices were low, farmers wanted to see railroad rates and industrial prices fall so that farm products would continue to exchange for other goods in a ratio to which they had been accustomed.

Following World War I, farm prices fell drastically again. Farmers were aroused and became more active politically. Old farm-pressure groups were strengthened and new ones formed to press for Federal aid. During the twenties there was wide disagreement among farm leaders concerning methods of achieving higher prices and farm prosperity. A conservative group held that legislation could do little to restore farm prices to higher levels; it felt that the remedy would come essentially through the interplay of natural economic forces. This group, however, thought that some things could be done.

1. It wanted the margin between prices paid by consumers and prices received by farmers reduced. Specifically, it recommended preferred legislation for farmers' cooperatives, an improved system of intermediate credit, improved warehousing facilities and supervision, reduction of freight rates, the establishment of better grades and standards for farm products, and better farm roads. Many of these recommendations were incorporated into Federal programs by Congress. Although they were good measures, it is doubtful whether marketing margins were reduced. To a considerable extent the bitter complaints about high middleman costs were emotional rather than analytically sound.

2. It wanted to help the farmer adjust his production to market needs by supplying him with economic information concerning supply and demand conditions. This resulted in the establishment of the "Outlook" services, an attempt to forecast supply and demand conditions, sponsored by the United States Department of Agriculture and other agencies.[29] Again, this was a sound idea but its significance is hard to measure.

3. It endeavored to find more foreign markets for farm products by an expansion of the foreign service functions of the Department of Agriculture. This was done but, helpful as it may have been, the problem of inadequate export demand still persists.

4. It favored the erection of higher tariffs on farm products in order to exclude foreign competition at home. This too was accomplished. The wisdom of the move has always been doubtful because the major commodities in surplus were ones which depended on an export market and whose price could not climb above the world market level.

Other farm groups, especially those from the hard-hit wheat districts, wanted much more direct aid through Federal legislation. They pressed hard for a program which would "dump" quantities of certain farm products on foreign markets. The domestic prices of these products would be held above world market prices by means of tariffs. Measures providing for such

[29] It may be noted that, if all farmers followed the advice of these forecasts, the end result might be the opposite of that anticipated. For example, suppose the forecast indicated that the outlook for hog production was profitable and, as a result, the great mass of farmers expanded their hog production. Feed prices would rise and hog prices would fall, bringing financial losses to farmers.

programs passed Congress twice in the twenties, but were vetoed by President Coolidge. However, export subsidies were eventually tried (in the late twenties) and found to be unfortunate in several respects. They were revived in the late fifties and caused anguish again.

Still other farm spokesmen thought the solution to the farmer's price difficulties could be worked out through his own cooperative efforts, and they believed in what was called "orderly marketing." Their idea was to set up large, nation-wide farmers' marketing cooperatives. If prices tended to sag, these marketing agencies would buy certain farm commodities in sufficient volume and place them in storage so as to elevate prices. Later, when prices were more favorable, these products would be sold. If production of some farm products appeared to be excessive year after year, the cooperatives were to advise farmers to alter their production plans. President Hoover favored this type of farm program and his administration set up the Farm Board, whose job was to help finance the marketing cooperatives in their stabilizing efforts. Soon after the establishment of the Farm Board, however, the depression of the thirties began. Prices of farm products fell badly in spite of the efforts of the marketing cooperatives and the Farm Board to halt the decline. The Farm Board asked wheat farmers to reduce their production in line with the lower market demand but farmers did not heed the request. The Board concluded that its price stabilization program would work only if it were accompanied by some sort of Federal production control.

In March 1933, the New Deal initiated new and bold measures to help agriculture out of the doldrums of low prices and low incomes. In meeting these problems, faith was no longer placed in the individual or cooperative efforts of farmers themselves. Instead, the coordinating power of the Federal government was used to accomplish needed programs. Legislation was passed which provided that farm income be elevated to a position of equality or "parity" with that of other large economic groups, a goal that was to be achieved by keeping agricultural prices up to a "fair" level. In contrast to the Hoover Administration's Farm Board, the method for attaining the desired goal was to be a system of direct production control.

Under this production control program, acreage allotments were determined for cotton, corn, wheat, rice, tobacco, potatoes, peanuts, and all other soil-depleting crops taken as a group. The national allotment was then broken down into allotments for the several states, and these, in turn, for counties and for individual farmers. In determining the size of these allotments, factors such as past production, type of farming, and kind of land were taken into consideration. Payments were made to those who participated in the acreage reduction program, payments which proved effective in eliciting the cooperation of farmers. Thus, paradoxically enough, a measure of national production planning was in a relatively short time established in the most individualistic and competitive sector of the American economy.

Why was it that socially enlightened statesmen advocated lower production and higher prices during a depression period when many people were in dire want? The basic argument on behalf of production control was rooted in the peculiar events and economic philosophy of the time. The New Deal officials believed that the way to bring back prosperity was to raise prices. Guided by this belief, the Roosevelt Administration launched many programs designed to raise prices by reducing competition. The farm program was but one aspect of a broader, over-all economic policy.

Other arguments were advanced to support the New Deal farm program. It was pointed out, for example, that the foreign demand for products such as cotton, tobacco, wheat, and lard had nearly vanished and that it was therefore unwise for farmers to continue producing these commodities in the usual quantities. Until world markets recovered from the devastating effects of the depression, a maintenance of output in the face of drastically reduced demand was considered an ineffective means of stabilizing income.

Furthermore, it was pointed out that farmers, in their search for economic security, should be allowed the same privileges as were already enjoyed by other important groups in the national economy. Other groups, it was said, had erected bulwarks to insulate themselves from the deflationary effects of competition in times of depressed business conditions. It was claimed that industry was protected from "excessive" competition by tariffs, patents, formal and informal agreements, etc. It was argued that many urban workers had devised ways and means of assuring themselves a "place in the sun" through collective bargaining, minimum wage laws, social security, etc. Did not social justice require that agriculture be guaranteed—with the help of the government—a "fair" share of the national income? After all, the effects of such a guarantee would benefit not only the selfish interests of the farm population, but would also serve social ends. Since a prosperous farm population constituted a necessary market for the output of manufacturing industry, it was essential—so the argument ran—to lift farm income in order to promote recovery in other sectors of the economy.

Aside from the pro's and con's of production control, acreage limitation did not accomplish the desired objective. During the first term of the New Deal, production was indeed held back, but this was chiefly due to the effects of two great droughts in 1934 and 1936. As the weather returned to normal in 1937 and in subsequent years, surpluses appeared (in spite of acreage reduction) with price-depressing effects. In the endeavor to support prices, the crop loan program under the Commodity Credit Corporation

(CCC) assumed large proportions. On January 1, 1941, there were about 11 million bales of cotton in storage which had been financed by CCC. This was almost twice the annual domestic consumption of cotton during the thirties. At that same date, there were in storage 370 million pounds of tobacco, 477 million bushels of corn, and 281 million bushels of wheat (519 million in 1942). These amounts in storage went beyond the requirements of a reserve for weather risk. It became a serious question whether the CCC could continue its support activities, or whether the effort would have to be abandoned, as was the case with the Farm Board earlier.

The outbreak of the war in Europe in 1939 prevented a crisis in farm policy. At first, the effect of the war on farm prices was slight. By 1941 and subsequently, however, the demand for agricultural products increased greatly as the United States experienced a fully employed economy and as exports were stimulated by war and postwar developments. Farm commodities held in storage during previous years, due to a lack of market demand, were utilized and their prices rose sharply. With few exceptions, they stayed above parity levels until the end of 1948. Late that year and in 1949 the CCC found it necessary again to vigorously support the prices of several commodities, and to spend about two billion dollars in doing so. But, in 1950 and 1951 the inflationary forces associated with the Korean War pushed prices generally above support levels, and some commodities moved out of storage, reducing the CCC's financial commitments.

Surpluses soon returned, and beginning in mid-1952 support activities were resumed on a substantial scale for corn, wheat, cotton, and butter. The surplus situation remained chronic despite stepped-up disposal measures, export subsidies, and an endeavor to restrain production via the new Soil Bank Program. The flood-tide rose, and by mid-1959 the CCC had about nine billion dollars invested directly and indirectly in stored crops.

Several times over the past twenty years, when a crisis in the price support activity appeared imminent due to enormous quantities of commodities bulging out of storage bins, some new world event would generate an upsurge in demand and thereby relieve the pressure on the CCC. Will some new upsurge in demand rescue the program again in 1960 or 1961? Or, will the bulging surpluses finally force a fundamental change in the Federal farm policy?

Weaknesses of Price Supports and Acreage Limitation

No matter how carefully parity price and acreage limitation legislation may be drawn, serious weaknesses will remain.

1. *Total Income May Not Be Increased.* If prices are pegged above the

free-market level, both theory and practice have demonstrated that the market will not absorb the whole crop. Surpluses must then be stored, or somehow disposed of. To prevent surpluses each successive year, the Secretary of Agriculture will probably ask for acreage reduction. Since total income is a result of quantity times price, under price pegging (if production is cut back) total income may not be significantly larger.[30]

2. *Production May Not Fall Under Acreage Limitation.* Of course, if acreage is cut back enough, production will certainly go down. Yet, acreage reductions of small magnitudes (such as 10 per cent) may not cause a reduction of crop output because average output per acre may rise enough to offset the smaller acreage. This has happened continuously since the thirties as efforts to hold back production by acreage limits have been thwarted by higher yields. Usually, the poorer acres on a farm are the ones removed from production. The use of more fertilizers and other technological improvements often result in striking gains in average yields per acre.

3. *Surpluses May Appear in Different Commodities.* When acres are withdrawn from corn, for example, the farmer will not let his land lie idle. Normally, he will plant those acres with a soil-improving crop such as legume hay which permits him to collect the soil conservation payment. When he gets a good crop of hay or pasture, he will expand his beef or dairy herd in order to make use of this roughage. Or he may plant another grain. After a few years, beef, pork, and dairy product supplies may become so large (with price depressing effects) that producers of these products will call for production control. Experience indicates that acres withdrawn from cotton have tended to go into corn, hay, peanuts, small grains, and pasture. The result has been larger supplies of chickens, hogs, poultry, dairy and beef cattle in the South.

In summary, our experience with acreage limitation shows that while production of a few crops may be held back, total agricultural output cannot be easily reduced. Partly this is because Congress has consistently left some loopholes in the control regulations.

4. *While Acreage is Limited in the Main Producing Areas, It May Expand in Other Areas.* For example, if the price of corn is supported near parity and its acreage is limited in the Middle West, deficit regions such as the East and South will likely expand their corn output. Laws could be enacted, perhaps, which would prevent an expansion of corn acreage outside the Corn Belt, but such laws would raise questions of discrimination and constitutionality. They would be very hard to administer and would be disliked intensely by farmers.

[30] This depends on the elasticity of the demand for the particular crop in question.

5. *Reduction of Production is Unpopular.* Farmers claim that they do not like anyone to tell them what they can or cannot do with their land. (However, their satisfaction with the tobacco program, which involves extensive controls, leads one to doubt their opposition.) The general public, desiring abundant supplies of farm products at low cost, frowns on attempts by the Federal government to reduce agricultural output.

6. *Farmers in Sufficient Numbers May Not Heed Requests for Reduced Production.* This is apt to be the case in years when market price looks attractive to farmers, even though it may be below parity level. As an example, in the fall of 1948, the Federal government asked wheat farmers to plant about 8 per cent less wheat than they had planted the previous season. Farmers, in general, paid little heed to this request. To meet a situation like this, the Department of Agriculture could ask farmers to vote on marketing quotas, and impose these quotas if most farmers agreed. However, marketing quotas cannot be enforced readily for crops which can be fed to livestock economically.

7. *High Prices Curtail Consumption.* In a time of depression, when parity prices would meet the situation for which they were essentially designed, the effect of the program tends to make it difficult for low-income families to purchase the essential farm products. And in normal times, high supported prices for butter and cotton have encouraged substitutes like oleomargarine and synthetic fibers to invade their markets.

8. *Misguided Production.* Prices supported above free-market levels may encourage an expansion of production in fields which, from a social point of view, ought to be contracted.

9. *Doesn't Help Farmers Who Need It Most.* Like any other program in which benefits are tied to volume of output, this one does not significantly help the small-scale farmer.

10. *Loss of Foreign Markets.* Foreign markets are important for tobacco, rice, cotton, and wheat. When prices are supported above the world price, foreign buyers tend to buy elsewhere.

11. *Inflated Land Values.* The value of farm land follows the value of crops which can be raised on it. Acreage limitation schemes make land the one scarce factor of production while supports tend to boost the value of output per acre. In consequence, support prices tend to become capitalized into higher land values, creating a windfall gain for the first owner, but making a higher overhead cost for the next one.

Other Proposals

A dozen years ago there was considerable interest in the idea of using *forward price floors*, instead of parity prices tied to a past period, as a device to assist farmers. It was suggested that a board of experts announce in advance each year a series of price floors for leading agricultural commodities, the notion being that production and consumption could be guided up or down by this means. (Other steps would have to be taken to make the price floors effective.) Interest in this approach is now slight because it is generally felt that the pressures for expanding agricultural production are so strong that announcing lower price floors would have no significant restraining influence. They would, therefore, fail to provide a check on the ever-mounting farm surpluses.

In 1947 a committee on agricultural price policy of the American Farm Economics Association recommended a "parity-income" approach.[31] Under this scheme the farm population would be assured a minimum *share* of the national income. Prices for commodities would be determined on free markets. In case farmers' income from marketing fell below parity, supplemental payments would be made directly to them from the Federal treasury to make up perhaps 80 or 90 per cent of the difference between computed parity and their actual income. Individual farmers would share according to the market values of their outputs. In order to avoid criticism that the government might be subsidizing the well-to-do, a sliding scale of payments tilted in favor of small producers would be utilized.

In practice this program would offer the least income protection to farmers whose products had fallen the most in price, it would not keep farm income at a desirable level in absolute terms, and it would not alleviate the small-scale farm problem. Moreover, from a farmer's point of view the program as suggested didn't offer much "support." The committee forwarding the plan was well aware of these criticisms and had valid reasons for shaping its recommendations the way it did. Farmers and their friends in Congress didn't take much interest in the proposal, however.

About ten years ago the "Brannan plan" aroused much discussion. For perishable commodities (which make up 75 per cent of total farm output) Mr. Brannan, then the Secretary of Agriculture, proposed free-market prices combined with production payments to farmers directly from the Federal government in case prices were below a parity level. In effect, the proposal amounted to a very high level of income support to farmers, while at the

[31] See article by this committee, "On the Redefinition of Parity Price and Income," *Journal of Farm Economics*, November 1947, Vol. 29, pp. 1358–77.

same time promising lower food prices to city people. The gimmick was that the cost to the Federal treasury would be enormous. With what amounts to a high price assured, American farmers would turn out an astounding volume of production. To keep Treasury outlays within reasonable bounds, strict production controls would have had to be implemented—an unsolved problem for which the Brannan plan had nothing new to suggest.

Increasingly, as crop surpluses have accumulated in mammoth proportions, the question arises whether there should be a return to *free-market pricing*, pure and simple, in order to get produced crops into consumption, preserve this nation's position in foreign markets, and presumably to let the price system tell farmers not to produce so much. The repercussions would be felt in the case of wheat, the most troublesome surplus crop, in that its price would have to fall to the point where it would compete with corn and other feeds for livestock; the secondary reaction would be lower prices for feed grains generally with a subsequent surge in livestock production and consequently lower prices for eggs, pork, milk and beef. Cotton production would probably fall off sharply, in the face of a drastically lower price, on thousands of marginal farms in the Southeast; production in the Delta region of the Mississippi and in certain Western states might expand.

As for the chief consequences of a return to the free market for agriculture as a whole, it is believed that: (1) total output would continue upwards, but at a slower pace than in recent years; (2) crop prices would fall more so than those for livestock; (3) net farm income would fall approximately 25 to 30 per cent, the impact varying widely among different groups; (4) farm land values would experience a sharp drop from their present high level; (5) the gap between the incomes of efficient and inefficient producers would widen.[32]

These consequences add up to a most bitter pill, indeed, for American farmers to swallow, and they are generally not ready for strong medicine. Professor Willard C. Cochrane, Professor of Agricultural Economics at the University of Minnesota, has stated this well: "Farmers generally do not realize the seriousness of their situation; they live by a myth—a myth of a 'sound,' healthy agriculture that is only a little out of balance. They live by this myth because they have been told repeatedly by politicians and their leaders that agriculture is basically 'sound'—that with a little 'fixing' this 'emergency' will pass and all will be well."[33] As long as farmers' political

[32] For a concise discussion of this subject see Fred R. Robertson, "Letting the Farm Income Problem Work Itself Out in the Open Market," *Increasing Understanding of Public Problems and Policies, 1958,* Chicago: Farm Foundation, 1958, pp. 74–80.
[33] Willard C. Cochrane, "The Supply Control Route," *Increasing Understanding of Public Problems and Policies, 1957,* Chicago: Farm Foundation, 1957, p. 87.

influence remains important, it seems safe to say that there will be no return
to the free-market system of pricing.

In view of the magnitude of disruptions which would now be involved,
economists who have thought long and rigorously about the farm problem
are hesitant to recommend the end of all supports and a return to free-market
pricing; but if they could turn the clock back and start ten years ago, it
is likely that many would advocate something approaching it. High supports
have by now become so deeply imbedded in land values that any marked
lowering of product prices will cause enormous capital losses to owners who
have acquired land in good faith in the last ten or fifteen years. Economists
do recognize more clearly than do most others that a *drastic* system of
production control must be enacted if high support prices are to be continued. For example, Professor Cochrane has set forth a "public utility"
approach which would involve the setting of national sales quotas for each
principal agricultural commodity in amounts which Federal authorities
estimate would clear the market at parity prices, and then the giving to each
farmer his pro rata share in the form of a marketing certificate.[34] A farmer
could not legally market more than the amount permitted by the certificate.
A new producer could enter the field only by purchasing a market certificate
from someone currently owning one. There are some features which are
easily recognized as unfortunate indeed in this program; its only virtues are
that it would hold production in line with consumption at prices farmers
consider "fair" and it would protect present capital values.

Presently all the old proposals considered since 1920, plus a few new ones,
are being given a new hearing, but none of them offers much promise of
achieving the results so devoutly wished for.[35] The Committee for Economic
Development, with the assistance of a prominent group of economists as
technical advisors, issued a thoughtful report on agricultural policy in 1956
in which it held that the high rigid-support approach, having been given an
adequate trial, was seriously defective in several respects.[36] As to an alternative, the CED did not advocate a return to a completely free market price
because that would expose farmers to "unnecessary risks and instability."
The group did emphasize, however, that "a satisfactory farm price policy
must retain as many of the desirable features of a freely functioning price

[34] Cochrane, *op.cit.*, pp. 85–92. For a very similar proposal see Stephen J. Brannan,
"Direct Restraints on Farm Marketing," *Increasing Public Understanding of Public
Problems and Policies, 1958*, Chicago: Farm Foundation, 1958, pp. 56–63.

[35] See especially the series of nine essays in the section "Approaches to Solving the
Income Problem of Commercial Agriculture," in the Farm Foundation's 1958 volume of
Increasing Understanding of Public Problems and Policies, previously referred to.

[36] *Economic Policy for American Agriculture*, New York: Committee for Economic
Development, January 1956.

system as is possible." Furthermore, the CED group indicated that the free-market price was a sort of norm from which the general level of agricultural product prices should not long depart.

To deal with the surplus problem the CED recommended continued price supports at gradually reduced levels combined with a program to pay farmers to take land out of crop production. To cope with the instability of prices it proposed a system of flexible price supports or income payments (the forward price floor idea) combined with a storage program (akin to the Ever Normal Granary); these devices were not to be expected to boost prices upward in the long run, but rather were to bring about stability and orderly marketing. As for the low-income segment of producers the CED report contained the usual suggestions whereby the operators would be aided in securing other kinds of employment and/or become more productive on their farms. A unique feature of the report was the recommendation to establish an Agricultural Stabilization Board whose members would be broadly representative of farm and nonfarm interests and who would serve for long terms on a "staggered" basis; the purpose in mind was to divorce the formulation of policy (especially the setting of price support levels) from short-run political demands—a commendable idea, indeed!

Experience since this report was submitted seems to indicate that efforts to hold agricultural production down by withdrawing land from production (the Soil Bank program) fail to dampen output as much as the CED apparently expected.

Conclusion

The role of the Federal government today in the affairs of American agriculture is unbelieveably large; the budget for fiscal 1958 contained more than five billion dollars for agriculture—an amount equivalent to more than 40 per cent of total realized net farm income for the entire nation in 1957! The chief element in this package of costs was for price-propping activities. Will interest in this expensive approach to the problem of low crop prices subside as has been the case with a half dozen or more other policies in the past? This could happen because the high support idea has not yet been subjected to a sustained acid test; bad droughts obscured the impact of the program in the midthirties, and upward surges in total demand came along at several points since 1940 to save the crop storage activities from complete embarrassment. Perhaps, in this dynamic and insecure world, this will continue to be the case, though it is to be doubted.

Standing in the way of finding a better approach than the current one is a serious conflict of objectives. What is it that is wanted? *Stability* in prices? *High* prices? Is *freedom of enterprise* important in agriculture? Why be so concerned about the maintenance of the freedom in farming when in other areas of the economy (business and labor) the concept has been modified so much? (Some may answer that with entry freedom restricted in other industries, there is more reason than ever to keep one great area, agriculture, open.) Regarding large subsidies for agriculture, even if it were granted that these subsidies were wrong in principle, should farmers abstain from seeking them when other groups within the ranks of business and organized labor have repeatedly sought to bolster their respective incomes through legislative devices?

If the chief objective of the program is to be *high* support, it is now clear that the government will find it necessary to curtail drastically the freedom of enterprise of farmers and would-be farmers. If, on the other hand, farmers should decide that they would be satisfied with a program which would give them a degree of price stability, moderate support, and considerable freedom of enterprise, these features may be had substantially via the program as amended in 1948.

Regarding the relative importance of the various objectives, farmers and their spokesmen are definitely divided. Evidence currently is conflicting as to what proportion would be inclined to surrender quite a bit of freedom of enterprise in exchange for assured high prices. Economists, on the other hand, appear to be much more anxious that economic freedom be maintained. In conclusion, it is apparent that the choice of a support program for agriculture hinges not only on economic but also on philosophical and political considerations.

SUGGESTED READINGS

M. R. Benedict, *Farm Policies of the United States* (New York: The Twentieth Century Fund, 1953).

———, *Can We Solve the Farm Problem?* (New York: The Twentieth Century Fund, 1955).

——— and O. C. Stine, *The Agricultural Commodity Programs* (New York: Twentieth Century Fund, 1956).

L. C. Gray, *History of Agriculture in the Southern United States to 1860*, 2 vols. (Washington: Carnegie Institution, 1928).

H. G. Halcrow, *Agricultural Policy of the United States* (New York: Prentice-Hall, 1953).

O. B. Jesness (ed.), *Readings on Agricultural Policy* (Philadelphia: Blakiston, 1949).

T. W. Schultz, *The Economic Organization of Agriculture* (New York: McGraw-Hill, 1953).

G. S. Sheppard, *Agricultural Price and Income Policy* (Ames, Iowa: The Iowa State College Press, 1952).

L. Soth, *Farm Trouble* (Princeton: Princeton University Press, 1957).

Bureau of Agricultural Economics, *Low Production Farms*, Agriculture Information Bulletin 108 (Washington: United States Department of Agriculture, 1953).

W. W. Wilcox and W. W. Cochrane, *Economics of American Agriculture* (New York: Prentice-Hall, 1951).

Chapter 2

IRWIN M. STELZER

The Cotton
Textile Industry

SECTION I: INTRODUCTION

The cotton textile industry is one of the largest of American industries. In 1954 the value of cotton broad-woven goods shipped was $2,790 million and that of cotton yarn $1,031 million, while thread mills shipped $184 million and narrow fabric mills $250 million worth of goods, respectively.[1] Of the 446 similar industry groupings included in the *Census,* cotton broad-woven goods ranked eleventh in terms of value of shipments.

In 1954 this industry employed approximately 602 thousand. It is estimated that the investment in cotton manufacturing facilities approximates five billion dollars.[2]

From the date of its introduction into the United States in 1790 the cotton textile industry has presented questions of major public policy importance. Its history provides a case study in the impact of geographic and techno-logical change upon a major industry; its structure provides, or has in the past provided, one of the closest approximations to the purely competitive ideal of the classical economist; the behavior of its prices has produced at least one classic study of the nature and impact of "cut-throat competition";[3] its recent wave of mergers and integration has provided a case study

---

[1] United States Department of Commerce, Bureau of the Census, *Census of Manufactures: 1954.* Volume II, "Industry Statistics," Part 1, p. 22B–5. Since about one-third of the yarn is used in cloth manufacture, addition of all these figures would involve some double counting.

[2] Edward L. Allen, *Economics of American Manufacturing,* New York: Holt, 1952, p. 371.

[3] Lloyd G. Reynolds, "Cut-Throat Competition," *The American Economic Review,* Vol. XXX, No. 4, December 1940, pp. 736 ff.

of the impact of structural changes on industry behavior; and its general performance—rate of technological change, ability to meet the competition of imports, reaction to the introduction of substitute products—has provided a basis for numerous studies on the efficiency with which a competitive industry adapts to and accepts change.

History

The present-day cotton textile industry is the result of a process of uneven growth and development which began in 1790, the year in which Samuel Slater established the first successful cotton mill in the United States with machinery constructed from memory. It is worthy of note that Slater's mill was equipped for spinning only, the spun yarn being distributed to families for weaving into cloth for their own use or for sale.

The growth of the industry was painfully slow for several years; by 1807 there were only 8,000 spindles in place in the entire country. In that year, however, came the first in a series of events which were to provide a tremendous stimulus to the American industry. The Embargo Act of 1807, followed in two years by the Non-Intercourse Act, and finally the War of 1812, meant that trade with England was virtually suspended. This interruption of commerce simultaneously removed many of the obstacles to the growth of the domestic textile industry. The South, now unable to sell its cotton to England, proceeded to flood the New England market with raw cotton, driving the price down by over 50 per cent. The simultaneous and virtually complete unavailability by English cloth drove products prices up from $.17 to $.75 per yard. Finally, the capital shortage which plagued the industry was solved when many New England merchants who had accumulated wealth in foreign commerce sought new outlets for their energies and funds.

By 1815 there were 130,000 spindles in the United States, and by 1820, 220,000. "The building of cotton factories," in the words of one student, "became one of the passions of the age." [4] This growth was accompanied by the integration of the spinning and weaving processes, under one roof, and the enlistment by the mills of the services of independent selling houses.

The resumption of Anglo-American relations brought with it the flooding of United States markets by British manufacturers anxious to recapture their lost market. Significantly, Congress responded to a New England clamor for tariff protection by inserting in the Tariff Act of 1816 a 25 per cent duty on

[4] Albert S. Bolles, *Industrial History of the United States,* Norwich, Connecticut: The Henry Bill Publishing Company, 1878, p. 41.

cotton goods. Prosperity and rapid expansion returned to the industry. By 1860 some 1,091 mills were turning out 115 million dollars in cotton goods on about 5.2 million spindles with the aid of some 122,000 employees.

This growth was accompanied by significant structural changes. Many mills, all constructed north of Boston, were built on the so-called "Lowell System," i.e., they were large-scale concerns, organized as joint stock companies by bankers rather than manufacturers, and designed for the mass production of highly standardized goods. By 1860 the number of spindles per mill had more than tripled as compared with 1831, with a resultant increase in efficiency, no matter how measured.

The growth of the industry received a further stimulus from the outbreak of World War I, which brought large Government orders as well as high prices. The immediate postwar period saw demand continue at record-high levels, and when a Republican Congress added to this already bright picture in 1922 by increasing the low tariff established by the Democrats in 1913, profits soared. This boom, however, did not last. In 1923 the number of active cotton spindles reached its peak, and the industry earned 91 million dollars, estimated to have been 11 per cent on its capitalization; in 1924 three million spindles stood idle, 65 per cent of the industry's firms showed no net profit, and the industry as a whole incurred a deficit of 40 million dollars.[5] Thus, "The cotton textile industry staged a private depression all its own long before American industry in general took to its bed in 1930." [6] Having achieved the unenviable status of a "sick industry" by the latter part of the roaring twenties, the industry was ill-prepared for the great depression. A trough in the percentage of capacity utilized (59.4 per cent) was reached in 1934, after which the industry recovered, so that by 1940 it was operating at 96.2 per cent of capacity.[7]

The outbreak of World War II brought with it a return of textile prosperity on a scale not seen for twenty years. Operations were consistently above 100 per cent of capacity, as rising consumer incomes and large government orders increased the demand for textiles to peak levels. Cloth production in the war period exceeded the 1935–39 levels by 34 per cent. The increased level of demand and activity during the war brought with it an increase in margins and earnings. As wartime production consisted mainly of yarns to meet military demands for bagging, jungle cloth, work clothes, and tents, a

[5] *Statistics of Income;* R. C. Epstein, *Industrial Profits in the United States,* New York: National Bureau of Economic Research, 1934, p. 254.
[6] Douglas G. Woolf, "The Modern Textile Industry," in John George Glover and William Bouck Cornell, *The Development of American Industries,* New York: Prentice-Hall, 1946, p. 237.
[7] Capacity figures are based upon total active spindles, and are computed on a 5-day, 2-shift, 80-hour week basis.

large backlog of consumer demand for finer goods was built up. Maintenance of a high rate of operations and profits in the postwar period made it possible for the industry to be discharged from its sick bed. Declines since World War II have proved to be relatively short-run phenomena from which the industry quickly recovered.

Organization of the Industry

The cotton textile industry includes all mills performing one or more of the functions involved in the preparation of raw cotton for processing, the spinning of cotton fibers into yarn, the weaving or knitting of yarn into cloth, and the finishing of the fabric. Thus the industry comprises all the stages of production and distribution from the opening of the cotton bale to the placing of the finished cloth in the hands of its final distributor, or the manufacturing of apparel and other products.

The raw cotton is first cleaned and straightened by either carding or combing. The latter process is employed when finer grades of yarn are to be manufactured, although recent progress in carding methods has minimized the difference in the medium-count range of yarns. After being combed or carded, as the case may be, the cotton is spun into yarn or thread. At the time of the last census there were 357 yarn mills which sold their product— known to the trade as "sales yarn"—to thread, twine, mop, and insulated wire manufacturers, and to household consumers who buy hand-knitting, crochet, and embroidery cottons. Most companies, however, own both spinning and weaving mills and weave the yarn that they turn out, rather than sell it as sales yarn.

Yarn which is to be further processed (this excludes the bulk of sales yarn) is woven into cotton cloth, or "gray goods" by some 582 cotton broadwoven fabric mills and some 513 narrow fabric mills, the former being of far greater importance than the latter. About a third of all the gray cloth produced goes without further processing to the manufacturers of industrial products such as bags and cordage. The balance is finished by being subjected to bleaching, dyeing, printing or, less commonly, mercerizing, sanforizing, etc. This work is done by about 725 finishing mills, almost all of whom work on a fee basis instead of taking ownership of the cloth.

The routes which the gray goods take in getting to the finisher vary. Some weaving mills do their own finishing; others sell all or part of their output through brokers; still others have selling houses do this work for them. These selling houses, otherwise known as commission houses and merchant houses, may sell directly to a buyer or, more frequently, through a broker.

The broker's function is to bring the converter and the mill sales representative, i.e., the commission house, together. He keeps converters informed as to what mills are offering and the mills informed as to converters' wants, and negotiates the prices at which goods are sold. The broker neither takes title to the goods nor handles them physically in most instances. He receives for his services a commission of 0.5 per cent of the sales value of the goods, this being paid by the selling house. Attempts by the latter to by-pass the broker have rarely been successful, as converters feel that only through using the services of the broker can they get goods at truly competitive prices.

The selling houses are specialists who handle the entire output of 5 to 75 mills for a commission of 2 to 5 per cent. In return for this commission the selling house finds customers for the produce of the mills it services, guarantees their credit and otherwise aids their financing, and advises the mills as to the types of cloth they should produce. Like the broker, the selling house rarely assumes ownership of the cloth. Occasionally, however, commission houses and brokers have the cloth finished on their own account, and sell it to (a) manufacturers of apparel and of other end-products that use cotton, known in the trade as "cutters," and (b) distributors, i.e., wholesalers and large retailers. More often, however, the cloth is sold in the gray to a special middleman known as a converter. The converter, called into being in the late nineteenth century by the rising importance of fashion and design, is the specialist who assumes the responsibility and the risk for the selection of styles and finishes for cotton fabrics. He purchases the gray cloth from the weaving mill or its representative, has it processed by a finishing mill according to his instructions, and then sells it to manufacturers of cotton products or distributors. Since the converter retains ownership of the goods —the finishing mill operating, as was said, on a fee basis—he assumes the risk inherent in finishing a good subject to the whims of fashion. Consequently, the converter must carefully follow market trends and constantly attempt to develop novelties, whereas the weaving mill which does its own finishing tends to concentrate on the so-called staples of the trade—checks, plaids, and so on.

Converters handle about half of all cotton goods which require finishing, the balance being finished by the weaving mills or by finishing mills on commission from the weaving mill, the final manufacturer, or the distributor. In 1948 there were estimated to be 1,151 converters, most of whom handled rayon as well as cotton goods. Only 6 per cent owned their own finishing plants. With little investment required in fixed plant, and with "factors" standing ready to relieve the converter of short-term credit liabilities, the amount of capital needed by a would-be converter is quite small. This, combined with rapid shifts in fashion trends which often leave converters with stocks of out-of-style goods on their hands at the end of a season,[8] explains the high turnover which has always characterized the converting trade.

This, then, is the way goods move through the industry from process to process and on into the hands of the consumer. The problems raised by this marketing structure are many, and will be discussed more fully below.

SECTION II: MARKET STRUCTURE AND PRICE POLICY

Market Structure

The market structure of the cotton textile industry has long been a subject of debate among economists. One author informs us that "despite its age, cotton textile production remains one of the most competitive industries in the country." [9] Another notes in the same vein that "The cotton textile industry is one of the few large American industries which still approximates the theoretical model of 'pure' competition." [10] On the other hand, Solomon Barkin reports that "the proportion of the industry now embraced by the large integrated organizations is so considerable as to make them the characteristic form of industrial organization." [11] Examination of the available data indicates that the truth lies somewhere between these extremes. This can be established by a consideration of the three relevant economic entities in the industry: the plant, the firm, and the interest group.

The 1954 Census of Manufactures reported the existence of 582 broad-woven fabric mills, 513 narrow fabric mills, 357 cotton system yarn mills, 97 thread mills, and 725 finishing plants. Only 86 of the 582 broad-woven fabric mills employed more than 1,000 persons; 381 of these mills employed less than 500 persons; and 174 employed fewer than 100 workers. On the other hand, those units employing over 1,000 persons accounted for over 50 per cent of the workers employed in cotton broad-woven fabric mills,

---

[8] The head of the merchandising department of a leading mill, when interviewed by the author, estimated that one-quarter to one-third of the styles introduced by a converter each year will not "move," and will have to be marked down and "sold out" at the end of the season.

[9] Allen, *op.cit.*, p. 370.

[10] Archibald M. McIsaac, "The Cotton Textile Industry," in Walter Adams, ed., *The Structure of American Industry*, New York: Macmillan, 1950, p. 1.

[11] Solomon Barkin, "The Regional Significance of the Integration Movement in the Southern Textile Industry," *The Southern Economic Journal*, Vol. XV, No. 4, April 1949, p. 395.

i.e., 15 per cent of these mills accounted for over half of the employment in that line. Similar concentration of employment existed in finishing, 12 per cent of the mills providing 63 per cent of the employment; the 44 largest cotton system yarn mills—the largest 12 per cent—accounted for 43 per cent of the employment.

Data available on the extent of concentration of output in firms, as opposed to plants, reveals a mixed picture. Multiplant firms, of course, are commonplace. In 1954 there were an average of nine plants per firm in cotton broad-woven goods and in cotton yarn, and two, three, and four plants for each narrow-fabric, thread, and finishing firm, respectively. Nevertheless, in 1947 the leading four manufacturers of cotton broad-woven fabrics accounted for only 13.1 per cent of the total value of cotton broad-woven goods shipped; [12] and the eight leading firms supplied only 22.2 per cent of the total. In that same year the four largest producers of narrow fabrics accounted for only 17.0 per cent of the total, and the eight largest only 25.0 per cent. The four largest cotton system yarn mills accounted for 13.2 per cent of the total value of output from these mills in 1947; the eight largest accounted for 22.1 per cent. Later data, for the year 1950, although available only as related to concentration of *employment*, indicate that the 1947 data were still applicable at that later date.[13] In the cotton textile industry considered as a whole, the leading four firms in 1952 accounted for only 14.3 per cent of the total spindles, and in 1955 for only 13 per cent of total industry employment.[14]

These over-all views of the industry may, however, tend to understate the extent of concentration in specific product lines. Thus the Federal Trade Commission found that in 1933 six companies sold the equivalent of 74 per cent of the tire cord manufactured in the United States. More recently, it was found that in 1947 the leading four companies produced 65.3 per cent of the thread shipped in this country, and that the production of many finished cotton products was highly concentrated.[15] The low level of the over-all concentration data must also be qualified by the fact that they ex-

---

[12] In terms of concentration, this industry ranks 412 out of 452 tabulated by the Census Bureau.

[13] Federal Trade Commission, *Report on Changes in Concentration in Manufacturing, 1935–47 and 1950*, Washington, 1954, p. 139.

[14] Simon N. Whitney, *Antitrust Policies: American Experience in 20 Industries*, New York: The Twentieth Century Fund, 1958, p. 525.

[15] The leading four firms accounted for 42.5 per cent of the work gloves, 52.4 per cent of the work shirts, 47.3 per cent of the men's and boy's underwear, and 45.7 per cent of the women's neckwear produced in 1947. Hearings before the Subcommittee on the Study of Monopoly Power, House Judiciary Committee, Serial 14, Part 2-B, Washington, 1949, pp. 1437–45. See also statement of Lazare Teper, Director of Research, International Ladies' Garment Workers' Union, *op.cit.*, Series 14, Part 1, p. 306.

hibit a marked increase in the percentage of the industry's facilities controlled by the four largest firms. Thus the share of the top four increased from 6.3 per cent of the industry's spindles in 1920 to 14.3 per cent in 1952, and to 16.8 per cent in 1955.[16]

The facts of concentration in specific product lines, and of increased over-all concentration, although not without significance, must be evaluated in terms of other available information. The ease of flow of productive resources from product to product which has always characterized the industry places an extreme limit on the monopoly power which the producer of even a relatively large share of a given product can exert.[17] And the significance of the increased over-all concentration is diminished somewhat by the fact that the composition of the four leading firms has changed constantly since 1920. Of the four largest firms in 1920, not one was left in the list by 1947. Two had disappeared from the list in 1930, another by 1937, and the last by 1947. It is also interesting to note that of the leading four firms in 1920, only one—Pacific Mills—ranks among the top ten at present. Furthermore, the firm which led the industry in 1937 now ranks eighth; the third largest in 1937 has since declined to eleventh position; and the fourth ranking firm in 1937 now ranks ninth.[18]

Those firms that have risen most rapidly in the list have as a rule advanced by acquiring already existing smaller firms. Thus Burlington began a long series of acquisitions when, in 1937, it acquired the Rayon Fabrics Corporation and the Dutchess Fabrics Corporation. In the following year it acquired the Cetwick Silk Mills and absorbed a former subsidiary, the Puritan Weaving Company; and in 1940 it acquired the E. M. Holt Plaid Mills via merger. Between 1940 and 1947 Burlington made twenty-four more acquisitions of other firms;[19] and more recently has acquired the May McEwen Kaiser Company (1948), Wheatley Fabrics (1948), Brighton Mills (1950),

[16] 1955 data derived by Whitney, *op.cit.*, p. 539, from data received from Research Department, Textile Workers Union of America. See also Jesse W. Markham, "Vertical Integration In The Textile Industry," *Harvard Business Review*, Vol. XXVIII, No. 1, January 1950, p. 86.

[17] William C. Kessler, "An Outline History of the Textile Industry in the United States," in E. C. Bancroft, W. H. Crook, and William C. Kessler, *Textiles: A Dynamic Industry*, Hamilton, New York: Colgate University, 1951, p. 16 (hereinafter, *Colgate Study*). For a broader discussion of the danger of defining the market too narrowly see Clair Wilcox, "On The Alleged Ubiquity of Oligopoly," *American Economic Review, Papers and Proceedings*, Vol. XL, No. 2, May 1950, pp. 23–25.

[18] Comparison drawn from data in Moody's. For a more sophisticated discussion of the implication of rank shifts see Jules Joskow, "Structural Indicia: Rank-Shift Analysis as a Supplement to Concentration Ratios," in *Review of Economics and Statistics*, Vol. XLII, No. 1, February 1960.

[19] Federal Trade Commission, *The Merger Movement, A Summary Report*, Washington: United States Government Printing Office, 1948, pp. 56–57 (hereinafter, *Merger Report*).

Worth Brothers (1951), and National Mallinson Fabrics, Sarfert Hosiery Mills, and Peerless Woolen Mills (these three all in 1952).

Berkshire, the second ranking firm in 1952, was not quite as active in acquiring other firms as was Burlington, but it did make nine acquisitions between 1929 and 1952. J. P. Stevens, currently third largest, is simply the product of a series of recent mergers, the first of which brought together eleven textile firms with thirty mills located both in the North and in the South. Finally, Cone Mills, although engaging in no merger activity until after World War II, has since that time made eleven acquisitions of previously independent firms.

Whatever the reason, it seems fairly clear that companies which have risen to the top of this industry have failed to maintain their positions for any very extended period of time. It is equally obvious that the main means of moving into the top group, i.e., of displacing firms already in it, has been by the acquisition of other, smaller units. This great importance of recent (i.e., post-1890-1904) mergers as a source of growth of leading firms in the textile industry is particularly interesting because it seems to contrast with the experiences of most other industries.[20]

Turning from the plant and the firm to a consideration of concentration of control in the hands of "interest groups," we find the lack of national data offset somewhat by Barkin's recent study, which indicates that in 1948, 58.1 per cent of Southern textile mill employees were employed by 42 interests which each controlled more than 3,000 spindles. In addition to the fact that the applicability of regional concentration data to an industry which sells in a national market can be challenged, the degree of concentration revealed by these figures, especially in view of the fact that the term "interests" is subject to varying definitions, is hardly alarming.

Any explanation of the foregoing material must, of necessity, be based upon an analysis of the relationship between efficiency and size in the cotton textile industry. Since availability of meaningful data on size and efficiency relate to the *plant*, conclusions about optimum *firm* size will be of a more qualitative nature.

A congressional study of carded yarn mills grouped on the basis of size as indicated by volume of sales in 1936 shows that in all years studied (1936, 1939, 1941, and 1944) the net operating profit of mills whose annual sales exceeded $500,000 came to a higher percentage of net sales than did the profit of mills with annual sales of under $500,000.[21] This was true even in

---

[20] See J. Fred Weston, *The Role of Mergers in the Growth of Large Firms*, Berkeley: University of California Press, 1953.

[21] It is unfortunate that available data break carded yarn mills into these two groups only, with $500,000 as the dividing line.

1944, when gross margins (net sales less net material costs) of the smaller mills exceeded those of larger mills, when expressed as a percentage of sales. Labor costs in the larger mills typically account for a smaller percentage of the sales dollar, and for the years studied averaged 21.8 per cent of sales for smaller mills compared with 20.4 per cent for the larger units. On the average, then, labor costs account for 1.4 percentage points, or 7 per cent, more of the sales dollar of mills with sales of under $500,000 per year than they do for larger mills. These larger mills also find that general and administrative expenses, being spread over a larger volume of sales, account for a smaller portion of their sales dollar.

As a result of all these advantages, the net operating profits of carded yarn mills with sales exceeding $500,000 per year, expressed as a percentage of the sales dollar, were 47, 60, 20 and 25 per cent above those of the smaller mills in 1936, 1939, 1941 and 1944, respectively. This was not true in the production of combed cotton yarns. In that field mills with annual sales of less than one million dollars consistently had higher net operating profits (expressed as a per cent of sales) than did larger mills. The higher general and administrative expenses of the smaller units were more than offset by the fact that their labor and manufacturing costs took a somewhat smaller portion of their sales dollar. The advantage of the smaller mills in this area is probably due to the fact that the production of the finer combed yarns requires a greater degree of skill, care and supervision than does the production of carded yarns. It must be remembered, of course, that almost 90 per cent of all cotton yarn produced in this country is carded, and that therefore the data relative to that branch of the industry must be given far greater weight.

Data available for the cotton print cloth industry seem to reveal a pattern similar to that characteristic of carded yarn. Labor costs, manufacturing expenses, and general and administrative costs claim a decreasing proportion of the sales dollar in larger print cloth mills. Mills with sales in excess of $1.5 million per year found labor costs taking an average of 24.6 per cent of net sales, while for smaller mills this figure was 25.6 per cent. Manufacturing expenses averaged 15.8 per cent of sales for larger mills and 16.2 per cent for smaller units; general and administrative expenses took 2.2 per cent of the sales dollar of mills classified as large and 2.4 per cent in mills with sales of less than $1.5 million.[22]

Finally, let us consider the wholesaling end of the industry. Figures for

[22] Computed from Hearings before the Special Subcommittee on Cotton of the Committee on Agriculture, *Study of Agricultural and Economic Problems of the Cotton Belt,* Washington, 1947, p. 146.

wholesaling firms engaged in selling yarn and for those engaged in selling cotton piece goods indicate that in both these areas operating expenses decline as a per cent of sales as the size of the wholesaling concern increases, although less consistently in the case of piece goods. Operating expenses for yarn wholesalers handling less than $10,000 in annual sales came to 21.1 per cent of sales; for firms handling over two million dollars worth of goods this percentage was only 5.5 per cent. For wholesalers of cotton piece goods these figures were 13.1 per cent for the smallest establishments (annual sales of under $10,000) and 6.7 per cent for the largest (sales of over one million dollars). In both lines the lower operating expenses of the larger concerns are due primarily to the fact that administrative and selling expenses decline as a percentage of sales as volume increases. There does seem to be somewhat of a difference between yarn and piece goods wholesaling, as is reflected in the fact that in the former field operating expenses decline steadily as a percentage of sales as volume increases, while in piece goods wholesaling all firms with sales of less than one million dollars seem to operate on a substantially equal basis as far as costs are concerned. This is because wholesalers' delivery and warehousing expenses do not decline with increased volume in the piece goods field.[23]

Unfortunately, the available data are such that it is impossible to say whether the higher net operating profits of the larger units simply reflect the fact that direct costs constitute a smaller, and overhead costs a larger, percentage of sales. There is also the possibility that the higher profit rates may mirror merely the higher unit prices received by the large units as a result of brand preferences. Finally, the separation at $500,000 of sales in the case of carded yarn and $1.5 million in the case of print cloth obviously lessens the usefulness of the data, as it is not at all clear that a relationship between size and efficiency actually exists at all levels of sales. It therefore becomes necessary to supplement the above data with information of a more qualitative sort. Many in the industry seem to feel that larger mills are the most efficient units,[24] and the steady increase in the size of the average mill (as measured by workers per mill) would seem to indicate that persons building new cotton textile facilities feel that larger units are more efficient than smaller plants.

The above data and information can be summarized as follows: The cotton textile industry is one in which there seems to be—at least within certain indeterminate limits—a relationship between plant size and operat-

---

[23] See *ibid.*, pp. 219 and 222.
[24] Interviews with the presidents of two leading cotton textile trade associations and with the Public Relations Director of a leading mill.

ing efficiency in most branches. The existence of *over-all* economies of scale at either the plant or the firm level cannot be established from the available data, however, although there is a general belief throughout the industry that such economies do exist. At any rate, it would seem that the differences in the efficiencies of large and small firms are not sufficient to explain even the slight degree of concentration which characterizes the production of cotton cloth, the growth of the leading firms having been accomplished largely through mergers. Such economies as are revealed in the data presented above certainly do not seem so great as to cause the competitive elimination of enough small firms to substantially reduce the force of competition in the industry; nor do they seem substantial enough to have erected formidable barriers to entry. Thus, even if the economies of scale realized by mills with annual sales in excess of $500,000 were far greater than the data indicate, such mills are small enough in relation to the total market to allow the existence of several hundred competing sellers.

Price Behavior

Most analysts of the cotton textile industry have, until very recently, emphasized the extent to which its price behavior conforms to the competitive pattern, citing the fact that changes in demand for cotton textiles are reflected quickly in corresponding price changes.[25] More recently, however, the behavior of textile prices has become the subject of considerable debate. On the one hand there are those who contend that in the postwar period, "either because of a realization of past errors or because of the growth of large units in the industry . . . and the high costs of producing for inventory, a fall in demand and price . . . resulted in sharp curtailment of production";[26] that integration has brought with it "the limitation of output rather than recourse to the older, customary, excessive output and cutthroat price competition";[27] that, "The level of productive operations are now more quickly adjusted to variations in the volume of sales than ever before."[28] On the other hand we have a group of scholars who contend that "there seems to be little if any evidence that . . . competitive forces are not continuing to play their traditional role" in the industry, and that it consequently "becomes extremely difficult to see any serious threat of monopoly power in the textile industry in the foreseeable future . . .";[29] and that

[25] See for example Whitney, *op.cit.*, pp. 549 ff.
[26] Kessler, *loc.cit.*, p. 39.
[27] Wilfrid H. Crook, "Corporate Concentration in the Textile Industry," *Colgate Study*, p. 5.
[28] Barkin, *loc.cit.*, pp. 409–10.
[29] Markham, *loc.cit.*, p. 88.

"the signs of diminution of price competition in the gray goods market as a result of the merger movement are not yet convincing." [30]

Examination of the available evidence would seem to support the contention that the changes in the industry's market structure have affected the behavior of prices, reducing their flexibility. First, an examination of the frequency of price changes in some of the more important series of cloth prices indicates a slight but perceptible downtrend. Print cloth prices, which changed an average of ten times a year in 1935–39, changed only an average of nine times in 1954–58; [31] sheeting prices changed an average of nine times a year in 1935–39, and only seven times in 1954–58; denim prices, which changed an average of eight times per year in the 1935–39 period, changed only once a year, on the average, in 1954–58.

Second, a detailed statistical study prepared by the author indicates that, particularly in recent years, the price of cotton cloth has become much less variable relative to production than was once the case. Thus, whereas in the 1935–39 period the variability of cloth prices around their average annual level equaled 64 per cent of the variability of cotton production around its annual average level, by 1953–57 the variability of cloth prices around their annual average equaled only 15 per cent of the variability of cotton textile production.

Finally, it appears that in the pre-World War II era there was a strong tendency for cloth prices to turn down *before* production when demand fell, and for production to turn up *before* price when demand recovered. It was not uncommon for falling prices to be associated with increased output, as declining mill margins and unit profits caused mills, ignoring the probable reaction of other firms, to expand output in an attempt to maintain total profit or minimize losses. In more recent years, on the other hand, production has tended to lead in downturns and to rise simultaneously with price (rather than before it) during a recovery. Periods of rising prices and falling production have become not uncommon. This combined behavior of prices, production and margins would seem to support the conclusion that in the change in market structure which resulted from the merger and integration movements lies an explanation of the change in the industry's price behavior.

The increased size of the productive unit, in part a result of the merger movement, has made entry into the industry more difficult. The increased capital required of a newcomer makes it easier for existing firms to con-

---

[30] Whitney, *op.cit.*, p. 552.
[31] Changes are computed on a monthly basis, with the maximum possible changes during a year totaling twelve.

tract output in times of falling demand, and to delay its expansion in periods of rising demand.

Integration has also increased the manufacturers' knowledge of market conditions. A slackening in consumer demand, when felt by a mill-owned sales outlet, is immediately made known to the mill. Previously, mills would continue producing for some time after demand had declined, the information relating to such a decline having to filter back from the retailer through the converters, brokers, commission houses, etc. To some extent, then, the more rapid adjustment of production to demand is a result of better information. To some extent, however, it is probably the result of the market control which is associated with large-scale enterprise.

A form of this market control has been the rise of product differentiation which has accompanied the appearance of larger units in the industry. Prior to World War II the industry engaged in little sales promotion, manufacturers making practically no attempt to increase consumption by more aggressive selling. The largest advertisers of textiles and allied products were the retail stores. This type of advertising gave very little attention to the manufacturer of the textile product, concentrating instead upon the store and its bargains, "usually with a very great emphasis upon price." [32] With the rise of large integrated units this situation has changed. Fabrics and finishes are being branded and advertised in an effort to reduce the elasticity of the individual firm's demand curve. Dan River's "wrinkle-shed" fabrics, Avondale's "companion colors" line, and Bates' "Picolay" are cases in point. Cone Mills recently inaugurated its first real advertising campaign, an upwards of $1,000,000 affair designed to popularize Cone fabrics with consumers.[33] It has been reported that many textile mills have begun to put pressure on garment manufacturers to force the latter to promote textile brands instead of their own business identities.[34] Thus woolens and worsteds produced by Pacific Mills are sold to clothing manufacturers under a written understanding that the finished garments will be identified with woven labels as made from Pacific fabrics. "This understanding applies regardless of whether the garment is a skirt to retail at $3.98 or an expensive coat and suit." [35] Stroock fabrics are also sold to a select group of manufacturers, each

[32] Reavis Cox, *The Marketing of Textiles*, Washington: The Textile Foundation, 1938, pp. 323, 326. By way of contrast Cox points out (and this was written in 1938) that "the larger rayon producers make strong efforts to popularize their products, not only by advertising to the manufacturers who use their yarn, but also by advertising to consumers in the hope that they will insist upon getting a particular yarn in the garments or fabrics they purchase" (p. 327).

[33] "Cone Mills: Old King Denim," *Fortune*, January 1953, p. 165.

[34] Statement of Lazare Teper, *loc.cit.*

[35] James C. Cummings, *Sales Promotion in the Textile Industry*, New York: Fairchild, 1946, p. 50.

of whom agrees to label the finished product with a Stroock woven label. The manufacturer and Stroock jointly select the stores that will retail the garment.[36]

The degree of control over price which such a campaign of winning consumer acceptance can yield is shown by the fact that Wamsutta Mills, with only a minute portion of the total sheet market, but with a vigorous merchandising and advertising department, did not change its wholesale price for a period of at least five years.[37] Thus, increased advertising and branding have led mills to believe that the public is more brand conscious than ever before, i.e., that the area of discretionary pricing has increased. Therefore, the decline in the flexibility of gray goods prices noted earlier has been accompanied with an even greater rigidity in prices of fabricated consumer goods such as sheets, bedspreads, and blankets.[38]

The increased importance of product differentiation has also tended to reinforce the increased capital requirements in making entry at the mill level somewhat more difficult. Thus, it was recently reported that manufacturers of unbranded muslin sheets receive about 25 per cent less for their goods than do manufacturers of branded sheets of the identical quality, while branded percales bring 10 to 25 per cent more than do nonbranded percale sheets.[39] This clearly illustrates the effectiveness of the advertising, branding, and product differentiation described above.

Increased vertical integration has led to greater price stability also by reducing the importance of the selling houses. The latter, receiving their compensation according to the volume of goods they sold, were strongly tempted to cut prices whenever demand fell off. A mill-owned outlet is much less likely to do this.

As changing market structure provides a partial explanation of changing price-production behavior, so differences in market structures provide some explanation of the difference between the behavior of denim and say, sheeting prices. Cone's dominance in denims—in 1953 it accounted for 30 per cent of the work-denim output in the United States—enabled it, for example, to hold the line on denim prices after the repeal of OPA so as to "discourage new producers from entering the field" and to "broaden further the already expanding denim market." [40]

The material presented above would tend to indicate that price behavior

[36] *Ibid.*, p. 27.

[37] Interview with company official who pointed out that to get more business Wamsutta, rather than cut prices, turns to the production of higher styled goods, such as "candy striped" sheets.

[38] For confirmation of this see Barkin, *loc.cit.*, pp. 409–10.

[39] *The New York Times,* April 25, 1954, Sec. 3, p. 1.

[40] *Fortune,* January 1953, p. 90.

in the cotton textile industry must be explained, in part, at least, in terms of industrial concentration. In this industry the number of sellers, the entry conditions, the degree of integration, and the extent of product standardization certainly do, as one economist puts it, "impinge on price."[41] One cannot accept without some qualms the statement that "there seems to be little if any evidence that . . . competitive forces are not continuing to play their traditional role" in the industry.[42]

SECTION III: PUBLIC POLICY

As indicated above, the public policy questions presented by events in the cotton textile industry are numerous—so numerous, in fact, that it is necessary to consider them separately.

Locational Shift

The early concentration of the textile industry in the New England area, and its subsequent massive shift to the South are well known. At the start of the Civil War almost 75 per cent of the spindles in this country were in the New England States;[43] by the beginning of the present decade approximately 80 per cent of the spindles were in the cotton-growing states. Portions of the industry, such as finishing, however, are still centered in New England and the Middle Atlantic States. The cotton cloth market is still heavily centered in New York, with Boston ranking second. Ninety per cent of the converters are located in New York, and the city remains the chief center of selling houses, mill sales departments, and the garment manufacturing industry.

The causes of the southward shift of most phases of the industry need be considered here only to the extent that they shed light on various public policy issues. First, much has been made of the wage differential which favored such a movement to the South. There can be no doubt that such a differential existed for an extended period of time; that the real labor cost differential was lower—due to the higher productivity of Northern workers, their lower absentee rates, and related factors—seems equally certain.[44] To

[41] John T. Dunlop, *Wage Determination Under Trade Unions*, New York: Augustus M. Kelley, 1950, p. 9.
[42] Jesse W. Markham, *loc.cit.*, p. 88.
[43] Computed from Melvin T. Copeland, *The Cotton Manufacturing Industry of the United States*, Cambridge: Harvard University Press, 1917, p. 8.
[44] It has been estimated that as late as 1914 hourly rates for men were 44 per cent higher in the North while hourly rates for women were 47 per cent higher than in the South. On the other hand, at about this time, the value of product per employee was $1,200 in Massachusetts, $1,010 in Georgia, $984 in South Carolina, and $937 in North

the extent that wage rate differentials are a function of economic forces beyond the control of legislative bodies, there is little point, from a public policy point of view, in exploring this aspect further. It is worth mentioning, however, that an important consideration inducing mills to move South was the wide differential which existed between Northern and Southern labor legislation.[45] New England mill owners were faced with hours restrictions for women workers, and a *relatively* less hostile climate toward trade unions.[46] The lesson here seems obvious: the existence of interstate markets makes it virtually impossible for individual states to establish and maintain labor standards. Only Federal intervention can prevent the movement of industry, other things being equal, to states which permit lower standards; "usurpation of States' Rights" replaces "cut-throat competition" for industry with uniformity.

Another factor important in the southward movement of the industry was the difference in local tax rates.[47] Southern communities not only offered lower tax rates but often provided water power, electricity, and rail facilities at very low costs, and even issued their own tax-free bonds to aid in the financing of new mills. To the extent that the establishment of such local differentials was made possible by features of the Federal tax laws, e.g., tax exemption of interest on municipal bonds, the serious-minded student must resolve this question: Should Federal policy be permitted to encourage an interregional competition for industry when such competition may result in serious social and economic dislocations, often further burdening the Federal taxpayer?

No discussion of the causes of the Southern migration of the textile industry would be complete without reference to the managerial laxity and

---

Carolina. See Malcolm Keir, *Industries of America—Manufacturing,* New York: Ronald, 1928, p. 354; and S. J. Chapman, *The Cotton Industry and Trade,* London: Methuen, 1905, pp. 149–50.

[45] At the time in which the Southern shift of the industry was occurring the Supreme Court's ruling that "The Commerce Clause was not intended to give Congress a general authority to equalize such [working] conditions" was the law of the land. *Hammer* v. *Dagenhart,* 247 U.S. 251, 1918.

[46] For a broader discussion of the effect of social legislation on New England's competitive position see *The New England Economy,* A Report to the President Transmitting a Study Initiated by the Counsel of Economic Advisors and Prepared by its Committee on the New England Economy, July 1951, pp. 76–77.

[47] It was estimated in the midtwenties that mills in the Piedmont and Carolina sections paid from four-sevenths to five-sevenths of the taxes paid in Massachusetts, and mills in Alabama, Georgia, and further South paid about three-sevenths of the tax paid by Massachusetts mills. See National Association of Cotton Growers, *Transactions, 1927,* p. 313. Contrasting views as to the effects of tax differences may be found in W. F. Doane, *The Flight of Capital and Industry from Massachusetts,* Philadelphia: Pennsylvania Manufacturers' Association, 1935, and Joe Summers Floyd, Jr., *Effects of Taxation on Industrial Location,* Chapel Hill: University of North Carolina Press, 1952.

conservatism which came to dominate New England textile management. This group evidenced an unwillingness to invest in new equipment, even when earnings were extremely high. For example, while Southern firms rushed to introduce the automatic power loom which had been invented in the latter part of the nineteenth century, Northern management hesitated. By 1929, 80.3 per cent of the plain looms and 66.6 per cent of the fancy looms in the South were automatic, as compared with 59.1 and 32.6 per cent, respectively, in New England.[48] To what extent New England's refusal to introduce the new looms was due to managerial laxity, to what extent it was due to the many interlocking directorates which then existed between the manufacturers of nonautomatic looms and the New England mills,[49] and to what extent it was due to the unwillingness to scrap old but still serviceable equipment [50] will probably never be known. Nevertheless, the legal prohibition against such interlocking directorates as tend to foreclose markets to purveyors of new idea and equipment would seem to have a basis in economic fact.

It would seem safe to say that the shift in spindlage has about run its course. New England governments have become aware of their past errors, and are taking steps to remedy them. Those mills that have remained in New England seem quite able to meet Southern competition. The adjustments required of New England were quite severe, partly because of the concentration of the textile industry *within* that area. Inhabitants of Lowell, Fall River, and other towns suffered from the shift of facilities and from the fact that theirs were primarily one-industry towns.[51] On the other hand, the coming of textiles to the South offered new opportunities for local labor and undoubtedly tended to lift standards of living in that area. What has been happening in American textiles is part of an over-all trend which has seen a lessening of interregional inequality of income distribution. While government programs to ameliorate the suffering caused by the relocation of the industry would have been desirable—such things as interest-free loans to aid Northern millhands to relocate, and government sponsored training to prepare Northern workers to assume useful places in other New England industries come to mind—it would seem that efforts designed to *prevent* this

[48] See William C. Kessler, "An Outline History of the Textile Industry in the United States," in *Colgate Study*, p. 24.

[49] Wilfrid H. Crook, "New England Textile Collapse. Area or Leadership at Fault?" in *Colgate Study*, p. 12.

[50] Seymour E. Harris, *The Economics of New England*, Cambridge: Harvard University Press, 1952, p. 292.

[51] Reynolds estimates that in 1937, 36 per cent of all gainfully employable persons in Lowell were totally unemployed, as were 35 per cent in Fall River, and 41 per cent in New Bedford. Reynolds, *loc.cit.*, p. 74, n. 22. See also *The New England Economy*, pp. 39–46.

shift would not have been of long-run benefit to the economy.[52] The working out of normal competitive forces has reestablished a workable equilibrium between the regions, and there has been little recent evidence of a further major southward shift of facilities. Thus the North-South wage differential has been considerably narrowed, there is an increasing threat of unionization facing Southern plants, and (as indicated above) New England governments have adopted more enlightened policies to encourage mills to remain in the area. As a consequence, New England's share of total textile production has remained virtually constant since 1947.[53]

Mergers and Vertical Integration

Having established above that the superiority of large textile units—plants and firms—is not so great as to warrant the *competitive* elimination of many small firms, we must now turn our attention to the elimination of these firms via integration and merger. The latter phenomena are so intimately related in the cotton textile industry that it is impossible to separate them. Consequently, they will be discussed together, as aspects of the same problem, and as results of similar causes.

To some extent vertical integration has always characterized the cotton textile industry. Francis Cabot Lowell's Boston Manufacturing Company integrated spinning and weaving so successfully that since 1814 nearly all mills have followed that example. As integration of these two processes came to be viewed as a necessity, it proceeded rapidly. By 1899 the 502 combined spinning and weaving mills owned 84 per cent of the industry's spindles and 96 per cent of its looms—figures which have remained virtually unchanged since that date.[54]

Many attempts at integrating still more stages of production went hand in hand with the merger and trust movements of the late nineteenth and early twentieth centuries. With the notable exception of the overpromoted Consolidated Cotton Duck Company,[55] many of the integrations and mergers

---

[52] This is particularly true because textile production is typically the first step in the industrialization of a region previously specialized along extractive lines. See Edgar M. Hoover, *The Location of Economic Activity*, New York: McGraw-Hill, 1948, pp. 192 and 194.

[53] The 1952 *Annual Survey of Manufactures* indicates that New England accounted for 23 and 22 per cent of the total value added in textile mills in 1947 and 1952, respectively.

[54] Jules Backman and M. R. Gainsbrugh, *Economics of the Cotton Textile Industry*, New York: National Industrial Conference Board, 1946, p. 39.

[55] This concern was organized by a group of promoters who expected to reap substantial profits from the sale of the securities of their consolidated organization. See Stephen J. Kennedy, *Profits and Losses in Cotton Textiles*, New York: Harper, 1936, p.

consummated in this 1890–1914 period were quite successful. Cannon Mills was established as a horizontal combination of twelve mills controlling 285,500 spindles and 3,734 looms, and later integrated forward by establishing its own sales agency in New York. The Amoskeag Company in New Hampshire acquired several neighboring mills, while the Parker group in the South provided a further early example of horizontal integration via merger by consolidating nine mills which operated 357,952 spindles. Vertical integration also made its appearance, both as the backward purchase of productive facilities by selling houses such as Deering, Milliken and Company, and Marshall Field,[56] and the forward movement of producing mills into the selling field. An example of the latter was the establishment of its own New York sales agency by B. B. & R. Knight, an organization which included seventeen mills, a print works, and a bleachery.

These early integrations, however, had very little effect on the great mass of textile firms. The pace was stepped up somewhat in the twenties as industry spokesmen came more and more to emphasize consolidation and integration as the solution to the industry's problems.[57]

In the latter part of the twenties many firms began to accept integration as the solution to their problems. Powdrell and Alexander expanded from the manufacture of curtain fabrics into curtain making; Kendall Company, a textile finisher, began producing and selling surgical gauzes; United States Rubber decided to produce its own tire cord. In 1929 Pacific Mills severed connections with its commission house and resorted to direct selling of its products, and the Berkshire Fine Spinning Associates was formed, this latter organization amalgamating five companies with a capacity of 600,000 spindles and 12,000 looms. In the following year Wamsutta Mills and the Nashua Manufacturing Company followed the lead of Pacific and adopted a policy of direct selling. Finally, the formation in this period of United Merchants and Manufacturers deserves mention.

We see, then, that even before World War II horizontal and vertical integration were not unknown to the industry. Movement in this direction, however, although dramatic at times, was not extensive. By 1930 only 10.2

20; Arthur Stone Dewing, *Corporate Promotions and Reorganizations,* Cambridge: Harvard University Press, 1930, pp. 334 ff.

[56] Copeland, *op.cit.,* pp. 161, 172, and 175.

[57] See for example Claudius T. Murchison, "Management Problems in The Cotton Textile Industry," in G. T. Schwenning, ed., *Management Problems,* Chapel Hill: University of North Carolina Press, 1930, p. 66. See also Murchison's *King Cotton Is Sick,* Chapel Hill: University of North Carolina Press, pp. 146 and 161; and Melvin T. Copeland and Edmund Learned, *Merchandising of Cotton Textiles: Methods and Organization,* Cambridge: Bureau of Business Research, Graduate School of Business, Harvard University, 1933, p. 5.

per cent of all cotton textile firms listed in Moody's had extended the scope of their operations to include some equipment at all the stages of production normally included in the industry, and only 43 per cent of all firms were acting as their own selling agents. In 1935 only 125 of the 1,042 mills reported by the Census had finishing plants as well as spindles and looms. Even at as late a date as 1939 only 9.5 per cent of total cotton broad goods, 5.1 per cent of narrow goods, and 3.5 per cent of the cotton yarns were sold by cloth manufacturers directly through their own outlets.[58]

The World War II period saw an acceleration of the trend toward integration which had become apparent in earlier years,[59] and once again integration and merger proceeded simultaneously. Between 1940 and 1946, 164 cotton textile companies were reported by the financial manuals to have changed hands.[60] These transfers involved 4.4 million spindles and more than 80,000 looms, or about 20 per cent of the industry's productive facilities. Only 23.7 per cent of the spindles transferred were acquired by new firms, the balance—with the exception of the 8.5 per cent of the total which machinery companies purchased for resale—changing hands as the result of integration by companies already in existence. Nearly half of the spindles acquired were involved in vertical acquisitions, with selling agents and converters the most prominent buyers, and about 18 per cent of the transfers represented horizontal combination. Independently compiled data for the South present a similar picture. Between January 1943 and November 1948, 211 Southern textile mills with approximately five million spindles and 90,000 looms changed hands, these recorded changes in ownership affecting about 22 per cent of the existing capacity of the region.[61]

Not only was the pace of integration stepped up,[62] but the nature of in-

[58] Markham, *loc.cit.*, p. 82; Backman and Gainsbrugh, *op.cit.*, p. 39; and Bureau of the Census, "Distribution of Manufacturers Sales," 1939, p. 77.

[59] It would seem correct to say that the period of the thirties witnessed a trend toward integration. Markham (*loc.cit.*) reports 494 textile mill acquisitions in that period, among them 220 horizontal integrations, 58 interfiber mergers, and 125 vertical integrations. Note that these figures refer to all textile fiber lines. The percentage accounted for by cotton textile firms is not known.

[60] These manuals, unfortunately, understate the total number of mergers because their coverage is quite incomplete for smaller firms. One study estimates the total number of mergers to have been 3½ times as large as those reported in the financial manuals. This of course, only strengthens any observations which may be made concerning the wide extent of the recent merger movement. See J. Keith Butters, John Lintner, and William L. Cary, *Effects of Taxation, Corporate Mergers,* Cambridge: Riverside Press, 1951, p. 242, n. 5.

[61] Federal Trade Commission, *Merger Report,* and Barkin, *loc.cit.,* p. 403. Note that these data refer to "recorded changes in ownership," and therefore are not a perfect measure of the extent of integration. Applying national data to the South, we can assume that one-fourth of the capacity which changed hands represented acquisitions by new firms, i.e., 3,750,000 Southern spindles and 67,500 looms were involved in integrations.

[62] Note that Markham records 492 mergers in all textile lines in the thirties; *Textile World* reported 542 such mergers in the first seven years of the forties.

tegration changed, with a moderate shift from horizontal to vertical acquisitions becoming evident. Whereas over one-half of a sample of mill transfers in the early thirties represented acquisitions of direct competitors and only 22 per cent represented vertical acquisitions, in the 1940–48 period 31.7 per cent of that sample were for horizontal expansion and 42.4 per cent were for vertical expansion.

The result of the movement was that by 1947, 33 per cent of the cotton textile firms listed in Moody's were fully integrated and almost 75 per cent were acting as their own selling agent, as compared with 10 per cent and 43 per cent, respectively, in 1930. Further, in 1946, 75 per cent of all broad goods sales were made by manufacturers through their own outlets,[63] as compared with 9.5 per cent in 1939. In 1952 one authority estimated that about two-thirds of all finished piece goods were produced by "integrated companies." [64]

The causes of this recent integration movement may be classified into the temporary and the permanent. One of the chief temporary reasons was the desire to participate in the higher profit margins allowed by the OPA on finished goods, a desire which led to a vertical movement forward into finishing.[65] Furthermore, price regulations were such that the producer could claim each of the mark-ups allowed on subsequent operations, i.e., the mill was allowed a certain mark-up over the price of raw cotton, the converter a mark-up over the price of gray cloth, and so on. With demand at record levels, acquisition of a new operation provided additional *guaranteed* profits, made doubly attractive by the fact that margins on these subsequent operations were handsome—at least relative to those on earlier processes.[66]

Another temporary reason for the recent integration movement was the shortage of gray goods which characterized the war and immediate post-war periods. This led to backward integration to assure sources of supply, as is shown by the fact that no less than 60 per cent of the vertical acquisitions which occurred between 1940 and 1946 were purchases of mills by selling

[63] Markham, *loc.cit.*, pp. 79–80, and 82.

[64] Claudius T. Murchison, "Vertical Integration in the Cotton Textile Industry," in Nugent Wedding, ed., *Vertical Integration in Marketing*, Bulletin 74, Urbana: Bureau of Economic and Business Research, College of Commerce and Business Administration, University of Illinois, 1952, p. 117.

[65] Kessler, *loc.cit.*, p. 37; Markham, *loc.cit.*, p. 82. This seems to be merely a special case of the general tendency of firms to move from low to high profit areas. In this instance entrance into the higher profit industry—converting—was affected by integration, indicating that in many instances diversification is a potent force for maintaining competition.

[66] This does not imply that it is always profitable to cumulate margins by adding functions, since these functions are by no means costless. In the case under discussion, however, these additional margins were (a) high relative to those already being earned, (b) fairly certain to remain high for some time, and (c) being earned in areas which existing firms could easily add to their lines.

houses and converters. The need for an assured source of supply was felt most strongly by large marketing organizations which had heavy financial commitments in a marketing program, e.g., J. P. Stevens, Ely and Walker, and Deering Milliken. This backward integration, in turn, added the danger of a thinning of markets to the mills' already strong incentive to integrate forward. So here as elsewhere integration by some led to counterintegration by others. Thus, forward integration by manufacturers into retailing often caused movement in the opposite direction by nonintegrated retailers.

Another temporary factor which tended to induce merger and integration was the shortage of machinery, which often made acquisition of other firms the only way to expand. A final temporary factor was the tax structure, which encouraged both the buyers and sellers in these transactions.

Permanent forces were also at work. The chaotic conditions that plagued the nonintegrated industry in the twenties and the early thirties were alone enough to cause some firms to desire integration, and to take action when wartime conditions made such a move even more desirable. Thus it had been found that commission houses often sold at prices uneconomic to the orig-inating mills. These houses, working on a flat commission basis, frequently tended to push sales whether or not the price received made such business profitable to the mills. Mills also complained that agents, more anxious to maintain the good will of buyers than to promote the interests of their mill-clients, were too lenient in permitting buyers to cancel orders and to return goods after prices had fallen. Various selling organizations, on the other hand, felt that too often their advice to mills about market conditions went unheeded.[67]

The desire to escape from these conditions was buttressed by an increased awareness that integrated firms could guarantee the quality of their products and demand consumer recognition—instead of the gray goods becoming completely buried in the "great inland sea" of the cloth market and so hidden in the finished product that the consumer could not possibly know who made it. This desire for quality control was, of course, mixed with a desire to reap the advantages of greater discretion over price which a successful campaign of product differentiation can yield. Thus one industry executive noted that once the nonintegrated mill sells its product it loses control over final quality and price, and another reported that one advantage his organization had obtained from integration was that it could now control quality and price right through the finished fabric. Both, obviously, sought greater control over price as well as quality. These twin goals made the acquisition of finishing

[67] Reavis Cox, *The Marketing of Textiles*, Washington: The Textile Foundation, 1938, pp. 146–8.

facilities by mills an important element in the integration movement. The combination of finishing and weaving facilitated quality control as it enabled mills to rectify such weaving defects as become apparent only in finishing; it at the same time allowed for product differentiation, witness the appearance of "companion color" and "frostee tone" sheets, and "wrinkle-shed" finishing.

A final advantage many saw in integration was that consumer preferences could more quickly be reflected in the production policies of a firm with its own market outlets than they could be in the case of a firm which had to wait for information to trickle back from converters, brokers, commission houses, etc.

It must be pointed out that there seems to have been a halt since 1947 in the trend toward merger and integration. Whereas *Textile World* reported an average of 68 cotton mergers per year in the years between 1940 and 1947 only approximately 21 such transfers were reported, on the average, in the years 1952–58. There has even been some tendency toward disintegration. Many of the war-inspired mergers turned out to be uneconomic and were liquidated. This is particularly true of those which involved the union of small converters and small mills, although as large a firm as Textron has found it necessary to sell its consumer goods enterprises and retreat to the manufacture of gray goods only. This latter move was apparently a result of Textron's inability to find an adequate substitute for the styling information provided by converters. In general, it has been found that the integrated mill lacks the flexibility of the converter, may lose heavily if it guesses wrong on styles with a big production program, and must as a rule confine its production to standard checks and plaids. It cannot, like the independent converter, buy lots of goods for short runs in the finishing mills.

The retreat from vertical integration by some firms was offset, however, by the fact that most of the large integrated organizations have continued to add to their facilities, both via acquisition and new construction. They have found that the opportunities for product differentiation and quality control presented by vertical integration have enabled them to build up a substantial consumer following. Further, the distribution of risk achieved by horizontal and interfiber integration has tended to stabilize the earnings of these companies.[68] Finally, these firms had also found that in many instances cost savings have arisen from the elimination of some handling operations and the avoidance of various intermediate sales expenses. Thus, expenses of wholesaling cotton yarn averaged 4.1 per cent of net sales for

[68] See "Financial Data on 22 Textile Mills," *America's Textile Reporter*, Vol. LXVIII, No. 7, February 18, 1954, p. 35.

manufacturers' sales offices and 8.9 per cent for independent wholesalers.[69]

It is generally believed in the industry that there will ultimately be a division of labor, with the independent converter taking the high style items on short runs and the integrated mills the less stylized and larger lots. This is a phenomenon not peculiar to textiles, and has led one economist to conclude that the result of the operation of both integrated and non-integrated firms "may be the survival of more than one pattern. . . ." [70] Further, the integrated units will probably remain only partially integrated, selling both direct and to converters in the case of mills which have integrated forward, and producing only part of their needs in the case of selling houses which have integrated backward. Thus, Lowenstein manufactures only about half the goods that it currently sells, and many integrated mills sell large quantities of goods to converters as well as to their own sales outlets.[71] Such partial integration is not characteristic of textiles alone, as vertically integrated firms in all industries do a good deal of supplementary buying and selling. Thus, some sort of structural equilibrium seems to have been reached at a new and higher level of integration. But, what has been the effect of the integration movement on the competitive opportunities of the nonintegrated firms? We have already suggested that the pattern of vertical integration of the large firms is sufficiently loose and incomplete, that there remain abundant niches into which the nonintegrated fit and may continue to fit. Since, however, as Corwin Edwards has pointed out, disproportionate integration involves the danger of price and availability squeezes, the question remains of whether the independents survive only by sufferance, and whether they may therefore remain a genuinely independent competitive force in the industry. The crucial test here is not whether they happen to buy from or sell to integrated companies. This fact might equally suggest that the integrated companies are dependent on the nonintegrated, as that the small exist at the sufferance of the big. The test is whether the nonintegrated continue to enjoy sufficient alternatives—a sufficient number of sources of supply, in sufficient volume, a sufficient variety and capacity of market outlets—to prevent their being squeezed.

To some extent the position of the independent converters seems to be

[69] Special Subcommittee on Cotton of the Committee on Agriculture, *op.cit.*, p. 218.

[70] Corwin D. Edwards, "Vertical Integration and the Monopoly Problem," *The Journal of Marketing*, Vol. XVII, No. 4, April 1953, p. 405.

[71] Various interviews. It should be noted that even partial integration supplies the firm which practices it with enough market information to enable it to avoid many of the disadvantages of the nonintegrated market structure described above. In addition it permits it to achieve such of the advantages of product differentiation as the market will allow it, selling unbranded and presumably at lower prices that portion of its output that it cannot dispose of under its own brand name. Partial vertical integration thus permits a species of market separation for purpose of price discrimination.

threatened. Companies with their own finishing plants tend to see that those units are kept operating at full capacity during periods of high demand, and to sell to the converter only whatever gray goods are left over. In periods of slack demand there is some tendency for integrated mills to solicit the customers of the converters who usually buy from these mills, justifying this on the ground that the converter's customers are *really* customers of the mills. This practice, however, is not too common as the mills, having found complete integration to be uneconomic, still must retain the good will of their converters, the latter being important suppliers for some integrated concerns and important customers of others.

Further, the problems alluded to above become acute only when monopoly power of some stage of the productive process falls into the hands of a vertically integrated firm. The possibility of anticompetitive effects is not too great so long as the integrated concern controls only a minor portion of the business done at each successive level of activity at which it operates. Fortunately, this is the case in cotton textiles, where the large, vertically integrated firms control only a small portion of the total cloth output, and where at least two-thirds of the firms do *not* possess equipment at all of the stages of production normally included in the industry. At any rate, there has been little evidence thus far of nonintegrated organizations having difficulty in securing supplies or markets.

Technological Progress

No appraisal of an industry would be complete without an analysis of the rate of technological progress which is characteristic of it. It is generally known that technical progress in the manufacture of cotton textiles, although not nonexistent, did not, for many years, proceed at a rapid rate. One student noted, in 1936: [72]

The textile industry has been unique . . . in that the fundamental characteristics of its manufacturing processes were stabilized years ago . . . no basic change in processes or machinery has taken place since the invention of the Draper loom about 1900. Such improvements as had occurred were largely in the form of refinements in existing machinery which could be made use of either by special machine attachments or by rebuilding the machinery.

Not only has progress been moderate, but what advances there have been have taken the form of *improvements* in processes, rather than in the de-

[72] Stephen Jay Kennedy, *Profits and Losses in Cotton Textiles*, New York: Harper, 1936, p. 161.

velopment of *new* processes or products. Further, what new developments there have been have stemmed, not from the textile manufacturing industry, but from the oligopolistic textile machinery industry.[73] The machinery companies have, in fact, repeatedly complained that the mills are content to leave the job of research to the machinery manufacturer.[74]

It would seem that the relative lack of technical advance in the cotton textile industry was due to the industry's market structure. Cotton textile manufacturers have rarely been possessed of the above-normal profits evidently required for research. Note that this indicates that research expenditures are considered by most mill-men to be a "frill," or a species of charity to be financed out of profits, rather than a necessary cost of doing business. In this attitude the textile industry is not alone. Even in research-conscious industries such as chemicals and electronics, manufacturers feel that research expenditures "come out of profit margins," and do not hesitate to curtail such expenses when margins fall. It is not surprising, therefore, that in 1940 a sample of cotton manufacturers spent only .0017 cents of each sales dollar on research and development. In recent years, i.e., since the growth of larger integrated units and the return of profitability to the industry, expenditures on research have increased to .12 cents of each sales dollar. That this increase has been due as much to the appearance of the larger units as to the return of profits is indicated by the fact that of the 738 research engineers and scientists employed by the textile mill products and apparel industries in January 1952, 660 (89 per cent) were in the employ of firms with more than 1,000 employees, and 422 (57 per cent) were with firms employing more than 5,000. Further, between January 1951 and January 1952 firms with fewer than 500 employees reduced their research staffs by 14.0 per cent, while firms with 500–4,999 employees added to them by 2.9 per cent, and firms with over 5,000 employees increased their research personnel by 4.5 per cent.[75] This research activity by the larger firms has led them to adopt air-conditioning to eliminate temperature changes and thereby facilitate quality control; to install electronic controls on slashers and in finishing

---

[73] For a long list of examples see Thomas R. Navin, *The Whitin Machine Works since 1831,* and George Sweet Gibb, *The Sacco-Lowell Shops,* both published in 1950 by the Harvard University Press at Cambridge.

[74] *America's Textile Reporter,* October 1, 1953, LXVII. But cf. Clifford D. Clark and Bernard M. Olsen, "Technological Change in the Textile Industry," *The Southern Economic Journal,* Vol. XXVI. October 1959, No. 2, p. 133.

[75] House of Representatives, *Study of Agricultural and Economic Problems of the Cotton Belt,* Hearings before the Special Subcommittee on Cotton of the Committee on Agriculture, eightieth Congress, 1st Session, 1947, p. 147; and United States Bureau of Labor Statistics in cooperation with Department of Defense, *Scientific Research and Development in American Industry,* Washington: Government Printing Office, 1953, p. 62.

plants; to adopt mechanical conveyors and material handling equipment; and to develop new finishes and fiber blends. Nevertheless, it is obvious that despite their research expenditures these large firms have contented themselves with discovering ways in which the developments of other industries could be successfully applied to textiles. Improved air-conditioning equipment and electronic controls are not products of textile research laboratories; nor are mechanical conveying devices. Even the development of new fiber blends simply represents the use of different combinations of fibers supplied by the chemical industry. This situation does, however, represent some improvement over pre-World War II days.

The experience of the cotton textile industry, therefore, sheds some light on the more general problem of the relationship of market structure to technological progress. The emphasis on research activity by the larger firms—possessed of the funds and of the knowledge that they will be in business for a rather long time—does indicate that present attitudes toward research expenditures require the existence of above-normal profits as a prerequisite to the financing of research on any appreciable scale. This does not mean, of course, that maximum progress will be achieved by concentration of market control and research effort in the hands of a very few large firms. The present situation in cotton textiles—large firms with funds for research, and the competition of smaller but vigorous competitors to keep them alert and forward looking—may perhaps turn out to be the most conducive to rapid advance.

Ancillary Government Measures

As is true in many cases, various policies adopted by the Government have tended to affect the well-being of the cotton textile industry. The New Deal antidepression policies are a case in point. On July 9, 1933, The Cotton Textile Code—the first approved under the National Industrial Recovery Act—was adopted. The code approved collective bargaining, limited hours of work to forty per week, required that there be no reduction in weekly pay, limited mill operations to two shifts of forty hours each, provided for the collection of statistics and accounting data, and prohibited installation of new machinery without permission of the National Recovery Administrator. The key provision, of course, was that which limited mills to eighty hours per week. This restriction worked strongly to the benefit of the Northern mills, which had earlier been forced onto a one shift basis by a lack of orders. Southern mills, which, until this time had been operating on a two shift, 110-hour week, had to reduce their operations sharply in order to comply with the NIRA code. When a brief flurry of prosperity brought a flood of new orders in 1933 (and the most profitable year the industry was to have between 1927 and 1936) New England mills were able to expand operations to a two shift basis while Southern mills were being forced to contract output.

New Deal legislation also influenced the industry through its effect on costs. The Bankhead Cotton Control Act of 1934 in effect made the Agricultural Adjustment Act of the previous year compulsory. The amount of cotton that a farmer could raise was limited by the imposition of a prohibitive tax of 50 per cent on ginnings in excess of the alloted quota. Those who refused to participate were given no allotment, and therefore had to pay a tax of 50 per cent on all the cotton they sold. Production was sharply reduced and raw cotton prices rose, more than doubling between 1932 and 1934. It does not follow, however, that cotton manufacturers were adversely affected by this increase in raw material costs. The crop restriction program tended to keep cloth production at somewhat lower levels than it might otherwise have reached and this, combined with a recovery of demand, caused cloth prices to increase sufficiently to bring mill margins in 1934 to 43 per cent above 1932 levels.

Other legislation passed under the New Deal regime tended to affect labor costs in textile manufacture. The National Industrial Recovery Act established a minimum wage of $.30 per hour for Southern textile labor and $.325 per hour for Northern labor. The Walsh-Healey Public Contracts Act of 1936 set minimum wages and maximum hours for firms manufacturing goods exceeding $10,000 in value for the Federal government. The Fair Labor Standards Act, passed a few years later, had a greater effect on the low-wage textile industry than on other industries. Even more important was the passage of the National Labor Relations Act, which greatly aided both the United Textile Workers (AFL) and the Textile Workers Union of America (CIO) in their organizing efforts.

It is probable, however, that these measures did not lead to increases in unit labor costs. One set of estimates shows an actual *decline* in these costs during the thirties,[76] indicating that higher rates of pay induced some increased efficiency of mill operation.

Thus, although the New Deal legislation did force an increase in raw cotton prices, it cannot be said that on balance New Deal antidepression measures proved detrimental to the cotton textile industry. The increase in the general level of industrial activity and employment attributable at least in

[76] Jules Backman and M. R. Gainsbrugh, *Economics of the Cotton Textile Industry,* New York: National Industrial Conference Board, 1946.

part to the over-all effects of such moves redounded to the benefit of the cotton textile industry. Per capita consumption of cotton rose from 21.14 pounds in 1930 to 21.53 in 1935 and 29.77 in 1940, and the level of productive operations in cotton textiles increased from 61.3 per cent of capacity in 1935 to 96.2 per cent in 1940. This improvement in the industry's condition was also reflected in the profit figures, which rose considerably during the period in which this legislation was in operation.

An area in which Government policy had perhaps greater influence on the ultimate shape of the textile industry concerns government procurement programs. During World War II and the Korean police action the army tended to place the great bulk of its textile contracts with the largest producers in the industry. Thus, in 1944 100.0 per cent of the Army Quartermaster Corps contracts for silesia went to the four largest contractors. The percentages for other important types of cloth were: herringbone twill, 95.4 per cent; uniform twill, 90.6 per cent; wind-resistant poplin, 82.0 per cent; unbleached drill, 77.4 per cent; sheeting, 69.3 per cent; netting, 55.8 per cent; and print, 53.9 per cent.[77] Scattered data reveal that a somewhat similar situation existed during the Korean emergency. The Department of the Army's list of its top one hundred contractors between July 1, 1950 and March 31, 1951 includes eight textile firms, six of which (J. P. Stevens, Burlington Mills, Pacific Mills, Dan River Mills, Mount Vernon-Woodberry Mills, and Cannon Mills) are among the giants of the industry.

Such heavy reliance on large contractors cannot be explained on the grounds that successful conclusion of a war must be society's first objective, and that this effort often calls for channeling contracts into the hands of a few large firms so as to assure the most efficient utilization of national resources. The dichotomy between the preservation of competition and the survival of the most efficient which such an argument implies ignores the fact that the survival ability of a substantial number of smaller textile firms has been demonstrated over the years. The concentration of Army textile contracts in the hands of a few large firms is more properly viewed as the result of the problems generally faced by small business in procuring defense contracts simply because they are small.

[77] Blair, Houghton, and Rowe, *Economic Concentration in World War II*, Report of the Smaller War Plants Corporation to the Special Committee to Study Problems of American Small Business, U.S. Senate, 1946, p. 246.

Antitrust Impact

There have been no suits of major importance brought against the textile industry. Further, some of those which have been brought do not seem to have achieved any real results.[78]

This should not be taken to mean that the industry has been totally unaffected by the antitrust laws. When malpractices have been uncovered, they have often, although not always, been eliminated (or at least weakened by being driven under cover). Furthermore, the threat of antitrust prosecution is one of the factors which often makes such prosecution unnecessary. In the final analysis, however, it is the competitive structure of the industry and its "antimonopoly" characteristics rather than the antitrust laws which remain of primary importance in protecting the consumer.

Summary

The public policy analyst has little to offer in the way of suggestions for improving the performance of this industry. The wave of mergers and integration which characterized the immediate postwar period have, on the one hand, had a tendency to reduce price flexibility; on the other hand, there has been some tendency to increase the rate of technological change and the rationality of business behavior. Perhaps all that can be said is that as little as possible should be done to interfere with the stimulating effect of such outside competitive forces as imports and competition of substitute products. The pressure of this competition, along with that which undoubtedly remains in this industry, should continue to produce results which the dispassionate economist cannot, particularly considering the problems raised in other chapters in this book, consider pressing.

SUGGESTED READINGS

Books and Pamphlets

J. Backman and M. R. Gainsbrugh, *Economics of the Cotton Textile Industry* (New York: National Industrial Conference Board, 1946).

[78] See, for example *United States* versus *Adolph C. Kluge*, Eq. 14–343, S.D., N.Y., 1917; *United States* versus *Interlaken Mills*, Civil 15–19, S.D., N.Y., 1918; *United States* versus *E. O. Barnard and Company*, Eq. 46–131. *Original Petition by the United States*, 1928; *United States* versus *E. O. Barnard and Company*, Eq. 46–131, S.D., N.Y., 1928; *United States* versus *Textile Refinishers Association*, Eq. 83–26, S.D., N.Y., 1936; Interview with a trade association official; *United States* versus *Wellington Sears Company*, Cr. 108–63, S.D., N.Y., 1940. See also *Tag Manufacturers Institute* versus *Federal Trade Commission*, 174 F. 2d 452.

E. C. Bancroft, W. H. Crook, and W. C. Kessler, *Textiles: A Dynamic Industry* (New York: Colgate University, 1951).

J. Keith Butters, J. Lintner, and W. L. Cary, *Effects of Taxation on Corporate Mergers* (Cambridge: Riverside Press, 1951).

Reavis Cox, *The Marketing of Textiles* (Washington: The Textile Foundation, 1938).

Hiram S. Davis, George W. Taylor, C. Canby Balderston, and Anne Bezanson, *Vertical Integration in the Textile Industries* (Philadelphia: Industrial Research Department, Wharton School of Finance and Commerce, University of Pennsylvania, and Washington: The Textile Foundation, 1938).

Corwin D. Edwards, *Maintaining Competition* (New York: McGraw-Hill, 1949).

Joe Summers Floyd, Jr., *Effects of Taxation on Industrial Location* (Chapel Hill: University of North Carolina Press, 1952).

Seymour Harris, *The Economics of New England* (Cambridge: Harvard University Press, 1952).

Edgar M. Hoover, *The Location of Economic Activity* (New York: McGraw-Hill, 1948).

Claudius T. Murchison, "Vertical Integration in the Cotton Textile Industry," in Nugent Wedding, ed., *Vertical Integration in Marketing*, Bulletin 74 (Urbana: Bureau of Economic and Business Research, College of Commerce and Business Administration, University of Illinois, 1952).

Richard Ruggles, "The Nature of Price Flexibility and The Determinants of Relative Price Changes in the Economy," in *Business Concentration and Price Policy* (Princeton: Princeton University Press, 1955).

J. Fred Weston, *The Role of Mergers in the Growth of Large Firms* (Berkeley: University of California Press, 1953).

Simon N. Whitney, *Antitrust Policies: American Experience in 20 Industries* (New York: The Twentieth Century Fund, 1958).

Government Publications

Hearings before the Special Subcommittee on Cotton of the Committee on Agriculture, "Study of Agricultural and Economic Problems of the Cotton Belt," 80th Cong. 1st Sess., 1947.

Journal and Magazine Articles

Solomon Barkin, "The Regional Significance of the Integration Movement in the Southern Textile Industry," *Southern Economic Journal*, Vol. XV, No. 4, April 1949.

Corwin D. Edwards, "Vertical Integration and the Monopoly Problem," *The Journal of Marketing*, Vol. XVII, No. 4, April 1953.

Jesse W. Markham, "Vertical Integration In The Textile Industry," *Harvard Business Review*, Vol. XXVIII, No. 1, 1950.

Lloyd G. Reynolds, "Cut-Throat Competition," *American Economic Review*, Volume XXX, No. 4, December 1940.

Chapter 3

JAMES B. HENDRY

The Bituminous
Coal Industry

SECTION I: INTRODUCTION

Coal is inextricably linked with any image of industrial America, but its role has been changing rapidly over the past generation. Other fuels have replaced or supplemented coal in important uses, with the result that coal has by and large failed to share in the enormous growth of the American economy. Whether this development be viewed with the same indifference attending the demise of the buggy whip and kerosene lantern industries, or as a critical weakness in a vital portion of our industrial economy, depends on how one interprets the underlying reasons which have brought this change.

Whatever the conclusion, it is clear that bituminous coal still holds a significant position, and a brief overview of the industry can quickly establish that fact. Production in 1957 totaled 492 million tons, with a total value, f.o.b. the mine, of over 2.5 billion dollars. The United States accounted for about 21 per cent of total world production, but did so with a labor force of slightly more than 200,000 miners that represented less than 1 per cent of its nonagricultural employees. The recoverable bituminous coal reserves of the United States, nearly all of them privately owned, are vast—estimated to be nearly 950 billion tons, or enough to last literally centuries at current rates of depletion. In contrast, reserves of petroleum and natural gas are reckoned in decades, although new discoveries have tended to more than match production in past years. Demand for coal is essentially an industrial demand, headed by electric utilities and closely followed by steel, both of

74

which have excellent growth prospects. On the other hand, retail deliveries, once an important part of the industry, have dropped below 10 per cent of total production, as have sales to the nation's railroads.

Despite its obvious importance to American industry, bituminous coal has long been regarded as a "sick" industry, vacillating between gluts and shortages, providing unstable profits and uncertain employment. Labor relations have been marked by long and often bitter clashes between miners and operators. Over the years the plight of the miners has been dramatically illustrated by recurring disasters in the mines, by the difficult, dirty conditions under which they have had to work, and by the drab, isolated mining communities in which they have had to live. More than any other industry, except for the traditional public utilities and the railroads, coal mine operations have attracted the active concern of Federal and state governments and have been the object of proposals to stabilize and strengthen the industry. For all these reasons, there are valuable lessons in tracing this industry's long-run contribution and its adjustment to the changing industrial structure of the nation.

SECTION II: MARKET STRUCTURE AND PRICE POLICY

The Supply Side

Geological Structure. Perhaps the best place to begin discussion of the supply side is with the nature of the product itself, for the geologic and physical conditions of a mine largely determine the cost of production. In this industry, cost does not determine the quality of the final product, since quality is inherent in the deposits themselves.[1] Although coal (anthracite, bituminous, or lignite) is found in almost all parts of the United States, the circumstances under which it is taken from the ground vary widely. Both the depth at which the deposits are found and the size of the coal seam have an important bearing on the costs of extraction. Further, the physical and chemical properties of bituminous coal determine its usefulness to consumers and therefore its ultimate marketability and price.

Deposits located deep underground can be mined only after relatively large investments have been made in mining facilities (shafts, lifts, mechanized loading and cutting equipment, ventilation provisions, maintenance shops, etc.). Such "deep" mines tend to require initial investments of up-

[1] TNEC Monograph No. 32, *Economic Standards of Government Price Control*, Washington, D.C.: Government Printing Office, 1941, p. 235.

wards of $5,000,000 for a Class I mine.[2] When the deposits lie closer to the surface it is possible to get at them directly with power shovels which remove the layers of earth and rock (overburden) covering the coal. This is called "strip" mining, and is generally less costly in terms of initial investment. It is sometimes even carried on in a small way with nonspecialized equipment, such as roadbuilding equipment, usable elsewhere when not engaged in strip-mining operations. Finally, some coal is also taken from abandoned deep mines by "punch operations," which involve small firms or families who invest little more than some dynamite, a few shovels, and their own effort to get out small quantities of coal.[3] A part of the cost structure therefore depends on the location of the deposit and the size of the investment needed to get at it. This can range from very expensive to nearly negligible amounts. While the more costly deep-mining and extensive strip-mining operations are initiated only where the deposits give promise of long-term exploitation, the easily started marginal strip or punch operations can add to total supplies on relatively short notice, and with very little in the way of investment expense to curb entry into the industry.

The size of the coal seam also affects costs, for narrow seams (less than three feet) make it difficult to use mechanized equipment, or force miners to work in awkward, difficult positions. If there is a high proportion of impurities mixed with the coal, more labor time is required to separate them out than in high-grade mines. On the other hand, seams that exceed the ideal thickness of six to eight feet require more timbering to protect against cave-ins, increasing costs both by adding to materials needed and by upping the time devoted to nonproductive underground work.

The process of cutting and blasting the coal from the seams breaks it into pieces of varying sizes, again depending partly on the nature of the deposit itself. Since different consumers demand coal of different sizes, mining operations often yield some quantities in shapes and sizes that are not as readily marketable as the bulk of the coal being mined at the same time. In general, the smaller sizes are the more difficult to sell, and this has led to occasional distress sales, or "dumping." The picture is further complicated by the fact that consumers are interested in such properties as volatility and ash and sulphur content which, in combination with the size of the coal, affect its saleability.

Thus, any consideration of the economic problems of the bituminous coal

[2] One current rule of thumb is that investments in underground mines run at a rate of $10 per ton of annual capacity, and that a minimum reserve of forty years is necessary to attract such investment. See Herbert Solow, "Soft Coal: How Strong a Comeback?" *Fortune*, October 1957, p. 236.

[3] Morton S. Baratz, *The Union and the Coal Industry*, New Haven: Yale University Press, 1955, pp. 2–3.

industry must start from the recognition that the physical location and nature of the deposits constitute data which inevitably set limits to the adjustments the industry will be able to make.

Entry. Ease of entry is one of the distinguishing characteristics of a competitive market, and represents a safety valve through which new firms may erode any market power exercised by firms already in the industry. The data for bituminous coal show changes in the number of mines in operation from year to year, and to this extent are a rough measure of entry. Increases in the number of mines may reflect new firms, new mines opened by existing firms, or the reopening of mines closed down at some earlier time. Moreover, any complete picture with respect to entry must take into account the growth of so-called "captive" mines, and also the historical influence exercised on entry by transportation rates. Finally, there are compelling economic forces which delay the exit of firms during periods of falling demand, and these also shape the nature and extent of competition in the industry. Conclusions as to the ease of entry, therefore, rest on the interpretation made of available evidence on each of these aspects.

The smaller strip and punch mining operations can be started with very small investments which means that marginal operators can quickly increase the number of mines in operation at times of rising prices. Thus, the short run—the period during which existing plant and equipment are assumed fixed—can be very short indeed. This is borne out by the fact that fluctuations in the number of mines in operation from year to year have sometimes been quite substantial. For example, the number of mines increased from 7,333 in 1946 to 8,700 in 1947, an increase of over 18 per cent, and total production increased by an equal percentage. (See Table 1.) This is not true of every year, of course, but it could be matched by other examples and by decreases of similar magnitude.

Much of this flexibility in the number of mines undoubtedly represents the reopening of mines, both large and small, previously kept idle. To develop a new mine of more than 500,000 tons annual capacity and equip it with modern equipment requires several years, and additions to supply by this means will not take place until long after the decision to invest in new capacity has been made. Much of the mining machinery in use today is made to special order, and even after it arrives at the mining site the process of assembly and installation can be very time-consuming. From the date of placing the orders for equipment to the date of full production may thus take as long as four years for a major strip mine and five to six years for an underground mine. To some extent, therefore, genuinely new entry may be slower and less frequent than the data suggest.

Change in the number of mines in operation does not necessarily mean an

TABLE 1

Domestic Production—Growth of the Bituminous-Coal and Lignite-Mining Industry
in the United States—1910–57

| Year | Production (net tons) | The Value of Production | | Number of Mines | Capacity at 280 Days (million tons) |
		Total	Average Per Ton		
1910	417,111,142	$ 469,281,719	$1.12	5,818	538
1911	405,907,059	451,375,819	1.11	5,887	538
1912	450,104,982	517,983,445	1.15	5,747	566
1913	478,435,297	565,234,952	1.18	5,776	577
1914	422,703,970	493,309,244	1.17	5,592	608
1915	442,624,426	502,037,688	1.13	5,502	610
1916	502,519,682	665,116,007	1.32	5,726	613
1917	551,790,563	1,249,272,837	2.26	6,939	636
1918	579,385,820	1,491,809,940	2.58	8,319	650
1919	465,860,058	1,160,616,013	2.49	8,994	669
1920	568,666,683	2,129,933,000	3.75	8,921	725
1921	415,921,950	1,199,983,600	2.89	8,038	781
1922	422,268,099	1,274,820,000	3.02	9,299	832
1923	564,564,662	1,514,621,000	2.68	9,331	885
1924	483,686,538	1,062,626,000	2.20	7,586	792
1925	520,052,741	1,060,402,000	2.04	7,144	748
1926	573,366,985	1,183,412,000	2.06	7,177	747
1927	517,763,352	1,029,657,000	1.99	7,011	759
1928	500,744,970	933,774,000	1.86	6,450	691
1929	534,988,593	952,781,000	1.78	6,057	679
1930	467,526,299	795,483,000	1.70	5,891	700
1931	382,089,396	588,895,000	1.54	5,642	669
1932	309,709,872	406,677,000	1.31	5,427	594
1933	333,630,533	445,788,000	1.34	5,555	559
1934	359,368,022	628,383,000	1.75	6,258	565
1935	372,373,122	658,063,000	1.77	6,315	582
1936	439,087,903	770,955,000	1.76	6,875	618
1937	445,531,449	864,042,000	1.94	6,548	646
1938	348,544,764	678,653,000	1.95	5,777	602
1939	394,855,325	728,348,366	1.84	5,820	621
1940	460,771,500	879,327,227	1.91	6,324	639
1941	514,149,245	1,125,362,836	2.19	6,822	666
1942	582,692,937	1,373,990,608	2.36	6,972	663
1943	590,177,069	1,584,644,477	2.69	6,620	626
1944	619,576,240	1,810,900,542	2.92	6,928	624
1945	577,311,053	1,768,204,320	3.06	7,033	620
1946	533,922,068	1,835,539,476	3.44	7,333	699
1947	630,623,722	2,622,634,946	4.16	8,700	755
1948	599,518,229	2,993,267,021	4.99	9,079	774
1949	437,868,036	2,136,870,571	4.88	8,559	781

| Year | Production (net tons) | The Value of Production | | Number of Mines | Capacity at 280 Days (million tons) |
		Total	Average Per Ton		
1950	516,311,053	2,500,373,779	4.84	9,429	790
1951	533,664,732	2,626,030,137	4.92	8,009	736
1952	466,840,782	2,289,180,401	4.90	7,275	703
1953	457,290,449	2,247,828,694	4.92	6,671	670
1954	391,706,300	1,769,619,723	4.52	6,130	603
1955	464,633,408	2,092,382,737	4.50	7,856	620
1956	500,874,077	2,412,004,151	4.82	8,520	655
1957	492,703,916	2,508,314,127	5.08	8,539	680

Source: U.S. Bureau of Mines, *Minerals Yearbook,* 1957, Vol. II, p. 49.

equal change in the number of firms either, because some firms operate more than one mine, just as it does not mean that all additional mines are newly opened. Still, the change in the number of operating mines from year to year does show fairly quick response to market stimuli on the supply side and, with the qualifications noted, entry does appear relatively easy.

The data in Table 1 also imply that entry and exit are equally flexible, but once a mine has been opened and is in operation there are strong pressures to maintain production. Production continues even in the face of falling demand and falling prices because the cost of maintaining idle mines may be very heavy. Theory tells us that sunk costs may be disregarded and that "bygones should be bygones," but any operator who intends to use his mine again in the future will find it necessary to make large expenditures to prevent deterioration of his equipment and the investment in shafts and tunnels already in existence. Mines must be kept dry, well ventilated, and structurally sound even when not in use, in addition to which there are the usual fixed charges any firm incurs such as taxes, insurance, and normal maintenance outlays.[4] Moreover there are limits to the length of time a mine can be maintained in complete idleness. After a two year period, corrosion and water damage will generally force the abandonment of an installation. For these reasons, operators may prefer partial production to complete idleness, with corresponding effects on the industry's ability to reduce supply in the face of adverse market conditions.

One would expect that the substantial changes which have taken place over time in the number of mines in operation would reflect the profitability of coal mining, drawing capital into the industry in periods of high earnings and forcing exit during periods of loss. The increase in the number of mines

[4] Baratz, *op.cit.,* p. 5.

which began about 1940, was, in fact, accompanied by general increases in the total profits earned by the industry over the decade 1940–50.[5] However, over the period 1928–50, there were only three years (1946–48) when less than 40 per cent of the corporations engaged in bituminous coal mining reported no net income, and in about two-thirds of the years during this period, at least half the corporations reported no net income.[6] This would indicate that any prosperity stemming from rising demands for coal is not spread evenly through the industry, and that cost and locational factors preclude a substantial number of firms from benefiting from it, even in the best years. It is also evidence of the tenacity with which firms continue in production over periods of loss.

A special entry problem is posed by the existence of "captive" mines, i.e., mines owned and operated by firms which are major consumers of coal. These firms may find it advantageous to own their coal supplies in order to insure continuous production and avoid delays, as well as to reduce fuel costs relative to prevailing market prices. Thus, for example, some steel firms provide coal from their own mines.[7]

"Captive" mines have exerted a twofold influence on the commercial operators by absorbing some of their market and undermining their position *vis-à-vis* labor. On the first point, the increased "entry" of mines that are part of integrated industrial production thins the market for the commercial coal operators, and this may become important if restricted to any one region. On the second, operators of the "captive" mines have been more willing to come to agreements in labor disputes than have the independent operators because they are anxious to avoid costly delays caused by shutdowns in any one part of the chain of integration. The independents' interest in resisting the wage pressure of the unions has thus been in sharp contrast to the interest of "captive" operators in maintaining production and avoiding work stoppages.[8]

At times entry has been deliberately encouraged by the pattern of freight rates established by the railroads. The latter have sought to utilize their own facilities as fully as possible and have carried coal from new fields at lower rates per ton mile than they charged for shorter hauls from established producing areas. Discriminatory rates of this kind have stimulated entry even

---

[5] *1952 Bituminous Coal Annual,* p. 188.

[6] Waldo E. Fisher and Charles M. James, *Minimum Price Fixing in the Bituminous Coal Industry,* a report of the National Bureau of Economic Research in cooperation with the Industrial Research Department, Wharton School of Finance and Commerce, University of Pennsylvania, Princeton: Princeton University Press, 1955, p. 328.

[7] U.S. Steel Corp. is currently the second largest coal producer in the nation.

[8] Baratz, *op.cit.,* p. 38.

during periods when existing producers were encountering major problems of declining demand for coal. The United States Coal Commission reported in 1925 that ". . . much of the soft coal that is now produced and consumed in this country is transported undue distances, in many instances on its way to market passing other fields producing coal of similar character. That these long-haul coals . . . are of high quality has added to the facility with which they have encroached on the natural markets of the older fields." [9]

Since the interests of the operators of fields distant from the main markets and the railroads serving those areas coincided, and since freight charges added an average of 72 per cent to the cost of coal f.o.b. the mine even in 1956,[10] the favorable freight rates on long hauls were a major factor in permitting the penetration of established markets. Moreover, railroad rates were set in some areas, notably along the Ohio River, in a way which substantially curbed the use of the normally lower-cost water transport which was competitive with it.[11] Controversy has centered on these freight differentials since the 1920's, and the industry has continuously sought to compete partially by obtaining favorable freight rates.[12] Railroads which derive large revenues from coal transportation and the producers favored by existing rates have naturally resisted any change, with the result that existing patterns of rates have been modified only slowly.

In recent years, the importance of rail transportation has been reduced, and shipments by water and by truck have greatly increased. For example, shipments by rail accounted for 87.9 per cent of total production in 1933, but this had dropped to 77.9 per cent in 1956. In that year, shipments by water that were trucked to water had risen to 10.1 per cent of the total, and shipments solely by truck were 9.9 per cent of the total. Over the period 1933 to 1956, shipments by water more than tripled, and although rail shipments also increased in terms of tonnage, the railroads' relative share in total transportation has been steadily declining. This development promises decreasing transportation costs for coal, for rates on water and truck hauls are generally lower than railroad rates on short hauls. There has also been some attempt to test the feasibility of transporting coal by pipeline. This would be of limited use because all coal consumers cannot use the pulverized coal

[9] *Report of the United States Coal Commission*, Washington, D.C.: Government Printing Office, 1925, p. 252.
[10] U.S. Bureau of Mines, *Minerals Yearbook*, 1956, p. 11.
[11] *Report of the United States Coal Commission*, op.cit., p. 254.
[12] For an account of revival of attempts to alter freight rates, see "War on Coal Shipping Rates," *Business Week*, July 14, 1956.

transported by this means, but it could become an important supplementary means of transportation and further alter existing freight rate structures significantly.

As a summary view of entry into the industry, there appears to be a good deal of flexibility upward due to the reopening of existing mines and the entry of marginal producers at times when demand increases, a flexibility accentuated by the heavy costs of idle capacity. Flexibility has also been enhanced in the past by the rate policies of railroads seeking to secure new markets for transportation services, and supplemented by major consumers of coal who have integrated coal production into their total operations. Despite the evidence of contraction in the number of operating mines at various times over the past fifty years, flexibility downward seems to be more "sticky" than flexibility upward, and this has been an important contributing factor to the numerous ills which have beset the industry.

The Problem of "Excess" Capacity. The relative ease of entry leads naturally to consideration of the problem of industry capacity. Many writers have concluded that the industry suffers from "excess" capacity, and that the underutilization of existing facilities explains much of the fierce competition in bituminous coal production. There is much to support this view, although it is difficult to reach firm conclusions on the extent of excess capacity. This is so because seasonal shifts in the demand for coal normally lead to fuller use of capacity at some times of the year than at others, in which case unused capacity at off-peak periods is not the complete economic waste implied in the term "excess." Making some allowance for seasonal requirements, the industry has still consistently been able to produce a great deal more coal than has been taken at existing market prices, and given the "stickiness" of the industry in contracting the number of mines in operation, a downward shift in demand has typically spread falling prices, losses, falling wages and unemployment throughout the industry.

For an initial look at this problem, comparison of the first and last columns of Table 1 shows actual production against the amount that could be produced if the existing capacity had been worked on a single-shift basis for 280 days during the same year. On this basis, production in recent years has been at roughly two-thirds of capacity. This 280-day figure assumes a work week of slightly more than five days of seven-hour shifts, but the average number of days worked per year has exceeded 250 days in only three years of the period 1890 to 1956.[13]

However, as indicated above, coal production is affected by seasonal changes in demand and, during the seasonal peaks, the capacity may be

[13] U.S. Bureau of Mines, *Minerals Yearbook*, 1956, pp. 48–9.

utilized more fully. One study has found that, ". . . when the capacity necessary to meet the year's peak demand is considered, the estimated single shift capacity on the 1937 operating basis does not appear so excessive or so far beyond reasonable stand-by capacity." [14] The storage of coal to meet such peak demands is inhibited by the difficulty of providing storage facilities at the mine, the expense involved, the dangers of spontaneous combustion, and the deterioration in the quality of the coal as a result of additional handling and reloading. Therefore, a certain amount of stand-by capacity is necessary, given the seasonal demand swings.

Although different measures of capacity usually assume single-shift operations, an assumption of two or three shifts daily would greatly increase estimates of capacity. Even if the markets would absorb production at these expanded levels at current prices (an assumption clearly contrary to fact), the available transportation facilities cannot move that much coal annually. Over 630 million tons have been moved in one year, 1947, but it is not known how much more could be transported. An earlier estimate placed the upper limits at possibly 700 million tons annually.[15] In any case, production beyond the single-shift capacity figure for 280 days would currently encounter severe transportation limitations, even if other factors permitted it.

Finally, some mines already operate more than one shift and, to the extent that strip mining continues to expand, this may become more common. There is also the fact that some authorities believe there are safety advantages in limiting production to no more than two shifts daily, leaving the "graveyard" shift for inspection and maintenance of machinery and mine conditions. Both reasons would cause some reduction in estimates of the upper limits of possible production through extra shifts.

On balance, it is safe to assume that excess capacity continues to exist in the industry in the sense that the industry could produce much more coal than it actually does. The continued existence of a substantial percentage of coal-producing corporations which earn no net income would indicate that some of the fixed factors in the industry probably would withdraw if they could transfer their fixed resources into other uses. The authors of the TNEC monograph on bituminous coal reached substantially the same conclusion, finding that actual capacity in the industry was not radically above reasonable stand-by capacity, although it was great enough to exert some downward pressure on the price structure.

Market Structure.   Up to this point, the survey of the supply side of the

---

[14] TNEC Monograph No. 32, *op.cit.*, p. 238. The capacity calculation used here, however, was based on an assumed 261-day year.

[15] *Ibid.*, p. 241.

market has examined some of the basic factors affecting entry, and has touched briefly on the problem of industry capacity. Normally, conditions such as those described lead to relatively low levels of concentration, and this tends to be the case in bituminous coal. There are signs that concentration is growing, but this it not as surprising as the fact that it has progressed as slowly as it has. Further, trends toward increasing concentration within the industry must be placed in the context of the growing importance of interfuel competition and the loss of major markets once served exclusively by coal.

One measure of concentration is by size of mines in operation, and Table 2 shows the relative share produced by Class 1 mines (those producing over

TABLE 2

Percentage of Number of Mines and of Production of Bituminous Coal and Lignite Mines in the United States, 1957

Size of Mine	Percentage of Total Mines	Percentage of Total Production
Class 1 (more than 500,000 net tons)	2.9	48.5
Class 2 (200,000 to 500,000 net tons)	3.5	21.3
Class 3 (100,000 to 200,000 net tons)	3.6	9.0
Class 4 (50,000 to 100,000 net tons)	5.5	6.7
Class 5 (10,000 to 50,000 net tons)	28.0	10.5
Class 6 (1,000 to 10,000 net tons)	56.5	4.0
Total	100.0	100.0

Source: U.S. Bureau of Mines, *Minerals Yearbook*, 1957, Washington, D.C.: Government Printing Office, 1957, p. 60.

500,000 net tons annually). An overwhelming proportion of these mines, 96.8 per cent of the total in Class 1, are located in the eight largest coal-producing states. In each of these states, which usually do not represent actual market areas, Class 1 mines provide an important share of the total state-wide production, ranging from a low of slightly less than one-third in Virginia to over 80 per cent in Illinois.[16]

The concentration ratios by firms show that in 1956 the 107 largest coal firms produced 68 per cent of all the soft coal mined, with the largest firm, Pittsburgh Consolidation, accounting for 8 per cent of the total. In recent years concentration in the industry has increased as a result of both mergers and a massive investment in production facilities. Thus, the ten largest firms increased their market share from 16 per cent of total production in 1946 to 26 per cent in 1956—in large part as a result of mergers.[17] Even with this

[16] U.S. Bureau of Mines, *Minerals Yearbook*, 1956, pp. 46–7.
[17] Solow, *op.cit.*, pp. 224, 229.

relative increase within the industry, concentration in bituminous coal continues to be very low by comparison with most major industries in the U.S.

In the numerous studies made of the industry, there has been no indication that the existing degree of concentration has led to price leadership or other types of imperfectly competitive market behavior. Despite the growing importance of the large firms and the largest mines in production, the market structure for coal is sufficiently complex to prevent domination of the industry or a restriction of entry.

This complexity is largely a reflection of the fact that coal is mined where it is found, that the geologic conditions vary greatly from place to place, that coal is a bulky substance which is costly to transport, and that the markets for coal can shift, even though the producers cannot. Table 3 il-

TABLE 3

Reported Costs, by Producing District, Minimum Price Area 1, Selected Years

Producing District	*Dollars per Net Ton, F.O.B. Mine*					
	1936 Average Costs	*Rank*	*1938 Average Costs*	*Rank*	*1940 Average Costs*	*Rank*
Eastern Pennsylvania	2.09	2	2.31	2	2.14	2
Western Pennsylvania	1.96	3	2.26	3	1.98	4
Northern West Virginia	1.63	8	1.78	8	1.65	7
Ohio	1.72	7	1.90	6	1.71	6
Michigan	3.59	1	3.90	1	3.90	1
West Virginia Panhandle	1.75	6	1.86	7	1.64	8
Southern Numbered 1	1.95	4	2.23	4	2.04	3
Southern Numbered 2	1.81	5	2.04	5	1.90	5

Source: Waldo E. Fisher and Charles M. James, *Minimum Price Fixing in the Bituminous Coal Industry,* Princeton: Princeton University Press, 1955, p. 329.

lustrates the diversity of average costs per ton in eight different production districts which were administratively lumped together in a single minimum price area under the Bituminous Coal Act of 1937. These average costs are unrelated to the marketability of the coal, for they reflect only the costs of getting it out of the ground and preparing it for sale, and these even fail to indicate cost variations between mines in the same producing district. However, they do point up the fact that the competitive cost position of a mine will depend in large part on its location, as well as its proximity to important markets and the transportation rates and transportation facilities which apply in its case. The opening of new mines or the degree of concentration in any state, therefore, may have limited impact on the markets for coal because not all markets will be affected by such developments in other producing areas. On the other hand, increased production in low-cost producing areas, if coupled with good transportation facilities and favorable freight rates, will have a competitive impact over a wide area.

Coal producers in relatively sheltered positions with respect to other mine operators have had to face growing competition from other fuels, however, for reasons which are discussed more fully below. At this point, it need only be pointed out that the attractiveness of natural gas and fuel oil has reduced coal's share in the fuel markets to approximately one-fourth of the total, as compared to over two-thirds of the total market in 1920. A shift of this magnitude strongly indicates the effectiveness of interfuel competition. While pockets of market power may still exist, the growing availability of alternative fuels has eroded such market power as individual operators, or combinations of operators, may once have had.

Labor. Most discussions of the bituminous coal industry accord an important role to labor. This is warranted by the fact that labor costs have typically represented better than 60 per cent of total outlays in the mines, and therefore anything that affects the markets for mine labor has a major bearing on mine operations. In addition, long and bitter labor disputes have frequently turned the spotlight on the industry's labor relations and on John L. Lewis, for forty years the colorful president of the United Mine Workers of America (UMW).

Employment in the mines, which rose quite consistently over the latter part of the nineteenth century and through the period of World War I, reached a peak of 704,793 men in 1923. After that date, the number of men employed began a steady decline that did not reverse itself until the depression year of 1932. Employment rose during the mid-thirties, dropped slightly just prior to World War II, and rose again during the early war years. From 1948, however, employment declined drastically so that the average number of men working daily in 1957 was less than half the number employed in 1942, the year of peak employment during the second world war. (See Table 4.)

On a national scale, the slightly more than 200,000 miners currently employed do not represent a significant segment of the nonagricultural work force. Wages and salaries in bituminous and other soft coal mining constituted less than .5 per cent of total United States wages and salaries in 1956. Only in two of the most important mining states (Kentucky and West Virginia) did mine employees constitute more than 3 per cent of the number of nonagricultural workers in 1956,[18] and there the percentages were only

[18] U.S. Department of Commerce, *Statistical Abstract of the United States, 1957*, Washington, D.C.: Government Printing Office, 1957, pp. 206–7.

TABLE 4

Employment and Productivity in the Bituminous Coal and Lignite Mining Industry
in the United States, 1923–57

Year	Men Employed	Average Number of Days Worked	Net Tons Per Man	
			Per Day	Per Year
1923	704,793	179	4.47	801
1924	619,604	171	4.56	781
1925	588,493	195	4.52	884
1926	593,647	215	4.50	966
1927	593,918	191	4.55	872
1928	522,150	203	4.73	959
1929	502,993	219	4.85	1,064
1930	493,202	187	5.06	948
1931	450,213	160	5.30	849
1932	406,380	146	5.22	762
1933	418,703	167	4.78	797
1934	458,011	178	4.40	785
1935	462,403	179	4.50	805
1936	477,204	199	4.62	920
1937	491,864	193	4.69	906
1938	441,333	162	4.89	790
1939	421,788	178	5.25	936
1940	439,075	202	5.19	1,049
1941	456,981	216	5.20	1,125
1942	461,991	246	5.12	1,261
1943	416,007	264	5.38	1,419
1944	393,347	278	5.67	1,575
1945	383,100	261	5.78	1,508
1946	396,434 [a]	214	6.30	1,347
1947	419,182 [a]	234	6.42	1,504
1948	441,631 [a]	217	6.26	1,358
1949	433,698 [a]	157	6.43	1,010
1950	415,582 [a]	183	6.77	1,239
1951	372,897 [a]	203	7.04	1,429
1952	335,217 [a]	186	7.47	1,389
1953	293,106 [a]	191	8.17	1,560
1954	227,397 [a]	182	9.47	1,724
1955	225,093 [a]	210	9.84	2,064
1956	228,163 [a]	214	10.28	2,195
1957	228,635 [a]	203	10.59	2,155

[a] Average number of men working daily.

Source: *Minerals Yearbook, 1957*, p. 50.

6.2 and 16.4 per cent respectively. Over the years, the numerical importance of the coal miners has therefore been reduced on both the national and state levels.

The picture of the industry presented by its employment record is, of course, a reflection of many other things, but, in this case an important part is due to policies pursued over the years by its major union organization, the UMW. Formed in 1890, the UMW was not the first attempt to organize the miners, but it was ultimately the most successful. The union's major concern in the very beginning was mere survival, but, by 1898, the Central Competitive Field Compact came into being and provided a vehicle for collective bargaining between miners and operators in Illinois, Indiana, Ohio, and the Pittsburgh Field in Pennsylvania, an agreement which remained in effect until 1927. Other compacts were formed in other areas, and some of these also lasted for many years. However, operators in eastern Kentucky, West Virginia, and Tennessee remained non-union during this time, providing an important competitive area that operated free of any contractual limitations on wages or working conditions.

The failure to organize the entire industry eventually spelled disaster for collective bargaining in the northern fields and brought the union to a low point in its history. Between 1900 and 1927, the southern operators' share of total production rose from about 12 per cent to 38 per cent, while the Central Competitive Field Compact operators' share dropped from over 40 per cent to only 25 per cent during the same period. This loss of relative market position, coupled with a general decline in the markets for coal, brought great pressures on the northern operators. To offset this, the operators turned increasingly to mechanization. According to one authority, the process works as follows:

> To offset [the relative loss in market position], the union operators turn to technological innovations, which at first counteract in part the encroachment of the nonunion operators. Unless geological conditions preclude such action, however, the nonunion competitors will also resort to mechanization. When mechanization in the nonunion operations catches up with that in the union operations, the situation becomes intolerable for the union producers. Unless the union will make concessions which will place the union operators in a competitive position, those operators must then decide whether they want to go out of business, or refuse to continue the bargaining relations with the union. The chances are good that they will decide upon the latter course of action.[19]

Thus, the Central Competitive Field Compact expired in 1927. Operators sought to meet the declining demand for coal by sharp cuts in wages and

[19] Waldo E. Fisher, *Collective Bargaining in the Bituminous Coal Industry: An Appraisal*, Philadelphia: University of Pennsylvania Press, 1948, p. 26.

prices. Even so, tonnage, profits, and miners' incomes dropped; unemployment spread in the coal fields, and membership in the UMW fell to 84,395 in 1929. This was less than one-quarter the membership in the prosperous year of 1920, and it reflected (1) the demoralization of men who were undergoing extreme hardship through prolonged periods of unemployment, (2) the successful efforts of the operators to crush union organization, and (3) the impotence of the union to maintain employment and earnings for its members in the face of severe deflationary forces.[20] Attitudes of miners and operators today still partially reflect the bitter clashes of that period.

Federal legislation affecting labor relations and the general economic recovery which began in 1933 brought a change in the fortunes of the UMW, and, armed with this support, the UMW organized the hitherto nonunion southern operators. Since 1933, then, a major part of all important producing areas have become included in collective bargaining contracts, and the UMW has consistently pursued policies which brought considerable benefits to a membership now spread through the industry. For example, although contractual wage rates on a piece-work basis still retain traces of the old north-south differentials (vestiges of the union-nonunion regional division), increased mechanization has enabled the UMW to institute similar time rates in all regions. Mechanization makes piece-work less attractive as incentive pay because the equipment rather than the man largely determines the rate of production. Therefore the widespread use of mechanized methods has meant, in fact, virtual elimination of the erstwhile north-south wage differentials.

Both of these developments—widespread organization and increased mechanization—have tended to stabilize the industry, as well as provide some protection to miners against the impact of "excess capacity." On its part, the UMW has taken steps to reduce the size of the mine work force by support of child labor legislation and enforcement of seniority provisions. As the need for mine labor is reduced because of increased mechanization, it is matched to some extent by the natural attrition in the number of miners through retirement. Technological unemployment is therefore minimized, but not entirely eliminated. Restriction on the entry of young men through seniority provisions reduces the supply of labor and strengthens demands for higher wages, since fewer men, working with mechanized equipment, can be paid higher wages due to the increase in their productivity.[21] In addition, the UMW has been able to obtain numerous fringe benefits, including paid

---

[20] For miner reaction to union efforts and other factors affecting his position during this period, see the interesting account in Homer L. Morris, *The Plight of the Bituminous Coal Miner,* Philadelphia: University of Pennsylvania Press, 1934, Chapter VIII.

[21] Baratz, *op.cit.,* p. 71.

vacations, a welfare fund supported by royalties on all coal mined, portal-to-portal pay, improved safety conditions, and a shorter work week.

It should not be inferred from the foregoing that the downward adjustment in the size of the mine work force has been accomplished without hardship. Many of the displaced miners have spent their entire working lives in the mines and find it difficult to move into other employment. The welfare benefits keep many in the mining communities, hoping for work, because rights to these benefits are lost if miners accept employment in other occupations. In some areas, reduced employment opportunities have turned mining centers into bleak communities of vacant houses, virtual "ghost towns." [22]

Still, the miners stand solidly behind their union, its leaders, and the policies it has pursued. Their loyalty and solidarity are reinforced by the isolation of the mining towns, the social isolation of the miners as a group, and the nature of the work they perform. The miners' confidence in the union's ability to improve their economic position, based on their interpretation of the union's efforts in the past, portend continuing acceptance of the social and economic strains which increased mechanization has brought to some of the membership. [23]

As in the period of the early 1920's the policies of the UMW in recent years seem to have resulted in rising earnings and wage rates, although, as already noted, the number of miners has declined to the lowest level since the turn of the century. Since the mid-thirties, average hourly earnings in bituminous coal mines have continued to rise faster than for all manufacturing, although average hourly earnings for the miners have generally been higher than in manufacturing since 1909. On an annual basis, earnings in manufacturing exceeded those in bituminous coal mining in all but four years, 1900–44, because manufacturing employees typically worked more hours per year than the miners. But from 1944, average annual earnings of the miners have exceeded those in manufacturing,[24] and this advantage of manufacturing employment disappeared.

Over the period 1939–50, average hourly earnings rose much more rapidly than output per man hour, or approximately 128 per cent for the former against 23.3 per cent for the latter.[25] Although not strictly comparable, data for a more recent period show that output per man day has increased by 69.4 per cent from the 1947–49 average to 1956, while weekly gross earnings

---

[22] Lawrence T. King, "Idle Mines, Idle Men," *The Commonweal*, May 29, 1959, p. 230.

[23] Bernard Karsh and Jack London, "The Coal Miners: A Study of Union Control," *Quarterly Journal of Economics*, Vol. LXVIII, No. 3, August 1954, pp. 432–3.

[24] Fisher, *op. cit.*, pp. 29–32.

[25] Baratz, *op. cit.*, pp. 96–7.

increased 57.8 percent for the same period. Prices for the period remained relatively steady.[26] On this showing, earnings increases subsequent to 1947 were in line with increases in output per man per day.

These developments have led one observer to the finding that "no other conclusion seems possible than that the greater gains of coal miners compared to other workers, union and nonunion, were directly attributable to the superior bargaining power and aggressiveness of the United Mine Workers." [27] This has meant that the union has not shrunk from using the weapon of the strike, or the threat of strike, in its efforts to improve the economic position of its members and "stabilize" the industry. These work stoppages, given the position of coal in the economy, have raised recurring fears in the minds of the public and of government officials over the "emergencies" thus created, and have contributed to pressures to subject the coal industry to a greater degree of control in the public interest.

It is doubtful that the public or the major consumers of coal have actually suffered from coal strikes in the past. Although time losses from labor disputes since 1942 have greatly exceeded the losses for any comparable period prior to that time, production also has exceeded all previous records. "No other nine-year period in the entire history of coal mining in the United States can match the record of 1942–50 either for dispute time losses or for production." [28] Since disputes do not occur suddenly, without warning, but rather fall predictably on the date on which the existing contract is due to expire, producers and consumers may anticipate their needs and prepare for cessation of production accordingly. This "time-shift offset factor" in anticipation of a strike is possible because of the existing excess capacity in the industry and the increasing importance of the highly productive strip mines, although it is limited to some extent by shortages of transportation facilities. Further, since only about 75 per cent of the tonnage from commercially sold production comes from unionized mines, even in this period of relatively high levels of union organization, it is also possible to continue to supply some needs from mines not affected by the dispute, or by what has been termed the "current-transfer offset factor." [29] Professor Christenson has summarized the impact of these offsetting capabilities in these words:

> The net effect of the operation of the offset factor in both its forms was to make it possible for U.S. coal production to reach levels considerably above those for

[26] Data provided through the courtesy of Boni, Watkins, Jason and Company, Inc.

[27] Baratz, *op.cit.*, p. 95.

[28] C. Lawrence Christenson, "The Theory of the Offset Factor: The Impact of Labor Disputes upon Coal Production," *American Economic Review*, Vol. XLIII, No. 4, September 1953, p. 519.

[29] *Ibid.*, p. 523.

earlier years, even while the amount of dispute time losses also was passing above the highest recorded magnitudes. So great was the output volume that it is extremely doubtful whether, taking the period as a whole, it would have been enhanced at all had there been no dispute time losses whatsoever. Certainly the claim that dispute time losses in the coal industry produce some kind of equivalent fall in output simply is not true.[30]

Added to this is the fact that over the period 1933–53, over 85 per cent of all time losses due to labor disputes came at times when demand for coal was declining either seasonally or because of business recession.[31] The needs for reserve stocks were therefore at their lowest levels, and offsetting consumers' requirements was made easier than if the disputes had occurred at times of peak demand. Considering the case of important consumers, such as the steel industry, it appears that "The largest reductions in steel output, also in consumption by coke ovens, have resulted from general recession forces or from labor disputes in the steel industry itself." [32] Altogether, then, much of the fear that coal strikes create national economic emergencies is based on failure to appreciate the flexibility with which the bituminous coal industry has been able to anticipate needs and provide for them. The miners, on occasion, have initiated deliberate slowdowns, designed to reduce the size of aboveground reserves by the date of contract expiration to a five-day "peril-point" supply. This has caused alarm to the point of threatened seizure of the mines by the federal government,[33] but the record above indicates this degree of concern may not be warranted.

From the dismal period of the late twenties and early thirties, when competitive wage and price cutting brought miners and operators no discernible benefits, the industry has moved into an era in which the UMW has successfully organized a majority of firms in the industry in all important producing regions and provided substantial opposition to any attempts to reduce wage levels. At the same time it has encouraged mechanization and restricted growth in the mine work force as a means of facilitating increasing wage rates and earnings for the members who remain.

Mechanization. The increased mechanization of mining has already been mentioned in connection with labor relations and as a factor affecting entry and cost structure. Though late in getting started, this development has been of critical importance to the growing competitive strength of bituminous coal in the major fuel markets. Whatever the chief reasons for the delay

---

[30] *Ibid.,* pp. 546–7.
[31] C. Lawrence Christenson, "The Impact of Labor Disputes upon Coal Consumption," *American Economic Review,* Vol. XLV, No. 1. March 1955, p. 88.
[32] *Ibid.,* p. 111.
[33] "Dilemma in Coal," *Fortune,* August 1952, p. 61.

—including lack of research, financial weakness of the many small firms, inertia, indifference—a trend toward highly mechanized operations is clearly established, fed by recognition that economic survival depends on their adoption.

This changing technology can be seen in the increase in the percentage of total underground production cut by machine, which rose from 60.7 per cent in 1920 to a postwar high of 92.8 per cent in 1952. It also shows in the increased percentage mechanically loaded (from zero in 1922 to 84.0 per cent in 1956) and the percentage mechanically cleaned (from zero in 1905 to 58.4 per cent in 1956). Strip mining, a highly mechanized operation which was capable in 1956 of producing two and one-half times the average tons per day possible in underground mines, now accounts for one-fourth the total output of bituminous coal. Another recent development has been the growth in auger mining, first used in 1945, which is being substituted in areas where strip mining has become impracticable because of the thickness of the overburden. The average tons per man per day in auger mines is even higher than in strip mines, but less than 2 per cent of total production was being mined in this way in 1956.[34] A "continuous miner," first used commercially in 1948, both cuts and loads coal at a rate of four tons per minute. Over 500 are in operation at the present time, but they still account for a relatively small proportion of total output.[35] Thus, although varying in degree and type, the process of mechanization has been widespread and rapid, bringing a very substantial increase in productivity.

Despite the tendency to picture this development as the operator's response to UMW wage policies, and the union's unabashed support for increased mechanization, the data show that mechanization has taken place steadily during periods of high wages and low. Clearly, wage rates have had some effect on management decisions. During the depressed period of the twenties, when wages were being cut in nonunion mines, union operators sought competitive advantage in mechanization. Still, underlying all is the fact that mechanized methods offer such economies that all operators are forced to follow the lead of those who first adopt them.[36] While a speculative opinion, it nevertheless seems quite probable that mechanization would have taken place, though perhaps at a slower rate, even without the presence of a strong UMW. Union policy, therefore, has simply hastened the inevitable.

Although the gains in productivity are unquestioned, certain factors tend

[34] U.S. Bureau of Mines, *Minerals Yearbook*, 1956, pp. 49, 74, 58–9.
[35] Solow, *op.cit.*, p. 229.
[36] Fisher, *op.cit.*, p. 35.

to inhibit the use of mechanized equipment in some cases. One of these has been the financial stringency bedeviling many operators. Another has been the fact that, until the mid-thirties, existing equipment could not be used in many of the mines. It was too large, or too bulky, or required auxiliary equipment that was not suited to the size of the coal seam. Since geological conditions vary from one mine to another, and each mine has problems not precisely like others, much of the mining machinery is made to special order. Many operators assist in the development of new designs, and the National Coal Association and the U.S. Bureau of Mines also foster research in this area. As a result of combined efforts, a breakthrough in machinery improvement seems to have been made in the thirties which has made mechanization feasible in more cases than was true in earlier periods.

A more complete view, therefore, is that mechanization has been spurred by cost considerations growing out of the rising wage rates, the increased availability of improved machinery, and the diffusion of technological change as competitors sought to maintain their relative positions. Inertia, resistance to change, financial stringency, and geological conditions may still deter mechanization in some cases, but elsewhere there is continued rapid change.

Cost Structure.   It is now possible to bring together the various elements affecting the supply of coal in a composite view of production costs. From what has gone before, it is clear that there can be a range in costs per ton, in some cases quite wide, both within and between coal fields. (See Table 3.) These in turn reflect the factors of geological formation, type of mining (underground, strip, auger, etc.), wage rate differentials, and degree of mechanization, all of which have been discussed to some extent. Cost differences may also reflect such things as state and local taxes, efficiency of labor and management, and the age of mines and equipment. Finally, production costs are affected by the amount of time a mine is actually in operation.

This latter point is important because it illustrates the way in which otherwise efficient mines may feel the pinch of prolonged shutdowns or disruptions of production, and explains why the operators are anxious to maintain production in the face of declining demand. When a small number of days per month is worked and total production is thereby curtailed, the relatively high fixed costs and costs of maintaining the mines in operating condition are spread over a small total tonnage. Increased mechanization may partially compensate for declines in the number of days worked by improving the tonnage per man per day through increased efficiency and by reducing the need for direct labor, the latter constituting over 60 per cent of total mining costs in the past. However, it also adds to the fixed costs which become so important at low levels of production.

Producers have therefore felt some compulsion to maintain production as long as they are able to more than cover their variable costs, thereby making some contribution toward meeting fixed charges. Because average total costs fall rapidly, leveling off over much of the output range, marginal costs tend to be fairly constant up to the point of capacity. "This means that the mine operator has a strong incentive to maintain a high level of output as long as marginal revenue exceeds marginal out-of-pocket costs. He may be minimizing his losses . . . by producing at capacity rather than by operating on only a part-time basis." [37] For some operators, consideration for the welfare of the miners will also provide incentives to maintain production in the face of falling demand, but the history of the industry suggests that this has not been a major factor.

On the whole, bituminous coal industry does not present a homogeneous picture with respect to costs of production. Geological advantages in one area may be partially offset by increased mechanization or by increasing the length of time in operation in others. Generally, though, the poorer coal seams are also the more difficult to mine by mechanical means, and eventually the preferred geological sites (and this would pertain with special emphasis to locations where surface mining can be undertaken) will regain the advantage. The behavior of costs, with heavy fixed charges and relatively stable marginal costs, encourages production, even when demand and prices are falling. We have now come full circle in a survey of the forces which draw firms or new mines into production, and which impede their exit under adverse market conditions.

The Demand Side

Coal Consumption. In broadest outline, the demand for coal at the present time is an industrial demand. (Electric utilities, the largest single user, accounted for 32.5 per cent of the total used in 1957. Coke ovens, steel works, and rolling mills accounted for an additional 22.9 per cent.) Annual consumption has increased in every decade except 1930–39 and although the industry has not suffered an absolute drop in demand for its product, it has lost ground relative to the competing fuels of natural gas and fuel oil, and has failed to expand at the same rate as the economy as a whole. (See Table 5.)

The secular change in demand is a reflection of many factors, some of

---

[37] Baratz, *op.cit.*, pp. 17–18.

TABLE 5

Total Percentage Consumption of Energy Fuels and Energy from Water Power in the Continental United States in Selected Years, 1920–57

Year	Bituminous Coal and Lignite	Anthracite	Crude Oil	Percentage Petroleum Products Net; E, except imported; I, imported	Natural-Gas Dry	Natural-Gas Liquids	Water Power
1920	67.4	11.0	15.3	E 2.0	4.2	0.2	3.9
1925	62.6	7.8	22.2	E 2.3	5.8	.6	3.3
1930	53.5	7.7	27.6	E 2.2	8.8	1.1	3.5
1935	48.9	6.8	30.4	E 1.6	10.3	.9	4.3
1940	47.2	5.2	32.1	E .7	11.4	1.0	3.8
1945	46.5	4.2	32.3	E 1.8	12.6	1.5	4.7
1950	34.8	3.0	36.0	I 1.2	18.0	2.3	4.7
1955	27.8	1.5	39.9	I .9	23.1	3.0	3.8
1956	27.0	1.4	40.5	I 1.0	23.4	2.9	3.8
1957	25.8	1.3	40.5	I .9	24.8	3.0	3.7

Source: Bureau of Mines, *Minerals Yearbook,* 1957, Vol. II, pp. 10–11.

them apparent from what has been said already. Clearly, price has been one consideration, and such cost-raising tendencies as higher wage rates have undoubtedly had a bearing on the market decisions of important consumers. However, the record shows that the shift from coal to other fuels has occurred in times of both rising and falling prices, with no consistent relationship visible between price changes and the relative share of bituminous coal in industrial markets. "We must conclude," say Fisher and James, "that forces other than the price of bituminous coal are more important in determining the rate at which the various types of energy are utilized by consumers." [38]

These "other" factors would, of course, include the price movements of other fuels. Natural gas, in particular, the wholesaling of which in interstate commerce is subject to regulation by the Federal Power Commission, was sold at average prices that remained stable or fell slightly over the decades of the thirties and forties. As such, it was an increasing bargain in relative terms. Further, a tremendous expansion in pipeline capacity and extension into new areas (strenuously opposed by the coal industry in proceedings before the FPC) made natural gas available to more potential customers than ever before. Since 1947–49 this picture has changed—the prices of natural gas industrial sales increased 48.1 per cent, 1947–49 to 1956, as compared to a rise of only 12.6 per cent in bituminous coal prices. [39] Even with the price increases, the cost of natural gas was still about three-fourths that of coal per 1,000 Btu's.

Although fuel oil prices have nearly paralleled those of bituminous coal, fuel oil use has also greatly expanded. For the period 1935–39 to 1950, coal prices rose 100.2 per cent compared to a rise in the price of fuel oil of 80.7 per cent. In addition, handling charges for coal were somewhat higher than for oil. Consumption of coal rose by only 11.5 per cent against an increase of 101.9 per cent for fuel oil. [40] The subsequent percentage increase in fuel oil prices (1947-49–1957) was nearly 7 per cent greater than coal. Further, average fuel oil cost per 1,000 Btu's was nearly 50 per cent higher than coal. On this finding, it appears that things other than relative prices make some competing fuels attractive in comparison with coal.

An important feature of coal use from a consumer's point of view is the fact that it requires storage space, which is expensive, or, alternatively, an uninterrupted supply. Since the latter has been notably lacking at various

---

[38] Fisher and James, *op.cit.*, p. 413.

[39] U.S. Department of Labor, Bureau of Labor Statistics, *Wholesale Prices Index*, and derived from American Gas Association, *Historical Statistics of the Gas Industry*, 1956, *1956 Gas Facts*, pp. 100 and 118, and *1957 Gas Facts*, pp. 101 and 118.

[40] Fisher and James, *op.cit.*, pp. 415–16.

times due to a variety of causes, storage space has been an important consideration. "Captive" mines have been one solution. Natural gas poses no storage problem, although industrial customers are often unable to get "firm" service. Electric power, like natural gas, avoids the storage problem. Fuel oil must be stored, but this can be done more easily and economically than in the case of coal. In addition, coal use involves an ash disposal problem which is not present in the case of competing fuels, and all of these competitors are cleaner and cause fewer smoke and air pollution problems than coal. Such considerations militate against continued use of coal by some consumers.

Most customers are unable to change from one fuel to another quickly in response to small changes in prices, although multiple fuel burning facilities are installed by some users. Fuel-burning equipment tends to be specialized and costly, and changeovers are generally not made frequently. Consequently, the change to competing fuels usually comes at time of replacement, and the replacement decision rests on estimates of future trends in relative prices and convenience and use factors more than it does on prices at the time of the change. The shift is therefore a long-term matter, and the fact that all replacements do not come at the same time accounts for the observed short-term inelasticity of demand in the face of price changes in coal.

Developments such as better insulation, better fire controls, better furnaces, better firing methods, have also led to economies in the use of coal and thus reduced the total demand. In some cases, innovations have shifted consumers into new fuels entirely, as, for example, the emergence of diesel locomotives on the railroads; these offer advantages in greater overall efficiency and not just in fuel savings alone.[41] Railroads have also improved the efficiency with which they use coal-burning steam locomotives in terms of gross ton-miles of freight and passenger train car-miles per net tons of coal.[42] In the steel industry, increased use of scrap has reduced the need for coking coal.

In contrast to these developments, recent research in the distillation of bituminous coal has opened a whole new world of products which can be obtained from coal. To mention a few, ammonia, benzene, carbide abrasives, vinyl plastics, naphthalene, nitric acid, and urea are produced through

[41] The impact of diesel use on railroads is seen in the fact that coal has dropped from 68.8 per cent of fuel costs of Class I railroads in 1941 to 6.5 per cent in 1958. Diesel fuel, on the other hand, has risen from 1.6 per cent of fuel costs in 1941 to 87 per cent in 1958. *Petroleum Facts and Figures*, Centennial Edition, 1959, New York: American Petroleum Institute, 1959, pp. 356–7.

[42] Bituminous Coal Institute, *Bituminous Coal—Facts and Figures*, 1948 edition, p. 76.

refining and re-refining. In turn, these and other basic chemicals are used in the manufacture of drugs, dyes, artificial flavorings, perfumes, explosives, synthetic fibers, and photographic chemicals. Adaptation of gas turbines to use solid coal is another development which may lead to further innovation in the railroads, and experiments are going forward with the underground gasification of coal and the manufacture of synthetic petroleum from coal and lignite.[43] The latter could be enormously important in view of the relative scarcity of petroleum reserves in the U.S. compared to reserves of coal. Unfortunately for the industry, these new demands, promising though they may be for the future, have not yet begun to increase to a point where they replace the fall in demand from other, more traditional users of coal in industry or for home heating.

The list of factors affecting the demand for coal is not yet complete. Coal demand reflects substantial seasonal influences which place heavy pressures on the transportation facilities. Given the storage problem, operators generally are unable to accumulate stocks against anticipated seasonal increases in demand, and therefore are unable to spread production evenly through the year. While summer months are the normal slump period for the industry as a whole, some districts register above-average production at that time, as in the case of districts which take advantage of the open-shipping seasons on the Great Lakes. Some districts are even able to avoid pronounced seasonal peaks but, for the most part, seasonal shifts do apply.

Cyclical changes in the demand for coal have been even more important economically. Because the bituminous coal industry produces such a large proportion of its total output for industrial consumers, decreases in production by these major customers due to cyclical downturns have a powerful impact on coal production. This "accelerator effect" has been pronounced during periods of recession in the past (e.g., 1920–21, 1929–32, 1937–38, 1948–49), and the industry has also experienced periods of rapidly rising demands during times of expansion (e.g., 1915–18, 1934–36, 1939–44, 1946–47). At times like these, changes in the rate of coal consumption exceed the rate of change for the economy as a whole.

There is, finally, the enormously complex demand with respect to coal of varying sizes and with varying performance and physical properties. Since different consumers have different requirements for the coal they purchase, there are really many submarkets for coal which give rise to different prices for the different sizes and qualities of coal. Coal as it comes from the mine

---

[43] For a brief survey of these results of research, see John G. Glover and William B. Cornell, eds., *The Development of American Industries,* New York: Prentice-Hall, 1951, pp. 305–311. Also, a description of the first coal-hydrogenation chemical plant in operation is given in "Coal Chemicals," *Fortune,* August 1952.

("mine-run") may satisfy the needs of some customers, but not all. It is therefore separated into desired sizes by a screening process and usually further treated by washing and cleaning to remove impurities and increase marketability. Since the properties of mine-run coal vary, even within a single mine, the costs of producing the various sizes and qualities are joint costs to a great extent. Producing marketable coal inevitably leaves a residual of jointly produced, but less desirable or less marketable, sizes— the "slack" and "screenings." Operators frequently dispose of this at any price which will move it out of the way, since it takes valuable storage or car space needed for the other sizes.[44]

To give some idea of the variety of coal as it is actually sold, several producing districts reportedly distinguished more than one hundred different sizes of coal, and some mines sell as many as forty different sizes.[45] The major classes, however, are lump or block, egg, nut, stoker, slack, and screenings. Added to the size classification are such characteristics as heat content, moisture content, ash content, ash-handling cost, sulphur content, ash-softening temperature, appearance, structure, friability, and special treatments given. Understandably, the administration of the Coal Act of 1937 faced an extremely complicated task when it attempted to classify coal into a manageable number of defined categories for the establishment of minimum prices. For purposes here, it is only necessary to be aware that "coal" is far from a homogeneous commodity as it is marketed, and that demand is affected by the special requirements of customers to a very marked degree.

Summarizing, then, the demand for coal is affected by pronounced seasonal fluctuations, and subject to accelerated fluctuations triggered by business cycles in the national economy. Relatively inelastic with respect to price in the short run, the demand of fuel customers has tended to shift away from coal in the long run as a result of price expectations related to coal and competing fuels, technological changes in consuming industries, convenience and use factors, relative dependability of supply, and storage problems. There are some indications that the shift from coal to other fuels may be ending and that technological developments in the industry which point to greater stability, more efficient use, and completely new uses may serve to reverse past trends.

[44] Fisher and James, *op.cit.*, p. 62.
[45] *Ibid.*, pp. 121–2.

Secular Changes in Prices and Production

It is now possible to pull together the various elements which have influenced the price and production performance of the bituminous coal industry over the first half of the twentieth century. In doing so, we have some basis for evaluating the performance of an industry that is, to all appearances, "workably competitive." [46] It is true that from 1937 to 1943 the industry was subject to minimum price regulation under the Bituminous Coal Act of 1937, and that wartime price controls were in effect on three other occasions. It is also true that some attempts had been made at earlier dates to coordinate marketing activities and to bargain collectively with the UMW. However, for much of the period since 1900, the collusive or price-fixing elements in the industry were of relatively minor importance.

The basic descriptive data were shown in Table 1, which summarized the chief elements of change over a fifty-year period. From those, it is possible to see with what degree of precision a workably competitive market transmits its guides to individual firm and employee action, and with what speed the industry makes the necessary adjustments to market signals. The heavy demand of World War I, operating with accelerated impact on coal operators, brought new mines into operation quickly, jumped output and employment, and more than doubled the average price per ton (1915–18). High average prices continued into the postwar period, and, although production dropped in 1921–22, it climbed again to wartime levels in 1923. Prices started to decline after 1922 as industry began to enter a more "normal" period and the demand for coal underwent a shift downward.

Market forces had thus brought about an allocation of coal reserves, labor, and capital into the coal industry through the lure of high prices and rising demand. Railroad rates had also encouraged opening distant mine fields by offering low ton-mile rates on long hauls. The demand shift of the early twenties, therefore, left more resources committed to coal production than consumers required at the old level of prices. The adjustment process required by the market was neither easy nor rapid. Operators faced strong incentives to maintain production, even in the face of declining demand; labor faced severe difficulties in moving into alternative kinds of employment, even, in fact, in leaving the mining communities. Operators could do

---

[46] "Workable competition is considered to require, principally, a fairly large number of sellers and buyers, no one of whom occupies a large share of the market, the absence of collusion among either group, and the possibility of market entry by new firms." Edward S. Mason, "The Current Status of the Monopoly Problem in the United States," *Harvard Law Review*, June 1949, p. 1268.

little to alter their fixed costs, which in some cases reflected investments made during boom times, but they could try to do something about their variable costs, of which labor cost was the most important. Their efforts to force wages down resulted in a breakdown of collective bargaining agreements in unionized areas. The nonunion areas had already reduced wages and were expanding sales. Competition was therefore "working," and it signaled a reallocation of resources by bankruptcy, falling wages, and unemployment. This was the "excess capacity" problem which drew increasing attention as the decade of the twenties wore on. The onset of the depression in 1929 accelerated the decline in demand, now essentially a cyclical force rather than an adjustment of changing technology and the competition of other fuels. The coal industry continued to reflect the pressures on it as hourly wage rates, annual earnings, and average number of days worked declined for employees; production, average prices, and the number of mines declined for the operators. Industry operators as a whole showed a net loss in income from 1925 to 1940.

Although these developments were presumably good for consumers and, in the long run, good for the remaining efficient operators and their employees who managed to weather the economic storms, this conclusion is subject to some doubt. Consumers were encountering difficulties of their own after 1929, and since there was no shift to coal from other fuels during this period, it is not evident that developments in the coal industry, welcome though they may have been to consumers, significantly benefited them. Moreover, for those in the coal industry, the period of adjustment to secular and cyclical forces lasted about fifteen years (1925–40), a period of time which constitutes a large portion of a man's working life. It is little wonder that contemporary observers were concerned over the possible harmful results of "cut-throat" competition, and that efforts were made to minimize it by the passage of minimum price legislation under the Bituminous Coal Act of 1937.

The concern for the industry, which had led to minimum price legislation, dissolved in the rising demand for coal fanned by the wartime needs of industry. When the Coal Act of 1937 expired in 1943, it was not renewed. It was replaced instead by the wartime maximum price controls then in effect for the entire economy. In the period since the end of World War II, the industry has gone through an adjustment which has been, in many ways, similar to that following World War I. One important difference has been the strong position maintained by the UMW, which has meant that competitive wage-cutting has not been an alternative open to the operators when faced with falling demand for coal. Postwar production reached a peak in

1947 (the largest volume of production in the history of the industry), fell sharply during the recession of 1949, rose during the Korean War years of 1950–51, then took another sharp turn downward in the recession year of 1954. (See Table 1.) Once again the accelerator principle seemed at work, leaving in its wake the familar problems of underutilization of capacity, unstable profits, and uncertain employment.[47]

Still, by the middle and late fifties, there were several signs that a half-century of rigorous competition had finally forced the kinds of basic adjustments within the industry that would permit it to face the future with some measure of confidence. For one thing, rapid mechanization had brought productivity in coal mining which surpassed even the most optimistic estimates of thirty years earlier, and far greater than that achieved anywhere else in the world. The accompanying stability in coal prices has made coal competitive again with other fuels and has brought some expectations that coal may begin to recapture part of its lost share in the total fuel market. Coupled with this have been the active research programs sponsored by producers' associations, some of the larger firms, and by the government, which seek new end uses for coal, new methods of using coal, new production methods, and new transportation means. Some of these research areas hold promise of substantially altering the convenience and use characteristics that have long served to turn consumers away from coal, while others may open entirely new markets.

Concentrating on known and proven markets, the picture is relatively bright. According to the President's Materials Policy Commission, the expanding economy will require vast amounts of electricity in the decades ahead, and this will mean expanding demand for coal.[48] Despite increased efficiency in use, coal consumption by electric utilities has been increasing over the period 1950–56, both in terms of absolute tonnage and relative proportion compared to oil and gas. Similarly in steel, where substantial increases in production are anticipated, more coal will be required. Although steel now uses 40 per cent less coking coal per ton than in 1933, an anticipated 50 million ton expansion of steel production capacity by 1975 will still mean rising demand for coal. Finally, exports of coal, especially to Canada and Western Europe, have been increasing in recent years. Growing shortages of soft coal of metallurgical grades in Europe will create esti-

---

[47] See, for example, "Recession Gets a Test Case," *U.S. News and World Report*, May 15, 1953; "When An Industry Gets Sick," *U.S. News and World Report*, July 23, 1954; "Living with Unemployment in a Coal Town," *Business Week*, January 8, 1955.

[48] Hearings before the Special Subcommittee on Minerals, Materials, and Fuel Economies, Committee on Interior and Insular Affairs, Eighty-third Cong., 2nd Sess., S., Pt. 8, p. 350.

mated needs of 55 million tons annually in 1975 to be met by imports from the United States. The increased efficiency in production in the U.S. opens this export market as a new and important supplement to domestic demand. Thus, electric power, steel, and exports provide a solid base for expectations of expanding markets for coal production.

There is finally the fact that, although employment has been curtailed sharply in the past decade, the welfare of those remaining in the mine work force is protected by high levels of earnings and substantial fringe benefits. Employment may drop still further, but the chances are good that it will do so at a decreasing rate. Just as the mining force is being trimmed down, there are signs that the marginal firms in the industry increasingly are being merged to form financially stronger and better-equipped larger firms. Small firms will certainly continue to operate within the industry, but the mechanization which is now increasingly possible requires larger outlays of capital and encourages combination. This development should impart some stability to the industry, while continued active competition from other fuels will set limits to the market power increased concentration might otherwise bring.

SECTION III: PUBLIC POLICY

The structural and cyclical difficulties of the bituminous coal industry have given rise to numerous suggested national policies to relieve the industry, most of which never pass beyond the discussion stage. The Supreme Court ruling in the *Appalachian Coals* case and the experience under the Coal Act of 1937 represent major expressions of national policy in the past, and a brief review of them will provide some basis for consideration of policy alternatives in the present. At the same time, it should be borne in mind that these are not the only "national policies" affecting the industry, and that legislation, court decisions, and executive action can work in contradictory ways from the viewpoint of one industry. For example, while the Bureau of Mines directly assists the industry by promoting research, the pipeline certification and rate decisions of the Federal Power Commission in natural gas cases permit the entry of a powerful new competitive fuel. Much the same could be said for legislation on tariffs and the depletion allowance for tax purposes as they apply to petroleum. What this means is that the nation has yet to develop a comprehensive and consistent body of policy decisions applying to the development, production and conservation of its fuel resources, replacing the piecemeal approach to the problems of individual industries. In the case of coal, public policy has usually meant attempting to strengthen the industry by permitting it to stabilize prices in some way.

The *Appalachian Coals* case provides an instance in which the Supreme Court approved the establishment of a private marketing agency formed by 137 producers located in eight different producing districts. These operators registered sales of only 11.96 per cent of all coal produced east of the Mississippi, but 74.4 per cent of that produced in the so-called "Appalachian territory." The marketing agency, known as Appalachian Coals, Inc., was formed to increase sales through improvements in distribution, advertising, research, marketing, and the elimination of "abnormal, deceptive and destructive trade practices." [49] It was also expected to establish standard classifications, to sell the coal of the owners at the best price obtainable, or, if necessary, to apportion orders among them. The operators disclaimed any effort to fix prices in the process, but the Department of Justice obtained an injunction against Appalachian Coals, Inc. as constituting a restraint of trade and attempted monopolization under Sections 1 and 2 of the Sherman Act, on grounds that it was an attempt to fix prices.

In a rare instance in which the "rule of reason" was applied to an alleged price-fixing agreement, the Supreme Court found the joint marketing arrangement a legally valid attempt to deal with the problems then plaguing the coal industry. The court went on to conclude that any restraint this agency could impose would not be "undue" because the "evidence as to conditions of the production and distribution of bituminous coal, the available facilities for its transportation, the extent of developed mining capacity, makes it impossible to conclude that defendants through the operation of their plan will be able to fix the price of coal in the consuming markets." This opinion was based on the probable impact of the marketing agency on prices. If actual practice proved otherwise, the court noted that the government was not precluded from seeking further remedy if "undue restraint" were exercised in fact.

Despite the policy precedent established by this opinion, the impact of this case on the industry cannot really be measured. Shortly after Appalachian Coals, Inc. began to operate, passage of the National Industrial Recovery Act of 1933 paved the way for the establishment of marketing agencies throughout the industry, subject to the approval of Code Authorities. Unlike Appalachian Coals, Inc., these agencies were expected to set minimum prices for coal, but they did not exercise any production controls. If no marketing agencies were proposed independently, the Code Authorities

---

[49] *Appalachian Coals, Inc., et al.,* versus *United States* (1933), 288 U.S. 344, p. 359.

themselves were to establish "fair prices." The task of fixing prices, even minimum prices, proved formidable, and violations of Code-approved prices were widespread by the time the NIRA was declared unconstitutional. The approach to industry health and stability by means of private marketing agencies thus failed to produce any satisfactory or conclusive body of evidence.

A more inclusive series of attempts to reduce the distress of the coal industry, this time by legislation, can be traced back to 1925.[50] These efforts eventually culminated in the Bituminous Coal Act of 1937.

The Act called for the creation of a National Bituminous Coal Commission in the Department of Interior, empowered to establish minimum prices in the coal industry, and responsible directly to Congress. It also launched the most exhaustive and complex attempt at price determination and stabilization that the U.S. economy has ever experienced.[51]

The intent of Congress in passing the Act was to provide a price floor that would recover the major operating costs, including the wage costs determined through collective bargaining. This would "protect" the interstate commerce in coal and eliminate the "unfair" competition Congress felt existed in the industry prior to passage. It does not appear that Congress was interested in preserving mine operators as such since income taxes, interest on investment, development costs, and other capital charges were eliminated from any computation of cost in arriving at minimum prices. The concern was essentially over the hardships which Congress assumed stemmed from the severe competition in the industry, and with the need to protect those associated with the industry from them.[52] The criteria contained in the Act for setting prices, many of which referred to the necessity of fixing prices that were "fair" and "equitable," were in some respects overlapping and contradictory, with the result that controversy over the Commission's decisions became inevitable. More important was the fact that the criteria tended to be backward-looking, based on the structure and practices in the industry as it existed, and therefore ". . . disregarded the impact of minimum price fixing on consumption, utilization, and capacity."[53] In short, the problems of the industry were essentially problems of adjustment to a changing world. In attempting to meet those problems by the price-fixing

[50] See Report of the United States Coal Commission, *op.cit.*, esp. pp. 265–9.
[51] This description and evaluation of the Bituminous Coal Act of 1937 relies heavily on the definitive work on this topic; Fisher and James, *op.cit.* Readers of this detailed volume cannot help but be impressed with the enormity of the task imposed on the Commission as it sought to meet the many requirements of the Act in the course of establishing several hundred thousand individual prices for bituminous coal.
[52] Fisher and James, *op.cit.*, p. 312.
[53] *Ibid.*, p. 322.

process, Congress failed to take into consideration the long-run implications of its policies or to make any basic reassessment of the contributions to be made by the different sources of fuel and energy in the future.

Although the work of the Commission in establishing and enforcing the minimum price schedules stands as an example of ". . . outstanding competence, persistence, and public service," [54] experience under the Act was disappointing in several respects. For example, because of the difficulty in estimating all the variables in a dynamic situation, there were "substantial" differences between determined costs and actual costs in some areas. There were wide variations in procedures followed by the District Boards, and the auditing of cost reports was not always effective. The method of estimating selling costs permitted inclusion of items not properly falling within this category, and the coordination process was essentially based on "judgment, negotiation, and compromise." These shortcomings were partly due to the procedures adopted by the Commission, but they were also due partly to the Act itself which failed in important respects to provide clear and workable criteria for the Commission to follow.[55]

What was the impact of minimum price-fixing on the industry? Unfortunately, the record does not tell us much because the industry began to experience the rejuvenating effects of a wartime economy shortly after the Act went into effect. Evaluations must, therefore, remain somewhat speculative. Fisher and James believe that price fixing may aggravate basic causes for instability in the industry, encourage even further overdevelopment, and reduce the long-run demand for coal. They see minimum prices acting to keep high-cost mines in operation, attracting production by marginal mines, and encouraging mechanization, all of which would stimulate overdevelopment, and they also see great difficulties in keeping abreast of a dynamic and changing economy. The prognosis for minimum price-fixing as a solution to traditional industry problems is therefore not very encouraging.

Policy Alternatives

We come finally to consideration of the various public policy alternatives, where individual predispositions toward one or the other will depend essentially on the interpretation placed on the historical performance of the industry—a record sketched in necessarily abbreviated form in the preceding sections. Ideally, public policy toward the coal industry should be part of a

[54] *Ibid.*, p. 402.
[55] *Ibid.*, pp. 400–1.

broader national policy encompassing development and use of all national fuel resources. This, in turn, involves a weighting of current needs and current rates of use against estimated needs and estimated resources in the future. At present we rely to a great extent on competition in the fuel markets to make the decisions on rates of current use, although there are important elements of production and price control by state and federal agencies in the petroleum and natural gas industries. Reliance on competitive markets (admittedly subject to some degree of regulatory control) to make these crucial decisions on conservation may be questioned, but this in itself is an important problem area beyond the scope of this industry survey. Here, we must limit ourselves to considering the problems of the bituminous coal industry and assume a continued commitment to a competitive fuels market as a mechanism for determining the current and future use of our national fuel reserves. Unlike the policy problems in many other industries, discussion has typically centered on whether or not this function was impaired by too much competition rather than too little.

Policy suggestions for bituminous coal range all the way from complete non-interference to nationalization of the mines, with the greatest demand for governmental intervention coming, naturally, during periods when the industry is experiencing severe difficulties. A brief listing of the alternatives may give some basis for consideration, although space does not permit a thorough discussion of any one of them.

To start at one end of the spectrum, nationalization offers certain distinct advantages, but is currently a politically unrealistic alternative. Much would depend, of course, on the manner in which a nationalized industry was administered, although in theory it could be run as though subject to competitive stimuli and restraints. To judge by British experience, there is little assurance that nationalization *per se* will bring an end to industry problems.[56] Legislative consideration of government ownership or control of coal production in the United States can be traced as far back as 1894, and proposals for government ownership or control have made on several occasions since that date. Conceivably, a government owned and operated in-

---

[56] The problems of the British coal industry are not precisely those of the U.S. (for example, coal seams are much thinner, the rate of mechanization was very slow before the war, there is trouble keeping miners in the pits, etc.), but one writer has concluded his study of nationalized coal by stating ". . . output would have been no higher and quite likely lower under private ownership; that prices would have been as high, and more probably higher; and that the basic problems of the industry would have been as great if not greater. If such a line of reasoning is correct, nationalization of the coal industry may be considered a success, but not an overwhelming one." William W. Haynes, *Nationalization in Practice: The British Coal Industry,* Boston: Graduate School of Business Administration, Harvard University, 1953, p. 391.

dustry would be able to reduce some of the excess capacity, eliminate the least efficient mines, force a rationalization of freight rates, maintain stability in supply, provide high average earnings for miners, conduct extensive research in new methods of production and new uses of coal, and maintain competitive price levels. One of the dangers in a solution of this kind would be that pressures may be exerted from many sources—consumers, competing fuels, miners—with the result that the industry would be directed toward special interest objectives. This need not happen, yet any realistic appraisal must account this a distinct possibility. Competition with fuels produced under private ownership would certainly lead to friction, and, perhaps, extension of nationalization into other fields. On balance, government ownership and operation provides one feasible alternative if conceived as a means to accomplish what the market has failed to bring about in terms of rationalizing the industry and making it more efficient. The probability of acceptance of this solution is slight because the present climate of opinion militates against it, particularly in light of the many signs that the industry is rapidly developing into a healthier, more vigorous competitor in the fuel markets than at any time since the early twenties.

A second alternative would be some form of government price-fixing, as provided, for example, under the Coal Act of 1937. Experience under that Act does not induce much optimism that this type of solution to the industry's problems is worth the enormous administrative effort involved. Unless the price-fixing agency is empowered to decide which mines are to continue operation and how the business will be divided among the firms remaining in production, price-fixing does no more than maintain the *status quo.* If the administrative agency is empowered to make these necessary decisions, it amounts to *de facto* nationalization, and it is difficult to see what advantages are gained by refusing to take that ultimate step. As long as price-fixing is essentially backward looking and firmly rooted in the existing industry structure, the administering agency cannot bring about the adjustments which become necessary in a changing economy. Administered minimum prices based on the average costs of existing mines, including the high-cost, less efficient ones, provide a protective umbrella which can only aggravate the familiar problem of excess capacity. Professor Donald H. Wallace has summarized the requirements in these terms:

. . . minimum price fixing in the coal industry can promote the objectives of decent wages and maximum economic consumption if the economic standards used in price fixing result in enough reduction in the number of working mines so that all of those remaining in operation receive in most years' revenues at least sufficient to recoup the variable operating expenses, if the regulatory agency exhibits a high order of judgment and of skill in applying the standards, and if the industry cooperates satisfactorily.[57]

It remains to be shown that any strictly administrative agency can achieve this refinement of direction and control.

· A third possibility is through the encouragement of marketing agencies on the model of Appalachian Coals, Inc., and those made possible under the NIRA and the Coal Act of 1937. On a limited basis, agencies of this kind may provide economies in marketing and advertising, in the use of transportation facilities, in standardization of coal sizes, and the facilitation of research. However, if they include only small percentages of the total market, and a large number of producers remain outside the agencies, their impact on prices and production is likely to be minimal. To this extent, they do not offer much prospect for stabilizing the industry. On the other hand, if the marketing agencies were to become large enough to acquire the market power to effectively control prices and production, they would then be operating in violation of existing antitrust laws, and some form of government supervision or control would become necessary to protect the public interest. In that event, there would seem to be little justification for the agencies' existence. Government control could be exercised more effectively if carried out directly.

The final alternative is to leave the industry basically in private hands, subject to private decisions on production and the play of market forces in pricing, but with some government intervention or concern designed to make the necessary structural adjustments somewhat easier. For example, efforts might be expanded to assist miners find alternative employment if the work force is further reduced. Major assistance might be given to basic research and to promote technological advance. The government could take a more active role in promoting revision of existing freight rates, eliminating features which encourage cross-hauling or discriminate against some producing areas. In short, the assumption here is that a competitive industry will manage its own major decisions and will, by and large, perform efficiently and in the public interest. Government policies would be limited in scope and directed toward complementing market forces rather than replacing them or shielding the industry from them.

These, then, appear to be the major policy alternatives, although other ideas have been put forth from time to time that fall somewhere between them. The important thing to bear in mind is that the enormously productive American economy is drawing upon its finite reserves of fuels of all

---

[57] TNEC Monograph No. 32, *op.cit.*, p. 471.

kinds at a very rapid rate, but because the reserves of coal are so vast, long-run plans for self-sufficiency in fuel must rest on them. Conservation needs, therefore, require that coal consumption be encouraged by efficient production and by widening the pattern of end-use to diminish the drain on our less plentiful reserves of other fuels. If a privately owned and operated competitive industry can achieve this, as the most recent developments in coal now give indications of doing, we may be witnessing a long-delayed vindication of the competitive market solution. However, if the old problems return to plague the industry again, the national interest will require a more comprehensive effort at social control than has been attempted to date.

SUGGESTED READINGS

Books

Bituminous Coal Institute, *Bituminous Coal Annual* (Washington, D.C., various years).

Percy W. Bidwell, *Raw Materials* (New York: Harper, 1958).

Morton S. Baratz, *The Union and the Coal Industry* (New Haven: Yale University Press, 1955).

Waldo E. Fisher, *Collective Bargaining in the Bituminous Coal Industry: An Appraisal* (Philadelphia: University of Pennsylvania Press, 1948).

Waldo E. Fisher and Charles M. James, *Minimum Price Fixing in the Bituminous Coal Industry* (Princeton: Princeton University Press, 1955).

Walton H. Hamilton and Helen R. Wright, *The Case of Bituminous Coal* (New York: Macmillan, 1926).

Herman R. Lantz, *People of Coal Town* (New York: Columbia University Press, 1958).

Homer L. Morris, *The Plight of the Bituminous Coal Miner* (Philadelphia: University of Pennsylvania Press, 1934).

Glen L. Parker, *The Coal Industry* (Washington, D.C.: American Council on Public Affairs, 1940).

Government Publications

U.S. Bureau of the Census, *United States Census of Mineral Industries: 1954* (Washington, D.C.: Government Printing Office, 1958).

F. E. Berquist *et al.*, *Economic Survey of the Bituminous Coal Industry Under Free Competition and Code Regulation* (Washington, D.C.: Office of National Recovery Administration, Division of Review [mimeo], 1936).

U.S. Coal Commission, *Report of the United States Coal Commission* (Washington, D.C.: Government Printing Office, 1925).

U.S. Bureau of Mines, *Minerals Yearbook* (Washington, D.C.: Government Printing Office, various years).

Temporary National Economic Committee, *Economic Standards of Government*

Price Control, Monograph No. 32 (Washington, D.C.: Government Printing Office, 1941).

President's Materials Policy Commission, *Resources for Freedom,* Vol. III (Washington, D.C.: Government Printing Office, 1952).

Articles

I. Bernstein and H. G. Lovell, "Are Coal Strikes National Emergencies?" *Industrial and Labor Relations Review,* Vol. 6, April 1953.

C. L. Christenson, "The Theory of the Offset Factor: The Impact of Labor Disputes upon Coal Production," *American Economic Review,* Vol. XLIII, September 1953.

C. L. Christenson, "The Impact of Labor Disputes upon Coal Consumption," *American Economic Review,* Vol. XLV, March 1955.

W. H. Hamilton, "Coal and the Economy: A Demurrer," *Yale Law Journal,* Vol. 50, February 1941.

B. Karsh and J. London, "The Coal Miners: A Study of Union Control," *Quarterly Journal of Economics,* Vol. LXVIII, August 1954.

J. P. Miller, "The Pricing of Bituminous Coal: Some International Comparisons," in C. J. Friedrich and E. S. Mason, ed., *Public Policy* (Cambridge: Harvard University Press, 1940).

R. J. Myers, "Experience of the UMWA Welfare and Retirement Fund," *Industrial and Labor Relations Review,* Vol. 10, October 1956.

H. Solow, "Soft Coal: How Strong a Comeback?" *Fortune,* October 1957.

G. G. Somers, "Effects of North-South Wage Uniformity on Southern Coal Production," *Southern Economic Journal,* Vol. XX, October 1953.

E. V. Rostow, "Bituminous Coal and the Public Interest," and "Joinder in Demurrer," *Yale Law Journal,* Vol. 50, February 1941.

Chapter 4

CARL BREHM

The Residential
Construction Industry

SECTION I: INTRODUCTION

Twenty-five per cent of America's housing is substandard. In any city or village one can find, even today, the dirty, littered streets, the junk-filled yards, the dilapidated and unpainted buildings that some people must call their home. Inside, families are crowded into one or two rat-infested, decayed, and ill-lighted rooms, equipped with one cold-water tap and a toilet that works part of the time. This is a glaring example of the "housing problem." It is the part of the market at the bottom of housing's "filter down" ladder.

Many factors besides the performance of the residential construction industry account for slums. Real estate restrictions and racial discrimination are two important factors which force part of our population into these ghettos. But over and above these considerations is the fact that private enterprise housing cannot provide livable units at prices which lower income people can afford.

During the postwar housing boom the industry was content to skim the cream from the housing markets. Little or no attempts are recorded of builders making serious efforts to reduce housing costs. Historically, productivity has increased at a slower pace in residential construction than it has in most other sectors of the economy. Even when the operative builder provides luxury housing for upper-middle income families the results are inadequate. Bernard P. Spring, writing on "Advances in House Design," states:

113

Among the most conspicuous of their shortcomings is a standardized form which becomes grotesque when repeated countless times on typical small lots. Such houses do not provide a harmonious neighborhood pattern; they offer neither continuity between house and site, nor privacy inside or out. The planning allows only either a rigid schedule of activities or a constant internal conflict. There is no real control over light or view. The forms and materials provided are unrelated to the way the family uses the house. In short, these houses are spruced-up versions of the very inadequate minimum houses of the past.[1]

This state of affairs, however, is not inevitable. Informed observers believe that the industry can improve its performance as well as its product. They call for a flexible building system making possible houses which are better adapted to the site and whose interiors are easily rearranged to fit the changing needs of a growing family. In this direction, schemes to assemble dwellings from premanufactured components—including all major parts such as foundations, walls, roof, plumbing, and mechanical equipment—hold the most promise. But present construction methods must be overturned if this goal is to be achieved.

What is the character of this industry which has always been the object of so much criticism? Professor Burnham Kelly has summarized it as follows:

. . . the essential character of the housebuilding industry has been determined by [its] diffused and localized [structure]. Ease of entry for new building organizations remains unusually great and so does competition among builders. To the typical builder, a wide availability of general and specialty subcontract facilities and local materials outlets for almost every aspect of building has meant that there is no need to maintain staff, equipment, or inventory. . . .

The system of construction and mortgage finance, the basis of building regulation and inspection . . . all derive their basic form from the premise that houses are and will continue to be assembled at the site by skilled craftsman under the direction of contractors. . . .

The labor force is mobile and flexible, unattached to any single employing organization, with individuals shifting status from employer to employee when the situation warrants. . . .

Innovation of all sorts is hampered by the fact that few companies dare to bring new channels of distribution and new building teams into play. . . . As a result, most builders have come to assume that present housebuilding conditions cannot change, and that the only way to deal with inefficiencies is through the liberalizing of financial terms and government supports.[2]

If this diagnosis is correct, what are the causes of the malaise? Why has the industry been so stubbornly backward? Why has it continued to rely on

[1] Burnham Kelly *et al.*, *Design and the Production of Houses*, New York: McGraw-Hill, 1959, p. 68.
[2] *Ibid.*, pp. 25–7.

craft skills and why has industrialization made such little headway? And finally, what of the future organization of the industry if it is to better serve the consumer?

Housing's Place in the Economy

Residential construction plays a significant role in the economy. The value of private nonfarm residential building accounted for about 4 per cent of gross national product. When compared to other broad groups in the GNP accounts, expenditures on new homes have averaged over 50 per cent of all spending on goods and services by state and local governments during the post-World War II period, and they have amounted to more than half of all business expenditures on new plant and equipment. In 1958 funds expended on new housing totaled 18 billion dollars, while new plant and equipment outlays totaled 30.5 billion dollars and payments by state and local governments had continued their postwar increase to 40.5 billion.[3] In contrast to other kinds of private construction activity, housing expenditures since 1946 have been double that of commercial, industrial, and institutional building. Moreover, housing volume exceeded spending on utilities and other construction activity by about the same margin, and money spent on public construction has ranged from one-half to four-fifths of private spending on new homes.

Dollars spent on housing, however, have an importance over and above their aggregate total. Expenditures on nonfarm residential construction have averaged slightly more than 25 per cent of gross private domestic investment, and about 50 per cent of all new construction activity.[4] Moreover, spending on residential construction leads to more investment. One authority estimates that for every dollar spent on residential building, $.50 more must be spent by public and private groups to provide such services as streets, shopping centers, schools, hospitals, churches, and utilities. In addition, new furniture and household durables are often purchased to furnish the new home.[5]

Broadly speaking, the volume of investment in an economy determines its level of income. Since housing accounts for about one-quarter of all investment, it is apparent that changes in building activity may play an important

[3] Department of Commerce, *U.S. Income and Output,* Washington: Government Printing Office, 1958, pp. 118–19, 191; *Federal Reserve Bulletin,* November 1959, p. 1414.

[4] *U.S. Income and Output, op.cit.,* pp. 118–19.

[5] Leo Grebler, "The Role of Residential Capital Formation in Postwar Business Cycles," in *Conference on Savings and Residential Financing,* 1959 Proceedings, The United States Savings and Loan League, 1959, p. 64.

role in the business cycle. On balance, during the postwar period changes in housing production have tended to be countercyclical. At times when the rate of spending on producers' plant and equipment slackened, expenditures on new homes tended to increase enough to partially offset the decline, thus moderating the downturn in income and employment. During the prosperity phase of the cycle a decline in housing investment has been a welcomed restraint on general levels of business activity.[6] While it is beyond the scope of this chapter to analyze this cyclical behavior, suffice it to say that residential construction has tended to be an antiinflation and antirecession force.

The Product

Quite obviously housing may assume many forms, including tents, house trailers, house boats, luxury hotels, motels, apartments, penthouse apartments, and the single-family, three-bedroom dwelling in suburbia. All of these units provide "housing," but the most important sector of the market is the single-family, nonfarm dwelling unit which accounted for 82 per cent of all privately built housing in 1958. During the period 1951–58 there was an average yearly output of 973,000 single family homes out of a total production of 1,112,000 residential units of all types.[7] Obviously, there are many kinds of family homes ranging from small cottages to palatial mansions but they all possess common characteristics which have affected the organization and structure of the building industry.

The size and structural complexity of the house reflects in many ways the civilization we share. Members of a nomadic culture like the Plains Indians of North America, for example, required a simple tent structure which could be easily moved and set up as it was needed. In the elaborate and complex civilizations of today houses must obviously supply more than simple shelter. Space for sleeping, preparation and consumption of meals, relaxation and play, and other activities must be provided. Facilities are also required for waste disposal, central heating and air conditioning, proper lighting, and storage of family possessions including the car. Given these needs, the house, of necessity, is bulky, highly complex, and durable and hence an immobile and expensive product.[8]

[6] *Ibid.*, pp. 65–69. For a discussion of factors affecting investment in housing see James S. Deusenberry, *Business Cycles and Economic Growth*, New York: McGraw-Hill, 1958, Chap. 7.

[7] *Federal Reserve Bulletin,* November 1959, p. 1407. Since 1951, 87 per cent of all housing produced was of the single-family type.

[8] Leo Grebler, *Production of New Housing*, New York: Social Science Research Council, 1950, pp. 12–14. Also Miles Colean and Robinson Newcomb, *Stabilizing Construction*, New York: McGraw-Hill, 1952, Chap. II.

Because the house, once completed, cannot be moved, the builder must produce the dwelling at the site where it is to be used. As a result, contractors tend to confine their activities to local markets where they are familiar with housing tastes and market conditions. They must limit production to what the locality can absorb because they cannot produce for shipment to other areas. Even manufacturers of prefabricated units find the extent of their market confined by transportation costs, and their dealers in turn restrict their activities to limited areas.[9] Product immobility, with its consequent restriction of production to localities, holds unique implications for the housing industry which will be discussed in Section II below.

Since the home must be sturdy enough to provide protection from the elements, it is generally durable enough to last an average of thirty years or more.[10] Moreover, its useful life may be extended with proper repair and alterations. There is, therefore, no large-volume replacement market similar to that for other consumer durables. While some existing units may be condemned or destroyed, most new housing is a net addition to the total stock.[11]

Finally, and of greatest importance to the consumer, the new dwelling is the most expensive purchase made by the average family. In many areas of the country, low priced housing with a lot will cost five times as much as a low priced car. Its value, when measured against the consumer's annual income, is two to three times as great. This high cost is the result of two equally strong forces. First, given present building techniques, the high cost of housing is traceable to the size, complexity, and durability of the structure; and second, conservatism and tradition limit the scope for technical innovation and cost reduction.

Immobility and expensiveness engender pressures on all sides of the market to reduce the risks associated with the production and ownership of houses. Most producers, financial institutions, and buyers are satisfied with familiar and widely accepted designs, constructed of materials whose performance can be accurately predicted. Dwellings of this type, because they enjoy a greater popularity, can be more easily sold and resold. Only the minority who can afford to experiment with radical designs and new materials is able to assume the risks inherent in innovation. Consequently, because producers and consumers, to minimize risk, insist on the old and familiar in housing construction, it is difficult to obtain wide acceptance of cheaper designs and materials.

With regard to the methods of construction, the product's complexity and immobility have encouraged the retention of site production using re-

---

[9] *Design and the Production of Houses, op.cit.,* pp. 169–71.
[10] Glenn H. Beyer, *Housing: A Factual Analysis,* New York: Macmillan, 1958, p. 46.
[11] Grebler, *op.cit.,* pp. 17–19.

lated, yet autonomous, craft skills. The house is assembled in stages through the cooperation of three distinct groups—contractors, materials dealers, and subcontractors. The contractor manages the erection of the house, including the preparation of the site and laying of the foundation; the framing and enclosing of the structure and its roof; the emplacement of interior walls; the installation of mechanical equipment; and the finishing of the interior and exterior surfaces. He depends on materials suppliers to provide the wide variety of constituent parts at the site as they are needed. In addition, he uses subcontractors who supply the diverse specialized skills needed to construct a home. As the house has become more complex additional trades skills have developed to provide necessary services to the contractor, and materials dealers have seen their inventories increase with wider varieties of building components and materials. How this loosely coordinated production system helps the builder reduce many of the market risks associated with housing production will be taken up in the next section.

SECTION II: MARKET STRUCTURE AND PRICE POLICY

There were almost 387,800 home builders counted in a 1949 survey of the industry, and of this total 110,000 were professional companies.[12] However, these large numbers tell us very little about the degree of competition in housing. Since construction is confined to the site and producers therefore tend to operate in local markets, the relevant questions about the industry concern the interrelationships of sellers in each locality. How many firms are there and how is the market shared among them? What kinds of price policies prevail in these limited markets? Answers to these questions will help us appraise the economic performance of the industry.

Housing Markets

Most of the structural characteristics of residential building may be traced to the limited nature of each market and the ease of entry into the industry. Less populous areas tend to have fewer producers and hence buyers face an oligopoly. As population increases so do the number of firms competing for customers in each trading area, and construction assumes more of the attributes of competition. Thus, there is a continuum of housing markets starting with oligopoly and changing by degrees to monopolistic competition. Whether a particular firm or group of firms dominates a market is im-

---

[12] Bureau of Labor Statistics, *Structure of the Residential Building Industry in 1949*, Bulletin No. 1170, Washington: Government Printing Office, 1954, Table 1, p. 21.

possible to predict since it is easy to imagine a wide variety of possibilities. Although there is little information on markets in nonmetropolitan areas, for metropolitan centers, where over 80 per cent of building is done, there exists some information on the number of firms and their relative size.

In the twenty-four metropolitan centers surveyed in 1949, each reported enough sellers to warrant the conclusion that substantial competition exists among residential builders. A look at Table 1 reveals that each city had a relatively large number of firms, ranging from 335 in El Paso, Texas, to 13,355 in New York City. Even when the owner-builder is excluded because he enters the market only once, the group remaining—the commercial builder—is still large. In the smallest city in the sample, Binghamton, New

TABLE 1

Number of Builders and Commercial Builders by City
and Number of Large Builders and Share of Output in each City

City	Total No. of Builders	No. of Commercial Builders [a]	No. of Commercial Builders Producing more than 100 Units Annually	Percentage of Production in Each City by Commercial Builders of 100 or more Units
Atlanta, Ga.	2,185	765	15	52
Binghamton, N.Y.	370	111	1	34
Boston, Mass.	3,010	1,204	n.a.	20
Chicago, Ill.	6,715	2,283	45	32
Cleveland, Ohio	2,565	898	9	29
Dallas, Texas	1,070	770	15	38
Dayton, Ohio	640	243	n.a.	18
Denver, Colo.	1,600	720	7	32
Detroit, Mich.	5,105	1,429	57	45
El Paso, Texas	335	134	3	27
Grand Rapids, Mich.	1,065	341	n.a.	6
Lancaster, Pa.	420	122	0	0
Los Angeles, Calif.	12,055	4,943	99	55
Miami, Fla.	2,920	1,080	21	46
Mobile, Ala.	430	129	3	34
New Haven, Conn.	1,160	348	n.a.	11
New York, N.Y.	13,355	7,078	142	50
Philadelphia, Pa.	3,240	1,393	42	54
Pittsburgh, Pa.	2,605	755	8	21
San Francisco, Calif.	2,700	1,593	32	47
Seattle, Wash.	2,415	821	8	38
Stockton, Calif.	345	155	2	33
Tulsa, Okla.	760	281	8	28
Washington, D.C.	1,700	799	48	79

n.a. = not available.
[a] Estimated by Author.

Source: *Structure of the Residential Building Industry in 1949, op.cit.*

York, there were 111 professionals reported, while in New York City they numbered almost 7,100 companies. Similarly, in every other city covered, substantial numbers of firms are found vying for the consumers' housing dollar. Moreover, there is no evidence to indicate that the same conditions do not prevail in other housing markets of the same relative size.

In each city, however, large firms producing more than 100 units annually, accounted for a disproportionate share of total output. Big builders (who constitute about 2 per cent of all professional contractors) started 36 per cent of all homes. But in some cities the number in this class was significant. Referring again to Table 1, four cities had fewer than five large firms; five had six to ten; and ten cities had more than eleven big producers—three of these cities reporting more than fifty firms in this group.[13] In general, the picture is one of relatively few firms having an important share of the market without attaining a dominant position. Thus residential construction, even when account is taken of the distribution of output by firms, has a competitive structure.

Moreover, the ease with which new firms and do-it-yourself builders can enter the industry provides an additional guarantee of competition. The large proportion of owner-builders and part-time contractors (roughly those completing less than five houses a year), found in all parts of the country, is evidence of the ease of entry. In the sample of twenty-four metropolitan areas owner-builders averaged 58 per cent of all producers and completed 14 per cent of all homes in 1949.[14] Likewise, the proportion of part-time firms was large, averaging 72 per cent of the professional group and starting 14 per cent of all dwelling units.[15] The high ratio of owner and part-time producers poses a threat to any restrictive combinations which large-scale commercial builders may attempt. Any time costs are pushed high enough nonprofessionals find it profitable and easy to enter the industry.

Free movement into residential construction is encouraged by the absence of any significant cost barriers. Capital requirements are low. Whenever heavy equipment is needed it may be leased for the job, and working capital may be obtained through trade credit, house buyers, or construction loans from financial institutions. The only constraint is that the contractor know something about building houses. Thus carpenters and other craftsmen with some knowledge of the industry find it easy to enter. In fact, most part-time producers come from this group, although persons employed in real estate, mortgage financing, or engineering, also are likely candidates. But we must

---

[13] Ten builders produced 1,000 or more homes in 1957. *House and Home,* March 1958, p. 45.

[14] *Structure of the Residential Building Industry in 1949, op.cit.,* p. 21.

[15] *Ibid.,* Tables 2 and 3, pp. 22–3.

not conclude that all of the market is competitive. Even though residential contractors compete among themselves, housing markets in many localities have been hamstrung by trade restraints and price-fixing agreements among materials manufacturers and distributors, subcontractors, and the building trades unions.

Competition in the manufacture and sale of materials has often been suppressed by agreements to fix prices and limit sales to authorized dealers. Prices fixed with the aid of patent licensing agreements and basing point systems have been evident in the past in gypsum products, lumber, electrical goods, plumbing fixtures, and cement and other building products. In the plumbing, heating, electrical, plaster, and tile setting trades, materials have been sold only on an installed basis. Moreover, subcontractors, when bidding on jobs to supply materials and labor, may agree among themselves to follow uniform pricing formulas, or use open bidding systems by revealing bids to each other, or abide by understandings which allocate work.[16] Fundamentally, this type of anticompetitive behavior rests upon the ability of sellers to exclude outsiders from the market.

Restrictions in construction markets are often abetted by strong local union organizations and city building codes.[17] Craft unions—by limiting entry, regulating work pace, and the kinds of power equipment used on the job—can increase their share of the housing dollar and the cost of the house as well. Moreover, outmoded building codes, which require specific types of materials or the employment of licensed mechanics, extend preferential treatment to the groups so favored. For example, wet plaster or electrical conduit have been made mandatory by some codes, thus benefiting plasterers and electricians. Consumers are denied free choice of materials and, furthermore, there is often a *de facto* limitation on their power to select among numerous competing firms when buying materials and labor.

However, market restrictions in some cases are subject to erosions through innovation. Union restrictions with respect to limiting output may become meaningless when a new material is developed that threatens the existence of the craft. For instance, plasterers adopted the plaster-gun when increased use of dry-board construction jeopardized the trade.[18] In addition, the widespread availability of most building products from large retail mail-order chains reduces the usefulness of trade restraints in local markets. Similarly,

---

[16] Colean and Newcomb, *op.cit.*, pp. 116–22.
[17] *Ibid.*, p. 118.
[18] William Haber and Harold Levinson, *Labor Relations and Productivity in the Building Trades,* Ann Arbor: Bureau of Industrial Relations, University of Michigan, 1956, pp. 113–27.

the development of materials requiring less skill to install and their wide-spread availability weakens the power of local craft unions and dealers. Finally, where building codes are responsible for increased costs builders can move outside the area in which the code applies. Hence, while periodic attempts may be made to limit competition in materials and labor markets, events may nullify the effects of these agreements.

Price Policy

There is no price policy in residential construction comparable to that found in more concentrated industries. Given the number of producers in major markets and the ease of entry, values are generally determined by competition. The present market structure makes it extremely difficult for any group of producers to sustain an administered price structure for an extended period of time. Consequently, consumer preferences (validated by a willingness to purchase new housing) together with the builders' productive efficiency have the greatest impact on consumer costs. Therefore, to understand what forces decide the amounts consumers spend on housing, we must analyze the factors underlying demand and supply in the housing market.

Demand

Like the demand for other products, demand for housing is subject to numerous and complex forces. The most important of these are (1) consumer income and liquid asset holdings, (2) the terms of finance, (3) product price, and (4) population size and the rate of family formation. Since the unit is expensive, income and the terms of finance have the greatest short-run influence.

(1) Past income must have been high enough to allow an accumulation of savings for the downpayment on a house. Current income must be sufficient to cover the monthly carrying charges and the other costs associated with home ownership. Therefore, a rise in wages and salaries tends to increase the rate of household formation as "doubling up" in dwellings is reduced and more people can afford the expenses of home ownership. A decline in earnings will have the opposite effect.

(2) Since most purchases are on credit, liberalized financing terms, such as a reduction in downpayments, will enable more buyers to enter the market. Similarly, a decline in the interest rate or lengthening of maturities will

reduce the monthly carrying charge, making it possible for people with lower incomes to qualify for credit to buy a house.

(3) Product price is, of course, an important variable. Most sellers believe that the demand for housing is price inelastic, i.e., a relatively small change in price will lead to a relatively smaller change in the number of units sold.[19] When demand is stimulated by other factors such as rising incomes or more favorable financing terms this may be true. But in the absence of these changes the question of whether variations in value will or will not affect the quantity demanded is difficult to answer. It is certainly true that any increase in consumer cost results in larger downpayments and monthly carrying charges. Consequently, a price rise would act either to exclude some buyers from the market or force them to purchase lower quality housing. If unit valuations decline, more families will be brought into the market. When consumers find they need and can afford a new home they will make their purchase unless they expect further price reductions in the immediate future.

Of course, present values of "old" houses and rental units will also affect the demand for new dwellings. Whenever the money outlay for older houses or rentals increases relative to the cost of new housing people may be induced to purchase the latter. At the same time, a rise in prices of existing houses means that the value of real assets held by home owners has increased, so that they are better able to buy improved housing. Changes in the relative values of old and new houses is one index the operative builder uses in assessing his market.

(4) Fundamentally, the number of people in the economy and the rate at which family units are formed provides the basic demand for housing. If population and the number of family units is increasing there develops a pressure for more living space. Likewise a migration from rural to urban areas or from the Midwest and Southwest to the Far West results in increased demand for new homes in the expanding areas. Although changes in the number of people and shifts from one region to another provides a basic demand for dwelling space, income, financing terms, and prices will determine how well their needs are fulfilled.

Inasmuch as the demand for new houses is most responsive to changes in income and financing terms—which are subject to variations in levels of business activity—it is not surprising to find that sales fluctuate from year to year. Cyclical and seasonal changes in demand have been among the most important factors influencing the organization of the residential construction

[19] *Ibid.*, p. 16.

industry. Because houses are highly durable, families may make do with what they presently have until income and/or availability of financing on acceptable terms makes it possible to enter the market. At the same time, the number of dwelling units may be augmented by conversion of single-family to multifamily units or, where necessary, families may "double-up" until they are able to obtain more housing. Thus, any improvement in living accommodations can be postponed with relative ease. Since the producer finds that market demand varies from year to year—straining his resources during some periods and at other times scarcely employing his services at all—his best strategy is to remain as flexible as possible. He is able to curtail building activity with a minimum loss when the market declines, and he can expand production quickly as demand increases.

Supply

The most important problem facing the industry is the continuing high cost of supplying new houses. Observers have noted time and again the persistence of archaic production methods founded on craft skills, and they feel that somehow productivity could be improved so that prices can be reduced. However, the path to lower building costs is not clear. Most of the confusion arises because insufficient account has been taken of the economics of housing supply.

In general, the supply of new residences arises in two ways, depending upon who initiates the project. In the past, most units were constructed at the behest of the owner. Today only about 30 per cent of all starts occur in this way.[20] Since World War II the operative builder, producing units for sale after completion, has become the most important factor in the market.

Custom building is a service performed for the owner. The contractor undertakes the job on a cost-plus-fixed-fee basis or, more frequently, he enters a lump-sum bid. His success requires that he be as efficient as his competitors in managing the erection of a house. Typically, he is a small builder producing less than twenty-five houses a year. He is geared to producing custom units with perhaps a few speculative homes and since he is called upon to produce units of widely divergent design the ability to solve a great variety of construction problems is very important.

In contrast, the operative builder specializes in the production of a large

[20] *Structure of the Residential Building Industry in 1949, op.cit.*, p. 21. See also Ralph J. Johnson, "Technological Changes in Residential Construction, 1961–70," in *Study of Mortgage Credit*, Eighty-fifth Cong., 2nd Sess., p. 130. Here the author estimates that contract construction accounted for only 15 per cent of commercially built housing while operative builders produced 85 per cent of output in 1958.

quantity of standardized units. He holds the initiative in augmenting the supply of housing. Since the units are expensive and immobile, the builder incurs some definite risks in site selection and improvement as well as the choice of an attractive house model. Consequently, he must take special pains to evaluate demand. Furthermore, when he produces many identical dwellings his methods of production tend to differ from those of the custom-builder. In the popular mind, the speculative builder is the developer who turns corn fields into large scale housing tracts of more or less identical units cramped on small lots. In the producer's mind, he is the creator of "communities."

Production technique varies with the firm's scale of operations. The small contractor doing primarily custom work finds the more traditional house-building methods suited to his limited output. On the other hand, the large builder producing 100 or more identical units has to employ different techniques and establish different relationships with materials dealers and subcontractors. By describing the operations of small and large producers we can explain why the traditional organization of production persists where there is low output and the significance of changes in construction techniques brought about by big builders, and, moreover, indicate what steps are necessary to bring new housing within the reach of more people.

The Small Builder

The small builder is ubiquitous. In both metropolitan and nonmetropolitan areas he outnumbers all other producers. His forte is his ability to take any set of plans and efficiently build a house. The materials may be wood, stone, brick, or poured concrete; the house may be a large mansion or a small cottage; whatever the building requirements, the small builder is prepared to meet the needs of the buyer. As long as buyers want custom-made units and as long as residential construction is local in character, the small builder will have a place in the industry.

Small builders are usually organized as a proprietorship or partnership. Total assets are on the order of $35,000 to $40,000 with some firms reaching $100,000.[21] Carpentry is the usual trade of the contractor, but he may also come from real estate, finance, or one of the other building trades. In the smallest firm he is a part-time manager, with his office in the cab of his pick-up truck. As his building operations become more extensive, he spends

[21] Sherman Maisel, *Housebuilding in Transition,* Berkeley: University of California Press, 1953, p. 39. Data are derived from a study of residential construction firms in the San Francisco Bay area.

a larger proportion of his time in purely management functions. The permanent work force consists of no more than one or two skilled carpenters and one or two unskilled laborers, with the contractor serving as a carpenter-foreman. Since some labor economies arise when a crew is kept together long enough to learn to work as a team, the builder tries to plan his jobs so that the work force is fully employed. An efficient and highly skilled carpentry crew is considered an essential ingredient for success.

Most subcontracting is let on a negotiated rather than on a bid basis. Both contractors and subcontractors seem to prefer this way of doing business, because bidding is an expensive and time consuming operation. Periodically, to be sure they are not being overcharged, builders will ask for bids from other subcontractors to test the market.

The practice of subcontracting is often criticized because it seems to introduce an unnecessary middleman into the house-building operation. It is argued that this method results in added costs because payment must be made not only for the direct labor of the subcontracted skills, but also for the services and mark-up on materials supplied by the subcontractor. In general, however, the skill offered by each subcontractor is only a small part of the total labor time required to complete a house. For example, a man can lay an asphalt tile floor in a modest-size unit in ten hours; a roof can be finished in eight to ten hours; and roughing in the plumbing may require as little as two days' work. A small builder producing twenty units a year could use a roofing crew for only about twenty days of the year, and plumbers for perhaps fifty or sixty days. While each contractor uses these skills for a relatively short period, the subcontractor can keep them fully employed by working for several builders. Furthermore, the subcontractor has the training and experience to evaluate and supervise the work of the particular trade, a skill not necessarily possessed by the builder. Therefore, it pays the contractor to buy the subcontractor's services and let him assume the responsibility for the job. Certainly, building costs would be much higher if the small builder had to maintain a work crew representing the great variety of skills required to complete a house. Hence, the subcontracting system contributes to the economical utilization of those skills used infrequently by each of many small builders.

Another much abused middleman in the building industry is the materials dealer. He also is charged with getting an "unearned increment" from the home buyer's pocket. But upon closer inspection we find that he too performs essential services for the small builder. Because house production is low, the producer's annual requirements for materials are modest. He must have lumber, millwork, fixtures and the like for only twenty-five or fewer houses. Moreover, he requires a diverse stock if he does custom building. The materials dealer carries an inventory from which the small builder may draw his needs.[22] Usually the dealer undertakes to cut materials to the builder's specifications, and to deliver them at the construction site as they are needed. Thus the builder does not have to store or handle materials before they reach the site, and he is able to get whatever items he needs to complete a house satisfactorily. He often obtains a builder's discount and credit as well, and the latter obviously is an important matter to a small firm with little capital of its own.[23]

Of course, the builder pays a higher price for the materials purchased from dealers than if he bought in carload lots from the manufacturer. But the small builder has no use for large quantities of materials. Volume purchases would make his total costs per unit much higher because he would have the expense of handling and storing the wide varieties of lumber and other products which he requires. Moreover, his capital needs would also be greatly increased by the large inventory on hand. Under these circumstances, it pays to use the materials dealer because these expenses can be spread over sales to a number of builders, and hence unit costs are minimized for individual customers.

Yet the question of whether materials prices are too high, even when account is taken of the services performed by the dealer, remains to be answered. The reply turns on the degree of competition found among materials dealers and among manufacturers. As long as competition is unfettered by restrictive agreements, prices in the long run should just cover costs including a normal return to the producer. In general, lumber, millwork, building paper, bricks, cast iron pipe, paint, lighting fixtures, furnaces, and hot-water heaters come from industries in which the eight leading firms account for 36 per cent or less of all sales. These products constituted 60 per cent of the value of all materials used in the construction of a house in the San Francisco area.[24] Building materials produced in industries with a high degree of concentration include gypsum products, plumbing fixtures, window shades, linoleum, window glass, and ceramic tile. In this group restrictive practices have been found—including basing points, price fixing agreements, and strong distributor tie-ups.[25] Except for these oligopolistic sectors of the

[22] His inventory may turn over no more than two or three times a year. To gain an idea of how extensive the materials market is, Sweet's, a catalogue of building products, is issued in ten volumes, contains 15,868 pages, and weighs 150 pounds, yet offers only a selected list of products. *Design and the Production of Houses, op.cit.,* p. 85.

[23] Maisel indicates that in the San Francisco area the builders discount is from 5 to 20 per cent depending upon the item. *Op.cit.,* p. 56.

[24] *Ibid.,* p. 136.

[25] See above, p. 121.

market, where higher than normal rates of return may be earned, the great bulk of building materials used in residential construction come from competitive industries.[26] Builders in larger markets find that they have enough alternative sources of supply to assure competitive prices.

Small builders are geared to producing custom-houses and a few speculative units. Each custom-built house poses its own problems—its dimensions, its materials, and layout are all unique, and consequently mass production techniques cannot be used. Parts must be measured and cut and nailed by hand. Power saws and drills may facilitate some of the work, but the operation will be basically handwork. Even when the small builder is engaged in a speculative project it will pay him to adopt only a limited amount of the yard and site prefabrication techniques used by larger builders. Of course there are some items—like cabinets and mounted door and window units— which the small builder can obtain in prefabricated form. He may also use limited site prefabrication of house frame and wall units.

However, where the number of units produced is small, the builder will continue to rely upon piece-by-piece, cut-and-fit building methods. In custom building and small speculative projects the cost of increased site prefabrication, i.e., the use of greater labor specialization, results in a marked increase in management costs not offset by any significant increase in labor productivity. The small builder's output is simply not large enough to justify the expanded overhead associated with more elaborate production methods.

Yet the small builder has a definite place in the residential building industry. Most of our local markets can support only small builders. Also, as long as some buyers insist on custom-built housing, the small builder will have a role in the industry. By using materials suppliers and subcontractors, he is able to attain a high degree of flexibility in his operations. In the words of one authority:

> This approach to house construction is as loosely knit as it can be and still be workable. It is ideally suited to handling localized and unpredictable orders and at the same time makes possible the maximum degree of individuality in any given house. Whatever the owner or the architect calls for can be produced; the necessary combination of skills and supplies can be had. No other house-building operation has this extreme flexibility.[27]

[26] Maisel, *op.cit.*, pp. 137–41.
[27] *Design and the Production of Houses, op.cit.*, p. 141.

The Large Builder

The operations of the large operative builder are markedly different. Those who have looked for industrialization of the building industry have found in the large building firm the closest approximation of their ideal. The firm is a partnership or closely held corporation. Often it consists of a number of related subsidiary companies, each responsible for one phase of the building project—land procurement and development, planning and engineering, materials purchasing, organizing and managing the building operation, and sales. Management functions are now split among the principal owners of the firm and the number of overhead personnel (those not working at the site) increases disproportionately to the number of houses built.[28] Consequently, the builder must discover and exploit economies of scale which will support the additional overhead.

Economies of scale are achieved by concentrating on producing large numbers of identical units, quantity materials purchasing, subcontracting, large scale land development, and financing. In any project the large operative builder will offer a limited number of models each with slight variations of trim and color to achieve relief from monotony. Once the house models are selected, a thorough study is made of each to eliminate any features which may increase cost. Prefabrication of component parts is used wherever possible to take advantage of the labor savings associated with the repetition of simple work tasks. The managerial staff must plan and arrange the flow of materials and prefabricated parts to the work site so that houses can be assembled with a minimum of costly delays. At the same time, the builder's work crews and subcontracting crews will be scheduled so that they may move in sequence from house to house without undue confusion and delay. Roofing crews, plumbers, electricians, furnace installers, painters, and flooring crews, must all be scheduled so that one does not interfere with the work of another. Consequently, the whole project must be planned with painstaking care.

The large operative builder achieves significant savings in the purchase of materials. Maisel estimates that these savings amount from $410 to $540 or almost 25 per cent of a small builder's materials cost for a typical house.[29] A summary of the comparative cost data is presented in Table 2. Purchases are made in carload lots directly from the manufacturer wherever possible. To be sure, the savings from such volume purchases are partially offset by

---

[28] Maisel, *op.cit.*, p. 102.
[29] *Ibid.*, p. 121.

TABLE 2

Costs of Building the Composite House by Builders of Different Sizes

Component	Size of Builder			Size of Builder		
	Small	Medium	Large	Small	Medium	Large
	(in dollars)			(in percentage)		
Labor						
Direct	1,485	1,300	1,100	16	14	13
Trade contractors	1,161	1,010	944	12	11	11
Subtotal	2,646	2,310	2,044	28	25	24
Materials						
Direct	2,235	1,925	1,825	24	21	21
Trade contractors	1,524	1,427	1,265	16	16	14
Subtotal	3,759	3,352	3,090	40	37	35
Trade contractors' overhead and profit	694	594	448	7	6	5
Builders' overhead and profit	741	1,334	1,608	8	14	18
Land	1,250	1,250	1,250	13	14	14
Financing and incidentals	410	410	310	4	4	4
Total	9,500	9,250	8,750	100	100	100
Subtotals						
Subcontracts	3,379	3,031	2,657	35	33	30
Direct costs [a]	7,509	6,666	5,892	79	72	68

[a] Does *not* include "builders' overhead and profit" and "land."

Source: Maisel, *op.cit.*, p. 197. Reproduced by permission of the University of California Press.

handling and storing expenses. But since the builder only orders for specific projects, the storage space and the variety of products in inventory is not as great as that required of materials dealers. By using specialized equipment, such as fork-lift trucks and sleds, he can minimize handling costs and, by placing materials in convenient places at the building site, reduce the amount of labor time used in moving materials to each house site. Another saving associated with large-volume purchasing is the ability of the buyer to get parts made on special order. For example, North Shore Supply, purchasing subsidiary for Levit, on an order of 200 sinks was able to have the manufacturer move the drain opening to one side to facilitate plumbing connections in the house.[30]

On a typical dwelling the large-scale builder pays about 22 per cent less for subcontractors than does the small builder. As Table 2 shows this sav-

[30] *Design and the Production of Houses, op.cit.*, p. 38.

ing breaks down to $259 in materials costs, $217 in labor costs, and $246 in overhead and profit. Savings in material costs are the result of large volume purchasing, and have already been discussed. Labor savings arise because the subcontractor is able to make use of some labor specialization among his crews, and a certain amount of preassembly of component parts can be done in the shop thus realizing savings in direct labor costs.[31] Furthermore, it is easier to supervise labor and establish standards of work performance for the subcontracting crews, permitting the builder to get the maximum amount of work from the labor force. In fact, the subcontractor, because he usually works for only one builder, functions as a crew foreman. Costs also are reduced because the subcontractor knows that his crews and equipment will be fully employed, which means that he does not have to allow for idle time when computing his overhead charges to the builder. In a word, the subcontractor can realize his own economies of scale on the large project and these savings are reflected in lower subcontracting costs for the large operative builder.

From the data in Table 2 it is apparent that direct labor costs for a large builder's own crews on a typical house amount to 26 per cent less than the labor costs of a small builder. The labor force is split into specialized crews with each man performing a limited number of operations. On one project, for example, sheathing a roof was broken down into a three-step job. One man took lumber from a stack and leaned it against the house; a second man on the roof drew the lumber up and cut it to size; the third man nailed the sheathing in place. Extensive prefabrication of subassemblies is used to increase labor productivity. Dormer roofs, roof trusses, window assemblies, bathrooms, walls, and stairwell assemblies may all be prefabricated on jigs. Other parts are cut to size and delivered in order of assembly at the construction site. Prefabricated parts of the house are thus produced in the shop under superior working conditions with a consequent improvement in labor productivity.[32]

While labor specialization permits the builder to utilize his work force more efficiently, labor productivity is increased by the more extensive use of power equipment. Power saws and drills, pneumatic hammers, tractors, power shovels, trenchers, and motorized trowels are examples of equipment which will help reduce direct labor costs on the large project. Another saving becomes possible by hiring crews which do not possess the same wide range of skills as are required by the small contractor. Instead of hiring master carpenters, for example, the large builder can use men whose skill

---

[31] Maisel, *op.cit.*, 194–6.
[32] *Design and the Production of Houses, op.cit.*, pp. 152–4.

consists of little more than cutting boards or nailing boards precut by someone else.[33] Also, since preassembly of components in the shop plus the need for scheduling work crews at the site requires the builder to establish minimum work standards, he tends to have better control of the work force and is able to extract from them productivity which the small contractor cannot attain. For these reasons—labor specialization, intensive and extensive use of power equipment, and improved control of work standards—the large builder has increased labor productivity.

Extensive development of raw land offers the large builder another cost cutting advantage. When developing large tracts of land he can use heavy earth-moving equipment to prepare building sites. Installation of sewers, water, electricity, gas, streets, and walks can be done in one operation and the costs spread over a substantial number of units. The cost of "legal overhead per house"—title fees, clearing the project for compliance with zoning and health ordinances, and other local regulatory hurdles—can be minimized in the big project. Many large developments also include commercial developments (such as shopping centers) which tend to increase the profitability of the entire project.[34] While it is hard to say exactly how important these economies are, it cannot be doubted that they represent a significant cost saving for the large builder.

In addition, size confers two kinds of financial advantages upon the large operative builder: (1) more efficient use of capital, and (2) greater availability and lower cost of capital. The large builder can achieve economies through more intensive use of working capital. The funds tied up in inventories can be kept to a minimum by cutting down the time it takes to complete a house and to deliver it to the buyer. Both materials inventory and house inventory are turned over at a more rapid rate so that working capital is utilized more intensively.[35] The second type of financial saving arises because the larger firm has better cost and accounting controls, better management, and greater stability. Hence financial institutions prefer to lend to these firms. Furthermore, size together with more able management helps the large operative builder find funds in diverse institutions at better rates

---

[33] Maisel, *op.cit.*, pp. 113–15.

[34] In the Park Forest, Illinois project the object of the developers was to provide housing at bargain prices while most of the profits would come from the water works and the developers cut (up to 10 per cent) of gross sales in the shopping center. See William H. Whyte, Jr., *The Organization Man*, Garden City, N.Y.: Doubleday, 1957, p. 312.

[35] Maisel, *op.cit.*, pp. 105–6. Maisel shows that the net worth of the larger firms in proportion to sales is lower than that shown by small builders. At the same time net profits as a percentage of sales and net worth tend to be greater for the large builder. See tables 31, 34, and 35, pp. 359–61.

of interest. These savings add to the advantages enjoyed by such builders.

All the major cost-reducing devices of the large builder have now been enumerated. Increased labor productivity, lower materials costs, lower sub-contracting costs, savings in land development and financing costs can be ascribed to the enterprise of the big building organizations. After totaling these savings, however, we find that they are offset to a great extent by an increase in overhead and profit for the bigger firm. Table 2 reveals that while direct costs declined 18 per cent, indirect costs rose by 117 per cent. Thus, on balance, a house that cost $9,500 when produced by a small builder cost $8,750 when produced by a large builder, or 8 per cent less. Overhead ranged from 2.5 per cent of the smallest builder's (1–9 units yearly) total cost to 4.3 per cent for firms completing 10 to 24 houses, while for the large builder the proportion was 8 per cent. Overhead expenditures per house by the large builder amounted to almost three times as much as in the case of the smallest builder. Profits averaged between 5.7 per cent of sales for the smallest firms and 6.7 per cent for small firms building between 10 and 24 units annually. For the large companies the rate averaged 10 per cent.[36]

These differences indicate that while the relatively higher overhead expenses of large builders yielded results in reduced labor and materials costs, the net gain was not as great as might have been expected. At the same time it is hard to say whether the higher profitability shown by the large builder is necessary to attract more "innovative" talent to the industry or whether it is windfall profit. Data on this facet of the industry is too sketchy for any solid conclusions, especially since it was collected in 1949 and 1950 (i.e., during the postwar surge in housing demand). Part of the profits accruing to the larger firms, therefore, may simply reflect temporary monopoly returns. At the time, big builders were in the best position to meet the demands of the mass market and until this need was met they were able to reap better than normal returns.[37] In the future, profit margins of the larger firms in the industry may be reduced if current conditions of free entry continue to prevail. At any rate, the large builder has been able to cut production costs and has, in fact, been able to achieve economies comparable to those gained by the largest factory prefabricators of housing.[38]

[36] *Ibid.*, pp. 208–13, Table 34, p. 360. Comparative cost data do not take account of any savings arising in land development.
[37] *Ibid.*, pp. 212–13.
[38] *Design and the Production of Houses, op.cit.*, pp. 31–2.

Economies of Scale

The question remains whether further economies could be achieved if production were expanded. The answer seems to be that such economies are not likely, given the present technology of home building. Maisel finds that optimum scale is reached at a production rate of 200 to 500 units annually.[39] At this level the amount of labor specialization has reached its limit. Profitable increases in labor productivity are limited, because mass construction of houses must be a combination of shop prefabrication and site assembly. Coordination of work crews becomes increasingly difficult as production is increased and there is a disproportionate expansion of overhead costs to keep the housebuilding process moving in an orderly fashion. For example, the weather can bring chaos to the best planned project. If it rains, some crews whose work is indoors can continue their tasks while outdoor crews must halt operations, thus upsetting the whole schedule. Therefore, some builders maintain their work programs on a blackboard so that the frequent changes may be reworked with a minimum of fuss. Any disruption can be handled by simply erasing the board and starting over in devising a new schedule. But this may not be feasible if output is expanded beyond 500 units. Problems may then grow faster than output.

Additional economies of scale are not likely to come from materials handling, unless further cost reductions could be realized either by purchases in greater quantities than are presently made or by vertical integration. The builder cannot drive the cost of materials below long-run cost. If the lumber mill cannot make a normal return on sales to the large builder, he will seek other customers or go out of business. Furthermore, it must be remembered that while the builder may save on materials prices by buying in larger quantities, he must stand not only the additional expense of capital tied up in inventories but also charges for storage and handling. Such costs may set limits beyond which larger quantity purchases do not pay, even if lower prices are available. With respect to vertical integration of builder and supplier, there might be some cost savings. For example, to gain better quality control, it might pay the builder to acquire some suppliers. This is especially true in lumber, but vertical integration does not mean that lumber becomes "free" to the builder; interest and profits as well as other economic costs must be earned.

With regard to subcontractors, economies of scale are closely associated with the technology of the craft. Once he is able to keep his force efficiently

[39] Maisel, *op.cit.*, Chap. 8.

employed, further expansion of output may lead to increasing unit costs. Again, there are indications that the big builder has already achieved the most important economies.[40] Increased productivity in this area must await, as in much of the industry, basic changes in housing technology. At the same time, vertical integration does not appear to offer a road to cost reductions—even though the biggest builders employ subcontracting crews full time. By not integrating many of the trades the builder can keep his direct overhead at manageable levels. Thus, he does not have to concern himself with keeping the skilled crews fully employed. If he finds it to his advantage to reduce output in any year, he may do so without considering any overhead which might be tied up in the specialty trades.[41] These reasons, plus the fact that operative builders apparently obtain subcontracting services at a minimum cost, indicate why further economies are impossible until there are fundamental changes in building methods.

Consequently, economies of scale at even higher levels of output do not appear to be forthcoming. Giant firms do not have a productive advantage in residential construction once they have reached the 200 to 500 output level. However, one economy—land development—has not been considered here. It may be that large building and land development organizations may have a cost advantage in the planning and development of land for large projects. But it is doubtful whether the savings achieved through such activity will mean substantial price reductions for the consumer in the absence of dramatic advances in housing technology.

Summarizing, then, the economic performance of the housing industry appears to be generally satisfactory. Builders, small and large, are organized to serve particular segments of the housing market. Small builders serve those markets where (because of a limited market or the type of house desired) the rate of output must be low. By combining the services of materials dealers, subcontractors, and his own work crews, the small builder can achieve the flexibility to meet at minimum cost the housing needs of these markets. Given the characteristics of the market, costs do not appear to be too high and, in addition, builders' profit rates have not been as high as those found in other sectors of the economy.[42] Large builders, capitalizing on the needs of urban mass markets, have been able to achieve economies by producing a large volume of identical units. Whether the product has been satisfactory to the buyer is a moot question. The fact remains, however, that homes were produced in large numbers at prices that consumers were

---

[40] *Ibid.*, pp. 204–5.
[41] Compare with "tapered integration" in the automobile industry, pp. 324 below.
[42] Maisel, *op.cit.*, p. 266.

willing to pay. Moreover, this sector of the industry discovered ways to cut costs by a certain amount of innovation, both in the methods of production and in design. Nevertheless, the lack of major innovation remains the chief failure of the residential construction industry.[43]

There can be little doubt that the industry has been very slow in developing different and better ways to produce housing. Repeating what was said in the preceding section, builders tend to employ traditional techniques and are, in fact, too small to sustain costly programs looking toward the development of novel housing designs or new construction methods. What innovation there has been has usually come from outside the industry—particularly materials suppliers and related industries and government agencies. But, even where advanced techniques and new materials did appear, builders were generally reluctant to assume the risks linked with them, although part of this reticence to try something unfamiliar must be laid to the innate conservatism of consumer tastes.

SECTION III: PUBLIC POLICY

In the most recent inventory of housing in the United States, in 1956, one-quarter of all units were found to be dilapidated—i.e., run down, structurally unsafe, or lacking in water, plumbing, or adequate heating facilities.[44] While this represents an improvement over the situation in 1950 when one-third of all units were substandard, it is a shocking performance for an economy as rich as ours. Besides the social waste—poor health, crime, and other welfare losses—there are direct money costs attributable to bad housing conditions. Studies of blighted neighborhoods have shown that it costs the community a disproportionate share of its income to take care of them. Tax revenues from these neighborhoods are low while city costs of maintaining fire and police protection, and providing welfare services, are higher than for the rest of the community. In short, the slum neighborhood is a net drain on our cities' resources.[45] The fact that dilapidated units continue to

[43] *Design and the Production of Houses, op.cit.,* p. 188.

[44] Reinhold P. Wolff, "Substandard Dwelling Units and Their Replacement, 1961–70," *Study of Mortgage Credit, op.cit.,* p. 45. Also see Housing and Home Finance Agency, *Eleventh Annual Report, 1957,* Washington: Government Printing Office, 1958, pp. 18–20.

[45] For example Mr. James W. Follin, a Federal Urban Renewal Commissioner, cited these examples: "An Eastern city, in one year, received $108 more in per capita revenue from good residential areas than it spent there, but its slums cost $88 more per person than they yielded. In one Southern city slum areas contributed only 5.5 per cent of the city's property taxes, but required 53 per cent of the city's health, police, fire, and other service facilities." It is estimated that the national cost of slums amounts to two billion dollars annually. Quotation and data from Oscar H. Steiner, "The Arithmetic of Slum Clearance," *New Republic,* November 16, 1959, pp. 9–11.

be occupied indicates that the housing industry has not been able to produce housing that is low enough in cost to make the slum unit unprofitable to operate.

In the past, public policy has attempted to solve this problem primarily by measures designed to stimulate demand rather than efforts to improve the production techniques of the construction industry. It has been tacitly assumed that given sufficient demand, mass production of housing would achieve economies of scale, or lead to new innovations which would lower costs. We have now had enough experience with the present policies to doubt these conclusions.

FHA and Public Housing

Demand has been sustained by programs designed to make it easier to own a house and by policies to stabilize income and employment at high levels. The principles of the former are embodied in the FHA mortgage insurance program. Full-employment policies have been more indirect in their contribution, but it is clear that higher stable levels of income enable more families to qualify for residential borrowing. At the same time, if government stabilizes employment, financial institutions are more willing to commit funds to the residential mortgage market.

Federally insured mortgages have played an important part in the housing market since 1934. In that year, the mutual insurance fund was set up under what is now the Federal Housing Administration. This fund provided insurance to the lender against default on mortgages for low and medium priced homes and for rental housing projects. Because the risk of financial loss is absent, lending terms are more liberal—lower down payments, longer maturities and lower interest rates—than on conventional mortgages. To qualify for FHA insurance the borrower must be credit-worthy, and the property must be appraised by FHA to assure that its value has not been overstated. And, most important, there must be a regular monthly amortization of the principle and interest on the mortgage. In sum, the program is geared to helping lower-income families make a home purchase under the best financial conditions.

A more direct method of assuring adequate housing for the underprivileged is the public housing project.[46] Usually a housing authority with rights of eminent domain and public funds can acquire land and construct units which are then leased at nominal rentals to the lowest income groups.

[46] Since 1950, public housing starts have averaged less than 4 per cent of all housing starts. Computed from data in the *Federal Reserve Bulletin*, September 1959, p. 1193.

Customarily, the objective is to eliminate slum housing and provide decent homes for poor families at prices they can afford. Thus, public housing is designed for families which would not otherwise be able to rent or buy. Hence, it does not compete with the commercial builder who produces houses for sale to the public.

While mortgage insurance and public housing programs have provided a stimulus to demand, the reach of these programs is limited. Mortgage terms cannot be extended much beyond present levels. With downpayments approaching zero, with mortgage maturities spanning the income-earning period of the borrower, and with the need to keep interest rates sufficiently attractive to command funds in the market, how much further can the program be liberalized without changing its basic nature?[47] The only alternatives are for the government either to lend funds directly at artificially low rates of interest, or to build houses and lease or sell them to low income groups at a loss.

With respect to direct public housing programs, any attempt to achieve a quick solution through vastly increased expenditures will have a serious impact on the new housing market. A large increase in expenditures for low-income units may simply bid up the cost of labor and materials in the short run and draw them away from the middle- and upper-income housing markets. The end result would be a change in the composition of output with an increase in the production of low-income housing and a smaller output of upper-income housing at higher prices. Eventually, if the program is maintained, we could expect new resources to flow into the industry, including materials suppliers, and an adjustment to the new conditions completed with an eventual increase in output. It would appear, therefore, that abrupt attempts to increase housing demand are likely to lead to costly short-run dislocations in the market.

The stimulus to demand given by FHA has made possible the mass building operations of the speculative builder. But it is obvious from the evidence that such firms have made relatively minor changes in building procedures and costs have not been significantly reduced. Since even the largest builder is small when compared to the giants of other industries, he lacks the resources to conduct extensive research into newer and cheaper building methods. Thus, innovation has been slow and painful. To gain better results some observers have argued for the organization of giant producers capable of amassing the resources needed for research and development. But despite the claims of institutional advertising, giantism is no guarantee of progress.

[47] Charles Abrams and Morton Shussheim, "Credit Terms and the Effective Demand for New Housing," *Study of Mortgage Credit, op.cit.,* pp. 81–6.

Indeed, most evidence indicates that successful research is not related to firm size.[48] Discovery and innovation may come from a firm of any size. In residential construction research will be costly and time-consuming and no group within the industry and related fields, at the present time, has the incentive and means to conduct the kind of unified research and development program necessary to cut housing costs.[49]

Moreover, to promote a greater concentration of producers in the market would sacrifice the competitive characteristics of the industry. In a free society competition is the best way to protect the consumer because it forces builders to construct the best possible houses at prevailing prices without the need for direct government intervention. Encouraging concentration removes one safeguard for the consumer.

Improving Industry Performance

Reducing production costs involves parts standardization, on the one hand, and increasing labor productivity through greater specialization and use of power equipment, on the other. At present, systems of dimensional coordination and prefabrication of major component parts of the house offer the most promise for the future.

A system to coordinate design and materials dimensions has already been adopted throughout the building industry. Called modular coordination, it attempts to establish a basic dimensional unit, the module, which is $4'' \times 4'' \times 4''$. All building materials are supplied in sizes that are multiples of the basic module. Architects and builders design and plan the construction of a house so that all dimensions—wall thicknesses, room dimensions, and wall openings such as doors and windows—are in multiples of the modular unit. As a result, waste is reduced and labor efficiency is improved because less time is consumed in cutting and fitting materials. For example, modular bricks laid in a wall scaled to modular dimensions

[48] Jacob Schmookler, "Bigness, Fewness, and Research," *Journal of Political Economy,* Vol. LXVII, December 1959, pp. 628–32.

[49] Privately supported research has generally been of a limited nature. Recently the National Association of Home Builders has sponsored research in better building techniques. Materials manufacturers and related firms have also developed newer construction methods and house designs, but these efforts are often directed to increasing the utilization of the companies' particular products. For example, all-steel, all-aluminum, or all-concrete houses are designed, or, on the other hand, an appliance manufacturer designs all-electrical (his electrical products) houses or all-gas houses. The objective is to pack the house with the manufacturer's products, and production costs of the house are a secondary consideration. See the discussion of experimental housing designs in Burnham Kelly, *The Prefabrication of Houses,* New York: The Technology Press of M.I.T. and Wiley, 1951, pp. 28–46.

materially reduces the amount of fitting which the bricklayer has to do to complete the wall. Moreover, where cutting of materials is necessary, the remainder from the cut is also of a modular dimension and can be more easily fitted into the structure. For materials dealers, modular coordination makes possible a reduction in the variety of sizes stocked, with a consequent cut in inventory costs. In short, dimensional coordination constitutes a first tentative step in the direction of the parts-standardization systems used in other industries.[50]

Although modular coordination may contribute to some lowering of costs, it is probably not sufficient to warrant any optimism about major cost reductions in the foreseeable future. The system still calls for the handling and assembling of a myriad of constituent pieces at the building site. More fundamental economies would require a reduction in the number of separate parts handled at the site by transferring most of the "pieces" of the house to the factory where they would be assembled into major components. Prefabrication of component parts permits more extensive use of power equipment and labor specialization, thus lowering costs. The component, completely factory finished and installed at the site, would need no more labor expended on it.[51]

Architects and builders would design houses using premanufactured component parts ordered from the factory in the quantities needed. Wall panels would be delivered with surfaces completely finished in the desired colors and including wiring and electrical outlets where needed. Roof panels, with roofing attached at the shop, would be assembled on the house. The builder, after fitting the wall and roof panels together, would then seal the joints to finish the frame. The mechanical core, including plumbing, heating, and kitchen equipment, would be installed as one unit and hooked up to the utility lines. In this way, inefficient site labor would be replaced by the efficiency of the factory.

With prefabrication, all major components of the house including foundation, exterior walls, interior walls, floors, ceilings, roof, and mechanical core would be purchased from manufacturers as specified in the house design. With components finished in the factory and assembled at the site, the traditional chain of materials dealers and trade subcontractors would be broken and the builder would simply serve as a parts assembler. The system would permit a variety of output so that both the custom-home buyer and

---

[50] Housing and Home Finance Agency, *Basic Principles of Modular Coordination,* Washington: Government Printing Office, 1953. For further refinements in dimensional coordination see *Design and the Production of Houses, op.cit.,* pp. 224–31.

[51] For an extended discussion of component systems in house design and building see *Design and the Production of Houses, op.cit.,* esp. pp. 68–72, 231–9.

operative builder could select units suited to the family's needs from a diversity of designs.

This building system is currently receiving much attention from industry representatives. However, given the structure of the industry, and the propensity of suppliers to push research in their own products, no agency is presently able to support the unified research program necessary to overcome the technical obstacles which impede a profitable reorganization of residential building. In industrial building, for example, curtain-wall construction has proved to be a cheap and economical building method. Yet its commercial development depended upon extensive experiments by customers large enough to bear the cost burden before the curtain wall could be widely used.[52] In general, no one in residential building is prepared to stand this kind of expense. It is imperative, therefore, that government provide the funds for reseach into the design and production problems associated with the development of lower-cost housing.

As in all other areas of knowledge, what we know about housing is minute compared to the challenge before us. For example, minimum structural standards for houses in various climates have never been systematically worked out.[53] Furthermore, the development of off-site manufacturing techniques needs experiment in housing designs which can utilize the technique and research into the best ways to break down the house into suitable component units. There are, also, a whole host of technical problems to be solved before components prefabrication can be undertaken on a large scale. Development of better and quicker ways to join pieces of wood together, i.e., glues and other bonding agents; durable interior and exterior finishes applicable in one coat at the factory; discovery of sealants and gaskets to make joints between component units weathertight and strong; wall panels and roofs which are strong and lightweight; easily installed foundation units; simplified mechanical cores—these are only a few of the many technical production problems which must be solved by or for the residential construction industry.[54]

Concurrently, government research can develop performance standards for house structures and materials. At present, little is known in this area and consumers and builders lack bench marks against which they can measure the in-place cost and performance of new structures and materials.

[52] General Motors Technical Center was one of the early examples of curtain-wall construction. Since cost was not so important a factor to GM it could afford the several attempts necessary to find the best bonding and caulking compounds for satisfactory performance. *Ibid.*, p. 93.

[53] Ralph J. Johnson, "Technological Changes in Residential Construction, 1961–70," *Study of Mortgage Credit, op.cit.*, pp. 140–1.

[54] *Design and the Production of Housing, op.cit.*, pp. 78–82, and Chap. 6 and 7.

To illustrate, without standards it is hard to judge whether a new wall panel is strong enough to perform adequately in a house or to know whether a new paint provides a better wearing surface than paints presently on the market. Furthermore, the establishment of performance standards and the devising of methods to test structures and materials furnish a foundation for the development of local building codes that do not obstruct progress in residential construction. Much discussion elsewhere has dwelt on the need to change local building codes if housing costs are to be reduced.[55]

How successfully we can cut housing prices no one can say. Past experience with research in many areas suggests that over time many technical problems can be solved with an adequate research program. Of course, the rate at which we move toward those goals depends upon how much of our resources we currently want to commit to achieve them. It is conceivable that a large enough program of research and development could give us a whole new housing industry within a short period of time. The rate of development we have presently chosen is very slow when compared with rates which might be achieved if a greater effort were to be made.

SUGGESTED READINGS

Books and Pamphlets

G. H. Beyer, *Housing: A Factual Analysis* (New York: Macmillan, 1958).

M. Colean and R. Newcomb, *Stabilizing Construction: The Record and Potential* (New York: McGraw-Hill, 1952).

L. Grebler, D. M. Blank, and L. Winnick, *Capital Formation in Residential Real Estate* (Princeton: National Bureau of Economic Research and Princeton University Press, 1956).

L. Grebler, *Production of New Housing* (New York: Social Science Research Council, 1950).

W. Haber and H. W. Levinson, *Labor Relations and Productivity in the Building Trades* (Ann Arbor: Bureau of Industrial Relations, 1956).

B. Kelly and Associates, *Design and the Production of Houses* (New York: McGraw-Hill, 1959).

B. Kelly, *The Prefabrication of Houses* (New York: The Technology Press of M.I.T. and Wiley, 1951).

S. J. Maisel, *Housebuilding in Transition* (Berkeley: University of California Press, 1953).

[55] Maisel, *op.cit.*, pp. 246–49. Also see *Design and the Production of Houses, op.cit.*, Chap. 9.

Government Publications

Bureau of Labor Statistics, *Structure of the Residential Building Industry in 1949,* Bulletin No. 1170 (Washington, 1954).

Housing and Home Finance Agency, *Basic Principles of Modular Coordination* (Washington, 1953).

Housing and Home Finance Agency, *Eleventh Annual Report, 1957* (Washington, 1958).

Subcommittee on Housing, Senate Committee on Banking and Currency, *Study of Mortgage Credit* (Washington, 1958).

Journal and Magazine Articles

F. E. Balderston, "Scale of Output and Internal Organization of the Firm," *The Quarterly Journal of Economics,* Vol. LXIX, February 1955.

Fortune, "Housing: The Stalled Revolution," Vol. LV, April 1957.

Fortune, "The Coming Changes in Housing," Vol. LX, August 1959.

Fortune, "The Industry Capitalism Forgot," Vol. XXXVI, August 1947.

House and Home, various issues.

J. Schmookler, "Bigness, Fewness, and Research," *Journal of Political Economy,* Vol. LXVII, December 1959.

O. H. Steiner, "The Arithmetic of Slum Clearance," *The New Republic,* November 16, 1959.

L. Winnick, "Housing: Has There Been a Downward Shift in Consumers' Preferences?" *The Quarterly Journal of Economics,* Vol. LXIX, February 1955.

Chapter 5

WALTER ADAMS

The Steel Industry

SECTION I: INTRODUCTION

America's steel industry is the most powerful in the world. Its plant capacity is almost double that of all "iron curtain" countries combined. Its product is the basic ingredient of our industrial civilization. Both in peace and war, the American economy depends on steel and is vitally affected by the policies and practices of the steel industry.

History

Before 1898, the steel industry was the scene of active and, at times, destructive competition. In this early period, various gentlemen's agreements and pools were organized in an effort to control the production of steel rails, billets, wire, nails and other products, but the outstanding characteristic of these agreements was the "frequency with which they collapsed." [1] Their weakness was that inherent in any pool or gentlemen's agreement, namely that "60 per cent of the agreers are gentlemen, 30 per cent just act like gentlemen, and 10 per cent neither are nor act like gentlemen." If production and prices were to be controlled, these loose-knit agreements had to be superseded by more stable forms of organization. The latter came upon the industry with a suddenness and intensity seldom paralleled in American industrial history.

From 1898 to 1900, a vast concentration movement took place in the steel industry. Large companies such as Federal Steel, National Steel, National Tube, American Bridge, and American Sheet Steel were organized. Dom-

---

[1] H. R. Seager and C. A. Gulick, *Trust and Corporation Problems*, New York: Harper, 1929, p. 216. This book is an excellent source on the early history of U.S. Steel.

144

inated by three financial interest groups—Carnegie, Morgan, and Moore—
these consolidations did not succeed in bringing "stability" to the industry.
In fact, a fight between the newly formed giants seemed unavoidable.

Since each of the major interest groups was peculiarly vulnerable in case
a "battle between the giants" materialized, and since cooperation promised
to be more profitable than competition, stubbornness yielded to reason. In
1901, with the initiative of Charles Schwab, J. P. Morgan, and a corporation lawyer named James B. Dill, the interested parties agreed to form the
"combination of combinations"—the U.S. Steel Corporation which at the
time of its formation controlled approximately 65 per cent of the nation's
steel capacity. The size of the $62,500,000 promotion fee which accrued to
the Morgan banking syndicate immediately aroused "the suspicion that
here, as in earlier combinations, the security issue was greatly inflated." [2]
Later investigation by the Commissioner of Corporations has justified this
suspicion, for it was found that of the corporation's total capitalization of
$1,402,846,817 only about half, $676,000,000, represented investment in
tangible property. The rest, i.e., $726,846,817 minus reasonable allowance
for good will, indicates, of course, the amount of excess capitalization or
stock watering [3] which, over a period of years, was eventually squeezed out
of the capital structure and replaced with tangible assets in the form of
mills and mines.

Considerable disagreement has attended discussions of the motives behind the organization of the U.S. Steel Corporation. The announced motives were to form a completely integrated steel company; to secure the advantages of the most advanced technical organization; and to develop an
extensive export trade. Judge Gary testified that the latter was the "dominating factor" favoring the creation of the corporation.[4] Most disinterested
observers, however, agree that the "intent to monopolize" played a significant and perhaps dominant role. The policies of the corporation, subsequent
to its organization in 1901, seem to bear out this opinion; for the corporation proceeded to acquire properties which would put it in a position to
dominate the steel industry. Especially significant was the acquisition of
essential raw material assets, particularly coking coal and iron ore mines.

By 1907, however, the corporation became concerned with more immediate problems than the long-run elimination of *potential* competition through

[2] *Ibid.*, p. 224.

[3] In his testimony before the Stanley Committee in 1911, Judge Moore defended such
stock watering as not at all unusual. Said the judge: "Everybody knows what they [sic!]
are getting when they get common stock. . . . They know they are not getting anything that represents assets."

[4] *Hearings before the House Committee on Investigation of the U.S. Steel Corporation,*
Vol. I, p. 104; hereafter referred to as *Stanley Hearings* (1911).

a monopolization of some raw material supplies. It had to face a spasm of *active* price competition which had been brought on by the business panic of that year. To meet this challenge and to restore price stability under its own leadership, it innovated the famous Gary dinners. The purpose of these dinners—in the words of the host, the president of U.S. Steel—was "to maintain to a reasonable extent the equilibrium of business, to prevent utter demoralization of business and destructive competition." [5] Mr. Gary *achieved* this objective by urging "his guests, who represented fully 90 per cent of the industry, that they cooperate in holding prices where they were." [6] He exhorted them like a Methodist preacher at a camp meeting to follow the price leadership of U.S. Steel. There was no need for any formal agreements, no need to force a group of reluctant competitors into a cooperative arrangement. U.S. Steel merely assumed the lead incumbent on a firm its size; its rivals followed, fully realizing the security and profitability of co-operation. Under these circumstances, the Gary dinners were a singular success and presented but another vivid illustration of Adam Smith's observation that "people of the same trade seldom meet together, even for merriment and diversion, but the conversation ends in a conspiracy against the public or in some contrivance to raise prices."

Available evidence indicates that the dinners were held at irregular intervals until 1911. However, when the government became increasingly suspicious of their price-fixing function and when it finally filed suit for the dissolution of U.S. Steel, the dinners were abruptly abandoned. But the damage had been done. The Corporation stood accused in the Federal courts as a monopoly, and the government demanded the extreme penalty—dissolution.

Due to the outbreak of World War I, the case was not decided until 1920 when the fervor of earlier trust-busting campaigns had died down. By a vote of 4 to 3, the Supreme Court decided against dissolution.[7] Without considering the effects of price quotation under the Pittsburgh-Plus system, the court declared that mere size was no offense. While conceding that U.S. Steel was guilty of an attempt to monopolize the steel industry, the court maintained that such a monopoly had never actually been achieved. However, if any one factor responsible for the court's rejection of the government plea were singled out, it would undoubtedly be the friendly attitude which U.S. Steel evidenced toward its competitors. This fact more than anything else probably explains why U.S. Steel was allowed to survive while

[5] *Stanley Hearings*, Vol. I, p. 264.
[6] Ida M. Tarbell, *The Life of Elbert H. Gary*, New York: Appleton, 1930, p. 205.
[7] *United States* v. *United States Steel Corp.*, 251 U.S. 417 (1920).

the Standard Oil Company and the American Tobacco Company were unceremoniously dissolved. This was a vindication of a policy very close to Judge Gary's heart, a policy over which there was considerable dispute with the corporation's board of directors; for Gary's "Directors, worthy men but of a cruder age, were honestly puzzled. It was bewildering to hear their Chairman preach the community of interests of all steelmakers, to see him consistently refusing to use the Corporation's size as a club over the rest of the industry. Destructive competition, they pointed out, had made hundreds of millions for Rockefeller's oil trust. But the day came when Gary could point out that the oil trust was busted and that the steel trust had survived, and that its survival was largely due to his policy of 'friendly competition.' " [8]

After 1920, U.S. Steel continued to dominate the industry, although its percentage control over total industry sales declined steadily. The corporation remained sufficiently big, however, to keep its competitors "in line" without threats and without displays of force. The friendly competition, which had paid such handsome dividends in the past, endured as the basic characteristic of the industry.

Then, in 1929, came the big depression. For the steel industry, it was a traumatic experience causing widespread unemployment and a terrific drop in production. Production decreased from 63 million tons in 1929 to 26 million tons in 1933, while employment during the same period fell from 440,000 to 213,000 men (four-fifths of whom were employed only part time). In 1932, plants were operated at 19.5 per cent of capacity. Under the pressure of a rapidly falling demand, individual firms began to grant unofficial and secret price concessions in order to increase plant utilization and thereby spread fixed costs over a larger volume of output. Even the formerly effective basing-point system seemed powerless to check the activity of panicky price cutters and "chiselers" with the result that the stable structure of uniform delivered prices broke down.

When anarchy seemed certain to gain control of the industry's price determination process, the National Industrial Recovery Act of 1934 was passed. Under the NRA code of fair competition—drafted by steel leaders and approved by the President—the steel industry was almost totally immune against antitrust attack. It could, for the first time in its history, fix prices legally—or quasi-legally at any rate. So enthusiastic were steel executives over this government sanctioned price-maintenance scheme that Charles M. Schwab, former President of the Bethlehem Steel Corporation, claimed

---

[8] "U.S. Steel: I," reprinted from *Fortune*, Vol. XIII, March 1936, p. 157, by special permission of the Editors. Copyright Time, Inc.

that never before in his fifty years' experience in the trade had he seen a year "when the business of the industry could be conducted on a common-sense basis." Little wonder can be expressed at this enthusiasm when it is considered that all price concessions under the NRA had to be approved by the Code Authority for the Steel Industry. This Code Authority consisted of none other than the Board of Directors of the American Iron and Steel Institute, the official trade association of the industry, in which the nine largest companies exercised majority (52 per cent) control.

Even government sanctioned price-fixing, however, could not provide more than a palliative for the depression ills of the steel industry. The fact remained that, given a low level of demand for producer goods, price rigidity alone could not solve the basic problems of the steel industry in the thirties. The one sure way of getting steel out of the doldrums was by restoring full employment in the economy as a whole. This occurred only when production was stimulated by the outbreak of World War II and by the eventual entry of the United States into that conflict.

During the war, the industry made great forward strides in production and employment and by 1943 operated at 98.1 per cent of capacity. Prices, of course, were carefully regulated by the OPA and intricate priority and allocation systems were worked out to govern the distribution of steel among essential users. After V-J Day it was generally expected that these regulations would be relaxed and the industry return to its "normal" methods of price determination. This expectation, however, never materialized simply because steel remained a scarce commodity during the postwar boom. A pent-up demand, generated during the war years, and the failure of an expected business recession to occur after the cessation of hostilities made the demand for this basic commodity far in excess of the industry's capacity to supply it. A gray market, which by 1948 reached $500,000,000 proportions,[9] developed due mainly to the insistence of industry leaders, the public, and the government that no substantial upward adjustment of steel prices take place. This decision by the large steel producers to pit their judgment against the judgment of the market in the valuation of steel necessitated the institution of a "private" OPA and allocation system to ration off the commodity's scarce supply. This, in turn, made it imperative that the government grant the industry temporary exemption from the antitrust laws to permit cooperation among the producers in the execution of the new allocation scheme. Eventually, with the outbreak of the Korean War in 1950, many of the detailed World War II controls were reimposed on the industry. But, with or without controls, the industry adhered to its basic pattern of rigid, administered prices.

[9] "That Daffy Gray Market," *Fortune*, Vol. XXXVII, May 1948.

SECTION II: MARKET STRUCTURE AND PRICE POLICY

Market Structure

The iron and steel industry is divided into four principal branches—iron ore mining, pig-iron production, steel making, and steel rolling. Depending on the function performed, the individual companies composing the industry are classified as integrated, semiintegrated, and nonintegrated. Integrated companies are those which operate in all four of the industry's branches. Semiintegrated concerns do not make their own pig-iron, but purchase it to make steel and rolled products. Nonintegrated producers either make pig-iron exclusively (these are the so-called merchant blast furnaces) or buy ingots or semifinished steel for rolling and further processing.

As is evident from Table 1, the steel industry today is—structurally speaking—an oligopoly and is dominated by a relatively few, large, integrated producers. These, taken together, own or control about 85 per cent of iron

TABLE 1

Productive Capacity of Major Steel Companies in the United States

Company	Pig Iron [a]		Steel Ingots [a]		Finished Hot-Rolled [b]	
	Net Tons	Per-centage of Total	Net Tons	Per-centage of Total	Net Tons	Per-centage of Total
U.S. Steel	31,093,700	32.9	41,916,000	28.4	28,293,910	27.3
Bethlehem	15,000,000	15.9	23,000,000	15.6	15,899,000	15.3
Republic	7,902,000	8.3	12,742,000	8.6	8,285,000	7.9
National	5,750,000	6.1	7,000,000	4.7	5,239,000	5.1
Jones & Laughlin	5,061,000	5.3	8,000,000	5.4	5,210,000	5.0
Youngstown	4,140,000	4.4	6,750,000	4.6	4,935,000	4.8
Inland	3,325,300	3.5	6,500,000	4.4	4,490,000	4.3
Armco	2,853,000	3.0	6,400,000	4.3	4,414,100	4.3
Wheeling	1,954,000	2.1	2,400,000	1.6	1,856,000	1.8
Kaiser	1,912,100	2.0	2,933,000	2.0	1,158,000	1.1
Colorado F & I	1,463,600	1.5	2,836,500	1.9	2,059,500	2.0
McLouth	1,239,220	1.3	2,040,000	1.3	1,154,810	1.1
Total for 12 largest	81,693,920	86.3	122,517,500	83.0	82,994,320	80.1
All others	12,940,930	13.7	25,116,170	17.0	20,627,910	19.9
Grand Total	94,634,850	100.0	147,633,670	100.0	103,622,230	100.0

[a] This column shows annual capacities as of January 1, 1959, and is based on statistics supplied by the American Iron and Steel Institute.
[b] This column shows annual capacities as of January 1, 1957, as reported in American Iron and Steel Institute, *Directory of Iron and Steel Works of the United States and Canada*, 1957. Unfortunately, accurate statistics of later date are not available on finished hot-rolled steel capacity by companies.

ore reserves [10] and account for 87.3 per cent of blast furnace capacity, 83.0 per cent of ingot and "steel for casting" capacity, and 80.1 per cent of finished hot-rolled capacity.

Since Table 1 measures concentration in the industry as whole, it seriously understates the degree of concentration in particular product lines and particular market areas. The reason is simple; not every steel company produces every steel product or sells in every section of the country. Thus, taking the industry as a whole, the four largest ingot producers account for roughly 55 per cent of the output, whereas in some product lines—like skelp, tube rounds, steel piling, electrical sheets and strip, axles, joint bars, etc.—the four largest supply 100 per cent of the total. Also, since different companies specialize in different market areas, the regional concentration ratios are higher than the national. In the case of hot-rolled merchant bars, for example, the four largest producers control only 65 per cent of the industry's national capacity but 75 per cent of the capacity in the Northeastern states. It is fair to say, therefore, that regional and product concentration are higher than Table 1 would lead us to suspect.[11]

Historically, the present pattern of concentration has been shaped by four sets of forces. One of these, the relative decline of U.S. Steel, has resulted in some deconcentration. The other three—the government's disposal of World War II steel plants, the concentration of iron ore reserves, and the forward integration of the majors—have tended in the opposite direction, viz. to fortify and extend the oligopoly of the large integrated producers vis-a-vis their smaller rivals.

The Decline of U.S. Steel. The relative position of U.S. Steel in the industry has been declining ever since its formation in 1901, but this trend became especially pronounced during the period between the wars. Several factors were responsible for this development. First, U.S. Steel did not want to become too big for fear of prosecution under the antitrust laws. Judge Gary was impressed with the William Jennings Bryan rule that no business should be allowed to control more than 50 per cent of an industry. Gary felt that if U.S. steel confined itself "voluntarily to a size approved by the

[10] "Management and operation of iron-mining properties is concentrated in a few large companies which are either partly or wholly owned by the large iron and steel producers or otherwise closely affiliated with them." (U.S. Tariff Commission, "Iron and Steel," *War Changes in Industry Series*, Report No. 15, Washington, D.C., 1946, p. 88.) See also TNEC, *Hearings*, Pt. 18, p. 10426; Lake Superior Iron Ore Association, *Lake Superior Iron Ores*; also the *Mining Directory of Minnesota*, Minneapolis: Mines Experiment Station, University of Minnesota. Data on iron ore holdings in Michigan can be obtained from the Department of Conservation, Lansing, Michigan.

[11] Senate Subcommittee on Antitrust and Monopoly, *Administered Prices in Steel*, Senate Report No. 1387, Eighty-fifth Cong., 2d Sess., 1958, pp. 67–72; hereafter cited as *Kefauver Committee Report*.

most popular and trusted of radicals, [it] surely cannot be attacked for monopoly." [12]

Second, starting in the twenties, the "independents" in the industry took part in an aggressive consolidation movement. In 1922, Bethlehem acquired all the properties of the large Lackawanna Steel Co. near Buffalo, N.Y.; it erected extensive modern facilities at Sparrows Point, Md.; it acquired the large Cambria Steel Co. (1923); and, in 1930, bought the assets of the Pacific Coast Steel Co. and the Southern California Iron and Steel Co. (Its attempt to merge with Youngstown Sheet and Tube, the nation's sixth largest steel producer, was blocked by judicial decree in 1958.) In 1930 another powerful independent arose when a merger between the Republic Iron and Steel Co., the Central Alloy Steel Corp., the Donner Steel Co., and the Bourne Fuller Co. was consummated. A third important merger during this period resulted in the formation of the National Steel Corp. (1929), which united steel plants in the West Virginia and Detroit areas and the blast furnace properties of the M. A. Hanna Co. of Cleveland.[13]

A third factor contributing to the relative decline of the U.S. Steel Corporation was the gradual transformation in the demand for steel from heavy products (such as rails, plates, and structural shapes) to lighter products (such as sheets and strips). This shift in demand had important repercussions on the position of U.S. Steel which was deeply committed, as far as plant capacity was concerned, to the production of heavy products. What made this shift in demand even more painful for the corporation was the geographic source of the new demand—especially that of the growing auto industry—which was often located at a considerable distance from the corporation's main plants. To the extent that the smaller companies were more flexible, they could, of course, accommodate themselves more readily to these changing patterns of steel consumption and thus improve their position relative to U.S. Steel.

A fourth factor affecting the position of the industry's giant was the impact of changing technology. Here U.S. Steel lagged significantly behind its integrated rivals. In 1926, the American Rolling Mill Co. bought the patents on the continuous rolling mill process which was the major American advance in steel technology during the interwar period. Republic Steel became the leader in the growing alloy steel field. Finally, technological innovations which permitted an increasingly large use of scrap in the production of steel ingots tended to reduce the value of U.S. Steel's heavy in-

[12] Tarbell, *op.cit.*, pp. 257–8.
[13] For a history of the merger movement in the steel industry, see "Steel—Acquisitions, Mergers, and Expansion of 12 Major Companies, 1900 to 1950," *Hearings before the House Small Business Committee,* Eighty-first Cong., 2d Sess., 1950.

vestment in iron ore mines and blast furnace capacity. The growing use of scrap also tended to shift the most advantageous location pattern for the industry away from coal-producing regions and toward consumption areas which were rich sources of scrap.[14] This technological change—reinforced as it was by a change in the type of steel products demanded—put U.S. Steel in an unenviable position. On the one hand it was difficult for the corporation to decrease its heavy investment in the Pittsburgh area; on the other hand, a relocation of some of the capacity concentrated there became imperative because technological change was rendering it—in part, at least —locationally anachronistic.

A final factor contributing to the relative decline of U.S. Steel was the depression of the thirties which made the maintenance of price conformity under the basing point system more difficult. The corporation was not completely successful in protecting its recognized position as the industry's price leader against the inroads of "chiselers" and secret price cutters.

Summing up, we can say that "the competitive significance of these relatively rapid changes was that a number of independents, either foreseeing the changes or recognizing their importance as they occurred, accommodated themselves to them. . . . In contrast, United States Steel was either unprepared to shift as markets shifted or did not see the necessity for doing so." The result was that the corporation lagged behind the industry as a whole in the competitive race, a lag which is best measured by the frequent failure of its profits to keep pace with those of the "independents." [15]

The Disposal of World War II Steel Plants. The second set of forces which has affected the structural organization of the steel industry was the government's policy in the disposition of surplus steel plants after World War II. Also important in this connection was the Supreme Court's decision in the *Columbia Steel* case.

At the end of the war—as of October 8, 1945—the War Assets Administration held the following steel and related facilities: (1) 29 plants, valued at more than five million dollars each, which were technically capable of disposal as independent operating units; (2) twenty plants, valued at more than five million dollars each, which were classified as "scrambled with privately owned facilities"; and (3) plants, costing less than five million dollars

---

[14] See W. Isard, "Some Locational Factors in the Iron and Steel Industry since the Early Nineteenth Century," *Journal of Political Economy,* June 1948; also W. Isard and W. M. Capron, "The Future Locational Pattern of Iron and Steel Production in the United States," *Journal of Political Economy,* April 1949.

[15] From E. B. Alderfer and H. E. Michl, *Economics of American Industry,* p. 76. Copyright 1942. Courtesy of the McGraw-Hill Book Co., Inc., New York. In recent years the Corporation has caught up by modernizing its plants and changing its product mix. Nevertheless, it has not improved its relative position in the industry.

each, which were classified as partly "scrambled." The lion's share of the government's investment in steel facilities was in the first category. It amounted to 770 million dollars and represented 59 per cent of the government's total investment in this area.[16]

Of the 29 larger plants capable of independent operation, four were integrated steel plants: the Geneva plant (erected at a cost of $202 million) whose wartime operator was U.S. Steel; a Chicago plant operated by Republic Steel during the war (costing $92 million); a plant at Houston, Texas, operated by Armco (valued at $37 million); and the Homestead, Pa., plant operated by U.S. Steel (valued at $124 million). These important plants, with the exception of Geneva, carried a purchase option by their wartime operators and two of the four might have been difficult to run by anybody else. Whatever the considerations which influenced the government's decision, however, the fact remains that these plants were sold to their wartime managers, i.e., to the large integrated producers of the industry. The effect of this action, whatever the justification for it, was to strengthen the hand of oligopoly in the steel industry and to encourage perpetuation of the status quo in the industry's economic structure. Especially significant is the fact that, in some areas—especially in the far West—the disposition of these plants allowed the major producers to increase considerably their percentage control of output in the local market. This is made clear when we consider that acquisition of the Geneva plant (built at a cost of $202 million to the government and sold to U.S. Steel for approximately $47 million) enabled U.S. Steel to increase its total capacity in the Pacific coast and mountain states from 17.3 to 39 per cent, and to bring its total of steel ingot capacity in the area up to 51 per cent.

The oligopoly structure of the steel industry was further strengthened by the Supreme Court decision in the Columbia Steel case.[17] This decision sanctioned the acquisition of a relatively small—small on a national scale —Pacific coast plant by United States Steel. The company in question (Consolidated Steel) accounted for 11 per cent of the total fabricated structural products made in the West. Together with United States Steel it would account for 25 to 30 per cent of total fabricated structural products produced in the eleven-state Pacific coast and mountain states region. The merger of Consolidated with U.S. Steel constituted—in the minority opinion of the Supreme Court—a "purchase for control, a purchase for control of a market for which United States Steel has in the past had to compete but which it no longer wants left to the uncertainties that competition in the West may

[16] U.S. Tariff Commission, *op.cit.*, p. 71.
[17] See *U.S. versus Columbia Steel Company et al.*, 334 U.S. 495 (1948).

engender." The effect of the merger was not only to encourage concentration in the newly developing markets of the West, but to permit the growth of a major company which, according to Justice Douglas, was "big enough."

The Concentration of Iron Ore Reserves. The concentrated ownership of iron ore reserves has also tended to fortify the oligopoly control of the integrated producers, and it appears rather unlikely that the development of new iron ore sources will in any way upset the status quo. In fact, the control over this vital raw material will, according to present indications, be more concentrated in the future than in the past, and thus have a profound influence on future competition in steel making. As the former Secretary of the Interior observed: "I do not think it would make any difference whether you had five companies in the steel business or 500 companies . . . if one or two companies controlled the source of raw material. The monopolistic features would be there in the controlling point." [18]

Today, the nine largest integrated steel producers and the four major iron ore merchants account for over 95 per cent of the "measured" reserves in the nation's richest iron ore area—the Lake Superior District. [19] This district contains the highest grade (lowest cost) ores, and yields approximately 85 per cent of our annual iron ore requirements. In the other iron ore districts—the northeastern, southeastern, and western—the integrated companies also exercise substantial control, at least with respect to high grade ores.

Of the nine major steel companies, only U.S. Steel has more than enough ore to support its steel making operations. Its competitors—including such companies as Bethlehem, Republic, Armco, Inland, Sharon, and Wheeling —lack adequate iron ore reserves and depend on the corporation for a portion of their supplies. The corporation is thus in an enviable position, for it can, if it desires, withhold strategic ore supplies from the market. "Whether exercised or not, this power to deprive competitors of ore is a potential weapon to bring recalcitrants into line and keep them there." Moreover, "as shrinking reserves, and a steadily tightening ore market enhance the importance of [the Corporation's] ore, the strategic position of United States Steel in this regard will be strengthened." [20]

[18] Subcommittee on the Study of Monopoly Power, House Judiciary Committee, *Report on the Iron and Steel Industry*, Eighty-first Cong., 2d Sess., 1950, p. 19; hereafter cited as *Celler Report.*

[19] Federal Trade Commission, *Report on the Control of Iron Ore*, 1952, p. 87; hereafter cited as *FTC Iron Ore Report.* For the entry implications of this concentration pattern, see Joe S. Bain, *Barriers to New Competition*, Cambridge: Harvard University Press, 1956, pp. 153–4.

[20] *FTC Iron Ore Report*, pp. 100–1. During the period of high steel production following World War II, the corporation's ore sales to outsiders have steadily declined. In 1945, the corporation sold 9,276,000 tons; in 1946, 7,400,000 tons; in 1947, 6,900,000

The four major ore merchants offer the small ore users and semiintegrated steel companies little hope of an assured iron ore supply. Nor are they likely to provide an open market in competition with the integrated majors. The fact is that, by 1948, the ore merchants had virtually become satellites of the major steel companies to whom they were tied by partnership arrangements, long-term supply contracts, and joint ownership. Approximately half of the ore handled by these houses went to the nine big steel companies under existing partnership arrangements. Almost all of the remaining ore was tied up under long-term contracts with the same nine companies. As a result, the spot market for iron ore, so far as sales by the ore merchants was concerned, has practically disappeared.[21]

These facts led the Federal Trade Commission to some rather grim conclusions regarding the long-range prospects of the nonintegrated ore users. According to the commission, the independents "who have survived have done so by digging in along the crevices of the industry. Their access to iron ore is not such as to give them encouragement in expanding their operations, though it is enough to keep them going at the present time. This kind of predicament breeds neither independence of outlook nor competitive behavior. To a considerable extent the smaller users of iron ore exist by sufferance; they are hardly in a position to be a vital element in competition." [22] Certainly, the dependence on major competitors (or on ore merchants affiliated with these competitors) weakens the independents in the steel market. It reduces their incentives to be nonconformists on prices or other matters of business policy. With the sword of Damocles over them, the independents tend to be congenial and cooperative—a small price, indeed, for the privilege of survival.

The position of the independent steel producer is not likely to be improved by impending changes in the ore situation. These changes—necessitated by the gradual depletion of high grade domestic reserves—involve a growing reliance on foreign ores and the beneficiation of domestic taconites. Both these developments may further aggravate the prospects of an assured raw material supply for the independent producer.

In the control of foreign ore deposits the major integrated companies seem to enjoy a commanding lead. The extent of their deposits is indicated by the following estimates of expected annual yields by the end of 1960:

---

tons; in 1948, 5,700,000 tons; and in 1949, 4,000,000 tons. This has led some ore purchasers to charge—and Mr. Fairless of U.S. Steel to deny—that the corporation has indeed *used* its power to withhold strategic ore supplies from its competitors. (*Celler Report*, p. 23.)

[21] See *FTC Iron Ore Report*, p. 82.
[22] *Ibid.*, p. 77.

(1) ten to fifteen million tons of Venezuelan ore controlled by U.S. Steel; (2) two to three million tons of Venezuelan ore controlled by Bethlehem; (3) two million tons of Liberian ore controlled by Republic; (4) ten million tons of Labrador ore controlled by the Iron Ore Company of Canada (a joint venture of Republic, Armco, Youngstown, National, Wheeling, and Hanna Ore Co.). An additional seven to eight million tons per year are anticipated from Canada, Chile, Sweden, Cuba, and other regions,[23] but these supplies are also expected to go largely to the integrated producers. The pattern of foreign ore holdings, therefore, is such as to offer little hope for a breach in the oligopoly control of the major steel companies.

A similar conclusion seems justified with regard to the beneficiation of domestic taconites. This development, involving an investment of $15 to $20 per ton of ore capacity, may yield an annual ore supply of 25 million tons by 1970. But here again, the majors appear to be far in the lead. U.S. Steel owns the largest high grade taconite holdings of any steel company, and its predominant position "cannot easily be threatened." [24] The other companies with interests in taconite development are associated in two major cooperative ventures. Wheeling, Armco, and Cleveland-Cliffs (an ore merchant) are joint owners of the Reserve Mining Company. Bethlehem, Youngstown, and Pickands & Mather (an ore merchant) are joint owners of Erie Mining Company. Given this controlling lead in the commercial use of low grade (taconite) ores, the prospects for the smaller steel companies are none too bright. The latter "neither own any substantial share of these deposits nor possess the capital necessary for their processing." [25]

In sum, the concentration of iron ore reserves—past, present, and future —helps explain the oligopoly structure of the steel industry, and the commanding role of its leader, the U.S. Steel Corporation. Whether recent technological innovations, or the substitutability of scrap for pig iron, or the availability of low grade (i.e., high cost) ores will change this picture, remains to be seen.

Forward Integration by the Majors. The forward integration by the major producers has also been a factor in the strengthening of the steel oligopoly. In the past, a good part of steel fabrication was left to the smaller independents—the semiintegrated and nonintegrated finishers. The dominance of the integrated companies in this branch of the industry was always much less than in the production of pig-iron, ingots, and semifinished steel. Since 1939, however, the situation has changed. Large steel producers have integrated forward; large steel consumers have integrated backward;

[23] *Celler Report*, p. 16.
[24] *FTC Report on Iron Ore*, p. 135.
[25] *Celler Report*, p. 20.

and independents have been subjected to at least one major vertical price squeeze. In periods of steel shortage, independent fabricators have also complained of a supply squeeze.

That the steel companies have, in fact, been extending themselves into the fabrication of finished products is apparent from the investigations of the Senate Small Business Committee. The committee found that the percentage of hot-rolled sheets, for example, that went to fabricating subsidiaries of large integrated companies rather than to independent fabricators increased from 5.7 per cent of the total output in 1940 to 10.5 per cent in 1947. The committee also reported that "since 1939 the United States Steel Corp. has purchased three steel-drum firms, an oil-well equipment company, a pump manufacturer, a wire-cloth fabricator, a prefabricated housing company, and a fabricator of structural steel, plates, bridges, and so forth. During this same period, Bethlehem Steel Corp. has acquired two steel-drum firms (including the purchase of 28.9 per cent of the stock of the extremely important Rheem Manufacturing Co.), three concerns in the oil-well equipment field, two shipyards, a forge company, and a tank company. Republic Steel Corp., third largest steel producer and a leading producer of alloys, has purchased during this interval a producer of steel drums, a manufacturer of wire and screens, a drawn-steel company, a metal window firm, and a culvert company. And Jones & Laughlin, fourth largest steel producer, has acquired two steel-drum companies." [26]

This forward integration—achieved largely through mergers and acquisitions—has, in some cases, resulted in the virtual disappearance of entire "small business" industries. Thus steel drum fabrication was almost completely absorbed by the basic steel producers, a process which *Iron Age* described as follows:

Long, long ago, in 1939, before the words postwar and planning were wedded, the manufacture of heavy steel barrels and drums was a rather volatile business firmly in the hands of a large number of highly individualistic entrepreneurs. Most of these fabricators had started on a precarious shoe string and were justifiably vocal in their pride of success in the classical Horatio Alger Pluck and Luck Tradition.

A few weeks ago, the purchase of Bennett Mfg. Co., Chicago, by the United States Steel Corp. pretty well completed the capture of the entire barrel and drum business by the major steel producers. Some 87 per cent of the business, representing about 435,000 tons of steel consumption yearly has been corralled by the mills and the remaining 64,500 tons of independent capacity will probably remain so for a variety of reasons.[27]

[26] Senate Small Business Committee, *Changes in Steel Distribution, 1940–1947,* Eightieth Cong., 2d Sess., 1948, p. 4.
[27] *The Iron Age,* September 21, 1944, p. 103; quoted in FTC, *The Merger Movement: A Summary Report,* 1948, p. 46.

The significance of such forward integration is twofold: it tends, on the one hand, to extend the oligopoly of steel making into steel fabrication; and, on the other, to tie up an increasing portion of the semifinished steel which formerly was available on the open market. As a result, nonintegrated steel users, dependent on the open market for their supplies, may be deprived of essential raw materials and find it increasingly difficult to stay in business.[28]

In this respect, the position of the independent fabricator is further aggravated by two other developments. Some major steel *consumers* have integrated backward, i.e., gone into steel making. Others have, in order to assure themselves of a more steady steel supply, entered into special contracts with steel producers. General Motors has, for example, granted a $28,000,000 loan to Jones & Laughlin and a $40,000,000 loan to Republic to finance the expansion of their Cleveland facilities. These companies have, in turn, obligated themselves to supply a portion of their increased steel output to General Motors. Other automobile companies have entered into similar contracts.[29] Whatever their purpose from the viewpoint of the automobile companies, the effect of these arrangements is to restrict further—especially in periods of steel shortage—the steel supply of the independent, nonintegrated fabricators.

One other aspect of the vertical integration movement in the steel industry is noteworthy, viz. the price squeeze. When forward integration by the majors is combined with a vertical price squeeze against the independents, there are likely to be fatalities. For, the nonintegrated fabricator—caught by the denial of supplies, on the one hand, and manipulation of his profit margin, on the other—may find survival unduly expensive, if not altogether impossible.

An example of how the vertical squeeze works is afforded by the price changes instituted in the spring of 1948. In February of that year, U.S. Steel raised *semifinished* steel prices by an average of $5 per ton, and other companies promptly followed. Three months later, in May, U.S. Steel led the industry to a price reduction on *finished* steel, concentrating primarily on products made by semiintegrated and nonintegrated mills. This move, which

---

[28] This is especially true in times of steel shortage, when the independents complain about the alleged increase in steel shipments to the steel companies' own fabricating subsidiaries; the alleged increase in steel shipments to the steel companies' own warehouses; and the alleged increase in the proportion of steel sold in the more expensive cold-rolled and other highly finished types at the expense of the less costly hot-rolled types. See FTC, *The Distribution of Steel Consumption, 1949–50,* 1952. On this point, see also Simon N. Whitney, *Antitrust Policies,* New York: Twentieth Century Fund, 1958, Vol. I, pp. 319–21.

[29] See "GM in Steel," *Business Week,* May 19, 1951, p. 26.

Iron Age characterized as "one of the most unusual in steel history,"[30] elicited the following conclusion from the Federal Trade Commission:

It is apparent that by raising the prices of semifinished steel in February and by cutting the prices on the products made therefrom in May, United States Steel Corp. applied a double squeeze on the smaller semi-integrated and nonintegrated mills. The leadership of United States Steel was followed by the other large integrated companies in both instances, though apparently somewhat more reluctantly on the second occasion. These companies were themselves caught in the squeeze when the prices of finished steel products were cut. However, their loss of revenue at the finished-steel level was partially offset by larger receipts for semifinished steel, whereas the nonintegrated companies, as a result of the double action, were squeezed at both the semifinished and finished levels.[31]

Such vertical price maneuvers are but one manifestation of the vertical integration movement, and the entry of the major producers into steel fabrication. The effect is to impose a serious handicap on the independent whose predicament arises from the fact that he is dependent on the integrated producers for his supply of raw materials, while simultaneously competing with them in the sale of finished products. The dangers implicit in this relationship were clearly set forth by *Iron Age*, the industry's own trade magazine. Said *Iron Age*:

For years, larger steel companies have sold huge quantities of semifinished steel to nonintegrated firms only to face competition from those companies in the sale of finished steel products. Now, with larger steel mills requiring semifinished steel for their own finishing mills, there is a marked disposition to drastically slash the tonnage of semifinished steel being shipped to the small, nonintegrated makers. For this reason, it is expected that unless management of the smaller companies can, like a few units in that category, find their own markets in the form of specialties or special services, the going may be so rough as to cause fatalities.[32]

As far as market structure is concerned, we can conclude therefore that, due to a variety of competitive forces, a single firm no longer dominates the steel industry; that this dominance is now shared by twelve large integrated producers who operate within an oligopoly framework. The companies follow a market strategy characteristic of oligopoly behavior, a fact which becomes more apparent from an analysis of the industry's price policy.

[30] *The Iron Age*, May 6, 1948, p. 125 B. That this was a price squeeze seems clearly to have been recognized by the late Senator Robert A. Taft who was then chairman of the Joint Committee on the Economic Report. See the interesting colloquy between Senator Taft and Benjamin Fairless, then president of U.S. Steel, in *Hearings before the Joint Committee on the Economic Report*, Eightieth Cong., 2d Sess., 1948, pp. 14–15. Some time after this hearing, Senator Taft is reported to have said that the power of the steel companies over prices seems to be such as perhaps to require some supervision in the public interest.

[31] FTC, *Monopolistic Practices and Small Business*, 1952, pp. 53–54.

[32] *The Iron Age*, January 3, 1946.

Price Policy

Price policy, especially in a basic industry like steel, is of crucial importance. It influences the amount of steel consumed in a given year and the extent to which capacity is utilized. It stimulates or retards steel-using industries. It sets a pattern for other basic industries, and thus plays a central role in the economy. Without too much exaggeration, one can say that "as steel goes, so goes the nation." Hence it is important to understand the industry's price policy and the underpinnings on which it rests, *viz.* basing points, price leadership, and price stability.

The Mechanics of Basing Point Pricing

Although it was officially abandoned in 1948, the basing point system is deeply imbedded in the philosophy of the steel industry and may again be used, at least in modified form, in times of recession. The mechanics are simple. Under the single-basing point (Pittsburgh-Plus) system, steel prices at any given delivery point were uniform—regardless of where the steel was shipped from. To achieve this uniformity, sellers did not have to meet in a smoke filled room or preview each others' bids. They simply had to adhere to the basing point formula of (1) uniform base prices, (2) uniform delivery charges, and (3) uniform prices for "extras" and "deductions."

(1) The base price was the charge for a ton of steel applicable at designated basing points and measuring up to standard specifications (gauge, thickness, length, chemical composition, and tolerance). Until 1924, Pittsburgh was the only basing point and all steel prices were quoted in terms of the Pittsburgh base plus the cost of transportation to the point of delivery. As a rule, base prices were set by U.S. Steel and widely publicized in the trade press, so that other companies would have no difficulty in following the leader.

(2) Transportation charges, the second element in the formula, had to be uniform in order to make delivered prices identical at any one destination. Obviously, the delivered price in Detroit would not be identical if one company charged an all-rail rate while its competitors charged a part-rail, part-water rate. Moreover, if one company charged the actual transportation costs while another collected "fictitious" freight charges, it would be impossible to maintain uniform delivered prices. For many years, therefore, the American Iron & Steel Institute published a book of freight rates showing the rail cost for transporting a ton of steel from Pittsburgh to every delivery point in the United States.

(3) Extras and deductions, the third element in the formula, were merely additions to, or deductions from, the base price—in order to make allowance for special variations from standard specifications. Here again, the objective was to assure uniform delivered prices and U.S. Steel, often after consultation with other companies, set up and publicized its schedule of extras which its rivals chose to follow with amazing regularity.

Here is a concrete example of how the Pittsburgh-Plus system operated: In 1920, the Pittsburgh price for steel was $40 per ton, and the freight charge from Pittsburgh to Chicago (then not a basing point) was $7.60. The delivered price in Chicago, therefore, was $47.60—regardless of where the steel was shipped from and regardless of which company happened to make the sale. In an extreme case, where steel was wheeled through a party wall opening from a Chicago producer to a Chicago consumer, the latter still had to pay $7.60 for transportation even though no transportation cost had been incurred. Such "phantom freight" came into being whenever steel was shipped from a mill nearer than the basing point to the place of delivery. The amount of phantom freight was measured by the excess of the "official" over the actual transportation cost.[33]

To carry our example a step further: If the Chicago producer shipped to a customer in Pittsburgh, he would get a delivered price of $40 (base price plus cost of transportation from the *basing* point to the point of delivery). He would be unable to collect any freight charges, even though it cost him $7.60 to transport the steel to Pittsburgh. He would have to "absorb freight"—the exact amount being the excess of the actual over the "official" freight charges. On this transaction, therefore, he would receive a mill net price of $32.40—in contrast to the mill net of $47.60 on his sale to the Chicago customer.[34] He would discriminate against the nearby (well-located) consumer and in favor of the distant (poorly-located) consumer.

In 1924, this Pittsburgh-Plus system was superseded by a multiple basing point system. The principle of quoting uniform delivered prices, however, remained intact. The only modification was to create new basing points like Chicago, Birmingham, and Sparrows Point, and to quote prices in terms of the *nearest* basing point (called the governing basing point) plus the transportation cost to the point of delivery. In Des Moines, therefore, the delivered price would be computed on a Chicago instead of a Pittsburgh

[33] Phantom freight also arose when a producer charged his customer an all-rail rate while actually using cheaper transport means, such as water or truck.

[34] Mill net is defined as the price received at the mill after the payment or allowance for the actual transportation from mill to destination has been deducted from the invoiced delivered price.

base, but all mills shipping into Des Moines would still quote identical prices at the point of delivery.

The Case for Basing Point Pricing

Steel industry executives have defended the basing point system with uncompromising consistency.[35] They have supported the efforts to legalize the system even after the Supreme Court declared it to be a violation of the antitrust laws. Their arguments are as follows:

(1) The basing point system is the quintessence of perfect competition, since it results in one price in one place at one time: "Competition is at its perfection of expression when all of the sellers are on the same level." [36]

(2) The system cannot be harmful because it does not work. Thus the president of U.S. Steel told a Congressional Committee that "[i]f base prices as announced were followed in every transaction, and . . . the nearest basing point to the consumer governed, and . . . rail freight was added from that point, and the delivered price actually arrived at in that manner, there wouldn't be any competition in the steel industry. It would be a one-price industry, pure and simple." [37] Industry spokesmen point out, however, that basing point prices are "fictitious"; they are prices "we want to get" —"prices that we feel fair." "We don't succeed in getting those prices because competition won't permit it," [38] the spokesmen contend. And, in times of slack demand, there is some truth in this argument. The deeper the recession, the greater is the pressure on steel firms to shade the list prices computed under the basing point formula.

(3) The basing point system, some say, is necessary—not to promote competition but to prevent its excesses. In the steel industry, overhead costs are a significant portion of total costs, and profits depend largely on the

---

[35] In this, they have had the support of some distinguished economists. See, among others, J. M. Clark, "Imperfect Competition Theory and Basing Point Problems," *American Economic Review*, Vol. XXXIII, June 1943, and "Law and Economics of Basing Points," *ibid.*, Vol. XXXIX, March 1949; A. Smithies, "Aspects of the Basing-Point System," *ibid.*, Vol. XXXII, December 1942; H. G. Lewis and T. O. Yntema in *TNEC Papers* (United States Steel Corporation), 1940.

[36] TNEC, *Hearings*, Part 5, p. 1882. To this argument, TNEC members replied that, under perfect competition, a single price in a given market at a given time is the result of an interplay of many buyers and sellers, whereas under the basing point system —by contrast—there prevails a single *bid* price at a point of delivery, a price quoted *outside* the market and then imposed *on* the market. It is further contended that this basing point price in fact results in variable mill net prices; that it is therefore, in effect, a discriminatory price based on a predetermined formula collusively derived. Compare: *Ibid.*, pp. 1862–63, 1873, 1882, 1911–13.

[37] TNEC, *Hearings*, Part 27, p. 14172.

[38] *Ibid.*, Part 19, pp. 10511–12.

extent to which capacity is utilized. As steel output goes up, average costs decline and profits increase. The converse is also true. It is imperative, therefore, that steel companies operate as close to full capacity as possible in order to maximize profits. And here is the rub. Given high overhead costs, and in the face of a slack demand, steel companies will be tempted to secure additional sales by offering price concessions. They will tend to accept additional orders at any price in excess of variable cost (out-of-pocket expenses). If one company does this, there are no adverse effects; but if all resort to the same solution of their overhead cost problem, the inevitable result is a devastating price war—waged without regard to average costs.[39] Such a war may cause prices on *all* sales to be cut below average total costs and may eventually result in a victory for the financially most powerful producers (those who can sustain short-run losses because of their financial staying power) rather than in the survival of the industry's most efficient firms. Such a war would only lead to cut-throat competition, the extinction of some producers, and a further tendency toward concentration in the industry.

At this point the clincher is applied to the overhead cost argument. Steel producers, it is said, are under constant pressure to spread their overhead costs over as large an output as possible. Since they dare not cut prices and thus invite certain retaliation and perhaps a disastrous price war, they have only one alternative—to discriminate.[40] By following the basing point system—by absorbing freight in their invasion of distant markets—steel producers can solicit additional sales without incurring the dangers of price competition. In order to stimulate volume, they can accept a lower mill net price on sales outside their "natural" market areas in the hope of solving their overhead cost problem. The only difficulty with this solution is that freight absorption has to be paid out of the consumer's pocketbook. Moreover, it may prove self-defeating if other producers resort to the same solution as they inevitably will and must.

(4) The basing point system, steel leaders point out, is a necessary in-

---

[39] This argument is based on the assumption of an inelastic and cyclically derived demand.

[40] J. M. Clark describes the paradox of price confronting a firm burdened by high overhead costs as follows: "If any business that would pay its own particular costs is refused because it will not pay its share of overhead, there is a loss. Yet prices must be charged, which will cover overhead, so long as industry depends on private enterprise. There is only one answer to this dilemma—discrimination. The overhead costs must be levied on such parts of the business as will stand the burden, while other parts of the business, which cannot otherwise be had at all, are charged whatever they can pay, regardless of overhead costs. However," Clark significantly concludes, "this is only a partial answer to the question, and creates more problems that it solves." *The Economics of Overhead Costs,* Chicago: University of Chicago Press, 1923, p. 23.

strument of price stability, because the demand for steel is highly inelastic; i.e., price cuts will not bring about a proportionate increase in steel consumption. To be sure, the individual producer faces an elastic demand schedule; if he cuts prices, he can increase sales. But, if all producers do the same thing, they cannot increase their sales sufficiently to overcome the inelastic demand for the industry as a whole. Therefore, it is argued, it is desirable to prevent price competition through some stabilizing mechanism like the basing point system.

Steel spokesmen cite the following evidence for the inelasticity of steel demand. *First,* they point to the fact that steel is a raw material the demand for which is derived from the demand for other products. Hence, if the aggregate demand for such items as automobiles and washing machines is depressed (because of a recession), cutting the price of steel is futile as a demand stimulant.

Second, they argue that "substitution of steel for other materials, or a reverse substitution, is not an important factor in the cyclical fluctuations in the demand for steel." [41] Since the substitution factor is not very important in the demand for steel, "price reduction would result in very little additional steel being sold as substitutes for other products, and a price advance, unless abnormal, probably would not result in additional competition from substitute products." [42]

Third, so runs the argument, the demand for steel is inelastic because steel generally constitutes a very small portion of the total cost of the products in which it is contained as a raw material. It is pointed out, for example, that, under 1948 conditions, "a $5 per ton change in the price of all steel products going into a $1,500 automobile would affect the cost of producing the automobile about $8; a $20 electric toaster would be affected by less than 1 cent; a $285 electric refrigerator by 61 cents; a $184 gas range by 49 cents; and a $130 washing machine by 25 cents while the cost of building a 35 story steel frame office building would be affected by six-tenths of 1 per cent." [43]

[41] Study by the United States Steel Corporation, Exhibit No. 1410, TNEC, *Hearings,* Part 26; reprinted in TNEC Monograph No. 42, *The Basing Point Problem,* p. 15.

[42] TNEC Monograph No. 42, *op.cit.,* p. 16. Comparative prices for other metals would tend to bear out this assertion. In 1947, according to *Iron Age,* the average price per pound for zinc was 11.02¢; for lead, 14.69¢; for aluminum, 15.00¢; for electrolytic copper, 21.30¢; and for tin, 77.97¢. By contrast steel sold for an average of 3.00¢ per pound during the same period. This argument is, of course, at loggerheads with the industry's contention, that steel is subject to intense interindustry competition.

[43] Statement by Arthur B. Homer, President of the Bethlehem Steel Corp., *Hearings before the Joint Committee on the Economic Report,* March 2, 1948. Cf. also T. Yntema, "A Statistical Analysis of the Demand for Steel, 1919–1938" in the United States Steel Corp., *TNEC Papers,* New York, 1939; General Motors Corporation, *The Dynamics of Automobile Demand,* New York, 1939.

It is for these reasons that industry leaders hold the demand for steel to be inelastic, and consider the price stabilizing functions of the basing point system to be vital to the preservation of a healthy price structure for steel products.

(5) Another favorite argument in defense of the basing point system alludes to the dangers of local monopoly in case the system were abandoned and replaced by f.o.b. mill pricing. F.o.b. mill prices, it is charged, "would put [the consumer] generally at the mercy of the nearest mill," because the latter could make the shipment of steel into its "natural" delivery area unprofitable to rivals. The nearest mill could eliminate competition in its immediate vicinity by setting a price so low that no competitor could meet it.[44]

The Case against Basing Point Pricing

In its legal skirmishes against the basing point system which lasted some thirty years, the FTC relied on the following major arguments:

(1) The system, according to the Commission, promotes collusion and results in the elimination of price competition. The system worked so well that companies located at widely separated points, and in ostensible competition with one another, would submit sealed bids to the federal government which were identical to the fourth decimal place.[45] At any given destination, there would be no price competition—regardless of which company made the sale or where the steel was actually shipped from.

The basing point formula, according to the FTC, is a more effective instrument of collusion than old fashioned price agreements. It is the eye which discovers the chiseler and the hand which wields the punishing whip.

[44] If it were the inevitable result of f.o.b. mill pricing, however, the consumer can certainly be no worse off than under the basing point system; for, if the local mill ever attempted to exploit its regional monopoly by charging exorbitant prices at a given point "A," producers located in nearby areas would again find it profitable to make deliveries at "A," thus destroying the potentially evil effects of local monopoly. A local monopoly in steel, therefore, would be no more serious than the monopoly enjoyed by the neighborhood grocer due to his strategic location in respect to the market. Under these conditions, "The mercy of the nearest mill might be preferable to the mercy of a whole industry united on one price." Compare: "U.S. Steel II: Prices," reprinted from *Fortune*, Vol. XIII, April 1936, p. 136, by special permission of the Editors. Copyright Time Inc.

[45] See TNEC, *Hearings*, Part 5, p. 1897. While the commission does not consider the basing point formula illegal per se (i.e., when used by *one* or a *few* producers independently), the formula is held to become unlawful when it serves to implement collusion and price-fixing among *all* the producers in an industry. (*Notice to Staff*, October 12, 1948, p. 2.) As such it is deemed illegal under Section 5 of the Federal Trade Commission Act, since the commission believes it to be "an obvious fact that the economic effect of identical prices achieved through conscious parallel action is the same as that of similar prices achieved through overt collusion." (*Ibid.*, p. 3.)

Under its rules price cutting does not pay and, in its enforcement, price cutting is not "necessary." Price cutting does not pay because the chiseler's reduced price immediately becomes the base price in his area and is "matched" by all his competitors. This means that "all delivered prices are identical again and the fellow hasn't gained anything by cutting his price except a headache." [46] Moreover, price cutting is not necessary because the steel industry's "live and let live" tradition makes for a protective umbrella that is high and wide enough for everyone—including the inefficient producers.

(2) The system, according to the FTC, is artificial and discriminatory. The customer located nearest to the production site from which the steel is actually shipped does not always get the lowest price and often "would be as cheaply supplied if the nearby mill did not exist." [47] Moreover, he suffers discrimination even if he is located right at the basing point. This is so, because base prices must be high enough to permit mills to absorb freight on sales to less fortunately located customers. Such discrimination would persist, even if all production points were to become basing points. While phantom freight would disappear, the system of uniform delivered prices would still result in freight absorption and hence differential (discriminatory) mill nets.

(3) The system, the FTC charges, results in wasteful cross-hauling—i.e., the reciprocal invasion of the "natural" market areas of steel mills producing identical products.[48] As Charles Schwab, former president of Bethlehem Steel Corp., candidly observed, it "is manifestly uneconomic for a steel manufacturer in Chicago to ship 100,000 tons of steel to Pittsburgh at a time when a Pittsburgh manufacturer is shipping a like quantity of like material from Pittsburgh to Chicago." [49] Not only is such cross-hauling self-defeating; it also dissipates part of the producer's revenue on unnecessary transportation and imposes an additional burden on the consumer who ultimately has to pay for this wasteful extravagance. Competition is diverted from base price reductions which would benefit *all* consumers to increased freight absorption which entails no price advantage to *any* consumer.

---

[46] TNEC, *Hearings*, Part 5, p. 1868.

[47] TNEC Monograph No. 42, *op.cit.*, p. 2.

[48] In this connection it is interesting to note the attempt of Professor Smithies of Harvard to show that a rational monopolist would certainly have eliminated the wasteful practice of cross-hauling. Smithies regards the preservation of cross-hauling under the basing point system as one item of evidence that the basing point system is not necessarily an instrument of collusion. A. Smithies, "Aspects of the Basing-Point System," *American Economic Review*, Vol. XXXII, December 1942, pp. 423–40.

[49] Quoted in C. D. Edwards, "Basing Point Decisions and Business Practices," *American Economic Review*, December 1948, p. 840.

(4) The basing point system is also said to result in uneconomic location of both steel producers and consumers. The latter may locate at an unfavorable site just to be close to a basing point, whereas under a different pricing system they might have chosen a better location near a steel mill which was *not* a basing point. Similarly, steel producers can afford to maintain their investment in anachronistic locations because "under the umbrella of a controlled price system the test of profitable plant location ceases to be essentially a matter of cost of production and distribution. . . . Plants thereby may be established at uneconomic points in terms of production costs." [50]

Why, some critics ask, should Detroit have only 5 per cent of the nation's steel capacity when Detroit industries consume nearly three times as much? Why should Pittsburgh produce almost twice as much steel as is needed in its market area? Can the present location of steel plants be explained purely in terms of proximity to raw materials and markets? Obviously not. The basing point system bears part of the blame for whatever distortion exists, because it allows "every steel mill to compete on a substantially equal footing for any piece of business anywhere in the country," thus tending to neutralize the advantages of location.

Price Leadership

Although most of these arguments against the basing point system are valid, it would be a mistake to carry them too far. In an industry like steel, geographic price discrimination and restraints on price competition can be explained not so much in terms of the basing point system but by the fewness of sellers, the homogeneity of steel products, the importance of overhead costs, the difficulty of entry, the substantial concentration on the buyer's side of the market, and the danger of cut-throat competition (especially when firms are hungry)—in short, by the structure of the industry. It is a fundamental fact that steel is an oligopoly and that its prices will therefore be "administered." This can be done "in many different ways. There may be no other technique of price administration that is so elegantly simple to operate as the basing point system, but there may be many others that will yield socially equivalent results." [51]

With or without a basing point system, price leadership is a pervasive characteristic of the steel industry. Typically, U.S. Steel sets the pace and

[50] Reprinted from David Lynch, *The Concentration of Economic Power*, p. 191. Copyright 1946 by Columbia University Press, New York.
[51] J. K. Galbraith, "Light on a Hot Subject," reprinted from *Fortune*, April 1949, p. 211, by special permission of the Editors. Copyright Time, Inc.

the other companies follow in lockstep—both in their sales to private customers and in their secret bids on government contracts. Often, steel producers shipping from different locations will quote delivered prices identical to the thousandth of a cent per pound. Mr. Blough, president of U.S. Steel, explained this phenomenon by citing a Naval Gun Factory contract as an example: "United States Steel offered a delivered price to meet the lowest delivered price it anticipated would be bid on this item. From its prior knowledge of dealings with the Naval Gun Factory and of the market, U.S. Steel could and did expect that Bethlehem would offer a bid on this invitation. Upon evaluation of these competitive circumstances, U.S. Steel found that if Bethlehem bid its announced price for the item at its producing mill at Sparrows Point, Md., from which it could be expected to offer to ship, plus freight from that mill to the Naval Gun Factory, its delivery price would be $0.07205 per pound. U.S. Steel accordingly reduced its own delivered price for shipment from its Fairless Works to the Naval Gun Factory by an amount which would enable it to meet the equally low price of its competitor." [52]

"Meeting competition" is the industry's euphemism to explain this price uniformity. On the downside this is understandable. Given the high degree of standardization of steel products and the negligible differences in quality, price cuts by one producer must quickly be matched by his competitors. "There isn't certainly any steel company in the first ten or in the first twenty," says the president of U.S. Steel, "that couldn't require us to change our prices overnight simply by taking action which is different than the action that we take." [53]

But what about "meeting competition" on the upside? Why do powerful companies like Bethlehem or National seldom challenge U.S. Steel's decisions to increase prices? Such price followership seems anomalous especially in those lines and those areas where these companies surpass U.S. Steel in production volume. In 1957, for example, Bethlehem held 72.2 per cent of the capacity for rolled steel piling (compared to U.S. Steel's 26.6 per cent), yet it dutifully followed U.S. Steel's price leadership. In the Northeastern states, National ranked first (18.9 per cent) and U.S. Steel sixth (7.2 per cent) in cold-rolled sheets capacity, yet National was not inclined to challenge the price leader.[54]

This price followership is also anomalous because different steel companies have different costs, and earn different profits. Both Bethlehem and

[52] *Kefauver Committee Report,* p. 122.
[53] *Ibid.,* p. 78.
[54] *Ibid.,* pp. 90–94.

National, for example, generally enjoy higher rates of return than U.S. Steel. For the forties, exclusive of the war years, Bethlehem returned 12.2 per cent on stockholders' investment after taxes compared to National's 16 per cent and U.S. Steel's 9.4 per cent. For the fifties, excluding the Korean conflict, the comparable figures were 14.2 per cent for Bethlehem against 14 per cent for National and 11.5 per cent for U.S. Steel.[55] Despite these differences in profits (which probably reflect, at least in this instance, differences in efficiency), U.S. Steel's price leadership seemed to remain inviolate. Its absolute size—rather than its relative market control or comparative efficiency—apparently insured the corporation's position as price leader and bellwether for the industry.

Meeting the price *increases* of a competitor is what the steel executives call competition. They liken it to the Gimbels-Macy's rivalry. But Senator O'Mahoney calls it "upside-down competition," and Senator Kefauver rejects the Gimbels-Macy's analogy: "Would New Yorkers," he asks, "have the benefit of greater competition, of greater freedom of choice, if the prices of Macy's and Gimbels were invariably identical? Would . . . competition . . . be greater if every price increase by Macy's was immediately matched by Gimbels? If Macy's and Gimbels turned to what we have heard here about the steel industry, then a new Macy's slogan might wave over Herald Square, 'Our prices are always exactly as high as Gimbels.'"[56] Price uniformity in a competitive industry is one thing. In an oligopoly, it is quite another.

Price Rigidity

This tendency toward price uniformity is reinforced by a tendency toward price rigidity. In comparison to other industries, where prices are more responsive to "automatic," "competitive" market forces, steel prices appear remarkably stable and inflexible. Contrast steel with textile and agricultural products, for example. In these industries, a cyclical change in demand tends to result in relatively drastic price changes without a similar effect on output and employment. In steel, the process is reversed. Production and demand are equated by an "administered" price which results in relatively wide output and employment fluctuations and proportionately smaller price fluctuations. In other words, price stability is obtained at the expense of instability in output. (See Figure 1.)

Such stability, of course, is not natural or inevitable, but the result of

[55] *Ibid.*, pp. 84–89.
[56] *Ibid.*, p. 100.

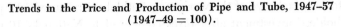

FIGURE 1

Trends in the Price and Production of Pipe and Tube, 1947–57
(1947–49 = 100).

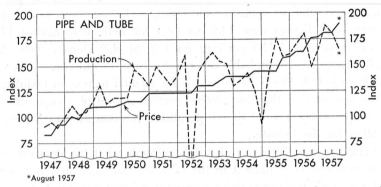

*August 1957

Source: Subcommittee on Antitrust and Monopoly, "Administered Prices: Steel,"
Senate Report No. 1387, 85th Cong., 2d Sess., 1958, p. 21.

conscious administrative direction. In the past, U.S. Steel has tended to resist substantial price increases in times of high demand and opposed any
marked reductions in times of slack demand. It has tried to hold prices
constant—often for months and years. In the case of Bessemer steel rails
—to take an extreme example—annual average prices fluctuated from $67.52
to $17.62 per ton between 1880 and 1901, i.e., during the competitive era
preceding the organization of U.S. Steel. From May 1901, however, less
than sixty days after the founding of the Corporation, a price of $28 per
ton was in effect until April 1916 (a period of 180 months). After some
fluctuations, a price of $43 per ton was announced in October 1922, which
remained in effect until October 1932 (a period of 121 months).[57] Other
steel products have experienced similar, though less pronounced, price
stabilization. "Unless impelled by sharp increases in direct costs or dangerous sniping by rivals," say Kaplan, Dirlam, and Lanzillotti, U.S. Steel has
generally preferred to resist "either price increases or decreases," and to
sacrifice stability "only when the decision [was] unavoidable." [58]

In recent years, however, this policy seems to have undergone some
change. According to the Kefauver Committee, steel prices have tended to
become more flexible—but flexible in an upward direction only. Since 1947,
the Committee reports, there has emerged a fairly consistent pattern of
"stair-step" price increases at regular intervals—with base prices usually
going up in midsummer and extra prices rising in midwinter. Moreover,

[57] See Burns, *op.cit.,* p. 205 ff.
[58] A. D. H. Kaplan, J. B. Dirlam, and R. F. Lanzillotti, *Pricing in Big Business,* Washington: The Brookings Institution, 1958, p. 175.

this upward flexibility has at times been achieved in the face of declining demand. Thus, between December 1955 and August 1957, the price index on cold rolled sheets rose 20 points while the production index declined 80 points; on cold rolled strip, the price index advanced 23.8 points, while the production index slumped 45.6 points; on hot rolled sheets, the price index rose 30.4 points, while the production index fell 58.6 points. Similar trends were observed in hot-rolled bars, pipe and tube, rails, plates, and other steel products.[59]

Since World War II, it seems, steel prices have not only shown a remarkable insensitivity to market conditions but risen with virtually unbroken regularity. They increased even when demand and production declined (as in 1949, 1954, and 1957). They continued their climb even when unit labor costs declined (as in 1950 and 1955). According to the Kefauver Committee, "no matter what the change in cost or in demand, steel prices since 1947 have moved steadily and regularly in only one direction, upward." The fact that prices were raised again in 1957, and that this increase was "made to stick" in the face of a general recession, was further "tribute to the perfection with which price leadership in the steel industry maintains price rigidity."[60]

Price Level and Profits

Industry spokesmen have attributed this upward trend of steel prices to two factors: trade union pressure and the "depreciation gap." On the one hand, they say, higher prices have resulted from higher wages and the operation of "wage push" inflation; on the other, they claim that higher prices (and profits) have been required to finance the replacement of outworn facilities and the building of new ones. Both these arguments have, at least, some merit.

It is true that since World War II hourly earnings in the steel industry have advanced faster than man-hour productivity, with the result that unit

---

[59] *Ibid.*, pp. 17–26. Prices of different steel products are, of course, adjusted to varying market elasticities. In general, prices and profit margins are highest on items facing less intense competition, like steel rails and cable. "Stainless steel, galvanized sheets, and tin plate, on the other hand, which are in direct or potential competition with substitutes from aluminum to lumber, had narrower profit margins." The same holds true for products like cold rolled sheets which are sold to buyers (e.g., automobile and farm equipment manufacturers) "who are able to exert strong pressures because of size and ability to threaten, at least, to make their own." See Kaplan, Dirlam, and Lanzillotti, *op.cit.*, p. 172 ff.

[60] *Kefauver Committee Report*, p. 129. Again, it should be noted that those prices subject to more intense competition or buyer pressures have increased less than others, but the composite index for *all* steel products has clearly risen.

labor costs have gone up. Between 1947 and 1958, average hourly earnings increased 100 per cent, while productivity rose only 26.6 per cent, so that unit labor costs increased 58 per cent. If we compare the years 1947 and 1955—both years in which the industry operated at 93 per cent of capacity —average hourly earnings increased 64.6 per cent, productivity 29.4 per cent, and unit labor costs 27.2 per cent.[61] To this extent, the industry's position is valid.

Before branding labor as the inflationary villain, however, the observed changes in wages, productivity, and unit labor costs must be compared with concomitant changes in the industry's prices. Such a comparison shows that, between 1947 and 1958, finished steel prices increased 103 per cent while unit labor costs rose only 58 per cent. Even with a generous allowance for the higher costs attributable to fringe benefits, it still appears that steel prices have gone up much more than the cost of steel labor.[62] Using a different base period, Secretary of Labor Mitchell arrived at the same conclusion. He found that, between 1940 and the fiscal year 1959, basic steel prices increased 178 per cent while employment cost per ton (including wages and fringe benefits) for wage employees rose 131 per cent, and employment costs for all employees rose 153 per cent. Concluded the Secretary: "The increase in average prices of steel products since 1940 has exceeded the rise in employment cost per ton of steel produced. This is true whether employment cost for wage employees alone is considered, or whether employment cost of all employees is taken into account."[63]

The 1957 wage-price adjustment affords a dramatic illustration of the inflationary spiral in the steel industry. In July of that year, the companies granted wage hikes and fringe benefits which, in the opinion of Dr. Gardiner C. Means, raised the cost of steel by $1.75 per ton. At the same time, they advanced base prices by $6.00 per ton—on the heels of a $5.00 increase in the price of extras a few months earlier. Given this $11.00 price rise in the face of a $1.75 cost increase, Dr. Means concluded, the industry was hardly justified in blaming labor for inflation.[64] On the contrary, its conduct reinforced the union's claim that in the postwar era the steel companies have raised prices by $3 for every $1 increase in labor costs.

Rising profit margins further weakened the industry's contention that steel prices go up only because they are *pushed* up by trade union pressure. As Table 2 indicates, the steel companies have not only been able to main-

---

[61] *Congressional Record*, June 30, 1959, p. 11164.
[62] *Ibid.*
[63] U.S. Department of Labor, *Background Statistics Bearing on the Steel Dispute*, August 1959, Section 14.
[64] *Congressional Record*, June 30, 1959, p. 11164.

TABLE 2

Steel—Relationship between Operating Rate and Rate of Return
on Net Worth after Taxes

Year	Steel Industry Operating Rate	Steel Industry Rate of Return	United States Steel Operating Rate	United States Steel Rate of Return	Year	Steel Industry Operating Rate	Steel Industry Rate of Return	United States Steel Operating Rate	United States Steel Rate of Return
1920	76.7	12.1	86.2	11.5	1936	68.4	4.8	63.4	3.8
1921	34.9	2.2	48.3	4.3	1937	72.5	7.2	71.9	7.0
1922	61.7	3.8	70.9	4.6	1938	39.6	.3	36.4	—.6
1923	77.3	9.4	89.1	10.9	1939	64.5	4.2	61.0	3.1
1924	64.6	6.5	72.2	8.4	1940	82.1	8.2	82.5	7.5
1925	75.4	7.6	81.7	8.6	1947	93.0	11.4	96.7	10.0
1926	84.1	9.3	89.1	10.1	1948	94.1	14.0	93.8	10.5
1927	75.4	6.6	79.8	7.4	1949	81.1	11.7	82.5	9.4
1928	84.6	8.4	84.6	9.0	1950	96.9	15.0	98.2	11.8
1929	88.7	12.1	90.4	12.6	1953	94.9	11.2	98.4	9.9
1930	62.8	5.1	67.2	5.8	1954	71.0	9.4	73.2	8.3
1931	38.0	—.3	37.5	.7	1955	93.0	14.7	90.8	14.8
1932	19.7	—4.5	17.7	—4.1	1956	89.8	13.2	85.2	12.8
1933	33.5	—2.2	29.4	—2.2	1957	84.5	12.5	85.2	14.3
1934	37.4	—.7	31.7	—1.3	1958	61.0	8.5	59.2	9.8
1935	48.7	1.4	40.7	.1					

Source: *Congressional Record,* June 30, 1959, p. 11165.

tain but to increase their return on investment at given levels of operation. Thus, in 1947, an operating rate of 93 per cent yielded profits of 11.4 per cent (after taxes) whereas in 1955 the same operating rate yielded a 14.7 per cent profit. In the absence of any radical shift in "product mix"—i.e., a shift to the production of more profitable steel products—this would indicate an improvement in cost-price margins. Table 3, which compares U.S. Steel's profit rates at various operating levels between 1954 and 1958, points to the same conclusion. Again the evidence would suggest a widening gap between unit costs and prices. It shows that the union may have the power to raise wages beyond gains in productivity, but it also shows that the companies had enough market power to raise prices in excess of cost increases. On the basis of this record, the companies could ill-afford to brand labor as an engine of inflation.

But what about the "depreciation gap"? Can recent increases in steel prices and profits be explained by the higher cost of replacing worn-out facilities? "Yes," is the virtually unanimous reply of steel industry officials. U.S. Steel's Robert C. Tyson, for example, claims that "because of inflation, to construct or purchase new plants or equipment today costs a vastly greater

TABLE 3

United States Steel Corporation—Comparison of Relationship between
Operating Rate and (a) Net Profit per Ton (after Taxes) and
(b) Rate of Return (after Taxes) on Net Worth
by Quarters, 1954–56 and 1957–58

Operating Rate	Net Profit per Ton		Rate of Return on Net Worth	
	1954–56	1957–58	1954–56 (percentage)	1957–58 (percentage)
50 to 60 per cent	$9.32 (III/56)	$15.41 (I/58) 17.19 (II/58) 18.81 (III/58)	5.4 (III/56)	8.3 (I/58) 9.8 (II/58) 10.0 (III/58)
60 to 70 per cent	9.88 (III/54)		7.9 (III/54)	
70 to 80 per cent	9.14 (II/54) 11.78 (IV/54)	17.62 (IV/57) 19.31 (IV/58)	8.7 (II/54) 10.1 (IV/54)	13.1 (IV/57) 12.1 (IV/58)
80 to 90 per cent	8.07 (I/54) 12.57 (I/55) 14.57 (III/55) 15.48 (II/56)	18.11 (II/57) 18.55 (III/57)	8.0 (I/54) 12.4 (I/55) 15.3 (III/55) 16.2 (II/56)	16.8 (II/57) 14.1 (III/57)
90 to 100 per cent	14.91 (II/55) 15.73 (IV/55) 15.23 (I/56) 15.89 (IV/56)	17.44 (I/57)	17.9 (II/55) 17.4 (IV/55) 16.1 (I/56) 16.2 (IV/56)	16.7 (I/57)

Operating rate:
  1954: I–80.8; II–70.7; III–66.3; IV–75.3.
  1955: I–85.5; II–94.4; III–86.8; IV–96.6.
  1956: I–98.0; II–89.4; III–55.6; IV–96.9.
  1957: I–95.7; II–89.5; III–81.1; IV–74.9.
  1958: I–54.1; II–53.0; III–57.1; IV–72.7.

Source: Congressional Record, June 30, 1959, p. 11165.

number of dollars than the plant or equipment being replaced cost twenty
or more years ago. Yet the depreciation of these old plants is required for
tax purposes to be based on the relatively small number of dollars paid for
them long ago. As a result depreciation currently allowed is quite insufficient
to equal what has to be paid out when the old facilities are modernized or
replaced." Between 1939 and 1956, Tyson estimates, his company alone has
incurred a depreciation deficiency of 904 million dollars—an experience
shared by other steel companies.[65]

Given this depreciation gap, the industry feels justified in raising its prices
and "paper" profits. U.S. Steel, for example, seems to have abandoned its
traditional price policy which was based on "the expectation of earning
over the years a net return, after taxes, of around 8 per cent.[66] In the past,

---

[65] Subcommittee on Antitrust and Monopoly, *Hearings on Administered Prices, Steel,*
Part 2, 1957, p. 246.
[66] Kaplan, Dirlam, and Lanzillotti, *op.cit.,* p. 169.

the company claims, this may have been adequate, but it no longer is. Since it presumably takes $2 in the form of higher prices (or lower costs) to compensate for every $1 of depreciation deficiency, the Corporation now aims for a higher profit target, and has raised prices to meet it—with the rest of the industry following suit. And, as Table 3 shows, the Corporation has apparently been successful, having earned more than 8 per cent in every year since 1947 and substantially more in periods of prosperity and labor peace.

There is, of course, some truth in the depreciation gap argument. It is undoubtedly true that the cost of replacing facilities has gone up since World War II. (According to one estimate, a ton of new steel capacity today costs $300 compared to $100 in 1939.) [67] After more than a decade of inflation, depreciation charges based on original cost are clearly inadequate. Nevertheless, the depreciation gap is not as serious as the industry would have us believe. Nor is the exercise of oligopoly power a happy solution for the problem. *First*, the facilities built today may cost more than those in 1939, but they are also more productive. They are not the same facilities, and cannot be considered "replacements" in the literal sense. *Second*, the cost inflation of which the steel industry complains is partly of the industry's own making. As Eckstein and Fromm point out, "If steel prices had behaved like other industrial prices, the total wholesale price index would have risen by 40 per cent less over the last decade and less by 52 per cent since 1953." [68] Steel has not only contributed to the postwar inflation, but benefited from it substantially. *Third*, there is no evidence that the depreciation gap has worked actual hardship on the industry. Between 1946 and 1958, for example, U.S. Steel has been able to finance a four billion dollar capital expenditure program (including replacement *and* expansion) with virtually no help from the capital market. That is, the Corporation succeeded in drawing 3.9 billion dollars from its depreciation, amortization, and retained earnings accounts to underwrite this tremendous building program.[69] *Finally*, the power of an industry to "tax" its customers in the form of higher prices to finance either replacement or expansion of facilities raises grave policy issues. Why should the steel industry be allowed to exercise its market power and, in effect, "repeal" the internal revenue statutes governing depreciation? If every other industry is compelled by law to base depreciation on original cost, why should steel be permitted to decide unilaterally to use a replacement cost standard and to impose this on the market? If original

[67] *Ibid.*, p. 170.
[68] "Steel and the Postwar Inflation," *Study Paper No. 2*, Joint Congressional Economic Committee, 1959, p. 34.
[69] *Congressional Record*, June 30, 1959, p. 11165.

cost is an improper gauge of economic depreciation, it is up to Congress to do something about it—not only for steel but for every other industry in the country.[70] It is questionable whether, in a democracy, we can tolerate an *imperium in imperio*—a system of private governments in concentrated industries.

Summary

Summarizing, then, steel is a concentrated industry. Its behavior conforms closely to the oligopoly pattern. Price uniformity is assured through price leadership (with or without resort to the basing point system). Price stability is attained, often at the expense of extreme fluctuations in production and employment. Price levels are geared to a break-even point of less than 40 per cent of capacity, and only remotely influenced by natural market forces. The industry leader sets prices like a public utility, aiming for a predetermined profit target (after taxes), and the other firms usually follow in lockstep. In short, the industry's performance hardly measures up to the standards of workable competition. As George Stocking correctly concludes, the industry's "structure contribute[s] to conduct incompatible with an effective interplay of market forces, and its structure and conduct [result] in unacceptable performance."[71]

SECTION III: PUBLIC POLICY

What should be the public policy toward the steel industry? Is the performance of the industry sufficiently good to justify a policy of noninterference? Could performance be improved by a change in structure, or is it enough to press for a rehabilitation of behavior? Above all, is effective competition in the steel industry possible, and/or desirable? If so, how can it be promoted?

Ever since the Supreme Court's refusal to break up U.S. Steel in 1920, the government has confined itself mainly to combating collusive, discriminatory, and exorbitant prices. For more than twenty years, the Justice Department and the FTC have battled in the courts—first to eliminate the single and then the multiple basing point system. These battles were eventually won. The Pittsburgh Plus system was proscribed in 1924, and

---

[70] My colleague, Abba P. Lerner, suggests that the depreciation gap may be a blessing in disguise. It forces the steel companies to resort periodically to the capital market, thus permitting the market to validate or veto their investment decisions.

[71] "The Rule of Reason, Workable Competition, and Monopoly," *Yale Law Journal*, July 1955, p. 1136.

the multiple basing point system and systematic freight absorption were banned in 1948. These rulings have not caused havoc in the industry. Nor have they assured the competitive pricing of steel products. Now, as before, price leadership and collusion in the economic sense are hallmarks of this industry.

As of today, the steel industry has operated for a dozen years under a modified sort of f.o.b. pricing. Despite the dire predictions of 1948, this has caused little, if any, hardship. Quite to the contrary, the industry has done amazingly well. It has expanded annual capacity by more than 50,000,000 tons; it has earned record profits; in short, it has demonstrated that there is little need for the collusive basing point practice in time of *prosperity*. The issue is far from settled, however. With a slackening in the demand for steel, there are bound to be renewed drives to legalize the basing point system. Given a major recession, the industry is almost certain to insist that stabilization of competition is imperative, and that such stabilization requires basing point pricing. In the face of such agitation it may be well to remember, however, that recessions cannot be cured by basing points, and competition cannot be achieved through collusion. In the light of our recent experience, it would be difficult to justify the return to a collusive, discriminatory, and wasteful pricing method. It would be difficult to justify a reversal from our present opposition to basing points and systematic freight absorption.[72]

On the other hand, it is unrealistic to suppose that mere abstention from the basing point system will achieve either price competition or price flexibility—a fact illustrated by the recurrent official inquiries into steel prices and profits. Congress has investigated, exposed, and condemned. The President has pleaded, admonished, and warned. Steel labor and steel management have been exhorted to exercise restraint and to forego desired wage and price increases in order to combat inflation and thus preserve the American way of life. "The response," as Ben Lewis observes, "has been not only less than spectacular; it has been imperceptible." Voluntary restraint, creeping admonitionism, and economizing by conscience have simply not worked. They have become, as Lewis says, "a symptom of, and not a cure for, organic disabilities which are beginning to be plainly discernible in our economic body."[73]

From society's point of view, the objective is not to keep steel prices

[72] This recommendation is supported by the findings of the most up-to-date and thoroughgoing study of the basing point problem. See F. Machlup, *The Basing Point System*, Philadelphia: Blakiston, 1949.

[73] "Economics by Admonition," *American Economic Review Proceedings*, May 1959, pp. 384–5.

low in prosperity and high in depression. The function of steel prices, as of all prices, should be to promote a proper allocation of society's resources —to channel resources into those uses where the consuming public most wants to have them. Thus, given a high demand for steel, an uncompetitively low administered price brings in its wake grey markets and allocation problems. Such a price is, in effect, a subsidization by the steel industry of steel-consuming industries. It distorts the allocation of resources in accordance with the dictates of the market. It strikes at the central nervous system of a free enterprise economy. The same is true in times of slack demand. At such times, the effort by the steel industry to stabilize prices and to maintain prices at higher levels than the market justifies again results in distortions of the allocation process. It represents an unwarranted tax on steel-using industries imposed by steel producers. It is an attempt to cure recessions by cartel-like restraints on the free market. Not only are such attempts futile, as history amply demonstrates, but they represent a crucial deviation from the fundamentals of free enterprise.

No! Creeping admonitionism, voluntary restraint, and the corporate soul are not likely to solve the basic problem. Nor will a conscientious adherence to f.o.b. pricing make the steel industry a paragon of competition. The problem goes deeper. It is inherent in the structure of the industry. It is the problem of "size," and any attack on oligopoly pricing without an attack on oligopoly structure will be no more effective than the treatment of a symptom instead of the disease itself. In other words, public policy toward this industry must concern itself with the basic problem of structure and how it can be changed. This, in turn, raises questions about the relation between the size of firms and technological efficiency—in short, the feasibility of increasing the number of competitors. If it is possible to increase the number of firms and thus create a more competitive industry structure, this would enhance the prospects for more competitive behavior and the likelihood of nonconformity in pricing and other aspects of business policy. Whether this can be done is the problem to which we now turn.

The Problem of Size

On the basis of information which is available it seems reasonable that iron and steel making requires firms of considerable size—firms which are not only significant horizontally (i.e., within any one branch of the industry) but which are also integrated vertically. Vertical integration seems economically justifiable due to the "geographic concentration of the industry, the magnitude of individual operations necessary for efficiency in mining and manufacture, and the economies obtained by continuous operation, which makes possible the immediate use of the end product of one stage of production as the material in the next stage." [74] Thus there are very definite economies to be obtained from a combination of the operations of blast furnaces and steel works. These economies are obtained (1) by transforming pig iron into steel by a continuous process without permitting the iron to cool, thus using it in a molten state; (2) by recovering the valuable by-product gases from blast furnaces and coke ovens; and (3) by avoiding the cost of transporting pig iron, a cost which is high in comparison to its value.

On the other hand, there is little evidence to indicate that firms must be of Brobdingnagian size to be efficient. Professor Bain, for example, estimates that an integrated steel mill of "optimal size" need have a capacity of not more than one to 2.5 million ingot tons. [75] Other studies indicate that (1) operational efficiency, (2) technological progressiveness, and (3) profitability might best be promoted not by preserving, but by reducing the size of some steel giants.

First, with respect to operational efficiency, it is interesting that the capacity of the giant steel companies is not concentrated in a handful of large *plants.* Thus, when a total of 51 steel making plants belonging to the 8 largest companies were classified according to size, it was found that only five had annual capacities of more than three million ingot tons; twenty-four had ingot capacities from one to three million tons; and the remaining twenty plants had capacities of less than one million tons. [76] These, remember, were plants owned by the eight largest steel companies.

Moreover, it is doubtful if the combination of spatially and functionally separate plant units yields any significant economies. To be sure, there are advantages in integrated steel production at Pittsburgh or Gary or Birmingham; but is there any technological justification for combining these three functionally independent *plant units* under the administration of one *firm?*

Consider for a moment that U.S. Steel's Gary plant alone is bigger than the total operations of Jones & Laughlin, National, Youngstown, Armco, and Inland. *One* plant of the nation's largest steel producer is bigger than *all* the plants of the fourth largest producer. This inevitably raises the question, whether Jones & Laughlin, National, and other companies of similarly substantial size are big enough to be efficient. If they are, then certainly U.S. Steel's Gary plant—standing on its own feet and divorced from the industrial

[74] U.S. Tariff Commission, *op.cit.,* p. 42.
[75] Bain, *op.cit.,* p. 236. On this point, see also *Celler Report,* p. 69, which corroborates Bain's estimate.
[76] Bain, *op.cit.,* pp. 236–37. The data are for 1952.

family of U.S. Steel—should also be capable of efficient operation. The same goes for the corporation's integrated units at Pittsburgh and Birmingham. Divorcement of these plants from the home office should hardly result in a loss of efficiency.[77]

In fact, such divorcement may result in more, not less, operational efficiency—at least, if the evidence in the hitherto unpublished Ford, Bacon & Davis report is reliable. This report was prepared by Ford, Bacon & Davis (a private management consulting firm) at the request of U.S. Steel itself, and was of course undertaken at the corporation's expense. Its findings, as summarized by Professor George Stocking before the Celler Committee, pictured the corporation as

. . . a big sprawling inert giant, whose production operations were improperly coordinated; suffering from a lack of a long-run planning agency; relying on an antiquated system of cost accounting; with an inadequate knowledge of the costs or of the relative profitability of the many thousands of items it sold; with production and cost standards generally below those considered everyday practice in other industries; with inadequate knowledge of its domestic markets and no clear appreciation of its opportunities in foreign markets; with less efficient production facilities than its rivals had; slow in introducing new processes and new products.

Specifically, according to the engineers, it was slow in introducing the continuous rolling mill; slow in getting into production of cold-rolled steel products; slow in recognizing the potentials of the wire business; slow to adopt the heat-treating process for the production of sheets; slow in getting into stainless steel products; slow in producing cold-rolled sheets; slow in tin-plate developments; slow in utilizing waste gases; slow in utilizing low-cost water transportation because of its consideration for the railroads; in short, slow to grasp the remarkable business opportunities that a dynamic America offered it. The corporation was apparently a follower, not a leader, in industrial efficiency.[78]

On the basis of the powerful indictment in this engineering report (as well as other evidence), Stocking concluded that "the Steel Corp. has lagged, not led"; that "it was neither big because it was efficient, nor efficient because it was big." [79] This conclusion was supported by the testimony of other leading economists who maintained that the dissolution of U.S. Steel into at least three separate integrated units was technologically quite feasible. They assured the committee that "one can be opposed to economic bigness and in favor of technological bigness in most basic industries without inconsistency." [80]

Second, with respect to technological progressiveness, it is noteworthy that the small- and medium-sized steel companies compare quite favorably with U.S. Steel. Thus it was Bethlehem which patented the sensational Gray beam; it was Republic which became the leader in alloy steels; it was Armco which patented the continuous rolling mill process (invented by Naugle and Townsend); it was the Cold Metal Process Co. which patented the Steckel reversing mill; and it was Republic which, in conjunction with the Babcock & Wilcox Co., developed the continuous casting process which promises to be among the more important technological developments of recent decades. Finally, it should be recognized that it was the German and not the American steel industry which became the leader in steel technology after World War I. It was Europe which taught us how to make stainless steels and how to save millions with by-product coke ovens.

Third, with respect to profitability, it is significant that some of the medium-sized companies have fared considerably better than the giant U.S. Steel Corporation.[81] To the extent that profit figures are valid as measures of efficiency, the record would show a balance in favor of the medium-sized firm. Moreover, multiplant companies seem to have performed no better than single-plant organizations. Thus, Professor Bain found that between 1936–40 and 1947–51 there was "apparently no significant relation of profit rate on equity to size of firm among the 15 largest steel firms in the United States, although these firms ranged in size from U.S. Steel, with about nineteen mills, down to single-plant firms. Although these profit-

---

[80] *Ibid.,* p. 996. This was the statement of Professor Stigler who argued that Bethlehem, and possibly Republic, might also be subjected to dissolution proceedings.

[81] For empirical efforts to measure the relation between size and efficiency, see TNEC Monograph No. 13, *Relative Efficiency of Large, Medium-Sized, and Small Business,* Washington, D.C., 1941, pp. 26–29, 106, 214–397; W. L. Crum, *Corporate Size and Earning Power,* Cambridge: Harvard University Press, 1939; R. C. Epstein, *Industrial Profits in the United States,* New York: National Bureau of Economic Research, 1934. Care must be exercised in making profit comparisons the measure of relative efficiency in corporations of different size. Profit rates often do not measure relative efficiency, since "the rate of profit is affected by bargaining advantages and various other factors as well as by efficiency of operation. Since bargaining advantage tends to grow with size, a corresponding increase of profits might be attributable to corporate power, whereas a failure of profits to increase, too, might be a persuasive indication that the level of efficient operation had been passed." From *Maintaining Competition* by C. D. Edwards, p. 119. Copyright 1949. Reprinted by courtesy of the McGraw-Hill Book Co., New York. For a general discussion on the relation between size and efficiency in multiple-plant enterprises, see Edwards, *op.cit.,* pp. 113–20.

rate data are not conclusive," says Bain, "they are consistent with the hypothesis that economies did not result from expansion beyond a single integrated plant with from one to 2.5 million ingot tons capacity."[82]

On the basis of the little authoritative information available, we can say that while large firms are necessary for efficient steel production, and while a considerable degree of vertical integration is imperative for maximum efficiency, the optimum size of firm is substantially smaller than that of the largest companies today. While there can never be enough firms in the steel industry—from the point of view of the technological and economic optimum—to assure even an approximation to perfect competition, there can nevertheless be enough firms to assure more intense competition than prevails today. There can be enough decentralization of power to assure a basic minimum of freedom for individual action "so that new ideas, new men, and new organizations will have the bona fide chance to introduce themselves."[83]

What makes the achievement of more effective competition in the steel industry so compelling is a consideration of the alternatives. Once we grant the unworkability of competition, the only alternatives seem to be: (1) a supervision of steel prices by a government commission (along the ICC pattern);[84] (2) a government counterspeculation agency;[85] (3) direct government participation in the steel industry; (4) industry self-government along NIRA lines, and (5) outright socialization. A perusal of the choice available should convince us that experimenting with the workability of competition is worthwhile. Only after fair trial and definitive failure, should we consider abandoning a competitive plan for the steel industry.

Conclusion

In conclusion, let us note that the steel industry today stands at an important cross-road. It is on the horns of the proverbial dilemma. If it con-

---

[82] Bain, *op.cit.*, p. 255. Medium-sized firms have an advantage especially in times of depression when an organization like U.S. Steel finds itself too big to limit its operations only to the successful branches of the industry. "When the current is adverse, smaller companies can make headway in the eddies, but the Steel Corporation must breast the main stream. Furthermore the bigger a company the harder to keep it operating at a satisfactory percentage of capacity, if for no other reason than that buyers of steel tend to divide their orders equally among steel companies rather than on a basis prorated to capacity." Reprinted from *Fortune*, March 1936, p. 170, by special permission of the Editors. Copyright Time, Inc.

[83] D. McC. Wright, "What's Best for the Competitive Enterprise System" in U.S. Chamber of Commerce, *op.cit.*, p. 205.

[84] This proposal was advocated by Judge Gary, former president of United States Steel, before the Stanley Committee.

[85] See A. P. Lerner, *The Economics of Control*, New York: Macmillan, 1944.

cedes that effective price competition is feasible, it must go out and play the capitalistic game according to its naked, shameless, yet vitalizing and invigorating rules. If, on the other hand, it follows Judge Gary's lead and insists that competition in steel is impossible, that competition must somehow give way to cooperation, the industry must then accept some form of government regulation to protect the public interest. In any event, the industry can hardly continue with a structural organization under which every price change becomes the subject of a congressional investigation; every labor dispute the cause of a national emergency; every refusal to expand capacity the invitation to threats of governmental competition. The brutal choice before the steel industry seems to lie between the painful rigors of competition and the anguished frustrations of bureaucratic regulation.

SUGGESTED READINGS

Books and Pamphlets

A. R. Burns, *The Decline of Competition* (New York: McGraw-Hill, 1936).

J. M. Clark, *The Economics of Overhead Costs* (Chicago: University of Chicago Press, 1923).

C. R. Daugherty, M. G. de Chazeau, and S. S. Stratton, *Economics of the Iron and Steel Industry*, 2 vols. (New York: McGraw-Hill, 1937).

F. A. Fetter, *The Masquerade of Monopoly* (New York: Harcourt, Brace, 1931).

F. Machlup, *The Basing Point System* (Philadelphia: Blakiston, 1949).

H. R. Seager and C. A. Gulick, *Trust and Corporation Problems* (New York: Harper, 1929).

United States Steel Corporation, *TNEC Papers*, 3 vols. (New York, 1940).

H. H. Wein, *Steel Mergers, Competition, and the Clayton Act* (East Lansing: Bureau of Business & Economic Research, Michigan State University, 1961).

Government Publications

Federal Trade Commission, *Report on the Control of Iron Ore* (Washington, 1952).

Hearings before the Subcommittee on Antitrust and Monopoly, Senate Judiciary Committee, *Administered Prices: Steel*, Parts 2, 3, 4 (Washington, 1957).

Hearings before the Subcommittee on the Study of Monopoly Power, House Judiciary Committee, *Steel*, Serial 14, Parts 4-A and 4-B (Washington, 1950).

Hearings before the Temporary National Economic Committee, *Iron and Steel Industry*, Parts 19, 20, 26, 27 (Washington, 1940).

Subcommittee on Antitrust and Monopoly, Senate Judiciary Committee, *Administered Prices: Steel* (Washington, 1958).

Subcommittee on the Study of Monopoly Power, House Judiciary Committee, *The Iron and Steel Industry* (Washington, 1950).

Temporary National Economic Committee, *Price Discrimination in Steel,* Monograph No. 41 (Washington, 1941).
————, *The Basing Point Problem,* Monograph No. 42 (Washington, 1941).
U.S. Tariff Commission, "Iron and Steel," *War Changes in Industry Series,* Report No. 15 (Washington, 1946).
U.S. versus *Bethlehem Steel Corp., et. al.,* 168 F. Supp. 576 (1958).

Journal and Magazine Articles

Fortune, "Basing Points: The Great Muddle," Vol. 38, September 1948.
Fortune, "Steel in the West," Vol. 31, February 1945.
Fortune, "That Daffy Gray Market," Vol. 37, May 1948.
Fortune, "U.S. Steel I:" Vol. 13, March 1936.
Fortune, "U.S. Steel II: Prices," Vol. 13, April 1936.
Fortune, "U.S. Steel III: Labor," Vol. 13, May 1936.
Fortune, "U.S. Steel IV:" Vol. 13, June 1936.
Iron Age, New York, various numbers.
A. Smithies, "Aspects of the Basing-Point System," *American Economic Review,* Vol. XXXII, December 1942.

Chapter 6

ROBERT F. LANZILLOTTI

The Aluminum Industry

Within a relatively short span of years aluminum has become a principal basic industrial material, rivaling steel's status and significance in both peacetime and wartime. An annual average growth rate of about 11 per cent since the early 1900's underscores the rather spectacular growth of world-wide aluminum production, particularly since World War II. Aluminum's economic significance is also illustrated by the fact that today twenty-five countries have fully integrated aluminum industries, and one or more stages of the productive process—from the mining of the basic material, bauxite, to the fabrication of aluminum products—have been established in many other areas of the world.

In recent years, the Soviet Bloc countries have emerged as important producers, and their estimated total production now exceeds that of Canada, which had long been the world's second largest producer. According to most recent estimates (1958), the percentages of world output accounted for by the U.S., Canada, and the Soviet Bloc countries were approximately 40, 15, and 20 per cent, respectively.

SECTION I: INTRODUCTION

The history of the aluminum industry in the United States is in very large part a study of the Aluminum Company of America, more commonly known as Alcoa. Until the post-World War II period, Alcoa represented the classic example of a virtually complete manufacturing monopoly in the U.S. The growth pattern and market behavior of the company included many of the activities customarily associated with monopoly—patent control, resource control, affiliations with international cartels, mergers and acquisitions, and the use of exclusionary tactics of various types, including the "squeeze" on

185

nonintegrated competitors and potential competitors. In its early growth, the company also experienced success in its skirmishes with the antitrust law, largely as a consequence of weak administration of the law, timid court interpretations, and weakly-drawn consent judgments.

Patents and Early Development

The early development of the industry in the U.S. was closely tied to patent control. The first economical technique for producing aluminum (i.e., extracting the aluminum from aluminum oxide) was developed independently in 1886 by Charles M. Hall in the U.S. and Paul L. T. Héroult in France. The Hall-Héroult electrolytic process for reducing aluminum from its compound with oxygen is still in use today, basically unchanged. The Pittsburgh Reduction Company (after 1907, Alcoa), backer of Hall's experiments, was formed in 1888 by Hall and several Pittsburgh industrialists. Another U.S. company, the Cowles Electric Smelting and Aluminum Company, had been producing aluminum alloys since 1885 (using the C. S. Bradley patent), but had failed in its attempts to produce commercially pure aluminum by a carbon reduction process. From 1891 to 1893 Cowles Electric produced aluminum using an electrolytic process essentially the same as the Hall process, but after losing a patent infringement suit to Pittsburgh Reduction, the Cowles Company shifted to aluminum fabrication. In 1903, however, Cowles won a countersuit on the alleged infringement, based upon the broad process patent issued to Bradley in 1892, which the Cowles Company had secured by a combination of luck, shrewdness, and persistent litigation. It was all too clear at this stage that the Hall and Bradley patents blocked one another, and the two firms reached a speedy agreement for the sale of the Bradley patents to Pittsburgh Reduction. The Cowles brothers, who were perhaps better able to enter into aluminum production than any other men in the U.S. at that time, decided to withdraw with a lump-sum payment and annual royalties and promised not to enter the aluminum field again. Thus, with the protection of the Hall patent until 1906 and the Bradley patents until 1909, the monopoly of virgin aluminum production in the United States was assured.

There were four European producers in existence at this time, using the Hall-Héroult process.[1] The threat of competition from these firms called for either an aggressive policy in dealing with foreign competitors or a regula-

[1] The Swiss Company Aluminum Industries, A.G. (AIAG), 1888; the French companies Société Electro-Métallurgique Française (1889), and Societé Industrielle d'Aluminum (1894), taken over by Compagnie des Produits Chimiques d'Alais et de las Camargue in 1896; and the British Aluminum Company (1896).

tion of the market. Pittsburgh Reduction tried both. It licensed a small established metal firm in 1895, openly challenging the established European aluminum producers, and in 1896 reached an accord with AIAG (the Swiss company) not to invade one another's domestic or "natural" market. Earlier, the appearance of Cowles, the competition from European producers, the cost reductions incident to perfecting the technique of production, and cheaper energy all helped to reduce the price of aluminum in the U.S. from $5 a pound in 1887 to 75 cents in 1893, and 33 cents in 1899. However, any serious threats from foreign competition were forestalled by a cartel agreement that closed the U.S. market to European producers, by the imposition of a tariff, and finally by the increasing demands of European home markets.

In this early period, a chief problem was the difficulty of finding markets for aluminum. In fact, until 1904–05 most of the aluminum output was consumed by the iron and steel industry for improving the quality of steel, cast iron, and wrought-iron products. With the exception of this market, aluminum could hardly be sold in ingot form. The marketing problem was further complicated during the 1890's as a result of attempted applications of the material to uses for which it was ill-suited or on which inadequate research had been done to develop suitable alloys. With aluminum rapidly developing a bad name in several industries, the Pittsburgh Reduction Company became convinced that fabrication of aluminum products was necessary to demonstrate the advantages of the metal in various uses.

After the mid-1890's a fairly distinct growth pattern can be traced for the company, which is best described as two-dimensional—mostly vertical integration moves from 1895 until around 1910, and horizontal expansion through the twenties and thirties. Beginning in 1895 the company pursued an active policy of *backward* integration with the acquisition of bauxite deposits, the development of hydroelectric projects, and the integration of ore refining and processing. At the same time integration was being effected *forward* into the manufacture of finished and semi-finished aluminum products. By 1910, Alcoa had become a very highly integrated concern. It owned bauxite deposits (the basic material from which alumina is extracted) in Georgia, Alabama, and Arkansas. These ores were processed through its crushing, grinding, and drying plant, converted into aluminum oxide at its East St. Louis plant, and then sent to its reduction furnaces at Niagara Falls and Massena, New York, and Shawinigan Falls, Quebec. Most of the electricity needed for reduction of aluminum was generated by Alcoa subsidiaries and carbon anodes and furnace linings were manufactured in its own plants. A large part of its ingot production was used for rolling sheets, rods, tubes, shapes, cooking utensils, wire, aluminum bronze powder, and other articles.

It is estimated that a substantial reduction in cost undoubtedly resulted from this vertical control.[2]

Horizontal Expansion and Market Control

1905–29. Development of aluminum markets and desire for greater efficiency soon gave way to market control considerations. Although the patent protection and other protective measures mentioned earlier had provided a solid foundation for Alcoa's monopoly position, these pillars had to be strengthened for the day when the basic patents expired, when a rupture might develop in the cartel agreements, or when a shift might arise in United States commercial policy. Accordingly, about 1905 when its vertical integration was essentially complete, the company embarked upon an extensive program of horizontal expansion including the aggressive acquisition of large reserves of foreign ores and power, purchase of foreign reduction plants, and the extension of fabrication facilities. The increase from $1,000,-000 in assets when commercial production began to $12,000,000 in capital and surplus in 1912, to $50,000,000 by 1915, and to $250,000,000 by 1928, reflects the magnitude of Alcoa's growth during this phase.

The company's expansion during the twenties dwarfed that of foreign producers. It added to its *bauxite* holdings in British and Dutch Guiana, acquired new reserves in France, Yugoslavia, Greece, and Istria. It expanded its *power* generating potential in Quebec, New York State, and on the Little Tennessee River; it also purchased power sites in Norway, Italy, the Pyrenees, and Southern France. In the *reduction* stage, it acquired a 50 per cent controlling interest in the reduction facilities of an important Norwegian firm which also possessed bauxite holdings in France and Surinam and a fabricating plant in France. It also acquired majority interest in a European company, which held important electrode patents as well as a substantial interest in the Tysse water power in Norway, and a one-third interest in another Norwegian company, giving Alcoa an equal share with British and French interests. At the *fabricating* level, Alcoa expanded its capacity in South America and constructed two large mills in New Jersey and Tennessee. Finally, the company expanded its railway and steamship interests.

The economic significance of Alcoa's policy regarding horizontal expansion generally and the acquisition of bauxite reserves in particular (variously estimated by the Department of Justice to constitute approxi-

[2] Donald W. Wallace, *Market Control in the Aluminum Industry*, Cambridge: Harvard University Press, 1937, p. 27.

mately 90 per cent of the known reserves at the time), was to perpetuate market control after the company's patent monopoly expired in 1909. All of the company's acquisitions and purchases were strategic for market control purposes—i.e., they entailed important patents and bauxite reserves, helped cement interests with foreign producers, and provided the leverage against the latter in maintaining Alcoa's market position in the United States.

Tariff Protection for Alcoa. A further barrier to potential competition in the United States market was the early and continuing restrictive tariff imposed by the U.S. on aluminum imports (Table 1). The Dingley Tariff of

TABLE 1

United States Duties on Aluminum, Ingot, and Fabricated Products, 1890–1939
(in cents per pound and percentage ad valorem)

Years	Ingot	Sheet	Foil	Utensils	Other Manufactures
1890–94	15¢	—	—	—	—
1894–97	10¢	*	*	35%	35%
1897–1909	8¢	13¢	*	45%	45%
1909–13	7¢	11¢	*	45%	45%
1913–22	2¢	3½¢	*	25%	20%
1922–30	5¢	9¢	35%	11¢ + 55%	40%
1930–39	4¢	7¢	40%	8½¢ + 40%	45%

* No separate classification on these items in the years indicated.

Source: U.S. versus *Aluminum Company of America,* 44 F., Supp. 97 (1941), p. 411.

1897 fixed a rate for semi-fabricated aluminum products (plates, sheets, bars, and rods), at 13 cents a pound, crude aluminum metal, at 8 cents a pound, and on miscellaneous aluminum manufactures not specially named at 45 per cent ad valorem. Since the price of aluminum was dropping steadily during this period, the measure of protection afforded by these duties assumed greater and greater importance. The 1905 duty on crude metal, for example, was an estimated equivalent of 33 per cent ad valorem, and on semi-fabricated products about 16 per cent. Duties were reduced slightly under the Payne-Aldrich Tariff of 1909 and the Underwood Tariff of 1913. Even under the apparent low rates of the 1913 Tariff, the ad valorem equivalent was about 16 per cent.

Southern Aluminum's Unsuccessful Attempt to Enter U.S. Market. The only determined attempt to enter the United States market before World War I was made by a group of experienced French producers possessing their own bauxite deposits and with help from several large French and Swiss banks. The new firm (Southern Aluminum) acquired property obtained earlier by an American group which had purchased control of a hydroelectric company on the Yadkin River in North Carolina. Just before the outbreak of war, Southern Aluminum ran into a financial bind, and with the onset of the war further financing from Europe became virtually impossible. The company turned to financial interests in the U.S., but without success. Faced with the entire loss of the investment already sunk (about $5,500,000), the company sold its facilities to Alcoa in 1915.

The significance of this episode is to illustrate the extremely difficult conditions facing potential entrants into the U.S. market at this time. Despite the mists of war uncertainty, the Southern Aluminum plant could not be removed to Europe and it was as safe as any other domestic company from foreign plunder. Nonetheless, there was an apparent unwillingness on the part of United States bankers to finance new American enterprise for entry into the aluminum industry.[3] No other attempts to enter the industry were made until after World War I, by which time the size and strength of Alcoa had been even further enhanced.

1930–39. The 1930–39 decade was a period of consolidation and cooperation among world producers. Alcoa had incorporated all of its foreign holdings (except some of its bauxite deposits and some minor assets) in 1928 under Aluminium, Limited of Canada (Alted), presumably as a move to strengthen the American-Canadian group in its dealings with the European Cartel. Aluminium Limited was an independent company in form only—four of its shareholders owning 41 per cent interest in Alcoa also owned 55 per cent of the common voting stock in Aluminium, Limited. The importance of the Canadian subsidiary is best illustrated by its role in the international aluminum cartels.

Alcoa and the International Cartels

The First Cartel (1901). The first international aluminum cartel was formed by the four European producers listed above and Northern Aluminum Company, a Canadian subsidiary of Alcoa. The agreement's terms were typical for any cartel: (1) home markets were reserved for domestic producers; (2) foreign markets were divided with each of the firms assigned a share of those markets; and (3) domestic as well as international prices were set by the cartel (domestic prices being set one cent higher than those

---

[3] There is reason to believe that the lack of interest shown by American bankers in financing competitive aluminum producers was a sign of deference to the Mellon family's financial interests in Alcoa. Cf. Wallace, *op.cit.,* pp. 113, 151; see also TNEC Monograph No. 29, *The Distribution of Ownership in the 200 Largest Nonfinancial Corporations,* Washington: 1940, p. 1489.

quoted in foreign markets to prevent third parties from buying up aluminum and reselling it in the open market). The result was higher prices both in Europe and the U.S. However, due to an imbalance between production and quotas among members, the growth of noncartel producers, and the general influence of the 1907–08 depression, all agreements were dissolved. The European price fell sharply and foreign metal began to pour into New York, causing a like drop in the U.S. price.

The Second Cartel (1912). An interim agreement of early 1912 to reserve markets was short-lived. The expiration of the Héroult patent, and the entry of seven new European producers not bound by the agreement, precipitated a price war, causing further declines in the U.S. price for ingots. At the same time sales more than doubled and Alcoa's net profits increased to 41 per cent of stockholders' equity in 1909 and 50 per cent in 1910.[4] Alcoa was eager to reestablish its monopoly in the U.S. by a new market stabilization agreement, and the second cartel was formed several months later, to run for ten years. A consent decree entered into by Alcoa on June 7, 1912 (five days before the new cartel agreement was ratified by the members) enjoined the company from entrance into any agreement curtailing importation of aluminum into the United States or affecting the domestic price. Alcoa got around this obstacle by using its Canadian subsidiary, Northern Aluminum, in the negotiations.

In general, the terms of the cartel agreement were similar to those of the first cartel: home markets were reserved and open markets (*other than the United States*) were apportioned on the basis of production quotas, with each member free to sell his quota where he chose. The United States market was not *expressly* reserved for Alcoa, but a specific clause limiting cartel restrictions to "sales outside the United States" afforded protection to Alcoa. Thus, world production was effectively limited and prices held rigid, subject to periodic revision.

Alcoa apparently was willing to take a chance that the loss of some of its market would be temporary, and in the event this proved wrong to use the foreign invasion as a plea for retention of tariff protection. Another part of Alcoa's market strategy at this time was to stabilize aluminum prices. Its reluctance both to lower prices in 1907–08 and to raise prices late in 1912, when a sudden spurt exhausted its stocks is indicative of its early disposition toward price stabilization which has continued down through the years. The stability of prices in 1912 might be explained further by the antitrust case and the desire of the company to appear in a favorable light before Con-

[4] G. W. Stocking and M. W. Watkins, *Cartels in Action*, New York: Twentieth Century Fund, 1951, pp. 233–7.

gressional committees, which might raise unpleasant questions about the company's activities at a time when the company was seeking tariff protection.

World War I. During World War I, all producers expanded capacity and some new producers entered the field. Between 1914 and 1920 Alcoa doubled its capacity until near the end of the War, when the War Industries Board required Alcoa to cut its price to 33.5 cents. Following the end of hostilities, the United States became the focal point of competition for international markets. European exports to the United States in 1920 and 1921 equaled almost one-half of total American production, and helped push the price of ingot down to around the prewar level of 19 cents a pound. Alcoa countered this invasion of the U.S. with the extension of its interests in European bauxite deposits, hydroelectric developments, and fabricating facilities.

The Third Cartel (1926). A price agreement among European producers in 1923 broke down within two years, so a more stringent cartel was reestablished in 1926 along the lines of prewar arrangements. The association's executive committee was empowered to periodically set standard delivered prices, uniform for all markets, "closed" or "open." The 1926 agreement also went one step further than earlier arrangements; it applied quota allocations both to ingot sales, sheet, and other fabricated shapes. The established quotas were enforced by heavy penalties for members exceeding their quota, while underquota members were reimbursed.

Although Alcoa was not formally a member of the 1926 cartel, the company generally cooperated with the cartel by observing its traditional policy of avoiding exports from the U.S. and scrupulously following the cartel-fixed prices in export sales through its Canadian subsidiary.[5] The absence of formal participation in the cartel by Alcoa, however, did not reduce the effectiveness of the control of international markets by any perceptible amount. Harmonious relationships were steadily maintained throughout the life of the agreement, with Alted representing Alcoa's interests when necessary.

The European-American "Alliance" (1931). With the worsening of the business conditions during the Great Depression of the thirties and the growing stocks of aluminum, more comprehensive control measures to stabilize aluminum markets were called for if prices were to be stabilized. The way had been paved for such a development just three years earlier with the formation of Alted and its emergence as a world power in aluminum

---

[5] Alcoa, for example, refused to sell to an Italian firm not a member of the cartel "lest it give grounds for suspicion that the North American companies were not loyally cooperating with the cartel." Its Canadian subsidiary refused to sell alumina to a Swiss concern which was not a cartel member, because "it would irritate members of the cartel." Cf. Stocking and Watkins, *op.cit.*, pp. 253–254.

production. Since Alcoa exercised control over 50 per cent of the world's productive capacity, it was important that it or Alted should take a leading role in any new schemes to broaden and strengthen the 1928 agreement. Alted took over the negotiations with European producers. The agreement signed in 1931 was the most effective of all the cartels mentioned due to the corporate structure and authority of the Alliance and the wide representation of world aluminum producers—nonmembers companies were those in Italy, U.S.S.R., Japan, and Alcoa in the U.S. Members of the Alliance were apportioned shares based upon 1930 production (one share equal to 100 tons of ingot), with respective quotas of whatever aggregate production the Alliance might set as follows: Alted, 28.6 per cent; French, 21.4 per cent; German, 19.6 per cent; Swiss, 15.4 per cent; and British, 15.0 per cent. Since production quotas were established and prices regulated for all sales, wherever made, effective control of world markets was insured, and no firm needed to fear an invasion of home markets by any member.

Alcoa's cooperation, of course, was crucial to the success of the cartel. Since the agreement made no express exception of the United States market, it seems to have been implicit that cartel members would "respect" Alcoa's dominant position in the U.S. Likewise it must be assumed that as a *quid pro quo* Alcoa would tacitly agree to some export control. The experience of the cartel bears out the "silent partner" relationship of Alcoa and the predominant influence Alcoa exercised through Alted in the operations of the alliance.

The new alliance was established for a period of 99 years, but its powers were weakened when Germany made known its plans to expand production (in line with the Nazi rearmament program). At first, the Alliance attempted to supply the increased demands of the German rearmament program within the cartel's proportional curtailment plans, but the incompatibility of the cartel's market strategy and the Nazi military program was soon evident. Thus, all quota restrictions were removed from German members with the proviso that German producers stay out of world markets, and as a result German annual production increased 200 per cent between 1933 and 1936, while American-Canadian capacity remained constant. By the end of 1937 German capacity exceeded that of the U.S. The importance of these developments for U.S. national security was all too clear shortly thereafter.

Magnesium Control: The Alcoa-I. G. Farben-Dow Cartel

Another weak link in Alcoa's market control strategy requiring attention was the threat from magnesium, the lightest known metal, which has many properties in common with aluminum. The potential substitution of the two metals in a wide range of uses, with cost constituting no great obstacle, meant that any program Alcoa developed for "rationalizing" or "monopolizing" aluminum would be effective only if similar measures were taken to control magnesium production.

The only two firms in existence after World War I were the Dow Chemical Company and American Magnesium Company (AMC), which was acquired by Alcoa in 1924. Dow's interest in the economical utilization of raw materials of its chemical operations and Alcoa's desire to protect its vested interest in aluminum provided special incentives for each to participate in the development of magnesium. Independent behavior under the duopoly was clearly an unacceptable relationship, and in 1927 purchase and cross-licensing agreements were signed. The peaceful co-existence arrangement was threatened by I. G. Farben (IG), then Germany's largest magnesium producer, thus creating a three-sided conflict of interest in magnesium. However, between 1931 and 1934, all conflicting interests were resolved and an international magnesium cartel was fully implemented.[6]

The economic significance of the cartel is to illustrate the role of inter-industry competition and how it can be suppressed. The tendency of the cartel to retard magnesium growth by its discriminatory policies assured Alcoa of a development of magnesium in accordance with its own plans, and in keeping the price of magnesium above the "volume parity" level as against aluminum.[7] During the thirties, aluminum and magnesium prices stood in nearly a 1 to 1.5 ratio; the price of magnesium did not dip below the margin theoretically protecting aluminum from competition until 1939.

In summary, the aluminum and magnesium cartels gave Alcoa essentially the edge it needed over potential competitors, both in the aluminum and magnesium fields. By controlling imports of aluminum into the United States and engaging in agreements to control magnesium fabrication, while simultaneously keeping the prices of aluminum and magnesium under control, Alcoa effectively restricted entry for many years into the aluminum industry and light metals generally.

Alcoa and the Law

In view of the circumstances surrounding Alcoa's control of the U.S. market, its relationships with the aluminum and magnesium cartels, and its

---

[6] For a detailed account of the negotiations among the three producers, see Stocking and Watkins, pp. 276 ff., and Charlotte F. Mueller, *Light Metals Monopoly*, New York: Columbia University Press, 1946.

[7] Magnesium, with a specific gravity approximately two-thirds that of aluminum, reaches "volume parity" in price with aluminum when magnesium sells at 1.5 times the price of aluminum.

tactics in dealing with potential competitors, it was almost inevitable that the company should run afoul of the antitrust laws. In retrospect, perhaps the most surprising thing is the small measure of success which the government realized through court action up to and including the landmark decision of 1945.

1912 Consent Decree. The first action against Alcoa was speedily settled by the consent decree of 1912 calling for (1) cancelling the 1908 cartel agreement with AIAG, (2) dropping the restrictive agreements which kept two firms, whose bauxite Alcoa had purchased, from producing aluminum, (3) enjoining Alcoa from taking part directly in agreements or mergers which had the effect of controlling output or price, and (4) discontinuing price and other discriminations against competitors (including refusal or threat of refusal to deliver raw materials for aluminum production). The ineffectiveness of the decree was well illustrated by the signing of the 1912 cartel agreement just a few days after Alcoa had signed the consent decree. The mere cancellation of restrictive agreements and the failure of the decree to specifically cover exclusionary tactics, while granting Alcoa permission to quote special prices and to refuse to deal with certain customers, did little to promote the cause of competition in aluminum. Moreover, weak enforcement by the government of the injunction against discriminatory practices resulted in making a mockery of the 1912 decree.

Federal Trade Commission Actions. The FTC likewise was unsuccessful in two separate actions brought against the company. The FTC was sustained in the first suit, charging that Alcoa's purchase of controlling stock in the Cleveland Products Company violated Section 7 of the Clayton Act, and Alcoa was ordered to sell its holdings. However, Alcoa reacquired Cleveland Products at a sheriff's sale, held to settle the heavy indebtedness of the company—a situation which arose in large part out of a supply contract with Alcoa for ingot in quantities and at prices that were ruinous under the government's wartime price-fixing of aluminum products. The FTC objected to the sale, but was overruled by the same judges who earlier had sustained the FTC in the case.

The other suit against Alcoa was based upon the FTC's 1924 report to the Congress disclosing repeated violations of the 1912 consent decree—e.g., by delaying of shipment of materials to competitors, forwarding of materials known to be defective, discrimination in prices, and hindering competitors from enlarging their operations.[8] However, when the Department of Justice issued a rebuttal in 1926 clearing Alcoa of the alleged charges,[9] the FTC

---

[8] FTC, Vol. 3, p. xxxii.
[9] *Aluminum Company of America*, Senate Doc. 67, Sixty-ninth Cong., 1st Sess., 1926, p. v.

was forced to dismiss its complaint (in 1930) admitting the charges could not be sustained by the available evidence.[10]

The 1945 Conviction of Alcoa. The major attack on Alcoa was filed by the Department of Justice in 1937 charging violation of both Section 1 and Section 2 of the Sherman Act, i.e., both conspiracy to restrain trade and monopolization. The specific charges, which read like a history of Alcoa, were as follows:

(1) conspiracy with foreign producers to restrain importation of aluminum into the U.S., to fix prices, limit production, and to allocate customers of alumina and aluminum products; and

(2) monopolizing the production and sale of aluminum and aluminum products (including castings, cooking utensils, pistons, extrusions, structural shapes, sheet, cable, foil, and miscellaneous other products), by (a) acquiring bauxite deposits, water power sites and plants in excess of its needs, and entering into restrictive agreements designed to prevent potential competitors from obtaining water power; and (b) "squeezing" independent fabricators (e.g., Baush) by fixing and maintaining the price differential between ingot and fabricated products at such levels as to suppress and exclude others from the production of aluminum products.

In 1941, three years after the court trial began, District Judge Francis G. Caffey ruled in favor of Alcoa on all charges. Relying to a large extent upon the decision handed down in the U.S. Steel case of 1920 and the International Harvester case of 1927, Caffey held that mere size, unaccompanied by abuses of power did not violate the Sherman Act. The Justice Department appealed to the Supreme Court, but four of the Justices disqualified themselves because of earlier participation in the case before appointment to the court. Congress then passed legislation to cover such situations by giving authority to the New York Circuit Court of Appeals to hear the appeal.

In 1945, Judge Learned Hand, speaking for the three judges, sustained Caffey on almost all charges, but held that Alcoa had in fact monopolized the market for primary (virgin) aluminum. The opinion was a milestone in antitrust history in unequivocally reversing the old dictum that mere size is no offense, and providing a more economically meaningful standard by which to judge monopolization under the Sherman Act. According to Judge Hand, size was not only evidence of violation, or of potential offense under the Sherman Act, it was the essence of the offense. Size—meaning market control—was what competition and monopoly were about.[11] He rejected the contention accepted by Judge Caffey that "secondary" aluminum should be included in determining Alcoa's share of the market. The decisive fact in

---

[10] Aluminum Company of America, Docket 1335, 13 FTC 333 (1930).
[11] Cf. Eugene Rostow, *A National Policy for the Oil Industry*, 1948, p. 127.

Hand's view was that many years after its patents had expired, Alcoa made, and then fabricated or sold, over 90 per cent of the *virgin* aluminum consumed in the United States.

Going further, Judge Hand held that Alcoa's arrangements with foreign companies for dividing world markets provided additional evidence of monopolizing.[12] The fact that it had engaged in deplorable tactics to prevent other firms from entering the industry compounded the offense. Abuse of power was found in the sale of fourteen gauges of sheet aluminum from 1925 to 1932 at too small a margin above ingot prices to allow adequate profit to independent sheet producers (such as Baush Machine and Tool and the Sheet Aluminum Corporation).

Regarding the all-important problem of appropriate relief, the court deferred to the exigencies of war and the promise of industry reconstruction through other means. The case was turned back to the District Court with instructions to withhold remedial measures until after the disposal of the government's surplus aluminum plants constructed during World War II. The court refused to decree immediate dissolution on the grounds that the disposition of the war plants would so alter the structure of the industry "it would be idle for the government to assume that dissolution would be proper, as it is for Alcoa to assume it would not be . . ."[13] Judge Hand's decision expressed concern about the possible loss of technical efficiency,[14] although he did not argue that such loss would prevent him from decreeing dissolution. In any event, the sharp contrast of the form of relief granted in relation to the court's ringing denunciation of the monopoly, serves to illustrate once again the reluctance of the courts to decreeing divestiture or dissolution. In this case, in particular, however, it is altogether surprising that a company which had monopolized the aluminum industry for almost fifty years was allowed to remain intact, the restructuring of the industry to be accomplished by "indirection."[15]

Disposal of Government Aluminum Plants. Tremendous expansion of aluminum production was required by the military needs of World War II

---

[12] He also enjoined Alted, although a foreign corporation, from further participation in cartels.

[13] *U.S. versus Aluminum Company of America*, 148 F. 2d 416 (2d Circuit, 1945), p. 446.

[14] On this score, there is no evidence that Alcoa's size at the time was justified by efficiency considerations. On the contrary, while some cost-reductions may have resulted from the combination of plants, the optimum size of *individual* plants and the *company* evidently had been reached by 1905. By 1914, at the latest, the aluminum industry was large enough to support at least three or four independent firms of optimum size, and by 1945 several times that number. Cf. Wallace, p. 202.

[15] Cf. Walter Adams, "The Aluminum Case: Legal Victory—Economic Defeat," *American Economic Review*, December 1951, pp. 914–22.

with the government undertaking a total investment of about $700,000,000 in aluminum and allied facilities. (See Table 2.) The magnitude of this investment is indicated by Alcoa's wartime expansion, nearly doubling its capacity between 1941 and 1944, with total assets of $475,000,000. Most of the government-owned plants were designed, constructed, and operated by Alcoa.

Disposal of the government-owned plants in conformance with the objectives of the Surplus Property Act [16] and the Hand decision was made difficult by a number of problems: [17]

1. Judge Hand's decision had limited the Surplus Property Board to a narrow course of action; the Board had no power to restructure Alcoa and it really could not sell the plants to many independent firms incapable of coping with Alcoa. This meant the Board had to create new producers large enough to compete with Alcoa.

2. Some of the plants were so poorly located and had such high power costs as to handicap disposal (Maspeth, Burlington, Los Angeles, Riverbank, and Massena—see Table 2).

3. Both the medium-grade domestic bauxite reserves and the high-grade supplies abroad were mainly under the control of Alcoa and its Canadian affiliate Aluminium, Limited (Alted).

4. An insured supply of electric power was necessary at rates which did not place new producers at a disadvantage vis-à-vis Alcoa, which generates much of its own power.

5. The enormous stockpile of excess aluminum (largely secondary metal and scrap), equal to ten times the 1939 demand for primary aluminum, had to be released without hurting the price level and operating rates of the new producers.

6. Although most of the aluminum patents had expired by the end of the war, the plants operated by Alcoa (The Hurricane Creek plant in particular), used equipment, techniques, or alloys protected by patents. Alcoa was willing to license but not to turn over its patents to any new producers.

7. Leases held by Alcoa were not due to expire until 1947 and 1948, which meant that the entire disposal program might fail unless Alcoa gave up its leases prior to 1947.

As matters turned out, Alcoa's leases were cancelled on technical grounds,

[16] The Act provided that government-owned property was to be disposed so as (a) to give maximum aid in the reestablishment of a peacetime economy of free independent enterprise, (b) to foster the development of the maximum of independent operators, (c) to discourage monopolistic practices, and (d) to strengthen the position of small business concerns.

[17] Cf. Walter Adams and Horace M. Gray, *Monopoly in America*, New York, 1955, pp. 126–132.

Alcoa agreed to make its patents available on a royalty-free basis, newcomers were promised access to the government's bauxite reserves, flexible power contracts were to be made available on public power (through the Tennessee Valley Authority and Bonneville Power Administration), secondary aluminum supplies were to be sold over a long period, and liberal terms of lease or sale of plants with prices to be determined by earning ability.

The disposal of war plants resulted in a drastic transformation of the aluminum industry—from a single-firm monopoly to a three-firm oligopoly. The first breach in Alcoa's control actually had been made in 1941, when the Reynolds Metals Company (the leading manufacturer of aluminum foil), with the aid of a Reconstruction Finance Corporation loan, began operating a new 30,000–ton fully integrated plant. While this was the first successful entry into primary aluminum production since 1893, Alcoa still owned or operated 96 per cent of alumina capacity, 91 per cent of primary (ingot-pig) capacity, and from 80 to 90 per cent of the important fabricated products such as shapes, sheets, bars, and extrusions. Reynolds rounded out its integrated operations by acquiring the alumina plant at Hurricane Creek, Arkansas, ingot plants at nearby Jones Mill and Troutdale, Oregon, and fabricating plants at Listerhill, Alabama, McCook, Illinois, and Grand Rapids, Michigan (Table 2). Kaiser got the government alumina plant at Baton Rouge, Alabama, reduction plants at Spokane and Tacoma, Washington, and fabricating mills at Spokane and Newark, Ohio (Table 2). The net result was that by 1948 aluminum reduction capacity was distributed as follows: Alcoa, 50 per cent, Reynolds, 30 per cent, and Kaiser, 20 per cent. The market power of Alcoa, though not destroyed, was substantially weakened.

Sequels to the Case. In 1947, Alcoa petitioned the District Court for a decree that the company had ceased to monopolize primary aluminum production, holding that competitive conditions prevailed. The government opposed this move in a petition filed in 1948, and requested the court to divest Alcoa of enough plants to create effective competition. Judge Knox ruled in 1950 that Alcoa still had the power to expand disproportionately and thus exclude competitors. But he denied the government's petition for divestiture stating that effective competition depended upon "balance" (i.e., countervailing power) in the market, and reducing the power of Alcoa through dissolution would hamper rather than promote competition. The court, however, required certain large stockholders of Alcoa to divest themselves of either their Alcoa stock or Aluminium Limited stock, and extended jurisdiction in the case for a period of five years. In June 1957, the government

TABLE 2

Government Alumina, Aluminum Reduction, and Fabrication Plants
(costing $5,000,000 or more)

Type of Plant and Location	Cost to the Government	Annual Capacity (short tons)	Wartime Operator	Sold or Leased to
Alumina plants:				
Hurricane Creek, Ark.	$39,331,000	777,500	Alcoa	Reynolds
Baton Rouge, La.	25,682,000	500,000	Alcoa	Kaiser
Reduction plants:				
Maspeth, Queens, N.Y.	32,571,000	148,458	Alcoa	Cannibalized
Jones Mills, Ark.	29,258,000	76,038	Alcoa	Reynolds
Los Angeles, Calif.	24,042,000	92,820	Alcoa	Cannibalized
Spokane, Wash.	22,270,000	109,392	Alcoa	Kaiser
Massena, N.Y.	19,081,000	53,874	Alcoa	Standby
Troutdale, Ore.	18,898,000	70,356	Alcoa	Reynolds
Burlington, N.J.	16,768,000	54,384	Alcoa	Cannibalized
Riverbank, Calif.	11,657,000	54,960	Alcoa	Cannibalized
Tacoma, Wash.	6,309,000	20,094	Olin	Kaiser
Fabrication plants:				
Spokane, Wash.	47,630,000	144,000	Alcoa	Kaiser
Chicago, Ill.	44,327,000	144,000	Alcoa	Reynolds
Cressona, Pa.	25,237,000	27,850	Alcoa	Alcoa
Newark, Ohio	23,198,000	150,000	Alcoa	Alcoa
Listerhill, Ala.	20,031,000	66,000	Reynolds	Reynolds
Los Angeles, Calif.	8,149,000	11,594	Bohn	Harvey
Grand Rapids, Mich.	6,775,000	11,466	Extruded Metals	Reynolds

Source: United States Department of Commerce, Materials Survey—Aluminum (November 1956), p. VII–22; Adams and Gray, op.cit., p. 127.

petitioned for another five-year extension, but was refused by District Court Judge Cashin, who ruled that the new entrants had thrived and could effectively compete with Alcoa, whose relative share of the market had declined appreciably.

SECTION II: MARKET STRUCTURE AND PRICE POLICY IN THE FIFTIES

Market Structure

The aluminum industry today consists of four principal groups of producers: (1) the "Big Three" integrated companies (Alcoa, Reynolds, and Kaiser) which produce alumina, primary metal, semifabricated shapes, and some finished products; (2) the new integrated companies—the "Little

Three," Anaconda, Harvey, and Ormet (Olin-Revere Metals Company), which produce primary metal and semifabricated shapes; (3) the secondary smelters who buy scrap and produce ingot for foundries, metallurgical and other uses (e.g., for oxidizing steel and making alloys); and (4) the non-integrated fabricators, who make semifabricated shapes. In terms of structure, therefore, the industry is best described as an oligopoly with a competitive fringe. The oligopoly core—Alcoa, Reynolds, and Kaiser—dominate the industry; together they account for over 90 per cent of alumina capacity, 88 per cent of ingot capacity, and from 40 per cent to 90 per cent of the market for aluminum mill shapes.

Alumina Capacity and Bauxite Reserves. As of December 1958, Alcoa had 36 per cent, Reynolds, 33 per cent, Kaiser, 22 per cent, and Ormet, 9 per cent of domestic alumina capacity. (Table 3.) With the completion of plants under constructure in 1959, Alcoa's capacity will increase to 41 per cent of the industry total.

The "Big Three" also are amply supplied with *bauxite* reserves for their alumina plants. Alcoa's main reserves are in Arkansas and Surinam, with a concession in the Dominican Republic and some low-grade reserves in Arkansas.[18] Reynolds relied on government bauxite stockpile for a few years and now has reserves of its own in Jamaica, Haiti, and British Guiana. Kaiser has a contract to purchase from Alcoa up to 500,000 tons a year until 1963,[19] and recently has developed bauxite deposits on a concession in Jamaica, which now constitute the major source of the company's supply. Regarding the "Little Three," Ormet gets bauxite under a long-term contract from Surinam, Anaconda has a long-term contract with Kaiser, and Harvey buys alumina under long-term contracts with two Japanese companies.

Primary Reduction (Ingot) Capacity. The dominance of the "Big Three"

[18] The bulk of the bauxite consumed in the U.S. is imported—86 per cent in 1958. The United States has only limited reserves of high-grade bauxite ore, and the high alumina clays found in Oregon and Washington are not economical to mine under present technology and prices. However, Anaconda expects to extract alumina from these clays in a few years on a mass-production basis at a cost less than the price at which bauxite can be purchased from others. Cf. United States Department of the Interior, "Quarterly Bauxite Report No. 52," *Mineral Industry Surveys* (April 7, 1959), Table 1, and *Aluminum Industry Hearings before Subcommittee No. 3 of the Select Committee on Small Business* [hereafter Yates Hearings (1958)] House of Representatives, Eighty-fifth Cong., 1st and 2nd Sess., Washington, 1958, p. 241.

[19] The Department of Justice objected to this arrangement but it was on the horns of a dilemma. If it attempted to prevent this interim dependence on Alcoa, Kaiser might have had difficulty securing an adequate supply. Conversely, the Department probably would have been forced to object if Alcoa had refused to supply its newly created competitors. As a result, the Department did nothing. Cf. testimony of L. J. Emmerglick, *Study of Monopoly Power,* Hearings before Subcommittee on Study of Monopoly Power, House Judiciary Committee (hereafter Celler Hearings), Eighty-second Cong., 1st Sess., 1951, Serial 1, Part 1, "Aluminum," pp. 654–5.

TABLE 3

Alumina and Ingot Capacity of Primary Aluminum Products, Selected Years, 1950-60
(thousands of short tons)

Company	1950 Amount	% of Total	1954 Amount	% of Total	1956 Amount	% of Total	1958 Amount	% of Total	1960 Amount	% of Total
ALUMINA										
Alcoa	910	35.9	n.a.	—	n.a.	—	1,406	36.2	2,156	41.1
Reynolds	878	34.6	n.a.	—	n.a.	—	1,278	32.9	1,460	27.9
Kaiser	750	29.5	n.a.	—	n.a.	—	850	21.9	1,280	24.4
Anaconda	—	—	—	—	—	—	—	—	—	—
Harvey	—	—	—	—	—	—	*		—	—
Ormet	—	—	—	—	—	—	345	8.9	345	6.6
Industry Totals	2,538	100.0	1,512	100.0	1,774	100.0	3,879	100.0	5,241	100.0
INGOT										
Alcoa	370	50.9	690	45.6	792	44.6	798	36.4	1,000	38.4
Reynolds	225	30.9	414	27.4	488	27.5	601	27.4	701	26.9
Kaiser	132	19.2	408	27.0	434	24.5	537	24.5	610	23.4
Anaconda	—	—	—	—	60	3.4	60	2.7	60	2.3
Harvey	—	—	—	—	—	—	54	2.5	54	2.1
Ormet	—	—	—	—	—	—	144	6.5	180	6.9
Industry Totals	727	100.0	1,512	100.0	1,774	100.0	2,194	100.0	2,605	100.0

* Imports Alumina from two Japanese firms, under long-term contracts.

Sources: 1950 data from United States v. Aluminum Company of America, 153F. Supp. 132 (Knox decision) pp. 366–74; data for other years from U.S. Department of Commerce, Business and Defense Services Admin., Aluminum and Magnesium Division.

in alumina carries over to the reduction (ingot) branch of the industry, as shown in Table 3. Alcoa's position has declined markedly in the postwar period, reaching a low point in 1958 of 36 per cent of total industry capacity, while Reynolds and Kaiser have accounted for about 27 per cent and 24 per cent of industry capacity, respectively. By 1960, however, when plant expansions currently underway are completed, Alcoa's position will increase to over 38 per cent of the industry total.

The importance of these statistics is to emphasize that entry conditions for the production of primary aluminum are still very difficult. This is due not only to the heavy capital requirements,[20] the limited amount of bauxite ores, and the availability of power, but also the firmly entrenched position of the three large integrated producers. Were it not for continuing government assistance to this industry in the form of periodic rapid amortization certificates (under which 85 per cent of plant investment is written off over a five-year period), government-guaranteed construction loans, long-term supply contracts for government stockpile, and supply of government electric power at low rates, it is doubtful that the newest producers would have attempted to enter this branch of the industry.[21] The combination of continued expansion of the established integrated producers and the encouragement given by the government to new primary producers have helped increase the percentage of U.S. aluminum supplied from domestic facilities. From a low point of approximately 60 per cent in 1950, U.S. primary production increased to 75 per cent of the 1958 total U.S. supply from all sources.

Secondary Smelters. A second important source of the U.S. supply of aluminum, in addition to that from bauxite, is the smelting industry, whose raw material is aluminum scrap. There are approximately 65 secondary smelters in the United States, supplying over 3,000 die-casters, permanent mold casters, *sand foundries,* steel mills, and fabricators. The smelters are essentially an industry within an industry, but their operations can have a significant effect on the primary aluminum market, and vice versa. To illustrate, secondary aluminum averaged 20 per cent of the total supply of aluminum to the United States over the last decade, but has been declining in importance in recent years—to about 15 per cent in 1958. The decline has occurred partly because obsolete scrap cycles have not had time to

[20] As of 1956 the capital investment per ton of pig aluminum were said to be about $1,000 compared with about $150 per ton of steel ingot (although more recently the costs were estimated at nearer $1,500 and $300 per ton, respectively, depending on where operations are started). In terms of value of output the capital investment relationship works out to about $1.56–$2.34 per dollar of steel ingot to about $2.33 for pig aluminum. Cf. *Materials Survey—Aluminum,* pp. IV–1 and IV–2, and Yates Hearings (1958), p. 37.

[21] See testimony of Lawrence Harvey, Yates Hearings (1958), p. 278.

develop from the volume of goods manufactured from the increased production of primary metal. Partly also, the decline has been due to the slowing down in the expansion of the *primary* aluminum producers, which has meant rougher competition for the secondary smelters. Today, secondary producers function largely as custom smelters, which is reflected in their business being limited to a rather narrow field—over 80 per cent of their shipments go to foundries and die-casters. This restricted scope of their operations make the smelters' position all the more precarious, especially when an important part of their business, e.g., automobile castings, is threatened by the integrated companies.

Imports. Another source of aluminum supply to the U.S. is imports, which constitute about 10 per cent of the total supply. Canada, the most important source of imports, supplies about 85 per cent of the total, with most of this being sold to the nonintegrated fabricators, some to Alcoa, Kaiser, and Anaconda under long-term contracts, and a small amount to foundries and secondary smelters. It is Aluminium, Limited's (Alted) policy to limit sales in the U.S. to aluminum *ingot only,* and not to compete in the end-product markets.[22] From Alted's viewpoint this policy provides the company with an outlet for its expanded capacity, and at the same time has helped supply the needs of the nonintegrated U.S. fabricators (see below). But it also has had other important effects on the structure of the aluminum industry in the United States. It has relieved some of the pressure on the "Big Three" in supplying the nonintegrated firms, thus permitting Alcoa, Kaiser, and Reynolds to supply more metal for their own fabrication and end-product facilities. Since Alted does not compete in the latter product markets in the U.S., Alted's policy thus has tended to help maintain and expand the position of the "Big Three" in the semifinished and end-product markets in the U.S.

Fabricated Products. Moving from primary metal production to the fabrication branch of the industry the structure changes, with a much larger competitive fringe around the oligopoly core in some product lines. Here again, however, the forward integration of "Big Three" and the backward integration of the "Little Three" have been an important factor in the solidification of the aluminum oligopoly. Alcoa, Reynolds, and Kaiser, but especially Alcoa, are highly diversified, as shown in Table 4. Sheets constitute the most important fabricated product of all three, although Alcoa and Kaiser each have twice the sheet capacity of Reynolds. Both Reynolds and Kaiser are still diversifying, which suggests the likelihood of their expanding

---

[22] See testimony of Nathaniel V. Davis, President of Alted, Yates Hearings (1958), p. 143 ff.

TABLE 4

Product Diversification of Alcoa, Reynolds, and Kaiser, as Shown by
Fabrication Capacity, 1958
(Amounts in thousands of short tons)

	Alcoa		Reynolds		Kaiser	
Product	Amount	Per-centage	Amount	Per-centage	Amount	Per-centage
Sheet	377	47.2	191	52.4	353	69.5
Extruded Shapes and Tubing	111	13.9	56	15.2	32	6.3
Wire, Rod, Bar, and Rolled Struct. Shapes	64	8.0	18	4.9	60	11.9
Electrical Cond. Cable and Acces.	67	8.3	39	10.6	30	6.0
Foil	40	5.0	52	14.3	16	3.1
Forgings	34	4.2	—	—	4	8.9
Powder and Paste	5	0.6	9	2.5	—	—
Welded Tubing	11	1.4	—	—	11	2.2
Sand Castings	16	2.0	—	—	—	—
Permanent Mold Casting	30	3.8	—	—	—	—
Other Misc. Prod. (die castings, rivets, screw machine products, collapsible tubes, impact extrusions and customers blanks, cooking utensils, and jobbing)	43	5.4	—	—	—	—
Totals	799	100.0	364	100.0	507	100.0

Source: *United States* versus *Aluminum Company of America*, 153 Supp. 132, pp. 149–50.

further into more end-product lines as Alcoa has done.[23] This, in turn, has had an important impact on the position of nonintegrated producers in both end-product and semifabricated lines.

Because of its importance for competitive relationships with other fabricators, it should be noted that the fabrication capacities of the "Big Three" exceeds that of their reduction establishments. This insures that, among the integrated firms, the bulk of sales—and therefore the locus of competition —will take place largely in the sale and distribution of fabricated products.[24] Moreover, any advantage held by an integrated producer at the

[23] Alcoa's diversification has not ended. In 1959, it acquired the assets of the Rome Cable Corporation, a wire and cable manufacturer, largely in copper lines.

[24] Fabricated products are more profitable than primary metal according to the primary producers, but custom extruders deny this. See Yates Hearings (1958), pp. 60 and 228–9.

fabrication stage will play an important part in permitting that company to maintain or enlarge its share of semifinished and end-product markets. Among oligopolists, this means that a tendency toward "market-sharing" is likely to develop, which has been the case on primary, and appears to be developing in the important fabricated products as well.

Nonintegrated Fabricators. In the fabricating stage, the integrated producers meet the competition of the nonintegrated companies, of which there are estimated to be (a) 60 to 75 mill-product manufacturers making sheet, foil, rod, bar, and extrusions, principally from *primary* pig or ingot; (b) 3,000 foundries or fabricators of castings producing castings, principally from scrap or secondary ingot; and (c) 14,000 end-product fabricators making such items as utensils, window frames, venetian blinds, and electrical cable, principally from sheet, rod, or extrusions. Only a very few of these nonintegrated firms produce the major mill products such as sheets, foil, tubes, and wire and cable—e.g., there are only about a dozen nonintegrated sheet producers, about the same number of tube and conductor-cable fabricators, and six nonintegrated foil manufacturers. Also four firms account for over 45 per cent of the die-casting business. Most of the nonintegrated firms in group (a) above are extrusions manufacturers.

Thus, despite the large number of nonintegrated fabricators their market influence is small and restricted. The integrated producers continue to dominate the markets for mill shapes, as shown in Table 5. The integrated producers account for the bulk of all shipments of the principal mill shapes listed in Table 5 (which amount to over 90 per cent of all mill shapes), with the exception of extruded shapes and drawn tubes. Furthermore, over the nine-year period covered by the table, the nonintegrated firms have increased their share in only sheet and plate (to 10 per cent) and extruded shapes (to 61 per cent) of total shipments. With the inclusion of the three new integrated producers in the 1958 shipments data for the integrated companies, the six integrated producers' share of these markets is even larger—the data on ACSR (aluminum conductor cable, steel reinforced) and other wire and cable products, in particular, are affected by this revision in coverage.

Maintaining Access to Primary Aluminum for Independent Fabricators. It should be clear from the foregoing discussion that the position of the nonintegrated fabricators depends, for markets, upon the over-all growth of the industry and new aluminum uses and, for supplies of aluminum, upon the integrated primary producers. That this dependency on the primary producers can be most unfortunate (for both the independent fabricators and the "Big Three") is attested by periodic Congressional hearings over the past decade into complaints of the independents against shortages of primary.

TABLE 5

Integrated and Nonintegrated Producers' Shares of Major Mill Shapes Markets, Selected Years, 1950–58
(percentage of total shipments)

Mill Shapes	1950 Integrated Cos. % of Total	1950 Non-integrated Cos. % of Total	1952 Integrated Cos. % of Total	1952 Non-integrated Cos. % of Total	1954 Integrated Cos. % of Total	1954 Non-integrated Cos. % of Total	1956 Integrated Cos. % of Total	1956 Non-integrated Cos. % of Total	1958 [a] Integrated Cos. % of Total	1958 [a] Non-integrated Cos. % of Total
Sheet and Plate	95.6	4.4	95.2	4.8	94.0	6.0	91.9	8.1	90.5	9.5
Foil	72.8	27.2	67.9	32.1	69.4	30.6	73.3	26.7	78.8	21.2
Bare Wire, Conductor and Nonconductor / Insulated or Covered Wire and Cable	n.a.	n.a.	60.7	39.3	56.9	43.1	56.7	49.3	66.4	33.6
ACSR [b] and Bare Cable	75.6	24.4	73.2	26.8	75.3	24.7	59.6	40.4	86.3	13.7
Extruded Shapes and Drawn Tube	65.4	34.6	60.4	39.6	46.8	53.2	39.0	61.0	44.5	55.5

[a] Includes as integrated for the first time: Anaconda, Harvey, and Ormet; hence, data *are not* directly comparable with earlier years.
[b] Aluminum Covered Steel Reinforced.

Source: U.S. Department of Commerce, Business, and Defense Services Administration, Aluminum and Magnesium Division.

The problem is complex, and there are many arguments offered on both sides of the controversy. For a variety of reasons, the integrated producers ordinarily prefer to utilize all their own primary output, but essentially it boils down to the profits in fabrication as against those in selling primary, and belief of the majors that captive fabrication facilities are necessary to protect primary capacity. Moreover, as already pointed out, the real market for aluminum is increasingly in end products, not primary aluminum.[25] In the view of the integrated firms, the industry growth thus calls for the development of new markets, requiring heavy financial investments for expanded research and promotional efforts, which only the large integrated firms can undertake. The primary producers, of course, would be glad to supply the independents under less-than-peak demand conditions, but prefer to supply themselves in good times. The reason is that the focal point of competition among the integrated firms has become largely a contest of timing the completion of new capacity and production to coincide with the rising demand for aluminum in prosperous times; but this also is precisely when the nonintegrated fabricators have the opportunity and desire to build up their own businesses.[26] In effect, this means that the development and control of end-product markets are as crucial to the integrated producers today as power and bauxite have been in the past.

Nevertheless, a substantial assured supply has been made available to the nonintegrated fabricators for several very good reasons: (1) the extended court jurisdiction through June 1957 in the Alcoa case; (2) continuing Congressional hearings into nonintegrated fabricators problems, which in part were responsible for (3) the Office of Defense Mobilization's continued encouragement to expansion of primary production, by granting accelerated amortization certificates and government supply contracts for stockpile. An important provision in the accelerated amortization agreements requires that a stipulated percentage of the expanded production be made available to the nonintegrated fabricators.[27] The effects of these actions are seen in Table 6, which shows that in recent years the nonintegrated

[25] Reynolds, Harvey, and Anaconda all entered primary production to insure primary supplies for their fabrication operations. Reynolds was principally a foil manufacturer until World War II, Harvey had made extrusions, structurals, and rods and bars from 1948 to 1957; and Anaconda has had a strong position in copper wire and cable products before its recent move into the aluminum field. See testimony of company officials in Yates Hearings (1955), pp. 229, 237–8, and 410; Yates Hearings (1958), pp. 237 and 278.

[26] Cf. Simon N. Whitney, *Antitrust Policies: American Experience in Twenty Industries,* New York: Twentieth Century Fund, 1958, Vol. II, p. 109.

[27] For the first five years from the time the new plants began production (through 1957), *two-thirds* of the output (minus military set-asides and government purchases) was to be made available to nonintegrated firms. In addition, for a period of fifteen

fabricators were receiving more metal from domestic primary producers than in the past (column 7), as well as a larger share of the total U.S. supply (column 8). The fact that the primary producers bought less scrap (secondary) in 1955, 1956, and 1957, compared with 1953 and 1954 (reflected in column 4), the continued imports from Canada, plus the general decline in demand for aluminum products with the onset of the 1957–58 recession, also were contributing explanations for the favorable supply position of the nonintegrated fabricators. Notwithstanding the influence of other factors, however, the role of government policy must be assigned the major credit in bringing about an improvement in the situation.

Price Policy

The character of market control in aluminum—fifty years under a single-firm monopoly and more than a decade under a three-firm oligopoly—has directly conditioned the pattern of cooperation and competition in the several stages of the industry. The high degree of concentration in the reduction and fabrication stages is conducive to a community of interests among the "Big Three" in dealing with one another (and with the new integrated producers), and in defending themselves against Congressional scrutiny and public criticism. In other branches of the industry, combined strength of the "Big Three" provides them with enormous potential economic power in dealing with outsiders.

The numerous nonintegrated fabricators, aluminum casters, and foundries are dependent upon and their operations are materially influenced by the policies and practices of the integrated primary producers. Economic theory and empirical study indicate that under this type of market structure the pattern of interfirm behavior will be ruled largely by conservative price policies designed to protect price and profit levels. For the most part, the pricing of aluminum and aluminum products by the "Big Three" has followed the expected pattern—price leadership, a delivered price system, and rigid prices—with some disruptions from small competitors at the periphery and in specialized product areas—and rivalry centering increasingly along nonprice lines.

Price Movements. Alcoa recognized very early the advantages accruing

---

years after the initial five-year period 25 *per cent* of the expanded production was to be offered for sale to nonintegrated users. In the Fall of 1957, this requirement was increased to 35 *per cent* by mutual agreement between the companies and the government. According to the Director of the Office of Defense Mobilization, these obligations alone would supply about 228,000 tons or almost two-thirds of the 1957 consumption of nonintegrated producers of *mill shapes.* Yates Hearings (1958), pp. 340–1.

TABLE 6

Nonintegrated Fabricators' Share of Total Aluminum Supply, 1947–57 (Thousands of Short Tons)

| | (1) | (2) | Sources of Nonintegrated Fabricators Supply | | | | (7) | (8) |
| | | | (3) | (4) | (5) | (6) | | |
Year	Total Supply (Domestic and Imports)	Output of Primary Producers	Purchases from Primary Producers	Secondary Metal	Imports from Canada	Total $3+4+5=6$	Percentage of Primary Producers' Supply Sold To Noninteg'd Fabricators $3 \div 2$	Percentage of Total U.S. Supply Used by Noninteg'd Fabricators $6 \div 1$
1947	946	572	97	266	1	364	17.0	38.5
1948	1,058	623	109	195	20	324	17.5	30.6
1949	898	603	88	120	10	218	14.6	24.3
1950	1,200	719	132	180	32	344	18.4	28.7
1951	1,270	837	121	220	58	399	17.6	31.4
1952	1,377	937	165	235	76	476	17.6	34.6
1953	1,946	1,252	194	264	124	582	15.5	29.9
1954	2,016	1,460	193	230	117	540	13.2	26.8
1955	2,168	1,566	376	281	114	771	24.0	35.6
1956	2,261	1,679	518	252	108	878	30.8	38.8
1957	2,246	1,648	464	252	98	814	28.2	36.2

Sources: Cols. (1) and (2), 1947–55 data from *Materials Survey-Aluminum, op.cit.*, p. VIII-1; 1956–57 data from Bureau of Mines, *Minerals Yearbook*, 1958. Cols. (3), (4), and (5), 1947–54 data from *Small Business and the Aluminum Industry*, Report of Subcommittee No. 3 on Minerals and Raw Materials to House Small Business Committee, Eighty-fourth Cong., 2nd Sess., 1956, pp. 14, 55, and 64; 1955–57 data computed from testimonies in Yates Hearings (1958), pp. 7, 73, 141, 210, 223, and 238. Nonintegrated fabricators' 1956 and 1957 purchases from primary producers partially estimated (i.e., portion from Alcoa).

to the company from an orderly reduction of aluminum prices over the years as necessary to penetrate new markets, coupled with a policy of stabilized prices between price reductions. The introductory price of $5 a pound in 1888 was reduced to 50 cents a pound by 1891 as a result of the short price war precipitated by the temporary appearance of the Cowles firm. For the next two years the price fluctuated around 75 cents; it came to rest at 33 cents in 1899, where it remained until the boom beginning in 1908. Alcoa attempted to stabilize at a 33-cent price, even though foreign producers continued to undersell and the American market loomed more and more attractive.[28] Alcoa was endeavoring to penetrate the electrical transmission market held by copper producers, and made a special price available of 29 cents a pound, which, with copper selling at 14 cents a pound, put the two metals on about a par with regard to cost.[29] The company did not wish to see the price pushed any lower than necessary to invade such markets, which partly explains its associations with the European cartels.

Alcoa was not able to maintain market prices during the 1908–09 recession, nor against the pressures of the 1920–21 recession, but by the twenties the company's position in the U.S. market and relationships with European producers was sufficiently developed to permit it to rationalize its operations, adjusting prices and investment to accommodate new demand and discourage potential competitors. The company was highly successful in its price-stabilization policy down to the end of World War II. Orderly price reductions, coupled with unfair methods of competition (price discrimination, delivery delays, etc.), were all a part of the company's policy of market penetration and broadening the uses of aluminum. This policy also served to discourage potential competitors. Between 1937 and 1942, for example, when prices were generally rising, Alcoa cut its prices from 20 to 15 cents a pound. Alcoa attributed this reduction to its traditional promotional price policy, but the influence of the government's pending antitrust suit and the emergence of Reynolds as a competitor in primary production must have weighed heavily in the company's pricing decisions.

The price of ingot remained at 15 cents until June 1948, after which it was increased thirteen times, reaching 28 cents in January 1957. As against this

---

[28] The low prices on imported metal temporarily defeated Alcoa's price-stabilization objective, but the company apparently preferred to take a chance that the loss of some of its market would be temporary, and whatever losses were incurred could be useful as supporting its (successful) plea for retention of tariff protection.

[29] The weight of an aluminum transmission line of equal conductivity is a little less than one-half (48 per cent) that of a copper conductor; hence, when the price of aluminum per pound is twice that of copper, a slight advantage exists for aluminum.

40 per cent increase over the 1937 level, the prices of other metals (steel, zinc, copper, and lead) have more than doubled or trebled.[30] Why? The "Big Three" apparently have been charging less than the traffic will bear. Other factors helping to keep aluminum prices at low levels have been the government's antitrust action, the nature of disposal of surplus aluminum plants to new firms, the periodic assistance in plant expansions of new producers, and continual Congressional hearings.

Production Costs of Primary Aluminum. The economies of large-scale production also have had some influence in bringing down the prices of aluminum and in keeping them at relatively low levels, but this factor can be easily overemphasized today. With reference to Kaiser Aluminum's Tacoma plant with a capacity of about 36,000 tons and its Chalmette plant with over 200,000 tons, a company vice-president explained: "But after you get to a certain size, there is very little efficiency accomplished by having a larger plant. The size of these plants to a large extent is controlled by the availability of power in the particular area." [31] This is consistent with the findings of Wallace cited earlier in connection with Alcoa's horizontal expansion. The significance of this long-run cost pattern for the industry today is that further duplication of plants by the "Big Three" must be due to potential savings in purchasing, advertising, marketing, research, crosshauling saving, plant specialization, and market strategy and market control considerations. However, since no evidence has been uncovered which shows that there are any important real economies at the level of the firm from having multiple aluminum plants at the primary stage, it would appear that reinforcement in market positions is controlling.

Short-run unit costs of producing aluminum pig are constant over a wide range of output. The reason for this is that it is possible to cut out one or more of the smelting furnaces (electrolytic cells or "pots") connected in a series (or "potline") used in aluminum production. When all the pots in a potline are being utilized, a particular combination of alumina and electric current will yield lowest average variable costs per pound of pig metal produced. It is possible to increase output by using more electricity and more raw material, with the same amount of labor; but the output per kilowatt hour increases to a maximum and then decreases as more current is ap-

---

[30] It is of interest to note that magnesium ingot prices have followed a pattern similar to those for aluminum, but with greater increases in the fifties, especially after 1954. Magnesium prices have continually remained above those of aluminum; just under the "volume parity" level of 1.5 to 1, discussed above. See Bulletin No. 141–142, "Selected Magnesium Statistics, 1928–1957," Table I, and *Iron Age* (July 30, 1959), p. 162; other information from the Department of Commerce, Aluminum and Magnesium Division.

[31] Yates Hearings (1958), p. 78.

plied.[32] In the plants consisting of several potlines, it is not only possible to maintain constant unit costs by cutting out individual *pots,* but also by cutting out and cutting in entire *potlines.*

The importance of the constancy of short-run marginal and average variable costs for pricing purposes is that variations in demand and resulting changes in output of primary aluminum will not affect the level of mill operating costs per pound of metal. This aspect of production costs has had an important effect on the pricing policies of the integrated producers—both in primary aluminum and fabricated products.

Per unit mill costs of the major primary producers have been approximately the same in recent years. The evidence originally presented in the Alcoa antitrust case, and further extended in the 1957 Cashin decision, discloses that as of 1956 Reynolds had the lowest and Kaiser the highest mill costs per unit, with Alcoa in the middle. (See Table 7, column 6.) It must be assumed, of course, that all primary producers have this information. More important for pricing purposes, is the fact that the primary producers all *believe* that their respective mill costs are approximately the same:

A *Kaiser* official testified in response to a question about differences in the cost of alumina to each of the "Big Three": "I do not think there is a great deal of difference in costs."

In response to a question regarding variance in cost among primary producers an *Alcoa* official testified: "Oh, I presume there are some slight differences; yes. There is not any great mystery in the production of aluminum today. Facilities are pretty much alike. There will be some slight differences, I suppose, as Mr. Rhodes [Kaiser Vice President] indicated yesterday, between a small plant . . . and a very large plant . . . but the general practice is to average those out, so that you wouldn't have one price in Louisiana adjacent to Chalmette and a different price in Tacoma and still a different price somewhere else."

An *Anaconda* official stated: "It is our belief that in 1956 our mill costs are comparable with those of Kaiser with the possible exception that Columbia Falls *total operating costs,* before depreciation, interest, and other charges are approximately 6 per cent higher due to our purchase of alumina from outside sources."

And finally, an official of Aluminium, Limited (Alted) testified: "As a general statement, it is our conviction that currently our costs and the costs of our American competitors are running approximately the same." [33]

Since mill costs are said to constitute approximately 75 per cent of total unit costs, moreover, the task of elimination of oligopolistic uncertainty on prices is made easier.

[32] See Leonard A. Doyle, *Economics of Business Enterprise,* New York: McGraw-Hill, 1952, pp. 152–5, and *Materials Survey—Aluminum, op.cit.,* pp. VI–6 through VI–11.

[33] Yates Hearings (1958), pp. 78, 135, 161, and 441.

TABLE 7

Aluminum Pig Mill Costs [a] of Alcoa, Reynolds, and Kaiser, Selected Years, 1947–56
(cents per pound)

(1)	(2)	(3)	(4)	(5)	(6)	(7)	(8)
						99%	Ratio of Mill Costs Per Unit
		Raw			Total	Pig Prices	to Pig Prices
		Material	Power	Mfg.	Average	(annual	(6) ÷ (7)
Year	Company	Cost	Cost	Costs [b]	Mill Costs	average)	(Percentage)
1947	Alcoa	3.71	1.73	3.96	9.40	14.0	67.1
	Reynolds	3.03	2.17	4.29	9.49	"	67.8
	Kaiser	4.93	1.90	3.55	10.38	"	74.1
1949	Alcoa	4.14	1.94	4.86	10.94	16.0	68.4
	Reynolds	3.56	2.28	5.60	11.44	"	71.5
	Kaiser	5.14	1.81	4.58	11.53	"	72.1
1951	Alcoa	4.02	2.70	5.57	12.29	18.0	68.3
	Reynolds	3.70	2.60	4.84	11.14	"	61.9
	Kaiser	5.36	1.85	5.09	12.30	"	68.3
1953	Alcoa	4.71	2.93	6.43	14.07	19.75	71.2
	Reynolds	4.63	3.16	5.42	13.21	"	66.9
	Kaiser	6.15	2.21	8.47	16.83	"	85.2
1955	Alcoa	4.44	2.93	6.06	13.43	22.0	61.0
	Reynolds	4.50	3.07	5.71	13.28	"	60.4
	Kaiser	4.85	1.88	7.13	13.86	"	63.0
1956	Alcoa	4.60	3.06	6.16	13.82	24.5	56.4
(9mo.)	Reynolds	4.56	3.05	6.02	13.63	"	55.6
	Kaiser	5.08	1.85	7.35	14.28	"	58.3

[a] These figures represent actual costs after deducting book profits on intracompany transfers and without allowance for return on investment.
[b] Includes labor and plant overhead costs directly bearing on the pig manufacturing process.

Source: Columns (1)–(6), *United States* versus *Aluminum Company of America*, 153 Fed. Supp. 132, Table VII further extended, p. 185; Column (7) from Table 9 and Column (8) computed by author.

Column (8) of Table 7 sheds some interesting light on the question of profitability of primary production, which was mentioned above. The data show that from 1947 to 1956, pig prices increased percentagewise more than mill costs per unit. In other words, the gross profit margin on pig production increased by about one-third (the complements of the percentages in column 8) over this period, i.e., 100 per cent minus 67.1 per cent, 100 per cent minus 56.4 per cent, etc.

Alcoa's Price Policy. For many years Alcoa's pricing has been based upon the objective of realizing a predetermined return of 20 per cent on investment, using an assumed average utilization of plant capacity of 70 per cent. The company has indicated that in following a target-price policy (a) *run-of-the-mill products* are usually priced to return the company target objective, (b) *fabricated products* (especially those subject to rigid specifications of customers) usually carry an increased profit-margin factor, (c) *jobbing-type products* (e.g., castings), where the company encounters competition from numerous foundries and die-casters, are not priced according to the target formula, and (d) *new products* (including those in competition with substitute metals) are priced "promotionally" i.e., on a small-margin basis initially, or enough below that of substitute metals (given weight-value equivalents) to penetrate the market.[34] A tabulation of the target costs and prices and actual costs for a fabricated product are shown in Table 8.

In pricing fabricated products Alcoa must take into consideration not only its own costs and profit target, but also its estimate of competitors' costs, in conformance with the 1946 judgment of the District Court, which states:

> The defendants are enjoined and restrained from selling aluminum ingot for the fabrication of aluminum sheet or aluminum alloy sheet at higher than fair prices, if the fabricator of such sheet is thereby prevented from fabricating and selling aluminum sheet or aluminum alloy at a reasonable profit, provided that such fabricator is efficient, well equipped, and otherwise able to fabricate and sell such sheet on a fully competitive basis; and further enjoined and restrained from selling aluminum sheet and aluminum alloy sheet . . . at prices below its selling prices for aluminum ingot, plus the cost of manufacturing and selling such sheet.[35]

The court mandate was directed specifically at the pricing of certain gauges of aluminum sheet (with some overtones for cable also), but is equivalent to stating that Alcoa must price to allow fabricators a reasonable profit. Alcoa gives the principle enunciated in the court ruling a general application since it believes an identical ruling probably would have been made by the court had a price squeeze been found on other fabricated products.

It is difficult to generalize on the total effects of the antitrust decree on Alcoa's price policies, but the impact is quite clear with respect to semifabricated and fabricated products. The company is now sensitive to the practical fact that both Alcoa's ingot and fabricated product prices must be

---

[34] See A. D. H. Kaplan, Joel B. Dirlam, and Robert F. Lanzillotti, *Pricing in Big Business*, Washington: Brookings Institution, 1958, pp. 31–6.

[35] *United States* versus *Aluminum Company of America et al.*, U.S. District Court for the Southern District of New York, Judgment on Mandate Against Aluminum Company of America *et al.*, Equity 85–73 (April 23, 1946), p. 18.

TABLE 8

Target Price and Performance on a Fabricated Aluminum Product,
Aluminum Company of America, 1956 [a]

	Target Price (cost estimate)		Actual Cost and Price	
Elements	Dollars per Pound	Percentage	Dollars per Pound	Percentage
Metal value (including commercial metals)	.261	29.0	.243	27.0
Prime Cost of Fabrication				
Direct labor	.038	4.2	.040	4.4
Direct material	.145	16.1	.167	18.6
Factory burden at standard rates	.125	13.9	.131	14.6
Total prime cost of fabrication	.308	34.2	.338	37.6
Transportation allowance	.015	1.7	.016	1.8
Allowance for idle facility cost [b]	.029	3.2	.032	3.6
Allowance for plant administrative expense	.032	3.6	.035	3.8
Total works cost	.645	71.6	.664	73.8
Allowance for general administrative and selling expense	.039	4.3	.040	4.4
Total cost	.684	76.0	.704	78.2
Allowance for profit margin	.216	24.0	.196	21.8
Price	.900	100.0	.900	100.0

[a] Figures rounded.
[b] For determining target costs and price, the norm is 70 per cent of full capacity. Since the itemized costs are figured on the basis of full capacity, a general allowance is made to spread the full burden of the facilities over output averaging 70 per cent of full capacity use.

Source: A. D. H. Kaplan, Joel B. Dirlam, and Robert F. Lanzillotti, *Pricing in Big Business*, Washington: Brookings Institution, 1958, p. 29.

subject to a consideration of competitors' costs. This consideration was more important on ingot pricing when Kaiser and Reynolds were getting established as primary producers, but it has recurred from time to time in recent years as extruders and other fabricators raised complaints about various alleged price squeezes by the "Big Three," which will be discussed below.

Price Leadership. Alcoa's role as industry price leader has never been seriously challenged, although on several occasions over the past decade Kaiser and Reynolds have taken the initiative on price leads, and in 1958 Alted initiated a cut in the price of pig (see Table 9). President Wilson of Alcoa frankly acknowledged Alcoa's leadership in testimony before the Celler committee in 1951:

THE CHAIRMAN. And you would say, then, Alcoa was the price leader in the field?

MR. WILSON. Well, if we are—and I think that may be a fair enough statement—but if we are, it is because the others are followers, and not because we are the leaders. We can only use our best judgment. I suppose when you have followers, that makes you the leader.[36]

Kaiser led increases in pig and ingot prices in January 1953, and March 1956. Reynolds unsuccessfully attempted to raise the price of ingot in July 1950, but led an increase in January 1956, after trade sources had insisted a few days before that if Alcoa did not take the lead there would be no increase.

The first real threat to Alcoa's price leadership came in March 1958, when Alted, customarily an obedient follower, announced a two-cent cut in the price of pig. The announcement followed a series of developments which had adversely affected Alted's position both in the U.S. and European markets.[37] Various forms of discounting had developed in the United States (e.g., generous freight absorption allowances, sale of premium-grade metal at regular-grade prices, advertising and display allowances, etc.). Also U.S. primary producers were buying less and less metal from Alted, their own capacity being adequate for the 1957–58 levels of demand, and Alted found itself relying more and more upon the nonintegrated fabricators for U.S. business. At the same time U.S. primary producers began moving into European markets.[38] On top of this, Russia was threatening Alted's European business with sales at reduced prices (actually the U.S.S.R. had only a limited amount of aluminum to sell and their exports declined in 1959). Alted thus had many motives in cutting the pig price. Prices did not remain at the 24-cent level for long, however. In August Alcoa resumed its traditional leadership by raising both pig and ingot to 24.7 cents; the others (including Alted) followed. (See Table 9.)

The tabulation of pig and ingot prices in Table 9 discloses the consistent uniformity of list prices among the major primary producers as well as the rigidity of prices between the periodic revisions. The concurrence of the other primary producers with the price stabilization policy of Alcoa also is evident from the table. Since company primary costs are similar and their prices identical at given times and over long intervals, competitive behavior has been channeled mainly into nonprice lines, with more and more

---

[36] Celler Hearings, p. 634.
[37] Cf. *Business Week*, August 1, 1959, p. 26.
[38] In January 1959, Reynolds won a share in control of British Aluminium, a leading British fabricator, and more recently Alcoa entered into an arrangement with Imperial Industries, Ltd., of England, for the operation of a joint fabricating subsidiary. *Business Week*, January 17, 1959, p. 59 and June 27, 1959, p. 34.

TABLE 9

Price Leadership Pattern on Aluminum Pig and Ingot Prices, 1950–58
(prices in cents per pound)

Year	Date	Company	Price	
			Pig	*Ingot*
1950	May 22	Alcoa	16.5	17.5
	23	Reynolds	16.5	17.5
	23	Alted	16.5	—
	25	Kaiser	16.5	17.5
	Sept. 25	Alcoa	18.0	19.0
	25	Alted	18.0	—
	28	Kaiser	18.0	19.0
	29	Reynolds	18.0	19.0
1952	Aug. 4	Alcoa	19.0	20.0
	4	Kaiser	19.0	20.0
	4	Reynolds	19.0	20.0
	7	Alted	19.0	—
1953	Jan. 22	Kaiser	19.5	20.5
	23	Alcoa	19.5	20.5
	23	Reynolds	19.5	20.5
	23	Alted	19.5	—
	Jy. 15	Alcoa	20.0	21.5
	20	Reynolds	20.0	21.5
	20	Kaiser	20.0	21.5
	21	Alted	20.0	—
1954	Aug. 5	Alcoa	20.5	22.2
	6	Reynolds	20.5	22.2
	6	Kaiser	20.5	22.2
	6	Alted	20.5	—
1955	Jan. 10	Reynolds	21.5	23.2
	12	Kaiser	21.5	23.2
	13	Alcoa	21.5	23.2
	14	Alted	21.5	—
	Aug. 1	Alcoa	22.5	24.4
	2	Kaiser	22.5	24.4
	6	Reynolds	22.5	24.4
	8	Alted	22.5	—
	Aug. 2	Alted	26.0	—
1956	Mar. 26	Kaiser	24.0	25.9
	27	Reynolds	24.0	25.9
	29	Alcoa	24.0	25.9
	31	Alted	24.0	—
	Aug. 10	Alcoa	25.0	27.1
	11	Kaiser	25.0	27.1
	13	Reynolds	25.0	27.1
	14	Alted	25.0	—

Year	Date		Company	Price	
				Pig	Ingot
1957	Jy.	30	Alcoa	26.0	28.1
		30	Reynolds	26.0	28.1
		30	Kaiser	26.0	28.1
	Aug.	2	Alted	26.0	—
1958	Mar.	28	Alted	24.0	—
		29	Alcoa	24.0	26.1
		29	Reynolds	24.0	26.1
		29	Kaiser	24.0	26.1
	Aug.	1	Alcoa	24.7	26.8
		1	Reynolds	24.7	26.8
		1	Kaiser	24.7	26.8
		1	Alted	24.7	—

Source: 1950–56 prices, *United States* versus *Aluminum Company of America,* 153F Supp. 132, p. 151; later years from *The New York Times* (July 30 and August 2, 1957; March 28 and 29, and April 1 and August 1, 1958).

emphasis going into brand names, quality differences, and development of new aluminum products, such as consumer products, building materials, and automotive parts and accessories.

Price competition in aluminum is limited principally to some of the fabricated product lines where the number of firms is large and cohesiveness among the various producers is loose—especially among casting companies, foundries, extruders, and utensil and miscellaneous aluminum building materials. The "Big Three" feel some of the backwash of this competitive behavior, but they generally do not vary their own prices until the sniping at list prices by the smaller companies gets out of hand and threatens market stability. In such cases the majors usually respond with "firming" cuts to match effective market prices, which is frequently followed with "firming" increases. However, as the following discussion will show, the "Big Three" have not completely abandoned price competition as an offensive weapon, both within and outside the established aluminum markets, as it suits their objectives. Their attempts to increase their present share of established markets and the backwash of their efforts to penetrate new markets have served to make the position of some independent fabricators more and more precarious. The most recent developments along these lines have been alleged price squeezes associated with primary prices and scrap prices, the pricing of certain mill shapes, and the so-called "hot-metal deals."

Price Squeezes. In recent years some of the secondary *smelters* have complained that they are being squeezed between a ceiling of *primary* aluminum prices and a floor determined by scrap prices. According to the Aluminum Smelters Research Institute, purchases of aluminum scrap by the primary producers provides "the leverage through which the smelting industry can be controlled."[39] The purchase by primary producers of 30 per cent of scrap in 1957, when metal was in long supply, is cited as an example of their pushing up the market price for scrap. Part of the motive for this practice is alleged to be the primary producers' "desire to force *secondary* ingot prices to an unnatural point" so that they can make special contracts more palatable to their customers, or as a means of extending unannounced price cuts on fabricated shapes through "conversion deals."[40] An Alcoa official has testified that "historically scrap had always been purchased, and had to be purchased in a certain ratio to primary production in order to take it off the market and in order to take care of your casting business."[41]

The nonintegrated fabricators' concern over shortages of aluminum have disappeared, but once again they are raising complaints about price squeezes —i.e., between the price they have to pay the integrated producers for pig and semifabricated shapes and the price at which the major producers sell *their own* fabricated products in competition with the independents.[42] In 1957 and 1958 new charges of price squeezes have been made before a Congressional committee by extruders, die-casters, and smelters.

The kind of "Big Three" practice which various aluminum *extruders* complain about is illustrated by the case of those making round, flat, and shaped wires for the slide-fastener ("zipper") industry. The basic material used in manufacturing these wires is called "5056 redraw rods," which have been available from only two sources—Alcoa and Kaiser.[43] In November 1957, a

---

[39] Yates Hearings (1958), p. 209.

[40] In these conversion deals, scrap is accepted by the fabricator as a credit on the purchase of mill products, but the allowance for the scrap may bear no recognizable relationship to the established market price for scrap. Instead, it is claimed to represent a surreptitious discount which encourages customers to make forays into the scrap market for additional supplies of scrap for conversion—and these conversions are always at premium prices for scrap. This activity is said to serve "as another disruption in the market for smelters' raw materials and end by placing just so much more of that raw material under the control of the primary producers." *Ibid.*, p. 210.

[41] *Ibid.*, p. 48.

[42] Price squeezes have been a long-standing complaint of the independent fabricators, and was a major issue in the antitrust case against Alcoa. See Findings 257–262 and 280–286, as amended, *United States* versus *Aluminum Company of America*, U.S. District Court for the Southern District of New York, Judgments and Orders of the Court (April 23, 1954).

[43] Extruders report Alcan (Alted's main subsidiary) manufactures this material, but will not sell to U.S. fabricators. This is in line with Alted's policy of not competing in end-product markets in the U.S. markets against the "Big Three." Yates Hearings (1958), p. 301.

Kaiser representative informed these extruders that 5056 *wire* would be cut 5 cents (about 8 per cent) immediately, and a few days later Alcoa announced it was meeting the cut. At the same time, however, the price of 5056 *rods* (from which the 5056 wire is made) remained unchanged. One extruder testified that two Kaiser officials informed him the reason for the price cut was to increase the company's market share:

Very frankly, Kaiser's position was that they did not feel that they were getting their fair share of the business in the metropolitan area of New York City, and this was a medium of attempting to get their fair share of the business.[44]

Another fabricator, who buys pig and ingot from the majors to make rods from which he, in turn, makes *electrical cable,* stated that he was placed in a similar squeeze under the same series of price cuts by Kaiser—specifically a cut from 34.6 to 28 cents on the aluminum rods for electric cable. With the price of pig at 24 cents (recently cut from 26 cents), and rods at 28 cents, the fabricator had only a 4-cent spread, which he said completely squeezed the profit out of his operations. No further comment from Kaiser was made on the first case, but in the latter case Kaiser stated that such price cuts instead of injuring the small fabricator would help him by promoting the use of aluminum. Moreover, the company said that it cut the price of redraw wire for cable to protect the position of those cable producers who use redraw wire as starting raw material, as against other producers (like the one referred to above) who produce *their own* redraw rods from pig and ingot.[45] Thus, here we have the strange situation of Kaiser taking on the role of protector of small fabricators against "semiintegrated" independent fabricators.

Apparently, the majors are definitely interested in promoting the use of aluminum in end-products, and they are prepared to undertake price reductions for promotional purposes. But, this does not ordinarily mean proportionate reductions in the prices of primary or semifabricated raw materials used by the nonintegrated firms. Even on the rare occasion when the price of *primary* is cut, as occurred in 1957, when Alted cut pig 2 cents to 24 cents, the independent fabricators are still caught in the middle. The "Big Three" met the 24-cent pig price in that instance, but they also cut the price of their fabricated products, so that the squeeze on the independents was not loosened.

"Hot Metal" Contracts. The "hottest" controversy of recent years centers around the contracts Reynolds has made with Ford and General Motors for the delivery of molten aluminum—called "hot-metal deals" by the trade. In

[44] *Ibid.,* p. 299.
[45] *Ibid.,* pp. 306–8, 319–20.

1955 and 1957, after several years of experimental work with molten metal sales, Reynolds worked out contracts with Ford and General Motors for the delivery of molten aluminum to be used in the auto companies foundries for the production of transmission parts. Alcoa signed a similar contract with GM early in 1960.

These contracts are of real moment to the smelters because in effect, they constitute sales of metal for castings (the major business of the smelters) at discount prices. The Ford contract, for example, calls for 10 per cent off the list price for pig, after deduction of a freight factor, plus an increment for the alloy content. The smelters maintain this discount is in excess of the cost of pigging aluminum, and thus places them under an unfair ceiling. In support of their position, they have presented evidence showing that independent smelters' costs of pigging run from about ¼ of a cent to not more than ½ of a cent, as against the 2½ cent discount of the Ford contract. The size of the discount is even more interesting in view of the additional costs of special molten metal transportation equipment and a large "holding" furnace for each alloy involved (to avoid production delays at either end).[46] The smelters, thus, maintain that the discounts contained in the Ford and G.M. contracts are preferential for the captive foundries of the auto companies, and therefore discriminatory.

At the same time, the *die-casters* see their very existence threatened by these hot-metal deals. The die-casters point out that they engineered the automatic transmissions for autos, and the automobile companies have been their biggest customers for years. They do not like to see these markets taken away and would like to bid on the auto contracts on the same basis as the primary producers, but the auto companies will not entertain bids on an equal basis. Under the Reynolds-G.M. contract, G.M. agreed to buy enough aluminum from Reynolds to make one-half of the transmission castings needed for total Chevrolet production. Ford and G.M. purchases of transmission die-casting from the die-casters differ somewhat, however; they are based on an estimated percentage of estimated purchasing requirements. Thus, in the hot-metal contracts the basis for bids is *production* requirements, and in the other *purchasing* requirements, which means that if G.M. sales drop the corporation may have no purchase requirements.[47] The die-casters would prefer to have an *assured* market for product requirements as Reynolds now has under its contracts.

The fundamental issue here is not simply a case of a reduction in the die-

---

[46] Testimony of Kaiser and Alcoa officials confirm the contention that it does not cost 2½ cents a pound to pig hot metal. Yates Hearings (1958), p. 214.

[47] Ford explains that it preferred to contract with primary producers in order to obtain an assured supply at a stable price. Yates Hearings (1958), p. 132.

casters' share of the market,[48] but the broader questions of possible price discrimination and equal access to markets. The primary producers have gone to some pains to establish molten metal as the fourth primary aluminum product, alongside of pig, ingot and billet. This, of course, is highly significant in that there are only two or three large buyers of the product, which on the surface circumvents price-discrimination complications. The implications of such contracts are far-reaching and will be considered further in Section III.

Change to Delivered-Price System. Ever since 1921, aluminum and aluminum products have been sold on a zone system of pricing geographically, with freight allowed to destination, i.e., an allowance granted to customers to cover the actual or equivalent cost of freight. In June 1959, Kaiser announced that effective on July 1, 1959 it would price all aluminum products on a *uniform delivered-price basis* nationally—in effect, a "postage-stamp" system, with the exception of forgings (which will continue to be sold on an f.o.b. foundry basis). Alcoa and Reynolds followed Kaiser, and there seemed to be little question that the new pricing system would immediately become industry-wide practice. In announcing the change to its customers, Alcoa stated that in part the change was due to abuses of the policy of making equivalent allowances on customer pick-ups at the point of shipment, resulting in "price discriminations beyond our [Alcoa's] control," for those customers who do not, or cannot, pick up their orders at the plant. This means that the delivered price to all buyers will be the same irrespective of their location with respect to producing mills or point of shipment; freight will be *paid*, but not *allowed*.

The underlying reasons for the change go much deeper, however. With the onset of the 1957–58 recession and the end of government stockpiling of aluminum, freight allowances became more and more important as a device for discounting quoted prices. These practices posed a real threat to the "Big Three's" price-stabilization policy for aluminum. Alcoa's justification for a postage-stamp system in aluminum follows lines similar to those frequently mentioned in support of basing-point systems: (1) the simplicity for pricing purposes; (2) the relatively small importance of freight as a cost element (it is said to average about 3 to 4 per cent of delivered price); and (3) the desire of the company to place aluminum fabricators on an even footing pricewise in the use of aluminum, irrespective of plant location.[49]

[48] Their share has dropped from 100 per cent to 50 per cent, although their total business doubled from 1952 to 1957. It should be noted also, that the ten largest die casters (four of which are divisions of large companies like National Lead) account for 43.7 per cent of the total die-casting business. Yates Hearings (1958), pp. 194–5.

[49] Cf. Kaplan, *et al., op.cit.,* p. 28.

The monopolistic significance of delivered-pricing systems, long recognized by economists, is evident in the reasons supporting the system and in the circumstances surrounding the change from a freight-equalization system. The new system will help insure geographic uniformity of prices among customers; it will result in price discrimination among buyers due to systematic freight absorption (evidenced by the varying mill-nets to producers from sales to differently situated *buyers*); it will entail what is essentially a wasteful practice, cross-hauling, and in time it will tend to result in an uneconomic location of both aluminum producers and consumers. Thus, it is difficult to defend a delivered-price system for aluminum except as a mechanism for insuring geographic price uniformity among producers to all buyers and a means for stabilizing industry prices against fluctuations in demand and supply. From the aluminum producers' point of view, a policy designed to stabilize industry prices seems necessary and justified; whether it is desirable from a public policy viewpoint, is something else again.

SECTION III: PUBLIC POLICY

The aluminum industry provides an excellent case for studying the impact of public policy measures upon market performance. Many important policy issues can be singled out for discussion, but the fundamental question is: Whether market results are altered significantly when an industry that was under monopoly control for fifty years is transformed into a three-firm oligopoly. Any attempt to evaluate the industry's performance under the new structure must, of course, take into consideration the influence of the District Court's extended jurisdiction over Alcoa down to 1957, and the continuing Congressional interest and industry assistance beyond that date. Thus, it is really too soon to evaluate the results under "unbridled" oligopoly, but we can assess the effectiveness of government policy to date and indicate the problems that require attention—in particular, the issues of high concentration, price squeezes and "hot-metal" contracts, price stabilization, and delivered-pricing.

Market Performance Under Oligopoly: Summary

Before turning to a discussion of the policy issues proper, let us briefly summarize the market results over the past decade under government-created and government-supervised oligopoly. To begin with, despite the concern expressed by the District Court, there never was any serious doubt that Kaiser and Reynolds would survive:

> Needless to say, Kaiser and Reynolds *will* survive and the *status quo* in the industry *will* be maintained during the next five years. This outcome seems certain because Alcoa—in order to forestall any future relief action by the Court—will refrain from expanding its share of the market. By exercising self-restraint, Alcoa will prove to the Court that Kaiser and Reynolds can maintain their market position, and possibly, improve it. By judiciously avoiding aggressive or expansionary activity, Alcoa can thus effectively bar the Government from showing the need for further relief in the crucial five-year period. By pursuing a "live and let live" policy—which has proved so effective in other industries—Alcoa can then insure the termination of the Court's jurisdiction by 1955.[50]

Both Reynolds and Kaiser have survived, and prospered, which is due in part to the continuing high level of demand for aluminum, but buttressed by government purchase agreements and other aid to primary producers, arising out of the Korean conflict and the stockpiling program for strategic metals.

The industry has made a good record over the past ten years: total capacity has been expanded almost fourfold and prices have remained low relative to other nonferrous metals and steel. These are noteworthy accomplishments for any industry, but they too are explainable to a large extent by the government's special interest in the industry, as reflected in the antitrust case, the nature of surplus property disposal, and various forms of assistance to increases in primary capacity.

The producer restraint implicit in the price movements of aluminum has not worked any real hardship on the "Big Three"; rather the policy has resulted in quite generous earnings, as shown in Table 10. The rates of return over the 1949–59 period have averaged 12.8 per cent, 18.5 per cent, and 20.8 per cent, *after taxes*, for Alcoa, Reynolds, and Kaiser, respectively. Alcoa and Reynolds' performance has been somewhat steadier than Kaiser's, which is due partly to differences in the methods of financing expansion and the resultant differences in capital structures. In view of the accelerated amortization privileges granted to the "Big Three" in connection with their expansions over this period, the rates of return are understated compared to what they would be under normal amortization rates. When all the rapid write-offs end, the companies will have higher tax liabilities (other things remaining equal), but because of the lag between expansion and full utilization, the rates of return are not likely to fall sharply.

[50] Adams, *op.cit.*, p. 920.

TABLE 10

Rates of Return After Taxes on Stockholders' Investment,
for Aluminum "Big Three" 1949–59

Years	Alcoa	Reynolds	Kaiser
1949	7.8	9.4	27.6
1950	14.5	20.7	33.7
1951	12.0	21.7	21.3
1952	13.6	19.4	20.2
1953	17.2	22.1	23.3
1954	16.1	23.6	28.8
1955	18.7	27.0	24.8
1956	16.5	22.5	21.6
1957	11.9	14.8	11.8
1958	6.0	11.7	9.0
1959	6.8	10.4	7.2
1949–59 Average	12.5	18.5	20.8

Sources: Alcoa and Reynolds (1949–56) and Kaiser (1954–56) from Federal Trade Commission, *Rates of Return for Identical Manufacturing Companies—Selected Manufacturing Industries, 1940, 1947–1955*, Washington (1957), p. 42; and *Rates of Return for Identical Manufacturing Companies—Selected Manufacturing Industries, 1940, 1947–1956*, Washington (1958), pp. 31 and 42; other figures computed by author using *Moody's Industrials* and the methods outlined on pp. 22–3 of the latter publication.

Some meaning is given to the size of the returns of the aluminum producers by comparing them with the rates of return of 34 steel companies over this period—about 12 per cent—as reported by the Federal Trade Commission. The aluminum industry is younger and in an earlier stage of its growth curve, which affords some basis for the more favorable showing of the aluminum producers. Theoretically, as more firms enter the industry the rates of return should tend to come down, but because of the degree of concentration still prevailing in primary production no trend in this direction is yet discernible. Rates of return were lower for all three companies in 1957 and 1958, but this was largely due to recessionary movements rather than fundamental economic changes in the companies' earning capacities.

Price Stabilization

It has been shown how the pricing of aluminum over the years has been influenced by Alcoa's market-development and market-penetration policy. In line with this general objective, Alcoa has assumed continuing responsibility for the general price structure of aluminum products, except for extrusions, foil, cable, and some items of rod, bar and wire. Alcoa justifies its price-stabilization policy on the grounds that (1) stable prices are not only preferred by the aluminum producers, but also by aluminum users who frown on the erratic price movements typical of some materials such as copper; (2) stable prices permit the aluminum producers to plan expansions of plant and equipment with the assurance of a "target" flow of profits needed to accommodate planned investment outlays; (3) stable prices avoid cutthroat competition; and (4) high ("unrestrained") prices tend to disturb the long-run industry equilibrium by bringing in unneeded capacity.

A policy of price stabilization is said to constitute a device for approximating market equilibrium, without the disruptions caused by cutthroat or exploitative pricing. However, the foregoing justification for price-stabilization policies via price-leadership conventions can be said to result in genuine market equilibrium only if the particular price levels involved are made equivalent to the judgments and decisions of the industry leader.

The disposition of Alcoa and the other integrated producers toward price stabilization is reinforced by the increasing tendency on the part of high government officials to appeal to industry price leaders to be "reasonable" in their pricing decisions. Such appeals are an obvious recognition of market power to administer prices. Firms are expected to avoid taking full advantage of profit opportunities, but precisely whose standards of reasonableness are to be used is not made clear. It would seem that in working toward economic stability and growth, reliance should be placed upon fiscal and monetary controls, rather than admonishing producers to set prices on the basis of what they believe would contribute to these national objectives. Such burdens should not be placed upon businessmen; in a free enterprise system, businessmen should be expected to act as businessmen and not as public policymakers.

Protecting the Independent Fabricators

The technology of aluminum fabrication is such that the industry can support a rather large number of relatively small firms without loss of efficiency. A recurring problem that has faced the nonintegrated fabricators over the past decade has been the scarcity of supplies of primary aluminum for fabrication. In recent years this shortage has been alleviated as a result of expansion of reduction capacity by the "Big Three" and the new producers, increased guarantees of aluminum sales to independents, and increased imports from Canada. Shortages in times of peak demand, of course, are almost inevitable, but this is not simply a problem of shortages. The position of the nonintegrated fabricators may be in jeopardy again if the continued expansion of the integrated producers into fabricated lines results in diversion of scarce supplies to their own captive facilities.

The basic public policy issue posed by this problem, in essence, is (1) the extent to which the integrated primary producers—subsidized by government loans, government purchase guarantees, access to low-cost federal power, and certificates for accelerated amortization of facilities—should be free to "select their own customers," and (2) the extent to which, and for how long, they should be required to guarantee supplies to the independent fabricators. Although the current supply situation is satisfactory, as a long-run matter there is need for a comprehensive program for assuring the independents access to primary aluminum on a nondiscriminatory basis, that is, if efficiency rather than sheer market power is to be the determining factor for the survival and growth of fabricators. The reductions in tariff duties to 1¼ cents a pound on crude aluminum in 1958 should give additional encouragement to imports of aluminum. Therefore, if imports continue to increase, they will help provide greater independence for the nonintegrated fabricators.

"Hot-Metal" Contracts

The "hot-metal" contracts raise questions regarding the possibility of price discrimination in the sale of aluminum. As a matter of policy there are no grounds for objection to cost reductions resulting from the development of more efficient means of processing basic aluminum metal. The policy issue here really concerns the side effects on the independents at both ends of these transactions: (1) the extent to which the size of discounts on molten aluminum are, in fact, justified by actual costs savings, and (2) whether the die-casters are being given equal opportunity to bid on the molten-metal business of the automobile manufacturers. Is aluminum-casting alloy of like quality and grade in molten form, in pig form, and in ingot form, to be considered as the same commodity or three different commodities? Reynolds maintains it has pioneered a new primary aluminum product, but the die-casters and smelters insist it is not a separate product. Since these forms are near perfect substitutes for each other—i.e., their cross-elasticity of demand is very high—it would seem that on economic grounds in any given alloy the three forms of aluminum should be considered as identical products. Thus, any differences in price should be justified by cost differences.

Isolating costs of sales to different customers is ordinarily a complex problem in price-discrimination cases, but since reduction facilities, holding furnaces, and transportation equipment are separate in this case, it should be possible to determine the cost differences for the aluminum in the three different forms without much difficulty. The service aspects of the supply contracts—e.g., continuous supply, variation in specifications of metal, and provision for converting metal into pig under certain contingencies—complicate the picture, but the experience in the determination of "extra" charges should minimize the complications.

The other aspect of the contracts concerning the impact on both the die-casters and smelters raises the question of whether the ties between the automobile companies and Reynolds constitute a form of exclusion from the market. If the die-casters are not being given an equal opportunity to bid on the aluminum-casting alloy business of the automobile companies, the transactions deserve careful examination. By the same token, if the prices established under the hot-metal contracts result in an artificial ceiling imposed on secondary alloys, a type of squeeze and exclusionary threat to the secondary smelters also may be entailed.

Delivered-Pricing

The change to a delivered-pricing system in aluminum is objectionable from a public policy viewpoint primarily because it promotes collusion among variously situated sellers and tends toward the elimination of price competition; and secondly, because it involves systematic geographic price discrimination in the economic sense. The circumstances surrounding the change to delivered-pricing make it clear that there was a general desire to curb price shading, extra allowances, etc.—that is, price competition. The uniformity among producers on quoted base prices evidently was not sufficient to guarantee stable prices under slack demand. The technique of delivered prices (if followed) will take care of this uncertainty by insuring that all sellers will quote *the same price to all buyers in any given market*. This suggests that the problem of geographic-pricing in aluminum is really the problem of oligopolistic uncertainty now facing the industry, of which delivered-pricing is only one aspect. From a public policy standpoint, therefore, the formalization of recognized interdependence of sellers means that the promotion of competitive pricing requires that attention be given to the source of the problem, namely, the market structure in aluminum.

Concentration and Size: Conclusion

This brings us to the central issue in aluminum, the high degree of producer concentration. Despite the restructuring after World War II and the recent entry of three new integrated producers, the aluminum industry today is still one of the most highly concentrated industries in the United States. The "Big Three" account for almost 90 per cent of primary capacity and the conditions of entry in this stage remain difficult. Moreover, the six largest integrated firms have 66 per cent to over 90 per cent of the market for principal mill shapes with the exception of extrusions and wire, where their share is 44 per cent, and they are continuing to expand present capacity and to diversify further into more fabricated lines.

This does not gainsay the fact that enormous changes have not taken place in aluminum. What it does mean is that under the close-knit oligopoly tacit concerted action has replaced unilateral monopoly action. Alcoa's monopoly power has been broken, but as the recognized industry leader its policies still guide the industry in large part via the convention of price leadership. Certainly there is more independent action in the industry today than under the monopoly rule. Competition is very keen in several areas: in foundry and die-casting products, extrusions, wire, and cable, and from substitute metals; and there are occasional outbursts of real competition at the primary level under conditions of temporary excess capacity. On primary aluminum and major product lines, however, as well as on basic producer policies, the "Big Three" stand as a fairly cohesive group.

Other firms are free to and do challenge Alcoa's decisions, at all stages of the industry, but the occasional attempts at independent action by other integrated producers or independent fabrication do not appear to have materially weakened the leadership of Alcoa. The point here is that in the aftermath of restructuring the aluminum industry oligopoly problems have arisen which require the same degree of care and attention given to the problems under the old monopoly.

The general lesson which this offers for public policy in aluminum is that the industry's structure and interfirm relationships be kept fluid by more entry, especially at the primary level. Direct government action has been undertaken in this industry from time to time, and if truly competitive conditions are desired ultimately, further restructuring will be required. The entry of more firms will avoid the danger of the aluminum industry following the pattern of steel, with all of its dilemmas.

Another lesson which the aluminum experience suggests, is that market situations having a history of firmly entrenched leadership may require divesting the leader of its residual monopoly power exerted through conventions such as price leadership. In brief, this means that in oligopolistic situations, by reducing the market power of the industry leader and fostering genuine rivalry for leadership or prominence in the industry, more fluid conditions will develop and more independence of decision-making is likely to prevail. This, of course, is the kind of remedial action that the courts have been generally reluctant to undertake. However, the aluminum case already has established a precedent in the postwar period for direct government assistance to potential aluminum producers. Continuation of this policy can be expected to further the cause of competition and perhaps should be considered more generally as a supplement to antitrust action. It is vastly preferable from the standpoint of antitrust policy in a free-enterprise system to have restructuring of industries undertaken where necessary by direct judicial action and court supervision. Nevertheless, the court's decision to provide a remedy in aluminum by direct government action has led to improved market results in this industry.

SUGGESTED READINGS

Books and Pamphlets

Walter Adams and Horace M. Gray, *Monopoly in America* (New York: The Macmillan Company, 1955).

Charles C. Carr, *Alcoa—An American Enterprise* (New York: 1952).

Louis Marlio, *The Aluminum Cartel* (Washington: Brookings Institution, 1947).

Charlotte F. Mueller, *Light Metals Monopoly* (New York: Columbia University Press, 1946).

George W. Stocking and Myron W. Watkins, *Cartels in Action* (New York: Twentieth Century Fund, 1947).

Donald W. Wallace, *Market Control in the Aluminum Industry* (Cambridge: Harvard University Press, 1937).

Simon N. Whitney, *Antitrust Policies: American Experience in Twenty Industries* (New York: Twentieth Century Fund, 1958), Vol. II.

Government Publications

U.S. Department of Commerce, *Materials Survey-Aluminum*, compiled for the Office of Defense Mobilization, Washington, November 1956.

U.S. Department of Commerce, "World Trade in Aluminum, 1954–57," Washington, 1958.

Hearings Before the Subcommittee on Study of Monopoly Power, House Judiciary Committee, "Aluminum," Serial No. 1, Part 1, Washington, 1951.

Hearings Before Subcommittee No. 3 of House Select Committee on Small Busi-

ness, "Aluminum Industry," Part I, Testimony Concerning Shortages and Other Matters, Washington, 1958.

Hearings Before Subcommittee No. 3 of House Select Committee on Small Business, "Aluminum Industry," Washington, 1958.

U.S. versus *Aluminum Company of America,* 44 F. Supp. 97, opinion of Judge Caffey, March 12, 1941.

U.S. versus *Aluminum Company of America,* 148 F. 2d 416, opinion of Judge Hand, March 12, 1945.

U.S. versus *Aluminum Company of America,* 91 F. Supp. 333, opinion of Judge Knox, June 2, 1950.

U.S. versus *Aluminum Company of America,* 153 Supp. 132, opinion of Judge Cashin, June 28, 1957.

Journal and Magazine Articles

Walter Adams, "The Aluminum Case: Legal Victory—Economic Defeat," *American Economic Review,* Vol. XLI, December 1951.

Fortune, "Kaiser Aluminum—Henry J.'s Marvelous Mistake," July 1956.

Fortune, "The Splendid Retreat of Alcoa," October 1955.

Fortune, "Look at the Reynolds' Boys Now," August 1953.

Fortune, "Aluminum Reborn," May 1946.

Business Week, January 17, June 27, and August 1, 1959; February 4 and 18, 1956; April 30, 1955; May 30 and August 14, 1954; and April 5, 1947.

American Metal Market, various numbers.

Chapter 7

ALFRED E. KAHN

The Chemical Industry *

SECTION I: SCOPE AND STRUCTURE

In the industry study, the economist uses the tools of price theory to help him describe, explain, and evaluate the operation of some specific market, supplying some specific product. But what is an industry, a product, a market? In 1959, the Federal Trade Commission, proceeding under the Textile Fiber Products Identification Act, issued a set of rules requiring that all artificial fibers made from cellulose be clearly labeled "rayon." The decree drew strong, but unavailing, protests from several manufacturers who claimed to have developed cellulose-derived fibers resistant to shrinkage and wrinkling, and were hoping to offer them for incorporation in wash-and-wear clothing with new, less invidious names.[1] The Celanese Corporation of America fought an equally futile fight years before, to lift the same incubus from its fibers and fabrics. Are Celanese or Courtauld's new "Lincron" distinct products, with distinct markets, or are they truly relatively unimportant variations of rayon? Obviously they are both. They are in some measure physically different from other rayons and from each other; and they are economically distinct because some buyers rightly or wrongly would consider them so. Yet each is in varying degree like other rayons and competes with them. Indeed, all products so labeled compete also in varying degrees

* Although it differs in substantial respects, the present chapter draws heavily on Chapters 9–11 of George W. Stocking and Myron W. Watkins, *Cartels in Action,* New York, Twentieth Century Fund, 1946. The present author prepared the first draft of those chapters, as a staff member working under the direction of Messrs. Stocking and Watkins. He wishes to express to them and to the Fund his appreciation for their permission for this use of those chapters. He wishes also to thank Professor William H. Martin for the opportunity to study the partially completed draft of his monograph on the chemical industries and Gail Stewart for her assistance.

[1] "Rayon is Rayon," *Business Week,* June 6, 1959, p. 32; *ibid.,* March 12, 1960, p. 114.

with natural silk, nylon, and other textile fibers in what must to some extent be conceived of as one great market.

But substitutability of products is not the only useful basis for delineating markets and industries. Steel companies produce thousands of products, most of them in no sense interchangeable. The cohesiveness and interdependence of these companies and of their various markets come largely from the supply side: from the fact that, working on common materials and with similar basic techniques, producers can move from supplying one product to another.

So it is with the "chemical industry," although the definition of this one is more arbitrary than of most others. Most of its products are not in any sense substitutes for one another, although it comprises numerous subindustries, like synthetic fibers, that do have this characteristic. (Many economists for this reason choose to refer to it in the plural, as the chemical *industries*.) It is the domain of a number of companies which history and business usage have marked as a fairly distinct group, because, employing a predominantly chemical technology, they have supplied the basic chemicals used in industry.[2] The membership is not stable, and there are many part-time members; but there is a definable, interdependent group which is worth studying as such.

We are not merely concerned, then, with the thousands of individual chemical markets or product groups: dyestuffs, synthetic fibers, explosives, plastics, synthetic rubbers, paints, fertilizers, pharmaceuticals, alkalies, solvents, antifreezes, or the vast numbers of heavy, light, fine, organic, and inorganic chemicals. We are primarily interested in all of them; that is to say, we are interested in the organization and market behavior of the companies that produce them, in their several markets.

This matter of defining the chemical industry is not a mere intellectual exercise; it is of pressing importance to those engaged in the trade. Chemical technology does not stop at the businessman's industry borders: as it grows and changes, developing new synthetic compounds competitive with established products in nonchemical fields (rayon and nylon for the traditional textiles, titanium and magnesium for other metals, synthetic detergents for soaps), tapping new, "nonchemical" sources of raw materials (the steel manufacturer's by-product coke oven, the petroleum refinery), it inevitably draws chemical companies into other realms, and nonchemical companies into chemistry (petroleum companies forward into synthetic ammonia, rubber, plastics, insecticides, and solvents, copper refiners into sulfuric acid

---

[2] It is the latter attribute essentially that distinguishes the chemical field from the manufacture of metals, petroleum, fuels, soap, glass, drugs, ceramics, cement, and paper, even though all these involve basically chemical operations, and even though many companies cross the boundaries between them and chemicals.

to make use of noxious waste gases, manufacturers of rayon, rubber tires, glass, paint, and photographic film backward into supplying their raw materials). The result is a complex and fascinating pattern of conflict and collaboration, competition and diplomatic negotiation and reconciliation.

The Prevalence of Oligopoly

Individual chemical markets tend each to be dominated by a relatively small number of sellers. The median of the 41 industries classified by the 1954 Census of Manufactures as falling within the group "chemicals and allied products" had 52 per cent of its shipments accounted for by the top four and 71 per cent by the top eight sellers. The ratio for all manufacturing industries that corresponds to the 52 per cent in chemicals was slightly under 37.[3]

What is true of individual industries is even more true of individual products. Before World War II, over 60 per cent of the total value of chemical and allied products were produced under conditions where the largest four concerns accounted for half or more of total production. A study of the production of 238 basic industrial chemicals during the first six months of 1945 found that 102 were produced entirely by four or fewer companies. Moreover, in 100, nearly three-fourths, of the remaining 136 products, the four leading producers accounted for 70 per cent or more of total output.[4]

[3] Computed from U.S. Senate, Committee on the Judiciary, Subcommittee on Antitrust and Monopoly, *Concentration in American Industry*, Eighty-fifth Congress, 1st Sess., 1957, pp. 20, 76–80. The following table distributes the value of shipments by each of the 41 chemical industries according to their concentration ratios for four leading companies, and compares the resulting distribution with all manufacturing industries:

Concentration Ratios (Percentage)	Chemical Industries ($000,000)	(% of total)	All Mfg. Industries ($000,000)	(% of total)
75 to 100	3,291	17.3	16,427	7.8
50 to 74	4,849	25.4	35,186	16.7
25 to 49	10,087	52.9	74,495	35.3
Less than 25	861	4.5	84,730	40.2
Total	19,087	100.0	210,838	100.0

Ibid., p. 24. The weighted average concentration ratios here (obtained by interpolation) are 46.5 for chemicals and 31.9 for all manufacturing.

[4] *Economic Concentration and World War II*, Report of the Smaller War Plants Corporation to Special Committee to Study the Problems of Small Business, U.S. Senate, 79th Congress, 2d Sess., Document No. 206, pp. 183, 192; see also Clair Wilcox, *Competition and Monopoly in the American Economy*, U.S. Temporary National Economic Committee, Monograph No. 21, Washington: Government Printing Office, 1941, p. 201. For a similar analysis, showing much the same results, of the 1,000-odd synthetic organic chemicals produced by du Pont in 1947, see Norman Bursler, *The Du Pont Industrial Group*, Association of American Law Schools, Industry Studies for Collateral Use in Courses in Antitrust Law, 1951, p. 38. Comprehensive studies of product concentration ratios for later years are not available.

It is impossible to state in general terms which of these concentration ratios—for industries or for products—is the more significant for market analysis. Some of the Census industry groupings are obviously too broad, embracing hundreds, even thousands, of essentially noncompeting products, and therefore understate the true concentration in individual markets, meaningfully defined.[5] On the other hand, the product classifications often overstate the true concentration of market power, because they are defined so as to exclude close substitutes.[6]

The Preponderance of Big Business

Although there is no single, overwhelmingly dominant firm, like Imperial Chemical Industries in England or I. G. Farbenindustrie A.G. in prewar Germany,[7] a relatively small number of great, diversified companies share the bulk of United States output in field after field, sometimes among themselves, sometimes with one or a few large and relatively specialized manufacturers.[8] This situation influences the pattern of competition and cooperation in all markets.

[5] The six leading (4-digit) chemical industries classified in note 3 above were organic chemicals not elsewhere classified, pharmaceutical preparations, plastics materials, paints and varnishes, inorganic chemicals not elsewhere classified, and synthetic fibers.
  [6] Thus 4-digit (industry) groupings like plastics materials, synthetic fibers, soap and glycerin, paints and varnishes may be at least as meaningful for identifying possible monopoly power as the individual product subgroupings thereof.
  A similar problem arises in deciding whether the appropriate concentration measure is of production or sales. Many companies make their own chemical raw materials, leaving open-market sales to one or a few of them. Production figures thus understate the concentration of market control; on the other hand, sales figures neglect the limitation on monopoly power inherent in the fact that many potential customers do, and others may be in a position to, produce for their own needs.
  [7] In 1948 I.C.I. alone accounted for just under 40 per cent of the output of the U.K. chemical industry. W. B. Reddaway, "The Chemical Industry," in Duncan Burn (ed.), *The Structure of British Industry, A Symposium*, Cambridge, England: Cambridge University Press, 1958, I, p. 224. The I. G. Farben share was about 40 per cent before World War II. Stocking and Watkins, *Cartels in Action*, p. 413.
  [8] It would be possible to document this statement at great length. A few examples should suffice: the preponderant share of du Pont, Allied, General Aniline, and American Cyanamid in dyestuffs; du Pont and Chemstrand (owned jointly by Monsanto and American Viscose) in synthetic fibers, Dow and Monsanto in styrene; American Cyanamid, Monsanto, and Union Carbide in acrylonitrile; du Pont, Rohm and Haas, and Celanese in acrylic resins; B. F. Goodrich, Union Carbide, and Monsanto in polyvinyl chloride; du Pont and American Viscose in cellophane; Dow and Monsanto in phenol; Union Carbide, Shell Oil, and Eastman Kodak in acetone; du Pont, Hercules, Atlas, American Cyanamid, and Olin Mathieson in explosives; Union Carbide and Air Reduction in oxygen and acetylene; du Pont, American Cyanamid, and National Lead in titanium dioxide; Monsanto, Food Machinery & Chemical, Victor Chemical, Hooker Chemical, and Olin Mathieson in phosphorus and phosphoric acid; du Pont, Celanese, American Viscose, and Eastman Kodak in filament rayon; and so on. Much of this information is from Standard and Poor's Corporation, Industry Surveys, Chemicals, *Basic Analysis*, October 23, 1958.

Table 1 lists and ranks by total assets the eleven largest of these companies, as of the end of 1935 and 1958; their leader, E. I. du Pont de Nemours, is the biggest chemical company in the world.

TABLE 1

The Leading Chemical Companies [a]

	1935			1958	
Rank	Company	Assets ($000,000)	Rank	Company	Assets ($000,000)
1.	E. I. du Pont de Nemours	667	1.	E. I. du Pont de Nemours	2,649
2.	Allied Chemical & Dye	400	2.	Union Carbide	1,530
3.	Union Carbide & Carbon	337	3.	Dow Chemical	875
4.	General Aniline & Film	71	4.	Olin Mathieson Chemical	787
5.	American Cyanamid	60	5.	Allied Chemical	748
6.	Columbian Carbon	49	6.	Monsanto Chemical	664
7.	Hercules Powder	40	7.	American Cyanamid	584
8.	Air Reduction	39	8.	Air Reduction	204
9.	Monsanto Chemical	36	9.	Hercules Powder	191
10.	Dow Chemical	27	10.	General Aniline & Film	169
11.	Mathieson Alkali	26	11.	Hooker Chemical	151

[a] In general, the identification of chemical companies is based on the grouping by Moody's *Industrials.* However several companies so listed by Moody's, producing large amounts of chemicals, are omitted here because their activities are primarily in other fields. Some attempt is made in the following table to indicate the order of magnitude of their chemical operations alone. Major omissions from both tables are drug companies like Parke Davis, Charles Pfizer and Merck, with assets of $188 to $212 millions, and producers of paints, soaps, steel (whose by-product coke ovens are important sources of industrial chemicals), and sulphur—the latter because theirs is essentially an extractive, rather than a chemical, operation.

There are many other important chemical companies. Several, with assets of $50,000,000 to $150,000,000 and typically more specialized than the giants listed above, bulk large in individual fields—alkali and chlorine producers like Diamond Alkali, Pennsalt Chemicals, and Wyandotte Chemicals; phosphate and fertilizer suppliers like International Minerals and Chemical, American Agricultural Chemical, and Virginia-Carolina Chemical; specialists like Atlas Powder, Rohm & Haas, and Publicker Industries; and others less readily classified, Commercial Solvents, Heyden Newport Chemical, Reichhold Chemical, Spencer Chemical, and Stauffer Chemical—the latter almost certainly attaining the tenth and possibly the ninth ranking on the above table by virtue of its 1959 acquisition of the $49,000,000 Victor Chemical. Moreover, there are a number of giant conglomerate firms with chemical divisions that must be counted as participating as importantly in this industry as some of the above-mentioned. Table 2 lists as many as possible of the more important of these companies with their total assets and with very rough estimates of their assets properly attributable to chemicals.[9]

TABLE 2

Leading Nonchemical Companies in Chemicals [a] with Assets at End of 1958
(in $000,000)

Company	Total Assets	Est. Assets in Chemicals [b]
W. R. Grace	498	250
Standard Oil (N.J.)	9,479	240
Phillips Petroleum	1,515	225
Eastman Kodak	762	200 [c]
Shell Oil	1,648	185
Standard Oil (Calif.)	2,451	180
National Distillers and Chemical	497	160
Food Machinery and Chemical	282	120
Goodrich Rubber	547	120
Celanese	340	110 [d]
Pittsburgh Plate Glass	561	110 [e]
Koppers	200	65 [f]

[a] The leading probable omissions, for lack of data, are U.S. Rubber and National Lead Co.

[b] In general, where more specific information is unavailable, the percentage which chemicals and allied products constituted of total sales (or in some instances of net operating revenue) is applied against total company assets.

[c] Excludes photographic film.

[d] Excludes fibers, mainly rayon, but includes chemicals used in the company's fiber operations.

[e] Excludes paint.

[f] Excludes most of tar products and products of wood preserving division (pressure treated lumber, building poles, treated wood).

Though their sheer bulk, power, and prestige are formidable, the major companies account for no such share of the sprawling and diversified chemical industry, taken as a whole, as the respective leaders do in individual markets. The top seven in 1958 accounted for perhaps 32 to 46 per cent,

[9] The estimates exclude the very large sales of rayon by Celanese, paint by Pittsburgh Plate Glass, and photographic film by Eastman Kodak, even though the assets of du Pont devoted to all these operations are included in Table 1. These are only peripherally chemical operations, and du Pont is virtually unique among chemical companies, as traditionally defined, in embracing them. For more authoritative estimates of petrochemical sales by the oil companies in this group, see "Petrochemicals Face New Challenges," *Business Week*, September 3, 1960, p. 63.

and du Pont alone for 11 to 14 per cent, of the sales of the industry, as we have been defining it.[10]

Still, it is mainly shifting groups of these diversified companies that account for the prevalence of oligopoly in one subindustry after another. Moreover, despite the unusually rapid growth and revolutionary changes in product mix that have characterized this industry in recent decades,[11] market concentration in general, and the domination by essentially the same giant firms in particular, has if anything become accentuated. First, while for manufacturing generally the share of total value added by industries with high concentration ratios (the top four producers accounting for 50 per cent or more of output) declined markedly between 1901 and 1947, from 32.9 to 24.0 per cent, in chemicals and allied products it increased during the same period from 24.3 to 33.7 per cent.[12] The latter trend apparently continued, but only moderately at most, in the following seven years.[13] Second, the share of the largest companies in total sales of chemicals and allied products seems definitely to have increased since 1935.[14]

Finally, the identities and relative positions of the leaders shown in Table 1 have, with a few readily explainable exceptions, been remarkably stable over the 23-year period. The significant declines in relative position have been suffered by Allied Chemical, General Aniline, and Columbian Carbon,

[10] The margin of error and judgment in this estimate is extremely wide. The main reason is the inevitable measure of arbitrariness involved in defining the industry. The higher concentration ratios result when we exclude from the total industry sales of chemicals and allied products, as reported in the *Survey of Current Business*, the output of rayon, pharmaceuticals, soap, cleaning and polishing products, paints, fertilizers, vegetable and animal oils, ink, toilet preparations, glue, carbon black, and salt—whose share in the total has been taken (somewhat arbitrarily) as equivalent to their shares in total plant shipments as reported in the 1954 Census of Manufactures. (Interplant shipments of their chemical raw materials are not removed.) In such a computation it is of course necessary to exclude the corresponding outputs of the top seven—notably du Pont's paints and rayon, and the nonchemicals production (including pharmaceuticals) of Olin-Mathieson and Union Carbide. The lower estimates come from putting back into the industry totals paint, detergents, rayon, and pharmaceuticals, on the ground that one or more of the seven produces each of these. Compare Simon N. Whitney, *Antitrust Policies, American Experience in Twenty Industries*, New York: Twentieth Century Fund, 1958, I, p. 190.

[11] According to the Federal Reserve index, chemical production has grown about twice as rapidly as industrial production generally in recent decades.

[12] M. A. Adelman, "The Measurement of Industrial Concentration," *Review of Economics and Statistics*, Vol. 33, p. 291 (1951).

[13] More industries in the chemicals group showed increases than showed decreases in concentration ratios in this period, U.S. Senate Judiciary Comm., *op.cit.*, p. 25; however, cf. p. 28.

[14] The three industry leaders accounted for 14.9 per cent of that total in 1935, 13.8 per cent in 1948 and 16.6 per cent in 1958. For some of the top seven one must rely on rough estimates for 1935, but it would appear their sales could not have been far from 19 per cent of the total in that year; it was 18.4 per cent in 1948 and 26.6 per cent in 1958. See also Whitney, *op.cit.*, pp. 226–7.

the significant rises enjoyed by Dow, Olin Mathieson, and Monsanto. These changes to some extent provide evidence of the dynamic character of the industry: a company like Allied, that until the fifties pursued a very conservative financial and product-development policy, found itself left behind;[15] and technologically aggressive companies like Dow and Monsanto forged ahead. But General Aniline has lost ground mainly because, German-owned before World War II, it languished for years under the control of the Alien Property Custodian; and Columbian Carbon never was a diversified chemical company but a specialist employing a primitive technology, whose branch of the industry did not grow as fast as the rest. And it was not primarily technological progressiveness but mergers that played the preponderant role in the dramatic rise of Olin Mathieson and Hooker, as well as in Air Reduction's success in holding its own.[16]

The relative stability in the composition of the industry's elite has been modified in two ways. First, leadership has come to be somewhat more evenly shared: the "Big Three" are more nearly merged now into a "Big Seven," as Table 1 shows. Second, chemical markets have been subject to invasion, on an increasing scale in recent decades, by a number of nonchemical companies, as we have already suggested. The Census of Manufactures shows this industry to be well above average in the extent to which it is subject to this kind of cross-filing.[17]

The entry of nonchemical companies has, however, not fundamentally transformed the structure of the industry. Many of them—notably Grace, National Distillers, Food Machinery, and Pittsburgh Plate Glass—have merely given their own names to the chemical companies they bought out.[18] Almost all of those listed in Table 2, or their predecessors, were already important chemical producers back in 1935. Other interlopers have entered

[15] "You'd Hardly Know Allied Chemical," *Fortune*, Vol. 50, October 1954, p. 119.

[16] Mathieson's expansion from a specialized, regional company with $49 millions of assets at the end of 1948 to the giant it is today was accomplished primarily by successive acquisitions of Southern Acid and Sulphur, Standard Wholesale Phosphate and Acid Works, E. R. Squibb & Sons (with assets at time of acquisition of $15, $10, and $107 millions, respectively) and its merger in 1954 with the $233 million Olin Industries. Monsanto's acquisition of the $148 million Lion Oil in 1955 is also worthy of note.

[17] I am indebted to Martin for this observation.

[18] W. R. Grace acquired the $59 million Davison Chemical, the $26 million Dewey and Almy Chemical, as well as some smaller producers. National Distillers bought U.S. Industrial Chemicals (formerly U.S. Industrial Alcohol), which had $44 millions of assets at the time; Food Machinery, a large number of companies, most prominently the $25 million Westvaco Chemical; and Pittsburgh Plate Glass had merged Columbia Chemical in 1920, formed Southern Alkali in 1931 jointly with American Cyanamid, then purchased the latter's interest for $19 million in 1951, and acquired Pacific Alkali in 1951. In each case the large acquisition was either the initial or the most important step by which the nonchemical company broke into chemicals.

the industry largely in collaboration with existing companies, as we shall see. And none of them approaches the stature in chemicals of the "Big Seven." [19]

Reasons for Big Business Domination

The growth of giant chemical companies has been the outcome of a variety of forces, and has had mixed results. The one distinctive conditioning influence has been technology: the enormous potentialities of applying chemical science to industry, exploited with increasing intensity during the last sixty years, have provided favorable conditions for growth in the scale of enterprise.

The major raw materials of chemical manufacture are themselves products of chemical reactions; and the chemical industry is its own most important market. Chemicals produced at any one stage ordinarily have a great variety of such raw materials, and serve as intermediates in a variety of successive operations. Experience and equipment in one line, similarly, may be useful in a variety of other branches of the industry. Finally, these raw materials, uses, processes, and end products have been changing and expanding at a virtually geometric rate.

So chemical companies, following the logic of their developing technology, have reached out backward, forward, and sideways to encompass in their own operations these varied processes, materials, and products. Du Pont went from nitrocellulose explosives backward into synthetic ammonia (in part to supply the basic raw material), forward and sideways into nitrocellulose lacquers, artificial leather, plastics, film, rayon, and cellophane; it went from synthetic ammonia into urea (fertilizers) and synthetic methanol (solvents, antifreezes), from coal tar dyestuffs into a wide range of synthetic organic chemicals, nylon, tetraethyl of lead, synthetic rubber, etc. The mushrooming activities of Dow and Union Carbide have had a similar rationale. Allied Chemical & Dye, in contrast, was the result of a mammoth merger in 1920 of five firms, each dominant in a basic branch of the industry. However, the chemical motivations and prospects seemed the same as elsewhere: Allied was a well-rounded, powerful combine, supplying its own heavy chemicals, and moving naturally from coke by-products (notably coal tar crudes and intermediates, and sulfate of ammonia fertilizer) into dyestuffs and synthetic ammonia.[20]

[19] According to the Chase Manhattan Bank's annual survey, the *gross* investment in petrochemicals by the 32 leading oil companies just passed one billion dollars in 1958. *Petroleum Industry, 1958*, p. 19; cf. the 1957 survey, p. 19.
[20] See the *Fortune* articles on Dow (Vol. 26, pp. 110–13, December 1942), Union Carbide (Vol. 23, pp. 60–68, Vol. 24, pp. 49–56, 57–67, June, July, September 1941),

Up to a point, size has made for greater efficiency in serving the public, for a number of reasons. Within limits, the large physical plant is more efficient than the small. Big stills, filter presses, evaporators, vats, the equipment required for highly mechanized and mechanically controlled operations, cost less, per unit of capacity, than small; certain installations—water supply and waste-disposal systems, boiler and power-generating plant, and so on—have to be made for plants of any sizes, and will therefore cost less per unit of capacity, the larger the plant.[21] By-product recovery, exceptionally important in chemical technology, is frequently feasible only when large scale operations make available, at a single point, sufficiently large quantities to justify the expense of recovery. The cost of new products has almost invariably declined with expanding scale of operation.

There are economies of scale in research as well as in production. These arise because of the increasing importance of expensive equipment, cooperative investigation by large staffs of professionals, and the frequently great length of time required to bring ideas to fruition—although assertions by large companies about the many millions they had to spend before getting a cent back from this or that product may have to be taken with several grains of salt.[22] A large investment in innovation may prove truly more efficient, in social terms, than a small one.

Moreover, chemical research and experience do not confine their results to one narrow product field or type of process. The ability that size gives a company to carry its technical skills, by-products or intermediates, and fruits of research over into new fields (and back) is obviously technologically advantageous. German superiority in synthesis of coal tar dyes laid the basis for leadership in synthesis of perfumes, flavorings, drugs, explosives, and ammonia as well. Highly diversified, integrated companies were the agencies and outcome of this development.

At the same time, it is not true that the size of chemical giants reflects only the dictates of technology. (1) First of all, it has resulted in no small

---

Allied (Vol. 20, pp. 44–51, October 1939), Monsanto (Vol. 19, pp. 54–58, January 1939), and du Pont (Vol. 42, pp. 87–118 ff., October 1950).

[21] See Jesse W. Markham, *Competition in the Rayon Industry,* Cambridge: Harvard University Press, 1952, Chap. 3; Reddaway, *op.cit.,* pp. 219–21, 225.

[22] What is misleading about such statistics is that they tend to lump research and development expenses, which may indeed involve gambles of a size that only large firms can afford, with initial investments in commercial plants, whose risks are of an entirely different order. The one most frequently cited example, du Pont's proclaimed "$27,000,000 gamble" in nylon, emerges from critical analysis at most $\frac{2}{27}$ in the former category and at least $\frac{25}{27}$ in the latter. See Willard F. Mueller, "A Case Study of Product Discovery and Innovation Costs," *The Southern Economic Journal,* Vol. 24, pp. 80–86 (1957). Still, du Pont's $60 million precommercial commitment to Orlon and $42 million to Delrin are impressive sums. See "Delrin: du Pont's Challenge to Metals," *Fortune,* Vol. 60, pp. 116 ff., August 1959.

measure from horizontal integrations of competing producers, motivated to a considerable extent by a simple desire for market control. Leading examples were the systematic gobbling up of independents (some 100 in all), accompanied by international cartel agreements, which gave du Pont by 1911 a virtually complete monopoly of American explosives manufacture and sale, and has left it, even after dissolution under the antitrust laws, with perhaps 40 per cent of that market; [23] the merger of twelve American sulfuric acid manufacturers in 1899 to form General Chemical; the numerous acquisitions in the coal tar derivative field which the Barrett Co. brought into Allied; the buying up of some 31 competitors, sometimes jointly, that gave Pure Carbonic and Liquid Carbonic 73 per cent of the national production of carbon dioxide by 1940; [24] the systematic acquisitions of industrial gas manufacturers by Air Reduction in the last thirty-five years. Most of these widespread horizontal mergers occurred several decades ago; but they made major contributions to company growth. It was du Pont's preponderant position in explosives, thus attained, that left it at the close of World War I with the enormous profits which in turn financed its large-scale subsequent diversification.[25] Hercules too owes its present dimensions in large measure to the size bestowed upon it by those same early du Pont mergers. General Chemical and Barrett became two of the key building blocks of Allied Chemical.

(2) When chemical companies have chosen to branch into new fields, and companies outside the chemical field proper have chosen to come in, they have done so almost invariably by joining with, or buying out, others al-

[23] See *U.S. versus E. I. du Pont de Nemours & Co.*, 188 F. 127 (1911), which led to the splitting off of Hercules and Atlas Powder Companies. Acquisitions made a major contribution to du Pont's expansion in explosives after 1920 as well. See Willard F. Mueller, *Du Pont: A Study in Firm Growth*, unpublished doctoral dissertation, Vanderbilt University, 1955, University Microfilms, Publication No. 14,981, pp. 163–5 and 283–4, citing in turn Edward W. Proctor, *Antitrust Policy and the Industrial Explosives Industry*, unpublished doctoral dissertation, Harvard University, 1951.

[24] *Monopolistic Practices and Small Business*, Staff Report to the Federal Trade Commission for the Subcommittee on Monopoly, Select Comm. on Small Business, U.S. Senate, March 31, 1952, p. 54. See also Whitney, *op.cit.*, pp. 198–9.

[25] The dividends it earned from its General Motors investment, one of the uses to which du Pont put these funds, accounted for over 50 per cent of its aggregate net income from all sources in the twenties, and about 36 per cent in the entire 33 years after 1920. In addition, du Pont clearly obtained some preferential access to General Motors as a customer for some of its products, and to chemical developments by General Motors technicians—notably tetraethyl of lead and Freon—although the extent of these preferences has of course been a subject of lengthy dispute. See Mueller, *Du Pont*, pp. 126–8, 140–5; George W. Stocking, "The Du Pont-General Motors Case and the Sherman Act," *Virginia Law Rev.*, Vol. 44, pp. 1–40 (1958); Joel B. Dirlam and Irwin M. Stelzer, "The *Du Pont-General Motors* Decision: in the Antitrust Grain," *Columbia Law Review*, Vol. 58, pp. 24–43 (1958); and *U.S. versus E. I. du Pont de Nemours and Co.*, 126 F. Supp. 235 (1954), 353 U.S. 586 (1957).

ready there or planning to enter. In heavy chemicals, the purchase of Grasselli Chemical and Roessler and Hasslacher by du Pont (the price for Grasselli alone was $70,000,000 of du Pont stock), Kalbfleisch by American Cyanamid, Merrimac Chemical and the Commercial Acid Co. by Monsanto, and Southern Acid and Sulphur and Standard Wholesale Phosphate and Acid by Mathieson are cases in point. Union Carbide's first move into plastics was apparently its acquisition of the $11 million Bakelite Company, a pioneer and leader in the field; American Viscose, the giant in viscose rayon, moved into cellophane by buying Sylvania Industrial; Monsanto's major step into petrochemicals was its $148 million purchase of Lion Oil; the "real push" in American Cyanamid's "getting closer to the consumer" was its merging of the $17 million Formica Company.[26] The critical role of acquisitions in the entries of Grace, Food Machinery, National Distillers, and Pittsburgh Plate Glass has already been mentioned.[27]

There is no question of the logic of this method of expansion and entry, from the standpoint of the companies involved. It avoids duplication of facilities, patent infringement difficulties, and competition;[28] it permits a pooling of managerial skills, financial resources, market connections, technical experience, and patents. Some of these motives and consequences are clearly related to efficiencies of scale and of integration. Others are not.

(3) The giant chemical companies all consist of a great number of separate operating departments; in several the larger merged satellites retain their corporate as well as functional identities. More important, the

[26] *Business Week*, February 11, 1956, pp. 54, 56.

[27] There have been a few attempts to measure the contribution of such "external" expansions to the growth of leading chemical companies; all of them suffer from the basic inadequacy that the contribution of past acquisitions to company size at some later date is inadequately measured by the absolute size of the assets at the time they were acquired. For example, according to the estimates of J. Fred Weston, external growth accounted for only 33–39 per cent of the growth of du Pont from 1903 to 1948 (*The Role of Mergers in the Growth of Large Firms*, Berkeley: University of California Press, 1953, pp. 138–40; for his other chemical companies, see pp. 132–7); yet for the 1903–39 period only, the 39 per cent figure changes to 62 per cent. (For these and other measures, see Mueller, *Du Pont*, Chapter 9.) The question is: had du Pont not engaged so heavily in acquisitions before 1939, and thus achieved the size and market position it enjoyed at that date, would it have experienced so great an absolute increase in its total assets after that date, by construction of new capacity, financed principally out of current profits? According to one of Mueller's measures, acquisitions accounted for 54.3 per cent of du Pont's growth over its entire life between 1803 and 1949, and no less than 73.3 per cent from 1803 to 1939.

[28] When, between 1908 and 1920, du Pont embarked on a program of diversification, in order to provide new outlets for its nitrocellulose capacity, it followed a deliberate policy of doing so by acquiring going concerns, as the means best calculated to avoid upsetting markets and to provide guaranteed customers. However, it is impossible to explain the growth of du Pont without emphasizing also the company's far-sighted and bold exploitation of the industrial potentialities of chemistry, as well as the sheer business acumen of its leaders. See Mueller, *Du Pont, passim.*

promised technological advantages of their corporate union has in case after case failed to emerge, simply because collaboration failed to reach down to the operating or research levels: Allied Chemical and Dye, American Cyanamid, Union Carbide, Olin Mathieson are outstanding examples.[29] The departments or subsidiaries specialize, it is true, and supply each other with materials. But this is an evidence of the efficiency of specialization, not of common ownership.

Size breeds size; it has a historical logic of its own, apart from considerations of efficiency. A big company becomes a magnet for any new inventions in its field: independent inventors and businessmen, even if fortified with patents, may be unwilling, or have insufficient financial resources, to risk the threat of infringement litigation, or to wage a competitive struggle with it for a share in the market. Other companies seeking to exploit a new process or product in its domain are likely to enlist its cooperation to avoid conflict—in expectation of a return of the favor when the situation is reversed. A big company usually has better access to capital markets, or is better able to finance expansion out of earnings. If raw materials are scarce, it is less likely to suffer, either because it produces them itself, or because suppliers are anxious to keep its good will. It is likely to be able to purchase supplies at preferential prices, or to induce reciprocal buying of its products by would-be suppliers. The chemical industries amply illustrate all these tendencies. Even where the giants have grown by "internal expansion" rather than by merger, they have done so in large measure on the basis of

[29] The unprogressiveness of Allied, disappointing the high hopes that attended its formation, has already been referred to; the architects of the grand union were financiers and businessmen, not chemists or engineers. See n. 15, above. In view of the crazy-quilt of 35-odd acquisitions, "a chemically unsophisticated program of mere expansion," ("American Cyanamid," *Fortune*, Vol. 22, September 1940, p. 106), that created the modern American Cyanamid, it should not be surprising that at least until the fifties that company "was a feudal state of autonomous kingdoms, each division concerned with its own problems, and without clear lines of authority." ("Rebuilding to Get Closer to the Consumer," *Business Week*, February 11, 1956, p. 55.) *Fortune* attributed Union Carbide's failure to achieve "a major research triumph since it opened the petrochemical field some thirty years ago," to "too much fragmentation" of both research and operations, the company's "historic bias toward developmental research" having been "accentuated by the fact that each of its research laboratories is attached to a particular operating division" ("Union Carbide Enriches the Formula," Vol. 55, February 1957, pp. 127–28, 180.) See finally *Fortune's* graphic picture of "Olin-Mathieson's Goat-Feathers" (Vol. 58, September 1958, p. 112), abounding with violent criticisms of this "loose confederation of tribal chieftains," for its excessive diversification, its lack of coordination, "orientation and central purpose," its "somnolence, slipshod planning . . . unbelievable carelessness and procrastination."

In each of these instances there have been efforts recently to improve the coordination of research and development efforts; but the fact that for years or decades these companies were able to operate as loose, uncoordinated federations, all the while growing with the industry, suggests that their present size owes but little to the technological advantages of integration.

patents or licenses acquired from others or simply by virtue of their being in a position, largely because of previous mergers, to take the major advantage of emergent market opportunities. For all these reasons big chemical companies have become bigger merely because they were big.

SECTION II: MARKET BEHAVIOR AND PERFORMANCE

The central economic characteristic of oligopoly is the recognition of interdependence: it makes it prudent for each seller to take into account all possible effects on the market and on other companies of his every contemplated action, whether it concerns output, price, investment, or entry. The distinctive characteristics of the chemical industry that above all others modify the influence of oligopoly are the versatility of the technology with which it works, and the extraordinary expansion of market opportunities to which the progressive exploitation of that technology has given rise. These circumstances continually engender possible conflicts with the sense of oligopolistic interdependence. The one counsels restraint in departing from established policies; the other offers rich rewards to the bold and the enterprising.

There is no simple way of summarizing or characterizing the combined effect of these two basically conflicting influences. The balance struck between them was quite different in the relatively stable environment of the thirties than in the exuberant early and middle fifties, and may again turn out quite different in the sixties. It seems most useful, for purposes of analysis, first to consider them separately.

Peaceful and Collaborative Coexistence

A situation in which a relatively small number of giant companies, with far-flung interests, meet each other in one market after another is conducive to conservatism, with respect both to "excessive" (from the private standpoint) investment, which may endanger satisfactory price and profit levels, and to price competition or similar unfriendly acts that might provoke retaliation, to the detriment of all concerned except the consumer. This fact, along with the ever-present threat of conflict in a dynamic industry, has given rise to a species of behavior in chemicals that can be likened only to diplomacy between national states of roughly comparable might. They avoid frontal assaults on one another. But they look to their sources of strength—their patents and technical capacities—and take what they can in neutral territories, or where they can do so without giving direct affront. They try to negotiate possible conflicts; but the division of the spoils reflects the underlying distribution of power.

Thus, market relations between sellers in the chemical industry are typically "friendly," if not collusive, and the preservation of such friendly relations becomes a primary objective of market policy. They have recognized "spheres of interest" and ordinarily trespass only to produce for their own requirements, or when they have some truly new product or process to exploit, or by buying up a company already operating in the field. Du Pont stayed out of nitrogenous fertilizers (dominated by Allied) as a matter of policy until it developed its synthetic urea; Union Carbide went into production of alcohols only on the basis of its pioneering work with petroleum and natural gases; [30] the numerous producers of plastics and synthetic fibers usually have come in with their own distinctive products. The same was true of synthetic rubber-like materials before the government-financed crash program during World War II. And even here, the operation of the plants was for a decade or more neatly divided to preserve traditional industry boundaries, with the oil companies supplying the butadiene, the chemical companies the styrene and acrylonitrile, and the tire manufacturers compounding the rubber—except for Jersey Standard's own product, Butyl.[31] The steel companies, whose coke ovens produce huge quantities of coal tar and its simple derivatives, have consistently refrained from moving into the highly profitable lines whose raw materials they remain content to supply.

In turn most of the recent incursions of chemical process industries backward into chemicals have been in order to produce their raw materials. And chemical companies have in general been content to supply raw materials to producers of glass, rayon, pharmaceuticals and detergents, and to fertilizer mixers. The exceptions hardly disprove the general rule. Du Pont came into rayon in the early 1920's upon expiration of the basic patent that had protected American Viscose's average annual returns of 77 per cent on investment in 1915–20; [32] rayon seemed one of the natural outlets for du Pont's capacities in cellulose chemistry. American Cyanamid and Mathieson became leaders in the ethical drug field, but only by major acquisitions—of

[30] "Before entering a new market, Carbide has always sought some clear edge in either raw-material supply or production process. Lacking such an edge, it hesitates to launch products that might seem to complement perfectly the company's existing lines." "Union Carbide Enriches the Formula," *Fortune,* Vol. 55, February 1957, p. 126.

[31] See "Government-Spawned War Baby Weighs in as a Healthy Industry," *Business Week,* September 7, 1957, p. 122. Also the annual reports of the Attorney General on *Competition in the Synthetic Rubber Industry,* as of July 1, 1956, 1957, 1958 and 1959.

[32] Markham, *Competition in the Rayon Industry,* p. 227.

Lederle Laboratories and Squibb, respectively. Monsanto went into direct distribution of its unique detergent, All, but withdrew and sold the venture to Lever Brothers, in part because it had found it embarrassing to compete with its customers, the soap companies.[33] General Aniline went into marketing liquid detergents only because the soap companies would not do so; then sold out its pioneering Glim to the B. T. Babbitt Company.[34]

The relationship between the oil and chemical industries is more difficult to characterize. Until the end of World War II, roughly, petroleum refiners stayed pretty much in the fuel business, and were content to sell their refinery and natural gases to chemical companies for further synthesis. They emphasized the fact that petrochemicals could not possibly absorb more than a per cent or two by volume of their oil and gas production; and took pains to assure chemical companies of their honorable intentions.[35] Even the notable and increasingly numerous exceptions were either joint ventures with chemical companies, or represented pioneering developments, like Shell's important synthesis of glycerine, or its use of natural gas as a source of hydrogen for ammonia synthesis, New Jersey Standard's Butyl rubber, and the toluene issuing from its new catalytic cracking processes, Phillips' pioneering work in synthetic rubber—and none of these competed importantly with chemical companies. The oil companies have moved into chemicals on so broad a front and on so large a scale since then, however, that it is no longer possible to regard nonintervention and nonencroachment as the general rule. There have been several, interrelated reasons for this development. First, over 56 per cent of the entire chemical industry's production by value now stems from oil and gas. Second, with the progressive adoption of catalytic cracking petroleum refiners have become producers of petrochemicals as well as practitioners of advanced organic chemical technology whether they wanted to or not. Third, the more rapid rate of expansion of the demand for chemicals than of oil, and the fatter profit margins that chemicals promised per barrel or per Mcf, created irresistible

---

[33] "Monsanto Yields Consumer Field," *Business Week*, June 1, 1957, p. 36. This was not the only reason, we shall shortly indicate. The Department of Justice in 1958 instituted a suit challenging the transfer as violating Section 7 of the Clayton Act.

[34] Martin, *op.cit.* (MS.), Chap. 4, p. 6.

[35] G. B. Walker, "Oil Companies Content to Be Chemical Suppliers," *Barron's*, September 16, 1946, p. 23. Similar expressions of solicitude appeared when I. G. Farben and Standard Oil began jointly to produce chemicals for the American market, through a joint subsidiary, Jasco. For example, according to I. G.: "If Jasco finds during the development of new processes that products or chemicals are produced which are manufactured in du Pont's sphere of interest, I. G. and Standard will discuss their plans with du Pont and endeavor to find a way by which utilization of such processes and products takes place to the greatest advantage of each of the three parties." *Patents, Hearings*, Committee on Patents, U.S. Senate, Seventy-seventh Congress, Second Sess., on S. 2303 and S. 2491, part 5, p. 2350. See also Bursler, *op.cit.*, pp. 104–18.

inducements to push forward into petrochemicals as a means of upgrading previously low-value refinery by-products and natural gas.[36]

Much of the restraint that chemical companies exhibit about encroaching on each other's domain can clearly be explained in terms that in no sense reflect adversely on their willingness to compete.[37] The fact that most producers of ammonia do not go into fertilizer mixing reflects the advantages of specialization and the unattractiveness of profit prospects in that field. There is logic, technologically speaking, to Union Carbide's producing acetic anhydride but not cellulose acetate rayon or film, ferro-alloys but not fabricated steel products. The failure of Allied to exploit its head start in synthetic detergents probably resulted from a lack of commercial vision rather than of competitive courage; and the failure of its Swerl, like Monsanto's troubles with All, probably proves that chemical companies are simply incompetent soap salesmen. One reason so many chemicals are produced by only one company is that their market is too limited to support any more.

But there can be no doubt that the restraint reflects also the dictates of oligopolistic diplomacy. The corollary of this rule is: where interests might otherwise conflict, collaborate. Collaboration among chemical companies, and between them and outsiders, takes various forms.

(1) They form joint ventures in fields which interest both: du Pont and National Distillers to manufacture ethyl alcohol; du Pont and Dow (Midland Ammonia) in synthetic ammonia; Ethyl and Dow (Ethyl-Dow) to manufacture ethylene dibromide; Texaco and American Cyanamid (Jefferson Chemical), Panhandle Eastern Pipe Line and National Distillers (National Petro-Chemicals), Tennessee Gas Transmission and Food Machinery (Petro-Tex), Standard of Ohio and Atlas Powder, to mention only a very few, in petrochemicals; du Pont and Procter & Gamble, and Jasco (owned jointly by Standard Oil and I. G. Farben) and Procter & Gamble, both in synthetic detergents; Dow and Corning Glass (Dow-Corning) in silicones; Monsanto and American Viscose (Chemstrand) in synthetic fibers; du Pont and Imperial Chemical Industries, Ltd. (the Duperial companies, and Canadian Industries, Ltd.) for the cooperative exploitation of selected foreign markets; American Viscose and Sun Oil (AviSun) in polypropylene; Hercules

---

[36] See Standard & Poor's, *op.cit.*, Chemicals, p. C32, and *Industry Surveys, Oil, Basic Analysis*, September 10, 1959, p.042. Also "Petrochemicals: Where the Growth Shows," *Business Week*, October 15, 1955, p. 78. Here again (see note 19, above), comments in the trade press may leave an exaggerated impression. According to the Chase Manhattan Bank, petrochemicals sales by the 32 leading oil companies were $785 millions in 1958; their total operating revenues were $29.5 billion. *Op.cit.*, 1958, pp. 19, 36.

[37] This is the view of Whitney, *op.cit.*, pp. 236–7.

Powder and ICI (Hawthorne) in methyl methacrylate plastics. The list could be extended almost indefinitely.

(2) They market products through established firms in the field. U.S. Industrial Chemicals contracted to market the solvents and other by-product petrochemicals produced by Standard Oil of Indiana and Texaco, and—years ago—the same company undertook to market any surplus alcohol produced by the joint du Pont-National Distillers company, mentioned above. U.S. Steel, which accounts for about 30 per cent of total American production of sulfate of ammonia (a by-product of its coke ovens, used mainly in fertilizers), has apparently marketed some or all of this through the Barrett Company, Allied's subsidiary.[38] Pure Carbonic, a subsidiary of Air Reduction, and Liquid Carbonic acted as exclusive marketing agents for some thirty other companies, giving them control over about two-thirds of national sales of dry ice in 1940.[39] Arrangements like these have probably become relatively rare since the successful antitrust suits against Barrett, the Carbonic companies, and the William S. Gray Co.[40]

(3) They engage or have engaged extensively in patent pooling, with implicit or explicit understandings to respect each other's recognized market or product areas. Such arrangements have the virtue of protecting major companies against sudden displacement as a result of the innovations of others; they give the participants preferential access in their recognized fields to any such new developments, and hence strengthen their entrenched positions (through the combined patents of all) against outsiders. Patent pooling also makes for efficiency by avoiding patent litigation—which is uneconomic for everyone but lawyers—and by making the best processes more widely available to all.

Particularly in the international field, the chemical industry came before

---

[38] Before World War II, and until restrained by an antitrust decree, Barrett marketed over 80 per cent of the total national output, as well as Allied's synthetic nitrate of soda, by far the largest synthetic nitrogenous fertilizer ingredient. *Cartels in Action*, pp. 149–50; *U.S. versus Allied Chemical & Dye Corp.*, Civil 14–320 (Southern Dist., N.Y.), filed May 29, 1941. See also FTC, *Report on the Fertilizer Industry*, Washington, 1950. Allied's ownership of a substantial bloc of U.S. Steel stock may have had some bearing on this arrangement. Allied disposed of part of these holdings in 1952; and in 1954 it also sold the approximately 10 per cent of the outstanding common stock of Air Reduction that it had held for many years. There have been other instances of intercorporate stockholding that may have contributed to market collaboration—notably du Pont's control over General Motors, already mentioned, and Air Reduction's 24 per cent share in U.S. Industrial Chemicals, later sold to National Distillers.

[39] Whitney, *op.cit.*, p. 198, citing *Pure Carbonic, Inc.*, Docket 5143, 44 FTC 1029 (1948), and *U.S. versus Liquid Carbonic Corp.*, Civil 9179 (E.D. N.Y., 1952).

[40] Gray acted as sales agent for the bulk of the hardwood distillation industry's output of wood alcohol. Civil 25–397 and 27–145 (S.D.N.Y., 1944); see also *Cartels in Action*, p. 393, n. 67.

World War II completely under the coverage of a comprehensive and inter-related network of international cartel agreements, most of them incident to such exchanges of patent rights and technical information; outstanding examples were the comprehensive collaborations between du Pont and I.C.I.; between Standard Oil of N.J. and I. G. Farben; the numerous agreements between I. G. and a great number of American firms; and the competition-eliminating cartel in titanium dioxide all over the world. The pervasiveness of these agreements, and the thorough way in which they suppressed competition cannot be fully appreciated except by an equally thorough tracing of their coverage and interrelationships; the pattern was too intricate to trace here.[41]

(4) They buy and sell chemical raw materials among themselves, frequently at preferential discounts. In this way, again, they avoid trespassing on each other's established fields, and sometimes obtain a competitive advantage in their own. Du Pont buys huge quantities of industrial gases from Air Reduction and Union Carbide, the two dominant suppliers. When Standard of New Jersey approached du Pont as a possible customer for its synthetic toluene, the latter cited its "close working arrangement" with U.S. Steel, at that time the major supplier, and its fear of "jeopardizing the preferred position" it enjoyed with that company.[42] During the late thirties, du Pont supplied Standard with methanol at a substantial discount below market price; the dyestuffs manufacturers regularly supplied each other with particular intermediates, at discounts. The disadvantages and competitive quiescence thus forced on smaller manufacturers, dependent on their larger rivals for this or that essential material, can readily be imagined.[43]

---

[41] See *Cartels in Action*, Chap. 3, 4, 9–11; Bursler, *op.cit., passim;* U.S. versus *National Lead Co. et al.*, 332 U.S. 319 (1947); *U.S. versus Imperial Chemical Industries, Ltd.*, 100 F. Supp. 504 (1951). On the ways in which a series of separate bilateral agreements inevitably interlock to constitute a consistent whole, see Corwin D. Edwards, "Economic and Political Aspects of International Cartels," U.S. Senate, Comm. on Military Affairs, Subcomm. on War Mobilization, *Monograph* No. 1, Seventy-eighth Cong., 2nd Sess., pp. 3–7.

[42] *Cartels in Action*, pp. 390–1.

[43] On the position of small explosives manufacturers, dependent on the large for blasting caps, see Mueller, *Du Pont*, p. 168; on the smaller manufacturers of dyestuffs, see *Cartels in Action*, pp. 405–6. An analogous practice with similar effect is the insistence by some large companies on reciprocal buying on the part of would-be suppliers of raw materials. See Stocking and Mueller, "Business Reciprocity and the Size of Firms," *Journal of Business of the University of Chicago*, Vol. 30, pp. 80–85 (1957). The president of a new chemical company says he encountered this obstacle in trying to market sulphuric acid: "several competitors let it be known that any customer who stopped buying their sulphuric acid could not expect them to continue purchasing the customer's end products. 'This sort of retaliation cost us plenty,' Mr. Dixon reported." *The New York Times*, December 27, 1959, p. F8.

Probably no other industry has come into conflict with the antitrust laws as frequently as this one. Since 1938 the Department of Justice alone has instituted on the order of fifty cases or groups of cases—the great majority successfully—charging conspiracies in restraint of trade and illegal monopolization of individual products. Even in the two major government defeats, in the case against du Pont charging monopolization of cellophane and a criminal suit against du Pont and Rohm & Haas in acrylics, the defendants had in fact enjoyed virtual monopolies in their respective fields, buttressed by patents and by agreements regulating both entry and output.[44] Antitrust activity directed against chemical companies has diminished since the forties. It is difficult to say to what extent this reflects a corresponding diminution in the industry's recourse to collaborative suppression of competition. The overt cartels have been dissolved, so far as the record shows. What is impossible to state with assurance is to what extent the earlier patterns of collaboration have persisted in altered guise. The writer can offer only his impression that thorough and comprehensive cartelization has diminished, but that the habit of market collaboration within the limits of the law as somewhat uncertainly drawn between the arrangements in titanium on the one hand and cellophane on the other [45] remains unimpaired.

Price Policy

Certain characteristics of the supply and demand for chemicals, in addition to fewness of sellers, engender a disinclination to engage in price competition. (1) Costs provide no clear-cut basis for pricing. The high degree of mechanization of chemical operations, the heavy expenditures on research and development, the high rate of physical deterioration and technological obsolescence of equipment all make for heavy overhead costs.[46]

---

[44] See *U.S. versus E. I. Du Pont de Nemours & Co.*, 351 U.S. 377 (1956), and *U.S. versus Rohm & Haas Co.*, Cr. 877–C and 878–C (D. N.J. 1942). A later civil suit against Rohm & Haas and du Pont was terminated by a consent judgment. Civil 9068 (E.D. Pa. 1948). See also Stocking and Mueller, "The Cellophane Case and the New Competition," *American Economic Review*, Vol. 45, pp. 29–63 (1955). In cellophane, du Pont was exonerated on the ground, essentially, that its market position was a consequence of its own progressiveness and a legitimate use of patents, and in any event conferred no monopoly power because cellophane was merely part of the broader flexible packaging materials market. On the nature of the patent interchange in acrylics, see Whitney, *op.cit.*, pp. 207–8.

[45] See the citations to the National Lead and du Pont cellophane cases in notes 41 and 44 above.

[46] In 1956, according to the Census of Manufactures, chemicals and allied products were surpassed only by petroleum and coal products, among all manufacturing industry groups, in their value added per production worker. See also the ratios of net fixed capital to output in Daniel Creamer, "Postwar Trends in the Relation of Capital to

The numerous joint products that issue from a single process, piece of equipment, or research laboratory make allocation of the fixed costs among individual products often highly arbitrary. The large spread between average variable costs of an individual product and total unit cost, considering all operations of a going concern, creates an irresistible temptation to price at full allocated cost, with an allowance for overheads permitting a quick recoupment of research and developmental expenses and making generous allowance for possible obsolescence.[47]

(2) A second factor is the belief, common in the industry, that total demand for most of its products is inelastic. Unless there are close substitutes available, the demand for individual materials or semifinished articles is usually less elastic than the demand for the finished products which embody them. A hundred per cent rise in the price of rubber has only a negligible effect on the price of rubber tires, and even less on the demand for tires, which are an essential but small part of the cost of automotive transport. Similarly, the demand for nylon or rayon tire cord, taken together, depends on the demand for tires, for caustic soda on the public's consumption of soap, textiles, paper, and gasoline—not, within very wide limits, on their price. Of course, demand for the products of any one alkali manufacturer would prove extremely elastic, if he alone were to alter his prices. But where there are few sellers of an essentially homogeneous product, price cuts by any one would certainly be met by his competitors; in these circumstances it is the elasticity of total market demand which is determining.[48]

Sales of chemicals are often on long-term contract to other manufacturers, who may value continuity of supply and precision of quality far more than price. This fact, like the fact that much production is for internal use, tends to constrict the open market at any given time and the number of sellers looking for business in that market, and to diminish both the incentive and the likelihood of their cutting prices to steal customers from rivals.

For these various reasons chemical pricing is typically "orderly." Wherever possible chemical companies try to sell new products on the basis of special properties, cutting prices sharply to take advantage of new processes

Output in Manufactures," *American Economic Review, Papers and Proceedings,* Vol. 48, May 1958, p. 253.

[47] For illustrations of costing and pricing formulas see the discussion of Union Carbide in A. D. H. Kaplan, Joel B. Dirlam, and Robert F. Lanzillotti, *Pricing in Big Business,* Washington: Brookings Institution, 1958, pp. 108–26.

[48] It may occur to the reader to wonder why, if sellers think demand is inelastic at the market price, they do not set their prices higher, where both total and net revenue as well would surely be higher. One possible explanation is that sellers do not individually maximize their profits. But it would seem a sufficient explanation that oligopolists may be unable to price at the level that would fully exploit the inelasticity of industry demand. See pp. 255–58, below.

or the economies of large scale production only when the possibility of a
mass market is established. In all other cases they price conservatively, with
as little regard as possible to short-run fluctuations in demand; and they
frown on price-cutting in quest of market advantage.[49] The leading "dis-
orderly" markets have been those in which supplies got out of control, because of excess capacity, or an uncontrollable flood of by-product supplies,
or the much lower costs of new, synthetic processes, or periodic break-
downs of cartel agreements. Notable examples have been caustic soda, ethyl
alcohol, nitrate of soda, and synthetic ammonia. But these are the exceptions,
precisely because with fewness of sellers and restricted entry overbuilding
is less likely to occur. Even the widely bemoaned excess capacity in synthetic ammonia that emerged after 1955 and, in a greatly deconcentrated
industry, led to price reductions, left prices still at remunerative levels.[50]
And the "serious overcapacity" of 1957–59 in synthetic rubber produced no
visible ripple whatever in domestic prices.[51]

The relative infrequency with which chemical price quotations are altered
is indicated by a Bureau of Labor Statistics study of the behavior of 1,789
wholesale prices during 1954–56. Of the 119 chemicals and allied products
included, the prices of 50.4 per cent changed zero to two times during the
three years; for all 1,789 commodities only 20.7 per cent changed so infrequently.[52] Their relative insensitivity to changes in demand is suggested by
the fact that the wholesale price index for chemicals declined only 13.2 per
cent between 1926 and 1933, compared with 29.5 per cent for all manufactures and 34.1 per cent for all commodities.[53] During the 1957–58 recession,

[49] For a typical illustration, see the admonition in a letter from a du Pont executive to
one of the company's Brazilian representatives, in Edwards, *op.cit.*, pp. 14–15.

[50] On the price-cutting in anhydrous ammonia from $85 to $72 a ton, in 1956–57, and
the observation that "even at the depressed price of $75 a ton this leaves a fairly wide
margin for distributing costs and profit," see *Wall Street Journal*, February 14, 1957,
p. 24. The price was back up to $88 a ton in 1957–58. See William H. Martin, "Public
Policy and Increased Competition in the Synthetic Ammonia Industry," *Quarterly
Journal of Economics*, Vol. 73, p. 388 (1959).

[51] See the Third and Fourth Reports of the Attorney General on *Competition in the
Synthetic Rubber Industry*. Open-market prices of butadiene and styrene did, however,
reflect this excess capacity.

[52] Joint Economic Committee, "Frequency of Change in Wholesale Prices, A Study of
Price Flexibility," Eighty-fifth Congress, 2d Sess., Joint Committee Print, 1959. Frequency distribution for chemicals supplied by the Bureau, by letter.

[53] See also Richard Ruggles, "The Nature of Price Flexibility and the Determinants of
Relative Price Changes in the Economy," in *Business Concentration and Price Policy*,
Universities-National Bureau Committee for Economic Research, Princeton: Princeton
University Press, 1955, p. 483. A better maintained demand for chemicals than for manufactures in general between 1926 and 1933 likewise contributed to the greater price
stability of the former. However, the greater importance of market control is indicated
by the fact that the chemicals whose prices showed the greatest cyclical flexibility—
packers' tallow, glycerin, tankage, oleic acid, copper sulphate, quebracho extract, palm

when the basic chemical industry's production dropped from an estimated annual rate of 82 to 72 per cent of capacity,[54] prices showed no cyclical trend whatever.

The relative insensitivity of chemicals prices to changes in demand operates on the up as well as the downside. So after the general recovery of the thirties, the 1937 and 1941 indexes, on a 1926 base, were once more virtually the same as those for all manufactures and all commodities. The industry shows marked restraint in refraining from charging all the traffic will bear in time of shortage: there were instances in the 1945–48 and 1950–51 inflations when "gray-market" prices and those charged by importers were several times the prices domestic producers quoted to their regular customers.

Such instances of forbearance in the short run are a reflection of long-run company policy. The unusually rapid increase of chemical sales in the last eighty years must be attributed in large measure to the ability of the industry to satisfy wants in new and more efficient ways, considering both unit price and performance. This fact clearly reflects a demand with a potential of rapid expansion, and also a demand for new products which is highly responsive to price, at least in the long run. The huge profits in rayon, cellophane, permanent antifreeze, synthetic alcohol, synthetic dyestuffs, penicillin, and plastics have come from the development of mass markets, and this has required secularly declining prices. Thus there have been numerous examples of new chemical products, or familiar products synthesized by new processes, having their prices drastically reduced, making possible the discovery of whole new areas of demand and large-scale production at low unit costs.[55] In consequence, chemical prices show a secular tendency to decline compared with industrial prices in general.

The tendency of oligopolists to price at cost plus some conventional mark-up in the short run, and to charge less than the traffic will bear in periods of shortage, has inspired the suggestion that big businesses today do not maximize their profits in any meaningful sense. These phenomena, plus the numerous instances of sharp price cuts on new products, have led some

---

niger oil, grain alcohol, ammonium sulphate—were ones whose supply was weakly controlled, either because they were by-products of other operations like meatpacking, copper smelting or coke manufacture, or because their production was in numerous, dispersed, and weak hands. Price flexibility ratings from National Resources Committee, *The Structure of the American Economy*, Washington, Government Printing Office, 1939, I, pp. 197–8, columns 19 and 20. See also Wilcox, *op.cit.*, p. 202.

[54] "Chemicals' New Era, Industry Overcapacity Slows Furious Growth, Heightens Competition," *Wall Street Journal*, May 1, 1959, pp. 1 f.

[55] For striking examples, see *The Chemical Industry Facts Book*, 4th ed., Washington: Manufacturing Chemists' Association, 1959, p. 21; also Kaplan, Dirlam and Lanzillotti, *op.cit.*, pp. 97–108, 114–17, 152.

observers to conclude further that there is no reason for concern about the oligopolistic organization of markets such as these. In my opinion, it would be an error so to interpret the record in the chemical industry, for the following reasons: [56]

(1) A policy of not raising prices rapidly with recovering demand is a necessary corollary of avoiding price cuts on the downside; stability of customer relationships would obviously be jeopardized if the two did not go together. One cannot emphasize the possible benefits of the former without giving equal consideration to the possible undesirability of the latter.

(2) Extortionate pricing in the short run has the further disadvantage, from the standpoint of the firm, of encouraging competitive entry. The necessity for considering this possibility (or of competitive circumvention by other products and other processes) demonstrates that monopoly power is not unlimited; it does not in itself prove that it is unimportant.

(3) The diverse and intense efforts by chemical companies to protect their market positions against competitive entry, by aggressive patent policies, by the various forms of market collaboration already described, in itself reflects the likelihood that entry would otherwise be greater, and prices and profits lower. Du Pont's resort to such policies to protect its high profits on cellophane provides the short and adequate answer to the conclusion of the U.S. Supreme Court majority that that product was not susceptible of monopolization, because of the high cross-elasticity of demand between it and other flexible wrapping materials.[57]

(4) Pricing on the basis of standard cost plus some target rate of return does not preclude wide variations in that mark-up depending on what the company conceives to be the elasticity of demand for its various products. One of the determinants of that elasticity is of course the availability of competitive sources of supply. Wide divergences in the rates of return individual companies earn on different products or in different markets are therefore the best possible evidence of a policy of charging what the respective traffics will bear.[58] Thus instances have come to light of extraordinarily high prices charged for particular products where tight monopoly control faced a highly inelastic demand.[59]

[56] See my "Pricing Objectives in Large Companies: Comment," *American Economic Review,* Vol. 49, pp. 670–78 (1959); also the article by Lanzillotti that inspired the comment, Vol. 48, pp. 921–40 (1958) and his response, Vol. 49, pp. 679–86 (1959).
[57] This point is developed at length by Stocking and Mueller, *op.cit.,* note 44, above.
[58] For examples in chemicals, see Kaplan, Dirlam and Lanzillotti, *op.cit.,* pp. 112, 113, 122, 150–55.
[59] See the striking examples of methyl methacrylate plastics, Monastral blue dyes, and the antibiotic chlortetracycline (Aureomycin)—all instances of patent-based monopoly and extreme price discrimination between high- and low-elasticity demands for the same

(5) Neither monopoly nor profit maximization are inconsistent with deep price cuts such as have occurred so frequently in chemicals, if demand and cost functions seem to be sufficiently elastic. The general distaste for price cutting has naturally been less intense when it appeared such reductions would enable a new product or process to supplant an old *produced by outsiders* who were in no position to retaliate—hardwood distillers, the indigo and rubber planters and silk growers of the Far East, the soap companies who supply glycerin, the cotton farmers in the South. Once the outside competitors were supplanted, the price cutting was typically arrested by oligopolistic self interest at levels that continued to provide ample margin above cost.

Still, the pricing record of this industry amply demonstrates, oligopoly is not the same as single firm monopoly, and noncollusive oligopoly with the possibility of competitive entry not the same as collusive oligopoly with entry effectively blocked. Oligopolists may be simply incapable of sustaining prices at the level that would maximize their combined profits, because some one might not follow,[60] or might at that price be tempted to cut,[61] or to enter the market. Entrants attracted by expanding market prospects and high profits in fact left this or that chemical industry in the late fifties with greater capacity than the market could absorb at preexisting prices. In certain instances, notably ammonia, competitive price cuts occurred. In others, where collective self-discipline was stronger, the idle capacity hanging over the market held prices in check in the face of rising input costs and recovering demand.

In sum, the pricing policies of chemical companies reflect such market power as they possess. When they enjoy monopoly power they exploit it, not to extract every possible cent of profit in any given month or year, but to get all the market will permit stably over time. The fewer the sellers, the closer their collaboration, and the higher the barriers to entry, the greater

---

products. See *Cartels in Action*, pp. 402–4 and Federal Trade Commission, *Economic Report on Antibiotics Manufacture*, 1958, p. 8.

[60] Goodrich-Gulf made the one attempt in the 1955–57 period to raise the price of GR-S synthetic rubber; no one followed, and after a month the company came back down. *Business Week*, September 7, 1957, p. 128.

[61] A price war broke out in 1959 between nylon and rayon tire cord, even though a relatively small number of companies produce each and the demand for the two combined is probably relatively inelastic, now that they have replaced cotton. Interestingly, du Pont, which started the 1959 cuts, had pioneered in, and was still a leading producer of rayon cord. The nylon producers clearly expect to take over a larger share of the market, as they already had been doing, even with rayon producers matching their reductions; du Pont converted at least one of its rayon plants to nylon cord. Significantly, these price reductions were not matched in textile rayon and nylon yarns. Obviously du Pont regarded their demand as less elastic.

is the probable degree of monopolistic exploitation.[62] But even a monopolist may find it profitable to reduce prices in the face of long-run decreasing costs and elastic demand, conditions often encountered in this industry, where new products and processes are usually substitutes for old. And in most chemical markets, the typical organization is not single-firm monopoly but oligopoly.

Price competition in chemicals is obviously not pure. How does one decide whether it is "workable"? Profits have been consistently above the average for all manufacturing in the last four decades. Earnings after taxes of 54 chemical companies reporting to the National City Bank averaged 4.9, 8.0, 11.8, and 12.9 per cent on net worth in 1932, 1933, 1935 and 1939, respectively, compared with −0.5, 2.5, 6.7, and 8.5 for all reporting manufacturing companies. During the period 1946–52 the chemical company average was 16.9, the all-manufacturing average 15.1 per cent; for 1953–58 they were 14.3 and 12.7, respectively.[63]

Continuously supernormal profits like these cannot be explained by inevitable lags in the flow of capital into a rapidly growing industry. Had entry been truly free, capital would long since have fully reacted to the unusual and well-advertised growth prospects in chemicals. Rather they reflect the ubiquitous presence of monopoly elements—fewness of sellers, collaboration, and barriers to entry, particularly into the most profitable lines. But high profits, reflective of highly impure competition, are not necessarily an index of unworkable competition. They may be a socially necessary reward for persistently successful innovation. One cannot thus evaluate the effectiveness of price competition in isolation.

[62] A striking illustration of these propositions is to be found in the divergent pricing histories and profit records of the various antibiotics—of penicillin, streptomycin, and dihydrostreptomycin, on the one hand, which were either unpatented or licensed to all applicants at a stipulated royalty, and of the broad spectrum antibiotics, on the other, whose patents have been tightly held and production highly concentrated. FTC, *Economic Report on Antibiotics Manufacture,* pp. 15–27 and Chaps. 6–8, *passim.*

[63] National City Bank, *Monthly Letters on Economic Conditions and Government Finance.* In 1956 and 1957, according to the latest FTC study, rates of return on stockholders' investment were highest in industrial chemicals (at 17.7 and 16.2 per cent respectively, after tax) of all the industries surveyed. *Report on Rates of Return for Identical Companies in Selected Manufacturing Industries, 1940, 1947–57.* On comparative profits in the twenties, see Stocking and Watkins, *Cartels or Competition?* New York: Twentieth Century Fund, 1948, p. 123. These profits, moreover, are after unusually generous allowances for obsolescence. According to Alderfer and Michl (*Economics of American Industry,* 3rd ed., New York: McGraw-Hill, 1957, pp. 251–3) it is customary in some branches of chemicals to write off equipment in two to three years. In a growing industry this practice will produce a consistent understatement of profits.

Innovation and the Possible Workability of Impure Competition

The fact scarcely requires elaboration that this is an extremely progressive industry. The efforts which under other circumstances might be devoted to high pressure selling, to frequent style changes, or to vigorous price competition are here devoted in large measure to the research laboratory. Chemical companies on the average spend an estimated 4 per cent of sales on research—a ratio three times that in manufacturing generally, and almost none of it is paid for by the government.[64]

Moreover these efforts are unquestionably competitive in both motivation and consequences. Continuous technological change makes the position of every chemical company in some measure precarious. One consequence is a code of business ethics among the giants which dictates an avoidance of the destruction of equities that a ruthlessly individualistic exploitation of new developments might involve. Another result, however, is to force all chemical companies—if they are to profit—into a test-tube rivalry. No firm may count on the generosity of others to guarantee it profits if it fails in this race. The result is a continuously renewed competition, in ever-changing combinations, between emerging and already emerged processes, products and industries—a competition in which comparative costs and prices as well as qualities are active determinants of success or failure.

This competition limits the significance of individual product and industry concentration ratios, more severely in chemicals than most other industries. The domination of acrylic resins by a few producers is rendered less significant by the competition of polystyrenes, polyethylenes, cellulose acetates, and so on; concentration in polyvinyls by-products as far removed as linoleum; in styrene and acrylonitrile by the fact that synthetic rubbers compounded from one or the other of these with butadiene competes with natural rubber, du Pont's Neoprene, Standard's Butyl, Dow's Thiokol, Phillips' and Montecatini's polybutadiene (dispensing with styrene), and most recently, completing the circle, Shell's synthetic polyisoprene, which virtually duplicates natural rubber itself.[65]

This does not mean that the concentration ratios have no economic significance. First, in many cases—in synthetic fibers, for example—concentration

[64] Standard & Poor's, *op.cit.*, *Chemicals*, p. C23; Alderfer and Michl, *op.cit.*, p. 251; "Chemical Makers Raising Research," *The New York Times*, January 4, 1959, p. F9. In contrast, of the estimated 6.5 billion dollars spent for research in American industry generally in 1956, the Federal Government paid 3.1 billion. National Science Foundation, *Reviews of Data on Research and Development*, May 1958.
[65] "More Rivals for the Rubber Tree," *Business Week*, March 28, 1959, pp. 85–6.

260 *The Structure of American Industry*

remains high even when the concept of the market is broadened to embrace the various substitutes. Second, the substitutes are in varying degree incomplete and ineffective. Cellophane, for example, could sell for seven times the price of the other leading flexible wrappings with which the District Court found it in active competition; its price could decline to two times their level without driving them from the market; and it could, at that doubly high price, which still yielded monopoly profits, still account for 17.9 per cent of their combined sales.[66]

The point, however, is this: that very often the high degree of market concentration and the high profits that it makes possible are themselves the product of innovation. Every true innovator is for a time a monopolist. His profits come, however, not from limiting the alternatives presented to buyers but from expanding them, not from weakening competition but intensifying it. In the process, therefore, high profits on older lines, themselves the product of earlier innovations, are eroded away, while the successes of the new line in turn stimulate competitive emulation. Rayon presents an excellent illustration of this kind of life cycle. American Viscose earned an average return on investment of 77 per cent annually in the last six years of its patent-protected monopoly. Expiration of the patent brought a number of entrants in the twenties and profits declined steadily, from 40–50 per cent in 1921–23 to 18–30 per cent in 1924–29, and 3–12 per cent in the thirties. By 1957, under the pressure of new fibers, the average return on stockholders' equity had dropped to 3.4 per cent.[67] The significance for the workability of competition of the fact that du Pont averaged no less than 25.9 per cent return on investment after taxes in the period 1947–55 cannot be appraised, therefore, without taking into account the company's boast that about one-half of its sales in recent years have consisted of products issuing from its own research, that it first introduced commercially in the last twenty five years.

The high profits *consequent* on innovation are particularly difficult to evaluate in view of the strong possibility that the prospect of earning them is an essential *stimulus* to innovation as well. To the extent that research and development require the commitment of large funds with an uncertain return from each individual venture, it is clearly necessary that the successful ones earn abnormally high returns if the expenditures are to be made in the first place. But does innovation require continuously supernormal returns on the totality of a chemical company's operations? The defenders of

[66] See the references in note 44, above. See also John M. Lishan, "The Cellophane Case and the Cross-Elasticity of Demand," *The Antitrust Bulletin*, July–August 1959, pp. 593–8.
[67] Markham, *op.cit.*, p. 227; FTC, *Report on Rates of Return*, *op.cit.*, note 63, above.

oligopoly would say that it does, because only stable and comfortable profit margins can provide the wherewithal to engage in continuous and costly research.

It has undoubtedly been the promise of high profits in chemicals that has spurred the widespread and impetuous entry into the industry in recent years—by the shipping, whiskey, farm machinery, and rayon companies in Table 2, by droves of oil and natural gas transmission companies, by food processors like Swift, Armour, and General Mills, paint manufacturers like Sherwin-Williams and Glidden, producers of rubber tires, and, as *Fortune* put it, "such wildly unclassifiable companies" [68] as General Electric, Minnesota Mining and Manufacturing, Borden, and the Philadelphia and Reading coal company. It was the same promise that attracted Eastman Kodak into cellulose acetate rayon and plastics, du Pont into film, Allied Chemical into nylon, Olin-Mathieson into cellophane, Koppers into styrene, Commercial Solvents into synthetic ammonia. And in this industry to enter is to innovate.

Ventures such as these have produced striking deconcentrations in synthetic ammonia,[69] synthetic rubber and its raw materials,[70] and in the enormously expanding plastics and fibers, polyethylene and polypropylene.[71] The effect of these developments on the relation of capacity to de-

[68] "The Chemical Century," Vol. 41, March 1950, pp. 70–71.

[69] Allied Chemical and du Pont accounted for 88.4 per cent of domestic capacity in 1939, and the industry had six members; as of the close of 1957 the top four companies accounted for but 39.1 per cent of a capacity eleven times as large, and controlled by 38 companies. Because of the importance of transport costs, regional oligopoly still remains the rule, but by any measure deconcentration has been spectacular. See Martin, *op.cit.*, note 50, above.

[70] The government disposed of its synthetic rubber plants for $285 millions. Within two years, the private owners had invested an additional $200 million, and newcomers another $100 million, doubling national capacity. "Government-Spawned War Baby Weighs in as a Healthy Industry," *Business Week*, September 7, 1957, p. 121.

[71] As early as 1954, about two years after the I.C.I. patents had become available, "at least eight companies . . . [had] placed their bets (amounting to a quarter billion dollars) on a single spin of the polyethylene wheel. Another half-dozen companies are standing by, waiting for an entry. . . ." "The Polyethylene Gamble," *Fortune*, Vol. 49, February 1954, p. 134. The later-developed, linear polyethylene, on which pioneer work had been done by du Pont, Phillips, Standard of Indiana, and Dr. Karl Ziegler, in Germany, had by 1958 the following companies licensed and/or in production: Phillips, Union Carbide, Grace, Celanese, Hercules Powder, Koppers, Allied Chemical, Dow, du Pont, Goodrich-Gulf, Monsanto, Esso, Spencer Chemicals, and Eastman Kodak. Several of the same companies then became actively involved in the even more recent linear polypropylene; other companies would have to be added to make up the latter list, notable among them the Italian Montecatini, which played a major role in developing the process. See "The New Breed of Plastics," *Fortune*, Vol. 55, February 1957, pp. 173–74 ff.; Standard & Poor's, *op.cit.*, *Chemicals, Basic Analysis*, October 23, 1958, pp. C37–38; "Tomorrow's Hot New Plastic?" *Business Week*, July 1, 1959, pp. 34–36.

mand and on price at least in the long run has already been suggested.[72] The process was assisted in ammonia and rubber by the Government's construction and then disposal of plants and its certificates of accelerated amortization; in polyethylene by an important antitrust decree; but this part of the story had best be reserved for Section III.

The various forms of market collaboration practiced in chemicals likewise make a positive contribution to risk-taking entry and innovation. Companies often move into new fields, we have noted, by acquiring firms already there, thus picking up technicians, experience, patents, and market connections ready-made. What if they would not otherwise move at all? And what if the new, combined ventures typically command greater financial, technical, and commercial resources than the acquired firms could possibly have mustered alone? An even stronger defense can probably be made of the joint ventures that have become so commonplace. They are almost invariably a method of pooling talents and interests for innovation and entry into some field adjacent to those in which the partners have been specializing. As for restrictive, anticompetitive covenants that have typically accompanied patents and processes agreements, would companies collaborate so wholeheartedly in innovation and in sharing its fruits if either were then free to use the knowledge thus obtained to the other's injury? [73] Finally, what *Fortune* calls the "tendency for chemical companies to huddle," synchronizing investments and product and material flows in integrated programs, is often by far the most efficient way of planning, achieving the advantages both of specialization and coordination.[74]

The fact that, even as they specialize, the major chemical companies can produce many of their own raw materials limits the monopoly power of their suppliers. Standard of New Jersey used the threat of manufacturing its own methanol to exact a large discount from du Pont for several years; [75] Dow had to offer Alcoa's American Magnesium a similar concession for a similar purpose.[76] Sharp reductions were posted during 1957–58 in the price of

[72] The price of polypropylene was 65 cents a pound at the end of 1957, and 42 cents in mid-1959. "Tomorrow's Hot New Plastic?" note 71, above. Also "Hot Competition in the Making," *ibid.*, November 1, 1958, p. 101.

[73] See the persuasive du Pont memorandum on the advantages of the I.C.I. relationship, reproduced in Bursler, *op.cit.*, pp. 89–93.

[74] See the striking description of "The Houston Complex," a chemical empire based on salt, sulphur, oil, gas, lime, and water, involving a "spaghetti bowl" of raw material and product interchanges among 25 to 30 companies. It is inconceivable that any of the companies involved could have undertaken the whole operation on its own, refusing to collaborate with the others, or that it would have been desirable to have it try. *Fortune*, Vol. 57, February 1957, p. 127.

[75] *Cartels or Competition?*, pp. 139–40.

[76] *Cartels in Action*, pp. 282–83.

rubber-grade styrene monomer, even though production was highly concentrated, "apparently to discourage the entry of rubber companies." [77] Linde Air Products (of Union Carbide) and Air Reduction have in recent years encountered strong competition from manufacturers of machinery that enables large users to make their own industrial oxygen.[78] Before the passage of the Robinson-Patman Act, it was possible for entrenched sellers to buy off the potential competition of large buyers by offering them special discounts the benefits of which were not passed on to smaller buyers or to the final customer. To the (probably limited) extent it has been effective, Robinson-Patman has denied sellers this relatively easy way out, and forced them instead to choose between the less palatable—and more competitive— alternatives of reducing their prices to all buyers or seeing the large customers turn into competitors.

So it is possible to make a formidable defense of the manifest impurities of competition in the chemical industry. Its interrelated elements may be summarized as follows: that business size and integration are necessary instruments for the perception, development, and exploitation of new ideas; that high profits provide both the incentive and the wherewithal for innovation, and are also its consequence; that collaboration between firms is the most effective means for achieving entry, innovation and growth; and that the process is highly competitive in the most creative way possible.

An Appraisal

Mere identification of the monopoly elements that pervade this industry clearly does not constitute a sufficient appraisal of its structure and performance. For example, Stocking and Mueller's convincing demonstration that du Pont enjoyed substantial monopoly power by virtue of its control over cellophane does not in itself justify their conclusion that the company was not selling that product "in an effectively competitive market." [79] That depends on whether this innovation, which made competition in flexible wrappings *more* effective, would still have been forthcoming in the absence

[77] Standard & Poor's, *op.cit.*, *Chemicals, Basic Analysis.* Dow and Monsanto had an estimated 61 per cent of national capacity in 1958, Koppers and Shell an additional 24 per cent. *Ibid.*
[78] "Battle is on for Oxygen's Future," *Business Week*, April 21, 1956, pp. 149–54. "Its machinery-building competitors . . . argue that for years, Linde's prices were too high —that it was the perfection of thoroughly reliable on-site generating machinery, available for sale or lease, that brought the price of oxygen down—to about 20 per cent of its level 30 years ago." *Ibid.* Reprinted by courtesy of the publisher.
[79] *Op.cit.*, note 44, above, p. 56; cf. Joel B. Dirlam and Irwin M. Stelzer, "The Cellophane Labyrinth," *The Antitrust Bulletin*, Vol. 1, pp. 643–47 (1956).

of the kind of patent system that gave rise to the monopoly in cellophane. Such a judgment would not be preposterous; but it is not self-evidently true either.

On the other hand, it is equally clear that the case for market impurities cannot by its own weight justify business size no matter how great, monopoly profits no matter how high or how achieved, and market collaboration no matter how pervasive and thorough.

The significant question, both for analysis and for policy prescription, is whether it is possible to separate the beneficial from the harmful market impurities or their manifestations. Can one decide, for example, *how much* and what kind of monopoly power, or how much monopoly profit is just enough and not too much? Or is it possible instead to conclude *what kinds* of impurities, what sources, manifestations, or exercises of market power are on balance desirable, which undesirable? It should be obvious that there are no simple, objective answers to these questions. But our study of the chemical industry supports the judgment that there is a point beyond which the positive contributions of monopoly are probably outweighed by its harmful effects, and that certain kinds or manifestations of monoply are inherently more objectionable than others.

This industry has in some ways passed the point of optimum balance. Its pricing is insufficiently competitive; its profits are too high. Output and investment have frequently been restricted and the introduction of new and better products or processes delayed—sometimes by explicit agreement, sometimes as the consequence of monopoly pricing or cartel agreements.[80] This has occurred in methyl methacrylate plastics (du Pont accepting a quantity limitation of output) and dentures, synthetic rubber, pour-point depressants (Standard Oil buying up and retiring from the market competitive products, including one which was admittedly cheaper and superior), synthetic methanol (du Pont's discount to Standard dissuading the latter from making its own, under I. G. patents), synthetic acetic acid and related chemicals (I. G. Farben closing down and dismantling the Jasco Baton Rouge plant in deference to Union Carbide and other companies), synthetic ammonia (I. G. abandoning plans to manufacture in the U.S. and refusing to license Hercules, both in deference to du Pont), synthetic fuels,[81]

[80] Most of these instances are presented in detail in *Cartels in Action* and *Cartels or Competition?* passim.

[81] Standard of New Jersey acquired broad patent controls in this field to defend its own interests in petroleum, and to "guide or restrict" development of these competitive processes. It pursued an explicit policy of "not stirring up interest" in them. According to its own president, development of these processes would have been more rapid had they not been controlled by oil companies. *Cartels in Action*, pp. 492–93.

magnesium, cellophane, and polyethylene.[82] These are only some of the more striking instances that have come to light—almost all of them as a result of antitrust prosecutions. This industry has been excessively monopolistic, at least in certain ways; and in the absence of the antitrust laws, it would have been far more so.

Were such instances of unmistakable retardation and monopolistic exploitation a necessary price of chemical progress? It is impossible to be certain; but they would seem to support the very opposite proposition: that it is not monopoly but competition that stimulates technological advance. If this industry is workably competitive, it is precisely because of its keen technological *rivalry*, which compels chemical companies to seek profits in the research laboratory. Competition is an organic process; an industry cannot go far in the direction of limiting its downward thrust on prices and profits without weakening the pressures it exerts in the direction of innovation as well.

"Countervailing power" is not an adequate substitute for competition in performing these functions. This power of the big buyer stems either from the existence of *competing* sellers to whom he can threaten to turn, or from the possibility of manufacturing for his own needs—again, a *competitive* step—or from the power to grant or withhold corresponding benefits in other transactions. In the absence of the competitive alternatives, there remains only the third; price concessions granted on such grounds as these far more often cement a noncompetitive alliance or community of interests than they hold down market prices or profits or stimulate innovation. In chemicals, there have been far too many instances of preferential discounts being extended to prevent competition, or as part of a pattern of collusion, and of big buyers actually proceeding to produce for their own account without breaking the rigid, noncompetitive market price, for one to be sanguine about countervailing power.[83]

One source of confusion about the relationship of monopoly to economic progress is the conception that monopoly profits are necessary somehow to "pay for" research. In this industry, competition makes the cost of conducting research an inescapable cost of doing business, if one wants to stay around for any length of time. Successful companies recoup this expense,

---

[82] The best evidence in the latter two cases is the desire of outside companies to enter the field and their inability to do so in the face of strong patent positions. On polyethylene see below, note 91.

[83] For examples in explosives and synthetic ammonia, see Mueller, *Du Pont*, pp. 173–74, 182. We have already mentioned similar instances in toluene, dyestuffs, methanol, and magnesium.

like the costs of rapid obsolescence, out of current revenues, themselves enhanced by the successful exploitation of past innovations. True, if prices on all chemical products were forced down by bitter price rivalry to bare out-of-pocket costs, research laboratories, long-range product development programs—and also institutional advertising and a number of vice-presidents—would have to be scrapped. But this is hardly an argument for monopoly profits, of whatever height, *over and above* those expenses.

There is a difference between the monopoly and profits which result from innovation and the lag of supply behind secularly expanding demand, and contribute to expansion, on the one hand, and those sustained by conscious oligopoly policy and resulting from restriction, on the other. One can hardly justify on the ground of their contribution to technological progress the monopolistic barriers erected to insulate profits against the threat of technological progress; or on the ground of facilitating market entry the agreements specifically proscribing mutual encroachment and the patent roadblocks painstakingly constructed and specifically exercised to prevent it; or, on grounds of enhancing competition, the resort to collaboration motivated largely by the desire to avoid it.

The association of monopoly and technological progress does not prove the one caused the other. Modern chemical science is not the exclusive handmaiden of American free enterprise, competitive or otherwise. In many ways the German industry, under Bismarck's paternalism and Hitler's totalitarianism far outstripped our own. The successes of scientists in harnessing the atom indicate that university research, and concerted, government-directed and -financed development programs are—in individual instances at least—more appropriate instruments of modern technology than private corporate research laboratories. It is not possible to give our present system of organization a clean bill of health simply because it has been progressive; in modern science it is difficult *not* to progress, whatever the system of organization. The only meaningful bench mark against which to test the achievements of the American industry is the potential inherent in chemical technology; but that potential is unknowable. A more limited test would be to compare accomplishments here with those of other countries. Such a comparison has yet to be made; but it is by no means a foregone conclusion that it would award the palm to the American industry, considering the advantages it has enjoyed.

In fact, by the supreme test, the ability to meet rival producers in open competition, the chemical industry is by the admission of its own spokesmen not an outstanding example of the superiority of American enterprise. They are among the leading advocates of high tariffs to protect themselves from the products of "cheap foreign labor." Yet in other American industries, where labor costs are an even higher proportion of total costs than in the chemical, the disadvantage of high wage rates is more than offset by labor's high productivity. It is of course not necessarily the "fault" of an industry's structure or policies if its technology is such that it is incapable of compensating in this fashion. But it is by no means clear that the chemical industry, with its typically high capital-labor ratios and far larger exports than imports, can offer such a defense for most of the high protection it enjoys.[84] As *Fortune* concluded in 1954:

> The once-feeble U.S. chemical industry has long since outgrown its swaddling clothes. . . . Those few strategic chemical lines in which the U.S. is a hopelessly high-cost producer, e.g. certain low-volume dyestuffs and drugs—should continue to receive some tariff protection . . . or direct subsidies. But for the rest, increased imports would serve to shake the industry loose from pricing practices that have no sanction other than tradition, and stimulate further cost reduction and product innovation.[85]

The latter verdict is similar to *Fortune*'s contention twelve years earlier that

> . . . a draught of old-fashioned price competition throughout the industry . . . would be an incalculable tonic for the economy. But a falling back into the soft competition of the last decade or more, with its recognized spheres and slowly graduated price reductions, would invite economic and political maladies. . . .
> A great new era can be built . . . if the industry supplies really free enterprise. Free price competition is the only incisive instrument of such enterprise. And the chemical industry, which has made a habit of earning somewhere around 20 per cent on sales before taxes, year in and year out, has a wide area in which to employ it.[86]

The blemishes on the record of the American chemical industry have not always been the product of domestic monopoly. Foreign ownership of American patents has at times forced American businessmen to come to terms which have had the effect of curtailing our production. Synthetic dyestuffs before 1914 and rubber before 1942 are cases in point. The fault at other times lay in government inaction, resulting in part from a naive faith (long ago abandoned in education, "infant industries," agricultural research, and

---

[84] The duties on numerous organic chemicals range between 20 and 50 per cent; and the effective rate, because the duties must be computed on the basis of domestic valuation, is far higher. See Percy W. Bidwell, *What the Tariff Means to American Industries,* Council on Foreign Relations, New York: Harper, 1956, pp. 189–94.

[85] "Tariff Cuts: Who Gets Hurt?" *Fortune,* Vol. 49, April 1954, pp. 216, 218. Reprinted by courtesy of the publisher. Also Bidwell, *op.cit.,* Chap. 8.

[86] "Dow Goes Down to the Sea." Reprinted from *Fortune,* Vol. 26, p. 194, December 1942, by courtesy of the publisher.

flood control) that every economic need, if it can be satisfied at all, can best be satisfied by competitive private enterprise.

The foregoing "appraisal" of the workability of competition in chemicals has not been a balanced or complete one. The reason is that the main question about workability is not has industry performance been "good," but is it improvable? The first question is almost meaningless, since there do not exist objective, valid bases for comparison. The answer to the second naturally emphasizes defects. It would be misleading, however, to conclude on a negative note. Though the comparison is in large measure meaningless, still one must observe that compared with others the chemical industry is efficient and progressive. And its efficiency and progressiveness are the product not of beneficent monopoly, but of a keen though highly imperfect competition. Is that competition improvable? That is a question of concrete alternative public policies, to the consideration of which we now turn.

SECTION III: PUBLIC POLICY

Social engineering is not an exact science. This fact would seem to dictate a program of reform which attempts to preserve and strengthen the forces that have been demonstrably successful in the past, while remedying their deficiencies. The following suggestions take as given the general American preference to entrust their economic fortunes principally to a system of competitive private enterprise. What follows is a list of possible ways of supplementing, preserving and strengthening competition in chemicals.

Government Research or Subsidy

The benefits to society of scientific research or of certain kinds of investment may not be adequately reflected in prospective profits for private business corporations in a market economy. Research and investment in synthetic dyestuffs (before World War I), synthetic rubber (before World War II), in fertilizer, titanium, atomic energy, medicine, and possibly synthetic fuels all depended heavily on or today require government subsidy or direct action. The case for such intervention is by no means confined to the interest of national defense; it consists in the unpredictably wide-ranging benefits conferred on the entire economy by advances in science and technology.

Government intervention can promote monopoly as well as competition; it is often as important to decide *how* it ought best to intervene as to decide whether it ought to at all. In the case of dyestuffs we chose the easy road of imposing protective tariffs: they were effective in accomplishing their purpose, but they also helped saddle the industry with monopoly. It was the consumer who in the end bore the burden of the heavy private expenditures required to develop the industry. Might it not have been cheaper for the government to have assisted or participated in the research directly, thus ensuring that the industry would remain truly independent (as in fact it did not) and that monopoly power would not result? [87] The successful development and deconcentrations achieved by government research, investment and disposal programs in synthetic ammonia and synthetic rubber in the end invigorated private competitive industry. Government subsidy of independent or cooperative commercial laboratories, offering their services for sale, might do the same, both promoting innovation and improving the competitive opportunities of small business.

Tariff Reduction

The time would certainly appear ripe for sharply reducing most of the tariff duties protecting this no-longer-infant industry. The ironic fact is that, according to a survey made in 1953, over one-half of the American chemical companies feel that their own exports would increase sharply but for foreign duties; and many felt they could cut their own prices but for American duties on some of their chemical raw materials.[88]

[87] Devising appropriate patent policies where the government merely foots the bill for private research is an especially difficult task. Most agencies permit private contractors to take out patents on the inventions issuing from such research, subject only to a nonexclusive grant to the government itself. Some critics have protested against the resultant monopolization of technology developed with public funds. See U.S. Senate, Select Committee on Small Business, *Patent Policies of Departments and Agencies of the Federal Government—1959, Hearings* before a Subcommittee, Eighty-sixth Cong., 1st Sess., 1960. On the other hand, Robert A. Solo concludes that the government-sponsored research program in synthetic rubber after World War II was a failure because the private contractors lacked commercial incentives to develop significant innovations, and the Government provided insufficient direction and leadership. "Research and Development in the Synthetic Rubber Industry," *Quarterly Journal of Economics,* Vol. 68, p. 70 (1954); see also his *Synthetic Rubber: A Case Study in Technological Development under Government Direction,* U.S. Senate Comm. on the Judiciary, Subcommittee on Patents, Trademarks, and Copyrights, Eighty-fifth Cong., 2d Sess., Study No. 18, Washington, 1959, esp. Chap. 9 and 11.
[88] "Tariff Cuts: Who Gets Hurt?" *Fortune,* Vol. 49, April 1954, p. 216. For an analysis of the probable effect on imports of the elimination of duties on a commodity-by-commodity basis, see Howard S. Piquet, *Aid, Trade, and the Tariff,* New York: Crowell, 1953, Chap. 10, pp. 79–346.

Compulsory Licensing in Specific Areas

The relationship between the patent laws and the general policy of preserving competition is inevitably an uneasy one. So long as patents do encourage innovation, it can hardly be concluded that the two policies are inherently in conflict; but it is equally clear that the patent privilege sometimes does give rise to excessive monopoly power, inhibiting not merely competition in general but innovation in particular. One obvious reform would be to require compulsory licensing in those instances where either the stimulus of the exclusive privilege seems less necessary to innovation, or the monopoly power it confers does more harm than good. What specific areas are logical candidates for such treatment?

One possibility is where the government has, by tariff, subsidy, or the financing of research already offered special inducements to investment and innovation. The problem here would be to avoid having the left hand of the government take away what the right hand is trying to confer; if special subvention is called for in the public interest, the purposes of subvention might be thwarted by diminishing the value of the patent inducement to those who respond to it.[89]

A minimum area would be foreign-owned patents that are not worked within the country. There is no reason to permit foreign business firms to tie up our chemical progress by taking out American patents and not exploiting them diligently.[90]

It has been suggested that because fields like medicine or atomic energy have so intimate a bearing on national welfare, all patent rights to these branches of technology ought to be made subject to compulsory licensing. The argument seems economically illogical. If the exclusive patent privilege is conducive to innovation it makes little sense to diminish the incentive it offers in the very fields where progress is most to be desired; if it is not, it ought to be modified in all fields. The particular importance of medicine is therefore a better argument for direct government research than for abolition or substantial modification of the patent system in this area.

Finally, the remedy is of course appropriate where, as in numerous anti-

[89] See note 87, above.
[90] Compulsory working provisions conflict with liberal international economic policies. Compulsory licensing at reasonable royalties seems less objectionable on such grounds: if it is uneconomic to work the patents within the host country, licensees will not appear, or if they do, will not survive. See Raymond Vernon, *The International Patent System and Foreign Policy*, U.S. Senate, Committee on the Judiciary, Subcommittee on Patents, Trademarks, and Copyrights, Eighty-fifth Cong., 1st Sess., Study No. 5, Washington, 1957, pp. 35–36.

trust decisions, it is found that patents have come to buttress an excessive concentration of market power. The major question is whether the antitrust laws are adequate detectors of excessive market power.

Enforcing Competition: Antitrust Policy

The numerous antitrust prosecutions beginning in the middle or late thirties made an important contribution to effective competition in chemicals. As presently formulated and interpreted, the law strikes at market power only when it has been acquired by combination or collusion or exercised to exclude competitors; but the flagrant instances of monopoly pricing and retardation in virtually every instance cited above did in fact require collusion or the illegal use of patents. And the prosecutions have helped pry open many markets to entrants previously excluded by such practices—notably in synthetic rubber, nylon, cellophane, titanium, polyethylene, polyester fiber (Dacron), methyl methacrylate, explosives, and metallic sodium.[91] The only difficult question is whether companies will be unwilling henceforth to collaborate technologically if they may not legally attach restrictive, anticompetitive conditions to their patents and processes agreements. It is difficult to believe that useful exchanges of technology require a market structure so closely approaching pure monopoly as the cartel partners erected, for example, in titanium; or that if it does the benefits are worth the costs. Since these decisions have made quite clear the illegality of such cartels, there seems to have been no diminution in the willingness of patent owners to engage in mutually beneficial technical collaboration, and certainly no diminution in the anxiety of foreign owners of American patents to see their inventions exploited in this market.[92]

Antitrust enforcement alone, without some basic change in the legal definition of monopoly, will never fully dissipate the practice of "live and let

[91] On some of these, see Whitney, *op.cit.*, pp. 195, 206–7, 214–5, 216–8, 225. Polyethylene provides the most dramatic example. Until the antitrust decree in *U.S. versus Imperial Chemical Industries, Ltd.*, 100 F. Supp. 504 (1951), du Pont had licensed only one company under I.C.I.'s American patents, and that was a special case. Polyethylene was "continuously in short supply." ("The Polyethylene Gamble," *Fortune*, Vol. 49, February 1954, pp. 135–36.) With Judge Ryan's decree, calling for compulsory licensing, "the race for polyethylene capacity started the next day" (*ibid.*, p. 166). Despite high license fees ($500,000 down and a royalty of more than 8 per cent of sales) five American licensees had signed up by the Spring of 1953, and there were eight companies in the field a year later (*ibid.*). I.C.I.'s later joint ventures in the U.S. market—with Hercules in methyl methacrylate and with Celanese in polyester fiber—both directly competitive with du Pont, would almost certainly not have occurred had the earlier arrangement between the two companies been permitted to stand.
[92] See Dirlam and Kahn, *Fair Competition, The Law and Economics of Antitrust Policy*, Ithaca, Cornell University Press, 1954, pp. 274–75, and Vernon, *op.cit.*, pp. 17–22.

272   The Structure of American Industry

live" in chemicals. It is incapable of attacking directly the power of the giant firm. And it could probably not be construed to prevent most of the mergers and joint ventures of the last fifteen years: seldom do they suppress pre-existing competition; and the collaboration typically produces stronger and more effective competitors. The case against them is ordinarily indirect and relatively remote: that firms that collaborate in particular joint ventures might otherwise have proceeded independently, or are henceforth unlikely to compete strenuously in other areas; that the large, conglomerate firm may have unfair advantages, unrelated to efficiency, over its nonintegrated competitors in purchasing, in being able to sell at narrow margins in certain fields, in raising capital; that an economy of such firms collaborating in various ways—an economy to which each merger, each joint venture makes its slight contribution—tends to be an economy of live-and-let-live rather than of intense competition.[93]

One might well conclude that satisfactory results can nonetheless be achieved in these circumstances. We have already sufficiently outlined the view that monopoly power in this industry issues primarily from innovation itself; that it is severely confined by technological rivalry, by interproduct, interprocess, and interindustry competition; and that such monopoly power as persists may be a small enough price for the consumer to pay for the industrial progress and efficiency it makes possible.

It is quite possible, however, that the present regime in chemicals falls considerably short of the best attainable result. Price competition is insufficiently pervasive or pressing to eliminate high profits. More important, competition that is feeble with respect to price may likewise be excessively restrained and gentlemanly with respect to innovation as well. The history of this industry discloses numerous individual instances of such retardation; whether the application of antitrust has sufficiently removed that threat is not clear.

Enforcing Competition: Compulsory Patent Licensing

The economic power of great chemical companies might be attacked at its source by removing the gunpowder from their patent arsenal: they might be required to license all applicants at reasonable royalty. Might corporations then cease to support research laboratories, engage in expensive programs of development, or disclose their employees' inventions? It is difficult

---

[93] For a lucid statement of this position, see Corwin D. Edwards, "Conglomerate Bigness as a Source of Power," in *Business Concentration and Price Policy* (note 53, above), pp. 331–52.

to predict. Chemical companies have to support research today for fear of falling behind in the technological race; to the extent that compulsory licensing intensifies competition it might strengthen this stimulus rather than weaken it. They frequently keep their "know-how" to themselves, even under present laws; to fail under a system of compulsory licensing to disclose what they now patent would expose them to the danger that other companies, working in the same areas, might take out patents on inventions previously made by their own technicians, thus obliging them to pay royalties to competitors on inventions originally developed in their own laboratories.

Still, there is a real question whether royalties would as well as monopoly profits repay research and developmental expenses, and whether it might not then pay a company simply to take out licenses under patents developed by others, rather than engage in continuous experimentation itself. In view of this danger, a more modest reform is worth considering: permit firms that have not fallen afoul of the antitrust laws to license out their own patent rights or not as they choose; but require all firms that purchase patents or cross-license with others to offer licenses under those patents to all comers on reasonable terms. Thus companies would be permitted to retain the full benefit, hence incentive, offered by the patents on their own inventions that stand on their own feet; but they would be prevented from resorting to patent diplomacy to forestall or settle possible conflicts with other patent owners in such a manner as to protect both against competition. Such a requirement might discourage wholesome patent cross-licensing; but companies would still have to do so where their patents could not stand alone; and if they chose not to do so, their patent position would have to face both more searching scrutiny by powerful competitors in the courts, and attempted circumvention by competitive research. And above all such a reform would prevent the kind of convenient settlement du Pont and Sylvania reached to their patent conflict that had threatened to expose both companies to unwanted competition in the cellophane field. As du Pont's patent counsel pithily summarized the Sylvania position before the companies settled their differences:

During the conference Mr. Menken stated that in his opinion the case should be settled. He said that they were very fearful of what the result would be to their company in the event they succeeded in having the claims of the patents which are involved in the litigation held invalid. He seemed to realize the old adage that the defendant can never win. . . . If the Du Pont Cellophane Company succeeds and the patents are held to be infringed, Sylvania . . . will be under injunction and will be obliged to stop manufacturing. . . . On the other hand, if they succeed in having the broad claims of the patents held invalid they will throw the art open, as far as the broad claims are concerned, to anyone and therefore will have additional competition.[94]

Enforcing Competition: Dissolution

The final attack on monopoly power would be to break up the chemical giants. This would probably not involve a great loss of efficiency. The operating departments of the major companies are even now largely independent. They could continue to supply each other with materials, by purchase and sale; if technological collaboration were desirable, it too could be continued through the various devices already widely employed.

On the other hand, the technical advantages of size, as we have seen, include the ability to finance large research and development programs, to bring to bear in one operating department, on occasion, the skills and knowledge of others. The president of du Pont has argued persuasively that only with a broad base of diversified skills can a company like his intelligently appraise the possibilities of commercial use of what its scientists discover.[95] It is extremely difficult to appraise an argument like this. Theoretically it is unassailable: technical cooperation between independent companies can seldom be as close as within the firm, in avoiding duplicative research, in profiting from the experience of others, in exchanging and perceiving the significance of seminal ideas well before they reach technical maturation and become appropriate subjects for patent licenses. And as a matter of historical fact it is possible to find in the history of du Pont numerous examples of innovations begun in one department, or springing from fundamental research in the company's Central Research Department, and developed or applied in another. Yet we have also seen that in practice interdepartmental technical collaboration has been sadly deficient in other giant firms, in many cases for decades after their formation. Nor, to return to an earlier theme, is it in fact clear that the giant American firms have been so proficient at self-insemination as they imply. Of du Pont's major new products of the last twenty years, for example, only neoprene synthetic rubber, nylon and orlon synthetic fibers, Duco and Dulux, and now perhaps Delrin were, so far as this writer is aware, the authentic products of original

[94] As quoted by Stocking and Mueller, *op.cit.*, note 44, above, pp. 42–43. It is difficult to escape the feeling that similar considerations motivated the settlements in 1956 of the infringement litigation over the very important antibiotic, tetracycline. See FTC, *Economic Report on Antibiotics Manufacture*, pp. 245–57.

[95] See House Committee on the Judiciary, Subcommittee on Study of Monopoly Power, *Hearings*, Eighty-first Cong., 1st Sess., Washington, 1950, Serial No. 14, Part 2–A, pp. 547–58, 552–3, 585.

du Pont research. This is not a negligible list. But the company got the basic patents and processes for rayon, cellophane, and synthetic ammonia from the French, lead tetraethyl and Freon refrigerant from General Motors, the superior ethyl chloride process for making lead tetraethyl from Standard of New Jersey, Lucite, Dacron, and polyethylene from I.C.I., and titanium oxide by acquisition of the Commercial Pigments Corporation. To the technical and commercial development of these ideas du Pont made contributions of enormous importance, but it is impossible to believe their foreign originators would not have made a major effort to exploit the rich potential American market in some other way, either by themselves or in partnership with other companies, had they been denied the possibility of alliance with du Pont; and it is doubtful that innovation would in that event have been slower.

Nonetheless, the size, integration and technological adventuresomeness of a du Pont, a Dow, or a Monsanto represent a potential for innovation, so often demonstrated in the past, that can not be lightly set aside. Proposals to do so surely must bear a heavy burden of proof—a burden heavier, in my judgment, than they can sustain. It would seem only prudent to try the other planks in the program of public policy outlined above before even considering the last.

SUGGESTED READINGS

Books and Pamphlets

N. Bursler, *The Du Pont Industrial Group,* Industry Studies for Collateral Use in Courses in Antitrust Law, Association of American Law Schools, 1951.

W. Haynes, *Chemical Economics* (New York: Van Nostrand, 1933).

E. H. Hempel, *The Economics of Chemical Industries* (New York: Wiley, 1939).

A. D. H. Kaplan, J. B. Dirlam, and R. F. Lanzillotti, *Pricing in Big Business* (Washington: Brookings Institution, 1958).

T. J. Kreps, *The Economics of the Sulphuric Acid Industry* (Stanford: Stanford University Press, 1938).

Manufacturing Chemists' Association, *The Chemical Industry Facts Book,* 4th ed. (Washington: Manufacturing Chemists' Association, 1959).

J. W. Markham, *Competition in the Rayon Industry* (Cambridge: Harvard University Press, 1952).

———, *The Fertilizer Industry* (Nashville: Vanderbilt University Press, 1958).

W. F. Mueller, *Du Pont: A Study in Firm Growth,* unpublished Ph.D. dissertation, Vanderbilt U. 1955, University Microfilms No. 14,981.

G. W. Stocking and M. W. Watkins, *Cartels in Action* (New York: Twentieth Century Fund, 1946).

———, *Cartels or Competition?* (New York: Twentieth Century Fund, 1948).

Government Publications

Attorney General, *Competition in the Synthetic Rubber Industry,* as of July 1, 1956, 1957, 1958, and 1959 (Washington: Government Printing Office, 1956, 1957, 1958, and 1959).

Federal Trade Commission, *Economic Report on Antibiotics Manufacture* (Washington, 1958).

————, *Report on the Fertilizer Industry,* Washington, 1950.

C. H. Greenwalt, testimony, *Study of Monopoly Power,* Hearings before the Subcomm. on Study of Monopoly Power, Comm. on the Judiciary, H. Rep., Eighty-first Cong., 1st Sess., 1949, Serial No. 14, Part 2-A, pp. 543–91.

R. A. Solo, *Synthetic Rubber: A Case Study in Technological Development under Government Direction,* U.S. Senate, Comm. on the Judiciary, Subcomm. on Patents, Trademarks, and Copyrights, Eighty-fifth Cong., 2d Sess., Study No. 18 (Washington, 1959).

U.S. versus *Imperial Chemical Industries, Ltd., et al.,* 100 F. Supp. 504 (1951).

U.S. versus *National Lead Co., et al.,* 63 F. Supp. 513 (1945).

U.S. versus *E. I. Du Pont de Nemours and Co.,* 118 F. Supp. 41 (1953), 351 U.S. 377 (1956).

Journal and Magazine Articles

W. H. Martin, "Public Policy and Increased Competition in the Synthetic Ammonia Industry," *Quarterly Journal of Economics,* Vol. 73, pp. 373–92 (1959).

G. W. Stocking and W. F. Mueller, "The Cellophane Case and the New Competition," *American Economic Review,* Vol. 45, pp. 29–63 (1955), reprinted in American Economic Association, *Readings in Industrial Organization and Public Policy* (Homewood: Richard Irwin, 1958).

Chapter 8

JOEL B. DIRLAM

The Petroleum Industry

SECTION I: INTRODUCTION

Petroleum in the U.S. Economy

The petroleum industry includes the production of crude oil and natural gas, their transport and refining, and the distribution of petroleum products to the consumer.* Changes in technology blur the outlines of the industry, as it becomes economically feasible to extract petroleum or its products from oil shale, gilsonite or tar sands, or to manufacture organic chemicals and plastics from petroleum. Petrochemicals, which account for about one-quarter of the total value of chemicals, are manufactured by oil companies, while chemical companies use natural gas and refinery products as raw materials.

Nevertheless, until the two industries effect managerial symbiosis, it is useful to speak of an oil company entering the chemical business, when Standard Oil (N.J.) produces plastics, or a chemical company moving into petroleum when Monsanto acquires Lion Oil. The technologies and, more important, the economic characteristics and behavior of the two industries are still distinct.

Petroleum has been a growth industry. A decline in demand for one product has been more than replaced by increases in demand for others. Petroleum refining has been sufficiently flexible, and petroleum engineers sufficiently ingenious, to permit the industry to be as powerful in the jet age as it was when it supplied oil for the lamps of China. From the end of World War I through 1956, the U.S. demand for petroleum grew at an

* The author wishes to express his appreciation to Professor Alfred E. Kahn for his critical comments and to Lila Abramson for research assistance.

277

annual rate of approximately 6 per cent, far exceeding the rise in Gross National Product. Dieselization of the railroads, mechanization on the farm, and the substitution of oil and natural gas home heating for coal have all contributed to the growth of the oil industry. But it has been the demand for gasoline as motor fuel that has contributed most. Until recently a U.S. phenomenon, it appears that the rush of mankind to self-propelled, wheeled vehicles has just begun. In a global context, petroleum demand may be expected to repeat, on a larger scale, U.S. experience.

Together, natural gas and petroleum products have accounted for about 65 per cent of the energy consumed in the U.S. in recent years.[1] This dominance is a result partly of superior efficiency—as in the diesel locomotive—partly of convenience, as in home heating where both fuel oil and natural gas are attractive. Most important, there is no substitute for gasoline.

Compared with the other American industries, the petroleum industry is of gigantic size. Its capital expenditures have made up about one-sixth of annual Gross Private Domestic Investment. Of the twenty-four manufacturing corporations with assets in excess of one billion dollars at the end of 1957, ten were oil companies.[2] The assets of the three largest oil concerns— Jersey Standard, Gulf, and Socony Mobil—were about four billion dollars in excess of the assets of the automobile companies represented, and $7.6 billion more than steel assets.

Continuing Problems of the Oil Industry

Two problem areas have plagued the oil industry since its inception. The first has been the necessity for arriving at and living with a competitive code, formal or informal, that would be compatible with the industry's economic peculiarities: a high proportion of fixed costs has made the industry especially sensitive to price-cutting. In spite of economies of scale in marketing and refining, niches provided for newcomers in a rapidly growing market have made it impossible for the large oil companies to duplicate the price stability of steel, automobiles, or aluminum. The bounty of nature in making crude oil available has created the second major problem.

The Standard Oil Trust. Shortly after "Colonel" Drake's well was spudded in at Titusville, Pennsylvania in August 1858, there were local squabbles between teamsters and pipelines. They were soon dwarfed by pitched battles between the Standard Oil Trust and independent producers

---

[1] U.S. Bureau of Mines, *Annual Petroleum Statement* No. 434, November 14, 1958, p. 18.

[2] First National City Bank Monthly Letter, September 1958, p. 105.

and refiners. For almost thirty years after 1883 (when it gobbled up the last independent pipeline) the Standard Oil monopoly bought, transported, refined, and marketed some 90 per cent of U.S. petroleum.

[Although managerial efficiency and economies of large-scale operation played a large part in its success, Standard's domination of the oil industry was abetted by unfair competition. It tried successfully to prevent independent pipelines from reaching markets or oil fields; it used its monopoly of crude pipelines and its domination of Eastern railroads to make crude oil prohibitively expensive to independent refiners; by threat of withdrawing its business, Standard not only got secret concessions on railroad rates but rebates on its competitors' shipments of oil; and, by the use of predatory local price-cutting, bogus independents and "fighting brands" the trust denied independent refiners and marketers access to the consumers.[3]

The customers and remaining competitors of Standard Oil called on the U.S. government, after extensive private and state litigation had proved unavailing, to redress the balance of power.[In a landmark decision, the Supreme Court in 1911 ordered the dissolution of Standard Oil. It held that Standard's habitual competitive methods were unreasonable restraints of trade and embodied a successful attempt to monopolize.] The dissolution decree could not immediately turn old business associates into aggressive competitors.[For a while the marketing companies kept scrupulously within their historic boundaries; refiners refrained from marketing, marketers did not refine. As time passed, the barriers were breached. Independents had appeared, sparked by new crude oil discoveries in Texas and California. Fed by the accelerating increase in demand for petroleum products, particularly motor fuel, they grew powerful. The old Standard Oil companies began to invade each other's marketing territories. They also integrated backward to crude oil production and forward to marketing.

As a consequence of these changes, the share of the gasoline market accounted for by members of the old Standard Oil empire has dropped, in their respective original territories, to about 20 per cent. On the other hand, backward integration has made them more significant in crude oil production, a field that John D. Rockefeller had regarded as too risky for heavy commitment of funds. And these Standard companies have remained the price leaders, or "reference sellers," in their respective territories, in quoting the key tank wagon gasoline price, even though some newcomers, such as Gulf and Texaco, are among the giants of the industry.

Controlling the Flood of Crude. During the twenties the industry was

[3] H. R. Seager and C. A. Gulick, Jr., *Trust and Corporation Problems* (New York: Harpers, 1929), Chap. VIII.

moderately prosperous but the collapse of 1929 brought serious trouble. Not only was there a sharp drop in the price of crude oil because of slackened demand, but the supply was increased with the discovery of new reserves, notably the gigantic East Texas field in 1930. The interests of some wild-catters and mavericks in unchecked production were ranged against the more conservative elements in the industry. It was not until 1933 that, after bitter legislative and court battles and several declarations of martial law, the Texas and Oklahoma legislatures were conceded the power to limit the flow of oil. But this was ineffective without Federal checks on interstate shipments of "hot oil," provided first through NRA, and then, after the demise of NRA, by the Connally Act. Under NRA, the industry attempted, with indifferent success other than in the oil fields, to check price cutting.[4]

Large integrated refiners in the Middle West, with the blessing of Secretary of the Interior Ickes, tried to support the market for gasoline by absorbing the output of small independents refining East Texas or other cheap crude. The majors selected one or more independents as "dancing partners." After a mammoth trial (requiring the enlargement of the court-room at Madison, Wisconsin) the Department of Justice obtained Supreme Court condemnation of the "dancing partner" program.[5]

A new threat to price stability and the profits of domestic producers was offered by rising imports of crude and products after 1950. The oil in-dustry is not united in its attitude toward imports. Some refiners would like to be able to buy unlimited quantities of Middle East crude oil at favor-able prices. Wholesalers on the East Coast would like to see cheaper imports of both crude and products. Companies like Gulf or Standard Oil (New Jersey) with heavy investments in Arabian production properties do not look favorably on import quotas. The so-called "independent producers" whose profits depend on U.S. production, however, are in favor of import restrictions. Politically powerful in the south and west, they have been able to call the tune on import policy. They have found an ally in the bituminous coal industry which, on most issues, does not see eye-to-eye with petroleum.

Technological Developments

The petroleum industry has experienced a rapid pace of innovation, espe-cially in refining. What is sometimes called "the octane race" has forced refiners continuously to redesign their equipment in an effort to produce the gasoline needed for engines with ever-higher compression ratios. Many

---

[4] See M. W. Watkins, *Oil: Conservation or Stabilization*, New York: Harper, 1937.
[5] *Socony-Vacuum Company* v. *U.S.*, 310 U.S. 150 (1940).

refining processes are available, which may be used in a variety of combinations. The design of a refinery will normally depend on its legacy of equipment from the past, the type of crude it expects to process, the proportion of residual fuel oil or coke believed profitable, and the grade of gasoline desired. The leading process for getting high octane gasolines is catalytic reforming,[6] commercially developed about 1950, but other techniques are available.

Improvements in transportation have taken the form of larger pipelines and tankers, and increased use of barges. Some tankers exceed 100,000 tons dead weight, carry enough crude to take care of one-seventh of the U.S. daily consumption and attain ocean liner speeds. Oil production has made rapid progress. Holes have been drilled ever deeper; in 1958, the 25,000 foot mark was exceeded for the first time. Only improved pipe and rigs permitted the achievement of this depth. At the same time, drilling and well completion has become commonplace in the Gulf of Mexico, ten miles off the coasts of Louisiana and Texas. The industry foresees, not far in the future, exploratory drilling on the Atlantic Coast, from Connecticut to Florida. On the horizon or already in operation are such advances as liquefied transport of natural gas by insulated tanker, subsurface combustion of shale oil, and wholly automatic refinery operation.

These changes have two aspects. On the one hand, they tend to reduce costs. It is cheaper to transport crude oil in the largest tankers or pipelines. The bigger refineries achieve somewhat lower refining costs. Offshore oil is often cheaper over the life of the field because huge reserves are discovered at relatively low cost per barrel. Yet the improved techniques require larger and larger investments. According to some oil company executives roughly $240,000,000 must be invested in refinery facilities to reach the optimum size, where unit costs will be at a minimum.[7] Giant tankers can cost $20,000,-000 apiece.[8]

SECTION II: MARKET STRUCTURE AND PRICING

The oil industry is dominated by a group of twenty companies, generally referred to as "majors," whose current roster by size of net U.S. crude produc-

---

[6] In catalytic reforming, gasoline that has already been "cracked"—that is, produced by distilling crude under heat and pressure usually in the presence of a metallic catalyst —is further processed by adding light fractions.

[7] J. S. Bain, *Barriers to New Competition* (Cambridge: Harvard University Press, 1956), p. 158. This estimate appears to be excessive, judging from the success of many small refineries, such as Aurora in Michigan, Northwest in Minnesota, and Frontier in Wyoming.

[8] *Petroleum Week*, November 7, 1958, p. 68.

TABLE 1

Major Oil Companies—Output and Revenue, 1958

Company	Net U.S. Crude Oil Production (bbls/day; 000's omitted)	U.S. Crude Runs to Stills (bbls/day; 000's omitted)	Net U.S. Production as Percentage of Crude Runs to Stills	Gross Revenue (000's omitted)
Texaco	387.3	598.7	64.7	$2,327,939
Standard Oil (N.J.)	375.7	749.0	50.2	7,543,571 [a]
Gulf Oil Corporation	316.9	485.0	65.3	2,769,377
Shell Oil Company	301.7	464.0	65.0	1,665,989
Standard Oil Co. (Calif.)	253.7	483.4	52.5	1,559,160
Standard Oil Co. (Ind.)	278.0	640.6	40.1	1,863,990
Socony Mobil	208.8	540.4	38.6	2,885,684
Continental Oil Company	136.5	148.8	91.7	596,503
Phillips Petroleum Co.	118.6	218.3	54.3	1,066,554
Sinclair Oil Corporation	114.5	420.6	27.2	1,190,377
Union Oil Co. of California	89.8	151.4	59.3	408,033
Sun Oil Company	89.1	212.1	42.0	721,773
Cities Service Company	90.4	251.8	35.9	1,015,317
Atlantic Refining Company	84.9	185.6	45.7	538,110
Tidewater Oil Company	79.2	192.2	41.2	552,944
Sunray Mid-Continent	74.0	103.1	71.8	372,285
Skelly Oil Company	64.1	48.9	131.1	253,790
Pure Oil Company	58.7	152.0	38.6	472,140
Richfield Oil Corporation	53.6	119.0	45.0	258,208
Standard Oil Company (Ohio)	25.8	128.1	20.1	358,001
Total, Twenty Majors	3,211.3	6,293.0		
U.S. Total	6,706.7	7,597.0		
Twenty Majors, Percentage of U.S. Total	47.5	83.0		

[a] This includes Standard's foreign as well as domestic operations.

Source: Petroleum Institute Projects, The Oil Record, 1959 edition. The Oil and Gas Journal, January 1959.

tion appears in Table 1. These companies are large and vertically integrated from production through wholesale marketing. As the table shows, they are by no means uniform in their degree of integration, measured by domestic self-sufficiency in crude. They differ in other respects as well; some have numerous scattered refineries, others concentrate their output. Some majors distribute a larger share of gasoline through owned service stations than other majors. All are giants, however, in terms of revenues and assets. While the difference between a "major oil company" and an "independent" is difficult to define precisely, and while independents, through growth, sometimes attain major status, it is the majors who are generally regarded as forming policy and the independents as upsetting it.

Production

The production of oil embraces the activities of geological and geophysical exploration, leasing, drilling, raising the oil to the surface, and processing it for transport. The gross amount invested in the production phase of the industry—estimated by F. G. Coqueron at about 28 billion dollars at the beginning of 1958—far exceeds the commitment to all other branches of the industry combined.[9] The weight of this investment helps to explain the oil industry's overriding concern with the price of crude.

It has been estimated that there are about 12,000 firms engaged in all phases of production. Although there are something over 6,600 producers, the output of crude is highly concentrated. In 1957, 33 oil companies or 0.5 per cent of the U.S. producers accounted for 56.5 per cent of the world's crude production and 63 per cent of U.S. production.[10] The twenty majors accounted for 47.3 per cent of U.S. production in 1958.

Production Costs

Exploration has been pushed to areas far from the continental United States—to the Sahara and Libyan deserts, Nigeria, northern Alberta and Alaska—and beneath the surface of the Gulf of Mexico. Even the bigger independents must join forces, as have Ashland Oil, Hancock, and Signal in operations in the Kuwait Neutral Zone, if they are to finance foreign or offshore production. A typical offshore well may cost $2,000,000, and the bonus paid to the state of Louisiana for the right to explore and drill on a single offshore tract can run into several million dollars.

Incremental cost per foot for 10,000 foot wells averages close to about $46 as compared with $12 for shallow, 4,000-foot wells.[11] Opportunities are limited today for wildcatters such as "Dad" Joiner, who, broke and in his late sixties, drilled the discovery well in the East Texas field with a second-hand rig, sporadically shutting down to collect a few dollars to hold his most

[9] *Annual Report, Petroleum Industry, 1957*, New York: Chase Manhattan Bank, 1958, p. 30.

[10] *Ibid.*, p. 6, and *Future Growth of the World Petroleum Industry*, New York: Chase Manhattan Bank, 1958, p. 34.

[11] American Petroleum Institute and Independent Petroleum Association of America, *Joint Association Survey of Industry Drilling Costs 1955 and 1956* (1959), p. 2.

voracious creditors at bay. Yet, an increase in total costs per well, which may seriously hamper small firms in efforts to produce, does not necessarily increase the average cost per barrel.

Those wells which barely cover production costs at prevailing price levels, producing four or five barrels of oil a day, are called "stripper" wells. Though numerous—there are over 370,000 of them—and hence politically powerful, strippers are responsible for less than a fifth of domestic production.[12] Most U.S. crude comes from supramarginal wells, of which about one-third are flowing under natural gas or water pressure. Two-thirds of the nonstrippers, however, require pumping or some form of artificial aid to the flow of crude, such as pressure injection of water or natural gas.

The small proportion of direct costs to current prices narrows the immediate response of most oil producers to changes in price. Variable expenses of producing from a flowing well are negligible. Natural pressures lift the oil. The heavy investment necessary to find and sink wells creates a strong financial incentive to rapid production. These incentives are especially effective with small producers. The supply of oil from flowing wells is therefore highly inelastic, unless price should fall to 1932 levels.

Wells under artificial lift have a somewhat more elastic response. Many of these wells, however, have called for heavy investment in secondary recovery techniques such as drilling of water injection wells.[13] Again, the owners anticipate that price will cover, in addition to direct, a heavy burden of fixed cost. In the short run, their production, too, will tend to be inelastic in supply. Economic theory indicates and sad experience confirms, that in the absence of state interference, oil will be produced in huge volume, even when its price is close to zero.

Looking further ahead, there is reason to believe that supply, in the long run, will be more responsive to price changes than in the short run. Oil men, even congenital gamblers lured by the dream of the "big strike," must anticipate that their activities will prove profitable or they will not explore and drill. Nevertheless, though shallow fields are difficult to find and though this may depress expectations, continuing advances in technology will prevent sharp increases in real costs per barrel. Higher prices for natural gas may also partially offset rising costs, and swell the resources available to carry on exploration.

The Federal tax system also serves to stimulate the discovery and production of oil by making the industry more attractive to investors than manu-

---

[12] *Petroleum Week*, March 13, 1959, p. 8.
[13] Secondary recovery brings oil to the surface, by methods other than simple pumping, after natural pressures are exhausted.

facturing or retailing. Oil producers can claim a percentage of total revenues as a depletion allowance every year, even though through such deductions they have long since recovered their exploration and development costs. In addition, they can deduct, annually, drilling and development costs up to about 75 per cent of all costs of bringing in a well. These costs may be offset against income arising from any source whatever; as a result corporations, or individuals with high income from activities other than oil production find oil investments almost equivalent to "a source of tax-exempt income. . . ." [14]

Conservation and Supply Restrictions

In those states with large oil reserves (other than California, which must import crude) production controls, called "prorationing," are imposed in the name of conservation. Policies of the Texas Railroad Commission, which administers the conservation statute in Texas, are strategic in prorationing.[15] About 50 per cent of U.S. production east of the Rockies flows from Texas wells. Output can not exceed MER—the maximum efficient rate of recovery, determined for each field by Railroad Commission engineers, that will yield the most oil with a minimum expenditure on secondary recovery. But the Commission may require a lower output than MER, if "market demand" is less. Market demand is a term inherited from the NRA Petroleum Code: it is designed to maintain price. Taking into account (1) forecasts of the U.S. Bureau of Mines, (2) nominations—or estimates of amounts they will purchase—submitted by large buyers for each field, and (3) the level of inventories, the Texas Commission fixes, in terms of number of days operation, each month's allowable output. There is no question that the primary goal of gearing output to market demand is to prevent the price of crude from falling.[16] On the other hand, to the extent that prorationing has raised or stabilized price, it has reduced the risks of production, made it creditworthy, and lowered capital costs. Through prevention of some of the pre-1933 wasteful production methods, such as allowing large quantities of natural gas to escape to the air, prorationing has also increased the ultimate recovery of oil through both primary and secondary methods.

[14] W. F. Hellmuth, Jr., "Erosion of the Federal Corporation Income Tax Base," in Joint Economic Committee, *Federal Tax Policy for Stability and Growth* (1955), p. 902.
[15] Five other states—Louisiana, Oklahoma, Kansas, New Mexico and Arizona—have similar statutes. *Second Report of the U.S. Attorney General* [on the operation of the interstate Oil Compact] (1957), p. 48 (hereinafter cited *Oil Compact Report*).
[16] Attorney General of Michigan, *Gasoline Price Investigation, 1955–1956* (hereinafter cited, *Gasoline Price Investigation*).

In spite of their attempts to limit output, state authorities have encountered increasing difficulties in checking the growth of inventories. Domestic crude has faced competition from the highly efficient wells of the Middle East and Venezuela. While cost estimates are not easy to come by, it seems safe to say that if Saudi Arabian oil could be freely imported into the U.S., it could undersell Texas crude at East coast refineries by almost 30 per cent. That it has not done so is attributable in part to the limitations, once "voluntary" and now mandatory,[17] on the volume of imports, and in part to the unwillingness of the large oil companies controlling Arabian and Iranian output to break the market for U.S. crude prices.[18]

How Crude Oil Is Priced in the Field

When the oil industry was in its infancy, crude was marketed by purchase and sale of certificates through organized exchanges, where the price changed frequently as demand and supply shifted. In 1895 Joseph Seep, Standard Oil's purchasing representative in the "Oil Regions," announced that producers would henceforth receive a fair price, not necessarily the price that prevailed on the exchange. Since producers could reach a market only through Seep's network of pipelines, the Titusville Exchange closed in 1896 never to reopen.[19] Crude oil is still purchased in most producing areas by much the same procedure as Seep's. Large buyers announce a "posted" price which they will pay for oil delivered into their gathering lines. They pay all sellers in the same field the same price, except for quality differences. If a seller is dissatisfied, he can switch to another buyer, although gathering lines must be made available. Changes in the field posted price usually are preceded by widespread undercover discounts or premiums, which are eventually recognized by a major oil company.[20] Thus, if crude is in short supply small refiners may offer premiums and induce some producers to switch connections.[21]

---

[17] *The New York Times*, March 11, 1959, p. 47.

[18] U.N., Economic Commission for Europe, *The Price of Oil in Western Europe* (1955); Federal Trade Commission Staff Report, *The International Petroleum Cartel* (1952), pp. 349–74.

[19] R. W. Hidy and M. E. Hidy, *Pioneering in Big Business, 1882–1911*, New York: Harpers, 1955, pp. 279–80. According to the Hidys, Standard Oil paid prices above those prevailing on the exchanges, thus making it more costly for nonintegrated competitors.

[20] A cut in crude oil prices in Oklahoma in October 1958, was initiated by Sunray-Midcontinent and Kerr-McGee, the two largest buyers in the state. *Petroleum Week*, October 17, 1958, p. 11.

[21] Standard Oil Co. (New Jersey) affiliates lost some 15,000 barrels of oil per day in 1947 because of premium prices offered by competitors. *Fuel Investigation*, Hearings Before House Committee on Interstate and Foreign Commerce, Eightieth Cong., 2d Sess. (1948), p. 1064.

But the price is sometimes increased by a big buyer even without the excuse of loss of connections to refiners offering a premium over the posted price. On January 3, 1957, Humble Oil (the source of domestic crude oil for Jersey Standard) raised its posted price by 25 cents a barrel, on the grounds that this was necessary to provide "an assured supply of oil." Texas at the time had a yearly average of 14.7 shutdown days per month, compared with 3.4 days in 1947,[22] and President Baker of Humble conceded that the price hike could not assist in making oil available to ease the Suez crisis.[23] Crude buyers apparently regard it as their responsibility to see that the level of prices is such as to provide long-term incentives to production, regardless of the immediate state of the market. Since the buyers are also heavily engaged in production, they are, in effect, paying themselves what they regard as a reasonable price.

There is another reason why integrated oil companies may not look unfavorably upon price increases for crude. They can deduct from taxable income 27.5 per cent of the value of crude production (up to 50 per cent of taxable income). The higher the price of crude, the larger the deduction which is available—even though the crude is not sold, but absorbed within the integrated firm, or exchanged.

Crude oil pricing behavior fails to conform to the competitive model. In the first place, the price of crude is quite rigid. The posted price of Mid-continent crude stood at $2.85 a barrel from June 1953 to January 1957. The prevalence of vertical integration makes it impossible to analyze the crude oil market as a typical oligopsony, where the most efficient firm would be the price leader. In effect a concensus among executives of the majors determines when prices are to be increased. Sometimes there is disagreement. The inelastic demand for gasoline and home heating oil leaves a margin for discretion in upward movements.[24]

Petroleum Products Markets

For convenience, the discussion of petroleum products will run mainly in terms of gasoline. More than 55 per cent of refiners' revenue come from gasoline sales. Refiners dispose of gasoline through three main outlets: (1) the bulk or cargo market, in tanker, barge or pipeline terminal lots to other

---

[22] *Oil Compact Report*, p. 86.

[23] Senate Committee on the Judiciary, *Petroleum, The Antitrust Laws, and Government Policies*, S. Rep. No. 1147, Eighty-fifth Cong., 1st Sess. (1957), p. 50.

[24] According to one study, the price elasticity of demand for gasoline was about 0.1. H. E. McAllister, *The Elasticity of Demand for Gasoline in the State of Washington*, Pullman: Washington State College, 1956, p. xiii.

refiners or terminal operators, (2) the terminal or refinery wholesale market, with fleet operators, industries, or large private brand marketers as customers and (3) their own tank wagon market selling mainly to retail dealers.

Refinery concentration data show that, on a national basis, the thirty largest refiners accounted for 84 per cent of output in 1957, while seventy refiners were responsible for almost all gasoline produced. The number of refiners selling in any one market is, however, much less than these totals would indicate.

There are three typical refinery locations. (1) Close to the source of crude, in the field; (2) at points where transportation is cheap and many sources of supply available, such as the New Jersey-Delaware Coast; and (3) in centers, such as Whiting, Indiana, from which a wide market can be conveniently served. The powerful integrated oil companies have joined their refineries to crude oil fields by pipeline, and they have reached markets likewise by products pipelines. Sometimes these lines are jointly owned, because there are savings to be derived from increasing pipeline size.

Influence of Refining Costs on Supply

Refining processes entail heavy fixed costs. In a representative case, during the years 1948–55, a large oil company made capital expenditures of $34.6 million on a middle-sized refinery unit. Its equipment was improved and its capacity raised from 35,000 to 50,000 barrels per day.[25]

To expand capacity usually requires several years of planning and construction; it can not be done overnight. Since shutdowns entail sizable costs, refineries will, if necessary, accept margins that fail to cover average cost once they are in operation. Moreover, incremental costs per barrel of crude oil processed are relatively low compared with average total costs of processing.[26] Integrated firms, with investments in production, transportation and marketing, will tend to maintain output even if refining is unprofitable. For these reasons, the supply of petroleum products tends to be maintained in the face of price declines. Nonintegrated refiners, who have to buy and sell on the market, are more likely to shut down in response to a squeeze on the margin between the price of crude, and the price of products.

In the short run there are technical limits to the proportion of crude that

---

[25] BLS Report No. 120, *A Case Study of a Modernized Petroleum Refinery,* U.S. Department of Labor (n.d.).

[26] According to an estimate for 1950, unit variable cost was 38 per cent of total cost (not including return on investment) for a 200,000 barrel a day plant, at capacity operation. J. G. McLean and R. W. Haigh, *The Growth of Integrated Oil Companies,* Cambridge: Harvard University Press, 1954, pp. 562–5.

can be converted to gasoline. As the demand for motor fuel has risen, refinery equipment has been designed so that today 45 or 46 per cent of the volume of output is gasoline, as against 25 per cent in 1918. With present equipment, an increase in this proportion would mean sacrificing other products which would have to be rerun, and combined with expensive high-octane fractions at sharply rising opportunity and processing costs. On the other hand, to reduce the volume of gasoline produced with a given crude oil throughout also imposes heavy costs on the refinery. A cold winter often results in raising motor fuel stocks higher than the industry would like because there is no way in which the proportion of gasoline output can be substantially reduced. In the short run, therefore, changes in the price of gasoline are unlikely to have much effect upon its output unless the total revenues from petroleum product sales decline so far as to leave a margin insufficient to cover the refinery's direct costs.[27]

The Refinery Market ←

The higher investment costs, required to keep them in the "octane race," have forced the demise of many small refiners. From 632 plants in 1936, the number of refineries declined to 350 in 1952 and 318 in 1958. Under pressure of vertical integration, the open market, where refinery sales are made in cargo lots, has gradually atrophied. On the Texas Gulf Coast, where once there was a lively market, less than eleven refineries made open market sales in 1954. One of these has since shut down.[28] In northern Texas and Oklahoma there are also concentrations of nonintegrated refineries—the "Group 3" refineries—which once sold largely on the open-spot market. Here, too, as on the Texas Gulf Coast, most gasoline is now disposed of on long-term contract.

The price is based either on quotations appearing in Platt's *Oilgram* (a trade paper) on day of shipment, or upon negotiation. When the spot market functioned, Platt's quotations reflected representative equilibrium prices. They now appear to be merely a collection of posted, or asking prices. Many

[27] The cost of gasoline, as a joint product, is unobtainable. Esso Standard has stated that it uses as a rough measure the cost of crude, less sales realization on fuel oil and refinery gases, plus processing costs to get a net figure for gasoline cost. The higher the price of fuel oil, the lower the cost of gasoline. A. D. K. Kaplan, J. B. Dirlam, and R. F. Lanzillotti, *Pricing in Big Business: A Case Approach*, Washington, D.C.: Brookings, 1958, p. 93.
[28] R. Cassady, *Price Making and Price Behavior in the Petroleum Industry*, New Haven: Yale University Press, 1954, p. 151, n. 23. Bureau of Mines, U.S. Department of the Interior, *Petroleum Refineries, Including Cracking Plants, in the U.S., January 1, 1958* (1959).

or most of the refineries quoting actually have no gasoline to sell on the open market. Processing margins equivalent to the difference between "the low of Platt's" for the most important products and the posted price of crude show wide variations, ranging in a few months from 2 to 25 per cent of the cost of crude, while the output of gasoline remains relatively constant. This seems to confirm the conclusion that the supply of gasoline at the refinery tends to be inelastic. Nevertheless, it is hard to know just how much weight to attach to margins, thus computed, when most of the gasoline is simply transferred from the manufacturing to the marketing division of an integrated company. Moreover, individual deals with independent marketers evidently take place at prices far below the quoted price.[29]

Because the demand for gasoline is inelastic, a single cargo of "surplus" or homeless gasoline thrown on a highly organized market might cause a severe price collapse. Hence, the industry has endeavored to narrow the scope of the open market, to hold surplus products in storage so they can be worked off at a later date, to integrate forward, and to sew up by contract much of the capacity of the independent refiners.

Tank Wagon Distribution

The larger part of the gasoline sold to retail gasoline dealers is delivered from tank wagons owned by refiners.[30] The balance moves through distributors or oil "jobbers" or large retailing chains, who buy in bulk from the refiners, either at terminals or more rarely the refinery itself. The distributors fall into two major groups. The branded distributor sells to retailers who market the gasoline under the refiner's name—as Shell, Gulf, or Texaco, etc. In most cases the branded distributor owns his own bulk storage plant and tank wagons although his supplier often helps to finance him. Often he owns service stations as well. The gasoline sold by the unbranded distributor is marketed under private brand names, or perhaps with no distinctive name at all.

Independent, nonintegrated refiners sell for the most part through unbranded distributors. The majors favor the branded distributors. There are differences among the majors, however, with respect to their reliance on

---

[29] At published prices for Oklahoma refineries prevailing over a six-month period, the reported delivered price at which gasoline was available in Chicago from Great Lakes Pipeline would not have covered transportation cost. S. M. Livingston, "The Limits of Private Price Policy," in Joint Economic Committee, *The Relationship of Prices to Economic Stability and Growth: Commentaries* (1958), p. 191.

[30] As of 1950, about 60 per cent of the gasoline moved to retailers in refiner-owned channels. American Petroleum Institute, *Petroleum Facts and Figures, 1956,* 12th edition, p. 293.

independent distributors. Shell, for instance, has about 1,500 branded distributors, Standard Oil of Indiana on the other hand, only 110. Standard Oil of Ohio is unique in marketing most of its gasoline through wholly company owned and operated retail stations.[31]

When a major oil company invades new territory or expands its refinery capacity it unsettles its customary balance between marketing and refining capacities. Standard of California shortly after World War II, and, more recently, Tidewater Oil acquired or built large-volume refineries on the East Coast. They could market the expanded gasoline output initially only by selling extensive amounts to unbranded or private brand marketers, such as Merit, or by offering unusually large discounts to lure branded distributors away from their usual source of supply.

Majors' contracts with distributors have typically quoted not a dollars-and-cents price per gallon but a discount below the price—either their own or that of the regional price leader charged on direct sales to retail dealers. Distributors' cost of gasoline is thus dependent on the ruling tank wagon price, set by the regional "leader."

While the total price to distributors could be regarded as a resultant of the distributors' demand for gasoline (which becomes highly elastic at prices exceeding the ruling quotation) and refiners' supply (which likewise becomes highly elastic at prices below the same customary price), it seems more helpful to consider the distributors as offering their marketing services for a price. This price is their "margin." For the branded distributor, the margin is a discount—usually 2.75 cents—below the prevailing tank wagon price to retailers. Unbranded distributors, who have to sell at lower prices, get correspondingly lower quotations, but may receive about the same margin. In the short run, the demand for distributors' services is probably quite inelastic downwards; refiners do not believe that with a lower margin more gasoline will be sold. At higher margins, they would prefer to take over the distribution function themselves. At lower margins, the distributors find it hard to cover their average costs, and eventually either sell out to their suppliers (usually at a fair price), or go out of business. Most adopt the first alternative. It seems fair to say that the distributor's margin represents something close to the cost of storing gasoline in bulk, selling it, and transporting it to retail dealers and to other wholesale customers.

[31] National Petroleum News, *Fact Book, 1959–1960* (1959), pp. 110–11.

The Price to Retailers

The behavior of tank wagon prices varies from place to place. According to data collected by Texaco in a 3½ year period the average tank wagon price in 50 cities showed 90 increases and 120 decreases.[32] When suppliers invade new territories the price of gasoline to retailers may be quite unstable. Efforts by a supplier to expand sales or to force its way into a market inevitably lead to lower prices, since total demand is quite inelastic. In other areas, independents selling at an established differential below the majors, may leave the prevailing tank wagon price unaffected.

[Tank wagon prices in each region have usually been established by a recognized price leader. The trade publication, *The National Petroleum News*, publishes the leader's prices in selected cities. Other marketers have generally followed the published price. On the whole, the prices have tended to increase with distance from the nearest source of large supplies of gasoline. On the East Coast, for instance, the price at New York or Boston tends to equal the cargo price at the Gulf plus transportation, terminal bulk plant storage and tank wagon delivery costs. At one time, the price at Chicago, St. Louis, or Minneapolis was arrived at by adding to "Group 3" refinery prices a differential to account for cost of moving the gasoline by tank car from Oklahoma refineries. Expansion of Western refining and gasoline transport through the Great Lakes Pipeline and the decline of the spot market, however, have made Group 3-Plus a thing of the past.

["Leadership" in tank wagon pricing is not of the so-called dominant firm type. The firm that initiates the change has no way of enforcing its decision on its competitors. Sentiment for an increase accumulates among the sellers, reinforced by evidence of increasing demand—as manifested by declining inventories—or by a higher cost level. At a propitious moment a large seller raises his price; other companies follow. This may be illustrated by events leading to a price increase in Michigan in 1955.

In Michigan, Standard of Indiana sells twice as much gasoline as the next largest marketer. In 1955, nine refiners enjoyed over 80 per cent of the wholesale gasoline sales; the largest four had 49 per cent of the business. Standard of Indiana increased its tank wagon price in the Upper Peninsula on May 6, 1955 by ½ cent per gallon. On May 9 it made a similar increase in the Lower Peninsula. This was the first change in tank wagon prices in Michigan in almost two years. The other major refiners selling in Michigan

---

[32] S. M. Livingston, *op.cit.* When the same change appeared in more than one city, only a single move was listed.

followed suit, raising their prices the next day. In response to inquiry by the Attorney General, the oil companies justified their price increase by pointing to a rise in labor costs and improvement in product, which had resulted in higher capital costs.

In spite of this example of leadership, Standard of Indiana, the nominal price leader in the Middle West, insists that it now sets its tank wagon price to meet local conditions. "Leaders" in other areas would undoubtedly make similar statements. Price leadership is of little importance when the tank wagon price is reduced. Price declines occur only when suppliers have to recognize inroads made by cut-rate or new suppliers; it makes little difference who first recognizes the threat.

What are the economics of tank wagon price behavior? There is nearly always a large stock of gasoline overhanging the market. Regardless of the companies' statements about cost impact, changes in the short-run marginal cost of producing gasoline—under the conditions of joint cost and the heavy fixed costs characteristic of refinery output—are unlikely to be reflected in changes in the supply of gasoline available to any given market. At the same time, if the large suppliers feel confident (as they did in Michigan in 1955) that a higher price will be accepted by each of them, demand becomes relatively inelastic, and it is worthwhile to raise the price. On the other hand, an aggressive firm that desired to expand its business would refuse to go along with the leader's price increase.

The modified price leadership that prevails in the different product markets has been under pressure in recent years. Accelerated expansion since 1950 has cut runs from close to 100 to well below 90 per cent of adjusted capacity though integrated firms have steadier rates of output than nonintegrated.

Profits of the refining segment are difficult to estimate, because such a large part of the industry is vertically integrated. A survey of firms engaged in both refining and marketing, but not wholly integrated, concluded that the long-term average return on investment was in the neighborhood of 6 per cent.[33] If the return on refining were actually as low as this, it seems doubtful that independent refiners would have expanded, as many of them have, in the past decade. Although there are no global data to show whether independent market outlets have grown commensurately, the majors are at least more aware of private brand competition than heretofore.[34] Census

---

[33] J. C. McLean and R. W. Haigh, *op.cit.*, p. 680.
[34] According to the marketing vice-president of Shell Oil Co., private brand marketers in Savannah, Georgia, had 37.3 per cent of the business in 1956, having increased their volume 15 per cent more than the general increase; in Detroit, private brand marketers had 18 per cent of the business, their volume being 20 per cent higher. He believed these percentages were representative for Shell's marketing territory. *Distribution Practices in*

data show independent jobbers and other bulk handlers doing about the same percentage of U.S. gasoline business in 1954 as in 1948.

Retail Marketing: Gasoline

Prior to 1935, the major suppliers owned and operated a large number of retail stations through hired attendants, who were told what price to charge. Since then however, operators of stations have ceased to be employees of majors in all but a few "training" stations. Standard Oil of Ohio appears to be the only large refiner that sells its branded gasoline exclusively through its owned stations. In New Jersey, Cities Service Co. has sold over 60 per cent of its gasoline through owned and operated stations. But these examples are exceptions. |Gasoline dealers are in theory "independent businessmen" who either own their stations, or lease them from their supplier or some other landlord. Fragmentary information [35] suggests that major suppliers channel the bulk of gasoline sales through their leased stations.|

When the station operator ceased to be an employee of his supplier, he became free to set the retail price. But this freedom has not been absolute. Suppliers have not lost interest in retail pricing. During price wars, they often "suggest" to their dealers that they cut their retail price to avoid losing gallonage to competitors. Suppliers usually require their dealers to accept a lower margin in these circumstances.[36] Dealers who refuse to cut are charged a higher tank wagon price than other dealers in the same marketing area. Conversely, Standard of Indiana and Ashland Refining have refused to give tank wagon reductions, available to other dealers, to any operator whom they can identify as the instigator of a price war. Under price-war conditions, some suppliers like Sunoco have gone further and simply placed gasoline "on consignment" for sale at a fixed price, giving dealers a fixed commission. In those states where gasoline is fair traded the suppliers fix a minimum retail price.[37]

The Petroleum Industry, Hearings Before House Select Committee on Small Business, 85th Cong., 1st Sess., Pt. I (1957), p. 328. The private brand marketer sells "20 to 30 per cent" of the service station gasoline in the Standard of Indiana marketing territory, and he has been growing. R. C. Gunness, "Gasoline Prices and Pricing Policy," speech, January 28, 1959, p. 16.

[35] Senate Small Business Committee, *Gasoline Price War in New Jersey,* Sen. Rep. No. 2810, Eighty-fourth Cong., 2d Sess. (1956), p. 9.

[36] Montana Trade Commission, *Gasoline Prices in Montana, Preliminary Report* (circa 1956), p. 13. In February 1959, when there was a price war in Los Angeles, the margin between the tank wagon official price and the typical service station price was 1.60 cents per gallon. At the same time the margin was 6.40 cents in Chicago.

[37] Atlantic and Sinclair sought injunctions in Pennsylvania in January 1959 against dealers selling below the fair trade minimum. *The Gasoline Retailer,* February 4, 1959, p. 1.

Why Price Wars?

⌊During a price war, gasoline is retailed at prices considerably below "normal" levels. The standards for normal are developed by assuming that a minimum amount is necessary to cover costs of each segment of the petroleum business, down to the cost of crude at the refinery. In an extreme Oklahoma price war, for instance, when gasoline sold at 21.9 cents a gallon the refinery netted less per gallon than the cost of crude after deducting state and Federal taxes and a 4.5-cent living allowance for the dealer.⌊Price wars are sometimes set off by a private brand marketer, who has bought his gasoline below the prevailing tank wagon price. But branded dealers may be responsible. There is a high cross-elasticity of demand among retail stations.⌋Marginal cost of pumping gasoline is negligible; station attendants are idle much of the time, and pumps are seldom occupied to capacity. An individual dealer who shades his margin, as many do, by giving undercover discounts to regular customers, may get higher profits by lowering his average cost per gallon. But he may bring retaliation in the form of open cuts by other dealers, and one slash is matched by another.

⌊In local markets there is usually a range of prices for branded gasoline, and a customary differential (usually about 3 cents) between the typical price for branded gas and the price of unbranded gas. If much gasoline is sold at the low end of the range for branded gasoline, a price war results.⌋ One study found a price range for branded gasoline of 5.7 cents in Chicago in 1950 while in Ithaca, New York, the range was 1.2 cents.[38] When the customary differential is disturbed, either because the branded dealers narrow the gap by cutting their price or the unbranded dealer enlarges it, by reducing his, price wars are likely to result.

⌊A dealer may be tempted to cut retail prices not only by excess capacity and high-demand elasticity, but because his average cost of operation is low.⌋ Individual negotiation between lessee and supplier results in a variety of arrangements involving rentals or payment for facilities such as pumps or lubrication equipment which may give one dealer his gasoline at a lower net cost than it is available to another operator selling the same brand. Large-volume, multipump stations, often selling unbranded gas, have lower average costs per gallon than small-volume stations. The smaller stations must meet the reduction in margins to maintain the normal differential between branded and unbranded gasoline.

---

[38] Cassady, *op.cit.*, p. 260; M. C. Howard, *The Marketing of Petroleum Products: A Study in the Relations Between Large and Small Business,* September 1951 (unpublished thesis, Cornell Library), p. 339.

The Retail Market: Heating Oil

Although the consumer as motorist is most familiar with the retail market for gasoline, as a householder he usually purchases large amounts of heating or furnace oil. The heating oil market has generated very few problems compared with the gasoline market; it is of interest to inquire why. For the most part, the large companies have not attempted to carry distribution of heating oils any closer to the consumer than the storage terminal. They have been relatively uninterested in attaching their brand names to furnace oil. Although branded distributors sell heating oils, they show less loyalty in purchasing oil than gasoline. A much smaller proportion of heating oil than gasoline goes through branded distribution channels.[39] Price to the consumer in most localities is therefore set by vigorous competition among branded distributors, unbranded distributors, and "peddlers" who have no bulk plants but shop around for their supply.

Two of the causes for friction in the retail gasoline market are therefore absent in the home heating oil market. In the first place, differentials are slight between nationally advertised and private brands, since to most consumers the oil is undifferentiated. Hence, private brands do not threaten the market share of the refiner's brands. Second, the nature of the sale precludes any supplier from being able to add substantially to his business by price cutting. Householders can shop around by phone to find the cheapest oil; there is little chance for a price cutter to take business away from a competitor before the competitor is on notice: he can meet the cut, and the price cutter's demand is therefore almost completely inelastic downwards. Variable costs of delivery and truck operation are also a larger part of total costs, leaving a smaller margin for manipulation, and less financial inducement to widen sales by reducing price.

SECTION III: PUBLIC POLICY

Prorationing

It has been argued forcefully that the present system of state prorationing, aided by the Connally "Hot Oil Act," has kept the price of crude far above its proper level. Admitting that some controls are necessary to insure, under the present system, that small, independent producers have an equal chance in each field to sell their oil to purchasing pipelines, there is said to be a

---

[39] In 1950, about 63 per cent of home heating oil was sold by independent distributors, as against 39 per cent of motor fuel.

superior alternative. If oil fields were unitized—that is, cooperatively managed—they could be produced at whatever rate the owners thought desirable.[40] No well owner then need feel that others were draining his land, or that his production would have to be wastefully stored above ground till he found a pipeline to take it off his hands. Thus the controls based upon market demand and justified by appeals for justice to the small producer under which Texas and other states set maximum days production for each field, would be unnecessary.

Would the unitized system result in lower prices? MER sets a ceiling to production in every state that now has conservation legislation. Under the unitized system, even this limit could be removed. It would be left to each operator in the light of current prices to weigh present against future production, or even diminished total recovery. Supply might increase and prices fall.

The oil producers have urged, however, that costs of exploration and production are so high that even current crude prices are scarcely remunerative. Thus, according to a representative group [41] the weighted average value of crude oil and natural gas at the wellhead had increased only 4 per cent from 1948 to 1959, while between 1948 and 1955 exploration, development and production costs had risen 62 per cent.[42]

Objective measures of the adequacy of current prices might include the profitability of the producers, or the extent of production activity. The first measure can not be effectively applied because of the capitalization of economic rent: oil bonuses and lease payments are costs to producing firms, though not to society. In the second place, oil producers enjoy special tax privileges which render it difficult to assess their reported earnings. A large proportion of developmental expense on productive wells can be directly charged to income. In addition, 27.5 per cent of market value of production is a deduction up to 50 per cent of taxable income, even though the cost of the oil may have been recovered many times over. Many giant oil companies pay little or no federal income tax.

The extent of production or exploration activity may be a better indicator of the reasonableness of the price of crude oil. From 1956, when there were

[40] E. V. Rostow, *A National Policy for the Oil Industry* (New Haven: Yale University Press, 1948), pp. 119–22.

[41] Cost Study Committee of the Independent Petroleum Association of America, "May 1959 Report on Cost Study."

[42] The petroleum industry has been unable to provide estimates of exploration, development, and production costs on an annual basis, which would be necessary if a reliable estimate were to be made of the cost of oil production. It is felt that data for the larger companies—presumably readily available—would be unrepresentative of the smaller operators, who usually assume the risks of wildcatting. *Report of the Cost Study Committee of the IPAA*, October 29–30, 1956.

16,173 exploratory wells drilled, there has been a steady decline to 13,199 in 1958.[43] On the other hand, reserves at the end of 1958 were higher than they were at the end of 1956.[44] Domestic production of oil and natural gas liquids averaged 7.5 million barrels a day in 1958 (a depression year) as against 8.0 in 1957 and 1956, but in 1959 the rate began once again to climb.

Even though domestic production has been rising year by year (apart from the set-back resulting from the 1957–58 recession), productive capacity has constantly exceeded it. Excess or shut-in capacity has been authoritatively estimated at 18 per cent of total capacity in January 1957, 26 per cent in January 1958, and about 25 per cent in January 1959.[45]

On balance, it must be concluded that there is little evidence that current prices of crude oil are too low. On the contrary, the presence of excess capacity shows that too many fields have been discovered. There is also good reason to believe that too many wells are drilled; on both scores, therefore, investment in the industry is excessive.

Additional evidence that the present level of crude prices in the U.S. is artificially maintained by restrictions is provided by our oil import policy. Following World War II, imports increased sharply, from 236 thousand barrels per day in 1946 to over 2 million barrels per day in 1958. Venezuelan crude and products accounted for the largest share of the imports but Canada and Kuwait occupied significant places by 1956.[46] Venezuelan transportation costs to East Coast refineries are less than those from the Gulf Coast. Nevertheless, Middle Eastern Oil is cheaper still. It would have displaced all other crude at East Coast refineries prior to the late fifties if the eight companies dominating Arabian production had not set prohibitive f.o.b. Persian Gulf prices.[47]

It seems probable that the big Middle East producers were afraid to antagonize the domestic oil producers. In 1949, under aegis of the Interior Department, the conflicting groups in the industry agreed ambiguously that imports should "supplement" not "supplant" domestic production. By 1955, however, the Office of Defense Mobilization yielded to pressure by the

[43] *Petroleum Week*, March 13, 1959, p. 11.
[44] *Idem*, March 20, 1959, p. 15.
[45] *Idem*, May 8, 1959, p. 12, and American Petroleum Institute, *Statistical Bulletin*, Vol. 40, No. 18, April 21, 1959.
[46] *United States Oil Imports*, Petroleum Industry Research Foundation (1958), Table 9, p. 95.
[47] The history of the Middle East Cartel may be traced through *The International Petroleum Cartel*, Staff Report to the Federal Trade Commission (1952); Economic Commission for Europe, *The Price of Oil In Western Europe* (1955) and OEEC, *Europe's Need for Oil* (1958). An unofficial estimate indicates that Middle East posted prices are set so high that no independent refiner or marketer could afford to purchase in the Eastern Hemisphere. W. Jablonski, "Petroleum Comments," *Petroleum Week*, March 20, 1959, p. 24.

domestic producers, and its Director called on importers to use more domestic crude. "Voluntary" quotas were set in 1957. Not all importers observed them, and on March 10, 1959, President Eisenhower put imports under mandatory curbs.[48] The Secretary of the Interior thereupon cut imports from 2.1 million to about 1.4 million barrels per day.[49] Crude quotas which had been alloted to some importing refiners on a historical basis, were now shifted to give all refiners, on a scale diminishing with size, the right to import a percentage of their total crude inputs. As a consequence, inland refiners who had quotas were able to sell them to East Coast refiners, permitting the latter—at a price—to realize the savings from importing cheaper oil.

⌊If there is one thing clear about our domestic crude oil policy, it is that it has never been frankly explained to the citizens who pay the price, nor fully debated by the Congress that has enacted, piecemeal, the legislation under which production is restrained, imports restricted, and exploration tax-subsidized. General appeals to conservation principles and national defense have sufficed to justify legislative and executive action. Since conservation purposes would obviously be much better served by unitization than by prorationing to market demand, and might be assisted by relying more rather than less upon imports, it must be concluded that the major purpose of our present policy is to increase the profits of domestic producers and royalty payments to landowners in the Southwest at the expense of consumers everywhere.⌉

Price Discrimination

Accusations of monopolistic price discrimination have rocked the oil industry since the early 1900's, when Waters-Pierce Oil Company knifed Standard Oil competitors by anticipating, with price cuts, the arrival of a shipment of independently refined kerosene.[50] A perennial complaint of jobbers has been that their suppliers underbid them on commercial business. Their problem was debated in drafting the Petroleum Code under NRA, and they threaten still now and then to appeal to Congress. Nevertheless, the jobbers actually seem reluctant to press their quarrel with the majors very far.[51]

Retailers have grievances against both refiners and jobbers. Their sup-

---

[48] 24 Federal Register 1781: *The New York Times,* March 11, 1959, p. 57.
[49] *Petroleum Week,* March 20, 1959, p. 18.
[50] P. H. Giddens, *Standard Oil Company (Indiana): Oil Pioneer of the Middle West,* New York: Appleton-Century-Crofts, 1955, pp. 93–94.
[51] M. C. Howard, "Interfirm Relations in Oil Products Markets," *Journal of Marketing,* April 1956, p. 359.

pliers sell branded—more frequently, unbranded—gasoline to large-volume
marketers at less than prevailing tank wagon prices. They have, on numerous
occasions, goaded the FTC into action under the Robinson-Patman Act. One
of the cases has become a *cause célèbre*.

In 1936 and 1937 Standard Oil of Indiana sold branded gasoline—Red
Crown—in Detroit to four large buyers, at jobbers' discounts of 1.5 cents
below the going tank wagon price. One of these buyers (Ned's) was simply
a large retailer which took advantage of its discount to cut the retail price
below what Standard's small retailers were then charging. Many of these
small dealers leased their stations from Standard and were therefore in no
position to switch suppliers. As justification for the concession to Ned's,
Standard alleged that other suppliers in Detroit, some of whom had approached Ned's from time to time, gave similar discounts to buyers who
purchased in large quantity, provided storage, and had good credit. After
the case had twice reached the Supreme Court on appeal, the Commission
finally, eighteen years after the complaint had issued, lost its fight to force
Standard to stop discriminating in favor of Ned's. The Court held that
Standard could meet competition, even if it discriminated in so doing.[52]

The Supreme Court's resolution of the "Detroit case" has met with a varying reception. Economists and lawyers who believe in what they call "hard"
competition have applauded the decision. Discrimination of the "Detroit"
type, they urge, breaks down what might otherwise be a monopolistic combination of dealers, jobbers, and refiners. The beneficiaries of the discrimination, by passing along their savings to motorists, undermine the price structure and, in the long run are responsible for making gasoline available at
minimum cost.

On the other hand, it has been argued that, by freeing the large supplier
to make discriminatory cuts to retain business, the "Detroit case" makes it
more difficult for a small refiner to break into hostile territory. Though he
may be selling at a lower, nondiscriminatory price, he knows that a giant
competitor can cut prices selectively to match him. Small refiners in such
circumstances may hesitate to bid for Standard's (or any large supplier's)
customers, and may be coerced into price followership.

The majors and the organized jobbers oppose any amendment to the
Robinson-Patman Act that would make it more difficult for a supplier to
justify a discriminatory price by pleading that he was meeting competition.
They are of the opinion that price cutters would flourish if the ability of the
large suppliers to meet local competition were restrained. For instance, the
sales vice president of Standard Oil Co. (Indiana) testified:

[52] *FTC* v. *Standard Oil Co.*, 355 U.S. 396 (1958).

. . . if we, as a supplier, can't help a dealer when his competit[or] across the street cuts prices, our dealer will be forced out of business. In such a case our dealer would lose. We would lose, too. Only the price cutter would gain.[53]

On balance it would seem that the market would be more flexible if large retailers could more easily qualify for a jobbers' discount, and if large suppliers had to make more general price cuts instead of selective discriminations. Imperfections in the market resulting from the tying of retail dealers to major suppliers should also be overcome, as far as possible. In price war territory, the oil companies have often reduced tank wagon prices or given rebates to their dealers. But they have not reduced the price to dealers who, in their judgment, do not suffer from price competition. Because the gasoline market is on wheels, some nonfavored dealers lose customers. An FTC examiner held that Pure Oil Co. violated the Robinson-Patman Act by granting special discounts to its retail dealers in Birmingham to enable them to meet price cutting dealer competition, while withholding discounts from other dealers.[54]

The suppliers fear that if the FTC supports the examiner's decision, it may thereforth prove impossible to cut the tank wagon price to protect dealers in a price war. Yet, if none of them can cut, either price wars will be short lived because dealers will not be able to get cheap gasoline, or nondiscriminatory, low-price suppliers will take over a larger share of the business. The latter consequence is certainly economically unobjectionable.

Price Collusion

⌞Is there collusion in setting tank wagon prices? It is not uncommon after price wars have continued for what they regard as an unconscionable time, for suppliers, to reach an informal agreement to bring them to an end.[55] The Antitrust Division regards such agreements as collusion.⌟After South Bend dealers had publicly stated that they had received identical instructions to raise prices on the same day from salesmen of several major suppliers the Antitrust Division obtained indictments.[56] Yet, oil men being talkative and highly gregarious, it would be absurd to imagine that they do not discuss

[53] *To Amend Section 2 of the Clayton Act, Hearings on S. 11,* Eighty-fifth Cong., 1st Sess., Senate Committee on the Judiciary (1957), p. 201.
[54] *Pure Oil Co.,* FTC Release 6640, February 20, 1959.
[55] At the tail end of a price war the writer was in the office of a distributor who, to prove this very point, called up representatives of several major oil companies (not simply his own supplier) to confirm the date on which the tank wagon price was scheduled to go up.
[56] *U.S. v. Standard Oil Co., et al.,* Criminal Action No. 2197, October 7, 1958, U.S. Dist. Ct., Northern Dist. of Indiana.

pricing problems whenever they meet. The difference between price leadership (such as that resulting in the May, 1955 increases in Michigan discussed earlier) and collusion, as in South Bend, is merely one of certainty of agreement. In both cases, the leading marketers thought it was time for an increase. The South Bend indictment should serve to warn them that they are not permitted to achieve absolute certainty in moving prices up. This is all to the good; otherwise the next step might be an agreement not to permit prices to be depressed.

In 1958 the Antitrust Division charged that 14 major oil companies had conspired in 1956 and 1957 to raise the price of crude oil.[57] In late 1956 most large oil producers believed, as always, and some of them publicly stated that the price of crude was too low. The Suez crisis provided a favorable atmosphere for taking action. Since at this time the Texas Railroad Commission was enforcing shut-downs of fifteen days a month (as compared with seven in 1952) the price increase was clearly not necessary to get more oil produced. It may have been required, however, to yield what the integrated oil companies regarded as a reasonable profit. In February 1960, the indictment was dismissed. The government failed to prove formal conspiracy among the defendants; telephone conversations and meetings of officials of top companies with their oil-purchasing subsidiaries was not considered sufficient to show illegal collusion—even though price increases were decided upon.

Even if the case had been successfully prosecuted, it is unlikely that crude prices would have been much affected. Unless horizontal dissolution is enforced, the big companies will continue to set the pace in upward movements of price. A return to the "oil exchange" system, with the independent pipelines and refiners purchasing their crude on a daily basis at spot prices, might eliminate the near-collusion that stems from the posted price system. But supply is, in the last analysis, limited by prorationing, not by collusion.

Gasoline Retailing

There are two principal policy issues other than price discrimination, in gasoline retailing. Gasoline retailers' associations have insisted that, because major suppliers have built too many gasoline stations, it is impossible for operators to make a profit. The number of gasoline stations has, as a matter of fact, remained almost unchanged at 185 thousand in recent years, increasing less than 2 per cent from 1950 to 1958. Sales per station rose 40 per cent

---

[57] *U.S.* v. *Arkansas Fuel Oil Corp., et al.,* Criminal Action No. 3450, May 29, 1958, U.S. Dist. Ct. for Eastern Dist. of Virginia.

in the same period.[58] There has been a high rate of turnover among station operators leasing from major oil companies. Approximately 20 per cent go out of business each year for reasons other than illness, retirement, death, or transfer to another station. The high failure rate may well be attributable to mistakes by majors in locating new stations, as well as poor business judgment of the operators. Until more data are available on the cause of failure and potential of the unprofitable stations, it is impossible to determine whether there are too many stations.[59] It is safe to say, however, that vertical integration inevitably stimulates station building, because when a major owns a station, it is assured of an outlet for its branded gasoline at a protected price.

Another retailing policy problem centers on gasoline price wars. Dealers' associations have inspired federal and state investigations of price wars almost continuously since the end of World War II. Operators have trooped to the witness stand to complain of losses suffered in price wars. They have tried to prevent price cutters from advertising lower prices by obtaining state or local legislation forbidding "circus signs." Several states have passed legislation providing that gasoline may not be sold below cost.

A Michigan statute, for instance, makes it unlawful to sell petroleum products at less than cost, cost being determined by a survey carried out by the dealers themselves.[60] To the extent that price wars are touched off by dealers, the statutes forbidding sales below cost may sometimes be effective. Partly under pressure from dealers, suppliers have directly fixed retail prices through taking advantage of state resale-price-maintenance legislation. It is more difficult for a dealer to breach the price in a contract with his supplier than to sell below an association-determined "cost." In Massachusetts, New Jersey, Connecticut, and North Carolina, where fair trade laws have not been held unconstitutional, suppliers have tried to use them to stabilize prices. Success has been spotty.[61]

The FTC has contributed to mitigating price wars by issuing complaints against companies that have given concessions to dealers in price war areas.[62] It has attacked a consignment plan by which it was alleged, Atlantic

[58] National Petroleum News, *Factbook 1958–1959* (1958), p. 182.
[59] API Study Shows 26 per cent Turnover at Lessee Stations," *The Gasoline Retailer*, May 6, 1959, p. 1.
[60] *Gasoline Price Investigation*, pp. 257–8.
[61] See *The Gasoline Retailer*, November 15, 1958, p. 1, March 4, 1959, p. 1, and April 1, 1959, p. 1. After fair trade was initiated in New Jersey in 1956, the number of independent stations increased from 165 to 600 by 1959. "Does Fair Trade Have A Future?" a speech by J. G. Jordan, Marketing Vice-President, Shell Oil Co., September 16, 1959, p. 15.
[62] *Pure Oil Co.*, Examiner's Opinion, 6640, February 20, 1959; *Sun Oil Co.*, Docket 6641, Opinion, January 5, 1959.

Refining forced down retail prices of dealers in price-war areas.[63] The FTC is also attempting to make the major oil companies preserve a 2 cent differential between the prices charged at retail for their branded gasoline and the prevailing unbranded gasoline price.[64]

It seems unlikely that retail prices and dealer margins can be protected forever against the superior efficiency of large-volume private brand marketers. In the short run, however, the result of common resort to resale price maintenance by dominant suppliers has been to raise prices to motorists by substantial amounts in New Jersey and Connecticut. The private brand marketers have moved up to maintain the customary differential.

Vertical Integration

According to one view, "the essential instrument of economic power in the oil industry is integration, and particularly the ownership by the major companies of transportation facilities. . . ."[65] It is alleged that vertical integration has permitted the companies to attain their present giant size and corresponding market influence. Only divorcement, by relieving independents at every level from squeezes by the majors, can restore competitive behavior.[66]

Pipelines. Control of crude oil pipelines by the Standard Oil trust was a key link in the power it exercised over both independent refiners and producers. Profits from pipeline operations—which measure the exploitation of these nonintegrated segments of the industry—were responsible for 41.6 per cent of the earnings of the Standard Oil combination, 1891–1911.[67] While Standard Oil no longer monopolizes pipeline facilities, 71 per cent of the crude oil and 96 per cent of the products pipeline mileage is owned by twenty large integrated companies.[68] Independent producers must sell their crude to these pipelines before shipment, and independent refiners with no other source of supply must purchase crude from pipelines owned by their competitors.

Legislative and litigative action has attempted, though with lethargy, to moderate the power of the pipeline owners. It was not until 1922 that the

[63] Complaint 7471, April 24, 1959.
[64] *The Gasoline Retailer,* May 6, 1959, p. 19.
[65] Rostow, *op.cit.,* p. 117.
[66] *Ibid.,* p. 123.
[67] Hidy and Hidy, *op.cit.,* p. 629.
[68] Antitrust Subcommittee of House Committee on the Judiciary, *Consent Decree Program of the Department of Justice* (1959), p. 127 (henceforth cited, *Consent Decree Program*).

ICC regulated tender requirements, using authority conveyed to it by the Hepburn Act of 1906 to permit independents to ship smaller quantities of crude. Not till 1934 did it initiate a rate investigation. In 1941, the Department of Justice, after attacking the majors' ownership of pipelines [69] as part of a broad (Mother Hubbard) antitrust suit against the oil industry, and questioning, under the Elkins Act, their receipt of allegedly illegal rebates in the form of dividends, entered into a consent decree that still governs pipeline activities. The decree provides that the lines can pay out as dividends no more than 7 per cent on the ICC valuation of their property.[70] In ordering a reduction in pipeline rates in 1940, the ICC found that 8 per cent on carrier investment was a reasonable return.[71] Apparently stirred by charges in a Congressional investigation that the pipelines had been paying excessive dividends, the Antitrust Division in 1957 filed motions to enforce the consent decree.[72]

Available evidence is far from demonstrating that pipeline rates are unreasonably high. Pipeline operating income ranged between 9.44 per cent and 6.29 per cent on borrowed and invested capital during the years 1945–51.[73] Part of the pipeline capital represented reinvestment of admittedly exorbitant returns in earlier years. A Congressional committee has charged that during 1952–56, the integrated pipeline owners received 30 to 300 per cent on their capital stock investment; but this on a base which includes neither reinvestment earnings nor borrowed funds.[74] Dividends from Arapahoe Pipe Line Co., jointly owned by Sinclair and Pure Oil, amounted to 52.6 per cent on original investment in 1955 and 72.7 per cent in 1957.[75] Most of the funds used in recent years to finance pipelines are borrowed from insurance companies, which permits a high return on the thin equity.

[Do independent refiners suffer disabilities from their failure to control sources of crude? Roughly 75 per cent of U.S. refineries' crude arrives via pipeline.[76] Independent refiners have not complained publicly about their dependence on competitors for their crude supply; [77] they seem, however, to prefer refinery locations like that of Ashland Oil at Catlettsburg or Crown Central at Houston where they will have access to barge or tanker trans-

[69] *U.S.* v. *A.P.I. et al.*, Civil Action No. 8524 (1940).
[70] *U.S.* v. *The Atlantic Refining Co., et al.*, Civil Action No. 14060, Judgment, Par. III.
[71] *Reduced Pipeline Rates and Gathering Charges*, 243 ICC 115 (1940).
[72] *Consent Decree Program*, p. 242.
[73] McLean and Haigh, *op.cit.*, Exhibit VII–8, p. 193.
[74] *Consent Decree Program*, p. 296.
[75] *Ibid.*, p. 190.
[76] *Petroleum Facts and Figures*, 12th ed., 1956, pp. 230–1.
[77] *Petroleum Week*, May 29, 1959, p. 19.

port.[78] It seems probable that the refinery pattern and the location of those independents who have survived has been long ago determined. The success of certain independents in the Northwest, who have access to Canadian oil, or Gulf Coast independents shows only that it is possible for some refiners to prosper without owning pipelines.

From time to time producers have complained that they were being "strangled" by pipelines. For instance, it has been alleged that integrated Pacific Coast producers, refuse in spite of a crude shortage to make the necessary commitments to purchase,[79] which would have permitted the financing of a pipeline from West Texas where many Permian Basin producers were left unconnected. Producers have also been aggrieved because pipelines have refused to accept from certain fields as much crude as the state prorationing commission has allowed to be produced—exercising, in effect, pipeline prorationing. Gulf has been accused of favoring its own wells in such pipeline prorationing.[80] Producers' claims have never been pressed before the ICC nor have they, apparently, been deemed worthy of serious consideration by the Department of Justice.

There are undoubted economies of scale that are realized with larger pipelines.[81] If an independent pipeline could not achieve these savings because the large refiners would not assure it the outlet for crude now provided by the vertically integrated operation, the community might be faced with higher transportation costs—were divorcement required. On the other hand, the refiners need the pipelines; they would scarcely build duplicating lines simply because they were forced to dispose of control of the existing ones. And the interconnections now available would permit an independent pipeline management to avail itself of more refinery outlets than are used now when each line serves only a select few.

Marketing Facilities. Independent retail and wholesale marketers allege that the majors while making money on crude production have deliberately been "taking a loss" on marketing (and refining). In its West Coast oil suit, the Antitrust Division asked that the large integrated companies be required to sell their wholesale and retail marketing facilities.[82] In 1949, a bill was introduced into Congress which would have made it illegal for a petroleum

---

[78] E. V. Rostow and A. S. Sachs, "Entry into the Oil Refining Business: Vertical Integration Re-examined," 61 *Yale Law Journal* 856, 892 (1952). However, cf. G. S. Wolbert, *American Pipelines* (1952).

[79] Senate Committee on the Judiciary, *Petroleum, The Antitrust Laws, and Government Policies,* S. Rep. No. 1147, Eighty-fifth Cong., 1st Sess. (1957), pp. 26–9, 66–8.

[80] *Third Report of the Attorney General as of September 1, 1958,* pp. 70–1.

[81] McLean and Haigh, *op.cit.,* pp. 183–90.

[82] *U.S. v. Standard Oil Co. of California, et al.,* Civil Action No. 11584–C, May 12, 1950.

marketer to be engaged in any other branch of the petroleum business.[83] Divorcement of marketing was suggested during hearings on the 1955 New Jersey price wars.[84] Jobbers object to competition from their own integrated suppliers.

[Marketing divorcement might lead to certain cost savings. There would be less likelihood that retail stations would be overbuilt, as they now are, in an effort by the majors to increase their share of a limited branded gasoline market. On the other hand, the major suppliers seem to have taken the lead in lowering distribution costs between the refinery and the dealer. They have consolidated and eliminated bulk plants, enlarged the size of transport trucks, and increased marketing efficiency. These developments might be slowed down if their ingenuity were checked at the marketing threshhold.

Conclusion. [Many of the arguments that have been advanced to justify integration rest upon the assumption that optimum size at almost every level of petroleum operations requires large investment. Pipeline costs per barrel-mile-hour shrink with increases in size of the line; refineries of less than 30,000 barrels per day capacity have high unit costs; exploration and production in offshore or foreign areas require ability to spend millions of dollars with little immediate return. Only an integrated company, it is argued, can so limit risk as to permit such heavy investments to be made at minimum cost.

It is also urged that vertical integration has enabled oil companies to offset variability in refining and marketing profits with steady earnings from transportation and production. By assuring them of outlets, vertical integration permits pipelines and refineries to operate at a higher percentage of capacity, and thus assures lower costs and higher profits. For instance, Gulf Oil Corporation in 1928–31 expanded forward via new refineries and acquisition of marketing outlets, because of a pressure of rising production of crude oil.[85] Atlantic Refining built transportation lines for crude oil during the same period because it became convinced it was paying excessive transportation costs to other majors for crude oil shipments.[86] A shortage of crude oil in 1948 helped to convince Sinclair that it should acquire more producing properties: when the refining margin was depressed, it had difficulty meeting the competition of companies with adequate supplies of crude.[87]

More generally, it is argued that vertical integration can not, by itself, call

[83] S. 572, Eighty-first Cong., 1st Sess.
[84] Senate Small Business Committee, *op.cit.*, note 36, p. 26.
[85] McLean and Haigh, *op.cit.*, pp. 96–7.
[86] *Ibid.*, pp. 194–7.
[87] *Ibid.*, pp. 382–3.

for action by antitrust authorities, or be of concern to the public. Vertical integration does not increase the percentage of a market controlled by a seller: acquisition of a pipeline does not give a refinery a larger share of the output of refined products. A vertically integrated refinery, it is asserted, would not change its pricing policy simply because of its ownership of marketing facilities. If there were monopoly at the refining level, then it would pay to charge a monopolistic price at that level, whether or not the firm were integrated. Divestiture of pipelines by refineries would accomplish nothing, as long as pipelines had monopoly power, because as rational businessmen the integrated firms must in any event have been extracting monopoly profits from the monopolized sector. Divestiture would not change or eliminate this market imperfection.[88]

It is not easy to appraise quantitatively the arguments for integration. Exactly how large does a firm have to be to justify its risking money in research? How large must a research laboratory be to be effective? While there may be a minimum efficient size for a refinery, does efficiency increase with size? While small independents have done little exploring or producing in Iraq, Iran or the Arabian Peninsula, it is not clear whether this is because they cannot finance the job, or because the greater power of the cartel members excluded them. There is much to show that the latter explains their small participation in Iran.

Savings from coordination of operations are even more difficult to measure. Some successful firms have managed to persist on an independent basis, at every level of the industry. Pure production companies such as Superior Oil and Amerada, protected by output limitations have made spectacular earnings year after year. Buckeye Pipeline Co., an independent, has had good earnings from its transportation of petroleum products. Ashland Oil was a highly successful independent refiner-marketer. Independent jobbers and private brand distributors have been able to survive and, according to some industry sources, expand their assets and market shares in recent years.[89]

Nor can we accept without reservations the thesis that vertical integration does not extend economic power from one stratum to another. A vertically integrated firm which faces more intense competition at one level than another may use the leverage available to hamper its nonintegrated competitors. Because of its control of pipelines in Pennsylvania and Ohio the

[88] R. Bork, "Vertical Integration and the Sherman Act: The Legal History of an Economic Misconception," 22 *University of Chicago Law Review* (1954), pp. 157, 194–201.

[89] The number of private brand outlets in the East has doubled in the past eight years. M. J. Rathbone, President of Standard Oil Co. of New Jersey, "The Challenge of Change," speech, September 10, 1958. Mr. Rathbone's company recently bought up Gasetaria, one of the leading independent marketers in Indiana.

Standard Oil Trust was able not merely to charge high rates to independent refiners, but to cut them off completely from their raw material. This forced them to capitulate to the Trust. While more recent moves toward forward or backward integration appear to have been designed more for defense than offense, they show that the businessman—be he producer, refiner, or marketer—regards integration as a method of buttressing his long-run position vis-à-vis powerful, integrated rivals.

Integration, of course, breeds more integration. Fearful of being dependent on a rival's pipeline or service stations, the independent finds security by tying up supply and customers. This in turn, makes it more difficult for the remaining independents.

If there were no crises of supply and markets, a vertically integrated firm might possibly do no more than exploit monopoly power already existing at each horizontal level. Dynamic, largely unpredictable change, however, is the essence of the oil industry and dominates its business policies.

Vertical integration of large firms leads, then, to defensive integration by smaller ones. The nonintegrated independent tends to find himself in greater difficulties in crisis situations. Mergers such as that between Sunray and Mid-Continent Oil Co., which gave a producer-refiner marketing outlets, or Kerr-McGee's absorption of Deep Rock's refinery, or the sale of Globe Refining (a leading independent refinery in Chicago) to Pure Oil were spurred in part by desire for security.

It is unlikely that vertical disintegration can be achieved without special legislation. Only if Congress decides, on other than conventional antitrust grounds, to set a limit on size, would the present pattern alter substantially. The Antitrust Division can chip away at practices such as exclusive dealing that extend vertical integration, but vertical integration by ownership, unless it is an instrument for unfair competition, is not illegal.[90] It has contributed to the vast size of the major oil companies. But size is not itself vulnerable to the antitrust laws; and besides, the giants are so numerous. Public policy would best be served by assuring maximum freedom for independents to enter and maintain themselves at every level of the industry where their efficiency warrants. The key figure is the independent refiner. Antitrust suits and Congressional investigations presently assure him a rough and ready protection against arbitrary limitation of supplies and exclusion from markets. As long as he has access to new oil fields—such as those in

---

[90] The judge hearing the West Coast oil suit (himself an owner of a service station) flatly refused, even before the end of the trial, to order divestment of retail assets by majors. *The Gasoline Retailer,* November 19, 1958, p. 1. The suit was settled by a consent decree, before trial, with the companies promising to avoid price fixing. *The Gasoline Retailer,* July 1, 1959, p. 1.

Canada—and to independent pipelines—like Great Lakes—he will survive —in other words, as long as the industry remains dynamic.

SUGGESTED READINGS

Books and Pamphlets

J. S. Bain, *The Pacific Coast Petroleum Industry*, 3 vols. (Berkeley: University of California Press, 1944–47).

M. W. Ball, *This Fascinating Oil Business* (Indianapolis: Bobbs-Merrill, 1940).

M. G. DeChazeau and A. E. Kahn, *Integration and Competition in the Petroleum Industry* (New Haven, Yale University Press, 1959).

P. H. Giddens, *Standard Oil Co. (Indiana): Oil Pioneer of the Middle West* (New York: Appleton-Century-Crofts, 1955).

J. C. McLean and R. W. Haigh, *The Growth of Integrated Oil Companies* (Boston: School of Business Administration, Harvard University, 1954).

E. V. Rostow, *A National Policy for the Oil Industry* (New Haven: Yale University Press, 1948).

M. W. Watkins, *Oil: Stabilization or Conservation?* (New York: Harper, 1937).

Government Publications

R. Cook, *The Control of the Petroleum Industry by Major Oil Companies*, U.S. Temporary National Economic Committee, Monograph No. 39, Washington, 1941.

W. S. Farish and J. H. Pew, *Review and Criticism on Behalf of Standard Oil Company (New Jersey) and Sun Oil Company of Monograph No. 39 with Rejoinder by Monograph Author*. U.S. Temporary National Economic Committee, Monograph No. 39-A, Washington, 1941.

Federal Trade Commission, Staff Report, *The International Petroleum Cartel*, Washington, 1952.

Articles

J. B. Dirlam and A. E. Kahn, "Leadership and Conflict in the Pricing of Gasoline," *Yale Law Journal*, Vol. 61, June–July 1952.

M. C. Howard, "Interfirm Relations in Oil Products Markets," *Journal of Marketing*, Vol. 20 (1956).

E. P. Learned, "Pricing of Gasoline: A Case Study," *Harvard Business Review*, Vol. 26 (1948).

Chapter 9

ROBERT F. LANZILLOTTI

The Automobile Industry

SECTION I: INTRODUCTION

Over the past half-century the automobile industry has introduced much more than a new form of transportation into American life—it has accounted for new work and living habits, new standards of comfort, style, and affluence, and vastly altered social attitudes and problems.* The automobile has influenced the lives of people and the organization of society to perhaps a greater extent than any other mechanical invention of the past century. Its total influence may yet rival that of the steam engine. Truly, the history, organization, and practices of the automobile industry cover the epic of the twentieth century's favorite child.

The pivotal position of the industry in the U.S. economy is underscored by such considerations as the following: One out of every seven workers in this country is said to be dependent directly or indirectly on the automobile industry;[1] the industry consumes about one-fifth of the nation's steel production, one out of every fourteen tons of copper, more than two out of every five tons of lead, more than one out of every four tons of zinc, one pound in seven of nickel, one-half the reclaimed rubber, almost three-fourths of the upholstery leather, and substantial proportions of total national output of glass, machine tools, general industrial equipment, and forgings.

In a very real sense the automobile is the prototype of the modern "durable" product. Regular model changes make it obsolete; it passes down the ladder of affluence in a "used" market; "gadgets" and decorative chrome

---

* Parts of this chapter are taken from Donald A. Moore's chapter on "The Automobile Industry" which appeared in a previous edition of this book. Both the author and editor are grateful to Professor Moore for this contribution.

[1] *Automobile Facts and Figures,* Automobile Manufacturers Association, 38th ed., 1958, p. 65.

311

relieve its standard design; it is purchased on installments, and its newness, novelty, and gadgetry distinguish the social status of its owner. In the words of a contemporary biographer, historian, and critic:

And to be on wheels was the desire of every American. The privilege of mobility was the criterion of happiness, the evidence of personal success. Was it not, therefore, more important than anything else? The conviction that it was had created the nation's most brutalizing industry, its most rebellious labor union, its largest corporation, its second largest fortune. And it had, besides, completely transformed the society and civilization in which Americans lived.[2]

History

As this volume makes abundantly clear, the development of many American industries has followed a well-worn path from many small, independent units to a few large producers, but the automobile industry is almost unique in the degree of concentration which has been reached. With the possible exception of the aluminum industry, the production of automobiles represents the Nation's most highly concentrated industry. Consider the bare statistics: (a) In the early 1900's, 181 companies manufactured and sold automobiles. (b) By 1927, 137 of these had retired from the industry. (c) Since 1939 only two new companies have ventured into the industry (both of which have since disappeared). (d) Today only five companies remain in business, of which the three largest account for over 90 per cent of total output. These facts pose some disturbing questions regarding the future structure and competitive behavior of the industry.

Broadly speaking, the history of the industry can be divided into several distinct stages with respect to growth patterns, market structure, and competitive behavior. For our purposes, the following stages have significance: the first, the period up to about 1910, was one of pioneering, experimentation, and early growth, during which numerous firms entered and withdrew, with no single firm able to sustain a position of prominence; the second, 1911 through the end of World War I, was the period of the development of a mass market, with Ford reaching prominence, but with the market structure remaining fluid as both new entrants and failures remained high; the third, the twenties and thirties, during which the number of producers declined sharply, and the industry's concentrated structure took its basic form; and the fourth, the post-World War II period, in which industry concentration reached new heights, and General Motors attained an increasingly dominant position.

[2] Lloyd Morris, *Not So Long Ago*, New York: Random House, 1949, p. 401.

Experimentation and Early Growth

It cannot be said that any one man invented the automobile. The idea is an old one, but more than a century of experimentation with power vehicles preceded commercial success. Early efforts began in Europe with steam vehicles, which provided regular "bus" service in Great Britain as far back as 1831. These did not prove to be popular, however, which was no doubt due in part to new restrictive legislation requiring that there be three operators and a man proceeding on foot with a red flag.[3] Probably the first gasoline-driven automobile was built by Siegfried Marcus in Vienna in 1865—a vehicle powered by a two-cycle hydrocarbon engine. Other vehicles developed around this period included: in France, Lenior's vehicle powered by a lighting-gas internal combustion engine (1860), and in Germany, Otto's model driven by a hydrocarbon four-cycle engine. Thus, by 1885, gasoline automobiles were being produced commercially in Europe, and, by 1893, were being exported to the United States.

In the United States, at about this time (1893), Charles and Frank Duryea successfully operated a buggy-like gasoline vehicle which is generally regarded as the first built in this country. There was some experimentation in the U.S. with steam vehicles, notably by Henry Ford and Ransom Olds, and some with electric, but most of the pioneers were attracted to the Otto four-cycle gasoline engine. Thomas Edison, the first to encourage Ford in his experiments, recommended gasoline power.

The early manufacturers not only designed and produced vehicles, but found it necessary both to demonstrate their sturdiness and utility and to continue the "good road movement" begun in the 1890's by the bicycle fans. Some interest in autos was generated by the moneyed aristocracy of the period, who imported and raced the European models at Newport, R.I., but these were expensive, dashing, and generally regarded as useless playthings —thus ideal for the socially ambitious. A few American racers appeared, including Ford's famous "999" driven by the legendary Barney Oldfield. People eagerly read about the races and new models and would gather anywhere to witness the passage of one of the stinking, noisy things; still only a few brave (and relatively wealthy) souls would buy them. Country physicians were among the first to find the vehicles useful in their work, but for most people they were too unreliable and the roads too poor. Early versions of modern-day endurance runs served to help break through consumer resistance: Winton attracted four buyers of his vehicle in 1897 fol-

[3] C. F. Kettering and Allen Orth, *The New Necessity,* Baltimore: Williams and Wilkinson, 1932, p. 4.

lowing a drive from Cleveland to New York (taking ten days), but the most impressive run of the era was made in 1900 by test driver Roy D. Chapin, who drove an Olds Runabout from Detroit to the nation's first automobile show in New York. The trip required seven and one-half days, many repairs, and the use of the Erie Canal tow-path. Nevertheless, it created such a sensation at the show that a dealer agreed to take 1,000 of them, and by 1903 25 per cent of the cars made in America were Oldsmobiles.[4]

Market Expansion and Mushrooming Entry

Between 1900 and 1910, demand expanded rapidly and total sales increased from 4,000 to 187,000. The competition to produce vehicles for this new market was vigorous as the number of new companies mushroomed. Between 1902 and 1909 the number of firms increased from twelve to 69 (Table 1).[5] This growth in the number of firms was achieved despite a relatively high rate of failures, as shown in the table. In 1910, the rate of failure reached 26 per cent, which was considerably higher than the rate that prevailed following the 1920 crisis and recession. There are several good reasons to explain this fluid structure. The steady increase in the number of firms reflected the relatively easy entry conditions in the early days—the nature of automobile manufacturing required only limited capital requirements to begin operations.[6] Manufacturing amounted to designing and assembling, with orders for engines, bodies, and other members and parts farmed out to many machine shops and carriage works then in existence. It was not unusual for an enthusiastic promoter to draw up an idea for an automobile, secure parts on 30- to 90-day terms, and contract with prospective customers to take the finished autos for cash. Assembly operations were often carried out in rented facilities, which further reduced the capital requirements.

Despite the rather large number of firms and ease of entry, the products offered were anything but standardized. Competition, from the beginning, ran partly in terms of product variation and vigorous selling effort. Price was an important selling point as soon as automobiles began to be advertised as

[4] See M. M. Musselman, *Get A Horse*, New York: Lippincott, 1950, Chaps. 3 and 5.

[5] Estimates of the number of early automobile manufacturing firms run to more than 1,000, but many of these were only "paper" firms, or companies that produced only one or two automobiles, or were essentially stock promotion schemes. The most reliable estimates are those of Epstein, who lists a total of 181 firms producing cars at some time between 1903 and 1926. See R. M. Cleveland and S. T. Williamson, *The Road is Yours*, New York: Greystone, 1951, pp. 270–91, and Ralph C. Epstein, *The Automobile Industry*, Chicago: Shaw, 1928, p. 164.

[6] The Ford Motor Company experience is typical: It was incorporated in 1903 with twelve people subscribing to $100,000 in stock, of which $51,000 was paid for with patents, machinery, and supplies. It is said that only $28,000 was actually paid in cash.

TABLE 1

Early Structure of the Automobile Industry

Year	No. of Entrants	No. of Exits	No. of Firms Remaining	Failures as % of Total
1902	—	—	12	—
1903	13	1	24	4
1904	12	1	35	3
1905	5	2	38	5
1906	6	1	43	2
1907	1	0	44	0
1908	10	2	52	4
1909	18	1	69	1
1910	1	18	52	26
1911	3	2	53	4
1912	12	8	57	12
1913	20	7	70	10
1914	8	7	71	9
1915	10	6	75	7
1916	6	7	74	9
1917	8	6	76	7
1918	1	6	71	7
1919	10	4	77	5
1920	12	5	84	6
1921	5	1	88	1
1922	4	9	83	10

Source: Ralph Epstein, *op.cit.*, pp. 176–7.

"pleasure cars" for the moderately well-to-do, but the models were individually priced for different purses and tastes. It was at this stage of development that a large number of well-financed dealers across the country was recognized as essential for survival—which helps explain both the importance of dealers in the present structure of the industry and many of the competitive practices now in use.

The increased failures around 1910 reflected another development—the changing conditions of auto manufacture. The trend to higher-powered engines, from the single- and two-cylinder to the four-cylinder, required redesigning the axles, transmission, and other parts, as well as the motor. The change to higher power also involved heavy expenses in order to buy new dies, jigs, and machinery. The resistance by many firms to undertaking the extensive changes involved in higher-powered motors resulted in loss of reputation and sales. The picture was further complicated by the uncertainty in the industry as to the kind of vehicle to produce and the best price class in which to place cars.

Early Attempt at Monopoly

An attempt at monopoly control of the industry was made in 1903, reflecting the general tone and industrial trend of the period. The effort centered around the formation of the Association of Licensed Automobile Manufacturers (ALAM) with 30 members by the Electric Vehicle Company. The Association's strength rested largely in the George Selden patent for the production and sale of the automobile granted in 1895. Members were required to pay royalties of 5 per cent (later reduced to 1.25 and 0.8 per cent) to the ALAM. Ford, refused admission to ALAM on the grounds that he was a "fly-by-night" operator, was promptly sued by the Association as an unlicensed operator. Ford joined a smaller association of eighteen producers (The American Motor Car Manufacturers' Association) whose function was to fight the ALAM. In 1909, when a court ruled against Ford in the patent suit, his association deserted him, and Ford was left alone to carry on the fight. In January 1911, however, a U.S. Circuit Court of appeals reversed the lower court's decision,[7] and as a result the ALAM disintegrated.

The ALAM episode left its mark upon the structure of the industry in several ways. First, the notion that patent rights should be allowed to cover such a generic commodity as the automobile became repugnant and, following the demise of ALAM, a new association was formed, Automobile Manufacturers Association, Inc., whose patent pooling practices enjoy the stamp of approval of the Federal Trade Commission.[8] Second, the early engineering activities of the defunct ALAM also resulted in the formation of the Society of Automotive Engineers (SAE), whose achievements in standardizing metals, metal fabrication units, screw and bolt threads, fuels, lubricants, and related items, has materially reduced costs for everyone connected with the industry. A third effect of the ALAM affair was to set Ford upon a maverick course of noncooperative behavior with respect to the rest of the industry. Although he and his engineers were members of the SAE, he spurned the AMA as an outgrowth of the hated patent monopoly. Ford's personality perhaps would have made him quite uncooperative in any case, but, as one historian put it, he "had a mad on," and was beginning to enjoy his public role as the champion of the little man. Ford's uncooperative attitude left its imprint on the industry in several important ways: he did not guard produc-

---

[7] The court held that Selden had used the Brayton two-cycle engine, while all current autos were using variations of the Otto four-cycle engine. Cf. 184 Fed. 893–916.

[8] See FTC, *op.cit.*, p. 62, where an officer of the AMA is quoted, tracing the practice of patent pooling to the lessons of the Selden case.

tion secrets and thus contributed much to the technology of the whole industry. More important was Ford's now famous announcement in 1909 that:

. . . in the future we were going to build only one model, that the model was going to be "Model T," and that the chassis would be exactly the same for all cars, and I remarked:

"Any customer can have a car painted any color that he wants so long as it is black."

I cannot say that anyone agreed with me.[9]

Formation of General Motors

Before turning to the effects of Ford's early pricing policy, one other significant development of this period should be mentioned: the formation of General Motors by William Crapo Durant, a financial genius who had previously reorganized and revived the Buick Motor Company. Durant believed that organization and finance were the prime requisites of a healthy automobile industry. In his opinion, the high mortality rate among auto firms at this time was due to the market's rejection of any one year's model; hence, a shakily financed firm could neither survive such reversal, nor could it survive a depression. A large firm, however, with adequate financial resources and many normally successful makes could, according to Durant, weather the storm and try again. With the objective of creating such a firm, Durant organized General Motors as a New Jersey holding company, which he hoped would eventually control all the principal auto manufacturers, in the manner of the great "trusts" of the period.

By the end of 1909, General Motors controlled more than twenty automobile and accessory companies (including Buick, Cadillac, Oldsmobile, and Oakland) and was bidding for Ford and others. Ford was willing to sell in 1908 for $3,000,000 in cash; and R. E. Olds—then with the Reo Motor Company—also demanded cash, which Durant was unable to raise. The following year, Ford again was willing to sell (this time for $8,000,000), but the terms were still cash. The General Motors Board of Directors approved the purchase, but Durant's Wall Street backers thought the Ford enterprise was not worth so big a cash risk. Thus, once again, Ford's intransigence had a decisive effect on the industry's structure.[10]

[9] Henry Ford, *My Life and Work*, New York: Doubleday-Page, 1923, p. 72.
[10] It has been observed that Ford and James Couzens (who together owned 68.5 per cent of Ford stock) still did not fully grasp the significance of their "Model T." (K. Sward, *The Legend of Henry Ford*, New York: Rinehart, 1948, p. 28.) This would appear to be correct, since the net earnings after taxes in 1911 were $7,579,334, and were to reach a peak of more than $120,000,000 in 1922. (FTC, *op.cit.*, pp. 634 and 645.) It might also be observed that Durant's backers did not fully appreciate the "Model T" either.

The General Motors Company was successful as a producer, but under Durant's leadership it often swallowed more than it could digest. In 1910, an investment banking syndicate came to the company's rescue with a large loan, ousted Durant from the presidency, and assumed control. Thenceforth, the company's production and financial policies were conservative until Durant regained control five years later.

1911–22: The Growth of Ford and General Motors

Producing for a Mass Market. This period witnessed the transformation of America to an "automobile society." The production, engineering, and selling genius of thousands of men contributed to the flow of vehicles into the hands of the people, who clamored for more. The cry "get a horse" was replaced by an occasional "look, Ma, there's a horse." Henry Ford had already turned his sights to what he called "the other 95 per cent of the market"—working men and farmers who could not buy the current models. He felt that the "Model T" was a utility vehicle, and by freezing its design, he could concentrate all his energies on mass production at low cost. Motor and chassis parts were completely interchangeable and remained so for all models from 1909 through 1926. By 1914, after five years of trial and error, the production men at Ford had a moving-belt production line fed by other moving belts with parts that were, in turn, mass produced. Other manufacturers employed the same principles, and the price of many automobiles declined rapidly. Ford's policy of reaching for larger total net profit through smaller margins on increased sales volume is shown in Table 2—the price of the Model "T" was reduced from $950 in 1909 to under $300 in the early twenties with the result that sales jumped from around 12,000 to almost two million or roughly 50 per cent of the market.

Noting Ford's success in reaching "the other 95 per cent" of the market, Durant joined Louis Chevrolet, who developed the small and "low-priced" Chevrolet Baby Grand. In 1915, Durant formed the Chevrolet Motor Company of Delaware, which acquired the stock of all other Chevrolet Motor Companies (including the original Michigan firm organized in 1911). Then Jonah swallowed the whale. Durant traded Chevrolet stock for General Motors stock until he had control of a majority of the outstanding common stock of G.M. When General Motors refused to take in the Chevrolet enterprise, Durant exercised his control and again became president of G.M. It was in this venture that the du Pont family of Delaware gave backing to Durant, and Pierre S. du Pont later became chairman of the board. At this point, the General Motors Corporations of Delaware, a holding company,

TABLE 2
Prices and Sales of the Model "T" Ford, 1909–25

Year	Price of Model T Touring Car	Total Ford Sales	Total Industry Sales	Ford Sales as % of Total
1909	$950	12,292	130,986	9.38
1911	690	40,402	210,000	19.24
1913	550	182,809	485,000	37.69
1915	440	355,276	970,000	36.62
1917	450	802,771	1,874,000	42.85
1919	525	782,783	1,934,000	40.48
1921	355	933,720	1,683,916	55.45
1922	298	1,351,333	2,655,624	50.88
1923	295	1,917,353	4,034,012	47.53
1925	290	1,771,338	4,265,830	41.52

Source: FTC, *op.cit.*, pp. 27, 632, except 1909 and 1922 totals; which are from Lawrence H. Seltzer, *A Financial History of the Automobile Industry*, Boston: Houghton Mifflin, 1928, pp. 75, 84.

was formed which dissolved many of the subsidiaries, making them divisions of an operating company. With this reorganization there was thus created what is essentially the present organization of G.M.

In 1917 and 1918, the du Pont Company invested $50,000 in General Motors, which provided some lucrative captive markets for du Pont products, and, years later, ample grounds for an antitrust suit. An important condition of the investment was that the du Pont Company would assume responsibility for the financial policies of G.M. and that Durant would assume responsibility for operations.[11]

Durant was not content with the marriage of Ford's idea (the mass-produced cheap car) and his own idea (diversification and financial backing); he wanted more. While Ford was integrating his operation by moving into the production of parts and basic materials, Durant sought to match this integration by *purchasing* parts-producing firms. In some instances he also secured key personnel by purchasing their firms—Alfred P. Sloan came with Hyatt Roller Bearing and Charles F. Kettering came with Delco. However, other acquisitions were markedly unsuccessful, and all of them required funds. In 1920 General Motors was caught with large inventories and short cash in declining markets for its many products. The firm was in trouble financially, and Durant personally attempted to support the price

[11] See *Report of the Federal Trade Commission on du Pont Investments*, February 1, 1929, pp. 15–23.

of G.M. stock on the market. The du Ponts, with the aid of the J. P. Morgan & Co. came to G.M.'s rescue, but Durant was forced out of the presidency and into permanent exile.

It was at this point that Pierre S. du Pont became chairman, and under the du Pont influence G.M. continued, although more cautiously, to "broaden the profit base." This policy has taken three forms: (1) the gradual assumption of parts manufacture, (2) the development of foreign markets, and (3) the development and manufacture of products other than motor vehicles. It has culminated in making General Motors the world's largest corporation.

The number of active producers continued to increase during this period, but the rate of failures remained high (Table 1). The level of concentration increased moderately despite this new entry, mainly as a result of Ford's successful price policy and the growth of General Motors.

The Twenties: Rise of the "Big Three"

Ford's relative position in the industry began to decline after 1921 (Table 2) although during most of the period from World War I to the end of the twenties it was the leading producer; more cars were manufactured by Ford than all other companies combined. Ford's product and price policies had paid off handsomely.[12] However, the failure of Ford fully to appreciate the changing nature of consumer demand in the twenties, lead to a weakening in its market position. With the choice between the economical and dependable, but ungainly, Ford and a Chevrolet—which for about $100 more offered not only a more pleasing style, but also greater speed, better transmission, cooling, lubrication, ignition, and springs—the public turned increasingly to the latter. Ford's market share fell from 55 per cent in 1921 to 41 per cent in 1925, and to slightly more than one-third in 1926. Ford resumed its leadership briefly with the changeover to the Model "A" at the end of the twenties. In 1929, Ford and G.M. each held about one-third of the market, and in 1930 Ford's share increased to over 40 per cent; but this proved to be the last year in which Ford was the leading auto producer. G.M. took the lead in 1931 with 43 per cent—a leadership position it has retained ever since.

Chrysler, the third member of the "Big Three," was formed in 1925. Walter P. Chrysler had revitalized the Maxwell Corporation for its banker-owners, who were willing to back an expansion of the company based upon a new design. The first Chrysler car, like the early Oldsmobile, created a sensation

---

[12] See Allan Nevins and Frank E. Hill, *Ford, Expansion and Challenge, 1915–33,* New York: Scribner's, 1957, p. 264.

at the New York Automobile show (or rather, nearby, since it was not admitted to the show). With a "high-compression" engine and four-wheel brakes, it was ahead of the field. Encouraged by this consumer response, Chrysler in 1928 acquired the estate of the Dodge Brothers from the investment banking firm Dillon Read & Company, which had outbid General Motors for the property two years earlier. The Chrysler line was completed in the same year with the introduction of the Plymouth and De Soto cars. Chrysler soon developed into a strong competitor, and the contest between what had become the "Big Three" worked hardship on the other producers in the industry. As in the case of the change to the Model "A" in 1928, Ford, again belatedly, abandoned the "A" for his "V-8" in 1932. By 1937, Chrysler had taken second place in the industry from Ford.

The Disappearance of the Independents and the Closure of Entry

Meanwhile, the number of firms in the industry declined sharply—partly because of combinations, but mainly because of failures. The attrition during the depressed thirties was only slightly greater than in the booming twenties. In any case, it seemed irreversible and left only a handful of firms in its wake. Of the thirty-eight companies which since 1895 had entered the competitive race, only six survived and of these, Willys Motors manufactures only jeeps, small utility vehicles, and station wagons, but no passenger cars. The defunct companies apparently failed because they were unable to make a dent in the market shares of the "Big Three." The most important single cause of failure can be attributed to the lack of capital. Evidently, the ubiquitous incursions by the "Big Three," with lines covering every price class, proved too much for the smaller producers with limited markets. The era of rapid market growth had come to an end and, in a depression-ridden economy, a product without an established reputation found the going extremely rough. Also, by 1940, the public was sufficiently conscious of trade-in values on different makes so that the industry was virtually closed to newcomers.

The depression decade gave rise to a new kind of rivalry among the few surviving producers. There were some price reductions,[13] but competition was confined mainly to other channels. The race for market share through model changes was intensified, and annual changes became the policy (with major changes every two or three years). In addition, great pressure was

---

[13] Ford's intransigence on prices persisted into the thirties. As an official of General Motors and the AMA pointed out in 1932, ". . . Mr. Ford, who won't play, is pretty much the price setter in this industry. I'll bet if Mr. Ford's cars were $50 higher, ours would be $50 higher. We care about Ford. We have been struggling with him for years." FTC, *op.cit.*, p. 33.

placed on cost reductions and the speed of the production line was considerably stepped up. Wages were cut, workers downgraded, and older men replaced. With long shutdowns for model changes, automobile workers learned the meaning of seasonal unemployment. These kinds of pressures on the labor force—while well known in the depression economy—were, according to the Henderson Report,[14] especially widespread in the automobile industry.

SECTION II: MARKET STRUCTURE AND PRICE POLICY

Survival of the Few

The growth of the automobile industry has been characterized by the concentration of production in progressively fewer hands, so that today there are only five domestic producers, the largest three of which account for 90 per cent of total industry output. (See Table 3.) Moreover, since 1931, when it gained the position as leading producer, General Motors usually has accounted for over 40 per cent of automobile registrations, and since

TABLE 3

Passenger Car Market Shares, by Company, Selected Years, 1950–59
(New Car Registrations as Percentage of Industry Total)

Company	1950	1952	1954	1956	1958	1959 [a]	Average (median) Percentage, 1946–59
G.M.	45.4	41.7	50.7	50.8	46.4	46.0	45.0
Ford	24.0	22.8	30.8	28.4	26.4	27.0	26.0
Chrysler	17.6	21.3	12.9	15.5	13.9	12.3	19.0
American Motors	4.9	5.3	2.1	1.9	4.3	5.5	4.8
Studebaker-Packard	5.4	5.4	2.4	1.8	1.1	2.0	4.5
Kaiser-Willys	2.3	2.7	.5	—	—	—	—
Foreign Makes	.4	.8	.5	1.6	7.9	7.2	.7 [b]

[a] 1959 percentages estimated by author.
[b] Based on years 1949–59 only.

Sources: Automotive News, 1958 Almanac Issue, p. 55; and 1959 Almanac Issue, p. 46; and Hearings before the Subcommittee on Antitrust and Monopoly of the Senate Judiciary Committee, Eighty-fifth Cong., 2nd Sess., *Administered Prices,* Pt. 6, "Automobiles," p. 2405. Hereinafter *Administered Prices* (Hearings).

[14] *Preliminary Report on Study of Regularization of Employment and Improvement of Labor Conditions in the Automobile Industry,* NRA, January 1935.

1950 its share has been from 45 to 50 per cent of total registrations, *including* all foreign makes. There has not been a successful new entry into the U.S. industry since the formation of the Chrysler Corporation after World War I.

For a considerable time prior to World War II the independents shared about 10 per cent of the market, and in the immediate post-World War II period their total share reached about 22 per cent of the market. That the independents' temporary resurgence was the result of the temporary shortage of new and used cars is all too clear today. The fifties saw the gradual disappearance of several of the independents and mergers among the others. Kaiser attempted to bolster its rapidly deteriorating position by the acquisition of Willys, but soon only the "Jeep" remained available; and in 1949 production of Kaiser passenger cars was discontinued. In 1954, Studebaker and Parkard merged, and Hudson joined with Nash to form American Motors—both mergers being approved by the Department of Justice and Federal Trade Commission on the premise that the new firms possibly would have a better chance of survival. It is also noteworthy that while American and Studebaker-Packard's market position appears stronger as of late 1959, the *gap* in size of firm and market share between the independents and the "Big Three" has remained persistently enormous (Table 3).

How can the rigidity of the automobile industry's structure, the increasing prominence of G.M., and the closure of entry into this industry be explained? Do the changes in the structural and operational aspects of the industry during the last three decades explain the inability of new firms to effect entry and of the remaining independents to make serious inroads on the "90 per cent" market of the "Big Three"? What reasons can be given for the failure of the relatively high profitability of the auto manufacturers to perform its traditional function of attracting new outside resources to this industry? In essence, what are the conditions for entry and survival in this industry, and to what extent are "natural"—i.e., economies of scale—as against "artificial" barriers responsible for the high degree of concentration that persists? [15] The principal barriers to entry and conditions for survival are: (1) size of operations necessary to realize the economies inherent in the mass production of cars; (2) large capital required for an optimum-sized operation; (3) the high degree of differentiation among the products of established sellers (which generally favors G.M. products over all others

[15] See Harold G. Vatter, "The Closure of Entry in the American Automobile Industry," *Oxford Economic Papers*, October 1952, pp. 213–34, and *Administered Prices: Automobiles*, Report of the Subcommittee on Antitrust and Monopoly of the Committee on the Judiciary, Eighty-fifth Cong., 2nd Sess., Washington, November 1, 1958 (hereinafter *Administered Prices: Automobiles*).

and "Big Three" products over the remainder); (4) need for a diverse product line covering a considerable range of prices; (5) the nature of resale value determination on used cars; and (6) the impact of government contracts and preferential treatment afforded established firms by suppliers of some basic materials.

Scale Economies and Optimum Plant Size

Economies of scale constitute a very important barrier to entry in automobile manufacture. It should be stressed that our interest here concerns "economic efficiency"; that is, ability of a firm to make the most economical use of resources and produce at the lowest possible unit cost. This is different, of course, from "business efficiency," or the ability of a firm to realize a high average rate of profits. A firm may be an efficient producer in both senses, but the former concept is the relevant one for economic analysis. Essentially, therefore, we wish to know how large an automobile manufacturing plant must be in order to realize optimum efficiency. For this purpose the appropriate unit for study is the plant, or integrated plant complex, i.e., "a related complex of facilities for manufacturing components [principally engines and bodies] normally integrated by the assembler and then assembling them." [16]

Some degree of integration in automobile production has proved strategically advantageous and has served also to broaden the profit base. In the interest of providing some immunity from total interruption in the supply of any one component or part, producers have developed what may be best described as "tapered integration," as contrasted with *complete* integration. Tapering means that producers will attempt to keep their parts factories operating at predetermined output rates, filling in additional supplies through "contract" suppliers. The automobile companies usually maintain at least two sources of supply for essential parts, and also reserve "shop rights" to manufacture given parts themselves in case a strike ties up the supplier.[17] This means that the parts suppliers are continuously placed in a very precarious position. Orders from the auto producers fluctuate with anticipated auto sales, to say nothing of some notorious "squeezes" that have been applied in the past by automobile companies. Moreover, there is a rather clear trend toward further integration in the automobile industry today.

---

[16] Joe S. Bain, *Barriers to Competition,* Cambridge: Harvard University Press, 1956, pp. 244–5.
[17] Simon N. Whitney, *Antitrust Policies: American Experience in Twenty Industries,* New York: Twentieth Century Fund, 1958, p. 497.

Whitney estimates that the percentage share of dollar sales of producers originating in outside purchases has been declining secularly.[18]

How important are economies of scale in automobile production under present technology? According to a recent study by Bain, the minimum size of auto plant—i.e., an integrated plant complex as defined above—necessary to realize lowest per unit costs would be 300,000 passenger cars per year, with some probably additional increase in efficiency up to 600,000 units. A plant complex of this size represents from five per cent to ten per cent of national output, assuming an industry total of 6,000,000 units. The economies of scale arise from greater efficiency in the production of major components, especially engines and bodies.[19] Scale economies are relatively unimportant in assembly operations; 60,000 to 180,000 units per year are considered to be an optimal size for assembly alone.

Similar estimates of optimum plant size were given recently by Mr. George Romney, President of American Motors:

Our studies based on our own experience and that of our competitors, is that optimum manufacturing conditions are achieved with a production rate of 62.5 cars per hour per assembly line. To absorb the desired machine-line and press-line rate, two final assembly lines would be required. . . .

A company that can build between 180,000 and 220,000 cars a year on a one-shift basis can make a very good profit and not take a back seat to anyone in the industry in production efficiency. On a two-shift basis, annual production of 360,000 to 440,000 cars will achieve additional small economies, but beyond that volume only theoretical and insignificant reductions in manufacturing costs are possible. It is possible to be one of the best without being the biggest.

. . . [My] point is that when you get up to 180,000 to 200,000 cars a year, the cost reduction flattens out, from a manufacturing cost standpoint, and from 360,000 to 400,000 on up it is a negligible thing.[20]

The Bain-Romney estimates relate to the minimum size necessary to attain optimum production efficiency, but do not indicate whether, once minimal optimum scale is reached, unit costs rise or remain constant. The most we can say about scale economies and diseconomies is that unit costs are fairly constant in the output ranges cited.

On the basis of these estimates, G.M., with an annual production in recent years of around 3,000,000 cars, is five to ten times the size needed for optimum efficiency, while Ford and Chrysler are several times the minimum

---

[18] The strength of the trend is underestimated, as Whitney points out, because the figures used included purchases of basic materials like iron and steel, transportation, and other services—none of which involves the parts industry. *Ibid.*, pp. 498–9.

[19] Bain, *op.cit.*, pp. 245–6, and *Administered Prices: Automobiles*, p. 85.

[20] *Administered Prices* (Hearings), p. 2851.

(Table 4). A comparison of the recent annual outputs of the respective divisions of the five producers with the Bain-Romney optimal range estimates (Table 4) discloses: (a) In G.M., the output of Chevrolet is two to three times the *maximum* of the range; all the other divisions, except Cadillac, fall within the optimal range. (b) In Ford, the Ford division production is more than twice the range *maximum;* Mercury is just above the range *minimum,* while Lincoln is considerably below the *minimum.* (c) In Chrys-

TABLE 4

Comparison of Annual Production Rates of Automobile Manufacturers and Estimated Optimum Plant Scale, by Makes, for Years 1956–58

Company & Model Name	1956–58 Output Range	Relation of Maximum Output to Optimum Scale (300,000–600,000)
G.M.:	2,169,000–3,235,000	
Buick	257,000–572,000	Within range
Cadillac	125,000–155,000	145,000 below minimum
Chevrolet	1,256,000–1,617,000	1,017,000 above maximum
Oldsmobile	311,000–485,000	Within range
Pontiac	219,000–406,000	Within range
Ford:	1,219,000–1,849,000	
Edsel	27,000–55,000	245,000 below minimum
Ford	1,039,000–1,469,000	869,000 above maximum
Lincoln	26,000–50,000	250,000 below minimum
Mercury	128,000–328,000	28,000 above minimum
Chrysler:	581,000–1,222,000	
Chrysler	50,000–121,000	179,000 below minimum
Desoto	37,000–118,000	182,000 below minimum
Dodge	114,000–292,000	8,000 below minimum
Imperial	11,000–38,000	262,000 below minimum
Plymouth	367,000–656,000	56,000 above maximum
American Motors	100,000–217,000	83,000 below minimum
Studebaker-Packard	57,000–105,000	195,000 below maximum

Sources: Production data from *Automotive News,* 1958 Almanac Issue, p. 31, and 1959 Almanac Issue, p. 25; other data computed by author.

ler, only the Plymouth is within the optimal scale, while other models are slightly below to substantially below the optimum. (d) American Motors is below the *minimum,* but probably reached that level in 1959. (e) Studebaker-Packard remains considerably below the *minimum.* Since several makes have production rates considerably below the estimated range for optimum efficiency, it is possible that the minimum estimates may be excessive, or that the range is somewhat wider than indicated.

Production rates for almost all of the individual makes of cars fall within the minimum efficient size for assembly operations—60,000 to 180,000 units. Since there are very important plant economies in both engine and body production, the apparent inefficiency in the production of some makes, e.g., Lincoln, DeSoto, and Chrysler, is offset as an operational matter by the utilization of common components for more than one make.

There is some evidence that extensive integration of parts manufacture— going well beyond the integration of bodies and engines assumed in the scale-economies estimated above—may provide additional absolute cost advantages to the established firms. Ford and G.M. are highly integrated on parts and they (G.M. in particular) also supply various parts to other car manufacturers. Thus, unless a firm can secure parts from independent suppliers it will likely experience increased parts costs. The alternative is integration of parts manufacture, which would mean that the minimum optimal scale would be higher, i.e., closer to the upper limit (10 per cent of the national market).

We may conclude from the foregoing that the *company* size of the "Big Three" automobile manufacturers, and G.M. in particular, are not explained by *plant-complex* efficiency alone. This does not mean that the companies are inefficient, or that they have necessarily run into diseconomies of scale. It does suggest rather that if scale economies justify the size of these producers, there must be other economies arising out of the operation of several plant complexes, due to plant specialization, mass buying, marketing, and advertising. No quantitative information is available on the importance of these types of savings in automobile manufacture, nor is there any evidence regarding the extent to which these economies of company size represent *real* cost-savings in the economic sense, or merely private savings or pecuniary gains (money "transfers" to the "Big Three" from various suppliers). Theoretically, there may be real economies, but these may be offset in part or in full by diseconomies resulting from excessive bureaucracy, inertia, difficulties in working out best scheduling of plants, and related problems.

Capital Requirements

Entry into the automobile industry is further impeded by large capital requirements. In the early days, very slender resources were necessary, which was a stimulus to new entry and at the same time provided much of the early innovation and competition. The original working capital requirements were supplied by firms other than the car manufacturers—i.e., parts suppliers who furnished credit, and dealers who made cash deposits and paid the balance on delivery. As the industry matured, these relationships were upset. Automobile companies which had been merely assemblers of purchased parts began making their own components and parts, and later moved into the credit field to finance the inventories held by dealers and installment buying by consumers. The installment finance capital, while essential to the industry, could well be supplied entirely by independently owned finance companies. There are, however, other factors which require an automobile producer to command sizable resources.

Bain estimates that a firm with a plant complex of efficient scale as previously described would require an initial investment of from 250 to 500 million dollars and might in addition need to invest another 150 million or more in "break-in" losses—all in the face of a substantial risk of ultimate failure.[21] Very similar estimates have been made by Mr. Romney, President of American Motors. According to Romney, a new company breaking into this industry for the first time, with an output of 250,000 cars per year would require 576 million dollars as of 1958, based upon reproduction costs for building, machinery, equipment, and standard tools and dies, plus organization expenses and estimated first-year losses.[22] An estimated additional 326.2 million dollars would be involved in establishing a system of dealers and distributors.[23] However, in the past these requirements have been supplied by the dealers themselves, so they should not appropriately be included in the total.

Just how much does a capital requirement of 576 million deter entry into this industry? The history of the Kaiser Motor Company is illustrative—bearing in mind that it started operating at a most propitious time (when there was a high backlog of demand which could not be satisfied by existing capacity of the established firms). It seems generally agreed that without the financial resources derived from many other Kaiser enterprises, augmented by a timely loan from the Reconstruction Finance Corporation, Kaiser could hardly have attempted entry into this industry. Apparently, the industry has passed the stage when a firm can start out small and grow in the manner of Ford. Kaiser's first two stock issues were successful in raising 53.5 million dollars capital, but this was inadequate to finance the period of losses while market acceptance was developing.[24] In 1950, when survival depended upon the launching of a new model, the old model was

---

[21] *Industrial Organization,* New York: Wiley, 1959, p. 254, and *Barriers to Competition,* p. 129.

[22] *Ibid.,* p. 17.

[23] The amount is distributed as follows: $262,500,000 for 3,500 domestic dealers, $18,750,000 for 350 Canadian dealers, and $45,000,000 for 3,000 export distributors. Cf. Romney testimony, *Administered Prices: Automobiles,* p. 16.

[24] *Fortune,* July 1951, p. 74.

still not selling in sufficient volume to finance the retooling costs. Moreover, the peculiar behavior of the investment banking firm of Otis & Company in 1948, and a refusal by California's Bank of America in 1949, sent Kaiser scurrying to the RFC for funds. This reluctance of bankers and investment houses to participate in the financing of new automobile concerns has been a typical experience of the industry, which means that the required capital must come from other financial intermediaries or from substantial retained earnings by an established concern in some other field. It will be remembered that the early participation of investment bankers in G.M. was obtained at the price of financial control, and that the Chrysler Corporation grew out of the Maxwell and Chalmers Motor Companies which Walter P. Chrysler was reorganizing for investment houses.[25]

Product Differentiation

Automobiles have been characterized by an extremely high degree of product differentiation, which constitutes an important barrier to entry and survival in the industry. The primary sources of product differentiation in autos are (a) physical design and related advertising outlays, (b) manufacturer's reputation among buyers, and (c) sales and service operations through a system of controlled dealers.[26]

(a) *Physical product differences* in body design, general appearance, engines, transmissions, suspension and braking systems, and the like have reached a position of primary importance in this market, and seem to gather increasing momentum over time. Strangely enough, while perceptible physical differences exist among various makes, the product policies of American manufacturers seem generally to be based on what Bain calls "protective imitation" in style, engine design, power, and other features. Similarities usually are more striking than the differences.

Changes in automobile design have become almost inextricably bound with advertising claims, and there is ample reason to assume that the emphasis on physical differences results in large part from the exaggeration of product differences in advertising claims. Along with the annual alteration in models, manufacturers feel obliged to make buyers forcibly aware of the new appearances of the models. Staggering sums are spent on various advertising media in an effort to impress the buyer with the unique appearance and features of what are fundamentally very similar products. A former president of the Bureau of Advertising, American Newspaper Publishers Association, has criticized these uninformative claims as follows:

[25] FTC, *op.cit.*, p. 551.
[26] Cf. Bain, *Barriers to Competition*, Chap. IV.

Last year the ads bristled with coined-name exclusive features. Today the glitter of chrome is equalled only by the glitter of generalities. The claims seem to come off the same copywriter's typewriter.

. . . Do automobile advertisement talk in terms of the prospects of daily needs and problems? With very few notable exceptions, the answer is negative. Apparently, automobile advertising isn't aimed at the consumer. Judging by what one sees and hears, the major objective of automobile advertising is to impress—and, preferably, frighten—one's fellow members at the Detroit Automobile Club.[27]

(b) The typical car buyer is poorly equipped to evaluate the respective properties and exaggerated claims concerning such a complex and expensive product, which forms the basis for a second source of product differentiation —*the tendency for buyers to rely upon the established reputations of manufacturers.* Since the average buyer is not in a position to make a decision on the basis of trial and error purchasing, he will lean toward the makes with long-established reputations, lest he find himself with an automobile orphan a few years hence. Consequently, automobile producers, and the "Big Three" in particular, tend to have a loyal group of buyers who buy on faith in their reputation. The psychology of conspicuous consumption, plus the fact that out of approximately 52 million cars on the road as of July 1, 1959, 25 million are General Motors products, 13 million Ford, and 10 million Chrysler, reinforce the tendency for buyers to go for popular brands. This, of course, helps maintain the market position of the large-volume makes.

(c) A third important source of product differentiation and an essential prerequisite for survival in this industry is a *national system of dependable, adequately-financed, and strategically-located dealers with service facilities.* In promoting sales and providing specialized maintenance and repair services the dealers provide further differentiation of the delivered product. The nature of the differentiation varies from community to community, and the degree of success in differentiation nationally will be a function of the scope and density of dealer representation. On this score, the "Big Three" have a decided advantage over the independents: as of February 1, 1959, G.M. had 20,023 dealers; Ford, 11,156; and Chrysler, 8,495. The number of dealers handling all other makes combined—including foreign cars—was less than 10,000.[28]

The pattern of consumer preferences resulting from these influences

[27] Harold S. Barnes, "Why Doesn't Detroit Bring Out a 1958 Model Marketing Philosophy?" *Advertising Age,* June 23, 1958, pp. 75–6.

[28] Since some of the dealerships involve dual franchises for different brands of a given manufacturer, these figures overstate the total number of individual dealers. If dual franchises are counted as one, the total number of dealers handling all makes, U.S. and foreign, is about 40,000. *Automotive News,* 1958 Almanac Issue, p. 182.

clearly provides each producer a preferred relationship with groups of buyers over time, and gives the "Big Three," G.M. in particular, a position of advantage over the independents. The market strength of the "Big Three" rests on many of the various factors cited earlier, but, as Bain observes,

. . . perhaps more largely on reputation, conspicuous-consumption motives, and superior strength and size of dealer systems than on demonstrable superiority in design or quality of products. Independents have generally encountered difficulties in keeping up with the Big Three in the matter of product design only after their market shares and profits had sunk so low that they had difficulty in financing periodic improvements and design changes in an adequate fashion.[29]

A Diversified Product-Line

Another condition for survival is a well-diversified product line. This was recognized by Durant when he formed General Motors, and by Chrysler in his firm's rise into the class of the "Big Three." To Ford, diversification was less important because of his early success in pioneering mass production. Since 1935, however, the Ford Company has introduced various models to complete its line. Mercury, and Lincoln to a somewhat lesser extent, have been successful, but the Edsel, introduced in 1957 and discontinued in 1959, was a failure. The independents have repeatedly attempted to cover wider segments of the market, with varying degrees of success. Such familiar but now defunct makes as the Terraplane (Hudson), and Lafayette (Nash), and the Rockne (Studebaker) attest to the futile efforts during the thirties to enter the low-price range. The sales volume of these makes was too low to meet the minimum conditions for economies of large-scale production and hence—despite increasing sales—they were discontinued or absorbed into the medium-priced lines. In recent years, American Motors and Studebaker again have made a bid for the low-price market, with stress on economy in operating costs.

The increasing emphasis upon product differentiation and maintenance of diversified lines has been accompanied by a narrowing differential between price classes. The price variety in automobiles in the twenties and thirties was startling compared to the situation today. Currently the "Big Three" have differentiated their products with regard to four rather loosely defined price classes (in terms of 1959 factory-suggested prices): (1) "low"—$2,000–$2,400; (2) "low-to-medium"—$2,500–$3,000; (3) "medium-to-high" —$3,200–$4,000; and (4) "high"—$4,400–$7,500. American Motors and Studebaker-Packard have concentrated more and more on the bottom two

[29] *Industrial Organization,* pp. 226–27.

price classes, while European producers continue to supply small cars in what must be regarded as a distinct fifth class and size—$1,500–$1,850 (1959 prices).[30] The success of the European makes in carving out and maintaining this fifth class seems reasonably certain at this writing, since the "Big Three" 1960 compact cars are priced around $2,000. Whether American Motors and Studebaker-Packard, with their limited lines, can succeed in an industry where product diversity seems so important will in the final analysis depend on their ability to attain sufficient volume, and on a favorable appraisal of their cars by the used car market.

Resale Value of Used Cars

It has often been observed that the market for new cars is supported by the used-car market. Since 60 to 70 per cent of all new car purchases involve trade-ins, the depreciation value of a used car in relation to the price of the new car is a major determinant of demand and a survival condition in the industry. If more rapid depreciation occurs in some makes than in others, brand loyalty—regardless of the impact of product differentiation and personal preferences—will be subjected to a most severe test. Among used cars of roughly comparable quality and age, whose new-car factory-suggested list prices were approximately identical, G.M. cars generally experience the lowest depreciation, with Ford and Chrysler somewhat larger, and the smaller producers taking the largest loss in value. To illustrate, the average retail prices for 1954 and 1955 Chevrolet, Ford, and Plymouth 6-cylinder sedans in various sections of the U.S. as of February 1958, were as follows: [31]

	Chevrolet 210 (6)	Ford Custom-line (6)	Plymouth Savoy (6)
Eastern Region:			
1954 Model	$ 795	$ 680	$ 675
1955 Model	1,035	980	995
Central Region:			
1954 Model	760	645	625
1955 Model	1,010	940	960
Midwest Region:			
1954 Model	830	715	705
1955 Model	1,070	1,030	1,030
Southern Region:			
1954 Model	790	670	645
1955 Model	1,025	965	985

[30] There is an even lower-priced (under $1,500) and smaller-size class—the "minicar" field, which includes the BMW Isetta, Fiat 500, NSU Prinz, Renault, Citroen 2CV, and the very interesting Goggomobil.

[31] From NADA Official Used Car Guide, National Automobile Dealers Used Car Guide Co., Vol. 25, No. 2 (February 1958), as shown in *Administered Prices: Automobiles*, p. 47.

In all eight instances, resale prices for Chevrolets were higher than for the other two makes. (In the higher-priced fields, G.M. cars enjoy a similar advantage.)

The differential between the prices of G.M. cars and the "minor" makes is even more pronounced. For example, the suggested retail list of the 1955 Studebaker 4-door sedan (Champion DeLuxe 6) when new was only $47 *below* the Chevrolet Bel Air 6; but by January 1958, the resale price of the Studebaker was $325 below the used Chevrolet price.

This preferential status in the average resale value of cars works in favor of the three principal producers, and G.M. in particular, in two important ways: (1) a higher trade-in value will tend to be allowed if the car is a G.M. product and (2) G.M. dealers can point out to the prospective buyer that a G.M. car ordinarily will be worth more in the future as a trade-in than competitive brands having approximately the same original price. These considerations provide G.M. and its dealers with a powerful competitive advantage in the market.

Other influences buttressing the advantages of established auto producers have been *government defense contracts and the preferential treatment afforded the Big Three by steel suppliers in times of shortages*. Defense contracts for both research and production provide a number of advantages to contractors, which among other things, (a) make it possible for a firm to keep its plant operating at most efficient (lowest cost) output rates; (b) if expansion of productive facilities is required, incentives are offered that are not normally available in private contracts; (c) marketing costs are reduced because of bulk sales; (d) financial risks are virtually eliminated; and (e) inestimable by-products are realized from research knowledge and patent rights associated with the defense work.[32]

There is reason to believe that as a result of loans and investments in steel companies General Motors and Chrysler have enjoyed preferential positions with respect to the supply of steel in times of shortage. In 1951, G.M. loaned 28 million dollars to Jones & Loughlin and $40 million to Republic Steel, while Chrysler made some investment in Pittsburgh Steel. The arrangement was for the automobile companies to be guaranteed a certain percentage of the increased capacity, under which the steel companies would pay back on a per-ton basis against those loans.[33]

---

[32] From June 1950 through June 1957, G.M. realized 4.5 per cent, Ford, 1.5 per cent, and Chrysler, 1.4 per cent of the net value of military prime contracts—ranking first, twelfth, and thirteenth, respectively, among the largest recipient companies. Moreover, the "Big Three," and especially G.M., have been among the largest beneficiaries of experimental, developmental, and research work—G.M. ranking twenty-fourth, twenty-ninth, and seventeenth in 1955, 1956, and 1957, respectively. Cf., *ibid.*, pp. 37–45.

[33] See *Administered Prices* (Hearings), pp. 2598–9 and 2855–7.

Conclusion on Entry Conditions

In summary, the importance of the economies of scale and the magnitude of capital requirements constitute very substantial barriers to entry, but by themselves would not appear to be sufficient reasons for the high degree of producer concentration in the industry. At present levels of demand, i.e., six to seven million cars annually, at least ten firms of efficient size are economically feasible. The main barriers to the attainment of an industry of this size would appear to be product differentiation—with all this implies regarding uninformed consumer reliance on established brand reputations, the "conspicuous-consumption" psychology of buyers, and widespread dealer organizations—and the crushing disadvantage in resale and trade-in values.

The only entry threat in many years which has a good chance of survival (assuming the revival of national protectionism does not spread) is that of the foreign producers in the "dinky" or "very small" car field. As of 1959, foreign makes have captured about 8 per cent of the market (compared to less than 1 per cent in 1955), and appear to be firmly entrenched. It is of special interest to note that sales of the leading import make, the German Volkswagen, were substantially above, and the second leading import, the Renault, were almost as large as those of Studebaker-Packard (see Table 5). The success of the imports in capturing this corner of the U.S. market reflects a number of factors, including the disenchantment of buyers with U.S. styling, size, planned obsolescence, quality of product, price, and cost of operation and maintenance. The fact that the import brands made large absolute as well as relative gains in the U.S. market during the recession years of 1958–59 is indicative of more than just transitory changes in demand. The introduction of the "Big Three" 1960 "compact" models would tend to support this observation.[34] The "compacts" actually are in a larger-size and higher-price class, and may encroach as much on the Chevrolet, Ford, and Plymouth as on the foreign brands. Nonetheless, it does not seem likely that the foreign producers will increase their share much further, and holding on to what they now have may become more and more difficult over time.

---

[34] The market strategy behind G.M. and Ford's belated entry may appear puzzling, but it should be noted that both had made provisions earlier against import penetration of the U.S. market by establishing subsidiaries in England and Germany—the English Ford and G.M. Vauxhall and Opel are among the top ten imports (Table 5).

TABLE 5

Foreign Car Sales in the United States, 1958

Make	Producing Country	Lowest-priced Model [a]	Sales	Percentage of Total Foreign Car Sales in U.S.
Volkswagen	Germany	$1,545	78,225	20.7
Renault	France	1,345	48,050	12.7
English Ford	England	1,442	33,425	8.8
Fiat	Italy	1,098	21,175	5.6
Hillman	England	1,699	18,900	5.0
Vauxhall (G.M.)	England	1,957	17,350	4.6
Simca	France	1,645	17,125	4.5
MG	England	2,462	16,250	4.3
Triumph	England	1,699	16,225	4.3
Opel (G.M.)	Germany	1,957	15,675	4.2
Volvo	Sweden	2,238	14,000	3.7
Metropolitan	England	1,626	12,325	33.3
Morris	England	1,745	9,075	2.4
All others [b]		—	57,948	16.9
Totals			377,548	100.0

[a] U.S. port of entry.
[b] Mercedes-Benz, Borgward, Austin-Healey, Jaguar, Peugeot, BMW Isetta, DKW, SAAB, Porsche, Lloyd, Goliath, Alfa Romeo, Austin, Tannus, Sunbeam, Citroen, Berkeley, Goggomobil, Skoda, Panhard, Toyopet, Rolls-Royce, Rover, Riley, Morgan, Wartburg, Maico.

Source: Automotive News (1959 Almanac Issue), pp. 16 and 174, and "Small Car Race," *Barron's* (January 12, 1959), p. 3.

Market Structure and Market Conduct

The oligopolistic structure of the automobile industry—literally competition among the few—means that fewness of sellers is crucial in determining market behavior. Since none of the producers can afford to ignore the actions and reactions of rival firms to given price or product policies, the pattern of interfirm behavior—under General Motors' leadership—has become largely a function of industry custom, convention, and tacit understandings. The activities of the Automobile Manufacturers' Association, the principal trade association of the industry, also serve to steer firms away from truly independent behavior. Trade associations generally provide avenues for cooperation and restrict the use of certain competitive devices; the AMA is no exception. Some activities, such as the cross-licensing agreements may have increased the degree of effectiveness of competition in the industry. On the other hand, the Sales Managers' Committee of AMA discusses such things as methods of quoting prices, used car problems, the "pack" to be allowed dealers,[35] and related matters. It is difficult to determine the net effect of the activities of these and other departments, but their very nature would seem to minimize the degree of truly independent decision-making on both price and nonprice policies. Much cooperative effort can be channeled through these committees without adversely affecting the consumer, but a solid front emanating from one of them could exceed the bounds of safety in the exercise of economic and political power by one manufacturing group.

Within this rather close-knit industry matrix is found a rather unique pattern of rivalry of both price and nonprice varieties. Interestingly, although there would appear to be a rather wide berth for price differences at the manufacturing level—reflecting advertised differences in quality and mechanical complexity—the existing form of rivalry has virtually eliminated price differences among firms on comparable models. Instead, there has been an ever-increasing emphasis on various forms of nonprice competition, particularly stylistic variations, and this has had an impact on the rigor of competition.

Demand

The demand for new automobiles is a complex phenomenon, reflecting the influence of many factors, including the prices of new and used cars, income of consumers, prices of other goods (both complementary and substitute goods), the stock of automobiles people own, availability and terms of credit, and the design of new models. Those that appear to be of greatest interest and importance in determining the level and responsiveness of demand are:

(1) *A new auto is a replacement for an old auto.* The demand for automobiles, like the demand for all durable goods, is essentially a replacement demand, i.e., a demand for "ownership," and thus does not follow any simple laws of demand.

(2) *Size of outlay.* The magnitude of expenditure involved for a new automobile is another distinguishing feature of demand. No other commodity, save the purchase of a home, entails such a large initial outlay in relation to the typical consumer's income and savings. This means that the average consumer may not be in a position to buy a new car unless credit is available at favorable terms.

---

[35] The "pack" is the amount of additional charges a dealer may add to the delivered price of a car. It has included a "handling" charge, a "mark-up" on the freight cost, a share of any freight saving realized through the use of cheaper transport medium, and a share of the finance company's charges.

(3) *A new auto is purchased out of "supernumerary" income.*[36] Although the automobile as such competes with all goods to one degree or another, the newness of a new car is a luxury for most buyers. As a result, purchase is considered only after provision has been made for other costs of maintaining minimum desired living standards. Thus the new auto is apt to be competing with a vacation trip, the remodeling of a home, or even a fur coat. The important thing here is that an automobile purchase involves some long-range planning by the household, so that anticipated changes in income and economic activity generally may be more important than actual changes.

(4) *A new automobile is a means of acquiring distinction and of expressing one's personality.* In a very real sense, an automobile, like clothing, has become part of a family's general appearance; to some, it may be more important than a fine house or attractive furniture. In our culture, the car owner's affluence and taste are judged by performance and gadgetry as well as by appearance. However, conspicuous consumption motives and tastes also tend, at any one time, to place a ceiling on possible new car sales; just as some people prefer undistinguished clothing and a generally humble appearance, there are some who cannot be seduced by stylistic changes in cars. If model changes are too rapid or extreme, to say nothing of the increased cost which results, these people may and have turned, in increasing numbers, to "economy" type models. Finally, as tastes have moved away from extreme ostentation, the most expensive cars have declined in relative importance.

Statistical studies of the elasticity or responsiveness of demand to price and income changes, both for the pre- and post-World War II periods,[37] are in substantial agreement in their findings with respect to price elasticity and income elasticity of demand:

Elasticity of New Car
Purchases With Respect to:

	Price	Income
Roos & Von Szeliski	−1.5	+2.5
Atkinson [a]	−1.4	+2.5
Chow [a]	−1.2	+3.0
Suits	−0.6	+4.2

[a] On a per capita basis.

[36] Supernumerary income has been defined as disposable income less subsistence living costs (rent, fuel, food, clothing, etc.). See C. F. Roos and Victor Von Szeliski, "Factors Governing Changes in Domestic Automobile Demand," in *Dynamics of Automobile Demand,* New York: General Motors, 1939, p. 41.

[37] The prewar studies were Roos and Von Szeliski, *op.cit.,* and L. Jay Atkinson, "Consumer Markets for Durable Goods," *Survey of Current Business* (April 1952), pp. 19–24. The postwar studies are Gregory C. Chow, *Demand For Automobiles in the*

Except for Suits' analysis, the results indicate a range of price elasticity between −1.2 and −1.5, and income elasticity in the range of +2.5 to +3.9.[38] Thus, as between the two most important variables affecting automobile demand, sales evidently are more responsive to changes in income than to changes in price.

A rough approximation of the responsiveness of demand to various possible price changes by the automobile industry, given various possible changes in income, is shown in Table 6 (based upon Chow's elasticities of

TABLE 6

Estimated Percentage Changes in Annual Purchase of Automobile as Related to
Percentage Changes in Income and the Relative Price of Automobiles
(per capita in constant dollars)

		Percentage Change in Income:						
		− 8	− 6	− 4	− 2	0	+ 2	+ 4
Percentage Change in Price:	+10	−36	−30	−24	−18	−12	− 6	0
	+ 5	−30	−24	−18	−12	− 6	0	6
	0	−24	−18	−12	− 6	0	6	12
	− 5	−18	−12	− 6	0	6	12	18
	−10	−12	− 6	0	6	12	18	24
	−15	− 6	0	6	12	18	24	30
	−20	0	6	12	18	24	30	36

Source: Testimony of Gregory Chow in *Administered Prices* (Hearings), p. 3193.

−1.2 for price and +3.0 for income). The data suggest that if income remains the same, a 5 per cent increase in price would mean a 6 per cent decrease in sales, while a decline in income of 2 per cent, coupled with a 5 per cent increase in price would produce a drop of 12 per cent in sales, and so on.

Costs and Supply

The most significant features of the supply of automobiles are the magnitude and structure of manufacturing costs. An estimated breakdown of the

United States, The Amsterdam: North Holland Publishing Co., 1957, and Daniel B. Suits, "The Demand for New Automobiles in the United States, 1929–1956," *Review of Economics and Statistics,* August 1958, p. 273.

[38] A reworking of Suits' study using the BLS index of retail prices of new cars (deflated by the Consumer Price Index) instead of the price series constructed by Suits, yielded a price elasticity coefficient of −1.2 and income elasticity coefficient of +4.2. See *Administered Prices: Automobiles,* pp. 142–4.

major cost components of the "average" General Motors car in 1957 is as follows: [39]

Overhead Cost	$ 550
Materials & other direct costs	950–$1,050
Hourly-rated labor cost	300– 400
Average Total Unit Cost	$1,750–$2,000

It can be seen that about 30 per cent of unit costs are overhead costs, of which more than one-half are depreciation and obsolescence, general selling and administration, and amortization of special tools (i.e., styling costs). Because of their magnitude, these overhead costs play an important role in the pricing of new automobiles; once incurred, they are "sunk" for a particular model year.

All of the major components of overhead costs have increased rapidly since 1950.[40] Altogether, the "Big Three" are spending approximately one billion dollars for model changes. Ford's "normal" expenditures for style changes have run around $350 million per year, Chrysler's have averaged around $200 million a year, and General Motors' are on the order of $500 million. The magnitude of these three components of overhead serves to emphasize the crucial role of volume in company pricing and production planning. On the basis of 1958 output, styling costs alone amounted to $250 to $300 per unit. Variation in volume will affect primarily overhead costs, and profits per unit. For example, the estimated overhead costs ($550) for G.M. listed above were for *actual* 1957 output volume. At 75 per cent of 1957 output, the overhead item would be $733, and at 125 per cent of 1957 output, $440. Evidently, short-run marginal costs are fairly constant within rather wide limits.

Price Making

The basic questions on automobile pricing that need to be examined are: How does each firm arrive at a price for each of its models? Do all firms follow a common procedure or objective in determining prices? What relation-

---

[39] *Ibid.*, p. 129.

[40] Plant and property depreciation and obsolescence have increased more than three-fold (from $3 billion to $9.4 billion, most of which has been due to very sizable expansion of productive capacity). Since 1950, selling and administrative expense (representing central office, as distinct from manufacturing overhead) have also jumped by about three-fold (from $450 million to $1.2 billion), due largely to the increase in advertising budgets. The other important portion of industry overhead costs, styling costs, have increased manufacturing overhead and have also inflated general selling and administrative costs, since styling and engineering efforts on model changes are general staff functions in each of the major companies. *Ibid.*, pp. 115–24.

ships exist between the pricing process among the various producers, the major producers in particular?

General Motors sets its prices on the basis *of cost-plus-profit*. But average total unit costs themselves are determined by the price decision. This interrelationship between costs and prices results from the method of price determination and the effects of price-induced changes in output on the company's overhead costs.[41] The pricing method employed by G.M., similar in many ways to rate setting by public utilities,[42] is as follows: Unit costs (i.e., direct labor and material costs plus unit overhead costs) are projected on the basis of "normal" or "standard" volume (generally set at around 80 per cent of capacity), and a profit margin per car is added to this "synthetic" unit cost to yield a predetermined total target rate of return to the company. The important thing to notice here is that *actual* costs are not used in pricing. The rate of return on which G.M. prices are based is 20 per cent on net worth. This is a long-run pricing objective of the company; no attempt is made to "maximize" the return in any given year. The target objective applied to the standard volume is basic in the pricing decision because long-run corporation planning of physical capacity and expansion are premised on a target flow of funds to support the investment plans.

G.M.'s approach implicitly makes certain necessary assumptions about (1) the percentage of capacity at which other producers operate—i.e., over time, G.M.'s capacity must be built with a view to rivals' expected sales. Thus, pricing will be partly a function of investment. (2) It assumes further that given rival producers' sales, G.M. will, on the average, be able to sell— at direct cost plus overhead (assuming 80 per cent of capacity), plus a margin to realize 20 per cent return on net worth—enough cars to realize the target return. (3) Hence, G.M.'s pricing assumes a share of the market. Is this share based upon assumptions regarding the level of rivals' costs (i.e., their marginal costs)? Evidently not; as we shall see, rivals' "costs" apparently do not determine their prices or sales, since they are price followers. G.M. must also assume that, given the price at which it intends to sell various models (determined as indicated above), it will realize 40 per cent to 50 per cent of the market. It has been able to assure itself of the target market share through stylistic changes and advertising—especially the former— which are reflected in cost. Therefore, the pricing problem for G.M. is one

[41] See A. D. H. Kaplan, J. B. Dirlam, and R. F. Lanzillotti, *Pricing in Big Business*, Washington: Brookings Institution, 1958, pp. 48–55 and 131–42, and *Administered Prices: Automobiles*, pp. 104–30.

[42] There is, of course, one important difference: A public utility is a regulated monopoly, whose costing and pricing practices are subject to governmental supervision and control. General Motors, on the other hand, has considerable economic power like a public utility, but is essentially free to set its own prices.

of simultaneous determination of target profits, in which some of the factors can be assumed to remain relatively constant—i.e., total industry demand, industry capacity, and respective market shares of producers.

Price Leadership and Price Uniformity

Chrysler and Ford executives have indicated that their companies do not have profits goals like G.M.'s which provide an objective for price determination, although Ford utilizes a "standard cost" procedure which is similar to G.M.'s—perhaps because Ford's chief operating executive is an alumnus of General Motors.[43] All three firms plan production of a new model with clearly defined cost targets based upon current prices of competitive makes. The primary concern in the early stages of production planning evidently is to make sure that a particular model can be mass-produced at costs which are considered suitable in relation to *current* prices. Final cost estimates are made on the basis of average volume of past years, after which production is started on the new model. The actual decision on prices, however, is not made until the last minute before models are placed on sale, so that ample time is available to study the actual or probable pricing action of rivals.

In view of the great emphasis placed upon product differentiation, one might expect independent discretion and action on prices; instead, the prices of "Big Three" models in given classes betray an intimate similarity, especially for the high-volume models, as hown in Table 7. The price differentials are very slight in almost all classes; in Class "A," less than $20; in class "B," less than $50; in class "C," $21 to $97; in class "D," $3 to $66; in class "E," $6; in class "F," $18 to $107; and in class "G," $54 to $60.

The absence of greater price differentials apparently is the result of deliberate market strategies of the major producers. There is no evidence of a consistent pattern of one firm announcing new prices first, with the others following; the role of first announcing price changes appears to have been about equally divided among the three companies. However, other evidence suggests that even where Ford or Chrysler announce new prices first, their basic aim is to anticipate the price actions of General Motors.[44] Perhaps the best evidence of the desire to keep prices in line with those of G.M. is Ford's famous "double shift" in pricing 1957 models. On September 29, 1956, Ford announced its suggested price list for 1957 models, averaging a 2.9 per cent increase, ranging from $1 to $104 over 1956 models. Two weeks later, General

---

[43] For a summary of Ford's standard cost procedures, see A. R. Oxenfeldt, *Industrial Pricing and Market Practices*, New York: Prentice-Hall, 1951, pp. 135–6.
[44] *Administered Prices* (Hearings), pp. 2777, 2683, 2785.

TABLE 7

Factory Suggested List Prices of 1958 Models of the "Big Three" [a]
(4-Door Sedan, 8 Cylinder Models)

Class	General Motors Models		Ford Models		Chrysler Models	
A.	Chevrolet		Ford		Plymouth	
	Delray	$2,262	Custom 300	$2,256	Plaza	$2,277
	Biscayne	2,397	Fairlane	2,409	Savoy	2,413
	Bel Air	2,547	Fairlane 500	2,562	Belvedere	2,547
B.	Pontiac Chieftain	2,638	Edsel Ranger	2,592	Dodge Coronet	2,637
C.	Buick Special	2,700	Edsel Pacer	2,735	Dodge Royal	2,797
			Mercury Mon-			
			terey	2,721		
D.	Pontiac Star		Mercury Mont-		DeSoto Fire-	
	Chief	3,302 [b]	clair	3,236 [b]	dome	3,305 [b]
E.	Oldsmobile				Chrysler Wind-	
	Super 88	3,343 [b]			sor	3,349 [b]
	Buick Century	3,316 [b]				
F.	Buick Super	4,033 [c]	Edsel Citation	3,926 [c]	Chrysler Sara-	
	Oldsmobile 98	4,023 [c]			toga	4,051 [c]
G.	Cadillac 62	4,891	Lincoln Capri	4,951	Chrysler Im-	
					perial	4,945

[a] Including Federal Excise taxes and suggested dealer handling charges and delivery charges.
[b] Includes automatic transmission for all four models since it is standard on some.
[c] Includes cheapest radio, cheapest heater, automatic transmission, power brakes and power steering for all models since some of these are standard on different models.

Source: Administered Prices: Automobiles, pp. 62–5.

Motors announced its new prices for Chevrolets, averaging 6.1 per cent over 1956 and ranging from $50 to $166 higher. One week later Ford revised its prices upward, with the result that on ten models the new price differences with Chevrolet were only $1 to $2, and on two models, $10 to $11. A week later Chrysler announced Plymouth prices, which conformed to the traditional Chrysler pattern of around $20 higher than Chevrolet.

Nonprice Competition

Planned Obsolescence versus *Standard Styling.* With the steady disappearance of price differentials on comparable models, "nonprice" competition has become increasingly intense. Greatest emphasis in recent years has been placed on design changes and advertising. At one time, model changes emerged from significant developments in technology, every four or five years; today they are largely merchandising devices designed to enhance sales. The industry custom is annual model changes—i.e., a complete retooling of the line every two years, with a "facelifting" in alternate years.

General Motors apparently has decided to increase the pace; beginning with its 1959 models, it is claiming all-new models every year.[45] John Keats puts it very succinctly:

> The basic shell is bent a little bit this way, this year, and is bent slightly that way next year. The headlights are higher one year, lower the next, or grow in double. . . . The door knobs are hidden, or recessed, or turned into buttons or bars. . . . Tail fins grow higher, or may be, grow in sidewise. A chiropodist has remarked that the [late] Edsel's fins resemble ingrown toenails.
>
> Meanwhile, no significant changes take place, except in price, and the change there is certainly significant. . . .[46]

The apparent objective of this kind of product variation, called "dynamic obsolescence" by G.M. executives, is to make sure that this year's models will become so unstylish in the next three or four years that owners will feel dissatisfied and trade them in for a new model. Standard styling, the hallmark of most foreign makes, is rejected on the premise that the public does not want it. It seems also that the "Big Three" have advertised themselves into a position where each must, or at least thinks it must, make a substantial annual model change in order to hold its position.

The magnitude of the cost of design changes perhaps can be appreciated by noting that the "Big Three" alone spend on the order of one billion dollars per year for restyling and retooling costs, or approximately $200 to $250 per car. Changes in design are closely interwoven with advertising, so that an annual model change entails at least $75 a car more (at the manufacturing level alone) to make the public aware of the new model and to broaden the public appeal. The effect of these costly annual model changes has been to doom the smaller companies in the industry. The steady increase in sales of the "standard styling" foreign makes suggests that to a large number of buyers an annual restyling is no longer a prerequisite. It remains to be seen if a significant segment of auto buyers will continue to support producers following a standard-styling policy.

Quality. An automotive consultant of Consumers Union (which has thoroughly tested over 250 cars since the end of World War II), holds that new car quality, in the sense of workmanship and freedom from mechanical imperfections at the time of delivery "is, on the whole, going downhill." [47] Evidently, this view of deterioration in quality and quality control by man-

[45] Cf. *Business Week*, June 21, 1958 and "GM Heads for Annual Retooling," *Iron Age*, May 22, 1958.
[46] *The Insolent Chariots*, New York: Lippincott, 1958, pp. 54–5.
[47] *Administered Prices:* Hearings before Subcommittee on Antitrust and Monopoly, Senate Judiciary Committee, Eighty-fifth Cong., 2nd Sess., Pt. 6, "Automobiles," pp. 3071–72 and 3086.

344 The Structure of American Industry

ufacturers was also held by a large percentage of buyers. An economist for one of the Big Three recently reported a survey disclosing that 22 per cent of potential car buyers believe European autos to be "mechanically more reliable" and 31 per cent say they have "better workmanship" than American cars. Moreover, a survey conducted by the National Automobile Dealers Association reveals that among buyers of cars priced in the $2,500 and up brackets, 71 per cent cited "better workmanship" as the reason for their purchase of a foreign car.[48] An occasional U.S. auto executive is willing to admit there is something to these impressions held by buyers and testing organizations, but the more typical reaction is that of G.M.'s E. N. Cole, General Manager of the Chevrolet Division, who is quoted as saying ". . . I can guarantee you that our quality will stand up against anything from Europe."[49]

Innovations. Innovations—their source and the speed with which they are adopted—are another aspect of nonprice competition significant for public policy. These are not matters that lend themselves to precise measurement, especially the relative values of different innovations; furthermore, several companies often claim credit for what is substantially the same development.[50] Not all of these claims are true "firsts" of the "Big Three," however. Most of the recent improvements have come from outside the large firms. Many, like the new suspension systems, were pioneered by small European concerns, and others, like the automatic transmissions and power steering, were largely the result of work by independent inventors.[51] Moreover, the small producers have done more than a proportionate share of pioneering.[52] They perform an important function in the market in this

[48] "Does Europe Top U.S. in Car Workmanship? Many Folks Think So," *Wall Street Journal*, August 20, 1959.

[49] *Time* magazine reports that hearing this, "Detroit wags recalled the time when Big Bill Knudsen, G.M.'s late president, boasted to adman Bruce Barton that a certain new-model Chevy was 'almost the perfect low-priced car—and it will really become perfect next year when we make one small change.' Barton bit hard. 'What change?' Deadpanned Bill Knudsen: 'We're just going to hang a small hammock under the chassis. Catch all the goddam parts that fall out.'" October 5, 1959, p. 92.

[50] See *A Study of the Antitrust Laws, Hearings before the Subcommittee on Antitrust and Monopoly, Senate Judiciary Committee,* Eighty-fourth Cong., 1st Sess., Pt. 7 "General Motors," pp. 3507–09, and *Administered Prices: Automobiles,* p. 23.

[51] For example, the original outstanding inventions in the development of the automatic transmission were made by an electrical engineer employed by a shipbuilding company. The principal contribution of G.M. was the development of a combination of converter-coupling and epicycling gearing. Cf. J. Jewkes, D. Sawers, and R. Stillerman, *The Sources of Inventions,* London: Macmillan & Co., 1958 and D. Hamberg, "Size of Firm, Monopoly, and Economic Growth," *Employment, Growth, and Price Levels,* Hearings Before the Joint Economic Committee, Eighty-sixth Cong., 1st Sess., Pt. 7 "The Effects of Monopolistic and Quasi-Monopolistic Practices," pp. 2342, 2354.

[52] The Automobile Manufacturers Association publication *A Chronicle of Automotive Industry,* Detroit, 1949, seems to confirm this merely by recording the origins of success-

regard, displaying a competitive vigor born of necessity. In fact, the high mortality rate among small firms has been partly due to a large amount of unsuccessful innovation.

With all this effort devoted to improving product performance, only little attention seems to be given to producing a somewhat safer product. The reluctance to produce a safe automobile no doubt is due to fear of hurting sales because of the psychological impact it might produce on buyers, as well as resistance to the drastic changes that would be required.[53] In sum, the innovative record of the automobile industry has been spotty, particularly over the past two decades. Professor Maclaurin has summarized it as follows:

> The automobile industry has certainly been one of the most vigorous new industries in America. Yet by the late 1920's the innovative characteristics of the industry began to change. There can be no simple explanation of this fact. But a partial answer lies in the quality of entrepreneurial leadership, the absence of a research conception, the explosive rate of previous growth, and the success of the established oligopoly.
>
> . . . If the automobile pioneers had believed in and understood research, they could have provided a more interesting innovative record since 1930.[54]

Profits

The rates of return on stockholders investment (after taxes) for the Big Three automobile companies have been exceptionally good both before and after World War II. As Table 8 shows, since the end of World War II General Motors has averaged around 25 per cent (after taxes), and only rarely has its return dropped below 20 per cent. Ford's return has generally been higher than Chrysler's, although both have been unsteady relative to General Motors. The independents have experienced the most variable returns, a fairly good performance in the late forties, but steadily deteriorating since 1950. Both American Motors and Studebaker-Packard have gone through a string of years with sustained losses, which have only recently shown signs of being reversed. The Government-approved mergers leading to the formation of American and S-P were made in the hope that the new

---

ful innovations. Among the innovations originating with or introduced by the smaller auto companies are all-steel body, noiseless rear axles, adjustable front seats, 4-wheel brakes, rubber engine mounts, overdrive, hydraulic valve lifters, turn signal indicators, and single-unit construction. Cf. *Administered Prices: Automobiles*, p. 24.

[53] See Keats, *op.cit.*, pp. 98–99.

[54] W. Rupert Maclaurin, "Innovation and Capital Formation in Some American Industries," *Capital Formation and Economic Growth*, National Bureau of Economic Research, Princeton University Press, 1955, pp. 554, 557.

TABLE 8

Rates of Return (after Taxes) on Stockholders' Investment
for Automobile Companies, 1940 and 1947–59

	General Motors	Ford	Chrysler	Eleven other Motor Vehicle Companies:			
					American Motors [a]		Studebaker-Packard [b]
Year				Average	Nash	Hudson	
1940	19.2	n.a.	22.1	4.2	3.7	− 6.6	8.9
1947	20.2	8.5	23.6	15.5	30.4	13.0	20.6
1948	27.1	12.1	26.2	19.8	28.1	25.1	34.3
1949	33.4	19.5	32.0	15.4	29.6	16.3	37.0
1950	37.5	24.3	26.7	16.1	28.4	17.3	24.3
1951	21.7	10.5	15.2	8.4	13.8	− 1.6	12.3
1952	20.0	9.1	16.7	8.7	10.4	11.4	13.4
1953	19.7	11.9	15.8	4.2	11.2	—	2.4
1954	24.5	15.0	5.8	− 6.1	− 6.1		− 16.0
1955	30.5	24.3	16.0	− 5.2	− 4.5		− 22.2
1956	18.9	12.3	3.1	−13.5	−23.4		− 64.4
1957	17.1	13.7	17.4	0.2	− 8.9		−110.9
1958	12.6	3.9	− 4.2	9.1	22.3		− 41.3
1959	16.3	19.6	− 7.8	n.a.	36.7		38.1

[a] American Motors formed in 1954 as a merger of Nash and Hudson.
[b] Studebaker and Packard merged in 1954. Data before 1954 for Studebaker only.
n.a. 1940 not available for Ford Motor Co.

Source: "Report of the Federal Trade Commission on Rates of Return for Identical Companies in Selected Manufacturing Industries, 1940, 1947–58"; 1959 data computed by author.

companies might have a better chance of surviving the costly competition of the times.

The rates of return of the "Big Three" as a group, and G.M. in particular, are significantly higher than for manufacturing industries as a whole. In the light of the foregoing analysis, there is a strong presumption that the earnings are related to the high degree of concentration, the importance of product differentiation and other entry barriers, and the apparent recognized interdependence among the Big Three on pricing and production policies.

SECTION III: PUBLIC POLICY

The high degree of concentration in automobile production and the market practices which emerge pose a number of public policy issues. At one time, even as two of the present giants were being formed, the industry was characterized by rather vigorous competition—a refreshing sight amid its "trustified" counterparts in American industry. Moreover, as of 1939, the Federal Trade Commission reported that:

Consumer benefits in the automobile manufacturing industry have probably been more substantial than in any other large industry studied by the Commission.[55]

A decade later, Professor Edward S. Mason, in commenting on the possibility of making informed judgments regarding a set of performance criteria for industry, concluded ". . . it is possible from the record of the last two or three decades to determine that the performance of the automobile industry is relatively good." [56] Another decade later, in 1958, Simon N. Whitney reached a similar conclusion.[57] But a 1958 report by the Subcommittee on Antitrust and Monopoly of the Senate Judiciary Committee offered contrary conclusions:

. . . The evidence adduced in the hearings at least affords indications that monopoly power is extant in the industry. . . . The subcommittee believes that the record of its recent hearings and those held in 1955 leaves little doubt that the hard core of the monopoly problem in the automobile industry is in the concentration of production and power held by G.M. This concentration appears neither compatible with nor conducive to a free market in which the public must buy automobiles. . . .[58]

How can these conflicting findings be reconciled? In part, it is a question of whether one focuses attention on the structure of the market or "performance" of the industry. An examination of performance alone, however, misses the significant question for public policy, e.g., whether the performance reflects the objective compulsions of the market, or strategic benevolence of managements. For competition to be workable or acceptable in any economically significant sense, the market and market processes should not only *permit* but, more important, must *compel* certain results to emerge.[59]

Problem of Concentration and Size

It will be recalled that Durant originally planned to extend his control over every producer of importance in the industry. Had events and personal-

---

[55] FTC, *op.cit.*, p. 1074.
[56] "The Current Status of the Monopoly Problem in the United States," *Harvard Law Review*, June 1949, pp. 1281–2. See also Mason, *Economic Concentration and the Monopoly Problem*, Cambridge: Harvard University Press, 1957, pp. 367–8.
[57] Whitney, *op.cit.*, p. 522.
[58] *Administered Prices: Automobiles*, pp. 182–3.
[59] See statements of Ben W. Lewis and Walter Adams, *Administered Prices, Hearings before the Subcommittee on Antitrust and Monopoly, Senate Judiciary Committee*, Eighty-sixth Cong., 1st Sess., Pt. 9 "Administered Price Inflation: Alternative Public Policies," pp. 4715–19 and 4782–83.

ities differed slightly, Durant might have succeeded and Ford, Chrysler, Reo, and Dodge could conceivably have become parts of a General Motors monopoly. The fact that only five domestic producers remain, with one's survival in doubt, raises the question whether the economics of the industry are such as to make the trend toward fewer and larger firms unavoidable. Given the mass production and consumption characteristics of the industry, Durant's logic would appear to be unassailable. There are definite and important scale economies associated with body and engine production and assembly operations. Yet, there is no reason why the industry had to be organized with only three firms producing 80 to 90 per cent of output for twenty years. The conditions bearing on operational efficiency discussed in Section II suggest that the present level of consumer demand would justify an industry consisting of *at least* ten firms of optimum size.[60] This estimate is a minimum, since a larger number would be feasible if firms could secure bodies and engines from other firms specializing in the production of these components. This pattern of production existed in earlier years, but it seems unlikely that any firm specializing in the production of engines and bodies could be assured of enough of a market today to make its operations profitable. As long as such specialty firms do not exist, an automobile manufacturer must perforce produce its own engines and bodies.[61]

The disappearance of producers over the years cannot be attributed solely to the economies of scale and the natural forces of competition, although their importance should not be minimized. The most important factor that caused the defunct companies to fail was the lack of capital to meet the increasing emphasis and staggering cost of frequent product changes and other product differentiation policies and practices of the "Big Three." Whether the degree of market power and the nature of interfirm behavior of auto producers violates Sherman Act or Clayton Act provisions has not been put to a court test. Yet, this question is certainly begged by Judge Hand's dictum in the 1945 Alcoa decision ("Size was not only evidence of violation, or of potential violation, . . . it was the essence of the offense") and the court's ruling in the 1946 *Tobacco* case ("Neither proof of the power

---

[60] G.M.'s automotive divisions alone could be divided into three or four efficient companies, Chrysler into two, and Ford into two. G.M. reportedly had a plan of its own for dividing its automobile divisions if required by antitrust action, under which separate companies would be formed of both Chevrolet and Buick, while Oldsmobile, Pontiac, and Cadillac divisions would remain as G.M. *Business Week*, February 7, 1959, p. 23.

[61] There are, however, some technological developments on the horizon that could reduce the minimum scale of plant for efficient operations and justify an even larger number of independent producers—e.g., the substitution of plastics for steel in body components and the use of an electric motor in place of the present internal combustion engine.

to exclude nor proof of actual exclusion of existing or potential competitors is essential to sustain a charge of monopolization under the Sherman Act").[62] The auto industry has never been charged with parallelism on price and product policies similar to those practiced by the "Big Three" of tobacco; but the market power, financial strength, large advertising expenditures, and general dominance of the three largest auto firms are the same kind of factors that underlie the finding of Sherman Act violation in the *Tobacco* decision. Thus, the crucial factors that would have to be weighed under present judicial interpretations would seem to be:

(1) whether the Big Three *have* the power (i.e., the *existence*, not the *exertion*) as a group substantially to influence the price of automobiles, and whether that power has been maintained for the purpose of enjoying and preserving the advantage of market position; and

(2) whether a "combination" can be inferred from a course of dealing or parallel action in response to stimuli of the market, or concerted action on such things as price, product, and distribution policies.[63]

Some students of antitrust law believe that even under the current interpretations recognizing the nature of oligopoly structures some abuse of power must be found in the form of predatory, exclusionary, or discriminatory practices. This history of concentrated industries generally discloses that market power is inevitably abused, intentionally or "unintentionally." The point is that if market power *can* be abused, it probably is. The automobile industry has not been an exception.

The majority of antitrust suits in the industry have been in the areas of parts and accessories and installment financing, involving charges of price fixing, price discrimination, coercion, exclusive dealing, allocation of territories, and tying clauses.[64] The most important cases against the auto makers proper have concerned certain practices that were alleged to harm the dealers, small finance companies, and independent parts manufacturers.

Auto Dealers

The dealers have suffered some of the most serious hardships of the industry and have raised frequent complaints against the practices of the auto manufacturers.[65] The principal charges have been "forcing" and arbitrary cancellation of franchises. "Forcing" takes several forms, e.g., the assign-

[62] *American Tobacco Company* versus *United States*, 328 U.S. 781 at 810 (1946).
[63] Cf. Eugene Rostow, "Monopoly Under the Sherman Act," 43 *Illinois Law Review*, 762–63.
[64] Cf. Whitney, *op.cit.*, pp. 435–52, for a detailed discussion of the cases.
[65] FTC, *op.cit.*, Chap. III–XI.

ment of new-car "quotas" to the dealer, with or without his consent, manufacturer's insistence that only "genuine" (i.e., the manufacturer's) parts and
accessories be stocked, forcing the dealers to accept a minimum "quota" of
parts and accessories, and requiring dealers to contribute an annual sum for
advertising (which, in the case G.M., allegedly exceeded the total advertising budget of the manufacturer).

The franchise creating the dealership and the conditions for cancellation
of franchises are other bones of contention. The franchise requires that the
dealer meet certain specified capital, character, and experience qualifications, and that he follow certain manufacturer-prescribed business and
accounting practices. Also, with only minor exceptions, the franchise establishes "exclusive" dealerships, i.e., it ties the dealer to a single manufacturer.
Franchises have been cancelled at the will of the manufacturer, without
hearing or for causes not clearly agreed upon by both parties. That very
little progress has been made in correcting the unreasonable exercise of
the one-sided powers of manufacturers and toward obtaining greater equity
for dealers is indicated by the testimony and many supporting letters of
protest by dealers and dealer organizations in 1955 before the Senate Subcommittee on Antitrust and Monopoly. It seems clear that in some cases
cancellations were based upon serious dealer malpractices, but in many other
cases cancellation was merely a reprisal against dealers refusing to accept
some type of forcing.[66]

Listening to an automobile dealer whine about his cruel fate at the hands
of a manufacturer would, as John Keats says, "ordinarily send a reasonable
man into gales of laughter." Sympathy for the small dealer doing business
with "giants" has been tempered by painful consumer experiences with
"sharp" dealer practices, especially the 1946–49 period when dealers had too
few cars to sell and sold them mercilessly, and the price-deception "pack"
of 1955 when the dealers had too many cars on hand. The difficulty here
is that the dealer finds himself in the uncomfortable position between the
powerful manufacturer on the one hand, and a demanding and not too
understanding public on the other. The public appears to gain from automobile forcing through lower prices more closely related to dealer's actual
cost, but may lose as much from parts and accessory forcing and from high
repair charges dealers use to offset low margins on new-car sales. Both

[66] Cf. *Hearings before the Subcommittee on Antitrust and Monopoly Senate Judiciary
Committee,* Eighty-fourth Cong., 1st Sess., Pt. 7, pp. 3156–89, and Pt. 8, pp. 4060–4143.
The weight of publicity on General Motors' practices led to a suspension of its dealer
advertising fund plan (regarding forced advertising contributions) and the extension of
one-year contracts for five years. *Ibid.,* Pt. 7, p. 3556, and Department of Justice announcement, December 3, 1956.

situations arise out of the degree of market power possessed by the car manufacturers, who have passed some of that power on to their dealers through exclusive franchise arrangements.

Installment Financing

Another area in need of reform, as reported by the FTC in 1939, is installment financing. There are several hundred relatively small finance companies, and a "Big Three" consisting of General Motors Acceptance Corporation (a G.M. subsidiary), Commercial Credit Corporation (owned by Chrysler until 1938), and Commercial Investment Trust (to which Ford sold its subsidiary Universal Credit in 1933). One aspect of the installment financing problem has to do with the advertising of finance costs. Most finance companies buy the customer's installment purchase contract from the dealers. In addition to carrying charges, dealers often add a "dealer's loss reserve" charge, and, in some cases, sell automobile insurance as a tie-in requirement. The last two items are excellent sources of dealer "packs."

In the thirties, the three large finance companies, on the insistence of the auto manufacturers, reduced or eliminated the "pack," and reduced carrying charges to 6 per cent of the full amount financed; the so-called "6 per cent plan." As originally advertised, this plan was misleading—actual simple interest amounted to nearly 12 per cent on the unpaid balance—later enjoined by the FTC. A related problem that prompted government action arose out of the auto manufacturers' forcing or encouraging the use of the "Big Three" finance companies through pressure on the dealers. In November 1939, General Motors, GMAC, and two other G.M. subsidiaries were found guilty of forcing GMAC financing on dealers and customers. Ford and Chrysler earlier voluntarily severed their relationships with installment finance affiliates under a consent decree arrangement. Recently, however, Ford has announced its intention to form a finance company, and Chrysler is expected to follow suit.

The basic problem here is not simply one of practices as such. It is part of the problem of concentration and the possibilities of distortion inherent in conglomerate integration; i.e., that credit terms and charges will be dictated not by the economics of financing, but by the exigencies of selling cars.[67] The situation points up something of a public policy dilemma in that

---

[67] See the hearings on two bills to prohibit auto manufacturers from engaging in financing and insuring automobiles, *Auto Financing Legislation, Hearings before Subcommittee on Antitrust and Monopoly, Senate Judiciary Committee,* Eighty-sixth Cong., 1st Sess., 1959, especially the testimonies of Thurman Arnold, former head of the Antitrust Division of the Department of Justice and Donald F. Turner, pp. 256–86, 363–71.

the competitive market for financing permitted excessive charges, while the "restrained" market reduced them. However, against this must be set the possibility that—even if savings are realized, and even if these savings should be passed on to the consumer—G.M. might offset this by charging a comparably higher price for its cars. Thus, the basic issue is the tight-knit oligopoly structure: If Ford and Chrysler reenter the installment finance business alongside of G.M., it seems reasonable to assume that oligopoly pricing of cars-plus-financing may make the consumer no better off, and probably worse off, than before.

Parts Suppliers

The precarious position of parts manufacturers has already been mentioned. By virtue of their vertical integration, the major auto companies are in a position to buy parts from (1) independent suppliers, (2) their own parts producing subsidiaries, or (3) "outside" firms that are closely tied to the auto companies through ownership or contractual arrangements. That this multiple relationship in the supply channels often results in an abuse of market power against the independent parts producers is indicated by a long list of cases tried by the Federal Trade Commission. For example, in July 1953, the FTC charged General Motors, Electric Auto-Lite, and Champion Spark Plug (who together produce around 90 per cent of the nation's spark plugs) with price discrimination in the sale of spark plugs to competing purchasers. The Commission also alleged that Champion and General Motors had induced distributors to agree to handle their lines exclusively. The latter was apparently a repetition of the 1939 violation under which G.M. and its A.C. Spark Plug Division were cited for forcing and maintenance of resale prices, requiring minimum inventories and purchases, and exclusive handling of their spark plugs and oil filters. The upshot of the spark plug cases was to enjoin all arrangements for exclusive dealing and Champion was ordered to justify, or cease and desist from maintaining, the extreme price differential between plugs for new cars (6 cents) and those for replacement use (21 cents and 31 cents).[68]

The prominence of price discrimination in many of these complaints calls attention to the possible effects of the intrafirm pricing system employed by integrated producers. Since the demand for a given automobile model tends to be more elastic than the demand for replacement parts, this may lead to marginal-cost pricing for component parts, with high profit margins on replacement parts sales, which in turn may reinforce the dealer practice

[68] FTC Dockets 3977, 5620, and 5624.

of trading down on new cars and holding up repair costs. Since all auto firms are not able to avail themselves of this technique, the commanding position of the larger manufacturers may be even greater than their size indicates, and the position of the small parts producers and dealers worse than in a more competitive situation.[69] In addition, when both integrated and independent parts producers agree on the same discriminatory pricing system, the consumer can hardly escape high charges for repairs and service.

The Du Pont-General Motors Case

The nearest thing to a direct attack on General Motors' size and market power was the recent Department of Justice suit decided in 1957 against du Pont and General Motors.[70] The Supreme Court ruled that du Pont's 23 per cent stock ownership gave du Pont what in effect was a monopoly of automotive paints and fabrics business of G.M., a reciprocity arrangement that was beneficial to both G.M. and du Pont. The central question of the case was whether the relationship between the two companies violated the presumption against bigness inherent in antitrust enforcement.[71] The control exercised by du Pont was found to cut off competition and exclude competitors from G.M. business; hence, it had not merely a potential but an actual anticompetitive effect.

Conclusion

In conclusion, it would seem that we are fast approaching, if not already beyond, the time for more direct action with respect to the structure of the automobile industry, and General Motors in particular. Muddling along as we have with occasional suits dealing with the symptoms of the problem have not resulted in any significant changes in past, nor likely to affect future, behavior of the "Big Three." No one can gainsay the benefits in automotive

---

[69] G.M., being the largest supplier of automotive parts and components to nonintegrated and partially-integrated firms, is in a much stronger position in this respect than any of its rivals. The corporation's policy is to price its parts so as to yield 20 to 30 per cent on capital invested in parts production, and results in larger over-all profits on G.M.'s integrated operations than those realized by less integrated competitors. This, of course, is nothing more than "normal, prudent" pursuit of the advantages inherent in G.M.'s integration, but it is just this sort of pricing policy that is one of the factors that tends to keep the independents of the auto industry weak and poor. Cf. Joe S. Bain, *Industrial Organization*, pp. 328–29.

[70] *United States* versus *E. I. du Pont de Nemours & Co.*, 353 U.S. 586 (1957).

[71] For a very penetrating analysis of the decision, see Joel B. Dirlam and Irwin M. Stelzer, "The du Pont-General Motors Decision: In the Antitrust Grain," *Columbia Law Review*, Vol. 58, January 1958, p. 24.

transportation provided by the industry over the years; but to look backward is to miss the main policy issue—maintaining the goal of competition. If the public is genuinely interested in making sure that an industry with such widespread ramifications on our economic and social life is subject to the objective compulsions of the market, then structural changes seem necessary. The traditional antitrust approach for dealing with corporate giantism indicates that the policy of competition is most likely to be realized in this industry through direct antitrust action for dissolution, divorcement, and divestiture—beginning with General Motors. The American Institute of Management put the issue very succinctly:

One cannot study General Motors' massive operations without experiencing an inescapable feeling—General Motors is too big. It is too big for the good of American businessmen who must deal with it and too big for the good of the country.[72]

The most salutary impact on the industry in recent years has been the appearance of the foreign economy models. The "Big Three's" rush to build compact models is a healthy sign, but should not blind policy-makers, the Congress, or the Courts to the cause of the industry's rejuvenation. In the interest of keeping this competitive influence alive, it would be desirable to reduce substantially or to repeal present tariff barriers on foreign automobiles—irrespective of any antitrust actions that may be initiated or contemplated. Particularly in highly concentrated industries, it would seem difficult to justify tariff protection, which serves to further support and insulate high, rigid prices and imitative product policies from the discipline of the market.

SUGGESTED READINGS

Books and Pamphlets

Automobile Manufacturers Association, *Automobile Facts and Figures*, Detroit (annual issues).
———, *A Chronicle of the Automotive Industry*, Detroit, 1949.
Automotive News, Detroit (annual Almanac issues).
ʼJoe S. Bain, *Barriers to Competition* (Cambridge: Harvard University Press, 1956).
R. G. Cleveland and S. T. Williamson, *The Road is Yours* (New York: Greystone Press, 1951).
P. F. Drucker, *Concept of the Corporation* (New York: Day, 1946).
R. C. Epstein, *The Automobile Industry* (New York: Shaw, 1928).
H. Ford, *My Life and Work* (New York: Doubleday, Page, 1923).

---

[72] "Profit Margins at General Motors: A Background Study in Management Action," *The Corporate Director*, Vol. VI, No. 3, July 1956, p. 4.

————, *My Philosophy of Industry* (New York: Coward-McCann, 1929).

General Motors, *Dynamics of Automobile Demand* (New York, 1939).

John Keats, *The Insolent Chariots* (New York: Lippincott, 1958).

C. F. Kettering and A. Orth, *The New Necessity* (Baltimore: Williams and Wilkins, 1932).

E. W. Lewis, *Motor Memories* (Detroit: Alved Publishers, 1947).

M. M. Musselman, *Get A Horse* (New York: Lippincott, 1950).

A. Nevins and F. E. Hill, *Ford, Expansion and Challenge, 1915–33* (New York: Scribner's, 1957).

Simon N. Whitney, *Antitrust Policies: American Experience in Twenty Industries*, Vol. 1 (New York: Twentieth Century Fund, 1958), Chap. 8.

Government Publications

Federal Trade Commission, *Report on the Motor Vehicle Industry* (Washington, 1939).

Hearings before the Subcommittee on Antitrust and Monopoly, Senate Judiciary Committee, *A Study of the Antitrust Laws*, Pt. 7 "General Motors," Eighty-fourth Cong., 1st Sess., 1957.

Hearings before the Subcommittee on Antitrust and Monopoly, Senate Judiciary Committee, *Administered Prices*, Pt. 6 "Automobiles," Eighty-fifth Cong., 2nd Sess., 1958.

Hearings before the Subcommittee on Antitrust and Monopoly, Senate Judiciary Committee, *Auto Financing Legislation*, Eighty-sixth Cong., 1st Sess., 1959.

Hearings before the Temporary National Economic Committee, *Investigation of Concentration of Economic Power*, Pt. 2, Seventy-fifth Cong., 2nd Sess., 1938.

Staff Report, Subcommittee on Antitrust and Monopoly, Senate Judiciary Committee, *Bigness and Concentration of Economic Power—A Case Study of General Motors Corporation*, Eighty-fourth Cong., 1st Sess., 1956.

Staff Report, Subcommittee on Antitrust and Monopoly, Senate Judiciary Committee, *Administered Prices: Automobiles*, Eighty-fifth Cong., 2nd Sess., 1958.

United States versus *E. I. du Pont de Nemours & Co.* 353 U.S. 586 (1957).

Journal and Magazine Articles

Fortune, "Success Story," December 1935.

————, "General Motors III," February 1939.

————, "SAE," August 1948.

————, "The Chrysler Operation," October 1948.

————, "The Used Car Deal," September 1949.

————, "Auto Sales and Capacity," April 1950.

————, "Kaiser-Frazer," July 1951.

————, "Lincoln-Mercury Moves Up," March 1952.

————, "A New Kind of Car Market," September 1953.

————, "Ford's Fight for First," September 1954.

————, "Super-Luxury Cars," June 1957.

————, "Will Success Spoil American Motors," January 1959.

The Corporate Director, "Profits Margins at General Motors: A Background Study in Management Action," Vol. VI, No. 3, July 1956.

E. S. Mason, "Current Status of the Monopoly Problem," *Harvard Law Review,* Vol. 62, June 1949.

H. B. Vanderblue, "Pricing Policies in the Automobile Industry," *Harvard Business Review,* Vol. XVII, Summer 1939.

H. G. Vatter, "The Closure of Entry in the American Automobile Industry," *Oxford Economic Papers,* Vol. 4, October 1952.

Walter Williams, "A Theory of the Declining Buick," *Current Economic Comment,* Vol. 21, November 1959.

Chapter 10

RICHARD B. TENNANT

The Cigarette Industry

SECTION I: INTRODUCTION

In 1958 the American people consumed 436.3 billion cigarettes for which they spent $5,700 million through normal channels of trade.[1] Another 33.7 billion worth $156 million were withdrawn free of tax for export or for use on ships at sea.[2] Cigarettes accounted for 1.3 per cent of the gross national product at market prices and for 4 per cent of all consumer expenditures for nondurable goods.

The importance of this activity to various sectors of the economy may be seen from the following approximate breakdown of total industry proceeds in 1958 (expressed in millions of dollars):

State Excise Taxes	$ 667
Federal Excise Taxes	1,580
Corporate Income Taxes	250
Total Taxes	2,662
Wholesale and Retail Margins	1,272
Farm Value of Tobacco Used	685
Other Manufacturing and Selling Costs	996
Interest	26
Net Profit of Manufacturers	215
Total	$5,856

[1] This chapter is based upon the author's book, *The American Cigarette Industry*, New Haven: Yale University Press, 1950. Recent brand statistics are based on H. M. Wootten's estimates published annually in *Printers' Ink*.

[2] Other tobacco products accounted for an additional $832 million in 1958.

357

Federal yields from cigarettes were larger than the proceeds of all internal revenue taxes for any year prior to 1918. Tobacco is the sixth most important cash crop in American agriculture and ranks first in Connecticut, Maryland, Virginia, North Carolina, and Kentucky. Cigarettes are distributed in all states by about 7,000 jobbers and 1.4 million retail outlets.

The economic importance of cigarettes is a relatively recent development. Two generations ago cigarettes were a minor branch of the tobacco industry, a branch which in point of value ranked below the plug, smoking and cigar branches but above snuff, fine cut chewing tobacco and little cigars. In 1900, cigarettes accounted for 3.4 per cent of the leaf tobacco consumed, for 6.7 per cent of tobacco tax receipts and for 4.1 per cent of the value of tobacco products. In 1958 the analogous figures were 88 per cent, 96 per cent, and 87 per cent. Total expenditure on cigarettes in 1900 was only $12.8 million, or about 0.2 per cent of sales in 1958. Cigarettes came into general acceptance among men during the First World War and the increasing growth since then has been based upon the spread of smoking among women, upon the progressive displacement of other forms of tobacco and upon the general growth in population.

Yet, although the great absolute growth of cigarette consumption has occurred during the twentieth century, cigarettes have a much longer history in the United States. They were first introduced to this country about the time of the Civil War and since 1870 have grown steadily in favor. In almost every year, the consumption of cigarettes has been higher than in the year preceding, and the industry was experiencing rapid percentage growth in the early years when absolute consumption was small.

Early History

Throughout its long history the output of the cigarette industry has been concentrated in a few firms. In the early 1880's four firms dominated the industry. Allen & Ginter of Richmond, Virginia; William S. Kimball & Co. of Rochester, New York; and Kinney Tobacco Company and Goodwin & Co., both of New York City, together produced about four-fifths of the national total. Between 1880 and 1885, the firm of W. Duke Sons & Co. which had previously produced only smoking tobacco secured a foothold in the industry through the extraordinary persistence and salesmanship of James B. Duke. The predominance of all these firms was based upon their ability to expand markets. The product was new and strange, and it was necessary both to educate consumers and to open distribution channels through tobacco jobbers and retailers so that goods would actually be available to satisfy the new demand. The position of the five leading firms was based upon their advertising ability and on their power to keep the channels of distribution open.

In these years, however, while the industry was young, even the leading firms were quite small, and it was probable that the existing concentration of output could not be long continued. At this time all cigarettes were made by hand, and a skilled workman could roll no more than 3,000 in a ten-hour day. Labor costs for hand rolling were about 75 cents per thousand in 1885, and the process of manufacture required the supervision of numbers of skilled workmen which would have caused difficulties in the operation of really large plants. As the industry continued its growth, the leading firms could maintain their position only by an equivalent increase in their own size, and if technological methods had remained unchanged, it seems unlikely that cigarette companies as large as those we know today could have grown up. The old firms would have found their expansion blocked by rising costs. New firms would have come in and much less concentration of output would have resulted.

In the early 1880's, however, a great technological change occurred with the invention of suitable cigarette-rolling machinery. The most successful of several inventions was patented in 1881 by James Bonsack and came into general use after 1884. The Bonsack machine could produce 200 to 220 cigarettes per minute and was usually rented complete with operator for 30 cents or 33 cents per thousand depending on whether a printing device was used. Even with these royalties the cost of fabricating was cut in half, and the labor cost alone was cut to 2 cents per thousand. With such significant cost savings it was inevitable that machine methods should supplant hand methods on all but the highest priced brands.

With the introduction of machinery the problem of supervising hand labor was removed, and the principal obstacle to continued industrial concentration disappeared. It was possible to increase the output of a firm simply by adding more machines, and the firm was free to expand to the extent that its sales would allow. In this purely negative sense the adoption of machinery removed potential barriers to the scale of enterprise.

Machinery also gave positive encouragement to increased concentration by the advantages which it conferred on particular manufacturers. James B. Duke was the first to adopt machines for his factory in spite of a general belief that consumers opposed machine-made goods. This gave him a considerable cost advantage over those firms which lagged in introducing the new methods. Moreover, in return for assuming the risk of consumer disfavor, he secured a secret contract with the Bonsack Machine Co. which provided for a rebate to reduce the net royalty to 20 cents per thousand whether printed or not, and a later clause guaranteed that the royalty charged Duke should always be 25 per cent less than that paid by anyone else.

This advantage itself was not so important as was the use which Duke made of it. The savings in costs were reinvested in the industry as was the major part of all operating profits. Duke spent large sums on advertising and on deals and inducements to jobbers and was himself extremely active in visiting the retail trade to promote his business. The resources which Duke commanded because of his secret contract and the extraordinary persistence and energy with which he applied them brought him rapidly to the front of the industry, and by 1889, W. Duke Sons & Co. was the largest cigarette manufacturer in the country.

The Tobacco Trust

The other companies found their businesses invaded and fought back as best they could, but Duke invested $800,000 in advertising in 1889 alone, and the struggle grew increasingly unattractive for the other companies. Unable to defeat Duke, they agreed to join him. In 1890, the American Tobacco Company was incorporated in New Jersey and exchanged its securities for the properties of the five leading companies.

The new company, which quickly became known as the "Tobacco Trust," controlled at the outset more than 90 per cent of the national output of cigarettes, and it maintained essential monopoly control for the next twenty years. The same aggressiveness which Duke had shown in forming the combination was used to preserve it and to expand its activities. The Trust at first secured exclusive rights to the Bonsack machine in return for royalty payments of $250,000 a year, bought up and sequestered patents on other machines, and sought to prevent the use of still other machines by suits for patent infringement. Adverse legal decisions removed this protection by 1895, but in any event it does not seem to have been a principal source of the Trust's power.

Such competition as arose was subjected to ruthless attack. The Trust cut prices drastically to discipline local competition. Thus, in 1900, the American Beauty brand was sold in North Carolina for $1.50 per thousand at a time when the internal revenue tax was $1.50. The Trust also secured favored treatment from jobbers, sought to deny wholesale facilities to competitors, fomented strikes in competing factories, bid up prices on local leaf tobacco markets where competitors secured their supplies, and in other ingenious ways made life difficult for independent manufacturers. The knowledge that measures of this kind would be used was a powerful deterrent to such potential competitors as might be attracted by the high level of Trust profits.

Perhaps the most important advantage of the Trust was the consumer loyalty to its many popular brands.[3] A large number of these were inherited from constituent companies and given further heavy advertising promotion. By 1898, one of the old Kinney brands, Sweet Caporal, accounted for more than 50 per cent of the total national consumption. Consumer loyalty and the market pressure which the Trust developed through advertising were probably even more effective than the various methods of unfair competition in maintaining the position of the Trust. By 1899, the Trust's output had risen to 95 per cent of the national total.

Most of the Trust's brands of cigarettes were made of straight domestic Virginia tobacco, and after 1900, a shift of public taste in favor of Turkish tobacco subjected the Trust to a temporary loss of business. Turkish cigarettes were relatively expensive on account of the imported leaf and were made by hand in small shops operated by Greeks, Egyptians, or other Levantine manufacturers.[4] The Trust had no established position in such brands and by 1906 its share of the national output had fallen to 80 per cent. However, the Trust redoubled its competitive efforts, bought up several of the leading independents and supported their brands with heavy advertising and with attractive prices to jobbers.[5] A number of completely new brands of Virginia tobacco or of blended Virginia and Turkish tobacco were also introduced.[6] By 1910, the independent Turkish manufacturers were no longer a threat and the Trust had regained complete dominance of the cigarette industry.

Although the Tobacco Trust was initially a combination of cigarette manufacturers, the Trust took early measures to invade the other larger branches of the tobacco industry. Using its large cigarette profits for heavy advertising and cutthroat price warfare and employing many other forms of market and financial pressure, the Trust secured dominant control of the

---

[3] The most important were Richmond Straight Cut, Pets, Virginia Brights, Duke's Best, Cameo, Sweet Caporal, Vanity Fair, High Grade, and Old Judge. The Trust produced about 100 brands of cigarettes in all.

[4] The leading independent brands were Natural, Melachrino, Milo, Condax, Rameses, and Philip Morris. These were manufactured in the order named by Schinasi Brothers, M. Melachrino & Company, Surbrug Company, Eli Condax & Company, Stephano Brothers, and Philip Morris & Company, Ltd.

[5] Trust Turkish brands included Pall Mall, Egyptian Deities, Murad, Mogul, Egyptian Straights, Helmar, and Turkish Trophies.

[6] The most important were Piedmont, Hassan, Mecca, and Fatima.

rest of the industry and around the turn of the century established the Continental Tobacco Company, the American Snuff Company, and the American Cigar Company to monopolize the plug, snuff, and cigar branches. By 1910, the Trust had achieved the following percentage control of various tobacco products:

Cigarettes	86.1 per cent
Plug	84.9 per cent
Smoking	76.2 per cent
Fine Cut	79.7 per cent
Snuff	96.5 per cent
Little Cigars	91.5 per cent
Cigars	14.4 per cent

The failure to achieve monopoly control of cigars stands in interesting contrast to the Trust's accomplishments with other tobacco products. In 1890, plug, smoking tobacco, and snuff were already concentrated in a moderately small number of firms, and it was possible for the Trust, by aggressive competition, to force them to combine further into single monopolies. The cigar industry, however, was not concentrated for reasons of technology. Adequate cigar-making machinery did not exist, and hand production methods involved serious administrative difficulties if large numbers of skilled workers were to be supervised. Cigar factories were characteristically small and remained so for many years. Even the aggressive tactics of the Trust were not sufficient to establish monopoly in cigars, and the Trust never enjoyed either the control or the profits which it had secured elsewhere. The persistence of industrial decentralization in cigars indicates the importance of the Bonsack machine in making possible the heavy concentration of the cigarette industry.

In the course of its expansion, the Trust absorbed some 250 companies operating throughout the world. Some were continued as subsidiaries, some were consolidated and some closed down. In 1909, 86 companies were doing business as members of the Tobacco Trust in the continental United States, Puerto Rico, and Cuba, and at least 33 companies were operating in other parts of the world. In addition to tobacco manufacture, the Trust had important interests in cigarette and cigar machinery, in licorice paste, in box manufacture, and in a large chain of retail stores.

The Trust was regarded with hostility by tobacco farmers, by distributors, by the competitors whom it suppressed, and by the public at large. There were several investigations of its affairs and a number of states instituted fruitless legal proceedings. At length the Federal Government intervened, and in 1911 the Supreme Court held the American Tobacco Company and all its subsidiaries and its affiliates to be in violation of the Sherman Act. A subsequent circuit court decree divided the assets and business among some sixteen "successor companies." The principal direct tobacco business of the Trust fell to only four companies: R. J. Reynolds Tobacco Company, Liggett & Myers Tobacco Company, P. Lorillard Company, and a much reduced American Tobacco Company. Reynolds had been a plug and smoking tobacco subsidiary of the Trust and was now removed from Trust control. Liggett and Lorillard, bearing names of companies acquired by the Trust, were newly organized for the express purpose of receiving a portion of the assets of the American Tobacco Company. Only these last three companies were engaged in the cigarette business.

The Camel Revolution

Scarcely had the new competitive regime been established when a second revolution occurred. In 1913 the R. J. Reynolds Tobacco Company which had not previously produced cigarettes introduced a new brand, Camel, which immediately swept the country. Reynolds expanded production as fast as it was able. New machines were added as rapidly as they could be obtained, and by 1917 Camel accounted for 35 per cent of the national output of cigarettes. By 1923 the proportion had risen further to 45 per cent.

A principal reason for this sudden popularity was the new blend of Virginia, Burley, Turkish, and Maryland tobaccos from which Camels were made. Burley had previously been used in smoking tobacco and in plug where its capacity to absorb quantities of sweetening sauces gave it an especial usefulness. This characteristic was now turned to account in the manufacture of cigarettes and appealed to the public taste.

There were also several contributory reasons for Camel popularity. Wartime shortages forced consumers to abandon their favorite Turkish brands and to try something new. By the end of the war, habit had reinforced natural liking. Camel was put up in a package of twenty like that in use today rather than in the cardboard slide and shell box commonly employed at the time. This new package had previously been used only on expensive blended cigarettes, yet Camel was priced at 10 cents compared with 15 cents for Fatima. Finally, Camel abandoned the use of redeemable coupons and prizes which had been a principal method of advertising in earlier years and which had increasingly come to be regarded as an unsatisfactory form of market pressure. Camel advertising was restricted to newspapers, magazines and billboards and on its pack was printed the slogan which it still bears, "Don't look for premiums or coupons as the cost of the tobaccos blended in Camel cigarettes prohibits the use of them." Reynolds was thus able both to abandon an unsatisfactory medium of advertising and to obtain an unfavorable implication regarding the quality of products which continued to use the older methods.

Whatever the reasons, Camel's success was overwhelming and revolutionized the industry. The American Tobacco Company and Liggett & Myers Tobacco Company brought out Lucky Strike and Chesterfield, respectively, made of similar tobacco blends and similarly packed and advertised. Although these retaliatory brands were quite successful from the start Camel held undisputed sway for several years. By 1925, however, the new brands as a group completely dominated the industry. Their combined sales were 82.3 per cent of the national total while the many brands inherited from the Trust steadily declined.

In 1925, George Washington Hill, one of the greatest advertisers of all times, became President of the American Tobacco Company and his subsequent advertising campaigns directed especially to women with the slogan "Reach for a Lucky instead of a sweet" caused a rapid increase in sales. In 1930, Lucky Strike first surpassed Camel in volume and for the next 25 years these two brands alternated the lead. For most of that same period, Chesterfield was sometimes in second and sometimes in third place.

Equally as dramatic as the rise of Camel was the decline of the Lorillard brands. This company had inherited most of the Trust's leading Turkish business, and in 1913 sold 22 per cent of the industry total. However, Lorillard developed no suitable answer to Camel and when the Turkish brands decayed, Lorillard's sales declined too, and by 1925 were only 1.9 per cent of the national consumption. The introduction of Old Gold in 1926 accompanied by unusually heavy advertising outlays was marked by a rise to 7 per cent of the national output in 1930 but this proportion was never again reached. For many years Old Gold enjoyed substantial success but remained in fifth place far behind the leaders.

By the end of World War I, the cigarette industry had achieved a new and apparently stable structure. The three leading companies had emerged in a position of complete dominance and three new leading brands had emerged which would not be seriously challenged during the interwar period. Advertising through national media had become the principal method of competition. The change from advertising by the package to general publicity on a national scale helped to reinforce the supremacy of the new brands, for the selling pressure developed in concentrated promotion of a single brand was greater than that developed by the same total expenditure scattered over a number of brands and dissipating much of its power in self-competition. The efficiency of large-scale advertising as an instrument of market pressure was sufficient for many years to maintain the supremacy of the major brands.

With secure market control there was little need for aggressive price tactics to restrain independents. Price discipline among the "Big Three" was strong and net profits as a percentage of equity were running at double the average rate for manufacturing corporations. Rapidly growing demand carried absolute profits to record heights. In terms of profits, prices, and extent of market control, it is difficult to see much difference between the old Trust and the new industrial regime which matured in the twenties.

A Pricing Error and New Competition

This comfortable state of affairs was disrupted by the Great Depression and by a major strategic error in pricing whose effects are still felt. In 1931, declining incomes were severely affecting consumer spending and cigarette consumption showed one of its rare declines below the level of the preceding year. Leaf tobacco prices were the lowest since 1905 and cigarette manufacturing costs were correspondingly reduced. Reynolds chose this time to raise the price of Camel to $6.04 per thousand net, the highest level in ten years, involving a rise of 1 cent per pack at retail. The other companies followed.

This interesting experiment in extreme monopoly pricing probably had little effect on the total consumption of cigarettes but it did make possible the rise of new competition. With the existing leaf prices an acceptable cigarette could be made for 10 cents per pack at retail and the difference between this and 14 cents or 15 cents for the standard brands made it possible to sell the new cigarettes. A number of brands were introduced of which Wings of the Brown & Williamson Tobacco Co. and Twenty Grand of the Axton-Fisher Tobacco Co. were the most important. By the end of 1932, sales of the 10-cent brands had risen to 23 per cent of the national total. Despite this invasion and despite the decline in total consumption, net profits for the "Big Three" companies were $100 million in 1932, or the second highest on record.

In January 1933, American cut the price of Lucky Strike to $5.29 net and the others followed. In February there was a second cut to $4.85. Efforts were made to see that the major brands were sold for 10 cents a pack at retail even though this allowed distributors a markup of only 15 cents a thousand. The 10-cent brands wilted under the attack and their sales fell to less than 10 per cent of the total. During the price war, both Lucky Strike and Camel were sold at a loss and when the enemy was under control, Reynolds, in January 1934, led a rise back to $5.38.

Although the 10-cent brands were repulsed, they were not eliminated, but recovered some ground when the extreme price pressure was removed. For most of the decade these brands sold around 11 per cent of the industry total. New 10-cent brands were introduced, and by 1939 the market share had increased to 13 per cent and the absolute quantity sold was more than twice as large as in 1932.

Other new competition began stirring in the thirties attracted partly by the price umbrella of the "Big Three" and partly by the growing national market which now had room for more than three brands, each receiving heavy advertising. In 1933, Philip Morris & Co., Ltd., Inc., an independent manufacturer of Turkish cigarettes in the days of the Trust, introduced a new blended cigarette which by 1939 was the country's fourth largest brand with 6.1 per cent of industry sales. The Brown & Williamson Tobacco Co., an independent plug manufacturer in the days of the Trust,[7] introduced a number of cigarette brands, Raleigh, filter tipped Viceroy, and mentholated Kool in addition to its 10-cent brands. From 1932 to 1942, Brown & Williamson was the fourth largest producer in the country with 10.6 per cent of industry sales in 1939, although none of the brands individually were of the first rank. Axton-Fisher was moderately successful with mentholated Spud. In 1938, the Riggio Tobacco Company, a newly organized firm, introduced Regents, the first successful king-size brand though its share of market was very small.

As a result of this new competition, the relative position of the "Big Three" weakened. Their market share declined steadily throughout the decade from 91 per cent in 1930 to 69 per cent in 1939. The control of the "Big Three" in 1930 had not in fact been as secure as it had seemed and the error of pricing beyond what their power would support imposed serious penalties.

Still further trouble arose from increased vulnerability to antitrust action. Largely as a result of this price behavior, the major companies in 1941 were convicted of conspiracy in restraint of trade and of monopolization under Sections 1 and 2 of the Sherman Act. This conviction was upheld by the Supreme Court in 1946.

Neither the direct business setback nor the antitrust conviction were seriously damaging in the short run. Despite the loss in market share, the major companies' absolute sales continued to grow as did total profits. Re-

---

[7] Since 1927 Brown & Williamson has been a subsidiary of the British American Tobacco Co., Ltd., one of the successor companies to the old Trust.

turn on equity, once the price war was out of the way, was well above the average manufacturing level. Moreover, part of the decline in market share was due to special depression conditions which made 10-cent cigarettes possible and helped to sell them. With higher incomes and leaf tobacco prices after the war, the cheaper cigarettes declined and by 1947 the market share commanded by the "Big Three" companies had recovered to 84.7 per cent. The pricing error reduced their sales and profits below what they might have been but the companies' basic power and profitability was not seriously hurt. The price war may even have served as a warning to smaller companies not to compete too aggressively and especially not through price.

The antitrust convictions also had limited direct effect. Fines of $250,000 were imposed, a matter of no particular moment in so rich an industry. At one time, it appeared that the government might seek to reform the industry through further proceedings in equity but fourteen years have passed without specific action and it seems unlikely that any will now come.

Yet for the long run both the business changes and the antitrust litigation have had important consequences. The unsettling of brand loyalties and competitive relationships in the thirties laid the basis for major industrial changes after World War II and the antitrust conviction has placed important limits on competitive behavior and profits. As was true of the first Tobacco Case of 1911, the second Tobacco Case of 1946 marked the end of an era in the cigarette industry.

King-size, Filters, and Cancer

Since 1946, the cigarette industry has seen a revolution in product and competitive standings comparable in importance to the earlier Camel revolution. The dominance of the three leading brands has been broken and the bulk of the market has been taken over by a proliferation of new brands—king-size, filtered, and mentholated. The share of the market accounted for by Camel, Lucky Strike, and Chesterfield regular has fallen from the post-war high of 82.5 per cent in 1947 to 27.5 per cent in 1959, and the share of the "Big Three" companies has fallen from 84.7 per cent to 68.8 per cent. Camel remains the leading brand but Lucky Strike and Chesterfield regular have fallen to fourth and tenth positions respectively. Reynolds and American are still the leading companies, but Liggett & Myers has declined so that its domestic sales are less than half as large as those of either of the other two. Lorillard and Brown & Williamson have trebled their market shares to overtake Philip Morris. The industry is now composed of a "Big Two" with domestic sales of over 120 billion cigarettes each, a "Second

Four" with sales in the range of 40 billion to 60 billion, and a few smaller companies with less than 2 billion, which supply 0.5 per cent of the market.

These changes were in large part the result of developments begun in the thirties. The growth of Philip Morris and of Brown & Williamson showed that it was possible for new brands to grow despite the concentrated promotion of the three leading brands. The growth of mentholated cigarettes like Kool, filter cigarettes like Viceroy, and king-size brands like Regents indicated that there was a market for new types of products and that if the leading firms did not supply them, other companies would.

The leading companies moved quickly to develop the market for king-size cigarettes. In 1939, American converted Pall Mall [8] to a king-size brand and later followed with Herbert Tareyton. Liggett & Myers converted its old brand Fatima, Lorillard brought out Embassy, and Philip Morris introduced Dunhill Majors. In 1949, Reynolds finally abandoned its policy of exclusive concentration on one brand by bringing out Cavalier.

Of all these brands, only Pall Mall and Herbert Tareyton were successful, accounting for 15.9 per cent of the total cigarette market by 1953. In 1952, the king-size Chesterfield was introduced and in 1953, Raleigh, Philip Morris and Old Gold appeared in the large size, thus attempting to capitalize on existing brand acceptance in a new market. Meanwhile, mentholated and filter sales had been growing. By 1953, the market share of the three leading brands had fallen to 54.3 per cent and the share of the three leading companies to 75.6 per cent.

How far or how rapidly these developments would have gone in the absence of new influences it is impossible to say. As it turned out, the process of change was slowed in some respects and accelerated in others by the well-known "cancer scare," beginning in late 1953. The charge by reputable medical authorities that cigarette smoking is an important factor in lung cancer and heart disease confronted the industry with major problems of public relations and competitive strategy.

The companies have disputed the validity of the medical charges and have moved simultaneously to bring out filter brands which yield less of the supposedly harmful tars and other combustion products. Filter brands rose from less than 1 per cent of the market in 1952 to 51 per cent in 1959 and 6 of the 10 leading brands in 1959 were filter cigarettes.

One of the first effects of the cancer scare in 1953 was to double the sales

[8] Pall Mall had been the leading Turkish brand of the old Trust and marked George Washington Hill's first great advertising and promotion success as a young man. Revived as a domestic blend in 1936 and entrusted to a subsidiary of the American Tobacco Company where it would not interfere with the promotion of Lucky Strike, Pall Mall showed moderate but satisfactory growth with very little advertising support.

of Viceroy, the old Brown & Williamson filter, and to sharply accelerate the growth of Lorillard's Kent, which had been introduced in 1952. Liggett & Myers introduced L&M in 1953. American's filter version of Herbert Tareyton, Reynolds' Winston, and Lorillard's Old Gold Filters all appeared in 1954. Philip Morris' Marlboro filter was introduced in 1955. In 1956, Reynolds and Brown & Williamson introduced menthol flavored filters in Salem and Kool filters respectively, and several companies have introduced competing brands in the last three years. Porous papers have been introduced to provide a "cooler" smoke.

The cancer scare stopped the rapid growth of plain king-size brands and since 1953 these brands have declined as a class though much less rapidly than the old regular brands. Pall Mall, however, has risen against the trend and is now the second leading brand with 13.6 per cent of the total cigarette market and 72.9 per cent of the king-size market. Chesterfield king has almost half the remainder of the king-size market, while Reynolds has not been successful.

In contrast, the filter market is much more actively disputed. Winston is the dominant leader with 19.8 per cent of the filter market and 10.6 per cent of the total cigarette market in 1959. Winston is the third largest cigarette brand of any type. Kent is not far behind with 16.4 per cent of the filter market, and L&M, Viceroy, and Marlboro all sell more than 20 billion. In the smaller and newer menthol filter market, Salem is the leader with about half the total, while Kool filters and Lorillard's Newport each have about one-sixth. American has no substantial position in filter cigarettes. Herbert Tareyton doubled in 1959, but still accounts for only 3.5 per cent of the filter market.

In the years prior to 1954, American was supported by its king-size brands and was industry leader by a substantial margin. Share of market fell only from 34.2 per cent to 32.6 per cent while Reynolds and Liggett declined more sharply. In the years since 1953, Reynolds has gained from its filter strength and the continued strength of Camel and has achieved industry leadership the past two years. Reynolds' share of market fell from 29.4 per cent in 1947 to 26.4 per cent in 1953 and rose to 30.2 per cent in 1959 for a net gain over the whole period. Liggett & Myers, with no outstanding success in any new type, saw its market share decline from 21.1 per cent in 1947 to 12.5 per cent in 1959. Meanwhile, the share of Philip Morris rose from 6.9 to 9.2 per cent, Lorillard from 4.3 to 11.7 per cent, and Brown & Williamson from 3.9 to 9.8 per cent.

The ultimate effect of the cancer problem is difficult to judge. The charges have so far produced only a temporary dip in cigarette consumption and it will take major confirming evidence and long exposure to the lesson for consumption to be seriously affected. Without additional evidence it is unlikely that existing smokers will reduce consumption substantially. Some threat to the industry's position is posed by the likelihood that fewer non-smokers will be converted.

It seems probable, however, that the multiplication of brands per company will be a permanent feature of the industry. Not only have old brands declined but it seems unlikely that new brands will enjoy the same exclusive dominance that was enjoyed by the "Big Three" in the twenties. With today's tremendously larger cigarette market, it is now possible for more than one brand per company to absorb large advertising expenditures with maximum efficiency, and the desire to appeal to more than one type of demand will probably ensure that each company maintains a full line. Ultimately, each product group will probably settle down with a stable set of brands, but continuous new product introductions are likely to be a feature of the industry for some time to come.

SECTION II: MARKET STRUCTURE AND PRICE POLICY

The present market structure of the cigarette industry is partly the result of historical development and accident. The personality of James B. Duke created the Tobacco Trust, the Supreme Court destroyed it and the character of the men who succeeded to control determined the pattern of power among the successor companies. Industry maturity and growth, specific pricing decisions, changes in public taste and the "cancer scare" have given rise to major changes in the product itself and in the methods of competition.

Market Structure

Yet in addition to accident and the heavy hand of the past there have been constant influences upon the industry throughout its history. In all phases of its existence the industry has shown a high concentration of output and marked similarities of competitive techniques and policies. The principal factors responsible have been the technology of cigarette manufacture and the nature of cigarette demand.

It has long been common knowledge that the demand for all tobacco products taken together is highly inelastic. Ever since the first discovery of the weed, tobacco has been a favorite object of taxation and of state or private monopoly because of the heavy charges which it can bear without appreciably diminishing consumption. The urgency of the wants which tobacco satisfies, the small cost even of relatively expensive tobaccos and the complete lack of substitutes make the volume of tobacco consumption independent of prices over a wide range.

For a single tobacco product like cigarettes other tobacco products are possible substitutes; pipes, cigars, plug and even snuff can be used in place of cigarettes and over the years wide shifts have occurred in the relative use of these various products. Between 1900 and 1958 the consumption of tobacco in the form of cigarettes rose from 3.4 per cent to 88 per cent of total tobacco consumption. Yet, it appears that in any short period of time very little substitution takes place in response to economic incentives. Changes in tobacco usage appear to be carried along on broad social currents of fashion and taste and do not seem to be greatly influenced either by relative prices of tobacco products or by advertising activity. In the longer study on which this chapter is based the author has demonstrated that the consumption of cigarettes is almost wholly insensitive to changes in price or in advertising pressures within the range of changes which can be observed.

In contrast the demand for individual brands of cigarettes is highly elastic in its response to price. In the thirties the major companies found that a difference of more than 3 cents per pack between the standard brands and the 10 cent brands was injurious to the business of the former and they tried to prevent the recurrence of so large a differential. This sensitivity existed despite real differences in product quality, for the leaf tobacco used in standard brands was sometimes more than twice as expensive as that in the cheaper cigarettes. Between brands of the same quality class, price sensitivity is even higher. In 1918, for example, Lucky Strike was sold for a short time at a higher retail price than Camel or Chesterfield and rapidly lost half its business. There were other occasions which indicated high sensitivity of demand for the standard brands to slight retail price differences.

Though individual brand demand is highly elastic there are some limits to this elasticity. Between different product types, i.e., regular, king size, filter, and menthol, there are significant physical differences which allow different prices. The leading brands in any one type are almost identical yet have slight differences in leaf blend and flavoring treatment. Customers show preferences for individual brands based in part on these differences and in part on intangible and even nonexistent qualities. The existence of irrational brand preference renders demand highly susceptible to advertising. The shifting fortunes of the leading brands within the same product type reflect both autonomous fluctuations in taste and the varying pressures of advertising.

These basic characteristics of cigarette demand give important market advantages to the large firm. It is possible to compete either through price cutting or through advertising and both methods have been used at one time or another. Whichever is used the large firm holds a competitive advantage over the small and it is to be expected that the industry will be dominated by large firms.

If prices are cut to gain business, as was the frequent practice under the Trust, it forces other firms to follow suit if they are not to lose a large portion of their business. This means that no firm can expect to gain customers by price cutting without inviting retaliation. But if prices are cut until all companies are losing money it is the largest and strongest which can hold out and endure losses until the small firms go under.

On the other hand, when competition is conducted through advertising its effectiveness depends largely on the total amount spent in promoting a given brand. Skillful salesmanship may allow one company to achieve the same results as another with only half the expenditures, for the persuasiveness of the advertising depends as much on the sales message as on the loudness with which it is shouted. Where advertising abilities are evenly distributed, however, the larger expenditures win and it is the big company which can afford these outlays.

Still another advantage to large companies arises from the requirements of distribution. With thousands of wholesalers and a million and a half retail outlets and with the heavy dependence of cigarette purchase upon convenient access, the maintenance of complete distribution requires expensive field sales activities. The major companies each employ many hundreds of salesmen to visit wholesalers and retailers for order taking, stock supervision, point of sales displays and other promotion. The expenses of such activities are more easily borne by large companies. A small producer can avoid some of these costs by accepting narrower distribution but he then reduces his market opportunities.

For all these reasons we would expect the output of the cigarette industry to be concentrated unless the large firm suffered a serious disadvantage in production costs. This does not appear, however, to be the case. The development of cigarette making machinery removed the technological impediments to the growth of the individual firm. Much of the process of manufacture is concerned with handling masses of tobacco in simple operations with close control of humidity and temperature. The machinery and equipment are readily adapted to quite small or very large factories. Cigarette making machines are highly complicated but the output of the individual machine is small with respect to that of the enterprise as a whole. A modern machine can product 750 to 1,600 cigarettes per minute and the American Tobacco Company was operating about 600 machines in 1942. The output of the firm can be quite small or very large simply by varying the number of machines; and while large firms may have significant cost advantages compared to very small ones there is no evidence of a significant cost advantage as between a moderately small or a very large firm. Since large firms are better able to apply market pressure they consequently expand until they have secured a large proportion of the national output.

Competitive Methods

The concentrated structure of the cigarette industry and the peculiarities of cigarette demand have a profound influence upon industry behavior. When firms are large they need not and in fact cannot, as in the theoretical model of perfect competition, accept the going market price and demand conditions as something given and outside their own control. Each firm must set its policy in the knowledge that its own action will affect the industry as a whole, and two entirely different types of behavior are possible. Policy may be directed either to eliminate weaker competitors by outright warfare or to ensure maximum profits on the assumption that all firms will survive. Price and advertising policies provide adequate tools for either task, and at various times in history both ends have been pursued and both tools have been used.

When Duke was a power in the industry, competitive measures were directed at injuring competitors so that they would either abandon business or agree to join forces. Usually extreme pressure by price cutting and advertising was combined with relatively generous offers to buy, and most competitors went out of existence by sale to the Trust rather than through the bankruptcy courts. Once control was achieved selling pressures were relaxed, and the Trust was able to enjoy a comfortable level of monopoly profits. So long, however, as control was incomplete, Duke used price and advertising primarily as weapons of commercial warfare rather than as instruments of short-run profit maximization.

After the dissolution on the other hand, competitive strategy was directed to increasing profits rather than to injuring competitors. The effect of the 1911 decree was to narrow the range of practicable business policy. There were now three or four major competitors, any one of whom possessed the resources to withstand prolonged price warfare. At the same time the decree forbade any recombination of the severed parts of the Trust. It was now possible neither to eliminate competitors nor to join them and the major successor companies were forced to adapt their policies to a situation in which each others' continued existence and independence must be taken for granted.

In these circumstances price cutting has serious disadvantages as a competitive weapon. These disadvantages stem from its very efficiency which would force competitors to retaliate, and from the small unit of sale which makes any retail price reduction a large percentage decline imposing a serious drain on profits. At present prices a reduction of one cent in the single package price would amount to 12 per cent of the manufacturer's net receipts excluding excise tax, and to more than the manufacturer's net profit after income taxes. A reduction in the price per carton can be more delicate but it is difficult to see how a price reduction attractive to consumers could also be attractive to manufacturers especially since competitors must cut in turn and no competitive advantage would result. A headlong drive to absorb losses may be useful for purposes of commercial warfare, but it is an unsatisfactory way of competing for business in normal times.

Advertising on the other hand can be a much less expensive method of competition. Even large changes in advertising outlays may be only a fraction of a cent per package. Advertising is as unlikely as price to change the total consumption of cigarettes, but competing advertising campaigns designed to change the division of the market need not result in a purposeless draw. The effectiveness of a given expenditure depends on skill and good fortune in discovering an effective sales message and each firm may hope to win. The frequent changes in relative position among the leading brands even during the period of "Big Three" supremacy testified to the erratic influence of advertising. Moreover, heavy advertising outlays by the leading firms make it more difficult for new competitors to grow and thus serve a function which is in the joint as well as in the competitive interest of the leading companies. For all these reasons it is evident why cigarette firms prefer to match prices and compete through advertising.

The disadvantages of using retail price as a competitive tool do not apply so strongly in the case of wholesale prices. Cigarettes are normally sold to jobbers at a price set by the manufacturer while the prices at which jobbers resell to retailers and the latter resell to the public are set by competition among distributors modified by occasional collusive agreements. Although a large change in the manufacturer's price will normally be reflected in a similar change at retail, a manufacturer's change of only a few cents per thousand may not be reflected in the retail price per pack but may be added to or subtracted from the distributors' margins. Thus, while the major firms almost always strive to maintain identical retail prices, it is possible that one of them may seek the goodwill of jobbers and retailers by shaving his net price. On the other hand, a slightly higher manufacturer's price by squeezing distributor's margins may make additional advertising funds available while leaving retail prices unchanged. Since both dealers' goodwill and advertising affect brand sales there may be a problem of deciding in which direction funds may be employed most profitably.

The greatest opportunities for the use of price as a competitive tool occur in connection with new product introductions. Consumer goodwill attaches to a brand rather than to the company which makes it, and hence a new and untried brand, even from a well known firm, is not equivalent to an established brand in the eye of the consumer. His willingness to try a new brand may not be greatly increased by a low price or prevented by a high price. In fact, since price is sometimes regarded as an indicator of quality, price incentives at some times or for some people may work in reverse. A new brand may be effectively promoted with prices which are below or above established brands. Once a brand is well known and accepted in a given class, interbrand elasticity becomes higher and uniformity of prices within the class is almost certain to be established.

Camel was introduced at 10 cents compared with Fatima, the nearest comparable brand at 15 cents. The directly competitive Lucky Strike and Chesterfield were introduced at the same 10 cent retail price but in the years before 1928 the price to jobbers of Lucky Strike was consistently several cents higher than the price of the other brands. At this time Lucky Strike sales were much smaller than Camel sales. As mentioned before, market position depends upon massive advertising expenditures, and if outlays on Lucky Strike were to be comparable in size to those on Camel, this required a higher level of expense per thousand. George Washington Hill's great skill in advertising and his even greater confidence in its value caused the company to set aside funds for that purpose, even though this involved a higher price and some distributor ill will. As sales increased, the necessity for additional funds declined and the dealer goodwill could be taken into account. After 1928, Lucky Strike was maintained at the same price as Camel. In 1922 experiments with Chesterfield prices above and below Camel indicated that a differential in either direction from the industry leader was not worth while and identical prices were thenceforth set.

The initial promotion of Philip Morris carried still further the price and advertising pressures which Lucky Strike had earlier employed. Philip Morris was introduced at a higher manufacturer's price and a higher retail price than the standard brands. An additional 1 cent per pack price to wholesalers made additional advertising funds available. A 2 cent higher price to consumers increased the dealers' interest which was important for a new brand. The higher retail price did not at first injure consumer demand because the new cigarette was named for an old expensive Turkish brand and by "trading down" on an established reputation was able to secure a special quality market. As the brand grew in size and was accepted as a counterpart of the standard brands the special quality appeal (which was due in part to the high price) no longer had validity and Philip Morris was brought to sell at the same wholesale and retail price as the other brands.

In normal competitive situations in the twenties and thirties when the major brands had achieved maturity and when all were selling comparable volumes, the major manufacturers were content to set identical wholesale prices, to strive through the auction markets to pay approximately the same prices for leaf tobacco, and to devote the difference between these two principal elements of receipts and costs to advertising outlays and to dividends as competitive pressures and stockholder requirements allowed. In this way price was not intended to serve the competitive function of shifting customers and the rise and fall of particular brands depended primarily on the use which the various companies could make of approximately equivalent advertising resources. The early behavior of Lucky Strike and Philip Morris represented departures from this pattern in order to compensate for lower sales as did the Old Gold effort to buy a market outright by sudden heavy expenditures financed through bond and stock issues.

The multiplication of brands since World War II has given many opportunities for price experiment, and the antitrust conviction has provided incentives to demonstrate price independence. With major new product classes assuming importance, it was necessary to establish workable differentials between them, and this involved testing and experimentation. The pattern of experimentation and some of the forces at work are seen quite clearly in the price record.

When price controls were abolished in 1946, all major brands bore the same price. In the first free price revisions, the manufacturer's net price of Camel was kept 3 cents per thousand below the prices of the other brands. The difference was small and made little sense in view of Camels' leading position, but was probably occasioned by the antitrust case. The companies protested bewilderment at what that case implied concerning their proper conduct, and this may have been an attempt to demonstrate noncollusive independence in pricing. In any event, the differential was eliminated in 1949.

In the early postwar period, Pall Mall was sold at the same net price as the standard brands but in 1950 was advanced to a differential of 4 cents per thousand above them. Cavalier, which had been introduced in 1949 at the standard brand price, stayed there while Pall Mall raised its differential to 9 cents in 1953 and to 44 cents in 1955. This attempt to win a market for Cavalier by a low price was unsuccessful and in 1956 Cavalier joined Pall Mall at 44 cents. Raleigh kings were introduced in 1953 at a 9-cent differential and held there when Pall Mall advanced in 1955. At the cheaper price Raleigh sales did not improve and in 1957 the price was raised to equal Pall Mall.

Meanwhile Chesterfield king was introduced in 1952 at a 47-cent differential while Pall Mall was at 4 cents. In 1953 the Chesterfield king differential was reduced to 30 cents when Pall Mall was at 9 cents. Philip Morris king and Old Gold king were also set at 30 cents when introduced in 1953. When Pall Mall's differential was raised to 44 cents in 1955 these other brands followed. In 1957 all king-size brands established a differential of 43 cents over the regular brand price, a differential which has lasted to the present time.

King-size brands thus showed both low- and high-price approaches to new market development. The low-price approach of Cavalier and Raleigh was ineffective and was dropped. The higher-price approach of Chesterfield and the others did not prove harmful and was taken over by the leader. Experiment had established a workable price structure, and identical prices once more ruled.

Filter cigarettes show an opposite type of behavior. Viceroy, as an old, small-volume brand, was priced in the early postwar years at various differentials between 45 and 62 cents over the standard brands. When Kent was introduced in 1952 it was priced $3.02 higher than the standard brands. This differential was reduced to $2.64 by a regular brand price rise in 1953. Viceroy stuck at 88 cents during this period. Liggett and Myers attempted to go along with the $2.64 differential when L&M filters were introduced in late 1953, but when Winston was introduced in early 1954 with massive promotion at an 88-cent differential, L&M capitulated at once and also established an 88-cent differential. Kent held on to the extra margin but lost more than half its sales in 1955 and joined the others in 1956. All other new filters were thereafter set at 88 cents until 1958 when the uniform differential was reduced to 53 cents. Even Parliament, an old premium brand acquired by Philip Morris, was reduced to the 53-cent level in 1958.

Thus the filter brands unlike the plain king-size brands saw the lower-price strategy win. For a time differentials rose moderately above the early Viceroy level, but the attempt of Lorillard and Liggett to get much higher margins was defeated. At the end of the period the differential above the regular brands was back to the early Viceroy range. Again experiment had established workable differentials and price uniformity ruled.

Apart from new product introduction and the price war of 1933, price has seldom been used as a competitive tool. Prices among brands in the same class are normally identical and price is not intended to affect the division of the market among competitors.

An interesting exception to this pattern occurred in 1928 when Reynolds led a price cut from $5.64 to $5.29 per thousand net. At this time Camel advertising was not proving effective while Lucky Strike advertising was having extraordinary success. The cut had the effect of reducing the advertising funds available to both firms and was probably designed to hobble the successful American campaign. Lucky Strike advertising did fall off but sales continued to expand and in 1929 Reynolds raised the price to $5.64 once again. This is one of the few cases in which price seems to have been used as a competitive tool among the major firms, though even here it is not the kind of tactic usually thought of in connection with the term "price competition."

Price Leadership

For many years the actual prices were determined by Reynolds. As the largest cigarette producer that company was in a position to enforce its will on other companies. In 1918 an attempt was made by American to lead a large price rise. Reynolds refused to follow and American was forced to retract. In 1921 American cut its price but Reynolds seized the initiative by cutting still further. Thereafter, Reynolds made the important changes with Liggett setting an identical price and American setting a related but slightly higher price. Reynolds led all later price changes until 1933 and all price rises until 1946. Since World War II, American as the largest seller most of the time has led most of the price increases. American has dominated the king-size price and Reynolds the filter price.

In 1956 Liggett & Myers attempted to lead a price rise of 50 cents per thousand on all brands. Liggett had never done this before and her executives had testified in the antitrust trial that they felt compelled by market forces to follow the lead of the other companies whether up or down. This contention was received skeptically by the courts and Liggett may have intended its lead as a declaration and demonstration of independence. Whatever the purpose, the attempt was a failure. The other companies refused to follow, and in two weeks Liggett retracted the rise.

Competition and Cooperation

The 1933 price war against the economy brands waged in a manner reminiscent of the old Trust was a highly unusual occurrence. Price policy in this industry since the Trust has normally been noncompetitive in character. For the most part price has been set with a view to good profits rather than to affect the division of the market.

This absence of price competition does not necessarily imply collusion by the manufacturers to fixed prices. It is clear that all have an interest in high prices and that there is no joint interest in low prices. The possible interest which each might have in cutting prices lower than the others is eliminated, except in some cases of new product introduction, by the certain knowledge that the others will follow any cut and that the net effect will be to the detriment of all without profit to any. As far as concerns price the interest of the leading firms is cooperative rather than competitive, and their small number makes effective price discipline possible without any need for outright collusion. As we have remarked before, the elimination or combination of the leading firms has not been a practicable object of market policy since the dissolution decree of 1911. Each firm must count on the continued existence of its competitors. Each firm need merely take into account the effect which its actions must inevitably have on the others, and in a mature market, judicious self-restraint will eliminate price competition as efficiently as would explicit agreement among them.

This common interest does not extend to all aspects of the firm's behavior. The major companies are in vigorous competition for the favor of consumers and for an increased share of the market. They have a joint interest in erecting advertising barriers against new competition but the difficulties of entry for a small firm are so great that little direct attention to this joint interest can be needed. In any event the companies' diverse interests in market shares induce them to make much larger advertising expenditures than they would if they were concerned solely to maximize the profits of the industry as a whole. The industry is unlike a monopoly in the resources it devotes to market competition through advertising and product innovation, but price behavior, once brands are well established, would probably not be very different if the major firms were governed by a single head.

Profits

The effects of noncompetitive pricing, of the 1933 price war, and of changing competitive patterns are clearly visible in the profit figures. The

FIGURE 1

Net Profits after Taxes as a Percentage of Equity

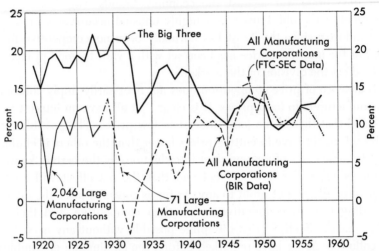

Source: Compiled from company reports; Bureau of Internal Revenue, *Statistics of Income*, 1931–47; R. C. Epstein, *Industrial Profits in the United States*, New York: National Bureau of Economic Research, 1934, pp. 56, 615; Federal Trade Commission-Securities and Exchange Commission, *Quarterly Financial Reports for Manufacturing Corporations*, 1948–58.

three leading companies earned yearly net profits after interest and taxes equal to 18 per cent on their average tangible net worth from 1912 to 1941 and the American Tobacco Co. earned 12.1 per cent on net sales over the same thirty-year period. Figure 1 presents a comparison between the percentage return on equity for the three principal cigarette companies and that for manufacturing corporations in general. American and Reynolds together earned 10.8 per cent on net sales from 1929 to 1941 while American manufacturing corporations as a whole were earning 3.8 per cent. In the twenty years before World War II, cigarette profits appear to have been at more than double the rate for manufacturing industry in general.

The superiority of cigarette earnings in the thirties partly reflected the stability of cigarette demand in the face of lower incomes. Even an industry characterized by flexible price competition would be expected to show superior profits if its demand were of this character. But in the twenties when most industries were prosperous the cigarette industry also earned at double the average level.

In the period since 1941 cigarette profits have been substantially lower and have generally been running at a rate about equal to that of manufacturing industry in general. This reduction can be explained by wartime price controls, by a cautious market policy probably induced by the monopoly conviction of 1941 and by the costs of the active multibrand competition of the past few years.

The rate of return on equity of course differs among the companies and Reynolds with its growing market share, rose to 18.7 per cent return in 1959. The industry did not suffer from the recent recession and it may be that earnings will rise in the future if the rapid pace of new product development slows down. For a remarkably long period, however, the three largest firms have had earnings near the average level and even American, first in sales much of the time and now second, has not secured unusually high profits.

Comparisons of profit figures over long periods of time are somewhat confused by changes in excise and corporate income taxes and by varying proportions of total corporate assets which are employed in direct cigarette manufacture. To avoid these complications and to provide a basis for comparison between the modern industry and the old Trust, Table 1 presents a series of average profit ratios for significant time periods.

TABLE 1

Selected Profit Ratios for the Trust and Three Successor Companies

	Trust	American	Liggett	Reynolds
Net earnings (before interest, after taxes) as percentage of net tangible assets:				
1890–1908	19.7			
1912–1941		15.1	14.7	20.0
1942–1947		8.9	8.9	12.0
1948–1958		7.4	9.3	8.5
Operating profit as percentages of net tangible assets in direct business:				
1890–1908	32.7			
1931–1941		20.8	17.3 [a]	23.8 [b]
1942–1947		17.0	15.8	20.1
1948–1958		14.3	13.6	18.7
Operating profit as percentage of net sales less tax				
1890–1908	25.8			
1931–1941		27.0	21.2 [a]	25.0 [b]
1942–1947		18.5	17.9	18.4
1948–1958		19.7	20.6	24.0

[a] 1933–41
[b] 1932–41

Sources: U.S. Bureau of Corporations, *Report on the Tobacco Industry*, Part II (1915); company reports.

It appears that though in the 1920's the leading successor companies enjoyed as high a return on sales as did the Trust, they had a somewhat lower return on tangible assets. Taking both of these measures of profitability together it appears that the rate of earnings of the successor companies was somewhat reduced by their competitive struggles and by the heavy advertising expenditures involved. Yet profits in the twenties remained remarkably high and testified to an almost unimpaired degree of market control.

Throughout the history of the industry profits have been limited by the possibility or actuality of outside competition. When the Trust was first organized and was enjoying its secure monopoly of cigarettes, profits were at the ample rate of 30 per cent of net sales less tax. Between 1894 and 1900 when successive price wars were extending the Trust's power over other branches of the tobacco industry, profits fell sharply to 20 per cent and below. Once the position of the Trust was consolidated the rate of profits on sales rose near its former level. Again in 1932 the operating profits of the American Tobacco Co. were 34 per cent of net sales less tax and this excessive margin allowed the 10-cent brands to prosper. Subsequent price cuts repulsed the invasion but reduced profit margins to around 25 per cent for most of the decade though they were back to 33 per cent in 1941. In the postwar period the slower growth in the total market, the increase in competition on new brands and a rising share of the market enjoyed by the three smaller companies, were reflected in substantially lower earnings.

From the usual analysis of nonaggressive oligopoly we would expect cigarette firms to maintain their prices as high as the elasticity of demand allows. The relevant elasticity which would make further price rises inadvisable in this case would not be the elasticity of demand for cigarettes as a whole but the long run elasticity of demand for the brands of the existing companies. The latter is influenced by the possibility of new entrants into the industry when the margin between cigarette prices and leaf costs becomes too wide. This seems to have been the basis of pricing during the long period between the two World Wars. In more recent years a variety of special influences have restricted prices below what the market probably would bear.

SECTION III: PUBLIC POLICY

Twice in its history the cigarette industry has been involved in major antitrust cases. Both cases have been important in the development of antitrust law and both have had significant effects upon industry structure and behavior. It is the purpose of this section to comment briefly on the nature of the antitrust cases and to consider the industrial reforms which have followed or which might follow in the future.

The 1911 Case

The 1911 Supreme Court opinion in *United States* versus *American Tobacco Co.* was a classic statement of antitrust principles and the subsequent Circuit Court decree was a classic example of industrial reform through dissolution. The courts were faced with a pattern of monopoly power deliberately created and predatorially used, and although this was one of the cases, along with the Standard Oil Case, in which the "rule of reason" was first developed, the pattern of industrial buccaneering was clearly outside the bounds of that rule. Legal remedy through dissolution—the breaking up of the monopoly into many segments—found one of its first applications here. The consequences for the industry were of fundamental importance.

The 1946 Case

The Supreme Court opinion in *American Tobacco Company* versus *United States* in 1946 had less clear effects either on antitrust law or on the industry than was the case with the 1911 decision. The problems involved may be indicated by a brief discussion of the case itself.

The leading companies and thirteen of their officers were convicted under Section 1 of the Sherman Act of a conspiracy or combination in restraint of trade and under Section 2 of conspiring to monopolize, of attempting to monopolize and of monopolizing the trade in cigarettes. The conviction in all its parts was based upon a finding by the jury that conspiracy or combination existed among the various defendants both to fix prices and to exclude competitors from the business.

Problems both for antitrust law and for effective remedy arise from the fact that no specific evidence was introduced during the trial to show that the defendants had gotten together or had made any explicit agreement on any important aspect of their businesses. Instead the conspiracy was to be inferred from a pattern of common behavior. As we have seen above the common price policy of the leading companies follows naturally from their individual interests and need not imply collusion.

Three possible interpretations of the jury verdict and the later Supreme Court opinion may be advanced.

1. The jury based its verdict on insufficient evidence. In the words of one of the defense attorneys the companies were "judicially lynched."

2. The kind of common action on price practiced by the industry and understood by all its members represented a kind of combination or conspiracy in restraint of trade without the need to prove an explicit agreement or without even the need for such an agreement to exist. Under this interpretation the cigarette industry is obviously monopolistic in economic terms and with new developments in legal thought, the fact of economic market power becomes nearly the same as legally defined monopoly.[9]

3. The jury convicted and the Supreme Court sustained the conviction because of a pattern of common oligopoly action lying quite outside the bounds of acceptable competitive behavior.

If interpretation 1 is correct, it implies a miscarriage of justice. For reasons to be developed below, this interpretation is not persuasive.

If interpretation 2 is correct, it raises peculiar problems of public policy for if rational oligopoly behavior is the same thing as illegal conspiracy or combination it makes futile a direct attack on the conspiracy itself. The conspiracy is merely symptomatic of a market structure which confers illegal power and the violation of the act arises from the structure of the industry itself not merely from deliberate illegality in the details of market behavior. This suggests that civil action to secure changes in the industrial structure would have been more appropriate than the criminal penalties on behavior actually enforced.

It seems doubtful, however, that interpretation 2 is valid either for the meaning of the law or as an explanation of the cigarette case itself. The appeals courts did not say that the pattern of common action on pricing was illegal but merely that a pattern of common action was grounds upon which a jury could properly infer conspiracy. It is doubtful that the jury was sufficiently impressed by common price behavior to bring a conviction on these grounds alone although the jury may well have entertained dark suspicions. In the cigarette trial, however, more than mere suspicion was present. There were clearly established indications of collusion on minor matters such as the sending of leaf buyers to market towns, and the price behavior from 1931 to 1934 indicated the presence of monopoly power and the use of that power for its own increase.

The 1931 price rise in the midst of depression clearly could have occurred only if the manufacturers had strong administrative discretion over their prices and were prepared to act cooperatively. It was the kind of use of monopoly power which popular thought has always opposed and feared.

---

[9] See E. V. Rostow, "The New Sherman Act: A Positive Instrument of Progress," *University of Chicago Law Review*, Vol. 14, No. 4 (June 1947), pp. 585.

So too the 1933 price war against the economy brands, while it indicated the actual weakness of this monopoly power, was a classic case of monopoly price raiding. The occasions of minor collusion and the aggressive use of monopoly power gave the jury something to strike at and probably served to increase the jury's willingness to infer collusion from a pattern of common price behavior.

It seems likely that interpretation No. 3 is nearest the truth and that the 1946 antitrust case penalized the abuse of power rather than its mere existence. Later antitrust cases have not made cooperative oligopoly pricing illegal *per se* and the cigarette conviction does not appear to have depended on such a principle.

Regardless of the explanation of the antitrust conviction itself, that conviction opened up a wide range of possibilities of industrial reform. Through further proceedings in equity the government could have sought to modify industry behavior. Structural reform through breaking up the existing companies into a number of smaller ones would have had a classic precedent in the cigarette industry itself. The fact that no further legal action has been taken raises some interesting questions. In what ways is the existing organization and behavior of the industry unsatisfactory? What opportunities for useful reform have been missed? What have been the effects of antitrust policy as it has actually worked?

Industry Behavior

An evaluation of the behavior of the cigarette industry might start from a consideration of the kinds of unsatisfactory behavior that traditional economic analysis leads us to expect from a monopoly. According to that analysis the economic results of monopoly are inferior in several respects to those which a perfectly competitive industry would yield. The monopolist sets prices higher than the competitive level and these high prices discourage consumption and result in the exclusion from the industry of resources which otherwise would be employed there. The monopolist operates on the downward sloping section of a U-shaped average cost curve so that excess capacity exists causing unit costs to be higher than they need be. The ability of the monopolist to do these things depends on the exclusion of outside competition and measures may be taken to reinforce the barriers to entry. The consequence is excessive profits. Thus the monopolist secures pay for the antisocial functions of restricting opportunity, increasing costs and disturbing the optimum allocation of resources.

At least one of the characteristics indicated by traditional analysis is true of the cigarette industry. For most of its history it has earned at about double the average profit rate. Market control has been reflected in high profits. In recent years, however, other pressures have forced cigarette profits to average levels and this may be accounted as one of the accomplishments of antitrust prosecution.

With this exception the failings attributed to monopoly do not seem to be characteristic of the cigarette industry. The extremely inelastic demand means that high prices and high profits do not reduce consumption. The firm does not exhibit a U-shaped cost curve, for the small producer is as efficient as the large and the long-run average cost curve is flat. Thus no burden of higher cost is imposed on the industry by its pricing practices and the excess capacity does not exist from any other cause than fluctuations in brand demand.

A question arises, however, whether large advertising outlays may not represent a special kind of waste in this industry. Considerable sums are involved and have been growing larger. In the early postwar years the industry spent around $50 million annually on advertising and between 1954 and 1958 total expenditure doubled from $74 million to $142 million.

A small part of this expense serves to inform consumers of what is available and thus to make possible a more intelligent choice. But most of the expenditure is for other competitive purposes. Some of it results in indirect entertainment benefits but this raises other issues concerning the organization and functioning of television and other communications industries which are beyond the scope of this chapter. Massive advertising also serves to strengthen large producers vis-a-vis small ones and is an important factor in maintaining the highly concentrated structure of the industry.

If advertising expenditures are to be accounted a waste it is important to note that they are wastes of competition. The expenditure is designed to capture the public attention and to foster brand loyalties. Advertising serves as a weapon in the competitive struggle and helps to shift customers among nearly identical commodities. This shifting may be on an irrational basis, but so long as competition exists some method for providing this shifting is necessary, and if advertising were not used in interbrand competition some substitute would have to be found. Other forms of sales promotion are also expensive. So long as the present structure of the industry exists, advertising appears a necessary expense, and while questions might be raised concerning the volume it is not easy to arrive at a judgment as to how much is superfluous and wasteful.

Industry Structure

Most cigarette industry behavior patterns are implicit in its present structure and any substantial change in the functioning of the industry would probably require a change in the number of firms and their relationships to each other. What kinds of structural reform might have been undertaken?

It should be noted at the outset that no possible reorganization of the cigarette industry could bring it close to the theoretical model of perfect competition. Perfect competition requires among other conditions that a commodity be homogeneous in quality and that marginal costs rise sharply at a small scale of output. Rising marginal costs keep the firm small while small size and homogeneous product yield a perfectly elastic demand curve for the firm. The perfectly competitive firm has no effect on price, no concern with price policy and no problem of sales. It can sell any amount it wishes at the going price and need only decide how large an output it is profitable to produce.

The cigarette industry obviously does not and cannot operate under such conditions. Long-run marginal costs do not rise and there is no limit to the size of the firm except that set by the market. The product of rival manufacturers although similar are not identical in the public eye and cannot be made so. The firm cannot merely sell at a going price all that it wishes but must fight for markets and this is the function of brand names, advertising, and other methods of distribution competition.

Since perfect competition cannot exist in the cigarette industry, all possible alternative forms of market structure which might be set up in place of the present oligopoly must contain some other kind or degree of monopolistic element. If the present firms were merged into one, reversing the 1911 dissolution, monopoly would result. If they were broken into very small segments the nonhomogeneous product would ensure a state of Chamberlinian monopolistic competition at least in the short run. A third possible situation in the industry would be a somewhat larger number of somewhat smaller firms yielding an oligopoly similar to the present but with the possibility of slightly different competitive relationships among the members.

If the cigarette industry were a complete monopoly under either private or government auspices the wastes of competition would disappear and there would be little need for advertising. This single possible advantage would be balanced by all the other disadvantages normally attributed to secure monopolies. Prices would be high and profits excessive unless restricted by regulation which has its own wastes and disadvantages. Government-run monopolies in other lands do not occasion confidence that full monopoly would be economically superior to the existing organization.

If the industry were composed of a large number of small firms profits would be expected to be at a competitive level which is about where they have been recently in any event. There is a serious probability that costs would be higher. There is no guarantee that an industry made up of small firms would have lower total advertising expenditures. Very small companies usually spend less per thousand, but this is partially because in the years when they have been successful they have mostly produced lower quality cigarettes selling to a different market where price was the primary appeal. A large number of small companies competing for the business of the present large companies would be just as likely to have equally high unit advertising expenditures.

Regardless of the effect on advertising, an industry with many small firms would probably have significantly higher total distribution costs. Non-advertising selling expenses would probably increase; the costs of field sales overhead are likely to be lower per unit for companies with large sales volumes. Moreover, other costs of distribution would probably be sharply higher. In 1910 when the Trust was promoting a large number of different brands the margins between the manufacturer's price and the retail price ranged from 22 per cent to 35 per cent of the latter and some years earlier when competition was more active the margins were as high as 42 per cent. In 1934 the NRA code established margins ranging from 10 per cent to 17 per cent of the retail price depending on whether the sale was by the carton or pack. In the early postwar years, the single pack margin excluding state taxes was about 20 per cent. This reduction in margin was possible because of the general growth of the business and because of the establishment of a few leading brands with a large steady volume of trade. Wholesalers' inventories normally turn over weekly and retailers retain only a few days' supply. Rapid turnover allows a small markup per package.

The multiplication of brands in the last few years has already been accompanied by some increase in distribution costs. Since 1952 wholesale and retail margins have risen by 49 per cent while total retail value has risen 33 per cent. If the cigarette industry were composed of a large number of small firms producing many brands it seems probable that inventories would be higher, storage space larger, bookkeeping more complicated and a larger portion of deliveries in broken cases and cartons. Distributors' costs would be higher and some widening of distributors' margins would necessarily occur.

If advertising expenditures were reduced in an industry with many small firms, the effects on distribution costs might be even worse. Other forms of sales promotion would probably expand and the selling activities of jobbers and retailers would become more important. Distributors' costs and margins would thus be increased not only by the greater mechanical complexity of distributing a large number of small brands but also by the necessity of resuming once more the functions of sales promotion which distributors used to fulfill in the days before national advertising was fully developed.

It is illuminating to compare the possible gains and losses from establishing a regime of monopolistic competition in the cigarette industry. In 1939 the three major companies earned net profits after taxes of $73 million. If we take this as twice the competitive level the possible savings from eliminating monopoly profits would have been $36 million. In the same years those companies spent $41 million for advertising. Distributors' markups on their sales were about $180 million. Thus, a rise of even 25 per cent in wholesale and retail margins would more than have erased the savings in monopoly profits. Any savings in advertising outlays would have been highly problematical and could easily have been offset if the rise in distributors' margins were larger than 25 per cent.

The situation in 1939 was more favorable to reform by dissolution than has been the case in recent years. Cigarette profits have been about at an average level so that a more competitive regime would produce no necessary savings. Distributors' margins have risen to $1,272 million in 1958 with the great growth of business and the active competition among an increased number of brands. The potential losses from wider unit margins if the industry were fragmented are accordingly much more serious.

A third possibility of creating a somewhat larger number of firms involves some of the same disadvantages as monopolistic competition though in less extreme degree. The relative rise in importance of the second three companies has already produced some of these results and a further increase in numbers would probably do more. There is no indication that the somewhat wider field of competition now existing has done much to eliminate conscious interdependence in setting price and there is no reason to expect greater differences in prices for comparable brands or a lower general level. Advertising expenditures have risen sharply with the active competition of recent years and a larger number of firms would probably increase them still further.

The present organization and behavior of the cigarette industry thus appear in relatively favorable light when compared with possible alternative market structures or alternative types of behavior. Perfect competition is not attainable. A full monopoly would offer doubtful savings and has other overwhelming drawbacks. Monopolistic competition or still looser oligopoly as a result of breaking up the present corporations would probably result in increased costs. On economic grounds there does not appear to be a case for serious reform in the structure of the cigarette industry and so long as the structure remains as it is, it is difficult to point to aspects of its behavior which need serious modification.

The major wastes in this industry are wastes of competition and they could not be removed without eliminating competition or seriously restricting it. At one time, the present author urged that a direct limit on the volume of advertising would be an effective way of loosening competitive relations and directly reducing waste. He does not now hold to this opinion. Quite apart from the political obstacles to imposing such a limit, we are without criteria for determining what it should be. If we accept competition as desirable in itself, we must accept associated costs and there are no obvious guides as to how much competition is too much or how much cost is excessive. In any event, this does not seem the kind of reform which would be appropriately sought as a remedy in antitrust proceedings.

There is one minor change in industry circumstances which might yield an improvement in its economic results. The present federal excise tax of $4.00 per thousand, or 8 cents per back, plus smaller state excises reinforce the least desirable features of the industry. The specific tax rate which is the same regardless of the price of the cigarette reduces the incentive to produce brands of different qualities with different prices. Some premium price brands are always sold, but it is unusual for cigarettes which are cheaper than the standard brands to have extensive sale. No savings which can be made either by shrinking profit margins or by lowering leaf quality and advertising costs can be enough to reduce price sufficiently to attract consumers when so large a fraction of unit costs is absolutely fixed. The replacement of a flat excise by an ad valorem tax would remove an artificial limit on product variety and give price variation a larger role in the industry's product and marketing activities.

The Influence of Antitrust

Twice in its history, the cigarette industry has been a party to spectacular Sherman Act proceedings. In view of the preceding analysis what can be said about the desirability and effectiveness of these applications of public policy?

It has long been an article of faith in American political thought that competition is desirable and monopoly and restraint of trade undesirable quite apart from narrow economic effects. The economist's view that monopoly is objectionable in distorting the proper allocation of resources has been an increasingly important element in antitrust thought, but the protection of the public and of other competitors against the tyranny and extortions of a monopolist have played a larger role in legal thought and in the political support for antitrust policy.

In terms of these objectives, the applications of the Sherman Act to the cigarette industry have been outstandingly successful. The old Tobacco Trust was not immune to the winds of competition but its power was too great and its exercise of power too tyrannical to survive a confrontation with the law. The second antitrust case thirty years later involved similar though smaller abuses of power and read a useful lesson on the limits of power in market behavior. The major companies are not likely to act in concert either explicitly or tacitly to exclude competitors in this generation.

Though the 1911 dissolution destroyed the overwhelming power of the trust, the successor companies retained strong market power and price discipline as the price and profit history of the twenties testifies. But the competitive struggles and loss in market share by the "Big Three" in the thirties indicated serious limits to their market power. These limits were further strengthened by the second Tobacco Case and the price and profit pattern since World War II indicates that the lesson has been learned.

One measure of the degree of competition in an industry is the ability of smaller firms to overcome larger and for industrial leadership to change. Immediately after the 1911 dissolution, the rise of Camel and the R. J. Reynolds Co. testified to a flexible competitive system. In the twenties it seemed that a new and stable competitive dominance had been established for the "Big Three," and the rise of Lucky Strike to equality with Camel could be interpreted merely as the expected revival of a company already well established in the industry and a member of the club. In the twenties, it appeared that the leadership of the three top companies was permanent and unchangeable.

In the thirties the rise of Philip Morris and Brown & Williamson from very small beginnings showed that competitive opportunities still existed, and the serious inroads by Philip Morris, Brown & Williamson and Lorillard in recent years indicate that the position of the leading companies is not automatically guaranteed by a position of superior power, but depends on the outcome of a competitive struggle which will go on into the future and on which the final returns may never all be in.

In terms of changing relationships among firms and in terms of the influences of competitive maneuvers upon profits the cigarette industry seems to be as competitive as many industries, and this is largely the effect of two important antitrust cases which changed the structure of the industry and set some *de facto* rules for competitive behavior.

Of course, throughout its history the number of leading firms has been quite small and it is not an easy industry for a small firm to enter and secure a substantial foothold. There are substantial economies of scale in marketing. It would require great antitrust pressure to force the industry into any other mold and in terms either of traditional antitrust objectives or narrower concerns with economic efficiency it is difficult to see why this should be done.

SUGGESTED READINGS

Books and Pamphlets

R. Cox, *Competition in the American Tobacco Industry* (New York: Columbia University Press, 1933).

W. H. Nicholls, *Pricing Policies in the Cigarette Industry* (Nashville: Vanderbilt University Press, 1951).

J. C. Robert, *The Story of Tobacco in America* (New York: Knopf, 1949).

R. B. Tennant, *The American Cigarette Industry* (New Haven: Yale University Press, 1950).

N. M. Tilley, *The Bright Tobacco Industry, 1860–1929* (Chapel Hill: University of North Carolina Press, 1948).

S. N. Whitney, *Antitrust Policies: American Experience in Twenty Industries* (New York: Twentieth Century Fund, 1958).

Government Publications

U.S. Bureau of Corporations, *Report on the Tobacco Industry*, 3 vols. (Washington: Government Printing Office, 1909–15).

U.S. versus American Tobacco Co., 164 F. 700 (1908); 221 U.S. 106, 328 U.S. 781 (1946).

Chapter 11

WILLIAM F. HELLMUTH, JR.

The Motion Picture Industry

SECTION I: INTRODUCTION

Who can you identify more easily? Van Johnson or Lyndon Johnson? James Monroe or Marilyn Monroe? Kirk Douglas or Paul H. Douglas? Mike Mansfield or Jayne Mansfield? Probably you picked the movie stars, even over senators or a former President. People know more about movie stars than about those who participate in any other business in the country. But there is much more to the motion picture industry than actors and pictures. This chapter shows some of its attractions for an economist: its brief but dynamic history, unique products, vertical integration, trade practices, effect of antitrust laws, and reaction to competition and technological change.

Motion pictures take in more paid admissions than any other industry in the United States. American consumers in 1959 spent 1.3 billion dollars to buy an average of 43 million movie tickets a week. This compares with only $265 million spent in 1955 on all spectator sports, including football, baseball, hockey, and basketball, and only $339 million spent on admissions to all other spectator amusements. Total revenues of American companies in the movie industry, including receipts from abroad and sales of popcorn and other refreshments, amount to about two billion dollars a year. The industry in the United States employs about 200,000 persons and represents an investment of about 2.7 billion dollars.[1]

History of the Industry

The first motion picture exhibited in the United States was shown in 1896, in New York City. For the first dozen years, almost perfect competition

[1] *Survey of Current Business* (July 1959), Tables II–4; VI–13; VI–17; "Silver Screens?," *Barron's*, January 11, 1960, pp. 5–6; *Film Daily Yearbook*, 1959.

393

prevailed. From 1909 to about 1930, a battle royal for control took place. From 1930 to 1948, despite depression, war, and inflation, the industry was characterized by the stability of the major companies which emerged victorious from the battle for control. Since 1948, the industry has been beset by change and trouble, resulting primarily from the success of the antitrust suit against the major companies, and competition from TV.

Competitive Small Business: 1896–1908. With the success of the first movies, motion pictures changed from a novelty to a business; aggressive businessmen replaced the inventors to seek maximum profits. Production, distribution, and exhibition practices were introduced which still characterize the industry.

Since the demand for equipment depended on the popularity of the pictures shown, movie equipment manufacturers began to produce films to attract large audiences. Edison, Biograph, and Vitagraph, the leading producers, joined in an effort to monopolize movie production through their control of United States patents. These attempts were unsuccessful; other cameras were available legally from abroad and illegally at home, and the prospective large profits were so alluring that they overwhelmed the fear of lawsuits over patent rights.

The only requisites for producing movies were a camera and money enough to buy film and pay the cameraman. At first, players and stories were unnecessary; anything which moved was a worthwhile subject—a moving train, Niagara Falls, and lunch hour at a factory were typical.

"The Great Train Robbery" (1903) introduced the story film, which quickly became the fashion. One reel of about 1,000 feet was standard length,[2] and the entire picture was ordinarily filmed in a day. Production was very profitable; there was complete freedom of entry.[3] Pictures were sold at a good price regardless of quality; speed of output was all that mattered. The increased volume of production necessitated more workers and specialization in acting, directing, photography, writing, and laboratory work, but no screen credits for anyone.

At the distribution level, producers at first sold films outright directly to exhibitors, who ordered by mail from a catalogue. Prices varied from $10 to $25 for a 100 foot film. This arrangement was expensive and wasteful for the individual exhibitor as each film purchased lost its value by exhausting the market at a single theater long before the film wore out. Exhibitors first sought a solution by exchanging films among themselves.

---

[2] It takes one minute to project 90 feet of film.
[3] For example, Kalem, a newcomer in 1905 with $600 of capital, was clearing $5,000 a week by 1908 from the sale of its weekly output of two pictures, produced at a cost of $200 apiece.

In 1903, the first film exchange appeared as an agency to buy films and to rent them to exhibitors at a percentage (25 per cent was usual) of the purchase price for limited periods of time. The function and profitability of film exchanges were evidenced by the appearance of 125 to 150 exchanges by 1907. For producers, the evolution of this distribution method meant a few large customers, each taking many pictures in order to have a wide variety to offer exhibitors. Exchanges in the same locality bid against each other with resulting higher revenue to producers. Also, an increased market for movies resulted because the exhibitors, paying less per picture under the new rental plan, were able to afford more pictures. And the exhibitors found that more frequent program changes stimulated movie attendance. Exhibitors began to bid against each other for prior rights on new films. Rental prices were graded by the run, with first run rights most valuable, and every run more valuable than a subsequent run. Dishonest distribution tactics such as "duping" and "bicycling" appeared early.[4]

The exhibitors cultivated the industrial workers in large cities, including large numbers of immigrants. Ten-cent tickets fitted the wage-earners' pocketbooks and visual appeal overcame language difficulties. No theater was needed to exhibit films; a large room, a screen, a projector, and all the chairs the room could hold were the only resources needed.

The nickelodeon, a new type theater to attract a larger audience, opened in Pittsburgh in 1905. A catchy name in electric lights, a pseudo-opera house interior, and piano music to accompany the picture typified the new movie houses. This first nickelodeon with 96 seats and a five-cent admission charge illustrated its wide appeal: shows of 20 to 30 minutes duration were offered continuously from 8:00 A.M. to midnight, seven days a week; total receipts exceeded $1,000 weekly, indicating average attendance above 90 per cent of capacity. Within three years, there were more than 100 nickelodeons in Pittsburgh alone and about 10,000 in the United States, usually located in the poorer shopping districts and slum neighborhoods.

Profits depended on quick turnover of customers which, in turn, meant short programs with frequent changes of pictures. This so boosted the demand for films that the production of movies became the most important branch of the industry.

This period was the high point of perfect competition; numerous small

---

[4] "Duping" was the practice of legitimately buying or renting a film, reproducing several negatives of the film, and renting both the original and the reprints to exhibitors as though all were originals. "Bicycling" was an exhibitor's trick to beat the distributor out of part of his rental fee. One exhibitor rented the film and he and his neighboring exhibitors so scheduled the showings that each exhibitor could show it several times on the same day—a bicycle being used to transport the film between theaters.

producers, distributors, and exhibitors, ease of entry into each field, and small investment requirements characterized the industry.

The Struggle for Control: 1909–1930. But this era of perfect competition did not last. In 1909, the ten leading producers of films and equipment combined in the Motion Picture Patents Company in an attempt to gain monopoly profits from their pooled patents. Only members were licensed to produce pictures; Eastman Kodak agreed to supply film only to licensees; confiscation of projectors and the loss of rights to licensed films were penalties for exhibiting any unlicensed picture. The patents trust organized its own nation-wide distribution system, the first vertical integration in the industry, which absorbed or forced out all other distributors except William Fox. Yet this attempt to monopolize production and distribution and gain predominant bargaining power over exhibitors failed. Antitrust suits harassed the trust but competition was more effective in denying it its goal.

Bitter competition between the trust and the independents lasted several years with four important results for the industry. (1) First, the independents improved the quality of their films in contrast to the trust's standardized, low-cost products. (2) Second, Adolph Zukor and the other independents began to publicize the leading players to attract patrons for their pictures. The first screen credits were given; fan mail, gossip columns, and movie magazines appeared. The public rated the stars on the basis of their salaries, giving each producer an incentive to have the highest paid star. Actors' salaries rose spectacularly; Charlie Chaplin received $100 a week in 1913; two years later, he was given a contract calling for $10,000 a week plus a $150,000 bonus for signing. Making stars became part of the motion picture business.

(3) A third result was the shift of the production center from New York to Hollywood. The independents moved to evade attacks—both legal and physical—by the Patents Company. The immediate advantage of the Los Angeles area was its accessibility to Mexico if a quick getaway was necessary. Long-run advantages of scenery, weather, cheap labor (until the thirties), and the ready cooperation of business groups have kept production in the Hollywood area. (The fifties witnessed a sharp decline in the importance of Hollywood as the industry's production center; in 1959, all or part of about half the features were filmed away from Hollywood.)

(4) The introduction of the feature picture was a fourth result of the competition between the Patents Company and the independents. The first multireel films shown in the United States were imports; their success led the independents to produce feature pictures but the trust stuck to the traditional one-reelers. These long-story films gained prestige for the movies;

they were the first pictures to be shown as the main attraction in first-class legitimate theaters and they appealed to the upper classes, as evidenced by the $1.50 admission charge in New York for the very profitable Italian feature, "Quo Vadis." By 1914 there was only a minor market for one-reel films.

Set back in each of these four areas, the Patents Company was unimportant after 1914. But the industry did not return to the perfectly competitive situation of 1908; instead other companies sought control by attempting to acquire dominant economic power.

With the star system and the feature film, production necessitated a large investment; to make profits, with heavy fixed costs, production had to be continuous. Producers acquired distribution facilities to market their output. At the exhibition level, the longer features reduced audience turnover and required higher film rentals. To meet the need for larger receipts, bigger theaters and higher admission prices were the answer. This led to a wave of theater building which began about 1914 and continued until the depression. These were not nickelodeons but movie palaces with elaborate lobbies, plush carpets, and upholstered seats to appeal to the middle and upper classes.

In 1917, Paramount (the leading distributor), Famous Players-Lasky (the major producer), and twelve lesser producers combined under Adolph Zukor, with the objective of obtaining the power to dictate terms to exhibitors. Paramount dominated production with the exception of Chaplin and Pickford films; Zukor took advantage of his control of the other stars to increase film rentals and to require "block booking." [5] Paramount released three or four features a week to 5,000 theaters.

To protect their bargaining position against the producer-distributors, the exhibitors combined into circuits to obtain pictures at low rentals. The First National chain, for example, expanded from 26 member theaters in 1917 to 639 in 1920, giving the circuit mass buying power.

The next move in the fight for control was complete vertical integration. To guarantee their own supply of films, First National contracted with Chaplin and Pickford to supply pictures. To keep in the race, Paramount extended its integration to the exhibition field, acquiring 303 theaters by 1921.

With both major companies fully integrated, the scene shifted to a competition for control of exhibition outlets. The competitors bought all the existing theaters which the independent owners could be persuaded or forced to sell; next was a race to construct new theaters. The more movie

---

[5] "Block booking" is the distributor's practice requiring an exhibitor to contract for several or all pictures of a given producer in order to get any.

houses the producing-distributing companies owned, the more certain they were of outlets for their pictures, bargaining strength in dealing with each other, and a share of the relatively large exhibition profits.

Paramount got the better of the competition for theaters, with the shrewdest move being Paramount's purchase of individual exhibitors and chains which comprised the First National organization. Goldwyn, Loew's, Metro, and Fox were other partially or fully integrated companies during the midtwenties. The Motion Picture Producers and Distributors of America, Inc. was established in 1922 as the trade association of major production companies, active in public relations, administration of the code of acceptable topics and dialogue, labor negotiations, foreign markets, and relations with independent producers and exhibitors.

In 1926, Western Electric offered sound equipment to the major movie companies, all of whom rejected it. Warner Brothers, a minor company, gambled on the sound equipment. The major companies decided to fight the adoption of sound; acceptance would make much of their equipment obsolete; long-term contracts with silent-picture stars might become costly liabilities; techniques would be revolutionized; conversion to sound would require the payment of royalties to Warner's, formerly a minor competitor, hurting their prestige as well as their pocketbooks.

Warner's released "The Jazz Singer," the first feature-length sound film, in 1927; Fox with its own patents also exhibited sound films the same year. The public response to talkies proved so enthusiastic that the majors were forced to switch from opposition to quantity production of sound pictures. Warner's headstart enabled it to expand its assets from 16 million dollars in 1928 to 230 million two years later; with its 500 theaters, it was second only to Paramount. Weekly attendance climbed from 60 million in 1927 to 110 million by 1929. The novelty of sound offset the reduction in purchasing power for the first two years of the depression; it was not until 1932 that box-office receipts turned downward.

The advent of sound resurrected the problem of patents in the industry. A.T. & T., which held patents for sound equipment through subsidiaries, signed exclusive long-term contracts to supply the major companies with sound equipment. R.C.A. appeared soon afterward with excellent sound equipment only to find the potential market bound to A.T. & T. To create a market for its equipment, R.C.A. founded Radio-Keith-Orpheum Corporation, a fully integrated motion picture company. With R.K.O.'s theaters as a wedge in the industry, R.C.A. charged A.T. & T. with unlawful restraint of trade; an agreement was reached out of court in 1935 which opened the sound equipment market. By 1943, R.C.A. was supplying about 60 per cent of all sound equipment.

Thus, sound clearly brought Warner Brothers and R.K.O. to important positions in the industry. Paramount had been a dominant company since 1917; Loew's and Twentieth Century-Fox emerged via expansion and combination as other major firms.

During the twenties, first the competition for expensive theaters and later the costly purchases of sound equipment necessitated financial help from Wall Street. All the major companies established alliances with leading banks and investment houses: Loew's with Liberty National Bank and General Motors; Paramount with Kuhn, Loeb & Co.; Chase National Bank, during the thirties at least, was the majority stockholder in Twentieth Century-Fox. The financiers, to oversee the use made of funds and to cement their contacts with a profitable industry, installed their representatives in important positions.

The largest financial interests in the country—Morgan through A.T. & T. and Rockefeller via General Electric and R.C.A.—held a powerful position in the industry. Lewis Jacobs summarized the situation in the mid thirties:

> The entire motion picture industry, therefore, through patent ownership, is indirectly under a monopoly control far beyond the early aspirations of the Motion Picture Patents Corporation. That control . . . is never for one moment basically deflected by the unceasing obbligato of government antitrust actions that enlivens its progress. The peak figures in American finance, Morgan and Rockefeller, either indirectly through sound-equipment control or directly by financial control or backing, now own the motion picture industry.[6]

As the production cost of the average feature in 1929 was $200,000 against $40,000 to $80,000 for the same length film a decade earlier, attention centered on making each picture a money-maker. To insure profits, advertising told the public to demand films with stars, large budgets, a story based on a famous book or play, and well known directors; producers were instructed to produce pictures to these specifications.

A Mature Oligopoly Industry: 1931–48. By the thirties, the erstwhile struggle for power had given way to an era of "good feeling" and cooperation. Paramount, Loew's, Warner Bros., Twentieth Century-Fox, and R.K.O. were dominant in the industry, and remained in control throughout this period. The depression caught up with the industry in 1932 but the box-office doldrums were brief and not too severe. The war and postwar boom brought the industry all-time record receipts; the movies had plenty

[6] L. Jacobs, *The Rise of the American Film,* New York: Harcourt, Brace, 1939, p. 421.

of shows to offer while personal incomes were high and other goods and services were in short supply. Wartime profits were restrained by the excess profits tax, but its removal made 1946 the industry's most profitable year ever.

Despite the publicity given to Hollywood, the nerve center of the industry has been in New York City. Lillian Ross put it this way: [7]

> Almost two years before, I had become interested in "The Red Badge of Courage" and I had been following its progress step by step ever since, to learn what I could about the American motion picture industry. Now, three thousand miles from Hollywood, in an office building at Forty-fifth and Broadway, I began to feel that I was getting closer than I ever had before to the heart of the matter.

To be sure, it was the Hollywood product which was sold in theaters but the product was made with budgets, top casting, and stories approved by the chief executives in New York.[8]

Period of Turmoil and Readjustment: 1949 to Present. The movie industry has been in a relative decline since 1946 in its competition for the time and money of the American consumer. As indicated in Table 1, personal consumption expenditures doubled between 1946 and 1958, while the amount spent for admissions to movies fell about 30 per cent. Annual figures record a steady decline in expenditures for movie admissions from 1946 to 1953, with stability at about 1.2 billion dollars a year since then.

Two major factors accounted for the changes. First and probably most important was the increasing competition for the consumers' recreation dollars. The closest competitor was television. The number of TV sets in operation in the United States increased from about 8,000 in 1946 and 1 million in 1948 to 20 million by 1952 and 44 million by 1958. About 88 per cent of all homes had TV sets by the end of 1958.

In addition other recreation and leisure time activities, such as sports, boats, and the chores and joys of suburban living, attracted increasing attention. Consumer expenditures for all recreation doubled between 1946 and 1958, while expenditures for movie admissions were falling.

The second factor causing major changes in the industry was the antitrust decision in 1948, which dates the end of the previous era. This decision led to the corporate divorce of the exhibition function from production and distribution, and ended the vertical integration which had characterized the industry since about 1920.

---

[7] *Picture,* New York, 1952, p. 247.

[8] "Paramount: An Oscar for Profits," *Fortune,* June 1947, p. 90; M. D. Huettig, *Economic Control of the Motion Picture Industry,* pp. 66–74.

TABLE 1

Movie Admissions Related to Disposable Income and Other Data, Selected Years, 1929–59

	1929	1933	1939	1946	1948	1954	1959
Personal disposable income (millions)	$83,120	$45,744	$70,444	$159,182	$189,300	$256,885	$337,266
Recreation (millions)	$ 4,331	$ 2,202	$ 3,452	$ 8,621	$ 9,808	$ 13,256	$ 18,304
Admissions to motion picture theaters (millions)	$ 720	$ 482	$ 659	$ 1,692	$ 1,503	$ 1,210	$ 1,278
Movie admissions to disposable income (percentage)	0.87%	1.05%	0.93%	1.05%	0.80%	0.47%	0.37%
National income originating in motion pictures (millions)	$ 440	$ 210	$ 449	$ 1,133	$ 893	$ 895	$ 821
Movie attendance per week (millions)	80	60	85	90	90	45	43
TV sets in operation (millions)	—	—	—	ᵃ	1	32	44
Percentage of homes with TV sets	—	—	—	ᵃ	3%	74%	88%

ᵃ Only 8,000 homes had TV in 1946.

Sources: U.S. Department of Commerce, *U.S. Income and Output*, Tables I-10, II-4; *Survey of Current Business*, July 1960, Tables 4, 8, 15; *Film Daily Year Book*; *Electrical Merchandising*.

SECTION II: MARKET STRUCTURE AND PRICE POLICY

Market Structure—1948

As of 1948, the "Big Five"—each with production, distribution, and exhibition facilities—dominated the motion picture industry in the United States. In addition, the "Little Three," consisting of Universal and Columbia (which were both producing and distributing companies) and United Artists (only a distributing company), were significant. Several other companies produced numerous feature pictures, mostly low-budget westerns.

Robert A. Brady summarized the industry situation in 1947:

The pattern . . . is one of monopoly in the more conventional sense of the term.

It is monopoly, however, not of the sort which serves readily to illustrate the curvilinear niceties of simon-pure monopoly as adumbrated in collegiate textbooks by experts in the economic didactics of applied geometry and elementary calculus. It is a type of monopoly that is difficult to define, that is frequently hard to trace and appraise, and, though more or less consistently evolved, that varies endlessly in methods of application and degrees of effectiveness. Practices under antitrust complaints may frequently, and without undue strain, be made to appear as the very essence of spirited competition. . . .

Nevertheless, the difficulty seems to be at least partly of terminological character. . . . One might regard the movie industry as dominated by a semicompulsory cartel, or even a "community of interests" of the type that typically stops short of the more readily indictable offenses under usual antitrust procedure.[9]

This community of interests of the major companies pervaded all three phases of the industry: production, distribution, and exhibition.

Production. The "Big Five" plus the "Little Three" were dominant in production. Production from 1930–31 to 1938–39 averaged 504 features annually, 329 of which were produced by the eight largest companies. But the number of films produced, taken by itself, grossly understated the importance of the largest producers. Practically all high revenue films originated with these eight. During 1948, for example, 89 of the 93 films which yielded rentals to their producers of $1,500,000 or more were produced by the eight majors.

Competition among the large companies took place in the production of pictures, the purchase of stories, and the development of new stars, but not

---

[9] "The Problem of Monopoly," *Annals of The American Academy,* November 1947, p. 125. (This abbreviated title refers to *The Annals of The American Academy of Political and Social Science.*)

for the services of established stars. The major studios lent their high-priced actors and technicians to each other on mutually satisfactory terms.[10]

Each of the "Big Five" produced 25 to 60 features annually. A neighborhood or small-town theater with a single-feature policy needed over 150 pictures a year; double-feature bills required more than 300 pictures a year. Columbia and Universal were useful to the majors in that these two companies supplied many low-cost pictures which facilitated frequent program changes and double features. United Artists distributed pictures made by independent producers with whom it had distribution contracts; most of these were high-quality features and were accepted by the majors for exhibition in their first-run houses.

Distribution. The eight major companies and several independents operate film exchanges to serve theaters in the 32 different distribution areas in the United States. The independent distributors handle low-cost domestic productions and most foreign films. It is at the distributor level that the critical decisions are made as to *when* an exhibitor gets a picture and *how much* he will pay. It was the trade practices used in this branch of the industry which were the prime target of the government's antitrust case. The power of the majors was even greater here than in the production phase. About 80 per cent of all features were released by the "Big Five" and an additional 15 per cent by Universal, Columbia, and United Artists; the same integrated distributors received 95 per cent of total film rentals.

This oligopoly in distribution had important ramifications for independents both in production and exhibition. For a picture to be shown in the large, downtown, metropolitan first-run theaters, the producer must have a contract with a major distributor. Exhibition in these theaters is necessary if the producer is to have a chance for high profits. Also a distribution arrangement with a major company is a prerequisite for a bank loan to provide working capital; [11] this is the normal method of financing half or more of the cost of a picture. The independent distributor was in a weak bargaining position

---

[10] TNEC Monograph No. 43, *The Motion Picture Industry—A Pattern of Control*, pp. 13–14.

[11] "If the producer has a good distributing contract . . . and that picture is distributed through a reputable distributing company that knows how to sell the picture, I might loan as high as the entire cost of production." Discussion by A. H. Giannini, President of the Bowery & East River National Bank, quoted in *Story of the Film*, edited by J. P. Kennedy, p. 87. Copyright 1927. Courtesy of McGraw-Hill Book Co., New York.

Donald M. Nelson verified this practice when he stated that banks will lend 60 to 70 per cent of the cost of a picture at 5 to 6 per cent interest if the collateral is acceptable. Such collateral consists of "a good story, commitments from one or more stars for the principal roles, a competent director, a studio where the picture can be shot, and a contract for the release of the picture with a good distributing company." "The Independent Producer," *Annals of The American Academy*, November 1947, p. 55.

since the distribution contract means life or death to him while, to the major integrated company, this is just one more picture. Also the big companies had their own productions and those of the other majors to show in their theaters; distributing the film of an independent created more competition for the majors' output.

Exhibitors must have access to good pictures on good playing dates for profitable operations. But for 80 per cent of the pictures, the independent exhibitor had to negotiate with distributors in competition with theaters affiliated with the distributor. The "Big Five" interchanged pictures among themselves, to the independents' disadvantage. The result was that independent exhibitors—especially small ones—existed largely by the whim of the integrated companies or under the sometimes inadequate protection of the courts.

Exhibition. The "Big Five" controlled 3,137 of more than 18,000 theaters in 1945, and this 17 per cent of all theaters accounted for 45 per cent of domestic film rentals. Next in importance and bargaining power were independent circuits of four or more theaters under common management, which operated 5,846 theaters. At the end of the line in economic strength were the 10,224 movie houses operated by small exhibitors with three or fewer theaters. The majors were especially important in first-run theater holdings in urban areas of the United States. The "Big Five" operated more than 70 per cent of the first-run theaters in the 92 cities with populations exceeding 100,000 and 577 of 978 first-run houses in cities of 25,000 to 100,000.[12]

The ownership of the major first-run exhibition outlets carried overwhelming economic power. Feature pictures must be shown in large downtown theaters with long operating hours and high admission prices in order to obtain high rentals; the advertising and prestige value of a downtown first-run showing is important for profitable exhibition elsewhere. To be certain of such outlets for their own pictures, the majors owned them. The greater the number of theaters owned, the larger the minimum market a producer was assured for each of his pictures. For example, Paramount, with the most theaters, averaged more screenings for its features than any other producer. "Big Five" productions played an average of 7,713 exhibitions per feature.[13]

Finally, control over exhibition outlets is significant because exhibition, under the 1948 scale of production costs and film rentals, generated by far

[12] Motion Picture Association of America, Inc., *Motion Picture Theatres in the United States,* 1948, Exhibit 1.
[13] Huettig, *op.cit.,* p. 72.

the most dollar profits for the motion picture business. *Variety* (January 5, 1949) reported that "easily 80 per cent of profits reported by the integrated companies were derived from exhibition."

The "Big Five" competed with each other at the first-run level in large cities. In the suburbs and smaller communities, however, the geographical location of their theaters was such as to eliminate effective competition between the "Big Five." For example, half of Paramount's 1,395 theaters were in the South, where the other majors owned only a handful of exhibition outlets, while most Fox theaters were in the Pacific Coast and Mountain states, and Warner's 500 theaters were largely in the mid-Atlantic states. Even when two majors had neighborhood theaters in the same state, these outlets were located in different areas.[14]

This wide noncompetitive ownership of theaters presented an excellent example of the community of interests between the major companies. Each major wanted to exhibit its own pictures all over the country. No one company had theaters all over the country, but together the majors spanned the area from Maine to California. Each company exhibited its pictures in its own theaters and rented its pictures to the other majors for exhibition in those areas in which they had outlets but the producing company had none. Thus a Fox theater in California showed all the Fox, Paramount, Warner, Loew's, and R.K.O. films in its bailiwick, while the Paramount theaters in Vermont and Texas likewise showed the films of all the majors. Only in some major cities were their theaters in competition with each other. This "happy family" of integrated companies gained whenever a family member produced a box-office hit—the producing company got the exhibition profits from its own theaters plus the rental income from all the theaters in which the film was shown. The company producing the most box-office hits did collect the most rental income, but shared exhibition profits with the other integrated companies.

Monopolistic Trade Practices

The marketing of motion pictures depends to a large extent on the nature of the product, the distributor-exhibitor relationship, and the bargaining power of the exhibitor. Each picture is copyrighted. The value of the film is perishable; the desirability of showing the picture while it is new makes priority in vending the film a most important consideration. The copyright and the perishable market for each picture have fostered many unusual trade practices.

[14] TNEC Monograph No. 43, *op.cit.*, p. 15.

Block booking and "blind buying" were trade practices prevalent in the industry until the late 1940's; "franchise," "formula deal," and "master agreement" were other widely used practices.[15] With block booking and blind buying, an exhibitor could be required to pay for a picture he did not want and might not even show. Both franchises and master agreements were used by the eight major distributors to establish minimum admission prices, restricting competition in theater admission prices to a range acceptable to the "Big Five." [16] The large circuits practiced "overbuying," i.e., renting more pictures than the exhibitor would use in their own theaters, with the intent of denying good films and good dates to their competitors. The small independents with the least bargaining power suffered most from these practices. Obviously, theaters affiliated with the distributors did not suffer, and the large independent chains had enough bargaining power to protect themselves.

In contracts with large exhibition chains, the major distributors included privileges not granted to small exhibitors, such as reduced rentals on pictures on double-feature programs, unlimited playing time, moveovers,[17] and permission to exhibit independent and foreign films.

Also, 214 theaters were operated under pooling agreements among two or more of the "Big Five" with the result of eliminating competition both in distribution and exhibition. An additional 1,287 theaters were operated under joint ownership and pooling agreements between the major companies and "independents." The Supreme Court described this situation very bluntly:

> The practices are bald efforts to substitute monopoly for competition and to strengthen the hold of the exhibitor-defendants on the industry by alignment of competitors on their side. Clearer restraints of trade are difficult to imagine.

[15] "Blind buying" was the procedure under which exhibitors rented films sight unseen. "Franchise" is an exhibitor-distributor contract covering rental terms and extending over a period of at least one motion picture season. "Formula deal" is an agreement between a distributor and a theater chain in which the chain pays a rental for a given feature amounting to a specified percentage of the picture's national gross receipts; this permitted the chains to allocate playing dates and film rentals among their theaters, with the high profits of the theaters in noncompetitive locations balanced against those in competitive situations, providing the chains a competitive advantage over small independents operating in the same market. "Master agreement" is a "blanket deal" between the distributor and several theaters, usually members of a circuit, covering the exhibition of features. *U.S. versus Paramount et al.*, 334 U.S. 131, 141–42.

[16] *Ibid.* In this case, the Supreme Court held an illegal price-fixing conspiracy existed horizontally between the major distributors and vertically between these distributors and their licensee-exhibitors.

[17] A "moveover" is a right given to an exhibitor to move a picture from one theater to another as part of a given run.

"Run," "clearance," and "zone" are unique provisions in contracts between movie distributors and exhibitors. "Run" indicates a theater's position in the sequence of exhibiting a newly released film. Allied with the run is the "clearance," expressed most frequently as the number of days which must elapse after the close of one run before any subsequent-run exhibitor in the area may show the same picture. Clearance may also limit the price differential between successive runs. "Zone" indicates the geographical area within which run and clearance restrictions apply.

The Los Angeles area exemplified these practices before antitrust action brought changes. First-run, metropolitan theaters, advertising on a grand scale with financial aid from the producer-distributor, raked in up to 60 per cent of the producer's rental and were (and are) crucial for the film's success in that locality. Clearances for other theaters varied according to the degree of competition with the first-run houses. Second runs in outlying towns, such as Pasadena, began seven days after the downtown first run closed. But fourteen days elapsed before the second run opened in near-by Beverly Hills and twenty-one days for Los Angeles proper. Clearances for subsequent runs increased from 35 days for the third run up to 133 days for the seventh run.[18]

Ownership of the neighborhood theaters also influenced the clearance situation. In Atlanta only the first-run theaters were affiliated with the majors; clearance was about sixty days between first and second runs. On the other hand, in Washington, D.C., Warner Brothers owned many neighborhood houses and the downtown houses were also owned by the majors; there clearance was only 28 days between the first two runs. Both of these arrangements seemed to fit the pattern of clearances designed to maximize the revenue of the "Big Five."[19]

These trade practices were frequently attacked as violations of the antitrust laws; the Supreme Court has ruled on these practices in several different cases, differentiating between "reasonable" and "unreasonable" clearance and zone provisions. The copyright owner may legally discriminate by renting the film on different terms at different times to maximize his profits; guaranteeing the first-run exhibitor that several days will elapse before any competing theaters show the picture makes the run more valuable and brings a higher rental. But using the copyright to restrict competition between exhibitors by price fixing and to establish a system of discriminatory clearances is regarded as an abuse of the copyright privilege.

[18] C. P. Skouras, "The Exhibitor," *Annals of The American Academy*, November 1947, pp. 28–29.
[19] TNEC Monograph No. 43, *op.cit.*, p. 43.

Costs, Prices, and Financing

The motion picture industry has geared itself to a mass market. Production expenses are large and can be recovered only by attracting millions of patrons to see each feature. In 1959, for instance, Hollywood produced 223 features at an average cost of about $1,500,000.[20] And once a movie has been filmed, all of its production costs are fixed, as are most of the distribution expenses. There is no way to avoid these costs if the picture is a "nix pix" at the box office.

Of the average $1.00 received at the box office, excluding any admission taxes, 65 cents stays with the exhibitor and 35 cents goes to the distributor. The distributor keeps 10 cents and pays the remaining 25 cents to the producer. With admission prices net of admissions tax averaging 60 cents, the producer's 25 per cent share amounts to about 15 cents. In practice, the picture companies now charge off about 60 per cent of production costs against film rentals in the United States and Canada, with the other 40 per cent of costs allocated as expenses against revenues from the rest of the world.[21] To recover the $900,000 average cost allocated to the domestic market, the average 1959 feature film would have to attract six million customers.[22]

To a large extent, the industry brought this reliance on a mass market on itself; back in silent picture days, it set cost as the measure of quality, so any low cost film is inferior by the industry's own yardstick. This dependence on a mass audience influences substantially the topics and presentation of American movies. Controversial current topics are usually taboo, because the industry does not wish to offend any numerically large group. The content of the movies is influenced by legal censorship, acceptability in foreign markets, and the interests of many pressure groups—such as the Catholic National Legion of Decency, the Protestant Motion Picture Council, the American Legion, congressional investigators, and professional, racial, and trade groups. Doctors, bankers, and policemen object to unsympathetic por-

[20] *Barron's*, January 11, 1960, pp. 5–6.
[21] "Loew's Incorporated," *Moody's Industrial Manual*, 1959. Before 1956, a larger proportion of costs (two-thirds) was charged against domestic film rental revenue.
[22] Of the other mass media, a publishing house can profit from the sale of 7,000 copies of a book, and newspapers or magazines can operate profitably with a 100,000 circulation. The need for a six million person audience for the producer to "break even" accounts for the content and form of the usual movie which appeals to the lowest common denominator among its potential patrons. And, unlike radio, TV, newspapers, and magazines, the movies receive no revenue from advertising, but on the contrary, incur advertising expenses of more than 50 million dollars per year. See L. C. Rosten, "Movies and Propaganda," *Annals of The American Academy*, November 1947, pp. 121–3.

trayals of members of their occupations; glass workers object to a scene showing canned beer.

After the exhibitor has paid the film rental, his biggest expenses are payroll; depreciation, property taxes, and insurance on the theater; and utilities and advertising. Total investment in theaters and equipment is above 2.5 billion (compared with only about 140 million in production and 25 million in distribution); this is all very specialized investment, with few alternative uses for a theater. This explains why many theaters operate in the short run so long as they are covering variable costs, since the chance of substantial recovery on fixed investment through liquidation is usually dim.

Major categories of expense at the studio are physical costs (set, costumes, music, lighting, cameramen), the cast, overhead (use of the studio, top executives, etc.), producer, director, and story and screen play. Inventory of completed and in process films is the largest single asset of the production companies. A picture is financed usually by a bank loan for a fraction of the cost in return for the first claim on the picture's earnings, perhaps a second, more speculative loan from a finance company or a wealthy individual in return for a share of the picture's profits, and third and most risky the production company's own funds. Independents normally use all three of these sources, the major producers usually only the bank and the company. Production costs are often reduced by granting the stars, producer, and director a share of the profits.

The effect of declining revenues on reported profits is large, especially for producing companies. The cost of a picture is amortized as an accounting expense over about a year following its release. A box-office slump always catches the producers with an inventory of high-cost pictures; and these high costs are written off against the reduced rental income over the year following release. This is equivalent to inventory losses for a merchandising company when selling prices fall. The exhibitors' profits are less unstable; they pay film rentals computed usually as a percentage of ticket sales; if sales are off, rentals automatically decline.[23] "Big Five" profits fell 50 per cent between 1946 and 1948, due to a 10 per cent drop in attendance and gross receipts.

---

[23] Paramount, for example, reported that its theater profits before taxes increased from five million dollars in 1940 to thirty million dollars in 1946 and fell to seventeen million dollars for the first nine months of 1948 while, for the same years, comparable profits for its production-distribution activities were two million dollars, twenty-nine million dollars, and five million dollars respectively. Paramount Pictures, Inc., *Proxy Statement, Special Meeting of Stockholders to Be Held April 12, 1949,* pp. 19, 24.

Foreign Markets

The decline in movie-going in the United States has made foreign markets even more important to the industry. Foreign markets account for about half the total receipts of American film companies, a welcome increase from the traditional one-third.[24] The Western European market has remained large, accounting for half of foreign receipts. Growth in foreign receipts is coming primarily in Latin America, the Middle East, and Asia. The foreign gross receipts of American films was about 300 million dollars in 1958, of which about 215 million was potentially available for remittance to the United States. There are about 90,000 movie theaters and an estimated weekly audience of 200,000,000 outside the United States, with American productions filling about three-fourths of the world's movie screen time.

Early in the postwar period, political and economic factors limited the receipts of American companies from the exhibition of films abroad. Communist-bloc countries barred American films for political reasons until the late fifties. American films were shown in Russia again, beginning in 1959, and somewhat earlier in several other countries of Eastern Europe.

Economic factors were and are also important. In the early postwar years, the world-wide dollar shortage was responsible for the low foreign revenues. When dollars and gold were scarce in most countries, movies had a low priority compared to vital imports such as food, machinery, and raw materials. In many cases, the restrictions were primarily on the conversion of foreign currencies into dollars. The American picture companies utilized their blocked foreign earnings in part to increase production abroad and to acquire foreign theater holdings.

Many countries, despite their improved balance of payments positions, continue to protect their domestic production companies with a variety of provisions. In some cases, barriers apply primarily to American films, but not to those of other countries. Moreover, the General Agreement on Tariffs and Trade (GATT) permits its members to use "screen quotas." Under a quota arrangement, a country requires that a percentage of the films shown, including features, must be domestically produced. Brazil, for example, requires that theaters exhibit Brazilian feature films at least 42 days a year, including two Saturdays and two Sundays in each calendar quarter. In addition, a Brazilian short subject or newsreel must be shown as part of every program. France limits the number of dubbed features which may be im-

[24] *The New York Times,* February 29, 1960.

ported in any year, in addition to setting a quota for screening French films. Other restrictions include special taxes for dubbing in the local language and release taxes which may run to thousands of dollars per feature film. Tariffs may be stated as so much per film or so much per foot. India charges the equivalent of $500 on a normal length feature. Australia, regarded as a high-tariff country by American producers, has a tariff of 6 cents a foot on positive film (ready for showing) and 9 cents a foot on negatives (unexposed). The American tariff rates are 1 cent per foot on positives and 2.7 cents per foot on negatives.

With its heavy reliance on foreign markets, the industry consistently supports government activities designed to reduce trade and currency exchange barriers in world markets.

SECTION III: PUBLIC POLICY

The motion picture industry in the United States was founded six years after the passage of the Sherman Anti-Trust Act establishing a national policy against monopoly and illegal restraints of trade. Despite this statute, the major movie companies since 1909 pursued the policy of restraining competition often with monopoly as their goal. The Temporary National Economic Committee's 1941 study of the industry stated: "The importance of the integration of production, distribution, and exhibition lies in the accomplishment, not of more closely knit operation but of virtual elimination of competition." [25]

Many factors in the movie industry facilitate monopolistic practices. The uniqueness of each picture, the star system, the fact that each theater is limited to offering one or two pictures on one bill are conditions inherent in the industry not subject to control. But ownership of the industry and trade practices may be controlled, if so desired, according to the goals of public policy.

The industry had occasional brushes with the Sherman Act prior to 1938. In that year, the Department of Justice instigated an antitrust suit charging the eight leading companies and their affiliates with monopoly and illegal restraint of trade in the production, distribution, and exhibition of motion pictures. After ten years during which there were thousands of pages of testimony and exhibits, two consent decrees, two lower court decisions, and one appeal, the Supreme Court—in a landmark victory for antitrust—held that the five fully integrated companies were parties to a combination which

[25] TNEC Monograph No. 43, *op.cit.*, p. 13.

had monopoly in exhibition in the large cities as a goal.[26] There was no finding of monopoly or illegal practices in the production of pictures.

To remedy the situation and guard against recurrence, the Court made the
four following findings: (1) Specific distributor trade practices, such as block
booking, master agreements, and price fixing were declared illegal restraints
of trade and their future use prohibited to all eight defendants. (2) The
Court ordered the termination of all joint interests and pooling arrangements
in theaters between the "Big Five" themselves or with other exhibitors. (3)
The trial court was directed to reexamine the "Big Five's" theater holdings
and order the divestiture of any theater the acquisition of which violated the
antitrust laws and/or reduced competition at the exhibition level. (4) The
Supreme Court rejected the lower court's solution of competitive bidding
to end unreasonable discriminations against small independent exhibitors;
competitive bidding, in the Court's view, did not promise the desired relief
from this favoritism and discrimination, might increase rather than reduce
the power of the conspirators, and involved the courts in the daily details of
business management. The findings of the District Court as to monopoly in
exhibition were set aside and the case remanded to make a fresh start on
the monopoly charge and its solution.

R.K.O. and Paramount, apparently tired of the effort, expense, and uncertainty of continued litigation, began negotiations for a consent decree.[27]
The Antitrust Division insisted on divorcement of theaters from production
and distribution interests, rejecting company proposals which called only for
divestiture of certain theaters. By early 1949, both R.K.O. and Paramount
agreed to consent decrees.[28]

Both decrees provided for four things: (1) Unfair distributor trade practices are prohibited, and each picture is to be rented on a picture-by-picture,
theater-by-theater basis, without regard for other pictures, exhibitor affiliation with other theaters, or past trade practices. (2) All theaters operated in
pools with other major companies and other theaters the ownership of which

---

[26] *U.S.* versus *Paramount Pictures et al.*, 334 U.S. 131, 170 (1948). In prohibiting certain trade practices, this decision was consistent with previous rulings condemning illegal
restraints by large independent circuits. See *Interstate Circuit* versus *U.S.*, 306 U.S. 208
(1939), and *Schine Chain Theaters* versus *U.S.*, 334 U.S. 110 (1948).

[27] Under a consent decree, the Antitrust Division of the Department of Justice and
a defendant in an antitrust suit agree on a solution; the court then approves the decree,
thereby making it a court order, and the trial is ended without any finding as to the
guilt or innocence of the defendant. For the defendant, the consent decree offers a
speedy, inexpensive settlement, with an opportunity to participate in shaping the terms
of the decree.

[28] U.S. District Court for the Southern District of New York, Equity No. 87-273,
Consent Decree as to the RKO Defendants (1948) and *Consent Decree as to the Paramount Defendants* (1949).

represented the fruits of the conspiracy, had to be divested within a stated period, usually three years. (3) Each existing company was to be divided into two separate companies, with the new theater company receiving the wholly owned theaters in the United States and the right to buy out partners in other theaters which the company owned jointly with independents. The production-distribution company received all studios and film exchanges. Other assets, such as foreign theaters, TV stations, and music publishing houses, could be assigned to either of the successor companies at the company's option; most of these assets have been assigned to the new production-distribution companies. In "closed situations," [29] the theater company had to dispose of one or more theaters to bring competition in exhibition to all areas where potential competitors exist. (4) Voting trusts were created to prevent the shareholders in the former integrated companies from exercising common control in both of the successor companies. And the directors and officers of each new company must have no financial ties with the other corporate descendant of the company subject to the consent decree.

Loew's, Twentieth Century-Fox, and Warner Bros. strongly disapproved the terms of these consent decrees. But the District Court directed the divorce of theater holdings from the business of production-distribution for these three remaining defendants. After the Supreme Court upheld this decision on appeal,[30] Warner and Twentieth Century-Fox in 1951 and Loew's in 1952 entered into consent judgments with basic requirements similar to those for R.K.O. and Paramount, differing only in that the number of first-run theaters to be divested was not fixed but depended on the extent to which first-run competition developed over a trial period.

Results of Divestiture

The results of the divorce of the production-distribution operations from exhibition are probably as clear now as they will ever be. The corporate separations have been in effect for several years and the last of the 1,200 theaters included in the consent decrees were divested by 1958.[31]

---

[29] "Closed situations" exist in localities in which there are two or more theaters, all under common management.

[30] 339 U.S. 974 (1950), on appeal from 70 F. Supp. 53.

[31] A fuller evaluation is to be found in S. N. Whitney, *Antitrust Policies*, Vol. II, New York: Twentieth Century Fund, 1958, pp. 160–86.

The staff of the Senate Small Business Committee summarized the results of the Paramount case as follows:

"The purpose of the Government's action was to protect independent theater owners against being forced either to sell out or to take a major as a partner if his location and policies proved profitable, against being relegated to subsequent runs behind long clearances, against paying a high price for poor pictures while the circuits paid a low

Competition in Exhibition. Clearly, more competition now exists at the exhibition level. The divorcements eliminate favoritism between distributor and exhibitor due to corporate affiliation and community of interest. No producer-distributor now owns any domestic theaters. The separate new theater companies have about 1,200 theaters, compared with the total of about 2,765 theaters operated by the "Big Five" before the consent decrees.[32] Divestiture of these theaters has brought competition at the exhibition level to more than 300 communities in which one of the "Big Five" formerly had a monopoly; much of this new competition is at the important and profitable first-run level in cities.

The individual exhibitor has more control over his own operations. His own policies, tailored to theater size, neighborhood and clientele, set admission prices and determine what pictures he seeks and when. He is no longer forced to buy many films to get one he wants, nor to take his place in a clearance-and-run system established by distributors and exhibitor chains, nor suffer from other discriminatory contract terms.

The aim is to match the earning power of each theater against the earning power of its competitors. Each theater negotiates for pictures according to the rental it will pay, not on the basis of its corporate affiliation with the distributor or its membership in a large circuit. This does not lead to equality of bargaining power; an 800-seat neighborhood theater will not be able to bid first-run rights from a 3,000-seat downtown house for a Cary Grant pic-

price for good ones under their special privileges, and against having to accept bad features as part of a block with good ones. These aims have to a large extent been realized. An independent theater owner today can demand and get equal treatment from the distributors, which was not the case before.

"These consent decrees were probably the Government's greatest economic victory in the entire history of the Sherman Act. It created a much freer market than existed before." *Motion-Picture Distribution Trade Practices—1956,* p. 242.

[32] The following tabulation shows the theater holdings for the "Big Five," before and 10 years after divestiture:

Before: (1948)		After: (1959)	
		American Broadcasting-	
Paramount	1,424	Paramount Theaters	496
Twentieth Century-Fox	588	National Theaters	250
Warner Bros.	441	Stanley Warner Co.	240
Loew's	188	Loew's Theaters, Inc.	111
R.K.O.	124	R.K.O. Theaters	89
	2,765		1,186

The "before" figures include some theaters operated but not fully owned by the companies and refer to the last year before each company agreed to a consent decree. The exhibition companies have fewer theaters now than permitted by the consent decrees. The less profitable properties have been sold or converted to other uses as the theater companies strive to increase the return on their investments. AB-Paramount Theaters were permitted 651 theaters by the consent decree but had pruned their holdings to 496 theaters by 1959.

ture. But it does mean that comparable theaters should be able to negotiate realistically with the best offer getting the picture. The small independents still fear the economic power of the large circuits, even though no circuit is any longer affiliated with a distributor, and each theater is supposed to bid individually for its pictures. They suspect that the large chains will use their financial resources to overbuy or to overbid, making it impossible for the independents to get pictures, thus eliminating competition. A few large chains, never owned by the "Big Five," have been required to divest some theaters gained by illegal practices or illegal intent.[33] More theaters have become first-run theaters. Neighborhood theaters find shorter clearance periods before the new features are available. These changes seem to be the result of the Paramount decision and the subsequent consent decrees, and to the *Jackson Park* case. In this case, an independent exhibitor in the Chicago area won treble damages from a Paramount affiliate for the losses suffered due to inequitable run and clearance arrangements.[34]

The exhibitors, however, are most unhappy with their situation in the late fifties. The distributor trade practices prohibited in the *Paramount* case are no longer being used. But the results have not been joy and prosperity for the exhibitors. They complain vigorously and often [35] about the way distributors decide which theater has made the best offer for a given run of a picture. The consent judgments required licensing of films "theater by theater, picture by picture, solely upon the merits and without discrimination in favor of affiliated theaters, circuit theaters or others." The criteria are specific only as to what is prohibited and do not indicate what formula or procedure a distributor should use to weigh the merits of bids from competing theaters.

The complaints are about clearance, run, and zone provisions, about price fixing, and about competitive bidding. The Supreme Court held that clearance, run, and zone arrangements are not illegal *per se*. They are lawful so long as the distributor does not act in agreement with other distributors, does not set up any fixed and uniform system of clearances, and so long as the clearance granted is reasonable for the protection of value of a theater's run.[36] This hazy distinction between reasonable and unreasonable clearances

---

[33] Examples are *U.S.* versus *Crescent Amusement Co.*, 323 U.S. 173, 188–89 (1944); *Schine Theatres* versus *U.S.*, 334 U.S. 110, 126–30 (1948).

[34] *Bigelow* versus *RKO Radio Pictures*, 327 U.S. 251 (1946); Whitney, *op.cit.*, p. 162.

[35] Representatives of the Antitrust Division reported about 1,000 complaints from movie exhibitors and estimated that "about one-third of the total correspondence of the Antitrust Division comprised motion-picture matters." U.S. Senate, *Report of the Select Committee on Small Business, Problems of Independent Motion-Picture Exhibitors*, p. 14.

[36] *U.S.* versus *Paramount Pictures et al.*, 334 U.S. 131, 144–48.

and the crucial importance of run, clearance, and zone to the profits of the theater owner have led to much litigation between exhibitors and distributors.

Competitive bidding is very controversial in the industry. This is used by distributors in only about 500 situations involving from 1,000 to 2,000 theaters. Distributors who ask for competitive bids say it is necessary to avoid disputes and lawsuits between comparable competitive exhibitors who ask for the same run on the same picture. Exhibitors claim it is used to make noncompetitive exhibitors bid against each other (which is a question of the reasonableness of a zone), as a "cloak to conceal favoritism and discrimination in the licensing of motion pictures" (by secrecy about the bids), and to foist on the industry a system which the Supreme Court has rejected.[37]

The exhibitors also complain that film rentals are higher and that fewer feature pictures are available than before the divorcements. Film rentals rose as a percentage of the box office receipts between 1947 and 1955.[38]

Film rentals have increased for several reasons. Exhibitors now bid more actively against each other for better pictures, earlier runs, and the more choice playing dates. True to one of the cardinal principles of economics, an increase in demand raises the price (i.e., the film rental).

With producer and exhibitor no longer part of the same corporation, the production-distribution companies had incentives to be more aggressive in seeking higher rentals. Producers now had to sell each picture on its merits, without block-booking and without their own theaters to assure a market for every film. This led to fewer pictures, generally more expensive and of better quality. The old grade-B pictures have disappeared from the theaters. Double-feature programs are offered less. Up to the mid-1940's, over 400 features were produced annually. Since 1954, American companies have produced only 200 to 250 features a year. The exhibitors face the reality that a decline in supply causes a rise in price. The neighborhood theater with three program changes a week requires over 150 features a year even on a single-feature policy. This requires the small exhibitor to have to bid for most of the features released each year.

The practice of road-show or prerelease runs of outstanding and expensive features has also raised film rentals. Frequently the rentals on these showings vary between 50 and 70 per cent of box-office receipts, against the usual 35 to 40 per cent on first-run showings.

---

[37] U.S. Senate, Report of the Select Committee on Small Business, *op.cit.*, pp. 8–10; *Motion Picture Distribution Trade Practices—1956*, Eighty-fourth Cong., 2d Sess., Senate Report No. 2818, pp. 40–41.

[38] *Ibid.*, p. 39; Whitney, *op.cit.*, pp. 168–71. Some data indicate a decline in rental percentages in 1955.

After assessing the many grievances of independent exhibitors against the distributors, the Senate Small Business Committee recommended (1) the establishment of a voluntary system of arbitration within the industry and (2) "a more forceful and more vigilant policy on the part of the Antitrust Division . . . in assuring compliance with the decrees resulting from the extensive litigation against the major motion-picture companies." [39]

Competition in Production

The divorce of domestic theaters and the prohibition of many distributor trade practices makes for more competition at the production level. Each picture must now be marketed on its own merits, not rented in a block with a hit picture, nor booked into a theater owned by the producing company. [40]

The production companies reacted to the changes in the industry by making fewer but better pictures. Before 1948, about 400 to 500 feature films a year were produced by American companies. Now the annual output is 200 to 250 features. Double features have diminished, as markets are not needed for so many pictures, and exhibitors no longer pay for pictures they do not want; and theatergoers have become more selective.

Independent producers and foreign films gained at the expense of the "Big Five." With integrated control of most metropolitan first-run theaters, independent producers previously gained access to these most profitable outlets only with the consent of the major companies, which had their own pictures to exhibit. Now, with all theaters independent of producers, it is in the exhibitors' interest to show the best pictures, regardless of what company produces them. All producers now have equal access to the best exhibition facilities, and competition between producers rests on the audience appeal of the individual picture. These changes benefit the consumer as well as the independent producer.

The effectiveness of antitrust action at the production level is modified by the foreign theater holdings retained by some of the divorced picture companies and possibly by their TV holdings, which in the future may supply the most important market for movies. Of the divorced production companies, Paramount controls over 400 theaters of the Famous Players-Canadian Corporation; Twentieth Century-Fox and Warner Bros. each controls over

[39] Report of the Select Committee on Small Business, *op.cit.*, pp. 16–17 (1953). See also the Committee's 1956 report, *op.cit.*, pp. 52–57, which continued the recommendation for arbitration but seemed to find Antitrust Division activity satisfactory.

[40] In 1936–37, for example, Paramount, the largest theater owner, was able to exhibit its least popular feature at 4,100 theaters. Loew's, with the fewest theaters of the "Big Five," had its poorest picture booked only 1,261 times. Huettig, *op.cit.*, p. 72.

400 theaters in Britain and other areas, either by direct ownership or by substantial stockholdings in foreign companies. So the advantage of affiliated exhibition outlets remains for these companies outside the United States and gives them a continued but reduced advantage over other producers. Clearly, the antitrust suits have created a competitive domestic market for new pictures and thereby substantially improved the opportunities of independent producers.

Other Results

The public seemed to gain access to better pictures and more convenient first runs. A wider choice of subject matter by producers and more exhibitor independence in screening foreign and off-beat pictures are other advantages.

Higher admissions prices reflecting the higher film rentals paid by exhibitors and the changing demand-supply relation would be one drawback. Whitney notes that movie admissions prices advanced faster than the consumer price index after 1949.[41]

The smaller number of features per year and the fewer attractions playing at any one time in many areas are other disadvantages to the public probably due to divorcement.

Corporate Changes

In addition to the new theater companies which were created to comply with the consent decrees, the disappearance of R.K.O. from movie production has been the major organizational change in recent years. R.K.O. Radio Pictures, the production company after the consent decree, was sold by Howard Hughes for 25 million dollars in July 1955 to General Teleradio, a wholly owned subsidiary of General Tire & Rubber Co. Later that year, General Teleradio was merged into R.K.O. Radio Pictures and the surviving company took the name of R.K.O. Teleradio Pictures, Inc. This company stopped production of motion pictures in 1958, and its business now is the ownership and operation of radio and TV stations.

R.K.O. Theaters, Inc. still operates over 100 theaters, mostly in the New York City area. Its corporate genealogy since divorcement has also involved name changes, sale, and mergers. Currently, it operates as a wholly-owned subsidiary of the Glen Alden Corp.

---

[41] *Ibid.*, p. 186. This compares with a change in admissions prices identical to the consumer price index over the 1935 to 1949 period.

The major companies are much less active as producers than they were a few years ago. They still produce some pictures on their own, but they also frequently participate with independents under various percentage of profit arrangements. In many cases the majors rent their lots and equipment to, and distribute pictures produced by, independent companies. Often the stars and directors form their own companies to produce one or more pictures, with distribution through a major company. Tax considerations as well as independence in choice and presentation of material make the independent company attractive.

Relapses from Competition

Since the initial burst of enthusiasm which greeted the consent decrees, some developments suggest that the successor companies are continuing their predominance in the industry. The boundary line between good business practice to improve a competitive position and unfair trade practices and unreasonable economic power is difficult to draw.

First, there were substantial delays in carrying out the decision. The final decree in 1950 set three and a half years as the maximum time for compliance. It was 1957, however, before the Paramount divestitures and 1959 before the Loew's divorcement were concluded, the latter twenty-one years after the case originated and eleven years after the Supreme Court decision.

Next, the original Paramount decree stipulated that stock in the theater company (United Paramount Theaters at first, later American Broadcasting-Paramount Theaters) should be held in trust while stockholders voted their stock in the new Paramount Pictures Corp. Theater company shareholders were to obtain voting rights only after they presented the trustee an affidavit that they did not own any stock in Paramount Pictures. The voting trust was to terminate when the number of shares remaining in trust had been reduced to one-third or less of the total theater company stock. In 1950, the trust was amended to allow holders of 500 shares or less to vote their theater company stock, regardless of their continuing ownership of Paramount Pictures stock. In March 1952, the owners of 39.7 per cent of the shares of United Paramount Theaters were also the owners of 54.4 per cent of the outstanding stock of Paramount Pictures Corp.[42] Only the owners of 500 or fewer shares were entitled to vote their shares. But the amendment to the voting trust seemed to compromise the requirement of the decree that control of the divorced theater company would be independent from control of the production company.

[42] FCC Docket No. 10031, p. 39.

Third, several of the new theater companies have integrated backward into the production of feature pictures. The U.S. District Court approved the production of fifteen Cinerama pictures during 1953–58 by Stanley Warner Corp. (the theater company resulting from the Warner Bros. consent decree).[43] The Department of Justice in 1956 approved the request of National Theaters to produce sixteen films in the Cinemiracle process, although the applicable Twentieth Century-Fox consent decree barred National Theaters from production and distribution. American Broadcasting-Paramount Theaters has also produced a small number of pictures.

Independent exhibitors have complained that the five theater companies created by the divorcements have been acquiring additional theaters. The implication is that these acquisitions reduce competition. From 1946 to 1955, the "Big Five" and their successor theater companies were prohibited from acquiring additional theaters. Most of the 5,000 drive-in theaters were built during this period, and none were for the theater companies involved in the Paramount case. The court's judgment in 1950 authorized the acquisition of theaters by these companies only upon a showing that each acquisition "will not unduly restrain competition in the exhibition of feature motion pictures." As the theater companies completed their divestitures of theaters which caused local monopolies, they became eligible to apply for additional theaters. Court hearings are held on each application with other exhibitors given an opportunity to present information. Four of the theater companies received approval to acquire a total of thirteen additional theaters in the first year after they were eligible to expand their theater holdings. The Antitrust Division did not oppose any of these acquisitions. It did, however, indicate informally that it would be likely to oppose certain proposed acquisitions and the theater companies have not attempted to secure court approval for these acquisitions.[44]

Acquisition of theaters by the large circuits is clearly an area of continuing controversy and concern. Another is in the relation of motion picture companies to television.

External Competition: TV and the Movie Industry

Since 1948, concurrently with the conclusion of the antitrust suit, the movie industry has faced serious competition from other industries. The effectiveness of this competition is indicated by attendance and profit figures: esti-

[43] *Moody's Industrial Manual 1959.* Stanley Warner liquidated its interest in Cinerama during 1959. Stanley Warner Corporation, *Annual Report 1959,* p. 5.
[44] *Motion Picture Distribution Trade Practices—1956,* pp. 743–6.

mated attendance—1946, 90 million weekly; 1959, 43 million weekly; profits before income taxes—1946, 309 million dollars; 1957, 4 million. With disposable personal income rising from 159 billion to 337 billion dollars over this period, the movie decline in the face of record prosperity for the whole economy shows the movies have been losing out in the competition for consumer spending.

The extent of the decline is partially due to the record level of prosperity enjoyed by the industry during and immediately following the war. While competing goods and services were unavailable or rationed, there were few restrictions on movie-making and none on movie-going, and the industry attained a record prosperity. So the post-1948 slump represented *in part* a normal readjustment from the abnormal prosperity, as consumers increased spending on houses, cars, appliances, and other recreation than movies to satisfy their postponed demands.

More than 5,000 theaters closed, due not only to a general drop in attendance but to poor accommodations, and to population shifts which left some neighborhoods "overseated." Drive-in theaters, catering to the mobile suburban family and solving the baby-sitter problem, mushroomed from 100 in 1945 to 5,000 in 1960, offsetting the closing of many older theaters. In addition more than a thousand new four-wall theaters have been built. Total theaters in operation in 1960 are 18,200, including the drive-ins.

Competition with TV. But the real villain for the movies is TV. In the early fifties, movie attendance had declined only about 10 to 15 per cent in non-TV areas but 30 to 40 per cent in communities with TV reception. In 1948, only 3 per cent of all homes had television. By 1952, 50 per cent of the homes had TV and by 1959, 88 per cent, as shown in Table 1. Movie attendance dropped steadily from 1946 to 1953, and then stabilized at about 40 million a week until 1958. Attendance in 1959 increased about 10 per cent over 1958 and the industry is hopeful that this heralds more prosperity and growth during the sixties. Apparently the spread of TV was accompanied first by a sharp drop in movie attendance, followed by a low level of attendance, and later by more movie going on a selective basis. The former steady moviegoer now gets his westerns and mysteries on TV, but is attracted to a theater by a high quality picture and perhaps by the desire for variety.

What is the natural reaction of any business to declining sales? (1) Become more efficient. (2) Improve the product. The motion picture industry is trying both these textbook solutions.

The industry has cut production costs by careful planning, rehearsals before shooting, cutting the number of actors, writers, directors, and technicians, and paying them on a per picture basis rather than straight salary, reducing executive salaries, putting executives and stars on a profit participation basis—rather than a fixed amount, more cautious bids for new books and plays, and sale of studio property.

New marketing techniques have been tried: advance showings of the best features at premium prices; saturation exhibition with simultaneous first-run showings at several theaters in a city; small and medium-sized "art houses" throughout the country offering selected domestic and foreign pictures usually appealing to a more adult clientele; use of TV to advertise movies; rehabilitation of selected older theaters, and drive-ins.

In addition to an effort to produce better pictures, the most spectacular moves to improve the presentation of the product has been the introduction during the fifties of the wide screen and stereophonic sound. Leading new techniques include Cinerama and CinemaScope.[45] Cinerama uses the widest curved screen, with three nonoverlapping cameras and three projectors needed to record and screen the whole range of action. CinemaScope projects its picture on a wide curved screen, with a ratio of 2.6 feet of width to 1 foot of height, using only one newly developed camera and one projector with special lenses which first compress and then expand the horizontal dimension. Stereophonic sound provides sound from several speakers throughout the theater to simulate directional sound and may be combined with any of the three new optical views or with conventional pictures. CinemaScope requires a new screen and other theater renovation at a cost of $5,000 to $25,000 per theater. Cinerama is most expensive; Stanley Warner Corporation paid $1,600,000 for equipment and installation in twenty theaters.[46]

These changes were the first major technological innovations in twenty years in the movie industry. Sound had been introduced in 1926; color in 1932. The wide screen was first offered by minor companies, Cinerama Productions and Natural Vision Corporation. This documents the lack of effective technical research and the unwillingness by the major studios to take risks on an innovation. This has been true throughout the history of the industry. Practically all innovations—the star system, multireel features, sound, and now wide screens—have been made by what were minor companies at the time. This illustrates well the point that effective competition requires many firms and freedom of entry for new firms and new ideas to best serve the consumers with quality pictures and technological improve-

[45] See *The New York Times*, April 12, 1953, p. X-5, for brief descriptions of eighteen of the many different wide-screen systems.
[46] *The New York Times*, July 7, 1953, p. 23. The number of Cinerama-equipped theaters in the United States has declined from a high of 24 to 6, reflecting the high operating costs of this process. *Ibid.*, January 13, 1960, p. 20.

ments. The large companies might be well advised to do more technical research and development.

Collaboration with the Enemy. But the industry has not only tried to compete with TV; it has followed the old adage, "if you can't whip 'em, join 'em." This collaboration occurs along four separate fronts.

(1) First and most obvious, TV provides a large market for movies. Practically all the pre-1948 features of the American producers have been sold for TV exhibition. The major companies sold their films during the 1955–58 period for many millions. Warner Bros. Pictures, Inc., for example, realized 15.3 million dollars' profit after taxes from the sale of its old films. Paramount Pictures sold approximately 700 features in 1958 for a guaranteed 35 million plus possible additional rentals of 15 million based on percentage of receipts until 1973. New companies, such as National Telefilm Associates, Inc., have bought film libraries for TV exhibition. The old films are rented to TV stations or networks, with the rental based on the economic strength of the renter and whether the screening is a TV first-run, or a subsequent run. These rental practices are very similar to those prevailing in distributor-theater transactions.

Picture companies are also producing films primarily for the TV market. This market was developed first by the small producers, such as Hal Roach and Walt Disney, and by new production companies established to produce for TV, such as Desilu.

The majors are now producing for this market which has a huge potential. Warner Bros. Pictures is leading the major companies in the production of films for TV. During the 1959–60 season, Warner Bros. is providing films which occupy eight hours a week on the ABC-TV network. Its products include "Maverick," "Cheyenne," "77 Sunset Strip," and "Colt 45," and also both educational and scientific films and commercials for TV. The 1959–60 TV programs double the Warner output of the previous year. Its TV revenue is estimated at 40 million dollars in 1960, compared with total revenue of 90 million from all sources in 1959.

Making available to TV films produced for theater exhibition is a complicated problem. TV cannot afford first-run rights to high quality features. This was well documented in the Paramount case before the FCC in 1952:

At the present time, television can pay a maximum of from 35 to 55 thousand dollars for the rights to telecast films nationally, even first quality films, and national television rights for the average film sell for from ten to twenty thousand dollars. The average cost of production of the 29 or 30 feature films released by Paramount in the 1951–52 season was approximately $1,400,000 each, excluding the cost of distribution and advertising. Even films which have been reissued for exhibition in theaters have produced revenue from $125,000 to $750,000. When films are seen by television viewers without cost, their value to theaters is substantially diminished, if not completely destroyed. Therefore, until the monetary return from licensing of films for television is comparable to that from theater television, Paramount cannot afford to release its films for television.[47]

The major companies initially were reluctant to produce films for TV or sell old films for TV exhibition. TV could afford only modest payments for programs. And these TV programs were competitive for the theater audiences. These audiences and the theater owners had been the bread-and-butter and cake too for the production companies. So the majors to safeguard their revenue needed to protect the theater film rentals or find some way to make TV showings more lucrative.

An antitrust case against most major production companies helped to remove the barriers to the sale of old films. The government asked that a limit be placed on the time that a production company could withhold its 16 mm. films (duplicates of its 35 mm. film for theater showing) from all uses including TV screening. Although the government lost the case in court, an accompanying consent decree helped to trigger the sale of old films to TV.[48] R.K.O. at about the same time sold its library of more than 700 features to TV. This started a scramble to sell most pre-1948 features by the major producers.

What is the effect of sale of old movies to TV on the rentals from new movies? The estimated sale value of 1948–59 movies to TV is 300 to 500 million dollars. Probably 60 per cent of this would be net profit. This potential revenue must be balanced against the rentals from current output, of about 360 million dollars a year. *Boxoffice*, a trade publication, cites estimated losses of current theater rentals of 71 million a year from 1957 through 1959, due to the TV exhibition of pre-1948 films.

(2) Pay TV offers the promise of large revenue from telecasts of quality films. Experiments are being conducted with different systems to deliver by wire programs to the home TV screen. International Telemeter Corp., a subsidiary of Paramount Pictures, is currently offering subscribers in a Toronto suburb the choice of three programs an evening. A coin box is attached to the set and the proper payment brings in the selected program. Wiring and special equipment costs $65 to $100 per TV set. Programs offered are largely first-run movies, but also include Toronto Maple Leaf

[47] FCC Docket 10031, p. 63.
[48] *U.S.* versus *Twentieth Century-Fox Film Corp.*, 137 F. Supp. 78 (S.D. Calif. 1955). See also Whitney, *op.cit.*, pp. 188–9.

hockey games and other entertainment features. The Telemeter system sends out its programs by wire and thus does not require FCC approval. Other toll TV methods, such as that of Zenith Radio Corporation, would send a signal over the air and thus would need FCC permission to use a channel.

The revenue potential here is enormous. Imagine several million families paying perhaps one dollar per family to see a first-run movie, or a championship fight. This would make production of quality, high-budget movies for TV economically attractive. Pay-TV would carry no commercials. The customer would be the boss directly, instead of indirectly through the sponsor and his advertising agency. The movie industry has mixed feelings toward subscription TV; the producers feel that it can only help them; exhibitors fear its success will doom many theaters.

(3) Theater TV is another TV offering with tremendous possibilities for the motion picture industry. Exhibitors and producers both welcome this innovation. Football, boxing, opera, and public service events have already been telecast directly on the large screen, usually in conjunction with the regular film program. Theater receipts gain from off-hour uses by education, nationwide companies, and other groups for simultaneous meetings in different localities. A divided screen and two-way communication are feasible. More than 100 theaters with over a quarter of a million seats are equipped for theater TV.

Theater TV may make obsolete the present distribution system which absorbs about one-third of film rentals. A central transmitting station could send films direct to the theater screen. The industry would need either its own TV channels, for which it has already filed with FCC (Docket 9552, 1952), or low rates for use of A.T. & T. cables.[49]

(4) Affiliation of movie interests with TV is another aspect of the "join 'em" program. The 1953 merger of United Paramount Theaters, the largest theater company, with American Broadcasting Company, one of the three major radio-TV networks, into American Broadcasting-Paramount Theaters (A.B.-P.T.) is only the most spectacular affiliation. Paramount Pictures Corporation owns 22 per cent of DuMont Broadcasting which broadcasts in radio and TV and manufactures TV equipment. DuMont, however, even with Paramount Pictures support, did not succeed as the fourth major TV network. Paramount Pictures also owns about 90 per cent of International Telemeter Corporation, which is developing the closed-circuit, coin-box sys-

---

[49] At present, A.T. & T. has a monopoly of the 35,000 miles of radio relay and cable facilities which connect TV stations into nationwide networks. This is comparable to its control over movie sound equipment about 25 years ago and puts A.T. & T. in a very strong position in the TV industry.

tem for pay-TV. These steps have been taken to strengthen the profit position and diversify the interests of companies in the movie industry, but they pose some tough questions for public policy.

Has the heart of the antitrust victory in the Paramount case been killed by the FCC decision in the new Paramount case? The FCC decision allowing the A.B.-P.T. merger and approving DuMont's TV station licenses, after recognizing that Paramount Pictures controls DuMont, goes a long way toward remarrying the movie production and exhibition interests. Paramount Theaters, the theater branch of the divorced Paramount, integrated horizontally by merging with ABC.

The Federal Communications Act (Sections 311, 313) makes antitrust violations a factor the FCC must consider in determining the eligibility of an applicant to hold a radio or TV station license. In the cases involving both Paramount Pictures Corporation and U.P.T., the FCC ruled that it would not consider activities of the applicants "where those activities took place in the relatively distant past (more than three years before the filing of said applications) and have not continued." [50] As the applications in this case had been filed in August 1951, the three-year cut-off barely eliminated the movie antitrust case which the Supreme Court decided May 3, 1948. The FCC recognized, but the majority disregarded, evidence of some violations continuing after August 1948, and decided in favor of the applicants. [51]

Theater companies seek protection by the acquisition of TV stations to reach the same audience through different means. In addition to A.B.-P.T., most other major theater chains are also in TV. National Theaters, the theater company created by the Twentieth Century-Fox divorcement, changed its corporate name to National Theaters and Television, Inc. in 1959 when it acquired National Telefilm Associates, owner of a nation-wide TV film distribution system and also of WNTA-TV in New York City and KMSP-TV in Minneapolis-St. Paul. National Theaters already owned WDAF-TV in Kansas City.

Other theater circuits also have TV stations. In 1956, 37 different motion picture theater interests had varying degrees of control in 52 TV stations, either in operation or under construction, out of about 596 such stations. Theater companies have acquired additional TV stations since then. [52]

[50] Memorandum Opinion and Order, August 1, 1952, quoted in Partial Dissent of Commissioner E. M. Webster, p. 11, FCC Docket No. 10031.

[51] *Ibid.,* pp. 11–13. Commissioner Webster cited one antitrust case decided against Paramount Pictures Corporation and noted that 190 such cases were pending at the time of the hearing.

[52] *Motion Picture Distribution Trade Practices—1956,* pp. 306–8; *Barron's,* January 11, 1960, p. 5. Paramount Pictures is apparently the only major production company with a

This horizontal integration certainly appears desirable from the theater companies' viewpoint. It protects them if the market for movies shifts from theaters to home TV. The Paramount case before the FCC raised the issue whether joint ownership of motion picture theaters and TV stations is compatible with competition in the consumer interest. Obviously a TV station and a movie theater have a conflict of interests.[53] There are also conflicts between TV broadcasting and theater TV; between subscription TV and theater exhibition; and between theater TV and movie production. With competition for the same audience, stories, and stars, how can a TV network combined with either a theater chain or a production company push both businesses aggressively in the consumer interest? Commissioner Hennock states in her dissent on the A.B.-P.T. merger: ". . . the effect of the proposed merger, in violation of Section 7 of the Clayton Act, may be substantially to lessen competition and tend to create monopoly within and between the fields of television broadcasting and motion picture exhibition." [54]

The merger strengthens the position of motion picture interests in the youthful TV industry during its formative years; these interests are successors to the ones which attempted to monopolize the movie industry, beginning in a stage of its development comparable to TV in the early fifties.

The public, the Antitrust Division, and the FCC should keep close watch over the continuing and developing trade practices and affiliations in both the movie and TV industries.

Conclusion

This is the third edition of this chapter. The eleven years since the first edition have been a period of trouble and readjustment for the industry. The industry has adjusted successfully to the 1948 antitrust decision and

---

TV station in the United States. Warner Bros. and Twentieth Century-Fox have substantial interests in TV and theater circuits in Britain and other areas.

[53] The merger of A.B.-P.T. puts that company in possession both of theaters and broadcasting (radio and/or TV) stations in 122 cities. Separate Views of Commissioner Hennock, p. 15, FCC Docket 10031.

[54] *Ibid.*, p. 1. For opposite view, see Decision, pp. 99–106, 125–6, where the majority held that the "autonomous operation of the ABC Division and the decentralized operation of UPT's theater subsidiaries and the obvious determination of the AB-PT officials to promote both media should serve to preclude the elimination of the competition for audience that probably exists between UPT theaters and ABC television stations and affiliates; on the other hand, we do not for a moment believe that some lessening of competition may not inevitably occur. However, we feel that there will not be any substantial lessening of competition, in view of the external competition facing UPT theaters and ABC radio and television stations and affiliates in every area . . . and in view of the reasonable expectation that this competitive situation will continue. . . ." *Majority Opinion,* paragraph 26.

the resulting decrees divorcing the theaters from the formerly integrated companies and changing trade practices in renting films for exhibition.

The economic adjustment to the decline and shifts in movie-going and to the competition of TV is continuing. Fewer but better pictures, rehabilitated theaters and new drive-ins, improved picture and sound, more production by independents, increasing affiliation with television, and continuing attention to foreign markets represent industry actions to adapt to changing markets.

With TV available for some years in practically all areas of the country, the market for free, home TV is almost saturated. TV-viewing usually declines after the novelty has worn off, and TV-set owners become interested in movies at theaters again, but on a more selective basis. TV has taken most of the habit-going audience from the theaters, especially for westerns and mystery films. The movie producers and theaters seem to have found a minimum weekly audience of 40 million or more by offering more quality pictures. Grade B pictures which used to account for the largest number of feature films have largely disappeared from the theaters. This market is now covered by films for TV. This is not to say that *all* current movie productions are high quality and *all* TV fare is grade B.

One theater circuit executive summarized the fifties as a decade of drastic change for the industry: "We don't buy pictures the same as we did; we don't show them in the same way and we don't have enough pictures to go around. Our equipment is different and our screens have become 24-sheets." [55]

The motion picture Oscar awards in April 1960 spotlight several current characteristics in the industry. "Ben Hur," the winner of eleven Oscars—an all-time high, is the epitome of the new style "blockbuster," the high budget, famous story, multistar, wide-screen, color spectacle. Its production costs are reported at a record high of 15 million dollars; it was filmed not in Hollywood but in Italy; its initial showings have been on a "special handling" basis in only 29 theaters in the largest metropolitan areas, with admission prices ranging up to $3.50 and two shows daily. (General release is expected about six months after the selective prerelease engagements, allowing the producer-distributor to develop first the most eager audience representing the most inelastic section of the demand curve.)

The Oscar for the best actress went to Simone Signoret in "Room at the Top." This award to a French actress in a British film documents the increasing popularity of foreign films in the American market.

And the motion picture industry, continuing the custom begun in 1958, sponsored the Oscar awards program to a nationwide *television* audience.

[55] *Boxoffice Barometer*, February 29, 1960, p. 10.

The movie industry is hopeful for prosperity during the sixties. The increasing population during the sixties, especially in the teen-age brackets—the movies' best customers—supports these hopes. The production companies with the alternative outlets for their products through theaters and TV have probably firmer basis for confidence in the future, than do the theater companies. The latter face the special long-run risk of loss of their audiences to pay TV, if pay-TV ever realizes the hopes of its more optimistic advocates.

Next time you go to the movies, or watch a movie on TV, ignore Cary Grant and Debbie Reynolds. Instead, concentrate on the producer-distributor-exhibitor relationships, the antitrust issues, the theater-TV competition, and the other economic and public policy problems of the motion picture industry.

SUGGESTED READINGS

Books and Pamphlets

I. Bernstein, Hollywood at the Crossroads (Hollywood: A.F.L. Film Council, 1957).

M. D. Huettig, *Economic Control of the Motion Picture Industry* (Philadelphia: University of Pennsylvania Press, 1944).

L. Jacobs, *The Rise of the American Film* (New York: Harcourt, Brace, 1939).

S. N. Whitney, *Antitrust Policies* (New York: The Twentieth Century Fund, 1958), Chap. 15.

Government Publications

Temporary National Economic Committee, *The Motion Picture Industry—A Pattern of Control,* Monograph No. 43 (Washington, 1941).

U.S. versus Paramount Pictures et al., U.S. District Court, Southern District, N.Y., Equity No. 87–273, 1938–49, 334 U.S. 131 (1948).

Eighty-third Congress, 1st Session, Select Committee on Small Business, U.S. Senate, *Problems of Independent Motion-Picture Exhibitors,* Report No. 835 (Washington, 1953).

Eighty-fourth Congress, 2d Session, Select Committee on Small Business, U.S. Senate, *Motion-Picture Distribution Trade Practices—1956,* Hearings before a Subcommittee (Washington, 1956).

Eighty-fourth Congress, 2d Session, Select Committee on Small Business, U.S. Senate, *Motion Picture Distribution Trade Practices—1956,* Senate Report No. 2818 (Washington, 1956).

Journal and Magazine Articles

G. S. Watkins (ed.), "The Motion Picture Industry," *The Annals of the American Academy of Political and Social Science,* Vol. 254, November 1947.

"The Derring-Doers of Movie Business," *Fortune,* May 1958, pp. 137 ff.

Chapter 12

CHARLES H. HESSION

The Metal Container Industry

SECTION I: INTRODUCTION

Our Prepackaged Civilization

Packaging in all its forms is an integral part of modern mass production and distribution. Packages are necessary to move the myriad products of our widely dispersed factories and farms to the points of consumption with dispatch and efficiency. In modern merchandizing, packages are all impor-tant in differentiating one's product from the thousands of others which seek to catch the customer's eye in supermarkets, department stores, or other retail outlets. The growing importance of packaging in the American econ-omy is strikingly demonstrated by the fact that in the last twenty years, while the nation's population has risen 30 per cent, the actual volume of packages sold has about tripled.

Today, the tin can industry [1] is by far the biggest supplier of rigid packages in the nation; its output of close to 42 billion cans in 1958 was approximately twice as large as that of its historic competitor, the glass con-tainer industry. In turning out this prodigious quantity of metal containers, the North American industry consumed about double the amount of steel for this purpose than all the rest of the world combined. On a per capita

---

[1] Actually, the tin can is mostly a steel container, disguised and protected by a thin coating of tin which is only about one-fortieth the thickness of a human hair; tin con-stitutes less than 1 per cent of the total weight of the average can. And, in some of its modern forms, there is no tin at all in the tin can!

For the early history of the industry, see E. C. May, *The Canning Clan*, New York: The Macmillan Company, 1937. A fuller treatment of some of the subjects of this chapter, especially for the period before World War II, will be found in the author's study, *Competition in the Metal Food Container Industry, 1916–1946*, Ann Arbor: Edwards Brothers, 1949.

430

basis, the average American family used 940 cans which added about $30 to its 1958 shopping bill.[2] The container often comprises more than 15 per cent the retail price of canned food. For example, of the 20 cents paid last year for canned peas, 3.3 cents was for the can.

In the last quarter century, the American consumer has been introduced to a number of successive innovations in canned products, most of which he has accepted enthusiastically. In the thirties fruit and vegetable juices made their debut in cans. In 1935, 160 million beer cans were put on the market; by 1957, eight billion cans for the frothy beverage were manufactured! Today, the beer can is the can industry's largest single production item. Since World War II, during which many new foods were packed in cans, the canning industry has offered such novelties as hamburgers, bacon, chicken stew with dumplings, and beef and gravy.

Many other nonfood products have made their appearance in cans in recent years; most notable among these have been oil, soft drinks, liquid detergents, and now a host of items in the new aerosol cans. These products

TABLE 1

**Shipments of Metal Cans in the U.S. by Type of Product Packed,
1947 and 1958, and Percentage Changes**
(Data are in short tons of steel consumed in
the manufacture of cans)

Type of Product	1947	1958	Percentage Change
Fruit and vegetables (incl. juice)	1,065,914	1,559,758	+ 46.4%
Evaporated and condensed milk	292,566	206,987	− 29.3
Other dairy products	38,191	35,678	− 6.6
Meat (incl. poultry)	110,072	135,961	+ 23.5
Fish and seafood	109,130	123,602	+ 13.3
Coffee	141,901	209,004	+ 47.2
Lard and shortening	57,402	109,811	+ 91.3
Soft drinks [a]	—	36,660	—
Beer	207,337	820,480	+295.7
Pet food	50,084	173,135	+245.7
Oil, open-top (1 quart and 5 quart)	195,029	271,960	+ 39.4
All other food (incl. soup and baby food cans)	331,425	494,060	+ 49.1
All other nonfood cans	357,065	583,608	+ 63.4
Total shipments	2,956,116	4,760,704	+ 61.0

[a] Separate figures on soft drink cans were first collected in 1954. In that year total shipments were 43,874.

Source: U.S. Department of Commerce, Bureau of the Census, *Facts for Industry,* Series M75D-07, June 2, 1948, p. 5; Series M34D-08, April 10, 1959, p. 2. Percentage changes have been calculated by the author.

[2] "Captive Cans," *Wall Street Journal,* April 8, 1958, pp. 1 ff.

have added substantially to the total production of what are called "general line" cans.[3] The changes in the end use of metal cans during the past decade are shown in Table 1. Inspection of this table should convince anyone of the fact that the can-opener has indeed become a *sine qua non* of modern, urban living and the tin can, as one historian of the industry has expressed it, "as much an emblem of our country as the American eagle!"[4]

History: The Industry's Changing Structure

What is the nature of competition in this industry? Are the market relations of the can producers such as to make the tin can a bottleneck of food production or a cornucopia which daily pours out the bounty of the world's farms, orchards, and fisheries upon the tables of American families? Has this industry, which is a classic example of oligopoly, operated in the public interest or against it? To answer these questions, let us first examine the changes in the industry's market structure in the last fifty years.

The modern history of the industry began in 1901 with the formation of the American Can Company. This was a combination of 95 leading can manufacturers which gave the newly formed company control of at least 90 per cent of the nation's can manufacturing capacity. Indeed, in its early years American Can was popularly referred to as "the 100 per cent trust," and the corporate financiers who dominated the new giant tried to capitalize on their monopolistic position by raising prices—and not by modest amounts. They succeeded merely in attracting a new and ultimately powerful competitor into the industry—the Continental Can Company which began business in 1904.

American Can had apparently attempted at the time of its formation to buttress its monopoly position by acquiring thirteen of the principal manufacturers of can-making machinery and by making exclusive selling contracts with three others. It had also obtained control of major patents on such machinery. In addition, it continued after 1901 acquiring new competitors and, most important, it received substantial rebates on its purchases of tin plate from the American Sheet and Tin Plate Company. Testimony in a later antitrust suit revealed that these rebates amounted to $9,000,000 over the years 1902–13 or, on an annual basis, an amount which was never below 20 per cent of the total net profit of the Company. Nevertheless, all these efforts to block newcomers from entering the industry largely proved to be

---

[3] Tin cans are customarily classified into two main types: (1) food, or packers' cans; (2) general line cans, such as those used to pack nonfood products which do not require heat treatment in the packaging process.

[4] J. H. Collins, *The Story of Canned Food*, New York: Dutton, 1924, p. 1.

in vain. Patent control was futile because most of the basic patents on can-making machinery had expired by 1901. The pace of technological development in the industry was so rapid that rivals were able to devise means of circumventing American Can's barriers. New entrants were also able, it would seem, to obtain their principal raw material—tin plate—on such terms as to make entry into the industry possible and even profitable. So it was that when the federal government finally brought suit in 1913 to dissolve the American Can Company, the erstwhile monopoly had only about 63 per cent of the business; Continental Can sold 11.8 per cent of the packers' and general line cans in that year. Nine other firms accounted for the remaining 24.8 per cent of the sales; only four of them manufactured a full line of products.

After a long trial which filled 8,700 pages of testimony and in the course of which 862 persons took the stand, a lower court judge was "frankly reluctant to destroy so finely adjusted an industrial machine as the record shows the defendant to be." [5] The court found evidence of an attempt to establish a monopoly, but decided that it had failed. Impressed by American Can's technical services to the canning industry and by its research activities, the court concluded: "In this case it appears probable that *all potential restraints upon free competition now imposed by the size and power of the defendant will pass away as speedily without as with dissolution,* and dissolution will cause far more loss and business disturbance than will attend the *gradual reestablishment of competitive conditions* by the play of economic forces." [6] This decision, upholding the legality of the defendant because of its "good" behavior (after a misspent youth) and stressing the inexpediency of dissolution from a business point of view, foreshadowed the line of argument in the more well-known case against the United States Steel Corporation.[7] But what of the court's prognostication of a "gradual reestablishment of competitive conditions" in this industry? Has time borne out its prediction? Or, was it simply another example of a naive faith in the beneficent working of laissez faire?

Analysis of the changes in the competitive standing of the major tin can companies since 1916 indicates a decided drift toward duopoly. By 1939, when allowance is made for its fiber can and other production, American Can still accounted for more than one half of tin container production (55.4 per cent of total sales of all types of cans). Continental Can, on the other hand, had increased its share of the business from 11.8 per cent in

---

[5] *U.S. versus American Can Co.,* 234 Fed. 1019.

[6] *U.S. versus American Can Co., Supplemental Opinion and Decree,* July 7, 1916, p. 6 (Italics in original).

[7] *U.S. versus U.S. Steel Corp.,* 251 U.S. 417 (1920).

1913 to more than one-fourth of the total sales in 1939 (28.3 per cent).[8] Together, the two leading companies appeared to be doing more than 80 per
cent of the business in the latter year. The remainder of the trade was
shared by much smaller companies, none of which accounted for more than
5 per cent of the sales.

In the years since World War II the duopoly position of the two leading
companies has apparently been strengthened slightly. Their combined percentage of the dollar shipments of the industry was 70 per cent in 1946,
72.5 per cent in 1951, 71 per cent in 1955, and "about 75 per cent" in 1957.[9]
In the latter year, the next two leading companies (aside from those manufacturing their own cans) were National Can, with about 6 per cent of the
industry's sales and the Crown Can division of Crown Cork and Seal, with
2 per cent. The Heekin Can Company had another 2 per cent of production
and the U.S. Hoffman Machinery Company, which purchased control of
four small concerns in 1955, had another 1 per cent of capacity. The process
of merger had eliminated some of the companies which had competed with
American and Continental in 1939; most notably, Continental Can absorbed
Owens-Illinois Can Co. in 1944 and National Can acquired the Pacific Can
Co. in 1954.[10]

American Can's expansion during the period 1916–55 was largely a
matter of internal growth, financed almost entirely out of profits. In 1956,
however, it broke with its long-standing policy of confining its efforts to
the production of metal containers and paper cartons by acquiring four
small companies with interests in plastic containers, closures, and collapsible
tubes. The following year, it also acquired the Dixie Cup and Marathon
Paper Companies. Its total physical plant, as of 1957, consisted of 66 metal
and composite container factories in the United States and abroad.

By contrast, Continental Can has grown to its present size by an ambitious
process of merger and purchase of other concerns. These consolidations
started in 1927 during the aggressive presidency of Carl C. Conway. Within
three years Continental had absorbed nineteen smaller companies, provid-

[8] U.S. Department of Justice, *Western Steel Plants and the Tin Plate Industry*, Seventy-
ninth Cong., 1st Sess., Document No. 95, p. LI.
[9] The 1946 figure is from *U.S. versus American Can Co.*, 87 F. Supp. 18, 21–22 (N.D.
Calif., 1949); data for 1951, 1955, and 1957 are from Standard and Poor's Corp.,
Industry Surveys, "Containers," Basic Analysis, April 2, 1953, p. C4–3, April 19, 1956,
p. C85, April 24, 1958, p. C83.
[10] The FTC's studies of economic concentration do not show much change in the tin
can industry during these years. The concentration ratio, as computed by the FTC for
the four leading companies in this industry, was 80.8 per cent in 1935, 77.8 per cent in
1947, and 79 per cent in 1950. FTC *Report on Changes in Concentration in Manufacturing, 1935 to 1947 and 1950*, p. 144, and FTC *Report on Industrial Concentration and
Product Diversification* in the *1,000 Largest Manufacturing Companies, 1950*, p. 213.

ing it with production facilities in the rapidly growing Pacific coast canning region and in other parts of the nation and further diversifying its output of general line cans. Starting again in 1942 the company launched upon a program of growth and diversification in which it acquired no fewer than 31 companies in the fields of paper and fiber cans, metal crowns and cork products, and plastic and polyethylene containers. Its merger in 1956 with the Hazel-Atlas Glass Co., third largest producer of glass containers in the nation, and the Robert Gair Co., a major producer of shipping containers, made it indisputably the largest enterprise in the container industry, with total sales exceeding those of American, its great rival of a half century ($1,010.3 million *versus* $978.8 million). Continental's rate of growth in recent years has been estimated to be "more than twice that for the economy as a whole as measured by the gross national product." Its net sales, swollen by its acquisitions outside the field of metal cans, have been at a rate twice that of American Can over the decade 1947–57. Continental's averred aim, as stated in a recent report, has been "to establish itself among the leaders in each of its packaging fields." [11]

In analyzing the foregoing concentration data, it must not be overlooked that sales figures on a national basis are not significant measures of the competitive standing of individual firms or indicative of the structure of an industry where the product is not sold in a nation-wide market. The unfilled tin can is a bulky commodity; it is not economical to ship it over long distances. Consequently, the market for such a product as packers' cans is in reality a number of separate, localized markets. In most major canning regions there are plants of two or more can manufacturers; as a whole, the structure of these local markets is decidedly oligopolistic.

The Buyers' Side of the Market

To achieve an understanding of the process of price formation in the can industry it is necessary to consider the structure of the industries which purchase metal containers. As Table 1 shows, the largest single user of such cans is the fruit and vegetable canning industry. Concentration of production and sales is much less pronounced in this industry than in the manufacture of cans. As of 1954, the Census Bureau reported that there were 1,461 packers of fruit and vegetables. These food packers vary greatly in financial strength, ranging from concerns with net tangible assets of as little as $15,000 to those with many millions of dollars—like California

[11] Quoted in H. F. Travis, "Battle for Leadership between Two Cans," *Magazine of Wall Street*, April 27, 1957, p. 184.

Packing Corporation (Calpak); Libby, McNeil and Libby; H. J. Heinz; and Stokely-Van Camp. In 1954, the four largest packers controlled 28 per cent of the output; the eight largest, 39 per cent; and the twenty largest, 52 per cent.[12]

The canning industry has been described as "the most harshly competitive industry in America." Actually each packer has a "monopoly" of his own brand, but brands are numerous and substitution easy. In addition, canned food must compete with frozen, dehydrated, and fresh products. Therefore, despite the relatively high degree of concentration which exists in the sale of some products, it seems reasonable to conclude that food canning is predominantly competitive. In general, the canning industry contrasts most sharply with that of can manufacture with respect to the number of producers and the concentration of sales. The bargaining power of most canners is probably weakened by their relatively small size, the peculiar risks of the industry,[13] the comparatively inelastic demand for its products, and the intense price competition which often characterizes their sale. On the other hand, the bargaining position of some canners, particularly the largest ones, has been enhanced by their ability to threaten to manufacture their own cans.

The brewing industry is also less concentrated than tin can manufacturing, but in its recent bargaining with the can companies it has shown an enviable degree of unity. In 1954, there were 263 brewers in the nation, but the four largest accounted for 27 per cent of the total value of shipments and the twenty largest, 60 per cent.[14] According to *Business Week*, "The canmakers' beer business is spread among a relatively small number of big-volume customers—and they have proved to be tough customers. . . . 'When it comes to cans, the boys [i.e., the brewers] don't compete,' says an industry expert. 'When one brewer wrangles a price concession, it's just about five minutes before the others are around asking for theirs, too.'"[15]

[12] *Statistical Abstract of the U.S.*, 1957, p. 794.
[13] Canners assume the risks of price fluctuations in their raw produce by their practice of contracting in advance of planting to take the grower's crop from a fixed acreage at a fixed price. In years of bumper crops, the relative inelasticity of demand for canned food creates a surplus (the "carryover") and low prices. If the crop is very short, the higher prices will usually not offset the packers' loss arising from the fixed costs of idle plant. The extrahazardous nature of this industry is reflected in the high annual rate of mortality among canners. During the eight years prior to 1958 the total number of fruit and vegetable canners declined about 25 per cent. The decline was concentrated among the small canner group. On the latter, see H. L. Stier, "The Relationship of Mortality to Size," *The Canning Trade*, February 9, 1959, p. 32.
[14] *Statistical Abstract, op.cit.*, p. 794.
[15] "Canners Profit from Price War," *Business Week*, February 14, 1959, pp. 54 ff.

SECTION II: MARKET STRUCTURE AND PRICE POLICY

Conditions of Entry in the Can Industry

In 1916, the American Can Company stood accused of efforts to block entry into this industry by acquiring monopolistic control of patents and can-making machinery. The Court concluded, however, that the company failed in its objective. What are the facts today? How free is entry into this industry? Is it free enough to impose effective limits on the prices and profits of the oligopolists? Is it free enough to make competition "workable"?

Restriction of entry into an industry is really significant only when excess profits can be earned, since new firms will not desire to enter unless the rate of profit exceeds the normal return on capital in enterprises of similar risk. In this connection, it is noteworthy that American and Continental earned slightly higher profit rates during the twenties than the average manufacturing corporation. American averaged 10.1 per cent and Continental 11.5 per cent on their respective capital investments for the years 1922–28 inclusive; the average for 2,046 manufacturing corporations during those same years was 9.7 per cent.[16] Furthermore, the profit rate of American and Continental showed greater stability in the depression of the thirties than that of the average manufacturing corporation; neither company earned less than 6 per cent on its capital investment during the worst years of that period.

Since World War II, however, the profit performance of the "Big Two" has been less favorable. Their profit margins have been narrowed by higher costs, price controls, and increases in taxes. A comparison of the net income of American, Continental, and Crown Cork and Seal with the net income (after taxes) of 378 industrial companies shows little advantage for the former, except in 1955 and 1956 when their combined incomes rose substantially. Financial commentators have expressed the view that competitive pressure on prices in 1958–59 would militate against dynamic growth in earnings from cans over the short term.[17]

Apart from the inducement of profits, another entry condition is the existence of persons or firms with the necessary, minimum "know-how." The manufacturers of general line cans who are relatively numerous (there were 85 of them in 1939) would seem to have the technological knowledge

---

[16] R. Epstein, *Industrial Profits in the United States,* New York: National Bureau of Economic Research, 1935, p. 56.

[17] Standard and Poor's Corp., *Industry Surveys,* "Containers," Current Analysis, June 4, 1959, pp. C90, C77.

required for packers' can production; the manufacturing methods used in making the two types of container are essentially similar. Yet, despite the apparent advantages in combining production of the two types of container, hardly any of the smaller general line producers undertook manufacture of packers' cans in the period 1916–58. As a matter of fact, there were just four new ventures in the latter field during those years—those of Crown Can, Owens-Illinois Can, Pacific Can, and the United States Hoffman Machinery Company. Crown Can has survived since its entry into the business in 1927; Owens-Illinois (a subsidiary of the glass container company of the same name), on the other hand, was sold to Continental in 1944, after eight years of unsuccessful effort to establish itself in the field. Pacific enjoyed a steady expansion of its sales and profits from 1934 until 1954 when the National Can Co. gained control of it. United States Hoffman Machinery Co. which entered the industry in 1955 by purchasing control of four small container manufacturers is not really a competitor of the major food container makers because its production of packers' cans is inconsequential.

The experience of the new entrants sheds a revealing light on the conditions affecting freedom of entry in this business. For example, Crown Cork and Seal, the parent concern of Crown Can, was forced to sustain heavy losses during the first three years of its existence (1936–39). These losses were attributed in the trade to the company's efforts to "buy its way" into the industry by quoting prices some 6 per cent below those of the leading companies. Owens-Illinois laid its failure partly to its "incompatible position in attempting to promote sales of both types of containers," though the opinion in the canning business at the time was that there were other, more substantial reasons. In 1950, the Government obtained identical court judgments against the two big can manufacturers which fundamentally affected the conditions of entry. We shall examine the terms and consequences of these decrees later, but it is important that we understand first the factors which apparently impeded entry in this industry in the years 1916–50:

(1) Control of patents or can-making machinery by the leading companies did not constitute an insuperable obstacle to entry. The three can-makers which entered the industry between 1916 and 1949 were obviously able to obtain the necessary can-making and can-closing machinery. Nevertheless, in view of the "Big Two's" dominant patent position, newcomers did not have access to the most up-to-date machinery and hence could not hope to produce at the same speed and efficiency as the "Big Two." (American Can boasted in its news magazine in 1937 that it had ten types of vacuum

machines, while no competitor had more than two.) Unless a new enterprise could match the large companies' research and development efforts, its continued existence in the industry must have been precarious indeed.

Developments in the industry since the 1950 decrees provide insight into this aspect of free entry. The big can-makers are alleged to regard technological improvements in can-making machinery as a possible deterrent to can-users manufacturing their own. As *Business Week* reports, "There's nothing to stop a big user of cans from deciding to make his own containers if he thinks he can do it cheaper [sic]. But he may think twice before getting into a technological race with can-making specialists. Canco's brand of planned obsolescence is not to bring out a new model of can every year, as Detroit does with automobiles, but to outdate can-making techniques as fast as improvements can be worked out. . . ."[18]

(2) A more serious obstacle to entry in the years before 1950 was the industry's practice of leasing its machinery on a "tying clause" basis. Many of the can companies leased their machinery only on the condition that the lessee purchase all the containers he needed from the lessor. While such leasing policies did not completely block new firms from entering the industry, they undoubtedly were major hurdles. These arrangements had the effect of emphasizing the type of nonprice competition in which American and Continental excelled. Closing machines require a considerable amount of servicing. In rendering such service—and the leading companies had elaborate service organizations—they could entrench themselves in their customers' favor and thus ensure the continued sale of their containers. The practice of leasing the closing machines enabled the dominant companies to sell more cans by stressing the value of these services rather than the relative prices of containers themselves. Entry into the industry was made more difficult because a new entrant, to be successful, had to offer his cans at competitive prices and also attempt to duplicate the expensive services of the established companies as well. The size of the initial investment required was also increased because a considerable capital outlay would have to be made for the machines which were leased to the canners.

(3) The long-term nature of the packers' can-sales contract probably also militated against new entry. This barrier to new competition became more effective in 1946 when American Can extended the length of its general supply contract for both metal and fiber cans from three to five years. Again, when the brewers turned in part from glass bottles to cans, American Can is reported to have insisted on ten-year contracts before it would invest in the new manufacturing facilities to make such cans. Deductive reasoning

[18] "Tin Cans Hustle to Hold Their Own," *Business Week*, May 11, 1957, p. 178.

suggests that the longer the term of contracts, the smaller the number that will expire in any one year is likely to be. The conclusion seems inescapable that extension of the term of the sales contract reduces the frequency with which a buyer reconsiders his source of supply and therefore narrows the opportunities for new firms.[19]

(4) Another factor affecting entry in this industry is the amount of capital required for successful operation. In any industry the size of the initial investment required depends upon whether very large plants are needed to secure the economies of large scale production and, secondly, whether there are economies of scale in the operation of multiple plants by one firm. In can manufacturing, reasonably efficient production is possible in small plant units. For example, it was reported in 1957 that a typical can-making line capable of producing 500 cans a minute would cost about one million dollars, including auxiliary equipment.[20] Further evidence of the fact that technology does not require huge plants for efficient can production is found in the policy of the can manufacturers dispersing their production in numerous plants throughout the nation. If efficiency were only possible in the very largest units, this decentralization of operations would be impossible. Incidentally, American Can is said to have followed the rule of thumb before World War II of erecting a plant if it could sell 75 to 100 million cans a year in a given locality.[21]

All this means that the technical requirements of production do not explain the present gigantic size of the leading firms in can manufacturing. Other factors are certainly involved. What advantages (other than proximity to markets) are obtainable by ownership of multiple plants which it would be impossible for a new entrant to achieve, unless he organized on a similar basis? Economic analysis suggests that there are several types of economy which a multiple-plant might obtain. Among these are: (1) larger quantity discounts in the purchase of raw materials; (b) savings in the cost of such "overhead" functions as research, financing, legal work, and advertising; (c) reduction of costs through ability to keep plants operating closer to capacity by meeting greater than peak demand in some localities by shipping from plants which have idle capacity.

[19] For a general discussion of the consequences of requirements contracts, see G. Shillinglaw, "The Effects of Requirements Contracts on Competition," *Journal of Industrial Economics*, April 1954, pp. 147 ff.

[20] "Tin Cans Hustle," *op.cit.*, p. 179.

[21] "American Can Company," *Fortune*, January 1941, p. 102. Professor Bain in his *Barriers to New Competition*, Cambridge: Harvard University Press, 1956, p. 237, states, on the basis of a questionnaire survey of the can industry, that the optimum size plant would seem to be from 0.33 to 2 per cent of the national total of production (packers' and general line cans together). This would be a capacity roughly from 100 million to 600 million cans, with specialization of plant by product line assumed.

Subsequent analysis will reveal that the two leading can companies have marked advantages over their smaller rivals and over potential new entrants in some of these very respects. The volume production of these multiple-plant firms has enabled them to demand maximum quantity discounts on their tin plate purchases, though the Robinson-Patman Act drastically curbed the granting of unwarranted price concessions. The amount of capital needed to finance distribution and research facilities at all comparable to those of American or Continental is also probably discouraging to new entrants. The economic barriers to entry in this industry were exceptionally formidable prior to the 1950 decrees which reformed many of the industry's market practices. On the favorable side, however, there was the fact that the marked secular increase in the demand for packers' cans offered more opportunities for new concerns to grow than might otherwise have been the case. In general, the imperfections in the markets for packers' cans before 1950, particularly as regards freedom of entry, definitely seem to warrant the conclusion that there were elements of monopoly profit in the earnings of the two major can companies.[22]

The San Francisco Judgments and their Impact on Market Structure

The so-called San Francisco judgments, resulting from civil suits instituted against American and Continental in 1946, had a fundamental bearing on the market structure, and especially the conditions of entry in this industry.[23] According to the government, a triple-threat combination of policies had destroyed competition in can manufacture and in the can-closing field. It was the defendant's policy, the government charged, to "lease machines only to customers, lease so far below cost that the customer must (in the economic sense) lease them, and contract with them on the basis of their total requirements for a long period of time. The intent and result: a monopolized market from which actual and potential competition are excluded."[24] By way of relief the government asked for cancellation of

[22] In a comparative study of entry conditions in twenty industries, Professor Bain classified the metal container industry as falling within his third group in which "entry is forestalled with prices moderately to slightly above minimal costs, and moderate to very low excess profits, . . ." rather than in group 1 in which entry was described as forestalled with resulting high prices and substantial excess profits. This classification of the tin can industry as falling within the group with the least restrictions on entry was a result, according to Bain, of the 1950 decrees referred to above. (Bain, *op.cit.,* p. 179.)

[23] 87 F. Suppl. 18 (1949). A consent decree containing terms identical with those in the American Can judgment was entered against Continental Can on June 26, 1950. It will be understood that the discussion above pertains to both companies.

[24] *Brief for the United States of America,* Civil Action No. 26345H, p. 264.

the offending machine leases and total-requirements contracts and, most important, for divestiture of the closing-machine part of the defendants' business.

In its decision the District Court upheld most of the government's charges. It concluded that the five-year requirements contract had unreasonably restrained trade in violation of the Sherman Act. It decided, however, contrary to the government's view, that a reasonable period for such contracts was one year. Further, such sales contracts in the future would have to be negotiated and executed on the basis of the individual plants of each customer; thus, it was hoped that the smaller can manufacturers would be able to bid at least for the business of a single plant of a multiplant concern.

The government regarded the machine leases of the can companies with their tying clause features as "the strategic bottleneck of the industry" and it asked for divestiture of this phase of the business from the sale of containers. But the court refused to divest the "Big Two" of their closing machines; instead it ordered the companies for a period of ten years to sell them to anyone and for five years to lease them to anyone other than a container manufacturer. Further, in order to facilitate entry of new, independent firms into the manufacture of closing machines, the defendants were required to issue royalty-free, nonrestrictive licenses on them to any applicant and also provide the necessary "know-how" at cost. If machines were leased, the rentals could not be less than reasonable under all circumstances and after January 1, 1954, they had to be compensatory to the lessor. Thus, below-cost rentals could no longer be used by the dominant can companies as an inducement to lease. The most important provision of the decrees regulating the selling practices of the two companies was that which prohibited the granting of any annual, cumulative-volume discounts for five years.

What were the effects of these judgments on entry and the structure of the industry generally? What happened to the machine leases and the plan to have the can companies sell closing equipment to the canners? Contrary to the District Court's expectations, most canners were willing to purchase the closing machines on the terms offered. This was not altogether surprising, since the price formula set by the court was well below the replacement value of the machines. With rents scheduled to rise to a compensatory level, it was logical for even the small canners to buy, which they did. By the middle of 1954, over 75 per cent of the closing machines of both American and Continental had been sold, and nearly all of them had been disposed of by the close of the following year. However, most of the buyers did not set up their own servicing departments, preferring to rely on those of the two big can manufacturers.

While fundamental changes have taken place with respect to the machine lease and other practices, no major outsiders have entered the commercial manufacture of packers' cans in the last eight years. According to one student of the decrees,[25] the large packers have been allocating their orders for cans to several suppliers, rather then dealing exclusively with one seller; there has been an enormous growth in open-order purchasing instead of on contract; and the smaller manufacturers have been able to detach "fragments" of business from the two principal suppliers of cans with the result that their market position has been greatly strengthened. Examination of the percentage share of the smaller manufacturers in the packers' can business would not suggest, however, that their status has improved as much as this optimistic survey implies.

The Economics of Vertical Integration in Canning

Perhaps the most important effect of the decrees thus far has been the apparent impetus which they have given to the manufacture of cans by concerns for their own use. In the early years of this century, a large proportion of cans were made in captive plants; for example, in 1913, an estimated 29.4 per cent were so made. The percentage of cans so manufactured declined over the years until in 1955 it amounted to only 12.8 per cent of the total; this decline in self-manufacture has often been cited as an indication of the can industry's efficiency and over-all performance. However, the enforcement of the Robinson-Patman Act with its ban on discriminatory prices led some users to change their methods of doing business. For instance, Campbell Soup, for long Continental's largest customer, began to purchase tin plate and allow the can company to manufacture it into cans under contract. After the 1950 decree, Campbell bought machinery and by producing for its own use became the nation's third largest can manufacturer. In general, it would seem that the 1950 decrees, by prohibiting cumulative quantity discounts, have stimulated a trend toward manufacture of their own cans by large users. Recently California Packing Corporation, packers of the Del Monte line, installed about five million dollars worth of equipment to make its own cans. "Cal-Pak's move is a direct result of the antitrust decree. It used to enjoy the maximum quantity discount—3 per cent on its purchases of cans—and wants to make up that differential, if

---

[25] J. W. McKie, "The Decline of Monopoly in the Metal Container Industry," *American Economic Review*, May 1955, p. 506.

possible, by savings on its canmaking venture." [26] The Minnesota Valley Canning Company, despite the seasonal nature of its operations, has been "rolling its own" for several years; Stokely-Van Camp, another of the nation's largest canners, reports "encouraging" results from its experiments in canmaking; processors of citrus concentrate in Florida are reported planning to pool resources to make cans; even Libby, McNeil, and Libby, which used to make its own cans forty years ago, has announced plans to manufacture them for its meat-packing business in Chicago, despite the fact that, according to the company, "the canmakers are trying everything to keep us from going into it." [27]

The big brewers have been the latest users to threaten to manufacture their own cans; they have been urged by the aluminum companies to make their own containers from that light metal and by using such threats they have wrung large concessions from the can-makers. "Customers in the less well-organized food-packing industry resent 'the favors that beer is getting' and talk of setting up their own canning operations." [28] Certainly, the "trend toward vertical integration" in the canning industry is on the upswing and trade sources estimate that can users might account for as much as 17 to 17.3 per cent of total can production in 1959. [29]

Further integration of can manufacture with food processing is a distinct possibility. It is clear from interviews with food processors that the main incentive pushing them into making their own cans is the need to cut costs. They cite the fact that can prices have about doubled since World War II. Some of them anonymously claim savings of as much as 10 to 20 per cent from self-manufacture, after depreciation. "A machinery supplier [not an impartial adviser, to be sure] claims the equipment pays for itself in as little as four years." On the other hand, the president of American Can ridicules expectations of such large economies. [30]

Two fundamental factors affecting the decision to "make or buy" containers are (1) the prospective annual volume of production and (2) the regularity of container requirements over the year. Without adequate volume, the initial investment in can-making equipment would not be justified and unless production is reasonably stable over the year idle plant and overhead costs would destroy the profitability of the operation. Despite these problems, many packers believe that they can achieve the necessary volume (40 million cans of one size per year), and that they can stabilize

[26] "Continental Can's Big Push," *Fortune,* April 1955, p. 122.
[27] "Canners Profit from Price War," *Business Week,* February 14, 1959, pp. 54 ff.
[28] *Ibid.*
[29] K. W. Bennett, "Tin Cans: Tensions in a Big Year," *Iron Age,* June 18, 1959, p. 56.
[30] "Captive Cans," *Wall Street Journal,* April 8, 1959, pp. 1 ff.

operations by packing a variety of crops with different picking seasons, by storing cans for later use, or by selling their surplus can production on the open market. Integration, they claim, is profitable because it yields the following economies: (1) Transportation costs are less because tin plate packages are compact and cost less to ship by railroad than bulky, easily damaged cans. (2) Handling costs are reduced. An executive of Stokely-Van Camp, for example, remarks, "We go direct from manufacturing right into production lines." (3) Canners also claim that they avoid some of the overhead costs which the commercial canmakers must add to their selling prices.

If the economies of integration are as large as claimed, the movement is likely to spread. Given the small margins of profit in food processing, "savings from can-making enjoyed by one firm tend to draw others into similar ventures." The big can manufacturers are, of course, aware of this possibility and they have taken a number of steps to counteract it. They have been locating new plants closer to their customers' in order to save freight costs and they have apparently also been offering extra services, such as free warehouse space, to hold their accounts. Their research and engineering work have been intensified to improve their own can-manufacturing methods and they have recently taken drastic action in the field of price policy to discourage the establishment of captive plants. The repercussions of these developments on the price front will be dealt with below. Here, we may simply note that the 1950 judgments have had the somewhat unforeseen effect of disturbing the industrial equilibrium of the can industry not so much by enticing new entrants to undertake commercial production of cans, but by encouraging integration by the large buyers.

Bilateral Oligopoly in the Tin Plate Market

The price of tin plate is of controlling importance in the economics of the tin can industry because that raw material is, by far, the principal item of cost in the manufacture of metal containers. As of April 1, 1958, for example, the cost of tin plate equaled about 64 per cent of can prices for that date. Prior to 1947, tin plate consistently equaled about 65 per cent of can selling prices—an indication of how decisive the price of tin plate is in the operations of the tin can industry.

The market for tin plate is especially interesting to economists because it provides a striking illustration of that much-debated phenomenon known as countervailing power. Indeed, as J. W. McKie has pointed out, "This whole industry from top to bottom is characterized by substantial buying power at each stage: the makers of tin plate are the chief buyers of tin, and purchase it from a cartelized industry; they sell in turn in an oligopolistic market, while the buyers of tin plate themselves face some influential purchasers among canners, and the canners are subject to pressure from chain stores. . . ." [31]

The "rung" of this ladder of buying power which is of immediate interest to us is that involving the sale of tin plate. This product, characterized by a high degree of concentration, is produced in the United States almost exclusively by the large integrated steel companies. In recent years, the four largest producers have shipped more than three-quarters of all the electrolytic tin plate made in this country. The sellers' side of the market, therefore, is definitely oligopolistic, while the concentration in the metal container industry makes for oligopsony (fewness of buyers). In short, tin plate is bought and sold under conditions of bilateral oligopoly.

In the pre-World War II period tin plate was sold on the basis of long-term contracts which usually ran for five or ten years. These contracts did not specify a definite price, but provided that it should be the seller's ruling current price at the time the order for the product was placed, less certain discounts. The price of tin plate was usually published about December 1 and it was effective for the following nine months; actually, it was good for twelve months. During that period, the price could not go any higher, but it might be lowered; in effect, it was a ceiling price.

The contracts under which the leading can companies secured their tin plate further stated that the price for the year should be "the officially announced domestic base price of the Carnegie Illinois Steel Corporation [a U.S. Steel subsidiary]. . . ." This was one of few cases in American industry in which a system of price leadership was embodied explicitly in the sales contracts, with the price leader specified as such. By this device the other tin plate producers partially abdicated their price-making function to the largest manufacturer of the product. (We say "partially" because there is evidence that in time of slack demand the smaller producers often shaded the leader's price.) The can companies, in turn, apparently delegated American Can to negotiate for them with Carnegie Illinois. In other words, the leadership principle was followed on both sides of the market.

What was the outcome of this peculiar process of price formation? The imperfect leadership of Big Steel's subsidiary, modified by the countervailing influence of American Can, seems to have produced two sorts of results: (1) a pattern of sporadic price discrimination which often led to a general price

---

[31] J. W. McKie, *Bilateral Oligopoly in Industrial Product Markets,* unpublished doctoral dissertation, Cambridge: Harvard University, 1951, p. 284. See also J. W. McKie, *Tin Cans and Tin Plates,* Cambridge: Harvard University Press, 1959, *passim.*

reduction. This usually came about because in a period of slack demand "the large buyer has an opportunity to exert pressure in a strategic way against any seller running substantially under capacity and exact concessions from him; and since buyers are alert and well informed, any concessions thus made will tend to spread over the market as other buyers exert pressure against their suppliers." [32] Thus, shading of the leader's price by one of the smaller tin plate producers could result in a uniformly lower price throughout the industry. (2) In other cases, persistent and systematic price discrimination seems to have been practiced with certain large buyers obtaining concessions from their suppliers which were not granted to all. This latter type of price discrimination existed in the industry before the passage of the Robinson-Patman Act of 1936.

Bargaining between the tin plate and tin can oligopolies for strategic advantage with respect to the price the latter paid for the product gave the market a fluidity which it otherwise would have lacked. The huge requirements of the big can-makers for tin plate and the possibility of reallocating their orders among the principal suppliers were a potent force in the thirties in keeping prices down and maintaining competitive pressures among the sellers; the buyers' bargaining advantages, however, were not such as to make the tin plate business unprofitable for the steel producers. In general, economic power was about evenly balanced, with the buyers having a slight edge in time of slack demand. In technological matters, the progress of the tin plate industry was "admirable" during these years, thanks, in the main, to "the constant needling of the large buyers and the stresses imposed on the sellers in competing in an oligopolistic market." [33]

In the years since 1946, inflationary pressures, strikes, and material shortages have generally made for a sellers' market. Buyers and sellers have negotiated with each other separately over the price of tin plate. The steel industry continued to announce tin plate prices annually until 1956, when it went on a six-month contractual basis, with prices published on May 1 and November 1. Later U.S. Steel announced that it was discontinuing the practice and that, after January 1, 1958, all revisions on tin mill products would be made not less than 35 days prior to the effective date of the changes. Buyers would pay the price in effect at the time of shipment. This departure from the traditional long-term pricing of tin plate reflected the need of producers for more flexibility to meet their changing costs. Can-makers had opposed the change, but their objections were of no avail.

Of much greater concern to the can manufacturers in these post-war years

[32] McKie, *Bilateral Oligopoly, op.cit.*, p. 275.
[33] *Ibid.*, pp. 300 ff.

has been the spiralling price of tin plate. Figure 1 which depicts the course of tin plate and tin can prices over the years 1939–59 graphically demonstrates this price upheaval of the postwar years. But the profit squeeze suggested by these figures is not the only worry of the can company executives. The inflation in the cost of their principal raw material, added to their own higher wage and other costs, has forced them to raise can prices so frequently that many of the large canners have threatened or actually begun manufacture of their own containers. These developments have led some can companies to take countermeasures in self-defense. For example, in the spring of 1956 officials of American Can vigorously opposed the new increases in tin plate prices and a few months later announced that in order to keep costs down they were installing 27 million dollars worth of new equipment at various plants in the United States to process tin and steel plate from coils.[34] Admitting that "it makes good sense for the container people to process their own coil," a leading steel publication added: "Behind the can companies' action is a threat that their customers—the packagers—will start making cans for themselves if prices go up again." [35]

The leading can companies have also sought to meet the problem of rising tin plate costs by intensified research with a view to reducing their use of tin or making containers from other materials, such as aluminum. All these developments illustrate the fact that, under conditions of bilateral oligopoly, business strategy is not limited to price policy, but may manifest itself in the nature of the product, the "product mix," production processes, marketing tactics, and even politics. Indeed, business competition under these conditions can perhaps be best understood by analogy to the waging of modern, total war.

Price Policy

Three phases of the price policy of the can industry will be treated in this section, namely (1) price leadership, (2) price discrimination, and (3) the stability of can prices.

(1) Price leadership has been one of the common practices resorted to by oligopolists to avoid the uncertainty and possible cutthroat competition which often prevail in that type of market structure. This pattern of con-

[34] "Tin Plate: Are Can Companies Revolting?" *Iron Age*, June 21, 1956, p. 61. American Can's program, now completed at a cost of 32 million dollars, comprises eight coil plants at which it can process about 85 per cent of its tin plate. Continental is also reported to be installing nine lines which will enable it to process about 90 per cent of its tin plate requirements. National Can has not undertaken any effort of this kind as yet.

[35] *Ibid.*, p. 164. The price differential between coils and cut sheets of tin plate is said to be about $.50 per base box.

current pricing, as it has been called, existed for many years in the metal container industry. For example, in the 1916 antitrust suit the court said: "The American Can Company practically establishes the market price for packers' cans. . . . The competitors of the American Can Company manufacturing packers' cans, as a rule, adopt the published prices." [36] The court qualified this finding by noting that Continental and Wheeling Can Companies had strictly adhered to American's prices, whereas the smaller companies frequently gave concessions of from 2 to 6 per cent off the leader's prices. American's published prices established the base line of competition, so to speak, for the minor concerns as well as for Continental, but because of the successful differentiation of product by the two leaders (especially in terms of service) the smaller companies had to resort to price reductions to obtain business.

In 1946, the federal government charged that the identity between American and Continental Can's prices in California was due to direct collusion rather than to the practice of price leadership. [37] The indictment alleged that the observed price uniformity was the result of "a continuing agreement and concert of action among the defendants" from approximately 1935 to 1946. American and Continental pleaded *nolo contendere,* and paid the maximum but insignificant fines that were imposed by the court: $25,000 for American and $20,000 for Continental.

While the prices charged by the two major can companies tended to be uniform in the years 1916 to 1946, indirect price concessions, such as liberal credit terms, generous treatment of customers' spoilage claims, low rentals for closing machines and the like, were common in time of slack business; but usually competition was diverted into nonprice forms and the close harmony on prices between the two giants of the industry was preserved.

In the postwar years and especially after the 1950 decrees, the rivalry between American and Continental became more intense—climaxed by the revolutionary price developments of 1958–59. For the first time in more than fifty years, American Can's price leadership was defied and rejected by its arch rival. It all started conventionally enough when U.S. Steel announced another increase in tin plate prices, 35 cents more per base box, effective November 1, 1958. In anticipation of this action, American had announced in September a 6 per cent increase on all can lines. At the same time, it stated that starting November 1, it would break with traditional industry pricing practice by establishing a policy under which changes would be made in can prices in direct relationship to the costs involved in each type of can.

---

[36] *U.S.* versus *American Can,* 234 Fed. 168.
[37] *U.S.* versus *American Can et al.,* Cr. 30323-S (N.D. Calif., 1946), par. 20.

Formerly, the company explained, a flat percentage increase had been applied. According to *Business Week*, "Instead of mirroring this price change, Continental announced it would impose only a 3 per cent increase. Then the price war began." [38]

American retaliated against its recalcitrant follower with a series of direct price cuts averaging 2 to 5 per cent, depending upon the size and type of can; these changes were estimated as saving buyers more than nine million dollars. Starting January 1, 1959, the new prices were to be based on separate f.o.b. quotations at each of its 68 plants for each type and size of can. (Previously, the industry had two general pricing areas—east and west of the Rocky Mountains.) Under the revised policy, American Can's prices were to be based on the actual transportation costs of steel and tin plate delivered to the company's plants, as well as the cost of delivery to the company's customers. Continental promptly matched these price changes, including the breweries in its concessions, and moved the effective date ahead two weeks. American, then, with equal promptness, matched its rival's earlier date.

According to some trade sources, the price cutting went on after this, though there was little mention of it in business journals. The president of the National Can Company, largest of the independents, was quoted as saying: "American and Continental are cutting their own throats—and ours along with them. Every price line has been cut at least twice; there have been six cuts in beer cans. And I'll be surprised if they don't cut down even further." [39]

These fears were soon realized. On April 2, 1959, general reductions of from 4 to 10 per cent in prices were made by American on packers' cans; Continental and National Can immediately announced similar reductions. American in large newspaper ads presented this action to the public as being its contribution to the fight against inflation as well as reflecting its efficiency and desire to have cans made by expert can-makers. A Continental Can spokesman frankly said its cuts were designed to keep packers from manufacturing their own cans.

A week later the president of American Can told reporters that the industry was not engaged in a price war, but conceded that the primary reason for the price reductions was to halt the growth of can manufacture by individual food processors. Terming self-manufacture "a very serious threat to the future of our can business," he disclosed that the company's January price reductions had staved off plans of six large customers to make their own cans.

---

[38] Canners Profit from Price War," *Business Week*, February 14, 1959, p. 54.
[39] *Ibid.*, p. 55.

Apparently not all can executives agreed on how to meet the crisis in their business. One of them commented: "It's a cold economic fact that some of the all-season packers can produce more cheaply than we can sell to them at some locations. I say, 'Let them go.' Don't wreck the whole business by trying to hold on to them. We are willing to show the packers, who could save money on making their own, how to go about it. . . . We'll trade our know-how, even turn out special can-making equipment for them, in exchange for first refusal on their business at those locations where we can offer them a clear economic advantage." [40]

We are perhaps too close to these unprecedented events to assess their significance, but some observations, however speculative, seem called for. In retrospect, it would seem that the price upheaval was due fundamentally to the abolition of aggregate price discounts under the terms of the 1950 decrees, the threats to integrate by the big users as container costs went up because of inflation, and American's adoption of the coil processing method. The latter step probably made its cost of plate sufficiently lower at specific plants relative to those of competitors that it was induced to establish its new method of price quotation.

It would be difficult to predict the effects of the new price structure upon competition and the price leadership practice. Talk of price war in this situation can undoubtedly be exaggerated. The disruption of price uniformity seems to have stemmed basically from disagreement between the "Big Two" as to the proper level of "limit pricing" they should follow to deter self-manufacture by their customers. This disagreement may readily be understood in terms of differences in the size of their respective customers and their related abilities to produce cans for themselves. The odds are against unrestrained price cutting; the financial cost to the principals is very obvious and the logic and tradition of price cooperation in this oligopolistic industry are very strong. In the future, the matching of price changes may be more evident on a local, market-to-market basis than on a national scale.

(2) The most important form of price discrimination in this industry has been the granting of excessive quantity discounts to large buyers. The adjective "excessive" is basic here, because discriminatory quantity discounts can only be said to exist when the varying amounts which a seller offers cannot be justified in terms of the identifiable production and marketing costs incurred in the handling of different sized orders. The economic conditions which are conducive to this form of price discrimination are pronounced in the canning industry; we refer to the great differences in size, bargaining power, and the consequent varying elasticity of demand of individual pack-

[40] *Business Week*, April 11, 1959, p. 57.

ers. The very large concerns, as we have seen, have real possibilities of choice in deciding whether to buy cans or to manufacture for their own use. This fact in itself makes their demand for cans potentially more elastic (at least in the long run) than that of the small canner, and makes the granting of price concessions to the former more probable.

American Can was the defendant in two suits involving price discrimination before the passage of the Robinson-Patman Act of 1936. In both of them, the courts held that a large packer had received discounts on its can purchases of 18 and 20 per cent respectively, which were prejudicial to its smaller competitors.[41] After the new law was passed, it is said that American was happy to be able to tell its large customers who were demanding "free closing machinery, credit without interest, freight rebates, and indiscriminate discounts" that such "wild cards" were now prohibited. At that time, the company discontinued its practice of giving discounts by private negotiation and published a schedule under which 1 per cent was allowed to firms buying $500,000 in a year, 2 per cent to those buying one million dollars, 3 per cent to those buying three million, and 4 per cent to those buying five million or more. The biggest buyers thus lost discounts which were later shown to have ranged up to 14 per cent. Concurrently, American cut its base prices to all customers by 8 per cent; this move was probably designed to prevent its large customers from manufacturing their own cans.

In 1946, American Can issued a new schedule of quantity discounts which applied, for the first time, to the smaller buyers. The revised list started with purchases of $50,000 on which .2 per cent was granted and rose gradually to 3 per cent on purchases of four million dollars and over.

In the postwar period American had to defend itself against two treble damage suits filed by small customers. In *Bruce's Juices*, the plaintiff eventually lost its appeal to the Supreme Court because of its refusal to pay for cans for which American was charging it more than it charged other competing firms.[42] In its treble damage action in Florida, however, Bruce's Juices was more successful; the District Court there found that American was evading the prohibitions of the Robinson-Patman Act[43] and the Court of Appeals sustained the decision.[44] In the second case,[45] American's discount system was ultimately held to be satisfactory by the courts, but the company

---

[41] *George Van Camp and Sons* versus *American Can Co.* 278 U.S. 245 (1929) and *American Can Co.* versus *Ladoga Canning Co.* 44 F. 2nd 763 (7th Cir., 1930).
[42] *Bruce's Juices, Inc.* versus *American Can Co.*, 330 U.S. 743 (1947).
[43] 87 F. Suppl. 985 (S.D. Fla. 1949).
[44] 187 F. 2nd 923.
[45] *Russellville Canning Co.* versus *American Can Co.*, 87 F. Suppl. 484 (W.D. Ark. 1949); *American Can Co.* versus *Russellville Canning Co.*, 191 F. 2nd 38 (8th Cir. 1951).

was vulnerable on another issue and hence made a private settlement of the suit.

In the long run, so far as price discrimination was concerned, these Robinson-Patman cases were much less important than the 1950 decrees which banned cumulative quantity discounts. Those prohibitions, as we have already noted, brought about revolutionary changes in the industry's price structure and contributed greatly to the recent trend toward self-manufacture.

(3) One of the obvious characteristics of the published prices of packers' cans prior to World War II was their relative stability over time. Can prices were much more stable between 1924 and 1939 than the selling prices which canners obtained for their canned fruit and vegetables. This stability was evident over the course of the canning season, i.e., for as long as a year, and for periods as long as three consecutive years prior to wartime price stabilization. Since the end of World War II can prices have shown little stability; rather they have moved upward steadily in response to the inflationary forces operating in the economy. The only period in which any stability was evident was the years 1954–55, when published prices remained the same for two years running. (See Figure 1.)

The major reason for the pre-World War II stability of can prices was a provision of the packers' can contract which tied the price of such containers to the price of tin plate with the result that the former displayed the same degree of price stability as the price of the raw material. The contract provision provided a formula in accordance with which the price of cans was adjusted each year to the opening price for tin plate as set by the Carnegie-Illinois Steel Corporation.[46]

The economic consequences of price stabilization depend very largely upon the duration of time over which stability is maintained. Officials of the American Can Company testified before the Temporary National Economic Committee in 1939 that the canners themselves desired price stability throughout the year.[47] The reasons given were these: The season for packing specific types of canned food varies from one canning region to another, yet the bulk of these products sell in the same national market. If the price of containers fluctuated from month to month, some canners might gain a competitive advantage by buying when the price was low. It has often been observed that where a raw material is subject to further fabrication, its pro-

---

[46] In the fall of 1939, American changed its policy in this respect and announced that henceforth it would publish its own basic price for tin plate. If the Company received concessions from this price during the course of the year, it agreed to make refunds to the canners to cover the difference.

[47] Temporary National Economic Committee, *Hearings*, Part 20, pp. 10761, 10762.

FIGURE 1

Published Prices of Tin Plate and Tin Cans, 1939–59
(Tin Plate per base box; tin cans per 1,000.)

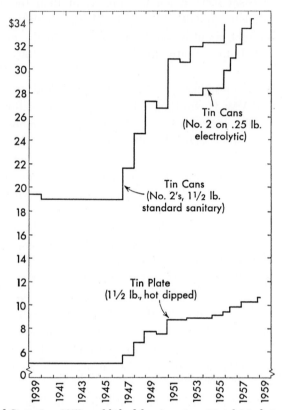

Source: Metal Statistics, 1959, published by American Metal Market, pp. 201, 203.

ducers are apt to be more concerned over price uniformity than the price
level. They wish merely to be on an equal competitive footing; this seems
to be the case with the canners, so far as the cost of containers is concerned.
Another point in favor of the practice is that price fluctuations during the
year would encourage speculative buying which, in turn, would disrupt and
disorganize the production schedules of the can-makers. All in all, it seems
that a good case can be made for seasonal price stabilization from the point
of view of both the canners and society as a whole.

The stabilization of can prices during a period of cyclical decline, such
as that of the thirties, has been a matter of greater controversy. Between
1929 and 1933, for example, the published price of American's No. 2 can
declined slightly less than 13 per cent, whereas the prices of canned vege-

tables and fruits fell 30 and 40 per cent, respectively. Actually, nearly all of the decrease in container prices over those years was due to the simultaneous reduction in tin plate prices. Critics of such price rigidity have frequently argued that the practice results, in a period of declining demand, in curtailment of production and employment, with their consequent adverse effects upon the whole economy. The relative inflexibility of some prices, it is likewise alleged, "throws the burden of further price adjustment on the flexibly priced commodities." The first criticism is not really applicable to the can manufacturing industry for two reasons: (a) the can producers cannot deliberately restrict production to maintain prices; under their total requirements' contracts they must supply the buyers' needs, whatever they may be; (b) even if can prices were drastically reduced in time of business depression, such a policy would probably not have a favorable effect on production and employment in can manufacturing or in canning because of the relative inelasticity of the demand for containers under such circumstances.

While the can manufacturer cannot administratively adjust his production to maintain price, he can control the size of the gross margin he charges for converting tin plate into tin cans. Calculation of the percentage change in the nominal gross margin of American Can from 1929 to 1933 reveals that the charge made for fabricating No. 2 tin cans from tin plate was cut by only a fraction more than 1 per cent between those years. The stability in the can manufacturer's gross margin, plus the effect of the relatively inelastic demand for cans during the depression years, readily account for the satisfactory financial records the major can companies made during that period, while small canners were failing by the hundreds and others were floundering in a sea of red ink. Recognizing the many factors which make the canning business extrahazardous, it still appears true that such extreme price rigidity had adverse effects upon the canners. Container prices, when added to other relatively rigid expense items, comprised as much as 50 per cent or more of the costs of canning in those years. When the price of canned products decline, the burden of these fixed costs falls on the canner's profit margin and the more flexible items of his expenditure. Granted that lower can prices would not stimulate additional sales of canned food in depression times, still they would distribute more equitably the incidence of the decline in business activity.

On the other hand, Simon Whitney argues that the can manufacturers were under no obligation to turn over to canners or consumers "the profit that continued high demand and failure of more firms to build competing can factories yielded to their line of business. . . ."[48] This argument blithely

[48] Whitney, *op.cit.*, pp. 207, 209.

ignores the barriers to new entry which the big container manufacturers erected in those years and which would seem to have had more than a slight influence on the profitability of the can-making business. While it is true, a 3 per cent reduction in can prices in those years would have "made up to them [i.e., the canners] something less than 10 per cent of the decline in their dollar sales between 1929 and 1932," the cut would have been highly desirable from the standpoint of equity.

The orthodox arguments against secular price stabilization (i.e., over periods of time longer than the average business cycle) apply with persuasive force to the price policies of the can manufacturers. During the twenties, for example, the "Big Two" maintained comparatively stable prices while the industry was undergoing a veritable revolution in terms of increased productivity. Technical changes doubled American's output from 150 cans per minute in the early twenties to 300 per minute by 1930. Productivity per worker in the industry as a whole rose 26.7 per cent between 1921 and 1929. Toward the end of that decade the introduction of electrical controls on the production lines permitted a reduction of the average number of workers per line from eleven to two and one half. Price stabilization, however, caused the greater part of these economies to be plowed back into expansion and modernization of plant or to be distributed as higher dividends rather than to be passed on to consumers in lower prices. The relative stabilization of can prices meant large income too for Continental Can whose expansion in the twenties via merger and purchase of competitors was mostly accomplished out of earnings. The steady profits which price stabilization made possible enabled the two leading companies to spend millions on research and other forms of nonprice competition; such expenditures strengthened their market position and made entry of new firms into the industry more difficult. In short, the twin policies of price leadership and price stabilization in the years between 1916 and 1946 seem to have fostered the drift toward duopoly in this industry.

Nonprice Competition

By nonprice competition economists mean the rivalry in service, advertising and in product development and improvement. This kind of competition is very common in oligopolistic industries and the tin can industry is no exception. In fact, a recent study of the pricing practices of big business found that "the clearest among those [companies] surveyed, in its emphasis on nonprice competition as a basis of price policy, was probably American Can. The policy of this Company of automatically transmitting to its customers increases or decreases in basic costs—tin plate and wages—removed its prices from the executives' roster of items with which they must have constant concern. Possibly even more important was the emphasis of this Company on routine and special services to its customers. American Can, having relegated price to the background, and having enjoyed a position as price leader, was able safely to concentrate on the provision of service and the devising of innovations. . . ." [49] (This summary was obviously written before the recent "unpleasantness" on price matters in the industry.)

With respect to innovations, an authoritative journal of the packaging trade has stated that the can industry's research and development facilities are "among" the finest and most extensive in the entire packaging field." [50] Indeed, it seems incontrovertible that the rivalry of the "Big Two" in these areas has been largely responsible for the sensational fifteen-fold increase in the demand for metal cans during the first half of this century. Consistently over the years, their engineers and scientists have made breakthroughs in chemical, metallurgical and mechanical research to produce numerous "firsts," such as beer cans, motor oil cans, baby food cans, etc.

Currently, in new enlarged laboratories, both American and Continental are working on substitute materials to free the industry from its dependence on tin, on welding and cementing processes, and on new containers and the machinery to make them. [51] It is estimated that the industry, as a whole, is presently spending 1.25 per cent of its income, or close to 40 million dollars, on research. Illustrative of the industry's progressiveness in this respect is its initiative in moving into the field of atomic energy research. Continental Can recently joined in a cooperative venture to establish the first irradiation center for research on the preservation of food by means of nuclear energy. It is also participating in the operation of the world's largest nuclear reactor owned and operated by private industry. [52]

As to service competition, it is widely recognized that the big companies are more thoroughly organized and equipped for customer service than most supplier industries. Their former practice of rental only of can-closing machinery contributed to their becoming the "technical assistant of the canning industry." It is significant in this connection that the abolition of

[49] A. D. H. Kaplan *et al., Pricing in Big Business,* Washington, D.C.: The Brookings Institution, 1958, pp. 260–1.

[50] *Modern Packaging,* January 1957, pp. 104–5.

[51] In June 1956, Continental opened a new seven million dollar research center in South Chicago which was said to employ 600 people, including 265 scientists and engineers. A year before American opened its new research center at Barrington, Ill. ("Research on Metal," *Modern Packaging,* July 1956, p. 174; D. A. Loehwing, "No Lid on Cans," *Barron's,* July 9, 1956, pp. 5 ff.; *The New York Times,* April 19, 1959, p. 14.)

[52] D. L. Thomas, "New Mettle in Cans," *Barron's,* December 8, 1958, p. 19.

compulsory rental of such machinery has not greatly diminished the importance of the can-makers' technical services to the industry.

The smaller can manufacturers have sought to compensate for their handicaps in nonprice competition with the two dominant companies by giving customers somewhat lower prices. Their policy of price competition is highly desirable from the social standpoint. It serves to hold down excessive nonprice competition, to reduce the cost of such competition, and to give the canners a wider range of choice. The virtues of nonprice competition in this industry have been appreciable, but without price competition there is the danger that the various services will be developed to an immoderate extent and become too costly.

Interindustry Competition

In appraising the prospects of a more workable competition than exists in many of our industries, Professor J. M. Clark some years ago suggested the possibility that technical progress might bring about closer and more general substitution of one product for another. "Indeed," he wrote, "it seems that the differences between substitute products, in costs of production and service value, are nowadays often no more serious than similar differences between different varieties of what we think of as the 'same' product." [53] Such substitution in the future, Clark held, might result in many of our large scale industries developing "the characteristics of fairly healthy and workable imperfect competition rather than those of slightly qualified monopoly." The development and use of numerous substitutes for tin cans during and after World War II raises interesting questions about the extent to which they have affected the price and other policies of the can manufacturers.

The competition of packers' cans with other types of food package and preservation process has become more severe in recent years. Even before Pearl Harbor, the competition among the container industries had become stronger—with the can manufacturers taking the aggressive role in the struggle for the beer, oil and milk container markets, among others. The war forced widespread substitution of glass, fiber, plastic, and other types of container material for tin plate and gave added support to the already rapidly growing frozen food industry. During those years, the can industry was faced with the greatest challenge in its history in the form of outside

[53] J. M. Clark, "Toward a Concept of Workable Competition," *American Economic Review,* June 1940, p. 247.

competition. Competition which in the past had been merely potential became active and aggressive.

The can-makers were successful in recapturing most of these markets during the postwar period, not so much by reducing their prices but through increased service to customers and a public relation program for the tin can. Aiding them in this effort was the fact that the tin can possessed the initial advantage of being cheaper for many uses than rival containers. Canned food was also less expensive than the increasingly popular frozen products. The can companies' knowledge of food packers' production problems and their excellent field service systems were other points in their favor.

During the postwar period the competition of the packaging materials and food processing techniques became more intense, especially in nonprice terms. Civilian consumption of frozen vegetables almost trebled and growth in per capita sales of frozen fruit was only slightly less. The glass container industry vigorously sought markets by spending more than ten million dollars annually on research and development—with an emphasis on the "lightweighting" of bottles, treatment by siliconing and other methods to reduce breakability, and redesigning of shapes and sizes.

Glass containers have been promoted most in such lines as baby food, soluble coffee, beer, soft drinks, applesauce, salad dressings, preserves of all sorts, etc. Interindustry competition would appear to be sharpest in some of these specific product lines where the alternative containers are close substitutes for one another in terms of price and technical characteristics. Plastic and paper containers have also registered large gains in the postwar years, but these packages are not competitive with tin cans where heat is required for the food preservation process.

Most recently, aluminum has made a bid to replace tin plate as a material for cans. Kaiser Aluminum has made aluminum cans for Kraft's grated cheese, Reynolds Metal Company is supplying Esso Standard with aluminum oil cans, and late in 1958 American Can itself began manufacture of aluminum cans for sardines. Draught beer has been packaged in aluminum cans by an enterprising Western brewer.[54] The big can companies have been studying aluminum's potentialities for their business for some time and they will be ready, if the price of the light metal warrants, to shift over to its use in the manufacture of containers.

Likewise, the can-makers have in part met the competition, active or potential, of other packaging materials by entering these fields either directly

[54] "Aluminum Cans," *Business Week*, November 2, 1957, p. 180, and "Coors Packages Draught Beer in Aluminum Cans," *American Brewer*, January 1959, pp. 33–7.

or through acquisition of others. Continental Can has gone furthest in the direction of diversification or "product integration"; in 1957, its metal can division accounted for only 53.6 per cent of its sales. Its paper division contributed 24.7 per cent of total sales and the glass and plastic division, 15.8 per cent. Other products accounted for the remaining 5.9 per cent. American, as already noted, has also expanded further into the paper and plastic field, although it contends that the products which have been acquired are not competitive with metal cans. Its billion dollar sales volume in 1957 came from the following sources: metal containers, 67 per cent; paper packaging and household paper products, 15 per cent; milk containers and composite containers, 9 per cent; paper drinking and food cups, 6 per cent; and other products, 3 per cent.

Thus, we see that the changing technology of the container industries is daily breaking down the walls which formerly separated them. In some cases substitute containers provide a greater degree of workable competition than exists in the metal can industry proper, but there are ways of circumventing or controlling this type of competition which should not be overlooked. For example, horizontal integration of the manufacture of substitute containers under the unified control of one or a few companies could greatly reduce the possibilities of competition of this sort.

SECTION III: PUBLIC POLICY

The Industry's Record in the Years 1916-49

The question can now be asked whether the changes in the metal container industry have justified Judge Rose's prediction, in the American Can case of 1916, of a "gradual reestablishment of competitive conditions." Judge Rose's decision, it must be understood, was predicated upon the assumption of a steady growth of American Can's competitors. "Continuance of the present conditions," he wrote, "may well result in the development of some of them [American Can's competitors] until competition will again control the market."

Our study discloses that in the earlier span of years some of American Can's competitors definitely grew, especially Continental Can. But American did not decline relatively, so that a condition of near-duopoly was created. While the resulting concentration in the industry's structure militated powerfully against price competition between the two leading companies, it did not diminish the tendency of the smaller concerns to shade the leaders' prices in order to obtain business. On the other hand, price leadership and price stabilization as practiced in these years tended to deny canners and consumers most of the savings made possible by technological progress. Furthermore, the stabilization of can prices during the 1929–35 cycle seems to have shifted an inequitable share of the burden of financial readjustment upon the canners.

Nonprice competition between American and Continental became much more vigorous over the years 1916 to 1949, as the latter grew larger, but there was the ever-present danger that some of its forms, such as expensive advertising and technical services, might be overdone. The duopolistic rivalry between the two leading companies in research produced a great many innovations in canned food and in general line containers during these years; it also brought about many desirable improvements in canning technology. All this was decidedly in the public interest. But there was an adverse aspect to it also; if the growth of the two leading firms was at the expense of the smaller firms, it would eliminate the partial check which the latter could exercise on excessive nonprice competition. There was much to be said then, as there is now, from a social viewpoint, for a diversified market structure in this industry, i.e., one composed of small as well as large enterprises.

It was the conduct of the two big companies, and particularly their use of the tying clause and excessively long-term contracts, which led Judge Harris to conclude in the 1949 suit against American Can that these practices operated as obstacles to entry and thus interfered with the maintenance of competition and the expansion of the smaller companies in the industry. Some economists who had studied can manufacturing in these years concluded also that, in terms of the criteria of structure, conduct and performance, this industry, as of 1949, did not meet the requirements of workable competition. They advocated the dissolution of the two leading companies as a necessary corrective of the industry's malfunctioning.[55]

The Industry's Performance since 1950

In retrospect, the 1950 antitrust decrees against American and Continental are rapidly assuming the character of legal landmarks in the evolution of

[55] Cf. the views of G. W. Stocking and M. W. Watkins, as expressed in *Monopoly and Free Enterprise*, New York: The Twentieth Century Fund, 1951, pp. 181–2; also G. W. Stocking, "The Rule of Reason, Workable Competition, and Monopoly," *Yale Law Journal*, July 1955, p. 1160, note 220; and the author's chapter in W. Adams, ed., *The Structure of American Industry*, rev. ed., 1954, pp. 440–41. The case against dissolution of these companies is presented in Whitney, *op.cit.*, Vol. 2, pp. 223–4.

public policy toward this industry. Indeed, one cannot deny the statement of the president of the American Can Company that these judgments "have brought about radical changes in the economic patterns and operations of the industry. . . ." [56] But, have these changes been fundamental enough to restore the industry to a state of workable competition?

On the positive side, it must be noted, first, that the purchase of the can-closing machines by the canners has given them a new degree of independence in contracting with the can-makers for containers; the big can companies can no longer use the leverage which they formerly derived from their control of this machinery to restrict the can buyer's freedom to purchase. Secondly, the decrees seem to have encouraged "an extensive breakdown of exclusive supplier-customer relations," with the probable result that price dickering and competition in nonprice terms have been stimulated. Third, self-manufacture of containers, or the threat of it, by large users has meant, in effect, that entry could not be blocked under the decrees and this has resulted in downward pressure on the industry's selling prices. Last, though the oligopoly structure of the industry remains pretty much intact, the price leadership pattern has been seriously disturbed, at least temporarily, to the consumer's advantage.

The negative aspects of the 1950 decrees from the standpoint of restoring effective competition may be summarized as follows: (1) The can-closing machines which have been purchased by the canners may turn out to be "white elephants," particularly for the smaller firms. We say this because the rapid obsolescence of these machines brought on by the big can companies' engineering improvements in such equipment may make the canners' investment a very costly one. Moreover, the continued reliance of many of these canners on American and Continental for service suggests too that the canners may not have as much independence of action as ownership of the machines might imply. Significant in this connection is a small survey of 44 canners undertaken by Whitney at the end of 1955: twenty-two of those questioned thought that their purchase of these machines was an unfortunate policy; fifteen believed that they had gained by the purchase of the closing equipment, and seven were indifferent whether they owned or rented. [57]

(2) Even the tendency toward self-manufacture which has worked to benefit all can buyers through the downward pressure it has exerted on the prices of the commercial companies may only be a temporary gain. If and when the can companies give up these big accounts as lost for good, this

[56] Quoted in Whitney, *op.cit.*, Vol. 2, p. 490.
[57] *Ibid.*, Vol. 2, p. 220.

salutary effect on the price structure will cease to operate. Many canners will probably be too small and specialized to consider container manufacture for themselves. They will then have to bargain without benefit of the countervailing power of the large canning companies.

(3) The most important reason for restraining one's optimism about the 1950 decrees is that, apart from the tendency toward backward integration by large users, the structure of the industry on the selling side is still decidedly oligopolistic. In fact, National Can's purchase of the Pacific Can Company in 1954 must have increased the concentration ratio, as measured by the four largest companies, in the packers' can field. With the industry so highly concentrated, will this not inevitably lead to the same cooperative practices which have characterized the industry in the past? Or, should we anticipate that some of the large canners who are now manufacturing for their own use will in time decide to sell their surplus production in the open market? Only the latter contingency would be likely to have a substantial effect on the industry's market structure and price behavior.

Performancewise, the can industry's postwar record appears to be somewhat better than in the years before 1945. The big companies have accelerated their efforts in the field of technology and product improvement and, in addition, they have priced their products in a difficult period of inflated costs at levels which have yielded them lower net incomes than in the decades before World War II. American Can, for example, had a mean rate of operating profit on sales of 12.1 per cent in the twenties, 13.7 per cent in the thirties, 10.5 per cent in the forties, and 10.0 per cent in the years 1950–55.[58] Further confirmation of this analysis is to be found in a government study of price-cost factors in the container industries during the years 1947 to 1956.[59] (See Table 2.) According to this study, "The generally consistent pattern of a lower rate of increase in the price of containers as compared with the cost of wages and materials can be attributed to many factors, primary of which are technological advances in container machinery and equipment, materials and production techniques, efficiency in operations, and keen, healthy competition not only within a particular industry but also between various industries in the broad packaging field."[60] This assertion as to the keenness of competition not only within the individual container industries but among them is interesting because of the increasing diversification of the two big can-manufacturing companies. Will the trend

[58] *Ibid.*, p. 211.
[59] U.S. Department of Commerce, Business and Defense Services Administration, "Packaging Statistics—A Look at Some Price-Cost Factors," pp. 1–8. The substance of this report is reproduced in *Modern Packaging*, Encyclopedia Issue for 1959, pp. 50 ff.
[60] *Ibid.*, pp. 3–4.

TABLE 2

Percentage Changes per Annum in Prices, Wages, and Cost of Raw Materials
of the Container Industries, 1947–56

Industry	Prices	Wages	Material Costs
Tin cans and other tinware	+5.5%	+8.3%	+7.0%
Glass containers	+3.9	+6.5	+3.9
Paperboard boxes	+2.3	+6.6	+3.8
Metal barrels	+2.5	+6.9	+6.8
Wooden boxes	+1.1	+4.8	+2.2
Textile bags	−0.5	+6.1	−3.3
Average	+3.2	+6.6	+4.1

Source: U.S. Department of Commerce, Business and Defence Services Administration, "Packaging Statistics," etc., *op.cit., passim.*

to diversification strengthen or weaken interindustry competition in the packaging field? And what will be its effect on competition within the tin can industry? These complex questions are at the heart of the Continental Can cases which are in process of trial as this book goes to press.

Public Policy Issues in the Continental Can Cases

The civil suits filed by the Government against the Continental Can Company in 1956, contesting its acquisition of the Hazel-Atlas Glass Company and the Robert Gair Company, Inc. involve policy issues of the utmost importance. In both suits the government charges that the mergers in question are in violation of Section 7 of the Clayton Act, as amended by the Celler-Kefauver Act of 1950. In the Hazel-Atlas action, the Government alleges that the effect of the merger by the second largest manufacturer of metal cans with the "second largest manufacturer of all glass bottles in the United States" will be that actual and potential competition between Continental and Hazel-Atlas in the sale of metal cans and glass bottles, plastic and glass bottles, and metal closures will be eliminated or substantially lessened. The merger of these two companies, it is further alleged, will give the resulting combination "a decisive advantage over its less diversified competitors" and will increase industry-wide concentration in the container field.

In refutation of these charges, Continental Can will undoubtedly contend that the products of the two companies are not, for the most part, in competition with one another and, where they are, competition will not be substantially lessened by the merger. Rather, by acquiring Hazel-Atlas and modernizing its plants and policies, competition will be strengthened. Further,

Continental's attorneys will probably argue that it is no longer merely a can company, but a seller of packaging. Its sales, including those of the acquired concerns, will be shown to be a relatively small percentage (maybe 10 per cent or less) of the total packaging market. Diversification, it will be stressed, is imperative for a progressive concern in the fast-moving packaging field of today. As *Business Week* states the case, "So many new container products and techniques are being developed that a company that sticks to one product line is likely to find itself left behind rapidly." [61]

The government's brief will no doubt seek to demonstrate that the Hazel-Atlas transaction should be regarded less as diversification for Continental and more as a merger of competitors. It will stoutly reject a global definition of the packaging market as not being relevant to the specific lines of commerce (types of canned or bottled product) or to the local markets in which competition may be threatened or eliminated by the merger. It will hold that interindustry competition will be weakened and relatively specialized can producers put at a disastrous disadvantage in competing with a "conglomerate" corporation such as Continental.[62] The court, in reaching its decision, will of necessity be concerned with definitions of the relevant markets, lines of commerce, and the doctrines of "reasonable interchangeability" and "quantitative substantiality"—concepts which were prominent in recent merger decisions.[63]

The Robert Gair case is not strictly within the scope of a survey of the metal container industry because it is concerned mainly with a merger of companies in other packaging fields. Here the government charged Continental with eliminating or substantially lessening competition in the paperboard, flexible packaging, and the paper container industries. ("The combined production in 1955 of defendant Continental and Robert Gair was the second largest in the industry in folding board and nonbending board; the fifth largest in the industry in container board; and third largest in the industry in the shipment of Kraft paper bags. . . ." [64]) Continental's acquisition of Robert Gair, the complaint points out, created a complicated interlocking ownership of stock in the container industries. Owens-Illinois, the largest domestic manufacturer of glass containers, had a 17 per cent stock

---

[61] "How Much Will the Law Allow?" *Business Week*, September 22, 1956, p. 88 ff. This article contains an interesting summary of the issues in the Continental Can cases and an analysis of diversification in the packaging industry as a whole.

[62] On the conglomerate combination, see C. D. Edwards, "Conglomerate Bigness as Source of Power," in *Business Concentration and Price Policy*, Princeton: Princeton University Press, 1955, pp. 331–52.

[63] *U.S. versus E. I. du Pont de Nemours and Co.*, 118 F. Suppl. 41 (D. Del. 1953) and *U.S. versus Bethlehem Steel Corp. et al.* (D.C. N.Y. 1958) 157 F. Suppl. 877.

[64] Complaint, *U.S. versus Continental Can Co.*, Civil Action 114–177, p. 6.

interest in the common stock of Robert Gair in 1955; so this merger made Owens-Illinois the beneficial owner of a significant amount of the outstanding stock of Continental. It has been reported since that Owens-Illinois is voluntarily disposing of this ownership interest in Continental. By way of summary it can be said that the government suit in the Gair matter is aimed at concentration and market power stemming from both horizontal and vertical integration.

Perspective on Public Policy in a Changing Society

Perspective on public policy and the shape it should take is difficult to attain in the swiftly-changing metal container industry. The effects of the 1950 decrees against American and Continental have not, as yet, fully made themselves felt; only a few years ago economists were debating the question of the dissolution of American, the top company in the industry. But already such discussions seem dated and stale; now Continental has become the largest company in the packaging field and its numerous mergers pose ever-new complexities for the public authorities. Obviously, the formulation of public policy must keep pace with the changing character of our dynamic economy.

SUGGESTED READINGS

Books and Pamphlets

American Can Co., *Fifty Years of American Can Company, 1901–1951* (New York, 1951).

J. H. Collins, *The Story of Canned Food* (New York: Dutton, 1924).

C. H. Hession, *Competition in the Metal Food Container Industry, 1916–1946* (Ann Arbor: Edwards Brothers, 1949).

J. W. McKie, *Tin Cans and Tin Plates* (Cambridge: Harvard University Press, 1959).

Standard and Poor's Corporation, Industry Surveys, "Containers," Basic Analysis.

S. N. Whitney, *Antitrust Policies* (New York: Twentieth Century Fund, 1958), Vol. 2, Chap. 16.

Government Publications

U.S. versus American Can Co. et al., 230 Fed. 859 (D. Md. 1916).

U.S. versus American Can Co. et al., 87 Fed. Sup. 18 (1949).

U.S. versus American Co. et al., Final Judgment, June 22, 1950.

U.S. Attorney General, *Western Steel Plants and the Tin Plate Industry* (Washington, 1945).

Temporary National Economic Committee, *Hearings*, Part 20, Washington, 1940.

Journal and Magazine Articles

"New Mettle in Cans," *Barron's*, December 8, 1958, p. 3.

"How Much Will the Law Allow?" *Business Week*, September 22, 1956, p. 88.

"Tin Cans Hustle to Hold Their Own," *Business Week*, May 11, 1957, pp. 178–80.

Fortune, "American Can Co." Vol. 23, January 1941.

Fortune, "Profits in Cans," Vol. 9, April 1934.

Fortune, "Continental Can's Big Push," April 1955.

J. W. McKie, "The Decline of Monopoly in the Metal Container Industry," *American Economic Review*, Papers and Proceedings, May 1955, pp. 499–508.

"Cans: Survey of a Supplying Industry," *Modern Packaging*, January 1957, pp. 102–6.

Chapter 13

HORACE M. GRAY

The Airlines Industry

SECTION I: INTRODUCTION

Since in air transportation government is a decisive organizational factor, a study of the structure of the commercial air transportation industry must perforce be largely concerned with a critical analysis of governmental policy. The standards of criticism by which that policy is to be judged are derived from traditional concepts of economic freedom, specifically: that men have an unrestricted right of access to the natural public domain—in this case the air—for conduct of their economic activities; that private monopoly of the airways, whether achieved by private action or by governmental sanction, is an abridgement of this basic right; that freedom of entry and free competition, to the maximum extent consistent with the general welfare, are essential requirements of economic freedom. One may quarrel with these standards of criticism. In fact, some will. There is a widespread disposition either to ignore the traditional ideal of economic freedom, or to disparage it as an unrealistic abstraction, or to challenge its applicability in given situations on grounds of economic and technological expediency. The latter is the case in air transportation; here men honor the principle but deny its application. Because of the confusion generated by this dichotomy it is well, before discussing the industry, to examine the principle.

Competition *versus* Monopoly

The advent of commercial air transportation as a major industry raises in a new form the ancient and perplexing question of which principle of organization—competition or monopoly—should prevail. This conflict between opposing principles of organization emerges at the point of entry. Shall ac-

468

cess to the air for purposes of transportation be free, or limited? Shall all who seek to engage in air transportation be free to do so, or shall entry into the field be restricted, either by private action or by government, or by the two in conjunction? Shall government intervene to preserve freedom of entry and competition, or to restrict entry and to promote monopoly? If the former, how may some satisfactory degree of order and stability be maintained? If the latter, how may the benefits of competition be attained and the evils of monopoly averted?

In the individualistic economy visualized by the classical English economists it was held that each individual should be free to engage in economic activity according to his inclination, capacity and interest, subject only to the reservation that in pursuit of his self-interest he avoid willful injury to others. Within this broad range of tolerance, the unrestricted pursuit of self-interest would operate to maximize the economic well-being of the community. Thus, each individual in seeking his own gain would inevitably promote the general welfare, even though that were no part of his original intention. The great force that would neutralize selfishness and transmute it into public good was competition; the central institution that would coordinate the manifold economic activities of individuals was the free, competitive market. This conception was so thoroughly consonant with the spirit of the time, when men sought greater liberty on every front, that freedom of entry, access to markets, free competition, and equality of economic opportunity came to be regarded as "natural" or "inalienable" rights beyond derogation by government or by any combination of private persons. These economic "rights" in time became embodied in the common law, in statutes, in constitutions, and in the folkways and traditions of our people.

When businessmen in pursuit of their self-interest restrict competition, whether by private action alone or with the aid of government, the scope of general economic freedom is reduced. Potential producers are either excluded from the market or admitted on disadvantageous terms. Suppliers of raw materials and intermediate products, which enter into monopolized end products, find their market opportunities restricted. Workers suffer from unemployment and reduced incomes. Consumers are denied the opportunity to purchase desired goods and services, which otherwise would be available, and are forced by necessity to buy at excessive prices those offered by monopolists. Thus, the generality of mankind suffer a loss of economic freedom, while those who control the market have the power to exploit their fellows. It is for this reason that from time immemorial men have resisted the encroachments of private monopoly; have condemned it as a crime against society; have struggled to suppress it; and have challenged the power of government to create private monopolies by grants of privilege. This anti-monopoly sentiment, long latent in the traditions and aspirations of the English people, came to full bloom in the eighteenth and nineteenth centuries when the great exponents of individual freedom incorporated it into their systems of philosophy, politics, economics, and law. Thenceforth, in their unremitting struggle against the persistent tendency of businessmen to contrive monopolies those who sought to maintain the principle of economic freedom would appeal to this body of social doctrine and would identify economic freedom with competition.

This public hostility placed the monopolist in extreme jeopardy. Like Ishmael, his hand was against every man and every man's hand against him. He was an outlaw; his activities were proscribed; he was under continuous surveillance; he was subject to severe penalties if apprehended and convicted. Consequently, he was forced to dissemble, to operate surreptitiously and to minimize his aggressions. Since he operated in an open market and his activities affected adversely the interests of others in the market it was impossible for him to escape detection for any considerable time. Obviously, this state of continuous jeopardy was not satisfactory to aspirants for monopoly power. They perceived that under such conditions the life of private monopoly was destined to be hard, short and full of trouble, its rewards uncertain and ephemeral. If it were to be established on a permanent, secure basis private monopoly must be "legitimatized" by being clothed in the sacred garments of "public interest." In short, the whole history of Anglo-American policy from the Elizabethan Statute of Monopolies in 1624 to the Sherman Act of 1890 must be reversed. This revolutionary transformation has been actively under way in the United States during the past fifty years. It has progressed to the point where it can now be said that for all practical purposes purely private monopoly, in the classical sense, has ceased to be socially significant and constitutes a minor irritant in the body politic. What we have instead is a vast structure of legalized private monopoly based on a complicated system of grants of privilege, all justified in one way or another on grounds of "public interest." In recent years there has been a proliferation of hybrid organizations in which public and private interests are functionally intermingled and virtually indistinguishable. These new institutions resemble the privileged corporations of Mercantilist England; although differing in detail they display the common characteristic of private monopoly buttressed by the legal sanctions of the State.

Of all types of monopoly, legalized private monopoly is the worst. A purely private monopoly lacks viability and permanence when confronted by the combined hostility of the market, the law and public opinion; its capacity for evil is definitely limited and vigorous prosecution can hold it to a tolerable minimum. But when society legalizes private monopoly it makes permanent what otherwise would be temporary; it subordinates the sovereign powers of the state to the service and protection of private monopoly; it creates a vested interest, which can neither be effectively controlled nor easily eradicated; it commits itself to subsequent restriction of the economic freedom of its citizens; it invites political corruption because the system is so thoroughly antithetical to the general welfare that the beneficiaries of such privilege—to protect themselves against hostile social action—must resort to corruption of the political state. They have no choice in the matter if they are to survive.

The experience of the past sixty years demonstrates that legalized private monopoly can never be reconciled with the public interest. The two are simply incompatible in a democratic society that aspires to maximum economic freedom. We have persistently deluded ourselves to the contrary, naively supposing that by the alchemy of public regulation such reconciliation is possible. Our lack of success in antitrust, railroad, public utility, and related forms of regulation, and with the techniques of special privilege and subsidization for private business, should dissipate this illusion and convince us that the basic theory is gravely defective. A growing awareness of this deep-seated institutional infirmity is evidenced by current criticism and investigation of regulatory commissions, and by numerous proposals for reform.

Is Air Transport a Public Utility?

Spokesmen for the major airlines, and to a lesser extent the CAB, when advocating restriction of competition, argue that air transportation is in reality a public utility—i.e., a legalized private monopoly. This is erroneous and misleading. Regulation of air transport, as provided in the Act of 1938, differs from traditional public utility regulation in several important respects:

(1) Historically, public utility regulation was predicated on a consumer oriented conception of public interest. It was assumed that the aggregate interests of consumers is synonymous with the public interest and that any derogation of the former militates against the latter. Therefore, to promote the public interest the State must intervene to protect consumers against exploitation at the hands of private monopolists. The basic obligation im-

posed by the state on public utilities runs to consumers—the duty to serve all, to provide adequate service, to refrain from discrimination, to charge reasonable rates.

In the case of air transport, however, the interest of consumers was not the principal objective of public regulation, but only one of several coordinate goals. Public interest was defined by the Act of 1938 to include objectives that heretofore had been no part of public regulation, such as: the present and future needs of foreign and domestic commerce, the postal service, national defense, the preservation of the inherent advantages of air transportation, the promotion of safety, the development of a sound air transport system, and the encouragement of civil aeronautics. These objectives, which are promotional, futuristic and nationalistic, indirectly involve consumer interests but the relationship is incidental and secondary.

(2) Public utility regulation was evolved to deal with already established monopolies—so-called "natural" monopolies—where for technological reasons competition is undesirable. In such situations society accepts private monopoly as a preferable form of organization, prohibits or severely restricts competition, and institutes public regulation as a substitute for competition. The Civil Aeronautics Act of 1938, however, did not conform to this traditional model. Provision was made for certain segments of the industry to be exempt from public regulation; competition in a restricted form was approved as a desirable principle of organization; service and rate regulation fell short of the standards customarily regarded as necessary in public utilities. Congress neither sanctioned monopoly nor imposed the type of regulation appropriate to a monopoly situation. Instead, it combined, in unspecified proportions, competitive and monopolistic elements, and delegated to the regulatory commission responsibility for reconciling conflicts between them.

(3) Public utility theory assumes that the going concern is a self-supporting, self-sustaining entity fully capable of deriving a revenue sufficient to cover all its costs, including a fair return on the capital employed in providing the service. In fact, it is assumed that in the absence of public restraint it would, by the exercise of its monopoly power, earn more than a fair return. The task of public regulation is to adjust revenues to costs so as to insure that consumers pay just enough—but no more than enough—to cover the costs of service.

In air transport, however, the basic assumption was quite different. It was assumed that the service was not then and for an indefinite time could not be self-sustaining; that public purposes, such as the postal service, national defense and the development of a sound air transport system, could not be attained under the cost-of-service principle commonly applicable to public utilities; that public subsidy would be necessary for an indefinite period; and that such subsidy was desirable to promote national objectives.

(4) Public utility regulation is essentially static in its basic conception. Its objectives are limited and relatively unchanging; it assumes stable techniques, markets, and geographic location of productive activities; it deals with established, mature, going concerns; it operates in areas of minimum risk where the relatively minor hazards of enterprise can be compensated for through slight variations in the rate of return; it assumes a slow rate of growth in which the principal element—new capital—can be had in sufficient quantities by appropriate adjustment of the allowed return; it contemplates a type of product or service that is sufficiently differentiated and unique to be immune from the external competitive pressure of substitutes.

Air transportation in 1938 was one of those extremely dynamic situations for which public utility regulation, in its traditional form, would have been totally inappropriate. Congress sensed this and wisely refrained from imposing public utility regulation on this young and rapidly developing industry. On the contrary it provided a promotional form of regulation. Subsequent events have confirmed the wisdom of this decision, for air transport has proven to be extraordinarily dynamic in every major respect—organization, capacity, market coverage, volume of business, equipment, service, rates, and operating efficiency.

(5) Public utility regulation, although originally consumer oriented, has undergone a subtle transformation of purpose with the result that today it is largely concerned with protecting going concerns—their markets, their revenues, their financial structures, their capitalized values. This policy is justified on grounds of practical necessity—the need to preserve the integrity and continuity of the going concern. Pushed to an extreme it results in a perversion of public regulation to private ends; instead of public utilities existing to serve consumers, consumers exist for the purpose of supporting the public utilities; in still more extreme cases, where consumers cannot or will not sustain this burden, taxpayers may be asked to lend a helping hand.

This protective philosophy was not incorporated in the Act of 1938, although the theory was well advanced in transportation and public utility circles at that time. The Congress instructed the Civil Aeronautics Board to consider as being in the public interest "the encouragement and development of an air transportation system properly adapted to the present and future needs of the foreign and domestic commerce of the United States," the fostering of "sound economic conditions" in air transportation, the promotion of "adequate, economical and efficient service." There is no suggestion that these positive objectives were to be attained by a negative policy of protecting established carriers in respect to their economic position. The spirit of the act was promotional and developmental rather than protectionistic.

These differences between public utility and air transport regulation are basic and very real. Air transport is not yet a legalized private monopoly, and the regulation is not yet public utility regulation. Whether it eventually becomes so remains to be determined. The pressure for legitimization of private monopoly is strong among the dominant firms; but competition, though restricted, is potentially viable, and both the economic and technological situations are fluid. It is thus theoretically possible to avoid the evil of legalized private monopoly in this industry.

SECTION II: MARKET STRUCTURE AND PRICE POLICY

Market Structure

Domestic Trunk-Lines, or Certificated Carriers. The most important division of the air transportation industry is the domestic trunk-lines, or certificated carriers. In 1938, when the Civil Aeronautics Act was passed, the industry was virtually limited to eighteen companies which were then carrying mail, passengers, and express over selected long distance routes between major cities; they had built up a considerable passenger business—1,197,100 revenue passengers, 479,843,978 revenue passenger-miles, and $25,000,000 of passenger revenue.[1] Congress recognized the established position of these companies by a "grandfather" clause in the Act of 1938, which provided that the CAB should confirm their operating rights and privileges by the issuance of certificates of public convenience and necessity. Under this provision twenty-three "grandfather" carriers were certificated, but mergers, changes in corporate name and one abandonment have reduced the number to twelve. These are: American Airlines, Inc., Eastern Airlines, Inc., Trans World Airlines, Inc., United Airlines, Inc., Braniff Airways, Inc., Capital Airlines, Inc., Continental Airlines, Inc., Delta Airlines, Inc., National Airlines, Inc., Northeast Airlines, Inc., Northwest Airlines, Inc., and Western Airlines, Inc.

Since 1938 the CAB has not issued a single new certificate. It has, however, extended and modified the original route pattern but it has not changed its

[1] Civil Aeronautics Board, *The Role of Competition in Commercial Air Transportation,* Report, Eighty-second Cong., 2d Sess., November 24, 1952, p. 8.

basic outlines or reallocated markets to correct the original imbalance in favor of the "Big Four"—American, T.W.A., United, and Eastern. The basic pattern was fixed by Congressional sanction of existing arrangements. The Board has consistently maintained that it has no general mandate or power to refashion that pattern, imperfect as it may be, except as it may succeed in doing so by piecemeal extension and modification.[2] These administrative adjustments have transformed certain monopoly routes into oligopoly routes, and thereby forced some sharing of the traffic, but they have not produced equality of competition or modified significantly the dominance of the "Big Four." In 1955 the latter still controlled 68.6 per cent of the revenue passenger miles and 73 per cent of the revenue ton-miles originated by the twelve certificated carriers.[3]

In the protected and lucrative markets thus assured to them the trunkline carriers have built up their volume of business very rapidly, particularly since World War II. During the twenty year period 1938–57 revenue passenger-miles have increased from 479,843,000 to 23,048,703,000—a 48-fold increase. Airmail ton-miles have increased from 7,449,245 to 94,749,000—nearly thirteen-fold. Express and freight ton-miles have increased from 2,182,420 to 286,446,000—over 130-fold. In all categories the increases in volume of traffic have been especially great since World War II, and particularly since 1950.[4]

Local Service, or Feeder, Lines. In 1946 the CAB authorized a new class of scheduled, certificated carriers—the so-called local service, or feeder, lines—to provide air transportation between smaller cities, and between these smaller cities and main terminals, where trunk-line service was not available nor practicable. Such carriers would fulfill two useful and desirable functions: (1) provide local service for communities and regions that otherwise would lack air transportation entirely; (2) provide connections at principal terminals so that people in smaller cities and more remote areas might have ready access to the large trunk-line systems. In respect to the latter function, they would serve as "feeders" for the main trunk-lines,

[2] As the Board says in its own defense: "Remember these routes and carriers were given to us on a platter by Congress. They were already determined. We didn't pick the carriers. We didn't pick the routes. They were the grandfather routes and certificates." (Testimony of Oswald Ryan, Chairman, Civil Aeronautics Board, in *Future of Irregular Airlines in United States Air Transportation Industry,* before a Subcommittee of the Select Committee on Small Business, United States Senate, Eighty-third Cong., 1st Sess., March 31, 1953, Hearings, p. 15.)

[3] *Airlines,* Report of the House Committee on the Judiciary, Eighty-fifth Cong., 1st Sess., 1957, p. 19.

[4] Select Committee on Small Business, *Future of Irregular Airlines,* Senate Report No. 822, Eighty-third Cong., 1st Sess., July 31, 1953, p. 22; and Civil Aeronautics Board, Annual Report, 1957, p. 40.

thus extending the coverage of air transportation service and transforming the existing system into a more truly national one.

The CAB has granted certificates of public convenience and necessity, on a temporary basis, to twenty-three local carriers, of which thirteen are in operation today. In 1955 Congress enacted a "little grandfather" clause to require permanent certification of local carriers operating on or after January 1, 1953.[5] During the thirteen-year period, 1945–57, these local service carriers have increased their revenue passenger-miles from 1,312,000 to 687,827,000—524-fold; their airmail ton-miles from 74,510 to 1,562,000—twenty-one-fold; and their express and freight ton-miles from 11,482 to 3,946,000—344-fold.[6] These high rates of growth are explainable by the fact that their volume of business in 1945 was very small. Despite this growth, their contribution to the total volume of commercial air transport business is still almost negligible, amounting to about 3 per cent of total revenue and 2.5 per cent of revenue ton-miles.[7] They have been sustained in large measure by airmail subsidies. In the seven-year period, 1951–57, these subsidies, as reckoned by CAB, amounted to $157,031,000, and in 1955 nearly 40 per cent of their total operating revenue was derived from subsidies.[8]

Large Irregular, or Nonscheduled, Airlines. The large irregular, or non-scheduled, airlines operate under letters of registration issued by the CAB. The chairman of the CAB fixed the number of such carriers at 61 in his testimony of March, 1953, before the Senate Committee on Small Business.[9] The irregular, or nonscheduled, carriers are peculiarly a postwar phenomenon. After World War II many new companies entered the air transportation business, some carrying passengers, others cargo, on an irregular, or demand, basis, at rates generally lower than those of the certificated trunk-line carriers. How many such operators there were immediately after the war will probably never be known for lack of complete records. The CAB had issued—as of August 8, 1948—147 letters of registration but there must have been many others who operated without benefit of CAB authorization. One responsible journal affirms that in 1947 there were 750 such operators in air cargo alone.[10] At any rate by 1948, when performance records became available, the irregulars (or "nonskeds," as they are called in the trade) carried 189,488 revenue passengers and flew 457,954,000 revenue passenger miles, less than 1.5 per cent of the passengers, but over 7.6 per cent of the revenue

[5] *Airlines*, p. 23.
[6] *Future of Irregular Airlines*, p. 23, and CAB, Annual Report, 1957, p. 40.
[7] *Airlines*, p. 24.
[8] *Ibid.*, pp. 23–24.
[9] *Future of Irregular Airlines*, Hearings, p. 8.
[10] Competitive Transportation Review, February 1953, p. 13.

passenger miles of the certificated carriers. By 1950 the number of passengers had risen to 498,799 and the revenue passenger miles to 795,569,000 —2.8 per cent of the passengers and nearly 10 per cent of the passenger miles of the certificated carriers.[11] In 1951 and 1952, despite the efforts of CAB to limit their operations and the aggressive competition of the trunk-lines in air coach service, the irregulars increased their volume of passenger business, reaching a total of 988.8 million passenger-miles in 1952. This was about 41 per cent of the air coach passenger-miles produced by the trunk-lines and about 8.2 per cent of the total passenger-miles (first class and coach) of the trunk-lines.

In addition to their passenger business, the irregulars carry a considerable amount of freight. Of 55 such concerns, reporting in 1950, 27 carried both passengers and freight, while 28 carried passengers only. The 27 freight carriers accounted for 26,869,667 cargo ton-miles.[12] A considerable proportion of this, however, appears to have been overseas rather than domestic cargo. Between 1947 and 1955 the CAB, in an effort to protect the trunk-line carriers from competition, imposed severe operating restrictions on the irregular, or nonscheduled, carriers, the effect of which was to reduce their number and limit their growth. By 1955 the number of such carriers had declined from an original 147 to 54. The latter, in 1955, produced 869,298,000 domestic revenue passenger-miles and 40,056,000 domestic cargo ton-miles.[13] This performance, as compared with 1952, represented a substantial decrease in passenger-miles and a fourfold increase in cargo ton-miles. In relative terms the nonskeds had less than 5 per cent of the domestic passenger business and less than 13 per cent of the domestic cargo business.

As matters now stand, then, the role of the irregulars, or nonskeds, in the national air transport system is a modest one. They operate on the periphery of the industry, supplying charter service, serving peak and seasonal demands, providing emergency service, shifting from one route to another as the demand warrants, providing low-cost coach service which the certificated carriers are unable or unwilling to supply. Whether this minor role can be expanded, or even maintained, is problematical because it depends on economic and technical factors, and on government policies. Their position is legally insecure and their place in the industry highly controversial.

Small Irregular Carriers, or "Air Taxi" Operators. This classification in-

[11] Select Committee on Small Business, *Role of Irregular Airlines in United States Air Transportation Industry,* United States Senate, Report, Eighty-second Cong., 1st Sess., July 10, 1951, p. 9.
[12] *Role of Irregular Airlines in United States Air Transportation Industry,* Hearings, 1951, p. 164.
[13] *Airlines,* p. 30.

cludes some 2,000 small, fixed-base operators using equipment with a maximum take-off weight of 12,500 pounds. They provide charter service on an irregular basis to off-line points and emergency service on demand. So long as they continue to operate within this limitation they are exempt from the economic regulations of the Board and not required to get either a certificate of public convenience and necessity or a letter of registration.[14]

Whether the small irregulars actually contribute any significant volume of traffic to the trunk-lines is not demonstrable by any available evidence. Neither can it be determined whether they provide an adequate service from points on airline routes to communities not now served by air transportation, or whether they operate in combination with certificated carriers as auxiliaries. In the absence of convincing evidence, one is entitled to infer that the policy reflects the general philosophy of the Board that this—as well as all other minor segments of the air transport industry—ought to supplement the main trunk-lines, which the CAB regards as the backbone of our national air transport system. What the future holds for these 2,000 small irregulars is not clear, but it may well be doubted that their principal function is to feed the trunk-lines. If left free to operate independently they may find in a greatly expanded air transport industry new opportunities for useful service quite different from their present limitations.

Certificated All-Cargo Carriers. In addition to mixed carriers (passenger, mail, and freight) there are three all-cargo airlines (Flying Tiger, Slick Airlines, and U.S. Airlines) which operate scheduled service over designated routes under certificates of public convenience and necessity issued by the CAB. These three all-cargo concerns accounted for approximately one-half of all air freight in 1952, and their total exceeded that of the trunk-line companies—122,798,000 ton-miles as against 115,514,000 ton-miles for the latter.[15] The certification of these all-cargo carriers developed from the chaotic postwar situation. Beginning in 1946 there was a great rush of new firms into air transportation, many of them specializing in air freight. By 1947 a number of them had filed application for certificates of public convenience and necessity with the CAB. Those who had so filed were

---

[14] The general theory underlying this policy was stated by Delos W. Rentzel, Chairman, Civil Aeronautics Board: "In issuing this regulation . . . , it was the Board's belief that these small-craft operations were primarily auxiliary to, and not in competition with those of the certificated carriers. . . . The small air carriers will perform basically an air-taxi-type service from points on airline routes to communities not now served by air transportation. We now believe that this activity should be permitted on a regular basis in order that the utmost advantages and usefulness may be obtained from the small irregulars in happy combination with our existing certificated air transport system." Testimony before the Subcommittee of the Select Committee on Small Business, United States Senate, Eighty-second Cong., 1st Sess., April 25, 1951, *Hearings*, p. 79.

[15] *Competitive Transportation Review*, March 1953, p. 11.

classified as *noncertified cargo carriers* and granted a temporary exemption authorizing them to engage in the transportation of freight without limitation as to regularity or frequency of service. In the meantime all such applications were consolidated in the Air Freight Case; after protracted proceedings the CAB eventually issued certificates to three of these applicants, thereby changing their status to that of *certificated cargo carriers* (Air Freight Case, 10 C.A.B. 572, July 29, 1949).[16]

The growth of Air Freight since World War II has been phenomenal. In 1941, after thirteen years of experimentation by the then existing carriers (1928–41), it amounted only to 5,258,551 ton-miles.[17] During the war years it increased substantially, reaching about 40,000,000 ton-miles in 1946.[18] After 1946, with the advent of the irregulars and the all-cargo specialists, and more vigorous promotion by the trunk-lines, greater availability of equipment, and drastic rate reductions, the total volume of air freight increased very rapidly, reaching a total of nearly 475,000,000 domestic ton-miles in 1957. Of this total, however, the all-cargo carriers accounted for only one-third.[19]

Estimates of future volume by 1960 range between 700,000,000 and 1,000,000,000 ton-miles.[20] These predictions, however, depend for their realization on a number of vital contingencies, such as: the availability at reasonable cost of specially designed, large capacity, all-cargo equipment, adequate airports and freight handling facilities at terminal centers, drastic reductions in the per ton-mile cost of air transportation—approaching the four cents per ton-mile objective of Gross and Haines. Even though air freight in this volume is potentially available, the practical obstacles to be overcome before it can actually be developed are so formidable that it appears doubtful this can be accomplished within the immediate future. But, whatever the rate of increase, it seems clear that the present pattern of air transport organization, which has been built primarily on the passenger business, is quite inadequate for an air freight movement of the magnitude contemplated. What new pattern may emerge will be determined primarily by economic and technological factors but governmental policy will play an important part in the evolution. Indicative of the probable course of future policy is the Monroney Plan, now under consideration by the Congress, for

[16] *Role of Competition in Commercial Air Transportation,* pp. 31–37.
[17] *Ibid.,* p. 32.
[18] R. Gross and W. W. Haines, "Freighters of the Future," *The Atlantic Monthly,* August 1952, p. 38.
[19] *CAA Statistical Handbook,* 1958, p. 97.
[20] The Civil Aeronautics Administration favors the lower estimate. See *Competitive Transportation,* February 1953, p. 13. Gross and Haines are more optimistic, predicting a total of 1,000,000,000 ton-miles by 1959; *op.cit.,* p. 38.

government subsidization of research to design a new low-cost cargo plane, and for loans and guarantees to finance their construction.

International Carriers. Three classes of carriers are involved in international air transportation to and from the United States: (1) Twenty domestic carriers certificated by the CAB to engage in regular international passenger service; (2) Twenty-one irregular or supplemental domestic carriers authorized by the CAB to engage in international service on an irregular basis—eleven for cargo only, four for passengers only, and six for both passengers and cargo; (3) Fifty-nine foreign carriers holding air-carrier permits from the United States. All these arrangements must, under the law, be approved by the President of the United States.[21]

During the twenty year period, 1938–57, United States international carriers have increased their revenue passenger-miles from 53,208,000 to 5,529,446,000—104-fold; their airmail ton-miles from 1,990,715 (in 1943) to 57,313,000—29-fold; and their express and freight ton-miles from 5,088,325 (in 1943) to 133,464,000—26-fold. In all categories the big upsurge in volume of business began in 1946 and has continued unabated. The big increase in freight ton-miles is largely a product of the last five years.[22]

The international passenger business to and from the United States is divided among three classes of carriers, as follows: twenty domestic certificated carriers 40.1 per cent of revenue passenger-miles; ten irregular carriers (four-passenger only, six-passenger and cargo) 4.4 per cent; and 59 foreign carriers 55.5 per cent.[23] The significant feature of this distribution is the failure of the irregular carriers to maintain their original share of the traffic (it was 9 per cent in 1952) notwithstanding the extraordinary increase in total air travel. This is due to restrictive action of the CAB, which since June 1947 has prohibited them from making flights on an individually ticketed basis, and since 1955 has permitted only charter flights on prior approval. The language of the CAB makes it clear that this restriction was imposed to prevent competition: "Once supplemental passenger service was authorized, the Board would be powerless to prevent extensive diversion by farecutting practices on the part of the supplemental air carriers."[24]

The general policy of the CAB is that competition must necessarily be more limited in the international than in the domestic field. This is ostensibly due to the relative thinness of traffic over international routes, the high cost of operation, and the restrictive landing privileges imposed by foreign

---

[21] *Airlines*, pp. 40–43.
[22] *Future of Irregular Airlines*, p. 23, and CAB, Annual Report, 1957, p. 40.
[23] *Airlines*, p. 39. Figures are for 1955.
[24] *Ibid.*, p. 41.

governments against American airlines. Although the CAB professes to believe in the abstract merits of competition in international air transportation —and points to its record in rejecting the *"chosen instrument"* theory and in granting parallel certificates over dense traffic routes (such as the North Atlantic)—nevertheless the Board appears to accept the view that "certain inherent characteristics of international air transport cast it in a different mold from its domestic counterpart." [25] This evaluation of the situation, so it is held, justifies restriction of entry into the international field, by denial of certification in the case of scheduled service and by denial of special permits in case of irregular or nonscheduled operations.

Indirect Carriers, or Freight Forwarders. Such concerns do not operate cargo planes or transport goods by air; rather, they operate a ground service, soliciting, collecting, and consolidating cargo for air shipment over the lines of regular air carriers, and effecting delivery at the point of destination. They publish tariffs of their own, setting out the charges for their complete service, including what they must pay the airline for the actual transportation of goods. While not engaged directly in air transportation they are an important factor in the movement of cargo by air. Because they hold themselves out to serve the public by providing air transportation of property for a stated compensation, they come within the purview of the Act of 1938 and are subject to regulation by the CAB.

The number of such forwarders operating in the air cargo field is not known exactly. Prior to 1948, the Railway Express Agency was the only concern engaged in air transportation as an indirect carrier. For some years it operated an air express service under contract with the certificated trunkline carriers and in 1948 handled nearly 30,000,000 ton-miles of air express.[26] In September 1948, in the *Air Freight Forwarder Case* (9 C.A.B. 473) there *"were more than 70 applicants, many of whom have substantial finances with large organizations and ample facilities."* [27] The Board decided that these applicants, and others who might qualify under the Board's exemption regulation, could obtain letters of registration, which would permit them to operate without limitation as to their numbers or to the point served. In addition to these registered indirect carriers, there are numerous other firms engaged in freight forwarding operations which do not come within the jurisdiction of the CAB and, hence, are not registered, or licensed. In fact, one authority states that the majority of freight forwarders by air are un-

[25] *The Role of Competition in Commercial Air Transportation*, p. 39. See pp. 38–47 for discussion of international and territorial service.
[26] *Role of Competition in Commercial Air Transportation*, p. 33.
[27] *Ibid.*, p. 38.

licensed.[28] He points out, further, that those licensed by CAB are handicapped by the lack of interest on the part of the direct air carriers in aiding the development of the consolidated freight-shipment business and by the competition of unlicensed forwarders.

Private Air Transport. An important, and growing, segment of the air transport industry is operated by private individuals and business corporations for their own account. It is estimated that some 10,000 business organizations own and operate 28,250 planes, and log 5.7 million hours of flying time yearly—double the amount a decade ago and some 1.5 million more flying hours than all domestic commercial airlines. The Civil Aeronautics Administration estimates that by 1965 the flying time of business planes will reach 7.8 million hours, or 51 per cent of all civilian flying. Sales of new business planes have increased from 3,000 in 1952 to 7,500 in 1959.[29] In addition to these business planes, there are, it is estimated, some 106,000 small private planes, up from 60,000 in 1952. The number of such small planes is increasing at the rate of between 6,000–7,000 per year.[30]

The magnitude of this private operation is obviously an important structural and competitive factor in the total air transport industry. It is significant that so many private individuals and business corporations have found it economically advantageous to own and operate their own planes rather than patronize the certificated commercial airlines. The rapid rate of increase in private air transport, and the intensive activity of aircraft manufacturers in designing and constructing planes suitable for such service, are indicative of competitive vigor in this area. The prospects for the future, however, are clouded by a shortage of air fields and air space for such craft. Unless government acts to provide adequate air fields and to insure a reasonable allocation of air space for private planes their growth will be restricted. Here again, the maintenance of competitive alternatives depends on governmental policy.

Military Air Transport Service. As an adjunct of its far flung military and national defense activities the Federal government operates "the free world's largest airline"—the Military Air Transport Service. MATS has 1,144 aircraft and 119,000 personnel, of which 526 aircraft and 36,359 personnel are assigned to transport functions, as distinct from other auxiliary services. It operates only outside the United States, carrying military personnel, supplies and equipment.

[28] L. A. Bryan, "Civil Aviation at Mid-Century," *Illinois Business Review*, June 1953, p. 9.
[29] *Wall Street Journal*, January 13, 1960.
[30] *Wall Street Journal*, October 15, 1959.

For many years the Air Transport Association, representing the commercial airlines, has waged a political war of attrition against MATS under the slogans of "free enterprise" and "getting the government out of business." Its aim is to restrict MATS to purely military operations—movement of troops and field equipment—and to force the transfer of all general passenger and cargo business to the commercial airlines. This pressure campaign has achieved a large measure of success. In 1955 the Defense Department paid to commercial airlines $4,500,000 for transportation of military personnel and cargo; by 1959 this figure had increased to $71,000,000; in 1960 it reached $85,000,000. In January 1960 the President was prevailed upon to order an additional transfer of business, estimated at $100,000,000, from MATS to the commercial airlines. The excess cost that would result from 50 per cent commercialization of MATS operations is estimated at $300,000,-000 per year; complete commercialization would involve excess costs of $649,000,000 annually.[31]

This liquidation of MATS will provide a bonanza for the commercial airlines at the expense of federal taxpayers. The government will be in the ridiculous position of maintaining a large air transport establishment for military purposes but will be denied the right to use its own equipment and personnel to carry military passengers and cargo. It will keep its own fleet in enforced idleness, while it shifts its own traffic to commercial planes. Instead of paying the low out-of-pocket, incremental costs of operating its otherwise idle planes the government will pay the much higher, noncompetitive rates demanded by private carriers. It would be difficult to conceive a worse bargain for taxpayers or a greater folly than for the government to forfeit its independence and thereby become dependent on private interests for the performance of an essential public function.

Price Policy

Rates for air transportation conform neither to the principle of competition, nor monopoly, nor cost-of-service. Instead, they represent a mixed system of pricing in which elements of competition, private monopoly and oligopoly, and public protection and subsidy are commingled. Within the protected markets assured to them by governmental restriction of competition, the trunk-lines set rates by joint agreement with a view toward maximization of profit. In addition, they get all they can from government

[31] Brig. Gen. Thomas R. Phillips, U.S.A. (Ret.), *St. Louis Post Dispatch*, November 8, 1959, and *Wall Street Journal*, February 10, 1960.

by way of free or partially requited services and air mail subsidies. The system of public regulation is not designed to insure service-at-cost but rather to promote the development of the industry.

Historically, passenger-rates, the most important revenue producer, have been geared to first class Pullman railroad fares—the most comparable alternative. Among upper income and business groups many would pay a premium for high-speed, long-distance air transportation; the problem of the airlines was to entice this patronage away from the railroads by quoting rates somewhat higher than Pullman fares but not in excess of the premium value of air service. It was a sure thing for the airlines, because if they succeeded they could keep the profits, if they failed the government would cover their losses by airmail subsidies. The record of average passenger revenue per passenger-mile, at standard fares, is as follows: [32]

	Cents		Cents
1929	12.0	1941	5.04
1930	8.3	1942	5.28
1931	6.7	1943	5.27
1932	6.1	1944	5.35
1933	6.1	1945	4.95
1934	5.9	1946	4.63
1935	5.7	1947	5.06
1936	5.7	1948	5.76
1937	5.6	1949	5.76
1938	5.18	1950	5.55
1939	5.10	1951	5.59
1940	5.07		

After 1948 the trunk-lines began to experiment with discount rates for round trips, excursion and vacation travel, and family flights on certain days of the week when traffic is normally light. These innovations, while successful in terms of volume and load factor, involved no new principle of rate making; the service was still geared to high-income patronage and rates to the premium valuations of this group. To the extent costs were determinative in rate making they were the costs of highly selective, de luxe service. The first real break came when the irregular carriers introduced coach service at rates approximately 65 per cent of standard trunk-line fares. This forced the trunk-lines to differentiate their service by providing coach service at comparable rates. They did so with phenomenal success, increas-

[32] *The Role of Competition in Commercial Air Transportation*, p. 15.

ing their coach and tourist business from 248,844,000 revenue passenger-miles in 1949 to 6,662,529,000 revenue passenger-miles in 1955—a 26-fold increase. Despite the inflation and the extension of coach and tourist service to thinner territory the average revenue per passenger-mile was 4.36 cents in 1955—well below the first class rate.[33]

The story is much the same in the area of express and freight. Since 1928 the trunk-lines have had an exclusive contract with the Railway Express Agency covering essential ground services in connection with air express. This contract originally provided that air express rates should be at least twice rail express rates; actually, however, they were maintained at five to seven times the rail level—i.e., about 80 cents per ton-mile as against 10 to 15 cents per ton-mile for rail express. This fantastic arrangement remained operative until 1943, when it was revised under threat of antitrust prosecution.[34] Under these excessive and artificial rates, which bore no relation whatever to actual costs of transportation, air express and air cargo were stifled. By 1941, air express amounted only to 5,258,551 ton-miles and accounted for only 3 per cent of total airline revenue; air freight was almost completely undeveloped.

During World War II the Military Air Transport Service demonstrated that air cargo could be moved in volume at relatively low cost, given appropriate equipment and operating organization. After the war, irregular carriers and all-cargo specialists entered the field at rates that reflected competitive costs. This competition forced the trunk lines to reduce their charges and air cargo rates were driven down from about 60 to 16 cents per ton-mile. At this juncture the CAB intervened to prescribe minimum rates in order to protect the trunk-lines from destructive competition.[35]

Competition for both passenger and freight traffic is distorted and jeopardized by the fact that the trunk-lines can utilize monopoly revenues and airmail subsidies to finance a war of attrition against competitive, nonsubsidized carriers. The CAB offers no protection against such discrimination. It is interested in protecting the trunk-lines, not in maintaining competition; it has done nothing to eliminate monopoly profit or to prevent such profits from being used to finance discrimination in the competi-

[33] *Airlines*, p. 92.
[34] A. C. Wiprud, *Justice in Transportation*, New York: Ziff-Davis Publishing Company, 1945, pp. 14–17.
[35] *Air Freight Rate Investigation*, 9 CAB 340 (1948). The prescribed minimum was 16 cents per ton-mile for the first 1,000 ton-miles of any shipment and 13 cents per ton-mile for all in excess of 1,000. This was done "to prevent the financial stability of the industry from being imperiled by unrestrained competitive pressures which drive the rate structure generally to unremunerative levels."

tive sectors; it construes the Act of 1938 to permit losses incurred on both passenger and freight operations to be covered by air mail subsidies.[36] So long as this equivocal policy persists the viability of competition remains precarious.

The House Judiciary Committee, after an extensive investigation, condemned severely the rate policy of the CAB. It has limited and restricted competition. During its entire existence, i.e., since 1938, it has never concluded a general investigation of passenger fares. It has not even determined standards or principles of rate making by which it might judge whether existing rates are unreasonable or discriminatory. It has started four general rate investigations but abandoned the first three and stalled the fourth since May 10, 1956. It has authorized service mail rates which are excessive by competitive standards. It has permitted air lines to charge first-class fares for flights in coach equipment. It has permitted a private cartel —the Air Transport Association—to fix rates and control service by private collusion. In short, the whole policy of the Board has been to protect the certificated carriers in respect to their routes, fares, services, and profit margins.[37]

International rates are fixed on a monopoly basis by an all-embracing international cartel—The International Air Transport Association, the private trade organization of the scheduled international air carriers. In 1946 the CAB endowed this cartel with a certain legal sanction by approving its rate-making system and extending to it immunity from the antitrust laws. The subsequent record has been one of uncontrolled monopoly pricing. The House Judiciary Committee found that rates were set at the highest level the traffic could bear; that in the interest of rate stability and uniformity the rate level was dictated by the minimum demands of the most determined and intransigent member; that the recommendations of CAB to IATA respecting rates have been ignored; that most of the pressure within IATA for uneconomic rates and practices has come from American companies; that price competition has been completely abolished; that wasteful, traffic-diverting service competition has been substituted for price competition; that tourist class revenues have been used to subsidize first class luxury service; and that excessive rates have prevented enlargement of the market for international air transportation. The CAB has tolerated this regime of

---

[36] *Braniff Airways, Inc., Mail Rates,* 9 CAB 607 (1948). This same principle was applied subsequently in the Delta and Capital cases. Later, in the "Big Four" case, the board declined to approve the underwriting of losses by airmail subsidies, not as a matter of law or principle but because it was not necessary for development purposes.
[37] *Airlines,* pp. 267–268.

private monopoly pricing for fear that disapproval of these industry agreements would result in the "economic chaos" of open competition.[38]

The breakdown of the recent Honolulu rate conference of IATA and the discussions at the recent Tokyo Assembly indicate that this cartel system of pricing faces a crisis and probable collapse. The introduction of high-cost jet planes with greatly enlarged capacity, the increase of low-rate chartered service, and the demonstrated success of "economy fare" flights on the North Atlantic run have convinced the more progressive leaders in the field that a drastic downward revision of rates and the extension of "economy fares" to all main routes are essential for profitable operation in the future. They want to move immediately in the direction of low-cost, mass transportation, but certain recalcitrant, monopoly-minded members of the organization will not agree. They refuse to heed the admonition of Sir William P. Hildred, Director General of IATA: "Our markets are inexhaustible so long as we keep the fares down. Our problem is to attain the highest possible economy of operation as the basis for the lowest possible price." [39] Although Sir William is Director General of a private cartel he speaks the language of competitive man. He merits an assist from the CAB in the form of action against American companies who refuse to follow his sound advice.

Airmail Subsidy

The air transportation industry is the beneficiary of two general classes of subsidies: (1) free or partially requited use of public property, such as investment in scientific research and development, airways, and airports; (2) direct payments from the Post Office under the guise of airmail compensation. The first, although very important, is omitted from the present discussion because it does not bear directly on the structure of the industry. The second, however, is a determinative organizational and price factor.

Payments by the Post Office on account of airmail assume two forms: (1) a so-called "service" rate for the actual transportation of airmail, now fixed at 45 cents per ton-mile for the larger certificated carriers and 53 cents per ton-mile for the smaller ones; (2) additional compensation sufficient, when combined with all other revenues, to enable the carrier to maintain and continue the development of air transportation adequate for the commerce of the United States, the postal service, and the national defense. In practice, the latter provision means whatever amount an individual carrier

[38] *Airlines*, pp. 275–8 and Chap. VI, pp. 217–35.
[39] *Wall Street Journal*, October 13, 1959.

can prevail upon the CAB to allow on the basis of its showing of financial need. In short, it is a commitment by the federal government to guarantee, through the guise of airmail payments, the financial integrity of the certificated carriers. Obviously, this arrangement has nothing whatever to do with the actual cost of transporting mail by air but is a direct subsidy designed to promote the development of air transportation.

In most discussions of this subject it is assumed that the "service" rate reflects the actual cost of transportation and is devoid of any taint of subsidy. This is the position of the CAB and the trunk-line carriers, both of whom refer to it as a "compensatory" rate. But this assumption is questionable. This "service" rate is not a competitive price determined in a free market, but rather a "negotiated" rate determined by the CAB on the basis of "cost" data supplied by the certificated carriers. Since these carriers are primarily concerned with passenger traffic of de luxe quality, their cost structure reflects the high cost incident to this type of business and has no necessary functional relation to the transportation of airmail. In fact, the 45 cents per ton-mile "service" rate for airmail received by the large certificated carriers is roughly about two-thirds of the passenger rate figured on a comparable basis. No one believes seriously that this differential reflects accurately the difference in cost between handling mail and first class passengers. The extreme artificiality of this "service" rate is indicated by the fact that air cargo rates, which are more comparable to airmail, range under 20 cents per ton-mile; that American Airlines recently offered to carry first class mail on its New York-Los Angeles run for 25 cents per ton-mile; [40] that the certificated cargo carriers recently offered to carry airmail, parcel post, and express at one-half the present airmail "service" rate, saving the Post Office an estimated $26,000,000 per year,[41] and that the Post Office has petitioned the CAB to approve a rate of 18.6 cents per ton-mile for ordinary first class mail between New York and Chicago.[42] If these figures are realistic indications of actual costs then it would appear that probably about one-half of all airmail payments at "service" rates are in the nature of a subsidy, being gratuitous and unnecessary for the performance of a public service.

This conclusion is confirmed by the findings of the Celler Committee and the Comptroller General. From 1939–56 the Post Office made total "airmail payments" of $1,337,986,000 to domestic airlines, $600,571,000 for "service" and $737,415,000 for "subsidy." For overseas airmail, during the same period, it paid $195,351,000 for "service" and $339,238,000 for "subsidy"—a total

[40] *Chicago Tribune,* July 22, 1953.
[41] *The New York Times,* May 2, 1952.
[42] *St. Louis Post Dispatch,* September 10, 1953.

of \$534,589,000. Thus, of the grand total airmail payments of \$1,872,575,000 "service" payments amounted to \$795,922,000 and "subsidy" to \$1,076,653,-000.[43] If, however, some one-half of the so-called "service" payment is actually a disguised subsidy, as the Celler Committee and the Comptroller General appear to believe, the real subsidy, over this period, amounts to about \$1,474,614,000, or about 75 per cent of the total airmail payments.

The record of airmail payments since 1938 indicates that, despite great increases in traffic and nonmail revenue, the actual amount of airmail subsidy has increased. There are several reasons for this. First, the so-called "service" rate is roughly twice the competitive rate, thereby creating a hidden subsidy the total amount of which increases with ton-miles of mail carried. Second, the openly labeled "subsidy" is significantly influenced by the heavy reliance of international carriers and local service lines on continued subsidization. Third, open "subsidy" is dependent on financial need, not on service performed in the transportation of mail. Since financial need is an undefined, variable concept, determined by administrative interpretation and the vagaries of uncontrolled private management, subsidy to meet financial needs may be increased for reasons totally unrelated to airmail service. The system being as it is, there is no basis for anticipating the early demise of airmail subsidies; on the contrary, they may well increase as airmail tonnage increases and new financial needs emerge. The only certain way to eliminate them would be to put the transportation of airmail on a competitive basis. As matters now stand, airmail subsidy has become a powerful vested interest and a principal obstacle to the more rational organization of the industry.

The CAB takes the position that it has a mandate to reduce and ultimately to eliminate airmail subsidies. Therefore, it reasons, competition must be vigorously suppressed lest it necessitate an increase of subsidies; passenger, mail, and cargo rates must be maintained at present levels lest revenues be impaired and subsidies raised; competition on international routes must be restricted if present large subsidies are ever to be reduced; all sectors of the industry must be integrated with the trunk-line carriers and required to serve them as auxiliary feeders in order to strengthen them and thereby reduce subsidies; new forms of air transport, such as low-cost coach service and air cargo, must be developed exclusively by the certificated carriers in order to enhance their revenues and thus reduce subsidies; the number of certificated carriers must be restricted and their routes carefully protected against any competitive dilution of traffic lest this require offsetting increases in subsidies. In short, everything competitive must be prohibited lest it in-

[43] *Airlines*, pp. 17, 24, 58–59, 268.

crease subsidies; everything monopolistic must be done in order to reduce subsidies. One wonders what the CAB would do if it lost this crutch!

Airmail subsidies are a fraud in the first place but the CAB compounds the evil when it predicates its whole attitude toward the organization and rate policy of the industry on this specious policy. The first fraud merely robs the taxpayers for the private benefit of a few privileged interests; the second perpetuates monopoly, frustrates the dynamic development of a new industry, and deprives millions of people of the potential benefits of low-cost air transportation. It is really fantastic to argue, as the CAB does, that the economic organization of an important industry should turn on the narrow financial issue of increasing or reducing a public subsidy, which is extremely questionable in the first instance. Furthermore, the eradication of competition and the establishment of monopoly will never, as the CAB fatuously supposes, eliminate airmail subsidies; it will only serve to strengthen and perpetuate them. The only sure way to eliminate them is by Congressional action to put the airmail service on a strictly cost basis, either by competitive private bidding or, failing that, by government operation. Subsidy may be justifiable on grounds of national interest, but it should not dictate the structure or price policy of the industry.

SECTION III: PUBLIC POLICY

Legislative Intent

The proponents both of competition and of monopoly profess to discover in the legislative history of the Civil Aeronautics Act of 1938 support for their respective contentions. Both interpret the somewhat obscure price policy declarations of the Act according to their reconstruction of congressional intent as that is revealed in the record of earlier statutes and in the hearings, reports, and debates of the Congress when the Act of 1938 was under active consideration. Subsequent investigation can never disclose congressional intent in the categorical sense claimed by advocates, but it illuminates the ceaseless struggle between the forces of freedom and privilege for control of the industry and it indicates the strategic points at which decisions once made become determinative for the future. A brief review of the legislative history of the Civil Aeronautics Act of 1938 will indicate how the Act settled none of the fundamental questions but merely transferred them to another arena.

In 1918 the United States Post Office launched an airmail service, using converted Army planes for this purpose. From 1918 to 1927 the airmail service was conducted exclusively by the Post Office.[44] A transition to private contract carriage, however, got under way after the passage of the Air Mail Act of 1925 (the so-called Kelly Act). This act authorized the Postmaster General to designate airmail routes and to enter into contracts with private companies for the transportation of airmail over these routes. Although the Kelly Act did not so prescribe, the Post Office followed the practice of letting contracts on competitive bid. No subsidy was provided; in fact, an attempt was made to preclude subsidy by limiting the payment for transportation to four-fifths of the revenue derived by the Post Office irrespective of the costs to the carrier.

The Post Office, however, experienced difficulty in placing such contracts and for a period of two years (1925–27) both the Post Office and private contractors carried airmail. The difficulty was that certain air transport companies wanted more than a mere temporary competitive-bid contract to carry airmail; they wanted exclusive operating rights on a permanent basis over selected air routes that offered promising potentialities for passenger and freight business. Their demands were partially satisfied by the airmail amendment of 1926, which authorized the Postmaster General to issue "airmail route certificates." By this action Congress converted a public service, competitive bid contract into something quite different—a private privilege of uncertain but potentially great value. Thereafter, the metamorphosis was rapid. Beginning as temporary service contracts for the performance of a public function on a competitive basis (1925), airmail contracts soon became "route certificates" (1926), then "route certificates good for 10 years" (1928), then "indefinite route certificates" (1934), then "grandfather routes" (1938), then, after 1938, certificates of public convenience and necessity.

Once airmail contracts were transmuted into route certificates, entitling the holder to exclusive operating rights over designated routes, they became valuable prizes eagerly sought by rival system builders. Fantastically low bids were submitted for transportation of airmail—even down to zero—merely to get control of routes where the prospects for passenger and freight business were attractive. Soon 21 of the 25 lucrative contracts in force had been cornered by three holding companies. By 1934 the Postmaster General had managed to place 90 per cent of the air transportation business in the hands of three large companies through the device of airmail contracts.[45]

---

[44] *The Role of Competition in Commercial Air Transportation*, p. 1. See also testimony of Hamlin B. Johnston in *Future of Irregular Airlines, Hearings*, 1953, pp. 118–19.
[45] Testimony of Hamlin B. Johnston, cited *ibid.*, p. 118.

The matter became a public scandal with charges of fraud and collusion in connection with the awarding of contracts. Following a Senate investigation, which substantiated these charges, the Postmaster General canceled all airmail contracts and President Roosevelt ordered the Army to fly the mail. Several fatal crashes of Army planes, however, led to the restoration of private operation on a temporary contract basis.[46] In the meantime Congress enacted the Airmail Act of 1934, which reestablished the private contract system and granted indefinite tenure to airmail contracts (route certificates) awarded by the Postmaster General.

In the Act of 1934 Congress sought to limit monopolization by prohibiting common control of airplane manufacturing and airmail transportation, interlocking directorates and merger of parallel routes. Moreover, it placed control of airmail rates in the hands of the Interstate Commerce Commission, thereby indicating its intention to put airmail contracts on a cost-of-service basis and to prevent their manipulation for purposes of route control and system building. It would thus appear that, at this stage, Congress was aware of the monopolistic tendencies in the industry and generally hostile to monopoly. However, its concern was primarily with airmail and it perceived only vaguely the larger problems involved in the development of a national air transport system. That Congress was aware of these larger problems, is nevertheless evidenced by the fact that—in the Act of 1934—it created a five-member Federal Aviation Commission to study and report on all questions of aviation policy.

The deliberations of the Federal Aviation Commission, of the various federal agencies concerned with aviation, of House and Senate committees, and of the air transport industry came to a focus in the drafting and consideration of what became the Civil Aeronautics Act of 1938. One of the most complete and fully documented summaries of antimonopoly thinking in Congress at the time is that prepared by former Senator Joseph C. O'Mahoney of Wyoming for the Select Committee on Small Business of the United States Senate.[47] Mr. O'Mahoney makes the point that the present dilemma over the issue of competition versus monopoly in air transport "comes from a misunderstanding of the purpose of the civil aeronautics law." He asserts that "throughout the debate in both the Senate and the House on the CAB law the meaning and intent of the Congress was to maintain freedom of entry into the air"; and he cites as evidence of this intent section 401 (J) to the effect that "no certificate shall confer any proprietary, property or ex-

---

[46] *Ibid.*, p. 119.
[47] *Future of Irregular Airlines*, pp. 283–301. See also O'Mahoney's testimony at pp. 253–72.

clusive right in the use of any air space, civil airway, landing area or air navigation facility." Freedom of entry, he says, was "a dominant theme" in all debates and hearings concerning the industry. The Federal Aviation Commission favored freedom of entry; both the Post Office and the Commerce Department objected strongly to certificates of public convenience and necessity, and to the "grandfather" clauses; an interdepartmental committee, appointed by the President and consisting of representatives of the various departments concerned with aviation proposed modifications to satisfy the objections of the Post Office, Commerce, and Justice; the subsequent debates in the House and Senate, and the explicit assurances of committee chairmen in response to interrogations, confirm the antimonopoly sentiments and intent of Congress; as Mr. O'Mahoney concludes, "the Congress did everything that could possibly be done in order to make it unmistakably clear that opportunities were to be accorded to newcomers to an extent never before paralleled in Federal regulation of transportation." This O'Mahoney interpretation was accepted as a valid and accurate portrayal of congressional intent by the Senate Small Business Committee under a Republican Chairman, Edward J. Thye of Minnesota.[48]

If such was the actual intent of Congress, the public policy declaration of the Act failed to make it clear and explicit. In Section 2, where Congress indicated the things to be considered in determining the "public interest" and "public convenience and necessity," it is provided that:

Sec. 2. In the exercise and performance of its powers and duties under this Act, the authority shall consider the following, among other things, as being in the public interest, and in accordance with public convenience and necessity—

(a) The encouragement and development of an air-transportation system properly adapted to the present and future needs of the foreign and domestic commerce of the United States, of the postal service and of the national defence;

(b) The regulation of air transportation in such manner as to recognize and preserve the inherent advantages of, assure the highest degree of safety in, and foster sound economic conditions in, such transportation, and to improve the relations between, and coordinate transportation by, air carriers;

[48] Senator Thye, in summarizing the evidence, stated: "The fundamental issue in this case involves the right of entry of new business into an industry. Freedom of opportunity has always been a basic American economic doctrine. Congress has placed limits on the freedom only with great reluctance. The Civil Aeronautics Act of 1938 represented a limit on that freedom. When that act was passed, the aviation industry was an infant industry with very shaky economic foundations. In order to develop this industry, Congress gave the Civil Aeronautics Board the right to protect the then existing companies from competition until such time as they became strong. *Never in the hearings nor the floor debate on the legislation was there any indication that Congress intended to bar all future entry into air transportation. In fact, the record is filled with repeated assurances that the door would still be open to new companies.*" (Italics supplied.) *Future of Irregular Airlines*, Senate Report No. 822. Eighty-third Cong., 1st Sess., 1953, p. 18.

(c) The promotion of adequate, economical, and efficient service by air carriers at reasonable charges, without unjust discriminations, undue preference or advantages, or unfair or destructive competitive practices;

(d) Competition to the extent necessary to assure the sound development of an air-transportation system properly adapted to the needs of the foreign and domestic commerce of the United States, of the postal service, and of the national defence;

(e) The regulation of air commerce in such a manner as to best promote its development and safety; and

(f) The encouragement and development of civil aeronautics.

The CAB, in defense of its administrative record, and the certificated carriers, in defense of their privileged position, place an entirely different construction on this language and on the events preceding the passage of the Act of 1938. They point out, and quite correctly, that from 1925 to 1938 government policy, as manifested by congressional legislation and decisions of the Postmaster General, favored "restricted competition," with the holders of airmail contracts enjoying exclusive operating privileges over routes awarded to them; that Congress in the Act of 1938 recognized and confirmed the established position of these carriers in the "grandfather" clause; that Congress sanctioned the use of certificates of public convenience and necessity as a device to regulate entry into the air transport business; that both the House and Senate reports, particularly the latter, called attention to the excess of competition then prevalent and to the desirability of restricting competition in order to protect the financial status of the carriers; [49] that Congress provided for airmail subsidies sufficient, when combined with all other revenues, to enable the carriers "to maintain and continue the development of air transportation to the extent and of the character and quality required for the commerce of the United States, the postal service, and the national defence." These acts, they affirm, reveal clearly the real congressional intent. That intent was to limit competition in the same manner and for the same reasons as in other public utility industries.

The Policy of the Civil Aeronautics Board

The Civil Aeronautics Board has consistently maintained that the original eighteen "grandfather" airlines, now reduced to twelve, constitute the backbone of the air transport industry in the United States. Moreover, the Board insists that it has a mandate from Congress to develop a sound and adequate national air transport system on this predetermined foundation. All other

[49] H.R. Rep. No. 2254, Seventy-fifth Cong., 3d Sess. (1938); Sen. Rep. No. 1161, Seventy-fifth Cong., 3d Sess. (1938).

segments of the industry must be integrated with this basic system, supplementing but not competing with the trunk-lines. From this point of view, free competition is a destructive force because it jeopardizes the financial integrity and service of the trunk-lines. Restricted or regulated competition, however, has some constructive value under special circumstances, but it must be used with circumspection and caution lest it undermine the basic foundation.

In appraising the implementation of this philosophy it should first be noted that the Board's efforts to correct the original imbalance among the "grandfather" carriers has been attended with but indifferent success. In 1938 the "Big Four" (American, Eastern, TWA, and United) accounted for 82 per cent of the total nonmail revenue of the trunk-lines and the remaining 18 per cent was distributed among fourteen other companies. At the end of 1951, after thirteen years of effort by the Board to strengthen the weaker trunk-line carriers and to achieve a more balanced system, the same "Big Four" had 67 per cent of the nonmail revenue and the remaining 33 per cent was divided among twelve other companies.[50] By 1953 the degree of concentration was more pronounced, the "Big Four" accounting for nearly 75 per cent of total domestic trunk-line operations and the "Big Six" for 83 per cent.[51] In 1955 the "Big Four's" share of total revenue ton-miles was 73 per cent.[52]

This lack of success is due to the failure of the Board to utilize either of two effective techniques: (1) reallocation of routes and (2) certification of additional carriers. It has not used the first because it claims to lack the necessary power; it has not used the second because it construes its congressional mandate to protect the trunk-lines against competition. Thus, since 1938 the Board has not issued a single new certificate of public convenience and necessity for a trunk-line carrier. While the Board has never said categorically that under no circumstances will it ever issue a new certificate, its language in a 1941 case goes almost that far.[53]

---

[50] *The Role of Competition in Commercial Air Transportation,* p. 9.

[51] Testimony of Hamlin B. Johnston, *Future of Irregular Airlines,* 1953, p. 119. Commenting on this situation, Mr. Johnston said: "We have again reached the point where the Congress must intervene to break up the monopolistic tendency which the Civil Aeronautics Board has fostered." (*Ibid.,* p. 119.)

[52] *Airlines,* p. 19.

[53] "The number of air carriers now operating appears sufficient to insure against monopoly in respect to the average new route case, and we believe that the present domestic air-transportation system can by proper supervision be integrated and expanded in a manner that will in general afford the competition necessary for the development of that system in the manner contemplated by the act. In the absence of particular circumstances presenting an affirmative reason for a new carrier there appears to be no inherent desirability of increasing the present number of carriers merely for the

The Board has relied on certain indirect or secondary techniques to correct the imbalance among the certificated trunk-lines. From 1938 to 1951, it extended the route mileage of certificated carriers from 30,000 to over 130,000 miles and increased the number of cities authorized to be served by the trunk-lines from 240 to 416.[54] Between 1941 and 1950, it authorized competitive trunk-line service between a number of principal cities, with the result that of 100 top-ranking pairs of stations 76 were competitive in 1950 whereas in 1941 only 30 pairs had been competitive. These 76 competitive pairs of stations accounted for 88 per cent of the passenger-miles produced by the 100 pairs of stations in 1950.[55] Of the first 25 pairs of stations, in terms of passenger-miles, all but one are served by two or more carriers. In 1955, in a series of decisions, the CAB opened twenty-one markets to competition for the first time and admitted small certificated carriers to thirteen major markets from which they had previously been excluded.[56] Neither of these policies—extension of route mileage or authorization of parallel service between principal traffic centers—can be regarded as truly competitive so long as they are confined to a limited number of certificated carriers. They merely convert a monopoly into an oligopoly, and effect a minor redistribution of traffic among the oligopolists. The larger air lines complain bitterly against this enforced sharing of traffic under this system of "multiple-competition," as they call it.[57]

The Board has sought to build up and strengthen the weaker carriers by admitting them to new markets, extending and consolidating their routes, approving traffic interchange agreements and eliminating restrictions that prevent them from competing effectively. More recently the Board has sought to improve the route pattern and to strengthen the weaker carriers by a positive program of mergers and consolidations.[58]

---

purpose of numerically enlarging the industry." (*Delta Air et al.*, Service to Atlanta and Birmingham, 2 CAB 447, 480, 1941.)

[54] *The Role of Competition*, p. 8.

[55] *Ibid.*, p. 10.

[56] *Airlines*, p. 21.

[57] Frederick F. Robinson, President, National Aviation Corporation, *Wall Street Journal*, February 5, 1960.

[58] This policy is rationalized as follows: "Any proposal for a national route plan taking into account the over-all needs of the country must have as a vital ingredient the possibility of mergers which will achieve a system of carriers whose size and other characteristics will permit more uniform cost levels; will avoid excessive competition detrimental to the system as a whole but at the same time preserve existing competition and increase the effectiveness of it; will improve service to the public through combinations of carriers whose routes logically integrate. For some period of time now the Board has given consideration to possible mergers that would achieve the foregoing objectives and has from time to time urged carriers to take steps to bring about such combinations. . . . It is the Board's intention to continue to pursue this policy of

The solicitude of the CAB to protect the certificated carriers against competition is dramatically illustrated by its treatment of the so-called "irregulars." In its Nonscheduled Regulation of 1938, the Board granted exemption from the economic regulations of the Act to all irregulars. The effect was to permit freedom of entry into the irregular sector of the industry so long as operations were irregular and intermittent. This attitude, however, changed quickly after the war. When the irregulars expanded the scale and frequency of their operations, particularly in the area of low-rate coach service, and began to constitute a competitive threat to the certificated carriers the CAB for the first time questioned the legitimacy of their status in the industry.

The first move was an investigation to assemble information concerning the operations of the irregulars. (Investigation of Non-Scheduled Air Service, 1946.) This investigation, however, was inconclusive and no significant changes in the regulations were made. In May 1947, the CAB revised its nonscheduled exemption by creating two classes of irregulars—large and small—the latter being defined as those operating craft under 12,500 pounds. The large irregulars were required to obtain *letters of registration* from the Board, although no showing of need or fitness was required, and the basic limitation on frequency of service, which heretofore had been only implicit, was stipulated in precise and detailed form. In August 1948, the Board ruled that no further letters of registration would be issued unless an application had been filed by August 6, 1948, and it commenced a vigorous program of enforcement of the exemption regulation, resorting to suspension orders without hearings, court injunctions, and proceedings to revoke letters of registration.[59] In May 1949, the blanket exemption of large irregular carriers, which had been in effect since 1938, was terminated, but it was provided that any carrier which by a specified date filed an application for an individual exemption could continue limited operation pending disposition of its application.

This campaign culminated in the sweeping order of May 25, 1950, in *Large Irregular Carriers, Exemptions* (11 CAB 609). Here the Board enunciated a policy of restriction to insure that irregular operations "will have no adverse effect upon the certificated carriers." It denied the applications for exemption of all irregulars that had been conducting what the Board called route services, i.e. "a pattern of operations which shows a concentration of relatively frequent and regular flights between a limited number of pairs of points." The Board also denied the applications of all holders

---

searching out and encouraging those transactions that will help to achieve the policies set forth by Congress in the act." (*The Role of Competition*, pp. 49–50.)

[59] *Report of Senate Small Business Committee*, 1951, p. 5.

of letters of registration who had not operated within the preceding year. Going further, it promulgated the drastic "3 and 8 rule" under which irregular carriers who were granted individual exemptions would be restricted to three flights in the same direction during any period of four successive calendar weeks between designated pairs of points (thirteen pairs of cities) and eight flights in the same direction in such period between any other pairs of cities.

Pursuant to this policy the Board granted nineteen applications, denied or dismissed 42, and was in process of acting on the remaining 46 when, on September 21, 1951, it suspended further processing of applications and instituted a general investigation of irregular carriers (Docket No. 5312). This investigation has been under way for two years and the Board estimates that it will require two more years to complete it.[60] In the meantime, the orders denying individual exemption have been suspended pending completion of this investigation. Likewise, the "3 and 8 rule" was suspended, first on the request of the Senate Small Business Committee and later in accordance with an injunction granted by the District Court for the District of Columbia.[61] But there has been no abatement of the enforcement program; in fact, it appears to have been stepped up during 1952 and 1953.[62]

Further evidence of the Board's attitude is found in the classic *Transcontinental Coach-Type Service Case* (Docket 3397, decided November 7, 1951). Here four large irregular carriers—Air American, Inc., California Eastern Airways, Inc., Trans-American Airways, Inc., and Great Lakes Airlines, Inc.—had applied for certificates of public convenience and necessity under Section 401, or exemption under Section 416, to render coach-type service on transcontinental routes. The Board denied the applications, both as to certificates of public convenience and necessity and as to exemptions from frequency restrictions. It said:

> We are influenced in large part by the fact that from three to four airlines are already certificated and operating between each of the points which the applicants propose to serve, and that the certification of additional air carriers offering unlimited air-coach service would result in unnecessary, excessive, and destructive competition. [p. 8] . . . It is our conclusion, therefore, that the existing carriers are fully capable of providing the scheduled regular and frequent air

[60] *Report of the Senate Small Business Committee*, 1953, p. 7.

[61] *American Air Transport Inc. et al., plaintiffs, v. Civil Aeronautics Board et al.*, defendants, Civil Action No. 1295–51, May 29, 1951.

[62] The Senate Committee on Small Business observes: "It is clear that the Board is moving rapidly in the direction of eliminating the major irregular carriers long before the completion of the overall hearings." (Senate Report No. 822, 83d Cong., 1st Sess., 1953, p. 7.)

coach services needed between the points which they are already serving, and that they have the necessary resources and facilities to insure the future growth and development of such low-fare services [p. 11].

Commissioner Joseph P. Adams dissented in part, confessing himself unable to reconcile the majority opinion with either the Act of 1938 or with previous decisions. He pointed out that the Board's fear of traffic diversion and loss of revenue as a result of low-cost coach services by irregular carriers was an illusion and wholly unsubstantiated. He attacked the Board's "theory of capability" respecting the ability and willingness of the certificated carriers to develop the air coach business, affirming that "this 'theory of capability' inevitably forces its proponent to the philosophy of 'preservation of the status quo'; a philosophy which at best is a strange one for the Board to adopt in the regulation and promotion of an industry as dynamic as the airline industry."

An even stronger dissent arose within the board in the Southern Service to the West Case (Docket No. 1102, decided January 30, 1951). Here Commissioner Josh Lee excoriated his brethren for what he regarded as their pro-monopolistic, anticompetitive propensity. He disagreed with the majority decision *"because it changes the policy of the Board from one that favors competition wherever it can be justified to one that opposes it wherever its refusal can be justified."* [63] He flatly accused the Board of violating the intent of Congress and repudiating its earlier decisions: "An objective reading of the Civil Aeronautics Act of 1938 leaves no doubt that the lawmakers considered competition a desirable thing which should be established wherever it could be justified. The Civil Aeronautics Board which was set up under its authority placed that interpretation upon it and during the earlier years of its existence certificated competitive services accordingly. . . . Immediately following the enactment of the law, while the debates and discussions leading up to its passage were still fresh in the minds of the members of the Civil Aeronautics Board and while the plain simple language of the Act itself was the principal guide to its meaning, there was no doubt but that the intent of the Congress was that the Board should give the public the benefits of competition wherever it could be justified" [p. 29]. Never, he says, until the present case has the Board announced a complete reversal of its original policy. The Board, he charges, has "built its own storm cellar against competition." He ends with a taunt at the Board's denial of competition because hard times might lie ahead: "If the majority will not agree to competition in good times, it is not likely that the majority would agree to

[63] *Ibid.*, p. 28 (italics by Lee).

competition during those hard times; so it would seem that the majority cannot find an appropriate time for competition." [64]

Investigations and Reports of the Select Committee on Small Business, United States Senate

This harrying of the irregulars by the CAB naturally evoked a storm of protest. The act that precipitated the explosion was the promulgation by the CAB of its drastic "3 and 8 rule." This was a death sentence for free enterprise and competition in air transport, and the irregular airlines petitioned the Senate Small Business Committee for relief. The committee, under the chairmanship of John Sparkman of Alabama, caused a staff survey to be conducted, requested the CAB to submit a report on its policies respecting competition, held hearings, and published two reports. [65]

The committee found "a certain identity of interest between the CAB and the more firmly established portion of the industry"; that the Department of Justice had protested strongly against the frequency restrictions on the grounds that they were calculated to put the irregulars out of existence, thereby violating the intent of the 1938 Act and the spirit of the antimonopoly statutes; that the Board, in cooperation with the certificated carriers, harassed the irregulars with suspensions, revocations, enforcement proceedings, and court injunctions; that the Board appears obsessed with the idea that low-cost operation by the irregulars will undermine the fare structure of the certificated carriers; that the Board was negligent in failing to develop a consistent policy appropriate to rapidly changing conditions in the industry; that the policy of the Board contravened the Act of 1938; that the Board has the power, if it would only use it, to authorize the irregulars to operate at a level of frequency that would enable them to survive and provide effective competition; that the Board clings to the view that air transportation "must perforce remain the exclusive franchise of the certificated carriers"; and that the Board views air transportation problems in much the same way as the established members in the industry. The committee reminded the Board of its public obligations and pointed out that if it failed to develop more constructive and appropriate policies its failure "would, indeed, lend credence to the charge that it is servile to the interests of the certificated carriers." [66] The committee made six specific recommendations of an interim

---

[64] *Ibid.*, p. 32.

[65] *Report on Role of Irregular Airlines*, Senate Report No. 540, Eighty-second Cong., 1st Sess., July 10, 1951. *Annual Report*, Senate Report No. 1068, Eighty-second Cong., 2d Sess., January 21, 1952, Chap. XII, pp. 243–53, and weekly staff reports, pp. 280–329.

[66] Senate Report No. 540, 1951, p. 18.

or transitional nature, which it hoped would alleviate the immediate crisis and eventually lead to some satisfactory compromise solution:

1. The CAB rescind its "death edict" limiting "nonskeds" to three and eight round-trip flights per month.

2. The CAB issue a temporary regulation permitting the "nonskeds" to fly sufficient flights for profitable operations.

3. The CAB issue a regulation which would established a procedure for existing and new irregular carriers to file for permanent authority to operate an unsubsidized second-class or coach-type route service without regard to regularity but limited as to the total allowable flights.

4. The CAB should act promptly to relieve the hardships it is imposing on Alaska through restricting flight from the United States and should recognize the special need for cargo transportation and lack of alternate forms of low-cost transportation. The report cited that the "nonskeds" had reduced the cost of air freight to Alaska from 68 cents a pound to 15 cents.

5. Legislation should be enacted to separate airline subsidies from compensation for the cost of carrying air mail.

6. The CAB should reassess its whole approach toward air transportation. Its restricted view, resulting in the use of subsidy to provide high-cost luxury air service for a small part of the population, needs re-examination. The operation of the nonscheduled air carriers has demonstrated that there is strong public demand for cheap air transportation on a vastly extended basis. Far from reaching a saturation point, air-coach service apparently has hardly scratched the surface of the potential market.

The committee waited patiently for nearly two years for the Civil Aeronautics Board to act. But the Board made no effort to carry out the recommendations; on the contrary, it proceeded with its campaign to eliminate the irregular airlines by administrative attrition. At length, in February 1953, the committee ordered new hearings, especially for the purpose of ascertaining why the CAB had failed to act on the previous recommendations. On July 31, 1953, it submitted a report in which it made sixteen specific findings and five recommendations.[67] This report sustained the previous position of the committee with respect to the role of competition in air transportation and was equally critical of the CAB; the findings and recommendations, while different in detail, conformed to the previous pattern and reflected the same conception of desirable public policy.

The committee noted with concern "the constant pressure by the Civil Aeronautics Board to put these small carriers out of business," "the constantly weakening long-term economic position of these airlines," and the fact that pending enforcement proceedings would eliminate lines accounting for 50 per cent of the irregular business. The committee condemned the

[67] Senate Report No. 822, 83d Cong., 1st Sess., 1953.

procedure in mild but pointed language: "the Board's deviation from the certification procedures provided for in the Civil Aeronautics Act was unfortunate. Your committee hopes that once the present problem is solved that the Board will grant all future permanent authorizations only through the procedures established in the act." [68] The committee was dissatisfied with the Board's evasion of the 1951 recommendations by the obvious dodge of instituting a general investigation of irregular airlines, which was calculated to stalemate the situation for four years while the irregulars were destroyed by administrative attrition. It reaffirmed the principle of economic freedom: "The fundamental issue in this case involves the right of entry of new business into an industry. Freedom of opportunity has always been a basic American economic doctrine . . . the door should be kept open in the development of our commercial air-transportation system." [69]

The findings and recommendations of the committee are as follows:

Findings

1. The certificated carriers are the backbone of our air transportation system and their economic stability should not be jeopardized.

2. The irregular carriers are a valuable asset to the Nation and should be preserved.

3. The irregular airlines were created as a result of economics demands that were not being met by the services approved by the Civil Aeronautics Board.

4. The irregular airlines were the first to offer low-cost coach-type service.

5. The aircoach service by these irregular airlines stimulated the entry of the certificated carriers into the coach field and thus aided the development of a low-cost mass air transportation system.

6. Aircoach service is destined to become the standard type of air travel. The innovators of it have a right to share in its success.

7. The unsubsidized irregular airlines serve as a valuable "yardstick" of airline cost.

8. The irregular airlines have not caused a diversion of traffic from the certificated carriers. While there is a duplication of routes between the irregular and certificated carriers, there is relatively little duplication of markets. The introduction of thousands of lower-income-bracket travelers to aviation should be attributed to the irregulars. Their pioneering, which has been along economic rather than geographic lines, has shattered the concept of a fixed, limited market for civil aviation. As a result, the question

[68] *Ibid.*, p. 3.
[69] *Ibid.*, pp. 18–19.

is no longer what portion of a fixed pie any company will get, but rather how much the entire pie can grow.

9. The importance of the irregular airlines as an airlift reserve for the Nation's defense is adequately demonstrated by their participation in the Berlin and Korean airlifts and in domestic troop movements.

10. The refusal of the Civil Aeronautics Board to certify any of these irregular carriers for international airfreight operations has tended to divert available traffic to foreign carriers.

11. The Civil Aeronautics Board has refused entry to new airlines into common carriage of passengers on the trunk routes, despite the fact that traffic over these routes is now twenty times greater than it was when the Board was established in 1938.

12. The Civil Aeronautics Board has instituted enforcement proceedings against a number of irregular carriers for flying too regularly, which, if successful, would put out of business the economically significant element of this industry within a short time.

13. The Large Irregular case, which is destined to determine the future of these carriers, has been in process almost 2 years and is expected to require at least another 2 years before a decision can be made. At the present rate of enforcement proceedings, there is considerable doubt how many of the irregular carriers will be in existence at the conclusion of the case to benefit from its findings.

14. The Civil Aeronautics Board has failed to exercise sufficient ingenuity in devising ways to integrate the irregular carriers into our air-transportation system.

15. A way should be worked out to keep the irregular airlines as vital going concerns in the air-transportation industry.

16. The Senate Small Business Committee is an entirely proper body to consider whether or not the nondominant elements of an industry are receiving unprejudiced consideration from a regulatory body of the Federal Government.

Recommendations

1. Issue a temporary regulation permitting the irregular carriers to fly fourteen round-trip flights a month between any two points, pending the conclusion of the Large Irregular case.

2. Grant temporary exemptions to the four and five irregular carriers or groups of irregular carriers to engage in a rigidly restricted route-type service.

3. Expedite the Transatlantic Cargo case (CAB Docket No. 3041).

4. Make every effort to expedite the Large Irregular case (Docket No. 5132) so that the future of this class of carriers can be clarified as soon as possible.

5. Authorize organizations to serve as air clearing houses for the irregular carriers in providing charter service and common carriage in order to pool the services of the carriers for the maximum benefit of the public.

These investigations, criticisms and recommendations have somewhat tempered, but not abated, the CAB's protracted war of administrative attrition against the large irregular carriers. Of 147 original holders of "letters of registration" only 54 remained in operation in 1956.[70] On November 15, 1955, the Board granted to 45 of these survivors a somewhat liberalized status as "supplemental carriers"; the remaining nine continued as irregular carriers.[71] The new arrangement removes original restrictions on charter flights, both passenger and cargo, but retains the ten-flights per month limitation on individual sale passenger flights. Under a proceeding initiated by American Airlines the order creating these "supplemental carriers" was remanded by the Appeals Court to the Board for further findings.[72] The performance record of the large irregular carriers under this restrictive regime has deteriorated relative to the industry as a whole. In 1951, their peak year percentage wise, they accounted for 7.49 per cent of total revenue passenger-miles and 21.41 per cent of total cargo ton-miles; by 1955 they were down to 5.42 per cent and 14.55 per cent respectively.[73] Although they pioneered low-rate passenger and cargo air transport immediately after World War II they have been denied the right to share equitably in the extraordinary growth of traffic which their competitive efforts generated.

Problems of the Future

The Federal Government is responsible under the law for planning a sound and adequate national air transport system. The public interest is paramount and should not be subordinated to the vagaries of private profit seeking, oligopolistic rivalries or special privilege. This planning should be directed toward the attainment of social ends, such as: full development of the potentialities of air transportation, maximum availability of service to all people and to all areas, reduction of costs and rates, technological progress, and maximum freedom of opportunity consistent with these goals.

[70] *Airlines*, p. 29.
[71] *Ibid.*, pp. 32–33.
[72] *American Air Lines* v. *CAB*, Civ. No. 13044, D.C. Ct. App., July 19, 1956.
[73] *Airlines*, p. 30.

Realization of these objectives depends on the solution of many perplexing problems only a few of which can be mentioned here.

One of the most urgent is the rearrangement of the route pattern. The existing "grandfather" pattern should be overhauled and routes reallocated to secure a more balanced system, more complete market coverage, and more intensive development of potential air traffic. Under the present system, the "Big Four" dominate the heavy traffic routes and make large profits by exploiting their high-value traffic potentials; but they avoid—insofar as they safely can—serving thin territory, smaller markets, and lower-value traffic. The latter service is provided on a limited scale by smaller trunklines and local feeder lines, sustained in large measure by public subsidies. In short, the "Big Four" skim the cream off the richest part of the total market while the taxpayers foot the bill to maintain limited service in the poorer sectors of the market. This situation might be corrected either by compelling the major carriers to serve all communities and all types of traffic within their respective areas on a public utility basis, or by opening the monopolistic and oligopolistic sectors of the market to free competition.

Competition, however, cannot survive unless the CAB suppresses discrimination by the certificated carriers. If they are free to use their monopoly and subsidy revenues to finance discrimination on selected routes and types of traffic, or in particular markets, they can destroy any competitor. Discrimination is a standard technique of private monopoly and is always bad; but it is doubly bad when financed in part by public subsidy. The CAB in its zeal to protect the certificated carriers has allowed them to use this weapon of aggression freely. This policy should be reversed.

A large increase in the volume of air transportation is projected for the immediate future. But this increased traffic cannot be handled unless the airport bottleneck is broken. Airports at main terminals are inadequate for present traffic; they cannot cope with the much heavier traffic of the future. Existing institutional arrangements for the financing of airport facilities are seriously defective; the cities and states are unable to assume this burden, the Federal aid program is too limited, the airline companies are unwilling or unable to provide the necessary capital. To escape from this dilemma, and because of the national interests involved, the Federal Government might appropriately undertake this investment program on a self-liquidating basis.

Another bottleneck that must be broken is that of equipment. Existing planes are appropriate for high-cost, limited service but quite inadequate for the low-cost, mass transportation of the future. Further refinement of the luxury liners at ever increasing cost is no solution; neither is the conversion of military planes or the use of equipment discarded by the major airlines. What is required is basic research and experimentation directed toward the perfection of planes suitable for low-cost, mass air transportation. Here, again, the problem is nobody's business; the certificated carriers are indifferent, the manufacturers busy with military and luxury liner orders, the competitive sector of the industry weak and disorganized, the CAB concerned with protecting the status quo. One of the most persuasive arguments for competition is that it would stimulate all interested parties to attack and solve this problem.

In a greatly expanded air transport industry, competition has an appropriate role. What that role may be is not presently known, but there is no technological or economic imperative that renders monopoly inevitable or even expedient. If government continues to defray the major overhead costs—technical research and development, airports and airways—service operations can for the most part be competitive, just as on waterways and highways. A possible exception is regularly scheduled, basic passenger service; here public convenience may necessitate service by a single company. But this exception is limited to basic passenger service; it does not apply to special movements, such as week-end, holiday, vacation, seasonal, and convention travel. Air freight can be separated from passenger traffic, and moved competitively in equipment especially designed for that purpose. Long-distance United States mail, including present airmail, first-class mail, and parcel post, could be transported at cost, either by the Post Office or by private contractors on a competitive bid basis. On international routes freedom of entry should prevail—both for passenger and freight business—to the extent permitted by foreign control of landing privileges. Economic and technological factors, then, appear sufficiently favorable to competition so that it becomes a practical possibility—provided we have the social wisdom to recognize it and the courage to maintain it.

Perhaps the most important and urgent piece of unfinished business is the reorganization of air transport regulation. The Act of 1938 is gravely defective and totally inadequate for the future. The policy of the Civil Aeronautics Board, based on its interpretation of the Act, serves to promote monopoly, to suppress competition, and to frustrate the dynamic development of the industry. The Board is trapped, partly by its own illusions, partly by its subservience to the certificated carriers, but basically by the terms of the Act itself—particularly the "grandfather" clause, the subsidy system, the certification requirements, and the lack of power over rates and services. Given these handicaps no Board, however able and public spirited, can succeed in developing a sound and adequate air transport system. The ultimate responsibility rests squarely on Congress; the present crisis cannot be resolved until Congress recognizes and acts on this responsibility.

For over forty years we have relied on improvisation, subsidy, privilege, monopoly and protective regulation to produce a national air transportation system. The result pleases none, except the privileged and subsidized. What we have in the main is a subsidized oligopolistic system the imperatives of which run in one direction only—more privileges, more subsidies, further concentration, extinction of residual competition, limitation of service, and maximization of profit. Such a system is compatible neither with our tradition of economic freedom, nor with our ideal of public service, nor with the economic and technological realities. Competition is technically possible and economically viable over large sectors of the industry; it should be exploited to its full potentialities. The public service function of regular passenger service between main centers, and to connecting subordinate centers, could be operated by public authority at cost. This combination of public operation of an essential utility service and private operation under free competition in areas where public interest is not so intimately involved would be preferable to subsidized private oligopoly over the entire industry. Since the people, as taxpayers and consumers, are going to pay the bill anyway, they should insist on a plan of organization that insures maximum service at minimum cost.

SUGGESTED READINGS

Books

W. Adams and H. M. Gray, *Monopoly in America—The Government As Promoter* (New York: Macmillan, 1955).

P. W. Cherington, *Airline Price Policy: A Study of Domestic Airline Passenger Fares* (Boston: Harvard University Graduate School of Business Administration, 1958).

J. H. Frederick, *Commercial Air Transportation,* 3rd ed. (Chicago: Irwin, 1951).

F. W. Gill and G. L. Bates, *Airline Competition* (Cambridge: Harvard University Press, 1949).

J. L. Nicholson, *Air Transportation Management* (New York: Wiley, 1951).

B. Schwartz, *The Professor and the Commissions* (New York: Alfred A. Knopf, 1959).

Transportation Association of America, *Sound Transportation for the National Welfare* (Chicago: 1953).

R. E. Westmeyer, *Economics of Transportation* (New York: Prentice-Hall, 1952).

G. L. Wilson and L. A. Bryan, *Air Transportation* (New York: Prentice-Hall, 1949).

A. C. Wiprud, *Justice in Transportation—An Expose of Monopoly Control* (Chicago: Ziff-Davis Publishing Company, 1945).

Government Publications

Civil Aeronautics Board, *Annual Reports,* 1939–
———, *Annual Airline Statistics, United States Certificated Air Carriers,* 1939–
———, *Decisions,* 1939–
———, *Economic Regulations,* 1947–
———, *The Role of Competition in Commercial Air Transportation.* Report to the Subcommittee on Monopoly of the Select Committee on Small Business. United States Senate, 82d Cong., 2d Sess., November 24, 1952.

United States House of Representatives, Committee on the Judiciary, *Monopoly Problems in Regulated Industries, Part 1—Airlines, Hearings* Vol. 1–4, 84th Cong., 2d Sess., 1956.

———, Committee on the Judiciary, *Report on Airlines,* 85th Cong., 1st Sess., April 5, 1957.

———, Select Committee on Small Business, *Role of Irregular Airlines in United States Air Transportation Industry, Hearings,* Eighty-second Cong., 1st Sess., 1951.

———, Select Committee on Small Business, *Report on Role of Irregular Airlines in United States Air Transportation Industry,* Senate Report No. 540, Eighty-second Cong., 1st Sess., July 10, 1951.

———, Select Committee on Small Business, *Annual Report,* Senate Report No. 1068, Eighty-second Cong., 2d Sess., January 21, 1952.

———, Select Committee on Small Business, *Future of Irregular Airlines in United States Air Transportation Industry, Hearings,* Eighty-third Cong., 1st Sess., 1953.

———, Select Committee on Small Business, *Future of Irregular Airlines,* Senate Report No. 822, Eighty-third Cong., 1st Sess., July 31, 1953.

Chapter 14

THEODORE J. KREPS

The Newspaper Industry

SECTION I: INTRODUCTION

Throughout modern times the newspaper has been the symbol and proof of free enterprise and a free press. The first in America, a three-page sheet called *Public Occurrences,* was published and promptly suppressed by the Massachusetts Legislature in 1690. Fourteen years later the *Boston Newes Letter* was regularly "published with authority." It later became the *Boston Gazette* which in 1741 consummated the first newspaper merger, absorbing the *New England Weekly Journal.* Five years earlier William Bradford with a two-newspaper chain in Philadelphia and New York, started the process of vertical integration by acquisition of a paper mill in New Jersey. The oldest newspaper still in business is the Hartford *Courant,* established in 1764.

Though 35 weekly newspapers had a circulation of 21,000 copies by 1776, as late as 1800 there were but two dailies, four pages in size, hand-printed, costing 6 to 11 cents a copy, with a total circulation of only 700. Printing presses were small and cheap, usually run by a single journeyman printer who required but little capital to set up his own shop as editor and publisher. Not until 1833 did the first one-cent newspaper appear: the *New York Sun,* a tabloid distributed by newsboys, with 32,000 circulation, a want-ad page, a theater and sports section, and marriage and obituary notices. By 1850 there were 200 daily and 2,300 weekly newspapers with a total of 1,000,000 circulation.[1]

The last half of the nineteenth century became the hey-day of the small, independent, crusading, small-town newspaper. It followed the frontier. It

[1] From an excellent historical study by Alfred McClung Lee, *The Daily Newspaper in America,* New York: Macmillan, 1939.

509

sought out and unflinchingly exposed business and political corruption. Its editorials were frank, individualistic presentations of the truth and the facts as the editor saw them. Vigorous competition in ideas implemented the democratic way of life.

During the twentieth century, however, newspapers became big business. The number of daily newspapers steadily declined from 2,461 in 1916 to 2,034 in 1931, 1,854 in 1947 and 1,762 in 1958. Yet daily newspaper circulation grew from 24 million in 1909 to nearly 58 million in 1957.

Though 2,060 new daily newspapers were started during the period from 1909 to 1948 (including those changing from weekly to daily), 1,957 suspended publication or became weeklies. 547 disappeared through merger or consolidation. At least 302 local combinations took place. In addition, the number of newspaper chains increased from thirteen publishing 62 newspapers in 1909 to 70 operating 386 newspapers in 1949 with over two-fifths of the daily circulation and one-half the Sunday circulation.[2]

In 1958 only 76 cities out of the total of 1,762 had competing daily newspapers. Thus 95.7 per cent of American cities with daily newspapers in 1958 were one-publisher towns as compared with 92 per cent in 1951 and 57 per cent in 1920. In fourteen states there is not a single city with competing daily newspapers. In 30 states not a single city enjoys competing Sunday newspapers. Altogether 40 per cent of newspaper circulation is "noncompetitive," [3] so far as other newspapers are concerned.

In 245, or roughly a sixth, of the American cities with newspapers there is likewise control by the only newspaper over the one or two local radio stations. Throughout the country 24 per cent of all AM broadcasting stations, 39 per cent of FM stations and 46.6 per cent of the TV stations were affiliated in 1949 with newspapers.[4]

The process of newspapers becoming big is still in full swing in all its forms. Every year brings new examples of horizontal integration whether as mergers and consolidations, as combinations of the one ownership (two or more newspapers in the same city jointly operated though sometimes with diametrically opposite editorial policy) or of the cartel variety (two ownerships but selling national and local advertising in combination or forming a third corporation to operate consolidated mechanical and business divisions), or as chains of newspapers (two or more newspapers under single

[2] These statistics are taken from *Concentration of Ownership and Control in the American Daily Newspaper Industry* by Royal Henderson Ray, unpublished MS. in Columbia University Library 1950, pp. 2, 138, 176, 223.

[3] Estimate made by authors of "Local Monopoly in the Daily Newspaper Industry," *Yale Law Journal*, Vol. 61, No. 6, June–July 1952, pp. 949, 950, 951.

[4] Agee, "Cross Channel Ownership of Communications Media," *Journalism Quarterly*, 1949, Vol. 26, pp. 410, 411.

ownership in different cities). Every year sees new and successful attempts at vertical integration whether backward, to make more sure of newsprint, of syndicated feature services, and of newsgathering services, or forward, e.g., paper companies acquiring stock ownership in newspapers. Every month there are reports that newspapers are meeting the competition of substitute services such as radio and television stations via ventures of their own, or through affiliations or other harmonious arrangements. The end result of such agglomerative activities is not yet in sight.

In 1954, the year of the most recent census, total receipts of the 8,445 companies in the newspaper industry amounted to $2,926 millions, and their employees numbered 321,000 of whom 159,000 were production workers. Of these, one out of seven worked for one of the four largest firms, some 19 per cent worked for the eight largest, and 27 per cent for the twenty largest. To use another measure of concentration, the four largest companies did 18 per cent of total business as measured by value of shipments. The eight largest did 24 per cent of all newspaper business, the twenty largest 34 per cent. The primary product specialization ratio (the extent to which they made their money out of newspapers) was 95 per cent.

The forces militating against new, small and independent enterprise in the newspaper industry are not only manifold but for the most part irreversible. They stem from modern technology, twentieth-century political upheavals, and changing business strategy.

Modern technology in printing and distributing newspapers has demanded heavy fixed capital investment, greater mechanical speed, newer and more complex processes. It has greatly extended the area from which news is expected, obtained and selected. It has created new technical requirements for excellence of copy, color, photographic reproduction and speed and regularity of delivery. It has brought the big city daily even to the rural mailbox, and radio and television news broadcasts into the home. Only the modern and strong newspaper can survive.

Political upheavals have likewise taken their toll. During both World Wars the rationing of newsprint, the draft of personnel, and other restrictions put hundreds of small dailies out of business. In fact, there occurred a net decline of 112 during World War I and 121 during World War II. Federal and state restrictions against the use of child labor, especially at night, the greater time and area over which transport can be used, and the preference of advertisers for evening papers brought about a severe drop in the number of morning newspapers,[5] coupled with a growth in circulation.

---

[5] Local Monopoly etc., *op.cit.*, p. 950. In the second quarter of this century the circulation of evening newspapers rose 47 per cent, that of morning papers 68 per cent. Yet the total number of the former dropped only 9 per cent, of the latter 25 per cent.

Competition in laxity among the States in their incorporation statutes together with personal liability and corporate tax advantages greased the skids toward merger, combination, lateral and vertical integration. Thus in 1939 over three-fourths of the newspapers were incorporated, somewhat less than 10 per cent were partnerships, and only 15 per cent remained the sole proprietorships so characteristic of the nineteenth century.

Among the changes in business strategy most productive of big newspapers in the twentieth century was the national shift in marketing methods to advertising. In 1900 only 96 million dollars were spent by advertisers in all newspapers, magazines, and other periodicals.[6] This burgeoned to a figure of 1,750 million in 1948 and 3,325 million in 1957. Newspapers now generally collect more than two dollars of revenue from advertisers for every dollar they get from subscribers.

During the last ten years, however, there has arisen a new, formidable competitor for the advertisers' dollar: television. While in the period, 1949–57 total advertising expenditures have doubled (from 5.2 billion to 10.4 billion dollars) the share of the newspaper take has declined from 36.6 per cent to 32.7 per cent. That of television has risen from 1.2 per cent to 12.3 per cent. The hardest hit has been the radio whose share of the pie decreased from 12.2 per cent in 1949 to 6.7 per cent in 1957. Of course, the fact should not be forgotten that nearly half of the television stations are owned by newspapers.

Since newspapers, like businesses in general, cannot make lucrative profits by displeasing their customers, the selection and presentation of news and opinions, while independent and not dominated by customers, is done with care. As big businessmen, newspaper publishers hold the same views as their advertisers tend to hold. Each reinforces the social philosophy of the other. As a result, newspapers instead of being defenders of competition in ideas, alert to give full play to all aspects of the truth (including those unfavorable to merchants and manufacturers) now shrewdly merchandise the opinions and news both consider "sound." Like the products advertised such news and opinions are sometimes nationally manufactured, designed to be "put over" or "sold" for a profit.

Thus a considerable decline has taken place in the ratio of space devoted to news. According to one authority the percentage of nonadvertising space went down from 60 per cent in 1941 to 42 per cent in 1947.[7] Instead of giving equally competitive coverage to equally important political figures and events, newspapers with notable exceptions are virtually house-organs of the

---

[6] Max A. Geller, *Advertising at the Cross-Roads*, New York: Ronald, 1952, p. 21.
[7] "Local Monopoly," *op.cit.*, p. 960.

business point of view. At times they have been so far removed from giving expression even to the majority sentiments of this democracy that Presidents, governors and large legislative majorities have been overwhelmingly elected and reelected at national and state levels who were opposed by over four-fifths of the national and local press.

But advertisers want attractive copy and circulation, both highly expensive. Attractive copy requires constant experimentation in printing techniques, color, photography—all involving heavy capital outlays pressuring for intensive utilization. To build up more circulation newspapers have put on frenetic promotional campaigns and contests, given premiums and insurance, printed ever more lurid comic strips, expanded their sports coverage, devoted more space to canned editorials, syndicated features, larger news pictures, and screaming headlines on "safe" items such as sex and crime. Individual newspapers have enlarged their circulations by consummating mergers, consolidations, combinations, chains—in short, bigger, and more expensive operations.

SECTION II: MARKET STRUCTURE AND PRICE POLICY

The market structure of the newspaper industry both in the procurement of resources and in marketing exhibits the familiar behavior patterns of local monopoly, monopolistic competition, oligopsony, and oligopoly. As buyers of newsprint, of syndicated features, of wire services, and of labor and equipment they use familiar competitive and monopoloid pressures to keep down costs. As sellers of space they practice the devices of imperfect competition: rigidity in advertising and circulation rates; discrimination where possible such that different advertisers and readers pay different rates at the same time for identical space or newspapers; product differentiation and nonprice discrimination; and until recently exerted pressure for "block" sales requiring advertisers to buy space in both morning and evening newspapers under single ownership.

Factor Markets

On the average a daily newspaper pays out for newsprint about one-third of its revenues, roughly the fraction it receives from subscriptions. The percentage of total revenues going for paper and ink naturally varies with circulation volume. In 1951 it was 15.88 per cent for newspapers of 10–25,000 circulation, 19.50 per cent for the 25–50,000 range, 28.90 per cent for the 50–100,000 category, and 38.12 per cent for circulations in excess of 100,000.[8]

[8] *Editor and Publisher*, April 12, 1952, p. 74.

Practically all newsprint is sold in carload lots on a three-to-five-, and recently even on a ten-to-twelve-year contract basis, mostly to large publishers. During World War II 55 per cent of the available newsprint was consumed by less than 3 per cent of American dailies.[9] Those for whom it may be impractical to make carload purchases, e.g., dailies with less than 10,000 circulation (in 1939 41.4 per cent of the total number) and those seeking to enjoy their theoretical right to freedom of entry may be able to buy at 10 per cent higher open-market prices from newsprint jobbers, brokers, and paper merchants. Sometimes spot market prices are two to three times as high as long-term contract quotations. Or they may scrounge around to find some contract buyer with a temporary surplus of newsprint not tied by the producer to printing editions of specific publications. Such end-use restrictions "to prevent resale at exorbitant prices" are not uncommon. If the new entrant tries to establish his own newsprint mill he will find both domestic and Canadian acreage of softwoods timberlands preempted through ownership in fee, or leasehold, or cutting rights.[10]

Nor will the potential practitioner of free enterprise be able to shop around. He will run into a uniform delivered pricing system within each of ten zones into which the United States is divided. He will find that publisher-newspaper integration [11] has not only tied up most domestic newsprint but a substantial portion of Canadian as well. There is consequently almost perfect industry-wide price uniformity.

The procurement of syndicated features and wire services is no less difficult for the new entrant. Most features are sold by four syndicates, 62 being offered by AP Newsfeatures in 1946, 148 by King Features (Hearst), 86 by NEA Service (Scripps-Howard) and 35 by United Features (also tied to Scripps-Howard). Most franchises provide for exclusivity of territory. The practice of package selling at a flat price enables large publishers to buy up the rights to more features than they print—a species of preemptive purchasing. An unexpectedly popular feature has sometimes been transferred to newspapers connected with the syndicate.[12]

Oligopoly is likewise the chief trait of the wire services, the three most important being Associated Press (AP), United Press (UP), and International News Service (INS). The AP is a cooperative which prior to federal

[9] Subcommittee on Newsprint, Senate Select Committee on Small Business, Eighty-second Cong., 1st Sess., *Supplies for a Free Press*, p. 5.
[10] Report by Federal Trade Commission, *Newsprint Paper Decree Investigation*, 1939, pp. 51–4.
[11] Subcommittee on Study of Monopoly Power of the House Committee on the Judiciary, Eighty-first Cong., 1st Sess., *Hearings* Pt. 6-B, p. 78; also Pt. 6-A, pp. 214–5.
[12] *Newark Evening News Publishing Co.* v. *King Features Syndicate, Inc.* 7 F.R.D. 645 (D.N.J. 1948).

antitrust action in 1943 could and did refuse membership to applicants who might compete in the same city and field with existing members.[13] As a result of the change in by-laws prescribed by the Supreme Court AP domestic membership increased from 1,274 in 1943 to 1,708 in 1949, and radio members from zero to 940. Its world-wide clients numbered 4,274 in 1949. Entry now is relatively equal for all papers, though there are standards of qualification with respect to size of paid subscription list, staff and plant and ability to reciprocate with local news.

Access to UP and INS is more difficult. A new competitor not only pays the standard service charges but an extra fee—ultimately received by the publisher with whom he plans to compete, that is, if the publisher has an "asset value" contract. In 1944 the UP had such contracts worth $25,000 each with 215 subscribers in 144 cities and the INS contracts worth $30,000 each with 64 subscribers in 62 cities. In 26 cities that year monopoly newspapers had UP and INS asset value contracts plus AP membership.

In buying labor the small plant pays the going union rate set in negotiations by all publishers with the International Typographical Union, the International Stereotypers and Electrotyper's Union, the International Photoengraver's Union, the International Printing Pressmen and Assistants Union, and for nonmechanical workers the American Newspaper Guild. Such union rates are often more easily paid by the large daily than the small one.

The primary problem is efficient utilization. At each deadline there is a peak of activity of men and machines followed by a wait. Press-clock-time is usually one to three hours. The larger the circulation the smaller the fraction that alternately hurries and loafs. Other ways of evening out the days work are to schedule off-peak processing of "nonline" news, feature stories and Sunday sections, to merge circulations, or combine an evening with a morning paper. The smaller the newspaper, the more inefficient the utilization of personnel and equipment.

The daily newspaper with large circulation thereby assures itself of lower costs, especially in its composing, advertising, and editorial departments (about 50 per cent of total costs). In addition to the advantage of lower costs of printing advertising, the larger newspaper can levy a higher differential charge for it on national advertisers. The table below [14] indicates the nature of the relationships found: The larger the circulation the lower the costs.

The point of increasing average and marginal costs is not known. As one

[13] *Associated Press* v. *U.S.*, 326 U.S. 1 (1945) affirming 52 F. Supp. 362 (S.D. N.Y. 1943).
[14] Compiled from "Local Monopoly," *op.cit.*, p. 975; computations from data of The Newspaper Audit and Research Bureau in *Special Statistical Report*, 1951.

expert observes "the scale of operation over which decreasing costs prevail
. . . is far beyond the needs of our largest communities." [15]

TABLE 1

Average Unit Cost in 1950 per 1,000 Eight-Page Unit for 95
Nonmetropolitan Dailies in Eleven Circulation Groups

Circulation (thousands)	Editorial Costs per Unit in Dollars	Advertising Costs per Unit in Dollars	Percentage Higher Charges Paid for 20,000 Advertising Lines by National Advertisers	Composing Costs per Unit in Dollars	Circulation and Mail Departments in Dollars
3–5	14.12	10.10	22	19.70	5.28
5–6	10.20	5.86	50	14.40	5.12
6–8	10.20	6.41	44	14.30	4.95
8–10	8.64	5.91	44	9.94	4.84
10–15	7.66	4.62	55	8.71	3.96
15–20	6.64	4.12	65	7.50	3.60
20–25	5.25	3.60	63	6.18	2.92
20–35	5.04	2.87	65	6.70	2.96
25–40	5.15	3.18	61	6.95	2.44
30–50	4.94	2.50	48	6.06	2.91
45–85	4.26	1.98	50	3.40	3.48

Chains of large newspapers have certain additional advantages, notably
in making wider use of editorial and feature writers, in obtaining new funds
from the capital market, in block merchandising of space to national advertisers, in centralized research, in bulk purchases especially of newsprint,
and in maximum use of specialized technical and managerial services.

Sales to Readers

Newspapers merchandise their news, opinions and space in segregated
markets deriving their revenues from two major sources: readers and advertisers. In 1954 they received $2,059 million from advertisers or 71 per cent
of their total revenues. The remainder of their revenue or $841 million (29
per cent) they obtained from subscribers. The stability of the 2 to 1 relationship has been remarkable. It is sometimes higher in boom years (in
1929 it was 74.3 per cent for advertisers versus 25.7 per cent for circulation)
and lower during depression (64.2 versus 35.8 in 1933).

In 1957 there were 309 English language *morning* papers with a total
circulation somewhat over 23 million. Six, with circulation in excess of a
half million—the New York *Daily News* (2,014,542), the New York *Mirror*

[15] For a series of engineering cost functions see Malone, "Economic-Technological
Bases for Newspaper Diversity," *Journalism Quarterly*, Vol. 28, pp. 320–22.

(834,066), the Chicago *Tribune* (900,895), *The New York Times* (633,106), the Philadelphia *Inquirer* (604,977) and the Chicago *Sun-Times* (539,090) served nearly a fourth of the nation's morning newspaper buying public. Less than one-sixth, 56 in number, with circulations of 100,000 or over sold about 68 per cent of the nation's morning papers.

In 1957 there were 544 *Sunday* papers with a total circulation of 47,044,-349. Nearly a fifth were sold by five newspapers with circulation over a million: the New York *News* (3,564,864), the New York *Mirror* (1,424,886), the Chicago *Tribune* (1,276,767), *The New York Times* (1,291,134) and the Philadelphia *Inquirer* (1,108,209).

The total number of morning and evening newspapers in 1957 was 1,755 with a circulation of 57,805,445. Over 30 per cent was concentrated in the three states of New York (8,676,084), California (4,600,095), and Pennsylvania (4,157,691). Another 29 per cent was concentrated in the six states of Illinois (3,999,426), Ohio (3,410,566), Massachusetts (2,508,265), Texas (2,806,316), Michigan (2,389,565), and Missouri (1,861,661).

Sales to Advertisers

The newspapers are but one of the media available to advertisers. Besides the 1,755 daily newspapers and 544 Sunday newspapers already mentioned there were 3,248 commercial radio stations in operation in 1957, of which a third, mostly the larger stations, were affiliated with four major networks: ABC, 284 stations, NBC, 207 stations, CBS, 207, and MBS, 435 stations. There were 555 TV and 541 FM stations in operation. In addition, the Magazine Advertising Bureau reported that in 1951 there belonged to the Audit Bureau of Circulation some 251 national magazines with a circulation of over 150 million. Not to be forgotten as advertising media are the thousands of weekly, small town, school, farm and trade papers, direct mail, movies, outdoor posters, point-of-sale displays, and so on. Of the six and one-half billion dollars which, according to the magazine *Printers' Ink*, were spent by advertisers in 1957 the newspapers garnered 32.7 per cent, direct mail 14.3 per cent, radio 6.7 per cent, magazines 8.0 per cent, television 12.3 per cent, business papers 5.3 per cent, outdoor advertising 2.0 per cent. The remaining 20 per cent was paid to miscellaneous other media.

Despite the wide choice of media open to advertisers, they buy newspaper space in an administered price market. Space sells at different rates to three more or less compartmentalized groups of customers: local advertisers, national advertisers, and the classified ads.

Most important are the local advertisers normally providing over 43 per cent of a daily newspaper's total revenue. The percentage varies inversely with circulation as is evident from the table below.

TABLE 2

Percentage of Total Revenues by Types of Advertisers in 1951

Circulation (thousands)	Percentage from Local Advertisers	Percentage from National Advertisers	Percentage from Classified Advertisements	Percentage from All Advertising
10–25	50.51	11.98	10.82	73.31
25–40	43.94	12.59	13.34	69.87
50–100	42.84	12.97	11.87	67.68
Over 100	37.24	16.98	14.60	68.82
Composite	43.51	13.63	12.66	69.80

Source: Editor and Publisher, April 12, 1952, p. 4.

Local advertisers consist primarily of retailers and service enterprises. Rates are quoted on a line and milline basis. The former states the cost per line, the latter gives the cost of bringing a line of advertising message to a million readers. The larger the circulation the lower usually the milline rate. The variation however is considerable even for newspapers of equal circulation.[16]

Though local advertisers have only one local newspaper in which to push their wares, their ability to pay is usually limited by the rigor of retail competition. They have to be cost sensitive, especially during periods of buyers' markets. Since the volume of business they do depends in part on the number of shoppers that pass their store, they need repetitive advertisements that attract and hold attention, which means large, continuous purchasing of display space. In the case of groceries and drug stores, the hundreds of items on their counters require full-page advertisements on weekends merely for price lists. They too must have low rates for space.

During periods of inflation or boom retailers tend to advertise freely. In such a seller's market they frequently scan costs less rigorously. But when their competitors are slashing prices, cutting inventories and pushing bargain sales, retailers often reduce their advertising outlays and look around for substitute media such as Shopping News handouts. The pressure for lowest possible advertising costs becomes intense.

Thus the rate and discount schedules announced on publisher's rate cards are tailored to the locality, the type of business involved, and even the in-

[16] See Senate Select Committee on Small Business, Eighty-second Cong., 2nd Sess., *Newsprint for Tomorrow,* Senate Report No. 1404, Washington, 1952, p. 79, *et seq.*

dividual advertiser. Preferential rate concessions abound, especially during slack periods of retail activity. These may be open or clandestine. They sometimes take the form of complimentary ads, or discounts on space bought direct from the ad salesman without use of an advertising agency. In fact, milline rates are even tailored to the edition, being higher for the evening edition and for the evening papers read at leisure at home which have greater advertising pull among the housewives.

National Advertisers

In general, the national advertisers are large manufacturers and distributors selling branded consumer products under conditions of oligopoly or monopolistic competition. Usually they pay from 50–65 per cent more than local advertisers for advertising space, especially in cities of over 100,000 population. The charges vary, to be sure, with the newspaper and with advertising specifications such as frequency, position, color, changes, classification and bulk. In contrast with retail rates, 90 per cent of which are "open," 80 per cent of general rate cards are "flat," that is, no volume and frequency discounts are given. Despite continuous efforts of national advertisers to lower the differential, it has risen from an average of 37.9 per cent in 1933 to 55.6 per cent in 1950. In Sunday editions the differential in rates has risen from 54.1 to 68.5 per cent.[17]

The reasons why large national corporations are unable to keep down the rates they pay to the local newspapers are complex. They unquestionably are charged rates based in part on ability to pay. Local publishers know that potential customers for a nationally distributed product probably comprise a larger fraction of their total circulation, especially where new products are concerned, or their city lies within an area of virtually exclusive distribution. Such factual or arranged division of territories characterizes, for example, large portions of the motion picture exhibitor's market. To charge higher rates to the absentee national advertiser or to his local distributor is easier and less embarrassing than explaining increases to the local independent merchants.

In addition there are said to be cost differences. National advertisers make more frequent requests for republication because of dissatisfaction with position. The newspapers incur the cost of belonging to the Audit Bureau of Circulation. They not only finance market research demonstrating the

---

[17] These figures represent the per cent by which general milline rates exceed daily retail rates for 20,000 line purchases from newspaper members of the Audit Bureau of Circulation in cities over 100,000 population. See graph in "Local Monopoly" *op.cit.*, p. 1009.

desirability of advertising in their city and pay the salaries and commissions of their own representatives who solicit the advertising but foot the rebate for commissions charged by the advertising agency handling the account. While electrotype plates or mats are cheap and can be used for general ads, retail insertions that are pre-composed frequently run into the traditional International Typographical Union's rule of "bogus" (compulsory resetting of type, correcting of proof, etc., of all local ads arriving at the print shop in matrix form) which prevents advantage being taken of a possible cut in labor costs from 2 to 5 per cent.[18]

Most of the nationally distributed items locally advertised—automobiles, tires, gasoline, household appliances, kitchenware, furniture, carpets and rugs, radios, television sets, toys, silverware, clothing, cigarettes, breakfast foods, motion pictures, and liquor—are sold at established price lines by only a handful of producers under conditions of monopolistic competition with emphasis on quality, performance, prestige, fear, snobbery, mother love, sex appeal—everything except price. Changes in price are infrequent, occurring as a rule only when product or model changes are made. Advertisers who themselves emphasize nonprice considerations, naturally determine in the same manner their total advertising expenditures in a newspaper. The question of rates is distinctly secondary.

The Special Role of the Advertising Agency

The key role in maintaining a discriminatory, relatively inflexible, administered price structure for national or general advertising rates, at least until 1956,[19] was played by the advertising agency. As the authors of the eminent study on *Local Monopoly in the Daily Newspaper Industry* pointed out:

It is the agency, not the advertiser, with whom dailies deal, and to whom publishers sell space and send bills. Three quarters of advertising agency revenues consists of commissions granted by advertising media. The commissions are based on a flat percentage of dollar billings placed by the agency; in the case of newspapers this rebate is 15 per cent. Hence, agency compensation depends not on quantity of space purchased but on size of clients' ad expenditures. . . . Promotional skill, integrity, reputation, and financial soundness, rather than promises of bargain rates are decisive factors in interagency rivalry. Agency campaign lists are largely impervious to rate concessions.[20]

[18] See the NLRB case on the International Typographical Union, 86 NLRB 1025–1027 (1949).

[19] In that year some of the practices sketched in the next few paragraphs were outlawed. See *U.S. v. American Association of Advertising Agencies, Inc.*, S.D. New York, Civil Action No. 100–309, May 22, 1956.

[20] See "Local Monopoly," *op.cit.*, pp. 983–4 and extensive literature there cited.

Advance announcement of rate changes and periodic open-filing of rate cards kept all newspapers informed and in line. Each month the Standard Rate and Data Service published a rate book with milline computations called *Newspaper Advertising Rates and Data.* Publishers granted commissions only to "recognized" agencies, those namely, that conformed to the agency code of ethics and refused to engage in practices (e.g., rebates to clients) which might "degrade the rate structure of publishers." Should national advertisers try to buy lineage direct or through a subsidiary they received no discount.

Thus, *bona fide* advertising agencies became the unavoidable channel through which space was procured. They listed the newspapers that would share in the campaign. Since expenditures were a function of space times milline rate, there was a pronounced tendency to favor newspapers with large circulation coverage—which were not the newspapers usually with high rates. Small dailies received smaller lineage allocations. New entrants represented a frank gamble, having neither established circulation nor experience concerning the buying habits of potential customers. Most national advertisers did not like to take the risk.

Advertising agencies in effect enabled publishers to set national or general advertising rates on the principle of what the traffic would bear. The local rates, yielding three-fifths their advertising revenues, were lowest because publishers had to live in the same community with local merchants able to make or break their reputation, with power to bring complaints immediately and directly. In a segregated market subject to much higher rates were advertisers with a relatively inelastic demand: purchasers of classified, legal, political, financial, theater and amusement ads. In a third disparate market were the general or national advertisers, the special wards of advertising agencies.

Most publishers were able even to compel package or forced combination sales, especially when one publisher owned both morning and evening dailies. As Roy A. Roberts, owner of the Kansas City Star admitted, "In 1903 the Star put into effect combined advertising rates for morning and afternoon on general and classified advertising." [21] So extensive was this type of "unit rate" that advertisers who might have sought to contact the nation-wide morning circulation of 21,222,525 in 1951 would have been compelled to buy space also in evening papers totaling 8,252,668 circulation. Those wishing to bring an advertising message to all the evening circulation that year (32,795,413) would have had to buy space also in 8,437,750 morning circulation.[22] General "package" milline rates were higher than those of

---

[21] Advertisement, *The Wall Street Journal,* January 13, 1953, p. 11.
[22] *Editor and Publisher Yearbook,* 1952, p. 19.

independently sold papers.[23] In addition many "forced combination" tie-in sales excluded advertisers from using other newspapers or other media, such as local radio and television stations not owned by, or affiliated with, the publisher.

Sometimes "package" selling was extended beyond the confines of a single city. Chains offered discounts to buyers using all member papers. Newspapers organized joint selling programs or appointed "special representatives" to sell space on an all-or-none basis.

The control over rates by publishers was not weakened, even when manufacturers granted allowances to promote cooperative advertising programs which plugged both the product and the local retail outlet. The retailer attempting to place the ad often found that he was charged the higher general advertising rate, especially the automobile dealer.

Due to four notable antitrust cases brought by the Department of Justice between 1952 and 1958 these facts are undergoing a gradual change. In 1952 antitrust action outlawed "forced combination" contracts, etc., as will be commented on toward the close of this chapter in connection with the *Times-Picayune, Kansas City Star,* and *Wichita Eagle* cases. In 1956 the American Association of Advertising Agencies, Newspaper Publishers, Business and Periodical publishers, etc., in a consent decree were enjoined from

. . . entering into, adhering to, or following any course of conduct, practice, or policy, or any agreement or understanding:

(1) Establishing or stabilizing agency commissions, or attempting so to do;

(2) Requiring, urging, or requesting any advertising agency to refrain from rebating or splitting agency commissions;

(3) Requiring, urging, or requesting any media to deny or limit credit or agency commission due or available to any advertising agency;

(4) Establishing or formulating or attempting to establish or formulate any standards of conduct or other qualifications to be used by any media or association of media to determine whether media should or should not do business with or recognize any advertising agency;

(5) Requiring, urging or requesting any media not to do business with, or not to recognize, any advertising agency;

(6) Establishing or stabilizing or advertising rates to be charged advertisers not employing an advertising agency, or attempting so to do;

(7) Requiring, urging, or requesting any media to adhere to published advertising rates or rate cards.[24]

---

[23] Raymond B. Nixon, "Concentration and Absenteeism in Daily Newspaper Ownership," *Journalism Quarterly,* Vol. 22, 1945, pp. 97, 112.

[24] *U.S.* v. *American Association of Advertising Agencies, Inc., et al.,* S.D. New York, Final Judgment, Civil Action No. 100–309, May 22, 1956.

In how far these legal victories may have changed business reality is unknown. Far too little time has elapsed. But in 1960 as a general rule competition in advertising rates is still largely limited to nonprice factors—research, merchandising services, copy preparation, special position, free publicity in the news columns. Prices continue to be tailored to different segregated markets, are openly filed, and seldom change. As in the great depression when milline rates remained unchanged and line rates receded but a shade,[25] stability continues.

The problem is simply that of the oligopolist faced with a kinked demand curve. He dare not raise rates unless sure that others will follow. If he lowers rates, the response of the entire newspaper fraternity will be angrily immediate so that he will get no benefit.

The small newspaper publisher is in a vise. He lacks the circulation to attract much of the higher priced lucrative national advertising lineage. He operates primarily in the lower priced retail advertising field. He does not have the volume necessary to get the benefit of lower composing, editorial, and advertising costs. As a result, he is disappearing. "The structure and organization of the circulation and advertising markets exert pressure on small competing papers to suspend publication, or to combine and achieve more efficient operations. This prospect, together with the difficulties of raising initial capital, will also discourage entry into the field by potential publishers. In short, the conditions for viable newspaper multiplicity hardly exist." [26]

SECTION III: PUBLIC POLICY

Summarizing the mass of evidence presented to them during months of inquiry, the Commission on Freedom of the Press, financed by Time, Inc. and the Encyclopaedia Britannica, made these observations:

The American people do not realize what has happened to them. They are not aware that a communications revolution has occurred. They do not appreciate the tremendous power which the new instruments and the new organization of the press place in the hands of a few men. They have not yet understood how far the performance of the press falls short of the requirements of a free society in the world today.

The agencies of mass communication are big business and their owners are big businessmen. . . . The owners of the press, like the owners of other big businesses, are bank directors, bank borrowers, and heavy taxpayers in the upper brackets.

[25] Kintner, "Rigidity of Advertising Rates in Depression and Boom Years," *Journalism Quarterly*, Vol. 24, 1947, p. 122.
[26] "Local Monopoly," *op.cit.*, p. 1001.

Monopolistic practices, together with the cost of machinery and the momentum of big, going concerns have made it hard for new ventures to enter the field. It would cost somewhere between five and ten million dollars to build a new metropolitan daily to success. The investment required for a new newspaper in a medium-sized city is estimated at three-quarters of a million dollars; for a small-town paper $25,000–$100,000.

Has the struggle for power and profit been carried to such a point that the public interest has suffered? Have the units of the press by becoming big business, lost their representative character and developed a common bias—the bias of the large investor and the employer?

The published charges of distortion in the press resulting from the bias of its owners fall into the categories that might be expected. In 1935 the American Newspaper Publishers Association condemned the proposed Child Labor Amendment. . . . Bias is claimed against consumer cooperatives, [and trade unions], against food and drug regulation, against Federal Trade Commission orders designed to suppress fraudulent advertising, and against F.C.C. regulations affecting newspaper-owned broadcasting stations. Other claims involve their affiliations with suppliers of raw paper stock and their affiliations with electric power companies. Still others arise from ownership of outside businesses by owners of the press. Many people believe that the press is biased in matters of national fiscal policy.[27]

Allegations of bias in the press have not diminished since the Commission published its report. Every group other than the press itself and business has been increasingly uneasy about suppression and distortion of the news. Numerous studies have weighed the activities of the press, for example, in the elections of 1952, and found them one-sided and partisan. Los Angeles newspapers, to cite but one instance, gave one of the two major political parties "only 36 per cent of the total column-inches devoted to the campaign, only 33 per cent of front page space, only 38 per cent of the photographs which, in turn, occupied only 32 per cent of the photographic space."[28] Some 94 American authors, including 24 Pulitzer prize winners in an open letter charged the press with "nationwide abuse of the written word."

The election of 1956 revealed in even more striking fashion, former editor James Wechsler observed, that the American press "is overwhelmingly owned and operated by Republicans who fix the rules of United States political debate." In terms of newspaper circulation, the Republican candi-

---

[27] Commission on Freedom of the Press, *A Free and Responsible Press*, Supplement to *Fortune*, April 1947, pp. 10, 12, 20. For extensive documentation of these charges see the report by the nine Nieman fellows at Harvard University in 1945–46 as compiled by Leon Svirsky in *Your Newspaper: Blue print for a Better Press*, New York, 1947. Also George Seldes, *Lords of the Press*, New York, 1946.

[28] For extensive statistical comparison see Phil Kerby, "The Partisan Press and the Campaign," *Frontier*, January 1953, pp. 5–9. See also comprehensive data for San Francisco and other areas in the same issue.

date received nine times the volume of endorsement given his Democratic opponent. In six states there was not a single newspaper favorable to Democratic candidates. There was likewise none in such large cities as Chicago, Los Angeles, San Francisco, Detroit, Boston, Cleveland, Dallas, Denver, Baltimore, Pittsburgh, Seattle, Des Moines, Columbus, and Cincinnati. In New York City the Republican advantage was 5 to 1.

In several of the populous states the percentage of newspaper readers urged by their newspapers to vote for Republican candidates ranged from 99.8 per cent in Michigan and 99 per cent in Minnesota to 96 per cent in Illinois, 93 per cent in California, 91 per cent in Maryland, 89 per cent in Pennsylvania, and 85 per cent in New York and Ohio.

Not merely editorial endorsement but according to one study "over 80 per cent of the nation's newspaper readers may be getting their news with some Republican flavoring." [29] This flavoring took all the known forms: more stories and pictures, bigger headlines, better location on the page, more favorable tone, twisted and verdict headlines, suppression, etc. In the United States there is not merely a one-party press but a double-standard press.

The events of recent years but reemphasize the findings of the Commission on Freedom of the Press in 1947 that: "The right of free public expression has therefore lost its earlier reality. Protection against government is now not enough to guarantee that a man who has something to say shall have a chance to say it. The owners and managers of the press determine which persons, which facts, which versions of the facts, and which ideas shall reach the people." [30]

What Can be Done?

1. Some suggest the withdrawal of government subsidies. At present under the classification adopted by legislation in 1879 newspapers are given the second class mailing privilege which a federal court has called "a form of subsidy." [31] This privilege is granted subject to four conditions, three pertaining to regularity and form of printing. The fourth stipulates that the newspaper "must be originated and published for the dissemination of information of a public character, or devoted to literature, the sciences, arts or some special industry, and having a legitimate list of subscribers, provided, however, that nothing herein shall be so construed as to admit to second-

[29] A. E. Rowse, *Slanted News*, Boston: Beacon Press, 1957. Rowse was copy editor for The Boston Traveler.
[30] *A Free and Responsible Press, op.cit.*, p. 4.
[31] See *Hannigan* v. *Esquire, Inc.* 327 U.S. 146, 66 S. Ct. 456, 90 L. Ed. 586 (1946).

class rates regular publications designed primarily for advertising purposes, or for free circulation or for circulation at nominal rates."

In the interest of diffusion of information, knowledge, and education, the government has consistently carried newspapers, magazines, etc., through the mails at a loss. For many years every dollar's worth of business the newspaper brought the post office cost the tax-payer four or five dollars or more. The total each year usually amounted to tens of millions and sometimes, indeed, over a hundred million dollars.[32] The total postal deficit in 1952 alone exceeded $600,000,000. Over the last two decades the subsidy to newspapers may have totaled roughly a billion dollars.

One of the sardonic ironies of history is that such subsidies were in effect pocketed by newspaper publishers, four-fifths of whom were castigating the administration for wasteful expenditure, for high taxes, for not balancing the budget, for "welfare statism," creeping socialism and subservience to special interests. Yet their own advertising, some of it just a shade removed from being frankly political, the source of over two-thirds of their revenues, was subsidized in two ways. It increased the postal deficit. It also was deductible as a business expense for tax purposes. An excess profits tax probably added to the stimulus given advertising expenditures. If government aid to the sick represents socialized medicine, then the twofold subsidy to advertising may fairly be called socialized advertising. Yet, the administration's heroic efforts each year to put the Post Office Department on a business basis were ruthlessly beaten down in the Congress, primarily by newspaper and business pressure groups and their lobbyists. Beaten down indignantly, one might add, as if limiting a subsidy involved infringement of civil rights. Wherever substantial increases in postal revenues were legislated, as in 1958, they were mostly obtained from increases in rates on first class and air mail, already paying their way.

Valid grounds for continuance of the subsidy to advertisers and publishers no longer exist. Newspapers and magazines carrying advertising are big business, especially the big ones getting most of the subsidy. In the critical state of federal government finances, newspapers, especially those able to tap the advertising gold mine, should pay their way.

Moreover, journalism has shifted emphasis from information to entertainment, from objective debate on vital issues to partisan propaganda, from

[32] For careful computations see *Cost Ascertainment Report* U.S. Post Office Department, 1945 as summarized in Senate Committee Print No. 17, Eightieth Cong., 1st Sess., *Survival of a Free Competitive Press*, The Small Newspaper, Democracy's Grass Roots, Washington: 1947, pp. 48–53. In 1945 daily newspapers paid the Post Offices $9,789,215. The service rendered cost $50,545,991. The subsidy was $40,756,776. To distribute *Time* and *Life* cost the taxpayer about twelve million dollars. The subsidy to the *Saturday Evening Post* roughly amounted to 4.5 million and to the *Reader's Digest* one million.

enlightenment to comic strips. Like professional baseball teams, of which there are usually but one to a city, they deserve no subsidy from the government. They no longer perform any special educational service for the public justifying taxpayer underwriting.

Finally, they are no longer the only means, nor even the major channel for conveying information, objective and nonobjective, to the public. Thousands of public schools, millions of radio and television sets, hundreds of scientific, trade, and service organizations and forums, millions of direct display facilities now exist within easy reach of every voter and householder. The day of the isolated farmer whose only contact with the outside world was his newspaper has long since gone, and with it, the validity of the educational argument for carrying through the mails at taxpayers' expense publications full of advertising and amusing features.

What is clearly needed here—and not too difficult scientifically to devise— is a rate schedule which will not result in a loss in carrying newspapers, which will make special provision for new and small ventures, e.g., those with circulation below 25,000, which will make large publishers pay for what they get without depriving rural or remote readers of access to the publications of giant newspapers, distributors, and manufacturers. The rates should help those who need it most. Compensating profits might be derived from the mail traffic of those publishers whose large circulation demonstrates the measure of their benefit from public policy. Their rates might be proportional to the extra benefit derived. Subsidies might be continued to newspapers and magazines carrying little or no advertising.

2. Another suggestion frequently made is that government help small newspapers to grow bigger and more efficient, especially those with less than 20 or 25,000 circulation. Government now helps small newspapers by making available in addition to the usual statistical and other services, the facilities of Small Business Administration loans and the special tax advantages contained in the Technical Amendments Act of 1958. It has been suggested that the Department of Commerce sponsor voluntary newsprint conservation and allocation programs on behalf of small newspapers upon proof of inability to secure supplies of newsprint. The U.S. Treasury might purchase space in small weeklies and dailies to advertise bonds and notes. The copyright monopoly might be lifted from all news material which is not offered for sale to all buyers at reasonable prices and at a fair profit to the dispenser.

But as the eminent philosopher, Dr. Scott Buchanan observes,[33]

All devices of this kind seem weak before the massive power of money and technology that now is identified with the processes of free speech and assembly.

[33] Scott Buchanan, *The Corporation and the Republic,* p. 27. New York: Fund for the Republic, 1958.

Mass communication at present is more and more massive and less and less communicative, partly because public communications have to pass through the physical facilities of giant unwieldy bodies politic, incorporated newspaper chains and broadcasting systems, whose public functions are not yet sufficiently distinguished from their private business interests. As we understand and practice *freedom of the press*, it should not be supported or controlled by either the private corporation for profit or the public corporation of government, but these are the only two organizations that have the economic power to operate the means. This would seem to be crucial problem in the general field of economic underwriting for the Constitution.

3. A third suggestion is intelligent antitrust activity. Newspapers have to grow large or go under. Actions such as that already mentioned against the Associated Press in 1945 which gain access for the new entrant to news, to syndicated features, to newsprint or other factors have been highly beneficial. In this connection the Department of Justice might well scrutinize UP and INS "asset value" contracts.

Similarly beneficial are actions such as that of *Lorain Journal Co.* v. *U.S.*[34] or *U.S.* v. *The Mansfield Journal Co.*,[35] both of which enjoined the newspaper from refusing to sell advertising space to local merchants who bought advertising time on a nearby radio station. The entire question of permitting newspapers to own or control radio and television stations should be carefully investigated by the Congress. Divorce and divestiture of existing tie-ups might preserve competition between media. Both radio and newspapers are well able each to stand on their own feet, if allowed to grow to optimum size and efficiency.

Equally clear is the public advantage derived from actions against "forced combination" contracts and "exclusive dealing" advertising contracts such as were outlawed by District Courts in *U.S.* v. *Times Picayune*,[36] *U.S.* v. *The Kansas City Star Company*,[37] and *U.S.* v. *Wichita Eagle Publishing Company, Inc.*[38]

----

[34] *Lorain Journal* v. *U.S.* 342 U.S. 143 (1951) *affirming* 92 F. Supp. 794 (N.D. Ohio 1950).

[35] *U.S.* v. *The Mansfield Journal Company*, Civil No. 28253, N.D. Ohio, January 15, 1952.

[36] *U.S.* v. *Times Picayune Publishing Co.*, Civil No. 2797, E.D. La., May 27, 1952.

[37] *U.S.* v. *The Kansas City Star Company*, Civil No. 7989, W.D. Missouri. Final Judgment, November 15, 1957. The Court ordered divestiture of Radio Station WDAF and WDAF-TV, nondiscrimination among advertisers with respect to space, location or arrangement of advertisements, or with respect to credit, special discounts and rebates. Judge Duncan permanently enjoined the Star from refusing, or threatening to refuse to publish, or to continue or renew contracts for publication of, advertisements unless advertiser refrains from using any other medium in metropolitan Kansas City or agrees not to place a larger ad elsewhere or agrees not to place any ad of a size disapproved by the Star.

[38] *U.S.* v. *Wichita Eagle Publishing Company, Inc.*, Civil Action No. W-1876, Final Judgment entered June 29, 1959.

But antitrust action, whether federal or state, should not outlaw local combinations nor mergers and consolidations.[39] These for small newspapers are an economic necessity. Needless to say, in all other respects the Sherman and Clayton Acts should be rigorously enforced, even if the newspapers are small.[40]

Nor does it seem likely that antitrust action can achieve anything more substantial than confusion, if attempts are made to outlaw the system of discriminatory pricing which maximizes profits in each of the segregated markets, general, national, and classified advertising. Nor does it seem wise to try to alter the functioning of presently independent advertising agencies, or to attack the inflexible, administered price structure. Antitrust action should from the beginning have a remedial price and industry behavior pattern in mind. More orders to cease and desist from the clearly oligopolistic practices characteristic of the newspaper industry will neither restore a competitive price structure nor put small newspapers on an equal footing with their larger competitors. Size *is* efficiency.

4. A final suggestion frequently heard with respect to the market structure of the newspaper industry is that the fact be recognized that newspapers are primarily businesses interested in maximizing profits, not torchbearers for truth. They are not educational institutions with recognized trusteeship obligations to the public and commensurate privileges of academic freedom and public support. Newspapers succeed only in the measure they provide their customers, which means primarily their advertisers, what both they and the advertisers want: larger patronage and increased profits from increased sales. They attract subscribers by comic strips, livelier sports write-ups, "human interest" features, and headlines, not by learned, well-balanced editorials on public issues nor by rigorously factual news stories. If the American people want the whole news, they will have to begin by paying for the whole cost of the newspaper instead of only one-third.

Newspapers as businesses can afford to be interested in the truth of opinions or news only insofar as truth attracts buyers of papers and space. The products which newspapers merchandise are news items and opinions;

---

[39] This means that the Kefauver-O'Mahoney Amendment to Sections 7 and 11 of the Clayton Act forbidding merger of competing enterprise by sale of assets should not be construed to apply to newspapers with circulations, say, of 35,000 or less.

[40] An interesting case in point is that of *U.S.* v. *Harte-Hanks Newspapers, Inc., et al.*, N.D. Texas, Dallas Division, Criminal No. 15393, filed September 10, 1958. The indictment charges that the defendants used one of its papers, the *Banner* with a circulation of roughly 4,000 to force the only other paper in Greeneville, Texas, the *Herald* with a circulation of roughly 5,000, to sell out by such tactics as intentionally operating the *Banner* at a loss, utilizing revenues from other Harte-Hanks newspapers to finance such losses, also by lower subscription and advertising rates and home mail delivery of the *Banner,* distribution of the *Banner* free of charge, curtailing credit resources available to the *Herald,* etc.

like all products, carefully selected and packaged to sell. It is not that advertisers control publishers or vice versa. They do not have to. Both belong to the same ideological fraternity. They already see eye to eye on economic, social, and political issues. Both dislike, deemphasize, and suppress the same types of views and news. Neither needs to be persuaded, cajoled, or compelled.

Unquestionably most newspapers, when it is to their advantage or falls in line with their own goals, make sincere attempts to live up to the ideals set forth by the Commission on Freedom of the Press, namely, to give a truthful, comprehensive, and intelligent account of the day's events in a context which gives them accurate meaning; to provide a forum for the exchange of comment and criticism; to convey accurate pictures of all the groups—political, racial, and economic, that are found in our society, and to present and clarify public goals and values. But if they fail to make a profit, all except those having a multi-millionaire for an "angel" will ultimately go out of business. To be a "responsible," "ideal," fair and impartial newspaper, it must first survive. In the words of Palmer Hoyt, editor of the *Denver Post* "in the remaining competitive towns, it is an obligation, it is part of the responsibility of the press for newspapers to stay in business. I firmly believe that." [41]

In short, modern technological and economic developments place squarely upon society the task of devising some new mechanism for achieving the services that used to be rendered by a free, competitive, responsible press. Outstanding suggestions have already been debated on many forums. The thirteen recommendations made by the Commission on Freedom of the Press deserve most careful study. [42] The daily newspaper industry, primarily as a result of the communications revolution and its basic price and market structure seems hardly capable of being restructured to provide either a free, a workably competitive, or a publicly accountable, responsible press.

[41] Page 9, "The Public and the People," No. 14 of *The Press and the People*, A Series of Television Programs produced by WGBH-TV, Mass., published by The Fund for the Republic, New York, 1959.

[42] Those recommendations in essence are, that government facilitate new ventures; foster the development of new techniques; maintain competition between the media and between large, efficient units; employ media of its own when private agencies are unable or unwilling to supply information about this country to foreign countries (Voice of America); and encourage newspapers to accept voluntarily the responsibilities of common carriers of information and discussion. They recommend that newspapers engage in vigorous mutual criticism, increase the competence, independence, and effectiveness of their staff; boldly pioneer new ventures; and adopt a comprehensive program of responsible self-government. The public, according to the commission, should encourage nonprofit institutions to undertake to supply the variety, quantity, and quality of press services required by world tensions; create academic professional centers of advanced study, research and publication; and establish a new and independent agency to appraise and report annually upon the performance of the press.

SUGGESTED READINGS

Books and Pamphlets

N. W. Ayer and Sons, *American Newspaper Annual and Directory* (Philadelphia: N. W. Ayer and Sons, Annual).

Zachariah Chafee, *Government and Mass Communications* (Chicago: The University of Chicago Press, 1947).

The Commission on Freedom of the Press, *A Free and Responsible Press* (Chicago: The University of Chicago Press, 1947).

Robert E. Cushman, *Keep Our Press Free*, Public Affairs Pamphlet No. 123 (New York: 1946).

Editor and Publisher, *International Year Book*, Annual.

Morris L. Ernst, *The First Freedom* (New York: Macmillan, 1946).

The Fund for the Republic, *The Press and the People*, a Series of Television Programs produced by WGBH-TV, Mass. (New York, 1958–59).

Max A. Geller, *Advertising at the Cross Roads* (New York: Ronald, 1952).

Alfred McClung Lee, *The Daily Newspaper in America* (New York: Macmillan, 1937).

Royal Henderson Ray, *Concentration of Ownership and Control in the American Daily Newspaper Industry*, Unpublished Doctoral Dissertation, Columbia University, pp. xx, 460, 1950.

Arthur Edward Rowse, *Slanted News* (Boston: Beacon, 1957).

George Seldes, *Lords of the Press* (New York: Julian Messner, 1946), pp. viii, 408.

Leon Svirsky, ed., *Your Newspaper: Blueprint for a Better Press*, by nine Nieman Fellows at Harvard University, 1945–46 (New York: The Macmillan Company, 1947).

Government Publications

Committee of the Judiciary, Subcommittee on Study of Monopoly Power, House of Representatives, Eighty-first Congress, 2nd Session, *Hearings*, Pt. 6-A and Pt. 6-B (Washington, 1950).

Department of Commerce, Bureau of the Census, *Census of Manufactures, 1947, Newspapers, Periodicals, Books and Miscellaneous Publishing, MC 27A* (Washington, 1949).

Senate Committee to Study the Problems of Small Business, Eightieth Cong., 1st Sess., *Survival of a Free Competitive Press: The Small Newspaper, Democracy's Grass Roots*, Senate Committee Print No. 17 (Washington, 1947).

Senate Select Committee on Small Business, Eighty-second Congress, 2nd Session, *Newsprint for Tomorrow*, Senate Report No. 1404 (Washington, 1952).

Supreme Court of the United States, *The Associated Press et al. versus U.S.* 52 Fed. Supp. 366, 1943; 57, 58 and 59 S. Ct., 326, 1944.

U.S. versus The Kansas City Star Company, Roy A. Roberts, and Emil A. Sees. U.S. District Court, Western District of Missouri, Criminal Action No. 18444 and Civil No. 7989, January 6, 1953.

U.S. versus *The Mansfield Journal Co. et al.,* U.S. District Court, Northern District of Ohio, Civil No. 28253, 1952.

U.S. versus *Western Newspaper Union et al.,* U.S. District Court, Southern District of New York, Civil No. 87–60, August 18, 1953.

Journal and Magazine Articles

Warren K. Agee, "Cross-Channel Ownership of Communication Media," *Journalism Quarterly,* **26:** 410, December 1949.

Max Ascoli, *et al.,* "What's Wrong with the Press," *The Reporter,* Vol. 7, No. 11, November 25, 1952, pp. 4–16.

George L. Bird, "Newspaper Monopoly and Political Independence," *Journalism Quarterly,* **17:** 207, September 1940.

Charles R. Butler, "Recent Economic Trends in Newspaper Publishing," *Journalism Quarterly,* **9:** 66, March 1932.

Mitchell V. Charnley, "Preliminary Notes on a Study of Newspaper Accuracy," *Journalism Quarterly,* **13:** 394, 1936.

Comment, "Local Monopoly in the Daily Newspaper Industry," *The Yale Law Journal,* Vol. 61, No. 6, pp. 948–1009.

W. H. Davenport, "Trends and Cycles in Daily Newspaper Circulation," *Journalism Quarterly,* **27:** 282, 1950.

Andrew Jacobs, "Analysis of Columns and Broadcasts of Leading Commentators," *Congressional Record,* August 21, 1950, pp. A6275–A6287.

Phil Kerby and Godfrey Lehman, "The Partisan Press," *Frontier,* Vol. 4, No. 3, January 1953, pp. 5–18.

Paul Neuroth, "One-Publisher Committees: Factors Influencing Trend," *Journalism Quarterly,* **21:** 230, September 1944.

Raymond B. Nixon, "Concentration and Absenteeism in Daily Newspaper Ownership," *Journalism Quarterly,* **22:** 97, June 1945.

Royal Henderson Ray, "Economic Forces as Factors in Daily Newspaper Concentration," *Journalism Quarterly,* **29:** 31, January 1952.

Chapter 15

WALTER ADAMS

Public Policy in a Free Enterprise Economy

When Congress passed the Sherman Act of 1890 it created what was then
—and what has remained to this day—a uniquely American institution.
Heralded as a magna carta of economic freedom, the Sherman Act sought to
preserve competitive free enterprise by imposing legal prohibitions on
monopoly and restraint of trade. The objective of the Act, according to
Judge Learned Hand, was not to condone *good* trusts or condemn *bad* trusts,
but to forbid *all* trusts. Its basic philosophy and principal purpose was "to
perpetuate and preserve, for its own sake and in spite of possible cost, an
organization of industry in small units which can effectively compete with
each other." [1]

---

[1] *U.S.* v. *Aluminum Company of America*, 148 F.2d 416 (C.C.A. 2d, 1945). In
elaborating on the goals of the Sherman Act, Judge Hand stated: "Many people believe
that possession of unchallenged economic power deadens initiative, discourages thrift
and depresses energy; that immunity from competition is a narcotic, and rivalry is a
stimulant, to industrial progress; that the spur of constant stress is necessary to counteract an inevitable disposition to let well enough alone. Such people believe that competitors, versed in the craft as no consumer can be, will be quick to detect opportunities
for saving and new shifts in production, and be eager to profit by them. . . . True, it
might have been thought adequate to condemn only those monopolies which could not
show that they had exercised the highest possible ingenuity, had adopted every possible
economy, had anticipated every conceivable improvement, stimulated every possible demand. . . . Be that as it may, that was not the way that Congress chose; it did not
condone 'good' trusts and condemn 'bad' ones; it forbade all. Moreover, in so doing
it was not necessarily actuated by economic motives alone. It is possible, because of its
indirect social or moral effect, to prefer a system of small producers, each dependent
for his success upon his own skill and character, to one in which the great mass of those
engaged must accept the direction of a few. These considerations, which we have suggested only as possible purposes of the Act, we think the decisions prove to have been
in fact its purposes." (*Ibid.*)

The Antimonopoly Laws

Specifically, the Sherman Act outlawed two major types of interference with free enterprise, viz. collusion and monopolization. Section 1 of the Act, dealing with collusion, stated: "Every contract, combination . . . or conspiracy, in restraint of trade or commerce among the several States, or with foreign nations, is hereby declared illegal." As interpreted by the courts, this made it unlawful for businessmen to engage in such collusive action as agreements to fix prices; agreements to restrict output or productive capacity; agreements to divide markets or allocate customers; agreements to exclude competitors by systematic resort to oppressive tactics and discriminatory policies—in short, any joint action by competitors to influence the market. Thus Section 1 was, in a sense, a response to Adam Smith's warning that "people of the same trade seldom meet together even for merriment and diversion, but the conversation ends in a conspiracy against the public, or in some contrivance to raise prices." [2]

Section 2 of the Sherman Act, dealing with monopolization, provided: "Every person who shall monopolize or attempt to monopolize, or combine or conspire with any other person or persons to monopolize any part of the trade or commerce among the several States, or with foreign nations, shall be deemed guilty of a misdemeanor, and . . . punished." This meant that businessmen were deprived of an important freedom, the freedom to monopolize. Section 2 made it unlawful for anyone to obtain a stranglehold on the market either by forcing rivals out of business or by absorbing them. It forbade a single firm (or a group of firms acting jointly) to gain a substantially exclusive domination of an industry or a market area. Positively stated, Section 2 attempted to encourage an industry structure in which

---

[2] *The Wealth of Nations,* Book 1, Chapter 10. Here it should be pointed out that businessmen engage in trade restraints and organize monopolies not because of any vicious and anti-social motives, but rather because of a desire to increase personal profits. As George Comer, former chief economist of the Antitrust Division, once observed, monopolies are formed "not because business-men are criminals, but because the reports from the bookkeeping department indicate, in the short run at least, that monopoly and restraints of trade will pay if you can get away with it. It will pay a large corporation to agree with its competitors on price fixing. It pays to operate a basing-point or zone-price system. If patent pools can be organized, especially with hundreds or thousands of patents covering a whole industry, the profits will be enormous. If an international cartel can be formed which really works, the very peak of stabilization and rationalism is reached. If the management of all the large units in an industry can get together with the labor unions in the industry, a number of birds can be killed with one stone. And finally, if the government can be persuaded to legalize the restrictive practices, the theory of 'enlightened competition' is complete." ("The Outlook for Effective Competition," *American Economic Review, Papers and Proceedings,* May 1946, pp. 154–55.)

there are enough independent competitors to assure bona fide and effective market rivalry.

As is obvious from even a cursory examination of the Sherman Act, its provisions were general, perhaps even vague, and essentially negative. Directed primarily against *existing* monopolies and *existing* trade restraints, the Sherman Act could not cope with specific practices which were, and could be, used to effectuate the unlawful results. Armed with the power to dissolve existing monopolies, the enforcement authorities could not, under the Sherman Act, attack the *growth* of monopoly. They could not nip it in the bud. For this reason Congress passed, in 1914, supplementary legislation "to arrest the creation of trusts, conspiracies and monopolies *in their incipiency and before consummation.*" [3] In the Federal Trade Commission Act of 1914, Congress set up an independent regulatory commission to police the industrial field against "all unfair methods of competition." In the Clayton Act of the same year Congress singled out four specific practices which past experience had shown to be favorite weapons of the would-be monopolist, viz. 1) price discrimination, i.e. local price cutting and cut-throat competition; 2) tying contracts and exclusive dealer arrangements; 3) the acquisition of stock in competing companies; and 4) the formation of interlocking directorates between competing corporations. These practices were to be unlawful whenever their effect was to substantially lessen competition or to create tendencies toward monopoly. Thus price discrimination, for example, was not made illegal per se; it was to be illegal only if used as a systematic device for destroying competition—in a manner typical of the old Standard Oil and American Tobacco trusts.[4] The emphasis throughout was to be on prevention rather than cure. The hope was that—given the

[3] Senate Report No. 695, 63d Congress, 2d Session, 1914, p. 1 (italics supplied).

[4] A Congressional Committee explained the background of the price discrimination provision of the Clayton Act as follows: "In the past it has been a most common practice of great and powerful combinations engaged in commerce—notably the Standard Oil Co., and the American Tobacco Co., and others of less notoriety, but of great influence—to lower prices of their commodities, oftentimes below the cost of production in certain communities and sections where they had competition, with the intent to destroy and make unprofitable the business of their competitors, and with the ultimate purpose in view of thereby acquiring a monopoly in the particular locality or section in which the discriminating price is made.

"Every concern that engages in this evil practice must of necessity recoup its losses in the particular communities or sections where their commodities are sold below cost or without a fair profit by raising the price of this same class of commodities above their fair market value in other sections or communities.

"Such a system or practice is so manifestly unfair and unjust, not only to competitors who are directly injured thereby but to the general public, that your committee is strongly of the opinion that the present antitrust laws ought to be supplemented by making this particular form of discrimination a specific offense under the law when practiced by those engaged in commerce." (House Report No. 627, 63d Congress, 2d Session, 1914, pp. 8–9.)

provisions of the 1914 laws to supplement the provisions of the Sherman Act —the antitrust authorities could effectively eliminate the economic evils against which the antitrust laws were directed.

The Charges Against Monopoly

What those evils were has never been clearly stated, and perhaps never been clearly conceived, by the sponsors of antitrust legislation. In general, however, the objections to monopoly and trade restraints—found in literally tons of antitrust literature—can be summarized as follows: [5]

(1) *Monopoly affords the consumer little protection against exorbitant prices.* As Adam Smith put it, "the price of monopoly is, upon every occasion, the highest which can be got. The natural price, or the price of free competition, on the contrary is the lowest which can be taken, not upon every occasion indeed, but for any considerable time taken together. The one is upon every occasion the highest which can be squeezed out of the buyers, of which, it is supposed, they will consent to give; the other is the lowest which the sellers can commonly afford to take, and at the same time continue their business." [6] The consumer is, under these conditions, open prey to extortion and exploitation—protected only by such tenuous self-restraint as the monopolist may choose to exercise because of benevolence, irrationality, concern over government reprisals, or fear of potential competition.

The monopolist can generally charge all the traffic will bear, simply because the consumer has no alternative sources of supply. The consumer is forced to pay the monopolist's price, turn to a less desirable substitute, or go without. His freedom is impaired, because his range of choice is artificially limited.

An example, while admittedly extreme, serves to illustrate this point. It involves tungsten carbide, a hard-metal composition of considerable importance in such industrial uses as cutting tools, dies, etc. In 1927, tungsten carbide sold in the United States at $50 per pound; but after a world monopoly was established by the General Electric Company and Friedrich Krupp A.G. of Germany, under which G.E. was granted the right to set prices in the American market, the price promptly rose to a maximum of $453 per pound. During most of the 1930's the price fluctuated between $225 and $453 per pound, and not until 1942—when an indictment was

[5] For a good summary of the charges against monopoly as well as the claims made in support of monopoly, see C. Wilcox, *Competition and Monopoly in the American Economy*, TNEC Monograph No. 21, 1941, pp. 15–18.

[6] Smith, *op.cit.*, Book I, Chapter VII.

FIGURE 1

Free Competition versus Price Fixing

GRAPHIC ASSOCIATES FOR PUBLIC AFFAIRS COMMITTEE, INC.

Source: Thurman W. Arnold, *Cartels or Free Enterprise?* Public Affairs Pamphlet No. 103, 1945; reproduced by courtesy of Public Affairs Committee, Inc.

issued under the antitrust laws—did the price come down. Thereafter, it fluctuated between $27 and $45 per pound.[7]

(2) *Monopoly causes a restriction of economic opportunity and a misallocation of productive resources.* Under free competition, it is the consumer who—through his dollar votes in the market place—decides how society's land, labor and capital are to be used. Consumer tastes generally determine whether more cotton and less wool, more cigarettes and less pipe tobacco, more aluminum and less steel shall be produced. Under free competition

[7] See C. D. Edwards, *Economic and Political Aspects of International Cartels,* Monograph No. 1, Senate Committee on Military Affairs, 78th Congress, 2d Session, 1946, pp. 12–13.

the consumer is in this strategic position because businessmen must, if they want to make profits, do as the consumer demands. Since a businessman, under competition, is free to enter any field and to produce any type and quantity of goods he desires, the tendency will be for him to do those things which the consuming public (in its wisdom or ignorance) deems most valuable. In short, under a truly competitive system, the businessman can improve himself only by serving others. He can earn profits only by obeying the wishes of the community as expressed in the market.

Under monopoly, by contrast, the individual businessman finds his freedom of enterprise limited. He cannot do as he pleases, because the monopolist has the power of excluding newcomers or stipulating the terms under which newcomers are permitted to survive in an industry. The monopolist can interfere with a consumer-oriented allocation of resources. He, instead of the market, can determine the type and quantity of goods that shall be produced. He, and not the forces of supply and demand, can decree who shall produce what, for whom, and at what price. In the absence of competition, it is the monopolist who decides what *other* businessmen shall be allowed to do and what benefits the consuming public shall be allowed to receive.

A good illustration of this is the Hartford-Empire Company which once was an undisputed monopolist in the glass bottle industry. Through its patent control over glass bottling machinery, Hartford-Empire held life-and-death power both over the producers already in the industry and those attempting to enter it. As one observer described the situation,[8] Hartford had become benevolent despot to the glass container. Only by its leave could a firm come into the industry; the ticket of admission was to be had only upon its terms; and from its studied decision there was no appeal. The candidate had to subscribe to Hartford's articles of faith; he could not be a price-cutter or a trouble-maker. He could not venture beyond his assigned bailiwick or undermine the market of his partners in the conspiracy. Each concern had to accept the restrictions and limitations imposed by Hartford. Thus the Buck Glass Company was authorized to manufacture wine bottles for sacramental purposes only. The Sayre Glass Works were restricted to producing "such bottles, jugs, and demijohns as are used for vinegar, ciders, sirups, bleaching fluids, hair tonics, barber supplies and fluid extracts." Knox Glass Bottle Company was allowed to make only amber colored ginger ale bottles. Mary Card Glass Company could not make products weighing more than 82 ounces. Baurens Glass Works Inc. was licensed to

[8] See W. H. Hamilton, *Patents and Free Enterprise*, TNEC Monograph No. 31, 1941, pp. 109–15.

provide bottles for castor oil and turpentine, but none to exceed 4 ounces in capacity. Here indeed was a shackling of free enterprise and a usurpation of the market—a private government more powerful than that of many states. Here indeed was a tight little island, where the law of the monopolist was supreme and unchallenged. Only through antitrust prosecution were the channels of trade reopened, and the Hartford dictatorship dissipated.[9]

(3) *Monopoly often restrains technological advances and thus impedes economic progress.* As Clair Wilcox points out, "the monopolist may engage in research and invent new materials, methods, and machines, but he will be reluctant to make use of these inventions if they would compel him to scrap existing equipment or if he believes that their ultimate profitability is in doubt. He may introduce innovations and cut costs, but instead of moving goods by price reduction he is prone to spend large sums on alternative methods of promoting sales; his refusal to cut prices deprives the community of any gain. The monopolist may voluntarily improve the quality of his product and reduce its price, but no threat of competition compels him to do so." [10]

Our experience with the hydrogenation and synthetic rubber processes is a case in point. This, one of the less illustrious chapters in our industrial history, dates back to 1926 when I.G. Farben of Germany developed the hydrogenation process for making oil out of coal—a development which obviously threatened the entrenched position of the major international oil companies. Soon after this process was patented, Standard Oil Company of New Jersey concluded an agreement with I.G. Farben, under which Farben promised to stay out of the world's oil business (except inside Germany) and Standard agreed to stay out of the world's chemical business. "By this agreement, control of the hydrogenation process for making oil outside Germany was transferred to the Standard Oil Co. in order that Standard's petroleum investment might be fully protected. In the United States, Standard licensed only the large oil companies which had no interest in exploiting hydrogenation. Outside the United States, Standard . . . proceeded to limit use of the process so far as the threat of competing processes and governmental interest [of foreign countries] permitted." [11] As a result this revolutionary process was almost completely suppressed except in Germany where it became an effective tool for promoting the military ambitions of the Nazi government.

[9] See *U.S. v. Hartford-Empire Co. et al.,* 323 U.S. 386 (1945).
[10] Wilcox, *op.cit.,* pp. 16–17.
[11] Edwards, *op.cit.,* p. 36. For a popular discussion of the I.G.-Standard marriage, see also G. W. Stocking and M. W Watkins, *Cartels in Action,* New York: Twentieth Century Fund, 1946, Chapter 11, especially pp. 491–505.

The development of synthetic rubber production in the United States was similarly retarded by the I.G.-Standard marriage of 1928. Since Buna rubber, under the agreement of 1928, was considered a chemical process, it came under the exclusive control of I.G. Farben—both in- and outside Germany. Farben, however, was not interested in promoting the manufacture of synthetic rubber anywhere except in Germany, and proceeded therefore— both for commercial (i.e. monopolistic) and nationalistic reasons—to forestall its development in the United States. In this purpose, Farben had at least the tacit support of its American partner. As a result, the outbreak of World War II found the United States without production experience or know-how in the vital synthetic rubber field. In fact, when the Goodrich and Goodyear tire companies attempted to embark on synthetic rubber production, the former was sued for patent infringement and the latter formally threatened with such a suit by Standard Oil Company (acting under the authority of the Farben patents). This happened in November, 1941, one month before Pearl Harbor. Not until after our formal entry into World War II was the Farben-Standard alliance broken under the impact of antitrust prosecution, and the production of vital synthetic rubber started in the United States. Here, as in the case of hydrogenation, monopolistic control over technology had serious implications not only for the nation's economic progress but also its military security.[12]

(4) *Monopoly contributes to the inequality in the distribution of income, because the monopolist is not compelled to pass on to consumers, suppliers, or laborers (in the absence of strong unions) the gains of improved technology.* Moreover, monopoly profits are not widely distributed, since the ownership of all corporate stock (in competitive as well as monopolistic companies) is highly concentrated, and since corporate dividends go mainly to the upper income groups. In 1929, according to one source, over 83 per cent of all dividends paid to individuals went to the top 3.28 per cent of the population filing income tax returns; 78 per cent of such dividends went to the top three-tenths of one per cent.[13] According to another source, 64.7 per cent of all dividends paid to individuals between 1919 and 1938 went to the top one per cent of the nation's income recipients.[14] While this distribution is gradually becoming less unequal over time, it is still true that

---

[12] See W. Berge, *Cartels: Challenge to a Free World*, Washington: Public Affairs Press, 1944, pp. 210–14; G. W. Stocking and M. W. Watkins, *Cartels or Competition*, New York: Twentieth Century Fund, 1948, pp. 114–17; J. Borkin and C. A. Welsh, *Germany's Master Plan*, New York: Duell, Sloan & Pearce, 1943. For a contrary view, see F. A. Howard, *Buna Rubber*, New York: D. Van Nostrand Co., 1947.

[13] Wilcox, *op.cit.*, p. 17.

[14] S. Kuznets, *Shares of Upper Income Groups in Income and Saving*, New York: National Bureau of Economic Research, 1950, pp. 9 and 34 ff.

the great bulk of all dividend payments goes to a relatively small percentage of the total population.

Since there is little reason to suppose that the dividends derived from "monopolistic" enterprises are any more widely distributed than the dividends of *all* corporations taken together, monopoly thus makes for economic inequality. As Wilcox puts it, "the laborers whose incomes may be limited by the monopolist's failure to pay wages equal to their productivity are numerous. The producers of materials whose incomes are depressed by the low prices that the monopolist sometimes pays may also be numerous. The consumers whose real incomes are reduced by the high prices that the monopolist charges are likewise numerous. The stockholders who share the unnecessarily high profits that the monopolist thus obtains are few in number. A more nearly perfect mechanism for making the poor poorer and the rich richer could scarcely be devised." [15]

(5) *Monopoly tends to impede the effectiveness of general stabilization measures and to distort their structural impact on the economy.* Monopolistic and oligopolistic firms, as Galbraith suggests, may insulate themselves against credit restrictions designed to curb investment and check inflation. They may do so by raising prices to offset higher interest costs, by raising prices to finance investment out of increased profits, or by resorting to the capital market rather than to banks for their supply of loanable funds. Competitive firms, by contrast, cannot raise prices to compensate for higher interest charges. They cannot raise prices to finance investment out of higher profits. They cannot readily turn to the capital market for funds. Their lack of market control makes them the weakest borrowers and poorest credit risks, and they must therefore bear the brunt of any "tight money" policy. In short, monopolistic and oligopolistic firms not only can undermine the effectiveness of monetary control in their sector of the economy, but also shift the burden of credit restrictions to the competitive sector and thus stifle its growth. The implications for concentration need not be belabored. [16]

---

[15] Wilcox, *op.cit.*, pp. 17–18. It is because of this accentuation of inequality in the distribution of income by monopoly that some economists consider monopoly to be one of the causal factors in the occurrence of depressions. The scientific evidence on this point, however, is rather meager.

[16] "Market Structure and Stabilization Policy," *The Review of Economics and Statistics,* May 1957, pp. 131, 133. For further discussion of "sellers' inflation," "administered price inflation," and "inflation in the midst of recession"—in short, the relation between market structure and general price stability—see also *Hearings before the Subcommittee on Antitrust and Monopoly, Senate Judiciary Committee, Administered Prices,* Part I (1957), and Parts 9 and 10 (1959); and *The Relationship of Prices to Economic Stability and Growth, Compendium of Papers submitted by Panelists appearing before the Joint Economic Committee,* 85th Cong., 2d Sess., 1958.

(6) *Monopoly threatens not only the existence of a free economy, but also the survival chances of free political institutions.* Enterprise which is not competitive cannot for long remain free, and a community which refuses to accept the discipline of competition inevitably exposes itself to the discipline of absolute authority. As Mutual Security Administrator Harold Stassen once observed, "world economic history has shown that nationalization and socialization have come when there has been complete consolidation and combination of industry, not when enterprise is manifold and small in its units. . . . We must not permit major political power to be added to the other great powers that are accumulated by big business units. Excessive concentration of power is a threat to the individual freedoms and liberties of men, whether that excessive power is in the hands of government or of capital or of labor." [17] The enemy of democracy is monopoly in all its forms, and political liberty can survive only within an effective competitive system. If concentrated power is tolerated, giant pressure groups will ultimately gain control of the government or the government will institute direct regulation of organized pressure groups. In either event, free enterprise will then have to make way for collectivism, and democracy will be superseded by some form of authoritarianism.

This objection to monopoly, this fear of concentrated economic power, is deeply rooted in American traditions—the tradition of federalism, the separation of church and state, the tripartite organization of our governmental machinery. It is the expression of a socio-political philosophy which believes in the decentralization of power, a broad base for the class structure of society, and the economic freedom and opportunity for new men, new ideas, and new organizations to spearhead the forces of progress. It stands in stark contrast to the European varieties of free enterprise which involve merely curbs on governmental powers without similar checks on excessive private power.[18]

[17] Address reprinted on *Congressional Record*, February 12, 1947, p. A545. See also H. C. Simons, *Economic Policy for a Free Society*, Chicago: University of Chicago Press, 1948; F. A. Hayek, *The Road to Serfdom*, Chicago: University of Chicago Press, 1945; R. A. Brady, *Business as a System of Power*, New York: Columbia University Press, 1943; G. W. Stocking, "Saving Free Enterprise from Its Friends," *Southern Economic Journal*, April 1953, pp. 431–44. Also relevant in this connection are the repeated warnings by the Federal Trade Commission to the effect that "the capitalist system of free initiative is not immortal, but is capable of dying and dragging down with it the system of democratic government. Monopoly constitutes the death of capitalism and the genesis of authoritarian government." (*The Basing Point Problem*, TNEC Monograph No. 42, 1941, p. 9.)

[18] This point was well made by Senator Cummins in 1914, when he pressed for adoption of the Federal Trade Commission Act and the Clayton Act: "We have adopted in this country the policy of competition. We are trying to preserve competition as a living, real force in our industrial life; that is to say, we are endeavoring to maintain among our

By way of illustrating this charge against monopoly some students contend that the rise of Hitler in Germany was facilitated by the pervasive cartelization of the German economy—by the absence of competitive freedom in German business and the lack of democratic freedom in German government. Similarly, they point out that unregulated private monopoly was the breeding ground for Italian fascism and Japanese totalitarianism. Whether or not these correlations are scientifically valid is difficult to determine. Certainly, the seriousness of a danger is not easy to evaluate. "Who can say whether any particular warning is due to overcautiousness, timidity or even superstition or, on the other hand, to prudence and foresight? . . . It is, of course, possible that 'monopoly' is merely a bugbear frightening the believers in free enterprise and free society; but it is equally possible that we have underestimated the danger and have allowed the situation to deteriorate to such a degree that only a very radical effort can still save our social and political system." [19]

The Extent of Concentration

Despite a recognition of monopolistic evils; despite the antitrust laws which were enacted to combat them, we find that American industry today is highly concentrated. No monistic explanation of this concentration pattern

business people that honorable rivalry which will prevent one from exacting undue profits from those who may deal with him. . . . We are practically alone, however, in this policy. . . . England long ago became indifferent to it; and while that great country has not specifically adjusted her laws so as to permit monopoly they are so administered as to practically eliminate competition when the trade affected so desires. France has pursued a like course.

"Austria, Italy, Spain, Norway, Sweden, as well as Belgium, have all pursued the course of permitting combinations and relations which practically annihilate competition, and Germany, our most formidable rival, so far as commerce is concerned, not only authorizes by her law the formation of monopolies, the creation of combinations which restrain trade and which destroy competition, but oftentimes compels her people to enter into combinations which are in effect monopolies. We are, therefore, pursuing a course which rather distinguishes us from the remainder of the commercial world.

"I pause here to say, and I say it emphatically and earnestly, that I believe in our course; I believe in the preservation of competition, I believe in the maintenance of the rule that opens the channels of trade fairly and fully to all comers. I believe it because it seems to me obvious that any other course must inevitably lead us into complete State socialism. The only monopoly which civilized mankind will ever permanently endure is the monopoly of all the people represented in the Government itself." (*Congressional Record*, June 30, 1914, p. 11379.) Since World War II, the contrast between the American and European approaches to the monopoly problem has been considerably reduced. Several nations in Western Europe have enacted restrictive practices legislation which, though not as far-reaching as the American prototype, nevertheless reflects a growing awareness of the problem. See European Productivity Agency, *Guide to Legislation on Restrictive Business Practices*, 2 vols., Paris, 1960.

[19] F. Machlup, *The Political Economy of Monopoly*, Baltimore: Johns Hopkins Press, 1952, pp. 77–78.

is possible, for many forces coalesced to bring it about. Suffice it to say, that the dominance of giant firms in many industries is primarily attributable to (1) modern technology which required, in the interests of efficiency, substantial capital investments in large-scale production, distribution, and research facilities; (2) the structure of the capital market which made funds more easily and cheaply available to large and established firms; (3) the efforts of financial interests to collect handsome promoter's fees and monopoly profits by organizing giant consolidations; and (4) the failure of government to promote competition vigorously and imaginatively,[20] i.e., the failure, by and large, to make antitrust more than a policeman looking the other way.

It is noteworthy that economists are by no means agreed on the direction or interpretation of the "concentration movement." Some believe that since 1890 concentration has, on the whole, increased. Others vigorously deny this.[21] All are agreed, however, that the present *degree* of concentration—regardless of its implications—is substantial. The T.N.E.C., for example, found that as of 1937 one-third of the total value of all manufactured goods was produced under conditions where the leading four producers of each individual product turned out from 75 to 100 per cent of the value of the product. Similarly, the Federal Trade Commission found that, as of 1947, the 113 largest manufacturing corporations (with assets in excess of $100,000,-000 each) owned approximately 46 per cent of all net capital assets (both corporate and noncorporate) engaged in manufacturing.[22] In the nonagricultural sector, as a whole, firms which constitute only one per cent of the business population account for 60 per cent of total business employment, while "small business" which comprises 99 per cent of the busi-

---

[20] Many students of the concentration movement, including the distinguished historian Charles A. Beard, feel that monopoly is to a considerable extent the creature of government action and inaction. Professor Beard explained his position to a Congressional Committee as follows: "I should like to emphasize the fact that our state and national governments have a responsibility for the corporate abuses and economic distress in which we now flounder. It is a matter of common knowledge that corporations are not natural persons. They are artificial persons. They are the creatures of government. Only with the sanction of government can they perform any acts, good or bad. The corporate abuses which have occurred, the concentration of wealth which has come about under their operations, all can be laid directly and immediately at the door of government. The states of the American Union and the Congress of the United States, by their actions and their inaction, have made possible the situation and the calamities in which we now find ourselves." (*Hearings before a Subcommittee on the Judiciary*, 75th Congress, 1st Session, 1937, Part I, p. 72.) See also W. Adams and H. M. Gray, *Monopoly in America: The Government as Promoter*, New York: The Macmillan Company, 1955.

[21] For conflicting views on the extent of concentration in the American economy, see M. A. Adelman, "The Measurement of Industrial Concentration," *Review of Economics and Statistics*, November 1951; and J. M. Blair, "The Measurement of Industrial Concentration: A Reply," *Review of Economics and Statistics*, November 1952.

[22] Federal Trade Commission, *The Concentration of Productive Facilities, 1947*, p. 14.

ness population accounts for only 40 per cent of total business employment.[23]

More significant than these measures of aggregate concentration is the extent of concentration in particular industries. Here the pattern shows the richest variation, ranging from "extremely high" to "relatively low" concentration. Among the "extremely concentrated" industries, where the four largest producers account for 75 per cent or more of total industry shipments, are: primary aluminum (100 per cent); electric light bulbs (93 per cent); flat glass (90 per cent); cereal breakfast foods (88 per cent); chewing gum (86 per cent); cigarettes (82 per cent); sewing machines (81 per cent); tires and inner tubes (79 per cent); and motor vehicles and parts (75 per cent).

"Highly concentrated" industries, where the four largest producers account for 50 to 74 per cent of total industry shipments, include: tractors (73 per cent); biscuits and crackers (71 per cent); beet sugar (66 per cent); distilled liquor (64 per cent); photographic equipment (63 per cent); vacuum cleaners (62 per cent); primary zinc (56 per cent); concentrated milk (55 per cent); scientific instruments (51 per cent); and electrical appliances (50 per cent).

"Moderately concentrated" industries, where the four largest producers account for 25 to 49 per cent of total industry shipments, include: wool carpets and rugs (49 per cent); aircraft (47 per cent); cigars (44 per cent); men's and boys' underwear (43 per cent); frozen fruits and vegetables (39 per cent); paper bags (32 per cent); periodicals (29 per cent); beer and ale (27 per cent); and toilet preparations (25 per cent).

Industries with "relatively low" concentration, where the four largest producers account for less than 25 per cent of total industry shipments, are represented by the following: radios and related products (24 per cent); metalworking machinery (22 per cent); sporting and athletic goods (21 per cent); newspapers (18 per cent); costume jewelry (14 per cent); concrete products (9 per cent); and women's suits, coats, and skirts (3 per cent).[24]

Certain caveats are recommended to guard against unwarranted conclusions based on the above figures. *First,* it is difficult to define an "industry," and high concentration in one industry may not be very significant if its product competes actively with that of another industry (i.e. where the cross-elasticity of demand is high). For example, concentration in the field of textile fibers taken as a whole may, for public policy purposes, be more

---

[23] G. Rosenbluth, "The Trend in Concentration and Its Implications for Small Business," *Law and Contemporary Problems,* Winter 1959, pp. 194–95.

[24] Subcommittee on Antitrust and Monopoly, Senate Judiciary Committee, *Concentration in American Industry,* 85th Cong., 1st Sess., 1957, table 44. All the statistics cited are for the year 1954.

relevant than concentration in silk, wool, cotton, rayon, nylon, orlon, acrilan, dynel, dacron, etc. taken separately. *Second,* some giant firms are listed as members of one industry, although their capital assets are spread over a number of other industries. General Motors, for example, is listed as an automobile producer, although some of its capital investment lies in such fields as diesel engines, electric appliances, refrigerators, etc.—a fact which results in partial overstatement of the degree of concentration in the automobile industry. *Third,* concentration must not be confused with monopoly. The mere fact that an industry is highly concentrated is not positive proof that the industry is monopolized or that its firms are in active collusion. Under extreme circumstances, it is even conceivable that as few as two companies are enough to provide effective competition in an industry. As Dexter Keezer, vice-president of the McGraw-Hill Company, points out: "If the heads of the two surviving firms were the hard-driving, fiercely independent type of businessman who has played such a large part in the industrial development of the U.S.A., two of them would be enough to create a ruggedly competitive situation. But," Dr. Keezer adds, "if the two were of the genteel, clubby and take-it-easy type which is also known in the high reaches of American business, two companies might get together and tend to sleep together indefinitely. When the number of firms involved is small, the chances of having the industry animated by vigorously competitive leadership also seem to me to be small." [25]

In view of the many controversial aspects of present-day concentration, this much perhaps can be asserted with some measure of confidence: there is substantial concentration in the American economy, especially in such segments as manufacturing, transportation, public utilities, and some areas of finance. Many industries—some of them basic industries—are concentrated in the sense that the Big Three, Big Four, Big Five, or Big Six control the lion's share of their output. Many firms are, in absolute terms, of gigantic size and possess, therefore, considerable economic and political power (both actual and potential). Many of these firms control vast industrial empires, extending over several industries, and are sometimes joined into informal interest groups encompassing large segments of economic activity.[26] The

[25] "Antitrust Symposium." *American Economic Review,* June 1949, p. 718.
[26] In 1935, the National Resources Committee found that there were eight major interest groups of large corporations closely knit together by interlocking directorships, stock ownership, family ties, joint financing, and other associations. These interest groups, which allegedly occupy a dominant role in American industry, were listed as the Morgan-First National group, the Rockefeller group, the Mellon group, the du Pont group, the Kuhn-Loeb group, the Chicago group, the Boston group, and the Cleveland group. In 1935, the largest of these (Morgan-First National) included 13 industrial corporations (headed by U.S. Steel), 12 utility corporations (headed by A.T. & T.), 37 electric gen

significance of all this is still the subject of violent controversy, and all we can say—as Machlup suggests—is that economists regard the current degree of concentration either as (a) desirable and avoidable; (b) desirable and unavoidable; (c) undesirable and avoidable; or (d) undesirable and unavoidable.

Public Policy Alternatives

Depending on which of these views is accepted, economists will then recommend one of the following policy alternatives with respect to concentrated industries: (1) maintenance of the status quo which, by and large, is regarded as satisfactory; (2) imposition of public regulation or public ownership; or (3) rejection of both private and public monopoly, and the promotion of vigorous competition under the antitrust laws. It is these policy alternatives which shall now be examined in greater detail.

The Status Quo

The defenders of the status quo generally advocate a policy of noninterference with respect to our concentrated industries. They seem satisfied with the prevailing industrial structure, either because they believe that bigness and concentration are now controlled by the "right" people or because they refuse to regard concentration as indicative of pervasive monopolization.

Three distinct, though related, facets of this position are discernible. One is the belief that the business leader of today is a far cry from the robber baron of yesterday; the belief that industrial statesmanship, social responsibility, enlightened self-restraint, and progressive labor, customer, and supplier relations have replaced the exploitative behavior, the sharpshooting competitive practices, and the "public-be-damned" attitude of a bygone age; in short, the belief that the present managers of giant corporate enterprise have demonstrated their capacity for exercising industrial stewardship.[27]

---

erating companies, 11 major railroads, and several important financial institutions. (National Resources Committee, *The Structure of the American Economy*, 1939, Part I, pp. 160–63.) For the capital assets controlled by these interest groups, before World War II, see Smaller War Plants Corporation, *Economic Concentration and World War II*, Senate Document No. 206, 79th Congress, 2d Session, pp. 353–56.

[27] David E. Lilienthal, in his *Big Business: A New Era* (New York: Harper & Brothers, 1953), argues that the antitrust philosophy is no longer applicable and that the antitrust laws are, in fact, crippling America. He feels that the newer type of American big businessman is in little need of the restraints imposed by the antitrust laws.

The second facet of the status quo position is the "workable competition" thesis.[28] Its supporters hold that bigness and concentration are no cause for alarm, because competition is present and *working* in an economy such as ours where constant technological progress is reflected in ever-increasing output, lower prices, and new and improved products. They urge that the effectiveness of competition be judged not in terms of market structure (i.e. the degree of concentration in particular industries) but rather by market results (i.e. performance in the public interest). They suggest that an industry is "workably competitive"—regardless of the fewness of sellers in it —if it shows, among other things, "a progressive technology, the passing on to consumers of the results of this progressiveness in the form of lower prices, larger output, improved products, etc." [29] The emphasis here is on performance and results rather than on structural organization which *compels* such performance and results.

The believers in workable competition usually buttress their position with the suggestion that "old-fashioned" competition—i.e. competition among sellers and among buyers *within* an industry—be replaced with a more dynamic concept of *inter*-industry or technological competition. Their argument is this: classical, intra-industry competition tends to promote maximum output, minimum prices, and optimum utilization of capacity; in short, it stimulates efficiency. But this efficiency is static and unprogressive in character. It makes no allowance for the research, development, and innovation required for economic growth. While it prevents concentration, it stifles progress. To have progress we need more, not less, concentration. Only bigness can provide the sizable funds necessary for technological experimentation and innovation in the industrial milieu of the twentieth century. Only

---

In contrast to Mr. Lilienthal's position, it is interesting to note that a distinguished Wall Street attorney, General William J. Donovan, disagrees. Mr. Donovan's warning, sounded in 1936, is still relevant today: "Those who would remove the inhibitions of existing law must recognize that the alternative is not between the Sherman Act on the one hand and the regulation of industry by industry on the other. The alternative is between the continuance of the competitive system as a proper safeguard to the public, and the closest supervision and control of industry by the government. The self-interest of business in such matters would often be antagonistic to the interest of the public as a whole. The recent experience under the NRA shows the abuses that may arise by vesting in business the power of self-regulation without at the same time providing for adequate and capable supervision and control by a government agency." (Address before the American Bar Association, 1936, quoted in V. A. Mund, *Government and Business*, New York: Harper and Brothers, 1950, pp. 628–29.)

[28] See primarily J. M. Clark, "Toward a Concept of Workable Competition," *American Economic Review*, June 1940.

[29] E. S. Mason, "Antitrust Symposium," *op.cit.*, p. 713. See also C. E. Griffin, *An Economic Approach to Antitrust Problems*, New York: American Enterprise Association, 1951.

monopoly earnings can provide the bait that lures capital to untried trails. While progress may thus require high power concentrations in many industries, this need not be a source of concern to society at large. Technological development will serve as an offset against any short-run position of entrenchment which may be established. The monopoly of glass bottles will be subverted by the introduction of the tin can; and the dominance of the latter will, in turn, be undermined by the introduction of the paper container. The consumer need not rely, therefore, on the static competition between large numbers of small firms as protection against exploitation. In the long run, he can find greater safety—and better things for better living to boot—in the technological competition of a small number of large firms who, through research and innovation, eventually destroy any position of market control which may be established.[30]

The third facet of the status quo position is the recently promulgated "countervailing power" thesis which concedes the pervasiveness of concentration and monopoly, but maintains that the dangers of exploitation are minimized by certain built-in safeguards in our economy.[31] According to this thesis, the actual or real restraints on a firm's market power are vested not in its competitors, but in its customers and suppliers. These restraints are imposed not from the same side of the market (as under classical competition), but from the opposite side. Thus "private economic power is held in check by the countervailing power of those subject to it. The first begets the second." [32] A monopoly on one side of the market offers an inducement to both suppliers and customers to develop the power with which they can defend themselves against exploitation. For example, concentration in the steel industry will stimulate concentration among the industry's customers (automobile manufacturers) as well as among its suppliers (steel workers). The result will be, so the argument runs, a balance of power within the economy—the creation of almost automatic checks and balances requiring a minimum of interference or "tampering."

The foregoing arguments in defense of the status quo are subject to a number of criticisms. As to the beneficence of industrial stewardship and workable competition, we should note that "results alone throw no light on the really significant question: have these results been *compelled* by the system—by *competition*—or do they represent simply the dispensations of

[30] See J. A. Schumpeter, *Capitalism, Socialism, and Democracy*, New York: Harper & Brothers, 1943, p. 79 ff.

[31] See J. K. Galbraith, *American Capitalism: The Concept of Countervailing Power*, Boston: Houghton Mifflin Company, 1952.

[32] *Ibid.*, p. 118.

managements which, with a wide latitude of policy choices at their disposal, happened for the moment to be benevolent or smart?" [33] In other words, what assurance do we have that the workable competition of today will not be transformed into the abusive monopoly or oppressive conspiracy of tomorrow? How, in the absence of competition or constant and detailed supervision, can we ever determine whether the performance of industrial giants does, in fact, serve the public interest and will continue to do so in the future? By what concrete yardsticks do we measure the workability of competition?

Secondly, with regard to the countervailing power thesis, it can be argued (1) that countervailing power is often undermined by vertical integration and top level financial control which blend the opposing sides of the market into one; (2) that the bilateral monopolies created through the countervailance process often conclude bargains prejudicial to the consumer interest (witness, for example, wage increases for the C.I.O. Steelworkers followed by price increases for the steel industry); (3) that the countervailing influence of technological or inter-industry competition is often subverted by a combination of the potential competitors (witness, for example, the merger between motion picture houses and television networks); (4) that any countervailance through government action is often undermined by unduly intimate affiliation between regulator and regulatee (witness, for example, the I.C.C. which seems to have degenerated into a lobby on behalf of railroad interests); and finally (5) that the whole thesis rests on the dubious assumption that industrial giantism is inevitable under modern technological conditions—an assumption which still awaits scientific validation.[34]

Public Regulation or Public Ownership

The advocates of public regulation or public ownership hope simultaneously to insure industrial efficiency and to avoid the abuses of private monopoly—not by the dissolution of monopoly but by its social control. Their argument runs along these lines: Competition in many basic industries is a thing of the past and has been replaced by trade agreements and price fixing, cartels and monopolies. While legislation to eliminate specific abuses of monopoly power can do some good, it cannot compel a return to competition in industries where it would be wasteful and undesirable. The facts of life

[33] Ben W. Lewis, "Antitrust Symposium," *op.cit.*, p. 707.
[34] For a more comprehensive critique of the countervailing power thesis, see W. Adams, "Competition, Monopoly and Countervailing Power," *Quarterly Journal of Economics*, November 1953.

are that efficient organization in mass production and mass distribution fields requires unification, coordination, and rationalization. Only monopoly can bring this about. But private monopoly is no guarantee of efficiency. By fixing prices, allocating production, imposing levies on the efficient to keep the inefficient in production, the general level of prices is kept high, and incentives to modernization may be lacking. Hence, if monopoly is inevitable, it is preferable that such monopoly be publicly supervised or publicly owned.[35]

Basic to this argument is the assumption that monopoly, or at least cooperation on a comprehensive scale, is necessary in many industries—the assumption that monopoly is inevitable under modern industrial conditions. It is this belief in the inevitability of monopoly which has led men of such distinguished position, unimpeachable integrity, and obvious sincerity as Judge Gary (former president of the U.S. Steel Corporation) to advocate a public-utility-type regulation for concentrated industries. Thus Judge Gary, as long ago as 1911, offered the following testimony to a Congressional committee investigating the steel industry:

> I realize as fully, I think, as this committee that it is very important to consider how the people shall be protected against imposition or oppression as the possible result of great aggregations of capital, whether in the possession of corporations or individuals. I believe that is a very important question, and personally I believe that the Sherman Act does not meet and will never fully prevent that. I believe we must come to enforced publicity and governmental control, even as to prices, and, so far as I am concerned, speaking for our company, so far as I have the right, I would be very glad if we had some place where we could go, to a responsible governmental authority, and say to them, 'Here are our facts and figures, here is our property, here our cost of production; now you tell us what we have the right to do and what prices we have the right to charge.' I know this is a very extreme view, and I know that the railroads objected to it for a long time; but whether the standpoint of making the most money is concerned or not, whether it is the wise thing, I believe it is the necessary thing, and it seems to me corporations have no right to disregard these public questions and these public interests.
>
> "Your idea then," said Congressman Littleton of the committee, "is that cooperation is bound to take the place of competition and that cooperation requires strict governmental supervision?"
>
> "That is a very good statement," replied the Judge.[36]

Unfortunately, Judge Gary's faith in independent regulatory commissions has, in the light of American experience, not proved justified. These com-

---

[35] For this formulation of the argument, see the work of the British socialist, E. Davies, *National Enterprise*, London: Victor Gollancz Ltd., 1946, p. 16.

[36] Special Committee to Investigate the United States Steel Corporation, House Report No. 1127, 62d Congress, 2d Session, 1911, quoted in W. Adams and L. E. Traywick, *Readings in Economics*, New York: The Macmillan Company, 1948, p. 223.

missions—the Interstate Commerce Commission,[37] the Civil Aeronautics Board,[38] the Federal Power Commission,[39] the Federal Communications Commission [40]—have at times failed to regulate their respective industries in the public interest. Often these commissions adopted regulatory techniques which did little to promote operational efficiency and innovative progress; which were ineffective, costly and debilitating; and which suffered from administrative incompetence, unimaginativeness, and dishonesty. Moreover, no satisfactory solution seems yet to have been found for the vexing problem of watching the watchers. (*Quis custodiet ipsos custodies?*) As ex-Senator Wheeler once sadly observed, "It seems to invariably happen, that when Congress attempts to regulate some group, the intended regulatees wind up doing the regulating." [41]

Dissatisfied with the past record of regulatory commissions, some groups have gone further and advocated the nationalization, i.e. outright government ownership, of concentrated industries. Typical of these groups is the British Labour Party which, in 1948, demanded nationalization of the steel industry on the grounds that the public supervision of private monopoly is unworkable. Said the Labour Party: [42]

A board controlling a private monopoly must in the long run be ineffective. Its activities must be negative. It can, for example, refuse to recommend a price increase, but it cannot force the industry to take steps to cheapen production. It has no power to make the monopoly spend money on new plant or scrap old plant. A supervised private monopoly can be prevented from doing the wrong things, but it cannot be forced to do the right things. In the future, the control of steel must be dynamic and purposeful, not negative and preventive. . . . There is no hope, then, in a supervised monopoly. The only answer is that steel must be made a public enterprise.

---

[37] See, for example, S. P. Huntington, "The Marasmus of the I.C.C.," *Yale Law Journal,* April 1952; and Senate Small Business Committee, *Competition, Regulation, and the Public Interest in the Motor Carrier Industry,* Report No. 1693, 84th Cong., 2d Sess., 1956.

[38] See Chapter 13 above; also Senate Small Business Committee, *Report on Role of Irregular Airlines in United States Air Transportation Industry,* Report No. 540, 82d Congress, 1st Session, 1951.

[39] See, for example, Federal Power Commission, *In the Matter of the Phillips Petroleum Company,* Opinion No. 217, Docket No. G-1148, August 16, 1951.

[40] See, for example, Federal Communications Commission, *In the Matter of American Broadcasting Company Inc. and United Paramount Theatres, Inc.,* Docket No. 10046, 1953; also B. Schwartz, *The Professor and the Commissions,* New York: Alfred A. Knopf, 1959.

[41] Quoted in B. Bolles, *How to Get Rich in Washington,* New York: Dell Publishing Company, p. 23.

[42] *British Steel at Britain's Service,* London, 1948, p. 15; quoted in Mund, *op.cit.,* p. 548.

According to the socialist, then, nationalization is preferable both to public regulation and to private monopoly. It is better than public regulation, because the latter has proved generally ineffective. It is better than private monopoly, because the power to control basic industries, and hence the economy, must be "democratized." [43] Such power must, according to the socialist, be held by the many and not as hitherto concentrated—without corresponding responsibility—in the hands of a few. There must be assurance that monopoly—a system which can be used for good or evil—will be used in the public interest. According to the socialist, a nationalized industry affords such assurance, simply because its management will be motivated by considerations of public service and not private profit.

The disadvantages of public ownership are fairly obvious: administrators in nationalized industries may easily succumb to the disease of security, conservatism, procrastination, and bureaucracy. Their enterprises, as a result of supercentralization and lack of competitive incentives, may come to suffer from inflexibility and inelasticity. Moreover, the public enterprise may develop a tendency of using its monopoly power as a cloak for inefficient operation by resorting to the ready device of raising prices to meet increased costs, and thus avoid showing a deficit. Finally, there is the distinct possibility that the very people in whose interest a particular industry may originally have been nationalized will eventually lose control of it. This result is probable for two reasons: (1) general elections are no substitute for the market as an agency of social control (because people cannot indicate their dissatisfaction with a *particular* public enterprise by means of the ballot); and (2) the public enterprise, if it is to operate efficiently, must be "taken out of politics" and put in the hands of an autonomous body—again with the result of removing such enterprise from the direct control of the electorate.[44]

[43] See Ben W. Lewis, *British Planning and Nationalization*, New York: Twentieth Century Fund, 1952, pp. 43–45.

[44] See F. A. Hayek, *The Road to Serfdom*, Chicago: University of Chicago Press, 1945; L. Von Mises, *Planned Chaos*, New York: Foundation for Economic Education, 1947; C. E. Griffin, *Britain: A Case Study for Americans*, Ann Arbor: University of Michigan Press, 1950. These criticisms of public ownership are confirmed by the distinguished British scholar, W. Arthur Lewis. In his "Recent British Experience of Nationalization as an Alternative to Monopoly Control" (a paper presented to the International Economic Association in 1951), Professor Lewis makes the following comments on Britain's experiment in socialism: "The appointment of public directors to manage an undertaking is not sufficient public control." "Parliament is handicapped in controlling corporations by its lack of time. . . . Neither have Members of Parliament the competence to supervise these great industries. . . . Parliament is further handicapped . . . by paucity of information . . . for example, less information is now published about the railways than was available before they were nationalized." "Except in the case of

In summary, public regulation and public ownership suffer from the same basic drawback as private monopoly, viz., the concentration of power in the hands of a few. Such power may be used benignly or dangerously, depending on the men who possess and control it. They may be good men, benevolent men, and socially minded men; but society still confronts the danger of which Lord Acton so eloquently warned: power corrupts, and absolute power corrupts absolutely.

The Promotion of Effective Competition

The advocates of promoting greater competition through vigorous antitrust enforcement reject both the Scylla of private monopoly and the Charybdis of public ownership. Believing that the preservation of competitive free enterprise is both desirable and possible, they point out that this does not mean a return to the horse-and-buggy age, nor a strict adherence to the textbook theories of "perfect" or "pure" competition. What they advocate is a structural arrangement in private industry characterized by decentralized decision-making and "effective" competition.

Among the ingredients necessary for effective competition, the following are considered of primary importance: [45] (1) an appreciable number of sellers and buyers for substantially the same product, so that both sellers and buyers have meaningful alternatives of choice; (2) the economic, as well as legal, freedom to enter the market and gain access to essential raw materials; (3) the absence of tacit or open collusion between rivals in the market; (4) the absence of explicit or implicit coercion of rivals by a dominant firm or a group of dominant firms; (5) the absence of "substantial preferential status within the market for any important trader or group of traders on the basis of law, politics, or commercial alliances"; [46] (6) the absence of diversification, subsidization, and political motivation to an extent where giant firms

---

transport, the British government has resisted proposals that public corporations should be treated in the same way [as private monopolies], with the result that the consumer is formally less well protected vis-à-vis public corporations than he was vis-à-vis private firms operating public utilities." "The [public] corporation's Board, though publicly appointed, has many loyalties in addition to its loyalty to the public. It has also a loyalty to itself, and to its own staff, which may well conflict with the interests of the consumer." "Public corporations have not found it easy to dismiss redundant workers, or even to close down inefficient units or to expand more efficient units in some other place (e.g. railways, mines). It may well turn out that public corporations are less able to promote this kind of efficiency than are private corporations, in the British atmosphere of tenderness towards established sources of income." (Quoted in Machlup, *op.cit.*, p. 50.)

[45] See C. D. Edwards, *Maintaining Competition*, New York: McGraw-Hill Book Co., 1949, pp. 9–10.

[46] *Ibid.*, p. 10.

may escape the commercial discipline of a *particular* market or a *particular* operation.

Some economists feel that the maintenance of this type of competition may, under modern conditions, be difficult if not impossible. They contend that antitrusters are faced with the dilemma of choosing between "(1) firms of the most efficient size but operating under conditions where there is inadequate pressure to compel firms to continue to be efficient and pass on to the consumer the benefits of efficiency, and (2) a system in which the firms are numerous enough to be competitive but too small to be efficient." [47] According to this view our choice is between monopoly and efficiency, on the one hand, and competition and relative inefficiency, on the other.

The supporters of vigorous antitrust enforcement deny that such a choice is necessary, at least in many of our highly concentrated industries. The following reasons are usually given for rejecting the ostensible conflict between competition and efficiency. *First,* large firms, while technologically imperative in many industries, need not assume the Brobdingnagian proportions of some present-day giants. The unit of technological efficiency is the plant and not the firm. This means that, while there are undisputed advantages in the large-scale integrated steel operations at Gary or Pittsburgh or Birmingham, there seems little technological justification for combining these functionally separate plant units into a single administrative giant.[48]

Second, it seems significant that many of our colossal firms were not formed to gain the technical advantages of scale, but organized instead to achieve monopolistic control over the market and to reap profits from the sale of inflated securities. Giantism in industry today is not unrelated to the investment banker's inclination of yesteryear to merge and combine competing companies for the sake of promoter's profits.

Third, there is mounting evidence that industrial concentration is not necessarily the result of spontaneous generation or natural selection, but often the end-product of unwise, man-made, discriminatory, and privilege-creating governmental action. In an era of "big government," when the structural

---

[47] A. R. Burns, "Antitrust Symposium," *op.cit.,* p. 603.

[48] In his definitive study of twenty representative industries, Joe S. Bain found that, in 11 out of 20 cases, the lowest-cost (most efficient) plant would account for less than 2½ per cent of the industry's national sales; in 15 out of 20 cases, for less than 7½ per cent; and in only one case, for more than 15 per cent. Moreover, in estimating multiplant economies, Bain concluded that in 6 out of 20 industries, the cost advantages of multiplant firms were "either negligible or totally absent;" in another 6 industries, the advantages were "perceptible" but "fairly small;" and in the remaining 8 industries, no estimates could be obtained. (*Barriers to New Competition,* Cambridge: Harvard University Press, 1956, pp. 73, 85–88 ff.) These findings hardly support the contention that existing concentration in American industry can be explained in terms of technological imperatives.

impact of federal activity is no longer neutral, the government's spending, taxing, proprietary, legislative, and regulatory powers have often been used —unintentionally, in some instances—to throttle competition and restrict opportunity. Especially in the regulated industries, government has become an instrument for promoting concentration far beyond the imperatives of technology and economics.[49]

Finally, to the extent that profit figures are valid as measures of comparative efficiency, it seems that in a number of cases medium-sized and small firms outperform their giant rivals. Moreover, a breaking down of huge firms does not necessarily have fatal effects on efficiency *or* profitability. In the public utility field, for example, the comprehensive dissolution program carried out under the Public Utility Holding Company Act of 1935 has resulted in increased efficiency and profitability among the successor companies. This was demonstrated in the above average appreciation in the security values of the successor companies which occurred despite declining utility rates, higher costs, and the inevitably higher taxes.[50] On the basis of experience, therefore, it may not be unreasonable to suggest, as *Fortune* does, that there are areas in American industry where an unmerging process among the giants can contribute both to increased efficiency and more vigorous competition.[51]

If such an unmerging process were to be accomplished through antitrust action, three types of market structure would have to be identified and dealt with, viz., horizontal, vertical, and conglomerate integration. (1) The horizontal size of *some* firms would have to be reduced, if competition is to be promoted, because an oligopolistic industry structure often results in conscious or unconscious parallelism among the giant firms. Price leadership, live-and-let-live policies, nonprice competition, etc.—in short, the type of gentlemanly behavior which imposes higher and more inflexible prices on the consumer—are common among firms of oligopolistic size, because each fears retaliation by its large rivals as punishment for independence and nonconformity. (2) Vertically integrated size would, in some cases, have to be reduced because the large integrated concern can apply the squeeze—both on prices and supplies—to its smaller rivals who are both its customers and competitors.[52] A case in point here would be a fully integrated aluminum firm which simultaneously supplies independent fabricators with aluminum

---

[49] See Adams and Gray, *op.cit.,* especially chapter III.
[50] See W. Adams, "The Dilemma of Antitrust Aims: A Reply," *American Economic Review,* December 1952.
[51] See editorials in *Fortune,* March and April 1938.
[52] Senate Small Business Committee, *Monopolistic Practices and Small Business,* 82d Congress, 2d Session, 1952, pp. 21–55; also, *The Distribution of Steel Consumption, 1949–50,* 82d Congress, 2d Session, 1952.

ingot and then competes with them in the market for fabricated products.[53] (3) Conglomerate integration would pose a problem, because the widely diversified giant can exercise undue power as a buyer of materials, energy, transportation, credit, and labor; and also because such a concern often enjoys special advantages in litigation, politics, public relations, and finance.[54]

In launching a comprehensive program against these forms of integration a case-by-case approach seems preferable to any absolute prohibition on size per se. Moreover, to avoid any major conflicts with vested interests, enforcement might at first be confined to new industries where the problem of concentration is not yet extreme and where structural arrangements have not yet been solidified. This may have significant results, since ours is a dynamic economy in which new industries—if they remain competitive— can substantially curb the power of older and more entrenched interests. Finally, to forestall any possible interference with industrial efficiency, antitrust prosecution might be confined to cases where the goals of competition and efficiency are not in conflict. Toward that end, the antitrust laws can be amended to provide that "any corporation whose size and power are such as to substantially lessen competition and tend to create a monopoly in any line of commerce shall be dissolved into its component parts, *unless* such corporation can demonstrate that its present size is necessary for the maintenance of efficiency." [55] Given a provision of this sort, the dilemma of antitrust may be resolved and our twin goals of competition and efficiency actively promoted.

Antitrust enforcement along the above lines, however, is not enough if competitive free enterprise is to be maintained. Competition must become the core of an integrated national economic policy.[56] It must be positively

---

[53] See *U.S.* v. *Aluminum Company of America*, 148 F. 2d 416 (C.C.A. 2d, 1945).

[54] See Edwards, *Maintaining Competition, op.cit.*, pp. 99–108. It has been said, for example, that General Motors has so much conglomerate power that it could successfully enter the ice cream industry and capture a predetermined share of the business. "It would matter little whether General Motors is an efficient ice cream manufacturer or whether its ice cream is indeed tastier than more established brands. By discrete price concessions, by saturation advertising, by attractive promotional deals, it could commit its gargantuan financial power to the battle until only so much competition as General Motors is prepared to tolerate would be left in the industry . . . Put differently, in a poker game with unlimited stakes, the player who commands disproportionately large funds is likely to emerge victorious." (Testimony of Walter Adams in *Hearings before the Subcommittee on Antitrust and Monopoly, Senate Judiciary Committee*, 86th Cong., 1st Sess., 1959, p. 4780.)

[55] Cf. Monopoly Subcommittee of the House Judiciary Committee, *Hearings*, Part 2-B, 81st Cong., 1st Sess., 1949, pp. 1311–39, 1600–25. For a recent endorsement of this general position, see C. Kaysen and D. F. Turner, *Antitrust Policy*, Cambridge: Harvard University Press, 1959.

[56] See House Small Business Committee, *United States versus Economic Concentration and Monopoly*, 79th Cong., 2d Sess., 1947.

promoted, rather than negatively preserved.[57] It must have an environment which provides opportunity for new men, and is receptive to new ideas. To create such an environment, a number of recommendations merit consideration:

(1) Defense contracts, accelerated amortization privileges, and other wartime bonanzas coming down the government pike should not be restricted to a favored few, but distributed to many firms so as to assure the nation of a broad industrial base for future defense efforts.[58]

(2) In the disposal of government property—whether war surplus, synthetic rubber plants, or atomic energy installations—to private industry, sales should be made in a manner calculated to encourage competitive newcomers rather than to rigidify existing patterns of industrial control.

(3) The corporate tax structure should be overhauled so as to remove present penalties on the growth and expansion of small business.[59]

(4) Government financing of small business should be more than polite encouragement for prospective hot-dog stands and gasoline stations.

(5) The patent laws should be revised so as to prevent monopolistic abuse of the patent grant without destroying the incentives for invention. This may entail compulsory licensing of patents on a *royalty-free* basis in cases involving violations of the antitrust laws; compulsory licensing of patents on a *reasonable-royalty* basis in cases of patent suppression and nonuse; and outright prohibition of restrictive and exclusive licensing provisions in private patent agreements. In any event, an invention made as a result of govern-

---

[57] As Vernon Mund observes, "a policy of individual enterprise and price competition is a highly elaborate and complex plan for organizing the conduct of economic activity. It is a plan, however, which is not self-enforcing. When the policy of competition is accepted, it must be implemented by positive measures to provide for its creation, maintenance, and preservation. Competition is a form of human behavior; and like other behavior it should be conducted according to good manners and morals. The big mistake which government has made with respect to economic regulation is in thinking that in the absence of direct price control (as in the case of public utilities) government intervention is not necessary. The lessons of history clearly show that we cannot have fair competition unless positive measures are taken to create and maintain it." (Mund, *op.cit.*, p. 642.)

[58] See, for example, Senate Small Business Committee, *Concentration of Defense Contracts*, Report No. 551, 82d Congress, 1st Session, 1951; House Committee on Expenditures in the Executive Departments, *Inquiry into the Procurement of Automotive Spare Parts by the United States Government*, 82d Congress, 2d Session, House Report No. 1811, 1952; Attorney General, *Report Prepared Pursuant to Section 708 (e) of the Defense Production Act of 1950*, 1950; Joint Committee on Defense Production, *Hearings on Tax Amortization*, 82d Congress, 1st Session, 1951.

[59] See Senate Small Business Committee, *Tax Problems of Small Business*, Report No. 442, 83d Congress, 1st Session, 1953; J. K. Butters and J. Lintner, *Effect of Federal Taxes on Growing Enterprises*, Boston: Harvard Business School, 1945; J. K. Butters, J. Lintner, and W. Carey, *Effects of Taxation: Corporate Mergers*, Boston: Harvard Business School, 1951.

ment financing or subsidy should become part of the public domain and not allowed to accrue as private property to the corporation doing the contract research.[60]

(6) Any further exemptions from the antitrust laws should be discouraged, and some existing exemptions re-examined.[61] We must stop what Leverett S. Lyon has called the "growing tendency in the United States for special groups to identify their limited good with the national good and to ask government for subsidy, support, or special protection rather than for laws which increase competitive opportunity."[62] Such laws as the Webb-Pomerene Act, for example, which exempts foreign trade associations from the Sherman Act, should be drastically revised or altogether repealed.[63]

(7) Protective tariffs which serve to shield highly concentrated industries

[60] In this connection the Attorney General has recommended that "where patentable inventions are made in the course of performing a Government-financed contract for research and development, the public interest requires that all rights to such inventions be assigned to the Government and not left to the private ownership of the contractor. Public control will assure free and equal availability of the inventions to American industry and science; will eliminate any competitive advantage to the contractor chosen to perform the research work; will avoid undue concentration of economic power in the hands of a few large corporations; will tend to increase and diversify available research facilities within the United States to the advantage of the Government and of the national economy; and will thus strengthen our American system of free, competitive enterprise." (*Investigation of Government Patent Practices and Policies*, 1947, Vol. I, p. 4). Obviously, it makes little sense to permit—as in the past—"publicly-financed technology to be suppressed, used restrictively, or made the basis of an exaction from the public to serve private interests." (*Ibid.*, p. 2.)

[61] The problem of exceptions from the antitrust laws is well illustrated in the following story about a Polish ghetto, told by Congressman Celler: "The rabbi of the synagogue said: 'There is a very poor family on the other end of the ghetto. They have not raiment, they have not food, and they have not shelter. You are too poor yourselves'—he said to his congregation—'to help them, but I have an idea. . . . On the Sabbath eve when you praise the Lord for the fruitage of the earth, and you praise him by drinking a glass of wine, do not drink the full glass of wine. Drink a half a glass of wine, and the next morning when you come to the temple, I will have a barrel, and as you all come in, you will pour the half glass of wine that you left from the night before in the barrel. The Lord will not mind being blessed by the drinking of half a glass of wine, and at a given time the barrel will be filled. I will sell the barrel of wine and give the proceeds to this poor family. You will not be hurt; nobody will be harmed, and even the good Lord will bless you for it.' At a given time the barrel was opened and lo and behold, it was all water, and the rabbi reprimanded every member in the congregation, and they all had this answer: 'We figured what difference would a half glass of water make in a full barrel of wine.' . . . That is what is happening here. If we keep whittling away, and whittling away, and everybody asks to be exempted, everybody asks to put the half a glass of water in the full barrel of wine, we will have a barrel of water, and we will have no antitrust laws left." (Subcommittee on the Study of Monopoly Power, *Hearings*, 81st Cong., 1st Sess., Serial No. 14, Part I, 1949, pp. 267–68.)

[62] "Government and American Economic Life," *Journal of Business*, April 1949, pp. 89–90.

[63] Committee on the Webb-Pomerene Act, American Economic Association, "The Webb-Pomerene Law: A Consensus Report," *American Economic Review*, December 1947, pp. 848–63.

from the potential inroads of foreign competition should be reduced or repealed.

(8) Incorporation and licensing laws should not be made a front for monopolistic privilege and restrictive practices.

(9) The advisability of a progressive tax on advertising—with a generous exemption of, say, $3,000,000—should be examined, in an effort to prevent excessive advertising expenditures from acting as an obstacle to free entry in some concentrated industries.[64]

Such steps as these—and the list is by no means complete—may serve to stimulate an environment favorable to genuine free enterprise. The task is not easy, for we must strike a delicate balance between the businessman's search for profit and economic security, and society's insistence on freedom and opportunity for the newcomer. But while the task is difficult, it is not insuperable. Given a comprehensive and imaginative economic policy, it is likely that competition can be maintained (or revived), for the record shows that free enterprise in our generation has not failed; it has never been tried.

A hard look at the choice before us is indicated because, in the absence of positive action, we can expect little but aimless drifting and a gradual erosion of our traditional values. As Stocking and Watkins point out, "either the people must call a halt to the concentration—whether in governmental or private hands—of economic power, or they must be prepared to give up a competitive economy, bit by bit, year by year, until it is beyond recall. They will then be obliged to accept some collectivistic alternative that may give more short-run basic security but in the long run will almost certainly provide less freedom, less opportunity for experiment, less variety, less economic progress, and less total abundance." [65]

---

[64] See W. H. Nicholls, *Pricing Policies in the Cigarette Industry*, Nashville: Vanderbilt University Press, 1951, pp. 412–15.

[65] G. W. Stocking and M. W. Watkins, *Monopoly and Free Enterprise*, New York: Twentieth Century Fund, 1952, p. 526. We might profit from British experience which the conservative London *Economist* has summarized as follows: "The fact is that British industrialists, under the deliberate leadership of the Tory Party in its Baldwin-Chamberlain era, have become distinguishable from British Socialists only by the fact that they still believe in private profits. Both believe in 'organising' industry; both believe in protecting it, when organized, against any competition, either from foreigners or from native newcomers; both believe in standard prices for what they sell; both unite in condemning competition, the one as 'wasteful,' the other as 'destructive.' If free, competitive, private-enterprise capitalism is to continue to exist, not throughout the national economy, but in any part of it, then it needs rescuing from the capitalists fully as much as from the Socialists." (*The Economist*, London, June 29, 1946, p. 22. Copyright *The Economist*. Reprinted by permission of the publishers.)

FIGURE 2

Public Policy Alternatives: "The Road Ahead"

GRAPHIC ASSOCIATES FOR PUBLIC AFFAIRS COMMITTEE, INC.

Source: Thurman W. Arnold, *Cartels or Free Enterprise?* Public Affairs Pamphlet No. 103, 1945; reproduced by courtesy of the Public Affairs Committee, Inc.

SUGGESTED READINGS

Books and Pamphlets

American Economic Association, *Readings in the Social Control of Industry* (Philadelphia: Blakiston, 1942).

J. S. Bain, *Barriers to New Competition* (Cambridge: Harvard University Press, 1956).

J. B. Dirlam and A. E. Kahn, *The Law and Economics of Fair Competition: An Appraisal of Antitrust Policy* (Ithaca: Cornell University Press, 1954).

P. F. Drucker, *Concept of the Corporation* (New York: Day, 1946).

C. D. Edwards, *Maintaining Competition* (New York: McGraw-Hill, 1949).

W. Fellner, *Competition among the Few* (New York: Knopf, 1949).

J. K. Galbraith, *American Capitalism: The Concept of Countervailing Power* (Boston: Houghton Mifflin, 1952).

C. E. Griffin, *An Economic Approach to Antitrust Problems* (New York: American Enterprise Association, 1951).

R. B. Heflebower and G. W. Stocking, *Readings in Industrial Organization and Public Policy* (Homewood: Richard D. Irwin, 1958).

C. Kaysen and D. F. Turner, *Antitrust Policy* (Cambridge: Harvard University Press, 1959).

D. E. Lilienthal, *Big Business: A New Era* (New York: Harper, 1952).

F. Machlup, *The Political Economy of Monopoly* (Baltimore: Johns Hopkins Press, 1952).

E. S. Mason, *Economic Concentration and the Monopoly Problem* (Cambridge: Harvard University Press, 1957).

J. A. Schumpeter, *Capitalism, Socialism and Democracy* (New York: Harper, 1942).

H. C. Simons, *Economic Policy for a Free Society* (Chicago: University of Chicago Press, 1948).

G. W. Stocking and M. W. Watkins, *Cartels in Action* (New York: Twentieth Century Fund, 1946).

————, *Cartels or Competition?* (New York: Twentieth Century Fund, 1948).

————, *Monopoly and Free Enterprise* (New York: Twentieth Century Fund, 1951).

S. N. Whitney, *Antitrust Policies* (New York: Twentieth Century Fund, 1958).

Government Publications

Business Advisory Council, Secretary of Commerce, *Effective Competition* (Washington, 1952).

W. H. Hamilton, *Antitrust in Action,* Temporary National Economic Committee, Monograph No. 16 (Washington, 1940).

Hearings before the Subcommittee on the Study of Monopoly Power, House Judiciary Committee, *Study of Monopoly Power,* Serial 14, Parts 1, 2-A, 2-B, 81st Cong., 1st Sess., 1949.

Hearings before the Subcommittee on Antitrust and Monopoly, Senate Judiciary Committee, Parts 1–10, 85th and 86th Cong., 1957–60.

S. Nelson and W. Keim, *Price Behavior and Business Policy,* Temporary National Economic Committee, Monograph No. 1 (Washington, 1940).

C. Wilcox, *Competition and Monopoly in American Industry,* Temporary National Economic Committee, Monograph No. 21 (Washington, 1940).

Journal and Magazine Articles

W. Adams, "Dissolution, Divorcement, Divestiture: The Pyrrhic Victories of Antitrust," *Indiana Law Journal,* Vol. 27, Fall 1951.

M. A. Adelman, "Integration and Antitrust Policy," *Harvard Law Review,* Vol. 63, November 1949.

R. Heflebower, "Economics of Size," *Journal of Business of the University of Chicago,* Vol. 24, April 1951.

D. Keezer (ed.), "The Antitrust Laws: A Symposium," *American Economic Review,* Vol. XXXIX, June 1949.

E. S. Mason, "Current Status of the Monopoly Problem," *Harvard Law Review,* Vol. 62, June 1949.

G. J. Stigler, "The Case Against Big Business," *Fortune,* May 1952.

G. W. Stocking, "Saving Free Enterprise from Its Friends," *Southern Economic Journal,* Vol. XIX, April 1953.

C. Wilcox, "On the Alleged Ubiquity of Monopoly," *American Economic Review,* May 1950.

Chapter 16

CHARLES C. KILLINGSWORTH

Epilogue: Organized Labor in a Free Enterprise Economy

"The labor of a human being is not a commodity or article of commerce." So declares the Clayton Act, thereby embedding in the statutes of the United States a half truth which underlies one of the great dilemmas of public policy. Labor is our basic resource. Labor services are more important than the product of any industry discussed in this volume. The price of labor is of basic concern throughout the economy. Therefore, there would seem to be a special interest in maintaining competition in the labor market. Yet the trend in public policy has been not only to exempt labor combinations from the antitrust regulations applicable to almost all important branches of industry, but even to encourage the development of combinations which have as their avowed purpose the fixing of the price of labor.

Since the days of Adam Smith, economists have generally held a presumption in favor of competition. Economic theorists can readily demonstrate that the free play of market forces under perfect competition will result in the most efficient possible distribution of resources, and consequently maximum output. Therefore restraints on competition are generally presumed to be contrary to the public interest. On this ground some economists have strongly criticized the policy of encouraging (or even permitting) labor combinations.[1] Less sophisticated critics have argued that it is simply unfair to exempt labor organizations from the antitrust laws that businessmen must obey.

[1] For example, see Henry C. Simons, "Some Reflections on Syndicalism," *Journal of Political Economy*, Vol. LII, March 1944.

564

This latter argument ignores the fact that there are many exceptions to, and exemptions from, the antitrust laws for business and other groups. Many aspects of agricultural policy are intended to modify the operation of competitive forces in markets for agricultural products. The so-called "fair trade" laws restrict competition. In such fields as public utilities and ocean shipping, little or no effort is made to insure competition. These facts undermine the rather naive inequality arguments. They do not meet the criticisms of those economists who are also critical of these other departures from antitrust policy unless justified by special circumstances, as in the case of public utilities. If the general desirability of competition is accepted as a premise, it is essential to examine carefully the merits of each departure from a policy of maintaining competition. The purpose of this chapter is to consider the merits of a policy of permitting or encouraging labor combinations. The thesis of the chapter is that perfect (or even reasonably effective) competition is unobtainable in labor markets even in the absence of labor unions, that collective action by workers is essential to offset some of the effects of imperfections of labor markets, that unions perform vital noneconomic functions, and that collective bargaining is preferable to any of the realistic alternatives to it.

Let us consider first the nature of competition and of labor markets. The idea of perfect competition generally implies several important assumptions. One is that men behave in such a way as to maximize their incomes. Applied to labor, this means that the worker seeks the highest wage in the market. Obviously, if workers are to behave in this way, they must have knowledge of the alternatives offered by the market, and they must also have the ability and willingness to move to take advantage of better opportunities. A further requisite for perfect competition in the labor market is that the buyers of labor services—employers—must not be in collusion with each other. Also, in making employment, output, and price decisions, employers must be motivated solely by the desire to maximize their net revenue. These are the major requisites of perfect competition in the factor market.

If we add to the foregoing the further assumptions of perfect competition in the product market, and the ability of the employer to estimate with reasonable accuracy the contribution that would be made to his total output by an additional worker, we have conditions that will result in optimum allocation of resources. Competition between employers will insure that the wage of the worker is equal to the value of the extra product attributable to him. The effort of the worker to secure the highest possible wage will lead him to work where his marginal productivity is highest. On the other hand, according to some exponents of this theory, wage rates which are "artificially" high (because of trade union action or government intervention) will cause unemployment and inefficient allocation of resources.[2]

The unreal nature of the assumptions underlying the foregoing type of analysis is obvious. While the belief in the efficacy of competition stems from Adam Smith, he clearly saw some of the realities of the labor market. For example, he wrote: [3]

> We rarely hear, it has been said, of the combination of masters, though frequently those of workmen. But whoever imagined upon this account that masters rarely combine, is as ignorant of the world as of the subject. Masters are always and everywhere in a sort of tacit but constant and uniform combination, not to raise the wages of labor above their actual rate. To violate this combination is everywhere a most unpopular action, and a sort of reproach to a master upon his neighbors and equals. We seldom, indeed, hear of this combination, because it is the usual, and one may say, the natural state of things which nobody ever hears of. Masters, too, sometimes enter into particular combinations to sink the wages of labor even below this rate. . . . Such combinations, however, are frequently resisted by a contrary defensive combination of the workmen who sometimes, too, without any provocation of this kind combine of their own accord to raise the price of their labor. But whether their combination be offensive or defensive they are always abundantly heard of.

Moreover, recent empirical studies have shown that workers simply do not behave according to the assumptions of economic theory. Workers have strong attachments to particular geographical localities, to occupations, even to specific jobs, often without regard to the economic advantage of such attachments. Most workers move from one job to another only when circumstances force them to; and they generally take the first job that is offered to them without much "shopping around." Their knowledge of wage rates being offered is often meager and inaccurate. While many workers are vaguely dissatisfied with their jobs, their inertia and their ingrained conviction that jobs are hard to find (even in boom times) keep them where

[2] See J. R. Hicks, *The Theory of Wages*, New York: Macmillan, 1935; D. H. Robertson, "Wage Grumbles," reprinted in *Readings in the Theory of Income Distribution*, Philadelphia: Blakiston, 1946. Only the most essential assumptions have been summarized. There are others that are not unimportant—for example, that all factors of production are substitutable, mobile, divisible, adaptable, etc. However, these assumptions can be modified without doing major damage to the basic framework set forth above. This is not true of the more essential assumptions set forth in the text. When these assumptions are substantially modified to make them more realistic, the theory becomes completely unverifiable and of questionable utility. Cf. F. Machlup, "Marginal Analysis and Economic Research," *American Economic Review*, Vol. XXXVI, September 1946.

[3] *An Inquiry into the Nature and Causes of the Wealth of Nations*, 1776, Book I, Chap. 8.

they are, especially after they have established a few years of seniority. Job security is a more important factor to most workers than a wage differential.[4] These characteristics of workers, perhaps as much as the "tacit combination" and the greatly superior financial resources of employers, give the latter a strong advantage in dealing with individual, unorganized workers.

Thus workers do not, and in many respects cannot, behave in such a way as to make labor markets competitive. They have neither the broad knowledge of alternatives, nor the ability and willingness to move, that are essential for the proper operation of competition on the sellers' side of the market. Moreover, competition on the buyers' side of the market rarely conforms to the assumptions of the theory of competition. In a great many communities, one or a few employers employ most of the workers. The tacit combination among employers noted by Adam Smith survives in full vigor in many areas. Employers usually find it extremely difficult to estimate the added product attributable to one or a few extra workers; indeed, experience suggests that such factors as different supervisory techniques may cause substantial variations in productivity even when men, machines and product are unchanged, and cyclical and technological changes—which are unremitting in most industries—compound the difficulties of estimating marginal productivity. Furthermore, the readers of this volume know that perfect competition in product markets is virtually unknown in reality.[5] Thus the most fundamental assumptions of the theory of competition prove to be quite at variance with the observable facts in labor markets.

Strong, literal enforcement of the antitrust laws in such a way as to stamp out or prevent unionism, or even merely to reduce union power, would not remove the most important impediments to perfect competition in labor markets. Therefore, such application of the antitrust laws to labor activities could not possibly yield the beneficent fruits of competition that some economic theories portray. In other words, it is unrealistic to think that a pos-

---

[4] See L. G. Reynolds and J. Shister, *Job Horizons*, New York: Harper, 1949; C. A. Myers and W. R. Maclaurin, *The Movement of Factory Workers*, New York: Wiley, 1943; L. G. Reynolds, *The Structure of Labor Markets*, New York: Harper, 1951; C. A. Myers and G. P. Shultz, *The Dynamics of a Labor Market*, New York: Prentice-Hall, 1951; E. Wight Bakke and others, *Labor Mobility and Economic Opportunity*, New York: Wiley, 1954; A. M. Ross, "Do We Have a New Industrial Feudalism?" *American Economic Review*, Vol. XLVIII, December 1958.

[5] Imperfect or monopolistic competition in product markets makes it unprofitable for the employer to pay the worker the value of the extra output attributable to him, and the delicately balanced mechanism for achieving optimum allocation of resources is distorted even if there is perfect competition in factor markets. See E. H. Chamberlin, *The Theory of Monopolistic Competition*, 5th ed., Cambridge: Harvard University Press, 1946, esp. Chap. VIII.

sible alternative to the present system of collective bargaining is the neat, automatic achievement of optimum efficiency through the unhampered operation of competitive forces.

One realistic alternative to collective bargaining is sometimes called "individual bargaining." It is more accurate to call this a system of unilateral determination (by the employer) of wages, hours, and working conditions. The ordinary individual laborer seldom has any opportunity to bargain with a prospective employer; the employer decides what he is going to offer and the laborer has the choice of taking it or leaving it. Indeed, it is hardly feasible for the employer of more than a few workers to try to make individual bargains with them. Under this system, given the nature of the market for labor services, it is extremely unlikely that there is any important tendency toward the happy state of maximum efficiency that is supposed to be the end result of competition. Moreover, the worker has little or no protection against unjust or arbitrary treatment.

Another alternative is governmental determination of wages, hours, and working conditions. This alternative sometimes takes the form of an industrial court system, sometimes compulsory arbitration, sometimes something else, but its basic principle is generally the same. It is that government officials or their appointees should decide on what terms and conditions men are to work for their employers. Government control of wages in democratic countries is almost always accompanied by price control. For wage control to be really effective in the long run, it is probably necessary for the government to have the power to control the movement of workers from one job to another. Moreover, it may become necessary to regulate the right of the employer to go out of business, particularly if workers are to be denied the right to strike. The implications of such far-reaching intervention are obvious. Governmental determination of wages, hours, and working conditions as a general policy is incompatible with a private enterprise system.

The weaknesses of individual bargaining and of government determination are not enough, however, to justify a policy of encouraging or even permitting collective bargaining if such a policy can be shown to have more serious shortcomings than its alternatives. Many critics of unionism insist that such is the case. These critics do not confine themselves to those aspects of collective bargaining that might be considered "purely economic"—i.e., related to the allocation of productive resources. Their criticisms cover a broad range of political and social, as well as economic, aspects of unionism. This is as it should be, for really sound policy conclusions are often impossible if one limits one's consideration to the matters encompassed by the narrow boundaries of a single academic discipline, such as economics. This is especially true in the evaluation of collective bargaining and its institutions. Not only professional economists, but politicians, journalists, employers and employer spokesmen, and even union members are among those who have strongly criticized unions and their policies in the last 20 years. These criticisms must be evaluated with care in reaching a conclusion concerning the compatibility of collective bargaining with a free enterprise economy. Only the key criticisms need be considered here. The following will be discussed:

(1) unions are dedicated to the destruction or the drastic modification of the free enterprise system;

(2) the growth of unionism has concentrated enormous power over the welfare of millions of people in the hands of a few irresponsible leaders;

(3) unions are undemocratically run, and so are an evil influence in our political life;

(4) unions are monopolies, and their restrictive working rules and their wage policies interfere seriously with the proper functioning of our economy.

We shall find that there is some justification for at least some of these charges. We should remember, however, that too often all that life offers us is a choice between degrees of imperfection. We shall finally turn, then, to the advantages of collective bargaining, particularly as compared with unilateral determination and government determination, and attempt to judge the relative merits of the three in the American context.

Are Unions Seeking to Destroy the Free Enterprise System?

Some critics of unionism argue that the basic philosophy of the American labor movement is antagonistic to the free enterprise system. It is important, therefore, for us to analyze this philosophy and its origins with some care. The analysis will help us to consider not only this criticism but also some of the others listed above.

The key to an understanding of American unionism is the concept of job consciousness.[6] This concept was developed in the last half of the nineteenth century by the first of the modern trades unions. These unions later federated themselves in an organization which became the American Federation of Labor. The leaders of these early unions became convinced that the chief

[6] In the development of this theme, the author has drawn upon the writings of S. Perlman, especially *A Theory of the Labor Movement*, New York: Macmillan, 1928. See also J. R. Commons and Associates, *History of Labor in the United States*, 4 vols., New York: Macmillan, 1918, 1935.

error of earlier efforts to organize American workers lay in the attempt to appeal to class consciousness. These leaders perceived that any program which was not founded on the assumption of a permanent working class was unrealistic; but they also saw that it was impossible to rely on class consciousness as a lasting cohesive force because of the peculiar characteristics of the American environment. While most of the workers in this country came from lands where class feeling was strong, such class antagonisms were usually forgotten in America. The unparalleled heterogeneity of the working force made racial and national antagonism replace class antagonism. Particularly in the nineteenth century, an abundance of opportunity—or at least the belief in it—also helped to prevent the development of any definite class lines. Horatio Alger's "rags to riches" fables summed up the thinking of the century. Horace Greeley's advice, "Go West, young man!" helps to explain this thinking, because the free land on the western frontier enabled some people to rise from humble status to substantial means. Therefore, programs of social reform which might bear fruit only in generations to come had very little appeal for the optimistic worker who often felt that not only his descendants but he himself would rise out of the working class.

Samuel Gompers, who became the leading spokesman for the AFL viewpoint, argued that—in view of these characteristics of the American environment—a labor movement could survive only by appealing to the "job consciousness" of the workers. Workingmen may not be interested in the long range prospects for the working class as a whole; but rare indeed is the workingman whose interest is not aroused by the prospect of higher wages, greater security and better working conditions on the job that he is holding at the moment. To paraphrase some familiar labor slogans slightly, you must offer the American workingman bread and butter in the here and now instead of pie in the sky in the sweet by and by.

When the labor organizer decides to base his appeal on job consciousness, certain consequences ensue. Obviously, the appeal to job consciousness will be most effective if workers are organized according to job lines—that is, in job groups—because the job problems and interests of teamsters will differ from those of teachers, those of steel workers will differ from those of retail clerks, and so on. In a job-conscious labor movement, therefore, workers are not organized along geographical or political lines; they are organized according to function. This basis of organization creates a difficulty of drawing and maintaining boundaries, in part because products, processes, and materials are constantly changing. One result is jurisdictional disputes, which have plagued the American labor movement from its beginning. Another important consequence of the appeal to job consciousness is the doctrine of craft or trade autonomy, under which each job group is free to formulate its own bargaining policies and demands without any central direction or control from outside the job group. This freedom rests on the theory that no one can know the desires and interests of a particular job group better than the workers in that group. The result is a type of particularistic bargaining that has sometimes been criticized. Since it has been criticized, it is important to understand the vital connection between craft or trade autonomy and the fundamental concept of job consciousness.

A further consequence of the appeal to job consciousness is a deliberate refusal to set up long range goals. Gompers and his associates observed that many of the early labor organizations in this country had been wrecked by doctrinaire debates on the details of the blueprint for the future. Such high-flown debates often interfered with what Gompers considered the real task of a labor movement: the immediate improvement of the lot of the workingman. Take care of today and tomorrow will take care of itself, he thought. Naturally this policy involved the acceptance of the existing order—that is to say, the "wages system," private ownership of property, and the underlying political and social institutions. No frontal assault was to be undertaken on the system; instead, the status of the workingman in the existing order was to be gradually improved.

The main body of the American labor movement has been guided by these principles down to the present day. The controversy which split the AFL in the middle thirties and resulted in the formation of the CIO was very largely a clash over personality and method rather than fundamental principles. The CIO was founded primarily for the purpose of organizing the great numbers of unskilled workers in mass production industries. It found industrial unionism more suited to this purpose than the craft form favored for many years by the AFL. Nevertheless, the CIO based its program on an appeal to job consciousness. In consequence, the CIO organized workers along functional lines, even though in industrial unions, and it never developed any program for really fundamental changes in our political institutions. In 1955, when the organization of the mass production industries was virtually completed and some of the controversial personalities of the thirties had passed from the scene, the AFL and CIO merged. Some serious internal stresses have developed in the merged federation, but there is no quarrel over the fundamental precepts of job consciousness.[7]

[7] For a discussion of the AFL-CIO split and the merger, by one of the chief architects of the latter, see A. J. Goldberg, *AFL-CIO Labor United*, New York: McGraw-Hill, 1956. There have been a few avowedly "revolutionary" unions, like the IWW, in American history, and some that have been led or controlled by Communists; but those in the latter group have generally pursued the same "bread and butter" objectives as the

It is important to understand that the basic conservatism of the American labor movement is the direct outgrowth of the movement's most powerful cohesive force. It may seem strange to many people that any labor movement should be considered "conservative." Are not unions always agitating for changes in the status quo? They generally are, of course, but present-day American unions do not seek basic changes in the economic and political framework. They seek to better the status of the workingman, but within the confines of the private enterprise system. In a majority of the important industrial countries of the world before World War II, at least some of the major unions were actively seeking to bring about fundamental changes in the economic environment in which they were operating. The necessity for concentrating on the appeal to job consciousness has prevented the development of any such program here. This does not mean that American unions are necessarily committed to a defense of the free enterprise system; it means only that, generally speaking, they operate entirely in the present, with no blueprint for the future.[8]

This kind of approach does not insure, of course, that unions will never pursue short-run policies that have the long-run effect of undermining the free enterprise system. As was noted above, this is one of the common criticisms of unions. In a later section we will turn our attention to the basic question of the effect of unionism and collective bargaining on the economy. At this point, it should be emphasized that there is no evidence that any major unions are pursuing policies deliberately intended to weaken or destroy the private enterprise system.

Do Unions Permit Undesirable Concentration of Power?
Are They Undemocratic?

These two charges are best discussed together—because they primarily involve internal union government. The tremendous growth of unions in the last three decades, the concentration of the bulk of union members in a few giant unions, the concentration of control over collective bargaining largely in the internationals,[9] and the control of these internationals by a

---

majority of American unions. See J. Barbash, *The Practice of Unionism*, New York: Harper, 1956, Chap. 14.

[8] Some union leaders—for example, Walter Reuther—undoubtedly have their own blueprints which they advocate from time to time as influential members of the community; but I do not know of any instance in which union bargaining power has been used in support of such long-range objectives, except possibly in the case of a few Communist-led unions.

[9] Most national unions in the United States are called "internationals" because they have a few foreign locals, mainly in Canada.

few men have alarmed many people. Labor leaders have been repeatedly denounced as arrogant, corrupt, ruthless, irresponsible dictators. More temperate observers have questioned whether such great concentration of power in private hands is compatible with democratic government, or any government at all. This is closely related to the charge that will be discussed in the next section, that the union (or union leader) is a monopolist *par excellence.*

Superficially, there is much evidence to support the viewpoint that unions represent a dangerous concentration of power. Three international unions —the International Brotherhood of Teamsters, the United Automobile Workers, and the United Steelworkers of America—all claim more than one million members each. At the other extreme, there are sixteen international unions that report memberships of less than one thousand. Nearly 70 per cent of all international unions in the United States claim fewer than 100,000 members. But it is the relatively few really large unions that are the great seats of power in the labor movement. While only about 30 per cent of the internationals have more than 100,000 members, about 80 per cent of all union members are enrolled in these large unions. Better than a third of all members are found in the six unions with membership of 500,000 or more.[10] Is it true, then, that the organization of the labor force has given a handful of labor leaders a stranglehold on our economy?

In order to answer this question, we must consider the extent to which authority is centralized in union government. The most important units of government, for our purposes, are the local union, the international union, and the national federation. There are about 75,000 local unions, varying in size from a local with six or eight members to the giant UAW Local 600, which claims more than 25,000 members. There are about 185 international unions. Of these, 135 are affiliated with the AFL-CIO. The unaffiliated unions are mainly in the railroad industry and government service where independent unionism has been more or less traditional.

At the top of the organization chart of the labor movement we find the national federation, the AFL-CIO. Samuel Gompers once characterized the American Federation of Labor as a "rope of sand." He meant that there was no force binding the affiliates of the federation to the central body. This statement is as true of the merged AFL-CIO as of the AFL in the days of Gompers. The affiliated international unions are, for most purposes, far more powerful and important units of the labor movement than the top federation.

---

[10] Membership figures are taken from *Directory of National and International Unions in the United States,* 1957, U.S. Department of Labor Bulletin No. 1222, Washington: U.S. Government Printing Office, 1957.

The only significant disciplinary authority that the top federation has over affiliated internationals is the power of expulsion. This power is of limited effectiveness. Major unions—such as the Machinists and the Mine Workers—have voluntarily withdrawn from federations without any serious loss of strength or membership. The Teamsters boast that they have greatly increased their membership since their expulsion from the AFL-CIO in 1957.[11] Thus the only significant control of the federation over the internationals is not particularly potent, especially in the case of the large, powerful internationals. Indeed, some of the important internationals have been able to influence federation decisions at times by threatening withdrawal, though many attempts of this kind appear to have been unsuccessful.

For many years, the only important restriction which the American Federation of Labor attempted to enforce on its affiliated internationals was that each should confine its organizing activities to its recognized jurisdiction—a restriction more easily enforced with regard to the smaller internationals than with regard to the large ones. More recently, the authority of the federation over its affiliates has expanded. In 1949–50, the CIO expelled eleven of its affiliates on the ground that they were Communist-dominated. In 1953, the AFL expelled the Longshoremen's Union on the ground that it had failed to eliminate criminals from its leadership. When the AFL and the CIO merged, the constitution of the new organization provided for a standing Committee on Ethical Practices. That Committee later proposed and the AFL-CIO adopted six Codes of Ethical Practices. In December 1957, the AFL-CIO convention formally expelled three unions from membership—the Bakers, the Laundry Workers and the Teamsters —on the ground that they had failed to eliminate corrupt leaders and practices. Although the area subject to the scrutiny of the federation has thus been expanded, it should be emphasized that today as in the past the federation does not attempt to regulate the collective bargaining programs of affiliates. The present-day AFL-CIO observes trade autonomy, as did its predecessors. The important point, for the purpose of this discussion, is that there is no power over the whole economy centralized in the top federation.

The relationship of internationals to their locals is quite different from the relationship of internationals to federations. All international unions exercise a considerable degree of control over many of the major activities of their locals. Some internationals exercise more control than others, but in

---

[11] Expulsion has been much more effective when—as in the case of the United Electrical Workers which was expelled from the CIO—the federation was able to set up a rival union with the same jurisdiction as the expelled union, and the newly created rival attracted a substantial part of the membership. Some small unions have accepted "monitorship" by the federation as an alternative to expulsion.

almost all cases the international is predominant. The control is generally maintained by constitutional provisions which permit the international union to take over the direction of the affairs of the local union or to dissolve the local and set up a new local in its place. Thus the international has much more drastic authority over the local than the federation has over the international.

Even those local unions that enjoy a great deal of autonomy generally accept some degree of guidance from the international union in collective bargaining matters. In some instances, indeed, the constitution of the international union requires the local to submit all collective bargaining agreements to the international union executive board for approval. In the more highly centralized unions, collective bargaining is carried on by the international union officers themselves—almost always, however, with local union representatives participating.

We can conclude that there is a considerable degree of centralization in a great many international unions, although generalization is difficult because historical background and structural differences between industries have caused considerable variation as between different internationals. Centralization of authority cannot be regarded as necessarily evil where the circumstances in a particular industry make it essential to the effectiveness of the union. We must also remember that, whatever the arguments may be against centralization, many of the abuses in the labor movement are attributable to local autonomy. Indeed, one eminent authority has argued that the internationals should delegate broad policy-making powers to the federations, thus greatly increasing the centralization of authority in the labor movement. Such a shift would promote greater emphasis on long-run considerations, he believes.[12]

This proposal points up the fact that it is the degree of responsibility associated with centralization and the uses to which the resulting power is put that really determine whether centralization is dangerous to the public. In other words, are unions democratic? Are their policies harmful?

Unions can be roughly grouped into three categories. First, there are some unions, usually small, in which policies are adopted only after quite extensive debate among the membership, and the members maintain a very close check on the work of the officers. A good example of this type is the National Maritime Union, particularly in recent years. In the second classification, which probably includes the majority of unions and practically all of the larger ones, are the unions in which the rank and file takes

---

[12] S. H. Slichter, *The Challenge of Industrial Relations: Trade Unions, Management, and the Public Interest*, Ithaca: Cornell University Press, 1947, pp. 175–6.

but little interest in the day-to-day administration of the union and often no particular interest in the larger issues of union policy so long as all is going well and the union is adequately handling shop grievances. However, when the union suffers a major reverse in collective bargaining, when the leadership is vigorously attacked, or when the membership is in some other way given an extraordinary stimulus, it takes a greater interest in union affairs and checks up more closely on the leaders. The third classification, which includes a minority of unions, is composed of those controlled by dictatorial methods. In such unions opposition is ruthlessly suppressed. Rival candidates for office are seldom permitted to complete their campaigns—they are expelled from the union or otherwise disqualified before the election. The membership may be kept in ignorance of what the leaders are doing with the funds of the union. At times there may even be secret under-the-table deals with employers. Even in this latter situation, however, if the union constitution provides some of the elements of democratic government, the union members—like the irate citizenry of a boss-ridden town—can sometimes rise up and eject their despotic leaders. Such incidents are not unknown in union history.[13] The problem may be different, and much more difficult, if control of the union has been seized by professional criminals.[14]

Even in the unions characterized by dictatorial control the wishes and aspirations of the great body of rank and file members cannot be entirely ignored by the leaders. This is particularly true in collective bargaining negotiations. Almost all unions have constitutional provisions that require a vote of the members to authorize a strike and that require officers to submit proposed agreements to the membership for ratification. In most unions with even a semblance of democracy there is an opposition group that is always ready to point out the shortcomings of any settlement proposed by the administration group. Union leaders, like political leaders, generally try to keep "an ear to the ground." There is usually a fairly steady flow of information on the thinking of the membership from shop stewards to local officers to international representatives or district officers to the top leaders of the union. The surest basis of lasting power within any union is the ability to interpret or to anticipate the needs and desires of the members.

---

[13] For an interesting description of such an event see H. R. Northrup, "The Tobacco Workers International Union," *Quarterly Journal of Economics*, Vol. LVI, May 1942.

[14] A distinction should be made between the legitimate union leader who "goes wrong" and robs the union, and the professional criminal who takes over a union and uses it for his own gain. Despite the publicity given to both of these problems during the McClellan Committee hearings, only a small proportion of unions have ever had either problem. There is reason to believe that the problems of embezzlement and control by criminals are no more widespread in unions than in business. This does not mean, of course, that the problem is unimportant in either area.

At the same time, the union leader must consider the survival and growth needs of his organization. While the interests of the members and the interests of the organization may often be identical, this is not always so, especially in the short run. The Cigar Makers' Union provides an excellent example of conflict of these interests. For many years the members of this union, who directly controlled its policies through extensive use of the referendum, refused to permit the use of new methods and machines in unionized shops. The officers of the union argued incessantly against this policy, but the members feared—no doubt correctly—that abandonment of the policy would expose their skills to quick obsolescence. The union lost members rapidly, declining from 53,000 members in 1916 to 23,000 in 1923 and 7,000 in 1934. Although the union was almost destroyed by this policy, some of the old-time cigar makers were able to continue working in their old way in those few shops that remained under the control of the union. Similarly, the National Window Glass Workers adamantly opposed the adoption of glass making machines in unionized plants for twenty years. The final result was the formal dissolution of the union, for lack of members, in 1928.[15]

The personal ambition and interests of union leaders may also have a considerable influence on union policy. After many years in office a union leader is likely to feel that no one else could do as good a job as he and that consequently the loss of his services would be a great blow to the union and to the members as well. Therefore the leader may feel that anything that is done to retain his personal control is really in the best interests of the union and the membership in the long run. In some cases such rationalization may be unnecessary; the leader may be ruthless and cynical, perfectly willing to follow a policy of rule or ruin. Moreover, the ambitions of a union leader may extend beyond the confines of his own organization. He may aspire to a position of prominence in the national federation, or in the world labor movement. He may be willing, therefore, to sacrifice the interests of his own union and its members in order to promote his personal prestige. Such tactics are often quite dangerous to himself, however, unless the leader is able to maintain an iron-clad dictatorship within his own organization. Dissatisfaction with his policies may bring about his ouster unless he is very firmly established.

Thus there are generally at least three important elements in the motivation of a union leader. He must, at the minimum, keep his members reasonably well-satisfied. At the same time, he must consider the survival and

[15] Slichter, *Union Policies and Industrial Management,* Washington: Brookings Institution, 1941, pp. 216–23.

growth needs of the organization which he heads. Finally, he must give some attention to the task of keeping personal political fences mended. There are times, of course, when all three of these elements conduce to the same general type of policy. For example, in a time of general prosperity a union leader would hardly ever make a mistake to press for substantial wage increases. But there are also times and circumstances when these motivations conflict. Which one gets priority then? The answer cannot be a general one. The order of priority will be determined in part by the particular circumstances and in part by the personality of the individual union leader or leaders who are responsible for making policy within the union. To some extent also the decision will be dependent on the extent of control exercised by union members over their leaders. The leader of a democratic union generally knows rather precisely what his members want, and he must make that his goal unless he can persuade his members to want something else. Other union leaders generally have a broader area of discretion. Still, however, almost no leaders ever succeed in completely ignoring the desires of the members, and few try.

There is no simple answer to the question, Are unions undemocratic? A few are obviously undemocratic; a few are obviously democratic, in the town-meeting sense. In the majority, the major objective is generally to keep the members satisfied. However, lack of information or inertia on the part of the members, quite as much as a lack of the forms of democratic government, may result in government by bureaucracy. This is not unusual in other types of organizations, of course; generally clubs, lodges, fraternities, cities, and even states are governed by the few who are willing to expend the necessary time and energy. There is room for great improvement in union government in this respect. We cannot reasonably conclude, however, that union government in general is so undemocratic as to be a menace to our political institutions. Quite the contrary; union government compares not unfavorably with our political government in this respect, and, as will be explained below, the over-all effect of unionism is to strengthen democratic institutions.[16]

Are Unions Dangerous Monopolies?

Probably the most frequently repeated charge against unions is that they are dangerous monopolies, mercilessly exploiting consumers and at times

---

[16] For a valuable discussion of this general problem, with a conclusion perhaps more pessimistic than mine, see W. M. Leiserson, *American Trade Union Democracy*, New York: Columbia University Press, 1959.

employers, and seriously interfering with the free-market mechanism of our economy. This is a favorite complaint not only of interest groups opposed to unions, but of well-known economic theorists.[17] The charge is the main basis for arguments that unions should be subject to the antitrust laws, or some appropriate modification thereof—which would mean, of course, that unions would be rendered almost wholly ineffective.[18] To evaluate this charge and this program, we must examine the total effect of unionism on the functioning of our economy. Do unions exploit other groups for the benefit of labor? Do they interfere with the efficient operation of our economy?

The economists who have studied the over-all effects of unions and collective bargaining on the economy fall into two main groups. One group has started with *a priori* assumptions and has made logical deductions from them. The other group has observed the actual behavior of unions, workers, and employers, and has analyzed the available statistical data. As might be expected, the conclusions of these two groups are quite different. The first group has typically assumed, either explicitly or implicitly, that union leaders are interested mainly in maximizing the employers' wage bill; that employers are generally powerless to resist union demands; that, without unions, we would have reasonably competitive labor markets; that employers are influenced only by profit considerations in making employment, output, and price decisions. When these assumptions are made, it is logical to conclude, as many have, that the economic effects of unionism are bad. According to this line of reasoning, unions undermine the free enterprise economy in two chief ways: by interfering with the efficient use of resources through distortion of the wage structure, and by causing chronic inflation through upward pressure on the wage level.[19]

[17] For example, see the Simons article cited in note 1 above; also F. Machlup, "Monopolistic Wage Determination as a Part of the General Problem of Monopoly," in *Wage Determination and the Economics of Liberalism*, Chamber of Commerce of the United States, January 11, 1947; Jacob Viner, "The Role of Costs in a System of Economic Liberalism," *ibid.*; C. E. Lindblom, *Unions and Capitalism*, New Haven: Yale University Press, 1949; E. H. Chamberlin, "Economic Analysis of Labor Union Power," in Chamberlin *et al.*, *Labor Unions and Public Policy*, Washington: American Enterprise Association, 1958. For excellent critiques of this general point of view, see R. A. Lester, "Reflections on the 'Labor Monopoly' Issue," *Journal of Political Economy*, Vol. LV, December 1947; L. G. Reynolds, *The Structure of Labor Markets*, New York: Harper, 1949, esp. pp. 248–56; John T. Dunlop, review of Lindblom's *Unions and Capitalism* in *American Economic Review*, Vol. XL, June 1950.

[18] For an explicit statement of such a program, see H. Gregg Lewis, "The Labor Monopoly Problem: A Positive Program," *Journal of Political Economy*, Vol. LIX, August 1951.

[19] See C. E. Lindblom, *op.cit.*, for a detailed demonstration of the way in which such conclusions can be deduced from the foregoing assumptions.

The other group of students of this problem criticize both the assumptions and the conclusions just described. They point out that because of the unique characteristics of labor markets (which were described earlier in this chapter), such markets would not be competitive even in the absence of labor unions. They also emphasize a fundamental error in the assumptions concerning union behavior: unions do not uniformly seek to maximize the employer's wage bill, regardless of other considerations. The conventional economic analysis of monopoly behavior simply cannot be applied to unions because they do not "sell" labor, nor can they adjust the amount offered for sale as business monopolists are assumed to do, and in many other ways they cannot or do not behave as monopolies.

The most thorough studies of the available statistical data provide very little support for the idea that unionism has significantly increased labor's share of national income over the long run. Unionism may have contributed in a minor way to changes in wage structure, including compression of wage differentials, but the major forces bringing about such changes probably would have produced about the same effect in the absence of collective bargaining. Many people assert confidently that unions are a major cause—if not *the* major cause—of inflation under conditions of high employment. Economists are sharply divided on this point, with some agreeing with the foregoing statement but with others arguing that the primary causes of inflation lie in monetary policies. Some investigators have even contended that, for a variety of reasons, unions may cause a "wage lag" in times of rapid inflation. Perhaps it is safe to conclude that under some circumstances collective bargaining may contribute to general inflation, but at other times its contribution to inflation is negligible compared to that of other factors.[20] One economist, after carefully analyzing the voluminous studies of the past decade bearing on these points, concluded as follows:

> To sum up, part of the economic power attributed to American unionism is more illusory than it is real. To the extent that it is real it carries more promise than it does menace.[21]

The idea that unions have had but little independent effect on either the overall wage structure or the general level of wages is a startling one to many

[20] For an excellent analytical summary of the voluminous literature on the subjects treated in this paragraph, see George H. Hildebrand, "The Economic Effects of Unionism," in N. W. Chamberlain, F. C. Pierson, and Theresa Wolfson, eds., *A Decade of Industrial Relations Research 1946–1956*, New York: Harper, 1958 (Publication No. 19 of the Industrial Relations Research Association). See also the papers by Albert Rees, Clark Kerr, L. G. Reynolds, and John T. Dunlop in *Wages, Prices, Profits and Productivity*, New York: The American Assembly, 1959.
[21] Hildebrand, *loc.cit.*, pp. 137–8.

people. How can we explain such a state of affairs? Isn't it the major function of unions to force wages up? Before undertaking an explanation, we will turn briefly to another aspect of the "labor monopoly" problem, which will help to shed light on the question. "Industry-wide bargaining," so called, has been attacked as one important device by which unions exercise their monopoly power. Pattern bargaining as practiced by the United Steelworkers of America has been identified as a form of industry-wide bargaining.[22] Under this practice, according to its critics, a giant union concentrates its strength to force concessions from one of the major firms in the industry and then compels the rest of the industry to conform to the pattern thus set. In addition, the argument runs, the Steelworkers compel an unrelated industry—steel fabrication—to follow the pattern.

Let us consult the facts. Most of the companies in basic steel do follow the pattern set by the United States Steel Corporation, the largest producer. However, this practice long antedated unionism and collective bargaining. In steel fabrication, on the other hand, the "pattern" becomes a target which is missed more often than not. In recent years, in a typical district of the union, a substantial majority of the steel-fabricating and miscellaneous units under agreement with the Steelworkers have settled for appreciably less in wages and fringe benefits than the so-called industry pattern.[23] Careful examination of a number of cases in which the union accepted less than the pattern shows that labor and product market considerations were usually quite important factors in the bargaining.

In this fact we find a clue to the apparent failure of unions to exert much independent influence on the wage structure or the wage level of the country as a whole. The underlying market forces that have long been an important influence in wage determination are still effective, although the institutional channels through which they operate have changed. If a wage increase would clearly cause unemployment, union representatives will frequently drop their wage demands.[24] If the union insists on the wage increase regardless of consequences, the employer is likely to resist, and the union may find itself unable to command the support of its members for a strike. The employer is still subject to most of the same economic forces that influenced his wage policies in pre-union days. Today, they help to determine his bargaining position and thus influence what the union has to accept as a wage

[22] For example, Leo Wolman, *Industry-wide Bargaining*, Irvington-on-Hudson, New York: Foundation for Economic Education, 1948.
[23] George Seltzer, "Pattern Bargaining and the United Steelworkers," *Journal of Political Economy*, Vol. LIX, August 1951.
[24] Seltzer, *loc.cit.*; George P. Shultz and Charles A. Myers, "Union Wage Decisions and Employment," *American Economic Review*, Vol. XL, June 1950.

settlement. At the same time, it must be remembered that the typical labor market is so full of rigidities and imperfections that purely economic forces must have been considerably diluted in their influence on wage determination even before the advent of unionism. The factual evidence suggests that collective bargaining has not significantly altered this influence, such as it is.

The foregoing discussion is not intended to suggest that unions are always and everywhere helpless pawns in the face of inexorable economic forces. Where the employer is sheltered from economic pressures, as for example by a patent monopoly, the union may be able to capture a share of the monopoly returns for its members. In addition, there are undoubtedly cases in which unions ignore economic pressures—perhaps even at the cost of putting the employer out of business. In other cases, where an employer has been paying substandard wages, the union may be able to get very substantial wage increases without any disruptive consequences. Similarly, a union may be able to bring about the correction of an intraplant or intra-industry wage structure that is badly out of balance without endangering the employer's competitive position.[25] On the other hand, the economic pressures on the union and the employer may be well-nigh irresistible where there is strong competition in the product market and the industry is only partly organized. If any generalization at all is possible concerning collective bargaining, it is that there is tremendous diversity in both situations and behavior. The point here is that purely economic forces have never been the exclusive factor in wage determination, and that unions generally have not succeeded in escaping those economic forces; in the aggregate, these forces appear to influence the wage settlements that unions accept about as much as they ever influenced employers' unilateral wage policies.

We should not leave this subject without a brief consideration of the relative importance of wages in the collective bargaining process. Often it is assumed, especially by economists, that money is the central or even exclusive concern of collective bargaining. This assumption is wrong in far more cases than it is correct. Wage bargaining almost always takes places in a context of bargaining over other related points. The components of the labor agreement are to some extent interchangeable in the bargaining process. A union may forego a part or all of a wage increase that it might otherwise get in order to obtain (for example) a union shop clause. The importance of noneconomic factors will be further discussed in the next section of this chapter. The point to be emphasized here is that few unions

---

[25] For example, see Jack Stieber, *The Steel Industry Wage Structure*, Cambridge: Harvard University Press, 1959.

have unlimited bargaining power; workers are frequently more interested in considerations other than money; hence unions must often concentrate their limited bargaining power on some of the things that are more important to their members than wages.[26]

Before concluding this section, let us examine briefly one more aspect of the monopoly charge against unions. Critics have frequently pointed to the "featherbedding" practices of unions as another harmful exercise of monopoly power. The varieties of featherbedding are numerous; they include the requirement of pay for work not done, opposition to more efficient methods of production, requirement of unnecessary work, restriction of output, and so on. Featherbedding rules are adopted most typically in an effort to enhance job security. Economists almost universally condemn this method of meeting the problem. Few people care to defend such practices. Yet the problem should be viewed in its proper perspective. Unions are by no means the only group in our society which attempts to protect its security in such a fashion. One early study concluded that unorganized workers, for example, practice restriction of output more extensively than union members.[27] Moreover, the economic burden of featherbedding is generally overestimated. Such practices are either unknown or relatively rare in most mass production industries, and in those industries where they are found they are likely to be "paid for" by wages that are lower than they would otherwise be.[28] Efforts to eradicate featherbedding by law seem doomed to failure.[29] The chief difficulty, as was once pointed out by the late Senator Taft, is that no one has yet succeeded in drafting a law that would eliminate the undesirable practices without also forbidding many that are generally conceded to be legitimate. For example, health and safety admittedly require some limitations on speed of work and minimum crew sizes; but at what point do such limitations cross the line between legitimate protection and featherbedding? Even an expert would find it hard to say. We must

[26] Studies of worker dissatisfaction and turnover show that manual laborers are primarily interested in these factors in addition to (and frequently more than) the wage level: the kind of work—whether monotonous and repetitive or interesting; the surroundings in which the work must be performed; the degree of independence from close supervision—workers dislike "a nosy boss," or one who is "always breathing down the back of your neck"; fairness of treatment on the job; and the security of the job. Cf. L. G. Reynolds and J. Shister, *op.cit.*; E. Mayo, *The Human Problems of an Industrial Civilization*, New York: Macmillan, 1933; S. H. Slichter, *The Turnover of Factory Labor*, New York: Appleton, 1921.

[27] S. B. Mathewson, *Restriction of Output Among Unorganized Workers*, New York: Viking, 1931.

[28] S. H. Slichter, *Union Policies and Industrial Management*, Washington: Brookings Institution, 1941, esp. Chap. VI.

[29] Benjamin Aaron, "Government Restraints on Featherbedding," *Stanford Law Review*, Vol. 5, July 1953.

conclude that legislation is not the solution; perhaps there is no immediate solution. Although featherbedding is not a serious threat to our economy, the practices are deplorable. They are an item on the debit side that must be weighed against the advantages of collective bargaining in judging its desirability.

We have seen that the American labor movement is not consciously striving to do away with the private enterprise system. While some unions are quite undemocratic and a great many could be more democratic, the whole picture of union government compares not unfavorably with our political government. There are dangers, both economic and social, in centralization of power in unions; but decentralization creates its own problems and centralized authority is essential in some unions. The real test of the social desirability of centralization in unions is the use to which the resulting power is put. There is no proof that unions have used their power to the serious detriment of our economy. On the contrary, the available data are consistent with the conclusion that unions have had but little independent effect on the distribution of the national income, the geographical and industrial wage structure and on the general wage level. Whatever influence economic forces have exerted in wage determination seems to have been relatively unimpaired, in the aggregate, by the advent of unionism.

The Positive Side

Up to this point, we have been considering the common criticisms of unions and have found only a modicum of justification for such criticisms. Let us now look at the other side of the coin. Are there any positive reasons for accepting the protection and encouragement of collective bargaining as public policy?

One needs only to talk to a few working people or union and management participants in collective bargaining to perceive that some of the greatest values of the institution have been ignored or unduly minimized by a great many critics. Perhaps the greatest single contribution of collective bargaining is to insure equitable treatment of the worker by his employer. Virtually all collective bargaining agreements provide a procedure for the consideration of worker grievances, and more than 90 per cent of the agreements now in force provide for the submission of most types of unsettled grievances to an impartial arbitrator for final and binding decision. Under such a system, a worker cannot be discharged or otherwise disciplined except for just cause. Thus most agreements provide a kind of industrial "Bill of Rights" for workers.[30] Most agreements also provide mutually acceptable procedures for layoffs and rehiring, and sometimes for promotions. Collective bargaining also contributes to the development of more rational intraplant and industry wage structures. More effective "two-way communication" between workers and management usually results from collective bargaining. Finally, and partly as a result of the foregoing, collective bargaining gives the worker a sense of participation in the decisions that vitally affect his working life. As Slichter puts it:

> Trade-unions have helped to reduce the scope of personal management, to make management a matter of rules instead of men, to cause rights as well as duties to be attached to jobs and due process of law to be introduced into shops where formerly the boss has been almost as unrestrained as an oriental despot. Trade-unions make men more self-assertive, more contentious, sometimes more difficult to manage, often more annoying to the boss, but more independent and self-respecting.[31]

More important, such a feeling of participation makes the worker a citizen of industry, rather than a subject; it makes him less inclined to revolt than a system that imposes conditions on him which he finds intolerable and cannot challenge. Thus collective bargaining strengthens the private enterprise system and democratic government as well.

Obviously, this does not mean that collective bargaining never creates any serious problems, or that unions can do no wrong. Some of the trouble spots have already been mentioned and others will be referred to below. The shortcomings of unions and collective bargaining are put in proper perspective, however, by the consideration that we must choose among three possibilities: unilateral determination, governmental determination, and collective bargaining. Of these, the third is clearly the most compatible with the private enterprise system. The case against labor combinations is built primarily on false analogies between product markets and labor markets, between business enterprises and trade unions. Elimination of unions would not make labor markets competitive; and economic analysis based on the assumption that unions and their leaders behave as business men are

---

[30] Cf. the statement of H. W. Anderson, then Vice President of General Motors: "Our experience with the Umpire machinery in our labor agreements shows that impartial review of Management's action in disciplinary situations protects employees from errors or unfair treatment and provides a fair and peaceful means of settling such disputes." "Management's Responsibility for Discipline," a talk before the Industrial Relations Section of the California Institute of Technology, Los Angeles, California, January 1947.

[31] From "Notes on Collective Bargaining," in *Explorations in Economics,* New York: McGraw-Hill Book Co., 1936, p. 290. Copyright 1936. Reprinted by courtesy of McGraw-Hill Book Co.

supposed to is dangerously misleading. Even on purely economic grounds, the case against unionism is refuted by the facts, which disprove the contention that union policies are undermining our economy. When we widen our focus to include other significant considerations, the balance in favor of collective bargaining becomes clear. The political and social values of this type of industrial government justify a public policy aimed at its protection and encouragement.

A Review of Public Policy

The policy of the federal government has not always been directed to this end. Its policy for many years can best be characterized as "grudging toleration" of collective bargaining. There were no statutes specifically regulating industrial relations during most of the nineteenth century; governmental policy was formulated and applied by the courts, which relied on common law doctrines. The courts found justification in these doctrines for numerous restrictions on and prohibitions of union tactics and objectives. However, the courts found no basis for interfering with the antiunion activities of employers.

Early in the twentieth century, the Sherman Act was held to be applicable to unions despite some evidence of a contrary intent on the part of Congress. Thereafter, this law provided an important new basis for proceedings against union activities. In the nineteenth century, damage suits and criminal prosecutions were the usual methods of proceeding against unions. In the Pullman strike of 1894, a new weapon was used with great success: the injunction. Thereafter, both federal and state courts issued injunctions in labor disputes with increasing frequency, reaching an all-time high in the twenties. Unfortunately, such injunctions were all too frequently issued with little regard for the common law principles on which they were supposedly based or for the procedural safeguards usually followed in our courts. Moreover, they were often extremely sweeping in their prohibitions. Labor protested bitterly against "government by injunction." [32]

In 1932 the use of federal injunctions in labor disputes was virtually eliminated by the passage of the Norris-LaGuardia Act. This law marked the beginning of a fundamental change in federal labor policy. By eliminating one of the most effective weapons used by employers in preventing union

---

[32] For the early history of labor law in the United States, see E. E. Witte, *The Government in Labor Disputes*, New York: McGraw-Hill, 1932; C. O. Gregory, *Labor and the Law* (second rev. ed.), New York: Norton, 1958; F. Frankfurter and N. Greene, *The Labor Injunction*, New York: Macmillan, 1930; E. Berman, *Labor and the Sherman Act*, New York: Harper, 1930; A. T. Mason, *Organized Labor and the Law*, Durham, N.C.: Duke University Press, 1926.

organization and thwarting collective bargaining, the Norris-LaGuardia Act indicated a friendlier governmental attitude toward unionism.[33] However, it left the employer with a formidable arsenal of antiunion weapons, including discrimination for union activity, blacklists, labor spies, company unionism, and other devices. The Wagner Act (more formally known as the National Labor Relations Act), which was passed in 1935, marked the emergence of a full-blown policy of governmental encouragement and protection of collective bargaining.[34] It completely outlawed all forms of employer interference with employee efforts to organize or assist unions, and it directed the employer to bargain collectively with any union that might win the support of a majority of his employees.[35]

From the outset, some people argued that the Wagner Act was decidedly "one-sided." This law placed numerous restrictions on employers but apparently did not limit unions in any way.[36] Its critics argued that the act should be "equalized" by the addition of some restrictions on unions. Few of these critics recognized that literal "equalization" would have been accomplished merely by forbidding unions to interfere with the efforts of employers to organize for collective bargaining, and by requiring them to bargain with any employer whose employees they represented. Such provisions certainly would have been consistent with the basic purpose of the act, and probably should have been included; but in 1935 there seemed to be no real need for such provisions. Those who criticized the Wagner Act

[33] The "new" labor policy was not completely new. It had been followed briefly during World War I, only to be abandoned with the "return to normalcy"; and the same general policy had been applied to the railroad industry in 1926.

[34] For developments under the Wagner Act, consult the Annual Reports of the National Labor Relations Board covering the period from 1935 to date; also J. Rosenfarb, *The National Labor Policy and How It Works,* New York: Harper, 1940; D. O. Bowman, *Public Control of Labor Relations,* New York: Macmillan, 1942; H. W. Metz, *Labor Policy of the Federal Government,* Washington: The Brookings Institution, 1945; H. A. Millis and Emily C. Brown, *From the Wagner Act to Taft-Hartley,* Chicago: University of Chicago Press, 1950.

[35] A somewhat later development was the almost complete exemption of unions from the antitrust laws by court interpretation. Such an exemption had apparently been granted by Congress in the Clayton Act of 1914, but the Supreme Court decided that no significant change had been made in the applicability of the antitrust laws to labor unions. *Duplex Printing Press Co.* versus *Deering,* 254 U.S. 443 (1921). In 1941, however, the Supreme Court held that when the Norris-LaGuardia Act and the Clayton Act are read together as "interlaced" statutes, the Congressional intent to exempt unions from antitrust proceedings is clear. The only exception is where unions are in collusion with employers to enable the latter to violate the antitrust laws. *United States* versus *Hutcheson,* 312 U.S. 219 (1941); see also *Allen Bradley Co.* versus *Local Union No. 3, IBEW,* 325 U.S. 797 (1945).

[36] Actually, the law was ultimately interpreted to place rather important obligations on unions acting as bargaining agents. See N. W. Chamberlain, "Obligations upon the Union under the National Labor Relations Act," *American Economic Review,* Vol. XXXVII, March 1947.

as one-sided did not want such minor additions, however. Most of the critics demanded changes that would have had the effect of considerably modifying the basic purpose of the Wagner Act.

The Taft-Hartley Act

These critics gained increasing support as unions became stronger and more belligerent during the late thirties. The first results appeared in the states. While a number of so-called "little Wagner Acts" had been passed by state legislatures in 1937, by 1939 the political climate had so changed that Wisconsin repealed its protective, Wagner-type law and substituted an "equalized" law which had as its primary purpose the restriction of unionism and collective bargaining. Thereafter most of the states that enacted labor relations legislation made it restrictive in nature, rather than protective.[37] It was not until 1947, however, that Congress changed the federal labor policy. In that year the Labor Management Relations Act, usually called the Taft-Hartley Act, was passed.

Unfortunately, the Taft-Hartley Act soon became a potent political symbol. According to most union leaders, it was a "slave labor act." According to most management spokesmen, it was a new Magna Carta for the workingman and a guardian of the public interest. The shrill exchange of charges and countercharges all but obscured the real facts about the Taft-Hartley Act and the Wagner Act as well. The atmosphere of partisanship and special pleading persisted during repeated efforts to amend or repeal the Taft-Hartley Act, all of which were stalemated until 1959. In that year Congress passed the Landrum-Griffin Act. This new law amended certain provisions of the Taft-Hartley Act and also enacted a number of supplementary regulations, most of which were intended to correct abuses disclosed by the McClellan Committee hearings.

The Taft-Hartley and Landrum-Griffin laws taken together are an extremely complex body of legislation, covering a great variety of subjects. This legislation is neither pure black nor pure white, as some partisans have argued. Any sound judgment concerning its merits must be based on a meticulously detailed analysis of its many provisions and of the decisions and interpretations arrived at thereunder. Space does not permit such a detailed analysis here, for which the reader should perhaps be thankful. The author assures the reader that the general conclusions that follow could

---

[37] See C. C. Killingsworth, *State Labor Relations Acts*, Chicago: University of Chicago Press, 1948.

be supported, if space permitted, by a great many illustrations and citations.[38]

In the first place, it is important to note that the Taft-Hartley Act retained virtually unchanged almost all of the important substantive provisions of the Wagner Act. With only one moderately important exception,[39] the restrictions on employer interference with efforts of his employees to form, join, or assist unions are still in the law. The employer must still bargain with a union that represents a majority of his employees. In addition, some of the provisions which were new in Taft-Hartley were long-overdue extensions of the basic principle of protecting and encouraging collective bargaining: for example, the prohibition of boycotts or other economic pressure designed to oust a certified bargaining agent or in furtherance of a jurisdictional dispute, and the requirement that unions, as well as employers, must bargain collectively in appropriate circumstances. Moreover, some of the other Taft-Hartley innovations, while not strictly necessary to the Wagner Act policy, are not in conflict with it: for example, the requirement that unions file financial and informational reports with the government, and provide financial reports to their members.[40] Finally, the national emergency disputes procedure provides machinery that, even though exceedingly clumsy and frequently ineffective, is not seriously harmful to unions, despite their violent protests against the role of the injunction in the procedure.

Thus there is much in the Taft-Hartley Act that a disinterested supporter of collective bargaining cannot object to, and some things that he should welcome. The same is true of the more recent Landrum-Griffin Act. This newer law covers a broad range of subjects and its provisions cannot be briefly summarized. Speaking very generally, the provisions cover such matters as union elections, procedures for disciplining members, rights of members within unions, trusteeships over local unions, "conflicts of interest," bribery, extortion and embezzlement of union funds.[41] If one accepts the

[38] There has been a great volume of periodical literature, and a few books as well, on the Taft-Hartley Act. Perhaps the most useful articles for the general leader are these: E. E. Witte, "An Appraisal of the Taft-Hartley Act," *American Economic Review, Supplement,* Vol. XXXVIII, May 1948; A. Cox, "Some Aspects of the Labor-Management Relations Act, 1947," *Harvard Law Review,* Vol. LXI, November–December 1948; S. H. Slichter, "The Taft-Hartley Act," *Quarterly Journal of Economics,* Vol. LXIII, February 1949. See also Millis and Brown, *op.cit.,* in footnote 34. At the time this is written, no comparable discussions of the 1959 legislation have appeared.

[39] The "free speech" proviso gives the employer considerably greater latitude in campaigning against unions than he had under the Wagner Act.

[40] The reporting requirements of Taft-Hartley were superseded by more elaborate requirements, some carrying criminal penalties, in the Landrum-Griffin Act of 1959.

[41] The Landrum-Griffin Act also includes several amendments to the Taft-Hartley Act, one of which was mentioned in the preceding footnote. The ensuing discussion refers to Taft-Hartley as amended by the 1959 law unless otherwise indicated in the text.

desirability of governmental regulation of the internal affairs of unions, many of these provisions are quite reasonable. In many respects, they simply prescribe for all unions what is already the practice of the best-run unions.

These affirmative aspects of the 1947 and 1959 labor laws should not obscure their negative aspects. The Landrum-Griffin Act, as of this writing, is so new and untested that there is some risk of premature judgment. But the detailed and complex regulations of this statute, plus numerous provisions for court proceedings concerning various aspects of union administration, seem to hold the threat of a flood of law-suits for many unions. The great majority of local union leaders are unpaid, part-time officials who have no legal training and sometimes little formal education of any kind. The AFL-CIO has contended that, under these circumstances, compliance with the multitude of requirements set forth in this law (some of them carrying criminal penalties) will be close to impossible for most unions and that the effort to comply may undermine their effectiveness. No doubt much will depend on the spirit in which the law is administered and on the readiness of dissident union members to haul their leaders into court. Whether this law will achieve its apparent purpose of strengthening membership control of the unions is debatable, as is the general approach of the law. The encouragement of self-regulation by means of public review boards like the one established by the UAW might well have produced sounder results. Even so, it seems safe to predict that unions and collective bargaining will survive Landrum-Griffin, just as they have survived other restrictive legislation in the past.[42]

Taft-Hartley, perhaps even more than Landrum-Griffin, must be classified as restrictive legislation. The provisions of this law which restrict union organizing activities, bargaining tactics, and objectives overbalance the provisions carried over from the Wagner Act and make the Taft-Hartley Act a law which tends to restrict, discourage, or displace collective bargaining. We turn now to a brief consideration of these provisions of Taft-Hartley.

The law contains a number of provisions which significantly limit union organizing campaigns. One of the most important of these is a prohibition of "coercion" of any employee to make him join (or not join) a union.

---

[42] As is true of the Taft-Hartley Act, not all of the provisions of Landrum-Griffin can be considered restrictive in nature. For example, one proviso changes what President Eisenhower once called a "strikebreaking" feature of Taft-Hartley. For ten years, that act made strikers who had been "permanently replaced" ineligible to vote in a collective bargaining election. An employer involved in a strike had the right to request an election, and the strike became illegal and subject to injunction if the striking union lost such an election. The Landrum-Griffin Act now provides that strikers (as well as their replacements) shall be eligible to vote in any election called within a year after the beginning of the strike.

Virtually identical language in the Wisconsin Employment Peace Act has been interpreted to outlaw "persistent solicitation," social ostracism, and the economic pressure resulting from fear of wage loss through reduced patronage of the employer's establishment.[43] Such a broad prohibition hits certain obviously indefensible organizing tactics. On the other hand, if strictly enforced it could cripple most organizing campaigns. The Eisenhower appointees on the National Labor Relations Board have gradually moved in the direction of stricter enforcement of these provisions. Certainly the growth of unions has slowed down since the passage of the Taft-Hartley Act, though it is unlikely that this is entirely attributable to the act and its administration.

Similar broad restrictions on boycotts (and thereby, under certain circumstances, peaceful picketing) also ban some practices that are clearly undesirable, but at the same time they substantially weaken the bargaining position and organizing capabilities of unions in certain industries such as building construction, retail trade, and light manufacturing.[44] Established unions in heavy industry are little affected because they are less dependent on the sympathetic activities of fellow unionists. The present boycott clauses rest on the proposition that "neutrals" should be protected against economic pressures in labor disputes. Yet it is not difficult to demonstrate that "neutrality" is extremely difficult to define in a complex, interrelated economy. It would be much sounder to prohibit those boycotts and other forms of economic pressure which seek *objectives* that are inconsistent with orderly collective bargaining—for example, the displacement of a certified bargaining agent during the life of an agreement.

The most important of the law's restrictions on union objectives are those relating to union security devices.[45] The closed shop, under which a worker must be a member of the union before being hired, is outlawed, and so are union hiring halls. The union shop, under which nonunion workers can be hired but must join the union in a stipulated period, is permitted, as are lesser forms of union security, provided certain requirements are met. The most important limitation on the union shop is that no employee can be dis-

[43] See Killingsworth, *op.cit.*, Chap. V.

[44] The boycott clauses, it may be noted, write back into federal law many of the important restrictions on unions that once were applied under the antitrust laws. See M. J. Segal, "Differences Among Secondary Boycotts and the Taft-Hartley Act," *Wayne Law Review*, Vol. 5, Spring 1959. Landrum-Griffin tightened up some alleged "loopholes" in the Taft-Hartley boycott provisions.

[45] Space limitations do not permit the discussion of other restrictions on union objectives. The most important are the regulation of welfare funds and the prohibition of certain types of "make-work" rules. It is also impossible to examine a number of other restrictions on unions, such as the prohibition of political expenditures, or the provisions relating to union liability for damages.

charged for losing membership in the union for any reason other than failure to pay dues. Unions may expel members for other reasons, but cannot secure their discharge by the employer for any other reason. Thus the power of unions to discipline their members for leading outlaw strikes, for disloyalty to the union, and similarly serious offenses, is in effect eliminated. A closely related limitation is the provision which gives primacy to those state laws which prohibit any type of union security agreement. Eighteen states now have such laws.

Attempts to enforce these Taft-Hartley provisions have substantially disrupted industrial relations in some industries; in other industries, notably building construction, the enforcement problem is well-nigh insurmountable. In an unknown number of cases, unions and employers have apparently agreed to ignore the requirements of the law.[46] These difficulties arise primarily from the fact that closed shop and union shop agreements and their variants are a well-established institution in some American industrial relations systems, and in some instances are basic to the whole relation between the employer and union (as in the West Coast maritime trades).

It is doubtful that the public interest is properly served by the Taft-Hartley restrictions on union security. The principal argument in favor of them is that individuals should be free to join or not to join unions as they see fit. While this argument cannot be examined here in detail, it should be observed that the prohibition of individual bargaining where there is a certified bargaining agent representing the majority of workers (which is a key provision of Taft-Hartley) is a greater subordination of individual freedom to majority desires than is a conventional union security agreement. The reason for the doctrine of "exclusive representation" is that it is essential for effective collective bargaining. The federal law is inconsistent in prohibiting the traditional union security arrangements in those industries where they have become an essential element in the particular industrial relations system. The inconsistency is even greater in giving primacy to the more restrictive state laws regarding union security. State law is not permitted to supersede federal law in any other area of industrial relations.

It is the Taft-Hartley restrictions on union organizing tactics, bargaining weapons, and objectives that justify the statement that this law is fundamentally different from the Wagner Act and has basically modified the policy embodied in the latter. These restrictions cover some practices that few would care to defend, but their language is so elastic that the same

---

[46] This has been a common practice under state laws imposing stringent restrictions on union security agreements. Landrum-Griffin eased the union security regulations for the building construction industry in an effort to meet this problem.

provision which outlaws physical violence can also be interpreted to outlaw disdainful glares or "persistent solicitation." Despite the protection that it gives to the right to organize, and despite some significant improvements on the Wagner Act, the Taft-Hartley Act makes it difficult to conduct an organizing campaign within the law; it substantially weakens the bargaining position of some unions; and it outlaws union objectives that in some situations are vital to the collective bargaining relationship.

Perhaps the most acute current problem in federal labor relations policy is that of delay in enforcement. It is a common saying that in labor relations especially, justice delayed is often justice denied. When an employer fights a union with unfair labor practices such as refusal to bargain, the union has usually had to wait for months and sometimes for as long as four or five years for a final adjudication of the case and an enforceable court order directing the employer to obey the law. By then, of course, the union may have gone out of existence. This problem is intensified by the provision that certain types of charges by employers against unions—for example, charges of secondary boycotts—must be given priority over all other cases. Furthermore, in these priority cases the NLRB must seek an immediate injunction, even before a hearing, if a preliminary investigation shows a likelihood that the union is violating the law. Such preferential treatment for this type of employer complaint cannot easily be justified.[47]

Toward A New Labor Policy

Supporters of the present federal labor relations policies stress the fact that they grant many new rights to the individual worker. This is presented as one of the most admirable aspects of the law. It could also be stressed that the law grants new rights to employers too. But it is generally impossible to grant rights to one group without limiting the rights of another group. When the rights and interests of organized workers, unorganized workers, and employers are in conflict, the question which we should ask is, what balance between those rights best serves the *public* interest? The present federal labor policy generally decides in favor of individual workers and employers. As a result, the law gives many advantages to those who wish to prevent the development or spread of collective bargaining. Estab-

[47] The Landrum-Griffin Act makes a rather half-hearted attempt to deal with this problem by providing a *secondary* priority for discrimination charges (whether directed against unions or employers), but it does not provide for a mandatory injunction in such cases. Moreover, cases of refusal to bargain normally involve at least as much urgency as discrimination cases. My conclusion is that this developing system of priorities is far less satisfactory and equitable than more expeditious handling of *all* cases.

lished bargaining relationships generally are not greatly affected by federal labor law; but employment is declining, both relatively and absolutely, in many of the industries where unions are now strongest. If collective bargaining fails to spread beyond those industries where it is already well-established, its relative importance in our economy will almost surely diminish as other industries and trades expand.

The key question in public policy toward labor relations is whether it is collective bargaining or some alternative to it that best furthers the public interest. The answer to this question must be our principal guide in attempting to balance the rights and duties of organized workers, unorganized workers, and employers. The thesis of this chapter is that, given our kind of economic system and our political milieu, and considering the public interest first, collective bargaining presently seems clearly superior to either of the two chief alternatives to it. This is not equally true of all industries, of course; and changing economic [48] or political conditions might require another conclusion. Nevertheless, at the present time the public policy that seems best designed to further the public interest is the protection and encouragement of collective bargaining. From this it follows that many provisions of the present federal labor laws should be substantially modified to make them consistent with that policy.

As was pointed out above, certain Taft-Hartley provisions represent a definite improvement over the Wagner Act, and they should be retained; other provisions of Taft-Hartley and of the Landrum-Griffin Act are not inconsistent with the public policy recommended here and could be retained without doing violence to that policy. There are some distinctive restrictions, however, which should be drastically modified or abandoned if we are to pursue a policy of protecting and encouraging collective bargaining. Let us summarize briefly the provisions which should be changed.

One of the aims of the present federal labor policy appears to be to insulate individuals from all forms of economic pressure intended to get them to accept collective bargaining. The Landrum-Griffin provisions which severely restrict organizational picketing are an example of the effort to achieve this aim. In a great many cases, this type of picketing is in reality a counterpressure intended to offset the effects of nonunion competition on collective bargaining. Hence, the law tries to prevent economic pressure

---

[48] Many of the chapters in this volume favor governmental policies that would bring about greater competition in product markets. Even assuming that this end could be achieved—no small assumption—this would have no significant effect on the conditions in labor markets that make collective bargaining desirable. Conversely, the encouragement of collective bargaining does not necessarily make the enforcement of competition in product markets more difficult.

(through picketing) on unorganized workers, but it provides no comparable protection against economic pressure (through the market) on organized workers. The principle of equal treatment as well as the principle of encouraging the growth of collective bargaining support the view that peaceful economic pressure by unions should be permitted in organizing efforts. It is not inconsistent with this idea to prohibit physical violence or threats of it, but the enforcement of order has traditionally been a local function. Certain clearly unjustified uses of the secondary boycott can be outlawed without stripping unions of the right of sympathetic action. In addition, obviously undesirable practices and objectives of unions that are peripheral to collective bargaining can be prohibited by language narrowly drawn for this limited purpose. However, the present restrictions on union security objectives are an unjustified interference with collective bargaining. Improvements in the administration of the federal labor law, and elimination of the unfair priority system, are essential to expedite decisions and to make the basic policies of the law more effective.

The problem of so-called "national emergency" disputes remains an extremely difficult one. There are undeniably a few industries in which the government simply cannot permit a strike of considerable length. But collective bargaining is impossible without at least the possibility of a test of strength through a strike. In those industries, therefore, we may find it necessary to devise some substitute for collective bargaining instead of encouraging it. At the same time, of course, we must attempt to improve in every way possible our machinery for the settlement of disputes in those industries where collective bargaining is practiced.

Conclusion

Many critics of organized labor in the United States overlook a basic fact. A labor movement like ours, which accepts the fundamental values of the society in which it functions, also acquires some of the characteristics of that society. It is shocking that some union leaders have stolen from their members; it is also shocking that some great corporations have been systematically looted by insiders. It is shocking that criminals have gained control of some unions; it is also shocking that some policemen in large cities have become criminals in uniform. Perhaps it is an exaggeration to say that there is a little larceny in everybody's soul, but it is true that there are usually a few larcenous individuals in any large group. Not only dishonesty, but complacency and materialism are characteristics which are common in many segments of our society. We find these characteristics in some labor groups. A great many people demand of the labor movement idealism, self-sacrifice and missionary zeal, but these qualities are hard to find anywhere. Collective bargaining in the United States might be regarded as a system of countervailing selfishness. Since the participants in it are, after all, the products of the society in which they live, the system has a number of vexatious imperfections. But it is often dangerous to judge social institutions like collective bargaining by absolute standards. Perhaps the greatest merit of collective bargaining in the United States is that no one has developed or even proposed a system of industrial government which is better.

SUGGESTED READINGS

Books

J. Barbash, ed., *Unions and Union Leadership* (New York: Harper, 1959).

C. O. Gregory, *Labor and the Law*, 2nd rev. ed. (New York: Norton, 1958).

C. C. Killingsworth, *State Labor Relations Acts* (Chicago: University of Chicago Press, 1948).

William M. Leiserson, *American Trade Union Democracy* (New York: Columbia University Press, 1959).

C. E. Lindblom, *Unions and Capitalism* (New Haven: Yale University Press, 1949).

H. A. Millis and Emily C. Brown, *From the Wagner Act to Taft-Hartley* (Chicago: University of Chicago Press, 1950).

C. A. Myers, ed., *Wages, Prices, Profits and Productivity* (New York: The American Assembly, Columbia University, 1959).

S. Perlman, *A Theory of the Labor Movement* (New York: Macmillan, 1928).

L. G. Reynolds, *Labor Economics and Labor Relations*, 3rd ed. (Englewood Cliffs: Prentice-Hall, 1959).

S. H. Slichter, *Union Policies and Industrial Management* (Washington: The Brookings Institution, 1941).

E. E. Witte, *The Government in Labor Disputes* (New York: McGraw-Hill, 1932).

Journal and Magazine Articles

R. A. Lester, "Reflections on the 'Labor Monopoly' Issue," *Journal of Political Economy*, Vol. LV, December 1947.

H. C. Simons, "Some Reflections on Syndicalism," *Journal of Political Economy*, Vol. LII, March 1944.

S. H. Slichter, "The Taft-Hartley Act," *Quarterly Journal of Economics*, Vol. LXIII, February 1949.

E. E. Witte, "An Appraisal of the Taft-Hartley Act," *American Economic Review*, Supplement, Vol. XXXVIII, May 1948.

Author Index

Aaron, B., 583
Abrams, C., 138
Adams, W., 197, 198, 200, 225, 231, 232, 347, 507, 544, 550, 556, 557, 562
Adelman, M. A., 239, 544, 562
Agee, W. K., 510, 532
Alderfer, E. B., 152, 258, 259
Allen, E. L., 42, 47
Anderson, H. W., 585
Arnold, T., 351
Ascoli, M., 532
Ayer, N. W., 531

Backman, J., 60, 62, 70, 72
Bain, J. S., 154, 179, 181–82, 281, 310, 324, 325, 328, 329, 331, 353, 354, 440, 555, 561
Bakke, E. W., 567
Balderston, C. C., 73
Balderston, F. E., 143
Ball, M. W., 310
Bancroft, E. C., 49, 73
Baratz, M. A., 76, 79, 80, 89, 90, 91, 95, 111
Barbash, J., 572, 596
Barkin, S., 47, 50, 53, 56, 62, 73
Barnes, H. S., 320
Bates, G. L., 507
Beard, C. A., 544
Benedict, M. R., 40
Bennett, K. W., 444
Berge, W., 540
Berman, E., 586
Bernstein, I., 112, 429
Beyer, G. H., 117, 142
Bezanson, A., 73
Bidwell, P. W., 111, 267
Bird, G. L., 532
Blair, J. M., 71, 544
Blank, D. M., 142
Bolles, A. S., 43
Bolles, B., 552
Bork, R., 308
Borkin, J., 540
Bowman, D. O., 587
Bowman, W. S., 180
Brady, R. A., 402, 542
Brannan, S. J., 38
Brown, E. C., 587, 589, 596
Bryan, L. A., 482, 507

Buchanan, S., 527
Burns, A. R., 183, 555
Bursler, N., 235, 248, 251, 262, 275
Butler, C. R., 532
Butters, J. K., 62, 73, 558

Capron, W. M., 152
Carr, C. C., 231
Cary, W. L., 62, 73, 558
Cassady, R., 289, 295
Chafee, Z., 531
Chamberlain, N. W., 580, 587
Chamberlin, E. H., 567, 579
Chapman, S. J., 58
Charnley, M. V., 532
Cherington, P. W., 507
Chow, G. C., 337
Christenson, C. L., 91, 92, 112
Clark, C. D., 68
Clark, J. M., 162, 163, 183, 458, 548
Cleveland, R. G., 354
Cochrane, W. C., 37, 38, 41
Cole, E. N., 344
Colean, M., 116, 142
Collins, J. H., 432, 466
Comer, G., 534
Commons, J. R., 569
Cook, R., 310
Copeland, M. T., 57, 61
Coqueron, F. G., 283
Cornell, W. B., 44, 99
Cox, A., 589
Cox, R., 55, 64, 73, 392
Creamer, D., 252
Crook, W. H., 49, 53, 59, 73
Crum, W. L., 181
Cummings, J. C., 55
Cushman, R. E., 531

Daugherty, C. R., 183
Davenport, W. H., 532
Davies, E., 551
Davis, H. S., 73
De Chazeau, M. G., 183, 310
Deusenberry, J. S., 116
Dewing, A. S., 61
Dirlam, J. B., 170–71, 174, 215, 216, 243, 253, 255, 256, 263, 271, 275, 289, 310, 340, 353, 561
Doane, W. F., 58

597

Donovan, W. J., 548
Douglas, W. O., 154
Doyle, L. A., 213
Drucker, P. F., 354, 561
Dunlop, J. T., 57, 579, 580

Eckstein, O., 175
Edwards, C. D., 66, 73, 166, 181, 251, 254, 272, 465, 537, 539, 554, 557, 561
Emmerglick, L. J., 201
Epstein, R. C., 44, 181, 314, 315, 354, 380, 437
Ernst, M. L., 531

Farish, W. S., 310
Fellner, W., 561
Fetter, F. A., 183
Fisher, W. E., 80, 85, 88, 90, 93, 97, 100, 106, 107, 111
Floyd, J. S., 58, 73
Follin, J. W., 136
Ford, H., 317, 354, 355
Frederick, J. H., 507
Fromm, G., 175

Gainsbrugh, M. R., 60, 62, 70, 72
Galbraith, J. K., 167, 541, 549, 561
Gary, E. H., 145, 146, 150–51, 551
Geller, M. A., 512, 531
Gibb, G. S., 68
Giddens, P. H., 299, 310
Gill, F. W., 507
Glover, J. G., 44, 99
Goldberg, A. J., 571
Gray, H. M., 198, 200, 231, 507, 544, 556
Gray, L. C., 40
Grebler, L., 115, 116, 142
Greene, N., 586
Greenewalt, C. H., 276
Gregory, C. O., 586, 596
Griffin, C. E., 548, 553, 562
Gross, R., 479
Gulick, C. A., 144, 183, 279
Gunness, R. C., 294

Haber, W., 121, 142
Haigh, R. W., 288, 293, 305, 306, 307, 310
Haines, W. W., 479
Halcrow, H. G., 19, 40
Hamberg, D., 344
Hamilton, W. H., 111, 112, 538, 562
Hand, L., 533
Harris, S. E., 59, 73
Harvey, L., 203
Hayek, F. A., 542, 553
Haynes, W., 275
Haynes, W. W., 108

Heflebower, R. B., 562
Hellmuth, W. F., 285
Hempel, E. H., 275
Hendrix, W. E., 7
Hennock, F., 427
Hession, C. H., 430, 466
Hicks, J. R., 566
Hidy, R. W. & M. E., 286, 304
Hildebrand, G. H., 580
Hildred, W. P., 487
Hill, F. E., 320, 355
Hoglund, C. R., 6
Hoover, E. M., 60, 73
Houghton, H. F., 71
Howard, M. C., 295, 299, 310
Hoyt, P., 530
Huettig, M. D., 400, 404, 417, 429
Huntington, S. P., 552

Isard, W., 152

Jablonski, W., 298
Jacobs, A., 532
Jacobs, L., 399, 429
James, C. M., 80, 85, 97, 100, 106, 107
Jesness, O. B., 40
Jewkes, J., 344
Johnson, R. J., 124
Johnston, H. B., 491, 495
Jordan, J. G., 303
Joskow, J., 49

Kahn, A. E., 256, 271, 277, 310, 561
Kaplan, A. D. H., 170–71, 215, 216, 233, 253, 255, 256, 275, 289, 340, 457
Karsh, B., 90, 112
Kaysen, C., 557, 562
Keats, J., 343, 345, 350, 355
Keezer, D., 546, 562
Keim, W., 562
Keir, M., 58
Kelly, B., 114, 139, 142
Kennedy, J. P., 403
Kennedy, S. J., 60, 67
Kerby, P., 524, 532
Kerr, C., 580
Kessler, W. C., 49, 53, 59, 63, 73
Kettering, C. F., 313, 355
Killingsworth, C. C., 583, 591, 596
King, L. T., 90
Kreps, T. J., 275
Kuznets, S., 540

Lantz, H. R., 111
Lanzillotti, R. F., 170–71, 174, 215, 216, 253, 255, 256, 275, 289, 340
Learned, E. P., 61, 310

Lee, A. McC., 509, 531
Lee, J., 499
Lehman, G., 532
Leiserson, W. M., 578, 596
Lerner, A. P., 176, 182
Lester, R. A., 579, 596
Levinson, H., 121, 142
Lewis, B. W., 177, 347, 550, 553
Lewis, E. W., 355
Lewis, H. G., 162, 579
Lewis, J. L., 86
Lewis, W. A., 553-54
Lilienthal, D. E., 547–48, 562
Lindblom, C. E., 579, 596
Lintner, J., 62, 73, 558
Lishan, J. M., 260
Livingston, S. M., 290, 292
Loehwing, D. A., 457
London, J., 90, 112
Lovell, H. G., 112
Lynch, D., 167
Lyon, L. S., 559

Machlup, F., 177, 183, 543, 554, 562, 566, 579
Maclaurin, W. R., 345, 567
Maisel, S., 125, 127, 129, 134, 142
Markham, J. W., 49, 53, 57, 62, 63, 73, 242, 247, 260, 275
Marlio, L., 231
Martin, W. H., 233, 248, 254, 261, 276
Mason, A. T., 586
Mason, E. S., 101, 347, 356, 548, 562, 563
Mathewson, S. B., 583
May, E. C., 430
Mayo, E., 583
McAllister, H. E., 287
McIsaac, A. M., 47
McKie, J. W., 443, 446, 447, 466, 467
McLean, J. G., 288, 293, 305, 306, 307, 310
Means, G. C., 172
Metz, H. W., 587
Michl, H. E., 152, 258, 259
Miller, J. P., 112
Millis, H. A., 587, 589, 596
Mises, L. v., 553
Moore, D. A., 311
Morris, H. L., 89, 111
Morris, L., 312
Mueller, C. F., 194, 231
Mueller, W. F., 242, 243, 244, 251, 252, 265, 274, 275, 276
Mund, V. A., 548, 558
Murchison, C. T., 61, 63, 73
Musselman, M. M., 314, 355
Myers, C. A., 567, 581, 596
Myers, R. J., 112

Navin, T. R., 68
Nelson, D. M., 403
Nelson, S., 562
Neuroth, P., 532
Nevins, A., 320, 355
Newcomb, R., 116, 142
Nicholls, W. H., 392, 560
Nixon, R. B., 522, 532
Northrup, H. R., 576

Olsen, B. M., 68
O'Mahoney, J. C., 492
Orth, A., 313, 355
Oxenfeldt, A. R., 341

Parker, G. L., 111
Perlman, S., 569, 596
Pew, J. H., 310
Phillips, T. R., 483
Pierson, F. C., 580
Piquet, H. S., 269
Proctor, E. W., 243

Rathbone, M. J., 308
Ray, R. H., 510, 531, 532
Reddaway, W. B., 236, 242
Rees, A., 580
Rentzel, D. W., 478
Reynolds, L. G., 42, 59, 73, 567, 579, 580, 583, 596
Robert, J. C., 392
Robertson, D. H., 566
Robertson, F. R., 37
Robinson, F. F., 496
Romney, G., 325, 328
Roos, C. F., 337
Rosenbluth, G., 545
Rosenfarb, J., 587
Ross, A. M., 567
Ross, L., 400
Rosten, L. C., 408
Rostow, E. V., 112, 196, 297, 304, 306, 310, 349, 384
Rowse, A. E., 525, 531
Ruggles, R., 73, 254
Ryan, O., 475

Sachs, A. S., 306
Sawers, D., 344
Schmookler, J., 139, 143
Schultz, T. W., 15, 18, 41
Schumpeter, J. A., 549, 562
Schwartz, B., 507, 552
Schwenning, G. T., 61
Seager, H. R., 144, 183, 279
Segal, M. J., 591
Seldes, G., 524, 531

Seltzer, L. H., 319
Sheppard, G. S., 41
Shillinglaw, G., 440
Shister, J., 567, 583
Shultz, G. P., 567, 581
Shussbeim, M., 138
Simons, H. C., 542, 562, 564, 579, 596
Skouras, C. P., 407
Slichter, S. H., 575, 577, 583, 585, 589, 596
Smith, A., 146, 534, 536, 566
Smithies, A., 162, 166, 184
Solo, R. A., 269, 276
Solow, H., 76, 84, 93, 112
Somers, G. G., 112
Soth, L., 41
Spring, B. P., 113
Steiner, O. H., 136, 143
Stelzer, I. M., 243, 263, 353
Stieber, J., 582
Stier, H. L., 436
Stigler, G., 180–81, 563
Stillerman, R., 344
Stine, O. C., 40
Stocking, G. W., 176, 180, 191, 192, 194,
    231, 233, 236, 243, 251, 252, 258, 274,
    275, 276, 461, 539, 540, 542, 560, 562,
    563
Stratton, S. S., 183
Suits, D. B., 338
Svirsky, L., 524, 531
Sward, K., 317
Szeliski, V. v., 337

Tarbell, I. M., 146, 151
Tennant, R. B., 357, 392
Teper, L., 48, 55
Thomas, D. L., 457
Thomsen, F. L., 18, 19, 22
Thye, E. J., 493
Tilley, N. M., 392
Travis, H. F., 435
Turner, D. F., 351, 557, 562
Tyson, R. C., 173–74

Vanderblue, H. B., 356
Vatter, H. G., 323, 356
Vernon, R., 270, 271
Viner, J., 579

Walker, G. B., 248
Wallace, D. H., 109
Wallace, D. W., 188, 190, 197, 231
Watkins, G. S., 429
Watkins, M. W., 191, 192, 194, 231, 233,
    236, 258, 275, 280, 310, 461, 539, 540,
    560, 562
Webster, E. M., 426
Wein, H. H., 183
Welsh, C. A., 540
Westmeyer, R. E., 507
Weston, J. F., 50, 73, 244
Whitney, S. N., 48, 53, 54, 73, 158, 208,
    231, 239, 243, 249, 250, 252, 271, 324,
    325, 347, 349, 355, 392, 413, 416, 429,
    455, 461, 466, 562
Whyte, W. H., 132
Wilcox, C., 49, 235, 255, 536, 539, 541,
    562, 563
Wilcox, W. W., 7, 41
Williams, W., 356
Williamson, S. T., 314, 354
Wilson, G. L., 507
Winnick, L., 142, 143
Wiprud, A. C., 485, 508
Witte, E. E., 586, 589, 596
Wolbert, G. S., 306
Wolff, R. P., 136
Wolfson, T., 580
Wolman, L., 581
Woolf, D. G., 44
Wooten, H. M., 357
Wright, D. McC., 182
Wright, H. L., 111

Yntema, T. O., 162, 164

Subject Index

Advertising
See Product Differentiation
Antitrust Laws, 533–36
  and aluminum, 194–97, 199–200
  and automobiles, 351–53
  and chemicals, 271–72, 274–75
  and cigarettes, 382–85, 390–92
  and coal, 104–05
  and containers, 433, 441–43
  and movies, 411–20
  and newspapers, 522, 528–29
  and petroleum, 279, 301–02
  and steel, 146–47, 153–54

Basing Point System
  in aluminum, 223–24, 229–30
  in newspapers, 514
  in steel, 160–67, 176–78
Brannan Plan, 36–37

Cartels
See Cooperation
Competition, Interindustry
  in aluminum, 193–94
  in chemicals, 248–49
  in coal, 95–99
  in containers, 458–60
  in movies, 420–27
  in newspapers, 512, 517
  in steel, 171
Competition, Non-price
  in automobiles, 329–31, 342–45
  in chemicals, 259–63
  in cigarettes, 373–75, 376, 386, 388
  in containers, 456–58
  in textiles, 55–56
Compulsory Licensing
See Patents
Concentration, 543–47
  in airlines, 474–83
  in aluminum, 200–07
  in automobiles, 322–24
  in chemicals, 235–41
  in cigarettes, 367–70
  in coal, 83–86
  in construction, 118–21
  in containers, 432–35
  in movies, 402–05
  in newspapers, 509–12
  in petroleum, 281–83

  in steel, 149–50
  in textiles, 47–50
Conspiracy
See Cooperation
Cooperation
  in airlines, 486–87
  in aluminum, 190–93
  in automobiles, 335–36
  in chemicals, 246–52
  in cigarettes, 373–78
  in movies, 423–27
  in petroleum, 301–02
  in steel, 146, 165–66
Cost Structure
  in aluminum, 212–14
  in automobiles, 338–39
  in chemicals, 252–53
  in coal, 94–95
  in construction, 129–33
  in movies, 408–09
  in newspapers, 513–16
  in petroleum, 283–85, 288–89
  in steel, 162–63
  in textiles, 50–52
Countervailing Power, 549–50
  in chemicals, 265
  in containers, 445–48
Cross-Hauling, 166–67

Demand
  in agriculture, 14–16, 17–19
  in automobiles, 336–38
  in chemicals, 253
  in cigarettes, 370–71
  in coal, 95–101
  in construction, 122–24
  in containers, 435–36
  in petroleum, 290
  in steel, 164–65
Depreciation Gap, 173–76
Dissolution, Divorcement, Divestiture
See Antitrust Laws

Efficiency and Size, 555–57
  in agriculture, 6–10, 26–29
  in aluminum, 212–14
  in automobiles, 324–27, 347–48
  in chemicals, 242
  in cigarettes, 372–73
  in construction, 128–36

Efficiency and Size (*continued*)
  in containers, 440–41
  in newspapers, 413–16
  in petroleum, 307–09
  in steel, 179–82
  in textiles, 50–53
Elasticity
  See Demand
Entry
  in agriculture, 12–14
  in airlines, 492–500
  in aluminum, 189–90, 203
  in automobiles, 314–15, 321, 323–35
  in chemicals, 247–49, 261–63
  in coal, 77–82
  in construction, 120
  in containers, 437–43
  in newspapers, 513–16
  in textiles, 54, 56

Government Disposal of War Plants
  in aluminum, 197–99
  in steel, 152–53
Government Ownership, 552–54
  in coal, 108–09
Government Regulation, 550–52
  in agriculture, 23–26, 33–36
  in airlines, 471–74, 494–500
  in coal, 105–07, 109–10
  in petroleum, 280, 285–86

Innovation
  See Technology
Integration, Horizontal
  in aluminum, 188–89
  in chemicals, 243–46
  in containers, 434–35
  in movies, 425–27
  in steel, 144–45, 151
  in textiles, 49–50
Integration, Vertical
  in aluminum, 187–88, 204–09, 221–23, 227–29
  in automobiles, 352–53
  in containers, 443–45, 464–66
  in movies, 402–05
  in petroleum, 304–10
  in steel, 154–59, 178–79
  in textiles, 60–67

Location
  in steel, 167
  in textiles, 57–60

Mergers
  See Integration

Monopolistic Practices
  in airlines, 485–86
  in aluminum, 219–21
  in automobiles, 349–53
  in movies, 405–07
  in newspapers, 521–23
  in petroleum, 279
  See also Cooperation and Discrimination

Oligopoly, Bilateral, 445–48

Patents
  in aluminum, 186–87
  in automobiles, 316
  in chemicals, 250–51, 270–71, 272–74
  in containers, 438–39
  in movies, 396–97
Price Discrimination
  in automobiles, 352–53
  in chemicals, 251–52
  in cigarettes, 360–61
  in containers, 451–53
  in petroleum, 299–301
  in steel, 166
Price Leadership
  in aluminum, 216–19
  in automobiles, 341–42
  in cigarettes, 378–79
  in containers, 448–51
  in petroleum, 292–93
  in steel, 167–69
  See also Cooperation
Price Rigidity
  in aluminum, 226–27
  in chemicals, 254–56
  in containers, 453–56
  in steel, 169–71, 177–78
  in textiles, 54
  ———, absence of, in agriculture, 10–11
Pricing, Target Rate of Return
  in aluminum, 214–16
  in automobiles, 339–41
  in chemicals, 256
  in steel, 174
Product Differentiation
  in automobiles, 329–31
  in cigarettes, 386, 388
  in textiles, 55–56
Product Diversification
  in automobiles, 331–32
  in chemicals, 238, 243–44, 248–50
  in cigarettes, 367–70, 388–89
  in containers, 434–35, 459–60
  in movies, 425–27

Index

Productivity
  See Efficiency
Profits
  in aluminum, 225–26
  in automobiles, 345–46
  in chemicals, 258, 265–66
  in cigarettes, 379–82
  in containers, 463
  in petroleum, 293
  in steel, 172–76, 181–82
  in textiles, 51

Research
  See Technology

Subsidies
  in agriculture, 23–26, 33–36
  in airlines, 487–90
  in aluminum, 203
  in chemicals, 268–69
  in newspapers, 525–27

Tariff
  in aluminum, 189
  in automobiles, 334
  in chemicals, 269
Technology, 539–40
  in aluminum, 186–87
  in automobiles, 344–45
  in chemicals, 241–42, 259–63
  in cigarettes, 359–60
  in coal, 92–94
  in construction, 139–42
  in containers, 457, 463
  in movies, 422–23
  in petroleum, 280–81
  in steel, 151–52, 181
  in textiles, 67–69

Unions, Role of, 564–96
  in coal, 86–92
  in construction, 121–22
  in steel, 171–73
  in textiles, 57–58